May 9–11, 2019
Tysons Corner, VA, USA



Association for Computing Machinery

*Advancing Computing as a Science & Profession*

# GLSVLSI'19

## Proceedings of the 2019 Great Lakes Symposium on VLSI


*General Chairs:*

***Houman Homayoun, George Mason University, USA***

***Baris Taskin, Drexel University, USA***

*Program Chairs:*

***Tinoosh Mohsenin, UMBC, USA***

***Weisheng Zhao, Beihang University, China***

Association for
Computing Machinery

*Advancing Computing as a Science & Profession*

**The Association for Computing Machinery**
**2 Penn Plaza, Suite 701**
**New York, New York 10121-0701**



**ISBN:** 978-1-4503-6252-8 (Digital)

**ISBN:** 978-1-4503-7060-8 (Print)

Additional copies may be ordered prepaid from:

**ACM Order Department**
PO Box 30777
New York, NY 10087-0777, USA

Phone: 1-800-342-6626 (USA and Canada)
+1-212-626-0500 (Global)
Fax: +1-212-944-1318
E-mail: acmhelp@acm.org
Hours of Operation: 8:30 am – 4:30 pm ET

# General Chairs' Welcome

Welcome to the 29th edition of the *Great Lakes Symposium on VLSI (GLSVLSI) 2019,* held between May 9-11, 2019 at Tysons Corner, VA in the Washington, DC metropolitan area. GLSVLSI is a premier venue for the dissemination of manuscripts of the highest quality in all areas related to VLSI, devices, and system-level design. The location of this year's GLSVLSI is Washington, DC, visiting the east coast of the US, not too far from the "Great Lakes" region of the USA, especially given the global stretch of GLSVLSI host cities within the past decade. Conference will be held at Tysons Corner Marriott located in Tysons Corner, VA, a short ride from downtown Washington DC.

ACM GLSVLSI 2019 is presented through the collaborative effort of a 15+ member organizing committee with 100+ technical program committee members. The Technical Program Committee Chairs, Tinoosh Mohsenin and Weisheng Zhao, have put together the 2019 installment of the traditionally strong ACM SIGDA GLSVLSI program. The program is structured around the following eight tracks, with GLSVLSI welcoming the International Conference on Microelectronic Systems Education (MSE) for GLSVLSI attendees as one of the tracks in 2019:

1. VLSI Design (Track Chairs Selcuk Kose, Inna Partin-Vaisband)
2. VLSI Circuits and Power Aware Design (Track Chairs Deliang Fan, Swaroop Ghosh)
3. Computer-Aided Design (Track Chairs Yanzhi Wang, Jianlei Yang)
4. Testing, Reliability, Fault Tolerance (Track Chairs Sandip Ray, Benjamin Schaefer)
5. Emerging Computing & Post-CMOS Technologies (Track Chairs Sorin Cotofana, Yue Zhang)
6. Hardware Security (Track Chairs JV Rajendran, Patrick Schaumont)
7. VLSI for Machine Learning and Artificial Intelligence (Track Chairs Philip Brisk, Amey Kulkarni)
8. Microelectronics Systems Education (Track Chairs Tina Hudson, Bradley Minch)

The conference will showcase a program based on these eight tracks and the special theme "In-Memory processing for Future Electronics". The packed three-day program features:

- Seven Technical Sessions, Two Poster Sessions,
- Six Special Sessions (Special Session Chairs Mahdi Nikdast, Muhammad Shafique),
- Two Panel Discussions (Panel Chairs Tosiron Adegbija, Michel Kinsy),
- The Microsystems Education (MSE) technical paper session and the MSE Workshop (Organizers Tina Hudson, Bradley Minch),
- Streamlined Logistics for Registration and Accommodation (Finance Chair Selcuk Kose, Web & Registration Chair Yi-Chung Chen),
- Local attractions, Dinner Banquet in Washington, DC area (Local Organization Chairs Xiang Chen, Naghmeh Karimi),
- Proceedings in ACM Digital Libraries (Publications Chair Ioannis Savidis),
- Publicity Services (Publicity Chairs Jingtong Hu, Miao Hu, Robert Wille),

- 3 keynotes from academic influencers and thought leaders spread over the 3 days of the conference,
- 2 DARPA Program Manager keynotes on the 2nd day of the conference.

The conference will showcase a program highlighted by the five keynote talks:

1. Marilyn Wolf, Farmer Distinguished Chair in Embedded Computing Systems and GRA Eminent Scholar, the Georgia Institute of Technology, delivering the keynote entitled "Thoughts on Edge Intelligence".
2. Serge Leef, Program manager in the Microsystems Technology Office, DARPA, delivering the keynote entitled "Automatic Implementation of Secure Silicon".
3. Keith Rebello, Deputy Director, the Office of the Deputy Assistant Secretary of Defense for Systems Engineering, DoD, delivering a keynote whose content and title are pending approvals at the time of this letter.
4. Onur Mutlu, Professor of Computer Science, ETH Zurich, delivering keynote entitled "Processing Data Where It Makes Sense in Modern Computing Systems: Enabling In-Memory Computation".
5. Swarup Bhunia, preeminence professor of cybersecurity and Steven Yatauro endowed faculty fellow, University of Florida, delivering keynote entitled "Innovations in IoT for a Safe, Secure, and Sustainable Future".

GLSVLSI 2019 will continue the best Program Committee Reviewer award initiated in GLSVLSI 2018, recognizing the outstanding service of a few program committee members in each track. The process is centered around the nomination of track chairs based on quality of reviews and participation in the track discussions in the paper selection process. It is essential to report the inherent challenge of the selection of individual(s) for this award due to the outstanding service of so many, and often times all, of our PC members. In the inspiring light of this recognition, we would like to thank the track chairs, each PC member, and the anonymous reviewers, for their service, and hope to continue the tradition of best PC member recognitions for the GLSVLSI community.

We trust that you will find GLSVLSI 2019 highly rewarding and exciting in terms of the technical quality, networking opportunities, as well as content and diversity of the whole program.

| **Baris Taskin** | **Houman Homayoun** |
|---|---|
| *General Chair* | *General Chair* |

# Table of Contents

## Tech Session 4: Next Generation Interconnect: Architecture to Physical Design



## Tech Session 5: Designing Robust VLSI Circuits. From Approximate Computing to Hardware Security



## Tech Session 6: Emerging Computing & Post-CMOS Technologies

## Tech Session 7: Physical Design and Obfuscation



## Tech Session 8: Quantum Circuits and Emerging Technologies



## Tech Session 9: Towards Fast, Efficient, and Robust Memory



## Tech Session 10: MSE

## Session: Poster Sessions I, II

## Special Session 1: In-Memory Processing for Future Electronics



## Special Session 2: Approximate Computing Systems Design: Energy Efficiency and Security Implications

## Special Session 4: Opportunities and Challenges for Emerging Monolithic 3D Integrated Circuits



## Special Session 5: Robust IC Authentication and Protected Intellectual Property: A Special Session on Hardware Security

## Special Session 6: Neuromorphic Computing and Deep Neural Network



## Session: Panelist Position Papers

# GLSVLSI 2019 Symposium Organization

**General Chairs:** Houman Homayoun (George Mason University, USA)
Baris Taskin (Drexel University, USA)

**Program Chairs:** Tinoosh Mohsenin (UMBC, USA)
Weisheng Zhao (Beihang University, China)

**Panels Chairs:** Tosiron Adegbija (University of Arizona, USA)
Michel A. Kinsky (Boston University, USA)

**Proceedings Chair:** Ioannis Savidis (Drexel University, USA)

**Finance Chair** Selcuk Kose (University of Rochester, USA)

**Local Chairs:** Xiang Chen (George Mason University, USA)
Naghmeh Karimi (University of Maryland Baltimore County, USA)

**Publicity Chair:** Miao Hu (Binghamton University, USA)
Jingtong Hu (University of Pittsburgh, USA)
Robert Wille (Johannes Kepler University, Austria)

**Web & Registration Chair:** Yi-Chung Chen (SUNY at New Paltz, USA)

**Steering Committee:** Jose Ayala (Univ. Complutense Madrid, Spain)
Iris Bahar (Brown University, USA)
Sanjukta Bhanja (University of South Florida, USA)
Erik Brunvand (University of Utah, USA)
Yehea Ismail (America University Cairo, Egypt)
Alex K. Jones (University of Pittsburgh, USA)
Fabrizio Lombardi (Northeastern University, USA)
Hai (Helen) Li (Duke University, USA)
Enrico Macii (Politecnico di Torino, Italy)
Martin Margala (University of Massachusetts, USA)
Ken Stevens (University of Utah, USA)
Gang Qu (University of Maryland, USA)
Yuan Xie (University of California Santa Barbara, USA)
Zhiyuan Yan (Lehigh University, USA)
Hai Zhou (Northwestern University, USA)

**Track Chairs:** Selcuk Kose (University of South Florida, USA)
Inna Partin-Vaisband (University of Illinois at Chicago, USA)
Deliang Fan (University of Central Florida, USA)
Swaroop Ghosh (The Pennsylvania State University, USA)
Jianlei Yang (Beihang University, China)
Yanzhi Wang (Syracuse University, USA)
Benjamin Schaefer (The University of Texas at Dallas, USA)
Sandip Ray (University of Florida, USA)
Yue Zhang (Beihang University, China)
Sorin Cotofana (Delft University of Technology, Netherland)
Patrick Schaumont (Virginia Tech, USA)
Jeyavijayan Rajendran (Texas A&M University, USA)
Philip Brisk (University of California Riverside, USA)
Amey Kulkarni (Velodyne, USA)
Bradley Minch (Olin College, USA)
Tina Hudson (Rose Hulman Institute of Technology, USA)

## Program Committees

**Track 1: VLSI Design:** Md-Amimul Ehsan (Intel)
Emre Salman (Stony Brook University)
Srinivas Katkoori (University of South Florida)
Amlan Ganguly (Rochester Institute of Technology)
Sudeep Pasricha (Colorado State University)
Matthew Ziegler (IBM)
Joseph S. Friedman (The University of Texas at Dallas)
Valerio Tenace (Politecnico di Torino)
Iraklis Anagnostopoulos (Southern Illinois University)
Massimo Poncino (Politecnico di Torino)
Sujay Deb (IIIT Delhi)
Mahdi Nikdast (Polytechnique Montreal)
Akash Kumar (TU Dresden)
Turbo Majumder (Intel)
Pasquale Schiavone (ETHZ)
Saraju Mohanty (University of North Texas)
Weize Yu (Old Dominion University)
Tinoosh Mohsenin (University of Maryland Baltimore County)
Domenik Helms (OFFIS Research Institute)
Guanming Huang (Synopsys)

**Track 2: VLSI Circuits, and Power Aware Design:**
Chaitanya Kshirsagar (Broadcom)
Mohamad Hammam Alsafrjalani (University of Miami)
Ioannis Savidis (Drexel University)
Shomit Das (AMD Research)
Vinayak Honkote (Intel)
Yingyan Lin (Rice University)
Michel Kinsy (Boston University)
Tosiron Adegbija (University of Arizona)
Mingjie Lin (University of Central Florida)
Yu Bai (California State University Fullerton)
Xue Lin (Northeastern University)
Abhronil Sengupta (The Pennsylvania State University)
Ann Gordon-Ross (University of Florida)
Sheldon Tan (University of California, Riverside)

**Track 3: Computer-Aided Design (CAD):**
Olivia Chen (Yokohama National University)
Wujie Wen (Florida International University)
Rickard Ewetz (University of Central Florida)
Li Zhang (Technical University of Munich)
Jia Wang (Illinois Institute of Technology)
Hailong Yao (Tsinghua University)
Ahmad Patooghy (University of Central Arkansas)
Tsung-Yi Ho (National Tsing Hua University)
Yu-Guang Chen (Yuan Ze University)
Pingqiang Zhou (ShanghaiTech University)
Yukihide Kohira (The University of Aizu)
Yasuhiro Takashima (University of Kitakyushu)
Hamed Tabkhi (University of North Carolina Charlotte)
Evangeline Young (The Chinese University of Hong Kong)
Xiang Chen (George Mason University)
Daniel Grosse (University of Bremen & DFKI)
Emre Salman (Stony Brook University)
Fan Yang (Fudan University)
Cheng Zhuo (Zhejiang University)
Wanli Chang (University of York)
Christoph Grimm (TU Kaiserslautern)
Shao-Yun Fang (National Taiwan University of Science and Technology)

**Track 6: Hardware Security:** Ujjwal Guin (Auburn University)
Qiaoyan Yu (University of New Hampshire)
Fatemeh Tehranipoor (San Francisco State University)
Ioannis Savidis (Drexel University)
Naghmeh Karimi (University of Maryland Baltimore County)
Fareena Saqib (University of North Carolina at Charlotte)
Yousef Iskander (Cisco)
Amro Awad (University of Central Florida)
Domenic Forte (University of Florida)
Hassan Salmani (Howard University)
Mehran Mozaffari Kermani (University of South Florida)
Yier Jin (University of Florida)
Kevin Kornegay (Morgan State University)
Guru Venkataramani (George Washington University)
Avesta Sasan (Qualcomm)
Chengmo Yang (University of Delaware)
Seyed-Abdollah Sohrab Aftabjahani (Intel)
Tinoosh Mohsenin (University of Maryland Baltimore County)
Chintan Patel (University of Maryland Baltimore County)

**Track 7: VLSI for Machine Learning and Artificial Intelligence:** Marco Domenico Santambrogio (Politecnico di Milano)
Abhilash Goyal (Unknown)
Kenneth O'Neal (University of California, Riverside)
Subhasis Das (Zoox)
Di Wu (University of California, Los Angeles)
Andrew Putnam (Microsoft)
Ryan Robucci (University of Maryland Baltimore County)
Ashutosh Gupta (Synopsys)
Rajat Subhra Chakraborty (IIT, Kharagpur)
Yu Wang (Tsinghua University)
Upasna Vishnoi (Marvell)
Harsh Patel (University of Virginia)
Ram Krishnamurthy (Intel)
Amir Rahmani (University of California, Irvine)

# Thoughts on Edge Intelligence

Marilyn Wolf
School of ECE, Georgia Institute of Technology
Atlanta GA 30332
wolf@ece.gatech.edu

## ABSTRACT

Machine learning methods have exploded in the past half-dozen years. Machine learning is being applied to a huge range of problems across the spectrum of applications. Initial results relied on server-oriented computations. But many applications will require deploying aspects of machine learning throughout the network hierarchy. Several factors motivate the development of Edge Intelligence architectures and algorithms: network bandwidth, power consumption, latency, privacy, etc. This talk will start the motivation for edge intelligence with several examples from manufacturing and health care and outline some important problems for VLSI systems.

## CCS Concepts/ACM Classifiers

• Very large scale integration design, sensor networks

## Author Keywords

Internet-of-Things, IoT, machine learning, VLSI, edge intelligence

## BIOGRAPHY

Marilyn Wolf is Farmer Distinguished Chair in Embedded Computing Systems and GRA Eminent Scholar at the Georgia Institute of Technology. She received her BS, MS, and PhD in electrical engineering from Stanford University in 1980, 1981, and 1984. She was with AT&T Bell Laboratories from 1984 to 1989 and was on the faculty of Princeton University from 1989 to 2007. Her research interests include cyber-physical systems, Internet-of-Things, embedded computing, embedded computer vision, and VLSI systems. She has received the IEEE Computer Society Harry Goode Memorial Award, the ASEE Terman Award, and IEEE Circuits and Systems Society Education Award. She is a Fellow of the IEEE and ACM.

*GLSVLSI '19, May 9–11, 2019, Tysons Corner, VA, USA.*

ACM ISBN 978-1-4503-6252-8/19/05.
DOI: https://doi.org/10.1145/3299874.3322802

# Automatic Implementation of Secure Silicon

Serge Leef
DARPA
Arlington, VA
serge.leef@darpa.mil

## ABSTRACT

Throughout the past decade, cybersecurity threats have evolved from attacks focused high in the software stack to progressively lower levels of computational hierarchy. With the explosion of popularity and growing deployment of internet connected devices, economic attackers and nation-states alike are shifting their attention to Application Specific Integrated Circuits (ASICs) that enable complex capabilities across commercial and military application domains. Despite growing recognition of the problem and a substantial body of research across multiple chip security areas, no common tools, methods or solutions are in wide use today. Modern synchronous digital ASICs are already very complex and expensive to design and incorporation of security is viewed as a burden with unclear economic benefits. The result is that the majority of today's ASICs are largely unprotected. Absence of automation makes incorporation of security a laborious, manual task that generally requires very specific design expertise not generally possessed by semiconductor companies. These dynamics can be altered with a novel chip design flow that aims to protect advanced ASICs from known attack strategies by streamlining inclusion of scalable defense mechanisms into an automated process that maximizes architectural exploration of security vs. economics trade-offs while improving design productivity. The effort and cost to incorporate a level of hardware security aligned with application requirements and economics will be significantly reduced so that incorporation of security at all levels of hardware design is feasible and affordable.

## Author Keywords

EDA, ASICs, SoC, Simulation, Synthesis, Security, Optimization.

## BIOGRAPHY

Mr. Serge Leef joined DARPA in August 2018 as a program manager in the Microsystems Technology Office (MTO). His research interests include computer architecture, simulation, synthesis, semiconductor intellectual property (IP), cyber-physical modeling, distributed systems, secure design flows, and supply chain management. He is also interested in the facilitation of startup ecosystems and business aspects of technology.

Leef came to DARPA from Mentor, a Siemens Business where from 2010 until 2018 he was a Vice President of New Ventures, responsible for identifying and developing technology and business opportunities in systems-oriented markets. Additionally, from 1999 to 2018, he served as a division General Manager, responsible for defining strategies and building successful businesses around design automation products in the areas of hardware/software co-design, multi-physics simulation, IP integration, SoC optimization, design data management, automotive/aerospace networking, cloud-based electronic design, Internet of Things (IoT) infrastructure, and hardware cybersecurity.

Prior to joining Mentor, he was responsible for design automation at Silicon Graphics, where he and his team created revolutionary, high-speed simulation tools to enable the design of high-speed 3D graphics chips, which defined the state-of-the-art in visualization, imaging, gaming, and special effects for a decade. Prior to that, he managed a CAE/CAD organization at Microchip and developed functional and physical design and verification tools for major 8- and 16-bit microcontroller and microprocessor programs at Intel.

Leef received his Bachelor of Science degree in electrical engineering and Master of Science degree in computer science from Arizona State University. He has served on corporate, state, and academic advisory boards, delivered numerous public speeches, and holds two patents.

*GLSVLSI '19, May 9–11, 2019, Tysons Corner, VA, USA.*

ACM ISBN 978-1-4503-6252-8/19/05.
DOI: https://doi.org/10.1145/3299874.3322803

# Processing Data Where It Makes Sense in Modern Computing Systems: Enabling In-Memory Computation

Onur Mutlu
ETH Zurich
Zurich, Switzerland
onur.mutlu@inf.ethz.ch

## ABSTRACT

Today's systems are overwhelmingly designed to move data to computation. This design choice goes directly against at least three key trends in systems that cause performance, scalability and energy bottlenecks: 1) data access from memory is already a key bottleneck as applications become more data-intensive and memory bandwidth and energy do not scale well, 2) energy consumption is a key constraint in especially mobile and server systems, 3) data movement is very expensive in terms of bandwidth, energy and latency, much more so than computation [1-3]. These trends are especially severely-felt in the data-intensive server and energy-constrained mobile systems of today.

At the same time, conventional memory technology is facing many scaling challenges in terms of reliability, energy, and performance [4-5]. As a result, memory system architects are open to organizing memory in different ways and making it more intelligent, at the expense of slightly higher cost. The emergence of 3D-stacked memory plus logic [6], the adoption of error correcting codes inside the latest DRAM chips [7-8], and intelligent memory controllers to solve the RowHammer problem [9-11] are an evidence of this trend.

In this talk, I will discuss some recent research that aims to practically enable computation close to data. After motivating trends in applications as well as technology, we will discuss at least two promising directions: 1) performing massively-parallel bulk operations in memory by exploiting the analog operational properties of DRAM, with low-cost changes [3, 12-14, 23], 2) exploiting the logic layer in 3D-stacked memory technology in various ways to accelerate important data-intensive applications [2, 15-22]. In both approaches, we will discuss relevant cross-layer research, design, and adoption challenges in devices, architecture, systems, applications, and programming models [1]. Our focus will be the development of in-memory processing designs that can be adopted in real computing platforms and real data-intensive applications, spanning machine learning, graph processing, data analytics, and genome analysis, at low cost [26]. If time permits, we will also discuss simulation and evaluation infrastructures that can enable exciting and forward-looking research in future memory systems, including Ramulator [24] and SoftMC [25].


*GLSVLSI '19, May 9–11, 2019, Tysons Corner, VA, USA.*

ACM ISBN 978-1-4503-6252-8/19/05.
https://doi.org/10.1145/3299874.3322805

## CCS Concepts/ACM Classifiers

• **General and reference~General literature** • Computer systems organization~Parallel architectures • Hardware~3D integrated circuits • Hardware~Semiconductor memory • Hardware~Emerging technologies

## Author Keywords

processing-in-memory; near-data processing; data movement; accelerators; memory systems; 3D-stacked memory; DRAM; analog computing; energy efficiency; virtual memory; cache coherence; computing paradigms

## BIOGRAPHY

Dr. Onur Mutlu is a Professor of Computer Science at ETH Zurich. He is also a faculty member at Carnegie Mellon University, where he previously held the Strecker Early Career Professorship. His current broader research interests are in computer architecture, systems, hardware security, and bioinformatics. A variety of techniques he, along with his group and collaborators, has invented over the years have influenced industry and have been employed in commercial microprocessors and memory/storage systems. He obtained his PhD and MS in ECE from the University of Texas at Austin and BS degrees in Computer Engineering and Psychology from the University of Michigan, Ann Arbor. He started the Computer Architecture Group at Microsoft Research (2006-2009), and held various product and research positions at Intel Corporation, Advanced Micro Devices, VMware, and Google. He received the inaugural IEEE Computer Society Young Computer Architect Award, the inaugural Intel Early Career Faculty Award, US National Science Foundation CAREER Award, Carnegie Mellon University Ladd Research Award, faculty partnership awards from various companies, and a healthy number of best paper or "Top Pick" paper recognitions at various computer systems, architecture, and hardware security venues. He is an ACM Fellow "for contributions to computer architecture research, especially in memory systems", IEEE Fellow for "contributions to computer architecture research and practice", and an elected member of the Academy of Europe (Academia Europaea). His computer architecture and digital circuit design course lectures and materials are freely available on YouTube, and his research group makes a wide variety of software and hardware artifacts freely available online. For more information, please see his webpage at https://people.inf.ethz.ch/omutlu/.

## REFERENCES


[1] Saugata Ghose et al., "Enabling the Adoption of Processing-in-Memory: Challenges, Mechanisms, Future Research Directions", Invited Book Chapter, 2019.

[2] Amirali Boroumand et al., "Google Workloads for Consumer Devices: Mitigating Data Movement Bottlenecks", ASPLOS 2018.

[3] Vivek Seshadri and Onur Mutlu, "Simple Operations in Memory to Reduce Data Movement", Invited Book Chapter in *Advances in Computers*, 2018.

[4] Onur Mutlu, "Memory Scaling: A Systems Architecture Perspective", IMW 2013.

[5] Onur Mutlu and Lavanya Subramanian, "Research Problems and Opportunities in Memory Systems", SUPERFRI 2015.

[6] Donghyuk Lee et al., "Simultaneous Multi-Layer Access: Improving 3D-Stacked Memory Bandwidth at Low Cost", ACM TACO 2016.

[7] Uksong Kang, et al., "Co-Architecting Controllers and DRAM to Enhance DRAM Process Scaling", Memory Forum 2014.

[8] Minesh Patel et al., "Understanding and Modeling On-Die Error Correction in Modern DRAM: An Experimental Study Using Real Devices", DSN 2019.

[9] Yoongu Kim et al., "Flipping Bits in Memory Without Accessing Them: An Experimental Study of DRAM Disturbance Errors", ISCA 2014.

[10] Onur Mutlu, "The RowHammer Problem and Other Issues We May Face as Memory Becomes Denser", DATE 2017.

[11] Onur Mutlu and Jeremie S. Kim, "RowHammer: A Retrospective", IEEE TCAD 2019.

[12] Vivek Seshadri et al., "RowClone: Fast and Energy-Efficient In-DRAM Bulk Data Copy and Initialization", MICRO 2013.

[13] Vivek Seshadri et al., "Fast Bulk Bitwise AND and OR in DRAM", IEEE CAL 2015.

[14] Vivek Seshadri et al., "Ambit: In-Memory Accelerator for Bulk Bitwise Operations Using Commodity DRAM Technology", MICRO 2017.

[15] Junwhan Ahn et al., "A Scalable Processing-in-Memory Accelerator for Parallel Graph Processing" ISCA 2015.

[16] Junwhan Ahn et al., "PIM-Enabled Instructions: A Low-Overhead Locality-Aware Processing-in-Memory Architecture", ISCA 2015.

[17] Kevin Hsieh et al., "Accelerating Pointer Chasing in 3D-Stacked Memory: Challenges, Mechanisms, Evaluation", ICCD 2016.

[18] Kevin Hsieh et al., "Transparent Offloading and Mapping (TOM): Enabling Programmer-Transparent Near-Data Processing in GPU Systems", ISCA 2016.

[19] Jeremie S. Kim et al., "GRIM-Filter: Fast Seed Location Filtering in DNA Read Mapping Using Processing-in-Memory Technologies", BMC Genomics 2018.

[20] Amirali Boroumand et al., "LazyPIM: An Efficient Cache Coherence Mechanism for Processing-in-Memory", IEEE CAL 2017.

[21] Amirali Boroumand et al., "CoNDA: Enabling Efficient Near-Data Accelerator Communication by Optimizing Data Movement", ISCA 2019.

[22] Ashutosh Pattnaik et al., "Scheduling Techniques for GPU Architectures with Processing-In-Memory Capabilities", PACT 2016.

[23] Kevin Chang et al., "Low-Cost Inter-Linked Subarrays (LISA): Enabling Fast Inter-Subarray Data Movement in DRAM", HPCA 2016.

[24] Yoongu Kim, Weikun Yang, and Onur Mutlu, "Ramulator: A Fast and Extensible DRAM Simulator", IEEE CAL 2016.

[25] Hasan Hassan et al., "SoftMC: A Flexible and Practical Open-Source Infrastructure for Enabling Experimental DRAM Studies", HPCA 2018.

[26] Onur Mutlu et al., "Processing Data Where It Make Sense: Enabling In-Memory Computation", MICPRO 2019.

# Innovations in IoT for a Safe, Secure, and Sustainable Future

Swarup Bhunia, PhD
University of Florida, Gainesville, FL, USA
swarup@ece.ufl.edu

## ABSTRACT

Internet of things (IoT) promises to usher in the fourth industrial revolution through an exponential growth of smart connected devices deployed in myriad application domains. It gives rise to new relationships between man and smart connected machines that might transform our everyday experiences. Such a transformation, however, builds on innovations at all levels in the IoT architecture – from edge devices to the cloud. In this talk, we will cover the IoT design practices and core technological challenges that need to be addressed to enable wide-spread deployment of IoT. We will focus on innovations in the areas of energy-efficiency, security, interoperability and intelligent decision making. Next, we will discuss several compelling applications of IoT that gives unprecedented capability to us. In particular, we will cover applications of IoT in addressing some of the critical safety, security, and sustainability issues in our society.

## Author Keywords

Keynote Talk


*GLSVLSI '19, May 9–11, 2019, Tysons Corner, VA, USA.*

ACM ISBN 978-1-4503-6252-8/19/05.
DOI: https://doi.org/10.1145/3299874.3322806

# Innovations in IoT for a Safe, Secure, and Sustainable Future

# LPN-based Device Authentication Using Resistive Memory

Md Tanvir Arafin
ECE Department
College Park, Maryland
marafin@umd.edu

Haoting Shen
ECE Department
Gainesville, Florida
htshen@ece.ufl.edu

Mark M. Tehranipoor
ECE Department
Gainesville, Florida
tehranipoor@ece.ufl.edu

Gang Qu
ECE Department
College Park, Maryland
gangqu@umd.edu

## ABSTRACT

Recent progress in the design and implementation of resistive memory components such as RRAMs and PCMs has introduced opportunities for developing novel hardware security solutions using unique physical properties of these devices. In this work, we utilize the faults in HfOx-based resistive RRAMs to design secure, lightweight device authentication protocols. To detail our design, first, we introduce the device breakdown problem due to high bias conditions in resistive memory and the physics behind non-recoverable resistive states. Then, using the concepts of learning with parity noise (LPN) based authentication protocols, we demonstrate that simple READ and WRITE operations on resistive memory cells with defects can perform necessary calculation required for LPN-based authentication schemes. Next, we design two simple authentication protocols using resistive memory based hardware and provide a detailed security analysis for these protocols. We find that these authentication mechanisms can offer significant improvement against its CMOS counterpart regarding the area and power budget. Finally, we provide detailed physical design requirements for the memory components. The resistive memory components that are capable of performing the proposed authentication protocols have also been designed and fabricated. From our analysis, we find that these memory dependent authentication protocols are lightweight, resistant to learning attacks from active and passive adversaries, and reliable under normal changes in operating conditions.

## CCS CONCEPTS

• **Security and privacy → Hardware-based security protocols.**

## KEYWORDS

Resistive Random Access Memory (RRAM), Learning Parity in the Presence of Noise (LPN), One-time Writable Memory, Device Authentication.



*GLSVLSI '19, May 9–11, 2019, Tysons Corner, VA, USA*

ACM ISBN 978-1-4503-6252-8/19/05...$15.00
https://doi.org/10.1145/3299874.3317970

**ACM Reference Format:**
Md Tanvir Arafin, Haoting Shen, Mark M. Tehranipoor, and Gang Qu. 2019. LPN-based Device Authentication Using Resistive Memory. In *Great Lakes Symposium on VLSI 2019 (GLSVLSI '19), May 9–11, 2019, Tysons Corner, VA, USA.* ACM, New York, NY, USA, 6 pages. https://doi.org/10.1145/3299874.3317970

## 1 INTRODUCTION

Resistive memory primitives such as phase change memory (PCM), resistive random access memory (RRAM) and memristors promises a significant breakthrough in next-generation computing by replacing volatile DRAMs with faster non-volatile main memory components. High speed, simple device geometry, high density, large ON/OFF ratio, low-power of operation, in-memory computation capability, and application in neuromorphic computation are driving current research in improving the yield, reliability, and fabrication of existing resistive memory designs. Non-volatile memory elements also offer unique physical properties useful in designing next-generation hardware dependent security primitives. Such hardware-based security and trust designs can provide low-power yet provably secure cryptographic schemes essential for progressing towards next-generation Internet-of-trusted-things.

Modern efforts on the design and implementation of the Internet-of-things (IoT) envision a future of wide-scale deployment of interconnected smart objects. Intelligence in such network of *things* is derived from observations made using a large number of end-node components such as sensors and data collection hardware. The computation power is mostly budgeted for information acquisition and communication, and security is often an afterthought for these end-node components. Common cryptographic protocols usually require a substantial amount of energy, and thus, become prohibitive for most of the resource-constrained devices. Therefore, the IoT infrastructure remains dependent on a large number of untrusted, insecure components that jeopardize the security of the entire network [19].

One of the primary challenges in securing low-power end-nodes in IoT is authenticating the devices used for data acquisition. In this work, we develop solutions for secure authentication of low-power devices using resistive memory components and cryptographic primitives derived from learning parity in the presence of noise (LPN) problems. LPN-based authentication protocols were first proposed by Hopper and Blum [10] that inspired further investigation of the hardness of LPN-problems, and design of authentication protocols effective against active and passive attackers [4, 16]. One attractive feature of LPN-based techniques is that they require straightforward computation. For example, the Hopper and Blum (HB) authentication protocol [10] and its derivatives HB+, HB++, *etc* discussed in [5, 14, 16] require only vector inner-product calculation, parity computation, and counting operation. Thus, LPN-based protocols can offer lightweight authentication solutions with provable security even in a post-quantum scenario. However, in extreme resource-constrained system, such protocols need to be optimized and redesigned to balance achievable security and the power-budget. This work presents research on optimized implementation of LPN-based shared-key authentication using the resistive memory components of a system. The main contributions of this work are detailed below:

(1) We study the breakdown mechanisms of resistive memory components in section 2 and explore the opportunity of intentionally introducing device failure for secure key storage.
(2) We demonstrate a non-conventional method of purposefully corrupting (one-time) memory components in designing LPN-based device authentication scheme in Section 3.
(3) We present fabrication and design details of resistive memory components capable of executing the authentication protocols presented in this work in section 4, and discuss the security analysis, opportunities and implementation challenges of these protocols in section 5.

It should be noted that the authentication scheme presented in this work apply not only to resistive memory primitives but also to any other memory technologies that can support the coexistence of one-time programmable components in the memory systems.

## 2 PHYSICS OF RESISTIVE MEMORY

Changes in the resistive states in memories such as RRAMs depend on the conductive filament formation in the metal-oxide thin films. These devices have a simple metal-insulator-metal (MIM) structure, with nanometer-thin metal-oxide layer within the top and bottom metal electrode.

### 2.1 Device Model

The current-voltage relation of an RRAM is determined by - (1) the internal state variable $g$ that represents the spatial distance between the conductive filament in the oxide and the metal boundary, and (2) the electron tunneling in metal-insulator boundary. The analytical model of the thin-film evolution in a $HfO_x$-based RRAM can be described using the following equation as [8]:

$$\frac{dg}{dt} = v_0 e^{-Ea,m/kT} sinh(\frac{qa\gamma V}{LkT}) \quad (1)$$

where , $q$ is the electron charge, $L$ is the device filament thickness, $V$ is the applied voltage, $T$ is the device temperature, $Ea, m, \gamma, v_0$ are device dependent physical parameters. Then, the current-voltage relationship is given by [8]:

$$I(g, V) = I_0 e^{-g/g_0} sinh(\frac{V}{V_0}) \quad (2)$$

where $I_0, V_0, g_0$ are device dependent physical parameters. For this work, we assume the binary memory operation of a resistive memory unit, *i.e.,* it can stay in a high resistive state (HRS) or a low resistive state (LRS). This state transition is determined by the conductive filament formation in the oxide and metal boundary.

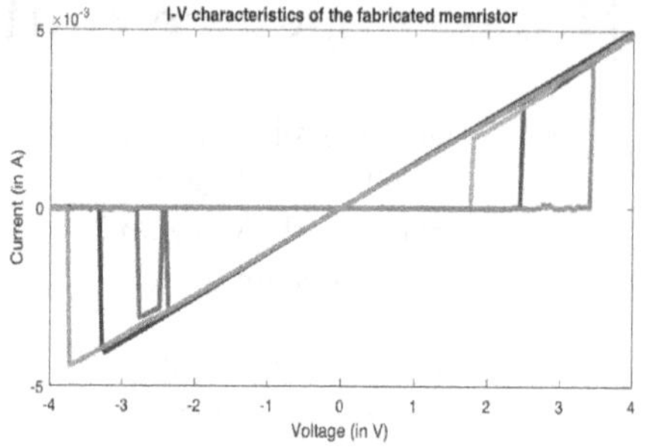


**Figure 1: Sample I-V curve of the fabricated memristor. Multiple READ-WRITE cycle of the memristor is provided. The violet, sky-blue and red lines represent a LRS to HRS transition when the voltage across a memristor at a low resistive state is varied from +4 to -4V. The green, yellow and dark-blue lines represent a HRS to LRS transition when the voltage across a memristor at a high resistive state is varied from -4 to +4V. Normal operating condition demonstrates the unbalanced SET-RESET voltage at around ±3*V*.**

### 2.2 Device Failure

From section 2.1 it is evident that RRAMs exhibit resistive switching and non-volatility due to the reversible nature of the conductive filament formation in the insulator film. High voltage biasing can break this reversible process and put the device in a fixed resistive state. Recent studies in Pt/TiOx/Pt/Cr-based devices suggest that such failure occurs due to either electrical or thermally assisted dielectric breakdown [6]. Experimental evidence of full crystallization oxide along with intrusion of the electrode metal (Pt) into the insulator layer has been found in the non-programmable RRAM devices [6]. It is evident that electrical or local thermal stressing of the insulator layer irreversibly breaks the programming properties of this devices [17]. This breakdown can be viewed as hard-failures of the memory elements. In this work, we utilize intentional high-voltage biasing to set a device in a non-recoverable resistive state.

Another mode of failure can occur due to the unbalanced SET-RESET operation of the resistive memories. Unbalanced SET-RESET causes accumulation (or depletion) of conductive filaments, and after multiple cycles, the devices gets stuck in a low (or high) resistive state. These failures are reversible in a sense that sufficient high voltage biases or current flow can *cure* the device by depleting (or accumulating) the conductive filaments. However, if there is no hardware support for *curing* the devices (*i.e.,* balancing the SET/RESET operation) in practice, the devices become non-programmable after a certain number of SET-RESET operation.

We have observed both modes of failure in an $HfO_x$-based memory unit as shown in Figure 1 and 2. Cycle-to-cycle variation in the SET-RESET voltage illustrates the need for proper READ/WRITE balancing for correctly writing a device to an HRS or LRS. Furthermore, Figure 2 depicts the irreversible hard-breakdown of the memory cell at a high RESET voltage applied with faster RESET time. After the hard breakdown, the device is stuck at the high resistive state. Further switching back has not been observed with SET voltages as large as 40V with 10mA currents through the device for multiple cycles. This represents a permanent breakdown of the reversible state-transition mechanism for the device.

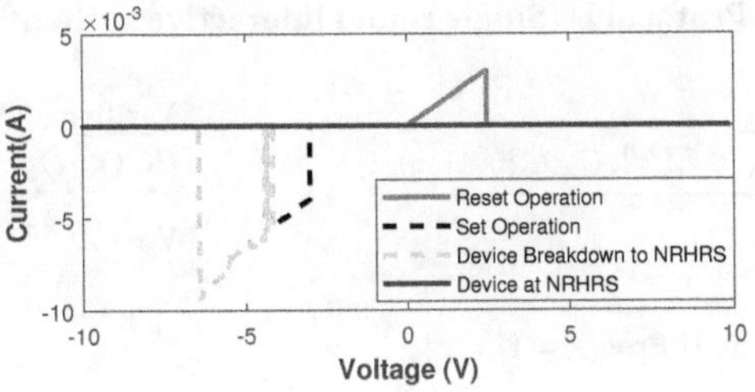


**Figure 2: Sample I-V curve for the SET/RESET operation and hard breakdown of the fabricated RRAM for this work. Hard dielectric breakdown occurs for the device when a larger RESET voltage with fast ramping is applied along the devices. After the breakdown, the device becomes incapable of switching to LRS even with larger SET voltages.**

# 3 AUTHENTICATION PROTOCOL DESIGN

## 3.1 Notations

In this work, the set of integers modulo an integer $q \geq 1$ is denoted by $\mathbb{Z}_q$. Matrices, vectors, and single elements over $\mathbb{Z}_q$ are represented by consecutively upper case bold letter, lower case bold letters and lower case letters such as $\mathbf{X}$, $\mathbf{x}$ and $x$. For a vector $\mathbf{x}$, the length of the vector is denoted by $|\mathbf{x}|$, $i^{th}$ element is represented by $\mathbf{x}[i]$ and $wt(\mathbf{x})$ denotes the Hamming weight (*i.e.,* the number of indices for which $\mathbf{x}[i] \neq 0$ ) of the vector $\mathbf{x}$. The Hamming distance between two binary matrices are denoted by $hd(\mathbf{A}, \mathbf{B})$ (i.e., the number of indices for which $\mathbf{A}[i][j] \neq \mathbf{B}[i][j]$). $hdp(\mathbf{A}, \mathbf{B})$ represents the parity of $hd(\mathbf{A}, \mathbf{B})$ (i.e, $hdp(\mathbf{A}, \mathbf{B}) = 0$ for even parity of $hd(\mathbf{A}, \mathbf{B})$ and $hdp(\mathbf{A}, \mathbf{B}) = 1$ for odd parity of $hd(\mathbf{A}, \mathbf{B})$). $\mathbf{0}^{\ell \times n}$ represents a $\ell \times n$ null matrix. The Hadamard product of two matrices $\mathbf{A}, \mathbf{B}$ is given by $\langle A \circ B \rangle$. Given two vectors $\mathbf{x}$ and $\mathbf{y}$, $\mathbf{z} = \mathbf{x} \oplus \mathbf{y}$ represents bitwise XOR operation of $\mathbf{x}$ and $\mathbf{y}$. $c \xleftarrow{\$} \{\mathbf{x} \in \mathbb{Z}\}$ represents a random sampling of $\mathbf{x}$. We denote *probabilistic polynomial time* (PPT) algorithms with upper case calligraphic alphabets such as $\mathcal{A}$. All the physical quantities such as voltage, current and device names are denoted with upper case letters.

## 3.2 Assumptions

Recent works have demonstrated that resistive memory hardware can assist simple authentication and secure key storage facilitates [1, 2]. To harness this potential, we present two learning parity in the presence of noise based authentication schemes that is provably secure against passive attacks. These schemes are derived from the Hopper and Blum (HB) authentication protocol that provides simple yet efficient authentication from hard learning problems [10, 16]. For our authentication protocol design, we will assume that an RRAM can be put into a non-recoverable high resistive state (NRHRS) using high current flow through the device as shown in Figure 2.

**Theorem 1**: Writing one bit to an RRAM, where the physical state of the RRAM can be either writable or NRHRS, is the same as performing the 2-input logic AND operation.

Proof: Assume that an RRAM in a high resistive state represents the storage of a binary '0' and the low resistive state represents '1', and the physical state describing whether the RRAM can be written is denoted by $y$ (*i.e.,* $y = 1$ meaning there will be successful state change if the data to be written is 1, $y = 0$ means there will not be a state change and the RRAM will stay at NRHRS). The existence of nor-recoverable high resistive state ensures that there will be RRAMs with $y = 0$. Then, if the incoming bit is represented by $x$ and the actual value stored after the WRITE operation is $z$, one can draw the truth table as shown in Table 1 From the truth table, it is evident that, $z = x \wedge y$.

**Table 1: Truth table describing the relation between the resistive state and the data stored**

| $x$ (Incoming Bit) | $y$ (Resistive State) | $z$ (Memory Content ) |
|---|---|---|
| 0 | 0(NRHRS) | 0 |
| 0 | 1(Writeable) | 0 |
| 1 | 0(NRHRS) | 0 |
| 1 | 1(Writeable) | 1 |

For device authentication protocols discussed in this work, we will also assume an interactive protocol between a single prover $\mathcal{P}$ (*i.e.,* the device) and a verifier $\mathcal{V}$. Both the prover and the verifier has some knowledge about a shared secret $\mathbf{x}$. The secret is generated through a key-generation procedure $KeyGen(1^\lambda)$,where $\lambda$ is a security parameter. The authentication protocol responds with the outputs accept or reject after a successful run of the protocol.

## 3.3 Description of Protocol I

The protocol uses an RRAM crossbar $M$ of size $\ell \times n$. The secret $\mathbf{X} \in \mathbb{Z}_2^{\ell \times n}$ for authentication is distributed using Algorithm 1. For authentication, multiple round of interactive authentication (as presented in table 2) is performed.

**Algorithm 1** Key Generation and Storage in RRAM Crossbar for LPN based Authentication

**procedure** $\mathbf{X} \leftarrow KeyGen(1^\lambda)$
  Sample $\mathbf{X} \xleftarrow{\$} \mathbb{Z}_2^{\ell \times n}$
  **return** $\mathbf{X}$
**end procedure**
**procedure** $KeyStorage(\mathbf{X})$
  **for all** $i \in \{1, \ldots, \ell\}$ **do**
    **for all** $j \in \{1, \ldots, n\}$ **do**
      **if** $\mathbf{X}[i][j] = 0$ **then, RESET** $M[i][j]$ to NRHRS.
      **end if**
    **end for**
  **end for**
**end procedure**

**Enrollment:** The verifier saves $\mathbf{X}$ for later authentication, the prover keeps the crossbar $M$, that is the device ultimately contains the crossbar for later authentication.

**Verification** The authentication is performed in $t$ rounds. The verifier finally authenticates the device if the response of the prover was wrong for fewer than $t\tau$ times.

## 3.4 Reduction of Protocol I to an LPN-problem

Hopper and Blum first proposed a simple authentication protocol (HB) [10] using the learning parity in the presence of noise (LPN) problem. The authentication protocol described in table 2 can be derived from the HB protocol. The reduction of Protocol I to an LPN problem is discussed below:

**Table 2: Protocol I: Single round interactive authentication**

| Prover($M, \tau$) | | Verifier(X) |
|---|---|---|
| | | $\mathbf{R} \xleftarrow{\$} \mathbb{Z}_2^{\ell \times n}$ |
| | $\xleftarrow{\mathbf{R}}$ | |
| $- e \in \{0, 1 \| Prob[e = 1] = \tau\}$<br>– Write **R** in $M$ using the following scheme:<br>If **R**$[i][j]$=0, **RESET** $M[i][j]$;<br>else **SET** $M[i][j]$<br>– Read back the corrupted value C from $M$ using the following scheme:<br>If $M[i][j]$=HRS, C$[i][j] = 0$<br>else C$[i][j] = 1$<br>$- z := e \oplus hdp(\mathbf{C}, \mathbf{0}^{\ell \times n})$ | | |
| | $\xrightarrow{z}$ | |
| | | $-\mathbf{P} = \langle \mathbf{R} \circ \mathbf{X} \rangle$<br>–If $z = hdp(\mathbf{P}, \mathbf{0}^{\ell \times n})$<br>accept |

**Definition 1 (LPN Problem)** Assume $\tau \in \mathbb{R}$ is a constant noise parameter where $0 < \tau < 0.5$, $t \in \mathbb{N}$ is the number of samples, **e** is a random binary vector such that $\mathbf{e} \xleftarrow{\$} \{\mathbf{x} \in \mathbb{Z}_2^t : wt(\mathbf{x}) \leq \tau t\}$ and **s** be a $\ell$-bit binary vector (i.e., $\mathbf{s} \xleftarrow{\$} \mathbb{Z}_2^{\ell}$). Given a random binary matrix $\mathbf{R} \xleftarrow{\$} \mathbb{Z}_2^{t \times \ell}$, and $\mathbf{z} = \langle \mathbf{R}, \mathbf{s} \rangle \oplus \mathbf{e}$, find an $\ell$-bit vector $\mathbf{x}'$ such that $wt(\langle \mathbf{R}, \mathbf{x}' \rangle \oplus \mathbf{z}) \leq \tau t$.

**Theorem 2** Assume $\mathbf{r} = vec(\mathbf{R})$ denotes vectorization operation that generates a vector $\mathbf{r} \in \mathbb{Z}_2$ of a matrix **R**. Then, the $hdp()$ calculation by the prover $\mathcal{P}$ returns the parity of $\langle \mathbf{r}, \mathbf{s} \rangle$ where $\mathbf{r} = vec(\mathbf{R})$, $\mathbf{s} = vec(\mathbf{S})$, **R** is the random challenge sent by the verifier and **S** is the matrix representing the writabilty of each RRAM in the crossbar (i.e., if $\mathbf{S}[i][j] = 0$, $M[i][j]$ is at NRHRS).

Proof: From Theorem 1, we can see that, after a writing operation the memory crossbar contains the corrupted value **C** which is equal to the binary Hadamard product of **R** and the physical state (S) of the crossbar (i.e., $\mathbf{C} = \langle \mathbf{R} \circ \mathbf{S} \rangle$). Then, if we consider $\mathbf{c} = vec(\mathbf{C})$, $\sum_i \mathbf{c}[i] \bmod 2$ will be equal to the inner product of **r** and **s** (i.e., $\sum_i \mathbf{c}[i] \bmod 2 = \langle \mathbf{r}, \mathbf{s} \rangle$). Since $hdp(\mathbf{C}, \mathbf{0})$ defines the parity of the Hamming distance between **C** and **0**, it effectively calculates the parity of the Hamming weight of **c** which is equal to $\sum_i \mathbf{c}[i] \bmod 2$. Therefore, $hdp(\mathbf{C}, \mathbf{0}) = \langle \mathbf{r}, \mathbf{s} \rangle$.

From theorem 2, it is evident that XORing an error $e$ to the response of the prover ($hdp(\mathbf{C}, \mathbf{0})$), one can construct an LPN problem with the shared secret **S** representing the physical state matrix of an RRAM crossbar as shown in the authentication protocol at table 2 .

We have shown that, Protocol I is secure against passive attackers in the Discussions section. However, an active adversary who pretends to be the verifier and provides chosen adaptive non-random **R** can learn the secret using polynomial time algorithms presented in [13]. Thus, the protocol I is insecure against active attacks. So, we improved the protocol in a similar fashion proposed at [16] in Table 3.

**Table 3: Protocol I+: Single round interactive authentication**

| Prover<br>($M, \mathbf{Q_v} \in \mathbb{Z}_2^{\ell \times n}, Q_z \in \{0,1\}, \tau$) | | Verifier<br>($\mathbf{X}, \mathbf{Q_v}, Q_z$) |
|---|---|---|
| | | $\mathbf{V} \xleftarrow{\$} \mathbb{Z}_2^{\ell \times n}$ |
| | $\xleftarrow{\mathbf{V}}$ | |
| $- e \in \{0, 1 \| Prob[e = 1] = \tau\}$<br>$- \mathbf{R} \xleftarrow{\$} \mathbb{Z}_2^{\ell \times n}$<br>$- \mathbf{Y} = \mathbf{Q_v} \oplus \mathbf{V}$<br>– Write **R** in $M$ using the following scheme:<br>If **R**$[i][j]$=0, **RESET** $M[i][j]$;<br>else **SET** $M[i][j]$<br>– Write **Y** in $M$<br>– Read back the corrupted value C from $M$:<br>If $M[i][j]$=HRS, C$[i][j] = 0$<br>else C$[i][j] = 1$<br>$- z := Q_z \oplus e \oplus hdp(\mathbf{C}, \mathbf{0}^{\ell \times n})$ | | |
| | $\xrightarrow{(z, \mathbf{R})}$ | |
| | | $-\mathbf{Y}' = \mathbf{Q_v} \oplus \mathbf{V}$<br>$-\mathbf{P} = \langle \mathbf{R} \circ \langle \mathbf{X} \circ \mathbf{Y}' \rangle \rangle$<br>–If $z = Q_z \oplus hdp(\mathbf{P}, \mathbf{0}^{\ell \times n})$<br>accept |

## 3.5 Description of Protocol I+

**Enrollment:** The prover and the verifier both shares additional information $\mathbf{Q_v} \xleftarrow{\$} \mathbb{Z}_2^{\ell \times n}, Q_z \in \{0, 1\}$ in the enrollment phase.

**Verification** The protocol is executed in $t$ rounds. The verifier finally authenticates the device if the response of the prover was wrong for fewer than $t\tau$ times.

# 4 HARDWARE DESIGN

The authentication scheme discussed in the previous section uses an $\ell \times n$ RRAM crossbar $M$. The key-storing process described by the procedure $KeyStorage(\mathbf{X})$ puts the RRAM element $M[i][j]$ to NRHRS for $\mathbf{X}[i][j] = 0$. This operation makes later LPN-based computation simpler to achieve with the resistive memory hardware. Experimentation on intentional device failure is performed using fabricated RRAM devices. The details of the fabrication for the *HfOx* based resistive memory components used for the experimental results presented in section 2.2 is given next.

## 4.1 Fabrication Details

The fabrication is performed on oxide cover Si wafer. The first metal layer (bottom) is prepared by lift-off photo-lithography processing, including Chromium (Cr, 10 nm), copper (Cu, 100 nm) and platinum (Pt, 10 nm) deposited subsequently, serving as the adhesion, conducting, and interface adjusting layer, respectively. Then, $HfO_2$ (10 nm) is coated by atomic layer deposition (ALD) at 200 °C. After that, the second metal layer (top) is prepared by lift-off again, including Pt (10 nm) and Cu (100 nm), serving as interface adjusting and conducting layer, respectively.

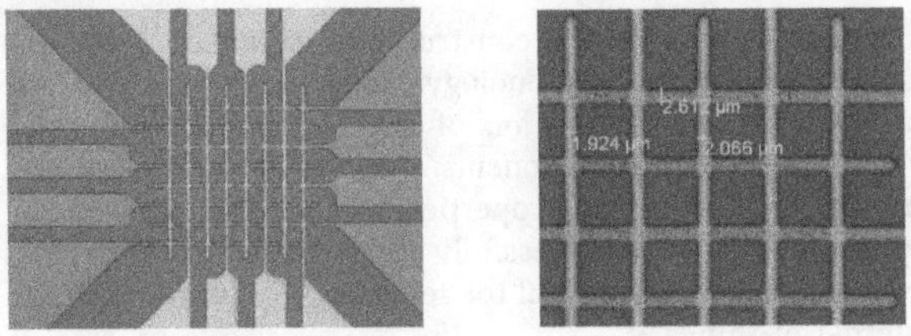

**Figure 3: Fabricated memristor and its dimensions. The top (light colored) and bottom (dark colored) electrode are seen as the gray crossbars. The width of the top and bottom crossbars are $2\mu m$ on average. In between the top and bottom crossbars, a 10 nm thin film of $HfO_x$ is deposited using atomic layer deposition.**

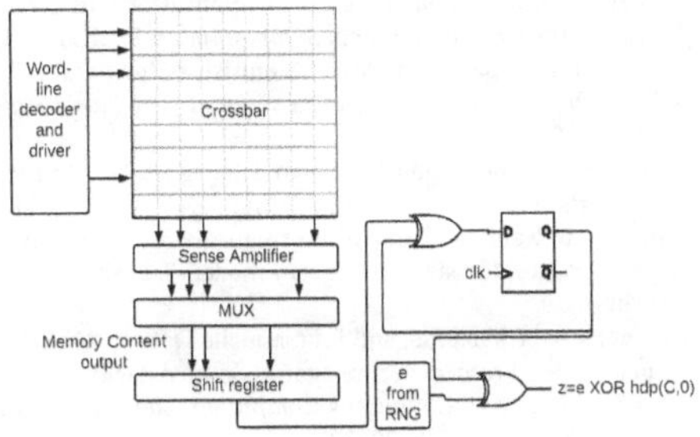


**Figure 4: Structure of RRAM crossbar with additional hardware for LPN-based authentication.**

## 4.2 Supporting Hardware

Protocol I is an extremely lightweight protocol that only requires the prover to calculate *hdp*() function and generate biased random number with a given $\tau$. Since, the READ/WRITE mechanism is fundamental to the memory systems, therefore, the driver design for READ/WRITE is trivial. The *hdp*() calculation can be supported in software, or can be implemented in hardware where *hdp*() function can easily be calculated using a finite state machine built with an $\ell$-bit shift register, a D-flip-flop and a two input XOR gate as shown in Figure 4.

Additionally, there have been several resistive memory-based true RNGs reported in the current literature [11, 12] that have passed NIST's RNG test-suites. These designs depend on the random resistance fluctuation of the memory elements. A construction of a biased-RNG with a fixed $\tau$ is given in Figure 5. It should be noted that, the sampling of $e$ in the protocols can also be performed in software where the system contains a TRNG source.

# 5 DISCUSSIONS

From our experiments with the fabricated devices and hardware design, we observe that the proposed LPN-based authentication schemes can be optimally implemented using the one-time programmable properties of resistive memory components. In this section, we discuss the physical implication of the design and our experimental observations.

## 5.1 Security Analysis

Protocol I is secure against random guessing attacks. It can be seen that for a single round of operation, a random guess on $z$

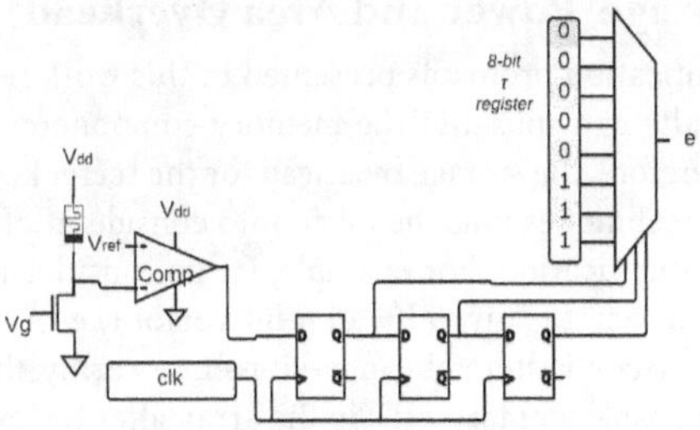


**Figure 5: Implementation of a biased RNG with $\tau = 3/8$. The value of $\tau$ is fixed by modifying the values of the $\tau$-register.**

has a probability of (1/2) to be correct. As the number of rounds $t$ increases, the chance of success (for correctly answering $z$) becomes $(1/2)^t \sum_{j=(1-\tau)t}^{t} \binom{t}{j} \leq e^{-t(3-2\tau)^2/6}$. Thus, the success of random guessing attack diminishes exponentially for Protocol I.

Furthermore, protocol I is secure against passive attackers, Let us assume that an attacker ($\mathcal{A}$) tries to learn the secret **X** by eavesdropping (**R**, $z$) over multiple rounds. It is shown in Section 3 that this learning problem for the attacker can be reduced to an LPN problem. LPN is an NP-hard problem [9], and it has been shown that in statistical query model, parity is not efficiently learnable in the random case [15]. The LPN problem is also known as the Syndrome decoding problem that tries to find the closest vector to a random linear error-correcting code, which is believed to be exponentially hard[3]. For $\tau > 0$, the BKW algorithm described in [4] gives a subexponential time algorithm that solves the LPN problem in $2^{O(\ell/log\ell)}$ time. Optimized implementation modified the BKW algorithm reported at [7] demonstrates how the efficient computation required for breaking LPN problems are memory-bounded, and it required about 15 days to solve for LPN instances with key-size $k = 243$ and $\tau = 1/4$. With $k \geq 790$ and $\tau = 1/4$ LPN can achieve 256-bit security on classical computers and 162-bit security on quantum computers with memory constrained to $2^{80}$-bits [7] which is sufficient for achieving NIST's post quantum call for security [18].

Protocol I+ also requires a solution for the LPN problem, and thus, it remains secure for random guessing attack and attacks from the passive adversaries with only eavesdropping capabilities. Therefore, let us assume an active attacker $\mathcal{A}$ who can query the prover $\mathcal{P}$ multiple times to learn about the shared secret, and then correctly answers the verifier $\mathcal{V}$ with finite probability $\epsilon$. Then to break protocol I+, the attacker needs to solve for **X**, $\mathbf{Q_V}$, and $Q_z$ with given instances of **V**, **R**, $z$. This requires the attacker solving for **P**. However, **Y**′ sample the random challenge **V** using $\mathbf{Q_V}$ and use this for computing **P**. Hence, solving for **P** and **X** essentially reduced to solving subset-LPN (SLPN) problem which is also a hard problem. Furthermore, since a chosen cipher-text by $\mathcal{A}$ always sampled using $\mathbf{Q_V}$ and the prover has control over the randomness of **R**, the overall response of each queries from an honest provider will not leak any information about the secret **X**. A detailed proof of security of such SLPN-based authentication can be found in [16]. Since the protocol does not leak any information about the secret even in chosen-ciphertext attacks, the protocol is secure against both active and passive attackers.

## 5.2 Storage, Power and Area Overhead

The authentication protocols presented in this work requires permanent faults in a subset of the memory components of a given device. Therefore, the storage overhead for the secret key and error correction techniques must be taken into consideration in designing this authentication. For example, let us consider in protocol I, the shared secret is given by an $n$-bit vector (*i.e.,* $n \times 1$ matrix). Then, if this secret is stored in an $m$-bit memory array, there will be $(m-n)$-bit usable memory cells in the array after the execution of Algorithm 1. However, as noted in the previous subsection, a key-length $n = 790$-bits can provide sufficiently secure implementation, and therefore, the storage overhead for the implementation will be extremely low on practical systems. Furthermore, the $(m-n)$-bit usable memory cell occurs in the worst case situation when all the secure bits are 0, requiring all $n$ -memory location to be set to NRHRS. However, on average $(n/2)$- memory location will be in writable state and additional $n/4$ memory location will contain a correct data. Thus, in average cases $(m-n/4)$-bits can be correctly stored in the an $m$-bit memory array. As $m$ grows, the adverse effect of the length of secret-key size $n$ diminishes for regular memory operations. If the system allows for approximate memory, with small memory error acceptance, then, one-time writing based key storage essentially would have zero overhead.

The main contribution in power consumption for protocol I and I+ comes from the writing operation of the resistive memory component. In practice, the WRITE operation requires significantly larger power than the READ operation ($E_{READ} \approx 1-5nJ$, whereas $E_{WRITE} \approx 10-20nJ$) [20]. Fabricated RRAMs reported in this work also shows similar properties, however, the READ/WRITE power are a magnitude larger due to the thicker filament, and larger low resistive state ( $1k\Omega$). Therefore, for $t$-rounds, the approximate energy consumption for the protocols would be $tE_{Write} + tE_{peripheral}$.

The proposed design is compact due to it's application of cross-point structure for memory design. The crossbar is controlled by external driver circuit, and thus, the area overhead is contributed mainly from the control circuits. If we assume that the crossbar is primarily used for memory operation, then from the hardware design in Section 4.2, it can be seen that the only area overhead results from the additional shift-register and D-filp-flops. Given the complete area requirement for the crosspoint memory driver circuits, the additional hardware requires a very small area overhead.

## 5.3 Noise Tolerance

It should be noted that, the authentication protocols relies on the correct memory operation of the underlying RRAM devices used for storing th secret key. Physical variation due to biasing, temperature *etc.* will not affect the authentication techniques as long as these variation does not push the RRAMs to the non-recoverable resistive state. On the other-hand, permanent fault due to aging or improper SET/RESET operation will lead a failure of the device authentication technique. However, it should be noted that, this is a trivial condition for strong security constructs where a single bit-flip should render the secure key void.

# 6 CONCLUSIONS

In this work, we have presented a secure and lightweight application of LPN-based device authentication technique in resistive memory based hardware. The constructs discussed are not bound only to the RRAM memory technology, rather, it is applicable in any memory system containing a mix of one-time and multiple-time programmable memory components. We have demonstrated that, integrating simple physical properties in simple yet secure cryptographic technique can successfully yield extremely lightweight authentication solutions useful for securing low-power nodes in the Internet-of-things.

# 7 ACKNOWLEDGMENT

This work was supported by AFOSR MURI under award number FA9550-14-1-0351. We also thank the reviewers for their valuable comments and feedback.

# REFERENCES

[1] Md Tanvir Arafin, Carson Dunbar, Gang Qu, N McDonald, and L Yan. 2015. A survey on memristor modeling and security applications. In *Quality Electronic Design (ISQED), 2015 16th International Symposium on.* IEEE, 440–447.

[2] Md Tanvir Arafin and Gang Qu. 2018. Memristors for Secret Sharing-Based Lightweight Authentication. *IEEE Transactions on Very Large Scale Integration (VLSI) Systems* 99 (2018), 1–13.

[3] ER Berlekamp, RJ McEliece, and HCA van Tilborg. 1978. On the inherent intractability of certain coding problems. (1978).

[4] Avrim Blum, Adam Kalai, and Hal Wasserman. 2003. Noise-tolerant learning, the parity problem, and the statistical query model. *Journal of the ACM (JACM)* 50, 4 (2003), 506–519.

[5] Julien Bringer, Hervé Chabanne, and Emmanuelle Dottax. 2006. HB++: a Lightweight Authentication Protocol Secure against Some Attacks. In *Security, Privacy and Trust in Pervasive and Ubiquitous Computing, 2006. SecPerU 2006. Second International Workshop on.* IEEE, 28–33.

[6] Daniela Carta, Peter Guttmann, Anna Regoutz, Ali Khiat, Alexander Serb, Isha Gupta, Adnan Mehonic, Mark Buckwell, Steven Hudziak, AJ Kenyon, et al. 2016. X-ray spectromicroscopy investigation of soft and hard breakdown in RRAM devices. *Nanotechnology* 27, 34 (2016), 345705.

[7] Andre Esser, Robert Kübler, and Alexander May. 2017. LPN decoded. In *Annual International Cryptology Conference.* Springer, 486–514.

[8] Ximeng Guan, Shimeng Yu, and H-S Philip Wong. 2012. A SPICE Compact Model of Metal Oxide Resistive Switching Memory With Variations. *IEEE Electron Device Letters* 33, 10 (2012), 1405–1407.

[9] Johan Håstad. 2001. Some optimal inapproximability results. *Journal of the ACM (JACM)* 48, 4 (2001), 798–859.

[10] Nicholas J Hopper and Manuel Blum. 2001. Secure human identification protocols. In *International Conference on the Theory and Application of Cryptology and Information Security.* Springer, 52–66.

[11] Chien-Yuan Huang, Wen Chao Shen, Yuan-Heng Tseng, Ya-Chin King, and Chrong-Jung Lin. 2012. A contact-resistive random-access-memory-based true random number generator. *IEEE Electron Device Letters* 33, 8 (2012), 1108–1110.

[12] H Jiang, D Belkin, SE Savel'ev, S Lin, Z Wang, Y Li, S Joshi, R Midya, C Li, M Rao, et al. 2017. A novel true random number generator based on a stochastic diffusive memristor. *Nature communications* 8, 1 (2017), 882–882.

[13] Ari Juels and Stephen A Weis. 2005. Authenticating pervasive devices with human protocols. In *Annual international cryptology conference.* Springer, 293–308.

[14] Jonathan Katz and Ji Sun Shin. 2006. Parallel and concurrent security of the HB and HB+ protocols. In *Annual International Conference on the Theory and Applications of Cryptographic Techniques.* Springer, 73–87.

[15] Michael Kearns. 1998. Efficient noise-tolerant learning from statistical queries. *Journal of the ACM (JACM)* 45, 6 (1998), 983–1006.

[16] Eike Kiltz, Krzysztof Pietrzak, David Cash, Abhishek Jain, and Daniele Venturi. 2011. Efficient authentication from hard learning problems. In *Annual International Conference on the Theory and Applications of Cryptographic Techniques.* Springer, 7–26.

[17] SB Lee, DH Kwon, K Kim, HK Yoo, S Sinn, M Kim, B Kahng, and BS Kang. 2012. Avoiding fatal damage to the top electrodes when forming unipolar resistance switching in nano-thick material systems. *Journal of Physics D: Applied Physics* 45, 25 (2012), 255101.

[18] NIST. 2017. Post-Quantum Cryptography. https://csrc.nist.gov/projects/post-quantum-cryptography

[19] Gang Qu and Lin Yuan. 2014. Design things for the internet of things: an EDA perspective. In *Proceedings of the 2014 IEEE/ACM International Conference on Computer-Aided Design.* IEEE Press, 411–416.

[20] Cong Xu, Xiangyu Dong, Norman P Jouppi, and Yuan Xie. 2011. Design implications of memristor-based RRAM cross-point structures. In *Design, Automation & Test in Europe Conference & Exhibition (DATE), 2011.* IEEE, 1–6.

# Leveraging On-Chip Voltage Regulators Against Fault Injection Attacks

Ali Vosoughi
mvosough@ur.rochester.edu
Department of Electrical and Computer Engineering
University of Rochester
Rochester, New York

Selçuk Köse
selcuk.kose@rochester.edu
Department of Electrical and Computer Engineering
University of Rochester
Rochester, New York

## ABSTRACT

The security implications of utilizing an on-chip voltage regulator as a countermeasure against fault injection attacks are investigated in this paper. The effect of the size of the capacitors and number of phases of the voltage regulator on the resilience of a cryptographic circuit against fault injection attacks are analyzed. The effectiveness of the proposed method in counteracting voltage glitch attacks is demonstrated with extensive simulations on the S-box of an advanced encryption standard (AES) cryptographic algorithm. Using a single phase on-chip voltage regulator, the number of faults generated by a voltage glitch attack is reduced by 5.45% as compared to unprotected S-box, and by 91.82% when number of phases increases to 32.

## CCS CONCEPTS

• **Hardware → Integrated circuits; Power and energy; Energy distribution; Power conversion; Robustness; System-level fault tolerance.**

## KEYWORDS

Hardware security; voltage regulator; fault injection attack; multi-phase voltage regulator

**ACM Reference Format:**
Ali Vosoughi and Selçuk Köse. 2019. Leveraging On-Chip Voltage Regulators Against Fault Injection Attacks. In *Great Lakes Symposium on VLSI 2019 (GLSVLSI '19), May 9–11, 2019, Tysons Corner, VA, USA.* ACM, New York, NY, USA, 6 pages. https://doi.org/10.1145/3299874.3317978

## 1 INTRODUCTION

Side-channel attacks are an important class of attacks aimed at breaking the secrets of a cryptographic circuit (CC) and threatening the security of cryptographic devices. In side-channel attacks, the physical emanations leaked from an integrated circuit is used to obtain the correct key that is stored within a CC [1–4]. For example, the correct key of an AES cryptographic algorithm can be obtained in a few minutes with a side-channel attack, however, using the supercomputers and the brute force search can take 149 trillion years to get the correct key [5].

Active side-channel attacks are a class of side-channel attacks to obtain the correct key by making transient (or permanent) changes to the CC and analyzing the output of the CC under those changes. In these attacks, which are known as fault injection attacks, the attacker causes a fault in the CC in various ways and exploits the fault analysis tools, such as differential fault analysis (DFA) [6], safe error analysis (SEA) [7], and collision fault analysis (CFA) [8] to obtain the key.

There are various methods for fault injection, such as injecting faults by voltage glitch injection, voltage starving, overvoltaging, injecting intentional temperature variations, white light, and laser radiation to the CC [9, 10]. Different methods require a different level of attacker skills and equipment [9, 10]. Voltage glitch attack (VGA) is a fault injection method that the attacker creates a fault in the CC through a sudden change, positive or negative, in the supply voltage of a CC [9–13]. VGA is used in a fault injection attack on the RSA device in the presence of countermeasures in [12]. VGA is exerted to inject the faults in unprotected RFID tags in [11].

Various techniques have been proposed to counteract fault injection attacks. Information redundancy-based techniques such as error correcting codes are a class of countermeasures against fault injection attack by encoding information flowing through the CC [14, 15]. Spatial redundancy-based countermeasures are a class of countermeasures which use the duplication/multiplication of the hardware of the CC to ensure the accuracy of the output through majority voting, and temporal redundancy based countermeasures verify the output through repetition of (part of) the cryptographic algorithm in time. Even though these countermeasures are advantageous in countering fault injection attacks, spatial, temporal, and information redundancies will lead to increased power dissipation of CC, reduced throughput, and increased area of the CC [9, 10, 12, 16]. Alternatively, analog countermeasures, such as voltage, temperature, and frequency sensors, are used to detect malicious fault injection activities and to protect a CC by ceasing the operations if such an activity is detected [9, 12, 17]. Detection of dynamic supply voltage variations has been used in [18]. Timing detectors are used to detect the glitches in [17] as a digital solution to counteract the VGA within a specific voltage and clock range. To the best of the knowledge of the authors, the on-chip VR has never been used as an inherent countermeasure against fault injection attacks. This paper is the first work to utilize the existing resources of an on-chip VR as a countermeasure against voltage glitch attacks where the implications of on-chip VR and the number of phases are investigated in counteracting voltage glitch attacks.


*GLSVLSI '19, May 9–11, 2019, Tysons Corner, VA, USA*

ACM ISBN 978-1-4503-6252-8/19/05...$15.00
https://doi.org/10.1145/3299874.3317978

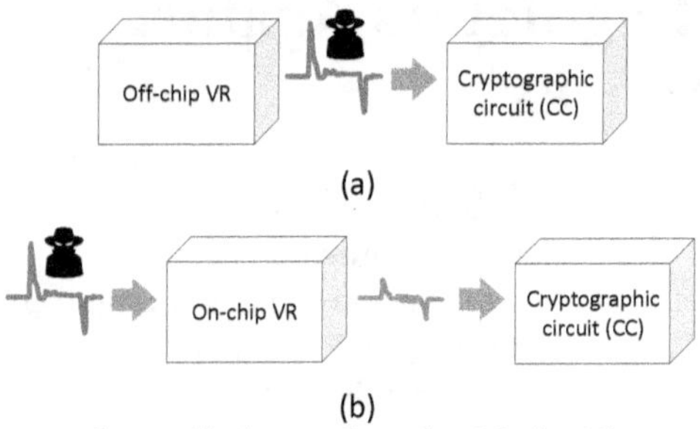


**Figure 1: A voltage glitch attack to the CC a) without on-chip VR and b) with an on-chip VR.**

The rest of this paper is as follows. In Section 2, the advantage of the on-chip VR on the resilience of CC against VGA is discussed and the effect of the capacitor size is analyzed. In Section 3, the effect of increasing the number of phases in the robustness of the CC to the VGA is investigated. In Section 4, extensive practical evaluations on the S-box of an AES with and without an on-chip VR is presented, followed by discussions on the overhead of the proposed countermeasure and conclusions.

## 2 ON-CHIP VR AGAINST VGA

An integrated circuit with an off-chip power supply is shown to be susceptible to side-channel analysis for key extraction [19]. The use of an on-chip voltage converter is shown to improve the security of CC against power and EM analysis attacks [20–24]. Intuitively, the on-chip VR is the first defense mechanism of a CC against side-channel attacks. Various topologies of VR, such as low-drop-out (LDO), buck, and switched capacitor (SC), have different responses against VGA based on the component selection and fabrication technology. These differences affect how the voltage glitch reaches the CC. Each VR, inherently acts as a low-pass filter that eliminates high-frequency inputs. A fault injection attack through voltage glitch to the CC in the presence of an on-chip VR and without on-chip VR is shown in Fig. 1. The $f_{-3dB}$ frequency of the VR and related frequency response depend significantly on the design of the VR and the number of effective reactive elements (*i.e.* inductors and capacitors). For example, a buck VR has two reactive components and thus is at least a second-order low-pass filter, as shown in Fig. 2a, while an LDO has only one reactive component and is inherently a first-order low-pass filter, as shown in Fig. 2b. Therefore, the expected amount of attenuation of high-frequency inputs in the stop-band of the buck VR will be higher than LDO. A switched-capacitor (SC) VR, has one or more number of effective capacitors depending on the configuration, as shown in Fig. 2c. The first-order low-pass filter is selected as the equivalent model of the low-pass behavior of a VR, as shown in Fig. 3.

The amount of energy transferred by the capacitor $C_{eq}$ to the output is equal to $\frac{1}{2}C_{eq}(\Delta V_{C_{eq}})^2$, where $\Delta V_{C_{eq}}$ is the voltage difference on the $C_{eq}$. If $C_{eq}$ increases, the amount of voltage glitch energy transferred through the VR to the CC also increases. Alternatively, with larger $C_{eq}$, the cutoff frequency $f_{-3dB} = (2\pi R_{eq}(C_{eq} + C_{out}))^{-1}$ of VR is reduced. However, this is provided that the glitch frequency is higher than the cutoff frequency of the VR. With larger $C_{eq}$, the cutoff frequency $f_{-3dB}$ is reduced and the filtering of the high frequency glitches is improved, while the amount of

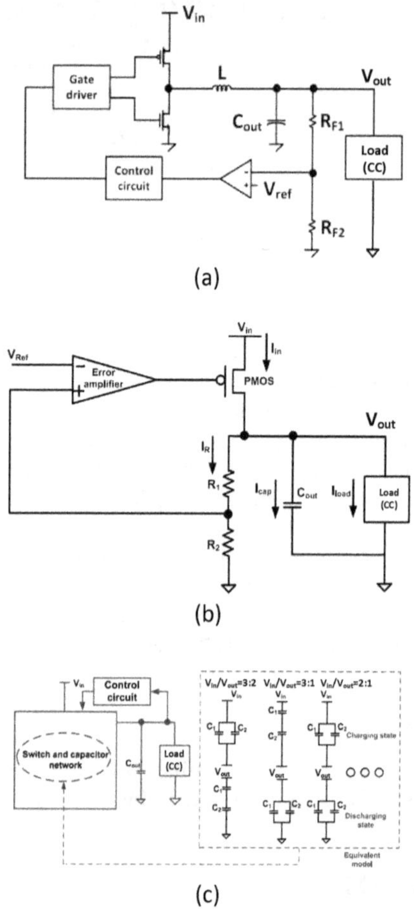


**Figure 2: Schematic of a) a conventional Buck VR with two reactive components, b) a conventional LDO VR with one reactive component, and c) a conventional SC-VR with a capacitor network.**

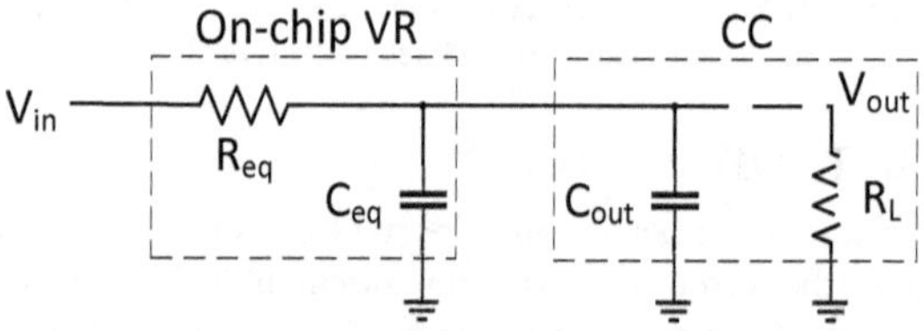


**Figure 3: A general, simplified first-order model for behavior of a VR as a low-pass filter (LPF) for input signals. $R_{eq}$ and $C_{eq}$ are equivalent resistive and capacitive impedance of on-chip VR.**

glitch energy transferred by the VR also increases with respect to $\frac{1}{2}C_{eq}(\Delta V_{C_{eq}})^2$. The relationship between the capacitance of the VR and the glitch energy transmitted to the CC is shown in Fig. 4.

## 3 MULTI-PHASE VR AGAINST VGA

In addition to the topology, component selection, and scaling, the number of phases of a VR has a significant impact on the resilience of a CC against a VGA. The amount of energy inserted into a CC during a VGA can significantly change the success rate of attack[17].

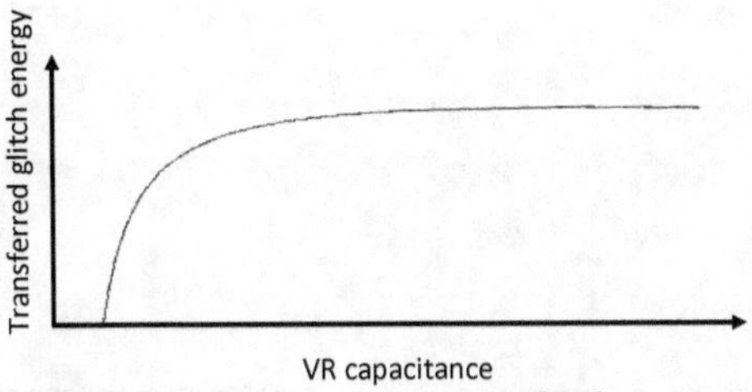


**Figure 4: Relation of $C_{eq}$ and voltage glitch transmitted to the CC. By increasing $C_{eq}$, the glitch transferred to the CC increases unto the cut-off frequency of the VR, where the increase of the $C_{eq}$ makes a negligible impact on the transferred glitch energy.**

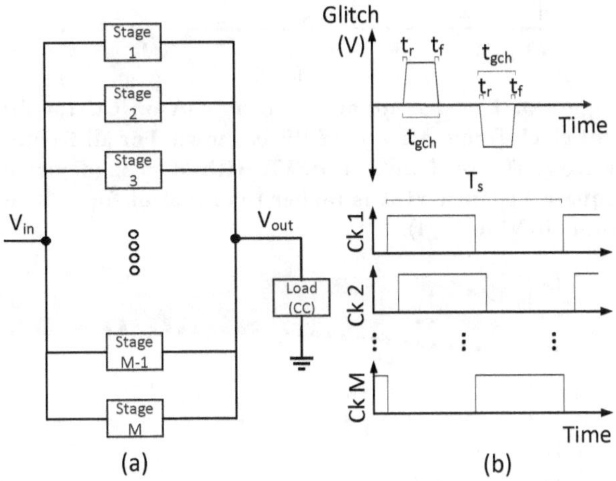


**Figure 5: Schematic of a) an MPVR with $M$ phases, and b) glitches of the VGA and clocks of the MPVR are depicted. The glitch has trapezoid shape with rise time $t_r$, fall time $t_f$, and duration $t_{gch}$.**

The amount of energy depends on the duration and amplitude of a glitch[17]. For a switching circuit, the duration of a glitch attack changes the effectiveness of an attack [25].

Multi-phase voltage regulator (MPVR) is a method in modern integrated circuits to increase the performance of power generation, power delivery and management of electronic systems, such as SoCs, and 3D integrated circuits. A block diagram of an MPVR with $M$ interleaved stages is shown in Fig. 5. An MPVR is a discrete time sampling circuit due to the clocking that causes consecutive connections and disconnections to and from the input of VR. Assuming $V_i^g$ as the voltage glitch when the stage $i$ is connected to the input of VR, the total glitch energy transmitted by the VR to the CC $E_{CC}^g$ at the end of period $T_s$ is

$$E_{CC}^g = \frac{C_{tot}}{2M} \sum_{i=1}^{M} (V_i^g)^2 \tag{1}$$

where $C_{tot}$ is total flying capacitance of an MPVR. The energy of the normal voltage of MPVR is not expressed in (1) since the effect of the normal output voltage is desirable for CC. If the glitch

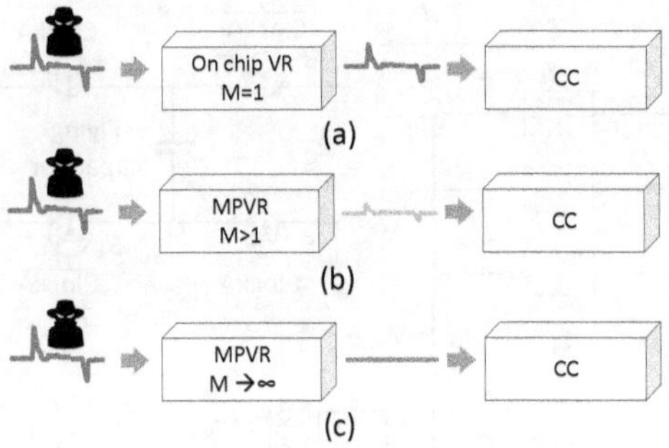


**Figure 6: The power of a CC is provided by an on-chip VR. Defeating the glitch is raised by increasing $M$ from a) $M = 1$, to b) $M > 1$, and further diminished by increasing to c) $M \rightarrow \infty$.**

duration is significantly less than $T_s$, such that $M \gg ||\overrightarrow{V^g}||_0$, then

$$\lim_{M \rightarrow \infty} E_{CC}^g \rightarrow 0. \tag{2}$$

The $f_{-3dB}$ frequency of an MPVR will decrease by increasing $M$[26]. As a result of the decrease in $f_{-3dB}$ frequency of MPVR, high frequency glitches at the input of MPVR will be reduced by increasing $M$. This smoothing in the voltage on CC results in reducing the effect of voltage glitch on CC, as shown in Fig.6.

## 4 PRACTICAL EVALUATIONS

Since the countermeasure is proposed against a VGA, the evaluation of the countermeasure requires the faults injected by voltage glitches. SCVR is a preferred choice over inductive counterparts due to the stability, area, and CMOS integrability considerations [27]. Moreover, an SC-MPVR with a high number of phases can be implemented by slicing larger capacitors and switches into smaller portions of capacitors and switches, and using a ring oscillator to generate interleaving clock phases [21, 27]. A 2:1 SC-MPVR is designed and simulated in Virtuoso Cadence at $60MHz$ ($T_s = 16.7\ nS$), $V_{in} = 2V$, $V_{out} = 1V$, and $M = \{1, \ldots, 32\}$. The schematic of the individual stages of VR, overall MPVR, and non-overlapping clocks are shown in Fig. 7. Switches $S_1, S_3$ are on for half of the period and switches $S_2, S_4$ are on for the rest of the period $T_s$. Furthermore, an S-box of AES [22] is implemented in 90 $nm$ predictive technology model of [28] using the Virtuoso Cadence. Average power dissipation of the S-box is 256 $\mu W$, where the minimum and maximum load power is between 156.3 and 387.22 $\mu W$. In Section 2, the effect of increasing the size of the capacitor in a VR on the transition of glitches to the CC is theoretically discussed. As shown in Fig. 8, by increasing the size of the flying capacitor from 500 $fF$ to 3 $nF$, the transferred energy of glitch into the CC is increased, however, this increase becomes marginal due to the filtering behavior of the VR.

The effect of increasing the switching frequency $f_s$ of the on-chip VR on the voltage glitch on the CC is shown in Fig. 9. The resilience of the CC against VGA increases by increasing the switching frequency of the VR, and for all $f_s$ frequencies, the resilience of the VR to VGA improves with increasing the number of phases.

When utilizing an on-chip VR, the security of the CC against VGA can be further enhanced by increasing the number of interleaved stages, as shown in Fig. 10. For a glitch with 10 ns duration

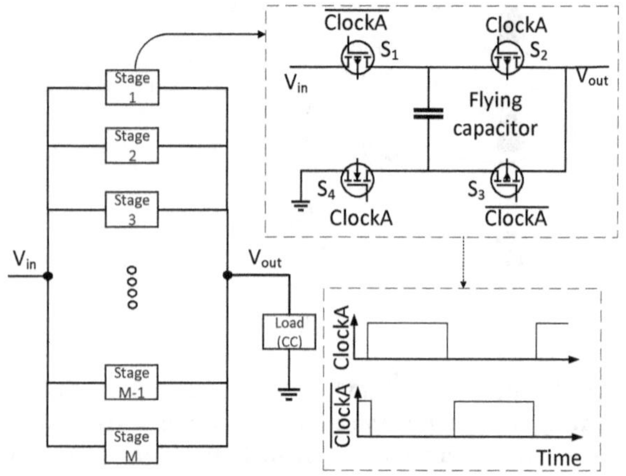


**Figure 7: A 2:1 SC-VR with $M$ stages is shown. Non-overlapping clocks A and B and switches $< S_1, S_3 >$ are connected for $T_s/2 - \epsilon$, and switches $< S_2, S_4 >$ are conducting for $T_s/2 - \epsilon$ remaining, where $\epsilon$ is the time assigned to ensure non overlapping clocks.**

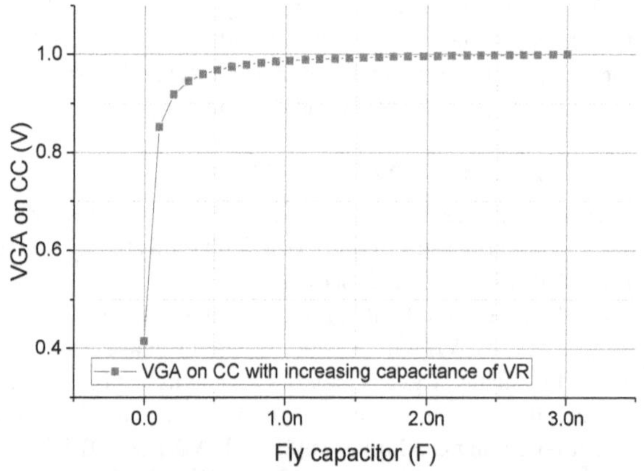


**Figure 8: Implication of the capacitive impedance of the on-chip VR on the glitch transferred to the CC. By increasing the size of fly capacitor, the voltage glitch transmitted to the CC is increased before up to $f_{-3dB}$ frequency of the voltage regulator.**

on an S-box operating at 100 MHz, the attenuation in the glitch amplitude is doubled with 32 interleaved phases, while the practical span of a voltage glitch on a CC is half the cycle of the operating frequency [25]. Except for the voltage-starving attacks, the proposed countermeasure increases the resistance of the CC to a wide range of glitch durations.

As shown in Fig. 11, by increasing the number of phases of an on-chip VR, the resilience of CC against fault injection attack is improved, as theoretically discussed in Section. 3. By describing the faulty output as any result at the output of CC other than the expected one, the success of the VGA on the CC is defined as [29]

$$\%Glitch\ attack\ success = \frac{\#\ Faults}{\#\ All\ tests} \times 100. \quad (3)$$

Using (3) and repeatedly simulating the VGA on the S-box of an AES and counting the number of the faulty outputs using a comparator

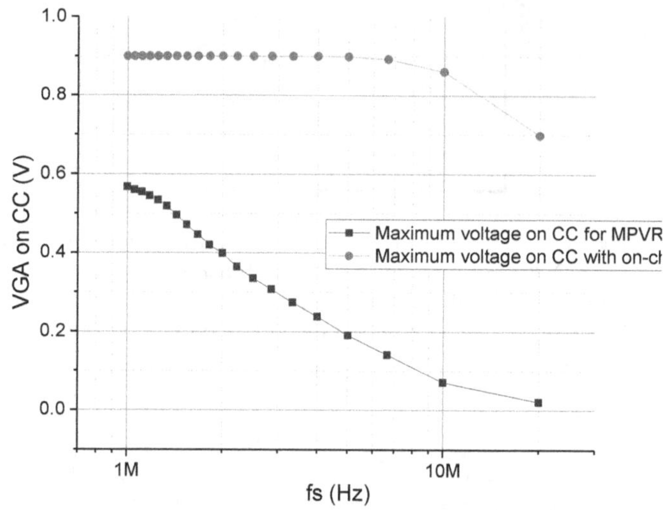


**Figure 9: The maximum effect of VGA on CC for different clock frequencies $f_s$ of VR is shown. For all frequency ranges, The resilience of MPVR with $M = 32$ (depicted by squares) against VGA is higher than that of for a CC with on-chip VR ($M = 1$).**

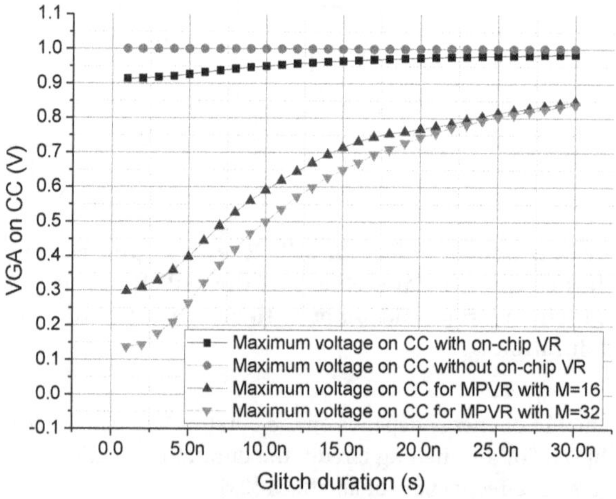


**Figure 10: Relation of glitch duration and maximum effect of VGA on CC with glitch duration $\{1ns, 3ns, \ldots, 31ns\}$, for CC with various MPVRs $M = \{1, 16, 32\}$ (depicted by triangles and squares), and for CC without on-chip VR (depicted by circles).**

and a counter [30], the success rate of fault occurrence in the presence of an MPVR is obtained, as shown in Fig. 12. The success of the VGA is reduced by increasing the number of phases. While the fault coverage for the unprotected S-box is 0%, the fault coverage is 5.45% with an on-chip VR, and the fault coverage reaches 91.82% with an increase in the number of phases to 32.

# 5 DISCUSSION

Assuming that the CC already has an on-chip VR, the throughput overhead on the CC is zero. Even though the increase in the number of phases of the VR is advantageous for the security purposes,

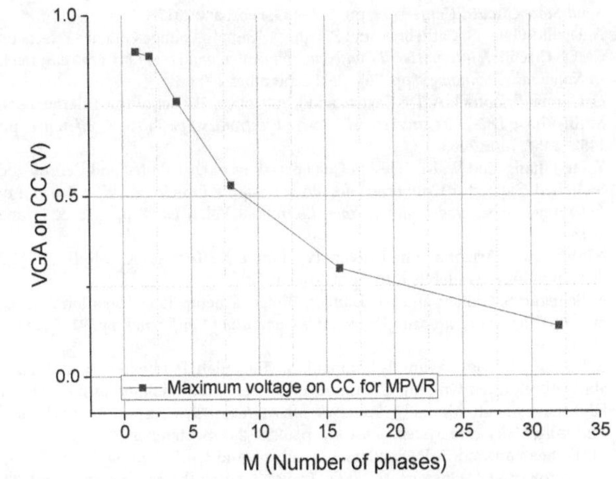


**Figure 11: VGA on CC with on-chip VR for $M = \{1, 2, 4, 8, 16, 32\}$, when a glitch with amplitude $V_{glitch} = \pm 2$, duration $t_r = t_f = 500ps$, and $t_{gch} = 1\ ns$ is applied.**

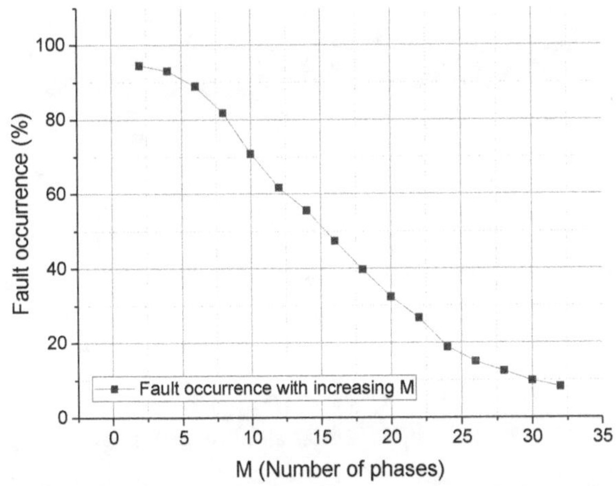


**Figure 12: Fault occurrence versus number of phases for an MPVR for various number of phases. Glitch input is applied to an S-box with MPVR and an S-box without MPVR, while the result is compared and number of faults is counted using a counter.**

with the increase in the number of phases the conduction losses in switches, buffers, and drivers will be increased [31]. Moreover, the design of clock generators with higher resolution is an overhead in the design of MPVR with higher $M$. Efficiency and area overheads of the on-chip VR with a various number of stages are listed in Table 1. The ripple at the output $V_{rip}$ is a function of output current, switching frequency of VR, the equivalent series resistance of capacitors of VR, and $M$, and decreases by increasing the number of phases [31]. Efficiency and area overheads of the on-chip VR with a various number of stages and ring-oscillator are listed in Table 1.

## 6 CONCLUSION

In this paper, the application of an on-chip VR as a countermeasure against fault injection attack is proposed as a solution to enhance the resilience of the CC against a VGA. The effect of the number of phases in the MPVR on the robustness of the circuit against VGA is analyzed. The effectiveness of the proposed countermeasure on an S-box of an AES is evaluated. The faults generated by the VGA on CC are reduced by 5.45% with a single phase on-chip VR, and by 91.82% with an MPVR with 32 phases, as compared to unprotected S-box of an AES device. The throughput, power, and area overhead of the proposed technique are negligible due to the utilization of the existing VR as a power supply, while the area and power overhead of the MPVR are increased, respectively, by 5.1% and 1% when the number of interleaved phases is 32.

**Table 1: Efficiency and area overhead of MPVR.**

| M | 1 | 2 | 4 | 8 | 16 | 24 | 32 |
|---|---|---|---|---|---|---|---|
| Ar.% | 0 | 2.62 | 3.93 | 4.58 | 4.9 | 5.02 | 5.07 |
| Eff.% | 84.4 | 84.54 | 84.68 | 84.9 | 85.56 | 86.0 | 85.41 |

## ACKNOWLEDGMENTS

This work is supported in part by the NSF CAREER Award under Grant CCF-1350451, in part by the NSF Award under Grant CNS-1715286, in part by SRC Contract NO: 2017-TS-2773, and in part by the Cisco Systems Research Award.

## REFERENCES

[1] F. Standaert, E. Peeters, G. Rouvroy, and J. Quisquater, "An Overview of Power Analysis Attacks Against Field Programmable Gate Arrays," *Proceedings of the IEEE*, Vol. 94, No. 2, pp. 383–394, February 2006.
[2] E. Karimi, Z. H. Jiang, Y. Fei, and D. Kaeli, "A Timing Side-Channel Attack on a Mobile GPU," *IEEE International Conference on Computer Design*, pp. 67–74, October 2018.
[3] H. Kumar *et al.*, "Towards Increasing the Difficulty of Reverse Engineering of RSFQ Circuits," *IEEE Transactions on Applied Superconductivity*, pp. 1–1, March 2019.
[4] M.A. Vosoughi and S. Köse, "Combined Distinguishers to Enhance the Accuracy and Success of Side Channel Analysis," *IEEE International Symposium on Circuits and Systems*, pp. 1–5, May 2019.
[5] M. Arora, "How Secure is AES Against Brute Force Attacks?," 2012. [Online]. Available: http://www.eetimes.com/document.asp?doc_id=1279619.
[6] G. Piret and J. J. Quisquater, "A Differential Fault Attack Technique Against SPN Structures, with Application to the AES and KHAZAD," *Cryptographic Hardware and Embedded Systems*, pp. 77–88, September 2003.
[7] S. M. Yen and M. Joye, "Checking Before Output May Not Be Enough Against Fault-Based Cryptanalysis," *IEEE Transactions on Computers*, Vol. 49, No. 9, pp. 967–970, September 2000.
[8] J. Blömer and V. Krummel, "Fault Based Collision Attacks on AES," *Fault Diagnosis and Tolerance in Cryptography*, pp. 106–120. October 2006.
[9] H. Bar-El, H. Choukri, D. Naccache, M. Tunstall, and C. Whelan, "The Sorcerer's Apprentice Guide to Fault Attacks," *Proceedings of the IEEE*, Vol. 94, No. 2, pp. 370–382, January 2006.
[10] A. Barenghi, L. Breveglieri, I. Koren, and D. Naccache, "Fault Injection Attacks on Cryptographic Devices: Theory, Practice, and Countermeasures," *Proceedings of the IEEE*, Vol. 100, No. 11, pp. 3056–3076, April 2012.
[11] M. Hutter, J. M. Schmidt, and T. Plos, "Contact-Based Fault Injections and Power Analysis on RFID Tags," *European Conference on Circuit Theory and Design*, pp. 409–412, August 2009.
[12] C. Aumüller *et al.*, "Fault Attacks on RSA with CRT: Concrete Results and Practical Countermeasures," *International Workshop on Cryptographic Hardware and Embedded Systems*, pp. 260–275, August 2002.
[13] K. Tobich *et al.*, "Voltage Spikes on the Substrate to Obtain Timing Faults," *Euromicro Conference on Digital System Design*, pp. 483–486, March 2013.
[14] A. Sarker, M. M. Kermani, and R. Azarderakhsh, "Hardware Constructions for Error Detection of Number-Theoretic Transform Utilized in Secure Cryptographic Architectures," *IEEE Transactions on Very Large Scale Integration (VLSI) Systems*, Vol. 27, No. 3, pp. 738–741, March 2019.
[15] M. M. Kermani and R. Azarderakhsh, "Reliable Architecture-Oblivious Error Detection Schemes for Secure Cryptographic GCM Structures," *IEEE Transactions on Reliability*, pp. 1–9, December 2018.

[16] S. A. Aftabjahani and A. Das, "Robust Secure Design by Increasing the Resilience of Attack Protection Blocks," *International Verification and Security Workshop*, pp. 13–18, July 2017.
[17] N. Beringuier-Boher *et al.*, "Voltage Glitch Attacks on Mixed-Signal Systems," *Euromicro Conference on Digital System Design*, pp. 379–386, August 2014.
[18] H. B. Le, X. D. Do, S. G. Lee, and S. T. Ryu, "A Long Reset-Time Power-On Reset Circuit with Brown-Out Detection Capability," *IEEE Transactions on Circuits and Systems II: Express Briefs*, Vol. 58, No. 11, pp. 778–782, November 2011.
[19] S. Saab, A. Leiserson, and M. Tunstall, "Key Extraction From the Primary Side of a Switched-Mode Power Supply," *IEEE Asian Hardware-Oriented Security and Trust*, pp. 1–7, December 2016.
[20] W. Yu, O. A. Uzun, and S. Köse, "Leveraging On-Chip Voltage Regulators as a Countermeasure Against Side-Channel Attacks," *Design Automation Conference*, pp. 1–6, June 2015.
[21] O. A. Uzun and S. Kose, "Converter-Gating: A Power Efficient and Secure On-Chip Power Delivery System," *IEEE Journal on Emerging and Selected Topics in Circuits and Systems*, Vol. 4, No. 2, pp. 169–179, June 2014.
[22] W. Yu and S. Köse, "Exploiting Voltage Regulators to Enhance Various Power Attack Countermeasures," *IEEE Transactions on Emerging Topics in Computing*, Vol. 6, No. 2, pp. 244–257, April 2018.
[23] A. W. Khan, T. Wanchoo, G. Mumcu, and S. Köse, "Implications of Distributed On-Chip Power Delivery on EM Side-Channel Attacks," *International Conference on Computer Design*, pp. 329–336, October 2017.
[24] M. Kar *et al.*, "8.1 Improved Power Side-Channel Attack Resistance of an AES-128 Core via a Security-Aware Integrated Buck Voltage Regulator," *International Solid-State Circuits Conference*, pp. 142–143, February 2017.
[25] A. Djellid-Ouar, G. Cathebras, and F. Bancel, "Supply Voltage Glitches Effects on CMOS Circuits," *International Conference on Design and Test of Integrated Systems in Nanoscale Technology*, pp. 257–261, September 2006.
[26] O. Garcia, P. Zumel, A. De Castro, and J. A. Cobos, "Effect of the Tolerances in Multi-Phase DC-DC Converters," *Power Electronics Specialists Conference*, pp. 1452–1457, June 2005.
[27] Y. Lu, J. Jiang, and W. Ki, "Design Considerations of Distributed and Centralized Switched-Capacitor Converters for Power Supply On-Chip," *IEEE Journal of Emerging and Selected Topics in Power Electronics*, Vol. 6, No. 2, pp. 515–525, June 2018.
[28] NIMO Group Arizona State University, "Predictive Technology Model (PTM)," 2008. [Online]. Available: http://ptm.asu.edu/.
[29] N. Selmane, S. Guilley, and J. L. Danger, "Practical Setup Time Violation Attacks on AES.," *Seventh European Dependable Computing Conference*, pp. 91–96, May 2008.
[30] E. Karimi, M. Haghbayan, A. Rahmani, M. Tabandeh, P. Liljeberg, and Z. Navabi, "Accelerated On-chip Communication Test Methodology Using a Novel High-Level Fault Model," *IEEE 9th International Symposium on Embedded Multicore/Many-core Systems-on-Chip*, pp. 283–288, September 2015.
[31] M. D. Seeman and S. R. Sanders, "Analysis and Optimization of Switched-Capacitor DC-DC Converters," *IEEE Transactions on Power Electronics*, Vol. 23, No. 2, pp. 841–851, March 2008.

# On the Theoretical Analysis of Memristor based True Random Number Generator

Mesbah Uddin
The University of Tennessee
Knoxville, Tennessee
muddin6@vols.utk.edu

Md Sakib Hasan
The University of Tennessee
Knoxville, Tennessee
mhasan4@vols.utk.edu

Dr. Garrett S. Rose
The University of Tennessee
Knoxville, Tennessee
garose@utk.edu

## ABSTRACT

Emerging nano-devices like memristors display stochastic switching behavior which poses a big uncertainty in their implementation as the next-generation CMOS alternative. However, this stochasticity provides an opportunity to design circuits for hardware security. There are several examples in literature where the stochastic switching time of memristors are used as the source of entropy to build true random number generators (TRNGs). Software-based pseudo-random numbers may not be random enough for many different applications where true random numbers are a necessity. In this work, we have analyzed traditional TRNG designs that utilize memristors' switching time and evaluated them in varying operating conditions and with process variation in mind. Specifically, we have mathematically formulated how large process variation and strong temperature and voltage dependence of memristors can degrade the performance of these TRNGs. Depending on these analyses, we also have proposed a new way of designing memristive TRNG based on difference between stochastic high resistance states of a pair of memristors. Using simple probabilistic mathematics, we have evaluated our proposed method with existing ones and shown that our proposed design is robust in unfavorable environmental conditions and in the presence of large process variation where traditional TRNG bit quality degrades rapidly.

## CCS CONCEPTS

• **Security and privacy → Embedded systems security; Hardware-based security protocols.**

## KEYWORDS

True random number generator; TRNG; RNG; memristor; Hardware security; memristor based RNG

**ACM Reference Format:**

Mesbah Uddin, Md Sakib Hasan, and Dr. Garrett S. Rose. 2019. On the Theoretical Analysis of Memristor based True Random Number Generator. In *Great Lakes Symposium on VLSI 2019 (GLSVLSI '19), May 9–11, 2019, Tysons Corner, VA, USA.* ACM, New York, NY, USA, 6 pages. https://doi.org/10.1145/3299874.3317981


*GLSVLSI '19, May 9–11, 2019, Tysons Corner, VA, USA*

ACM ISBN 978-1-4503-6252-8/19/05...$15.00
https://doi.org/10.1145/3299874.3317981

## 1 INTRODUCTION

With the emergence of billions of smart interconnected devices (Internet of things or IoT), hardware security is becoming more important that ever because of its ability to provide very lightweight and unique hardware specific secucirty solutions. Most, if not all security implementations require secret keys. Key generation software usually follows some complex algorithms to generate their secret keys randomly. However, these software-generated keys are at best pseudo-random in nature and may not fulfill randomness requirements of many applications. Therefore, there is a growing need for true random number generators (TRNGs) that can produce a stream of true random bits from hardware for cryptographic applications [5]. Using some stochastic and random physical phenomena within a circuit, these TRNGs produce a stream of random bits. True random numbers (TRN) are different from pseudo random numbers (PRN) where a seed is usually needed and the same stream of bits are produced if the initializing seed remains the same. A TRNG should ideally be insensitive to environmental variation, i.e. the source of entropy that produces the random bits should not be a strong function of temperature or supply voltage. Process variation should also have a small impact so that it doesn't disturb the randomness of the TRNG circuit. Naturally occurring random circuit phenomena are used to build TRNGs. These phenomena include clock jitter, random telegraph noise (RTN), thermal noise, metastable state, any quantum phenomena, etc.

Recently, stochasticity in novel nano-devices like memristors [11] is being explored to build TRNGs [4, 16]. Memristors display probabilistic switching behavior, i.e. their switching time or memristive states can have different values at different periods of time [9]. Researchers have tried to use this as a source of randomness to build different hardware security primitives specifically physical unclonable functions (PUF) [12, 14], sneak-path based tag generation [7], random number generator [16] etc. In [16], probability distribution of memristors's OFF and ON states based on the switching time is used to design the MTRNG (memristor-based TRNG). In [6], researchers have utilized a differential readout scheme to harvest the RTN (random telegraph noise) in memristors along with LFSR (linear feedback shift register) to implement a TRNG. The differential nature of this circuit improves performance against varying temperature and power supply noise. Switching variability in memristor's set process is used to extract random numbers in [1]. In [4], authors have proposed TRNG design where the random switching time of a diffusive memristor is used as the source of entropy and is shown to produce true random numbers without any post-processing. This diffusive memristor is different than common metal-oxide memristors, does not require forming and reverts to its high resistance state spontaneously. However, this self-OFF switching ($\approx 1ms$) property makes these memristors very slow.

The main purpose of this work is to analyze the underlying mathematical basis for traditional memristor based TRNGs. We have analyzed one such design and formulated how temperature, supply voltage change and process variation could affect the TRNG performance. To improve robustness against process variation and environmental changes, we have suggested a TRNG design that leverages the variability of high resistance state (HRS) of a memristor. This design uses relative measurements, i.e. the HRS of one memristor is compared with another to generate a random bit. Since HRS usually has shown higher variability compared to other memristor parameters [10], we have chosen HRS as the source of randomness for our design. The differential nature of this design makes it robust against process and environmental variation.

The contributions of this paper include

- Formulation of conventional memristor based TRNG design,
- Mathematical formulation of changes in performance of conventional design with outside effects,
- Proposition of a new twin memristor based TRNG design,
- Evaluation of both existing and proposed design against environmental changes,
- Evaluation of both design against process variation.

The paper is organized as follows: section 2 first presents a short introduction to memristor and its stochastic behavior. Section 3 derives the relationship of existing TRNG design with temperature shift and supply voltage and process variation. Section 4 presents and discusses our proposed design and again derives the relationship of this design with temperature, supply voltage and process variation. Section 5 presents the simulation results and explains the difference between these two designs. Finally, future prospects and concluding remarks are provided in section 6 and 7, respectively.

## 2 BACKGROUND

### 2.1 Introduction to Memristor

The memristor or ReRAM/RRAM (resistive random access memory) is one of the most promising post Moore-era devices because of their non-volatility, CMOS compatibility, low energy operation among other features [11]. Metal oxide memristors (metal-insulator-metal or MIM layer) are more common among various types of memristors. They are usually bi-polar, i.e. they have two stable resistive states namely high resistance state (HRS) or the OFF state and the low resistance state (LRS) or the ON state. Applying a minimum threshold voltage for a minimum amount of time switches a memristor from LRS to HRS or from HRS to LRS depending on the direction of applied voltage. The minimum threshold voltage and minimum time to switch from HRS to LRS are called positive threshold voltage and positive switching time, respectively, where from LRS to HRS, they would be called negative threshold and negative switching time, respectively. The transition from LRS to HRS is known as RESET where the transition from HRS to LRS is called SET. As memristors display RTN (random telegraph noise) i.e. their final HRS and LRS values along with threshold voltages and switching times are stochastic over time. Also, due to their nano-scale size and relatively immature fabrication process, memristors display a large die-to-die process variation [10, 15].

### 2.2 Stochasticity in Memristor

As mentioned before, in metal-oxide memristors, threshold behavior is observed. This means when the applied voltage is larger than a threshold voltage for at least the minimum switching time, the memristor switches its state from one memristive (or resistive) state to another. Because of large manufacturing process variation, memristors display a wide range of characteristics. Also, because of their underlying physical nature of switching mechanism, they also display varied characteristics in time. Thus their switching process is stochastic i.e. the value of their memristive states, switching time and threshold voltages can display variation across time. Over a larger number of clock cycles, their stochastic behavior can be approximated as Gaussian or Normal distribution [17]. A memristive TRNG would try to extract the uncertainty in their switching over different cycles to generate stream of random bits.

## 3 EFFECT OF ENVIRONMENTAL AND PROCESS VARIATION ON CONVENTIONAL DESIGN

As mentioned in earlier sections, most of the existing memristor based TRNG designs take advantage of the stochastic switching time. Memristors display cycle-to-cycle variation in their characteristics. The switching time (positive or negative) of a memristor can be approximated to have a normal distribution over many cycles. This is formulated as:

$$\mathbf{t_{swn}} = N(\mu_{tswn}, \sigma_{tswn}) \tag{1}$$

and,

$$\mathrm{P}(t \leq \mu_{tswn}) = \mathrm{P}(t > \mu_{tswn}) = 0.5 \tag{2}$$

To reiterate, equation 1 describes that the switching time of a memristor is a Gaussian (Normal) random variable with mean $\mu_{tswn}$ and standard deviation $\sigma_{tswn}$. Therefore, equation 2 expresses the probability that a random switching time, $t \in \mathbf{t_{swn}}$ to be less than or equal to the mean which is 0.5 or 50% according to the property of a Gaussian distribution. Thus if we determine the mean of that switching time ($\mu_{tswn}$) and apply a voltage greater than its threshold voltage to a memristor repeatedly for many cycles, then half of the time, memristor would switch to its other state and the other half of the time, it would not. This is the basis for most memristor based RNG where memristors's stochastic switching time is the source of entropy.

This method requires a precise pulse with pulse width being approximately equal to the mean switching time. Any clock jitter/skew or other source of noise could change this pulse width which may drastically change the overall switching probability. The switching time also depends heavily on the applied voltage magnitude across the memristor. Thus, any power supply noise would also strongly affect the switching time as well. Again, since the memristor's threshold voltages and memristive states are functions of temperature, temperature change would also affect the switching time and thus the overall switching probability. Thus any change in any of these factors would bring a change in the probability of switching and thus equation 2 would not hold for the changed distribution. Then the produced bit stream from that memristor could be heavily biased towards either a '1' or a '0'. In the next few subsections, we are going to formulate the change in switching time distribution for these factors.

## 3.1 Supply voltage variation

To simplify our analysis and to get an approximate idea how voltage variation can affect the random number generator performance, we have considered a linear model for a memristor which was developed first by Mcdonald *et.al.* [8] and later improved in [12, 13]. The RESET of a memristor (i.e. from LRS to HRS) is governed by this equation [13]:

$$M(t_{i+1}) = M(t_i) + \frac{R_{diff}\Delta t V(t_{i+1})}{t_{swn}V_{tn}}, \quad (3)$$

where, $t_{swn}$ and $V_{tn}$ are negative switching time and negative threshold voltage of a memristor, respectively. $R_{diff}$ is the difference between HRS and LRS. $M(t)$ presents the memristance and $V(t)$ represents the applied voltage across the memristor at a time instant, t. Equation 3 can be written as:

$$\Delta M = \frac{R_{diff}\left|V_{applied}\right|}{t_{swn}V_{tn}} * \Delta t, \quad (4)$$

By integrating this equation 4, we can establish a relationship between switching time and applied voltage. Let's assume that the applied voltage remains the same for one switching cycle, from equation 4, we can estimate the actual switching time for any applied voltage:

$$\int_{LRS}^{HRS} dM = \frac{R_{diff}\left|V_{applied}\right|}{t_{swn}V_{tn}} * \int_0^{t_{sw,actual}} dt \quad (5)$$

$$\implies t_{sw,actual} = t_{swn} * \frac{V_{tn}}{\left|V_{applied}\right|} \quad (6)$$

The resulting relationship between applied voltage and actual time to switch is found to be proportional which is expected from a linear switching model of a memristor. If the change in applied voltage is limited (max ±10% here), then a linear equation should provide reasonable accuracy. If $V_{applied}$ equals to the threshold $V_{tn}$, then the actual switching time is equal to the minimum switching time. However, from equation 6, a ±10% change in $V_{applied}$ from $V_{tn}$ would result in a (≈ -9%,+11%) change in actual switching time.

## 3.2 Temperature variation

Temperature directly affects memristive states and threshold voltages and thus in turn affect the actual switching time. From [2, 3], we can see threshold voltage magnitude decreases with increasing temperature within the range ≈$[0, 100]^0$C and we can approximate the change with a linear equation as:

$$V_{tn}(\theta) = V_{tn0}[1 + \alpha_{V_{tn}}(\theta - \theta_0)], \quad (7)$$

where, $V_{tn0}$ is the threshold voltage at room temperature, $\theta_0$=25$^0$C. From [3], the temperature coefficient for negative threshold voltage is calculated as ≈-0.007/$^0$C. Therefore, for a $\Delta\theta$ temperature change, the new $V_{tn}$ would be:

$$V_{tn}(\theta) = [1 - 0.007 * \Delta\theta] * V_{tn0}, \quad (8)$$

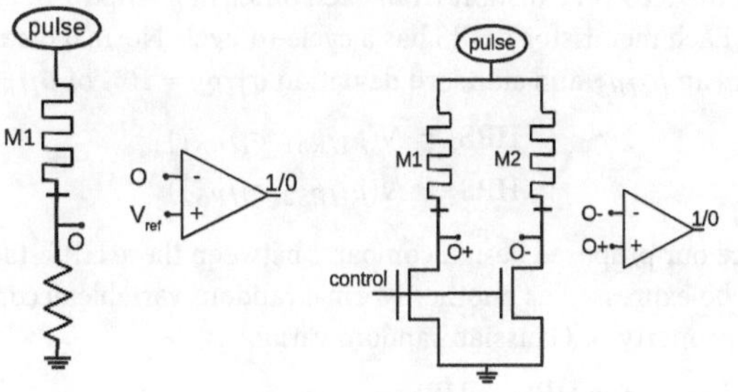


**Figure 1: Conceptual circuit diagram of (left) conventional switching time based single memristor TRNG, and (right) the proposed twin memristor TRNG**

The modified switching time would then be:

$$t_{sw,actual} = t_{swn} * \frac{[1 - 0.007 * \Delta\theta] * V_{tn0}}{V_{applied}} \quad (9)$$

## 3.3 Process variation

Because of large process variation of an emerging devices like memristor, all of its major parameters display a relatively larger variance. For existing RNG designs which are based on switching time, we are only interested in the variation of switching time. For this purpose, we have considered a 5% standard deviation ($\sigma_{tswn}$) on negative switching time, $t_{swn}$.

$$\mathbf{t_{swn}} = N(\mu_{tswn}, \sigma_{tswn}), die - to - die \quad (10)$$

where $\sigma_{tswn}$ = 0.05*$\mu_{tswn}$. Thus for a 1$\sigma$ variation of this switching time, the shifted mean of this distribution would be:

$$t_{sw,actual} = \begin{cases} 1.05 * \mu_{tswn}, & 1\sigma \text{ above mean} \\ 0.95 * \mu_{tswn}, & 1\sigma \text{ below mean} \end{cases}. \quad (11)$$

# 4 PROPOSED TRNG DESIGN

We have seen that process variation, temperature change and supply voltage variation can affect and thus shift the switching time distribution of a memristor. Therefore, any TRNG design based on the initial distribution of cycle-to-cycle switching time around the mean of this distribution would create biased proportion of ones and zeros and thus degrade the RNG performance. In this work, we are instead proposing a RNG design based on relative distribution of HRS. In this design, the main source of entropy is the cycle-to-cycle HRS variation of a pair of memristors. With equal voltage bias of a fixed duration, the memristive states of two memristors are compared to generate random bit streams. Figure 1 displays the high level circuit diagram of the existing switching time based single memristor TRNG and the proposed relative HRS based twin memristor TRNG. Temperature, voltage change and process variation have smaller effect on this proposed TRNG performance as we'll analyze now.

Suppose we have two memristors which are physically close in a circuit layout and their mean HRS values are 1$\sigma$ = 1% (mismatch) apart from each other where the variance of HRs is considered 10%. It is justified to consider much smaller mismatch variation between any two devices if they are physically close in a chip compared to two devices very distant from each other in a chip or in different die. Each memristor's HRS has a cycle-to-cycle Normal distribution of mean $\mu_{HRS}$ and standard deviation $\sigma_{HRS}$ = 10% of $\mu_{HRS}$.

$$\begin{aligned} \mathbf{HRS_1} &= N(\mu_{HRS1}, \sigma_{HRS1}) \\ \mathbf{HRS_2} &= N(\mu_{HRS2}, \sigma_{HRS2}) \end{aligned} \tag{12}$$

Since our proposed design compares between these HRS states, this can be expressed as another Normal random variable according to the property of Gaussian random variable.

$$\begin{aligned} \mathrm{Z} &= \mathbf{HRS_1} - \mathbf{HRS_2} \\ &= N((\mu_{HRS1} \sim \mu_{HRS2}), \sqrt{\sigma^2_{HRS1} + \sigma^2_{HRS2}}) \end{aligned} \tag{13}$$

If $\mu_{HRS2} > \mu_{HRS1}$ and thus $\mu_{HRS2}$ = 1.01*$\mu_{HRS1}$ (1% larger) and $\sigma_{HRS1}$ = 0.1*$\mu_{HRS1}$, $\sigma_{HRS2}$ = 0.1*$\mu_{HRS2}$ (10% standard deviation), then equation 13 becomes:

$$\begin{aligned} \mathrm{Z} &= N(.01 * \mu_{HRS1}, \sqrt{(0.1 * \mu_{HRS1})^2 + (0.1 * 1.01\mu_{HRS1})^2}) \\ &\approx N(.01 * \mu_{HRS1}, 0.1 * \sqrt{2} * \mu_{HRS1}) \end{aligned} \tag{14}$$

Since **Z** doesn't have a mean of zero, the ratio of ones and zeros wouldn't be the same. However, it should be close to zero as can be deduced using a Z-table. The z-score of this normal distribution to find the probability of a randomly chosen value to be less than 0 is:

$$\begin{aligned} z = \frac{x - \mu}{\sigma} &= \frac{0 - 0.01 * \mu_{HRS1}}{0.1 * \sqrt{2} * \mu_{HRS1}} \\ &= -0.0707 \end{aligned} \tag{15}$$

where, z represents a Normal random variable of mean 0 and standard deviation 1, transformed from **Z** to calculate the probability using a z-table.

From z-table, the probability of getting a '0' value for z-score of -0.0707 is:

$$\mathrm{P}(x \in \mathrm{Z} \leq 0) = 0.4718 \tag{16}$$

It should be noted that if the mean HRS between two memristors are less than $1\sigma$, then the the probability number in equation 16 would be even closer to the ideal value of 0.5. Thus our proposed design inherently has some bias. But this provides us with a better robustness against environmental changes compared to existing designs as we'll analyze now.

## 4.1 Supply voltage variation

Changing the voltage applied across the memristors would change the switching speed. However, in our design, we chose a large enough switching time so that memristors would always switch, since we are only interested in variation in the final HRS values, not the switching probability itself. Therefore, due to rail voltage variation ( $\approx \pm 10\%$), the time to generate a valid bit from the proposed TRNG changes slightly, but the value of that bit itself is assumed to be unaffected.

## 4.2 Temperature variation

Temperature would change the HRS of both memristors in our design. For a relatively small temperature window $[0 - 100]^0$C, this change is approximated by a linear equation, similar to threshold voltage change. Suppose, the temperature increases by an amount of $\Delta\theta$. Then from equation 7, we can find the two changed HRS as:

$$\begin{aligned} HRS1'(\theta) &= HRS1[1 + \alpha_{HRS} * \Delta\theta] \\ HRS2'(\theta) &= HRS2[1 + \alpha_{HRS} * \Delta\theta] \end{aligned} \tag{17}$$

where, $HRS_1$ and $HRS_2$ represent HRS at room temperature for these two different memristors. $\alpha_{HRS}$ is the linear temperature coefficient of HRS and approximated as -0.008/$^0$C. The die-to-die standard deviation of HRS considered here is $\sigma_{HRS}$ = 0.1*$\mu_{HRS}$ (10% of HRS).

Now, let's use the term $C_{\Delta\theta} = 1 + \alpha_{HRS} * \Delta\theta$. Thus we can rewrite equations 12 for these new HRS values at a different temperature. The standard deviation (and variance) is considered unchanged.

$$\begin{aligned} \mathbf{HRS'_1} &= N(\mu_{HRS1'}, \sigma_{HRS1'}) \\ &= N(\mu_{HRS1} * C_{\Delta\theta}, \sigma_{HRS1}) \\ \mathbf{HRS'_2} &= N(\mu_{HRS2'}, \sigma_{HRS2'}) \\ &= N(\mu_{HRS2} * C_{\Delta\theta}, \sigma_{HRS2}) \end{aligned} \tag{18}$$

and

$$\begin{aligned} \mathrm{Z'} &= \mathbf{HRS'_1} - \mathbf{HRS'_2} \\ &= N(C_{\Delta\theta} * (\mu_{HRS1} \sim \mu_{HRS2}), \sqrt{\sigma^2_{HRS1} + \sigma^2_{HRS2}}) \end{aligned} \tag{19}$$

Thus equation 18 and 19 actually represents scaled versions of the normal distribution of equation 12 and 13, respectively. Now we can find the new distribution of our proposed design by using equation 18 with equations 13 and 14. The z-score of this scaled normal random variable is:

$$\begin{aligned} z = \frac{x - \mu}{\sigma} &= \frac{0 - C_{\Delta\theta} * 0.01 * \mu_{HRS1}}{0.1 * \sqrt{2} * \mu_{HRS1}} \\ &= -C_{\Delta\theta} * 0.0707 \end{aligned} \tag{20}$$

For 50$^0$C temperature increase, $C_{\Delta\theta}$ = (1-.008*50) = 0.6 and thus the z-score would be z = 0.0424. The probability of getting 0:

$$\mathrm{P}(x \in \mathrm{Z} \leq 0) = 0.4831 \tag{21}$$

This value is very close to the value in equation 16. Thus changing the temperature does not bring in a significant change on the ratio of 1's and 0's and the RNG performance does not degrade with changing temperature.

## 4.3 Process variation

In last subsection, we observe that temperature change creates a scaled version of the original HRS distributions. Process variation would cause the HRS values to be different from the die-to-die mean HRS value, causing a shift in the distribution. However, since we are taking the difference among two memristors, the resulting distribution would just display a scaled mean and scaled standard deviation of the original distribution.

$$\begin{aligned} \mathrm{Z} &= \mathbf{HRS''_1} - \mathbf{HRS''_2} \\ &= N((\mu_{HRS1''} \sim \mu_{HRS2''}), \sqrt{\sigma^2_{HRS1''} + \sigma^2_{HRS2''}}) \\ &\approx N(.01 * \mu_{HRS1''}, 0.1 * \sqrt{2} * \mu_{HRS1''}) \end{aligned} \tag{22}$$

**Table 1: Percentage of 0's to the sum of 0's and 1's for different operating conditions**

| *Design with varying conditions* | Ideal/No change | Temperature variation +25$^0$C | Temperature variation -25$^0$C | Voltage variation +10% | Voltage variation -10% | Process variation +1 $\sigma$ | Process variation -1 $\sigma$ |
|---|---|---|---|---|---|---|---|
| Single-memristor | 50 | 4.01 | 95.99 | 18.16 | 86.67 | 69.15 | 30.85 |
| Proposed (twin memristor) | 47.18 | 47.76 | 46.62 | 47.18 | 47.18 | 46.90 | 47.46 |

Suppose, $\mu_{HRS1''}$ is $1\sigma$ larger than the mean $\mu_{HRS1}$. Thus $\mu_{HRS1''}$ = $1.1^*\mu_{HRS1}$ and the z-score of this would again be:

$$\begin{aligned} z = \frac{x-\mu}{\sigma} &= \frac{0 - 0.01 * \mu_{HRS1''}}{0.1 * \sqrt{2} * \mu_{HRS1}} \\ &= \frac{0 - 0.01 * 1.1 * \mu_{HRS1}}{0.1 * \sqrt{2} * \mu_{HRS1}} \\ &= -0.0778 \end{aligned} \quad (23)$$

The probability of getting 0 for $1\sigma$ variation of HRS is thus:

$$P(x \in Z \leq 0) = 0.469 \quad (24)$$

Thus the ratio of 1's and 0's change by a very small amount with process variation. This is an excellent result since it states that we do not need to change any design parameters even if memristors show a large variance across different die as the RNG performance should remain very close to optimum operating condition.

## 4.4 Output Correction

Since our proposed design inherently has a small percentage of bias i.e. amount of 1's and 0's produced are not equal even in ideal condition, some form of post processing could be useful to improve the data quality. In this design, we have proposed to use simple Von-Neumann correction which can be implemented very easily with minimum hardware overhead. Von-Neumann correction discards when two consecutive RNG output bits are both '1' or '0'. But if the bit sequence is '10' then it becomes a '1', and if the sequence is '01' then it becomes a '0'. It helps to remove simple bias and reduce correlation between consecutive bits. By employing some 'whitening' technique, the the quality of the output bit can be improved too. XORing of two TRNGs is one such technique. If output from two TRNGs are not correlated, then XORing them could help to improve randomness in the output. XORing the TRNG output with the output from a PRNG could also improve randomness.

# 5 RESULTS AND ANALYSES

First, we have analyzed both the conventional single memristor based TRNG design and proposed twin memristor based TRNG design in terms of the proportion of 1's and 0's with respect to varying operating conditions. We have used a MATLAB version of Mcdonald model, developed in [14] for simulation. We have calculated the percentage of 0's compared to the sum of 1's and 0's in normal operating condition, at temperature $\pm 25^0C$ change compared to room temperature, applied voltage with ±10% variation and with $1\sigma$ process variation. This $1\sigma$ process variation for single memristor design corresponds to the negative switching time variation and is assumed to be 5%. For the proposed design, the variation corresponds to of HRS and is assumed to be 10% as HRS displays higher variation than switching time or other memristor characteristics. Table 1 displays the result. As expected, process variation

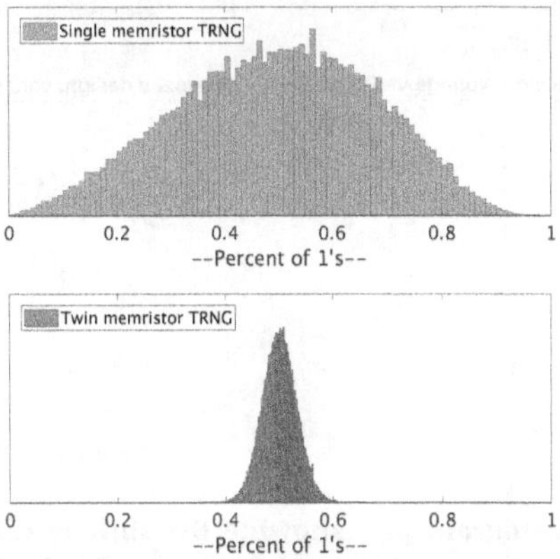


**Figure 2: Histogram of bit bias with process variation for (top) existing single memristor design and (bottom) proposed twin memristor design**

and temperature variation strongly affect switching time and thus the single memristor based design shows a large bias towards 1's or 0's except for normal condition. The proposed design is based on relative measurement of HRS and because of mismatch, inherently has a small bias i.e. the proportion of 0 is not 50% ideally. However, due to its relative nature, our proposed design only show a small change in performance in varying operating conditions. Thus our design can be considered robust against environmental changes or against large process variation. Table 1 lists the performance of this two designs for different conditions. As expected, performance of the proposed design doesn't show a large deviation from ideal condition where a single memristor TRNG performance could be affected severely.

To better understand the effect of process variation, we have run Monte Carlo analysis with 10,000 different chips and generated 5000 random bits from each chip. Figure 2 shows the percentage of 1's for different chips for both existing and proposed TRNG design. A TRNG should ideally have 50% of 1's i.e. the mean should be 0.5. As expected for our theoretical analysis, existing switching time based TRNG design shows a wide distribution with process variation with a standard deviation of 0.1805. But our proposed twin memristor design only has a narrow distribution over die-to-die process variation with a standard deviation of only 0.0322. This result shows our proposed design is robust against process variation and eliminates the need to redesign for every circuit instance.

We have also run Monte Carlo to visually show how the histogram shifts from ideal for a $\pm 10^0C$ change in temperature and for a ±10% change in supply voltage. This result is shown in Figure 3. Conventional single memristor based design shows a large deviation from ideal (i.e. with a mean of 0.5) distribution for both

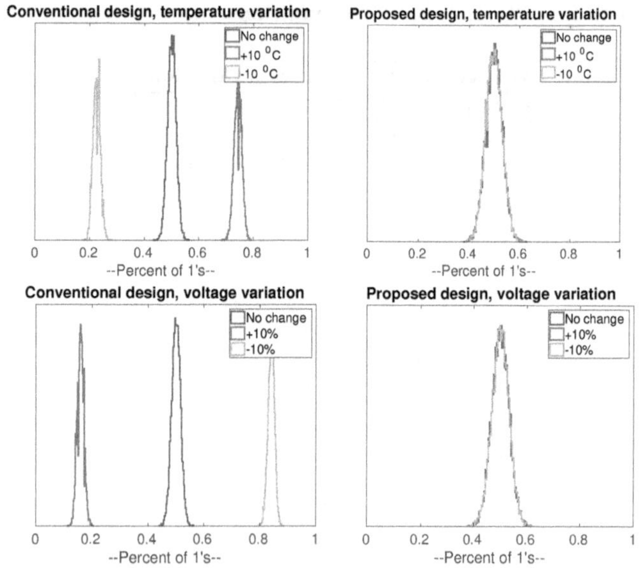


**Figure 3: Histogram plot showing the shift in distribution with temperature and voltage variation for both conventional and proposed design. Conventional design displays a wide variation while proposed design almost unchanged.**

increasing and decreasing temperature and supply voltage. But our proposed design shows almost zero or very negligible change.

## 6 FUTURE WORK

In this work, we have provided with a general idea about what to consider when designing a TRNG using memristor's stochastic switching behavior. However, different memristor materials would have different relationships with temperature and voltage as well as different variance of their parameters, one needs to characterize them first with corresponding temperature coefficients and switching equation to build a TRNG. Finally, our design is based on theoretical analysis only and thus other source of randomness (like noise) of a circuit might also affect the performance. Therefore, our immediate step would be to build our design using actual memristors and then evaluate it. The design of a good comparator to compare the memristive states is another important task. Finally, since our results are based on simplified mathematical model based simulation, any statistical random number tests are not shown in this work as software can only produce pseudo-random numbers.

## 7 CONCLUSION

We have used statistical distribution of random numbers to analyze the theoretical strength of existing TRNG designs against process, temperature and supply voltage variation. We have proposed our twin memristor based TRNG design which theoretically performs better than existing designs in these varying conditions. It also doesn't require sophisticated pulse width control to generate random bits and thus complexity of input signal generation circuit is reduced. However, as we know memristor is a novel device and its fabrication technology is still not mature, many different memristors consisting of many different materials with different underlying physics are out there. Thus the actual performance of a particular TRNG design would be very dependent on its underlying materials and their characteristics.

## ACKNOWLEDGMENT

The authors would like to thank Md. Badruddoja Majumder and other members of our SENECA research group at the University of Tennessee for interesting discussions related to this topic.

This material is based upon work supported by the Air Force Office of Scientific Research under award number FA9550-16-1-0301. Any opinions, finding, and conclusions or recommendations expressed in this material are those of the authors and do not necessarily reflect the views of the United States Air Force.

## REFERENCES

[1] Simone Balatti, Stefano Ambrogio, Zhongqiang Wang, and Daniele Ielmini. 2015. True random number generation by variability of resistive switching in oxide-based devices. *IEEE Journal on Emerging and Selected Topics in Circuits and Systems (JETCAS)* 5, 2 (2015), 214–221.

[2] T. Cabout et al. 2013. Temperature impact (up to 200C) on performance and reliability of $HfO_2$-based RRAMs. In *5th IEEE International Memory Workshop*. 116–119. https://doi.org/10.1109/IMW.2013.6582112

[3] Z. Fang, H. Y. Yu, W. J. Liu, Z. R. Wang, X. A. Tran, B. Gao, and J. F. Kang. 2010. Temperature Instability of Resistive Switching on $HfO_2$ -Based RRAM Devices. *IEEE Electron Device Letter* 31 (May 2010), 476–478. Issue 5.

[4] Hao Jiang, Daniel Belkin, Sergey E Savelév, Siyan Lin, Zhongrui Wang, Yunning Li, Saumil Joshi, Rivu Midya, Can Li, Mingyi Rao, et al. 2017. A novel true random number generator based on a stochastic diffusive memristor. *Nature communications* 8, 1 (2017), 882.

[5] Benjamin Jun and Paul Kocher. 1999. *THE INTEL© RANDOM NUMBER GENERATOR.* Technical Report. CRYPTOGRAPHY RESEARCH, INC. WHITE PAPER PREPARED FOR INTEL CORPORATION. 8 pages.

[6] J. Kim, T. Ahmed, H. Nili, N. Duy Truong, J. Yang, D. S. Jeong, S. Sriram, D. C. Ranasinghe, and O. Kavehei. 2017. Nano-Intrinsic True Random Number Generation. *ArXiv e-prints* (Jan. 2017). arXiv:1701.06020

[7] M. B. Majumder, M. Uddin, G. S. Rose, and J. Rajendran. 2016. Sneak path enabled authentication for memristive crossbar memories. In *2016 IEEE Asian Hardware-Oriented Security and Trust (AsianHOST)*. 1–6. https://doi.org/10.1109/AsianHOST.2016.7835568

[8] Nathan R. McDonald. 2012. *Al/Cu$_x$O/Cu Memristive Devices: Fabrication, Characterization, and Modeling.* Master's thesis. College of Nanoscale Science and Engineering, University at Albany, Albany, NY.

[9] Rawan Naous, Maruan Al-Shedivat, and Khaled Nabil Salama. 2016. Stochasticity modeling in memristors. *IEEE Transactions on Nanotechnology* 15, 1 (2016), 15–28.

[10] P. Pouyan, E. Amat, and A. Rubio. 2014. Reliability challenges in design of memristive memories. In *5th European Workshop on CMOS Variability (VARI)*. 1–6. https://doi.org/10.1109/VARI.2014.6957074

[11] Dmitri B. Strukov, Gregory S. Snider, Duncan R. Stewart, and R. Stanley Williams. 2008. The missing memristor found. *Nature* 453 (May 2008), 80–83.

[12] M. Uddin, M.B. Majumder, H. Manem, K. Beckmann, Z. Alamgir, N. Cady, and G.S. Rose. 2017. Design Considerations for Memristive Crossbar Physical Unclonable Functions. *Journal of Emerging Technology in Computing System (JETC)* 14, 1, Article 2 (sep 2017), 23 pages. https://doi.org/10.1145/3094414

[13] M. Uddin, M.B. Majumder, G.S. Rose, H. Manem, K. Beckmann, Z. Alamgir, and N. Cady. 2016. Techniques for Improved Reliability in Memristive Crossbar PUF Circuits. In *IEEE Computer Society Annual Symposium on VLSI (ISVLSI)*. 212–217.

[14] M. Uddin, M. B. Majumder, and G. S. Rose. 2017. Robustness Analysis of a Memristive Crossbar PUF Against Modeling Attacks. *IEEE Transactions on Nanotechnology* 16, 3 (May 2017), 396–405. https://doi.org/10.1109/TNANO.2017.2677882

[15] Christian Walczyk et al. 2011. Impact of Temperature on the Resistive Switching Behavior of Embedded $HfO_2$ -Based RRAM Devices. *IEEE Transaction on Electron Devices* 58 (September 2011), 3124-3131. Issue 9. https://doi.org/10.1109/TED.2011.2160265

[16] Chaofei Yang, Beiye Liu, Yandan Wang, Yiran Chen, Hai Li, Xian Zhang, and Guangyu Sun. 2016. The applications of NVM technology in hardware security. In *Proceedings of the 26th edition on Great Lakes Symposium on VLSI (GLSVLSI)*. ACM, 311-316.

[17] Cong Ye, Jiaji Wu, Gang He, Jieqiong Zhang, Tengfei Deng, Pin He, and Hao Wang. 2016. Physical mechanism and performance factors of metal oxide based resistive switching memory: a review. *Journal of Materials Science & Technology* 32, 1 (2016), 1–11.

# Control-Lock: Securing Processor Cores Against Software-Controlled Hardware Trojans

Dominik Šišejković[1], Farhad Merchant[1], Rainer Leupers[1], Gerd Ascheid[1] and Sascha Kegreiss[2]

[1]Institute for Communication Technologies and Embedded Systems, RWTH Aachen University, Germany

{sisejkovic, merchantf, leupers, ascheid}@ice.rwth-aachen.de

[2]Hensoldt Cyber GmbH, Germany, sascha.kegreiss@hensoldt.net

## ABSTRACT

Malicious circuit modifications known as hardware Trojans represent a rising threat to the integrated circuit supply chain. As many Trojans are activated based on a specific sequence of circuit states, we have recognized the ease of utilizing an instruction sequence for Trojan activation inside a processor core as a significant security issue. To protect against this threat, we propose Control-Lock: a novel methodology for securing inter-module control signals against software-controlled hardware Trojans, even if the signals are known to the adversary during fabrication. We demonstrate the approach with a RISC-V processor infected with a denial of service Trojan. We evaluate different Control-Lock encryption schemes with regards to the security-cost trade-off. Our results show that protecting a processor against a software-controlled hardware Trojan exploiting code execution implies an area overhead of only 4.75% as well as a negligible delay and power overhead.

## CCS CONCEPTS

• **Security and privacy → Hardware attacks and countermeasures**; *Security in hardware*; *Malicious design modifications*;

## KEYWORDS

Hardware Trojans; Logic Encryption; Denial of Service; RISC-V

**ACM Reference Format:**

Dominik Šišejković, Farhad Merchant, Rainer Leupers, Gerd Ascheid and Sascha Kegreiss. 2019. Control-Lock: Securing Processor Cores Against Software-Controlled Hardware Trojans . In *Great Lakes Symposium on VLSI 2019 (GLSVLSI '19), May 9–11, 2019, Tysons Corner, VA, USA.* ACM, New York, NY, USA, 6 pages. https://doi.org/10.1145/3299874.3317983

## 1 INTRODUCTION

Outsourcing the fabrication of Integrated Circuits (ICs) to external untrusted foundries has given rise to malicious IC modifications known as *hardware Trojans* [12]. These modifications can lead to catastrophic repercussions, including Denial of Service (DoS) attacks, data theft, circuit aging alternation and others [7].

Logic encryption (locking) is a popular choice to ensure the integrity of an IC [8, 14]. It relies on the insertion of additional gates to lock the original gate-level netlist based on a secret key. The key is stored in a tamper-proof memory after fabrication. Since the key is known only to the design owner, logic encryption conceals a hardware design, thereby protecting it against hardware Trojan injection, IP piracy and counterfeiting while being in hands of external parties [11]. Therefore, the primary objective of an adversary is to uncover the correct key to unlock the design.

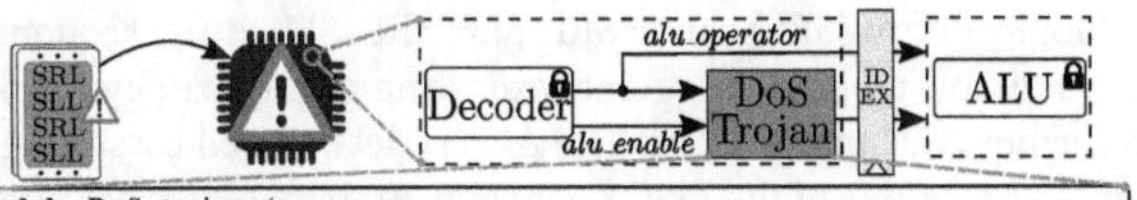


```
module DoS_trojan (
        input alu_enable,
        input [6:0] alu_operator,
        output alu_enable_modified
);
 int mode = 0;                                                          Trigger
 always_comb begin : trojan_trigger
   if ((mode == 0) && (alu_operator == 7'b0100101)) begin // SRL
     mode = 1;
   end else if ((mode == 1) && (alu_operator == 7'b0100111)) begin // SLL
     mode = 2;
   end else if ((mode == 2) && (alu_operator == 7'b0100101)) begin // SRL
     mode = 3;
   end else if ((mode == 3) && (alu_operator == 7'b0100111)) begin // SLL
     mode = 4; // Activate Trojan
   end else begin
     mode = 0; // Incomplete sequence; reset
   end
 end
 assign alu_enable_modified = (mode == 4) ? 1'b0 : alu_enable;  Payload
endmodule
```

**Figure 1: Example of denial of service RISC-V Trojan**

Existing logic encryption methodologies are usually applied to isolated design components [8, 9], that we refer to as *modules*. Often, it is assumed that hardware Trojans are embedded inside a module, and therefore, a *full recovery* of the key is required to perform a Trojan insertion. However, modern processor cores typically consist of multiple modules, such as an instruction decoder, Arithmetic Logic Unit (ALU), controller and others. Consequently, in this work, we focus on the following attack scenario: *by only identifying a few control signals indicating the instruction type (e.g., opcode) between processor modules, an adversary is able to insert a hardware Trojan that can exploit software-dependent signal behavior and launch a DoS attack resulting in a complete system failure.*

**Trojan Scenario:** To better understand the attack scenario, let us consider the concrete Verilog Trojan shown in Figure 1. The Trojan is located between the decoder and the ALU of the four-stage 32-bit processor known as the RI5CY core [3]. This processor is one implementation of the open-source RISC-V Instruction Set Architecture (ISA) [4] within the PULPino System-on-Chip (SoC) [3]. In this core, the opcode is exposed in the form of the *alu_operator*: a 7-bit signal generated in the decoder and used to control the ALU. The DoS Trojan follows a straightforward attack scenario; the adversary is able to identify the decoder output signals representing the *alu_operator* selection, even if the decoder or the ALU are encrypted. This operator is constructed based on the *opcode* and *funct3* fields of an instruction, both described in the RISC-V ISA. The *alu_operator* is forwarded through pipeline registers from the Instruction Decode (ID) stage to the ALU in the Execution (EX) stage to control which instruction should be executed in the next cycle. A Trojan can utilize the *alu_operator* to detect a predefined *rare sequence* of instructions. We selected a sequence of logical left (SLL)



*GLSVLSI '19, May 9–11, 2019, Tysons Corner, VA, USA*



ACM ISBN 978-1-4503-6252-8/19/05...$15.00

https://doi.org/10.1145/3299874.3317983

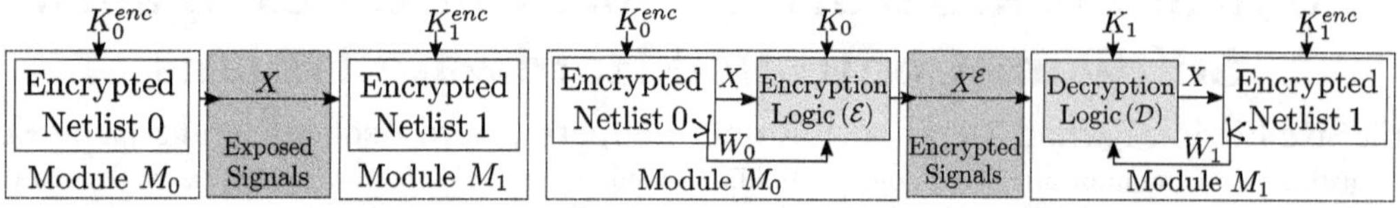


(a) Exposed signals (b) Encrypted signals

**Figure 2: Example of exposed and encrypted signals**

and logical right (SRL) shifts: SRL, SLL, SRL, SLL. If the sequence is detected, the Trojan is triggered, executing its payload by blocking all further ALU instructions. The ALU is deactivated by setting the signal *alu_enable* of the RI5CY core to 0. By remotely executing the instruction sequence on the infected core, an adversary can trigger this Trojan to execute a targeted DoS attack at a *time of the adversary's choice* to maximize the impact of the Trojan. This can lead to dangerous consequences, specifically in the context of military, medical and automotive electronics. Even though many signals can be used for Trojan activation, the opcode of a processor is a major target since it is easily exploitable and controllable through code execution. Therefore, protecting this subset of control signals can significantly increase the security of a processor design.

**Threat Analysis:** We identified software-controlled Trojans in processor cores as particularly alarming due to the following reasons. We assume that this powerful Trojan can be implemented *without the need to fully unlock the logically encrypted modules*, as the Trojan utilizes only inter-module signals and does not change the internal functionality of a module. Therefore, even if logic encryption assures an incorrect behavior of the identified signals for incorrect keys, a Trojan will still function correctly after the IC is activated as it relies on the *expected behavior* of the utilized control signals. Furthermore, the expected behavior of the opcode can easily be found in, e.g., an ISA manual, making processor cores very vulnerable to software-controlled attacks. Moreover, it stands to reason that it is easier to identify and understand inter-module control signals than internal signals within one module [10].

**Contributions:** To offer an additional layer of security apart from logic encryption, we introduce *Control-Lock*; a key-dependent encryption methodology for inter-module control signals. Control-Lock encrypts a set of *critical control signals* (wires) by modifying the output and input logic of a selected source and destination module, respectively. The main contributions of this paper are:

- A methodology and multiple schemes for encrypting control signals between design modules; *the signal values between the modules are always corrupted, even when the correct keys are applied.* Therefore, the design is protected against software-controlled hardware Trojans as the correct behavior of control signals (e.g., opcode) is corrupted and cannot be anticipated by an adversary. To the best of our knowledge, this is the *first work* on protecting inter-module control signals against software-controlled hardware Trojans.
- A randomized key-dependent netlist generation flow.
- Evaluation of the proposed methodology on a RISC-V processor core case study.

## 2 BACKGROUND

**Hardware Trojans:** A hardware Trojan is defined as an intentional, undesirable and malicious modification of an integrated circuit [5, 6]. Trojans can be inserted into the hardware design on multiple abstraction levels, including the Register-Transfer Level (RTL), gate-level and layout. Hardware Trojans typically consist of two elements: the trigger and the payload. The trigger of a Trojan is a set of signals indicating a value or state that, when encountered, activates the Trojan. After activation, the Trojan executes its malicious functionality known as payload.

**Threat Model:** In this work, we focus on hardware Trojans exploiting software-dependent control signals in processor cores as *a trigger source*. The payload can be manifested in various ways, including a DoS attack blocking all further code execution. In addition, the threat model is defined as follows [8]: (*i*) the personnel and tools in the design house are trustworthy, (*ii*) the foundry is untrusted and (*iii*) the adversary has access to both an activated IC to use as oracle from the semiconductor market and an encrypted netlist from reverse engineering.

**Security Model:** Both logic encryption and Control-Lock are applied to a netlist before the design is sent to the foundry. Since the design is activated by the design owner *after fabrication*, the security of Control-Lock depends on the secret key.

## 3 THE CONTROL-LOCK METHODOLOGY

**Design Concept:** The general idea of Control-Lock is presented in Figure 2. Initially, the two selected modules $M_0$ and $M_1$ consist of their logically encrypted netlists with the keys $K_0^{enc}$ and $K_1^{enc}$. In this scenario, Module $M_0$ outputs a set of signals represented as $X = \{x_0, \ldots, x_{n-1}\}$. Every element $x_i \in X$, where $0 \leq i < |X|$, denotes a 1-bit signal, i.e., one output signal of $M_0$. $X$ acts as a set of control signals for module $M_1$. Without the application of Control-Lock (Figure 2 (a)), $X$ is exposed to an adversary even if the correct activation key is not found, acting as a potential trigger for hardware Trojans.

To protect $X$, Control-Lock generates a randomized encryption ($\mathcal{E}$) and decryption ($\mathcal{D}$) logic. As shown in Figure 2 (b), the set of output signals $X$ of module $M_0$ is modified by the encryption logic $\mathcal{E}$, generating the encrypted set of signals $X^{\mathcal{E}}$, before being forwarded to module $M_1$. Therefore, $\mathcal{E}$ is appended to module $M_0$. As $X^{\mathcal{E}}$ needs to be decrypted before it can be processed, the decryption logic $\mathcal{D}$ is integrated at the inputs of module $M_1$. As Control-Lock encrypts the control signals between $M_0$ and $M_1$, $X^{\mathcal{E}}$ cannot easily be utilized for Trojan insertion, even if identified. After resynthesis, both $\mathcal{E}$ and $\mathcal{D}$ are structurally merged into the netlists of $M_0$ and $M_1$, respectively. Thereby, the original $X$ is no longer identifiable as it becomes an internal module signal.

**Implementation Concept:** The encryption $\mathcal{E}$ and decryption $\mathcal{D}$ are manifested as key-dependent *sets of encodings* of $X$ to $X^{\mathcal{E}}$ and vice versa: every key value defines a randomized encoding/decoding. Only if the correct key is provided for both $\mathcal{E}$ and $\mathcal{D}$, a correct encoding and decoding is performed. $\mathcal{E}$ is represented as a netlist depending on three inputs: the selected signals $X$, the set of key inputs $K_0 = \{k_0, \ldots, k_{j-1}\}$ and a set of randomly selected wires from the original netlist $W_0 = \{w_0, \ldots, w_{l-1}\}$. As before, all elements

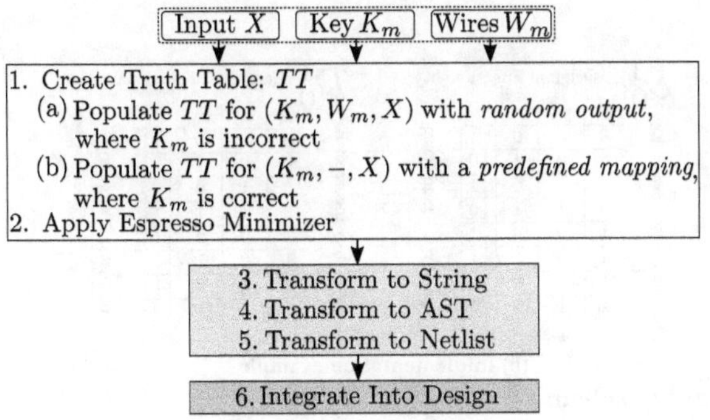


**Figure 3: Key-dependent netlist generation flow**

of $K_0$ and $W_0$ are 1-bit signals. $\mathcal{E}$ defines how $X$ is encrypted and mapped to the corrupted counterpart $X^{\mathcal{E}}$ based on the sets $K_0$ and $W_0$ for module $M_0$:

$$\mathcal{E} : (K_0, W_0, X) \rightarrow X^{\mathcal{E}}. \quad (1)$$

Consequently, the decryption logic $\mathcal{D}$ decrypts the corrupted set of signals $X^{\mathcal{E}}$ back to the original values of $X$, based on the set $K_1$ and $W_1$ for module $M_1$:

$$\mathcal{D} : (K_1, W_1, X^{\mathcal{E}}) \rightarrow X, \text{where } K_1 \neq K_0. \quad (2)$$

The signals in $W_1$ must be selected to prevent circular dependencies in the design of $\mathcal{D}$; preferably from a set of wires near the netlist inputs of $M_1$ and not positioned in the output cone of $X^{\mathcal{E}}$.

In the following, we discuss the design objectives and implementation details of different Control-Lock encryption schemes.

## 3.1 Design Objectives

To maximize the security and applicability of Control-Lock, we define the following design objectives: (*i*) key-dependent corruption, (*ii*) indistinguishability of the encryption and decryption logic compared to the original netlist and (*iii*) compatibility with any logic encryption algorithm.

**Key Dependency:** The key dependency of Control-Lock is fulfilled due to its basic design concept; the output of $\mathcal{E}$ and $\mathcal{D}$ depends on a set of keys. Correctly set keys imply that both $\mathcal{E}$ and $\mathcal{D}$ are able to encrypt and decrypt the given signals. If at least one of the keys $K_0$ or $K_1$ is incorrect (Figure 2 (b)), where $K_0 \neq K_1$, the encryption fails and *the overall design functionality* is corrupted.

**Indistinguishability:** The indistinguishability property assures that $\mathcal{E}$ and $\mathcal{D}$ cannot be structurally divided from the original netlist of a module so that removal-attack resilience is achieved. Control-Lock fulfills this property based on the fact that $\mathcal{E}$ and $\mathcal{D}$ depend on a set of chosen *original* wires $W_0$ and $W_1$ from the initial netlists. For example, the encryption logic $\mathcal{E}$ in Figure 2 (b) depends on the set $W_0$. Therefore, the functionality of $\mathcal{E}$ is partially driven by the set $W_0$, i.e., the original logic. After resynthesis, $\mathcal{E}$ and $\mathcal{D}$ are integrated into the module netlists. This has another important benefit; the adversary is not able to differentiate which key inputs are used for $\mathcal{E}$ or $\mathcal{D}$ and which for the actual logic encryption.

**Compatibility:** The compatibility objective is inherently fulfilled as Control-Lock can be applied to a netlist before or after the actual logic encryption has been done without affecting the security of the logic encryption algorithm.

In the following, we only exemplify the implementation of the encryption logic, as the decryption counterpart is designed using the same principles.

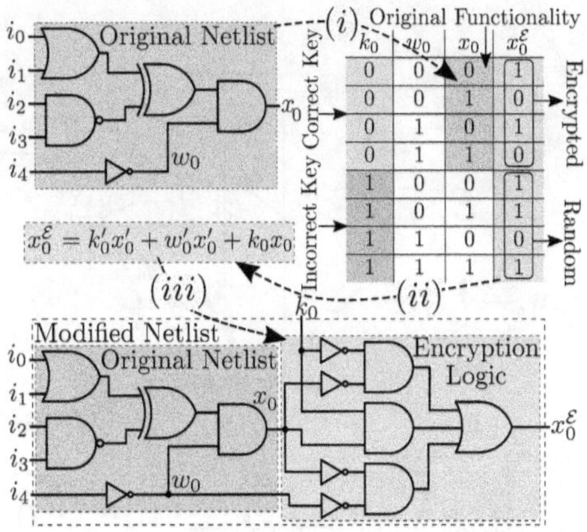


**Figure 4: 1-bit encryption logic example:** (*i*) **TT generation,** (*ii*) **minimization and** (*iii*) **transformation and integration**

## 3.2 Key-Dependent Netlist Generation

To maximally obfuscate the selected $X$, $X^{\mathcal{E}}$ should behave randomly for any incorrect key. For correctly set keys, $\mathcal{E}$ and $\mathcal{D}$ must perform a valid encryption of $X$ and decryption of $X^{\mathcal{E}}$. For this purpose, we introduce the key-dependent netlist generation flow presented in Figure 3. The input of the flow is a set of signals $X$, a selected key $K_m$ and a set of randomly selected signals (wires) $W_m$ from the module $M_m$, where $m$ is the module identifier. The flow consist of three phases: Truth Table (*TT*) generation, Boolean function transformation and netlist integration.

In the first phase, the *TT* is initialized. The input of *TT* is defined with the group of signals $(K_m, W_m, X)$. Where $K_m$ *is incorrect*, a random output is assigned for every $(K_m, W_m, X)$. Where $K_m$ *is correct*, a selected encoding is generated and inserted into *TT* for every $(K_m, -, X)$. In case of a correct key, the encoding does not functionally depend on the values of $W_m$. Afterwards, the *TT* is minimized using the *espresso logic minimizer* [2], offering compact Boolean functions that result in a low area overhead.

The second phase concerns the transformation of the *TT* into a generic netlist. In the first step, the *TT* is transformed into a *string* representing the Boolean function (e.g., sum of products). In the next step, this string is parsed into an Abstract Syntax Tree (AST). The AST is a suitable structure for generating 2-input gates representing the Boolean function. The final netlist is stored in plain Verilog. Finally, the generated netlist is embedded into the original design by coupling all necessary wires to drive $\mathcal{E}$ and $\mathcal{D}$.

A simple generation example for a 1-bit output where $|K_m| = 1$, $|W_m| = 1$ and $|X| = 1$, is presented in Figure 4. The selected output $x_0$ is encrypted by inverting its value when a correct key is applied. Otherwise, for an incorrect key, the encryption logic generates a random output. After minimization, the additional logic is integrated back into the netlist. After resynthesis, the structural boundaries between the original netlist and the encryption logic disappear (not shown in example). The same concept is repeated for the decryption logic to reverse $x_0^{\mathcal{E}}$ back to $x_0$.

## 3.3 Signal Grouping Schemes

So far, we considered that every bit $x_i$ can be encrypted and decrypted individually, as shown in Figure 4. However, in order to achieve a larger encoding/decoding space for a given key to strengthen the encryption, we introduce the concept of *signal*

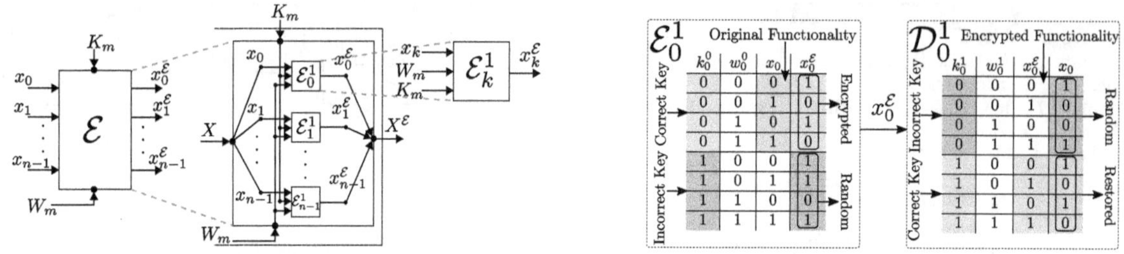


(a) Design concept

(b) Implementation example

**Figure 5: 1-bit signal grouping scheme**

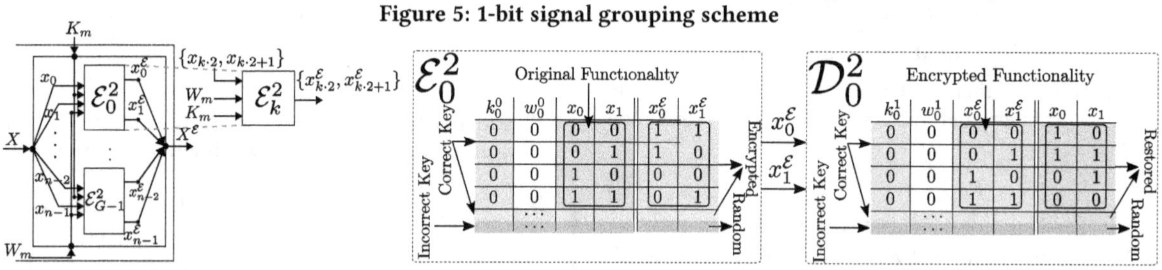


(a) Design concept

(b) Implementation example

**Figure 6: 2-bit signal grouping scheme**

*grouping schemes.* A grouping scheme defines how $X$ is divided into groups of signals. All signals in a group are jointly encrypted. A grouping scheme can be defined as follows:

$$\mathcal{E} = (\mathcal{E}_0^{N_0}, \dots, \mathcal{E}_{G-1}^{N_{G-1}}), \tag{3}$$

where $G$ is the number of groups $X$ is divided into and $N_k$ the number of bits in a group $k$, where $0 \le k < G$ and $\sum_{k=0}^{G-1} N_k = |X|$.

**1-bit Grouping:** Let us first consider the simplest case of a 1-bit grouping scheme where every $N_k = 1$, shown in Figure 5 (a). The encryption $\mathcal{E}$ is implemented as the grouping scheme $\mathcal{E} = (\mathcal{E}_0^1, \dots, \mathcal{E}_{G-1}^1)$. Every $\mathcal{E}_k^1$, where $0 \le k < G$, defines the encryption of a single $x_k$ individually, i.e.:

$$\mathcal{E}_k^1 : (K_m, W_m, \{x_k\}) \to \{x_k^{\mathcal{E}}\}. \tag{4}$$

Therefore, $G = |X|$ and $x_i = x_k$. The 1-bit grouping can be implemented as shown in Figure 5 (b); pairs $(\mathcal{E}_k^1, \mathcal{D}_k^1)$ for every $x_k$ are implemented with a separate $TT$. In this example, we assume that the correct 1-bit keys are $K_0 = \{0\}$ and $K_1 = \{1\}$, for $\mathcal{E}_0^1$ and $\mathcal{D}_0^1$ respectively. Since every $x_k^{\mathcal{E}}$ depends only on its original $x_k$ (apart from $K_m$ and $W_m$), one $TT$ per $x_k$ is generated.

To correctly generate $\mathcal{D}_k^1$, the information about how the encryption affects $x_k$ must be transfered. For example, if $\mathcal{E}_k^1$ inverts a selected $x_k$, than $\mathcal{D}_k^1$ has to invert it back to restore the original value. The 1-bit grouping scheme implements one functionality for every $x_k$: the signal is *forwarded* or *inverted* for a correct key.

**N-bit Grouping:** To utilize a stronger encryption, one $\mathcal{E}_k^{N_k}$ can jointly encrypt multiple $x_k$ ($N_k > 1$), creating a mutual dependency between the selected signals. For simplification, let us assume that $X$ is divided into $G$ groups of the same size, i.e.: $\forall N_k = N$. This additional dependency enables a new encryption strategy: for a selected $K_m$ and $W_m$, a mapping of a sequence of values can be defined, i.e.:

$$\mathcal{E}_k^N : (K_m, W_m, \{x_{k \cdot N}, \dots, x_{k \cdot N+(N-1)}\}) \\ \to \{x_{k \cdot N}^{\mathcal{E}}, \dots, x_{k \cdot N+(N-1)}^{\mathcal{E}}\}, \tag{5}$$

for every group $k$ where $0 \le k < G$. In general, any group of $N$ elements from $X$ can be selected to mutually depend on each other. As before, the correct mapping information must be transfered from $\mathcal{E}_k^N$ to $\mathcal{D}_k^N$. For example, let us consider the 2-bit grouping shown in Figure 6 (a). In this example, $X$ is partitioned into subsequent groups of $N = 2$ elements, i.e., every group of two encrypted signals $\{x_{k \cdot 2}^{\mathcal{E}}, x_{k \cdot 2+1}^{\mathcal{E}}\}$ depends on two inputs $\{x_{k \cdot 2}, x_{k \cdot 2+1}\}$, apart from $K_m$ and $W_m$. One implementation is shown in Figure 6 (b). For simplification, we assume that the correct key values are $K_0 = \{0\}$ and $K_1 = \{0\}$. Moreover, only a small part of the truth tables is presented. Since the selected $x_0$ and $x_1$ depend on each other, we can define the mapping $\{x_0, x_1\} \to \{x_0^{\mathcal{E}}, x_1^{\mathcal{E}}\}$, for all correct and incorrect keys. Afterwards, $\mathcal{D}$ needs to map all encrypted values $\{x_0^{\mathcal{E}}, x_1^{\mathcal{E}}\}$ back to the original form $\{x_0, x_1\}$ for a correct key. This joint encryption has the benefit that the single $x_0$ cannot be correctly decrypted without simultaneously considering the value of $x_1$, and vice versa. However, a higher grouping can lead to a higher area, delay or power cost.

Furthermore, the decryption logic $\mathcal{D}$ can have different implementations for the same $X^{\mathcal{E}}$ (if $X$ is an input to multiple separate modules). This is also one aspect of Control-Lock in favor of removal-attack resilience.

Note that a selected $X^{\mathcal{E}}$ can also be forwarded through registers (e.g., a pipeline). This however has no impact on the Control-Lock scheme as long as $X^{\mathcal{E}}$ connects $\mathcal{E}$ and $\mathcal{D}$.

# 4 EVALUATION

This section evaluates multiple Control-Lock schemes based on a RISC-V case study and the DoS Trojan described in Section 1.

## 4.1 Experimental Environment

To evaluate Control-Lock, the RI5CY core was selected [3]. RI5CY is an open-source single-core microcontroller based on the open-source RISC-V ISA [4]. For RTL and post-synthesis gate-level simulation the ModelSim HDL simulator by Mentor Graphics was used.

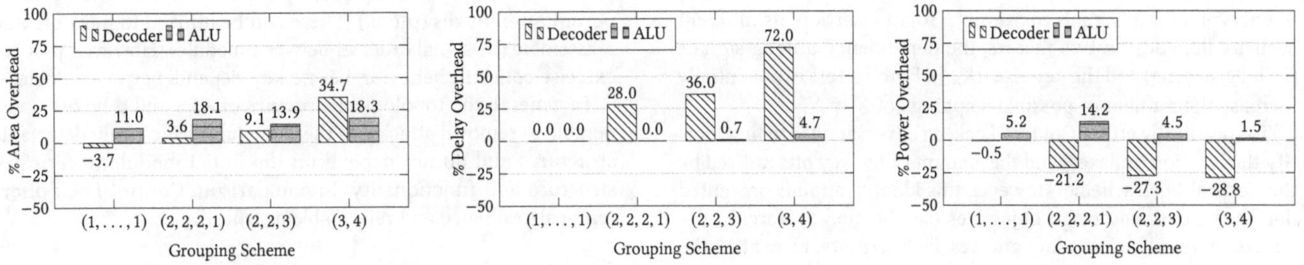


(a) Area overhead

(b) Delay overhead

(c) Power overhead

**Figure 7: RISC-V case study: overhead increase for selected grouping schemes**

**Table 1: Initial module area, delay and power**

| Module | Area [GE] | Min. Delay [ns] | Power [mW] |
|---|---|---|---|
| Decoder | 1,330 | 0.25 | 1.59 |
| ALU | 9,646 | 1.50 | 4.13 |
| RI5CY Core | 47,000 | 2.25 | 300 |

The logic synthesis was performed with Synopsys Design Compiler and the Faraday 90 nm technology library. Control-Lock was implemented using C++ and Python. The PyEDA library was used for Boolean function transformations [2].

## 4.2 RISC-V Case Study

Since Control-Lock is based on random behavior for incorrect keys, it becomes a challenge to fully predict the additional area, delay and power impact for a concrete implementation. Therefore, we selected two modules out of the RI5CY core: the decoder (ID stage) and the ALU (EX stage). This selection was based on the Trojan mentioned in Figure 1.

In this case study, an encryption unit $\mathcal{E}$ is appended to the decoder, while a decryption unit $\mathcal{D}$ is integrated at the inputs of the ALU. The initial post-synthesis area, delay and power evaluation for the modules without any encryption and the total core is presented in Table 1. The area is measured in Gate Equivalent (GE) for easier comparison. The values correspond to performance optimized designs. The ALU is more than seven times larger than the decoder, offering a suitable difference for evaluation.

The 7-bit *alu_operator* signal was selected for encryption with Control-Lock. We evaluated four different bit grouping schemes in the form of $(N_0, N_1, \ldots, N_{G-1})$, including: $(1, \ldots, 1)$, $(2, 2, 2, 1)$, $(2, 2, 3)$ and $(4, 3)$. Every number indicates one selected $N_k$-bit grouping, where $\sum_{k=0}^{G-1} N_k = |alu\_operator|$. The area, delay and power overhead per evaluated grouping scheme is shown in Figure 7. All evaluations consider the fastest achieved implementation. Furthermore, we assume $|W| = 1$ and $|K| = |X|$.

The highest grouping $(3, 4)$ generates an area overhead of up to 34.7% for the decoder and 18.3% for the ALU (Figure 7 (a)). While the area overhead increases for the decoder with higher groupings, the area overhead for the ALU does not change significantly. Interestingly, the lowest grouping $(1, \ldots, 1)$ has even decreased the total area of the decoder by 3.7%. In this case, the synthesis was able to find a more optimized mapping for the integrated logic.

The ALU has marginally been affected by Control-Lock in terms of the delay (Figure 7 (b)); only up to 4.7% for the highest grouping $(3, 4)$, while the delay overhead for the decoder reaches up to 72%. However, the more significant area and delay increase for the decoder for higher groupings is expected. For a selected grouping, approximately the same amount of gates is generated for $\mathcal{E}$ and $\mathcal{D}$. As the ALU is significantly larger than the decoder, the additional logic has a lower impact on its design.

Even though the delay overhead seems high for some groupings for the decoder, we need to take two factors into account. First, the high delay impact is only manifested in the relatively small decoder. Secondly, we need to consider the *critical path delay* of the RI5CY core to place the generated Control-Lock overhead into the right context. In fact, the critical path delay of the core is around 2.25 ns and it is placed in one of the peripherals and not in the core itself. Therefore, the delay overheads implied by Control-Lock in this scenario, *have no impact on the throughput of the core.*

The power has been evaluated by providing the correct Control-Lock key *after synthesis* (Figure 7 (c)). The power overhead of the ALU reaches up to 14.2% for the grouping $(2, 2, 2, 1)$, but decreases to only 1.5% for the highest grouping $(3, 4)$. Here, the synthesis was able to find a mapping that yields a lower power overhead, but increases the delay (4.7%). The power overhead for the decoder is negative for all evaluated groupings (up to -28.8%). Even though this is generally not expected, we have to consider the delay overhead to understand this effect (Figure 7 (b)). On one hand, some of the additional logic was placed on the critical path of the decoder, resulting in an increased delay. On the other hand, the longer critical path enabled more room for optimization on the shorter paths.

In general, the total area overhead for the *complete core* for the highest grouping is only 4.75% for the selected control signals, while the total power is even decreased due to the optimized decoder. Moreover, the delay overhead is not affecting the critical path. Since a higher grouping offers a more secure design and a reasonable overhead (especially for larger modules), *it should be prioritized.*

# 5 DISCUSSION

This section provides a discussion on the security analysis, optimization aspects and limitation of Control-Lock, thereby indication future improvements and research opportunities.

## 5.1 Security Analysis

We have to consider two security aspects of Control-Lock: the *overall* and the *inherent* security. The overall security depends on the security of the selected logic encryption algorithm due to the following reasons. First, the Control-Lock key is integrated into the logic encryption key, making it indistinguishable from the rest of the encryption. Secondly, Control-Lock changes the original functionality of the selected modules, i.e., *the activated design (oracle) is corrupted as well.* Therefore, the primary goal of an adversary is to first find the logic encryption key with a logic decryption scheme [8], before being able to reason about the encrypted control signals. However, as the goal of Control-Lock is to encrypt a set of signals to prevent Trojan insertion, its inherent security depends on two factors: the dependency among signals ($N$-bit grouping) and the key size ($|K_m|$). Both factors exponentially increase the number of possible mappings of $X$ to $X^{\mathcal{E}}$.

To specifically attack Control-Lock, an adversary has to first identify the location (indexes) and the amount of the key bits utilized by the Control-Lock scheme. However, this identification is prevented due to the defined design objectives (see Section 3), forcing the adversary to rely on random guesses. Furthermore, even after the correct key is identified, the signals are still encoded, making it difficult to isolate and identify the correct control signals.

In the context of the DoS Trojan described in Section 1, even if the adversary is able to identify the correct *alu_operator* signals without the need to unlock the whole circuit, a simple Trojan insertion remains unfeasible as the adversary cannot rely on the expected behavior of the software-controlled signals. Therefore, Control-Lock secures the selected $X$ by *excluding the direct utilization of the signals as Trojan triggers and forcing the adversary to first decrypt the overall design*, i.e., all modules affected by Control-Lock.

### 5.2 Optimization Aspects

Control-Lock can be applied to any control or even data signal in a processor core. However, to hamper the overhead cost, this methodology should be limited to protecting *critical signals* that are *easily exploitable* through instruction execution and can lead to serious consequences, e.g., a targeted system failure. The identification of security-critical signals in processors is left for future work.

To lower the overhead of Control-Lock, the random netlist generation can be adapted by carefully steering the output randomness to result in low-overhead functions as well as express better cryptographic properties. This is however susceptible to security flaws and must be further evaluated.

In this work, we assume that $|X| = |X^{\mathcal{E}}|$. However, this is not a fixed requirement. In fact, Control-Lock can be utilized to generate a set of encrypted signals where $|X^{\mathcal{E}}| > |X|$. Hereby, some of the signals are redundant, but cannot be identified as such, offering a higher security level.

### 5.3 Limitations

Control-Lock cannot protect against Trojans that are driven by internal module signals, as these Trojans act within the interfaces of one module. However, we assume that understanding the internal signals within one module is more complex than reasoning about its interfaces. Moreover, protecting against hardware Trojans in infected third-party IP blocks is beyond the scope of this work.

## 6 RELATED WORK

To the best of our knowledge, Control-Lock is the first technique to protect against hardware Trojans exploiting inter-module control signals in multi-module designs. However, we mention several alternative solutions for comparison.

One option to secure control signals is to utilize fully fledged (data) encryption, e.g., an Advanced Encryption Standard (AES) cipher [1]. Even though this is currently the most secure solution, it implies having one cipher module for each $\mathcal{E}$ and $\mathcal{D}$. Since hardware implementations of AES often exceed 20,000 gates and the computation requires multiple cycles, this method yields high area, power and delay overheads [13]. A simpler solution is provided by permutation boxes (p-box). These can be utilized to permute and reassemble the signal order in-between modules. However, p-boxes exercise constant behavior, i.e., no key-dependency is available.

In general, the topological structure of AES and p-boxes is vulnerable to removal attacks, as these modules have easily detectable structures and do not depend on the initial module in terms of structure and functionality. In comparison, Control-Lock offers removal-resilience and reasonable overhead.

## 7 CONCLUSION

In this paper, we presented Control-Lock, a novel methodology for thwarting software-controlled hardware Trojans exploiting inter-module control signals in processor cores. The signals are encrypted and decrypted between modules based on the proposed randomized key-dependent netlist generation flow. The design and implementation concepts of different grouping schemes have been described. The applicability was demonstrated on a RISC-V processor case study, assuming a denial of service Trojan. The experimental results were analyzed according to the security-cost trade-off. A comparison to alternative solutions was provided, indicating the benefits of Control-Lock. The results of the highest evaluated grouping scheme on the larger design show a limited area overhead (18.3%) as well as negligible delay (4.7%) and power (1.5%) overheads. Furthermore, the total area overhead for protecting against a major attack exploiting the opcode in a processor is only 4.75%. With Control-Lock, we encourage more research on protecting against software-controlled Trojans in processor designs. In future work, we plan to perform further security evaluations as well as extend the methodology in regards to the mentioned optimization aspects.

## REFERENCES

[1] Joan Daemen and Vincent Rijmen. 2002. *The Design of Rijndael.* Springer-Verlag, Berlin, Heidelberg.
[2] Chris Drake. 2015. Pyeda: Data Structures and Algorithms for Electronic Design Automation. In *Proceedings of the 14th Python in Science Conference.* 26–31.
[3] A. Traber et al. 2016. PULPino: A Small Single-Core RISC-V SoC. In *3rd RISCV Workshop.*
[4] A. Waterman et al. 2014. The RISC-V Instruction Set Manual. *volume I: User-level ISA, version 2.0, EECS Department, University of California, Berkeley, Tech. Rep. UCB/EECS-2014-54* (2014).
[5] B. Shakya et al. 2017. Benchmarking of Hardware Trojans and Maliciously Affected Circuits. *Journal of Hardware and Systems Security* 1, 1 (01 Mar 2017), 85–102. https://doi.org/10.1007/s41635-017-0001-6
[6] H. Salmani et al. 2013. On Design Vulnerability Analysis and Trust Benchmarks Development. In *2013 IEEE 31st International Conference on Computer Design (ICCD).* 471–474. https://doi.org/10.1109/ICCD.2013.6657085
[7] K. Xiao et al. 2016. Hardware Trojans: Lessons Learned after One Decade of Research. 22 (05 2016), 1–23.
[8] M. Yasin et al. 2017. Evolution of Logic Locking. In *2017 VLSI-SoC.* 1–6. https://doi.org/10.1109/VLSI-SoC.2017.8203496
[9] M. Yasin et al. 2017. Provably-Secure Logic Locking: From Theory To Practice. In *Proceedings of the 2017 ACM SIGSAC (CCS '17).* ACM, New York, NY, USA, 1601–1618. https://doi.org/10.1145/3133956.3133985
[10] P. Subramanyan et al. 2014. Reverse Engineering Digital Circuits Using Structural and Functional Analyses. *IEEE Transactions on Emerging Topics in Computing* 2, 1 (March 2014), 63–80. https://doi.org/10.1109/TETC.2013.2294918
[11] S. Amir et al. 2017. Comparative Analysis of Hardware Obfuscation for IP Protection. In *Proceedings of GLSVLSI 2017 (GLSVLSI '17).* ACM, New York, NY, USA, 363–368. https://doi.org/10.1145/3060403.3060495
[12] S. Bhunia et al. 2014. Hardware Trojan Attacks: Threat Analysis and Countermeasures. *Proc. IEEE* 102, 8 (Aug 2014), 1229–1247. https://doi.org/10.1109/JPROC.2014.2334493
[13] Ingrid Verbauwhede. 2011. AES and Other Secret Key Implementations. https://www.cosic.esat.kuleuven.be/ecrypt/courses/albena11/slides/ingrid_verbauwhede_aes_implementations.pdf Accessed September 2018.
[14] D. Šišejković et al. 2018. A Unifying Logic Encryption Security Metric. In *2018 SAMOS.*

# Lightweight Authenticated Encryption for Network-on-Chip Communications

Julian Harttung
Technische Universität Dresden
Chair of Computer Graphics and Visualisation
julian.harttung@tu-dresden.de

Elke Franz
Technische Universität Dresden
Chair of Privacy and Data Security
elke.franz@tu-dresden.de

Sadia Moriam
Technische Universität Dresden
Vodafone Chair Mobile Communication Systems
sadia.moriam@tu-dresden.de

Paul Walther
Technische Universität Dresden
Chair of Privacy and Data Security
paul.walther@tu-dresden.de

## ABSTRACT

In recent years, Network-on-Chip (NoC) has gained increasing popularity as a promising solution for the challenging interconnection problem in multi-processor systems-on-chip (MPSoCs). However, the interest of adversaries to compromise such systems grew accordingly, mandating the integration of security measures into NoC designs.

Within this paper, we introduce three novel lightweight approaches for securing communication in NoCs. The suggested solutions combine encryption, authentication, and network coding in order to ensure confidentiality, integrity, and robustness. With performance being critical in NoC environments, our solutions particularly emphasize low latencies and low chip area.

Our approaches were evaluated through extensive software simulations. The results have shown that the performance degradation induced by the protection measures is clearly outweighed by the aforementioned benefits. Furthermore, the area overhead implied by the additional components is reasonably low.

## CCS CONCEPTS

**• Security and privacy → Embedded systems security; • Networks → Security protocols; Network on chip; • Computer systems organization → System on a chip.**

## KEYWORDS

Network-on-Chip, Hardware trojans, integrity, availability

**ACM Reference Format:**
Julian Harttung, Elke Franz, Sadia Moriam, and Paul Walther. 2019. Lightweight Authenticated Encryption for Network-on-Chip Communications. In *Great Lakes Symposium on VLSI 2019 (GLSVLSI '19), May 9–11, 2019, Tysons Corner, VA, USA.* ACM, New York, NY, USA, 6 pages. https://doi.org/10.1145/3299874.3317990

This work is partly supported by the German Research Foundation (DFG) in the CRC 912 "Highly Adaptive Energy-Efficient Computing" and within the Cluster of Excellence "Center for Advancing Electronics Dresden".


ACM ISBN 978-1-4503-6252-8/19/05...$15.00
https://doi.org/10.1145/3299874.3317990

## 1 INTRODUCTION

The increasingly growing number of processing cores on a chip led to the domain of so-called multi-processor systems-on-chip (MPSoCs) [8]. As a result, efficient and reliable communication between potentially thousands of cores became a crucial task that cannot be tackled by bus-based systems. Hence, packet-switched Network-on-Chip (NoC) has established itself as a promising solution for the challenging interconnection problem [3, 10].

NoCs scale better with the number of cores and aim to overcome the drawbacks of traditional buses. However, the rise of NoCs also implies an increased interest of adversaries to compromise systems that implement them. Particularly due to the trend of chip manufacturers integrating a growing number of third party components, the threat of hardware itself being compromised due to the injection of hardware trojans (HTs) becomes increasingly relevant as a major attack vector [2, 4, 22]. An HT can be triggered to perform different kinds of attacks. We focus here on attacks on data transmission, namely eavesdropping and modifying or dropping flits.

In recent years, various approaches for securing NoC communication have been published. Among them, there are suggestions on how to prevent an attacker to trigger an HT [2, 22]. Another direction of research is to detect and suppress HTs [11, 15, 22]. However, protection against all different types of HTs cannot be guaranteed [4]. Hence, protection mechanisms need to be integrated into the system. The basic requirements on these mechanisms are that they are effective against the considered attacks and efficient so that they can be integrated into a NoC. Since a NoC is an environment with very strict requirements on low computational and communication overhead as well as low transmission delays, common protection mechanisms cannot directly be integrated.

To prevent modifications of transmitted data, Boraten and Kodi suggested the use of algebraic manipulation detection codes [6]. While the authors assume that sensitive or encrypted data may be sent, they do not explicitly consider encryption in their design. Kapoor et al. focused on ensuring both confidentiality and integrity by means of authenticated encryption [14]. However, they consider the use of AES-128 as the cryptographic primitive, which is heavyweight in both latency and area requirement. Hence, it is considered inapt given the challenging requirements in the NoC context.

The use of network coding [1] for NoC communication was shown to provide promising performance benefits [19]. The key idea of network coding is to compute and send linear combinations of data blocks. Hence, throughput, energy efficiency, and robustness against packet loss can be increased. As an additional protection against active attacks, two lightweight schemes were introduced in [20]. These schemes allow for an authentication of flits and, thus, for a recognition of modifications. Nevertheless, confidentiality was still not covered.

In this paper, we make the following *contributions*: We (1) introduce three lightweight approaches for the protection of *confidentiality and integrity*, (2) evaluate the efficiency of the suggested solutions by means of *comprehensive simulations*, (3) evaluate the influence of *ARQ limits*, and (4) investigate the *performance impact* entailed by security including a discussion of area requirements. Our results show that it is possible to obtain strong security with reasonable costs.

The paper is structured as follows. Section 2 describes our system model and the attacker model. The concept is introduced in Section 3. In Section 4, we evaluate our approach and present and discuss the results. Section 5 summarizes our findings and gives an outlook.

## 2 ASSUMPTIONS

### 2.1 System Model and Communication Model

Within this work, we assume a 2D mesh network with $n \times n$ nodes as the underlying NoC topology. Each node consists of a processing element (PE), a network interface (NI), and a router. PEs execute applications and require the ability to communicate with other PEs. Usually, messages to be sent are split into packets, which are then further divided into flits (flow control units) of a fixed length. Since we focus on the protection of communication, we simplify this process and assume that PEs generate flits that need to be transmitted to their respective receiving PEs. The flit size is assumed to be approximately 150 bits.

We focus on the transmission of single flits, i.e, each flit contains several header fields and a payload. From point of view of communication overhead, sending single flits represents the worst case. Alternative communication models like burst mode only reduce the communication overhead. Basic header fields that are found in all our protocol variants are a burst bit (reserved for future work), the $x$ and $y$ coordinates of source and target PE (altogether 16 bits), a mode field (4 bits) that specifies the flit type, and an address field for memory accesses (32 bits, reserved for future work). The size of the payload is 64 bits.

We consider two basic communication schemes: uncoded transmission (UC) and network coded transmission (NC) implemented according to [9]. Since metadata like address information is needed in plain, linear combinations are only computed from the payload fields of flits. Computations are done in finite fields where the payload of flit $f_i$ is represented by a vector $\vec{p}_i = (p_{i,1}, p_{i,2}, \ldots, p_{i,n}) \in \mathbb{F}_q^n$ with $q = 2^m$. According to [20], we assume $m = 4$.

The sender organizes the payload vectors of flits to be sent to the same destination into generations of size $G$. We assume $G = 2$ in order to achieve average latencies comparable to uncoded transmission [19]. A unit vector $\vec{\beta}_i \in \mathbb{F}_q^G$ that represents the global encoding vector (GEV) is prepended to each payload vector $\vec{p}_i$. Hence, the resulting generation is given by:

$$\begin{pmatrix} \vec{p}_1 \\ \vec{p}_2 \end{pmatrix} = \begin{pmatrix} 1 & 0 & p_{1,1} & p_{1,2} & \cdots & p_{1,n} \\ 0 & 1 & p_{2,1} & p_{2,2} & \cdots & p_{2,n} \end{pmatrix} \tag{1}$$

For each generation, the sender computes $C$ linear combinations $\vec{c}_k = \alpha_1 \cdot \vec{p}_1 + \alpha_2 \cdot \vec{p}_2$ with randomly selected coefficients $\alpha_i \in \mathbb{F}_q$. Intermediate nodes merely forward the flits to prevent them from being burdened with additional effort. Since the coefficients are applied to all symbols of $\vec{p}_i$, the GEV reflects all operations. This enables the receiver to decode the original data by solving a system of linear equations if it received at least $G$ linearly independent combinations of a generation. The receiver needs to know to which generation a combination belongs; hence, a 24-bit generation identifier *gid* is included in the flit. The *gid* has to be unique to prevent the reinjection of intercepted flits (replay attacks). In case of UC, the *gid* field contains a flit identifier $fid$ of the same size. Hence, the overall flit size equals 141 bits for UC and 149 bits for NC.

For our investigations, we worked with $C = 3$ and $C = 4$. Thus, there are three basic communication schemes: **UC**, **G2C3** (NC with $G = 2, C = 3$), and **G2C4** (NC with $G = 2, C = 4$).

### 2.2 Attacker Model

We consider PEs and NIs to be trustworthy while routers may be infected by HTs. This attacker model is based on the assumption that the use of third party components is more likely for routers since they do not contain specialized business logic. This may open up a way for injecting HTs into the NoC.

HTs may execute both passive and active attacks. Passive attacks threaten the confidentiality of the transmitted data. Regarding active attacks, we focus on HTs that modify or drop flits, thereby jeopardizing integrity and also availability since the receiver does not obtain the original data.

For simulation of active attacks, a number of routers is selected as malicious. A malicious router attacks all types of flits with a certain attack probability $p_a$. We assume $p_a < 1$ to complicate detectability of malicious routers. In case of an attack, the flit is either modified or dropped, with both cases being equiprobable. Security measures are integrated into the NIs that are assumed to be trustworthy.

### 2.3 Assumptions Regarding Protection Measures

The NoC context entails challenging requirements regarding performance. Despite the fact that security measures always imply additional costs, a feasible solution must neither cause significant overhead in terms of computation or communication nor a substantial increase of average path latencies. Hence, we emphasize lightweight solutions. Confidentiality and integrity are enforced in an end-to-end manner to eliminate computational overhead for intermediate nodes. However, each NI needs to be equipped with the necessary functionality for encryption/decryption and authentication since every PE can act as both sender and receiver.

Encryption is employed to prevent passive attacks that threaten confidentiality from succeeding. Authentication is used to enable the detection of modifications. We use only symmetric cryptography since it provides significantly better performance than asymmetric cryptography.[1] If the receiver detects a modification, it discards the corresponding flit.

An active attacker can also drop flits. A receiver can recognize such flit losses through the use of timers that are started after the arrival of a flit. A timeout occurring before the arrival of the next related flit indicates a flit loss. To allow for retransmissions of lost or discarded flits, we employ ARQs.

# 3 CONCEPT

## 3.1 Cryptographic Primitives

Cryptographic operations induce the highest latencies in our suggested schemes. In order to prevent them from becoming a bottleneck in the system, we integrate multiple crypto modules in each NI so that several flits can be processed in parallel.

In addition, we make use of lightweight ciphers. They are specifically designed to enable secure but efficient hardware implementations with low area and power requirements as well as small computational delays. In preliminary investigations [13], we thoroughly explored various hardware-optimized algorithms like PRESENT [5], mCrypton [17], and PRINCE [7]. All these algorithms are block ciphers with a block length of 64 bits. A dedicated FPGA implementation of each algorithm was used to allow for a fair comparison. PRESENT was found to occupy the least chip area, while PRINCE managed to be the fastest with only one clock cycle per block, albeit at a lower clock frequency than its competitors. Additionally, our results confirmed the large discrepancy of AES to the lightweight algorithms, corroborating its ineptitude in the NoC context.

We decided to use PRINCE since low latencies are considered to be especially important. Further, an algorithm with higher latencies implies a larger number of parallel crypto modules needed to prevent the cryptographic operations from becoming a bottleneck. Hence, the required total area might become even larger than with an algorithm with lower latencies but higher area requirements.

The ordering of encryption and authentication influences security as well as performance. We opted for Encrypt-then-MAC, i.e., the sender first encrypts the plaintext before he computes a MAC over the resulting ciphertext. This method provides integrity on the received ciphertext and, consequently, also on the plaintext. The receiver can compute the MAC for verification and in parallel start decryption. In case of an integrity breach, ARQs can be issued earliest as the verification is performed directly after the flits arrive.

In all communication schemes, confidentiality is achieved by encrypting the payload. If the sender encrypted all flits intended for the same receiver individually, this would correspond to the electronic codebook (ECB) mode [21] where encryption of identical plaintext blocks results in identical ciphertext blocks. To overcome this problem, we employ PRINCE for encryption in counter mode (CTR) [21]. In CTR, the block cipher is used to encrypt a counter. The resulting ciphertext block is used as a pseudorandom key for the actual encryption of the message by bitwise XOR. The counter must not be repeated as long as the same key is in use. In our scenario, the counter needs to be known to sender and receiver even in case of flit loss or if the ordering of flits was changed during transmission. Hence, the flit identifier (padded with zeros to get a block of 64 bit length) is used as counter.

[1]The use of cryptography requires a secure and efficient key management, however, this topic is beyond the scope of this paper.

## 3.2 Communication Protocols

In this paper, we extend the two lightweight solutions called (S1) and (S2) for authentication of communication introduced in [20]. In both schemes, the sender authenticates individual combinations. Additionally, we consider the authentication of all uncoded flits of a generation. Hence, we investigate the following three approaches: Individual Authentication (based on (S1)), Interwoven Authentication (based on (S2)), and Full Generation Authentication.

**Individual Authentication (IDA):** In case of UC, the payload of each flit to be sent is encrypted in the first step. Since the size of the payload matches the block size, this requires only one encryption operation. Next, the flit is authenticated by computing a MAC over the entire flit. This ensures that any modification can be detected. The MAC is computed using PRINCE in cipher block chaining (CBC) mode [21] with the CBC-MAC scheme. Since the total length has to be a multiple of the block length, the last block is padded with zeros. The computed 64 bit MAC is transmitted in a new flit with the same header fields except for the mode that indicates that this is a MAC flit. Both flits are sent to the receiver, while copies are held in a retransmission buffer (RTB).

When a flit arrives at a node, the mode field is evaluated first. If the flit is an ARQ, the requested flit(s) are retrieved from the RTB and resent. If the requested flits cannot be found in the RTB, the ARQ is just discarded. If the flit is a MAC flit, it is stored in NI buffers until the verification process is completed. Remaining flits are data flits that contain an encrypted payload. They are first duplicated so that they can be processed in two pipelines. One copy is used for the computation of the MAC, the other one is decrypted. When the MAC computation has finished, integrity is checked by comparing the computed to the received MAC. Any difference between them indicates a modification. In this case, the verification fails and an ARQ is sent to request a retransmission of both data and MAC flit since it cannot be decided which one was altered. In case of a successful verification, the decrypted data flit is delivered to the PE.

In the NC case, processing is similar despite the fact that the computation of linear combinations is done after encryption. Hence, MACs are computed over each combination. On the receiver side, the MACs for verification also have to be computed for the received combinations. Thus, this process can start as soon as a flit arrives. Before decryption, network decoding has to take place which requires $G = 2$ flits from the generation to have arrived. If verification fails, all already decoded and decrypted flits of the corresponding generation have to be discarded since one corrupted flit implies incorrect decoding. If possible, decoding is repeated with other successfully verified combinations.

**Interwoven Authentication (IWA):** In contrast to IDA, payload and MAC are included in the same flit so that only one flit is needed for verification. After encryption, the payload is split into two halves of 32 bits each. A new flit is created with the same header fields except for the mode field that is used to distinguish between the two halves. In UC, a MAC of 32 bits is computed for each flit using an Authentication Code [23]. For details of this step, we refer to [20]. The pseudorandom 64 bit key that is needed for the computation of the MAC is produced by encrypting the header fields (77 bits) of the flit in CBC mode. This step requires two encryption operations since there are two input blocks.

The receiver again first checks the mode of arriving flits. ARQs are handled as described above. The payload of other flits is split into data and MAC. Verification starts immediately while the flit carrying the second half of the data has to arrive before decryption of the merged payload parts can start. If verification fails, already decrypted flits are discarded and an ARQ is triggered. Otherwise, the merged and decrypted payload is delivered to the PE.

In case of NC, the two flits with the encrypted and split payload establish a generation. The sender computes $C$ combinations out of them. MACs are generated for the combinations and appended to the encrypted data. Processing at the receiver side is similar to UC. The only difference is the additional decoding step before the resulting $G$ payload parts of 32 bits can be merged and decrypted.

**Full Generation Authentication (FGA):** In contrast to IDA and IWA, this protocol only exists for NC since it presumes the existence of a generation for authentication. The aim of FGA is to reduce communication overhead. After encryption of $G$ flits, a MAC is computed over these uncoded flits. The MAC is inserted into a new flit with the same header fields except for the mode field that is set to MAC type. Afterwards, $C$ linear combinations are computed out of the $G$ encrypted data flits. The resulting encrypted and encoded flits and the MAC flit are sent to the receiver.

Arriving ARQ flits are handled in the usual way. MAC flits are buffered until verification is possible. Before verification, $G$ data flits have to arrive. Using these flits, decoding is performed first before the MAC is computed over the resulting decoded flits. In parallel, decryption begins. In case of a successful verification, the two decoded flits are delivered to the PE. Otherwise, they have to be discarded. If more than $G$ data flits have arrived, decoding and verification is reattempted with another set of flits. In parallel, an ARQ is issued requesting the retransmission of the complete generation together with the MAC flit since it cannot be decided which of the flits have been modified.

# 4 EVALUATION

## 4.1 Simulation Settings and Performance Metrics

The performances of the proposed protocols were evaluated by means of simulations. We implemented a simulator[2] in C++ based on the OMNeT++ discrete event simulation framework [18]. Parameters and their value ranges are given in Tab. 1. The flit creation rate in the PEs was adapted to meet the injection rate $\lambda$. For IDA-UC and IWA-UC, a pair of flits intended for the same receiver is necessary before decoding can start. To allow for a fair comparison between all schemes, flits are always generated in pairs, i.e., when one flit is created, another one with the same destination is created in the next clock cycle.

The NoC's global clock was set to 500 MHz since this is a common speed in NoC-related research like [11, 12]. However, the chosen cryptographic algorithm PRINCE cannot run at this high frequency.

[2] Source code is available at https://github.com/huljar/noc-ae-simulator.

**Table 1: Overview of simulation parameters.**

| Parameter | Value |
|---|---|
| Topology | 2D mesh of size 8×8 |
| Routing | Deterministic, dimension-ordered XY |
| Clock frequency | 500 MHz |
| Arbitration | Uniform random |
| Injection rate | $\lambda = 0.2$ |
| Communication models | IDA-{UC,G2C3,G2C4}, IWA-{UC,G2C3,G2C4}, FGA-{G2C3,G2C4} |
| Malicious routers | 8 (randomly selected) |
| Attack probability | $0.02i,\ i \in [0, 10] \cap \mathbb{N}$ and $0.1i,\ i \in [3, 5] \cap \mathbb{N}$ |
| Simulation run time | 50000 cycles (+500 cycles warmup/cooldown time) |

The authors of PRINCE achieved 212.8 MHz using speed-optimized synthesis strategies and 45 nm technology. For this work, we assume the use of 28 nm technology according to [12]. Under this premise, a frequency of at least 250 MHz should definitely be possible. The use of different clock domains is enabled by the *globally asynchronous, locally synchronous* (GALS) paradigm [16]. To simplify matters, we used only one global clock in our simulations and assumed that a crypto module processes one input block in two cycles of that global clock. The total number of cycles for encryption/decryption and computation of the MAC depends on the number of blocks to be processed. For network encoding or decoding, we assume one cycle per flit. Further, we assume single cycle routing as it was proven to be both feasible and practical [24].

The maximum number of retransmissions and, likewise, ARQs is limited per transmission unit. A transmission unit contains a set of flits with the same $fid$ or $gid$. For UC, this refers to data and MAC flits in case of IDA and to the two split flits in case of IWA. With NC, all combinations of one generation as well as the corresponding MAC flits in case of IDA and FGA constitute a transmission unit. We assume that a modification of an ARQ simply prevents a retransmission and, hence, is treated like a lost ARQ.

In comprehensive prior simulation runs, we determined further simulation parameters. Thus, the ARQ timeout is set to 12 cycles and each NI is equipped with 3 encryption/decryption and 9 authentication modules that are used in parallel to ensure low waiting times of flits for a free crypto module. Given our settings, these numbers provide a good trade-off between latency and area.

To evaluate the performance, the following metrics were used:

- **Acceptance rate:** Average number of flits injected into the network by each node per clock cycle including ARQs and retransmissions; indicator for network load.
- **Information rate:** Quotient of the amount of flits created by PEs and the total number of flits injected into the network; indicator for protocol overhead.
- **Residual error probability:** Portion of flits created by PEs that are not successfully transmitted to the destination PE despite exhausting the maximum allowed number of ARQs; indicator for reliability and resilience.
- **Average end-to-end latency:** Mean transmission time of flits from creation in the source PE to delivery to the destination PE; indicator of transmission and processing delays.

## 4.2 Simulation Results

Using the settings given in Tab. 1 and the metrics defined above, the communication models were evaluated (Fig. 1). The acceptance

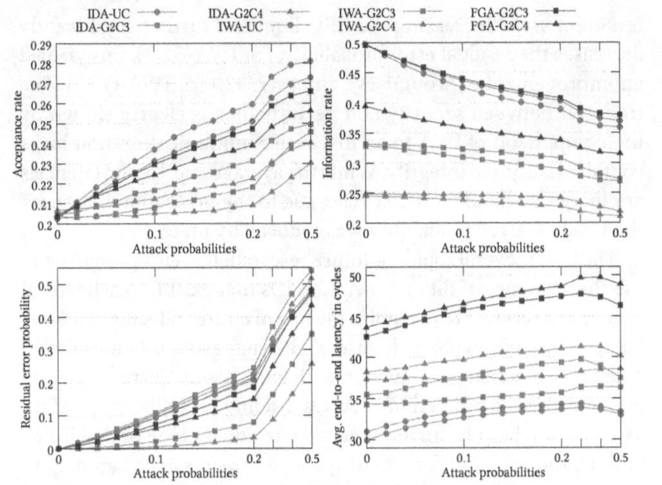


**Figure 1: Simulation results for all protocol variants.**

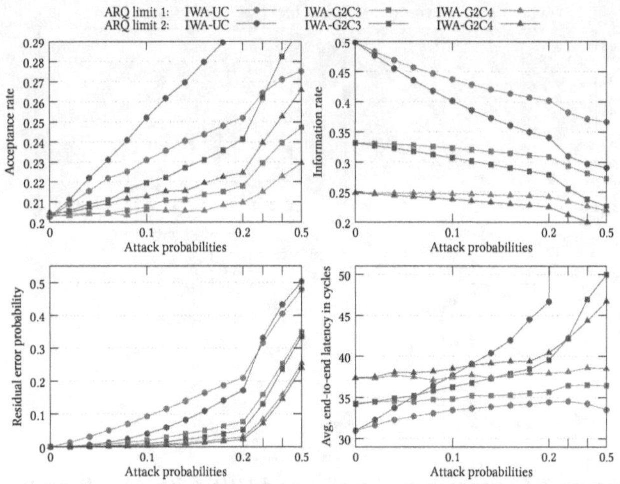


**Figure 2: Comparison of ARQ limit 1 and 2 for IWA.**

rate rises with increasing attack probabilities as more ARQs and retransmissions become necessary. The strongest growth is observed for the UC variants since they cannot recover from flit loss or modifications without issuing an ARQ. Similarly, FGA always entails an ARQ when a MAC flit is attacked. IDA and IWA with NC require significantly less ARQs as no single flit loss or modification within a generation can force a retransmission.

The information rates also reflect the portion of ARQs and retransmissions in the total traffic. Additionally, they show the overhead imposed by NC and authentication. For IDA-UC, IWA-UC, and FGA-G2C3, this overhead is lowest with 100%, while IDA-G2C4 and IWA-G2C4 display a 300% increase of flits.

The residual error probabilities show that IWA with NC mitigates the impact of attacks best, having significantly less residual errors than the other communication models. Peculiarly, IDA with NC performs worse than its UC counterpart. This happens due to the number of ARQs being limited per transmission unit, and IDA-UC having notably smaller transmission units.

Average end-to-end latencies increase with the number of combinations. Since FGA authenticates two flits at once, CBC-MAC takes almost twice as long as for the other schemes. The decrease for high attack probabilities is caused by the high number of flit drops – with less flits being present in the network, the successful transmissions are slightly faster.

Since the ARQs and retransmissions are just as vulnerable to attacks as the initial flits, we investigated increasing the ARQ limit to 2 per transmission unit. There, a further timer is started after the first ARQ is issued. The timeout of this timer depends on the Manhattan distance between source and target node to account for the round trip time of ARQ and retransmissions. Upon expiration, or if unrecoverable modifications are encountered in the retransmissions, the second ARQ is sent out. We chose IWA for this experiment as it performed best so far. Results are given in Fig. 2.

The acceptance rates are significantly higher and the information rates notably lower in the presence of attackers; both phenomena are explained by the additional secondary ARQs and retransmissions injected into the network. On the other side, a substantial improvement in terms of the residual errors was achieved. However, for high attack probabilities, the improvement vanishes quickly since the secondary retransmissions are likely to fail as well while still increasing the network load. The average end-to-end latencies rise due to the additional time the secondary retransmissions take. The skyrocketing value for UC coincides with high acceptance rates, indicating that the network becomes unable to handle the high traffic volume and experiences heavy congestions. All in all, for the NC versions, the increased ARQ limit proves to be advantageous, rendering the transmissions substantially more reliable.

Lastly, we compare these results to a baseline NoC simulation without security measures (NoSec). There, the NIs contain no crypto modules and no RTBs. Results are depicted in Fig. 3.

Acceptance rate and information rate were omitted as they are constant 0.2 and 1.0, respectively. Due to the lack of authentication, modified flits can reach the destination PEs undetected, hence an additional metric was included that shows the portion of modified flits from the total number of flits delivered to their destination PEs.

The results show that our security measures successfully reduce the number of residual errors by a large portion. While the number of corrupted arrivals is relatively low for NoSec, these cases still pose a serious threat that is fully mitigated by all our communication schemes. The cost of this is reflected in the latencies, which are significantly lower for the NoSec scenario.

### 4.3 Area Overhead

To give an impression of the chip area overhead required for our protocols, we have investigated the sizes of the additional components. The results are given in Tab. 2.

**Table 2: Additional chip area required per NI (ARQ limit 2).**

| | |
|---|---|
| Crypto modules | 99120 GEs |
| Network encoders/decoders | 8496 GEs |
| Retransmission buffers | 373 bytes |

Most of the additional chip area is occupied by the PRINCE modules. With 8260 GEs per module according to [7], a total of $12 \cdot 8260 = 99120$ GEs is required per NI (for 3 encryption/decryption and 9 authentication modules). The network encoders can be realized through look-up tables (LUTs) containing all product values

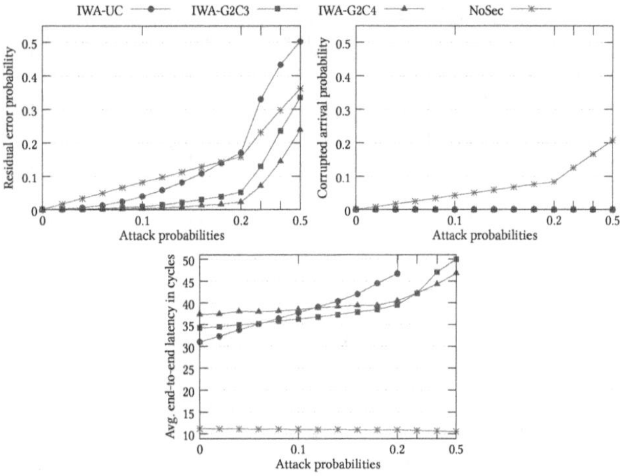


**Figure 3: Comparison of NoSec and IWA with ARQ limit 2.**

for the GF($2^4$) domain. According to [20], 36 LUTs are necessary to compute a combination within a single clock cycle. Furthermore, each LUT has a size of 118 GEs. Thus, 4248 GEs are occupied by the encoder. The decoders, which have to compute inverses of 2×2 matrices in GF($2^4$), are assumed to be of the same size. The RTB needs to be able to store flits long enough for them to still be present when a corresponding ARQ arrives (assuming a FIFO caching strategy). For an ARQ limit of 2, an initial ARQ timeout of 12 cycles, and NoC dimensions of 8×8, it was found that the secondary ARQ may arrive up to 96 cycles after the transmission of the initial flits. With an injection rate of $\lambda = 0.2$, 19.2 further flits enter the network during this timespan. Hence, for flits to not be replaced during this time, the RTBs need to be able to store 20 flits. With 149 bits per flit, this results in $\frac{20 \cdot 149}{8} \approx 373$ bytes.

Compared to a state-of-the-art reference MPSoC such as [12], which consists of 24.43 million GEs and 844 kB memory, the overhead constitutes only 4.4% and 0.24% in terms of GEs and memory, respectively. Since they employ a smaller NoC, the RTBs only need to store 11 flits.

# 5 SUMMARY

Within this paper, we introduced three lightweight secure communication schemes that ensure both confidentiality and integrity. They are based on NC and employ the lightweight cryptographic algorithm PRINCE in order to achieve a good trade-off between security and implied overhead. The approaches introduced in [20] consume about half the chip area of our proposed solutions since they use the lightweight cryptographic algorithm mCrypton that requires significantly less space than PRINCE. However, those approaches provide no confidentiality and are slower by a factor of about 6.5.

Our results have shown that especially an integration of data and MAC within one flit (IWA) in combination with the redundancy introduced by NC achieves good results. Given an attack probability of 0.2, IWA-G2C4 was able to reduce the network load by up to 17% and the residual error rate by up to 86% in comparison to IWA-UC. These benefits come at the cost of a reduction of the information rate of around 40% and an increase of the average end-to-end latencies of around 10%. Despite this performance impact, the provided security is a great asset. Increasing the ARQ limit to 2 further significantly decreases the residual error probability. For IWA-G2C4, this yielded an improvement of around 23% and even 32% for IWA-G2C3. The trade-off between security and performance is clearly shown by the comparison of IWA to an insecure communication that lacks confidentiality and integrity. While the average end-to-end latencies are increased by at least 20 cycles due to the protection measures, the residual error probability was reduced by up to 85%.

There are several topics of future research. It seems promising to use the sequence of flit or generation IDs that exist for each pair of sender and receiver to recognize the loss of entire transmission units. Further, we will explore the use of the suggested schemes for an efficient protection in conjuction with burst mode. Currently, we do not consider the protection of ARQs. Adding redundancy to ARQs as well may help to further decrease residual error probabilities. Finally, the use of different paths for retransmissions can help to circumvent malicious routers.

# REFERENCES

[1] R. Ahlswede, N. Cai, S.-Y. R. Li, and R. W. Yeung. 2000. Network information flow. *IEEE Trans. on Inf. Theory* 46, 4 (2000), 1204–1216.
[2] Dean Michael Ancajas, Koushik Chakraborty, and Sanghamitra Roy. 2014. Fort-NoCs: Mitigating the Threat of a Compromised NoC. In *Proc. of DAC.* 158:1–158:6.
[3] L Benini and G De Micheli. 2002. Networks on chips: a new SoC paradigm. *Computer* 35, 1 (Jan. 2002), 70–78.
[4] Swarup Bhunia, Michael S. Hsiao, Mainak Banga, and Seetharam Narasimhan. 2014. Hardware Trojan Attacks: Threat Analysis and Countermeasures. *Proc. of the IEEE* 102, 8 (2014), 1229–1247.
[5] A. Bogdanov et al. 2007. PRESENT: An Ultra-Lightweight Block Cipher. In *CHES 2007*, Pascal Paillier and Ingrid Verbauwhede (Eds.). Springer, 450–466.
[6] Travis Boraten and Avinash Karanth Kodi. 2016. Packet Security with Path Sensitization for NoCs. In *Proc. of DATE.* 1136–1139.
[7] Julia Borghoff et al. 2012. *PRINCE - A Low-latency Block Cipher for Pervasive Computing Applications (Full version).* Technical Report 529.
[8] Shekhar Borkar. 2007. Thousand Core Chips: A Technology Perspective. In *Proc. of DAC.* 746–749.
[9] Philip A. Chou, Yunnan Wu, and Kamal Jain. 2003. Practical Network Coding. In *Proc. Annual Allerton Conf. on Comm., Control, and Computing.*
[10] W.J. Dally and B. Towles. 2001. Route packets, not wires: on-chip interconnection networks. In *Proc. of DAC.* 684–689.
[11] J. Frey and Qiaoyan Yu. 2015. Exploiting State Obfuscation to Detect Hardware Trojans in NoC Network Interfaces. In *Proc. of IEEE MWSCAS.* 1–4.
[12] Sebastian Haas et al. 2017. A Heterogeneous SDR MPSoC in 28 nm CMOS for Low-Latency Wireless Applications. In *Proc. of DAC.* 47:1–47:6.
[13] Julian Harttung, Elke Franz, and Paul Walther. 2018. *Evaluation of Lightweight Cryptographic Algorithms.* Technical Report. Dresden University of Technology. ISSN 36629-211X.
[14] Hemangee K. Kapoor, G. Bhoopal Rao, Sharique Arshi, and Gaurav Trivedi. 2013. A Security Framework for NoC Using Authenticated Encryption and Session Keys. *Circuits, Systems, and Signal Processing* 32, 6 (2013), 2605–2622.
[15] Paul Kocher et al. 2004. Security as a New Dimension in Embedded System Design. In *Proc. of DAC.* 753–760.
[16] S. Kumar, A. Jantsch, J. P. Soininen, M. Forsell, M. Millberg, J. Oberg, K. Tiensyrja, and A. Hemani. 2002. A network on chip architecture and design methodology. In *Proc. of IEEE Computer Society Annual Symposium on VLSI. New Paradigms for VLSI Systems Design.* 105–112.
[17] Chae Hoon Lim and Tymur Korishko. 2006. mCrypton – A Lightweight Block Cipher for Security of Low-Cost RFID Tags and Sensors. In *WISA 2005.*
[18] OpenSim Ltd. 2019. OMNeT++ Discrete Event Simulator. https://omnetpp.org/
[19] Sadia Moriam et al. 2015. Resilient and Efficient Communication in Many-Core Systems using Network Coding. In *Proc. of IEEE IPCCC.*
[20] Sadia Moriam et al. 2018. Protecting Communication in Many-Core Systems against Active Attackers. In *Proc. of ACM GLSVLSI.*
[21] NIST Special Publication 800-38A. 2001. Recommendation for Block Cipher Modes of Operation – Methods and Techniques. U.S. DoC/NIST.
[22] Simha Sethumadhavan et al. 2015. Trustworthy Hardware from Untrusted Components. *Comm. of the ACM* 58, 9 (Aug. 2015), 60–71.
[23] Gustavus J. Simmons (Ed.). 1991. *Contemporary Cryptography – The Science of Information Integrity.* IEEE Press.
[24] Sneha N. Ved, Ankit Bhange, Aparna Arya, and Joycee Mekie. 2017. Route-on-Fly: A Single Cycle Router. In *Proc. of SPIN.* 109–114.

# Design of a Low-power and Small-area Approximate Multiplier using First the Approximate and then the Accurate Compression Method

Tongxin Yang
Graduate School of Information and Control Systems
Fukuoka University
Fukuoka, Japan
td166502@cis.fukuoka-u.ac.jp

Tomoaki Ukezono
Department of Electronics Engineering and Computer Science
Fukuoka University
Fukuoka, Japan
tukezo@fukuoka-u.ac.jp

Toshinori Sato
Department of Electronics Engineering and Computer Science
Fukuoka University
Fukuoka, Japan
toshinori.sato@computer.org

## ABSTRACT

Recently emerging applications, such as convolution neural networks (CNNs), which process thousands of convolutional computations, require a large amount of power. Multiplication is the key arithmetic in these applications and an approximate multiplier has the potential to reduce both power and area. In this study, first, we propose the approximate and, then, the accurate compression method for an 8-bit multiplier. The proposed compression method single handedly reduces eight rows of partial products into three and, then, thoroughly processes the rows into two. Comparison of the conventional Wallace tree multiplier demonstrates that the proposed approximate multiplier with the compression reduces power and area by 73.7% and 60.3%, respectively. In addition, compared with two existing low-power approximate multipliers, the proposed multiplier achieves higher reductions than these state-of-the-art multipliers relative to power, area, and delay, with undegraded accuracy. These improvements can be also found from the results of a popular CNN application.

**CCS CONCEPTS:** •Hardware → Circuits power issues; Hardware → Arithmetic and datapath circuits

**KEYWORDS:** Approximate computing; low-power multiplier; small-area multiplier; first approximate and then accurate

**ACM Reference format:** Tongxin Yang, Tomoaki Ukezono, and Toshinori Sato. 2019. Design of a Low-power and Small-area Approximate Multiplier using First the Approximate and then the Accurate Compression Method. In *Proceedings of 2019 Great Lakes Symposium on VLSI (GLSVLSI'19). ACM, New York, NY, USA, 6 pages.* https://doi.org/10.1145/3299874.3317975

## 1 Introduction

Many image processing and recognition applications are computationally demanding, and a large number of computations lead to unprecedented challenges to power consumption. Applications wherein powerful computing resources are easily accessible may not present substantial challenges. However, applications that are performed on embedded platforms are subject to stringent areas and power constraints owing to limited resources. Many of these applications have an inherent feature, which is insensitive to computational accuracy. Approximate computing can trade off accuracy of power for these applications [1].

Multiplication is a fundamental arithmetic function for many of these applications, and a number of approximate multipliers were proposed [2-8]. In this study, we focus on an 8-bit multiplier design because it is extensively used in such image processing and CNN applications. Our primary contribution is achieving low-power and small-area by using first the approximate and then accurate compression method. The proposed method compresses the partial products (PPs) simultaneously and roughly; thus, its delay path is minimized and its circuit complexity is simplified. After the tough compression, eight PP rows are reduced to three. Then, carry saved adders (CSAs) were used to thoroughly reduce the rows to two. To clarify the superiority of the compression, we used the compression method to construct an 8-bit approximate multiplier. We implemented the proposed and conventional Wallace tree multipliers and verified the improvements relative to power, area, and delay. Comparison of the conventional Wallace tree multiplier showed that the power and area of the proposed approximate multiplier are reduced to 73.7% and 60.3%, respectively, with Mean Relative Error Distance (MRED) of 1.23%. We provided a crosswise comparison of the existing approaches. Two low-power approximate multipliers were implemented to evaluate their improvements. The experimental results showed that the proposed multiplier outperforms the existing multipliers relative to power, area, and delay, with undegraded accuracy. We also evaluated the power and accuracy of these multipliers for the CNN application.

## 2 Related Work

A low-power approximate multiplier with a static error recovery vector was introduced in [2]. It ensures that the designers can determine the bit-width of the recovery vector at a design stage. A method with dynamical voltage scaling was proposed in [3]. It truncates some lower bits to release path slack and, then, reduces the voltage supply to achieve low power. In [4], a low-power multiplier with an approximate tree compressor and approximate 4-to-2 compressors was proposed to reduce the eight PP rows into two. Moreover, a 16-bit approximate multiplier design was proposed in [5]. It detects the position of the leading one bit of the input operands, and calculates the following k bits by using a smaller k-bit accurate


*GLSVLSI '19, May 9–11, 2019, Tysons Corner, VA, USA*

ACM ISBN 978-1-4503-6252-8/19/05...$15.00
https://doi.org/10.1145/3299874.3317975

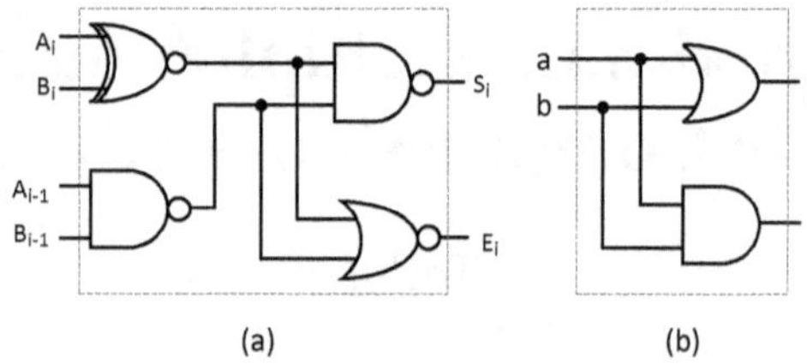


**Figure 1:** (a) Approximate adder in [2] and (b) approximate adder in [4].

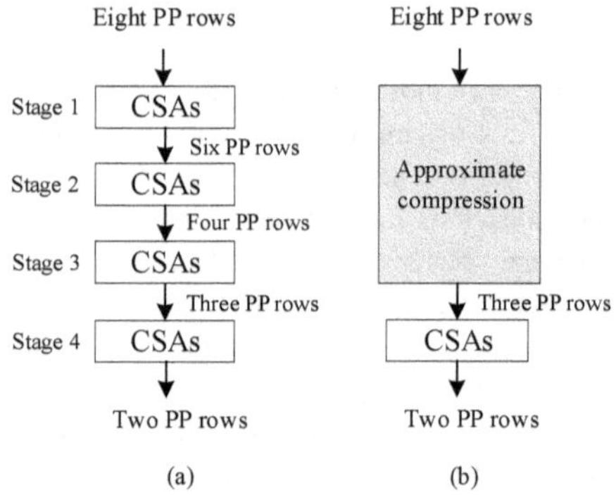


**Figure 2:** (a) Wallace tree multiplier PP reduction and (b) proposed compression.

multiplier. Three 4-to-2 compressors with relatively high accuracy were described in [6]. Dynamically accuracy-controllable approximate multipliers were proposed in [7][8]. In [7], a carry-maskable adder was utilized for accuracy control by dynamically masking the bits of the carry chain. A quality-configurable approximate multiplier by cutting off the power supply of some logic circuits was introduced in [8].

Approximate multipliers with different targets and design policies will lead to various results from the hardware aspect. In this study, we focus on the structure design of a low-power 8-bit approximate multiplier, and, then, we discuss our multiplier, as well as two existing low-power multipliers.

Liu et al. [2] introduced a previous relatively low-power approximate multiplier. They proposed an approximate adder (Fig. 1(a)) and used it to reduce PPs in parallel. As the figure shows, the approximate sum $S_i$ and the error recovery vector $E_i$ are generated from $A_i$, $B_i$, $A_{i-1}$, and $B_{i-1}$, where i is the bit position, $A_i$ and $B_i$ are the PPs at the bit position i, and $A_{i-1}$ and $B_{i-1}$ are the ones at the bit position $i-1$. Eight PP rows are reduced by the adders and OR gates to one approximate sum and one error recovery vector finally. To simplify the circuit complexity for the PP reduction, Yang et al. [4] proposed a small approximate adder cell (Fig. 1(b)) with only one AND and one OR gates. Unlike in [2], this adder cell generates an approximate sum p and a recovery vector q without the lower bit values (the $A_{i-1}$, and $B_{i-1}$ values in Fig. 1(a)), thereby reducing the design area. Eight PP rows are reduced to five via a tree compressor, which is constructed by using the adders. Then, the approximate 4-to-2 compressors and OR gates are used to further reduce the remaining rows into two.

The result shows that only the approximate components are used to reduce the PPs from eight into two rows in [2][4]. Moreover, at the beginning stages of their PP reductions, both of them compress PPs

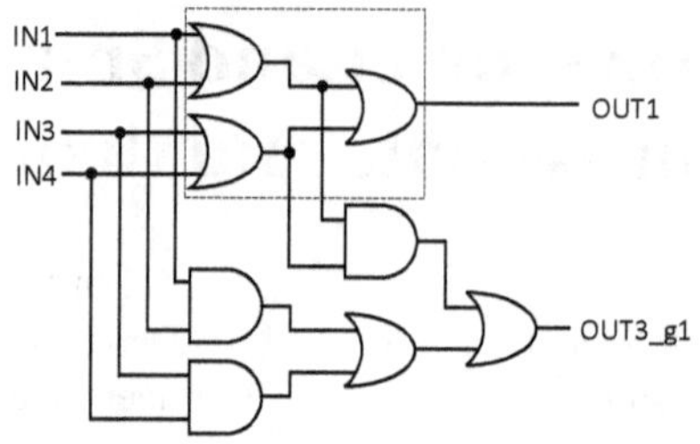


**Figure 3:** Compression circuit for group 1 with four inputs.

with error distances as short as possible. This consideration results in their circuits for the PP reduction complex. Our motivation is identifying a new compression method to render the circuit for the PP reduction smaller and simpler with an undegraded accuracy of the approximate multiplier. We propose a compression method that first approximately reduces eight rows into three by using simple circuits and, then, accurately collects the three rows using CSAs.

# 3 Approximate Multiplier

## 3.1 Proposed Compression Method

A conventional 8-bit Wallace tree multiplier consists of three parts, namely, (i) generating eight PP rows by using AND gates, (ii) reducing eight PP rows into two by using CSAs, and (iii) producing final result by using the carry propagation adder (CPA). To reduce eight PP rows into two in (ii), CSAs are used four times, and the number of PP rows is reduced as follows: 8 – 6 – 4 – 3 – 2 (Fig. 2(a)). Although the number of PP rows and PPs are reduced when stages go deep by the order from stage 1 to stage 4, each stage has no accuracy loss. Based on this fact, we consider that the later stage is more important for the approximate multiplier from the accuracy aspect. Based on this consideration, we retain the last stage (Stage 4 with three PP row inputs) for accuracy and roughly compress eight PP rows into three to simplify the circuit complexity from the design area aspect, as shown in Fig. 2(b).

As we discussed above, the eight PP rows must be compressed into three. Given that the highest number of PPs at a bit position in an 8-bit multiplier is eight, we use eight inputs to explain the compression method. The eight inputs are denoted by IN1, IN2, ..., and IN8 and the three outputs are denoted by OUT1, OUT2, and OUT3. We divide the eight inputs into two groups (denoted by groups 1 and 2), and each group consists of four inputs. We use OR gates to collect the four inputs roughly and each group generates one output. Therefore, two outputs are obtained and the equations are expressed as follows:

$$\mathrm{OUT1} = \mathrm{IN1}\ \mathit{OR}\ \mathrm{IN2}\ \mathit{OR}\ \mathrm{IN3}\ \mathit{OR}\ \mathrm{IN4} \tag{1}$$

$$\mathrm{OUT2} = \mathrm{IN5}\ \mathit{OR}\ \mathrm{IN6}\ \mathit{OR}\ \mathrm{IN7}\ \mathit{OR}\ \mathrm{IN8} \tag{2}$$

As Equations (1) and (2) show, OUT1 and OUT2 have been generated by OR gates. In this condition, two "1"s are present in each group, and the generation of OUT3 is defined as follows:

$$\mathrm{OUT3\_g1} = (\mathrm{IN1}\ \mathit{AND}\ \mathrm{IN2})\ \mathit{OR}\ (\mathrm{IN3}\ \mathit{AND}\ \mathrm{IN4})\ \mathit{OR}\ ((\mathrm{IN1}\ \mathit{OR}\ \mathrm{IN2})\ \mathit{AND}\ ((\mathrm{IN3}\ \mathit{OR}\ \mathrm{IN4})), \tag{3}$$

$$\mathrm{OUT3\_g2} = (\mathrm{IN5}\ \mathit{AND}\ \mathrm{IN6})\ \mathit{OR}\ (\mathrm{IN7}\ \mathit{AND}\ \mathrm{IN8})\ \mathit{OR}\ ((\mathrm{IN5}\ \mathit{OR}\ \mathrm{IN6})\ \mathit{AND}\ ((\mathrm{IN7}\ \mathit{OR}\ \mathrm{IN8})), \tag{4}$$

$$\mathrm{OUT3} = \mathrm{OUT3\_g1}\ \mathit{OR}\ \mathrm{OUT3\_g2}, \tag{5}$$

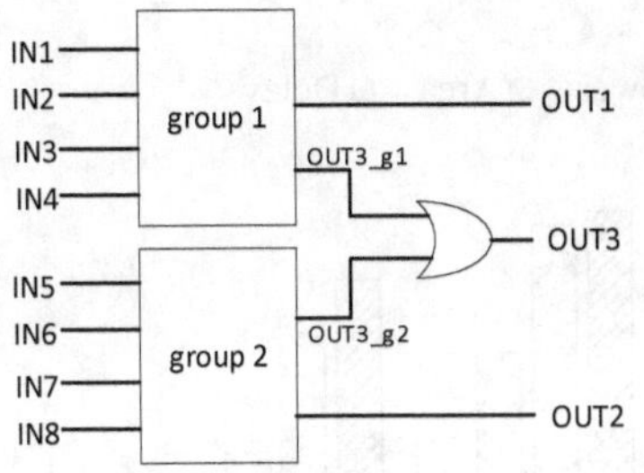


**Figure 4:** Compression circuit with eight inputs.

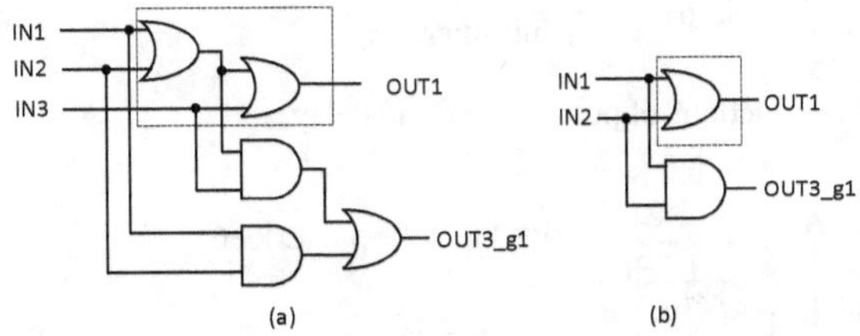


**Figure 5:** (a) Compression circuit for three inputs and (b) two inputs.

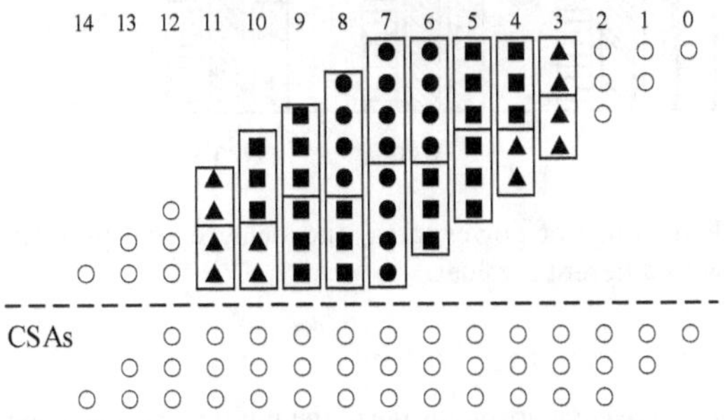


**Figure 6:** Structure of the proposed compression method.

where OUT3_g1 and OUT3_g2 represent the outputs from groups 1 and 2, respectively. Note that the generation of OUT3 can also be expressed in other forms. In this study, we reuse some OR gates in Equations (1) and (2) to generate OUT3.

Figure 3 shows the circuit of group 1 following Equation (3). By using Equation (5), we can obtain the structure of the compression circuit for eight inputs with two groups (Fig. 4). Note that the three outputs have the same bit position as the eight inputs and the compression circuit is the same for equal number of inputs. As Fig. 4 shows, OUT1, OUT2, and OUT3 have the same bit position as IN1, IN2, ..., and IN8, and the circuits of groups 1 and 2 are the same because both have four inputs.

To simply construct the compression circuit, we omit a few conditions with small probability. Consider that when the inputs of group 1 are three or four "1"s and those of group 2 are four "0"s, after the above compression, OUT1 = 1, OUT2 = 0, and OUT3 = 1 are obtained. From the maximum collection aspect for "1"s, if we add some circuits and use OUT2 to collect the "1" inputs of group 1, then, the accuracy will be better. However, such conditions occur only when four inputs of one group are all "0"s and three or four inputs of the other group are "1"s. Therefore, the probability of such conditions is very small; thus, we omit it.

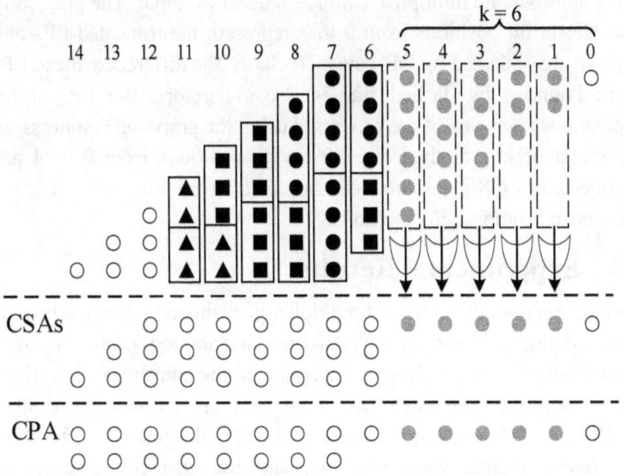


**Figure 7:** Structure of the proposed multiplier with k = 6.

The probability of the omitted conditions can be obtained as follows:

$$P_{omit} = \frac{2\times(C_4^3 + C_4^4)}{2^8}, \tag{6}$$

where $P_{omit}$ is defined as the probability of the omitted conditions and is 3.91%. We suffer from this accuracy loss to obtain more efficient hardware.

Similar compression circuits apply to other numbers of inputs. When the number of inputs reduces, the compression circuit becomes simple. Figures 5(a) and 5(b) show the compression circuit for three and two inputs, respectively. The circuit in Fig. 5(b) is the same as that of Fig. 1(b) [4]. However, ours is simplified from Fig. 5(a).

We use these compression circuits to construct the proposed first approximate and then accurate compression for an 8-bit multiplier. Figure 6 presents the detail of the proposed compression method. As the figure shows, the approximate compression part is above the dashed line and the black solid triangles, squares, and circles represent the PPs that are compressed by using the compression circuits with two, three, and four inputs, respectively. In addition, the rectangles represent the groups in each bit position. For example, at bit position 4, three black solid squares and two black solid triangles and two rectangles are present, and the three squares belong to group 1 and are compressed by using the compression circuit with three inputs. Moreover, the two triangles belong to group 2 and are compressed by using the compression circuit with two inputs. The empty circles at bit positions from 0 to 2 and from 12 to 14 in the approximate compression part are not necessarily compressed. After the compression, three PP rows are left below the dashed line. These rows are accurately collected by using CSAs.

## 3.2 Implementation

We use the proposed compression method to implement an approximate multiplier. Because the lower bits are usually not significant, we truncate some lower bits to further reduce the area and power.

The truncated bits at the lower bit positions are not processed using the proposed compression circuit but collected using the OR gates. k is defined as the length of the truncated bits; hence, the PPs at the bit positions from 0 to k-1 are truncated. Figure 7 shows the structure of the approximate multiplier with k = 6 as an example. The gray solid circles at bit positions from 0 to 5 represent the truncated PPs and those are collected by OR gates. To clarify the difference, these PPs are bounded by dashed frames also. Therefore, the PPs at bit positions from 6 to 14 are processed using the proposed compression method. If k = 5, then, the PPs at bit positions from 0 to 4 are collected by OR gates and those from 5 to 14 are processed using the proposed compression method.

## 4 Experimental Results

In this section, the proposed multiplier is evaluated regarding power, area, delay, and accuracy. To clarify the contributions of the proposed multiplier, we implemented and evaluated the conventional Wallace tree multiplier and other two low-power approximate multipliers [2][4]. In [2], two approximate multipliers that use 10- and 8-bit recovery vectors were proposed and the accuracy and power comparisons, respectively, were evaluated. Because the multiplier that uses an 8-bit recovery vector consumes less power than the one that uses a 10-bit recovery vector, the multiplier with the 8-bit recovery vector was adopted for this evaluation and is referred to as AMER8b. In [4], ATCM1 consumes less power than ATCM2; thus, ATCM1 was utilized. The CPA in each multiplier was implemented using a ripple-carry adder.

### 4.1 Experimental Setup

Verilog HDL was used to code all the approximate and Wallace multipliers. We used the Design Compiler to synthesize the multipliers at 0.5 GHz (2.0 ns max delay) timing constraint with the NanGate 45 nm Open Cell Library [9]. From the aspect of integrated circuit design, we determined the timing constraint wherein all the multipliers can be synthesized without timing violations. We used the switching activity interchange format files generated from VCS simulator to evaluate the power of all the multipliers. All the multipliers were 8 bits and were synthesized and optimized by using the default balanced synthesis option. We also used VCS to simulate the accuracy of the multipliers. The total possibilities of the input sets of the 8-bit multiplier were 65,536.

For accuracy metrics, we used error rate (ER), mean error distance (MED), MRED, and worst error distance (WED) to evaluate the approximate multipliers. The ER is the percentage of inaccurate outputs among all outputs generated from all combinations of inputs. Error distance (ED) is defined as the arithmetic difference between the accurate product (S) and approximate product (S′). MED is the average of EDs for a set of outputs (N). Relative ED (RED) is the ED divided by the accurate output, and MRED is the average of REDs. Meanwhile, WED is the maximum ED. These metrics can be obtained as follows:

$$\mathrm{ED} = |\mathrm{S} - \mathrm{S}'| \quad (7)$$

$$\mathrm{RED} = |\mathrm{S} - \mathrm{S}'|/\mathrm{S} \quad (8)$$

$$\mathrm{MED} = (\Sigma_1^N \mathrm{ED})/\mathrm{N} \quad (9)$$

$$\mathrm{MRED} = (\Sigma_1^N \mathrm{RED})/\mathrm{N} \quad (10)$$

$$\mathrm{WED} = \mathrm{ED}_{\max} \quad (11)$$

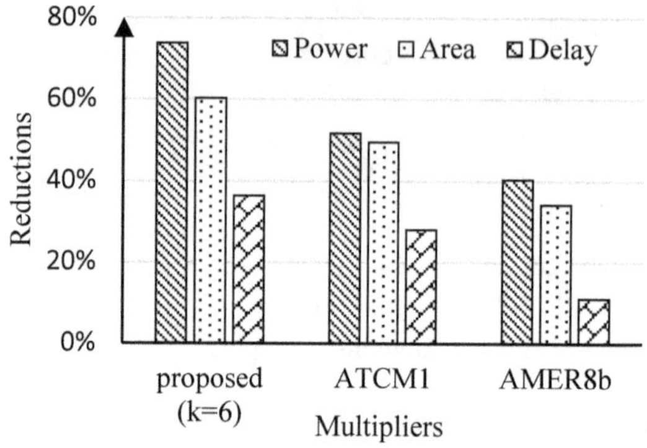


**Figure 8:** Reductions of power, area, and delay.

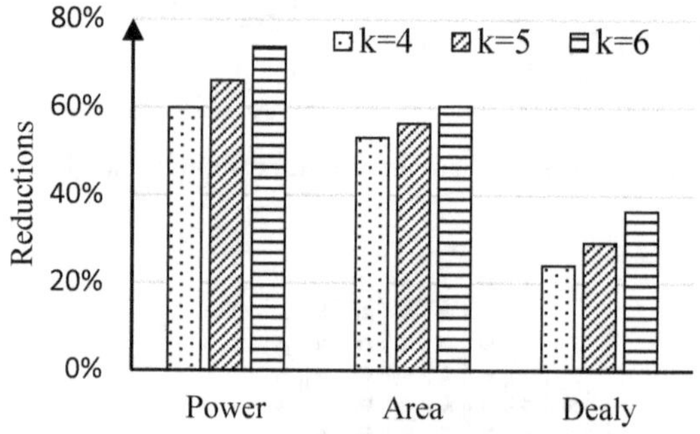


**Figure 9:** Reductions of power, area, and delay of the proposed multiplier with different k values.

### 4.2 Power, Area, and Delay

Figure 8 shows the comparison results of the multipliers. The x-axis is the evaluated multipliers, whereas the y-axis is the percentage in reduction from the conventional Wallace tree multiplier. Large values represent better results. The bars in each multiplier represent the reduction of power, area, and delay from left to right. Figure 8 plots the results of the proposed multiplier with k = 6. As shown in the figure, the proposed multiplier delivers the largest reduction of power, area, and delay among all the multipliers. The power saving of the proposed multiplier is approximately 73%. It is much larger than that of the other two approximate multipliers. Furthermore, the reduction of the design area of the proposed multiplier reaches 60%. The power and area improvements of the proposed multiplier benefit from the proposed compression method. Although the improvement of the critical path delay of the proposed multiplier is not as significant as that of power and area, it still reduces the delay by 36.4%. Moreover, the proposed multiplier with k = 6 can be synthesized without timing violations by the timing constraint reduced to 0.8 ns. ATCM1 is better than AMER8b among all the results of power, area, and delay, and its reduction of power and area are approximately 50%. AMER8b reduces power and area by approximately 40% and 35%, respectively.

We evaluated the proposed multiplier with different k values relative to power, area, and delay and, then, plotted the results in Fig. 9. The axis is the hardware metrics of power, area, and delay. The bars in each metric are for k = 4, k = 5, and k = 6 from left to right,

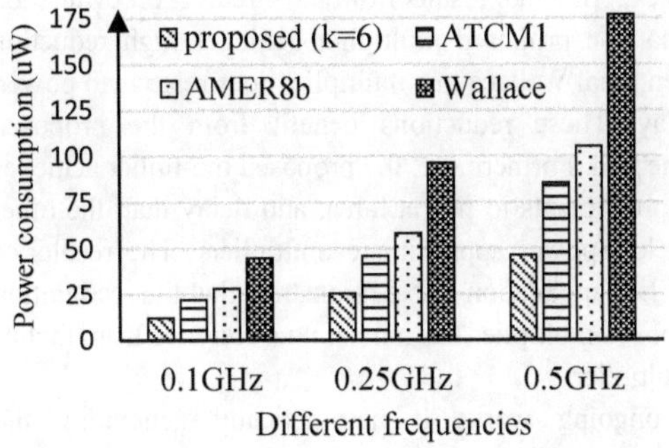


**Figure 10:** Power consumptions with the test patterns generated at a frequency of 0.1, 0.25, and 0.5 GHz.

**Table 1:** Static power consumptions of the multipliers.

| Power | Proposed(k = 6) | ATCM1 | AMER8b | Wallace |
|---|---|---|---|---|
| uW | 4.2 | 5.15 | 6.9 | 9.7 |

**Table 2:** Accuracy results of the multipliers.

| Metrics | Proposed | | | ATCM1 | AMER8b |
|---|---|---|---|---|---|
| | k = 4 | k = 5 | k = 6 | | |
| ER (%) | 41.08 | 51.26 | 61.97 | 55.44 | 51.42 |
| MED | 126.38 | 133.78 | 153.69 | 184.30 | 153.56 |
| MRED (%) | 0.68 | 0.86 | 1.23 | 1.64 | 1.16 |
| WED | 7714 | 7746 | 7810 | 7748 | 7072 |

respectively. The y-axis is the percentage of reductions. Note that k is defined as the number of truncated bits. As expected, when the value of k increases, the reductions improve. The proposed multiplier with k = 6 demonstrates superior results among all that with different values of k. In addition, from the comparison results of Figs. 8 and 9, the reductions of power and area of the proposed multiplier with k = 4 and k = 5 are found to be larger than those of ATCM1 and AMER8b, respectively.

We also evaluated the power consumptions of the multipliers with test patterns generated at different frequencies in Fig. 10. We explicitly show the absolute values of power consumption. The x-axis is the frequency, whereas the y-axis is the power consumption value. The bars in each frequency represent the multipliers. As expected, the power consumptions of all the multipliers become large from frequency of 0.1 to 0.5 GHz. Compared with Wallace tree multiplier, the power reductions of each approximate multiplier with the test patterns generated at 0.25 and 0.5 GHz frequencies are about the same. However, the power reductions of the multipliers at 0.1 GHz are a little smaller than those at 0.25 and 0.5 GHz. After checking the synthesis results, we found the static power consumption cannot be omitted when the frequency is slow (0.1 GHz for this comparison) and we summarized the static power consumptions of the multipliers in Table 1. Note that the test patterns generated from different frequencies have no effect on static power consumption. In fact, we can also locate a rough area comparison from the static power results of the multipliers.

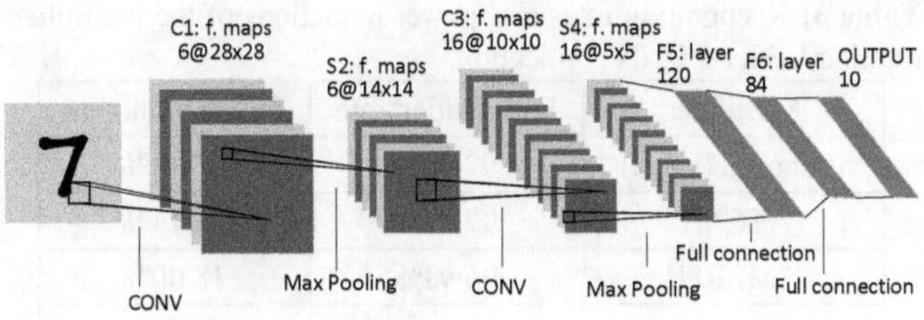


**Figure 11:** Structure of the LeNet-5 CNN application.

## 4.3 Accuracy

Table 2 summarizes the accuracy results of the proposed multiplier with different values of k, ATCM1, and AMER8b. Four accuracy metrics (i.e., ER, MED, MRED, and WED) are used to evaluate the approximate multipliers, where smaller values indicate better results. As indicated in the table, when k of the proposed multiplier increases, the results become worse. Except for the WED, the proposed multiplier with k = 4 and k = 5 shows better results than ATCM1 and AMER8b do. Note that the power and area results of the proposed multiplier with k = 4 and k = 5 are also better than those of ATCM1 and AMER8b, respectively. This finding demonstrates that the proposed first approximate and then accurate compression method significantly reduces circuit complexity while maintaining high accuracy.

For the WED, we can observe that the results of the proposed multiplier with different values of k are comparable to that of ATCM1 because both the proposed multiplier and ATCM1 omit the lower bits and only execute compression with the PPs at the same bit position to simplify the compression circuit. Meanwhile, the structure of the PP compression of AMER8b requires lower bits (Fig. 1(a)). From the comparison results of the proposed multiplier with k = 6, ATCM1, and AMER8b, the ER and WED of the proposed multiplier with k = 6 are slightly worse than those of ATCM1 and AMER8b. However, the results of the four metrics of these multipliers have generally no significant difference.

# 5 CNN Application

This section provides the power and accuracy evaluation for the multipliers by using the LeNet-5 CNN [10] with the MNIST database [11]. Figure 11 shows the architecture of the slightly variational LeNet-5. The LeNet-5 consists of two convolutional layers (C1 and C3), two max-pooling layers (S2 and S4), and two fully connected layers (F5 and F6) in the architecture. Given that the most popular non-linear activation function is the rectified linear unit (ReLU) [12], we also consider ReLU as the activation function in this evaluation. The MNIST database is for handwritten digit classification, and it consists of 60,000 training and 10,000 test images with 10 classes. The recognition rate is used as the metric in evaluating accuracy.

We coded the LeNet-5 CNN by using Verilog HDL to execute recognition. For the weights and biases, we used Python language to construct the LeNet-5 CNN on the TensorFlow framework [13] to obtain the trained weights and biases. The training was performed using 32-bit floating-point operations, and we normalized the 32-bit floating point data with boundary from -128 to +127 to an 8-bit

**Table 3:** Recognition rates and power reductions of the multipliers running LeNet-5 CNN application.

| Multiplier | Recognition rate | Power reduction |
|---|---|---|
| Proposed (k = 6) | 97.16% | 49.43% |
| ATCM1 | 97.07% | 25.14% |
| AMER8b | 96.93% | 18.00% |
| Wallace | 97.40% | 0.00% |

integer. We evaluated the proposed multiplier with k = 6, ATCM1, AMER8b, and Wallace tree multiplier. Because all these multipliers are unsigned, we used the two's complement numbers for negative weights and products to handle the negative numbers of weights. Note that only the power consumptions of the multipliers (excluding the circuit for generating the two's complement number) are considered in this evaluation.

Table 3 presents the results of recognition rates and power reductions with 10,000 test images of the multipliers. The recognition rates of the Wallace tree multiplier (8-bit integer) were found to be 97.40%. For instance, the recognition rate obtained from TensorFlow (32-bit floating point) is 98.28%. The recognition rate of the proposed multiplier with k = 6 is 97.16%. When the proposed multiplier is compared with the Wallace tree multiplier, the difference is only 0.24%. Compared to the other two approximate multipliers, the proposed multiplier obtains the highest recognition rate. The recognition rates of all these approximate multipliers have almost no difference from that of the Wallace tree multiplier. Therefore, the accuracy of these approximate multipliers is sufficient to perform the recognition in the LeNet-5 CNN with the MNIST database.

As presented in Table 3, the power reduction of the proposed multiplier with k = 6 is the largest among the multipliers. Compared with Fig. 8, the power reduction of each approximate multiplier is smaller. The possible reason is that the activation function ReLU generates many "0"s and these "0"s are the inputs of the multipliers in LeNet-5. The power consumptions of the approximate multipliers are not very different from that of the Wallace tree multiplier at such conditions. Although the reduction value of each approximate multiplier is mitigated, the power improvement of each multiplier is still observed.

Compared with the Wallace tree multiplier, the proposed multiplier with k = 6 achieves approximately 50% power saving with only 0.24% difference of recognition rates when executing recognition. Moreover, its area reduction is 60%. Note that the area and delay are not affected by various inputs. These results demonstrate that the proposed multiplier significantly contributes to reducing power and area.

## 6 CONCLUSION

This study proposed an approximate multiplier by using the first approximate and then accurate compression method. The compression significantly reduces the circuit complexity for the PP reduction. The experimental results from the circuit level evaluation demonstrate that the proposed multiplier achieves high reduction from the conventional Wallace tree multiplier does relative to power, area, and delay. These reductions benefit from the proposed compression method. Furthermore, the proposed multiplier achieves remarkable improvements to power, area, and delay than the other state-of-the-art low-power approximate multipliers. The results of the evaluated CNN application also demonstrate that the recognition rate of the proposed multiplier has almost no difference from that of the accurate multiplier.

One of our ongoing works is automatically generating the approximate arithmetic circuits. The proposed compression method in this study has a potential to simplify the autogeneration scheme.

## ACKNOWLEDGMENTS

This work was supported by JSPS KAKENHI Grant Number JP17K00088 and by funds (No.175007 and No.177005) from the Central Research Institute of Fukuoka University. This work is supported by VLSI Design and Education Center (VDEC), the University of Tokyo in collaboration with Synopsys, Inc.

## REFERENCES


[1] S. Venkataramani, V. K. Chippa, S. T. Chakradhar, K. Roy, and A. Raghunathan. "Quality programmable vector processors for approximate computing," in 46th Annual IEEE/ACM International Symposium on Microarchitecture (MICRO), pp. 1-12, Dec. 2013.

[2] C. Liu, J. Han, and F. Lombardi, "A Low-Power, High-Performance approximate multiplier with configurable partial error recovery," in Design, Automation & Test in Europe Conference & Exhibition (DATE), Mar. 2014.

[3] B. Moons and M. Verhelst, "DVAS: Dynamic Voltage Accuracy Scaling for increased Energy-Efficiency in approximate computing," in IEEE/ACM International Symposium on Low Power Electronics and Design (ISLPED), pp. 237-242, Jul. 2015.

[4] T. Yang, T. Ukezono, and T. Sato, "Low-power and high-speed approximate multiplier design with a tree compressor," in IEEE 35th International Conference on Computer Design (ICCD), pp. 89-96, Nov. 2017.

[5] S. Hashemi, R. I. Bahar, and S. Reda, "DRUM: A Dynamic Range Unbiased Multiplier for approximate applications," in IEEE/ACM International Conference on Computer-Aided Design (ICCAD), pp. 418-425, Nov. 2015.

[6] Z. Yang, J. Han, and F. Lombardi, "Approximate compressors for Error Resilient multiplier design," in IEEE International Symposium on Defect and Fault Tolerance in VLSI and Nanotechnology Systems (DFTS), pp. 183-186, Oct. 2015.

[7] T. Yang, T. Ukezono, T. Sato, "A Low-Power High-Speed Accuracy-Controllable Approximate Multiplier Design," in 23rd Asia and South Pacific Design Automation Conference (ASP-DAC), pp. 605-610, Jan. 2018.

[8] V. Mrazek, Z. Vasicek, and L. Sekanina, "Design of Quality-Configurable Approximate Multipliers Suitable for Dynamic Environment," in 2018 NASA/ESA Conference on Adaptive Hardware and Systems (AHS), pp. 264-271, Aug. 2018.

[9] Silicon Integration Initiative, Inc. NanGate FreePDK45 Open Cell Library, https://projects.si2.org/openeda.si2.org/projects/nangatelib, [Accessed on December 14, 2018].

[10] Y. LeCun, L. Bottou, Y. Bengio, and Patrick Haffner, "Gradient-based learning applied to document recognition," in Proceedings of the IEEE, Vol. 86, No. 11, pp. 2278–2324, Nov. 1998.

[11] Y. LeCun, C. Cortes, and C. J. C. Burges, "The MNIST Database of handwritten digits," http://yann.lecun.com/exdb/mnist/ [Accessed on December 14, 2018].

[12] Y. LeCun, Y. Bengio, and G. Hinton, "Deep learning," in Nature, Vol. 521, pp. 436-444, May 2015.

[13] TensorFlow, https://www.tensorflow.org/ [Accessed on December 14, 2018].

# GraphiDe: A Graph Processing Accelerator leveraging In-DRAM-Computing

Shaahin Angizi and Deliang Fan
Department of Electrical and Computer Engineering, University of Central Florida, Orlando, FL 32816
angizi@knights.ucf.edu,dfan@ucf.edu

## ABSTRACT

In this paper, we propose *GraphiDe*, a novel DRAM-based processing-in-memory (PIM) accelerator for graph processing. It transforms current DRAM architecture to massively parallel computational units exploiting the high internal bandwidth of the modern memory chips to accelerate various graph processing applications. *GraphiDe* can be leveraged to greatly reduce energy consumption and latency dealing with underlying adjacency matrix computations by eliminating unnecessary off-chip accesses. The extensive circuit-architecture simulations over three social network data-sets indicate that *GraphiDe* achieves on average 3.1× energy-efficiency improvement and 4.2× speed-up over the recent DRAM based PIM platform. It achieves ~59× higher energy-efficiency and 83× speed-up over GPU-based acceleration methods.

**ACM Reference format:**
Shaahin Angizi and Deliang Fan. 2019. GraphiDe: A Graph Processing Accelerator leveraging In-DRAM-Computing. In *Proceedings of Great Lakes Symposium on VLSI 2019, Tysons Corner, VA, USA, May 9–11, 2019 (GLSVLSI '19),* 6 pages.
https://doi.org/10.1145/3299874.3317984

## 1 INTRODUCTION

Nowadays, reaching high bandwidth of graph processing on top of Von-Neumann architectures suffers from various challenges [6], such as long memory access latency, intensified congestion at I/Os, humongous data communication energy, and large leakage power consumption for storing graph parameters that result in over 90% bandwidth degradation on CPU-DRAM hierarchy [18]. In order to tackle these challenges, Processing-in-Memory (PIM), as a potentially viable way to solve the memory wall challenge, has been put forward [4, 11, 16]. The key idea of PIM is to realize computation units inside memory to process data by leveraging the inherent parallel computing mechanisms and exploiting large internal memory bandwidth. Therefore, total memory bandwidth for computation units scales well by increase memory capacity leading to a significant reduction in latency and energy overheads of data communication [3]. PIM architectures ideally should be capable of performing bulk bit-wise operations which is needed in many graph processing applications [12]. However, this has been limited to basic logic operations such as AND, OR and XOR so far [12, 16], which are not necessarily applicable to a wide variety of tasks except by imposing multi-cycle operations [5, 16] or large in-memory computational units [11] to realize specific functions such as addition.


*GLSVLSI '19, May 9–11, 2019, Tysons Corner, VA, USA*

ACM ISBN 978-1-4503-6252-8/19/05...$15.00
https://doi.org/10.1145/3299874.3317984

The proposals for exploiting SRAM-based [2, 9] PIM architectures can be found in recent literature. However, PIM in context of main memory (DRAM- [3, 11, 15–17]) has drawn much more attention mainly due to larger memory capacities and off-chip data transfer reduction as opposed to SRAM-based PIM. Ambit [16] shows DRAM-based graph processing acceleration by realizing a majority function between every three rows and so can implement 2-input logic after saving operand data in reserved rows to avoid data-overwritten. GraphH [6] and Graphpim [14] present new designs based on Hybrid Memory Cube (HMC) to accelerate large-scale graph processing tasks at architectural level.

From graph processing algorithm perspective, network topology analysis can help us better understand the intricate connectivity of complex networks in practical problems. For instance, degree centrality is often used to measure the importance of a vertex. In social networks, people with more connections tend to have more significant influence in the community. The matching index is another basic topology parameter characterizing the similarity between two vertices in a network. It measures the ratio of common neighbors for pairs of vertices. Evaluation of these network properties plays an essential part in potential applications, such as social network analysis and traffic flow control. The main ***goal*** of this paper is to develop a parallel and energy-efficient PIM architecture that could simultaneously work as main memory and realize a high performance accelerator for such data-intensive graph processing applications. The main contributions of this paper are summarized as follows: (1) We propose a novel DRAM-based in-memory accelerator, *GraphiDe*, based on set of novel microarchitectural and circuit-level schemes. *GraphiDe* can perform any bulk bitwise operation inside DRAM exploiting DRAM structure, and therefore requiring low cost on top of commodity DRAM chip area. (2) We provide case studies of how important graph processing workloads can be partitioned and mapped to our architecture and how they can benefit from it. (3) We evaluate our proposed scheme using a variety of real-world social network graph data compared with other state-of-the-art accelerators i.e. DRAM, HMC, and GPU.

## 2 PROCESSING-IN-DRAM BACKGROUND

A DRAM cell basically consists of two elements, a capacitor (storage) and an Access Transistor (AT) (Fig. 1b Ⓑ). The drain and gate of the AT is connected to the Bit-line (*BL*) and Word-line (*WL*), respectively. DRAM cell encodes the binary data by the charge of the capacitor. It represents logic '1' when the capacitor is full-charged, and logic '0' when there is no charge. Technically, accessing data from a DRAM's sub-array (write/read) has three consecutive steps

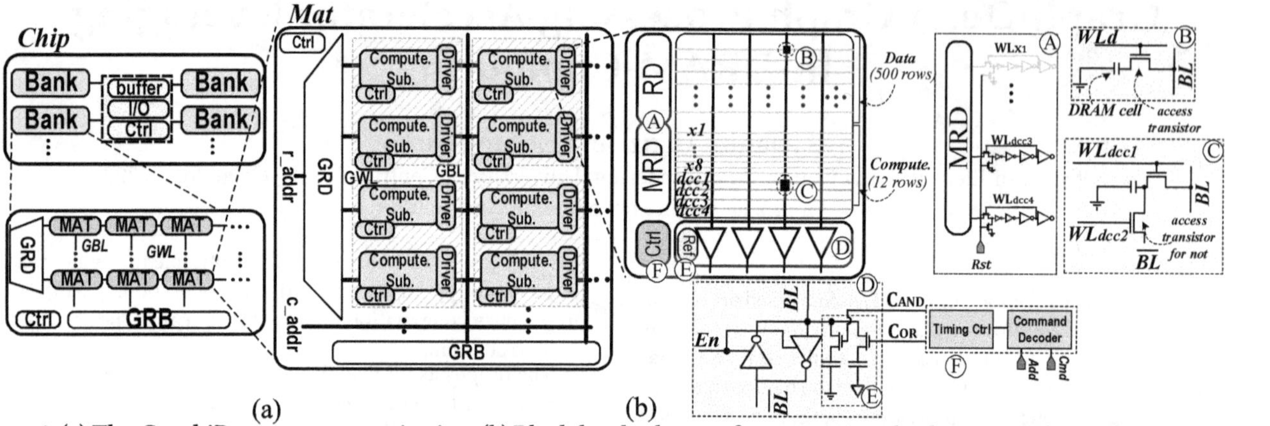


**Figure 1: (a) The *GraphiDe* memory organization, (b) Block level scheme of computational sub-array and peripheral circuitry.**

[15, 16]. During the first step (i.e. ACTIVATE), activating the specified row, data is copied from the DRAM cells to the Sense Amplifiers (SA). Then in the next step, such data can be accessed from the SAs by a READ or WRITE command. In addition, multiple READ/WRITE commands can be issued to an identical row. Afterwards, the activated row is precharged by issuing PRECHARGE command.

Following the aforementioned DRAM mechanism, series of circuit-level design have been presented, that enable design opportunity of applying PIM strategy to DRAM cell arrays. *RowClone* [17] presents an innovative mechanism to realize fast and efficient copy operation within DRAM sub-arrays without need to send the data to the processing unit. In this scheme, two back-to-back ACTIVATE commands to the source and destination rows without PRECHARGE command in between, leads to a multi-kilo byte in-memory copy operation. *Ambit* [16] extends the idea by realizing a 3-input majority function (Maj3)-based operation in memory by issuing ACTIVATE command to three rows simultaneously followed by a single PRECHARGE command so-called *Triple Row Activation (TRA)* method. Considering one row as the control, initialized by '0'/'1', Ambit can readily implement in-memory AND2/OR2 function. The NOT function has been also carried out in different works employing Dual-Contact Cells (DCC) [13, 16] with issuing two back-to-back ACTIVATE commands. DCC (Fig. 1b Ⓒ) first activates the $WL_{dcc1}$ of input DRAM cell, and reads the data out to the SA through *BL*. It then activate $WL_{dcc2}$ to connect $\overline{BL}$ to the same capacitor and so writes the negated result back to DCC. *Dracc* [7] implements a carry look-ahead adder by enhancing Ambit to accelerate convolutional neural networks.

## 3 GRAPHIDE DESIGN

*GraphiDe* is designed to be an independent, high-performance, energy-efficient accelerator based on main memory architecture. The main memory rank is a set of DRAM chips. Each chip is divided into multiple Banks. Banks within the same chip typically share I/O, buffer and banks in different chips working in a lock-step manner. Each bank consists of multiple memory matrices (mats). The general mat organization of *GraphiDe* is shown in Fig. 1a. Each mat consists of multiple computational memory sub-arrays connected to a Global Row Decoder (GRD) and a shared Global Row Buffer (GRB). According to the physical address of operands within memory, *GraphiDe*'s Controller (Ctrl) is able to configure the sub-arrays to perform data-parallel intra-sub-array computations. Our design is motivated by Ambit [16] PIM method, which leverages charge sharing among different rows to perform logic operations, but with significant modifications. We divide the *GraphiDe*'s sub-array row space into two distinct regions as depicted in Fig. 1b: 1- Data rows (500 rows out of 512) that include the typical DRAM cells Ⓑ connected to a regular Row Decoder (RD), and 2- Computation rows (12), connected to a Modified Row Decoder (MRD) (Fig. 1b Ⓐ), which enables bulk bitwise in-memory operations between copied operands. Eight computational rows ($x1, ..., x8$) include typical DRAM cells and four rows ($dcc1, ..., dcc4$) are allocated to special DCCs Ⓒ enabling NOT function in every sub-array. In the following, we propose dual-row in-memory AND-OR and addition operations that further enhance Ambit to perform graph processing tasks.

### 3.1 Dual-row in-memory logic

With a careful observation on Ambit's TRA method, we notice that it imposes an excessive latency and energy to memory chip which could be alleviated by rethinking about the process. Given R=A*op*B function ($op \in$ AND2/OR2), Ambit takes 4 consecutive steps to calculate the result as: 1-RowClone data of row A to row $x1$ (Copying first operand to a computation row to avoid data-overwritten), 2-RowClone of row B to $x2$, 3-RowClone of ctrl row to $t3$ (Copying initialized control row to a computation row), 4-TRA and RowClone data of row $x1$ to R row (Computation and Writing-back the result). As a matter of fact, every RowClone command imposes ~80ns [17], therefore TRA method takes averagely 320ns to perform in-memory operations. Our key idea to perform dual-row bit-line computing in *GraphiDe* is still based on majority function but by selecting different thresholds (references) when performing the charge sharing between selected memory cell(s). The proposed reconfigurable SA, as depicted in Fig. 1b Ⓓ, consists of a regular SA with two

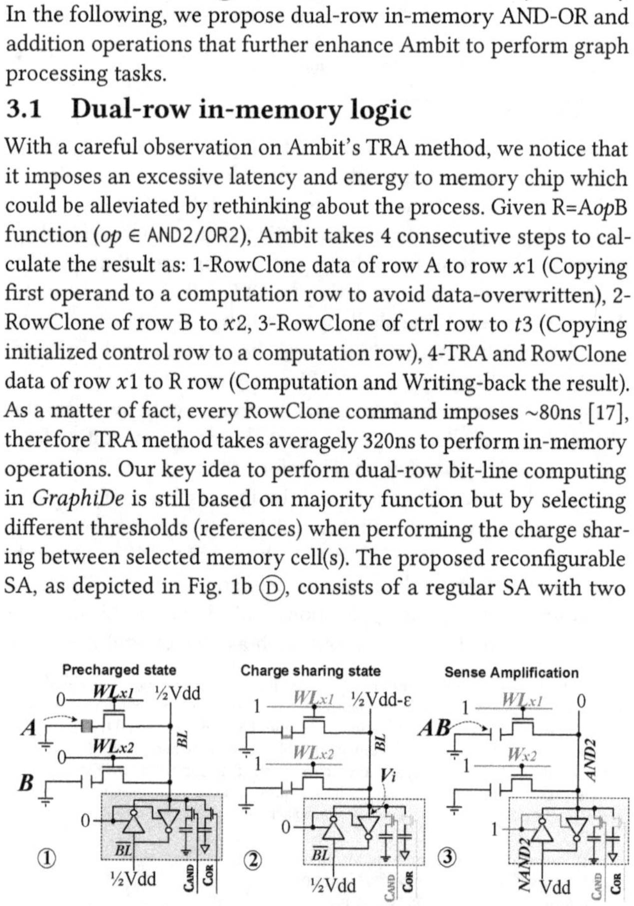


**Figure 2: Realization of AND2 function within *GraphiDe*.**

back-to-back inverters connected to two fixed reference-capacitor branches Ⓔ that can be selected by control bits ($C_{AND}$, $C_{OR}$) by the sub-array's Ctrl Ⓕ. This design basically forms a capacitive voltage divider between two selected cells by MRD and the activated reference (connected to either GND or $Vdd$), driving a CMOS inverter, to implement AND2 or OR2 functions, respectively.

*GraphiDe*'s Dual Row Activation method (DRA) eliminates the need for the third RowClone step in Ambit's AND2/OR2 operations and saves two initialized memory rows used for controls per sub-array at the cost of adding two low-overhead reference capacitors in SA unit. Fig. 2 shows the realization of AND2 operation in *GraphiDe*'s sub-array. Consider $A$ and $B$ operands are RowCloned from Data rows to $x1$ and $x2$ rows ① and both $BL$ and $\overline{BL}$ are precharged to $\frac{V_{dd}}{2}$. The DRA simultaneously activates two $WL$s and the corresponding reference ($C_{AND}$) for charge-sharing ②. During sense amplification ③, with the similar capacitance ($C_c$) of memory cells and the reference, input voltage of first inverter ($V_i$) in SA is simply derived as $V_i = \frac{n.V_{dd}}{C}$, where $n$ denotes the number of DRAM cells storing logic '1' and $C$ represents the total number of unit capacitors ($C_c$) connected to the inverter. Thus, the inverter acts as a threshold detector by amplifying deviation from $\frac{V_{dd}}{2}$ and realizes a NAND2 function on $\overline{BL}$ and consequently AND2 function ($AB$) on $BL$. *GraphiDe* can perform such DRA-based operations in ~240ns by eliminating the need for the third RowClone step in Ambit's operations. In this work, we use Ambit's TRA method just to directly realize in-memory majority function (Maj3) and AND2/OR2 operations are realized through DRA method.

## 3.2 In-memory adder

Here, we also propose Quintuple Row Activation method (QRA), as an extension for the TRA method, realizing 5-input (Maj5) operation. In this method, *GraphiDe*'s MRD (Fig. 1b Ⓐ) helps to activate five $WL$s, simultaneously. During the precharged state as shown in Fig. 3 ①, both $BL$ and $\overline{BL}$ are connected to $\frac{V_{dd}}{2}$. By activating the five $WL$s ($WLx1$ to $WLx5$), the memory cells storing input operands start to charge sharing ②. In this case, since three of the five cells are initially in the charged state, charge sharing results in a positive deviation on the $BL$. Therefore, by activating the Enable ($En$), such deviation from $\frac{V_{dd}}{2}$ is amplified ③ and the SA drives the $BL$ to $Vdd$ and accordingly, fully charges all the five cells. Based on Maj3 and Maj5 schemes, we now present a parallel in-DRAM computation and mapping method for addition (add) operation to accelerate a wide spectrum of graph processing tasks. Assume $D_i$, $D_j$, and $D_k$ as input operands, the carry-out ($C_{out}$) of the Full-Adder (FA) can be generated through $MAJ3(D_i, D_j, D_k) = D_iD_j + D_iD_k + D_jD_k$ using TRA method. Moreover, the $Sum$ can be readily carried out through $MAJ5(D_i, D_j, D_k, \overline{C_{out}}, \overline{C_{out}})$ with only writing back the $\overline{C_{out}}$ into memory (leveraging two DCC rows) and then applying QRA method. This will be further elaborated in subsection 3.3.

## 3.3 ISA support

While *GraphiDe* is meant to be an independent high-performance and energy-efficient accelerator, we need to expose it to programmers and system-level libraries to utilize it. From a programmer perspective, *GraphiDe* is more of a third party accelerator that can be connected directly to the memory bus or through PCI-Express lanes rather than a memory unit, thus it is integrated similar to that

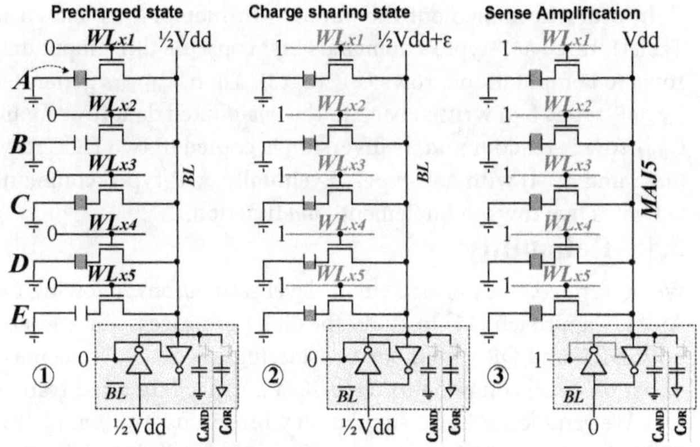


**Figure 3: Realization of MAJ5 function within *GraphiDe*.**

of GPUs. Therefore, a virtual machine and ISA for general-purpose parallel thread execution need to be defined similar to PTX [1] for NVIDIA. Accordingly, the programs are translated at install time to the *GraphiDe* hardware instruction set discussed here to realize the functions tabulated in Table 1. The micro and control transfer instructions are not discussed here.

*GraphiDe* is developed based on ACTIVATE-ACTIVATE-PRECHARGE command referred to as AAP primitives. As thoroughly explained in Ambit [16], most bulk bitwise operations involve a sequence of AAP commands. There are five types of AAP primitives supported by *GraphiDe* that only differ from number of activated source or destination rows, 1- AAP (src, des) that runs the following commands sequence: ACTIVATE source address; ACTIVATE destination address; PRECHARGE. This is manly used for copy and NOT functions as indicated Table 1. 2- AAP (src, des1, des2) that is designed to copy the result of an operation simultaneously to two destination rows. 3- AAP (src1, src2, des, Ctrl) that performs DRA method by activating two source addresses along with a control input ('0' for $C_{AND}$/ '1' for $C_{OR}$) and then writes back the result on the destination address. 4- AAP (src1, src2, src3, des) that performs TRA method by activating three source rows simultaneously and writing back the MAJ3 or MIN3 result on the destination address. 5- AAP (src1, src2, src3, src4, src5, des) that performs QRA method on five sources and write the result back to the destination address.

**Table 1: The basic functions supported by *GraphiDe*.**

| Function | Operation | Command Sequence | AAP Type |
|---|---|---|---|
| copy | $D_r \leftarrow D_i$ | AAP($D_i, D_r$) | 1 |
| NOT | $D_r \leftarrow \overline{D_i}$ | AAP($D_i, dcc2$) | 1 |
| | | AAP($dcc1, D_r$) | 1 |
| AND2 | $D_r \leftarrow D_i.D_j$ | AAP($D_i, x1$) | 1 |
| | | AAP($D_j, x2$) | 1 |
| | | AAP($x1, x2, D_r, 0$) | 3 |
| OR2 | $D_r \leftarrow D_i + D_j$ | AAP($D_i, x1$) | 1 |
| | | AAP($D_j, x2$) | 1 |
| | | AAP($x1, x2, D_r, 1$) | 3 |
| XOR2 | $D_r \leftarrow D_i \oplus D_j$ | AAP($D_i, x1, dcc2$) | 2 |
| | | AAP($D_j, x2, dcc4$) | 2 |
| | | AAP($x1, dcc3, x4, 0$) | 3 |
| | | AAP($x2, dcc1, x5, 0$) | 3 |
| | | AAP($x4, x5, D_r, 1$) | 3 |
| Addition | $Sum \leftarrow D_i \oplus D_j \oplus D_k$<br>$C_{out} \leftarrow MAJ3(D_i, D_j, D_k)$ | AAP($D_i, x1$) | 1 |
| | | AAP($D_j, x2$) | 1 |
| | | AAP($D_k, x3$) | 1 |
| | | AAP($x1, x2, x3, C_{out}$) | 4 |
| | | AAP($C_{out}, dcc2, dcc4$) | 2 |
| | | AAP($x1, x2, x3, dcc1, dcc2, Sum$) | 5 |

In order to implement the addition-in-memory, as shown in Table 1, three AAP-type1 commands first copy the three input data rows to computational rows ($x1, x2, x3$). Then, $C_{out}$ is generated by AAP-type4 and written back to the designated data row. Again, $C_{out}$ row is readout and its inversion is copied to two DCC rows ($dcc2$ and $dcc4$) with AAP-type2. Eventually, AAP-type5 command activates five rows to implement *Sum* function.

## 3.4 Reliability

We performed an extensive circuit-level simulations following the Ambit's approach [16] to study the effect of process variation on both DRA and QRA methods considering a worst-case scenario variation in all components (cell/$BL$/$WL$ capacitance and transistor). We ran Monte-Carlo simulation with 45nm PTM library [21] (DRAM cell parameters were taken from Rambus [8] model) under 10000 trials and increased the amount of variation from ±0% to ±20% for each method. Table 2 shows the percentage of the test error in each variation. We observe that even considering a significant ±10% [16] variation, the percentage of erroneous DRA or QRA across 10000 trials is just 0.12% and 0.39% which is consistent with what Ambit reports. Therefore, *GraphiDe* shows an acceptable reliability in performing PIM operations. Note that DRA method is less vulnerable to capacitance variation effects as opposed to TRA, due to its third fixed-voltage branch. By scaling down the transistor size, the process variation effect is expected to get worse [16, 17]. Since *GraphiDe* is mainly developed based on existing DRAM structure and operation with slight modifications, different methods currently-used to tackle process variation can be also applied for *GraphiDe* (e.g., spare rows). Besides, just like Ambit, *GraphiDe* chips that fail testing due to DRA, TRA, and QRA methods can potentially be considered as regular DRAM chips alleviating DRAM yield.

**Table 2: Process variation analysis.**

| Variation | ±0% | ±5% | ±10% | ±20% |
|---|---|---|---|---|
| DRA | 0.00% | 0.00% | 0.12% | 11.43% |
| QRA | 0.00% | 0.08% | 0.39% | 18.92% |

Regarding the error correction, many ECC-enabled DIMMs rely on calculating some hamming code at the memory controller and use it to correct any soft errors. Unfortunately, such a feature is not available for *GraphiDe* as the data being processed are not visible to the memory controller. Note that this issue is common across all PIM designs. To overcome this issue, *GraphiDe* can potentially augment each row with additional ECC bits that can be calculated and verified at the memory module level or bank level. Augmenting *GraphiDe* with reliability guarantees is left as future work.

## 3.5 Virtual memory

*GraphiDe* has its own ISA with operations that can potentially use virtual addresses. To use virtual addresses, *GraphiDe*'s Ctrl must have the ability to translate virtual addresses to physical addresses. While in theory this looks as simple as passing the address of the page table root to *GraphiDe* and giving *GraphiDe*'s Ctrl the ability to walk the page table, it is way more complicated in real-world designs. The main challenge here is that the page table can be scattered across different DIMMs and channels, while *GraphiDe* operates within a memory module. Furthermore, page table coherence issues can arise. The other way to implement translation capabilities for *GraphiDe* is through memory controller pre-processing of instructions being written to *GraphiDe* instruction registers. For instance, if the programmer writes instruction AAP $add0, add1$, then the memory controller intercepts the virtual addresses and translate them into physical addresses. Note that most systems have near memory controller translation capabilities, mainly to manage IOMMU and DMA accesses from I/O devices. One issue that can arise is that some operations are appropriate only if the resulting physical addresses are within specific plane, e.g., within the same bank. Accordingly, the compiler and the OS should work together to ensure that the operands of commands will result physical addresses that are suitable to the operation type. To avoid the complexity of virtual memory when using *GraphiDe*, system architects can opt for designating a continuous physical range that can be used by *GraphiDe* and the user/application can use physical addresses for operands. Directly operating on physical addresses can limit multi-tasking on *GraphiDe*, however, we leave supporting multi-tasking in *GraphiDe* through virtual memory support as future work.

# 4 APPLICATION: GRAPH PROCESSING

The *GraphiDe*'s parallel operations can be easily utilized to accelerate a wide variety of graph processing tasks. For the sake of limited space, we briefly explain two widely-used tasks so-called *matching index* and *degree centrality*.

**Matching index:** The matching index $M_{i,j}$ quantifies the *similarity* between two vertices ($V_i$ and $V_j$) based on the number of common neighbors shared by vertices as $(\frac{\Sigma \text{ common neighbors}}{\Sigma \text{ total number of neighbors}})$. The main task here is to find the common and total number of neighbors which can be implemented and accelerated by *GraphiDe*. Fig. 4 provides a straightforward example to elucidate the mapping and acceleration method of *GraphiDe*. Initially, the sample four-vertex network is converted to adjacency matrix and stored in 4 consecutive rows of sub-array. To find the common neighbors of two particular vertices (e.g. V1, V2), *GraphiDe* performs parallel AND2 on the rows and SA's outputs determine the matches (here, V4). In addition, the total number of neighbors is found by performing OR2 operation on the same rows. Then, *GraphiDe*'s add operation can readily process the summation operation as explained earlier. Afterwards, the only remaining operation is to divide these numbers that can be done utilizing a off-chip processing unit to generate corresponding index matrix.

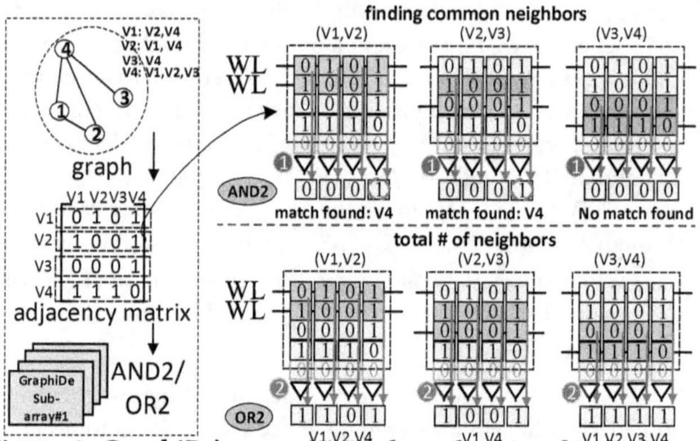


**Figure 4: *GraphiDe*'s mapping and acceleration for finding matching index.**

**Degree centrality:** One of the most important graph processing tasks is degree centrality. This task deals with massive number of add operation which basically counts the number of valid links connected to a vertex. Fig. 5 shows an intuitive example of hardware mapping and acceleration of such operation performed by *GraphiDe* for a small graph. Initially, the designated graph is converted to adjacency matrix and mapped to consecutive rows of *GraphiDe*'s sub-arrays. Now, in the first step, every three rows are activated through $WLs$ sequentially (here, (1) and (2)) to perform parallel add operation based on command sequence tabulated in Table 1 and generate initial Carry (C) and Sum (S) bits. In the second step, the results are written back to the memory reserved space. Then, next steps ((3) and (4)) only deal with multi-bit addition of resultant data starting bit-by-bit from the LSBs of the two words continuing towards MSBs. There are 2 steps for every bit-position computation. In the first step of (3), 2 $WLs$ (accessing to LSBs of 6 elements) and one $WL$ (accessing the reserved row initialized by zero) are enabled to generate the sum and carry. The SAs use these 3 words to generate sum and carry. During second step, two $WLs$ are activated to save back the sum and carry bits. This process continues to MSB. At the end, the degree of each vertex is stored in memory (e.g. 4 determines the degree of vertex 1 in Fig. 5).

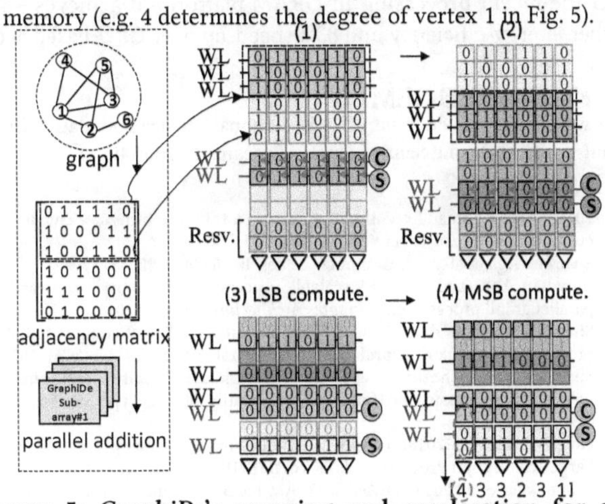


**Figure 5: *GraphiDe*'s mapping and acceleration for add-based graph processing operations. Here we take degree centrality computation as an example.**

# 5 EXPERIMENTAL RESULTS

We compare *GraphiDe* with other possible graph processing acceleration solutions based on DRAM, HMC, and GPU. We configure the *GraphiDe*'s memory sub-array with 512 rows and 256 columns, 4×4 mats (with 1/1 as row/column activation) per bank organized in H-tree routing manner, 16×16 banks (with 1/1 as row/column activation) and 512Mb total capacity. As mentioned earlier, enlarging the chip area provides a higher performance for *GraphiDe* and other PIM designs due to the increased number of computational sub-arrays, though the die size directly impacts the chip cost. Therefore, an identical physical memory size (512Mb) is considered for all implementations henceforth. To evaluate the performance of accelerators, we take three social network data-sets as tabulated in Table 3. Then, we map and run three graph processing tasks i.e. degree centrality, matching index, and Breadth First Search (BFS) on them that seek most of *GraphiDe*'s operations.

**Table 3: Social Network data-sets.**

| Dataset | Nodes | Edges | Graph Information |
|---|---|---|---|
| ego-Facebook | 4,039 | 88,234 | profiles & friends lists from Facebook [10] |
| dblp-2010 | 326,186 | 1,615,400 | scientific collaboration network |
| amazon-2008 | 735,323 | 5,158,388 | similarity among books reported by Amazon store |

## 5.1 Accelerators' setup

***GraphiDe:*** To evaluate the performance of *GraphiDe* as a new PIM platform, a comprehensive circuit-architecture assessment framework and two in-house simulators are developed. 1- At the circuit level, we developed *GraphiDe*'s sub-array with new peripheral circuity (SA, MRD, etc.) in SPICE 45nm PTM library [21] to verify the proposed design methods and achieve the performance parameters. 2- An architectural-level simulator is built on top of Cacti [20]. The circuit level results were then fed into our simulator. It can change the configuration files corresponding to different array organization and report performance metrics for AAP-based PIM operations. The memory controller circuits are designed and synthesized by Design Compiler [19] with a 45nm industry library. 3- A behavioral-level simulator is developed in Matlab to calculate the latency and energy that *GraphiDe* spends on different graph processing tasks. In addition, it has a mapping optimization framework to maximize the performance according to the available resources. Real world graph consists of millions of vertices and edges that need to be processed. To efficiently map such graphs into *GraphiDe* architecture, graph partitioning methods are used. Here, we adopt interval-block partitioning method to balance workloads of each *GraphiDe*'s chip and maximize parallelism. We use hash-based method [6] to split the vertices into $M$ intervals and then divide edges into $M^2$ blocks. ***DRAM:*** We developed an Ambit-like [16] accelerator for graph processing. Ambit implements logic function using capacitor-based majority functions. We accordingly modified CACTI [20] for evaluation of DRAM's solution. The controllers were synthesized in Design Compiler [19]. ***Baseline HMC:*** We used a conventional architecture presented in [14] using HMC as main memory without instruction offloading functionality. Due to the lack of space, we refer the readership to above-mentioned papers for the detailed configuration of each accelerator. ***GPU:*** We used the NVIDIA GTX 1080Ti Pascal GPU. The energy was measured with NVIDIA's system management interface. We scaled the achieved results by 50% to exclude the energy consumed by cooling, etc.

## 5.2 Energy and Delay

Figure 6 shows normalized energy consumption of the four accelerators on various graph processing tasks. *GraphiDe* achieves the highest energy-efficiency in different tasks compared to others owning to its low-energy and reduced-cycle operations. We observe that *GraphiDe* consumes on average 3.1× less energy than that of Ambit accelerator. The main reason here is the energy-efficiency of basic operations in *GraphiDe*; as discussed earlier, *GraphiDe* can finish the operations (such as addition) in less number of cycles using DRA and QRA methods. Fig. 6 shows that *GraphiDe* solution saves on average 3.9× and 58.6× energy compared to that of HMC and GPU solutions, respectively. It is worth pointing out that HMC and GPU designs are not capable of implementing fast bulk addition and therefore impose excessive energy consumption to memory chip in addition-intensive tasks such as degree centrality analysis. To realize such operation in Ambit platform, we considered multi-cycle majority-based implementation presented in [5].

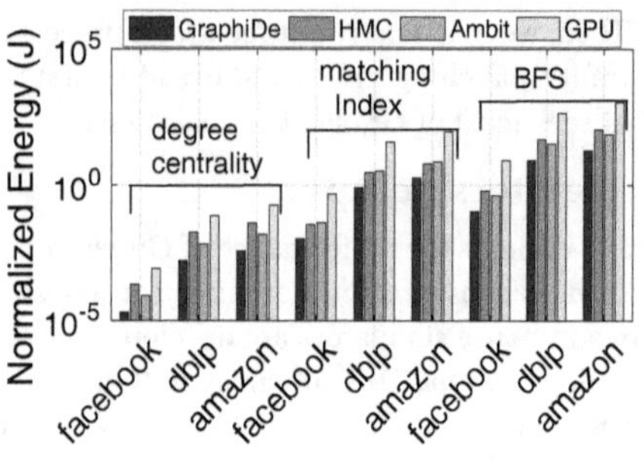


**Figure 6: Normalized log-scaled energy of accelerators.**

However, HMC solution shows a relatively equal energy-efficiency in matching index task compared to Ambit.

Figure 7 plots execution time of the *GraphiDe* and other accelerators on different graph processing tasks. We observe that *GraphiDe* solution is on average 4.2× faster than that of Ambit solution and 5.6× faster than HMC. This is mainly because of fast and parallel in-memory operations of *GraphiDe*, specifically for implementing add operation. Additionally, we see that *GraphiDe* is 83.4× faster that GPU solution. As can be seen, this directly translates to large performance improvements for the discussed applications that seek bulk bitwise operations.

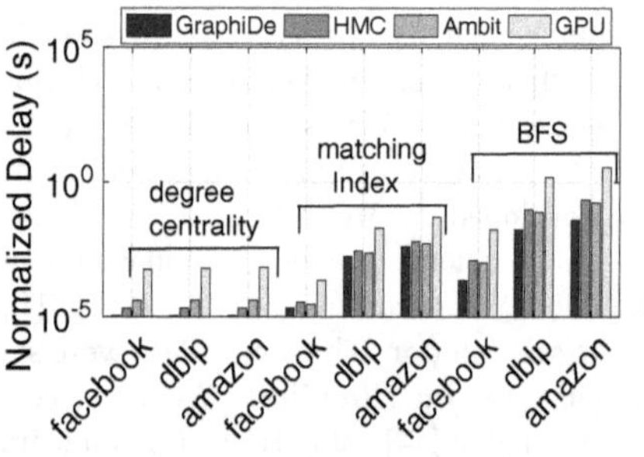


**Figure 7: Normalized log-scaled delay of accelerators.**

## 5.3 Memory bottleneck

Figure 8a reports the Memory Bottleneck Ratio (MBR), i.e. the time fraction at which the computation has to wait for data and on-/off-chip data transfer obstructs its performance (memory wall happens) running matching index task on two data-sets. The evaluation is performed according to the peak throughput for each platform considering number of memory access. The results show the *GraphiDe*'s efficiency for solving memory wall issue. We observe that *GraphiDe* along with other PIM solutions spend less than ~20% time for memory access and data transfer. However, GPU accelerator spends more than 90% time waiting for the loading data. The less memory wall ratio can be interpreted as the higher Resource Utilization Ratio (RUR) for the accelerators which is plotted in Fig. 8b. We observe that *GraphiDe* can efficiently utilize up to 70% of its computation resources. Overall, PIM solutions demonstrates a high ratio, which reconfirms the results reported in Fig. 8a.

## 5.4 Area overhead

*GraphiDe* is developed on top of Ambit [16] (with the area overhead of <1%). We have modified the controller and MRD circuits as well as SAs by adding two reference branches per column. Such enhanced SAs and peripheral circuitry in *GraphiDe*'s sub-array occupy less than 15% of area. Therefore, the overall area overhead of *GraphiDe* is ~1.3% over the commodity DRAM.

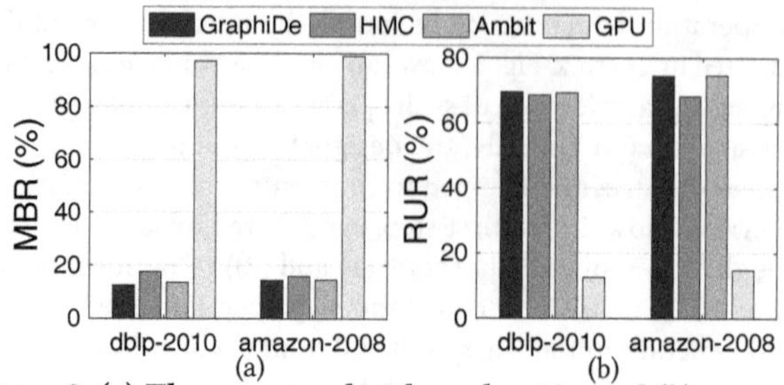


**Figure 8: (a) The memory bottleneck ratio and (b) resource utilization ratio.**

## 6 CONCLUSION

In this paper, we presented *GraphiDe*, which transforms current DRAM sub-arrays to massively parallel computational units to reduce energy consumption dealing with graph processing tasks and eliminate unnecessary off-chip accesses. The simulation results on three social network data-sets show *GraphiDe* can roughly achieve 3.1× energy-efficiency improvement and 4.2× speed-up over the recent processing-in-DRAM platform. It achieves ~59× higher energy-efficiency and 83× speed-up over GPU-based acceleration methods.

## ACKNOWLEDGEMENTS

This work is supported in part by the National Science Foundation under Grant No. 1740126 and Semiconductor Research Corporation nCORE.

## REFERENCES

[1] 2018. Parallel Thread Execution ISA Version 6.1. (2018). http://docs.nvidia.com/cuda/parallel-thread-execution/index.html
[2] Shaizeen Aga et al. 2017. Compute Caches. In *HPCA*. IEEE, 481–492.
[3] Junwhan Ahn et al. 2016. A scalable processing-in-memory accelerator for parallel graph processing. *Computer Architecture News* 43 (2016).
[4] Shaahin Angizi et al. 2018. CMP-PIM: an energy-efficient comparator-based processing-in-memory neural network accelerator. In *55th DAC*. ACM, 105.
[5] Shaahin Angizi, Zhezhi He, et al. 2017. Design and evaluation of a spintronic in-memory processing platform for non-volatile data encryption. *IEEE TCAD* (2017).
[6] Guohao Dai et al. 2018. GraphH: A Processing-in-Memory Architecture for Large-scale Graph Processing. *IEEE TCAD* (2018).
[7] Quan Deng et al. 2018. DrAcc: a DRAM based accelerator for accurate CNN inference. In *55th DAC*. ACM, 168.
[8] 2010. DRAM Power Model. https://www.rambus.com/energy/. [n. d.]. ([n. d.]).
[9] Charles Eckert et al. 2018. Neural Cache: Bit-Serial In-Cache Acceleration of Deep Neural Networks. *arXiv preprint arXiv:1805.03718* (2018).
[10] Jure Leskovec and Julian J Mcauley. 2012. Learning to discover social circles in ego networks. In *Advances in neural information processing systems*. 539–547.
[11] Shuangchen Li et al. 2017. DRISA: A DRAM-based Reconfigurable In-Situ Accelerator. In *Micro*. ACM, 288–301.
[12] Shuangchen Li, Cong Xu, et al. 2016. Pinatubo: A processing-in-memory architecture for bulk bitwise operations in emerging non-volatile memories. In *DAC*. IEEE.
[13] Shih-Lien Lu et al. 2015. Improving DRAM latency with dynamic asymmetric subarray. In *MICRO*. IEEE, 255–266.
[14] Lifeng Nai et al. 2017. Graphpim: Enabling instruction-level pim offloading in graph computing frameworks. In *HPCA*. IEEE, 457–468.
[15] Vivek Seshadri et al. 2015. Fast bulk bitwise AND and OR in DRAM. *IEEE Computer Architecture Letters* 14 (2015).
[16] Vivek Seshadri et al. 2017. Ambit: In-memory accelerator for bulk bitwise operations using commodity DRAM technology. In *Micro*. ACM, 273–287.
[17] Vivek Seshadri, Yoongu Kim, et al. 2013. RowClone: fast and energy-efficient in-DRAM bulk data copy and initialization. In *46th Micro*. ACM, 185–197.
[18] Linghao Song et al. 2018. GraphR: Accelerating graph processing using ReRAM. In *HPCA*. IEEE, 531–543.
[19] Synopsys Design Compiler. Product Version 14.9.2014. Synopsys, Inc. [n. d.]. ([n. d.]).
[20] Shyamkumar Thoziyoor, Naveen Muralimanohar, Jung Ho Ahn, and Norman P Jouppi. 2008. *CACTI 5.1*. Technical Report. Technical Report HPL-2008-20, HP Labs.
[21] Wei Zhao and Yu Cao. 2006. New generation of predictive technology model for sub-45nm design exploration. In *ISQED*. IEEE Computer Society, 585–590.

# An Efficient Time-based Stochastic Computing Circuitry Employing Neuron-MOS

Tati Erlina
Nara Institute of Science and Technology (NAIST)
Nara, Japan
tati.erlina.su4@is.naist.jp

Yan Chen
Nara Institute of Science and Technology (NAIST)
Nara, Japan
chen.yan.cw3@is.naist.jp

Renyuan Zhang
Nara Institute of Science and Technology (NAIST)
Nara, Japan
rzhang@is.naist.jp

Yasuhiko Nakashima
Nara Institute of Science and Technology (NAIST)
Nara, Japan
nakashim@is.naist.jp

## ABSTRACT

A compact and low energy circuitry of time-based stochastic computing (TBSC) have been designed. In the TBSC theory, stochastic numbers (SNs) are represented by duty-cycle of periodic signals. Additionally, multiplication and addition operations of the SNs require the signals to be in-harmonic and uncorrelated in frequency. In order to dynamically tune the frequency, a current-starved structure is applied in a three-stage inverter chain type of oscillator with the neuron-MOS mechanism. By feeding the pulses to a neuron-MOS based inverter with adjustable switching threshold, arbitrary duty-cycle for representing any specific SNs can be generated with the accuracy of 96%. In this manner, the implementation cost of the stochastic number generator (SNG) is reduced by avoiding the use of complex frequency-programmable-oscillator and comparator which are exploited in the conventional TBSC circuit. From circuit simulation results, multiplication and addition operations can be retrieved by proposed TBCS circuits with the accuracy of about 97%. The entire circuitry utilizes 210 CMOS transistors, and consumes the energy of 2.5*pJ* for one computation, which is 14% and 36.7% of conventional TBCS circuit, respectively.

## CCS CONCEPTS

• **Computer systems organization**; • **Hardware** → *Integrated circuits*; *Very large scale integration design*;

## KEYWORDS

time-based stochastic computing, current-starved ring oscillator, neuron-MOS, duty cycle detector

**ACM Reference Format:**
Tati Erlina, Yan Chen, Renyuan Zhang, and Yasuhiko Nakashima. 2019. An Efficient Time-based Stochastic Computing Circuitry Employing Neuron-MOS. In *Great Lakes Symposium on VLSI 2019 (GLSVLSI '19), May 9–11, 2019, Tysons Corner, VA, USA.* ACM, New York, NY, USA, 6 pages. https://doi.org/10.1145/3299874.3317985


*GLSVLSI '19, May 9–11, 2019, Tysons Corner, VA, USA*

ACM ISBN 978-1-4503-6252-8/19/05...$15.00
https://doi.org/10.1145/3299874.3317985

## 1 INTRODUCTION

Stochastic computing (SC) [1, 5, 8] paradigm has been considered as one of the potential solutions to the growing concern of computation efficiency. The concept has been implemented in a variety of complex applications as an alternative approach to the conventional binary computing paradigm, including in image processing [2], deep neural network [13, 17], and vector quantization [16]. The nature of number representation in the SC offers an inherent advantage of error tolerant [6] because every single bit is equally weighted. Therefore, a bit flip in any location of the stream contributes a small uniform variation to the value being represented. Another advantage of SC is the ability to solve complex arithmetic operations using a simple combinational circuit. For example, a multiplication of unipolar SNs can be done by a simple logic AND. This leads to a reduction in hardware cost and low power consumption.

However, SC paradigm also brings some shortcomings. For example, it needs a more extended bit stream compared to binary representation. Accordingly, to acquire a better accuracy level, longer computation time is needed. Besides, an SNG circuit which exploits a linear feedback shift register (LFSR) and a comparator, lessens the low cost advantage of the SC. This due to a significant amount of hardware cost consumed by the SNG. Hence, the SNG constitutes a large portion of power consumption [12] in an SC circuit.

In literature, a variety of methods have been explored to diminish the weaknesses of the SC. Considerable portions of these methods, however, concentrate solely on reducing the cost of SNG. For example, in [11] the authors proposed a method that incorporates an LFSR with a non-linear S-box function. While in [3], the authors proposed a method that exploits a D flip-flops to produce approximately independent SNs from a single random source. Other authors in [7] replaces the LFSR part in the SNG by Sobol sequence to reduce bit stream lengths and improve the accuracy of the stochastic computation. One of essential works to suppress the shortcomings of the SC, which offers not only a novel method in SNs generation but also SNs representation, is called TBSC [9]. Such an approach, although quite efficient, works on the current mode that fits better in special purpose computing like image processing. It also involves a comparator circuit which is complicated to implement and relies on inverters in adjusting the frequency. Therefore, a large number of inverters needs to be placed in the circuit even though it would not be used entirely in every operation.

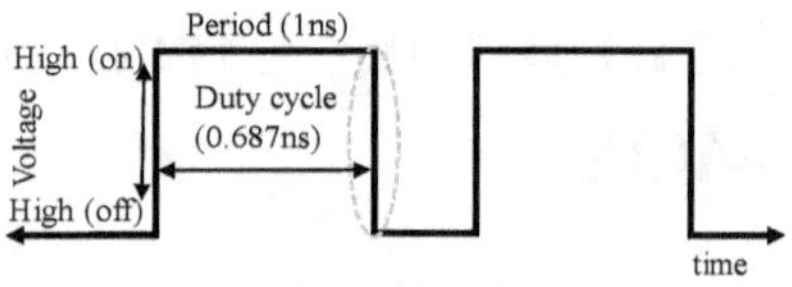


**Figure 1: time-based stochastic number representation [9].**

This paper proposes a compact and low energy circuitry to implement TBSC. By means of voltage mode, this circuit is expected to fit better in general purpose computing. The employment cost is reduced by exploiting current-starved structure and neuron-MOS mechanism, avoiding the use of complex frequency-programmable-oscillator and comparator which is employed in the conventional TBSC circuit.

## 2 TIME-ENCODED STOCHASTIC COMPUTING

Conventionally, the stochastic computing represents a number by the probability of 1s in the sequences of a random bit stream, recognized as SNs [15]. The SNs have two kinds of formats; unipolar and bipolar. The range of number x that can be represented in unipolar and bipolar format are [0 <= x <= 1] and [-1<= x <= 1], respectively. The same bit strings are interpreted differently in both formats. As an illustration, in the unipolar format, the 10-bit SN 1010100001 denotes 0.4, whereas the same bit sequence designates value -0.2 in the bipolar representation. In this sense, the length of bit streams and the position of 1s in stochastic numbers do not need to be fixed. Hence, a particular value such 0.2, can be represented in a number of possible ways such as 10000, 00100 or 0100010000.

Unlike its conventional SC, the value of data in the TBSC approach is encoded in time domain. More specifically, SNs is represented by the duty cycle, which is the ratio between pulse width (on) and the period of a pulse width modulation (PWM) signals [9]. If a PWM signal which has 1 ns period, for instance, is to be used to represent a value of 0.687, then the pulse width of the signal needs to be 0.687ns or 68.7% duty cycle, as illustrated in Fig. 1.

In the baseline reference [10], the time-encoded stochastic number is generated using a specific SNG that so called a low-cost PWM generator. The circuit creates a stochastic number by enabling frequency tuning and duty cycle adjustment of the PWM signals. There are three main parts of the PWM generator, namely a ramp generator, a clock generator, and an analog comparator, as shown in Fig. 2. The ramp generator accepts analog signal input from sensors and produces a relevant sawtooth waveform. The analog comparator then receives the waveform through its positive input and obtains control voltage in its other input port, the negative input. The duty cycle of the PWM signal produced by the circuit is controlled by the amount of current from the sensor. Meanwhile, its frequency is adjusted using a clock generator which is built based on a structure of ring oscillator. The number of inverters activated in the clock generator influences the frequency of the PWM signal. For instance, to produce a periodic signal which has 1ns period, as many 89 as inverters are required.

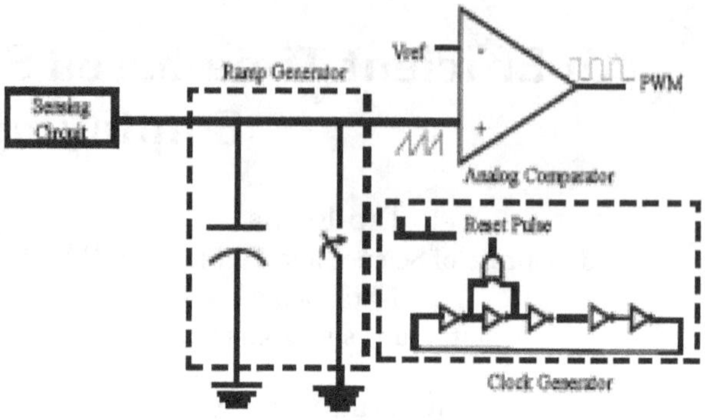


**Figure 2: Design of PWM generator [10].**

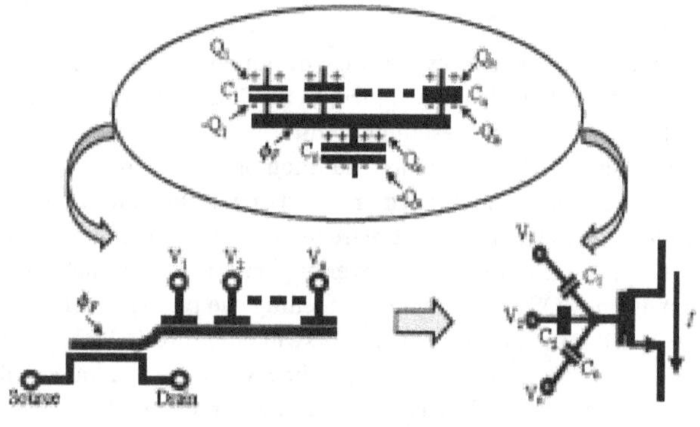


**Figure 3: Structure of neuron-MOS transistor[18].**

## 3 PROPOSED CIRCUIT

### 3.1 Principles of Neuron-MOS Transistor

Neuron-MOS is a MOS transistor which has electrically floating gate[14]. The gate is connected to multiple input terminals, $V_1$, $V_2$, ..., $V_n$, which are coupled with multiple capacitors, $C_1$, $C_2$, ..., $C_n$, as illustrated in Fig. 3. $C_0$ signifies capacitance value between the floating gate and the substrate, while the $Q_1$, $Q_2$, ..., $Q_n$ denotes electronic charge accumulated on the coupling capacitors. The value of the floating gate potential, $\phi_F$, is a linear combination of the multiple input voltages and its couple capacitance. Thus, it is calculated as:

$$\phi_F = \frac{C_1V_1 + C_2V_2 + \cdots + C_nV_n}{C_{tot}} \tag{1}$$

.

The value of $\phi_F$ is relative to the transistor threshold value and determines the on or off state of the transistor. Apparently, the structure of the neuron-MOS enables the potential on the gate to be dynamically tuned by applying different voltage on the input terminals according to specific capacitance ratio. This allows the use of the smallest capacitor size possible to reduce the chip area. Hence, neuron-MOS concept has been leveraged in various work including quaternary FPGA designs [19] and differential edge-triggered Flip-Flops [4].

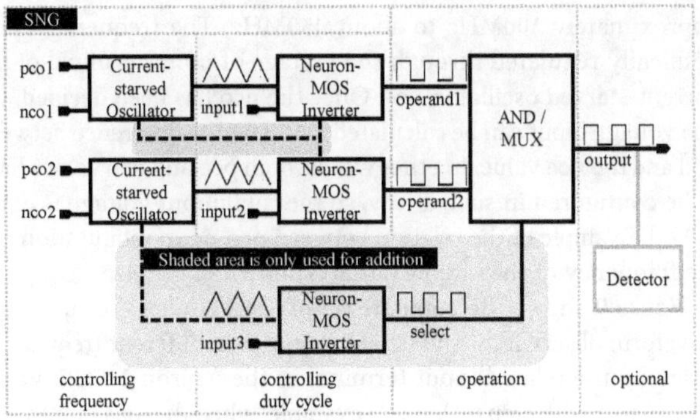


**Figure 4: Overall structure of two-operand multiplication/addition.**

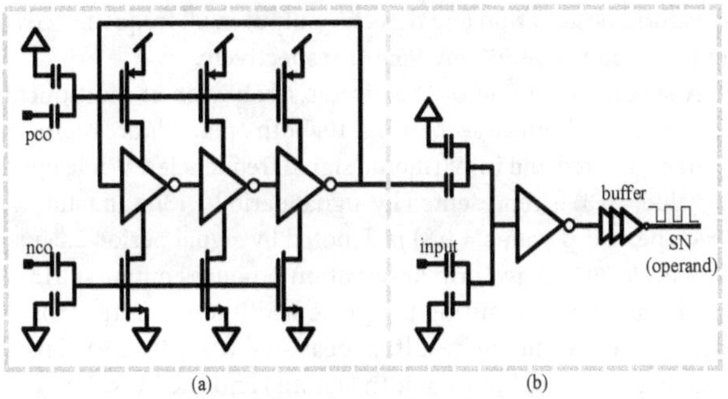


**Figure 5: Architecture of the proposed SNG, (a) Current-starved oscillator, (b) Neuron-MOS inverter.**

## 3.2 The architecture of the proposed circuits

High level view of the proposed TBSC circuit for multiplication and addition operation is shown in Fig. 4. SNs is generated by SNGs within two stages. First, a current-starved oscillator produces a periodic wave which frequency is specified through the combination of voltage in its two input terminal, pco and nco. Next, the neuron-MOS inverter accepts the oscillation and adjusts it duty cycle based on the voltage of its other input terminal. The output of the second stage is a PWM signal which duty cycle represents the value of the time-based SN or an operand of the intended operation.

Multiplication or scaled addition operations are performed using an AND gate or a MUX gate, respectively. Since the SNs (operands) of the multiplication operation in TBSC need to be represented by in-harmonic and uncorrelated frequency, both operands should be generated by different SNGs. On the contrary, the correlated signal frequency between operands is preferable in scaled addition [10]; uncorrelation is only mandatory between frequency signals which represent operands and select input of MUX. As the consequence, two operands of the scaled addition can be produced by an SNG which uses a single current-starved oscillator but with two different neuron-MOS inverters (as shown by upper shaded connecting line) in Fig. 4. Select input, however, needs to be produced by another SNG (shaded area). The use of detector in the circuit is optional since the detector functions specifically to ease the measurement of the duty cycle of the output signal.

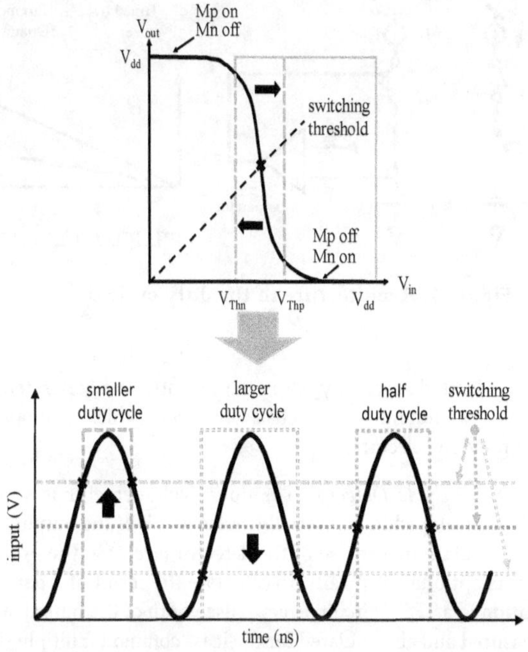


**Figure 6: Enabling flexible adjustment of duty cycle through shifting the switching threshold of the neuron-MOS inverter.**

3.2.1 *Current-starved Oscillator.* Design of the proposed SNG involves (a) current-starved oscillator, and (b) neuron-MOS inverter. The schematic circuit in Fig. 5(a), illustrates that the current-starved oscillator is mainly comprised of three inverters. Instead of linked directly to a voltage source and ground like conventional inverters, each of the inverter in this circuit is connected to a pair of pMOS and nMOS transistor which function as current sources. These transistor pairs function to limit the current available to each inverter. Thus, the inverters become current-starved and dissipate minimal power.

Furthermore, in order to restrict the current flow to the inverters more flexibly so that the charging and discharging speed of the inverters can also be regulated more loosely, every transistor that functions as a current source is constructed as neuron-MOS. The mechanism allows these transistors' gate potential to be bendable based on each input voltage which is coupled with capacitance value, as in formula (1). This construction, in the end, enabling reasonably flexible control of oscillation frequency output of the current-starved oscillator.

3.2.2 *Neuron-MOS Inverter.* The second part of the SNG in the proposed circuit is the neuron-MOS inverter as shown in Fig. 5(b). The inverter has a floating gate which potential is determined by output of the current-starved oscillator, one input voltage and their coupled capacitance. This structure of input allows the circuit to accept interaction from outside. Using neuron-MOS structure in this inverter enables shifting the switching threshold, $V_{\text{Thp}}$, of pMOS transistor and $V_{\text{Thn}}$, of the nMOS transistor flexibly, as shown in Fig. 6. Consequently, the circuit produces a signal which duty cycle can

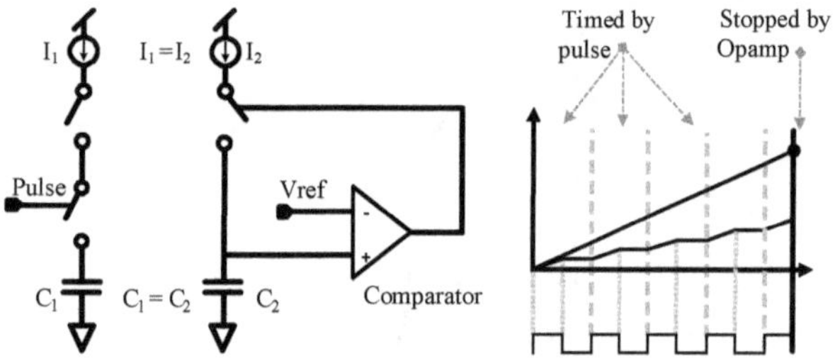


**Figure 7: Architecture of the duty cycle detector.**

also be adjusted amenably. More importantly, the generated duty cycle covers a full range of stochastic numbers, which is comparable to the previous circuit.

*3.2.3 Duty Cycle Detector.* The duty cycle detector is a circuit which is developed to measure the pulse width of the output signal of the calculation. The use of the detector circuit in the proposed circuit is optional. Typically, to calculate the result of a particular operation in a TBSC circuit, every pulse width of the output signals is measured and accumulated for the least common multiply (LCM) time of its operand's periods. This can be done by observing the simulation signals from a particular software. Unfortunately, this method is error prone due to inaccuracy and inconsistency of the measuring location of duty cycle of the observed signal. Besides, the manual measuring takes a long time to complete. Indeed, the simulation software provides a facility to measure the pulse width automatically. However, a close to maximum or minimum duty cycle value (0 or 1) of a duty cycle, which is cut because it intersects with the LCM of the output signal, is automatically skipped (not measured) by the software. Consequently, it contributes to the error rate of the operation output. For these reasons, the existence of the duty cycle detector is very convenient.

Mechanism of the duty cycle detector circuit exploits the concept of the current mirror where the identical current sources charge two identical yet separated capacitors as shown in Fig. 7. The first capacitor states; charging and remaining, are timed by PWM signals which duty cycle is being measured. Specifically, the length of pulse width (on) of the signals would determine the charging time of the capacitor while the length of off state would keep the capacitor remaining in the same previous capacitance level. Simultaneously, the second capacitor is charged until the positive input voltage of the connected comparator reaches about the same level as the reference voltage. The voltage measured in the first capacitor, at the moment the second capacitor charging is stopped, is the duty cycle of the output signal.

# 4 CIRCUIT SIMULATION RESULTS

## 4.1 Verification of Behavior

In order to verify the operations and the performance of the proposed circuit in SNG, multiplication and addition operation level, the circuitry in Fig. 4. were implemented in HSPICE. The simulations were carried out in a 180nm CMOS technology and generated signal displayed in CSCOPE. Based on the experiments, the neuron-MOS oscillator can produce a signal with a frequency ranging from approximately 100MHz to about 450MHz. The frequency is dynamically regulated through the voltage of input terminal of the current-starved oscillator, nco. Once the nco has been decided, the pco voltage input can be calculated based on the difference between Vdd and the nco value. In other words, both pco and nco values have to be configured in such a way, so the total input voltage is equal to Vdd. Example of the relation between pco-nco configuration and the frequency of the output signal is shown in Fig. 8.

Figure 9 shows the comparison of SNG circuit's ideal output, waveform observation and detector output in different frequencies based on the related input terminal in the neuron-MOS inverter (from 0 to 1 with step 0.1). As an example, when the bias input value is 0.4V, the SNG circuit is expected to produce signal with duty cycle 40%, representing ideal value 0.4. In this case, however, a slightly different average output is produced through waveform observation (0.426) and detector circuit (0.413). On average, the accuracy of waveform observation and detector output in all frequency covered by the circuit is 96.9% and 96.4%, respectively.

A specific example of the circuit's behavior in multiplication operation level can be seen in Fig. 10. Both operands are represented by uncorrelated and in-harmonic signal frequencies. While operand A (value = 0.3) is represented by signal period 3.13ns and duty cycle 30%, operand B (value = 0.8) is denoted by signal period 2.24ns and duty cycle 80%. Waveform observation produces output 0.215. This is calculated by measuring the pulse width of the output for LCM time. In this sense, the result is measured from 10ns to 17ns. The ratio between total pulse width (1.48ns) and the LCM (7ns) is the final output (0.21). As for output according to the detector circuit, the result is directly shown by the voltage level which is 0.235.

In the same fashion of multiplication, Fig. 11 shows a particular example of scaled addition operation. Since uncorrelated frequencies between signals representing operands is not suggested, both operands is denoted by the same frequency signal (period = 3.13ns). Utilizing uncorrelated signal as select input (period = 2.24ns) allows measuring result of the scaled addition at the same time as multiplication operation. Duty cycle observation gives of 0.6, while detector shows result of 0.66. This differs slightly from ideal scaled addition result, 0.7.

Overall circuit simulation result in operation level are illustrated in Fig. 12 and Fig. 13. Both operations involve 121 pairs of SNs (covering all possibility of SNs from 0 to 1 with step 0.1). The operands on multiplication are uncorrelated and inharmonic (produced by a different set of SNGs with period = 3.13ns and 2.24ns). However, Correlated in signal period is preferable in scaled addition operations. Therefore, both operands are represented by the same signal period (3.13ns) while select input is represented by signal period 2.24ns. Compared to the ideal output, the proposed circuit simulation result of the multiplication and scaled addition 121 pairs of SNs have almost the same accuracy, i.e., 97% of its ideal output.

## 4.2 Comparison

Table 1 shows a comparison of hardware implementation of the proposed circuit shown in Fig. 4 with the TBSC circuit in [10], where SNs are represented in the unipolar format. in the current work, all of those information derives from the simulation result in HSPICE using signal period 3.13ns and 2,24ns. For a fair comparison, data

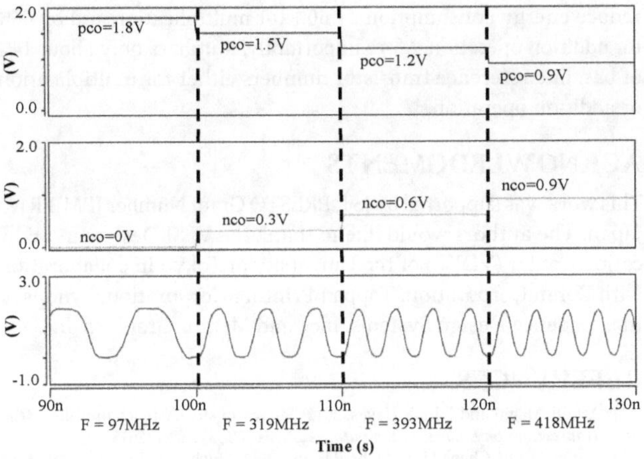


**Figure 8: Example of input configuration and their related output frequency.**

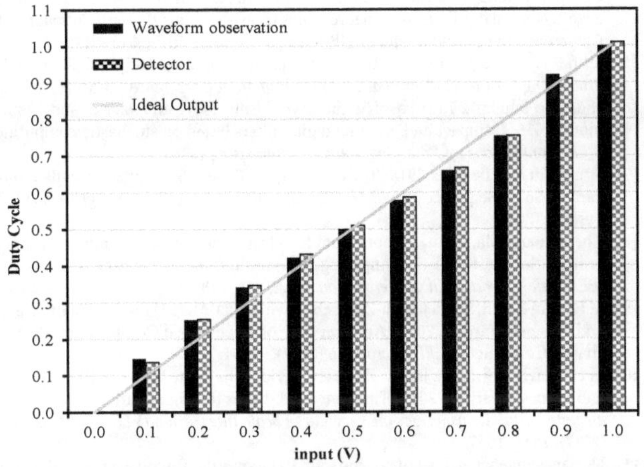


**Figure 9: Comparison of SNGs ideal output, waveform observation and detector based on input voltage of the neuron-MOS inverter.**

on all relevant parameters of comparison are taken from either available explicitly or assumed based on other relevant information in the previous reference. For example, the number of transistors needed for each operand in the previous TBSC circuit is calculated from the number of inverters used to generate operand for each period (89 inverters for 1ns period).

## 5 CONCLUSION

Based on design and simulation results, it can be concluded that the proposed circuit can retrieve the work of baseline reference utilizing current-starved oscillator and neuron-MOS inverter. The circuit is much simpler without involving comparator which is complicated to implement. Conducting operations on operands with the same signal frequency (period), the proposed circuit accuracy in multiplication and addition is only slightly lower (less than 2%) than the baseline reference. On the contrary, the proposed circuit

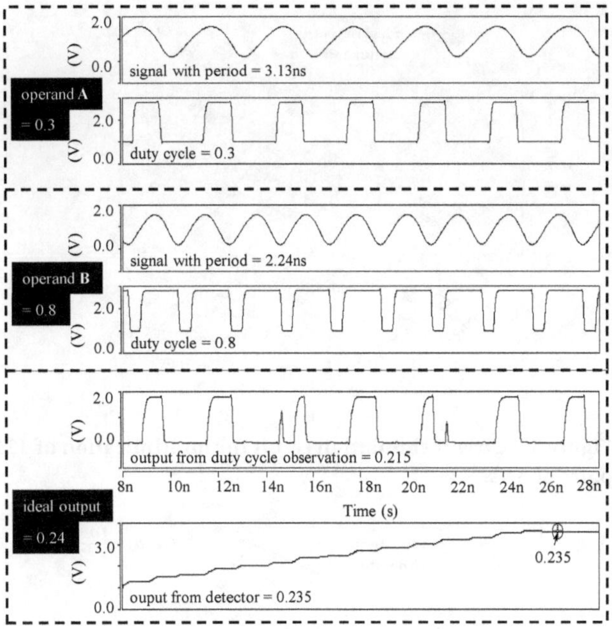


**Figure 10: Sample of multiplication between two operands (0.3 and 0.8) represented by signal period 3.13ns and 2.24ns.**

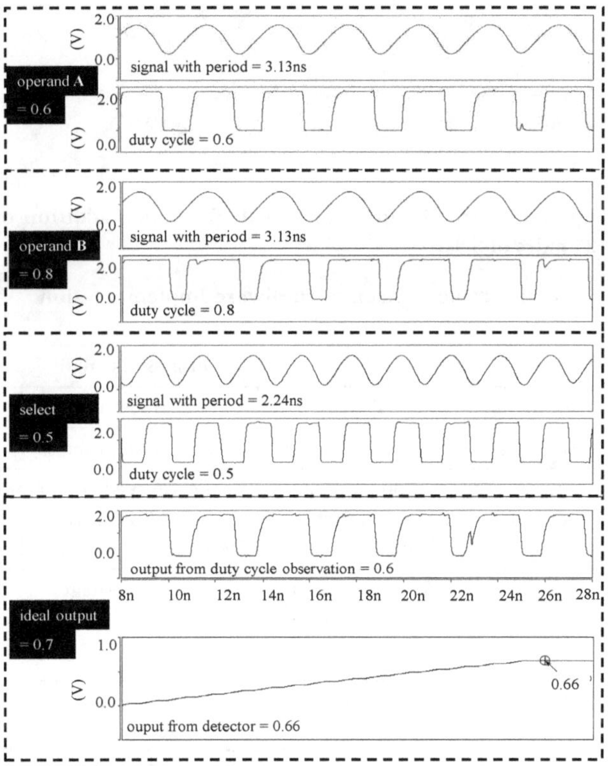


**Figure 11: Sample of scaled addition between two operands (0.6 and 0.8) represented by signal period 3.13ns.**

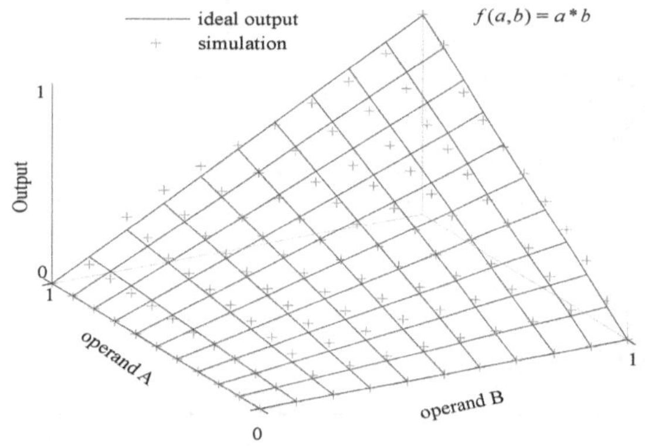


**Figure 12: Circuit simulation result for multiplication of 121 pairs of SNs.**

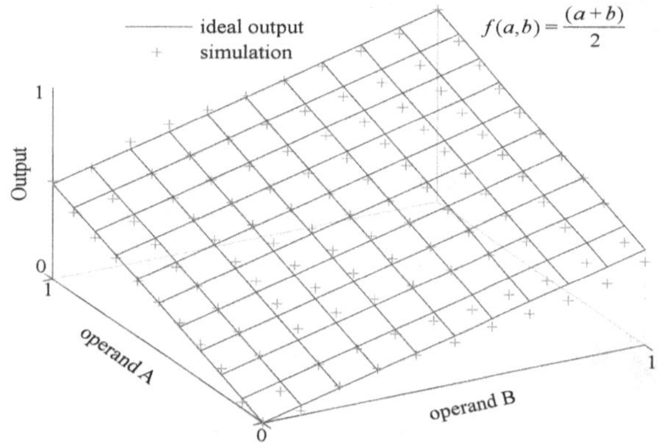


**Figure 13: Circuit simulation result for scaled addition of 121 pairs of SNs.**

**Table 1: Comparison of Hardware Implementation**

| | [10] | Proposed Circuit |
|---|---|---|
| Technology | 45nm | 180nm |
| Strategies | time-based values | time-based values |
| Components (of SNG) | Comparator<br>Ramp Generator<br>Clock Generator | Current-starved Oscillator<br>Neuron-MOS Inverter<br>PWM Detector (optional) |
| Input | Analog Current | Analog Voltage |
| Speed (ns) | 7 (mul.)<br>7 (add.) | 7 (mul.)<br>7 (add.) |
| Accuracy (%) | 98.6 (mul.)<br>98.6 (add.) | 96.6 (mul.)<br>96.7 (add.) |
| # of trans. | 967 (mul.)<br>1512 (add.) | 140 (mul.)<br>210 (add.) |
| Energy (pJ) | 4.5 (mul.)<br>6.8 (add.) | 1.8 (mul.)<br>2.5 (add.) |

reduce energy consumption by 60% for multiplication and by 66% for addition operation. More importantly, it utilizes only about 14% of baseline reference transistor numbers either for multiplication or addition operation.

## ACKNOWLEDGMENTS

This work was supported by JST, PRESTO Grant Number JPMJPR18M7, Japan. The authors would like to thank the VLSI Design and Education Center (VDEC) of the University of Tokyo in collaboration with Rohm Corporation, Toppan Printing Corporation, Synopsys, Inc., Cadence Design Systems, Inc., and Mentor Graphics, Inc.

## REFERENCES

[1] Armin Alaghi and John P Hayes. 2013. Survey of stochastic computing. *ACM Transactions on Embedded computing systems (TECS)* 12, 2s (2013), 92.
[2] Armin Alaghi, Cheng Li, and John P Hayes. 2013. Stochastic circuits for real-time image-processing applications. In *Design Automation Conference (DAC), 2013 50th ACM/EDAC/IEEE*. IEEE, 1–6.
[3] Te-Hsuan Chen and John P Hayes. 2014. Analyzing and controlling accuracy in stochastic circuits. In *Computer Design (ICCD), 2014 32nd IEEE International Conference on*. IEEE, 367–373.
[4] Guoqiang Hang, Xiaohui Hu, Hongli Zhu, and Xiaohu You. 2013. Differential edge-triggered flip-flops using neuron-mos transistors. In *2013 Ninth International Conference on Computational Intelligence and Security*. IEEE, 313–317.
[5] John P Hayes. 2015. Introduction to stochastic computing and its challenges. In *Proceedings of the 52nd Annual Design Automation Conference*. ACM, 59.
[6] Hideyuki Ichihara, Tatsuyoshi Sugino, Syota Ishii, Tsuyoshi Iwagaki, and Tomoo Inoue. 2016. Compact and accurate digital filters based on stochastic computing. *IEEE Transactions on Emerging Topics in Computing* (2016).
[7] Siting Liu and Jie Han. 2018. Toward Energy-Efficient Stochastic Circuits Using Parallel Sobol Sequences. *IEEE Transactions on Very Large Scale Integration (VLSI) Systems* (2018).
[8] Chengguang Ma, Shunan Zhong, and Hua Dang. 2012. Understanding variance propagation in stochastic computing systems. In *Computer Design (ICCD), 2012 IEEE 30th International Conference on*. IEEE, 213–218.
[9] M Hassan Najafi, Shiva Jamali-Zavareh, David J Lilja, Marc D Riedel, Kia Bazargan, and Ramesh Harjani. 2017. An Overview of Time-Based Computing with Stochastic Constructs. *IEEE Micro* 37, 6 (2017), 62–71.
[10] M Hassan Najafi, Shiva Jamali-Zavareh, David J Lilja, Marc D Riedel, Kia Bazargan, and Ramesh Harjani. 2017. Time-encoded values for highly efficient stochastic circuits. *IEEE Transactions on Very Large Scale Integration (VLSI) Systems* 25, 5 (2017), 1644–1657.
[11] Florian Neugebauer, Ilia Polian, and John P Hayes. 2017. Building a Better Random Number Generator for Stochastic Computing. In *Digital System Design (DSD), 2017 Euromicro Conference on*. IEEE, 1–8.
[12] Weikang Qian, Xin Li, Marc D Riedel, Kia Bazargan, and David J Lilja. 2011. An architecture for fault-tolerant computation with stochastic logic. *IEEE Trans. Comput.* 60, 1 (2011), 93–105.
[13] Ao Ren, Zhe Li, Caiwen Ding, Qinru Qiu, Yanzhi Wang, Ji Li, Xuehai Qian, and Bo Yuan. 2017. Sc-dcnn: Highly-scalable deep convolutional neural network using stochastic computing. *ACM SIGOPS Operating Systems Review* 51, 2 (2017), 405–418.
[14] Tadashi Shibata and Tadahiro Ohmi. 1992. A functional MOS transistor featuring gate-level weighted sum and threshold operations. *IEEE Transactions on Electron devices* 39, 6 (1992), 1444–1455.
[15] Paishun Ting and John P Hayes. 2017. On the role of sequential circuits in stochastic computing. In *Proceedings of the on Great Lakes Symposium on VLSI 2017*. ACM, 475–478.
[16] Ran Wang, Jie Han, Bruce F Cockburn, and Duncan G Elliott. 2016. Stochastic circuit design and performance evaluation of vector quantization for different error measures. *IEEE Transactions on Very Large Scale Integration (VLSI) Systems* 24, 10 (2016), 3169–3183.
[17] Aidyn Zhakatayev, Sugil Lee, Hyeonuk Sim, and Jongeun Lee. 2018. Sign-magnitude SC: getting 10X accuracy for free in stochastic computing for deep neural networks. In *2018 55th ACM/ESDA/IEEE Design Automation Conference (DAC)*. IEEE, 1–6.
[18] Renyuan Zhang and Mineo Kaneko. 2014. A feasibility study on robust programmable delay element design based on neuron-mos mechanism. In *Proceedings of the 24th edition of the great lakes symposium on VLSI*. ACM, 21–26.
[19] Renyuan Zhang and Mineo Kaneko. 2015. A feasibility study of quaternary FPGA designs by implementing Neuron-MOS mechanism. In *2015 IEEE International Symposium on Circuits and Systems (ISCAS)*. IEEE, 942–945.

# Monolithic 8x8 SiPM with 4-bit Current-Mode Flash ADC with Tunable Dynamic Range

Vikas Vinayaka
Department of Electrical and Computer Engineering
University of Nevada, Las Vegas
Las Vegas, NV USA
vinayaka@unlv.nevada.edu

Sachin P. Namboodiri
Department of Electrical and Computer Engineering
University of Nevada, Las Vegas
Las Vegas, NV USA
puruss1@unlv.nevada.edu

Shadden Abdalla
Department of Electrical and Computer Engineering
University of Nevada, Las Vegas
Las Vegas, NV USA
abdals1@unlv.nevada.edu

Bryan Kerstetter
Department of Electrical and Computer Engineering
University of Nevada, Las Vegas
Las Vegas, NV USA
kerstett@unlv.nevada.edu

Francisco Mata-carlos
Department of Electrical and Computer Engineering
University of Nevada, Las Vegas
Las Vegas, NV USA
matacarl@unlv.nevada.edu

Daniel Senda
Department of Electrical and Computer Engineering
University of Nevada, Las Vegas
Las Vegas, NV USA
sendad1@unlv.nevada.edu

James Skelly
Department of Electrical and Computer Engineering
University of Nevada, Las Vegas
Las Vegas, NV USA
skellj1@unlv.nevada.edu

Angsuman Roy
Freedom Photonics, LLC
Santa Barbara, CA USA
aroy@freedomphotonics.com

R. Jacob Baker
Department of Electrical and Computer Engineering
University of Nevada, Las Vegas
Las Vegas, NV USA
r.jacob.baker@unlv.edu

## ABSTRACT

A monolithic photon-counting receiver consisting of an integrated silicon-photomultiplier and a current-mode analog-to-digital converter (ADC) was designed, simulated and fabricated in the AMS 0.35 $\mu$m SiGe BiCMOS process. The silicon photomultiplier (SiPM) consists of 64 avalanche photodiodes (APD) arranged in an 8x8 pattern with integrated 236 kΩ quenching resistors. This silicon-photomultiplier exhibits peak responsivity at 490 nm and is intended for atmospheric and oceanographic light detection and ranging (LIDAR) applications. The current-mode ADC is used to directly convert photocurrent from the silicon-photomultiplier into a 4-bit word. The maximum sampling rate achieved in simulation is 100 MS/s. The measured differential nonlinearity (DNL) and integral nonlinearity (INL) for the ADC are 0.5 LSB and 0.17 LSB respectively. The dynamic range of the ADC is tunable based on the reference current and varies from 5 $\mu$A – 80 $\mu$A to 30 $\mu$A – 480 $\mu$A. The whole system covers an area of 0.375 mm$^2$. The fill factor of the silicon photomultiplier is 12.6 %.


GLSVLSI '19, May 9–11, 2019, Tysons Corner, VA, USA

ACM 978-1-4503-6252-8/19/05...$15.00.
https://doi.org/10.1145/3299874.3318005

## CCS CONCEPTS

Hardware~Data conversion • Hardware~On-chip sensors

## KEYWORDS

Silicon Photomultiplier (SiPM); Flash ADC; current-mode; analog to digital converter; photosensor; SiGe; avalanche photodiode (APD); bubble correction; tunable dynamic range; LIDAR

**ACM Reference format:**

Vikas Vinayaka, Sachin P. Namboodiri, Shadden Abdalla, Bryan Kerstetter, Francisco Mata-carlos, Daniel Senda, James Skelly, Angsuman Roy, R. Jacob Baker. 2019. Monolithic 8x8 SiPM with 4-bit Current-Mode Flash ADC with Tunable Dynamic Range. In *GLSVLSI '19: 2019 Great Lakes Symposium on VLSI, May 9-11, 2019, Tysons Corner, VA, USA. ACM, New York, NY, USA, 6 pages.* https://doi.org/10.1145/3299874.3318005

## 1 INTRODUCTION

Photon-counting has numerous applications such as medical imaging, time of flight (ToF), high energy physics, and LIDAR. The interest in LIDAR has been particularly high due to the advent of autonomous vehicle systems. With much of the focus in automotive applications, other uses for LIDAR have been neglected by the market. One such use of LIDAR is in atmospheric and oceanographic mapping [1]. The wavelengths of interest for this application are in the blue-green spectrum, between 460 nm and 532 nm, a band where there is a lack of low cost commercially available components and systems. The vast majority of LIDAR components are in the 1550 nm band for automotive LIDAR. One unique strength of LIDAR in the 460 nm to 532 nm band is that silicon photodetectors can be used which opens the possibility for a fully monolithic optical receiver solution instead of the current discrete component systems available on the market today. We propose a novel SiPM read-out circuitry consisting of a silicon-photomultiplier (SiPM) with a current-mode ADC implemented in a standard 0.35 $\mu$m SiGe BiCMOS process to address the need for low-cost atmospheric and oceanographic LIDAR applications.

An avalanche photodiode APD is a photodetector that is typically used for low-light level detection. It is usually realized by a reversed bias p-n junction. When the reverse bias voltage applied across the APD is in the "knee" of the break down curve, photocurrent gain can be achieved (due to impact ionization and avalanche multiplication). This is the linear mode of operation used in most APD applications. An alternate mode of operation is operating the APD in Geiger-mode, where the device is biased beyond breakdown. In this mode, the output of the APD can either be the dark current level or a saturation current level set by the quenching resistor. A Geiger-mode APD (Gm-APD) can break down due to thermally generated carriers (a dark count) or due to incident light (a light count). The fundamental method of quantifying the light level incident on a Geiger-mode APD is by counting the number of pulses in a certain time interval.

An extension of a Geiger-mode APD is the silicon-photomultiplier, which is an array of Gm-APDs arranged in a grid and connected in parallel. The output from a SiPM is a current pulse whose amplitude is an integer multiple of the current level from a single Gm-APD, with a maximum current level determined by the number of Gm-APDs in the SiPM array. This current output is then typically amplified by a transimpedance amplifier (TIA) and then digitized with an ADC in order to be processed by a digital system. This work offers a current-mode ADC as a solution to directly interface to a SiPM without a TIA, leading to simplicity and robust design.

The design and development of optical receivers for photon counting have recently gained considerable interest [2]. Many designs have been reported in the literature aiming for the development of efficient SiPM read-out circuitry [3,4]. However, most of the designs are mainly focused for biomedical imaging applications such as PET, SPECT, etc. The commonly used SiPM read-out circuits follow the conventional approach of using transimpedance amplifiers to convert the current output from the SiPM to a voltage signal and then digitized by an ADC for further data processing [5]. This has many advantages as well as limitations in terms of dynamic range, bandwidth, power consumption and simplicity. Another technique that has been used is the implementation of "digital SiPM", where the output of each APD is digitized [6]. The main advantage of a digital SiPM is that it can improve the noise of the system. However, the design turns out to be complex and covers more layout area and power consumption.

The SiPM read-out can also be implemented by using the current-mode technique. By using this approach, a high bandwidth as well as a large dynamic range can be achieved compared to voltage-mode topologies. The design in [7] makes use of this approach by incorporating current buffer along with SiPM array. The main challenge with this approach is that the matching of the current source is very critical. The mismatch in the device size can lead to degradation in the overall performance of the whole read-out circuit.

In this paper, we present a novel fully integrated SiPM read-out system using a 4-bit current-mode ADC implemented in AMS' SiGe 0.35 $\mu$m technology fabricated through the MOSIS service. The sensor (SiPM) is comprised of an 8x8 array of APDs. Since the output of the SiPM is a current signal, it will be directly fed into a current-mode ADC and thus bypassing a transimpedence amplifier and other circuitry that are conventionally used for an SiPM read-out. The ADC also offers the freedom of tuning the dynamic range and thereby can accommodate for different SiPM bias voltages. Section 2 of this paper discusses the overall system architecture. Section 3 reports the experimental setup and the measured results. Section 4 concludes the paper along with the scope for future work.

## 2 SYSTEM DESCRIPTION

Figure 1 shows the overall block diagram of the SiPM read-out circuit. It consists of the SiPM coupled with the current-mode 4-bit ADC. The SiPM outputs a current signal whose amplitude depends on the number of APDs triggered. This output current is then fed to the 4-bit current-mode ADC which produces a digital output. The SiPM and current-mode Flash ADC blocks are described in the subsequent sections. The output of ADC is available off-chip for further data processing using a DSP or FPGA.

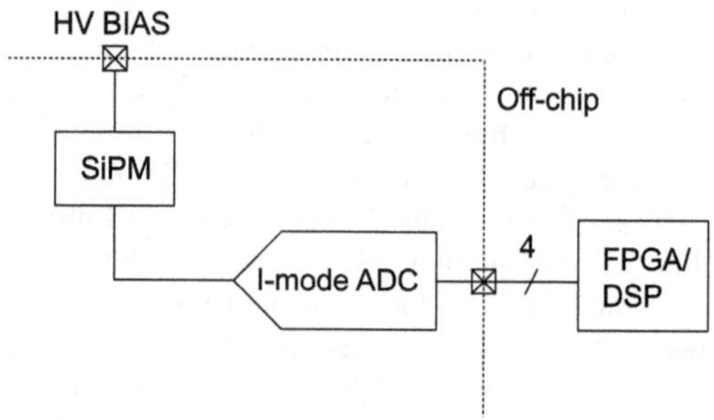


**Figure 1: System architecture.**

### 2.1 SiPM array

The SiPM is a photosensor whose output is a current whose value can be a set of discrete amplitude levels. The SiPM consists of an array of avalanche photodiodes (APDs) that are connected in parallel. Figure 2 shows the internal schematic of the SiPM and its equivalent electrical model. The anode of all the APDs are connected, ensuring the summation of each APD current output. The APDs are operating in Geiger-mode, which requires a quenching resistor, $R_{quench}$ placed in series as seen in the figure. All APDs are pre-charged above the breakdown voltage with a high voltage (HV) supply, typically 11V-15V. A single cell of the array showing a serpentine quench resistor wrapped around the APD is displayed in Figure 3. The layout of the 8x8 SiPM array in the AMS' 0.35 µm SiGe process is illustrated in Figure 4.

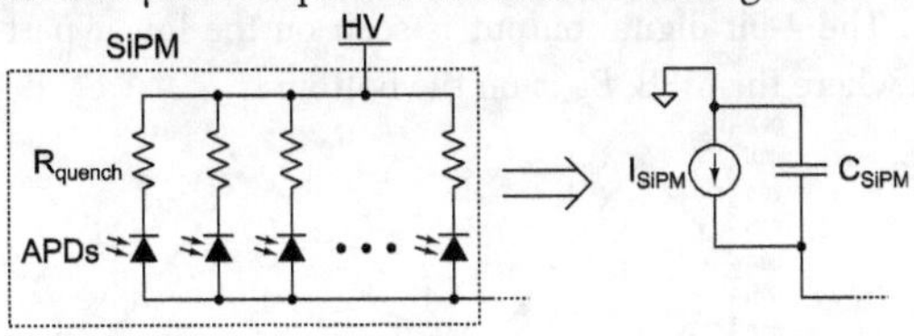


**Figure 2: Circuit and simple electrical model of SiPM.**

The main benefit of a SiPM as compared to a single APD is that it can detect multiple photons at the same time [8]. The significance of this is that the SiPM has a higher count rate and dynamic range than other photon-counting detectors.

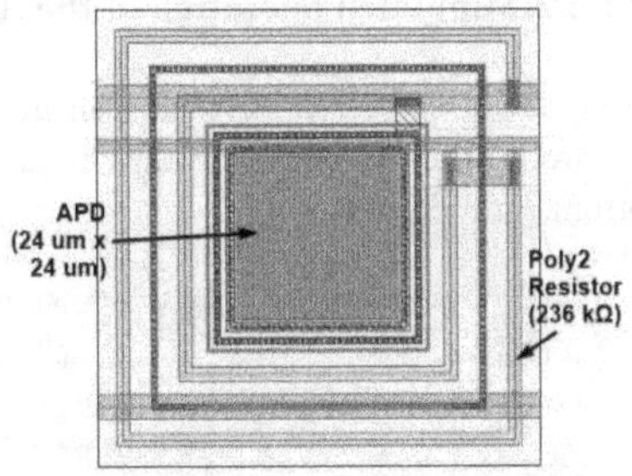


**Figure 3: Single APD cell of SiPM**

The SiPM array needs a bias voltage higher than its breakdown voltage which is much higher than the supply voltage (VDD) of other circuits on the chip. In this fabrication process, the APDs have a breakdown voltage of about 12 V whereas VDD is 5 V. When the SiPM is connected to the ADC, the ADC input has a bias voltage which reduces the voltage across the SiPM. As a result, the SiPM bias voltage must be offset by the average value of the voltage on the ADC input. The voltage on the input of the ADC is discussed in the next section.

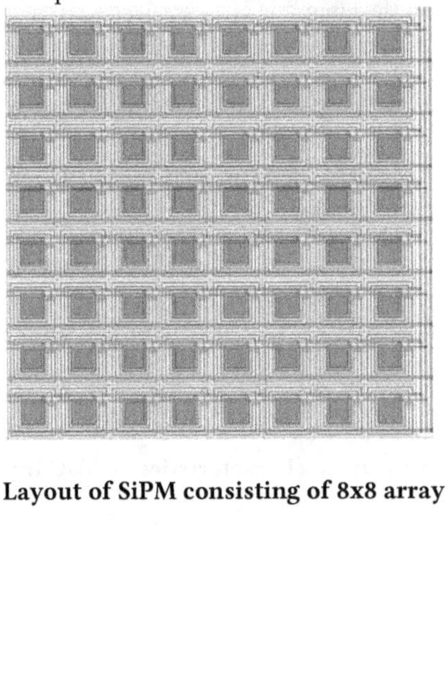

**Figure 4: Layout of SiPM consisting of 8x8 array of APDs**

## 2.2 Current-mode Flash ADC

The output of the SiPM is connected to the input of the current-mode Flash ADC. The ADC converts the incoming current to a 4-bit digital value. The output of the ADC is asynchronous and can be retimed using an off-chip clock if needed. Figure 5 shows the circuit of the 4-bit current-mode Flash ADC implemented in this work.

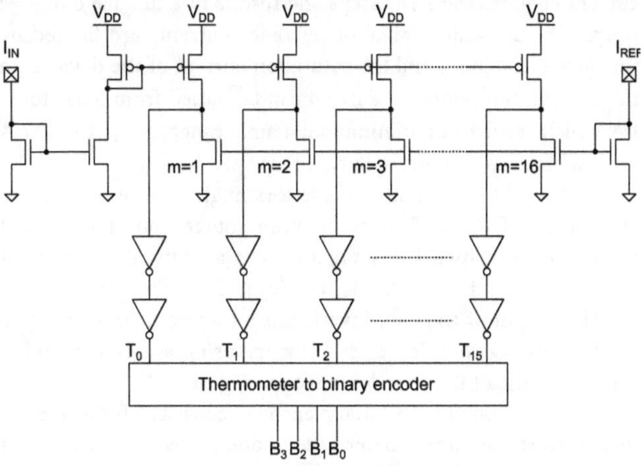


**Figure 5: Schematic of 4-bit current-mode Flash ADC**

The ADC mainly consists of current comparators, gain inverters and thermometer to binary encoder blocks.

In the Figure 5, the current comparator is seen on the top. It has the input current, $I_{IN}$ input on the left side and the reference current, $I_{REF}$ on the right side. The current comparator consists of PMOS current sources and NMOS current sinks in series. The current comparator operates as follows: The voltage at the junction point of the current source/sink (the drains of the PMOS/NMOS) is dependent on the current flow through the devices. If the current source value is higher than the current sink value, the voltage at the junction point is pulled up to VDD. Conversely, if the current sink value is higher than the current source value, the voltage at the junction point is pulled to ground. This is the mechanism of current comparison. The PMOS current sources are mirrored from the input current. The NMOS current sinks are scaled and mirrored from the reference current. The PMOS current is compared against each multiple of the reference current corresponding to all the ADC steps. The output of the current comparator array is a thermometer code.

The speed of the current comparator is limited by the current available to drive the gain inverters. The most significant current limitation occurs during conditions where the current source and current sink values are similar. This limitation can also be viewed as occurring near regions where the output code would transition to the next value.

The current comparator mainly relies on matching between the current mirror devices for proper operation. The device lengths are chosen to be four times the minimum length of CMOS devices in the fabrication process. This ensures good matching and increases the output resistance of the devices, which results in better gain and resolution of each ADC step. The length could be increased further to improve resolution, however there is a tradeoff of speed because of increased capacitance of all the devices. Also, increase in length for matching produces diminishing returns after a point where random mismatch and threshold voltage mismatch dominate [9].

Since the current comparators compare the input current against multiples of reference currents, changing the reference current changes the ADC steps and results in a tunable dynamic range. The allowable range of reference currents are limited by the device matching and the saturation current of the devices. In this design, the reference current can be varied from 5 $\mu$A to 30 $\mu$A which results in a minimum dynamic range of 5 $\mu$A – 80 $\mu$A up to a maximum 30 $\mu$A – 480 $\mu$A respectively.

The output of current comparators might not be resolved to logic levels if the difference between source and sink current values are too low. The gain inverters amplify the output of current comparators to standard logic levels.

The output of the gain inverters is a thermometer code of 16 levels. This is converted to 4-bit binary using a digital encoder. The schematic of the encoder is seen in Figure 6.

The thermometer to binary encoder consists of AND gates that convert the thermometer code to one-hot code. The one-hot code is converted to binary using the binary encoded ROM pattern. This generates the 4-bit binary output which is buffered and sent out off-chip.

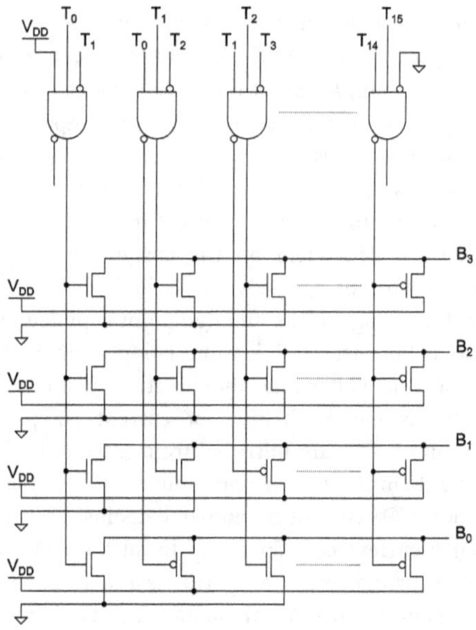


**Figure 6: Schematic of thermometer to binary encoder**

The thermometer code from the comparator output is prone to errors (bubble) that must be addressed while designing the encoder. This is usually caused by metastability of the comparator. The 3-input AND gate eliminates bubble errors [10]. If a spurious 0 is present in a string of 1's or a spurious 1 in a string 0's, it will be corrected at the output of the AND gate. The scheme used here can only correct a single isolated spurious code. If there are two or more spurious 0's or 1's in a string of complementary bits, more advanced schemes would be needed to correct it.

The simulation results of the Flash ADC are seen in Figure 7. This shows a triangle wave input current and the corresponding analog representation of the digital output on the top part of the figure. The 4-bit digital output is seen on the lower part of the figure where the MSB, $B_3$ is on the bottom.

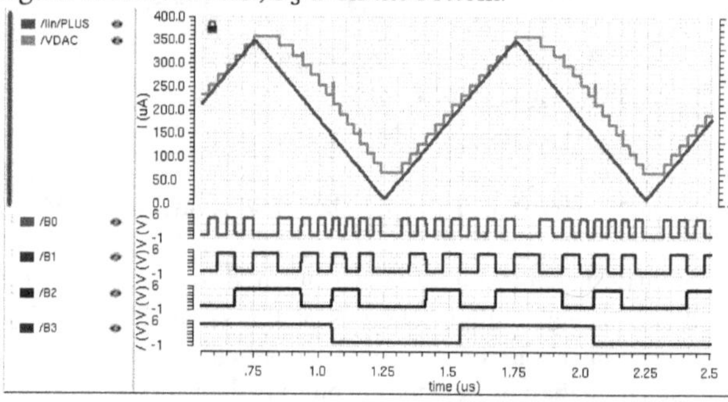


**Figure 7: Simulated operation of the ADC**

Complete layout of the Flash ADC is seen in Figure 8. The current inputs are on the left edge and the digital 4-bit outputs are on the bottom-right corner.

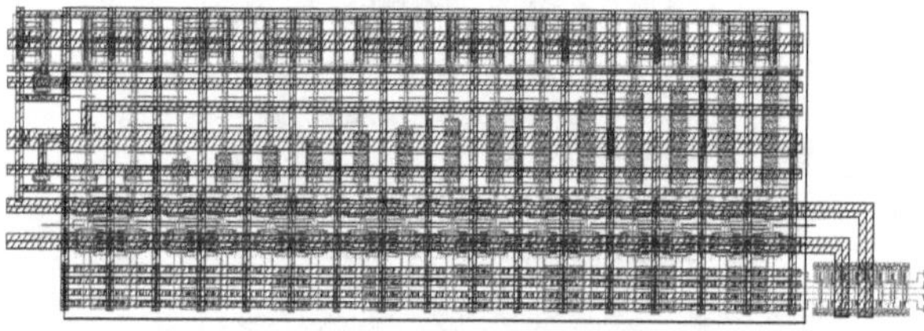

**Figure 8: Physical layout of ADC**

## 2.3 SiPM and Flash ADC

The input of the Flash ADC is a gate-drain connected NMOS as seen in Figure 5. As a result, an increase in input current also causes an increase in input voltage. This characteristic is seen in Figure 9 where the x-axis is the input current and the y-axis is the voltage on the input.

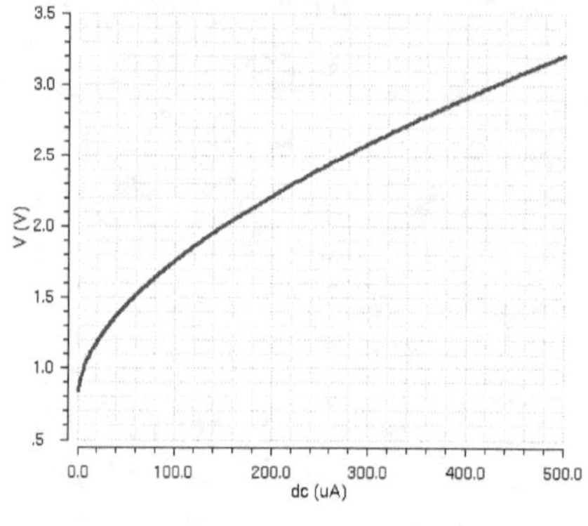


**Figure 9: I-V characteristics of ADC input**

Since the anode of the SiPM is connected to the ADC input, the voltage across the SiPM is the difference between the SiPM high-voltage bias applied to the SiPM cathode and the voltage on the input of the ADC. The SiPM bias voltage must be increased to compensate for the increase in ADC input voltage. This has a side effect that a higher bias voltage appears across the SiPM for lower currents and vice versa.

The variation in input voltage due to input current could be decreased by increasing the device widths used. However, this would put stricter requirements on the device matching due to reduced gate to source voltages. As a result, there is a trade-off between input offset voltage reduction and improved device matching.

## 3 MEASUREMENT RESULTS

The micrograph of the fabricated chip is seen in Figure 10. The chip has dimensions of 2 mm x 2 mm. As annotated in the figure, the SiPM array is at the center of the chip and the ADC is on the top-right corner of the chip. The output of SiPM is connected to the input of ADC using internal pad to pad bond wires. This was done to facilitate ease of testing; in future designs the SiPM and ADC can be directly connected with on-chip metal layers.

The test setup is implemented as follows: The chip is bonded on a TO-8 package and mounted on a PCB. The TO-8 package without a lid is inserted into one end of a copper tube. An LED driven by a constant current source is mounted on the other end of the copper tube. This results in a dark condition for the chip when the LED is off. The LED is activated using a square wave signal and the resulting digital output change is observed using a logic analyzer.

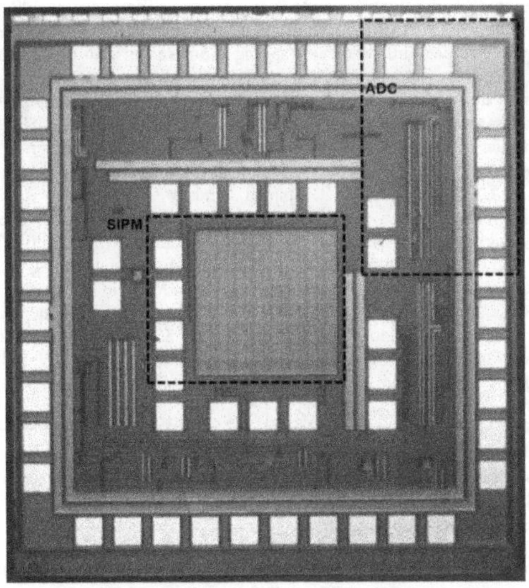


**Figure 10: Chip photomicrograph**

The measured output is seen in Figure 11. The LED control signal is seen on the top and the 4-bit digital output is seen on the bottom part of the oscilloscope capture image. The LED turns on when the LED control signal is high. The digital outputs increase when the LED is on. Since the SiPM generates pulses with pseudo-analog levels which are proportional to the amount of light incident on it, this results in the pulses seen on the output of the ADC. In this plot, the ADC reference current is 10 $\mu$A and SiPM bias voltage is 13 V.

The measured current-mode ADC transfer characteristics are seen in Figure 12. In this plot, the x-axis is the input current and the y-axis is the output digital code. This measurement is with the standalone ADC excluding the SiPM. The input current and reference current were directly applied to the ADC input using a sourcemeter to measure the characteristics. These characteristics are measured with a reference current of 10 $\mu$A.

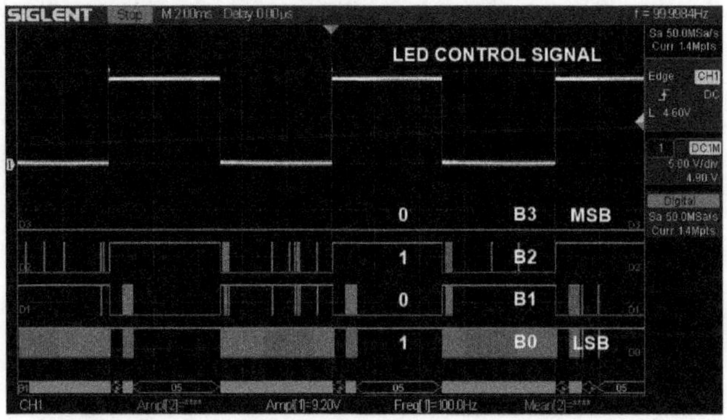


**Figure 11: Measured response of the system**

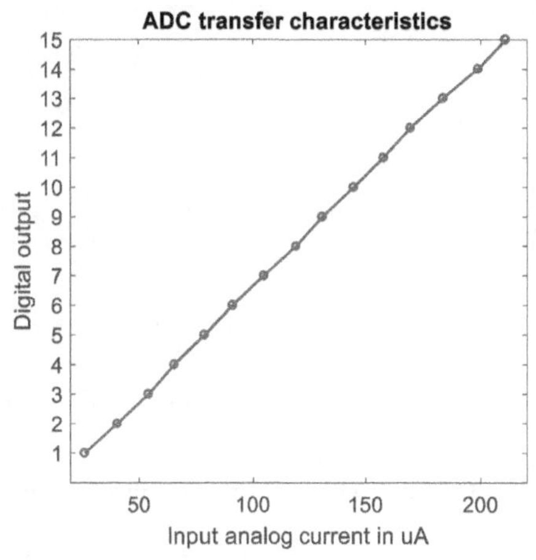


**Figure 12: ADC static transfer characteristics**

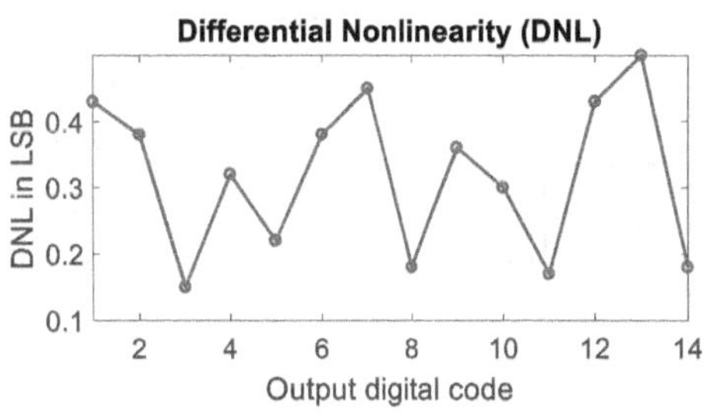


**Figure 13: Measured DNL**

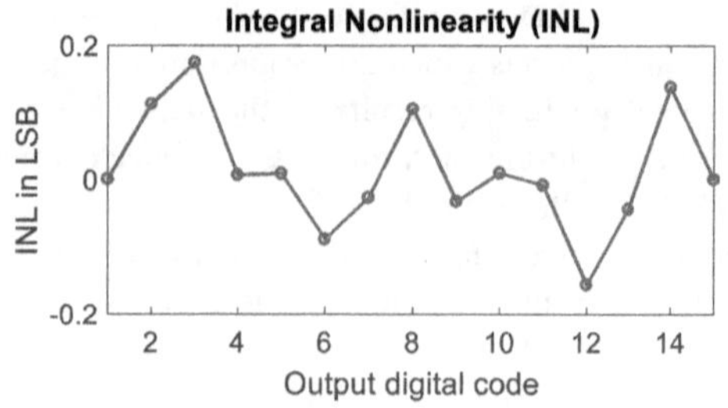


**Figure 14: Measured INL**

The differential non-linearity (DNL) and integral non-linearity (INL) are derived from the transfer characteristics and seen in Figure 13 and Figure 14. Observing these characteristics, we see that the maximum DNL is 0.5 LSB and maximum INL is 0.17 LSB. The ADC also has a gain error of 13.18 $\mu$A/bit and offset error of 26.1 $\mu$A. The ADC I-V input characteristics are measured and seen in Figure 15. The voltage on the ADC input varies from about 0.8 V to 3.3 V for an input current change from 1 $\mu$A to 500 $\mu$A. The SiPM bias voltage needs to be increased correspondingly in order to apply the required breakdown voltage across the SiPM.

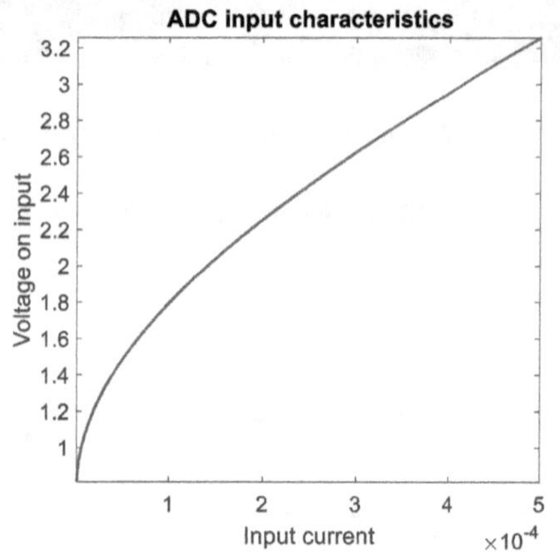


**Figure 15: Measured characteristics of ADC input**

**Table 1: Comparison of current-mode ADC**

| | This work | [11] |
|---|---|---|
| Technology | AMS 0.35um SiGe | 90nm CMOS |
| Supply voltage | 5 V | 1.2 V |
| Resolution | 4-bit | 3-bit |
| DNL/INL | 0.5 LSB / 0.17 LSB | 0.24 LSB / 0.24 LSB |
| Dynamic range | 30 µA – 480 µA | Not reported |
| Sampling rate | 100 MS/s * | 2 GS/s |
| Power | 14.3 mW * | 3.1 mW |

* Simulated value

# 4 CONCLUSION

In this work, an 8x8 SiPM is interfaced with a current-mode 4-bit Flash ADC. Both blocks reside on the same monolithic chip which results in an integrated system which is novel in this work. The whole system occupies an area of 0.375 $mm^2$ on the die. The current-mode ADC standalone results are summarized and compared with similar work [11] in Table 1. The ADC has DNL, INL, gain error and offset errors which are caused by device mismatch due to process variations. The read-out operation of the SiPM and ADC has been demonstrated. This work can be extended by developing a complete photodetection system which would need an on-chip digital signal processing depending on the appropriate application. The proposed monolithic photon counting system combining a SiPM with a current-mode ADC can significantly reduce the cost of LIDAR systems for atmospheric and oceanographic applications.

# ACKNOWLEDGMENTS

We are grateful for the support provided by Richard J. Hare and his team at NASA Langley Research Center. This work was supported by NASA under contract number 80NSSC18P2022.

# REFERENCES

[1] NOAA. What is LIDAR. Retreived from https://oceanservice.noaa.gov/facts/lidar.html
[2] Matteo Perenzoni. 2018. Single-Photon Avalanche Diode-Based Detection and Imaging: Bringing the Photodiode Out of Its Comfort Zone. IEEE Solid-State Circuits Magazine, 10(3), 26-34.
[3] S. Gundacker, E. Auffray, B. Frisch, H. Hillemanns, P. Jarron, T. Meyer, K. Pauwels, and P. Lecoq. 2012. A Systematic Study to Optimize SiPM Photo-Detectors for Highest Time Resolution in PET. IEEE Transactions on Nuclear Science, 59(5), 1798 – 1804.
[4] Salleh Ahmad, Julien Fleury, Christophe de la Taille, Nathalie Seguin-Moreau, Frederic Dulucq, Gisele Martin-Chassard, Stephane Callier, Damien Thienpont, and Ludovic Raux. 2016. Triroc, a Versatile 64-Channel SiPM Readout ASIC for Time-of-Flight PET. In Proceedings of the IEEE Nuclear Science Symposium, Medical Imaging Conference and Room-Temperature Semiconductor Detector Workshop, Strasbourg, France.
[5] Manuel de Medeiros Silva, and Luis B. Oliveira. 2014. Regulated Common-Gate Transimpedance Amplifier Designed to Operate with a Silicon Photo-Multiplier at the Input. IEEE Transactions on Circuits and Systems—I: Regular Papers, 61(3), 725-735.
[6] Leo H. C. Braga, Leonardo Gasparini, Lindsay Grant, Robert K. Henderson, Nicola Massari, Matteo Perenzoni, David Stoppa, and Richard Walker. 2014. A Fully Digital 8×16 SiPM Array for PET Applications with Per-Pixel TDCs and Real-Time Energy Output, IEEE Journal of Solid-State Circuits, 49(1), 301-314.
[7] Paolo Trigilio , Paolo Busca, Riccardo Quaglia, Michele Occhipinti, and Carlo Fiorini. 2018. A SiPM-Readout ASIC for SPECT Applications. IEEE Transactions on Radiation and Plasma Medical Sciences, 2(5), 404-410
[8] P. Eraerds, M. Legré, A. Rochas, H. Zbinden, and N. Gisin. 2007. SiPM for fast Photon-Counting and Multiphoton Detection. Optics Express, 15(22), 14539-14549.
[9] M. S. Bhat, Rekha S, and H. S. Jamadagni. 2004. Design of Low Power Current-Mode Flash ADC. In Proceedings of the IEEE Region 10 Conference TENCON 2004, IEEE, Chiang Mai, Thailand.
[10] Michael J. Delmer. 1991. High-Speed Analog-to-Digital Conversion. Academic Press Inc., San Diego, CA, USA.
[11] C. Park, H. M. Geddada, A. I. Karsilayan, J. Silva-Martinez and M. Onabajo. 2013. A current-mode flash ADC for low-power continuous-time sigma delta modulators. In *Proceedings of the IEEE International Symposium on Circuits and Systems (ISCAS2013)*, Beijing, 141-144. DOI: 10.1109/ISCAS.2013.6571802.

# A Systolic SNN Inference Accelerator and its Co-optimized Software Framework

[1]Shasha Guo, [1]Lei Wang*, [1]Shuquan Wang, [1]Yu Deng,
[1]Zhijie Yang, [1]Shiming Li, [2]Zhige Xie, [1]Qiang Dou
[1]College of Computer Science and Technology, National University of Defense Technology
[2]Joint Operations College, National Defense University
[1]Changsha, Hunan, P.R.China, [2]Beijing, P.R.China
guoshasha13@nudt.edu.cn,arrowya@gmail.com

## ABSTRACT

Although Deep Neural Network (DNN) architectures have made some breakthroughs in computer vision tasks, they are not close to biological brain neurons. Spiking Neural Network (SNN) is highly expected to bridge the gap between artificial computing systems and bio-systems. And it also shows great potential in low power computing. This paper presents a low power hardware accelerator for SNN inference using systolic array, and a corresponding software framework for optimization. First, we give the hardware design which adopts systolic array inspired by explorations of SNN. Then we ensure correct data mapping for systolic array for the sake of computational correctness. Next, we use compression methods for decreasing both the runtime and memory footprint. Finally, we make the systolic array size-configurable to adapt to different input, so as to reduce computational overhead. We implement the accelerator on Xilinx FPGA V7 690T. The experimental results show that SNN inference on our scheme suffers little loss on accuracy (less than 0.1%) on MNIST and Fashion-MNIST, and the runtime of the time-consuming layers decreases. The total power of our scheme is 0.745 W at 100 MHz.

## KEYWORDS

spiking neural network, systolic array, compression, size-configurable

**ACM Reference Format:**
Shasha Guo, Lei Wang*, Shuquan Wang, Yu Deng, Zhijie Yang, Shiming Li, Zhige Xie, Qiang Dou. 2019. A Systolic SNN Inference Accelerator and its Co-optimized Software Framework. In *Great Lakes Symposium on VLSI 2019 (GLSVLSI '19), May 9–11, 2019, Tysons Corner, VA, USA.* ACM, New York, NY, USA, 6 pages. https://doi.org/10.1145/3299874.3317966

## 1 INTRODUCTION

Spiking Neural Networks (SNNs) are the new generation of neural networks which aim to mimic the behaviors of neurons in the brain. SNNs shows great potential in improving low power neuro-based computing and get more and more attention from researchers. SNNs are naturally suitable for processing input from event-based sensors, and it is also proved to be accurate, fast, and efficient for classical frame-based machine vision tasks such as object recognition or detection, in particular when implemented on neuromorphic hardware platforms [1–3].

There are some well-known large scale models of neuromorphic neural systems, such as SpiNNaker, TrueNorth, NeuroGrid, Brain-Scales [4] and DYNAPs [5]. SpiNNaker represents a remarkable platform for fast simulations of large-scale neural computational models. It improves the performance of software simulations by integrating 18 processors onto a single die. It can support networks with arbitrary connectivity and various kinds of neuron, synapse, and learning algorithms. TrueNorth is a fully functional ASIC chip with 1 million spiking neurons and 256 million synapses. Unlike previous two systems, NeuroGrid, BrainScales and DYNAPs all use a combination of analog circuits and digital circuits to build the system.

SNN training typically does not use spike-based learning rules, but instead starts from a conventional DNN, fully trained with backpropagation, followed by a conversion of the rate-based model into a spike-based model with simple spiking neurons. This DNN-to-SNN conversion theory has shown that SNNs are almost as accurate as their analog counterparts [6–8]. Therefore, a balance between power consumption and task accuracy can be achieved by using SNN.

This paper proposes a low power SNN inference hardware accelerator and the corresponding optimized software framework. Based on the computational characteristics of SNNs converted from CNNs, we adopt systolic array in the accelerator and propose several techniques for joint optimization. Our contributions include:

(1) We propose and implement a new SNN inference hardware accelerator which uses systolic array. We implement a size-configurable $32 \times 32$ systolic array on Xilinx FPGA V7 690T.
(2) We propose and implement a software framework as the assistance of the hardware. The software framework enables data mapping for systolic array. During the data mapping, the framework will compress data quantity and numerical precision for runtime optimization.

We validate our design on 2 datasets, MNIST [9] and Fashion-MNIST [10] with 4 SNNs. The results show that SNN inference on our scheme suffers little loss on accuracy, less than 0.1% and the runtime of the time-consuming layers decreases. The total power of our scheme is 0.745 W at 100 MHz.


*GLSVLSI '19, May 9–11, 2019, Tysons Corner, VA, USA*

ACM ISBN 978-1-4503-6252-8/19/05...$15.00
https://doi.org/10.1145/3299874.3317966

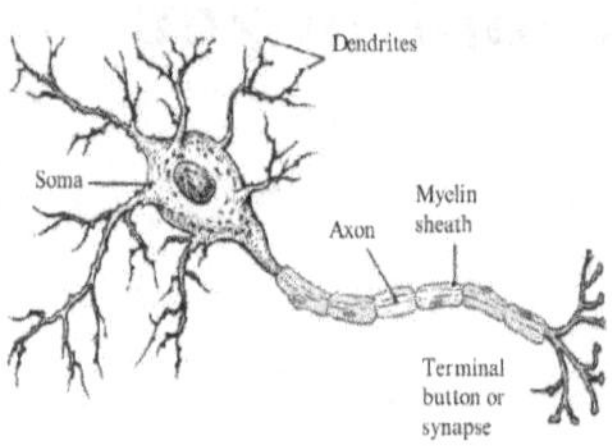


**Figure 1: Componenets of a simple biologic neuron [11].**

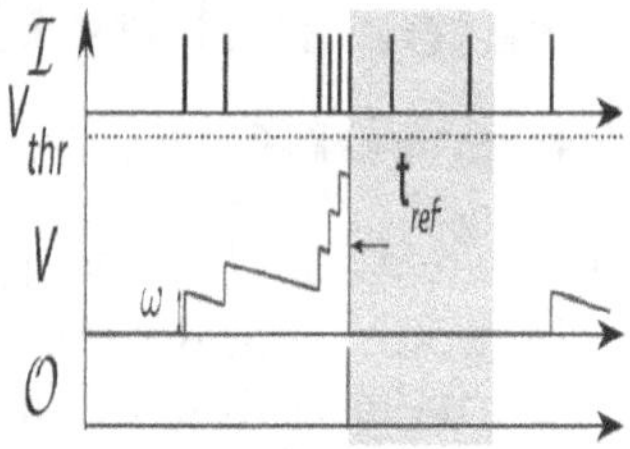

**Figure 2: Behavior of a LIF neuron. $I$ is the input spike train and $O$ is the output.**

## 2 BACKGROUND

### 2.1 Spiking Neural Networks

*2.1.1 IF Neuron Model.* A biological neuron consists of dendrites, soma, and axon (as shown in Figure 1). Two neurons are connected by synapses to transmit information. Dendrites receive spikes from pre-synapse neurons, and pass it to the soma later. The soma produces a corresponding membrane potential change based on the spikes, which is similar to a weighting process and the synaptic plasticity is just like the weight. When the membrane potential exceeds a threshold, the neuron generates a spike. After generating a spike, the neuron will enter into the refractory period and spikes arriving in this period will be ignored. Figure 2 shows the process.

The biological process of a neuron is usually represented by differential equations. Many models have been developed for explaining various spiking behaviors of real neurons, such as Hodgkin-Huxley (HH) Model, Leaky Integrate and Fire (LIF) Model, Izhikevich Model (IM) and so on [12]. The LIF neuron is the most widely used and best-known model of threshold-fire neurons. The membrane potential of the neuron leaks over time when there is no spike coming. A variety of LIF model is IF model with no leak which is the model used in this paper.

Based on the biological process, the calculation process of an IF neuron at every time step can be divided into three steps, input stimulus accumulation, spike generation and membrane potential update as following.

$$z_j^l(t) = \sum_{i=1}^{n^{l-1}} \left(w_{i,j}^l a_{i,j}^{l-1}\right) \tag{1}$$

$$a_j^l(t) = \theta\left(V_j^l(t-1) + z_j^l(t) - V_{thr}\right), \theta(x) = \begin{cases} 0, & \text{if } x < 0 \\ 1, & \text{if } x > 0 \end{cases} \tag{2}$$

$$V_j^l(t) = \left(V_j^l(t-1) + z_j^l(t)\right)\left(1 - a_j^l(t)\right). \tag{3}$$

Where $V_j^l(t)$ is the membrane potential of neuron $j$ in layer $l$ at time step $t$. And $z$ is the accumulation of input stimulus, $a$ is the output of the neuron, either 1 or 0, indicating the presence of spike or not. And $n^{l-1}$ is the number of neurons in layer $l-1$. The output of the previous layer is the input of the next layer. $w_{i,j}^l$ represents the synapse weight between neuron $j$ in layer $l$ and neuron $i$ in layer $l-1$. $V_{thr}$ represents the threshold.

Since the activation consists of only 0 and/or 1, Equation 1 can be rewritten as 4. This is also the basis of our work.

$$z_j^l(t) = \sum_{i \in S} w_{i,j}^l \tag{4}$$

where $S$ is the indices set of all pre-layer neurons that spike.

Based on these computing patterns, we adopt systolic array and eliminate multipliers for a low-power hardware.

### 2.2 DNN to SNN Conversion

As for SNN training, the conventional backpropagation algorithms for DNN training cannot be applied directly, as the derivative of a binary-valued neuron is ∞ at 0 and 0 everywhere else, which is not suitable to backpropagation [3]. There are some temporal rule for training SNN. The representative of unsupervised methods is Spike Timing-Dependent Plasticity (STDP). Supervised methods include SpikeProp, Tempotron, ReSuMe and so on [12].

Despite the existence of these learning rules, there is no effective training method for SNN that can provide better performance than second-generation networks. Generally, training spiking deep networks does not use spike-based learning rules, but instead starts from a conventional DNN [7, 8]. These systems first train DNN with traditional machine learning methods such as backpropagation, followed by a conversion of the DNN model into a SNN model consisting of simple spiking neurons. In SNN, the input image is presented to the network for a certain simulation duration, which is measured by time steps of typically 1 ms per time step.

Our work is based on the spiking-relu-conversion (SRC) project [7]. And we focus on two representative DNN types, Fully Connected Neural Network (FCN) and Convolutional Neural Network (CNN). Although the network topology in SNN is the same as the pre-trained DNN, there are differences between them in inference process. In DNN, the result of one inference only needs one forward process. However, in SNN, the result of one inference requires multiple forward processes, and the output layer accumulates these results to complete the classification.

### 2.3 Systolic array

The concept and architecture of systolic array was first proposed in 1978 by H.T. Kung [13], which is a one-dimensional (1D) or two-dimensional (2D) array composed of multiple isomorphic processing elements (PE). It does not depend on the complex functions of PE but improves performance at the system level by configuring a large number of simple PEs working in parallel. Each PE only exchanges data with their neighbors. The input data is pulsed from the memory toward the interior of the array using the pipeline method.

There are three kinds of data flow in a systolic array, namely, input stationary, weight stationary and output stationary. There are always two data flowing and one staying in the PE unit. In this paper, we adopt the third one, i.e., the output stays in the PE unit and the other two flow through the array.

Previous works give us an intuition that systolic array might be applied for accelerating the inference of large-scale SNN which is time-consuming, because there are some similarities in the computational process between SNNs and DNNs.

## 3 ARCHITECTURE

Figure 3 gives the overall diagram of our design. In the hardware accelerator, based on the matrix operation and binary data flow in SNN, we adopt systolic array and low-precision operators in order to reduce hardware complexity. We use a size-configurable systolic array to accelerate the inference process of SNN which achives the

**Table 1: Definitions of matrix variables**

| variables | description |
|---|---|
| Ar | rows of activation matrix A |
| Ac | columns of activation matrix A |
| Br | rows of weight matrix B |
| Bc | columns of weight matrix B |
| Mr | rows of systolic array |
| Mc | columns of systolic array |
| $Ar_i$ | rows of activation block of the $i_{th}$ computing round |
| $Bc_i$ | columns of weight block of the $i_{th}$ computing round |

low computational cost and low latency. In the optimized software framework, we adopt several techniques, such as data mapping and compression to allocate and optimize the SNN inference process on systolic array. We also implement a simulator to mimic hardware behaviors so as to help accelerate the design and implementation of hardware.

## 3.1 Hardware design

Figure 4 shows the hardware design which consists of six parts: input memory, output memory, weight memory, controller, AXI interface and systolic array. The input memory and the weight memory are implemented with block RAMs which are offered by the FPGA. The activation used as the input of a PE is 1 bit and the size of the activation memory is 8 KB. The weight is 32 bit and the size of the weight memory is 256 KB. The systolic array is responsible for computing process and it gets data from the corresponding memory to fulfill the need of calculation. The systolic array size is set to be 32 × 32 due to resource limitation of FPGA we used. The computing result is put in the output memory. Among these modules, the most important part is the controller and it controls the data to flow in a right way.

*3.1.1 PE unit.* Based on Equation 4, we know that PE unit for SNN inference do not need calculate multiply-and-accumulates (MAC) which is typical in DNN. The design of a single PE unit is shown in Figure 5. There is no need to add additional decision logic to check whether input activation is 1 or 0. Instead, we make the input as the enable signal for the adder. Adder needed for accumulates is cheaper than multiplier needed for MAC [8]. The two operands of the adder are the weight and the partial sum maintained in the PE unit.

*3.1.2 Configurable size.* Table 1 gives the symbols used here and in the rest of the paper. As shown in Figure 6, we explore the runtime a matrix multiplication needed using systolic array of different size. The runtime is measured by clock cycles (clocks for simple). We generate two random matrices of the same size 100×100 as the input of matrix multiplication, called $A$ and $B$. And we find that when $Mr$ and $Mc$ are close to $Ar/2$ and $Bc/2$, the runtime changes rapidly. To make it clear, we selects 8 configurations with $Mr$ being $Ar/2$ and the results are shown in Figure 7. We find that runtime is minimum when $Mc$ is $Bc/2$.

In conclusion, if the systolic array size is smaller than the matrix size, the best configuration is that $Mr$ and $Mc$ equal to $Ar/2$ and $Bc/2$ respectively. And if the array size is around that, larger is better than smaller. For example, when $Mr = 50$, it can be clearly seen that $Mc < 50$ is more time-consuming than $Mc > 50$.

To reduce the overhead incurred by zero padding, we decide to make systolic array size configurable with respect to different matrix size. And we don't make more because that will incur too much complexity in hardware.

Due to the resource limit of the experimental platform, the base systolic array is a square one with 32 × 32 PE units, and the other size is 32 × 16, which is a part of the square array. The key is when to shuffle between the two configurations. Once the decision logic finds that $Bc_i$ is less than 16 (i.e., the columns of second configuration), the control logic will change the size of systolic array from square to rectangle. This design could reduce overhead due to zero padding as it decreases the amount of 0 padded and the computing cycles of one round.

## 3.2 Software design

*3.2.1 Data mapping for systolic array.* Data mapping is important for using systolic array, not only to ensure correctness but also to improve the utilization.

Matrix operation is straightforward to allocate in systolic array. And the operations in converted SNNs are actually matrix multiplications. For the fully connected layer, the operation is a matrix-vector multiplication when there is only one input image and it is a matrix-matrix multiplication when there are multiple input images. For convolution layer, the convolution operation can be converted into matrix operation by im2col method [14] and thus the convolution operation turns into matrix-matrix multiplication.

We split the matrices into blocks and each pair of blocks need a computing round. And we make the block zero-padding if it is smaller than the size of systolic array. Although zero-padding will incur some overhead, this could eliminate complex control logic for mapping output data.

**Algorithm 1:** Compression.

**Require:** The input matrix, $A$ and $B$;
**Ensure:** Compressed matrix, $nA$ and $nB$;
1: repeat for each *column* in A;
2: repeat for each *element* in the *column*;
3: check if *element* is 1: if *element* is 1, record the column index and continue step 1; else continue step 2;
4: After all columns checked, select the corresponding columns into nA and corresponding rows into nB;
5: **return** $nA$ and $nB$;

*3.2.2 Compression for the sparse input.* Due to the inherent characteristics, spike input in a SNN is usually sparse. We propose a novel compression method for sparse input where weight pruning methods such as [15] are not suitable because the sparsity distribution in input is not stationary as that in weights. The method is described in algorithm 1.

There is no need for encoding or decompressing procedure for computation in our method, while most of the previous compressing methods [15] contain them. The compression is conducted in software framework. After applying our method for input and weight matrix, the slimed input and weight matrix are transferred

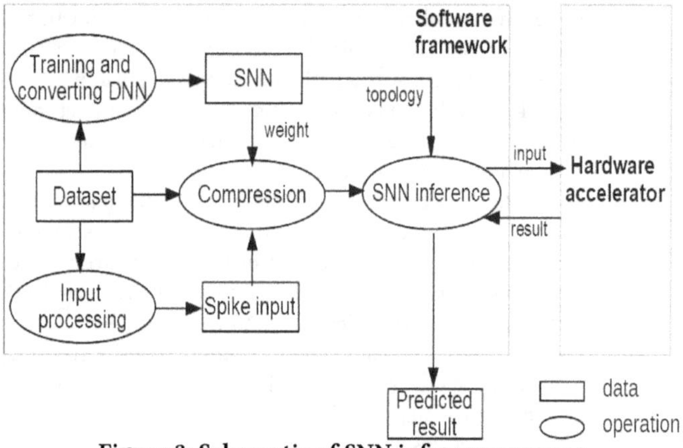

**Figure 3: Schematic of SNN inference process.**

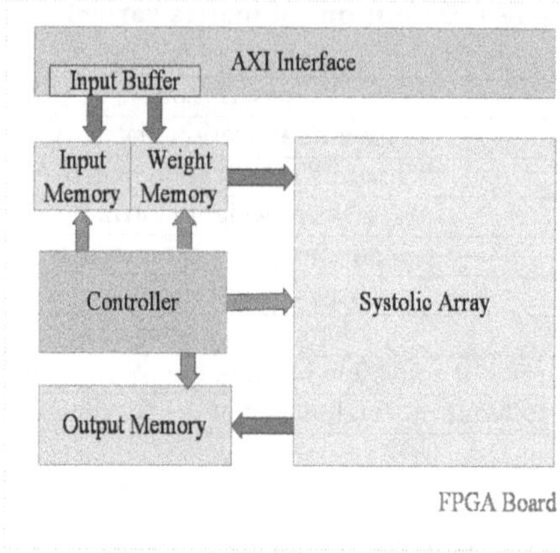

**Figure 4: Hardware design.**

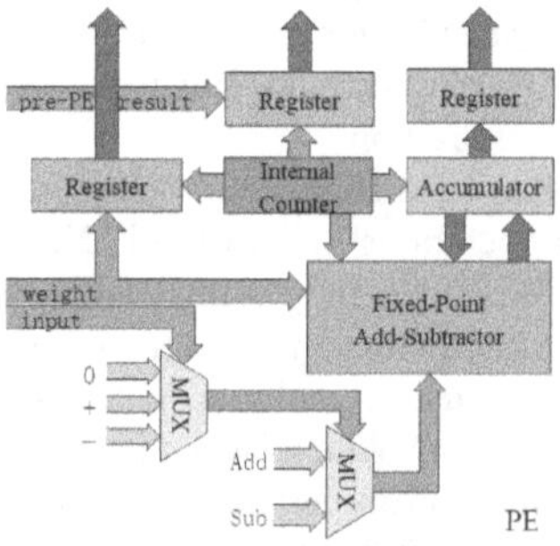

**Figure 5: Single PE design.**

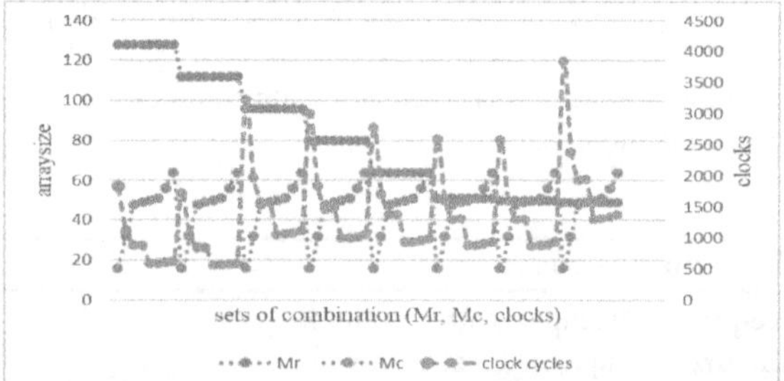

**Figure 6: Change of runtime with different systolic array size. $Mr$ and $Mc$ are the rows and cols of the systolic array. And *clocks* represents the runtime. The left vertical axis measures $Mr$ and $Mc$, and the right is for *clocks*.**

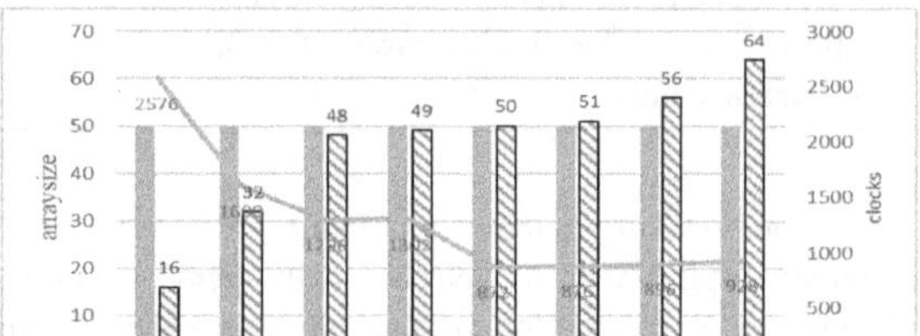

**Figure 7: Change of runtime with $Mr$ being $Ar/2$.**

into the accelerator to conduct the apparent matrix multiplication. The results from the systolic array are the final result. Our method does not require reconstruction to form the correct data layout for the next layer because the compression only decreases the dimension $Ac$ and $Br$ of the input matrices, which does not influence the generation of each element in result matrix which is $Ar \times Bc$. Our method can be seen to some extent as a variation of structural pruning based on the characteristics of spikes.

Compression has two advantages, reducing computing time and memory footprint. We denote the ratio of compression as ROC, which is $Dc/Ac$ and $Dc$ is the columns of compressed matrix $nA$. Before compression, the time required for the systolic array to complete a round of calculations is $Ac + Mr - 1 + Mc - 1$ (the time for data outflow is not counted), and the time required after compression is $Dc + Mr - 1 + Mc - 1$. The speedup is $\frac{Ac+Mr-1+Mc-1}{Dc+Mr-1+Mc-1}$.

The software framework also helps to decide the proper systolic array size from the available configurations for different input size.

**Table 2: utilization**

| resource | utilization | available | utilization % |
|---|---|---|---|
| LUT | 53461 | 433200 | 12.34 |
| FF | 100252 | 866400 | 11.57 |
| BRAM | 65 | 1470 | 4.42 |
| IO | 106 | 600 | 17.67 |
| BUFG | 2 | 32 | 6.25 |

# 4 IMPLEMENTATION & EXPERIMENT

## 4.1 Implementation

*4.1.1 Hardware.* We use Verilog for hardware design and Vivado 2016.4 for evaluation. The accelerator is implemented using Xilinx's FPGA V7 690T. The computational module is a size-configurable 2-dimensional systolic array. The two configurations are $32 \times 32$ and $32 \times 16$ respectively. There are two estimation modes in Vivado environment. One is called vector mode which requires Switching Activity Interchange Format (SAIF) files or VCD files. Another is non-vector mode which only requires simple parameters. We use the second method to estimate the power consumption of the $32 \times 32$ fixed-point systolic array with buffer size of 130 $32 \times 32$b (dual buffer for input, weights and output) and the result is 0.745 W. And table 2 gives the utilization details of the chip in this case. As we just implement fixed-point adders and operators, the number of DSPs is not listed in the table.

*4.1.2 Software and Simulator.* All simulations of the software framework discussed in this paper are conducted in the MATLAB environment. A simulator written in Python which mimics the temporal logic of the hardware accelerator is connected with the software framework via Python interface to MATLAB.

## 4.2 Experiment setup

We validate our design on two datasets with four networks. Table 3 shows the experiment setup. *Model* shows the network architecture. *TestAcc.* means training accuracy of the pre-trained DNN (with the same architecture) on the test set of the dataset.

The SNN is represented by the number of neurons or the computing feature of each layer. Take SNN3 for example, the input is $28 \times 28$, followed by 12 convolution kernels of size $5 \times 5$, followed by a $2 \times 2$ averaging pooling layer. All networks have a 10-node fully connected output layer corresponding to the 10 classes of input.

Before running the SNNs, one needs generate spike trains from the pixels for SNN. Neural responses follow a Poisson distribution [16]. A popular method for generating Poisson distributed spike trains for SNN is based on inequation [6, 7] which we use here.

**Table 3: Experiment setup.**

| | Dataset | Model | Test Acc. |
|---|---|---|---|
| SNN1 | MNIST | 784-1200-1200-10 | 98.84% |
| SNN2 | Fashion-MNIST | 784-1200-1200-100-10 | 87.56% |
| SNN3 | MNIST | 28x28-12c5-2s-64c5-2s-10 | 98.98% |
| SNN4 | Fashion-MNIST | 28x28-64c5-2s-64c5-2s-100c5-10 | 88.32% |

## 4.3 Results

The baseline is the original framework [7] without weight normalization.

*Accuracy and time comparison.* SNN inference using our scheme without and with compression do not impact the inference accuracy compared with the baseline. Figure 8 gives an example, which shows the inference results of SNN3 on 50 images from MNIST test set and that of SNN4 on 50 images from Fashion-MNIST test set. The convergent curves at each case are not exactly the same because the input spike train is generated randomly following the Poisson rates.

Figure 9 shows the runtime comparison of layers in SNNs corresponding to configurations in Table 3. And it shows that just using systolic array is computing effective.

*Compression result.* An example of input sparsity is shown in Figure 10. As we can see, the input is extremely sparse and it is similar in other networks in this paper. Applying compression does not impact the inference accuracy according to our experimental results of SNN3 and SNN4 as shown in Figure 8. Figure 11 shows the compression ratios of each round for hidden layers in SNN1. The ratios are mostly ranging between 0.3 and 0.5.

*Size-configurable systolic array.* For MNIST dataset, taking FCN-based SNN as an example, the weight matrix connecting the output layer is $1200 \times 10$, i.e., $Bc = 10$, corresponding to the 10 labels. As we

**Table 4: Runtime comparison of two configurations. Config1 is the full systolic array of $32 \times 32$ and Config2 is $32 \times 16$.**

| Cases | Ar | Ac(Br) | Bc | clock cycles (Config1/Config2) |
|---|---|---|---|---|
| case1 | 100 | 1200 | 10 | 5048/4984 |
| case2 | 1000 | 1200 | 10 | 40384/39872 |

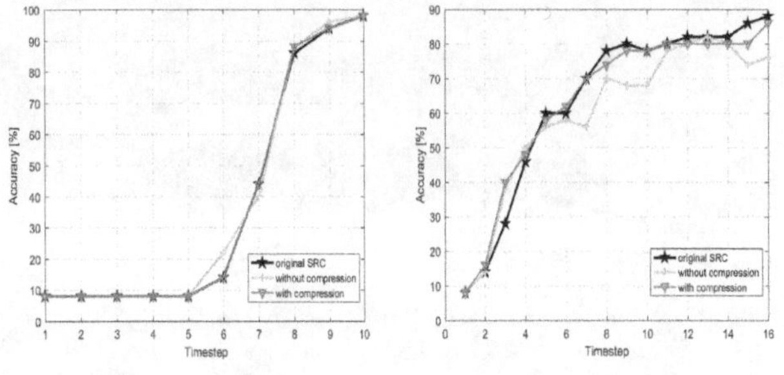


(a) Inference of SNN3. (b) Inference of SNN4.

**Figure 8: The inference accuracy on different cases. Legend *Without compression* in green means using systolic array hardware accelerator and our software framework without the compression step. And legend *with compression* in purple means using systolic array hardware accelerator and our software framework with the compression step.**

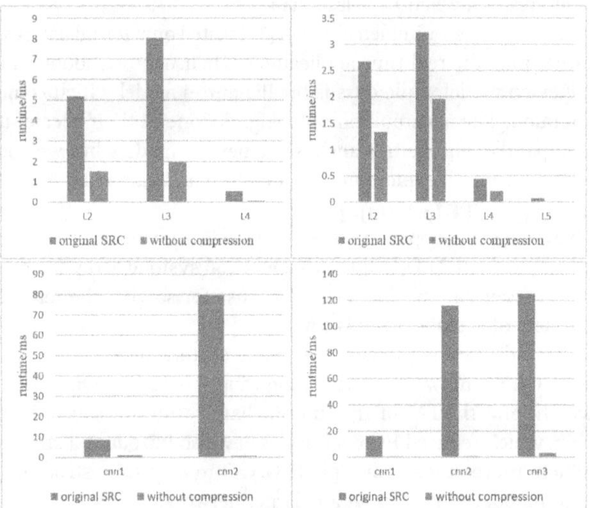


**Figure 9: Runtime comparison of "matrix multiplication" w.r.t. Table 3's configurations. The top results are from SNN1 and SNN2. The bottom are from SNN3 and SNN4. The vertical axis measures the runtime.**

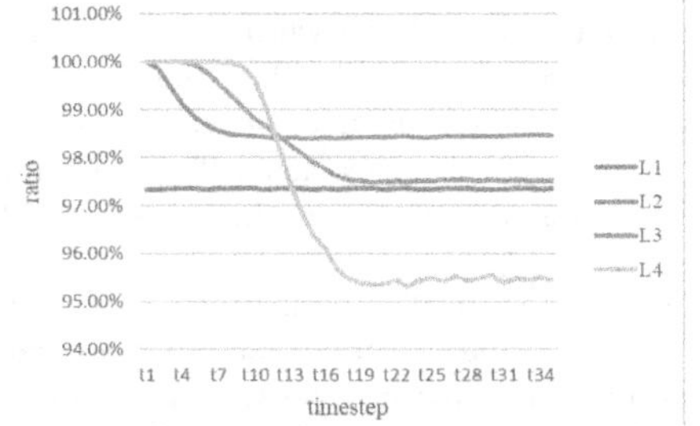


**Figure 10: Ratio of zeros of SNN1 on MNIST. The x-axis is the simulation time. The y-axis is the ratio of zeros.**

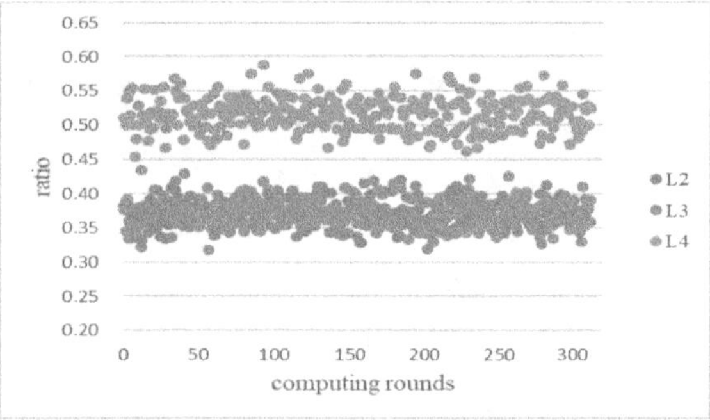


**Figure 11: ROC of hidden layers in SNN1. The x-axis is the number of computing rounds. The y-axis is the compression ratio. Each point represents a computing round.**

can see from Table 4, rectangle configuration is better than square configuration when $Bc$ is less than $\frac{Mc}{2}$.

The accelerator implemented in [17] tested only toroidal network rather than the real-time applications. Their neuron module is the Izikevich model while ours is the IF neuron model which is more common. The accumulation of weights done in their accelerator is in parallel via multi-branches in a neuron module but we adopt systolic array to explore more parallelism and data reuse.

## 5 RELATED WORK

There are many applications using systolic array to accelerate computing. Recent TPU [18] uses a 256 × 256 systolic array for calculation acceleration. The method we use for solving the mapping problem of systolic array is similar to [19].

In [20], they implement a scalable systolic accelerator of the binary CNN network of which the weight is binary. Only the I/O weight and the FM of the intermediate result are saved on the chip, which reduced I/O overhead. They also introduce a structure which interconnects multiple FPGAs into a systolic structure to accommodate larger input and larger networks.

For SNN, in 2009, [21] proposed an accelerator that simulates physical neurons. The neuron model they use is the Izhikevich Model, which maps the entire network to the chip. The PE unit of the systolic array compute, but also stores the results of the PE and the results of the weight. Ultimately, it can accommodate up to 800 neurons on the FPGA model, which does not meet the scale of today's deep neural networks. But they came up with the idea of simulating larger networks by interconnecting multiple FPGAs.

In this work, we implemente a simple IF model. But it is enough because the SNN is converted from a high-precision DNN.

## 6 CONCLUSION

In this paper, we implement a SNN inference hardware accelerator using systolic array and a corresponding software framework for optimization based on the high possibility of wide use of SNN. The use of systolic array is inspired by the inner characteristic of SNN. The systolic array is size-configurable and consists of 32 × 32 processing units. The PE is different from PE in conventional DNN accelerators, which does not have a multiplier inside. This simple PE could reduce power cost and area cost. And the systolic array is configurable. The software framework serves as assistance of the hardware accelerator. First, the software framework provides SNN for hardware accelerator by training DNN with traditional machine learning methods and converting the pre-trained DNN into SNN. Second, the software framework makes data mapping for systolic array, as well as compressing operands size and numerical precision for runtime optimization. We implement the accelerator on Xilinx FPGA V7 690T. The experimental results validate the correctness of our design. The time and memory footprint cost reduced are obvious. The total power of our scheme using 32-bit fixed-point precision is 0.745 W at 100 MHz.

In the future, we will apply our design to deeper SNNs. And we will further optimize the hardware design, including decreasing power and increasing the systolic array scale.

## ACKNOWLEDGEMENT

This work is supported by HGJ2017ZX01028103 and the National Natural Science Foundation of China (Grant No. 61802427). The authors thank the anonymous reviewers for their precious comments.

## REFERENCES

[1] Neil Dan. Minitaur, an event-driven fpga-based spiking network accelerator. *IEEE Transactions on Very Large Scale Integration Systems*, 22(12):2621–2628, 2014.
[2] Evangelos Stromatias, Daniel Neil, Francesco Galluppi, et al. Scalable energy-efficient, low-latency implementations of trained spiking deep belief networks on spinnaker. In *International Joint Conference on Neural Networks*, pages 1–8, 2015.
[3] Steven K. Esser, Paul A. Merolla, John V. Arthur, and others. Convolutional networks for fast, energy-efficient neuromorphic computing. *Proceedings of the National Academy of Sciences*, 113(41):11441–11446, 2016.
[4] C. D. Schuman, T. E. Potok, R. M. Patton, et al. A survey of neuromorphic computing and neural networks in hardware. arXiv:1705.06963, May 2017.
[5] S. Moradi, N. Qiao, F. Stefanini, and G. Indiveri. A scalable multicore architecture with heterogeneous memory structures for dynamic neuromorphic asynchronous processors (dynaps). *IEEE Transactions on Biomedical Circuits and Systems*, 12(1):106–122, Feb 2018.
[6] Yongqiang Cao, Yang Chen, and Deepak Khosla. Spiking deep convolutional neural networks for energy-efficient object recognition. *International Journal of Computer Vision*, 113(1):1–13, 2015.
[7] P. U. Diehl, D. Neil, J. Binas, et al. Fast-classifying, high-accuracy spiking deep networks through weight and threshold balancing. In *2015 International Joint Conference on Neural Networks (IJCNN)*, pages 1–8, July 2015.
[8] Bodo Rueckauer, Iulia-Alexandra Lungu, Yuhuang Hu, et al. Conversion of continuous-valued deep networks to efficient event-driven networks for image classification. *Frontiers in Neuroscience*, 11:682, 2017.
[9] Y. LeCun, L. Bottou, Y. Bengio, and P Haffner. Gradient-based learning applied to document recognition. *Proceedings of the IEEE*, 86(11):2278–2324, 1998.
[10] Han Xiao, Kashif Rasul, and Roland Vollgraf. Fashion-mnist: a novel image dataset for benchmarking machine learning algorithms. 2017.
[11] Neil Carlson. *Foundations of Physiological Psychology*. 1992.
[12] J. Hu, H. Tang, K. C. Tan, H. Li, and L. Shi. A spike-timing-based integrated model for pattern recognition. *Neural Computation*, 25(2):450–472, Feb 2013.
[13] H. T Kung and Charles E Leiserson. Systolic arrays (for vlsi). *Proc Sparse Matrix Conf*, pages 256–282, 1978.
[14] Yangqing Jia, Evan Shelhamer, Jeff Donahue, Sergey Karayev, Jonathan Long, Ross Girshick, Sergio Guadarrama, and Trevor Darrell. Caffe: Convolutional architecture for fast feature embedding. pages 675–678, 2014.
[15] Han Song, Huizi Mao, and William J Dally. Deep compression: Compressing deep neural networks with pruning, trained quantization and huffman coding. *Fiber*, 56(4):3–7, 2015.
[16] Dr. D. J. Tolhurst, J. A. Movshon, and I. D. Thompson. The dependence of response amplitude and variance of cat visual cortical neurones on stimulus contrast. *Experimental Brain Research*, 41(3-4):414, 1981.
[17] Kit Cheung, Simon R. Schultz, and Wayne Luk. *A Large-Scale Spiking Neural Network Accelerator for FPGA Systems*. Springer Berlin Heidelberg, 2012.
[18] Norman P. Jouppi, Al Borchers, Rick Boyle, Pierre Luc Cantin, Clifford Chao, Chris Clark, Jeremy Coriell, Mike Daley, Matt Dau, and Jeffrey Dean. In-datacenter performance analysis of a tensor processing unit. pages 1–12, 2017.
[19] Junzhong Shen, You Huang, Yuran Qiao, et al. Towards a multi-array architecture for accelerating large-scale matrix multiplication on fpgas. 2018.
[20] Renzo Andri, Lukas Cavigelli, Davide Rossi, and Luca Benini. Hyperdrive: A systolically scalable binary-weight cnn inference engine for mw iot end-nodes. 2018.
[21] Kit Cheung, S. R. Schultz, and P. H. W. Leong. A parallel spiking neural network simulator. In *International Conference on Field-Programmable Technology*, pages 247–254, 2009.

# Dynamic Beam Width Tuning for Energy-Efficient Recurrent Neural Networks

Daniele Jahier Pagliari, Francesco Panini, Enrico Macii and Massimo Poncino
Politecnico di Torino
Turin, Italy
name.first_surname@polito.it

## ABSTRACT

Recurrent Neural Networks (RNNs) are state-of-the-art models for many machine learning tasks, such as language modeling and machine translation. Executing the inference phase of a RNN directly in edge nodes, rather than in the cloud, would provide benefits in terms of energy consumption, latency and network bandwidth, provided that models can be made efficient enough to run on energy-constrained embedded devices.

To this end, we propose an algorithmic optimization for improving the energy efficiency of encoder-decoder RNNs. Our method operates on the Beam Width (BW), i.e. one of the parameters that most influences inference complexity, modulating it depending on the currently processed input based on a metric of the network's "confidence".

Results on two different machine translation models show that our method is able to reduce the average BW by up to 33%, thus significantly reducing the inference execution time and energy consumption, while maintaining the same translation performance.

## CCS CONCEPTS

• **Computing methodologies → Neural networks**; • **Hardware → Power estimation and optimization**; • **Computer systems organization →** *Embedded software.*

## KEYWORDS

Energy Efficiency; Neural Networks; Deep Learning

**ACM Reference Format:**

Daniele Jahier Pagliari, Francesco Panini, Enrico Macii and Massimo Poncino. 2019. Dynamic Beam Width Tuning for Energy-Efficient Recurrent Neural Networks. In *Great Lakes Symposium on VLSI 2019 (GLSVLSI '19), May 9–11, 2019, Tysons Corner, VA, USA.* ACM, New York, NY, USA, 6 pages. https://doi.org/10.1145/3299874.3317974

## 1 INTRODUCTION

Deep learning models are increasingly being used in many machine learning applications [1]. In particular, Recurrent Neural Networks (RNNs) are now able to deliver state-of-the-art performance in sequence modeling tasks such as machine translation and image captioning [2]. Unlike traditional feed-forward deep neural networks, RNNs have memory and can handle variable-length inputs and outputs.

The high quality of the results achieved by these models, however, comes at the cost of high computational complexity. Currently, the execution of deep learning models is mostly performed in the cloud, using multicore CPUs and clusters of GPUs which consume hundreds of watts of power [3, 4]. On the other hand, there is an increasing demand for intelligent behavior in "edge" nodes (mobile devices, IoT sensors, wearables), which are typically battery-powered and have limited energy budget and computational power. Implementing neural networks directly on the device would provide clear benefits in terms of network bandwidth, response latency and ultimately energy consumption [1]. This applies in particular to the *inference* phase, i.e. the actual classification, whereas the *training* can conveniently be left to the cloud, as a unique (or sporadic, in the case of re-training) task [1, 5] As a result, the energy-efficient design of neural networks and the development of optimized inference methods are acquiring a key role for the development of new applications [4, 6].

In literature, many works have tackled this problem proposing different solutions [1, 3–15]. However, the great majority of these works focuses on Convolutional Neural Networks (CNNs), while only few consider RNNs [6, 14].

One approach that has proven effective for CNNs is to exploit the trade-off between quality of results (e.g. classification accuracy) and model complexity. Complexity reductions can be obtained in different ways, ranging from bit-width reductions in data and computations to algorithmic optimizations. Most of these studies propose *static* solutions, in which the complexity is kept constant throughout the whole inference. However, recent works have shown that a static approach is suboptimal, since for most classification tasks not all inputs are equally difficult to process. *Dynamic* solutions have therefore been devised to exploit this data dependency: here, the complexity of the model is adapted to the currently processed data at runtime, based on some metric of the "confidence" of the output produced by the network [3, 5, 7].

In this work, we take a similar approach, but we apply it for the first time to RNN models, focusing specifically on encoder-decoder networks for Neural Machine Translation (NMT). We propose a method to dynamically tune one of the main parameters of the network, the so-called Beam Width (BW), depending on the currently processed data. Increasing the BW is beneficial for the quality of the translations produced by a RNN, but also has a strong impact on the computational complexity of the inference task. In order to optimize this trade-off, we propose to monitor the translation "confidence" in each decoding step, and adapt the BW accordingly.


*GLSVLSI '19, May 9–11, 2019, Tysons Corner, VA, USA*

ACM ISBN 978-1-4503-6252-8/19/05...$15.00
https://doi.org/10.1145/3299874.3317974

This allows to reduce the average BW by up to 33% with respect to a fixed-BW baseline, while producing comparable or even better outputs. Considering a single-threaded SW implementation of the target RNNs, i.e. the most common scenario for embedded devices, this corresponds to a 25% reduction of the average inference execution time, which in turn translates into significant energy savings for a fixed translation throughput.

# 2 BACKGROUND AND RELATED WORK

## 2.1 Background

*2.1.1 Encoder-Decoder RNNs.* A comprehensive description of the existing types of deep neural network can be found in [16]. Herein, we only focus on Recurrent Neural Networks based on the encoder-decoder structure, i.e. the main targets of this work, which are state-of-the-art models for sequence modeling and translation tasks [2].

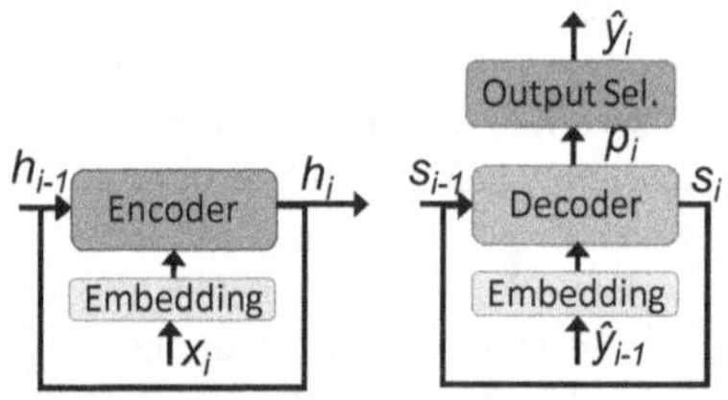


**Figure 1: Architecture of an encoder-decoder RNN.**

A high-level diagram of the architecture of an encoder-decoder RNN is reported in Figure 1. The *Encoder* and *Decoder* blocks contain two separate neural networks, with one or more layers of neurons each. The internal structure of these neurons is typically different from that of feed-forward networks; common models include the so-called *Vanilla RNN*, the *Gated Recurrent Unit* (GRU) and the *Long-Short Term Memory* (LSTM). The details of these models are immaterial for our method, and the reader is referred to [16] for the details. The *Embedding* layers at the input of both RNNs are typical in NMT applications; they are used to map words from the input/output vocabularies (e.g. English and German in the following example) onto a compact representation as arrays of floats, while respecting semantic similarities (i.e. similar words produce similar embeddings).

To perform a sequence-to-sequence mapping, first the Encoder and then the Decoder are executed multiple times. This process is described herein with the terminology of NMT (sentences, translations, etc.), but the same concepts apply also to other applications. To translate a sentence, initially the Encoder is iteratively fed with all input words $X = x^{<1>}, ..., x^{<T>}$ in order. In each iteration, the Encoder updates its *hidden state* vector ($h$), which is then fed-back to the network in the following step (similar to a FSM). This feedback, also present in the decoder, provides RNNs with memory and is their peculiarity with respect to feed-forward networks. When the last word has been processed, the corresponding Encoder hidden state contains a fixed-length representation of the input sentence, generally called *context* (C).

The context is then used to initialize the hidden state ($s$) of the Decoder, whose task is to produce the *predicted* output sentence $\hat{Y} = \hat{y}^{<1>}, ...., \hat{y}^{<T'>}$. Specifically, besides updating its internal state, the Decoder also produces an output $p^{<i>}$ at every step. This is an array of the same size as the output vocabulary, containing in its $k$-th position the likelihood of a sentence that contains all words predicted in previous steps, and that has the $k$-th word from the vocabulary as its $i$-th element. This likelihood is conditioned on the input sentence, represented by the context vector. Mathematically: $p^{<i>} = [p(\hat{y}^{<1>}, ...\hat{y}^{<i-1>}, y^{<i>} = y_k|X)], \forall k$. To model the dependency on previous predictions, the Decoder is also fed with the latest predicted word $y^{<i-1>}$, initialized at NULL in the first iteration. The block labeled *Output Sel.* is in charge of selecting the predicted output word(s) based on the likelihoods in $p^{<i>}$, as detailed in Section 2.1.2.

An example of the functionality of this type of RNNs is depicted in Figure 2a, where horizontal copies of the Encoder and Decoder represents executions of the *same* network in different iterations. In general, input and output sentences may have different lengths, so their termination is typically signaled by a special *End of Sentence* (<*EOS*>) value. During training, the parameters of the Encoder and Decoder RNNs are tuned to maximize $p(y^{<1>}, ..., y^{<T'>}|X)$, where $y^{<1>}, ..., y^{<T'>}$ are the elements of the *target* output sentence [16].

Several variations of this basic scheme have been proposed in order to improve performance. Notable examples include *bidirectional* RNNs, in which the hidden state can capture information coming both from previous and following words and *attention-based* RNNs, in which an additional layer is used to weigh the "importance" of each input element for the generation of a given output [2, 16]. The detailed description of these advanced models is out of the scope of this paper.

*2.1.2 Beam Search.* Basic encoder-decoder RNNs, such as the one of Figure 2a, produce output sentences using the so-called *Greedy Search* algorithm. That is, the predicted word at every iteration is selected simply as the one that generates the "partial sentence" with the largest likelihood. While this method produces good-enough outputs on average, it can be proven mathematically that the most likely partial sentence at a given decoding step does not necessarily correspond to the beginning of the most likely sentence overall [16]. Finding the most likely translation is actually a NP-complete problem, which involves searching through all possible word combinations. In practice, most real applications of RNNs utilize an intermediate solution called *Beam Search* [16]. Rather than greedily picking a single word, Beam Search considers a fixed number of most likely partial sentences as translation candidates in each decoding step; this number is called the *Beam Width* (BW). Once the decoding phase has completed (i.e. all sentences in the "beam" have reached <EOS>), the final translation is selected as the candidate with the highest joint probability.

An example of Beam Search decoding for BW = 3 is depicted in Figure 2b, where the encoding phase is not reported, being identical to that of Figure 2a. As shown, Beam Search corresponds to expanding a tree of possible translations, adding a level at each iteration and keeping the number of vertices in each level equal to BW. The Embedding and Decoder blocks are identical to those of Figure 2a, but they are both executed BW times per iteration. The main difference is in the output selection, which now takes the probabilities generated by the BW Decoder executions, and selects the words that generate the BW most likely partial sentences. The

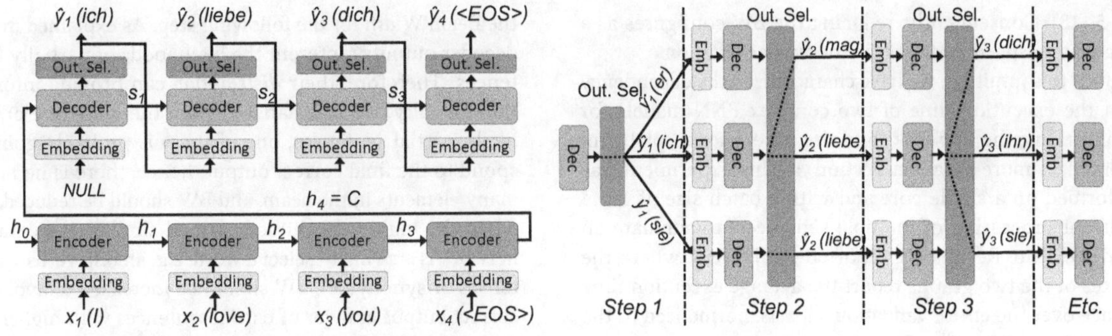


(a) Translation example with greedy search.

(b) Beam search with BW = 3.

**Figure 2: High-level view of an encoder-decoder RNN.**

latter can be generated by any combination of the decoders, as shown by the dashed lines in the figure.

## 2.2 Related Work

A popular approach to improve the energy efficiency of neural networks inference consists in designing dedicated hardware accelerators for FPGAs [14, 15] or ASICs [3, 6, 8–10]. These designs combine algorithm-level, architecture-level and circuit-level techniques to optimize the most energy consuming operations in the network. The vast majority of these solutions, however, focus solely on feed-forward models and in particular on Convolutional Neural Networks (CNNs) for image recognition. Despite their importance from an application perspective, fewer efforts have been devoted to improving the efficiency of RNNs by acceleration [6, 14].

Despite its effectiveness, hardware acceleration is mostly destined to high-end devices, that can afford specialized SoCs. Vice versa, lower-end embedded systems typically execute RNN inference on general purpose CPUs. While our work focuses on the latter scenario, the proposed algorithmic optimization is agnostic of the underlying platform, and would be equally effective even if applied to the hardware of [6, 14].

At the algorithm level, many studies (again mostly focusing on feed-forward models) apply *approximate computing* techniques to reduce neural networks complexity, exploiting their intrinsic *error resilience*, which allows the injection of significant approximations without dramatically impacting output quality [1, 4, 12, 17]. Common approaches include *quantization*, i.e. the replacement of floating-point data with reduced bit-width fixed-point [4, 11] and *pruning*, in which redundant computations (e.g. entire neurons) that do not affect output quality are eliminated [12, 13]. The former approach is brought to the extreme by Binarized Neural Networks[8, 17] , in which most arithmetic computations are replaced by bit-wise operations, while still retaining good output quality.

All aforementioned works implement *static* energy-vs-quality tradeoffs, in which the amount of approximation (e.g. the fixed point bit-width or the amount of pruning) are decided at design time. More recently, *dynamic* approaches have been proposed [3, 5, 7], starting from the observation anticipated in Section 1 that a static approach may be sub-optimal when inputs are not all equally hard to process. In such cases, a static network would either over-approximate complex inputs, hence producing poor results or under-approximate simple ones, resulting in a waste of energy.

Most dynamic techniques work at the algorithm-level and are hardware independent. The authors of [7] propose a sort of "Big/Little" network, in which two CNNs of different size and complexity are used for an image classification task. When a new input is received, at first the "Little" (least complex) network is executed. According to the confidence of the classification produced, the result is committed as is, or the "Big" network is triggered to provide a more accurate classification. As long as the larger network is employed rarely, total energy consumption is reduced. However, the total model size (number of weights to be stored) increases significantly, and the training effort is substantially doubled. To cope with these limitations, in [3], "Little" networks are generated starting from "Big" ones and using only a portion of each layer. Finally, in [5], a similar dynamic solution is adopted for tuning the bit-width of fixed-point operations depending on the considered input complexity. These dynamic approaches are the most similar to our proposed methodology, yet they are focused on CNNs; to the best of our knowledge, this work is the first to apply data-dependent optimizations for energy efficiency on encoder-decoder RNNs.

# 3 PROPOSED METHODOLOGY

## 3.1 Motivation: RNNs Execution Time Analysis

In this work, we focus on optimizing the execution of the inference process on *single thread* CPUs, i.e. the most common computational devices available in edge nodes. As mentioned in Section 2, encoding and decoding in RNNs are iterative processes, involving multiple calls to the same network. Since each step involves the same operations, the power consumption of a CPU will remain approximately constant throughout each phase. Therefore, the most straight-forward way to improve the energy efficiency of the network at the algorithm level is to reduce its execution time.

Based on the analysis of Section 2.1.2, the Beam Width parameter is expected to strongly influence the overall execution time of the decoding phase. In fact, a BW of $k$ corresponds to performing the $k$ decoding operations at each step (Figure 2b); in a single-threaded CPU, these $k$ executions must be carried out sequentially. Typical values of BW found in state-of-the-art models are in the range of 3 to > 5 [18]. Consequently, reducing the BW configures as a promising way to speed up the entire network execution.

To confirm this intuition, we have characterized the dependency on BW of the execution time of two complex RNN models for NMT applications; the networks and the experimental platform are presented in more detail in Section 4. This experiment has been performed on a single core and with a batch size of 1 (i.e. no concurrent processing of multiple sentences) to simulate an embedded scenario. Results are reported in Figure 3, where the vertical axes of the two graphs report the average execution time per sentence over the entire validation subsets, normalized to the result of greedy decoding (i.e. BW=1).

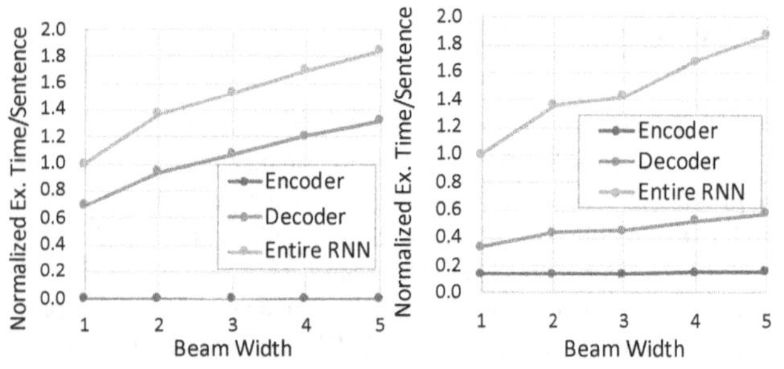


(a) EN-DE (b) DE-EN

**Figure 3: CPU execution time vs. Beam Width for two RNNs.**

A first observation is that the execution time of the encoding phase, which is expectedly independent from BW, is also negligible with respect to decoding. This gives even more value to the choice of BW as our target. Vice versa, the decoder accounts for a significant portion of the total execution in both networks, and is significantly influenced by BW. The dependency is not perfectly linear due to optimizations in the adopted computational framework; nonetheless, going from BW=1 to BW=5 causes an increase of 84% (EN-DE) and 87% (DE-EN) in the *total* execution time of the networks.

## 3.2 Input-Dependent Beam Width Tuning

In standard implementations of encoder-decoder RNNs, the Beam Width is kept constant throughout the inference phase. Therefore, this parameter is typically chosen conservatively, so that good enough translations are generated even for the most complex sentences. In consideration of the results presented in Section 3.1, however, the BW should be reduced as much as possible to contain the inference computational cost.

In order to do so without sacrificing translation performance, we propose a novel dynamic Beam Search algorithm, in which *the BW is varied according to the evolution of a translation.* This allows the network to self-tune, at each step, the effort required to produce a good translation. Our method is based on the intuitive concept that not all inputs, sentences or part of them, are equally difficult to translate. For easier, unambiguous sentences, a small BW could be sufficient, and vice versa.

More specifically, we propose to evaluate the outputs of the decoder at each step, and use them as an indicator on how to adjust the Beam Width for the following step. As explained in Section 2.1, decoder outputs represent the likelihoods of partially formed sentences. Therefore, their *distribution* can provide information on the difficulty of a translation. When there are one or few highly likely partial sentences, one of them is probably going to correspond to the final correct output; hence, there is no need to keep many elements in the beam, and BW should be reduced. Vice versa, when the highest likelihoods are all similar (indicating that the network is striving to select a word, e.g. among verbs with different tenses or synonyms), BW should be increased to avoid losing the correct output in favor of partial sentences with higher temporary probability. The details of our proposed policy for mapping decoder outputs to the next BW are presented in Section 3.3.

Figure 4 shows an example of the proposed Dynamic Beam Search, where the blocks labeled *Out. Sel. + Policy* encompass the selection of the predicted word(s) and of the next BW. For example, during Step 2, the decoder may have produced an output with much higher probability than all others, so the policy sets a BW of 1. Then, in Step 3, the distribution of the likelihood is more uniform, so the policy increases the BW to 3.

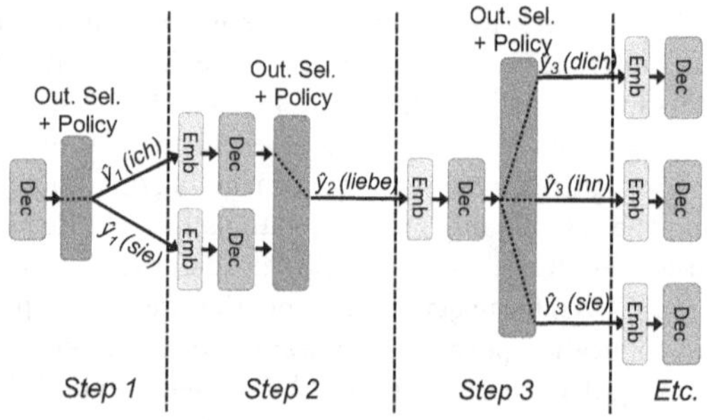


**Figure 4: Dynamic Beam Search example.**

With this dynamic strategy, we aim at reducing the execution time of the Decoder, while producing comparable or even better results with respect to a standard implementation using a fixed BW. Notice that, although this idea is inspired by previous work on CNNs [3, 5, 7], the knob used to adapt the complexity versus performance trade-off (i.e. the BW in our case) is completely different, as well as the proposed decision policy and off course the type of neural network.

## 3.3 Beam-Width Selection Policy

Many different policies can be used to map the decoder outputs to a value of BW. In this work, we introduce a simple yet effective approach based on analyzing the distribution of the largest likelihoods; more advanced policies will be object of future work.

The proposed policy considers at each steps the top-$k$ scores produced by the decoder, where $k = BW_{max}$ is the maximum allowed BW and is a parameter of the algorithm. The standard deviation $\sigma$ of these scores is then computed to evaluate their dispersion; large values of $\sigma$ correspond to large differences among the top-$k$ scores, and therefore will be mapped to smaller values of BW, and vice versa. Specifically, the mapping is performed using a piece-wise linear equation having $\sigma$ as the independent variable, shown in Figure 5.

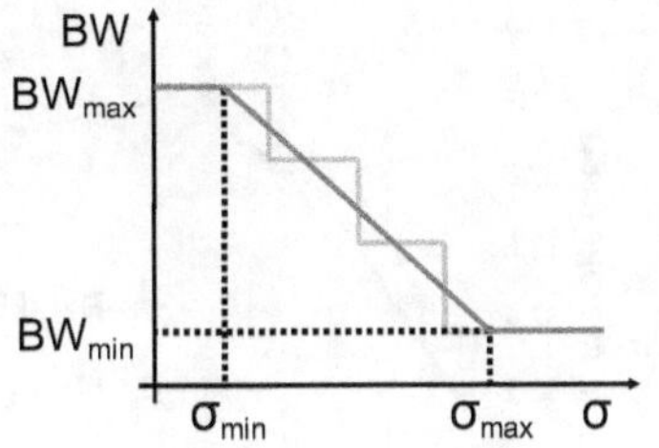


**Figure 5: Beam Width selection policy.**

Between a minimum and a maximum standard deviation value ($\sigma_{min}$ and $\sigma_{max}$) BW is decreased proportionally to the increase of $\sigma$ (red diagonal curve). Clearly, BW can not assume fractional values, hence it is rounded to the nearest integer, producing the blue stair-like curve. For values of $\sigma$ smaller than $\sigma_{min}$ or larger than $\sigma_{max}$, the BW is saturated to $BW_{max}$ and $BW_{min}$ respectively.

The range of allowed Beam Widths can be set depending on the target application: a reasonable value for $BW_{min}$ is 1 (although this is not mandatory), whereas $BW_{max}$ can be set to any value typically adopted in the target domain. For identifying good minimum and maximum values for $\sigma$, instead, designers should collect the standard deviation of the top-$k$ likelihoods produced by the original (fixed BW) network when inferring on representative data. The distribution of these standard deviations can provide a good starting point for exploring the parameters space. For example, selecting as initial $\sigma_{min}$ the 5-th percentile of the collected standard deviations corresponds to using $BW_{max}$ only in the $\approx$5% most difficult cases; similarly, a $\sigma_{max}$ equal to the 50-th percentile corresponds to using $BW_{min}$ in $\approx$50% iterations. Tuning these parameters requires some exploration, which however can be done offline using multi-core CPUs or GPUs.

# 4 EXPERIMENTAL RESULTS

## 4.1 Setup

We have tested our methodology on two complex encoder-decoder RNNs for NMT applications, using the *OpenNMT* framework in its PyTorch implementation [18]. This choice was motivated by the fact that the dynamic computational graph model of PyTorch makes it easier than in other frameworks to dynamically change the BW at runtime. The two selected RNNs perform English to German (Deutsch) and German to English translation, and are hereafter referred to as EN-DE and DE-EN respectively. Both networks are made available by OpenNMT online as pre-trained models. The EN-DE network is composed of a total of 6 layers, each composed of 512 LSTM neurons, whereas the DE-EN network is composed of 2 layers of 500 LSTM neurons. More details on the network architectures and datasets can be found in [18]. The default Beam Width for both models is set to 5.

Parameter explorations have been performed on a workstation equipped with a NVIDIA Titan XP GPU, whereas the measurement of execution times with and without our dynamic Beam Width mechanism have been performed on a laptop equipped with an Intel Core i7 CPU and 32GB of RAM. This choice is due to the fact that no porting of the OpenNMT framework onto embedded devices is currently available. However, in order to get a more accurate estimate of the execution times benefits obtainable on an embedded node, we have constrained all executions to use only one CPU thread and a batch size of 1. Therefore, while absolute execution times collected would not be representative of the actual implementation on an embedded CPU, relative trends should be a reasonable proxy. All tests have been performed on the validation sets of each network. Translation quality has been evaluated using two common machine translation scores, i.e. the *BiLingual Evaluation Understudy* (BLEU) and the *Perplexity* (PPL) [16].

## 4.2 Comparison with Fixed Beam Width

As we do not have dynamic BW tuning methods to compare against, we use as reference a standard RNN inference using a fixed Beam Width. Specifically, we have compared against BWs ranging from 1 (greedy) to 5.

The results of this comparison are shown in Figure 6. For each RNN we report three graphs; the leftmost two show the trade-off among the average inference execution time per sentence over the validation set, and the average BLEU and PPL scores. Execution times are normalized to the one of the original network with BW = 1. The rightmost graph shows on the horizontal axis the *average Beam Width* over all decoding iterations. For fixed BW inference, this value simply corresponds to the selected BW, whereas for our method, it is the result of the choices made by the mapping policy. This plot has particular relevance since it reports a platform-independent result, which does not depend on the target CPU. Similar plots for the PPL score are not reported for sake of space.

As expected, on the original network (blue curve), increasing the BW generally has a positive effect on both BLEU (for which larger is better) and PPL (smaller is better). It is worth emphasizing that, although the absolute differences in the two scores for the extremes of the range (BW=1 and BW=5) appear to be relatively small, they correspond to significant improvements of the translation quality. As a matter of fact, most state-of-the-art models use BW in the range 3 to 5, indicating that even such small improvements in the metrics are relevant. However, even a small increase of these metrics requires a large increase of execution time. For instance, for the EN-DE network, increasing the BLEU of 0.6 requires a 40% longer execution on average (from BW=1 to BW=2). In contrast, our proposed dynamic BW tuning allows to obtain many more fine-grain settings. This is shown by the orange triangles in the figure, which correspond to some of the Pareto points obtainable by experimenting with policy parameters. The numerical values of the selected parameters ($BW_{min}$, $BW_{max}$, $\sigma_{min}$ and $\sigma_{max}$, described in Section 3.3) and the corresponding results are reported in Table 1.

Most importantly, the figure shows that our method allows to consistently achieve a better trade-off compared to a fixed BW solution, thanks to the fact that the BW is automatically tuned to the "difficulty" of the current translation. In practice, comparable or even better performance can be achieved (according to both scores) while requiring a lower BW on average. For example, for the EN-DE model, an average BW=3.33 is sufficient to reach a BLEU score of 33.13, superior even to the one achieved by the standard network with BW=5 (33% reduction). On the target platform, this causes a reduction of the average execution time of $\approx$25%, for the same performance. Similarly, on the DE-EN network, a PPL of 1.61 is obtained with an average BW of 1.69 as opposed to a fixed BW of 2,

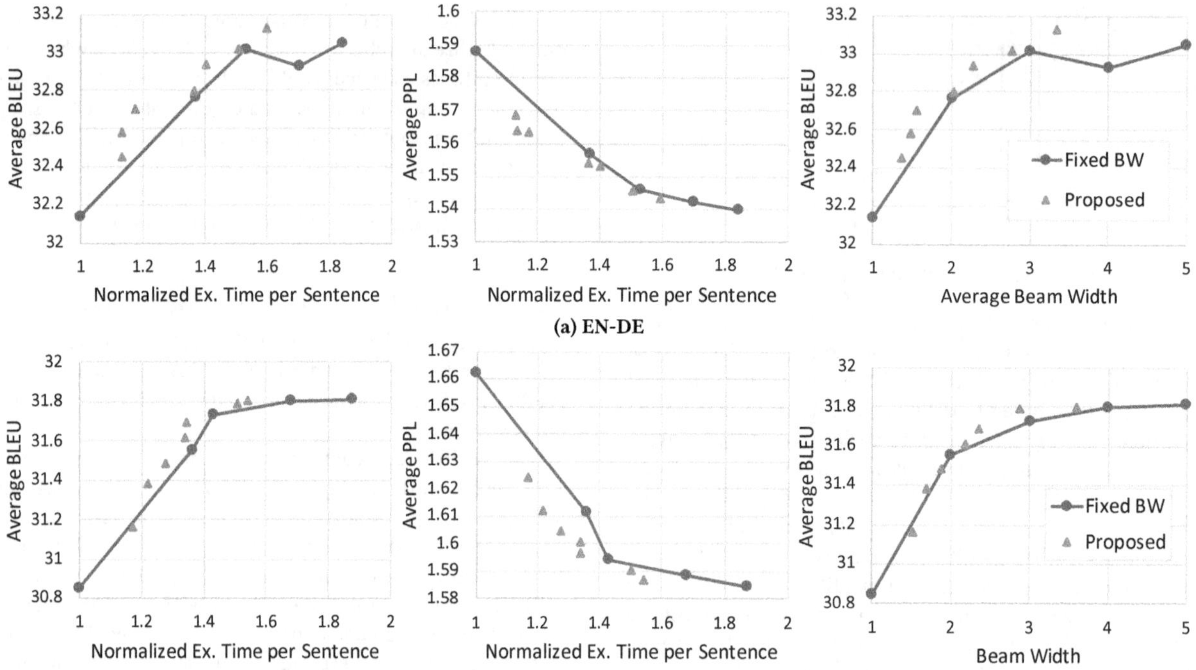


(a) EN-DE

(b) DE-EN

**Figure 6: Comparison with a fixed Beam Width approach.**

| RNN | $BW_{min}/BW_{max}$ | $\sigma_{min}/\sigma_{max}$ | Avg. BW | Ex. Time | BLEU | PPL |
|---|---|---|---|---|---|---|
| EN-DE | 1/2 | 0.1/2.2 | 1.36 | 1.13 | 32.45 | 1.568 |
| | 1/2 | 0.1/3.1 | 1.55 | 1.17 | 32.70 | 1.563 |
| | 1/3 | 0.1/1.7 | 1.48 | 1.13 | 32.58 | 1.564 |
| | 1/3 | 0.1/3.1 | 2.02 | 1.37 | 32.80 | 1.554 |
| | 2/4 | 0.1/1.7 | 2.27 | 1.40 | 32.94 | 1.552 |
| | 2/4 | 0.1/1.3 | 2.77 | 1.51 | 33.02 | 1.545 |
| | 2/5 | 0.1/1.7 | 3.33 | 1.59 | 33.13 | 1.543 |
| DE-EN | 1/2 | 0.1/2.2 | 1.51 | 1.17 | 31.16 | 1.623 |
| | 1/2 | 0.1/3.1 | 1.69 | 1.22 | 31.38 | 1.612 |
| | 1/3 | 0.1/2.2 | 1.88 | 1.27 | 31.48 | 1.605 |
| | 1/3 | 0.1/3.1 | 2.19 | 1.34 | 31.61 | 1.596 |
| | 2/4 | 0.1/0.6 | 2.35 | 1.34 | 31.69 | 1.600 |
| | 2/4 | 0.1/1.7 | 2.86 | 1.51 | 31.79 | 1.590 |
| | 2/5 | 0.1/1.7 | 3.59 | 1.54 | 31.80 | 1.586 |

**Table 1: Numerical results.**

causing an execution time reduction of ≈11%. As mentioned in Section 3, these execution time reductions correspond to proportional energy savings.

## 5 CONCLUSIONS

We have proposed a methodology for reducing inference complexity in an encoder-decoder RNN, by dynamically tuning the Beam Width depending on the currently processed input. By applying this technique, we have been able to significantly speedup the translation process (hence also reducing its energy consumption) while achieving comparable or even better output quality. Importantly, our approach can be applied to existing networks without re-training. In future work, we plan on experimenting with more policies for setting the Beam Width, and on integrating our approach with other knobs for exploring the energy-quality trade-off (e.g. quantization).

## REFERENCES

[1] V. Sze et al., "Efficient processing of deep neural networks: A tutorial and survey," *Proc. of the IEEE*, vol. 105, no. 12, pp. 2295–2329, 2017.
[2] A. Vaswani et al, "Attention is all you need," *Proc. NIPS*, 2017, pp. 5998–6008.
[3] H. Tann et al., "Runtime configurable deep neural networks for energy-accuracy trade-off," *Proc. IEEE/ACM CODES + ISSS*, 2016, pp. 1–10.
[4] B. Moons et al., "Energy-efficient convnets through approximate computing," *Proc. IEEE WACV*, 2016, pp. 1–8.
[5] D. Jahier Pagliari, E. Macii, and M. Poncino, "Dynamic bit-width reconfiguration for energy-efficient deep learning hardware," *Proc. IEEE/ACM ISLPED*, 2018, pp.47:1–47:6.
[6] F. Silfa et a., "E-pur: An energy-efficient processing unit for recurrent neural networks," *arXiv:1711.07480*, 2017.
[7] E. Park et al, "Big/little deep neural network for ultra low power inference," *Proc. IEEE/ACM CODES + ISSS*, 2015, pp. 124–132.
[8] R. Andri et al., "Yodann: An architecture for ultralow power binary-weight cnn acceleration," *IEEE TCAD*, vol. 37, no. 1, pp. 48–60, 2018.
[9] J. Zhu et al., "Sparsenn: An energy-efficient neural network accelerator exploiting input and output sparsity," *Proc. DATE*, 2018, pp. 241–244.
[10] Y. Chen, J. Emer and V. Sze, "Eyeriss: A Spatial Architecture for Energy-Efficient Dataflow for Convolutional Neural Networks," *Proc. ACM/IEEE ISCA*, 2016, pp. 367–369.
[11] F. Sun, J. Lin and Z. Wang, "Intra-layer nonuniform quantization of convolutional neural network", *Proc. WCSP*, 2016, pp. 1-5.
[12] T. Yang, Y. Chen and V. Sze, "Designing Energy-Efficient Convolutional Neural Networks Using Energy-Aware Pruning," *Proc. IEEE CVPR*, 2017, pp. 6071–6079.
[13] Y. Guo, A. Yao and Y. Chen, "Dynamic Network Surgery for Efficient DNNs", *Proc. NIPS*, 2016, pp. 1379–1387.
[14] C. Gao et al., "DeltaRNN: A Power-efficient Recurrent Neural Network Accelerator," *Proc. ACM FPGA*, 2018, pp. 21–30.
[15] C. Zhang et al, "Optimizing FPGA-based accelerator design for deep convolutional neural networks," *Proc. ACM FPGA*, 2015, pp. 161–170.
[16] G. Ian, B. Yoshua, and C. Aaron, *Deep Learning*, MIT Press, 2016.
[17] I. Hubara et al, "Binarized neural networks," *Proc. NIPS*, 2016, pp. 4107–4115.
[18] G. Klein et al, "OpenNMT: Open-source toolkit for neural machine translation," *arXiv:1701.02810*, 2017.

# Efficient Softmax Hardware Architecture for Deep Neural Networks

Gaoming Du, Chao Tian, Zhenmin Li, Duoli Zhang, Yongsheng Yin, Yiming Ouyang
HeFei University of Technology
dugaoming@hfut.edu.cn

## ABSTRACT

Deep neural network (DNN) has become a pivotal machine learning and object recognition technology in the big data era. The softmax layer is one of the key component layers for completing multi-classification tasks. However, the softmax layer contains complex exponential and division operations, resulting in low accuracy and long critical paths in hardware accelerator design. In order to solve the above issues, we present a softmax hardware architecture with proper accuracy, good trade-off and strong expansibility. We summarize the classification rules of neural network and balance the calculation accuracy between resource consumption. On this basis, we proposed an exponential calculation unit based on the group lookup table, and improve a natural logarithmic calculation unit based on the Maclaurin series and the data preprocessing scheme matching them. The experimental results show that the softmax hardware architecture proposed in this paper can achieve the calculation accuracy of 3 decimal fraction and the classification accuracy of 99.01%. Theoretically, it can accomplish the classification task of infinite categories.

**ACM Reference Format:**
Gaoming Du, Chao Tian, Zhenmin Li, Duoli Zhang, Yongsheng Yin, Yiming Ouyang. 2019. Efficient Softmax Hardware Architecture for Deep Neural Networks. In *Great Lakes Symposium on VLSI 2019 (GLSVLSI '19), May 9–11, 2019, Tysons Corner, VA, USA.* ACM, New York, NY, USA, 6 pages. https://doi.org/10.1145/3299874.3317988

## 1 INTRODUCTION

Today, DNN is one of the most prevalent deep learning technologies in recognition area such as object detection [15] and speech recognition [2]. DNNs have varying functions and structures, but usually share the same basic component layers (e.g., convolution layer, pooling layer, fully connection layer and softmax layer). Recent researches on hardware implementation of convolution layers [12], pooling layers [5] and fully connection layers [7] have greatly improved the performance and reduced the inference time of DNNs. However, few works focused on softmax layer hardware design.


*GLSVLSI '19, May 9–11, 2019, Tysons Corner, VA, USA*

ACM ISBN 978-1-4503-6252-8/19/05...$15.00
https://doi.org/10.1145/3299874.3317988

According to the location and function of softmax layer, the following three main design points are important: 1) Proper accuracy: classification accuracy refers to the correctness of Top-1 and Top-5. Calculation accuracy is expressed by the error of the corresponding probability of the hardware and the software model. As a state-of-the-art method, a common classification result of DNN is the probability of one category is much higher than that of the other. This means that in most cases, low calculation accuracy ensures high classification accuracy. However, we cannot ignore the need for high calculation accuracy in very few special cases; 2) Good trade-off: high speed, low power consumption and small area are the main trends of current Artificial Intelligence(AI) chip design. In order to be successfully integrated into existing chip architectures, softmax hardware design must follow above three design trends; 3) Strong expansibility: LeNet [14] only needs 10 categories, while AlexNet [13] has up to 1000 categories. With the development of DNNs towards richer function and stronger performance, the number of categories further increase trend is foreseeable.

In [23], Bo Yuan first proposed a hardware architecture of softmax layer. It utilized domain transformation technique and down-scaling approach to reduce hardware complexity and critical path delay. However, this architecture has the following weaknesses: 1) This architecture does not provide technical details and performance parameters; 2) The mathematical principle changed the softmax original formula and could not implement the classification function; 3) The data preprocessing scheme cannot give full play to due functions.

Aiming at the above weaknesses, we correct the algorithm and propose efficient softmax hardware architecture(ESHA). In the design process, we make full use of the general rule of DNN classification to balance the calculation accuracy and the usage of hardware resources. ESHA can ensure that no matter high or low calculation accuracy will not affect the correctness of Top-1 and Top-5. The synthesis results show that even if ESHA is integrated into an existing AI chip, the overall layout and resource usage will not change significantly.

Our contributions are summarized as follows:

- We proposed a preprocessing scheme based on the amount of valid data. This is not only an essential basis for ESHA to implement, but also enables ESHA to theoretically accomplish infinite classification of categories.
- We proposed an accuracy-selectable exponential calculation unit with high accuracy for distinguishing similar

pictures and low accuracy for reducing computational complexity.

- We improved a natural logarithm function algorithm based on the first two terms of the Maclaurin series, which effectively reduces the range of accuracy and improves the stability of the algorithm.

The rest of the paper is organized as follows: Section II summarizes the related works about neural network accelerators, exponential calculation units and logarithmic calculation units. Section III analyzes the existing softmax architecture and introduces the motivation for this paper. Section V evaluates the softmax hardware models proposed in Section IV in terms of accuracy, match ability and expansibility. Section VI concludes this paper and points out future directions of softmax hardware design.

## 2 RELATED WORK

Artificial Neural Network (ANN) is a research hotspot in the field of AI since the 1980s. In recent years, the emergence of neural network accelerators (e.g., DaDianNao [8], Eyeriss [9] and TPU [11]) have greatly promoted the hardware implementation of ANN. In the hardware design of the softmax layer, efficient implementation of exponential calculation unit and the hardware-friendly conversion of division are two critical issues.

The efficient implementation of the exponential unit is an important basis for improving the calculation accuracy of the softmax layer. Pouyan [19] proposed a parabolic synthesis method for exponential unit, which proved its performance over the coordinate rotation digital computer (CORDIC) algorithm. Nilsson [17] and Lin [16] proposed exponential models based on Taylor formula, which achieved less hardware resource consumption. However, the common feature of the three schemes is that the calculation accuracy and resource use cannot be well balanced.

The logarithm calculation unit can convert the division into a hardware-friendly subtraction operation. Brabec [4] proposed a logarithm unit based on the principle of continuous logarithm, which shows a significant improvement over the software implementation. Hormigo [10] proposed a hardware algorithm for variable-precision logarithm which combines iterative techniques, LUTs and polynomial approximation techniques. Aroutchelvame [3] proposed a pipeline structure based on Maclaurin series. The algorithm uses only the first two terms of the Maclaurin series to calculate the logarithmic function. Under the premise of ensuring accuracy, the last solution has a simpler circuit structure but has a large range of precision variation. In this paper, the original non-equal interval LUT is optimized into an equal interval LUT, which reduces the range of precision variation and reduces the usage of two-thirds of the LUTs.

In this paper, we propose a softmax hardware architecture combining the accuracy-selectable exponential calculation unit, low precision variation nature logarithmic calculation unit and data preprocessing schemes based on the number of valid data, respectively.

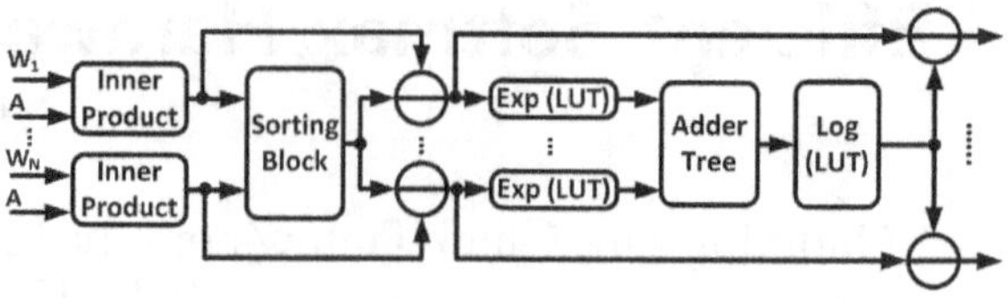


**Figure 1: Traditional hardware architecture in [23].**

## 3 BACKGROUND AND MOTIVATION

The softmax function is widely used in multiple classification tasks. Specifically, the calculation of the $i$-th neuron in softmax layer can be described as below:

$$P(belong\ to\ L-th\ category) = \frac{e^{W_m \cdot A}}{\sum_{L=1}^{N} e^{W_L \cdot A}} \quad (1)$$

where $W$ means the weight of the $m$-th neuron, $A$ denotes the activation of neuron, $\cdot$ represents inner product, and $N$ is the number of categories.

In [23], Bo Yuan utilizes the domain transformation technique and down-scaling approach to achieve the softmax model. Using the sorting block to compress the exponential function values to the interval (0,1], then introducing logarithmic LUTs to convert division into simple subtraction. The design block diagram is shown in Fig. 1.

This work laid a solid foundation for softmax layer hardware design. However, this work has three weaknesses: 1) The architecture is only an early exploration of the efficient hardware design of the softmax layer, without giving the technical details and performance parameters of the hardware implementation; 2) All dot product are sequentially subtracted from the maximum value of the dot product and the logarithmic value. The output data has no practical meaning, which is not numerically different from the input data, and different input data cannot be effectively distinguished; 3) Data preprocessing scheme cannot completely solve the calculation accuracy issue, because after the sorting block and the EXP(LUT) module, the range of the data is adjusted to (-∞, 0] and (0, 1], respectively. Adjusting a large amount of input data into a small interval will inevitably require more binary data bits to distinguish different data, resulting in a large waste of hardware resources.

## 4 SOFTMAX ARCHITECTURE

For input $X$, the corrected mathematical principle can be expressed by the following formula:

$$P(Lth\ category) = e^{(X_L - X_{max}) - ln(\sum_{L=1}^{N} e^{(X_L - X_{max})})} \quad (2)$$

Directly mapped into a circuit by equation (2), the architecture of the softmax is represented by Fig. 2. The softmax architecture can be divided into four parts: data preprocessing part, calculation part, probability output part, and control part. Specifically, the input data are mapped to the [-4, 4] interval in the preprocessing part and the calculation part mainly calculates the exponential function. The probability output part mainly calculates the logarithmic function and

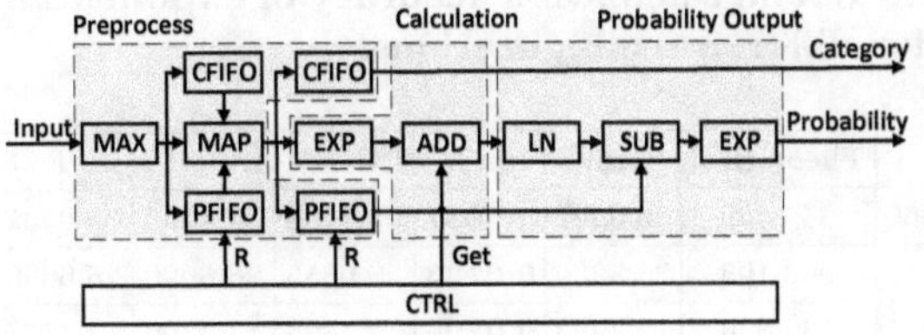


**Figure 2: softmax hardware structure and data path.**

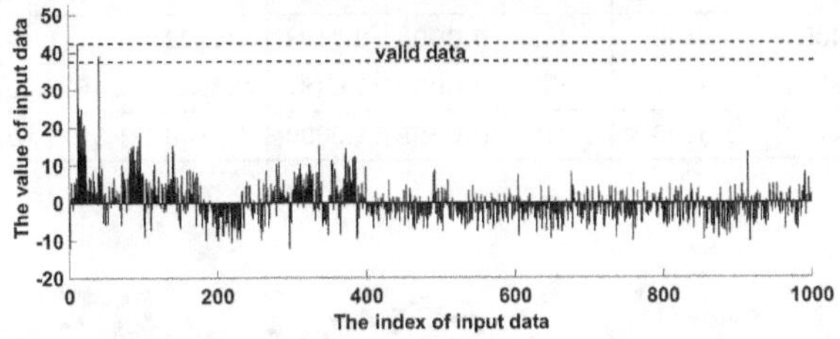


**Figure 3: The example of softmax input in AlexNet.**

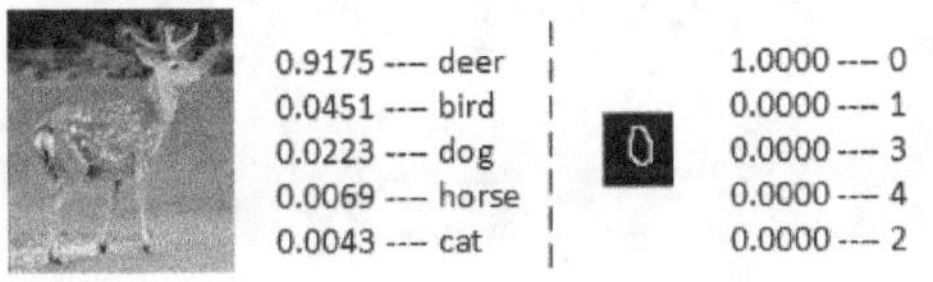


**Figure 4: Test examples on CIFAR-10 and MNIST.**

the control part is responsible for coordinating the other three parts of the work sequence.

## 4.1 The data preprocess part

DNN is a highly accurate image classification tool, so the probability of certain categories is significantly higher than other categories. for example, taking a set of data in AlexNet, the input data of the softmax layer is as shown in the Fig. 3. The example shows that the number of large value in input data is limited. More experiments confirm this conclusion, just as Fig. 4. After the exponential unit, big input data become bigger, while small input data become smaller, which is small enough to be ignored. In this paper, the data in the range of [Maximum-8, Maximum] is defined as valid data and other data is defined as invalid data. There are two reasons for this definition: 1) $e^8 \approx 2980.958$, when the difference between an input data and the largest input data after exponential calculation is about 3000 times, it is deemed safe to ignore this small value; 2) Using the formula $outputdata = inputdata - maximum + 4$ to evenly distribute the interval on both sides of origin 0 can effectively save hardware resources.

Based on the fact that the amount of valid data is limited, we only need to preprocess the valid data. Even if the invalid data is ignored, it will not affect the results of Top-1 and Top-5. In particular, in the case of only one valid data, softmax will directly output the category and corresponding probability (100%) without subsequent calculations. In other cases, the position and value of valid data are temporarily stored in the Category FIFO (CFIFO) and Probability FIFO (PFIFO), respectively for the next calculation.

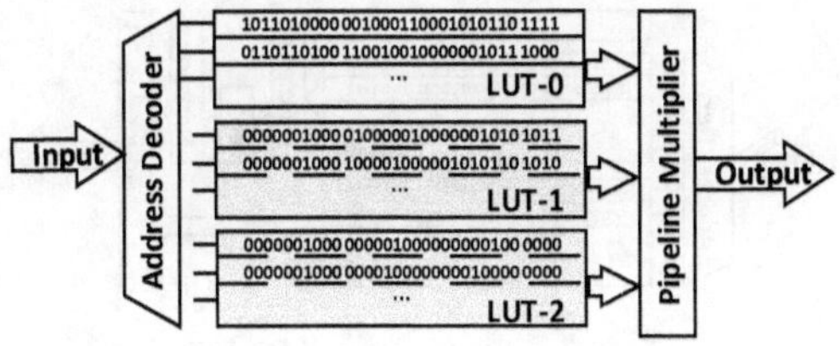


**Figure 5: Optional-accuracy EXP unit with GLUTs.**

## 4.2 The exponential unit (EXP)

In the exponential function calculation rule, assuming $x = x_1 + x_2 + x_3$, the following equation is true :

$$e^x = e^{x_1} \times e^{x_2} \times e^{x_3} \tag{3}$$

After preprocessing, the range of input data is limited to the interval [-4, 4]. $e^{x_1}$, $e^{x_2}$ and $e^{x_3}$ are pre-stored in the LUTs and $x_1$, $x_2$ and $x_3$ are addresses to fetch the corresponding value. The more LUTs that participate in the calculation, the higher the calculation accuracy. Because the data in the lookup table is stored in groups of four bits, we name this method group lookup table(GLUT). The exponential unit is shown in Fig. 5.

However, the three lookup tables do not always work together. The classification rule of neural network is that the probability of a certain category is much higher than that of the other in most cases. Excessive calculation accuracy does not affect the results of Top-1 and Top-5, but it will increase the burden of the circuit. To balance computational accuracy and resource usage, we set enable signals on all three LUTs. The LUTs are enabled sequentially according to how close the input data is. To be clear, it is possible to get the probability directly without LUTs. When all three lookup tables are enabled, the calculation accuracy can be achieved 25-bit binary fraction.

## 4.3 The natural logarithmic unit (LN)

In [3], Aroutchelvame proposed an algorithm which utilizes only the first two terms in Maclaurin series to compute natural logarithm function. This algorithm can be expressed as

$$ln(x) = lnR + ln(\frac{x}{R}) = lnR + ln[1 + \frac{x-R}{R}] \tag{4}$$

$$ln[1 + \frac{x-R}{R}] \approx \frac{x-R}{R} - \frac{(\frac{x-R}{R})^2}{2} \tag{5}$$

The equation (5) uses the first term of Maclaurin series to approximate calculation. The algorithm is simple but needs at least six LUTs. At the same time, the hardware implementation process of the algorithm inevitably produces precision loss, which is manifested by the large range of accuracy of the output data. In order to reduce the range of precision variation and resource consumption, we set the

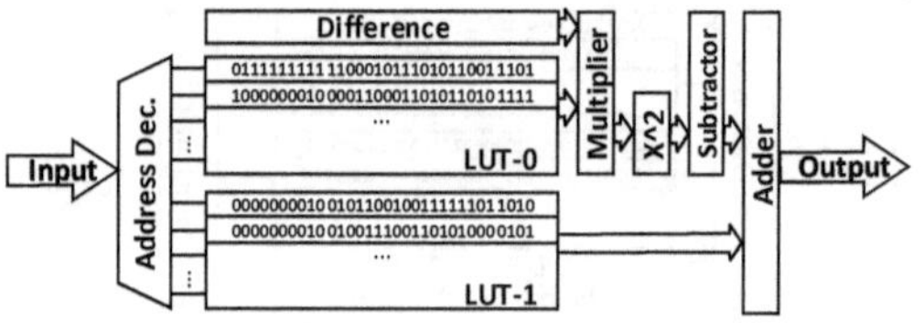


Figure 6: LN unit with equal intervals.

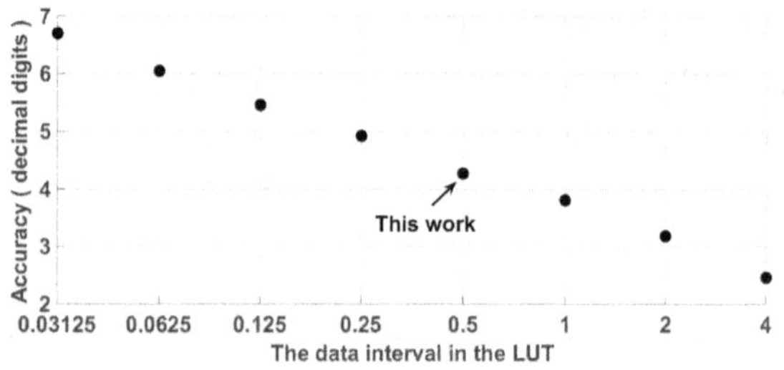


Figure 7: Relation between interval and accuracy.

data in the lookup table to equal intervals. The improved logarithmic calculation unit is represented in the Fig. 6.

In order to determine the optimal data interval in LUTs, we conduct further experiments with the architecture in [3]. We limit the number of input and data interval in LUTs to 200 and [54.5, 128], respectively. The experimental results is shown in Fig. 6.

A serial of test data shows that when the data interval is 0.5, the corresponding precision is a 4-digit decimal fraction. With this configuration, the amount of data in the LUTs is optimally balanced with the calculation accuracy.

## 5 EXPERIMENT

We perform experiments for the following purposes: (1) proving that the exponential calculation unit based on GLUTs can achieve the much higher and stabler accuracy than the algorithm in [16]; (2) proving that the improved logarithmic unit based on equal interval LUTs has a more stable accuracy change than the architecture in [3], and (3) comprehensively evaluating of the softmax hardware architecture using the metrics of accuracy, match situation and expansibility.

### 5.1 Accuracy comparison of EXP

The input value range of the exponential calculation unit in this paper is any value within the interval [-4,4]. But in [16], only the calculation results of integer values in the interval [-7, 8] are provided. In fact, the input to an exponential calculation unit cannot always be an integer or a negative number. In order to compare the calculation accuracy of the two circuits in detail, we implementation its core circuit and select randomly the data in the interval [0,4] as the test data. The results are shown in Table 1.

Looking at the data in the Table 1, there are two important points to note. Firstly, the premise of only using LUT-0 is that the input data is very different. Therefore, although the calculation error is very large, it will not affect the classification results of Top-1 and Top-5. As the difference between the input data decreases, LUT-1 and LUT-2 enable one after another. This greatly improves the accuracy of the calculation. Secondly, the three error values that look like zero are 0.000063, -0.000092 and -0.000059. Therefore, computational accuracy of exponential unit in this paper is approximately 5 decimal decimals, which is significantly higher than that of 2-3 decimal decimals in [16].

In terms of the use of computational resources, the number of multiplier used in [16] is a fixed value, which is 2. The GLUTs-based scheme uses two multipliers in extremely special cases, while in most cases only one multiplier is used, or even the multiplier is not required.

Table 1: The calculation accuracy of exponential unit under different configurations.

| input | Theoretical | [16] | error | LUT *1 | LUT *2 | LUT *3 | error |
|---|---|---|---|---|---|---|---|
| 3.5566 | 35.0439 | 35.0402 | **0.0037** | 33.1155 | 34.1666 | 35.0432 | **0.0007** |
| 3.2813 | 26.6103 | 26.5380 | **0.0723** | 20.0855 | 26.6090 | 26.6090 | **0.0013** |
| 2.6055 | 13.5380 | 13.4985 | **0.0395** | 12.1825 | 13.3799 | 13.5376 | **0.0004** |
| 2.3086 | 10.0603 | 10.0563 | **0.0040** | 7.3891 | 9.7889 | 10.0603 | **0.0000** |
| 1.7070 | 5.5124 | 5.5077 | **0.0047** | 4.4817 | 5.4059 | 5.5122 | **0.0002** |
| 1.4395 | 4.2186 | 4.2182 | **0.0004** | 2.7183 | 4.2102 | 4.2181 | **0.0005** |
| 0.8984 | 2.4557 | 2.4550 | **0.0007** | 1.6487 | 2.3989 | 2.4557 | **0.0000** |
| 0.2773 | 1.3196 | 1.3188 | **0.0008** | 1.0000 | 1.2840 | 1.3196 | **0.0000** |

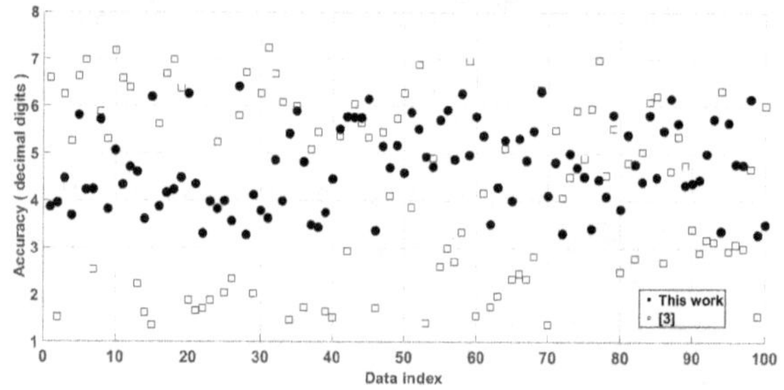


Figure 8: Comparison of the accuracy range.

### 5.2 Accuracy range comparison of LN

In [3], only the algorithm and architecture are given, but no more experimental data is provided. In order to compare the calculation accuracy of the two circuits in detail, we also implement its core circuit. The input data of this experiment is 100 random numbers in the interval [54, 128], which is expressed as 32-bit fixed point binary numbers. The experimental results are shown in Fig. 8.

We can find that the reproduced logarithmic unit has a range of accuracy is from 2 to 8 decimal decimals, and our improved logarithmic unit is from 4 to 6 decimal decimals. The accuracy range of the improved logarithmic calculation unit in this paper is significantly smaller than that of the recurring scheme but the overall average accuracy is not much different.

**Table 2: Comparison between various classification method implementations on MNIST dataset.**

| Method | Accuracy | Method | Accuracy |
|---|---|---|---|
| [6] SVM | 59.27% | [6] ES-based softmax | 88.74% |
| [6] softmax classifier | 82.29% | [6] EFACV | 91.87% |
| [18] FPGA(8 bits) | 95.00% | [21] GPUSVM | 95.00% |
| [21] GTSVM | 95.30% | [21] FPGA(4 bits) | 95.20% |
| [21] $SVM^{light}$ | 95.40% | [21] FPGA(4+8 bits) | 95.20% |
| [21] heterogenous classifier | 98.96% | [18] cascade classifier | 98.95% |
| software model | **99.25%** | ours | **99.01%** |

From the position of the logarithmic calculation unit in the ESHA, the accuracy does not depend on the highest precision that can be achieved but the range of precision variation. Logarithmic unit is used only once, and input data cannot be predicted. Assume that the maximum accuracy of the logarithmic unit is 8 bits, but only 2 bits can be achieved in a calculation. There is no doubt that the calculation accuracy of ESHA cannot be more than 2 bits. In other words, the calculation accuracy of the logarithmic unit depends on the lowest accuracy, not the highest.

## 5.3 Performance evaluation of ESHA

The synthesis tool is Xilinx ISE 14.7 and the development FPGA platform is Virtex5-XC5VLX110T. The accuracy and scalability results were obtained on it. The target technology and synthesis tool are 65nm and Synopsys Design Compiler respectively in Application Specific Integrated Circuit (A-SIC). The frequency, area and power consumption data were obtained by ASIC synthesis.

*5.3.1 Classification accuracy and calculation accuracy.* The true value of softmax layer hardware can only be evaluated when it is embedded the entire DNN hardware architecture. However, our current work is limited to the implementation of the softmax layer hardware architecture. In order to still be able to evaluate the accuracy, we adopted two schemes: 1) For classification accuracy, we used LeNet as an experimental platform and collected 10,000 groups of test set inference data as input data for ESHA. According to the output of ESHA, the classification accuracy of Top-1 and Top-5 is obtained; 2) For calculation accuracy, we select randomly three of above 10,000 groups of test set inference data to evaluate the calculation accuracy of the hardware model. The all classification accuracy test results are shown in Table 2.

All tests in Table 2 are performed on the mnist data set. The neural network model on the software platform consists of two convolutional layers, two dropout layers and two full connection layers. Both CPU and GPU are important computing platforms for training neural networks, but GPUs can effectively reduce training time due to their powerful parallel computing capabilities. Therefore, this experiment selects GPU (NVIDIA GTX 1070Ti) as the training platform. After 12 epochs of training, the accuracy of the neural network model is 99.25%. According to the above first scheme, the classification accuracy of ESHA is 99.01%, which is higher than the classification accuracy in the current work, and even close to the software model.

**Table 3: Softmax hardware architecture calculation accuracy evaluation under three kinds of accuracy.**

| Group | input data | software | LUT *1 | LUT *2 | LUT *3 | Error |
|---|---|---|---|---|---|---|
| No.1 | 0.2055 | 0.0137 | 0.0180 | — | — | **0.0043** |
| | 14.7945 | 0.9863 | 0.9820 | — | — | **0.0043** |
| No.2 | 11.2672 | 0.7042 | — | 0.7085 | — | **0.0043** |
| | 0.0832 | 0.0052 | — | 0.0052 | — | **0.0000** |
| | 4.6512 | 0.2907 | — | 0.2863 | — | **0.0044** |
| No.3 | 9.4572 | 0.5254 | — | — | 0.5259 | **0.0005** |
| | 8.5428 | 0.4746 | — | — | 0.4751 | **0.0005** |

**Table 4: Suppose softmax hardware architecture is integrated into AI chip for nearly three years.**

| ESHA | Frequency: **500** MHz | | Area: **0.64** $mm^2$ | | Power: **0.82** mW | |
|---|---|---|---|---|---|---|
| works | Freq | Technology | Area | Proportion | Power | Proportion |
| [9] | 200 | 65nm CMOS | 12.25 | 5.22% | 278 | 0.29% |
| [20] | 3-86 | 65nm LP | 9.61 | 6.66% | 1.8-7.8 | 10.51% |
| [22] | 10-200 | 65nm LP | 19.36 | 3.31% | 4-447 | 0.18% |
| [1] | 400 | 65nm GP | 3.90 | 16.40% | 600 | 0.14% |

The calculation accuracy comparison results of ESHA are shown in Table 3. Three sets of test data correspond to three different processing strategies. The first set of probabilities are so different that using only one LUT for calculation is enough. As the probability approaches closer and closer, the second and third groups must use more LUTs for calculation. The errors in the three sets of results were not exactly the same, but they remained at a lower order of magnitude.

All three computing strategies can guarantee the accuracy of classification, but the computing resources are different. The usage of computing resources increases with the improvement of calculation accuracy. For example, the first strategy requires one LUT and zero multiplier, while the second strategy requires two LUTs and one multiplier. Even though the third strategy requires three LUTs and two multiplier, we have to invest a lot of resources for calculation to ensure the correct classification results.

The error of ESHA mainly comes from the truncation operation in the hardware calculation process and the quantification of the input data, and the latter has a greater impact. Hardware calculation errors are unavoidable, but quantization errors can be reduced by increasing the width of the input data.

*5.3.2 Frequency, Area and Power.* In terms of synthesis frequency, ESHA is higher than the mainstream neural network accelerators of the last three years, just as Table 4. Pipeline technology effectively shortens the critical path length, thereby increasing the frequency. The synthesis report shows that critical path of ESHA is in the exponential calculation unit. We designed a seven-stage pipeline structure in this unit,

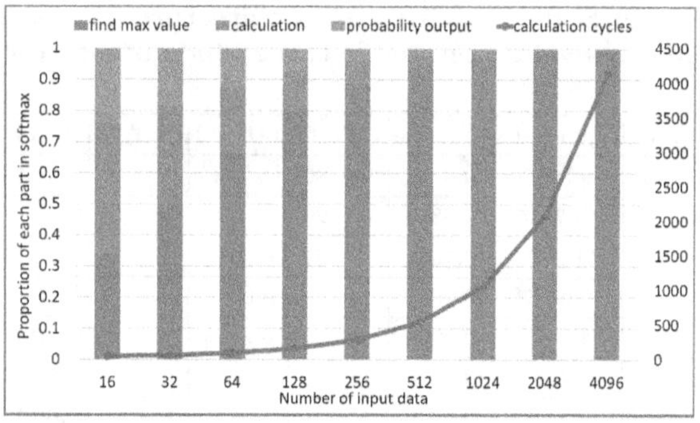


**Figure 9: The extensibility for 4-4096 input data.**

which extends the cycle but effectively reduces the computation time.

For area, note that the target neural network is a binary network and a ternary network in [1]. In both neural networks, the multiplier is replaced by an XNOR gate, and the adder is replaced by a counter. Both simple cells require less area, but ESHA is not optimized for quantized networks.

In addition to [20], the other three power consumption percentages are all less than 1%. ESHA mainly adopts gated clock technology to reduce power consumption by turning off functions unavailable clock. A speech recognition chip is proposed in [20]. The feature of speech recognition task is that the chip only starts to work when the user wakes up the recognition task. It's not hard to see why this chip has such low power consumption.

*5.3.3 Scalability.* ESHA has excellent scalability ability, which can handle large amounts of input data. To fully illustrate this feature, we select 16-4096 input data. The total and calculation cycle of each part are shown in Fig. 9. As the number of input data increases, the total computing period increases exponentially. At the same time, the proportion of the part looking for the maximum is gradually increasing, so that it far exceeds the other two parts. This phenomenon also points the way for our future work.

# 6 SUMMARY AND CONCLUSIONS

In this paper, we proposed a softmax hardware architecture with optional calculation accuracy and stable classification accuracy. In order to achieve optional calculation accuracy, we summarize the classification rules of neural network and effectively manage the usage of hardware resources. We propose a data preprocessing scheme according to the characteristics of softmax data and improve natural logarithm calculation unit to keep the classification accuracy stable. Future works are planned towards the following directions: 1) integrate the softmax layer into the entire DNN hardware structure and perform joint optimization at the architecture level; 2) modify the design so that softmax architecture can meet the accuracy requirements of different quantitative networks.

# REFERENCES


[1] Kota Ando. 2018. BRein Memory: A Single-Chip Binary/Ternary Reconfigurable in-Memory Deep Neural Network Accelerator Achieving 1.4 TOPS at 0.6 W. *IEEE Journal of Solid-State Circuits* 53, 4 (April 2018), 983–994.

[2] Ebru Arisoy. 2014. Converting Neural Network Language Models into back-off language models for efficient decoding in automatic speech recognition. *IEEE Transactions on Audio, Speech and Language Processing* 22, 1 (Jan. 2014), 184–192.

[3] S.M. Aroutchelvame. 2005. An efficient algorithm and architecture for natural logarithm using Maclaurin series. *IEEE International Conference on Electronics, Circuits and Systems* (Dec. 2005).

[4] Tom Brabec. 2006. Hardware Implementation of Continued Logarithm Arithmetic. *GAMM-IMACS International Symposium on Scientific Computing, Computer Arithmetic and Validated Numerics* (Sept. 2006).

[5] Luis Camunas-Mesa. 2011. A 32 x 32 Pixel Convolution Processor Chip for Address Event Vision Sensors With 155 ns Event Latency and 20 Meps Throughput. *IEEE Transactions on Circuits and Systems I: Regular Papers* 58, 4 (April 2011), 777–790.

[6] Siyi Chen. 2016. Image classification with stacked restricted boltzmann machines and evolutionary function array classification voter. *IEEE Congress on Evolutionary Computation* (July 2016), 4599–4606.

[7] Tianshi Chen. 2014. DianNao: a small-footprint high-throughput accelerator for ubiquitous machine-learning. *International Conference on Architectural Support for Programming Languages and Operating Systems* (March 2014), 269–283.

[8] Yunji Chen. 2015. DaDianNao: A Machine-Learning Supercomputer. *Annual IEEE/ACM International Symposium on Microarchitecture* (Jan. 2015), 609–622.

[9] Yu-Hsin Chen. 2016. Eyeriss: A Spatial Architecture for Energy-Efficient Dataflow for Convolutional Neural Networks. *International Symposium on Computer Architecture* (Aug. 2016), 367–379.

[10] Javier Hormigo. 2000. A Hardware Algorithm for Variable-Precision Logarithm. *IEEE International Conference on Application-Specific Systems, Architectures, and Processors* (July 2000), 215–224.

[11] Norman P. Jouppi. 2017. In-Datacenter Performance Analysis of a Tensor Processing Unit. *Annual International Symposium on Computer Architecture* (June 2017), 1–12.

[12] Sung Su Kim. 2004. Hardware implementation of a real time neural network controller with a DSP and an FPGA. *Proceedings - IEEE International Conference on Robotics and Automation* (April 2004), 4639–4644.

[13] Alex Krizhevsky. 2012. ImageNet classification with deep convolutional neural networks. *Annual Conference on Neural Information Processing Systems* (Dec. 2012), 1097–1105.

[14] Yann Lecun. 1998. Gradient-based learning applied to document recognition. *Proc. IEEE* 86, 11 (Nov. 1998), 2278–2323.

[15] Xi Li. 2016. DeepSaliency: Multi-Task Deep Neural Network Model for Salient Object Detection. *IEEE Transactions on Image Processing* 25, 1 (Aug. 2016), 3919–3930.

[16] Kaiwen Lin. 2017. Design and optimization of exponential function based on Taylor expansion. *Application Research of computers* (Oct. 2017).

[17] Peter Nilsson. 2015. Hardware implementation of the exponential function using Taylor series. *NORCHIP Conference* (Jan. 2015).

[18] Markos Papadonikolakis. 2012. Novel cascade FPGA accelerator for support vector machines classification. *IEEE Transactions on Neural Networks and Learning Systems* 23, 7 (2012), 1040–1052.

[19] Peyman Pouyan. 2011. A VLSI implementation of logarithmic and exponential functions using a novel parabolic synthesis methodology compared to the CORDIC algorithm. *European Conference on Circuit Theory and Design* (Aug. 2011), 709–712.

[20] Michael Price. 2017. A scalable speech recognizer with deep-neural-network acoustic models and voice-activated power gating. *IEEE International Solid-State Circuits Conference* 60 (March 2017), 244–245.

[21] Mudhar Bin Rabieah. 2015. FPGA based nonlinear Support Vector Machine training using an ensemble learning. *International Conference on Field Programmable Logic and Applications* (Oct. 2015).

[22] Shouyi Yin. 2017. A 1.06-to-5.09 TOPS/W reconfigurable hybrid-neural-network processor for deep learning applications. *Symposium on VLSI Circuits* (Aug. 2017), C26–C27.

[23] Bo Yuan. 2017. Efficient hardware architecture of softmax layer in deep neural network. *IEEE International System on Chip Conference* (April 2017), 323–326.

# HSIM-DNN: Hardware Simulator for Computation-, Storage- and Power-Efficient Deep Neural Networks

Mengshu Sun
Northeastern University
Boston, Massachusetts
sun.meng@husky.neu.edu

Pu Zhao
Northeastern University
Boston, Massachusetts
zhao.pu@husky.neu.edu

Yanzhi Wang
Northeastern University
Boston, Massachusetts
yanz.wang@northeastern.edu

Naehyuck Chang
Korea Advanced Institute of Science and Technology
Daejeon, South Korea
naehyuck@cad4x.kaist.ac.kr

Xue Lin
Northeastern University
Boston, Massachusetts
xue.lin@northeastern.edu

## ABSTRACT

Deep learning that utilizes large-scale deep neural networks (DNNs) is effective in automatic high-level feature extraction but also computation and memory intensive. Constructing DNNs using block-circulant matrices can simultaneously achieve hardware acceleration and model compression while maintaining high accuracy. This paper proposes HSIM-DNN, an accurate hardware simulator on the C++ platform, to simulate the exact behavior of DNN hardware implementations and thereby facilitate the block-circulant matrix-based design of DNN training and inference procedures in hardware. Real FPGA implementations validate the simulator with various circulant block sizes and data bit lengths taking into account accuracy, compression ratio and power consumption, which provides excellent insights for hardware design.

## CCS CONCEPTS

**• Computing methodologies → Neural networks; • Hardware → Emerging simulation; • Software and its engineering → Simulator / interpreter;**

## KEYWORDS

Deep neural network; hardware simulator; block-circulant matrix; FFT; hardware acceleration

**ACM Reference format:**
Mengshu Sun, Pu Zhao, Yanzhi Wang, Naehyuck Chang, and Xue Lin. 2019. HSIM-DNN: Hardware Simulator for Computation-, Storage- and Power-Efficient Deep Neural Networks. In *Proceedings of Great Lakes Symposium on VLSI 2019, Tysons Corner, VA, USA, May 9–11, 2019 (GLSVLSI '19)*, 6 pages.
https://doi.org/10.1145/3299874.3317996


*GLSVLSI '19, May 9–11, 2019, Tysons Corner, VA, USA*

ACM ISBN 978-1-4503-6252-8/19/05...$15.00
https://doi.org/10.1145/3299874.3317996

## 1 INTRODUCTION

Deep learning based on deep neural networks (DNNs) has experienced breakthroughs in recent years in broad areas, such as computer vision [11, 18] and speech recognition [14]. Deep learning applications have been migrating to smart objects like mobile and Internet-of-Things (IoT) devices [1, 20], which can compose the smart world and ubiquitous intelligence. Modern DNNs tend to consist of multiple cascaded layers with at least millions of parameters [18] that contribute to high computation accuracy through high-level feature extraction. Nonetheless, the growing model size also increases the computation and memory complexity, which becomes the key challenge of DNN applications especially in smart world. Aiming for higher scalability, performance and energy efficiency in deep learning systems, two contradictory trends in research and development for DNNs have emerged, namely *hardware acceleration* and *model compression*.

Hardware acceleration based on FPGAs or ASICs yields higher performance and better energy efficiency than that based on general-purpose computing systems like CPUs and GPUs. Representative works include Google's Tensor Processing Units (TPUs) [16], IBM's TrueNorth chips [9, 22], and optimization related to memory transfers [3, 4], dynamic-precision data quantization [23], processing dataflow [5], weight sharing [10], bit-serial computation [17], etc. Most designs of this type suffer from frequent accesses to off-chip DRAM, which may consume over 100× energy than capacity-limited on-chip SRAM[10, 12, 13], and easily dominate power consumption of the entire system.

Model compression has been realized by several algorithm level techniques, including weight quantization [7, 21, 26, 27], connection pruning [12, 13], and low rank approximation [15, 25]. A special case of quantization is the low precision fixed-point representation [21], which is prevalent in hardware like FPGAs and ASICs, only using one or two bits for representation in extreme cases [7, 27]. Connection pruning removes all connections with weights below a threshold [12, 13], and low rank approximation represents CNN filter banks using a low rank basis of filters that are separable in the spatial domain [15, 25]. Although these approaches offer reasonable parameter reductions with less data storage and transfer and minor accuracy loss, they have respective limitations. Quantization achieves the compression ratio in a fixed-point form but requires the gradients to be denoted in floating-point numbers in the training process. Pruning typically causes the network structure to be irregular, thereby limiting the compression ratio and performance, and both pruning and low rank approximation are likely to increase the training complexity. Moreover, the compression ratios achieved by all these approaches are heuristic and cannot be precisely controlled.

A distinct method in [6] explores parameter redundancy of DNNs by imposing a circulant structure for weight representation of fully-connected layers. This work proposes corresponding accelerated inference and training algorithms for fully-connected layers. Such a method is generalized for both fully-connected layers and convolution layers in [8], based on block-circulant weight matrices considering the trade-off between the accuracy degradation and compression ratio or computation acceleration. It provides a cross-platform hardware design and optimization solution for deep learning systems.

DNN hardware implementations are constrained by limited hardware resources, i.e., the computing and storage units in FPGAs or the tapeout area in ASICs, and it is time- and labor-consuming work to fit the DNN architectures into available resources while meeting the accuracy and power requirements. On the other hand, software simulators for deep learning, such as Caffe and Tensorflow, could not produce exact hardware results that are restricted by precision and computing resources in hardware implementations. Therefore, this paper proposes HSIM-DNN, an accurate hardware simulator that simulates the behavior of DNN hardware implementations for both training and inference procedures on the C++ platform. This simulator accelerates the design and optimization cycles of DNN hardware implementations by testing and checking the feasibility of the hyperparameters (variables) in the hardware design. It thus serves as a transition from pure software descriptions to hardware description languages like VHDL and Verilog.

The main features of HSIM-DNN are as follows:

*1)* HSIM-DNN produces fast and exact results with high accuracy for DNN hardware implementations, and detects the existence of data overflow of computations in hardware, allowing to avoid overflow and improve the design at an early stage.

*2)* HSIM-DNN provides the energy/power performance under different parameter configurations, and serves as the starting point for future hardware platform-specific functional modules, such as power and timing estimators.

*3)* HSIM-DNN supports online training of DNNs in hardware by analyzing and verifying the feasibility and performance, which is currently a technical difficulty for DNN hardware implementations.

## 2 BACKGROUND

### 2.1 Basics of Deep Neural Networks

DNNs may take various architectures, whereas they are all constructed by cascading multiple functional layers for feature extraction at multiple abstraction levels. The most fundamental types of functional layers in DNNs are *fully-connected layers, convolution layers* and *pooling layers.*

***Fully-connected (FC) layers*** are the most computation- and storage-intensive layers in DNNs [10, 23], due to the fully-connectedness between adjacent layers. The computation for an FC layer consists of matrix-vector arithmetic (including multiplication and addition) and activation transformation, described as

$$\mathbf{y} = \psi(\mathbf{W}\mathbf{x} + \theta), \tag{1}$$

where $\mathbf{x}$ is the input of the FC layer, $\mathbf{y}$ is the output, and $\mathbf{W} \in \mathbb{R}^{m\times n}$ is the *weight matrix* of the synapses (i.e., connections) between the $m$ neurons in the FC layer and the $n$ neurons in the previous layer, $\theta \in \mathbb{R}^m$ is the *bias vector*, and $\psi(\cdot)$ is the *activation function.* The multiplication calculation $\mathbf{Wx}$ determines the total computational complexity, and the remaining calculation in this equation contributes to a lower complexity of O($n$). The most widely utilized activation function in DNN applications is the Rectified Linear Unit (ReLU), given by $\psi(x) = \max(0, x)$.

***Convolution (CONV) layers*** extract features from the input data with a set of *kernels* (i.e., *filters*) [19] mainly by multi-dimensional convolutions, and the output *feature maps* are fed into the subsequent layers for higher-level feature extraction. The input data of a CONV layer can be images or feature maps from the previous layer. Specifically, the convolution of an input map and a kernel is generated by moving the kernel through the input map. With multiple kernels, a CONV layer is often associated with multiple input and multiple output feature maps. The CONV computation can be expressed in the form of *tensor computation*, as

$$\mathcal{Y}(a,b,d) = \sum_{i=1}^{r}\sum_{j=1}^{r}\sum_{c=1}^{C}\mathcal{F}(i,j,c,d)\mathcal{X}(a+i-1,b+j-1,c), \tag{2}$$

where $\mathcal{X} \in \mathbb{R}^{W\times H\times C}$, $\mathcal{Y} \in \mathbb{R}^{(W-r+1)\times(H-r+1)\times D}$, $\mathcal{F} \in \mathbb{R}^{r\times r\times C\times D}$ represent the input, output, and *weight tensors* of the CONV layer, respectively. There are $C$ input maps and $D$ output maps, and each kernel of size $r \times r$ is applied to each input map with the spatial dimensions $W$ and $H$ to generate an output map.

***Pooling (POOL) layers*** subsample the extracted features to reduce data dimensions and mitigate overfitting problems. The dominant pooling strategy in state-of-the-art DNN applications is *max pooling* because of the high overall accuracy and high convergence speed [4, 5].

Among these three types of layers, CONV and FC layers are responsible for the majority of computation, and a POOL layer has a lower computational complexity of O($n$). The storage requirement of DNNs originates from the weight matrices $\mathbf{W}$'s for FC layers and the convolution kernels represented by the tensors $\mathcal{F}$'s for CONV layers. Therefore, FC and CONV layers become the major research focus for efficient DNN implementations.

### 2.2 Block-Circulant Matrix-Based Weight Representation

A block-circulant matrix is constructed by arraying equal-sized square circulant sub-matrices in two dimensions, each circulant matrix being considered as a block. A circulant matrix with $k \times k$ elements has only $k$ free elements, so the size of the block is defined as $k$, which indicates the compression degree. Particularly, there is no compression for blocks with $k = 1$. Fig. 1 gives an example of a block-circulant matrix $\mathbf{W}$ with the calculation process with regard to a certain circulant sub-matrix $\mathbf{W}_{ij}$. The calculation of $\mathbf{Wx}$ can then be reduced to the calculation of $\mathbf{W}_{ij}\mathbf{x}_j$, which can be performed through the "FFT → element-wise multiplication →

IFFT" procedure according to the *circulant convolution theorem* [2], which is elaborated in Section 3.

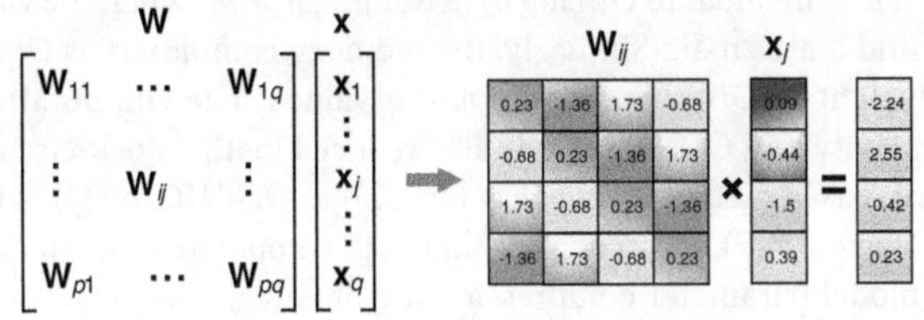


**Figure 1: Illustration of a block-circulant matrix.**

# 3 SIMULATOR IMPLEMENTATION

In the proposed simulator HSIM-DNN, the block size (size of the circulant matrix) and data precision (bit length) are considered as two fundamental hardware optimization variables that are chosen to balance the accuracy, the model compression ratio and the hardware utility rate. A higher block size results in a greater compression ratio with more computation acceleration but degrades the accuracy. Increase in the bit length improves the accuracy but requires more storage and computation resources.

The computation and validation process of HSIM-DNN is illustrated in Fig. 2. The image data and weights are first preprocessed, i.e., they are quantized according to the bit length and segmented based on the block size. After that, the FFT-based circulant multiplication is done for all circulant blocks. The outputs from the blocks are then reformulated to generate the overall result, which is checked on the correctness and overflow to give a feedback to adjust the block size and bit length. The software validation provides insights into the hardware design with much less effort and time compared with hardware validation.

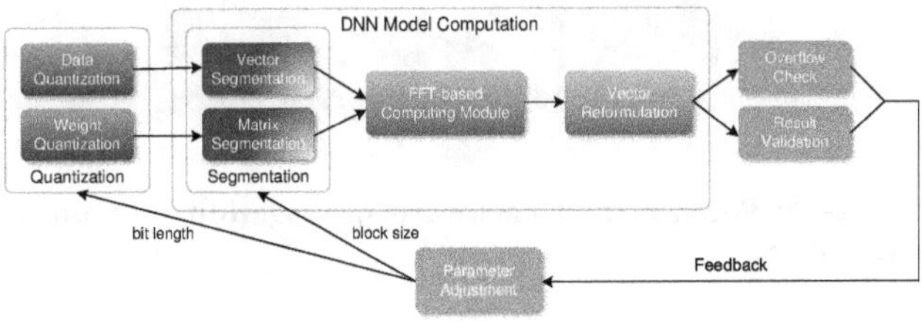


**Figure 2: Computation and validation of HSIM-DNN.**

The data in hardware is represented in the form of fixed-point binary numbers, i.e., in 2's complement, in order to fit the limited hardware resources. Therefore, the simulator contains a data conversion module to convert decimals to fixed-point binary numbers, and then it manages all operations based on fixed-point binary numbers to simulate the actual calculations in DNN hardware implementations. A fixed-point binary number consists of an integral part and a fractional part. More integral bits can represent data in a wider range and avoid overflow, and more fractional bits can provide higher precision and better accuracy. An overflow detection mechanism is added to report if the data value exceeds the acceptable data range and leads to computation errors.

The simulation procedure of HSIM-DNN has two main phases, simulating DNN training and DNN inference in hardware, respectively. The FFT-based computing module serves as the core calculation kernel for both phases.

## 3.1 FFT-Based Computing Module

As mentioned in Section 2.2, the calculation of $\mathbf{W}_{ij}\mathbf{x}_j$ can be performed through the "FFT → element-wise multiplication → IFFT" procedure, which is the basic computation in FC and CONV layers in both training and inference. This procedure can be expressed as

$$\mathbf{W}_{ij}\mathbf{x}_j = \text{IFFT}(\text{FFT}(\mathbf{w}_{ij}) \circ \text{FFT}(\mathbf{x}_j)), \tag{3}$$

where $\mathbf{w}_{ij}$ denotes the first row vector of $\mathbf{W}_{ij}$, and $\circ$ denotes element-wise multiplication. An FFT-based computing module is designed for HSIM-DNN to execute this calculation as shown in Fig. 3. This module can be split into an FFT submodule and an IFFT submodule, the latter based on the former, as an IFFT can be realized by an FFT with conjugate operations on the input and output.

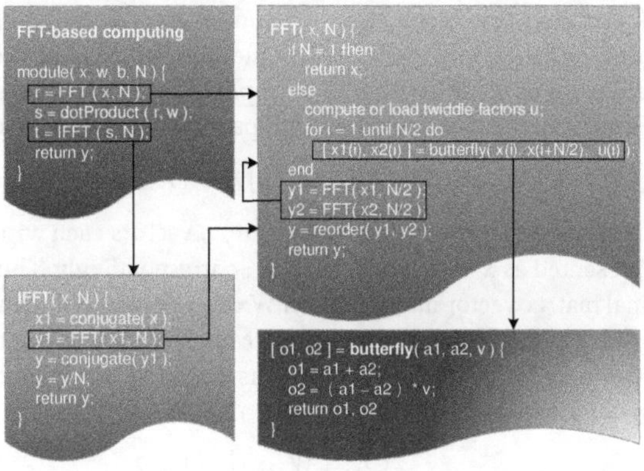


**Figure 3: Algorithm of FFT-based computing module.**

A recursive FFT is implemented by the radix-2 decimation in frequency (DIF) algorithm as illustrated in Fig. 4. More specifically, an $n$-size FFT with $n$ inputs and $n$ outputs can be separated into two FFTs each with size $n/2$ and one additional level of butterfly calculation, and an $n/2$-size FFT can be further divided into two $n/4$-size FFTs with one butterfly calculation level. A large-scale FFT can be calculated by recursively performing FFTs on the same computing module, and multiple small-scale FFTs can be calculated on several computing modules in parallel. This recursive property of FFT calculation is the key for hardware to accommodate DNN models of different types and sizes on relatively small hardware footprints with appropriate control logic and memory storage organization. Compared with the FFT computation, the rest of computations including component-wise multiplication, ReLU activation and pooling have little time complexity and memory overhead, which can be ignored.

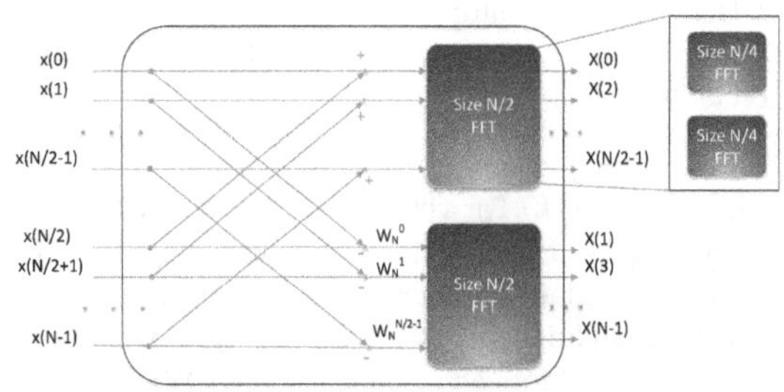


**Figure 4: Recursive FFT computation.**

## 3.2 Inference of HSIM-DNN

HSIM-DNN applies block-circulant matrix-based calculation in FC and CONV layers in the training and inference phases to mitigate the computation and storage burdens owing to the large amount of matrix-vector multiplication. The simulator first trains the DNN model through forward-propagation and backward-propagation to optimize parameters, and then it performs inference to make predictions for new input data. The inference phase is first introduced since it is similar to the forward-propagation step in training.

*3.2.1 Inference of FC layers.* The original weight matrix $\mathbf{W} \in \mathbb{R}^{m \times n}$ of an FC layer can have an arbitrary size. To obtain a block-circulant weight matrix, $\mathbf{W}$ is partitioned into equal-sized square sub-matrices, i.e., blocks. Each block $\mathbf{W}_{ij}$ is a circulant matrix with $k \times k$ elements (the block size is $k$), and $\mathbf{W}$ contains $p \times q$ blocks where $p = \lceil m/k \rceil$ and $q = \lceil n/k \rceil$. If the division of $m$ or $n$ has a remainder, zero padding should be applied for $\mathbf{W}$ to make every block square. The weight matrix with partition is represented as

$$\mathbf{W} = [\mathbf{W}_{ij}], \quad i \in \{1, \ldots, p\}, j \in \{1, \ldots, q\}. \tag{4}$$

The input vector $\mathbf{x}$ is also partitioned into $q$ vectors each with size $k$, represented as $\mathbf{x} = [\mathbf{x}_1^{\mathrm{T}}, \mathbf{x}_2^{\mathrm{T}}, \ldots, \mathbf{x}_q]^{\mathrm{T}}$, correspondingly. Thus the original matrix-vector multiplication $\mathbf{Wx}$ can be replaced with multiple sub-matrix-vector multiplication calculations. The inference process in an FC layer, omitting the bias and ReLU components in (1), is described as

$$\mathbf{a} = \mathbf{Wx} = \begin{bmatrix} \sum_{j=1}^{q} \mathbf{W}_{1j}\mathbf{x}_j \\ \sum_{j=1}^{q} \mathbf{W}_{2j}\mathbf{x}_j \\ \cdots \\ \sum_{j=1}^{q} \mathbf{W}_{pj}\mathbf{x}_j \end{bmatrix} = \begin{bmatrix} \mathbf{a}_1 \\ \mathbf{a}_2 \\ \cdots \\ \mathbf{a}_p, \end{bmatrix}, \tag{5}$$

where $\mathbf{a}_i \in \mathbb{R}^k$ is a column vector. Furthermore, each block $\mathbf{W}_{ij}$ can be denoted only by its first row $\mathbf{w}_{ij}$, and the calculation of $\mathbf{W}_{ij}\mathbf{x}_j$ can be implemented by (3).

*3.2.2 Inference of CONV layers.* For a CONV layer that is associated with multiple input and output feature maps, the convolution computation might be executed in multi-dimensions, namely in tensor form, as mentioned in (2). The concept of block-circulant structure is here generalized to a rank-4 tensor $\mathcal{F}$, with all slices of the form $\mathcal{F}(i, j, \cdot, \cdot)$ being circulant matrices. The tensor needs to be reshaped into a 2D matrix to fit the block-circulant matrix-based method. Specifically, the tensor computation in (2) is reformulated as the matrix multiplication $\mathbf{Y} = \mathbf{XF}$, where $\mathbf{X} \in \mathbb{R}^{(W-r+1)(H-r+1) \times Cr^2}$, $\mathbf{Y} \in \mathbb{R}^{(W-r+1)(H-r+1) \times D}$ and $\mathbf{F} \in \mathbb{R}^{Cr^2 \times D}$. The element $\mathcal{F}(i, j, c, d)$ is reformulated as $f_{C(i-1)+Cr(j-1)+c,d}$ in $\mathbf{F}$, making $\mathbf{F}$ a block-circulant matrix. Hence the fast multiplication approach for block-circulant matrices can be applied to implement $\mathbf{Y} = \mathbf{XF}$, leading to computation acceleration.

*3.2.3 Complexity Analysis.* An FFT of size $k$ has computational complexity of $O(k \log k)$. For a block $\mathbf{W}_{ij}$ of block size $k$, the replacement of the original matrix-vector multiplication by the FFT-based computation can reduce the computational complexity from $O(k^2)$ to $O(k \log k)$. In addition, only the first row vector $\mathbf{w}_{ij}$ or FFT($\mathbf{w}_{ij}$) requires to be stored for each circulant matrix $\mathbf{W}_{ij}$, reducing the memory complexity from $O(k^2)$ to $O(k)$.

Provided an $m \times n$ block-circulant matrix with the block size of $k$, the computational complexity of an FC layer is $O(pqk \log k)$, which is equivalent to $O(n \log n)$ (assuming $n > m$) when the values of $p$ and $q$ are small. Similarly, the memory complexity is $O(pqk)$, equivalent to $O(n)$ for small $p$ and $q$ values. The computational complexity of a CONV layer is also reduced by the block-circulant matrix-based method, from $O(WHr^2CD)$ to $O(WHQ \log Q)$, where $Q = \max(Cr^2, P)$. It can be seen that both computation acceleration and model parameter compression are obtained.

## 3.3 Training of HSIM-DNN

The purpose of training is to optimize the DNN parameters including weights and biases to minimize the loss, namely the gap between the prediction results from the DNN and the original correct results given by the training dataset. In image classification problems, the original results are labels indicating the category to which each image belongs. The training process consists of two steps, i.e., forward propagation and backward propagation. Forward propagation is similar to the inference process, where the DNN receives input image data and makes a prediction, and the only difference from inference is that a loss function is evaluated by comparing the results from forward propagation and the original labels. Backward propagation, also called backpropagation, calculates the derivatives of the loss with respect to weights and biases, which are then updated sequentially from the last layer to the first layer. Forward propagation and backward propagation are performed alternately until the loss decreases to an enough small value. The forward and backward processes are shown in Fig. 5.

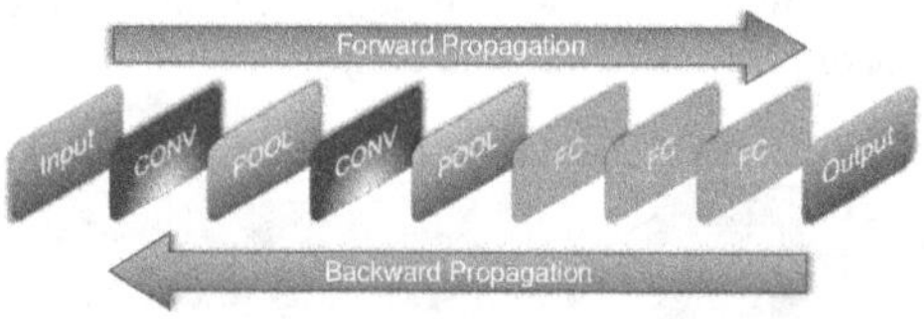


**Figure 5: Forward and backward propagation in a multi-layer DNN.**

Letting the loss function be denoted by $L$, the weight matrix $\mathbf{W}$ is updated in the backward propagation as

$$\mathbf{W} = \mathbf{W} - \epsilon \frac{\partial L}{\partial \mathbf{W}}, \tag{6}$$

where $\epsilon$ denotes the learning rate. Subtracting the derivative of $L$ with respect to $\mathbf{W}$ moves $\mathbf{W}$ to decrease the loss and thus improve the accuracy. Usually the derivative $\frac{\partial L}{\partial \mathbf{W}}$ cannot be computed directly, so the chain rule would be applied to obtain the derivatives sequentially from the last layer to the first layer, expressed as

$$\frac{\partial L}{\partial \mathbf{w}_{ij}} = \frac{\partial L}{\partial \mathbf{a}_i} \frac{\partial \mathbf{a}_i}{\partial \mathbf{w}_{ij}} = \sum_{l=1}^{k} \frac{\partial L}{\partial a_{il}} \frac{\partial a_{il}}{\partial \mathbf{w}_{ij}}, \tag{7}$$

$$\frac{\partial L}{\partial \mathbf{x}_j} = \sum_{i=1}^{p} \frac{\partial L}{\partial \mathbf{a}_i} \frac{\partial \mathbf{a}_i}{\partial \mathbf{x}_j} = \sum_{i=1}^{p} \sum_{l=1}^{k} \frac{\partial L}{\partial a_{il}} \frac{\partial a_{il}}{\partial \mathbf{x}_j}, \tag{8}$$

where $a_{il}$ represents the $l$-th output element in $\mathbf{a}_i$. Since $\mathbf{W}_{ij}$ is a circulant matrix, $\frac{\partial \mathbf{a}_i}{\partial \mathbf{w}_{ij}}$ and $\frac{\partial \mathbf{a}_i}{\partial \mathbf{x}_j}$ are also circulant matrices, defined respectively by the base vector $\mathbf{x}_j' = [x_{j,1}, x_{j,k}, x_{j,k-1}, \ldots, x_{j,2}]'$, and the base vector of $\mathbf{W}_{ij}$. And then $\frac{\partial L}{\partial \mathbf{w}_{ij}}$ and $\frac{\partial L}{\partial \mathbf{x}_j}$ can be calculated using the "FFT → element-wise multiplication → IFFT" procedure to reduce the computational complexity of each layer. The vectors $\mathbf{w}_{ij}$'s, composing the circulant blocks $\mathbf{W}_{ij}$'s of each layer, are trained directly so that the trained network naturally follows the block-circulant structure. The key advantage is that no additional steps are required in training and inference.

*3.3.1 Training Acceleration.* The FFT-based computing module is improved to enhance the simulator performance in the following three steps: (a) *Encapsulating the FFTW++ library* [24], which provides a simple interface for FFTs of 1D, 2D, and 3D complex-to-complex, real-to-complex, and complex-to-real Fast Fourier Transforms with automation of memory allocation, alignment, wisdom, and communication on both serial and parallel architectures and with support in in-place and out-of-place multithreaded transforms of arbitrary size. (b) *Changing the structure of FFT implementation* to perform FFTs iteratively instead of recursively to save overhead of implicit calls on the stack and to enable fine-grained memory management. (c) *Implementing multi-threads or multi-cores* to compute the inference and training individually in each batch.

## 3.4 Energy/Power Performance

The energy/power performance of DNN hardware implementations is another important concern in addition to the computation speed and accuracy, and it is affected by two optimization variables, the block size and bit length, as well as the hardware device type. Overall, large-scale devices dissipate more power, and they are needed to accommodate large block sizes and long bit lengths, which add more to the power dissipation. The power dissipation of FPGA devices is composed of dynamic power dissipation, static power and I/O power, with the first two terms as the main components. To assist the DNN implementations, the power dissipation is measured with several typical combinations of block sizes and bit lengths.

# 4 EXPERIMENTAL RESULTS

The HSIM-DNN design is tested for each module in DNN implementations in the Altera Cyclone V GT FPGA development kit, to validate the accuracy, compression ratio and power performance of the simulator. The training and inference of HSIM-DNN adopt the representative benchmarks MNIST and CIFAR-10. The effects of varying the block size and bit length are compared between the proposed simulator and the original uncompressed DNN models based on the software framework Caffe.

## 4.1 Results of MNIST and CIFAR-10 Datasets

Table 1 displays the accuracy and compression ratio of designed with different block sizes, with the integral bit length fixed at 8 and the fractional bit length fixed at 12. The compression ratios are obtained by comparing with the uncompressed DNN models in software with 64-bit floating-point data. The degradation in accuracy and increase of compression ratio can be observed as the block size increases. Specifically, compression for the block size of 32 is around 100× with accuracy degradation of 1.6%.

Table 2 describes the accuracy and compression ratio when optimizing the bit length and fixing the block size at 64. Generally, increasing the bit length will improve the accuracy. Overflow can occur when the integral bits are not enough, e.g., when the bit length is (6, 8), accompanied by a low accuracy. The low accuracy with bit length (7, 4) originates from the low fractional precision with 4 bits.

**Table 1: Comparison on various block sizes for MNIST**

| Block Size | Accuracy | Compression Ratio |
|---|---|---|
| 1 | 97.9% | 3.2 |
| 32 | 96.3% | 98.9 |
| 64 | 95.2% | 191.0 |
| 128 | 93.3% | 357.5 |
| 256 | 92.1% | 633.8 |

**Table 2: Comparison on various bit lengths for MNIST**

| Integral Bits + Fractional Bits | Accuracy | Compression Ratio |
|---|---|---|
| (6, 8) (overflow) | 91.5% | 272.8 |
| (7, 4) | 77.8% | 347.3 |
| (7, 5) | 94.4% | 318.4 |
| (7, 8) | 95.0% | 254.7 |
| (7, 10) | 95.1% | 224.7 |
| (8, 10) | 95.1% | 212.2 |
| (8, 12) | 95.2% | 191.0 |

Furthermore, the storage space for weights can be reduced by using less bits to represent weights in storage. Table 3 shows that 15 bits in computation can be reduced to 8 bits in storage with slight accuracy degradation.

**Table 3: Accuracy for storage with less bits**

| Bit Length for Computation | Bit Length for Storage | Accuracy | Compression Ratio |
|---|---|---|---|
| (6, 6) (overflow) | (5,3) | 92.0% | 381.0 |
| (6, 8) (overflow) | (5,3) | 91.2% | 444.5 |
| (7, 8) | (5,3) | 94.4% | 476.3 |

The results from CIFAR-10 dataset with different bit lengths and fixed block size of 128 are given in Table 4. Longer bit length also results in better accuracy.

**Table 4: Comparison on various bit lengths for CIFAR-10**

| Integral Bits + Fractional Bits | Accuracy | Compression Ratio |
|---|---|---|
| (4, 8) | 77.8% | 453.3 |
| (5, 8) | 78.0% | 378.5 |
| (5, 10) | 80.2% | 317.7 |
| (5, 11) | 80.5% | 287.5 |

## 4.2 Results of Power Measuring

The power data of DNN hardware implementations are obtained from tests on the same Cyclone V FPGA device, with the dataset CIFAR-10 as the benchmark. This process can be generalized to different datasets on various platforms. The Cyclone V devices dissipate much less static power than other Altera devices like Stratix V, which helps to implement DNN applications with low power consumption. The power measuring results with varying block sizes and bit lengths are described in Table 5. Without loss of generality, the integral bit length is fixed at 4, and the fractional bit length changes from 6 to 9, as the accuracy and power performance are more sensitive to the fractional part.

**Table 5: Power Comparison on various block sizes and bit lengths for CIFAR-10 (Unit: mW)**

| Bit Length \ Block Size | 32 | 64 | 128 |
|---|---|---|---|
| (4, 6) | 1103.07 | 1322.59 | 1899.50 |
| (4, 7) | 1180.63 | 1494.39 | 2158.22 |
| (4, 8) | 1244.73 | 1640.22 | 2347.46 |
| (4, 9) | 1289.36 | 1739.61 | n/a |
| (4, 10) | 1328.70 | 1845.50 | n/a |

The total power dissipation of the Cyclone V device can be approximated as

$$P_{tot} = 0.1647 + 0.06064 \cdot t + 9.294 \times 10^{-4} \cdot s \cdot t \quad (9)$$

where $s$ is the block size and $t$ the total bit length of integral bits plus fractional bits. The last term of this equation implies the correlation of the block size and the bit length. If one of the two variables is fixed at some value, the total power will grow almost linearly with the other variable.

# 5 CONCLUSION

This work implements a hardware simulator HSIM-DNN that visualizes the exact behavior of DNN hardware implementations on a software platform to facilitate the corresponding block-circulant matrix-based approach in terms of acceleration and compression for both training and inference phases. Simultaneously, the proposed simulator provides the hardware power data to help predict the power consumption under different parameter settings, thus creating excellent insights for more energy-efficient DNN implementations on embedded platforms. Real FPGA hardware implementations validate the whole design.

# ACKNOWLEDGMENTS

This work is supported by the National Science Foundation CCF-1733701.

# REFERENCES


[1] Sourav Bhattacharya and Nicholas D Lane. 2016. From smart to deep: Robust activity recognition on smartwatches using deep learning. In *Proceedings of the IEEE International Conference on Pervasive Computing and Communication Workshops (PerCom Workshops)*. 1–6.

[2] Dario Bini and Victor Y Pan. 2012. *Polynomial and Matrix Computations: Fundamental Algorithms*. Springer Science & Business Media.

[3] Tianshi Chen, Zidong Du, Ninghui Sun, Jia Wang, Chengyong Wu, Yunji Chen, and Olivier Temam. 2014. Diannao: A small-footprint high-throughput accelerator for ubiquitous machine-learning. *ACM Sigplan Notices* 49, 4 (2014), 269–284.

[4] Yunji Chen, Tao Luo, Shaoli Liu, Shijin Zhang, Liqiang He, Jia Wang, Ling Li, Tianshi Chen, Zhiwei Xu, Ninghui Sun, et al. 2014. DaDianNao: A Machine-Learning Supercomputer. In *Proceedings of the 47th Annual IEEE/ACM International Symposium on Microarchitecture*. 609–622.

[5] Yu-Hsin Chen, Tushar Krishna, Joel S Emer, and Vivienne Sze. 2017. Eyeriss: An Energy-Efficient Reconfigurable Accelerator for Deep Convolutional Neural Networks. *IEEE Journal of Solid-State Circuits* 52, 1 (2017), 127–138.

[6] Yu Cheng, Felix X Yu, Rogerio S Feris, Sanjiv Kumar, Alok Choudhary, and Shi-Fu Chang. 2015. An Exploration of Parameter Redundancy in Deep Networks with Circulant Projections. In *Proceedings of the IEEE International Conference on Computer Vision*. 2857–2865.

[7] Matthieu Courbariaux, Itay Hubara, Daniel Soudry, Ran El-Yaniv, and Yoshua Bengio. 2016. BinaryNet: Training Neural Networks with Weights and Activations Constrained to +1 or âĹŠ1. *CoRR* abs/1602.02830 (2016).

[8] Caiwen Ding, Siyu Liao, Yanzhi Wang, Zhe Li, Ning Liu, Youwei Zhuo, Chao Wang, Xuehai Qian, Yu Bai, Geng Yuan, et al. 2017. CirCNN: Accelerating and Compressing Deep Neural Networks Using Block-circulant Weight Matrices. In *Proceedings of the 50th Annual IEEE/ACM International Symposium on Microarchitecture*. 395–408.

[9] Steve K Esser, Rathinakumar Appuswamy, Paul Merolla, John V Arthur, and Dharmendra S Modha. 2015. Backpropagation for Energy-Efficient Neuromorphic Computing. In *Proceedings of Neural Information Processing Systems*. 1117–1125.

[10] Song Han, Xingyu Liu, Huizi Mao, Jing Pu, Ardavan Pedram, Mark A Horowitz, and William J Dally. 2016. EIE: Efficient Inference Engine on Compressed Deep Neural Network. In *Proceedings of the 43rd Annual International Symposium on Computer Architecture*. 243–254.

[11] Pu Zhao, Sijia Liu, Yanzhi Wang, and Xue Lin. 2018. An ADMM-Based Universal Framework for Adversarial Attacks on Deep Neural Networks. In *Proceedings of the 26th ACM International Conference on Multimedia*. 1065–1073.

[12] Song Han, Huizi Mao, and William J Dally. 2015. Deep Compression: Compressing Deep Neural Networks with Pruning, Trained Quantization and Huffman Coding. *CoRR* abs/1510.00149 (2015).

[13] Song Han, Jeff Pool, John Tran, and William Dally. 2015. Learning both Weights and Connections for Efficient Neural Networks. In *Proceedings of the 28th International Conference on Neural Information Processing Systems*. 1135–1143.

[14] Geoffrey Hinton, Li Deng, Dong Yu, George E Dahl, Abdel-rahman Mohamed, Navdeep Jaitly, Andrew Senior, Vincent Vanhoucke, Patrick Nguyen, Tara N Sainath, et al. 2012. Deep Neural Networks for Acoustic Modeling in Speech Recognition: The Shared Views of Four Research Groups. *IEEE Signal Processing Magazine* 29, 6 (2012), 82–97.

[15] Max Jaderberg, Andrea Vedaldi, and Andrew Zisserman. 2014. Speeding up Convolutional Neural Networks with Low Rank Expansions. *CoRR* abs/1405.3866 (2014).

[16] Norman P Jouppi, Cliff Young, Nishant Patil, David Patterson, Gaurav Agrawal, Raminder Bajwa, Sarah Bates, Suresh Bhatia, Nan Boden, Al Borchers, et al. 2017. In-Datacenter Performance Analysis of a Tensor Processing Unit. In *Proceedings of the 44th Annual International Symposium on Computer Architecture*. 1–12.

[17] Patrick Judd, Jorge Albericio, Tayler Hetherington, Tor M Aamodt, and Andreas Moshovos. 2016. Stripes: Bit-serial deep neural network computing. In *Proceedings of the 49th Annual IEEE/ACM International Symposium on Microarchitecture*. 1–12.

[18] Alex Krizhevsky, Ilya Sutskever, and Geoffrey E Hinton. 2012. ImageNet Classification with Deep Convolutional Neural Networks. In *Advances in Neural Information Processing Systems*. 1097–1105.

[19] Yann LeCun, Léon Bottou, Yoshua Bengio, and Patrick Haffner. 1998. Gradient-based learning applied to document recognition. *Proc. IEEE* 86, 11 (1998), 2278–2324.

[20] He Li, Kaoru Ota, and Mianxiong Dong. 2018. Learning IoT in Edge: Deep Learning for the Internet of Things with Edge Computing. *IEEE Network* 32, 1 (2018), 96–101.

[21] Darryl Lin, Sachin Talathi, and Sreekanth Annapureddy. 2016. Fixed Point Quantization of Deep Convolutional Networks. In *Proceedings of the 33rd International Conference on International Conference on Machine Learning*. 2849–2858.

[22] Paul A Merolla, John V Arthur, Rodrigo Alvarez-Icaza, Andrew S Cassidy, Jun Sawada, Filipp Akopyan, Bryan L Jackson, Nabil Imam, Chen Guo, Yutaka Nakamura, et al. 2014. A million spiking-neuron integrated circuit with a scalable communication network and interface. *Science* 345, 6197 (2014), 668–673.

[23] Jiantao Qiu, Jie Wang, Song Yao, Kaiyuan Guo, Boxun Li, Erjin Zhou, Jincheng Yu, Tianqi Tang, Ningyi Xu, Sen Song, et al. 2016. Going Deeper with Embedded FPGA Platform for Convolutional Neural Network. In *Proceedings of the ACM/SIGDA International Symposium on Field-Programmable Gate Arrays*. 26–35.

[24] SourceForge. 2010. FFTW++: Fast Fourier Transform C++ Header/MPI Transpose for FFTW3. http://fftwpp.sourceforge.net/

[25] Cheng Tai, Tong Xiao, Yi Zhang, Xiaogang Wang, and Weinan E. 2015. Convolutional neural networks with low-rank regularization. *CoRR* abs/1511.06067 (2015).

[26] Jiaxiang Wu, Cong Leng, Yuhang Wang, Qinghao Hu, and Jian Cheng. 2016. Quantized Convolutional Neural Networks for Mobile Devices. In *Proceedings of the IEEE Conference on Computer Vision and Pattern Recognition*. 4820–4828.

[27] Chenzhuo Zhu, Song Han, Huizi Mao, and William J Dally. 2016. Trained Ternary Quantization. *CoRR* abs/1612.01064 (2016).

# An Area-Efficient Iterative Single-Precision Floating-Point Multiplier Architecture for FPGA

Sunwoong Kim
University of Illinois at Urbana-Champaign
Urbana, Illinois 61801 USA
sunwoong@illinois.edu

Rob A. Rutenbar
University of Pittsburgh
Pittsburgh, Pennsylvania 15260 USA
rutenbar@pitt.edu

## ABSTRACT

Approximate multipliers have been widely used in critical applications, such as machine learning and multimedia, which are tolerant to approximation errors. This paper proposes a novel single-precision floating-point (SPFP) multiplication algorithm and its architecture. The proposed work approximates only one of the operands to reduce the number of logic blocks and iteratively compensates the approximation error to achieve acceptable error ranges in applications. To reduce the accuracy degradation by the single operand approximation, a rounding scheme and an operand selection scheme are additionally introduced. Compared with the widely-known previous iterative Mitchell design, our proposed SPFP multiplier design decreases the numbers of look up tables (LUTs) and flip flops (FFs) by 55% and 59% respectively, and shows two cycles shorter latency. The accuracy of our design becomes close to that of the iterative Mitchell design as the number of iterations increases, and it always meets the error tolerance of 1% when the number of iterations is four.

## KEYWORDS

Approximate computing, floating-point multiplier, FPGA

**ACM Reference format:**
Sunwoong Kim and Rob A. Rutenbar. 2019. An Area-Efficient Iterative Single-Precision Floating-Point Multiplier Architecture for FPGA. In *Proceedings of Great Lakes Symposium on VLSI 2019, Tysons Corner, VA, USA, May 9–11, 2019 (GLSVLSI '19)*, 6 pages.
https://doi.org/10.1145/3299874.3318002

## 1 INTRODUCTION

Since floating-point (FP) arithmetic provides a wider dynamic range than fixed-point arithmetic, specific applications such as scientific computations often use FP operators. Even in machine learning applications where fixed-point numbers are widely used, training still requires much more precision [1]. Nevertheless, the FP operators have critical issues such as significant circuit area, long latency, and excessive power consumption. In general, FP multiplication is one of the most common and expensive arithmetic operations [2], [3].


ACM ISBN 978-1-4503-6252-8/19/05...$15.00
https://doi.org/10.1145/3299874.3318002

To alleviate the critical issues, *approximate multipliers* have been widely used in critical applications, such as machine learning and multimedia, which are tolerant to the approximation error [1]-[7]. The error tolerance is due to various reasons such as the imperfection of human sensory systems and data redundancy, and the approximation error often does not significantly impair the overall performance of the applications [4].

Typically, acceptable error ranges of each application is different, and therefore approximate multipliers with fixed accuracy have limitations [5]. To resolve this issue, multiplication algorithms that enable us to configure accuracy while trading for area, latency, and/or power consumption have been presented [2], [5], [6]. Zhang *et al.* apply Mitchell's algorithm [8] to the mantissa multiplication of FP numbers and design to configure the accuracy [5]. However, there are only two configuration modes, and the errors always occur due to Mitchell's algorithm. The configurable FP multiplier proposed by Imani *et al.* discards one of the input mantissas and directly uses the other when the discarded mantissa does not exceed a threshold [2]. However, when the discarded mantissa exceeds the threshold, the existing mantissa multiplication is still executed. Babic *et al.* present a multiplier architecture based on Mitchell's algorithm [6]. Since it iteratively compensates approximation errors using the same circuits, various accuracy levels are provided. However, the architecture is only for integer multiplication, and therefore an optimized architecture for FP numbers is still needed.

The main contributions of this paper are as follows:

- We present an iterative single-precision FP (SPFP) multiplier architecture where the appropriate tradeoff between accuracy and latency is configurable.
- We approximate only a single operand to reduce the number of logic blocks, and introduce novel rounding and operand selection schemes to reduce the accuracy degradation.

The rest of this paper is organized as follows: Section 2 reviews background for this paper. Our proposed iterative SPFP multiplier architecture is presented in Section 3 and evaluated in Section 4. Lastly, Section 5 concludes this paper.

## 2 BACKGROUND

In the IEEE 754 SPFP format [9], each number is represented by 32-bits, which is composed of 1-bit for sign, 8-bits for exponent, and 23-bits for mantissa. The mantissa has a hidden most significant bit that is always set to 1. An SPFP number $x$ is represented as follows:

$$x = \pm 1.m \times 2^{e-127},\ 0 \le m < 1 \tag{1}$$

where $m$ and $e$ represent mantissa and exponent, respectively.

Typically, conventional SPFP multipliers generate results in the following order: 1) Add exponents of two numbers and then subtract it by the bias that is 127; 2) Multiply mantissas; 3) Calculate the sign by XORing [10]. Since the second step accounts for the bulk of hardware resources, many studies have focused on approximation of the mantissa multiplication [3], [5], [11]. However, in general, the error generated by this approach increases exponentially as the number of truncated bits increases.

Mitchell's algorithm is in the family of logarithmic multiplication methods, which is advantageous in terms of accuracy compared with other approximate methods [8]. First, it calculates logarithms of two operands using (2).

$$\log_2 x = l + \log_2(1 + r) \tag{2}$$

where $l = \lfloor \log_2 x \rfloor$ and $r$ is a rational number satisfying $0 \leq r < 1$. The multiplication of two numbers is then represented using (3).

$$\begin{aligned} x_1 \cdot x_2 &= 2^{l_1+l_2} \cdot (1 + r_1) \cdot (1 + r_2) \\ &= 2^{l_1+l_2} \cdot (1 + r_1 + r_2 + r_1 \cdot r_2) \end{aligned} \tag{3}$$

To substitute the multiplication with a shift and additions, the term of $r_1 \cdot r_2$ is omitted from (3), and the multiplication is approximated as follows:

$$x_1 \cdot x_2 \approx \begin{cases} 2^{l_1+l_2} \cdot (1 + r_1 + r_2), & r_1 + r_2 < 1 \\ 2^{l_1+l_2+1} \cdot (r_1 + r_2), & r_1 + r_2 \geq 1 \end{cases} \tag{4}$$

When the discarded $r_1 \cdot r_2$ is large, Mitchell's algorithm produces a sizeable error. To reduce the error, an iterative scheme was proposed [6]. In this scheme, the multiplication is represented as follows:

$$\begin{aligned} x_1 \cdot x_2 &= (2^{l_1} + x_1^{[1]}) \cdot (2^{l_2} + x_2^{[1]}) \\ &= 2^{l_1+l_2} + 2^{l_1} \cdot x_2^{[1]} + 2^{l_2} \cdot x_1^{[1]} + x_1^{[1]} \cdot x_2^{[1]} \end{aligned} \tag{5}$$

where the number in square brackets represents the current iteration index and $x^{[1]} = x - 2^l$. During the first iteration, the first three terms of (5) compose the partial result $P_1(x_1 \cdot x_2)$ that is implemented using shifters and adders. During the second iteration, the last term of (5), which is the first iteration *error*, is approximated with the same way as follows:

$$x_1^{[1]} \cdot x_2^{[1]} = P_2(x_1 \cdot x_2) + x_1^{[2]} \cdot x_2^{[2]} \tag{6}$$

The approximate multiplication result up to the second iteration is the sum of $P_1(x_1 \cdot x_2)$ and $P_2(x_1 \cdot x_2)$. The generalized formula is shown in (7).

$$x_1 \cdot x_2 \approx \sum_{i=1}^{n} P_i(x_1 \cdot x_2) \tag{7}$$

As the number of iterations $n$ increases, the number of partial results increases and the error is reduced. Since it enables us to trade off latency against error on the same circuit, this scheme can be used efficiently in various applications.

Fig. 1 shows an architecture of the basic block for iterative integer multiplication [6]. The basic block is based on a 4-stage pipeline, and therefore generates a partial result after 4 cycles. It comprises 2 leading one detectors (LODs), 2 shifters, 3 adders, and other components. Note that the adders in the first stage can be implemented using XOR gates, so they are not counted. To accumulate the partial results, one more adder and register are required. Since Babic *et al.* only present the iterative multiplier architecture for integers [6], an architecture for SPFP numbers is proposed in this paper.

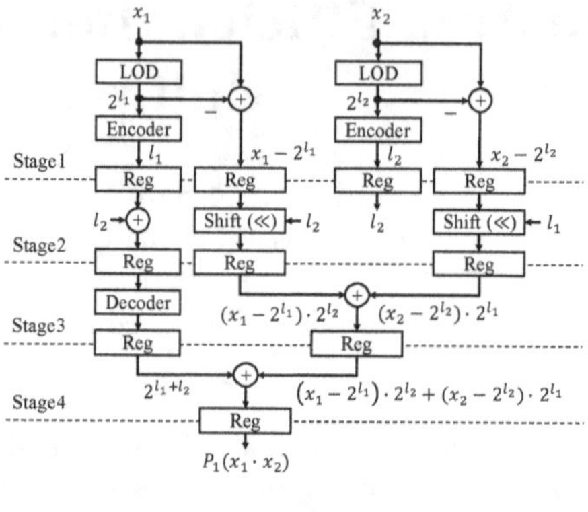


**Figure 1: Architecture of the iterative integer multiplier [6].**

**Algorithm 1: Approximate operand with a rounding scheme**

1 $error \leftarrow$ magn($x$) and $ap \leftarrow 0$
2 **for** $k = 1$ *to* $n$ **do**
3   **if** $error = 0$ **then**
4     Break
5   **else**
6     $f \leftarrow \lfloor \log_2|error| - \lfloor \log_2|error| \rfloor \rceil$
7     $l \leftarrow f \times \lceil \log_2|error| \rceil + (1 - f) \times \lfloor \log_2|error| \rfloor$
8     **if** $error < 0$ **then**
9       $error \leftarrow error + 2^l$
10       $ap \leftarrow ap - 2^l$
11     **else**
12       $error \leftarrow error - 2^l$
13       $ap \leftarrow ap + 2^l$
14     **end**
15   **end**
16 **end**
17 AP$_n(x) \leftarrow$ sign($x$) $\times$ $ap$

# 3 ITERATIVE SPFP MULTIPLIER

This section proposes a novel iterative SPFP multiplication algorithm and its architecture.

## 3.1 Rounding Scheme

The most intuitive scheme (we call it a *baseline*) is to iteratively add power-of-two numbers that are the closest to and less than an error ($= x_1 \cdot x_2 - \sum P_i(x_1 \cdot x_2)$). When the number of iterations is $n$, the shift amount $l_n(\cdot)$ and the approximate value on input $x$ are calculated using (8) and (9), respectively.

$$l_n(x) = \lfloor \log_2(|x| - \sum_{i=1}^{n} 2^{l_{i-1}(x)}) \rfloor \tag{8}$$

$$\text{AP}_n(x) = \text{sign}(x) \times \sum_{i=1}^{n} 2^{l_i(x)} \tag{9}$$

In (8), the initial $2^{l_0(x)}$ is 0. Even though the errors are compensated by this scheme, their values are still large. To reduce these errors, we propose a rounding scheme, which is shown in Algorithm 1. First of all, a fraction of $\log_2|error|$ is calculated (line 6). If its round number $f$ is 1, a shift amount is set to $\lceil \log_2|error| \rceil$. Otherwise,

**Table 1: Approximation example of SPFP number 0.4656868***

| $n$ | $f_n(x)$ | $l_n(x)$ | $t_n(x)$ | $z_n(x)+1$ | Normalization | | | $AP_n(x)$ |
|---|---|---|---|---|---|---|---|---|
| | | | | | $m_{n+1}(x)$ | $e_{n+1}(x)$ | Next $\lvert error\rvert$ | |
| 1 | 1 | $125-126=-1$ | $(0).00\mathbf{1}0001100\ldots1_2$ | 3 | $(1).0001100\ldots0_2$ | $125-3=122$ | 0.03431320 | 0.50000000 |
| 2 | 0 | $122-127=-5$ | $(0).000\mathbf{1}100\ldots0_2$ | 4 | $(1).100\ldots0_2$ | $122-4=118$ | 0.00306320 | 0.46875000 |
| 3 | 1 | $118-126=-8$ | $(0).0\mathbf{1}1\ldots1_2$ | 2 | $(1).1\ldots0_2$ | $118-2=116$ | 0.00084305 | 0.46484375 |

* $e_1(0.4656868) = 125$ and $m_1(0.4656868) = (1).11011100110111010000000_2$

$\lfloor \log_2 |error| \rfloor$ is used for the shift amount (line 7). In (8), the error $(= |x| - \sum 2^{l_{i-1}(x)})$ is always zero or a positive number. However, the error in Algorithm 1 can be a negative number as well. Therefore, the error and the intermediate approximate value *ap* are updated differently from the baseline. Specifically, if the error is a negative (positive) number, the error is added (subtracted) by $2^l$ and *ap* is subtracted (added) by $2^l$ (lines 8-14). After all iterations, the output value is calculated by multiplying *ap* and the sign of $x$ (line 17).

The proposed approximate algorithm processes SPFP numbers represented by the IEEE 754 SPFP format [9], which makes the architecture different from that for integer numbers. First of all, we propose a scheme to efficiently calculate the $f$ in Algorithm 1. The integer portion of binary logarithm is only related to the exponent of an FP argument. On the other hand, the fractional portion is influenced by the mantissa. Therefore, we can know whether the fractional part of $\log_2 |error|$ in Algorithm 1 is larger than or equal to 0.5 using the mantissa. As an argument increases, its binary logarithm increases. In addition, the argument satisfying that its binary logarithm is 0.5 is $\sqrt{2}$, and the mantissa of $\sqrt{2}$ is $(1).0110...11_2$. Therefore, when the mantissa of an FP number is larger than or equal to $(1).0110...11_2$, $f$ is set to 1. To make the circuit simpler, we use $(1).1000 \ldots 00_2$ instead of the $(1).0110 \ldots 11_2$, which means that the 22nd bit from the least significant bit of the mantissa is used as $f$. The approximate $f$ has little effect on accuracy.

As shown in Algorithm 1, rounding-up occurs when $f$ is 1. In this case, $l$ is increased by 1 and the absolute value of the next error is not $|error| - 2^l$ but $2^l - |error|$. In other words, $l$ and the next error are calculated differently depending on the $f$ value. When $f_n(x)$ represents the $f$ for an SPFP input $x$ and the iteration number $n$, a shift amount is calculated using (10).

$$l_n(x) = \begin{cases} e_n(x) - 127, & \text{if } f_n(x) = 0 \\ e_n(x) - 126, & \text{otherwise} \end{cases} \quad (10)$$

where $e_n(x)$ represents the exponent during the $n$-th iteration. Suppose that $m_n(x)$ represents the mantissa during the $n$-th iteration, and $t_n(x)$ refers to the mantissa of the difference between the error and $2^{l_n(x)}$ before normalization. If $f_n(x)$ is 0, $t_n(x)$ is set to $m_n(x)$ except that the hidden bit becomes zero (see the third row of Table 1). On the other hand, if $f_n(x)$ is 1, $t_n(x)$ is set to $-m_n(x)$ (see the second and fourth rows of Table 1). Note that $-m_n(x)$ is approximately implemented using a complement operator in this paper. The update (or normalization) processes for mantissa and exponent are shown in (11) and (12), respectively.

$$m_{n+1}(x) = t_n(x) \times 2^{(z_n(x)+1)} \quad (11)$$

$$e_{n+1}(x) = e_n(x) - (z_n(x) + 1) \quad (12)$$

where $z_n(x)$ refers to the number of bit 0s before the first bit 1 appears in $t_n(x)$. Since the hidden bit of $t_n(x)$ is always zero, the mantissa and exponent are normalized using "$z_n(x) + 1$".

Table 1 shows an approximation example for the SPFP number 0.4656868. In this table, binary numbers are represented by subscripts. The initial $e_1(0.4656868)$ and $m_1(0.4656868)$ values are 125 and $(1).11011100110111010000000_2$, respectively. Since $f_1(0.4656868)$ is 1, $l_1(0.4656868)$ is calculated as -1 using (10). The first bit 1, represented in bold, appears at the 20th bit of $t_1(0.4656868)$, $z_1(0.4656868)$ is set to 2. Using (11) and (12), $m_2(0.4656868)$ and $e_2(0.4656868)$ are set to $(1).0001100...0_2$ and 122, respectively. During the second iteration, $l_2(0.4656868)$ is calculated as -5. Meanwhile, $z_2(0.4656868)$ is set to 3 because the first bit 1 appears at the 19th bit of $t_2(0.4656868)$. Consequently, $m_3(0.4656868)$ and $e_3(0.4656868)$ are set to $(1).100...0_2$ and 118, respectively. The $e_3(0.4656868)$ sets $l_3(0.4656868)$ to -8. After the iteration number of 3, the SPFP number of 0.4656868 is approximated to 0.46484375 $(= 2^{-1} - 2^{-5} - 2^{-8})$. Note that the baseline approximates 0.4656868 to 0.4375 $(= 2^{-2} + 2^{-3} + 2^{-4})$.

## 3.2 Operand Selection Scheme

Since our multiplier approximates only a *single* operand, its architecture is simpler than the iterative Mitchell. On the other hand, it cannot beat the iterative Mitchell in accuracy because one more term in (5) is basically omitted. However, the accuracy degradation can be reduced by *choosing* the operand that has lesser approximation error.

If our rounding scheme is not used, it is easy to calculate the error because $n-1$ ones in the mantissa always survive (e.g., the mantissa of the approximated 0.4375, presented in the previous section, is $(1).110...0_2$ and the error starts from the third one of $(1).110\mathbf{1110011011101}0...0_2$). However, when our rounding scheme is applied, it is hard to know how many ones survive in advance (e.g., the mantissa of the approximated 0.46484375 is $(1).1101110...0_2$), which makes the error prediction difficult.

To resolve this issue, regular bit-patterns in the mantissa are analyzed and utilized in the proposed design. Table 2 shows the mantissa prediction table when $n$ is three. In the second column, RD and RU are abbreviations of rounding-up and rounding-down, respectively, and G*i* represents the *i*-th group of successive 1s. In the third and fourth columns, "0..." and "1..." represent successive 0s and 1s respectively, and $*$ refers to the remaining bits (don't-care term). There are four bit-patterns checked in this table: 010, 011, 101, and 100. As explained in the previous section, bits in the mantissa $t_n$ are flipped when rounding-up occurs. If the bits are flipped an even number of times, the next 010 or 011 pattern is searched. The middle 1 of the pattern becomes a hidden bit and the next bit is used as the next $f$ after normalization. On the other hand, if the bits are flipped

**Table 2: Mantissa prediction table when $n$ is three**

| $(f_1, f_2, f_3)$ | Function | Input mantissa | Output mantissa |
|---|---|---|---|
| (0, 0, 0) | RD @G3 | (1).0...010...010∗$_2$ | (1).0...010...010...0$_2$ |
| (0, 0, 1) | RU @G2 | (1).0...010...011∗$_2$ | (1).0...010...100...0$_2$ |
| (0, 1, 0) | RU @G2 | (1).0...011...101∗$_2$ | (1).0...011...110...0$_2$ |
| (0, 1, 1) | RD @G2 | (1).0...011...100∗$_2$ | (1).0...011...100...0$_2$ |
| (1, 0, 0) | RU @G3 | (1).1...101...101∗$_2$ | (1).1...101...110...0$_2$ |
| (1, 0, 1) | RD @G3 | (1).1...101...100∗$_2$ | (1).1...101...100...0$_2$ |
| (1, 1, 0) | RD @G3 | (1).1...100...010∗$_2$ | (1).1...100...010...0$_2$ |
| (1, 1, 1) | RU @G2 | (1).1...100...011∗$_2$ | (1).1...100...100...0$_2$ |

| | Ex1. Mantissa of 0.4656868 | Ex2. Mantissa of 0.3361206 |
|---|---|---|
| Input mantissa: | (1).1**1011100**1101110100000000 | (1).**0101100**0000110000000000 |
| | G1 G2 G3 G4 G5 | G1G2 G3 |
| | ↓ Rounding-down | ↓ Rounding-up |
| Output mantissa: | (1).11011100000000000000000 | (1).01100000000000000000000 |
| \|Error\|: | (0).00000000110111010000000 < | (0).00000111110100000000000 |

**Figure 2: Example of mantissa prediction on two operands.**

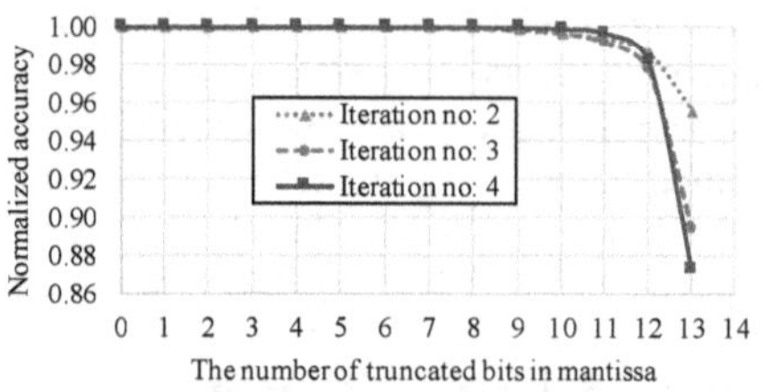


**Figure 3: Normalized accuracy depending on the number of truncated bits in mantissa.**

an odd number of times, 101 or 100 pattern is searched because a bit-flip changes 010 and 011 into 101 and 100, respectively. Fig. 2 shows an example of the mantissa prediction on two operands using Table 2. The mantissa of 0.4656868 satisfies the seventh row of Table 2, and the output mantissa is (1).1101110...0$_2$, which is the same result of Table 1. On the other hand, the mantissa of 0.3361206 satisfies the third row of Table 2, and the output mantissa is (1).0110...0$_2$. Since the absolute value of the error of 0.4656868 is smaller than that of 0.3361206, 0.4656868 is selected as the operand to approximate. Note that the error of 0.3361206 is smaller than that of 0.4656868 in the baseline, which makes the opposite selection result.

This operand selection scheme assures the almost-optimal result but requires rather many logic blocks and a long path delay. Especially, it needs multiple mantissa prediction tables for each iteration number because functions (and output mantissas) of the tables are different. To alleviate the hardware-related issue, two additional sub-schemes are proposed. First, only a *single* type of table is deployed while sacrificing accuracy. In our design, a prediction table for $n$ of 2 is empirically chosen. The details are explained in Section 4.1. Second, mantissas of input operands are truncated, which affects the number of logic blocks and the critical path delay of the entire design as well. Fig. 3 shows normalized accuracy depending on the number of truncated bits. The normalized accuracy

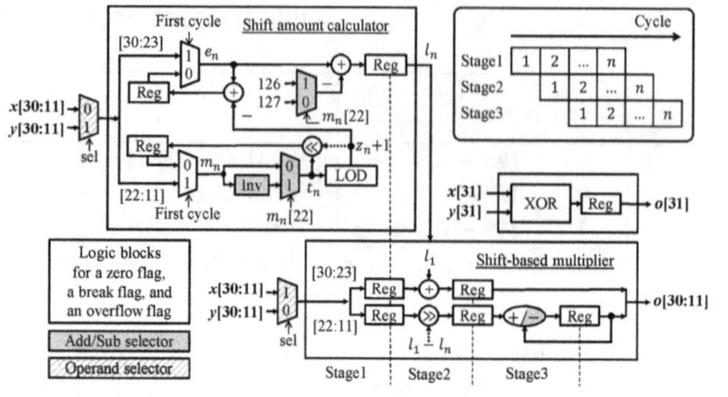


**Figure 4: Overall architecture of our SPFP multiplier.**

is calculated as the ratio of multiplications satisfying error < 0.1% with truncation to that without truncation. Since the normalized accuracy is larger than 0.99 until an 11-bit truncation, our design truncates the least significant 11-bits of two input operands from the beginning. To further reduce the number of logic blocks and the path delay, the least significant 5-bits of input mantissas for the prediction table are additionally truncated (the most significant 7-bits of input mantissas are used for prediction), which sacrifices the prediction accuracy. The details are described in Section 4.1.

## 3.3 Overall Architecture

Fig. 4 shows the overall architecture of our iterative SPFP multiplier where blocks represented by grey color and diagonal lines refer to additional logic blocks for the proposed rounding scheme and operand selection scheme, respectively. The detailed logic blocks for a *zero* flag (when input operand(s) is(are) zero), a *break* flag (when the intermediate mantissa becomes zero), and an *overflow* flag (when an overflow occurs in the adder/subtractor; the exponent increases or decreases by 1 and the mantissa is additionally right- or left-shifted by 1) are omitted for the sake of simplicity. The proposed architecture is based on a 3-stage pipeline. In Stage1, the sign bit is simply calculated using an XOR gate and stored in a register. In addition, the operand to approximate is chosen by the operand selector. The shift amount calculator generates $l$ values of the selected operand using (10), (11), and (12). In the shift-based multiplier, the exponent and mantissa of the other operand are stored in registers. In Stage2, the shift-based multiplier calculates the exponent and mantissa corresponding the $l$ values. As the number of iterations increases, the number multiplied by $2^l$ has a smaller exponent. Since mantissas are aligned based on the mantissa with the largest exponent, the first $l_1$ value is only added to the exponent and the mantissa is aligned by a shifter with the shift amount of "$l_1 - l_n$". In Stage3, the shifted mantissa is added to or subtracted from the accumulated mantissa by an integer adder/subtractor. A selecting signal for the adder/subtractor is generated in the add/sub selector, and it is reset to 0 (Add) and flipped whenever $f_n(x)$ is 1.

For example, to calculate 0.4656868×0.3361206 with the iteration number of 3, 0.4656868, which is selected as shown in Fig. 2, generates $l$ values of -1, -5, and -8 in the shift amount calculator (see the third column of Table 1). The numbers of 0.3361206, shifted by the $l$ values in the shift-based multiplier, are 0.1680603, 0.01050376875, and 0.00131297109375, respectively. To match the exponents of

**Table 3: Accuracy comparison of previous and proposed SPFP approximate multipliers with 200 million inputs**

| *n* | Algorithm | Correct (%) | | | | |
|---|---|---|---|---|---|---|
| | | Error < 0.1% | Error < 0.5% | Error < 1.0% | Error < 5.0% | Error < 10.0% |
| 1 | Mitchell [8] | 0.99 | 4.17 | 7.69 | 31.22 | 56.25 |
| 2 | Iterative Mitchell [6] | 19.14 | 47.37 | 65.13 | 99.13 | 100.00 |
| | Proposed BASE | 1.20 | 4.80 | 8.62 | 32.24 | 55.56 |
| | Proposed BASE+RND | 4.97 | 17.70 | 29.46 | 79.32 | 100.00 |
| | **Proposed BASE+RND+TRNC+SEL** | **9.30** | **32.12** | **50.01** | **95.58** | **100.00** |
| 3 | Iterative Mitchell [6] | 70.52 | 95.52 | 99.43 | 100.00 | 100.00 |
| | Proposed BASE | 6.36 | 19.79 | 31.06 | 75.00 | 94.45 |
| | Proposed BASE+RND | 28.92 | 65.89 | 84.72 | 100.00 | 100.00 |
| | **Proposed BASE+RND+TRNC+SEL** | **43.94** | **83.01** | **95.03** | **100.00** | **100.00** |
| 4 | Iterative Mitchell [6] | 98.03 | 100.00 | 100.00 | 100.00 | 100.00 |
| | Proposed BASE | 20.19 | 47.57 | 64.17 | 97.37 | 100.00 |
| | Proposed BASE+RND | 74.00 | 99.25 | 100.00 | 100.00 | 100.00 |
| | **Proposed BASE+RND+TRNC+SEL** | **86.69** | **99.81** | **100.00** | **100.00** | **100.00** |

Error (%) = 100 × |ideal result − approximate result| / ideal result
BASE: Baseline, RND: Rounding scheme, TRNC: Truncation, SEL: Operand selection scheme

these three numbers to 124 that is the biggest value among them, mantissas of 0.01050376875 and 0.00131297109375 are right-shifted by 4 (= (−1) − (−5)) and 7 (= (−1) − (−8)), respectively. Then, the shifted mantissas are added to or subtracted from the accumulated value depending on the selecting signal.

## 4 EVALUATION

This section evaluates the proposed iterative SPFP multiplier in terms of accuracy, and offers experimental results of hardware implementation on an FPGA.

### 4.1 Accuracy

Accuracy of the previous and proposed SPFP approximate multipliers is compared in Table 3. For evaluation, 200 million multiplications on random SPFP numbers between 0 and 1 are executed as presented in [5]. Rows represent different multiplication algorithms; columns show the percentage of these 200 million multiplications accurate within the specified tolerance (denoted as Correct (%)) as presented in [6]. We compare against the conventional Mitchell [8] and the iterative Mitchell [6] in this experiment. Originally, the iterative Mitchell is designed for integers, but extended to an SPFP multiplier in this section. There are three proposed designs in Table 3: baseline (denoted as BASE), baseline with the rounding scheme (denoted as RND), and baseline with the rounding scheme and the operand selection scheme (denoted as SEL) where input mantissas are truncated by 11-bits (denoted as TRNC). As shown in the second row, the conventional Mitchell shows low accuracy. On the other hand, the iterative Mitchell algorithm significantly improves the accuracy as the number of iterations increases. As shown in the fifth, ninth, and thirteenth rows, our rounding scheme significantly improves the accuracy compared with when it is not applied. Our operand selection scheme further enhances the accuracy. Specifically, the rates satisfying Error < 0.1% of which iteration numbers are 2, 3, and 4 are increased by 87%, 52%, and 17%, respectively.

Table 4 shows experimental results to select the type and input bit-width of the prediction table. The third, fourth, and fifth columns of this table show prediction accuracy compared to the optimal selection. The last three columns present the correct percentage satisfying Error < 0.5%. As represented by underlines, using their own prediction table and 12-bit input shows the best prediction accuracy. When a single prediction table is used and an additional truncation to this table is applied, using the prediction table with *n* of 2 and 5-bit truncation shows reasonable results in general. Therefore, we choose them in the proposed design.

**Table 4: Prediction accuracy and correct percentage (Error < 0.5%) depending on the type and size of the prediction table**

| | Input size | Pred. accuracy (%) | | | Correct (%) | | |
|---|---|---|---|---|---|---|---|
| | | *n* = 2 | *n* = 3 | *n* = 4 | *n* = 2 | *n* = 3 | *n* = 4 |
| **Pred. Table (*n*=2)** | 12 | 95.28 | 79.63 | 77.09 | 32.16 | 83.01 | 99.81 |
| | 8 | 95.14 | 79.57 | 77.05 | 32.16 | 83.01 | 99.81 |
| | **7** | **94.77** | **79.38** | **76.96** | **32.12** | **83.01** | **99.81** |
| | 6 | 93.64 | 78.70 | 76.65 | 31.36 | 83.01 | 99.81 |
| Pred. Table (*n*=3) | 12 | 79.70 | 95.77 | 82.68 | 30.68 | 88.13 | 99.90 |
| | 8 | 75.20 | 91.99 | 81.74 | 27.22 | 88.13 | 99.90 |
| | 7 | 69.45 | 85.69 | 78.63 | 23.55 | 87.91 | 99.90 |
| | 6 | 60.11 | 74.15 | 72.63 | 20.00 | 82.31 | 99.90 |
| Pred. Table (*n*=4) | 12 | 73.59 | 82.63 | 90.81 | 28.98 | 83.90 | 99.99 |
| | 8 | 55.75 | 58.36 | 72.12 | 19.18 | 71.66 | 99.99 |
| | 7 | 50.49 | 52.24 | 62.57 | 17.95 | 66.55 | 99.92 |
| | 6 | 50.16 | 51.87 | 59.15 | 17.68 | 66.04 | 99.24 |

### 4.2 Hardware Implementation Results

Table 5 compares hardware implementation results of the iterative Mitchell [6] and the proposed multipliers (BASE, BASE+RND, BASE+RND+TRNC, and BASE+RND+TRNC+SEL). As described in Section 4.1, the iterative Mitchell is extended to an SPFP multiplier. Its architecture is similar to ours. However, the number of shift amount calculators is two (2 LODs and 2 shifters for the mantissa). In addition, the shift-based multiplier has 5-stages: Stage1 to wait

**Table 5: FPGA (Virtex UltraScale) implementation results**

| | Iterative | Proposed | | | |
|---|---|---|---|---|---|
| | Mitchell [6] | BASE | +RND | +TRNC | +SEL |
| No. LOD(s) | 2 | 1 | 1 | 1 | **1** |
| No. Adder(s) | 2 | 1 | 1 | 1 | **1** |
| No. Shifters | 5 | 2 | 2 | 2 | **2** |
| $f_{max}$ (MHz) | 450 | 510 | 440 | 560 | **500** |
| LUT | 685 | 317 | 397 | 237 | **308** |
| FF | 241 | 142 | 144 | 100 | **100** |
| Latency | $n$+4 | $n$+2 | $n$+2 | $n$+2 | $n$+2 |

for shift amounts; Stage2 to calculate the second and third terms of (5), which requires 2 shifters for the mantissa; Stage3 to sum up the two terms (1 adder for the mantissa); Stage4 to normalize the sum to the first term (1 shifter for the mantissa); and Stage5 to accumulate the final output (1 adder for the mantissa).

All previous and proposed designs are implemented in Verilog HDL, and synthesized and placed-and-routed using Xilinx Vivado Design Suite (2016.4). The target device is Xilinx Virtex UltraScale FPGA (xcvu190-flgc2104-2-e) that has 1,074,240 look up tables (LUTs) and 2,148,480 flip flops (FFs). As shown in the second, third, and fourth rows, our proposed designs use one fewer LOD and adder for the mantissa, and three fewer shifters for the mantissa than the iterative Mitchell. The fifth, sixth, and seventh rows present the maximum frequency, the numbers of LUTs and FFs, respectively. Compared with the iterative Mitchell, our proposed design with the rounding scheme decreases the numbers of LUTs and FFs by about 42% and 40% at the similar frequency, respectively. As shown in the fourth and fifth columns, the 11-bit truncation increases the maximum frequency from 440MHz to 560MHz, and reduces the numbers of LUTs and FFs by 40% and 31%, respectively. The operand selector for higher accuracy re-increases the critical path delay and the number of LUTs and FFs. However, compared to the iterative Mitchell, the maximum frequency is 50MHz higher, which assures a higher throughput, and our design uses only 45% of LUTs and 41% of FFs. The eighth row of Table 5 shows the latency. Since all designs in Table 5 are based on iteration, they can trade off latency against accuracy without changing logic blocks. The latency of our proposed design is two cycles shorter than that of the iterative Mitchell. Note that the truncation scheme is not used in the original iterative Mitchell. However, applying the 11-bit truncation reduces the number of LUTs and FFs. For example, assuming that its hardware resources are reduced at the same rate as our design, it uses 409 LUTs and 167 FFs, which means that it needs 33% more LUTs, 67% more FFs, and two cycles longer latency than our work (BASE+RND+TRNC+SEL).

Our design shows lower accuracy than the iterative Mitchell. However, in applications which have a long interval of input data (e.g., 4 cycles), we can reduce the difference in accuracy by increasing the number of iterations while having the better hardware properties. Fig. 5 shows normalized accuracy, latency, and hardware resource comparison when $n$ values are 2, 3, and 4. Since the normalized rates of LUT and FF are not changed, they are only presented in Fig. 5(c). The normalized correct percentages satisfying Errors < 0.5% of our design becomes close to that of the iterative

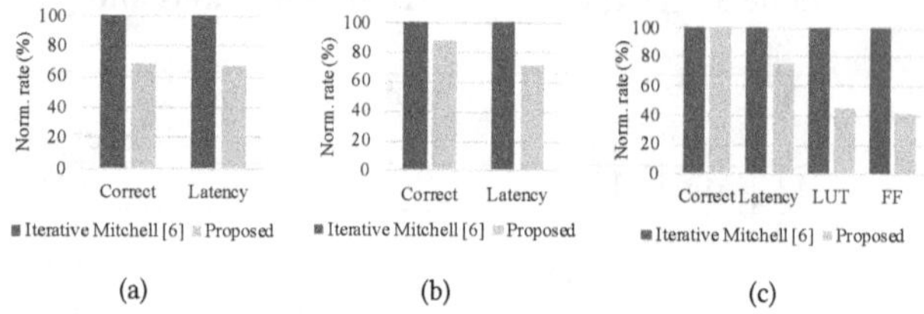


**Figure 5: Normalized accuracy (Error < 0.5%), latency, and hardware resource comparison. (a) $n$ is 2, (b) $n$ is 3, (c) $n$ is 4.**

Mitchell as the $n$ value increases while our design only uses about 43% of the hardware resources and shows about 71% of the latency.

## 5 CONCLUSION

This paper proposes an area-efficient SPFP multiplier architecture that can trade off accuracy against latency. We did not consider using digital signal processing (DSP) slices in this paper. Typically, the number of DSP slices is much more limited than those of LUTs and FFs on FPGAs. In systems where an extremely large number of multipliers are needed or other operators exploit DSP slices, a design only using LUTs and FFs is useful. Compared with the Xilinx LogiCore IP block for an SPFP multiplier [12], our design reduces the numbers of LUTs and FFs by 46% and 81%, respectively, and improves the maximum frequency by 19% when the pipeline depth of the LogiCore block is five and DSP slices are not utilized. Of course, this comparison is not completely fair because the LogiCore block is not an approximate and iterative design. Nevertheless, it implies that our design can be efficiently utilized in some applications where hardware resources are limited and approximation errors are tolerated. In future work, we hope to apply our iterative multiplier to applications that can be improved when the iteration number is allowed to be adaptively adjusted.

## REFERENCES

[1] M. S. Kim, A. A. Del Barrio, R. Hermida, and N. Bagherzadeh, "Low-Power Implementation of Mitchell's Approximate Logarithmic Multiplication for Convolutional Neural Networks," in *Proc. ASP-DAC*, Jan. 2018.

[2] M. Imani, D. Peroni, and T. Rosing, "CFPU: Configurable Floating Point Multiplier for Energy-Efficient Computing," in *Proc. DAC*, Jun. 2017.

[3] P. Yin, C. Wang, W. Liu, and F. Lombardi, "Design and Performance Evaluation of Approximate Floating-Point Multipliers," in *Proc. ISVLSI*, Jul. 2016.

[4] S. Hashemi, R. Iris Bahar, and S. Reda, "DRUM: A Dynamic Range Unbiased Multiplier for Approximate Applications," in *Proc. ICCAD*, Nov. 2015.

[5] H. Zhang, W. Zhang, and J. Lach, "A Low-Power Accuracy-Configurable Floating Point Multiplier," in *Proc. ICCD*, Dec. 2014.

[6] Z. Babic, A. Avramovic, and P. Bulic, "An Iterative Logarithmic Multiplier," *Elsevier Microprocessors and Microsystems*, vol. 35, no. 1, pp. 23-33, Feb. 2011.

[7] V. Sze, Y.-H. Chen, T.-J. Yang, and J. Emer, "Efficient Processing of Deep Neural Networks: A Tutorial and Survey," *Proceedings of the IEEE*, vol. 105, no. 12, pp. 2295-2329, Dec. 2017.

[8] J. N. Mitchell, "Computer Multiplication and Division Using Binary Logarithms," *IRE Trans. Electronic Computers*, vol. EC-11, no. 4, pp. 512-517, Aug. 1962.

[9] IEEE, "IEEE Standard for Floating-Point Arithmetic," *IEEE Std* 754-2008, pp. 1-58, Aug. 2008.

[10] M. Al-Ashrafy, A. Salem, and W. Anis, "An Efficient Implementation of Floating Point Multiplier," in *Proc. SIECPC*, Apr. 2011.

[11] J. Y. F. Tong, D. Nagle, and R. A. Rutenbar, "Reducing Power by Optimizing the Necessary Precision/Range of Floating-point Arithmetic," *IEEE Trans. Very Large Scale Integr. Syst.*, vol. 8, no. 3, pp. 273-286, Jun. 2000.

[12] Xilinx, "LogiCORE IP Floating-Point Operator v7.1 Product Guide (PG060)," [Online] https://www.xilinx.com/support/documentation/ip_documentation/floating_point/v7_1/pg060-floating-point.pdf.

# An Automatic Transistor-Level Tool for GRM FPGA Interconnect Circuits Optimization

Zhengjie Li, Yuanlong Xiao, Yufan Zhang, Yunbing Pang, Chengyu Hu, Jian Wang, Jinmei Lai*
State Key Lab of ASIC and System, School of Microelectronics
Fudan University , Shanghai, China
{18112020031, 14210720101, 17212020060, 17212020033, 15110720009, wjian, jmlai}@fudan.edu.cn

## ABSTRACT

Due to its dominance in FPGA area and delay, the interconnect circuit is traditionally designed and optimized in full customized fashion, which can be extremely time consuming. In this paper, we propose an automated transistor-level sizing optimization method for the widely-used General Routing Matrix FPGA interconnect circuits with the following three features: (1) an area model that takes into account the commonly used diffusion sharing, transistor folding and inputs sharing techniques in order to have an accurate area predication; (2) an accurate and effective non-linear delay model that treats the wire within a circuit and the wire between interconnect circuits separately; (3) a multi-thread acceleration method and the Minimum-Final-Delay algorithm to speed-up the simulation. The global optimization cost is measured by the product of the interconnect circuit area and the representative path delay based on our proposed models. The cost reduces 10.9%, when we use 65nm CMOS process chip for evaluation. The simulation time for different transistor sizing combinations is improved by 9X and 15X when 10 and 50 threads are used, respectively, faster than single-thread. Compared with the manual design method, our proposed optimization approach explores a larger design space and reduces the optimization time from months to hours.

## KEYWORDS

Transistor-Level Optimization; Area model; Wire load model; Minimum-Final-Delay Algorithm; Multi-thread acceleration

**ACM Reference format:**

Zhengjie Li, Yuanlong Xiao, Yufan Zhang, Yunbing Pang, Chengyu Hu, Jian Wang, Jinmei Lai. 2019. An Automatic Transistor-Level Tool for GRM FPGA Interconnect Circuits Optimization. In *Proceedings of 2019 Great Lakes Symposium on VLSI (GLSVLSI '19), May 9-11, 2019, Washington, D.C., USA. ACM, New York, NY, USA, 6 pages.* https://doi.org/10.1145/3299874.3318003.


*GLSVLSI '19*, May 9–11, 2019, Tysons Corner, VA, USA

ACM ISBN 978-1-4503-6252-8/19/05...$15.00
https://doi.org/10.1145/3299874.3318003

## 1 Introduction

A typical FPGA chip usually contains interconnect circuits, IOBs and logic block such as CLBs, BRAM, and DSP. Research result indicates that the interconnect circuit's area, power and delay contribute to more than 50% of total FPGA chip [1][2]. General Routing Matrix (GRM) interconnect is the prevalent architecture used by most state-of-the-art FPGA chips because it is diversified, flexible, and unified [3].

GRM interconnect circuits are often designed by full custom method, which is a time-consuming search type of process [2]. It may require months to obtain a high quality solution by iterative transistor sizing. The solution is often not optimal because only limited solution space will be explored. Finally, during this manual optimization process, it is hard to predict the overall area and delay of FPGA chip before the layout.

Therefore, a rich body of research efforts has been spent in automatic transistor sizing methodology for FPGA chip design [4-7], which we will survey in details in the next section. In this paper, we propose a transistor-level optimization method for GRM FPGA interconnect circuits design based on the popular COFFE algorithm [6].

We use an architecture description file to describe all FPGA resources (interconnect circuits and logic block) and their connections between each other. From this file, we get the netlist of all interconnect circuits and wire load. The our method will explore the transistor sizing to optimize the GRM FPGA interconnect circuit design with the area-delay produce as the optimization cost function.

The contributions of this paper are summarized as follows:

1. the input of our tool is FPGA architecture description file. From the file, we get the netlist to be optimized and wire load.

2. we have developed accurate and effective area model and wire load model for GRM FPGA which guide the optimization.

3. we have proposed a minimum-final-delay (MFD) algorithm for the optimization and a multi-thread acceleration method.

4. we have demonstrated the effectiveness of the proposed method on a fabricated FPGA chip using 65nm technology.

## 2 Related work and rationale of our approach

Automatic transistor sizing tool has been widely studied [4-7]. TILOS [4] treats the transistor sizing problem as a convex optimization problem and can terminate with a suboptimal solution. Kuon and Rose [5] enhance TILOS with a two-phase algorithm, which still suffers in accuracy because the linear model it uses. COFFE [6] transistor sizing algorithm uses two techniques, namely divide-and-conquer and inverter rise-fall balancing, to avoid using the linear model. Fpresso [7] is an architecture exploration tool which uses modified COFFE to build library. It is not suitable for transistor-level optimization.

We propose a Minimum-Final-Delay (MFD) algorithm instead of using COFFE's inverter rise-fall balancing technique for the following reason. Interconnect circuits use two-level MUX followed by two-stage buffer and level-restorer and sometimes an initial pull-up PMOS [3][8]. The signal gets weaker after passing the two-level NMOS. Thus it is not suitable to use inverter rise-fall balancing. We propose to optimize interconnect circuits as a whole, not separated parts. In this way, we can find minimum delay of interconnect circuit and decrease numbers of simulation.

The optimization objective in Kuon's and Rose's sizing tool is $Area^{b}Delay^{c}$ [5]. It optimizes along a representative path, which is the sum of delay of each subcircuit's delay multiplied by their weights. Similarly, our optimization goal is to minimize a global cost, which is the product of total area and delay. Through this way, we evaluate the FPGA interconnect circuits overall performance. In order to get accurate global cost value, we must provide accurate assessment of area and delay [5].

The minimum width transistor area model is widely used in FPGA research [2]. COFFE finds it is not accurate and improves it for area evaluation [6]. But Khan and Ye [9] argue that COFFE's area model overestimates the layout area of full adders by 13% and underestimates the layout area of multiplexers by a maximum of 58%. GRM interconnect circuit contains many types of multiplexers, so we need more accurate and effective model to evaluate interconnect circuit area. Our area model achieves this by considering GRM interconnect circuit's topology and layout's characteristics such as diffusion sharing, inputs sharing, transistor folding and design rules.

There are many different delay models. TILOS [4] uses Elmore delay model for optimization. Kuon and Rose [5] adopt a hybrid approach, which includes two steps. The first step uses linear models to get the approximate sizes of all the devices. The second step uses SPICE simulation to further optimize those sizes got from first step. COFFE [6] uses time-domain HSPICE simulation instead of linear models, which avoids inaccurate models to increase computation accuracy. It models all wire loading even including the relatively short metal connecting two transistors inside a multiplexer. This leads to computational complexity, and long simulation time.

Since wire delay becomes more and more important in advanced process nodes, our optimization method uses two schemes to build wire model. One is for the wire within a circuit and the other one is for the wire between interconnect circuits. Such model can keep precision of simulation and decreases computation complexity.

# 3. Problem description and solution

## 3.1 GRM FPGA interconnect circuits

Modern FPGA usually uses GRM architecture for a couple of reasons. Compared to the CB-SB FPGA interconnect, GRM interconnect is more diversified because it has abundant global and local interconnect; it is more flexible because it can go to any direction and can make a turn. A GRM FPGA is composed of repeated TILEs, refers to Figure 1. Though FPGA chip is usually very large, it can use the unified GRM interconnect to connect logic block, such as CLB, BRAM, DSP, etc.

A TILE is composed of interconnect circuits and logic block. Interconnect circuits includes global interconnect and local interconnect. Global interconnect transmits signal across different TILEs. Local interconnect transmits signal between global interconnect and logic block. Usually in GRM FPGA, the height of GRM interconnect circuit is the same as the height of CLB, which can be referenced as the basic unit. Large blocks like DSP or BRAM use four or more GRM interconnect circuits . Figure 2 shows the interconnect and a CLB logic block. The global interconnect usually includes three kinds of circuits: long line circuits, intermediate line circuits and short line circuits. The local interconnect circuits usually includes several kinds of interconnect circuits: IMUX, OMUX, CLK, BYP, FAN, CTRL, and etc. (see Table 1 for more detailed description).

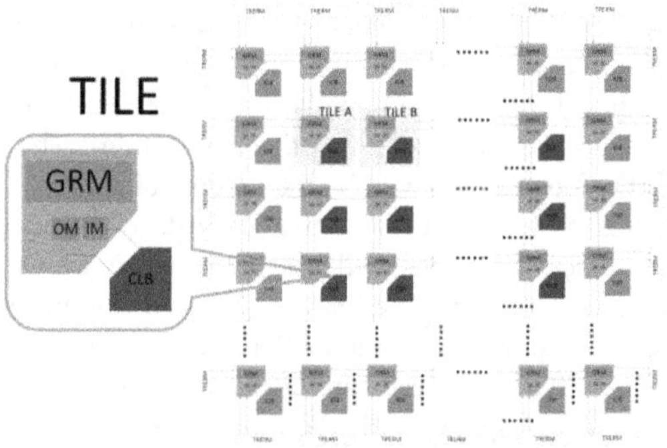


**Figure 1: GRM FPGA**

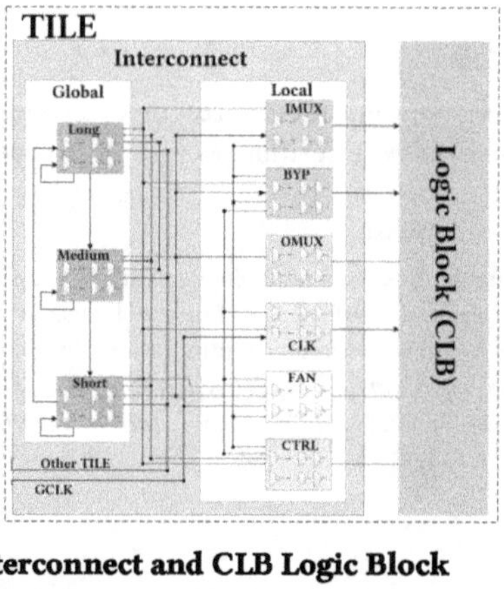


**Figure 2: Interconnect and CLB Logic Block**

Interconnect circuits is a bunch of wires and multiplexers which drive the wires. Each type of global interconnect wire can connect in any of the four directions (north/south/east/west). In addition, the middle long global interconnect wires can make diagonal connections. Table 1 describes the detailed attributes of global interconnect wires. Each type of local interconnect wire connects global interconnect and logic blocks. Depending on the ports of CLB/DSP/BRAM that local interconnect wires connect to, there are several different types of local interconnect circuits Table 2 describes the details.

**Table 1: Parameter for Global interconnect**

| Parameter | Description |
|---|---|
| Direction | Where wire goes to, use E/W/S/N indicates ease, west, south and north. In some situation the wire will turn during transmit, we use two letter NE/NW/SE/SW. LH/LV means horizontal long line and vertical long line. |
| Length | How many tiles wire traverse, if it is a double line, Length = 2. |
| Port | Input/ Output port of a wire within a tile. We use A/ B/ C/ D/ E/ BEG/MID/END, etc. For example, BEG means wire start point, END means wire end point. |
| Bus No. | One type of interconnect circuit has more than one wire, it is a bus. Bus number indicates the index within a bus. |
| Extent | In order to provide more connection ability, after END point, it can extend one tile more. Use E/W/S/N indicates extent direction. |

**Table 2: Parameter for Local interconnect**

| Parameter | Description |
|---|---|
| Type | IMUX provide data input to LUT; BYP provide data input to Carry Chain; CLK provide clock signal to the register; CTRL provide reset signal to the register; FAN provide clock enable signal to the register. |
| Bus No. | One type of interconnect circuit has more than one wire, it is a bus. Bus number indicates the index within a bus. |

The source of an interconnect wire is driven by a multiplexer. We assume that the multiplexer uses two-level topology, as it is described in commercial architectures [3][8], and it occupies small silicon area and has small delay [9] as shown in Figure 3. Using NMOS to transmit signal not only saves the space between different active areas, but also reduces the parasitic parameters. Depending on the type of the interconnect circuit, the driver has three structures: buffer structure as shown in Figure 3, inversion structure or tri-state structure as shown in Figure 8. For example, horizontal and vertical long line interconnect circuit has tri-state structure. CLK and CTRL interconnect circuit has inversion structure.

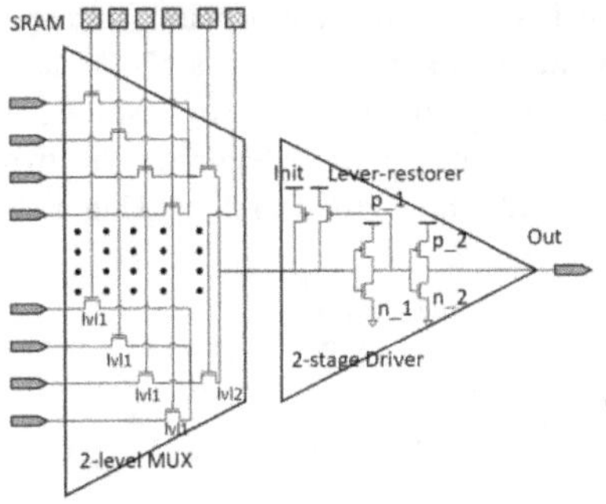


**Figure 3: A multiplexer using two-level topology [3][8].**

An architecture description file includes parameters of global interconnect (Table 1) and local interconnect (Table 2) to describe all FPGA resources (interconnect and logic block) and their connections between each other. From architecture description file we can get all the netlist of GRM interconnect circuit and wire load, and they are the inputs of our optimization methodology depicted in Figure 4. The outputs of Figure 4 are optimized transistor size and overall report about area, delay and cost.

## 3.2 Optimization methodology flow

Figure 4 shows the GRM FPGA interconnect circuit optimization methodology flow. The input to the flow is the process information and the connectivity description file which uses parameters of global and local interconnect. Then we get the netlist of all interconnect circuits. The most important part is Subcircuit Sizing Algorithm (section 3.3) which iteratively optimize each GRM interconnect circuits. The algorithm uses Minimum-Final-Delay algorithm and multi-threads acceleration, see Figure 5.

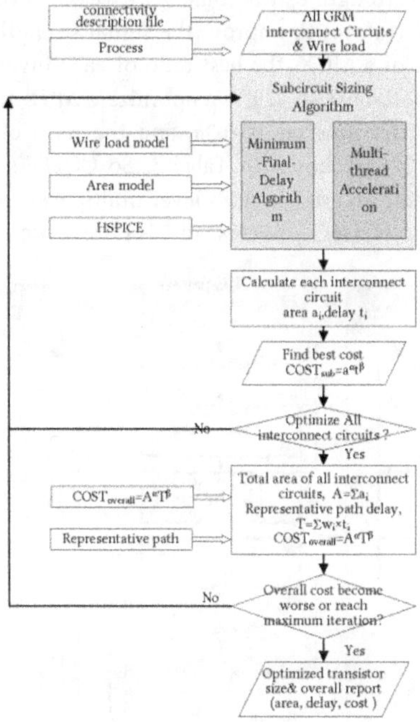


**Figure 4: Flow of the proposed optimization method.**

In each interconnect circuit optimization iterative process, this paper uses area model (section 3.4) to get area $a_i$ and uses HSPICE and wire model (section 3.5) to get delay value $t_i$. Then we find which transistor size combination can generate the minimum cost for each interconnect circuit, the $COST_{sub} = a^{\alpha}t^{\beta}$, where a is the area of subcircuit and t is the delay of subcircuit.

After finish optimizing all interconnect circuits. The optimization methodology can calculate overall cost. The $COST_{overall} = A^{\alpha}T^{\beta}$, the default value of α and β is $\alpha = 1$, $\beta = 1$. A is the total area of each interconnect circuits $a_i$, $A = \sum_{i=1}^{n} a_i$; T is the delay value of representative path, which is sum of delay of each GRM interconnect circuits' delay $t_i$ multiply by their weights $w_i$.

$$T = \sum_{i=1}^{n} d_i \cdot w_i \quad (1)$$

There are at least two rounds of optimization of all interconnect circuits. When the cost become higher or the maximum number of iterations has reached, the optimization process will terminate. Finally, we get the report size, area, delay of each interconnect circuit. We also get the global cost, which is the product of total area and the representative path delay.

## 3.3 Subcircuit Sizing Algorithm

Our subcircuit sizing algorithm is based on COFFE's[6] algorithm. We make two improvements, Minimum-Final-Delay algorithm and multi-thread acceleration, as shown in Figure 5.

### *3.3.1 Minimum-Final-Delay Algorithm*

COFFE's algorithm uses inverter rise-fall balancing technique, which has some drawbacks. As described in section 3.1, the interconnect circuits use two-level multiplexer (Figure 3). It uses two level NMOS to transmit the signal, when the signal reaches the driver, its strength can become very weak. So the driver has a PMOS level-restorer to improve the signal strength. Because of this structure of a MUX, the best ratio of each inverter may not keep Trise/Tfall close to 1. If we optimize a MUX manually, the ratio of the first inverter is 0.36, and the ratio of the second inverter is 1.22, as shown in Table 3. So COFFE's approach of equalizing each inverter of two-level multiplexer to keep each inverter's ratio (Trise/Tfall) close to 1 is unrealistic.

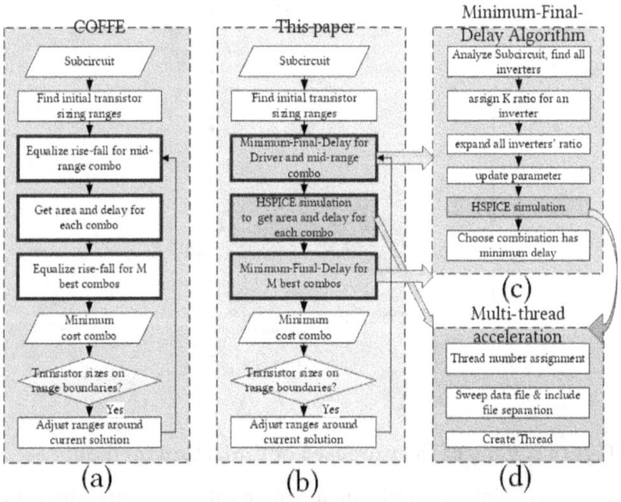


**Figure 5: The Subcircuit Sizing Algorithm. (a) COFFE[6] (b) This paper (c) Minimum Final Delay algorithm (d) Multi-thread acceleration.**

**Table 3: Size from manual optimization**

| p_1 /um | n_1 /um | p_2 /um | n_2 /um | tfall_1/ps | trise_1/ps | tfall_2/ps | trise_2/ps | Tratio1 | Tratio2 |
|---|---|---|---|---|---|---|---|---|---|
| 1.8 | 2.4 | 6 | 4 | 108 | 296 | 433 | 353 | 0.36 | 1.22 |

Therefore, we propose the Final-Minimum-Delay method to optimize interconnect circuits as a whole, not as separated parts, see Figure 5(c). First we analyze the subcircuit, and find all the inverters. Then we give each inverter K ratios (for example, 10 different ratios [0.4, 0.5, 0.6, 0.7, 0.8, 0.9, 1, 2, 3, 4]). Next, we expanse all inverter's ratio, so two inverters has 100 ratio combinations. Next we update sizing parameter according to the ratio combination, we do multiple times (e.g. 100) of simulation to find out the minimum delay of an interconnect circuit. The minimum delay of an interconnect circuit is the maximum value of Negative edge delay and Positive edge delay. We use minimum delay combination's ratio as inverter's final ratio.

### *3.3.2 Multi-thread acceleration*

COFFE [6] uses HSPICE simulation to get delay value. When the number of sizing combination is large, the simulation time will be long. We propose a multi-tread acceleration strategy. COFFE uses sweep function in HSPICE simulation, and puts the data need to be swept in the sweep_data.l file. Figure 6(a) shows HSPICE sweep function. Figure 6(b) shows sweep_data.l file, which includes 100 sizing value of two inverters. Because there is no data sharing between sweep data, multi-thread is suitable for parallel simulation to reduce simulation time, see Figure 5(d).

For example, if we use one thread to do HSPICE simulation, it needs one grm_double_mux.sp spice file, one includes.l file and one sweep_data.l file. If we have 10 threads, we separate these files into ten groups of files; see Figure 6(c). And each thread simulates with one group of files as input.

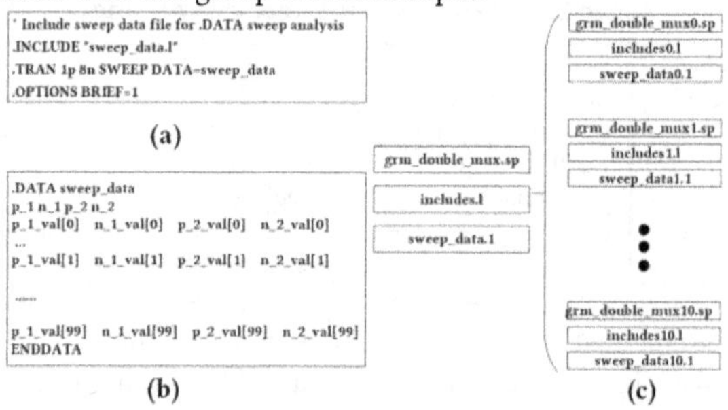


**Figure 6: The multi-thread simulation. (a) HSPICE sweep function (b) sweep_data.l file (c) File separation for multi-thread simulation.**

## 3.4 Area model

As described in section 3.1, the interconnect circuits use two-level multiplexers. Diffusion sharing and transistor folding are commonly used techniques when design multiplexer [9].

We found it is common that a pair of interconnect circuits shares the same inputs, in this way a NMOS layout can share dual ends, one end is the input for two NMOS, another end is output of two NMOS. So we categorizes the two-level NMOS pass transistors into three groups, refers to Figure 7.

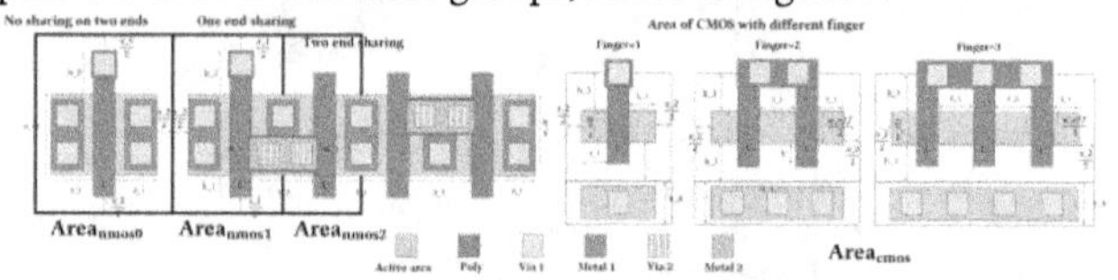


**Figure 7: Area model of NMOS and CMOS**

When transistors in a CMOS driver have large size, area model considers transistor-folding technique. In order to prevent the latch-up effect, we frequently add pickup in the CMOS driver. So area model considers the Pickup area, refers to Figure 7. At last, the SRAM areas also need to be added to the area model.

$$Area_{total} = \sum Area_{nmos0} + \sum Area_{nmos1} + \sum Area_{nmos2} + \sum Area_{cmos} + \sum Area_{SRAM} \quad (2)$$

## 3.5 Wire model

From architecture description file, we can get wire load of all interconnect circuits. We use two schemes to build wire model, one for wires within a circuit and the other one for wires between interconnect circuits.

*3.5.1 Interior wire model*

When the interconnect circuits use two-level multiplexer, we find that within an interconnect circuit, the capacitance of the wire has more impact on delay than resistance. Therefore, inside the interconnect circuit, our wire model ignores wire resistance parameter and just uses capacitance parameter. This will reduce simulation time with little impact in the accuracy.

From experiment, we only need put two parasitic capacitors in front of each inverter as shown in Figure 3, to simulate interior wire load. For driver that has inversion and tri-state function, we need three parasitic capacitors, the location are shown in Figure 8.

The wire capacitance equals to the sum of the size of each transistor followed by the wire multiply by a coefficient K.

$$\text{Capacitance}_{\text{interior wire}} = K\sum \text{Size}_{\text{transistors}} \quad (3)$$

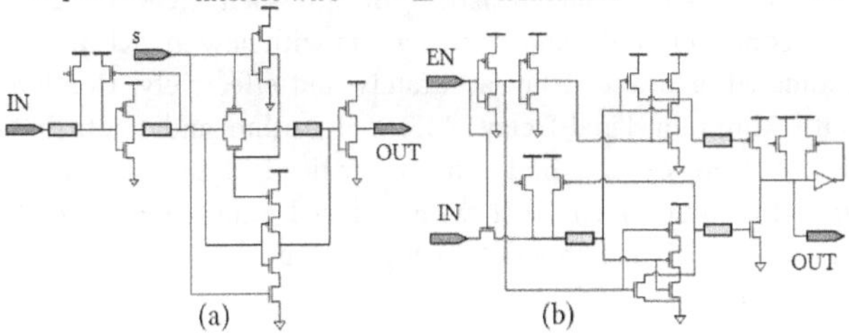


**Figure 8: Interior wire model. (a) inversion, (b) tri-state.**

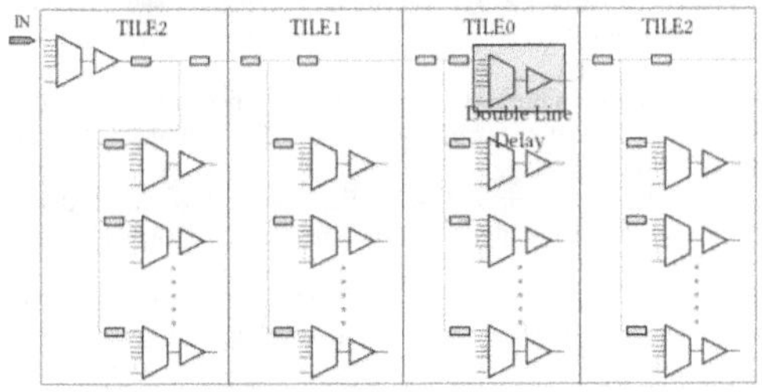


**Figure 9: Exterior wire model.**

*3.5.2 Exterior wire model*

FPGA's global interconnect traverse several tiles and can go to any direction. Figure 9 is a double line topology. We use average load method to estimate an interconnect circuit's exterior wire load. An exterior wire load is the sum of all different types of interconnect circuits average load (equation (4)). For one type of interconnect circuit average load, we calculate the total number then divide it by the total number of exterior wire (equation (5)).

$$\text{Load}_{\text{exterior wire}} = \sum \text{Load}_{\text{average}} \quad (4)$$

$$\text{Load}_{\text{average}} = \sum \text{Number}_{\text{load}} / \sum \text{Number}_{\text{exterior wire}} \quad (5)$$

## 4. Experimental results

We have previously designed and fabricated with 65nm process technology an FPGA chip, GRM Chip-A, using GRM architecture, logic block includes CLB/DSP/BRAM, etc. The total layout area is 6800um × 5000um, see Figure 10. The chip test results show that each function of the chip is correct, the electrical and switching parameter meets the specification requirement [10].

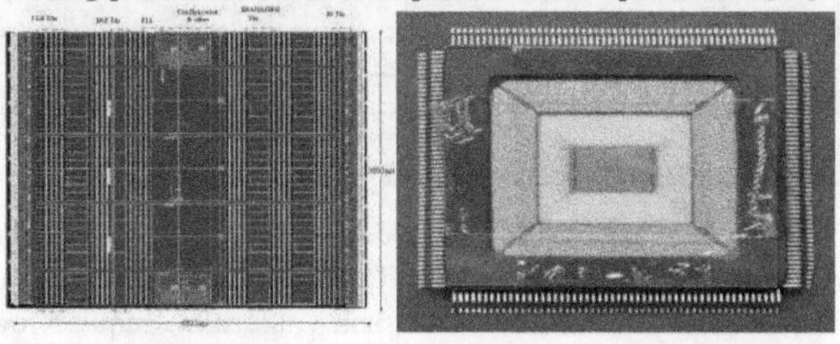

**Figure 10: GRM Chip-A layout and the fabricated chip**

In our experiment, we apply the proposed optimization method on the GRM Chip-A design and compare area model, wire load model, algorithm and multi-thread acceleration with actual data from the fabricated GRM Chip-A.

## 4.1 Area model and wire model

We get area of all interconnect circuits of GRM Chip-A by our area model equation (2). From Figure 11(a), compare to Minimum Width Transistor model [2] and COFFE's model [6], we find our area model is closer to actual layout than other models.

From simulation comparison we get K = 6E-19fF/nm in the equation (3). From GRM CHIP-A, we get exterior wire load. For example, a double line at MID node, there are 9 types of loads. So in equation (4) it is the sum of 9 items and IMUX is one of them. The total number of IMUX is 320 and the total number of double line is 40 (each direction has 10 lines), so in equation (5), the average load of IMUX is 320/40=8. It means that each double line interconnect circuit has 8 IMUX loads.

From Figure 11(b), our interior and external wire load model delay value are close to internal and external post-sim delay value of GRM Chip-A. The delay deviation is less than 10%, which means our interior and external wire load model is close to the actual chip's wire load.

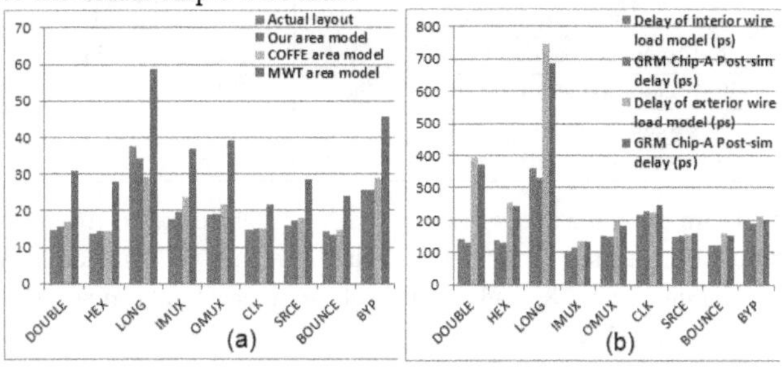


**Figure 11: Area model and wire model comparison (a) Area model comparison (b) Internal wire model and External wire model delay and post-sim delay comparison.**

We get weight of an interconnect circuit from benchmark circuit. After benchmark circuits are placed and routed, weights $w_i$ can be obtained from STA analyzer's report. We use circuits from MCNC benchmarks [11] and IWLS 2005 benchmarks [12]. Table 4 shows weights $w_i$ of each interconnect circuits, and weights $w_i$ is apply to equation (1) in section 3.1.

**Table 4: Weight of interconnect circuits**

| No. | Subcircuit | Weight | No. | Subcircuit | Weight |
|---|---|---|---|---|---|
| 1 | DOUBLE | 0.3048 | 6 | CLK | 0.0027 |
| 2 | HEX | 0.0704 | 7 | SRCE | 0.0027 |
| 3 | LONG | 0.0214 | 8 | BOUNCE | 0.0023 |
| 4 | IMUX | 0.1801 | 9 | BYP | 0.0363 |
| 5 | OMUX | 0.1380 | | | |

## 4.2 Minimum-Final-Delay Algorithm

We makes a comparison between COFFE subcircuit sizing algorithm and our proposed one. The results are shown in Table 5. It demonstrate our subcircuit sizing algorithm require fewer number of HSPICE simulation, a 38% [=(3506-2152)/3506] reduction from COFFE. The cost (area-delay product) of two algorithms are similar, 0.156318 (ours) vs. COFFE's 0.158144.

**Table 5: Subcircuit Sizing Algorithm Comparison between this paper and COFFE**

| | This paper | COFFE |
|---|---|---|
| Initial value | Same | Same |
| Mux type | Switch box | Switch box |
| Simulation No. | 2152 | 3506 |
| COST | 0.156318 | 0.158144 |
| AREA | 892.392 | 888.95 |
| DELAY | 1.752e-10 | 1.779e-10 |
| Ratio of Inv_1 | 0.4 | 1 |
| Ratio of Inv_2 | 0.4 | 1 |

## 4.3 Multi-thread acceleration

We use 1, 10 and 50 threads and compare their corresponding simulation time [unit: second(s)]. The number of sizing combinations shows how many number of different transistor sizes needs to be simulated with HSPICE. The acceleration performance is displayed in Table 6.

**Table 6: Multi-thread and Single-thread Comparison**

| Thread | No. of sizing combinations | | |
|---|---|---|---|
| | 256 | 1372 | 2401 |
| 1-thread simulation time | 718s | 3582s | 6199s |
| 10-threads simulation time | 79s | 388s | 653s |
| 10-threads acceleration ratio | 9.09 | 9.23 | 9.49 |
| 50-threads simulation time | 56s | 214s | 356s |
| 50-threads acceleration ratio | 12.82 | 16.74 | 17.41 |

From the table above, we see that 10 or 50 threads can reduce simulation time. Compared to single-thread, 10 threads can accelerate near 9X and 50 threads can accelerate near 15X [=(12.82+16.74+17.41)/3].

## 4.4 Overall optimization

The GRM Chip-A was fabricated with 65nm process technology, and we apply the proposed optimization method to optimize the GRM interconnect circuits of the GRM Chip-A. The representative critical path delay is the sum of delay of each GRM interconnect circuit's delay multiplying by their weights, $T = \sum_{i=1}^{n} d_i \cdot w_i$. The total area includes all kinds of GRM interconnect area, $A = \sum_{i=1}^{n} a_i$. We can get $COST_{overall} = A^{\alpha}T^{\beta}$, the default value of $\alpha$ and $\beta$ is $\alpha = 1, \beta = 1$.

**Table 7: Before/After optimization of interconnect circuits of a TILE**

| | Representative Critical Path Delay (ps) | Interconnect circuits' Area (um^2) | Cost (area^1 x delay^1) |
|---|---|---|---|
| Actual value of GRM Chip-A | 227.74 | 4556.81 | 1.0377 |
| Results after optimization | 184.02 | 5022.26 | 0.92417 |

From Table 7, we can see that the GRM Chip-A's manually designed interconnect circuit has room for improvement. After using our transistor-level optimization method, the global cost can be reduced by 10.9% [=(1.0377-0.92417)/1.0377)], which is the result of a 19.2% [=(227.74-184.02)/227.74] reduction on delay and a 10.2% [=(5022.26-4556.81)/4556.81] of area overhead. This improvement comes from the fact that we use automatic optimization method which, compared to the manual full custom design, can search more solution space for better solutions.

## 5 Conclusion

We develop an automated transistor-level optimization method that considers characteristics of prevalent GRM FPGA's interconnect circuits and layout, along with new models that can estimated area and delay accurately and effectively. Combined with Minimum-Final-Delay (MFD) algorithm and multi-thread acceleration, our method can automatically size the transistor and find best global cost with reduced simulation time. We validate our claims on a GRM Chip-A chip fabricated with 65nm technology.

## REFERENCES

[1] Vaughu Betz, Johathan Rose, Alexander Marquardt. 2000. Architecture and CAD for Deep-Submicron FPGAs. Kluwer Academic Publishers, Norwell, MA, USA.

[2] Benton Highsmith Calhoun, Joseph F. Ryan, Sudhanshu Khanna. 2010. Flexible Circuits and architecture for ultralow power. Proceedings of the IEEE, Vol. 98, No. 2(Feb 2010), 267-282.

[3] Xilinx Inc. 2017. 7 Series FPGAs Data Sheet: Overview. Retrieved from https://www.xilinx.com/support/documentation/data_sheets/ds180_7Series_Overview.pdf

[4] J. P. Fishburn and A. E. Dunlop, "TILOS: A Posynomial Programming Approach to Transistor Sizing," in ICCAD 1985, pp. 326–328.

[5] Ian Kuon and Jonathan Rose. 2011. Exploring Area and Delay Tradeoffs in FPGAs With Architecture and Automated Transistor Design. TVLSI, 19(1), 71-84.

[6] Charles Chiasson and Vaughn Betz. 2013. COFFE: Fully-automated transistor sizing for FPGAs. In Proceedings of the IEEE International Conference on Field Programmable Technology(Dec 2013), 34-41.

[7] G. Zgheib, M. Lortkipanidze, M. Owaida, D. Novo, and P. Ienne. 2016. FPRESSO: Enabling express transistor-level exploration of FPGA architectures. In Proceedings of the 24th ACM/SIGDA International Symposium on Field Programmable Gate Arrays, pages 80-89, Monterey, Calif., Feb. 2016.

[8] D. Lewis et al., "The Stratix II™ Logic and Routing Architecture," in FPGA 2005, pp. 14–20.

[9] Farheen Fatima Khan, Andy Ye. 2018. An Evaluation on the Accuracy of the Minimum Width Transistor Area Models in Ranking the Layout Area of FPGA Architectures. ACM Transactions on Reconfigurable Technology and Systems, 11, 1(March 2018), 1-23.

[10] Lei Li. 2015. Research and Implementation of High Performance and Low Power FPGA Interconnect Resources. Ph.D. Dissertation. Fudan University.

[11] YANG S, YANG S. Logic Synthesis and Optimization Benchmarks User Guide Version 3.0 [R]. Microelectronics Center of North Carolina, P . O. Bo x 12889, Research Triangle P ark, NC 27709. 1991, 4(4): 206-7.

[12] Albrecht, Christoph. "IWLS 2005 benchmarks" in International Workshop for Logic Synthesis (IWLS) [EB/OL] : http://www. iwls. org. 2005.

# Low Voltage Clock Tree Synthesis with Local Gate Clusters

Can Sitik
Drexel University
Philadelphia, PA 19104, USA
as3577@drexel.edu

Weicheng Liu
Stony Brook University
Stony Brook, NY 11794, USA
weicheng.liu@stonybrook.edu

Baris Taskin
Drexel University
Philadelphia, PA 19104, USA
bt62@drexel.edu

Emre Salman
Stony Brook University
Stony Brook, NY 11794, USA
emre.salman@stonybrook.edu

## ABSTRACT

In this paper, a novel local clock gate cluster-aware low voltage clock tree synthesis methodology is introduced. In low voltage/swing clocking, timing closure is a challenging problem due to tight skew and slew constraints. The clock gating makes this problem more challenging due to the high delay mismatch between the gated and the non-gated sinks. The proposed methodology preserves the power savings of the clock gating and exploits low swing clocking to further reduce the power consumption, while maintaining the same skew and slew constraints as the full swing counterpart. Experimental results performed on the large circuits of ISCAS'89 benchmarks operating at 1.5GHz in the 45nm technology node demonstrate that the proposed methodology can provide 38% power savings as compared to a full swing gated clock tree, achieving an additional 12% savings as compared to a low swing *non-gated* clock tree.

**ACM Reference Format:**
Can Sitik, Weicheng Liu, Baris Taskin, and Emre Salman. 2019. Low Voltage Clock Tree Synthesis with Local Gate Clusters. In *Great Lakes Symposium on VLSI 2019 (GLSVLSI '19), May 9–11, 2019, Tysons Corner, VA, USA.* ACM, New York, NY, USA, 6 pages. https://doi.org/10.1145/3299874.3318004

## 1 INTRODUCTION

Clock distribution networks are vital for timing closure [17]. Comprising generous resources to deliver this timing closure, the power consumption of the clock network and the clock sinks constitute 30% and 40% of the total IC power dissipation, respectively [18]. Thus, the tradeoff between the performance (i.e. timing) and the power consumption of the clock distribution networks is well-studied [12, 19]. Modern microprocessors satisfy tight timing constraints through the use of clock spines and clock mesh topologies, whereas low power ASICs target a tight power budget through various low power methodologies, including clock gating [7, 9, 11, 12, 19, 24] as well as the low voltage/swing clocking methodologies [1, 8, 15, 16, 20–23]. In this paper, a local clock gate cluster-aware low swing clock tree synthesis (CTS) methodology is introduced, while preserving the connectivity and placement of clock gates, determined at the synthesis and placement stages, respectively. Despite significant delay changes, the proposed low swing CTS methodology featuring this traditional clock gating flow is adept at preserving the local path timing. The preservation of local path timing is manifested by the newly synthesized low swing clock tree satisfying the same clock skew and clock slew constraints as those of a full swing clock tree. To accomplish this goal, local clock trees are synthesized for each clock gate cluster (sourced from the clock gate location) and buffer insertion, if necessary, is performed with a bounded skew (< $skew_{const}$). After each local tree is synthesized, the top level clock tree is generated by exploiting a useful skew approach to deliver the clock signal to the clock gate inputs as well as non-gated clock sinks. The useful skew approach provides the flexibility to handle different variations of local clock tree insertion delays (induced by the varying fanout sizes of clock gates) as well as the flexibility to balance the skew between gated and non-gated local trees. The outcome of this two stage CTS proposal is a bounded skew, gated, low swing clock tree. The proposed methodology is minimally invasive in not changing the synthesis or placement stages of the design flow. The experimental results performed on five largest circuits of ISCAS'89 benchmarks at 1.5GHz show that the proposed methodology achieves: (1) More power savings than the useful skew methodology in [4] via algorithmic improvement: 38% vs. 27%; (2) more power savings than a low swing non-gated clock tree methodology in [20] via efficient use of clock gating: 38% vs. 26%. Furthermore, the same clock skew (50ps) and clock slew (100ps) constraints are satisfied. Thus, the CTS methodology of this paper efficiently combines the power savings of clock gating and low swing clocking for a more power efficient solution.

The rest of the paper is organized as follows. The relevant previous work on low swing clocking and clock gating is discussed in Section 2. The preliminaries and the background of the proposed work are provided in Section 3. The methodology of this work is introduced and explained in detail in Section 4. The experimental results are presented in Section 5. The paper is finalized with concluding remarks in Section 6.


*GLSVLSI '19, May 9–11, 2019, Tysons Corner, VA, USA*

ACM ISBN 978-1-4503-6252-8/19/05...$15.00
https://doi.org/10.1145/3299874.3318004

## 2 PREVIOUS WORK

### 2.1 Previous Work on Low Swing Clocking

Low swing clocking is the method of scaling clock voltage to obtain power savings, with a possible overhead on the timing performance. In literature, low swing clocking has been exploited with different enablers, i.e. by using a fully low swing clock tree synchronizing low-swing-clock-aware DFFs running with a full swing data [8, 20], or using level-shifting cells at the first and the last level of the clock tree to interface with a traditional full swing clock source and traditional full swing DFFs at the sinks [1, 15]. However, each methodology fails to consider at least one of the three primary challenges of i) the degradation of the local timing, ii) the increase in the DFF power, iii) the decrease in the expected power savings due to level-shifting and/or lack of clock gating. For instance, the approach presented in [15] proposes to use level-shifting cells at the input and the last level of the clock tree. However, the last level of the clock tree has a substantial amount of the clock tree capacitance, failing to consider (iii). Another approach, presented in [8], proposes a custom-built DFF cell that can interface with a lower swing clock input, while running full swing data. However, the clock-to-q delay of this topology is significantly higher than traditional DFFs, therefore it is only applicable to low performance-demand designs and fails to address (i). A third approach, presented in [23], starts with a full swing clock tree, and gradually decreases its clock swing until a power-optimal point is identified [23]. The low swing clock tree is directly interfaced to a DFF running at full swing, therefore the high short circuit current in the DFF cell introduces a large overhead, failing to address issue (ii). In addition, clock slew, due to voltage scaling, increases the clock-to-q delay of the DFF cell, leaving issue (i) unaddressed. Another approach, presented in [20], proposes the combination of low swing clocking and a custom low-swing-aware DFF design, addressing the issues (i) and (ii). However, clock gating methodology is not considered, limiting its practical use as well as potential power savings through clock gating. In this paper, a local clock gate cluster aware low swing CTS methodology is proposed in order to preserve the existing clock gating cells while exploiting low swing clocking.

### 2.2 Previous Work on Clock Gating

Clock gating introduces an additional challenge in low swing clocking due to the insertion delay mismatch between the gated and the non-gated clock paths. In order to highlight this mismatch, a motivational example is presented in Figure 1. In Figure 1, 4 sinks on the left are gated [with one common integrated clock gating cell (ICG)] and the other 4 on the right are non-gated. A two-level local clock tree is built for the gated portion sourced at the top-level ICG cell. After local CTS, there are 5 sinks for the top level clock tree with non-equal target delays: 4 non-gated sinks on the right that have no children, and consequently, no insertion delay, and 1 ICG gate on the left that has the insertion delay of the local clock tree. Two recent approaches address this delay-mismatch challenge by type-matching [3] and delay-matching [7]. The type-matching approach proposes to swap clock buffers on the last level of the non-gated clock paths (not shown in Figure 1) with always-on clock gates in order to match the delay with the clock gate delays on the gated clock paths. The problem with this approach is the assumption of

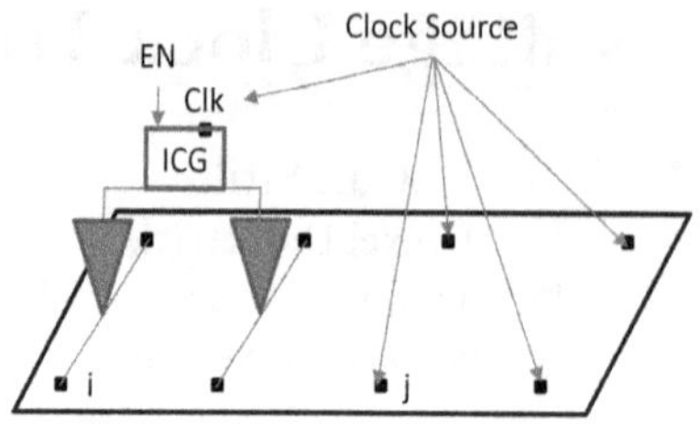


**Figure 1: Motivational example: 4 sinks on the left are gated and 4 sinks on the right are non-gated. Thus, this results in 5 sinks with different initial delays.**

having balanced loads at the clock gate outputs. The type-matching approach solves unbalanced load problem with a load-matching algorithm [13] so as to efficiently use type-matching. However, the clock gate clusters are defined depending on the activity patterns and enable timing before the CTS, therefore the number of DFFs and their placement can vary significantly. This variety makes it impractical to match the load of clock gates due to a wide range in the number of sinks and the wire capacitance. It is important to note here that this mismatch is more significant in low swing operation, resulting in high delay variance even when the same type of ICGs is used. An alternative (and more practical) approach to balance this mismatch is to exploit useful skew at the top-level clock tree. To this end, a useful skew CTS algorithm is used in this paper at the top-level in order to balance this mismatch and satisfy an overall bounded clock skew.

## 3 PRELIMINARIES

The effects of low swing operation on the timing and the power trends are presented in this section. When the clock voltage is scaled for low swing operation, the output current of a clock buffer decreases. Thus, the power consumption of the clock buffer decreases while the delay and the output slew of the clock buffer increase [10]. The same is true for the clock gates. The respective increases in the output slew of buffers and clock gates accumulate through (e.g. clock branch) interconnects potentially causing slew violations. Inserting extra buffers in order to avoid slew violations results in higher power consumption, degrading the power savings obtained through low swing clocking. In order to investigate this trade off, four clock tree cases on s38584 of ISCAS'89 benchmarks are considered. Cases 1 and 3 are constructed as baselines for comparison, establishing the current state of design where low swing novelties proposed in this paper are lacking, causing slew violations. Cases 2 and 4 are constructed to embody novelties proposed in this paper. These four cases are: (1) Low swing clocking is performed on the non-gated clock tree synthesized for full swing (100%), permiting slew violations, (2) Non-gated clock tree is re-synthesized at each voltage level to satisfy the slew constraint, (3) Voltage scaling is performed on the gated clock tree synthesized for full swing (100%), permitting slew violations, (4) Gated clock tree is re-synthesized at each voltage level to satisfy the slew constraint. These four cases are generated using 45nm technology at 1.5GHz while clock voltage is scaled from 100% to 70% of its nominal value (0.9V for this technology) with 5% decrements. In case 1 and case 2, the clock trees are synthesized using the low swing (non-clock gated) method

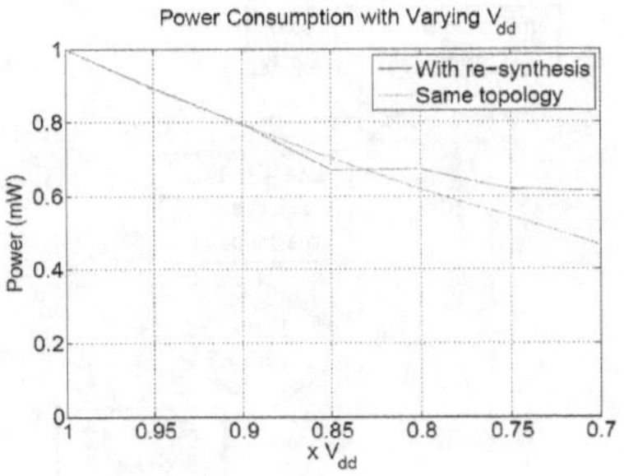


**Figure 2: Power consumed by non-gated clock tree with and without resynthesis, normalized to *non-gated* clock tree at full $V_{dd}$.**

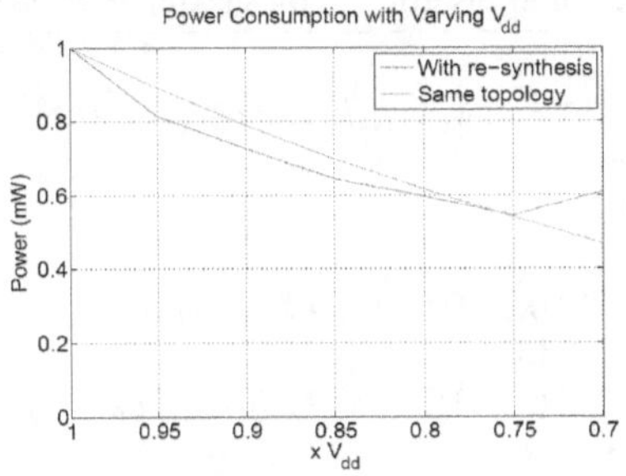


**Figure 3: Power consumed by gated clock tree with and without resynthesis, normalized to *gated* clock tree at full $V_{dd}$.**

in [20], as traditional synthesizers do not easily accommodate low swing clocking. In Case 3 and Case 4, the clock trees are synthesized using the CTS algorithm proposed in this paper. The power consumption comparison between Case 1 and Case 2, demonstrating the impact of low swing clocking with proposed novelties on a clock tree without clock gates, is shown in Figure 2. It is shown in Figure 2 that the power consumption decreases significantly when the clock voltage is scaled down on the same topology (with slew violations) whereas the power savings start leveling after some point due to the extra buffers inserted to satisfy the slew constraint. The same comparison is performed between Cases 3 and 4 for clock trees with ICGs, shown in Figure 3. It is shown in Figure 3 that the gated clock tree has the same conclusion as the non-gated case in Figure 2: The power savings level after some point due to the extra buffers inserted to satisfy the slew constraint. This trend is preserved despite the lower power dissipation in Figure 3 compared to Figure 2, as expected, thanks to the existence of clock gating. As the power dissipation values are normalized in each figure, this fact is not visible; yet note that clock gating provides close to 20% power savings on this experimental setup. More important for the presented analysis is the trend of the tradeoff between power savings and voltage scaling, which does not exist both in the gated and non-gated clock trees, and have similar criticality that need addressing. Considering the trend in Figure 3, the low swing voltage level is selected as 75% of $V_{dd}$ for the experimental setup of this paper, as further scaling the clock voltage does not provide additional power savings. Nonetheless, the proposed algorithm is independent of the low swing supply $V_{dd,low}$ and can be re-purposed as desired.

**Algorithm 1** Traditional DME Algorithm used in [4, 6, 20] for CTS

```
1: Cost_curr=∞
2: for i in Nodes do
3:     for j in Nodes do
4:         if Cost(i,j) < Cost_curr && Feasible(i,j) == 1 then
5:             Cost_curr=Cost(i,j)
6:         end if
7:     end for
8: end for
9: if Cost_curr != ∞ then
10:    Perform merging to initialize new node k=T_i,j
11: else
12:    for i in Unmerged Nodes do
13:        Insert buffer to fix violations.
14:    end for
15: end if
```

## 4 PROPOSED METHODOLOGY

The methodology proposed to synthesize low-swing clock trees with local gate clusters has a bottom-up flow, based on modified deferred-merge-embedding (DME) method described in Section 4.1, with two stages. The first stage, described in Section 4.2, is local CTS for a fixed set of ICG connectivity and placement determined at the logic and physical synthesis stages, as customary in physical design flow. The second stage, described in Section 4.3, details the top-level CTS with useful skew to accommodate the timing challenges caused by low swing clocking as well as clock gating. The time complexity of the algorithms is presented in Section 4.4, demonstrating the scalability of the proposed CTS tool in theory, as benchmarks large enough to empirically demonstrate scalability are not available publicly.

### 4.1 DME Method with New Cost Metric

Deferred-merge-embedding (DME) is a well-known methodology that is used for zero skew [2] and bounded skew [5] routing whose buffered versions are adapted for CTS [4, 6, 20]. The DME method provides a flexible framework adopted by various CTS methodologies [4, 6, 20], outlined in Algorithm 1. The traditional DME framework is adopted for zero skew [6], useful skew [4] and low swing clocking [20] by using different cost metrics (Line 5) and feasibility metrics (Line 4). In [6], cost is defined as the distance between two nodes, and in [4, 20] the cost metric is defined as the distance added with the potential wire snaking between two nodes to consider the delay differences. As for the feasibility metric, [4, 6] and [20] use maximum capacitance and constraint and [20] considers the maximum slew constraint, the exceeding of which is infeasible.

In this paper, the traditional DME method is adopted with feasibility metric defined as the maximum slew constraint (as in [20]) and a modified cost metric that is proposed so as to be appropriate for both zero skew (at local clock trees) and useful skew (at top-level clock tree). The purpose of such a cost metric is to satisfy a bounded skew among all sinks (both gated and non-gated). The cost metric is defined considering the actual delay difference (i.e. skew) and the resistive path (instead of distance) to enhance the quality of results.

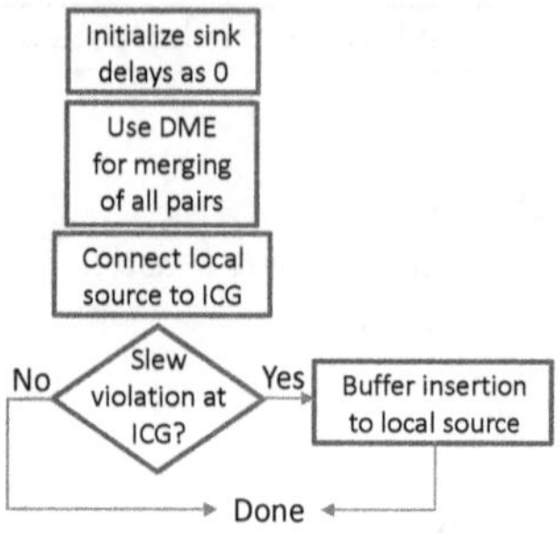


**Figure 4: The flowchart for the local clock tree synthesis.**

In particular, the merging cost for a node pair $i$-$j$ is defined as:

$$Cost(i,j) = max\_parent\_to\_node\_delay(i,j) + max[skew(i,j) - skew_{const}, 0] \quad (1)$$

where $k$ is the merging point of $i$-$j$ pair, maximum delay of $D(k,i)$ and $D(k,j)$ is $max\_parent\_to\_node\_delay(i,j)$, and $skew(i,j)$ is defined as the difference between the maximum insertion and the minimum insertion delays from $i$ and $j$ to their respective sinks. The first term in Eq. (1) considers the maximum of the two node delays $D(k,i)$ and $D(k,j)$, assuming two nodes are merged at location $k$ in order to account for the maximum resistive path. The purpose of using delay as the cost metric instead of the resistance itself is to make it consistent with the second term (so that they can be added together). The second term in Eq. (1) considers the skew between two nodes. In particular, the term is the excess of the skew between two nodes and the skew constraint of the design if the difference is larger than 0. If not, the term is equal to 0, as a skew smaller than the constraint does not cause a violation.

## 4.2 Local Clock Tree Synthesis

The local clock trees for each clock gate cluster are synthesized using the flow in Figure 4, based on the modified DME flow explained in Section 4.1. Furthermore, this novelty is introduced in the last step in the form of buffer insertion to satisfy the slew constraints. At the first step, the algorithm initializes each clock sink within the clock gate cluster with zero insertion delay. At the second step, DME algorithm, presented in Algorithm 1, is used with the proposed cost metric [Eq.( 1)]. After the local clock tree source is determined, it is connected to the corresponding clock gate in the third step. In the final step, it is checked whether the clock gate can drive the capacitive load without a slew violation. If this is the case, no buffer insertion is necessary and the algorithm terminates. Otherwise, the minimum size buffer that can drive the capacitive load without a slew violation is inserted at the local source node. Here, it is important to note that selecting the correct buffer size is critical when the size of clock gate clusters (i.e. number of fanout) varies, as the previous works either assume a balanced capacitive load [3] or use only one type of buffer [4, 20]. The procedure is followed for each local clock gate cluster.

## 4.3 Top-Level Clock Tree Synthesis

After the local clock trees are synthesized and the ICG cells are connected, the top-level clock tree is synthesized with the flowchart shown in Figure 5. The three step flow utilizes the modified

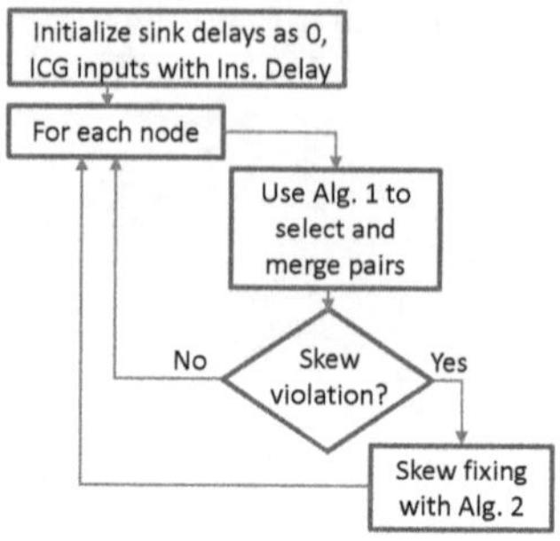


**Figure 5: The flowchart for the top-level clock tree synthesis.**

**Algorithm 2** Buffer insertion/Wire snaking to fix skew violations.

```
1: for b in B do
2:   if Slew(b) < slew_const(k) × slew_factor then
3:     Insert b
4:   end if
5: end for
6: while D^max(k) - D^min(k) > skew_const do
7:   for b in B do
8:     if D^max(k) - D^min(k) - D(b) < skew_const × skew_factor
       then
9:       Insert b, found=1
10:    end if
11:  end for
12:  if found==0 then
13:    if Inserting max size buffer improves skew then
14:      Insert max size buffer from B
15:    else
16:      Insert wire snaking, break;
17:    end if
18:  end if
19: end while
```

DME algorithm described in Section 1 and a novelty is introduced in the third step in the form of buffer insertion/wire snaking to satisfy the skew constraints. In the first step, the insertion delay of the clock gate inputs is initialized as the insertion delay of their corresponding local trees, and the insertion delay of the non-gated sinks is set to 0. In the second step, the DME algorithm, shown in Algorithm 1, is used to construct the top-level clock tree. As different initial delays are defined for each node in the first step, a useful skew approach is considered at the top-level in order to bound overall skew. Thanks to the new merging cost defined in Eq. (1), the merging pairs with small insertion delay differences are selected as the minimum cost pair. However, there may be cases, especially at higher levels in the clock tree, where the insertion delay difference between two nodes is larger than the skew constraint $skew_{const}$. Thus, a buffer insertion and/or wire snaking methodology, presented in Algorithm 2, is proposed to bound the overall clock skew in the third step. In Algorithm 2, the minimum size buffer that can drive the capacitance without a slew violation is inserted at the first step (Lines 1-5). Here, the violation is defined to be smaller than the actual slew constraint (i.e. $slew_{factor} \times slew_{const}$,

$slew_{factor}$<1.0) in order to provide an extra capacitance margin for possible wire snaking. For the experimental setup of this paper, this factor is set to 0.95, which provides a 5ps $[(1-0.95)\times slew_{const}]$ margin assuming a 100ps slew constraint. The purpose of inserting minimum size buffer (that can drive the capacitive load) is the fact that i) higher device resistance of a smaller size buffer provides a higher delay when driving the same capacitive load, ii) smaller size buffer potentially consumes less power. If the insertion of the minimum size buffer degrades the skew, wire snaking is preferred. After the insertion of the first buffer, the buffer insertion is continued (at the fan-in of the first buffer) with the maximum size buffer that improves the skew (Lines 6-19). Theoretically, this approach selects the maximum size buffer from the buffer library until the delay difference is small. However, the solution can be stuck at a local minimum (that causes an impractically large wire snaking) due to the large delay change caused by the maximum size buffer at the low swing operation. Thus, a more relaxed approach is proposed here. The buffer insertion is performed with the following condition: If a buffer can decrease the skew to a margin closer to the skew constraint (i.e $skew_{factor}\times skew_{const}$,$skew_{factor}$>1.0), that buffer is inserted (Lines 7-11), otherwise the maximum size buffer in the library is inserted if it decreases the skew (Line 14). For the experimental setup of this paper, this factor is set to 1.4, which provides a 20ps $[(1.4-1.0)\times skew_{const}]$ margin assuming a 50ps skew constraint. With this flexibility, buffers with different size are exploited in order to avoid large wire snaking that possibly results in a slew violation. If buffer insertion is not capable of decreasing the skew below $skew_{const}$, wire snaking is used at the last step (Line 16). It is important to note here that the wire snaking is not necessary if the target buffer library has enough granularity of buffer sizes (i.e. small delay difference in adjacent buffer sizes). In such a case, the factors $slew_{factor}$ and $skew_{factor}$ can be set to 1.0 as the granularity of the buffer sizes provides the necessary delay change. If such a library is not present, the $slew_{factor}$ can be set to a number slightly smaller than 1.0 (like 0.95), and the $skew_{factor}$ can be set to generate enough margin for the insertion of the minimum size buffer: In this paper the insertion of the minimum size buffer in the library provides ≈70ps delay change, thus the factor is set to (70-$skew_{const}$)/$skew_{const}$=1.4.

## 4.4 Complexity Analysis

Given $N$ sinks with $n$ clock gate clusters, the algorithm in Figure 4 selects one sink in the cluster and iterates through other $(\frac{N}{n-1})$ sinks and merges the minimum cost pair. This operation continues until only 1 node is left, which is the input of the clock gate. Thus, the complexity of this algorithm is $O(\frac{N^2}{n^2})$ per clock gate cluster, resulting in an overall complexity of $O(\frac{N^2}{n})$. After clock gates are connected, the algorithm in Figure 5 iterates through each pair of $n$ clock gates, therefore the complexity of this algorithm is $O(n^2)$. The total complexity of the proposed methodology is $O(\frac{N^2}{n})+O(n^2)$ when the design has $N$ clock sinks and $n$ clock gate clusters. Non-gated implementations of the previous works presented in [4, 20] have a complexity of $O(N^2)$, as all $N$ sinks are considered once. Thus, the gated implementation presented in this work exploits the natural partitions (i.e. clock gate clusters) to improve the run time.

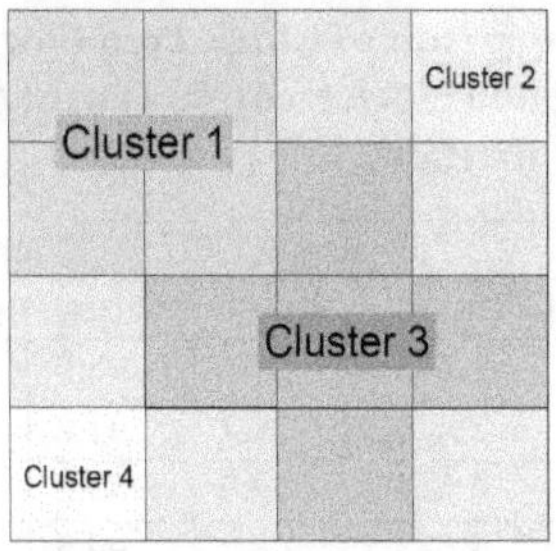


**Figure 6: The clock gate layout assumed for each benchmark circuit. The gray areas are the non-gated clock sinks.**

**Table 1: The number of clock sinks at each clock gate cluster and the percentage of gated clock sinks vs. total number of sinks using the configuration shown in Figure 6.**

| 2* Circuits | Number of Sinks in Each Cluster | | | | Gating |
|---|---|---|---|---|---|
| | Clus. 1 | Clus. 2 | Clus. 3 | Clus. 4 | % |
| s13207 | 141 | 43 | 165 | 44 | 66% |
| s15950 | 117 | 25 | 145 | 44 | 65% |
| s38584 | 316 | 73 | 380 | 102 | 70% |
| s38417 | 309 | 90 | 572 | 39 | 69% |
| s35932 | 426 | 115 | 540 | 112 | 69% |

## 5 EXPERIMENTAL RESULTS

The proposed algorithm is implemented as a *Perl* script and the generated clock netlists are simulated using HSPICE of *Synopsys* with 45nm technology from FreePDK library [14]. Five largest circuits from ISCAS'89 benchmarks (that have >500 sinks) are used for experimental analysis. The logic synthesis of RTL-level netlists is performed using *RTL Compiler* of *Cadence* and the physical placement of DFFs is performed using *SoC Encounter* of *Cadence*. The buffer library has 5 buffers with various driving strengths (from X2 to X32), and wire model has per unit values of R=2Ω/$\mu$m and C=0.1$fF/\mu m$ at the metal layer. The clock skew constraint is set to 50ps (7.5% of the clock period) and the slew constraint is set to 100ps (15% of the clock period) at the worst PVT corner (0.9V, 125C, SS transistors). The purpose of using worst case corner is to maintain the reliability of low swing operation even at the most extreme conditions (i.e. in lieu of a variation analysis). For a technique such as low swing clocking, which exploits the design margins, it is more appropriate to pinpoint the worst case operating point, as opposed to the nominal conditions with variations. It is well-known that nominal operating conditions would give better results and the variation analysis on the nominal corner would lead to result not any worse than reported in the experiments of this paper. The low swing DFF designs are used to interface low swing clock tree to full swing data paths, similar to [20]. In order to generate a clock gating structure with various fanout sizes, each design is partitioned into a hypothetical 16 grids, and each grid is assigned (or not assigned) to a clock gate as shown in Figure 6, and the clock gate is assumed to be placed at the geometrical center of the sinks of each cluster with a 50% activity. Relevant information is presented for each benchmark circuit in Table 1.

**Table 2: The comparison of Clock Tree Power (CP), Clock Skew (Sk.) and Clock Slew (Sl.) of a full swing gated clock tree (GCT), low swing non-gated clock tree (NCT) using [20], low swing gated clock tree (GCT) using [4], and the proposed low swing gated clock tree (GCT) method.**

| 2* Circuits | Full Swing GCT | | | Low Swing NCT with [20] | | | Low Swing GCT with [4] | | | Proposed Low Swing GCT | | |
|---|---|---|---|---|---|---|---|---|---|---|---|---|
| | CP(mW) | Sk.(ps) | Sl.(ps) | CP(mW) | Sk.(ps) | Sl.(ps) | CP(mW) | Sk.(ps) | Sl.(ps) | CP(mW) | Sk.(ps) | Sl.(ps) |
| s13207 | 2.435 | 29.2 | 98.9 | 1.603 | 10.2 | 90.8 | 2.272 | 37.8 | 89.5 | 1.787 | 47.6 | 87.7 |
| s15850 | 2.271 | 37.7 | 91.2 | 1.518 | 22.9 | 93.0 | 1.875 | 45.5 | 88.7 | 1.499 | 49.3 | 90.8 |
| s38584 | 4.911 | 39.0 | 83.2 | 3.580 | 15.4 | 89.3 | 3.589 | 48.1 | 98.0 | 2.917 | 40.0 | 99.0 |
| s38417 | 5.878 | 48.2 | 99.5 | 3.956 | 34.8 | 91.9 | 3.476 | 49.8 | 96.0 | 3.136 | 37.9 | 89.6 |
| s35932 | 5.004 | 45.6 | 91.3 | 4.496 | 36.4 | 95.0 | 3.814 | 49.2 | 87.2 | 3.435 | 37.7 | 92.2 |
| Normal. | 1.00 | <50 | <100 | 0.74 | <50 | <100 | 0.73 | <50 | <100 | 0.62 | <50 | <100 |

In order to present the independent and mutual impacts of clock gating and low swing clocking, the proposed methodology is compared against three cases: i) A full swing gated clock tree synthesized using the proposed methodology, ii) A low swing non-gated clock tree synthesized using the method in [20], and iii) A low swing gated clock tree synthesized using the useful skew method in [4] at the top-level clock tree, presented in Table 2. Comparing to a full swing gated clock tree, the *non-gated* low swing clocking methodology presented in [20] provides 26% power savings thanks to low swing clocking. This algorithm in [20], however, cannot handle clock trees with clock gates. Despite the inclusion of the clock gating cells to low swing clocking for an additional boost to low power operation, the useful skew methodology from [4] only obtains marginally better results, with power savings of 27%. This marginal improvement proves that the useful skew methodology of [4] does not exploit the useful skew efficiently, and therefore, the savings through clock gating does not improve power savings at the desired levels. Alternatively, the proposed methodology of this paper achieves 38% power savings, compared to the full swing gated clock tree. This 38% improvement is substantially higher than the improvement of 26% of the non-gated implementation. Thus, the CTS methodology of this paper efficiently combines the power savings of clock gating and low swing clocking for a more power efficient solution. Note that all cases are synthesized with the same clock skew (50ps) and clock slew (100ps) constraints, and no violation is observed in any case, as described in Section 3.

## 6 CONCLUSION

A novel local clock gate cluster-aware low swing CTS methodology is introduced. The proposed methodology synthesizes local clock trees for each clock gate cluster while preserving the clock gate locations in order not to degrade local timing. The top-level clock tree is synthesized by considering the insertion delay mismatch between the gated and the non-gated clock sinks with a useful-skew-based approach. The proposed buffer insertion scheme is shown to be effective to achieve a bounded clock skew. The proposed methodology is implemented within the IC physical design flow, therefore it is highly practical for automation purposes.

## REFERENCES

[1] H. A. Asgari, F., and M. Sachdev. 2004. A low-power reduced swing global clocking methodology. *IEEE Transactions on Very Large Scale Integration (TVLSI) Systems* 12, 5 (May 2004), 538–545.

[2] K.D. Boese and A.B. Kahng. 1992. Zero-skew clock routing trees with minimum wirelength. In *Proc. of IEEE Int. ASIC Conference and Exhibit.* 17–21.

[3] Chia-Ming Chang, Shih-Hsu Huang, Yuan-Kai Ho, Jia-Zong Lin, Hsin-Po Wang, and Yu-Sheng Lu. 2008. Type-matching clock tree for zero skew clock gating. In *Proceedings of the ACM/IEEE Design Automation Conference (DAC).* 714–719.

[4] Rishi Chaturvedi and Jiang Hu. 2005. An Efficient Merging Scheme for Prescribed Skew Clock Routing. *IEEE Transactions on Very Large Scale Integration (TVLSI) Systems* 13, 6 (Jun 2005), 750–754.

[5] Jason Cong, Andrew B. Kahng, Cheng-Kok Koh, and C.-W. Albert Tsao. 1998. Bounded-skew Clock and Steiner Routing. *ACM Trans. Des. Autom. Electron. Syst. (TODAES)* 3, 3 (Jul. 1998), 341–388.

[6] M. Edahiro. 1993. A Clustering-Based Optimization Algorithm in Zero-Skew Routings. In *ACM/IEEE Design Automation Conference (DAC).* 612–616.

[7] Shih-Jung Hsu and Rung-Bin Lin. 2011. Clock gating optimization with delay-matching. In *Proc. of the IEEE Design, Automation Test in Europe (DATE).* 1–6.

[8] C. Kim and S. M. Kang. 2002. A low-swing clock double-edge triggered flip-flop. *IEEE Journal of Solid-State Circuits* 37, 5 (May 2002), 648–652.

[9] W. Liu, E. Salman, C. Sitik, and B. Taskin. 2015. Clock Skew Scheduling in the Presence of Heavily Gated Clock Networks. In *Proceedings of ACM Great Lakes Symposium on VLSI (GLSVLSI).* 283–288.

[10] Weicheng Liu, Can Sitik, Baris Taskin, and Emre Salman. 2019. SLECTS: Slew-Driven Clock Tree Synthesis. *IEEE Trans. on Very Large Scale Int. (TVLSI) Sys.* (2019), 1–11. https://doi.org/10.1109/TVLSI.2018.2888958

[11] Shih-Chuan Lo, Chih-Cheng Hsu, and Mark Po-Hung Lin. 2014. Power Optimization for Clock Network with Clock Gate Cloning and Flip-flop Merging. In *Proc. of the ACM Int. Symp. on Physical Design (ISPD).* 77–84.

[12] Jingwei Lu, Wing-Kai Chow, and Chiu-Wing Sham. 2012. Fast Power- and Slew-Aware Gated Clock Tree Synthesis. *IEEE Transactions on Very Large Scale Integration (TVLSI) Systems* 20, 11 (Nov. 2012), 2094–2103.

[13] A.D. Mehta, Yao-Ping Chen, N. Menezes, D.F. Wong, and L.T. Pilegg. 1997. Clustering and load balancing for buffered clock tree synthesis. In *Proceedings of the IEEE International Conference on Computer Design (ICCD).* 217–223.

[14] NCSU 2011. *FreePDK 45nm Library v1.4.* NCSU.

[15] J. Pangjun and S.S. Sapatnekar. 2002. Low-power clock distribution using multiple voltages and reduced swings. *IEEE Trans. on Very Large Scale Integration (TVLSI) Systems* 10, 3 (June 2002), 309–318.

[16] M. Rathore, W. Liu, E. Salman, C. Sitik, and B. Taskin. 2015. A Novel Static D Flip-Flop Topology for Low Swing Clocking. In *Proceedings of ACM Great Lakes Symposium on VLSI (GLSVLSI).* 301–306.

[17] Emre Salman and Eby G Friedman. 2012. *High Performance Integrated Circuit Design.* McGraw-Hill Professional.

[18] R.S. Shelar and M. Patyra. 2013. Impact of Local Interconnects on Timing and Power in a High Performance Microprocessor. *IEEE Trans. on Computer-Aided Design of Integrated Circuits and Systems* 32, 10 (2013), 1623–1627.

[19] Weixiang Shen, Yici Cai, Xianlong Hong, and Jiang Hu. 2010. An Effective Gated Clock Tree Design Based on Activity and Register Aware Placement. *IEEE Trans. on Very Large Scale Int. (TVLSI) Sys.* 18, 12 (Dec. 2010), 1639–1648.

[20] Can Sitik, Leo Filippini, Emre Salman, and Baris Taskin. 2014. High Performance Low Swing Clock Tree Synthesis with Custom D Flip-Flop Design. In *Proceedings of the IEEE Computer Society Annual Symposium on VLSI (ISVLSI).* 498–503.

[21] Can Sitik, Weicheng Liu, Baris Taskin, and Emre Salman. 2016. Design Methodology for Voltage-Scaled Clock Distribution Networks. *IEEE Transactions on Very Large Scale Integration (TVLSI) Systems* 24, 10 (October 2016), 3080–3093.

[22] Can Sitik, Emre Salman, Leo Filippini, Sun Joon Yoon, and Baris Taskin. 2015. FinFET-Based Low Swing Clocking. *ACM Journal on Emerging Technologies in Computing Systems* 12, 2 (August 2015), 13:1–13:20.

[23] C. Sitik and B. Taskin. 2013. Skew-bounded low swing clock tree optimization. In *Proc. of ACM Great Lakes Symp. on VLSI (GLSVLSI).* 49–54.

[24] W. Liu, E. Salman, C. Sitik, and B. Taskin. 2016. Exploiting Useful Skew in Gated Low Voltage Clock Trees for High Performance. In *Proceedings of IEEE International Symposium on Circuits and Systems.* 2595–2598.

# TOIC: Timing Obfuscated Integrated Circuits

Mahabubul Alam
Electrical Engineering
Pennsylvania State University
State College, PA
mahabubul.alam@psu.edu

Swaroop Ghosh
Electrical Engineering
Pennsylvania State University
State College, PA
szg212@psu.edu

Sujay S. Hosur
Electrical Engineering
Pennsylvania State University
State College, PA
ssh29@psu.edu

## ABSTRACT

To counter the threats of reverse engineering (RE) and Trojan insertion, researchers have considered gate-level obfuscation in integrated circuits (IC) as a viable solution. However, several techniques are present in the literature to crack the obfuscation with varying degree of success raising the concern about their secrecy. In this article, we have presented TOIC (Timing Obfuscated Integrated Circuits), a novel technique where sequential elements are obfuscated to hide the true timing paths in the design. TOIC can act as a standalone countermeasure against IC reverse engineering or can be incorporated with existing gate camouflaging techniques to maximize adversarial RE effort. Previous research has shown that limiting access to internal nodes can improve the adversarial RE effort at the cost of poor testability. *TOIC can impose prohibitively large decamouflaging time complexity by limiting the controllability and observability over the internal nodes in an IC while preserving complete testability.*

## KEYWORDS

Reverse Engineering, Camouflaged Flip-Flop, Threshold-defined Switch, SAT, Timing Obfuscation.

**ACM Reference Format:**
Mahabubul Alam, Swaroop Ghosh, and Sujay S. Hosur. 2019. TOIC: Timing Obfuscated Integrated Circuits. In *Great Lakes Symposium on VLSI 2019 (GLSVLSI '19), May 9–11, 2019, Tysons Corner, VA, USA.* ACM, New York, NY, USA, 6 pages. https://doi.org/10.1145/3299874.3318001

## 1 INTRODUCTION

Reverse engineering (RE) of integrated circuits (IC) is the process of gaining a full understanding of the functionality to a point where it can be manufactured with little effort. *In optical RE, an attacker delayers the chip, take images of each layer and use image processing techniques to reconstruct the functional netlist of the IC from these images [1].* Vendors e.g., Chipworks and Degate advertise their ability to perform these tasks. Smaller ICs that are manufactured with mature technology nodes are at a higher risk of being reverse engineered as they are easy to delayer. *However, recently Holler et. al have successfully constructed the layout of a silicon ASIC (Intel 22nm) in a non-invasive manner using X-ray ptychography [2].* With such capabilities available to an attackers disposal, it is gradually becoming easier to reverse engineer and manufacture ICs with no design cost.

***Current State-of-the-Art:*** Researchers have considered gate obfuscation as a viable option to thwart RE. In a gate obfuscation, the layout of the gates are designed in such a fashion that the true functionality is hidden from an attacker during optical RE [3]. However, SAT-based and VLSI test-based attacks have been proven successful against obfuscation of combinational design irrespective of the obfuscation methodology chosen or the number of obfuscated gates in the design [4, 5]. *Although the validity of such attacks on large-scale sequential circuits is debate-able, the authors have justified the attacks based on the following argument: for any sequential design with full scan-access, we can divide the design into multiple camougflaged combinational logic blocks (CCLB) from one sequential stage to another, and decamouflage the CCLB's with the proposed attack methodologies.* The flow to RE a gate obfuscated sequential design is shown in Figure 2. The camouflaged gates do not affect the controllability and observability provided by the scan chain which makes this technique vulnerable to these query based attacks (SAT/VLSI test).

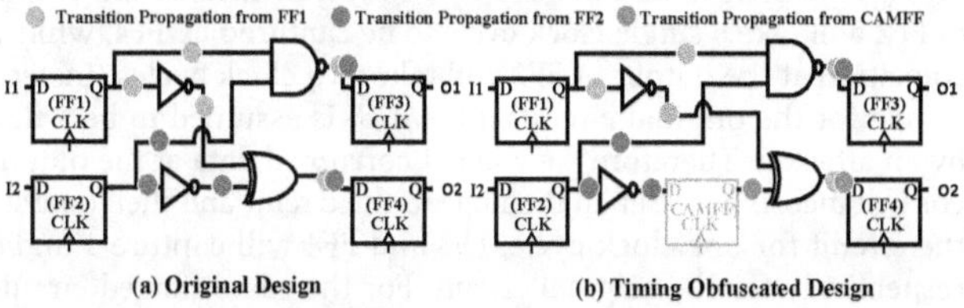


**Figure 1: (a) Oracle sequential circuit; (b) Timing obfuscated circuit.**

In [6], Zhang et al. proposed a technique to obfuscate the timing between successive flip-flops (FF) using unconventional timing. Using the concept of wave pipelining, they have shown that timing paths can be created in the design that looks like a single cycle timing path in a netlist, however, they work as a multi-cycle paths in the chip. Flip-flops are removed from the design selectively to create the multi-cycle paths. In modern chip design, flip-flops provide the desired controllability and observability over the internal nodes through scan access which is an integral part of post-fabrication chip testing and validation. The removal of flip-flops can lead to reduced controllability and observability over the design and significant increase in test time. As very few SAT-based attacks on sequential circuits are known, the timing obfuscation technique was thought to be resistant against these attacks. However, Li et al. showed that with a little modification in the netlist (circuit unrolling), decamouflaging attacks (as shown in Figure 2) can be applied to the timing obfuscated circuit that provides full scan access to an attacker [7]. In [8], Karmakar et al. proposed an encrypted flip-flop which can have inverted or non-inverted output in the fabricated chip based on a secret key. The design is vulnerable to path sensitization attack if the input of the flip-flop is directly accessible through the scan access or any primary input of the chip. Protection from such attacks requires additional scan-chain locking strategies at the cost of significant design overhead. Moreover, the design requires additional secure NVM storage to protect the secret key which can significantly increase the cost of the chip.

***Timing Obfuscation:*** In digital circuits, FFs operate as sequential elements to hold intermediate states between operations. The combinational arc between any two FFs is called a timing path. Data has to travel from start to end of a timing path within a single clock period. In a pipelined design, even a single failing path can corrupt the data transfer between successive stages. As a result, the output of the pipeline can be corrupted.

For a gate obfuscated sequential circuit, all the timing arcs are known to an attacker. *In this paper, we have proposed a novel circuit*


*GLSVLSI '19, May 9–11, 2019, Tysons Corner, VA, USA*

ACM ISBN 978-1-4503-6252-8/19/05...$15.00
https://doi.org/10.1145/3299874.3318001

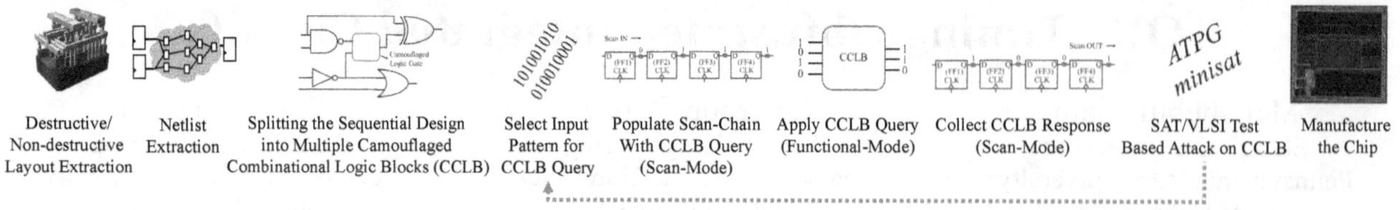


**Figure 2: Reverse engineering of gate camouflaged sequential circuits.**

*obfuscation technique where the actual timing paths are obfuscated through the use of camouflaged FFs. We call it timing obfuscation.* We have presented a design for a camouflaged FF which can act as a sequential or a non-sequential delay element in the circuit based on the threshold voltage ($V_t$) of a few selected NMOS pass transistors. *Replacing some FFs with camouflaged sequential elements, and sparingly deploying non-sequential camouflaged delay elements, we can obfuscate the true timing paths in the design from an attacker.*

In Figure 1(a), the following timing paths exist: FF1→FF3, FF1→FF4, FF2→FF3, and FF2→FF4. FF1→FF3 and FF2→FF3 interfere with each other as they share a common gate (*NAND2*). Because of the presence of the camouflaged FF (*CAMFF*) (Figure 1(b)), the timing arc between FF2→FF4 has been divided into two possible timing arcs (FF2→CAMFF and CAMFF→FF4). A transition at the output of FF2 will take a single clock cycle to be captured by FF4, while a transition at the output of FF2 will take two clock cycles (instead of one for the original circuit) if *CAMFF* is assumed to be a flop by an attacker. Therefore, he will get corrupted data at the output. For instance, if we reset all the flops in the circuit and then operate the circuit for one clock cycle, FF3 and FF4 will capture 1 and 0 respectively for the original circuit. For the camouflaged circuit, if *CAMFF* is considered as a flop, FF3 and FF4 will both capture 1 which is different than the original circuit. *The security of the design will lie on the difficulty for an attacker to identify the true and dummy sequential elements in the design.*

***Contibutions:*** (a) Three novel *CAMFF* designs have been presented and analyzed under temperature and process variations. (b) A novel circuit obfuscation technique where the true timing paths are obfuscated from an attacker through the use of *CAMFF's*. (c) Analysis of the *CAMFF* in the design and scan-chain. (d) Analysis of the security of TOIC based on several known and expected attacks. (e) A secure scan architecture based on the attack scenarios.

The rest of the article is organized as follows: we have discussed the design of the *CAMFF* in Section 2. The design obfuscation strategies with camouflaged flip-flops are discussed in Section 3. The security assessment of TOIC is presented in Section 4. Finally, we have presented the simulation results in Section 5.

## 2 PROPOSED CAMOUFLAGED FLIP-FLOPS

***Basic Building Block:*** In modern planar MOS fabrication technology, the threshold voltage of individual transistors in the design can be controlled by manipulating the doping concentration [10]. The technique can be used to realize threshold voltage defined switches (*TDS*). The NMOS switch can be fashioned by using either a high threshold voltage ($V_{HVT}$) or low threshold voltage ($V_{LVT}$) NMOS transistor biased at a voltage in between those two thresholds ($V_{SN}$) (shown in Figure 3(a)). If LVT is assigned to the switch during fabrication, it will conduct in the presence of the bias voltage ($V_{SN}$). For HVT, the switch will always be in the cut-off region. Using threshold defined PMOS and NMOS switches together, we can also build threshold defined CMOS switch (*TDCS*) as shown in Figure 3(f). Both the NMOS and PMOS switches are asserted LVT during fabrication for closed switch operation and HVT for open switch operation in the chip.

Although the *TDS* switches are easily identifiable in a layout, it is not straightforward for an attacker to identify the threshold voltages. *Threshold voltages of each of the transistors cannot be determined from the images of a delayered chip. While useful, micro-probing on thousands of transistors in a large scale integrated circuit is a prohibiting task.* Utilizing the secretive property of the *TDS*, camouflaged gates are fabricated in 65nm process [11]. In [9], the switches are used to realize threshold voltage defined muxes (*TDM*) which is shown in Figure 3(b). *D*0 is asserted to the output as the lower $V_t$ of *NMOS*1 turns it on when a voltage higher than its $V_t$ (but less than the $V_t$ of *NMOS*2) is applied to the gate ($V_{SN}$). *TDM* and *TDCS* are the basic building block for the proposed camouflaged FFs.

***Design of the Proposed Camouflaged FFs:*** We have used two and four input *TDM's* and regular D-flip-flop building blocks (N/P-latches) in *Design* − 1 and *Design* − 2. *TDCS* and inverter's with varied driving strengths are used in *Design* − 3. In general, all three designs can act as sequential (D-flip-flop) or non-sequential (buffer/inverter) elements in the fabricated chip based on the asserted threshold voltage of selected transistors.

*Design* − 1 : The *Design* − 1 of camouflaged FF is shown in Figure 3(c). We have split the connection between the P-latch and N-latch in a FF and inserted two threshold defined *mux* (*M*1&*M*2) [9] to create 4 logical paths between *Data_in* and *Data_out*. Based on the doping concentration of transistors *M*1 and *M*2, the device can act as a camouflaged FF (CFF), or inverted P-latch (CPL), or inverted N-latch (CNL), or buffer (CB). If LVT is assigned to the NMOS devices at A and C during fabrication, the *CAMFF* acts as *CB*. If LVT is assigned to the NMOS devices at B and D, the camouflaged FF acts as *CFF*.

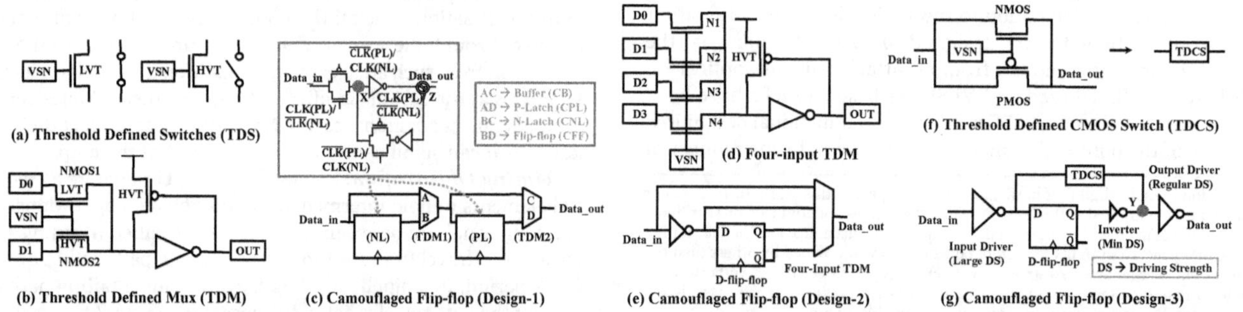


**Figure 3: (a) Threshold defined NMOS switches; (b) Pass transistor based 2:1 threshold defined mux [9]; (c) Schematic of the camouflaged FF (*Design* − 1); (d) Pass transistor based 4:1 threshold defined mux; (e) Schematic of the camouflaged FF (*Design* − 2); (f) Threshold Defined CMOS Switch; (g) Schematic of the camouflaged FF (*Design* − 3).**

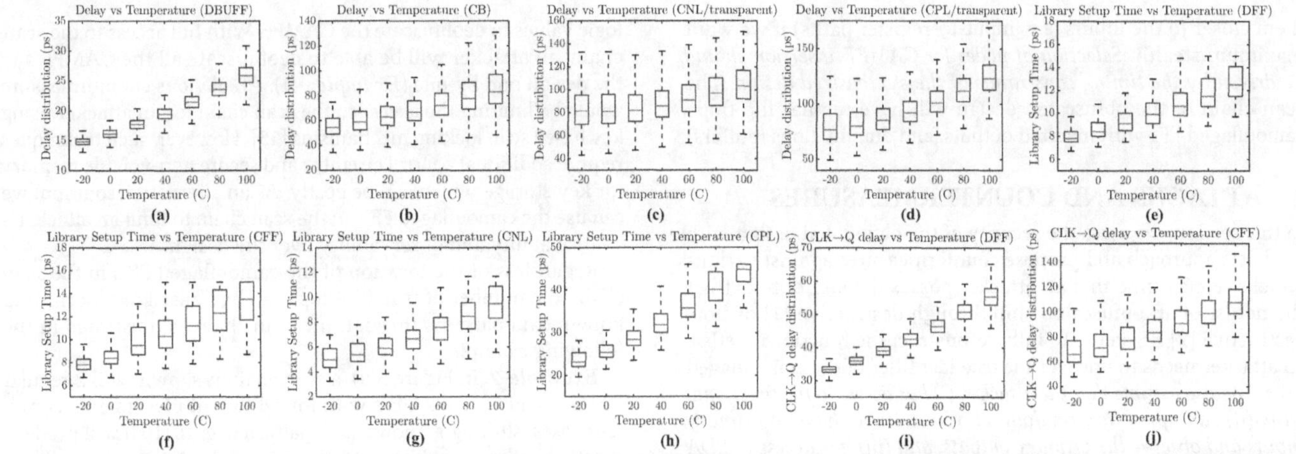


**Figure 4: Delay distribution (*Design* − 1) for (a) delay buffer (DBUFF), (b) camouflaged buffer (CB), (c) camouflaged N-latch (CNL), and (d) camouflaged P-latch (CPL); Library setup time distribution for (e) regular flip-flop (DFF), (f) camouflaged flip-flop (CFF), (g) camouflaged N-latch (CNL), (h) camouflaged P-latch (CPL); Clock→Q delay distribution for (i) DFF, and (b) CFF.**

*Design* − 2 : The *Design* − 2 is shown in Figure 3(e). A four-input *TDM* (as shown in Figure 3(d)) is placed in front of a regular D-flip-flop. Based on the assertion of the *LVT* transistor among the four *TDS's* (N1, N2, N3, and N4) in the four-input *TDM*, the *design* − 2 can act either as a buffer, or an inverter, or a flip-flop, or an inverting flip-flop.

*Design* − 3 : Regular flip-flops are generally isolated with input and output driver inverters. In our *Design*−3, we have connected an additional inverter between the D-flip-flop output (Q-point) and the output driver with minimum driving strength. The input driving inverter is upsized so that it has significantly larger driving strength than the minimum sized inverter. A *TDCS* is placed between the outputs of the input driver and minimum sized inverter. The gates of *TDCS* are driven by *VSN* (approximately half of the VDD). *TDCS* acts as a closed switch if LVT is asserted during fabrication for both the NMOS and PMOS devices. A contention exists between the input driver and the minimum sized inverter. Larger driving strength of the input driver enables it to overpower smaller inverter, and hence node Y follows the inverted input and the output driver follows the non-inverted input all the time (similar to a buffer). If HVT is asserted, *TDCS* acts as a closed switch and the *Design* − 3 operates as a regular flip-flop with inverted output.

***Design Analysis:*** We have simulated the performance of the camouflaged FF's using 32nm planar MOSFET technology with a nominal supply voltage of 0.9V [12]. The NMOS/PMOS pass transistors in *TDM*/*TDCS* (in Figure 3(b), (d), and (f) ) are biased (*VSN*) at 0.5V. The $V_t$ of the LVT NMOS/PMOS and HVT NMOS/PMOS devices are set around 200mV/-200mV and 750mV/-750mV respectively. The CMOS inverter following the NMOS pass transistors in *TDM* is left-skewed to restore the value to CMOS logic levels. The weak keeper PMOS device is used to accelerate 0→1 transition at the inverter input.

*Design*−1 has an area overhead of nearly 70% than a conventional flip-flop (*DFF*). The average power consumption can be 3X higher (all flip-flop power consumption calculated at 1GHz clock frequency with activity factor of 0.4). The simulated value of the CLK→Q delay distribution for a conventional *DFF* and *CFF* is shown in Figure 4(i)&(j). We have considered 10% variation in $V_t$ and a temperature variation from -20°C to 100°C. On an average, the CLK→Q delay of *CFF* is around 2X higher than *DFF* due to the presence of two *TDM* in the critical path of the flip-flop. The setup time of the *CFF* and *CNL* are similar to *DFF*. However, the *CPL* setup time can be 3X higher. This is because the setup time depends on the master stage delay from the input (D) to node M which remains the same for *CFF*, *CNL*, and *DFF*. For *CPL*, the additional delay for the *TDM* accounts for the large difference in the setup time. The hold time of *CFF*, *CNL*, and *CFF* are similar/smaller than *DFF* values due to the additional diffusion capacitance at node *Z*. In Figure 4, we have summarized the setup time of *CAMFF* under process (10% variation in $V_t$) and temperature variations for 1000 points monte carlo simulations. The delay of *CB*, *CNL*, and *CPL* (transparent mode) can be 5X higher than conventional delay buffer (Figure 4(a)-(d)).

*Design* − 2 has a similar area overhead to the *design* − 1. The average power consumption is approximately 2.5X to a regular D-flip-flop. The CLK→Q delay is approximately 50% higher than the regular D-flip-flop. The library setup and hold times are similar to a conventional flop as the master latch stages are identical. The buffer variant has area, power, and delay overhead of approximately 6X, 1.73X, and 1.62X to a conventional delay buffer. The inverter variant has area, power, and delay overhead of approximately 12X, 4.13X, and 1.74X to a conventional inverter.

*Design* − 3 has an area overhead of approximately 15% to a regular D-flip-flop. The average power consumption is approximately 20% higher than a regular D-flip-flop. The CLK→Q delay is approximately 35% higher than the regular D-flip-flop. The library setup and hold times are similar to a conventional flop. The buffer variant has area, power, and delay overhead of approximately 5X, 12X, and 1.25X to a conventional delay buffer.

## 3 DESIGN OBFUSCATION WITH CAMOUFLAGED FLIP-FLOPS

In this section, we present the basic strategies to obfuscate the design with camouflaged FFs. We pick *Design* − 3 for the demonstration purpose. We refer its inverted flip-flop variant as *CFF* and buffer variant as *CB* in the subsequent sections. The design obfuscation should be incorporated in a post-synthesized design that already meets all the timing requirements. Any *DFF* in the design can be replaced by a *CFF* as long as the additional CLK→Q delay does not create any setup violations in any timing path involving the *DFF* (fanins and fanouts). As the *CFF* output is inverted, an inverter has to be added to the design as well. A *CB* can be used as a delay element at any node in the design as long as all the timing paths involving that node have safe setup slack. We generally use delay buffers to fix hold violations. Instead, we can use *CB's* to provide extra security to the design in addition to fixing hold violations. During deobfuscation, any wrong assumption about the identity of the CFF's and CB's in the design may possibly lead to output corruption.

In a sequential design, switching at a node closer to the inputs have a lesser probability to propagate to the primary outputs than the nodes closer to the outputs. Hence, we can insert the camouflaged flops near the end stages of the pipeline (e.g. register-to-out paths) to ensure maximum output corruptibility, and we can put them closer to the inputs (e.g. input-to-register paths) if we want maximum stealth. *Selection of nodes for CAMFF insertion should be driven by the timing constraints of the synthesized design.* The scan-chain of the obfuscated design will have regular flip-flops, camouflaged FFs with inverted outputs, and dummy flops (buffers).

## 4 ATTACKS AND COUNTERMEASURES

In this section, we asses the security of the obfuscated design with the basic approach and propose countermeasures against various attacks. We assume that an attacker posses the ability to extract the netlist of an obfuscated chip through destructive [1] or non-destructive [2] RE steps. To fully reconstruct the functional netlist, an attacker needs to uncover the true identities of the camouflaged cells. *We also assume that the attacker, (i) has access to the functional chip, (ii) can apply any random set of queries to the chip primary inputs and observe the primary outputs, and (iii) has access to EDA tools for functional simulation of the obfuscated netlist.*

The output of any camouflaged FF in the design will be uncontrollable as long as its true identity is hidden from an attacker. Replacing all the flops in the design with camouflaged flip-flop could make all the internal nodes in the design uncontrollable except those directly accessible through the primary inputs(PI) and/or the scan access. However, it is impractical due to the associated design overhead. Selective camouflaging can leave many nodes in the design controllable for an attacker. He can utilize this advantage to deobfuscate the camouflaged flops in the design which is illustrated in the following example.

***Example-1:*** In Figure 5(a); nodes A, B, C, D, and DFF1-Q are controllable and DFF2-Q is observable for an attacker. CAMFF is a camouflaged FF in the timing path from DFF1 to DFF2. An attacker sets A, B, and D to 0, C to 1, and DFF1-Q to any logic value ('x'), and checks the value captured at DFF2-Q after two clock cycles. If CAMFF is a buffer, DFF2 will capture 1 and if its a flip-flop with inverted output ($Design-3$), it will capture 0. Using this two-cycle test, an attacker can successfully reveal the identity of the CAMFF as shown in Figure 5(b). For $Design-1$ and $Design-2$, dual two cycle tests will be required to deobfuscate the CAMFF which is shown in Figure 5(c).

At this point, we may consider placing camouflaged buffers (CB) at node A, B, C, and D, and replace DFF1 with another CFF to make all these nodes uncontrollable for an attacker. We may also replace DFF2 with a camouflaged FF to limit observability over CAMFF-Q. However, such an approach can be impractical for a commercial design because the design may not work for the desired clock frequency anymore due to the delay added by the camouflaged FF's.

For a large sequential design, the CAMFF can be located at any sequential depth. Node A, B, C, and, D can be the outputs of different flops if the CAMFF is at a higher sequential depth and directly not accessible through the PI's. Controlling these nodes using the PI's can be impossible for a large design in presence of other camouflaged FF's. In such a scenario, an attacker will have to use the scan access to set desired values at these nodes and observe desired node logic values to deobfuscate the CAMFF. With full access to the scan-chain, an attacker will be able to deobfuscate all the CAMFF's in the design one-by-one ($Example-1$). An obvious countermeasure would be limiting the access to the scan chain for an attacker using key based scan locking mechanisms [13]. However, such techniques require additional control circuitry and secure non-volatile memory for key storage which can be costly. As an alternative solution, we can use the camouflaged FF's in the scan chain to limit an attacker's controllability and observability over the design.

Regardless of the location of the camouflaged FF's in the scan chain, the number of true flip-flops can be figured out by shifting known data patterns through the scan chain as illustrated in the following example.

***Example-2:*** In Figure 5(d), a scan chain is shown with 2 regular DFF's, 2 CFF's, and 2 CB's with four different placements. For all four cases, shifting a known data pattern (e.g. 101100) will produce exactly similar scan digest at the scan output. An attacker will see 4 cycle delay at the output for all possible input data patterns. As the scan chain already has two regular flops, the attacker will know that there are two flops among the four camouflaged FF's. The rest of the camouflaged FF's are dummy buffers.

If all the camouflaged cells are placed at one edge of the scan chain, the number of clock cycles required to shift any desired data pattern from scan input to any regular flop of the scan chain (and from the output of the regular flop to the scan output) can be easily resolved ($Example-2$). In other words, an attacker would have the necessary controllability and observability over the regular flops of the design to apply the attack demonstrated in $Example-1$. An intuitive approach of obfuscating the scan chain would be placing them at both edges of the scan chain as shown in Figure 6(a) which we call the edge obfuscated scan chain (*EOSC*). The security of *EOSC* against the reset and shift attack [14] and pattern shifting is illustrated in the following example.

***Example-3:*** In Figure 6(a), 2 camouflaged flops are placed at the left edge, 2 at the right edge, and 2 regular flops at the middle of the scan chain. A global reset will generate a logic 1 at the scan output. However, it does not reveal the identity of CFF2. If we reorder CFF2 and CB2, the scan output logic will still be 1 after a global reset (buffer driven by an inverting flip-flop). A single cycle shift will generate a logic 1 at the output. If we reorder CFF2 and CB2, we will still get a logic 1 after 1 cycle shift at the scan output. Due to similar scan output for different scan chain ordering (aliasing), an attacker can not resolve the true identities of the camouflaged FF's in this manner. Applying the attack demonstrated in $Example-2$, an attacker will know the total number of dummy buffer among the camouflaged flops in the design. However, the number of flops at the left edge and right edge of the scan chain are still unknown. Without this knowledge, he will not have the required controllability and observability over the regular flops in the scan chain to apply the attack discussed in $Example-1$.

An attacker can gain controllability and observability over the regular flops of the *EOSC* using the primary inputs (only if the

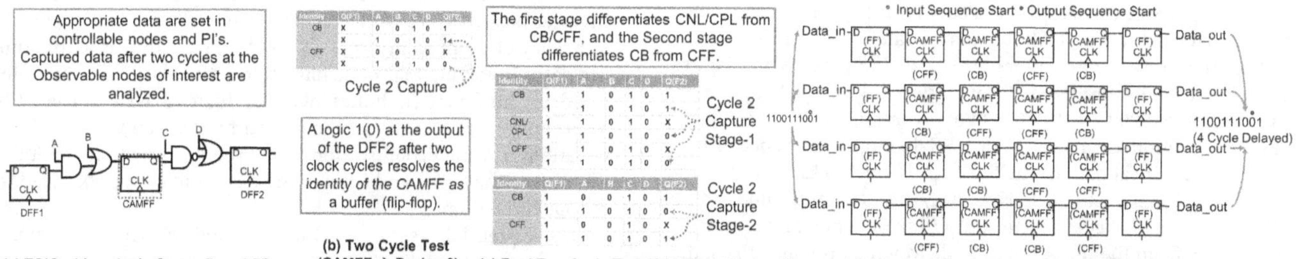


(a) TOIC with a single Camouflaged FF (b) Two Cycle Test (CAMFF → Design-3) (c) Dual Two Cycle Test (CAMFF → Design-1) (d) Aliasing Effect on Scan Chain Pattern Shifting

**Figure 5: (a) A timing obfuscated circuit with a single camouflaged FF; Deobfuscation of the camouflaged FF using (b) two cycle test when $Design-3$ is used, (c) dual two cycle test when $design-1$ is used as the CAMFF; (d) Pattern shifting through the scan-chain.**

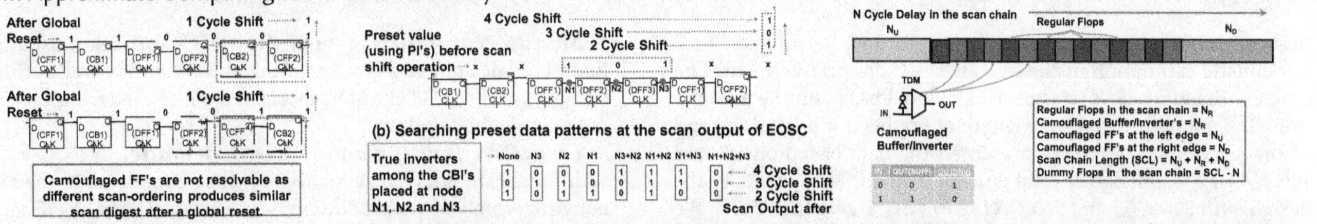


(a) Edge Camouflaged Scan Chain (EOSC) (c) Shifted patterns vary based on the true identities of the inserted CBI's (d) Edge Obfuscated and Camouflaged Scan Chain (EOCSC)

**Figure 6: (a) Camouflaged flops at both edges of the scan chain; (b) Gaining controllability over the edge obfuscated scan chain (*EOSC*) using PI's; (c) Effect of camouflaged buffer/inverter insertion in the *EOSC*; (d) Edge obfuscated and camouflaged scan chain (*EOCSC*).**

regular flops in the original design can be controlled through the primary inputs) which is demonstrated in the following example.

***Example-4:*** The *EOSC* shown in Figure 6(b) has two camouflaged flops at the left edge, two at the right edge, and 3 regular flops at the middle. We assume PI's can be used to control the regular flops at the middle of the *EOSC*. An attacker runs the chip in functional modes in the cycle with carefully chosen values at the PI's. At the end of the functional period, the DFF1, DFF2, and DFF3, hold logic 1, 0, and 1 respectively. Then he turns on the scan mode, shifts the data out of the scan chain, and looks for the data patterns captured at the controllable flops at the end of the functional period. He gets a logic 1 at the output after two cycle shift, logic 0 after three cycle shift and logic 1 after four cycle shift. Seeing the preset data pattern at the output, he determines that there are two flops at the right edge of the scan chain. With this knowledge and the knowledge gained from the attack demonstrated in *Example* – 2, he also understands that there is no flop at the left edge of the scan chain. Therefore, he regains controllability and observability over the regular flops in the *EOSC* to apply the attack discussed in *Example* – 1.

We can address the vulnerability demonstrated in *Example* – 4 by inserting camouflaged logic gates in the scan chain which we call *scan chain camouflaging*. We propose to insert camouflaged buffer/inverter at the output of every regular flops in the scan chain. *By putting an inverter between the D0 and D1 of TDM, we can convert it to a camouflaged cell that can act as a buffer or inverter based on the $V_t$ of the NMOS pass transistors (Figure 6(d)).* Note that, the inserted camouflaged buffer/inverter can be power gated during functional operation of the chip and only powered on during scan operation (as they are part of the scan path exclusively) and hence, they will add no power overhead to the design. However, there will be an area overhead. The presence of these camouflaged cells in the scan chain will provide security against the attack stated in *Example* – 4. We illustrate the solution with an example below.

***Example-5:*** In a similar setup of the *Example* – 4 with camouflaged buffer/inverter at the end of each regular flops in the scan-chain, the data pattern that the attacker has to look for at the scan output can be one of possible 8 based on the true identities of the camouflaged buffer/inverters as shown in Figure 6(c).

We term this scan chain with obfuscated flops at the edges and camouflaged buffer/inverters after every regular flop as edge obfuscated and camouflaged scan chain (*EOCSC*). *EOCSC* can effectively limit an attacker's controllability and observability over the design which ensures the security of *TOIC*. *EOCSC* can also protect standard gate camouflaged designs from the attacks shown in Figure 2. To gain controllability and observability over any flop in an *EOCSC* (Figure 6(d)), an attacker needs to find out (i) the number of true flip-flops at the left and right edges of the scan chain, (ii) the number of inverters between the scan input and the target flop, and the target flop and scan output. If we distribute the camouflaged flops equally on both edges of the scan chain, then $N_U = N_D$ which we call the obfuscated edge length (*OEL*). The number of true flip-flop at both edges of the scan chain can vary between 0 to *OEL*. The number of possible scan chain configurations can be $(2^{N_R} * 2^{N_U+N_D})$ for a brute force attack.

To fully de-obfuscate the *EOCSC*, an attacker has to identify the dummy sequential cells which act as delay elements. The de-obfuscation problem will be similar to diagnosing multiple hold-time failures in the scan-chain which itself has been proven a complicated problem to solve in the past [15]. *The state-of-the-art procedures can only come up with an upper bound and lower bound for the faulty FF in the scan chain in the presence of a single scan-chain failure [16]. The difficulty of the problem lies in the fact that multiple scan-chain failures will produce similar digest (scan-output), and thus they will mask each other.*

***Considerations for Design-1 and Design-2:*** As the camouflaged elements can exhibit more functionalities for *Design* – 1 and *Design* – 2, the brute force attack complexity will be significantly higher. The total number of possible circuit combinations for the obfuscated scan chain will be $(2^{N_R} * 4^{N_U+N_D})$ for both *Design* – 1 and *Design* – 2. The aliasing effect will also be pronounced more in the scan chain. However, the design overhead in terms of additional CLK→Q delay, area, and power overhead will be higher than *Design* – 3.

***SAT Attack on TOIC:*** Without controllability over any internal node of the sequential design, an attacker will have to convert the whole circuit into a combinational circuit using time-frame-expansion for a SAT attack [7]. Such an attack can be applied to the circuits without any feedback paths between the sequential elements. The number of time-frame-expansions required will depend on the sequential depth of the circuit. Li et al. showed that the necessary number of time-frame-expansion can have an exponential relation with the decamouflaging time [7]. However, practical circuits will have feedback paths which will create combinational loops during complete circuit unrolling. Existing SAT attacks are ineffective on circuits with combinational loops.

***Static Timing Analysis Attack:*** An attacker can partially de-obfuscate TOIC through a static timing analysis (STA) based attack. In this attack scenario, an STA of the RE generated obfuscated netlist has to be performed with a logic library that has similar timing profile for all the logic gates that are used in the original chip fabrication. If the summation of any two timing path to and from a camouflaged FF is greater than the chip operating clock period, its identity can be resolved as a flip-flop. However, a designer can intentionally create false paths to and from a camouflaged FF to thwart such attack. If the summation of the most delayed timing paths to and from a camouflaged FF is less than a clock period, the camouflaged FF can either be a dummy flop or the timing paths are indeed very short paths.

## 5 SIMULATION RESULTS

To estimate the design overhead of TOIC, we have synthesized ITC'99 sequential benchmarks [17] using ibm32nm gate library at 500 MHz clock frequency. The area and power of the *CAMFF's* have been interpolated based on their respective ratio that we have found from simulation with ASU 32nm planar MOSFET models [12] (based on *Design* – 1). We have chosen *Design* – 1 as it has the highest overhead among the three designs and, hence gives us a pessimistic estimation of the overall *TOIC* design overhead. The scan chain length (*SCL*) has been calculated based on the assumption of equal obfuscated edge length at the beginning and the end of the scan chain. We have presented the data based on 5% and 10% $CAMFF's$ among the total possible sequential elements in the design with 50% *CFF* and 50% $CNL/CPL/CB$ among the $CFF's$. We have excluded the camouflaged BUFF/INV power data from the chip power calculation considering them to be power gated during normal operation.

For reasonably large circuits, e.g. b19, TOIC will add a power overhead of only 1.6% for 5% *CAMFF* insertion, and nearly 3.27% for 10% *CAMFF* insertion which is significantly low. The associated area overheads are 15.40% and 15.84% respectively. The camouflaged buffer/inverter between the regular FFs accounts for the majority of the area overhead. The area overhead remains constant with the $CAMFF's$ which is evident from the results. For 10% *CAMFF* insertion, the possible number of circuit configuration is $4^{304}$ and scan chain configurations can be as large as $(4^{304} * 2^{5899})$ which can not be solved using brute force in any reasonable time-frame.

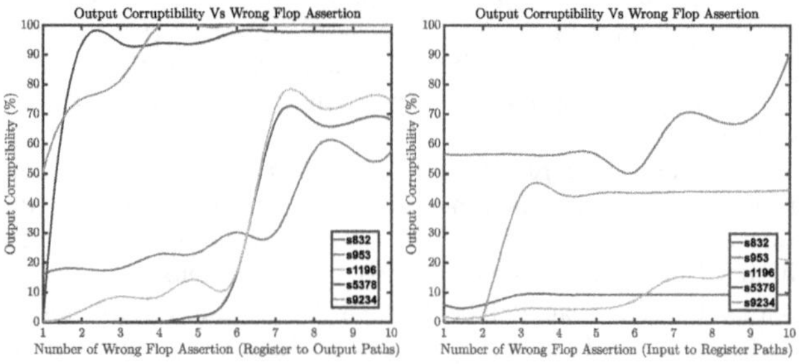


(a) Near REG2OUT Paths
(a) Near IN2REG Paths

**Figure 7: Output corruptibility of ISCAS'89 benchmarks for 12000 random inputs based on wrong flop assertion near (a) reg2out and (b) in2reg timing paths.**

We have simulated the ISCAS'89 benchmarks [18] for 12000 random inputs with randomly inserted $CAMFF's$ in the input-to-register and the output-to-register paths respectively and compared them with the original netlist to measure output corruptibility of TOIC. Simulation shows that even a single wrong flop assertion during de-obfuscation of the circuit can produce significantly corrupted output. For instance, for s832, even two wrong flop assertions can attain 100% output corruptibility. Moreover, the insertion of *CAMFF* near output-to-register paths can result in greater output corruptibility as they are closer to the PO's (Figure 7(a)&(b)).

## 6 DISCUSSION

***Testability of TOIC:*** The controllability and observability is greatly reduced for an attacker as long as the true identities of the camouflaged FF's and the camoufaged $BUFF's/INV's$ in the chain are hidden. From the test perspective *all the $CFF's$ and $DFF's$ in the obfuscated scan chain are controllable and observable to ensure similar testability as the original design*

***Manufacturability:*** State-of-the-art IC fabrication use multi-thres-hold designs to assist in timing closure and power optimization [10]. Hence, TOIC can be fabricated without altering the existing manufacturing flow.

***Clock Tree Routing and Power Distribution Network:*** The additional camouflaged sequentials will be connected to the clock network which will add additional routing overhead. A DC signal *VSN* has to be routed to the camouflaged cells which can use some tracks of the power distribution network.

## 7 CONCLUSION

We presented TOIC, a novel circuit obfuscation technique using camouflaged sequential elements. We also demonstrated a scan chain obfuscation methodology using these sequential cells and additional camouflaged buffer/inverters. By restricting the scan access as well as ensuring significant output corruptibility for wrong assertions during de-obfuscation, TOIC can provide substantially greater security than contemporary gate camouflaging techniques.

## ACKNOWLEDGMENT

This work is supported by SRC (2847.001), NSF (CNS- 1722557, CCF-1718474, DGE-1723687 and DGE-1821766) and DARPA Young Faculty Award (D15AP00089).

## REFERENCES

[1] R. Torrance *et al.*, "The state-of-the-art in ic reverse engineering," in *Cryptographic Hardware and Embedded Systems-CHES 2009.*
[2] M. Holler *et al.*, "High-resolution non-destructive three-dimensional imaging of integrated circuits," *Nature*, vol. 543, no. 7645, p. 402, 2017.
[3] J. Rajendran *et al.*, "Security analysis of integrated circuit camouflaging," in *Proceedings of the 2013 ACM SIGSAC.* ACM, 2013, pp. 709–720.
[4] M. El Massad *et al.*, "Integrated circuit (ic) decamouflaging: Reverse engineering camouflaged ics within minutes." in *NDSS*, 2015.
[5] C. Yu *et al.*, "Incremental sat-based reverse engineering of camouflaged logic circuits," *IEEE TCAD*, vol. 36, no. 10, pp. 1647–1659, 2017.
[6] G. L. Zhang *et al.*, "Timingcamouflage: Improving circuit security against counterfeiting by unconventional timing," in *DATE 2018.*
[7] M. Li *et al.*, "A synergistic framework for hardware ip privacy and integrity protection," Ph.D. dissertation, 2018.
[8] R. Karmakar *et al.*, "Encrypt flip-flop: A novel logic encryption technique for sequential circuits," *arXiv preprint arXiv:1801.04961*, 2018.
[9] J.-W. Jang *et al.*, "A novel threshold voltage defined multiplexer for interconnect camouflaging," Penn State, Tech. Rep., 2017.
[10] S.-L. Wu *et al.*, "Method to fabricate dual threshold cmos circuits," Aug. 1 2000, uS Patent 6,096,611.
[11] A. S. Iyengar *et al.*, "Threshold defined camouflaged gates in 65nm technology for reverse engineering protection," in *ISLPED 2018.*
[12] W. Zhao *et al.*, "Predictive technology model for nano-cmos design exploration," *ACM JETC*, vol. 3, no. 1, p. 1, 2007.
[13] J. Lee *et al.*, "Securing scan design using lock and key technique," in *DFT 2005.* IEEE, 2005, pp. 51–62.
[14] D. Hely *et al.*, "Scan design and secure chip." in *IOLTS*, vol. 4, 2004, pp. 219–224.
[15] Y. Huang *et al.*, "Survey of scan chain diagnosis," *IEEE Design & Test of Computers*, vol. 25, no. 3, 2008.
[16] Y.-L. Kao *et al.*, "Jump simulation: A technique for fast and precise scan chain fault diagnosis," in *ITC-2006.* IEEE, 2006, pp. 1–9.
[17] F. Corno *et al.*, "Rt-level itc'99 benchmarks and first atpg results," *IEEE Design & Test of computers*, vol. 17, no. 3, pp. 44–53, 2000.
[18] F. Brglez *et al.*, "Combinational profiles of sequential benchmark circuits," in *IEEE International Symposium on Circuits and Systems 1989.*

**Table 1: Design Overhead for Timing Obfuscation**

| Bench-mark | Std Cells | Flip-flops | Area ($um^2$) | Power ($uw$) | 5% *CAMFF* with 50% Dummy Flops | | | | | 10% *CAMFF* with 50% Dummy Flops | | | | |
|---|---|---|---|---|---|---|---|---|---|---|---|---|---|---|
| | | | | | Area | Power | SCL | OEL | CBI | Area | Power | SCL | OEL | CBI |
| b13 | 147 | 51 | 676 | 22.4 | 950.07 | 24.92 | 53 | 2 | 48 | 974.07 | 27.48 | 55 | 4 | 46 |
| b15 | 2846 | 417 | 10884 | 309 | 13036 | 316.5 | 423 | 6 | 410 | 13109 | 323.9 | 429 | 12 | 404 |
| b17 | 8707 | 1317 | 33431 | 931 | 40216 | 951.8 | 1334 | 17 | 1299 | 40422 | 972.6 | 1351 | 34 | 1282 |
| b18 | 32545 | 3020 | 110989 | 3085 | 126540 | 3131 | 3058 | 38 | 2981 | 127000 | 3177 | 3096 | 76 | 2943 |
| b19 | 58911 | 6042 | 201993 | 5595 | 233120 | 5686 | 6118 | 76 | 5965 | 234040 | 5778 | 6194 | 152 | 5889 |

* IBM 32nm technology library, SCL - Scan Chain Length, OEL - Obfuscated Edge Length , CBI - Camouflaged Buffer/Inverter.

# Design for Eliminating Operation Specific Power Signatures from Digital Logic

Md Badruddoja Majumder, Md Sakib Hasan, Aysha Shanta, Mesbah Uddin, Garrett Rose
University of Tennessee, Knoxville
{mmajumde,mhasan4,ashanta1,muddin6,garose}@utk.edu

## ABSTRACT

Conventional digital logic operations have distinguishable power signatures. Side channel power analysis combined with classification algorithm can reveal unknown logic operations. Revealing the underlying operations is the main task in reverse engineering an application. In this paper, we propose an unconventional way of overcoming this vulnerability by using chaos based reconfigurable logic operations. The chaos gate used in this paper is built from a simple 3 transistor chaotic oscillator capable of generating aperiodic states starting from a suitably chosen initial condition. We propose a design methodology using chaos gate to implement different logic operations with very similar power profiles. Therefore, it becomes significantly harder to distinguish logical operations built with chaotic logic gates in contrast to the conventional static CMOS logic gates. In addition, we show a mixed implementation of bitwise logic operations using different proportions of chaos and conventional gates resulting in a significant reduction of total overhead.

## CCS CONCEPTS

• **Security and privacy → Side-channel analysis and countermeasures**; • **Hardware → Reconfigurable logic applications**; **Evolvable hardware**.

## KEYWORDS

Chaos, Security, Side channel, Power analysis, Logic

**ACM Reference Format:**
Md Badruddoja Majumder, Md Sakib Hasan, Aysha Shanta, Mesbah Uddin, Garrett Rose. 2019. Design for Eliminating Operation Specific Power Signatures from Digital Logic. In *Great Lakes Symposium on VLSI 2019 (GLSVLSI '19), May 9–11, 2019, Tysons Corner, VA, USA.* ACM, New York, NY, USA, 6 pages. https://doi.org/10.1145/3299874.3318006

## 1 INTRODUCTION

Side channel power analysis is one of the major vulnerabilities in computing. Power profiles contain non-trivial information about computation and thereby pose a major threat to security. Power traces can be leveraged to determine processor instructions leading to software reverse engineering. Every operation in a digital system has its own power signature and can be distinguished from each other. It has been shown that side channel power analysis can be performed to reverse engineer machine code executed by a processor [10, 11, 13] .

Different mitigation schemes have been proposed against side channel power attack in different levels of abstraction starting from very low level hardware based approaches to high level code obfuscation [1, 11]. Two of the most common techniques in eliminating power signature from a computation are hiding and masking. Most of these approaches focus on eliminating data dependency of an operation from its power trace while the operation still can be recognized.

Earlier research pointed to chaos based logic design for power profile obfuscation [2, 12]. However, none of them was very specific about the type of vulnerabilities that it may help to resolve. A chaos based arithmetic logic unit (ALU) design was presented in [9] that can prevent power analysis based template attack to reverse engineer its instructions.

In this paper, we present a security aware logic design approach using a chaotic oscillator where each logic operation exhibits almost identical power traces to prevent power analysis assisted operation reverse engineering. In this design approach, a logic operation leaks minimal information about the type of operation it is performing since each operation exhibits very similar power signature. We perform machine learning based classification among the power traces of a set of logic operations implemented using the proposed method and a conventional method to compare their immunity to reverse engineering. We also perform a scalability analysis of the proposed design method up to 64-bit bitwise logic operations along with a mixed implementation technique using different proportions of chaos and conventional CMOS logic instances.

The remainder of the paper is organized as follows. Chaos based logic design technique is presented in Section 2. Section 3 describes the proposed security aware design methodology. Signal to Noise ratio (SNR) of the power traces is analyzed in Section 4 to quantitatively assess the similarity of power traces. Power analysis based classification results of both chaos and CMOS logic operations is presented in Section 5. Section 6 presents the mixed implementation method and its effectiveness against the attack. Section 7 discusses about the implementation overhead of the proposed chaos based logic. Finally, the paper is concluded in Section 8.

## 2 LOGIC USING CHAOS

Chaos computing refers to the idea of using nonlinear dynamics of chaotic systems for computation. Chaotic system produces aperiodic sequence over time dependent on the initial condition. Generation of a pattern from a chaotic system over time starting with an initial condition is called chaotic evolution. Evolution of a


*GLSVLSI '19, May 9–11, 2019, Tysons Corner, VA, USA*

ACM ISBN 978-1-4503-6252-8/19/05...$15.00
https://doi.org/10.1145/3299874.3318006

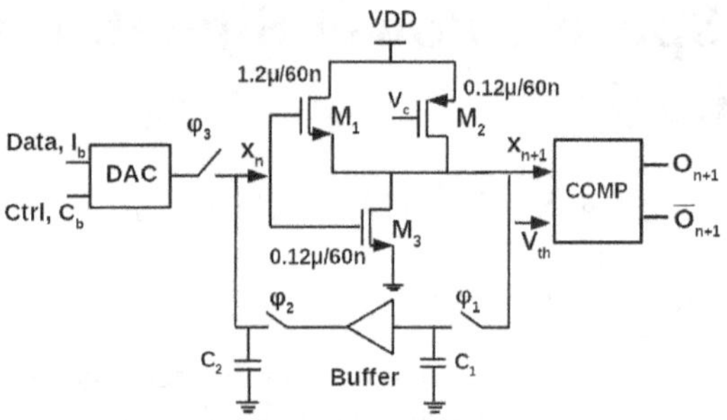


**Figure 1: Logic gate built from a discrete time chaotic map circuit.**

**Table 1: Evolution of chaotic output ($V_C$=0.68 V, $C_b$ = 1).**

| $X_0$ (V) | $X_{n+1}$ (V) | | | | |
|---|---|---|---|---|---|
| | $i=1$ | $i=2$ | $i=3$ | $i=4$ | $i=5$ |
| 0.171(00) | 1.19 | 0.52 | 0.40 | 0.93 | 0.36 |
| 0.514(01) | 0.41 | 0.88 | 0.34 | 1.15 | 0.49 |
| 0.857(10) | 0.33 | 1.16 | 0.50 | 0.49 | 0.52 |
| 1.2(11) | 0.52 | 0.40 | 0.94 | 0.37 | 1.06 |

chaotic system may occur either in the continuous time domain or the discrete time domain. Chua's circuit is an example of continuous time domain chaotic system [3]. On the other hand, the logistic map, tent map and shift map are examples of the discrete time domain chaotic system [7]. In discrete time chaos generator, chaotic patterns are generated in an iterative process. In each iteration output of the previous iteration becomes the input of the present one and thus evolves in discrete time. Dudek *et al.* proposed a 3 transistor non-linear circuit that works as a discrete time chaotic map [5]. This chaotic map circuit can be used to implement reconfigurable boolean functions [8].

In this work, we design a 65nm scaled version of the design presented in [8] for security aware chaos based logic design as shown in Fig.1. Similar to the basic functionality of any discrete time chaotic map, the output of the non-linear circuit is fed back to the input and iteratively generates a sequence of voltage. In addition to the non-linear map circuit, the chaos gate requires two sample-and-hold circuits controlled by the non-overlapping clocks, $\phi_1$ and $\phi_2$. When $\phi_1$ is high, the output, $X_{n+1}$ of the map circuit is sampled onto $C_1$. When $\phi_2$ is high, $X_{n+1}$ is sampled onto $C_2$ so that it becomes the input of the map circuit in the next iteration. A digital to analog converter is used to map the digital input, ($C_b$, $I_b$) to analog input, $X_n$ of the chaos gate. Control bit, $C_b$ is used for reconfigurability of the logic functions.

Initially, the circuit takes external input to start the operation which is controlled by the clock, $\phi_3$. In subsequent iterations, the output is fed back to the input to continue chaotic operation. Bias voltage, $V_c$ determines the voltage sequence of the chaotic evolution from this circuit. Output of the chaotic circuit is digitized using a comparator so that it works as a digital logic gate. Threshold voltage, $V_{th}$ of the comparator also works as a control parameter for this logic gate. Thus, different boolean functionalities are generated at different iterations depending on 4 control parameters:

**Table 2: Example chaos gate configuration for different operations.**

| Parameter | Instruction | | |
|---|---|---|---|
| | AND/NAND | OR/NOR | XOR/XNOR |
| $V_c$ (V) | 0.68 | | |
| $C_b$ | 1 | | |
| $V_{th}$ | 0.46 | 0.41 | 0.66 |
| $n$ | 2 | 5 | 2 |

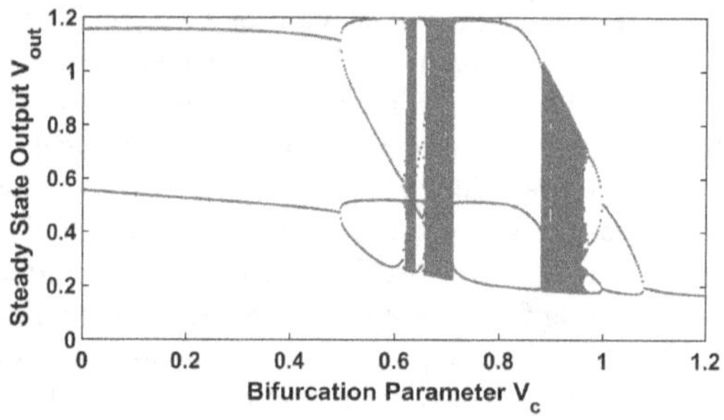


**Figure 2: Bifurcation diagram for the 3 transistor chaotic map circuit.**

bias voltage, $V_c$, control bit, $C_b$ , iteration number, $n$ and threshold voltage, $V_{th}$. The comparator used in this design is a dynamic comparator having both non-inverted and inverted output [6]. Any control parameter that produces a particular logic function also produces its inverted version. Therefore, AND/NAND, OR/NOR, XOR/XNOR, these functions are generated as pairs. Table 1 shows example analog output voltage sequences of the proposed design of chaotic gate for all possible input combinations with $V_c$=0.68 V and $C_b$=1. Chaotic circuit shown in Fig. 1 can work as 6 logic functions with appropriate threshold voltage, $V_{th}$ and sampling iteration, $n$. which is demonstrated in Table 2. For instance, if we digitize the output analog voltage at $2^{nd}$ iteration from Table 1 with a threshold voltage of 0.66 V, we get the XOR/XNOR functionality. Similarly, other functionalities can also be verified using the information provided in Table 1 and 2.

## 3 DESIGN FOR SECURITY

The goal of this work is to construct logic operations exhibiting very similar power profiles such that minimal information is leaked through power side channel. This can be achieved by proper choice of parameters in the proposed chaos based logic design. Proposed logic design method provides a large design space to choose its design parameters due to chaos dynamics. Design space is reduced by imposing different design constraints led by security goals and performance criteria. In this section, we discuss these constraints and how to apply them to achieve our desired design for security.

### 3.1 Security Constraints

There are four parameters in the chaos circuit that we can vary to realize different logic functions. These parameters are: control bit, $C_b$, bias voltage, $V_C$, threshold voltage, $V_{th}$, and sampling iteration,

**Table 3: Performance metric for different geometry of chaotic oscillator.**

| Index | Geometry | | | Metric |
|---|---|---|---|---|
| | $W_1(\mu m)$ | $W_2(\mu m)$ | $W_3(\mu m)$ | $\frac{mV}{fJ.\mu m^2}$ |
| 1 | 4.8 | 0.48 | 0.48 | 0.85 |
| 2 | 4 | 0.15 | 0.15 | 5.1 |
| 3 | 4 | 0.12 | 0.12 | 7.1 |
| 4 | 6 | 0.15 | 0.15 | 3.5 |
| 5 | 2 | 0.15 | 0.15 | 4.7 |
| 6 | 1.2 | 0.12 | 0.12 | 7.2 |
| 7 | 2.4 | 0.24 | 0.24 | 2.1 |

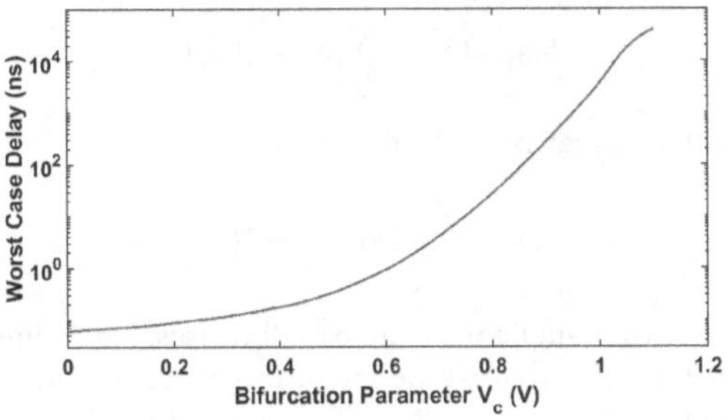


**Figure 3: Illustration of worst case delay vs. bifurcation parameter.**

$n$. In this chaos circuit, $C_b$ and $V_c$, respectively controls the initial input and the sequence of chaotic output which effectively dictates the power trace. For the type of security desired in this paper, power profiles of all logic operations need to be alike. In order to have maximum similarity of the power profiles among different operations, we keep $C_b$ and $V_c$ same for all functions with varying $V_{th}$ and $n$. Due to differences in $V_{th}$, the comparator has some operation specific signatures in the power profile. However, this variation is negligible to distinguish the operations based on their power profile which will be presented in later sections of the paper. We use a delay stage at the comparator output to make the final output available at the same time which helps in hiding the time induced power signature of all the operations.

## 3.2 Performance Constraints

Bifurcation diagram of a chaotic map circuit plots the possible outputs with respect to a bifurcation parameter. Fig. 2 is the bifurcation diagram of the chaotic oscillator shown in Fig. 1 where the bifurcation parameter is $V_c$. Chaotic operation occurs in a region in the bifurcation diagram where the outputs are densely populated within a certain range. The geometry of the circuit is chosen based on an empirical analysis as analytical approach is very complex and out of scope of this paper. We choose 7 different test geometries for the circuit and rank each of them based on a performance metric. The performance metric (PM) is formulated as

$$PM = \frac{C^{w1}}{A^{w2}.P^{w3}.D^{w4}} \tag{1}$$

where C=width of chaotic region in bifurcation diagram and A, P, D are the average area, power and delay of the chaotic map circuit, respectively. $w1$, $w2$, $w3$ and $w4$ are corresponding weight for these factors which are considered 1 in this work, i.e. $w_1 = w_2 = w_3 = w_4 = 1$. However, depending on applications we may modulate these weights to prioritize particular factors in the performance metric. As width of chaotic region in the bifurcation diagram contributes to the large functionality space of the chaotic gate, it is kept as the numerator in the performance metric. On the other hand, quantities contributing to design overhead such as area, power and delay are kept in the denominator. Table 3 shows the performance metric for each of the 7 geometries. Geometry 6 which has the highest performance value is chosen in the final design used in this work. $W_1$ , $W_2$, $W_3$ represents the width of transistors $M_1$, $M_2$ and $M_3$ in Fig. 1. Length of the transistors are chosen as $60nm$ which is the minimum length of the $65nm$ process.

For the chosen geometry, there are two distinct regions of $V_c$ that causes chaotic operation as can be seen in the bifurcation diagram. The first one is 0.62 V to 0.71 V and the second region is 0.88 V to 0.96 V. Primarily, $V_c$ is chosen from one of these two regions for having the maximum functionality space of chaotic operations. Investigating the circuit, it is found that the delay is maximum when the input makes a transition from VDD to 0. This worst case delay for chaotic gate increases with $V_c$ as shown in Fig. 3. The first region of $V_c$ results in considerably less delay than the second one. Therefore, we constrain the $V_c$ to the first region only.

Chaotic operations are sensitive to initial condition. Small perturbation can cause significant deviation in its evolution over time and amount of deviation increases with time. However, we can avoid this problem by restricting the iteration of the chaotic circuit within a certain limit that the deviation in the chaotic evolution is negligible and the circuit can function reliably. Furthermore, longer iteration time results in longer delay. In this design, we consider 5 iterations to choose the logic functionality from the chaotic circuit.

## 3.3 Design flow

In the first step of our design flow, we generate a set of possible configuration parameters for each of the logic functions individually. While generating this set of configuration parameters, we keep the iteration number, $n$ within 5. After that, a subset of this parameter set is considered based on common $V_C$ and $C_b$ which is our security constraint described earlier. We further reduce the set based on the worst case delay criteria mentioned earlier where $V_C$ is constrained between 0.62 V and 0.71 V. Such a combination of the parameters is shown in Table 2 for the proposed design of logic gates. It is to be noted that this particular combination is arbitrarily chosen and is one of many which satisfies all the constraints.

Fig. 4 and 5 shows the power profile of different operations for the same operand implemented using CMOS and chaos logic, respectively. It can be seen from visual inspection that power traces in CMOS logic are different from each other while they are almost indistinguishable in the proposed chaos logic. In order to compare the degree of difficulty in distinguishing the power trace of different logic operations, quantitative analysis such as signal to noise ratio (SNR) and machine learning based classification are performed in the following sections.

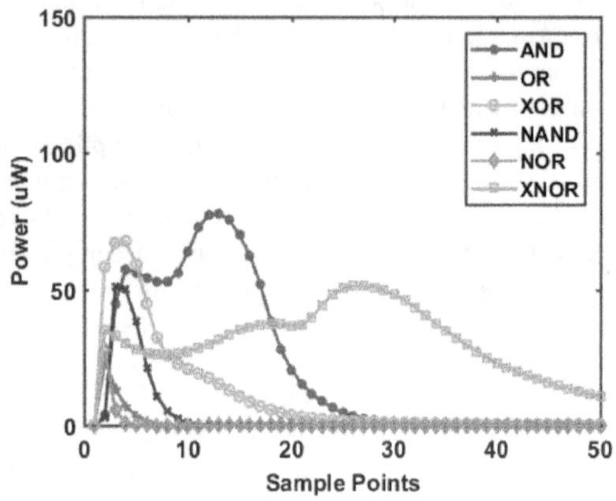


**Figure 4: Power trace of CMOS logic operations.**

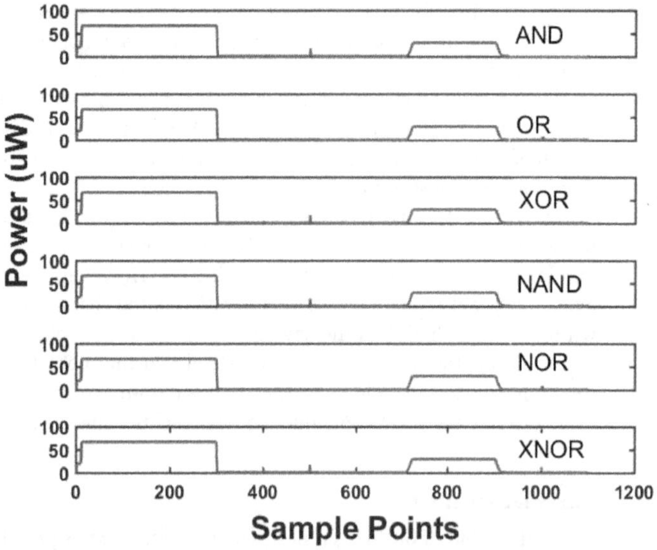


**Figure 5: Power trace of chaos logic operations.**

## 4 SNR ANALYSIS

In this work, we are interested in measuring the distinguishability of the power traces corresponding to different logic operations. The more the power traces are scattered among different operations, the more distinguishable they are. On the contrary, they are less distinguishable if the power traces are scattered more within operations due to different operands. In order to measure the SNR in this work, inter- and intra-operation scattering, $S_{inter}$ and $S_{intra}$ are considered as the signal and noise, respectively.

Since unnecessary dimensions affect distinguishability, we estimate the signal to noise ratio for the power traces with reduced dimensionality using linear discriminant analysis [4]. In this method, original data is projected to a lower dimensional space using a linear transformation. Let $X$ be a set comprising $C$ (number of classes) subset of $D$, $N$-dimensional power traces. $X$ is transformed to $Y$ where each power trace has a reduced dimensionality $N_r$. For Fisher's linear discrimant analysis, $N_r = C - 1$.

$$Y_i = X_i W, \tag{2}$$

where $W$ is a $N$ x $N_r$ transformation matrix.

We can calculate inter-class and intra-class scatter matrix, $S_{inter}$ and $S_{intra}$, respectively for the original $N$-dimensional power traces.

Intra-operation scatter matrix for each class is as follows.

$$S_{intra}(X_i) = \sum_{x \epsilon C_i} (x - m_i)^t (x - m_i), \tag{3}$$

where $m_i$ is the N-dimensional sample mean for power traces of each class. Overall intra-operation scatter matrix is then

$$S_{intra}(X) = \sum_{i=1}^{C} S_{intra}(X_i). \tag{4}$$

Inter-scattering matrix can be defined as,

$$S_{inter}(X) = \sum_{i=1}^{C} D(m_i - m)^t (m_i - m). \tag{5}$$

where, $m$ is the sample mean across all classes. Now, inter- and intra-scattering matrix can be found for the data with reduced dimension.

$$S_{intra}(Y) = W^T S_{intra}(X) W. \tag{6}$$

$$S_{inter}(Y) = W^T S_{inter}(X) W. \tag{7}$$

Criterion function for maximum distinguishability can be defined as,

$$J(W) = \frac{det(S_{inter}(Y))}{det(S_{intra}(Y))}. \tag{8}$$

According to our definition, the best case SNR of the power traces from different logic operations is

$$SNR = J(W_{max}) = \frac{det(W_{max}^T S_{inter}(X) W_{max})}{det(W_{max}^T S_{intra}(X) W_{max})}. \tag{9}$$

For the analysis of SNR, we simulate each logic operation both for the conventional CMOS design and chaos based design in Cadence Spectre circuit simulator. A power trace for a particular logic operation depends on its input data transition. There are 16 possible input data transitions for a 2 input logic operation covering all cases. We consider 6 logic operations for this work. Each operation has 16 different power traces. Dimension for power trace is 100 and 1100 for CMOS and chaos gates, respectively. More sampling points are required for chaos gate since it requires larger operation time. Using Eq. 9, SNR in the power traces for CMOS and chaos logic operation is found to be $1.265x10^{-5}$ and $3.384x10^{-11}$, respectively. Power traces of chaos logic is significantly harder to distinguish as its SNR is 6 orders smaller than that of CMOS logic.

## 5 CLASSIFICATION ATTACK AND RESULTS

We demonstrate power analysis based classification attack on a set of logical operations AND, OR, XOR, NAND, NOR, XNOR implemented using conventional CMOS logic gates and proposed chaos based logic gates. Based on the results of the attack, we can compare the resiliency of both implementation against power analysis.

**Table 4: Power analysis based classification accuracy of logic operations.**

| Method | Logic | Classification Accuracy(%) | | | | | | |
|---|---|---|---|---|---|---|---|---|
| | | AND | OR | XOR | NAND | NOR | XNOR | **Overall** |
| (K=1)-NN | CMOS | 98 | 97 | 99 | 97 | 93 | 99 | **97** |
| | Chaos | 23 | 38 | 24 | 24 | 37 | 24 | **28** |
| (K=3)-NN | CMOS | 98 | 96 | 98 | 97 | 91 | 99 | **96** |
| | Chaos | 23 | 33 | 22 | 22 | 32 | 23 | **26** |
| (K=)5-NN | CMOS | 97 | 95 | 98 | 97 | 89 | 99 | **96** |
| | Chaos | 21 | 32 | 20 | 20 | 31 | 22 | **24** |

## 5.1 Attack Method

The attack performed to distinguish each operation from a set of logic operations uses a classification algorithm. The classifier is trained using power traces from known operations. In the work flow of the attack method, we collect training power traces, reduce the dimension of data and finally apply the classification algorithm on the test data set. These steps are explained here.

*5.1.1 Data Collection.* We perform classification on bitwise logic operations of different bit sizes. In this work, bitwise logic operations of arbitrary operand size is implemented by using multiple 2-input single bit instances of the desired functionality. For example, an N-bit AND operation uses N copy of single bit AND gate. If instantaneous power profiles of the single bit gate is known for each possible input transitions, we can estimate the power profile of an arbitrary sized operation by adding up the profile of each logic instance for respective input transition. For this work, instantaneous power profiles of each of the six 2-input single bit logic gate are pre collected for all 16 possible input transitions using Cadence Spectre simulator for both CMOS and chaos based implementations.

*5.1.2 Dimensionality Reduction.* It is a common practice to reduce the dimensionality of data in order to make the classification more efficient in terms of computation and at the same time avoid the noise created by irrelevant points. From [10], it was found that principle component analysis (PCA) gives the best result for classifying instructions in a microcontroller using power traces and that is why PCA has been used in this work. In PCA, original data is projected orthogonally into a subspace with lower dimension. The projection subspace is chosen mathematically in such a way that maximizes the variance among projected data. Here,the first 30 principal components have been used since they contain more than 95% of the total variance.

*5.1.3 Classification Algorithm.* There are various algorithms that can be used for pattern classification such as K-nearest neighbor (KNN), multivariate Gaussian, support vector machine, etc. From the previous work on instruction classification presented in [10], KNN was found to be the most efficient in classifying different operations performed by a microcontroller. We, therefore, choose KNN with K=1, 3 and 5 as the classification algorithm to be used in this work. In KNN algorithm, the classifier calculates the distance between the test sample and all training samples and choose the K training samples having the least distance. Among these K samples, the class that most of these samples belong to is treated as the class of the test sample. Distance between two samples has been calculated using Euclidean distance function in this work.

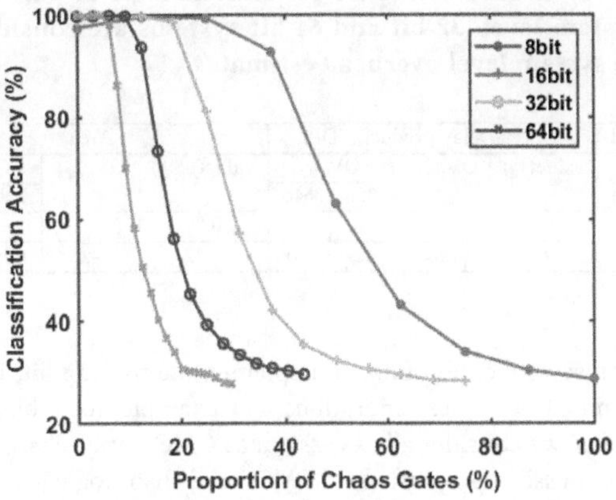


**Figure 6: Classification accuracy of bitwise logic operations for different operand sizes and different proportions of chaos gates.**

## 5.2 Attack Results

In order to test the recognition rate of the classifier, we used 60% of the total collected data for training and the remaining 40% data is used for testing the classifier. The set of training and testing samples are shuffled among the total collected sample space to cross validate the classifier. We choose a total data set of 4000, 8000, 16000 and 32000 samples for performing the classification attack on 8 bit, 16 bit, 32 bit and 64 bit operations, respectively. Classification accuracy for both conventional and chaos based implementation of 8 bit logic operations are tabulated in Table 4. For the conventional implementation of considered logical operations, overall accuracy of classification based on power profile is found to be 97%, 96%, 96% for nearest neighbor approach with K=1, 3 and 5, respectively while it is only 28%, 26% and 24% for the proposed chaos based design. Such reduction in classification accuracy reflects that proposed chaos logic operations are designed in a way that they carry minimal distinguishing features from each other in the power profiles which is consistent with the result of SNR analysis in section 4.

# 6 SCALABILITY AND MIXED IMPLEMENTATION

Logical operations in general purpose computing systems are performed bitwise on different operand size as machine instructions. As we described earlier, we can implement the operation of arbitrary bit size using multiple copies of the 1 bit instance. Using the simulated power data, we can perform the classification attack on any arbitrary bit size. In order to demonstrate the scalability of our design technique while preserving its immunity against the classification attack, we choose 8 bit, 16 bit, 32 bit and 64 bit logic operations.

An interesting aspect of the security with chaos based logic is that for bitwise operation in larger system, all single bit instances do not require to be implemented using chaos logic. Rather, a mixed implementation where only a fraction of total instances implemented using the proposed chaos logic is sufficient to defend against side channel attack. This significantly reduces the overhead of the entire system. In order to demonstrate this, we perform the classification

**Table 5: Overhead estimates for chaotic logic in gate level and system level. 32 bit and 64 bit systems are considered for the system level overhead estimates.**

| Method | Power-Delay product (PDP) | | | | Area | | | |
|---|---|---|---|---|---|---|---|---|
| | value(fJ) | $OV_{gate}$ | $OV_{sys}$ | | value($\mu m^2$) | $OV_{gate}$ | $OV_{sys}$ | |
| | | | 32b | 64b | | | 32b | 64b |
| CMOS | 54 | - | - | - | 0.29 | - | - | - |
| Chaos | 95 | 1.8x | 1.2x | 1.1x | 1.22 | 4x | 1.9x | 1.6x |

attack on several cases of mixed implementations for 8 bit, 16 bit, 32 bit and 64 bit logical operations. For example, for 8 bit logic operations, we consider all cases such as CMOS only, chaos only and other possible proportions of CMOS and chaos logic instances. For this analysis, we only consider nearest neighbor with K=1 using PCA as it can classify with higher accuracy.

The results of mixed implementations are demonstrated in Fig. 6. Here, number of chaos gate=0 refers to the CMOS only implementation. It can be seen that in the CMOS only implementation, classification accuracy is close to 100%. With the increase of chaos gate proportion, signature of CMOS instances in the power profile diminishes and the classification accuracy drops. At a certain proportion of CMOS and chaos gates, the classification accuracy reaches around 30% which is a significant improvement over the traditional design. The effectiveness of this mixed implementation technique lies in the fact that the implementation cost is reduced significantly in the design of proposed side channel resistant logic operations in larger computing systems.

## 7 OVERHEAD ANALYSIS

In conventional design of digital logic, operation performed by a logic gate can be revealed through the power measurements. Proposed logic design using chaotic dynamics prevents information leak about the operation of a logic gate through the power trace and helps mitigate these vulnerabilities. Design for security comes with a cost of implementation overhead as compared to conventional design technique. Here, we compare the overheads of our proposed design with conventional static CMOS logic design. Comparisons are made based on the average of area and power-delay product (PDP) of different types of logic gates. Overhead estimates are given in Table 5. Proposed chaos based logic requires approximately 1.8x PDP and 4x area per gate as compared to standard CMOS logic gate. CMOS gates considered here for comparison are designed in 65 nm process where the basic gates (NAND, NOR) are equivalent to an inverter having an aspect ratio of 480nm/60nm and 240nm/60nm for the PMOS and NMOS, respectively.

Due to the mixed implementation capability discussed earlier in this paper, proposed chaos logic can be more efficient while implemented in larger computing system as bitwise logical instructions. In a mixed implementation, bitwise logic operations are built with a proportion of chaos and standard CMOS gates and hence, the overhead can be reduced. If $k$ is the proportion of chaos gates for the bitwise implementation of a $n$ bit system, implementation overhead can be calculated as

$$OV_{sys} = \frac{(1-k)G_D + kG_C}{G_D} \tag{10}$$

where $G_D$ and $G_C$ are the implementation cost associated with each standard CMOS gate and chaos gate, respectively. Eq. 10 can be represented in terms of per gate overhead of chaos gate compared to the digital gates.

$$OV_{sys} = 1 + k(OV_{gate} - 1) \tag{11}$$

where $OV_{gate} = \frac{G_C}{G_D}$.

Area and PDP overhead for bitwise chaos logic for 32 and 64 bit system is tabulated in Table 5. From Fig. 6, proportion factor, $k$ of chaos gates in 32 bit and 64 bit logic operations are calculated as 0.3 and 0.2, respectively considering a maximum classification accuracy of 30%. Now, the mixed implementations of bitwise logic in 32 bit and 64 bit system exhibit a PDP overhead of 1.2x and 1.1x, respectively and area overhead of 1.9x and 1.6x, respectively.

## 8 CONCLUSION

Chaos based logic design shows great promises for application in security against side channel power analysis. A logical instruction set having very similar power profiles can be designed according to the proposed method which helps mitigate power analysis based instruction reverse engineering. Mixed implementation overheads associated with bitwise logic operations scale down significantly with the operand size and thus outweighs the per gate overhead. This paper mainly focused on application of the proposed design in hiding the logic operations from the power profile. Since this design methodology can be implemented using any discrete time chaotic map circuit, other circuit implementations can be explored in the future to reduce the overhead.

## REFERENCES

[1] Jude Angelo Ambrose, Roshan G Ragel, and Sri Parameswaran. 2007. RIJID: random code injection to mask power analysis based side channel attacks. In *Proceedings of the 44th annual Design Automation Conference*. ACM, 489–492.
[2] James Bohl, Lok-Kwong Yan, and Garrett S Rose. 2015. A two-dimensional chaotic logic gate for improved computer security. In *Circuits and Systems (MWSCAS), 2015 IEEE 58th International Midwest Symposium on*. IEEE, 1–4.
[3] Leon O Chua and G-N Lin. 1990. Canonical realization of Chua's circuit family. *IEEE transactions on Circuits and Systems* 37, 7 (1990), 885–902.
[4] Richard O Duda, Peter E Hart, and David G Stork. 2000. Pattern classification (pt. 1). *Danvers, MA: Wiley Interscience* (2000).
[5] P Dudek and VD Juncu. 2003. Compact discrete-time chaos generator circuit. *Electronics Letters* 39, 20 (2003), 1431–1432.
[6] Bernhard Goll and Horst Zimmermann. 2009. A comparator with reduced delay time in 65-nm CMOS for supply voltages down to 0.65 V. *IEEE Transactions on Circuits and Systems II: Express Briefs* 56, 11 (2009), 810–814.
[7] Behnam Kia, John Lindner, William L Ditto, et al. 2015. Nonlinear dynamics based digital logic and circuits. *Frontiers in computational neuroscience* 9 (2015), 49.
[8] Behnam Kia, John F Lindner, and William L Ditto. 2016. A simple nonlinear circuit contains an infinite number of functions. *IEEE Transactions on Circuits and Systems II: Express Briefs* 63, 10 (2016), 944–948.
[9] Md Badruddoja Majumder, Md Sakib Hasan, Mesbah Uddin, and Garrett S Rose. 2018. Chaos computing for mitigating side channel attack. In *2018 IEEE International Symposium on Hardware Oriented Security and Trust (HOST)*. IEEE, 143–146.
[10] Mehari Msgna, Konstantinos Markantonakis, and Keith Mayes. 2014. Precise instruction-level side channel profiling of embedded processors. In *International Conference on Information Security Practice and Experience*. Springer, 129–143.
[11] Thomas Popp, Stefan Mangard, and Elisabeth Oswald. 2007. Power analysis attacks and countermeasures. *IEEE Design & test of Computers* 24, 6 (2007).
[12] Garrett Steven Rose. 2014. A chaos-based arithmetic logic unit and implications for obfuscation. In *VLSI (ISVLSI), 2014 IEEE Computer Society Annual Symposium on*. IEEE, 54–58.
[13] Dennis Vermoen, Marc Witteman, and Georgi Gaydadjiev. 2007. Reverse engineering java card applets using power analysis. *Information Security Theory and Practices. Smart Cards, Mobile and Ubiquitous Computing Systems* (2007), 138–149.

# Non-Uniform Temperature Distribution in Interconnects and Its Impact on Electromigration

Ali Abbasinasab, Malgorzata Marek-Sadowska
ECE Department, University of California, Santa Barbara, Santa Barbara, CA 93106
{ali, mms}@ece.ucsb.edu

## ABSTRACT

We investigate the effect of electrically induced thermal load on interconnect reliability and aging. We propose new models for uniform and non-uniform temperature evolution and its steady state distribution in interconnects considering Joule heating and heat convection. The models are verified by comparing the results against those of finite element experiments. We apply our models to study material migration induced aging and failures. We discuss how different non-uniform temperature profiles affect interconnect lifetime. We propose new formulas for accurate temperature aware assessment of the mortality of interconnects. We demonstrate that neglecting thermal effects in modern technologies may lead to incorrect conclusions about interconnect mortality. We also provide a method for modeling the true mean time to failure based on underlying physics.

## KEYWORDS

Aging, lifetime, reliability, interconnect, electromigration, thermomigration, stress migration, EM

**ACM Reference format:**

Ali Abbasinasab, Malgorzata Marek-Sadowska. 2019. Non-Uniform Temperature Distribution in Interconnects and Its Impact on Electromigration. In *Proceedings of 2019 Great Lakes Symposium on VLSI (GLSVLSI'19).* ACM, New York, NY, USA, 6 pages. https://doi.org/10.1145/3299874.3317973

## 1. INTRODUCTION

Many papers are devoted to studying temperature distribution of conductors in VLSI chips. They mostly present analytical models that consider the effect of ohmic heating generated in wires by electric current [1-3]. However, most of them only consider this single source of heating without correctly considering the effects of vias and miscellaneous heat distributions and transfers due to various external settings. In reality, temperature is not distributed uniformly along the wire. Vias play the role of heat sinks or heat sources, transferring the heat between the layers. Assuming, in a common case, that vias transfer heat from the layers closer to device to the layer closer to the heat sink (ambient temperature), the temperature profile measured in the experiments are usually of upside-down shape (i.e. ∩). [2] takes the effect of via into account and proposes an analytical model for a single end-to-end wire. However, they assume that the temperatures at both ends are the same, which might not be true especially for long wires passing over several blocks. More advanced works such as [1] present a similar idea. However, their model cannot be readily incorporated into the aging problem due to their assumption on substrate temperature. Our novel model is later used for interconnect aging due to mass transport. The model considers Joule heating and heat convection with respect to arbitrary external settings.

The effect of temperature rise produces temperature gradients which generate thermomigration affecting other failure mechanisms namely electromigration and stress migration [22][23]. There are some similar efforts on modeling thermal effect and electromigration such as [24]. However, to our knowledge, the mutual interaction between them has not been discussed. Since the thermal effect on aging can no longer be neglected for modern technologies [4-6], we present novel formulas for mortality of interconnects under thermal load. We provide a comprehensive study using our models to see how various thermal profiles influence material migration through hydrostatic stress analysis. Many interesting and useful conclusions are drawn on any specific non-uniform temperature distribution. We also propose a set of useful tools for designer to potentially exploit the design opportunities provided by thermal effects. We perform extensive experiments to verify the correctness of our models by comparing them against detailed finite element experiments.

There are orthogonal works [1][7], that due to lack of correct physics-based models, use empirical external data and large-scale statistical analysis methods under various experimental temperatures and apply a corrective constant fixed temperature increase or fluctuation ($\Delta$T) to the average operating temperature or attempt to fit an exponent in Black's MTF equation [8]. We also present a method for calculating the true interconnect mean time to failure.

## 2. TEMPERATURE IN INTERCONNECTS

The evolution and steady state of temperature in interconnects has been studied very well. The existing models, however, are developed based on simplified initial and boundary conditions. In the well-known and widely adopted model in [1][2][9] the temperature distribution and evolution of temperature is studied only for uniform external temperatures and a specific boundary condition. In other words, they assumed that temperatures at both ends are the same, which is invalid for long wires with different layers of metal and devices underneath. We revisit the heat conduction in metallic interconnects and solve the heat equation for arbitrary shape interconnects and all possible boundary conditions.

Given by the first law of thermodynamics, the transient thermal behavior of a solid in a given region over time is [10]:


*GLSVLSI '19, May 9–11, 2019, Tysons Corner, VA, USA*

ACM ISBN 978-1-4503-6252-8/19/05...$15.00.
DOI: https://doi.org/10.1145/3299874.3317973

$$\rho_m c_p \frac{\partial T}{\partial t} + \nabla q = Q \quad (1)$$

where $\rho_m$ and $c_p$ are the mass density and specific heat, respectively, $q = -k\nabla T$ is due to the heat flux described by the Fourier's law, $Q = Q_{jh} + Q_{con}$ is due to various heat generation processes including Joule heating ($Q_{jh} = j^2\rho = \Delta V^2/\rho L^2$) and heat convection $Q_{con} = k(T_0 - T)/\Gamma^2$ where $\Gamma$ is the thermal characteristic length determined by the geometry and topology of surrounding interconnects. In this paper we use the model in [9] for $\Gamma$ which matches perfectly with FEM experiments. It can be shown that $\Gamma$ can be properly approximated by:

$$\Gamma^2 = t_{Cu} t_{ILD} \frac{k_{cu}}{k_{ILD}} \quad (2)$$

where $t_{Cu}$ and $t_{ILD}$ are the thickness of the wire and the dielectric and also $k_{cu}$ and $k_{ILD}$ are thermal conductivity of the wire and dielectric, respectively.

Note that $\Gamma$ can be modeled differently depending on layout topology. While we used the model in [2][9], the proposed model is not limited to $\Gamma$ as stated in (2) – any other model for the thermal characteristic length can be plugged into and handled by our new models.

Under stationary condition the solution to (1) for a wire ($-L/2 < x < L/2$) with initial conditions of $T(-L/2) = T_1$ and $T(+L/2) = T_2$ is obtained as:

$$T(x) = T_0 + T_m\left[1 - \frac{\cosh\left(\frac{x}{\Gamma}\right)}{\cosh\left(\frac{L}{2\Gamma}\right)}\right] + T_n\left[\frac{\sinh\left(\frac{x}{\Gamma}\right)}{\sinh\left(\frac{L}{2\Gamma}\right)}\right] \quad (3)$$

where $T_0 = (T_1 + T_2)/2$, $T_n = (T_1 - T_2)/2$ and $T_m = j^2\Gamma^2\rho/k$ is the maximum temperature rise. For the simple case where the anode and cathode have the same temperature ($T_0$), (3) matches the solutions in [2][3][9].

To verify the correctness and accuracy of the model proposed in (3), we compared it against detailed finite element experiments. Not only the model can be used for a single end-to-end wire, it can readily be used for any complex structure with given initial conditions (e.g. external temperatures). Figure 1 (a), for example, demonstrates the application of the new model to a complex structure. In principle, the model presented in (3) is solved for all individual node to node segments. The complicated multi-branch structure shown in Fig 1 is a small part of a large intermediate-length net from IBM benchmark [11]. The entire circuit is analyzed using SPICE which provides the corresponding current density to our FEM experiments. Branches carry current densities of the order of 1MA/cm². The segment is then properly constructed in COMSOL Multiphysics [12]. The values for geometrical, electrical, mechanical and

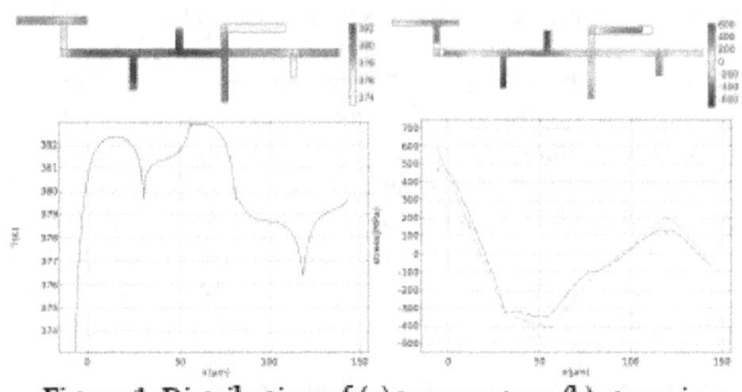

Figure 1: Distribution of (a) temperature (b) stress in a complex net

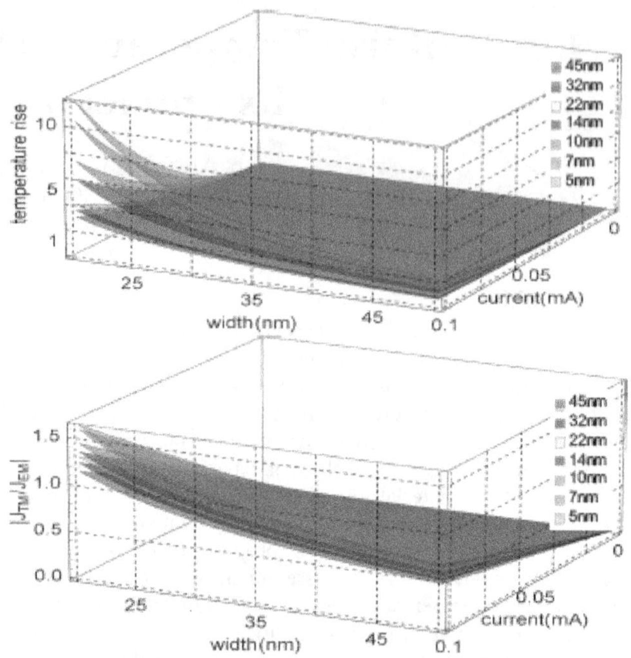


Figure 2: Effect of current, width and technology scaling on (a) temperature rise; (b) The TM flux to EM flux ratio.

thermal properties of technology are obtained from various recent reports of major foundries for 10nm [4-6][13-17]. Via effect which explains the inter-layer heat transfer is also employed for realistic and accurate modeling [1][9]. The external ambient temperatures for sournding layers 4, 5 and 6 are assumed to be 373.15K, 376.65K and 379.65K, respectively. The temperature evolution due to Joule heating and heat convection is obtained by detailed finite element methods. The temperature distribution is depicted for the steady state in Fig 1 (a) which agrees with the results obtained by the model proposed in (3).

The proposed model is independent of the underlying technology (geometry and material properties) or external settings. In other words, any arbitrary electrical and thermal settings can be properly fed to and accommodated by (3).

Fig. 2 shows the significance of temperature in contemporary technologies. In Fig 2 (a), the temperature rise is shown versus technology scaling (which includes all enforced factors: such as thickness, aspect ratios, minimum pitch, thermal and electrical properties) and design elements (such as current and width). Current density is not directly employed as it is partially technology dependent (through thickness) and thus is non-distinguishable in terms of design and technology. However, the corresponding current and the interconnect width are used appropriately. The mean values for the parameters are obtained from recent experimental reports on modern manufacturing processes of major foundries [4-7][13-17]. Due to the space limit, the effects are shown for local interconnects only; similar observations can be made for other layers. present a method for calculating the true interconnect mean time to failure.

## 3. MATERIAL MIGRATION

A metallic line is considered reliable if material concentration is almost constant across the wire within a specific period of time (i.e. several years). The change of atom concentration $C$ due to atomic fluxes is described as follows:

$$\frac{\partial C}{\partial t} = -\nabla . \vec{J} \quad (4)$$

where $J = \overrightarrow{J_{EM}} + \overrightarrow{J_{TM}} + \overrightarrow{J_{SM}}$ is the atomic flux composed of several different fluxes due to electromigration, stress migration, and thermomigration (left to right) described as:

$$\vec{J} = -\frac{DC}{kT}(eZ\nabla V + \Omega\nabla\sigma - QT^{-1}\nabla T) \quad (5)$$

where $D$ is the diffusivity, $k$ is Boltzmann's constant and $T$ is the temperature, $e$ is the fundamental electron charge, $Z$ is the effective charge $\rho$ is the resistivity and $j$ is the current density, $\sigma$ is the hydrostatic stress and $\Omega$ is the atomic volume and $Q$ represents the specific heat of transport of metal. [18] presents an analytical model that eliminates the intangible concentration quantity based on a relationship between hydrostatic stress and concentration (using $\delta\sigma/B = -\delta C_a/C_a$ where $B$ is the bulk modulus):

$$\frac{\partial\sigma}{\partial t} = B\nabla.\left(-\frac{D}{kT}eZ\rho j + \frac{D}{kT}\frac{Q}{T}\nabla T - \frac{D}{kT}\Omega\nabla\sigma\right) \quad (6)$$

As a result, studying concentrations of atoms can be done by analyzing stress evolution. The presented model is similar to the one proposed in [19]. The distinction, however, is that the current model captures all material migration factors whereas the model in [19] assumes fixed temperature and no TM.

Fig 2 (b) shows the relative significance of thermomigration flux w.r.t. electromigration flux which has roughly the same order of magnitude and can no longer be ignored. It confirms that impact of thermal effect compared to electromigration and stress migration on the overall material migration process is not negligible. Such overall effect is aggravated by technology scaling and larger current density. The mean values for the parameters are obtained from recent experimental reports on modern manufacturing processes [4-7]. This model confirms that for novel technologies [12-17], neglecting the temperature evolution and its impact on interconnect reliability and their lifetime may lead to wrong conclusions or catastrophic failures.

The steady state of a system under material migration is achieved when all atomic fluxes cancel each other out (i.e. $J_{EM} + J_{SM} + J_{TM} = -\frac{eZ}{\Omega}j\rho + \nabla\sigma - \frac{Q}{\Omega T}\nabla T = 0$) . By integration, the steady state of model in (4) can be described as follows:

$$\sigma(x) = \frac{eZ\rho}{\Omega}jx + \frac{Q}{\Omega}\ln T(x) + c \quad (7)$$

where constant c is readily obtained by boundary conditions.

# 4. ACCURATE CRITERIA FOR RELAIBILITY DUE TO MATERIAL MIGRATION UNDER NON-UNIFORM TEMPERATURE

Having (5) and the principle of atom conservation (i.e. $\int_{-L/2}^{+L/2} \Delta C dV = -\frac{C_0 HW}{B}\int_{-l/2}^{+L/2}\sigma dx = 0$) [20], yields:

$$\sigma_c - \sigma_a = \frac{eZ\rho}{\Omega}jL + \frac{Q}{\Omega}\Delta\ln T \quad (8)$$

$$\sigma_c + \sigma_a = -\frac{eZ\rho}{\Omega}j^2\mathcal{L}^2 \quad (9)$$

where $\mathcal{L}^2 = \frac{2Q}{eZk}\left(\frac{T_0}{T_aT_c} - \frac{2\Gamma}{T_0 L}\tanh\left(\frac{L}{2\Gamma}\right)\right)\Gamma^2 \approx \frac{2QT_0\Gamma^2}{eZkT_aT_c}$.

These criteria capture the effect of temperature, stress and current density for assessing the mortality of a wire. Having the critical stresses for voiding and hillock, $\sigma^v_{\text{crit}}$ and $\sigma^h_{\text{crit}}$, we can define new critical terms including temperature effects $\tau^v_{\text{crit}} = \frac{2\Omega}{eZ\rho}\sigma^v_{\text{crit}} - \frac{Q}{eZ\rho}\Delta\ln T$ and $\tau^h_{\text{crit}} = \frac{2\Omega}{eZ\rho}\sigma^h_{\text{crit}} + \frac{Q}{eZ\rho}\Delta\ln T$. Solving (8) and (9), the conditions for immortality under non-uniform temperature distribution can be stated as:

$$jL - j^2\mathcal{L}^2 < \tau^v_{\text{crit}} \quad (10)$$

$$-jL - j^2\mathcal{L}^2 > \tau^h_{\text{crit}} \quad (11)$$

This model is similar to Blech's conditions [3][21], yet it considers the effect of thermal load. The new model offers various extended criteria. The maximum current density for a wire with given length and initial temperatures is obtained by:

$$j^v_{\max} = \frac{-L + \sqrt{L^2 - 4\mathcal{L}^2\tau^v_{\text{crit}}}}{2\mathcal{L}^2} \quad (12)$$

$$j^h_{\max} = \frac{+L - \sqrt{L^2 + 4\mathcal{L}^2\tau^n_{\text{crit}}}}{2\mathcal{L}^2} \quad (13)$$

Also, the model implies more precise length criteria reflecting the effect of temperature and does not suffer from pessimistic voiding and optimistic hillock predictions of other models. Defining a relative temperature rise, $\theta = T_m/T_0$, yields useful tools for guiding physical design as follows:

$$L^v_{\max} = \left(1 + \frac{Q}{\Omega}\frac{\theta}{\sigma_v}\right)L \quad (14)$$

$$L^h_{\max} = \left(1 - \frac{Q}{\Omega}\frac{\theta}{\sigma_h}\right)L \quad (15)$$

The models presented in (14-15) imply that taking the temperature effect into account for any current density $j$, the maximum length for void-immune and extrusion-safe wire can be relaxed or tightened by $Q\theta/\Omega\sigma$, respectively. This also means designers can take advantage of a more accurate short length effect and apply significantly larger current densities.

## 4.1 Extrema

A metallic line The models presented in (10)-(15), in their core, check the hydrostatic stress against the critical stress on the end points of a wire where stress have the extreme values (i.e. the max tensile and compressive stresses occur in the cathode and anode, respectively). However, the exact positions of the extrema depend on temperature profile and may no longer happen in the wire ends. The maximum stress can be found by solving the following equation:

$$\frac{\partial\sigma}{\partial x} = \frac{eZ}{\Omega}j\rho + \frac{Q}{\Omega T}\frac{\partial T}{\partial x} = 0 \quad (16)$$

Plugging equation (3) into (15), yields a very accurate approximation for the maximum stress as follows:

$$x_s = \Gamma\cosh^{-1}\left(\frac{eZT_0k}{Qj\Gamma}\cosh\left(\frac{L}{2\Gamma}\right)\right) \quad (17)$$

where $t_{Cu}$ and $t_{ILD}$ are the thickness of the wire and the surrounding dielectric and also $k_{cu}$ and $k_{ILD}$ are thermal conductance of the wire and the dielectric, respectively.

The location for maximum stress under EM, TM and SM can be found based on the geometrical, electrical and thermal characteristics of a wire and dielectric which are readily available. The stress distribution under temperature effect for a complex net is shown in Fig 1 (b). The maximum stress within two end points may not necessarily occur at ends.

## 4.1 Mean Time to Failure

A metallic line The models The mean time to failure of an interconnect is often evaluated by the well-known Black's equation [8] as follows:

$$\mathrm{MTF} = Aj^{-n}e^{\frac{E_a}{kT}} \tag{18}$$

where $A$ is a constant and $n$ is a model parameter which are obtained empirically. Yet, determining the current density exponent is a crital task which may vary for interconnects with different electrical, thermal and mechanical loads. We propose to determine a true mean time to failure based on the atomic flux divergences. In other words, the parameters in Black's model can be determined readily by the following method.

As it was discussed before, the key to determine the depletion or accumulation of atoms in a region is to look at the overall intake and outtake of atoms due the multiple fluxes. This quantity can be measured accurately by atomic flux divergence. Therefore, it can be stated that

$$\mathrm{MTF} \propto \frac{1}{\nabla.\vec{J}} \tag{19}$$

It can be shown that the total flux divergence presented in (2) can be written as follows:

$$\nabla.\vec{J} \approx \left[\frac{E_a}{kT}\frac{\nabla T}{T} + \frac{\nabla^2 V}{\nabla V}\right].\overrightarrow{J_{EM}} + \left[\frac{E_a}{kT}\frac{\nabla T}{T} + \frac{\nabla^2 T}{\nabla T}\right].\overrightarrow{J_{TM}} + \left[\frac{E_a}{kT}\frac{\nabla T}{T} + \frac{\nabla^2 \sigma}{\nabla \sigma}\right].\overrightarrow{J_{SM}} \tag{20}$$

Plugging the fluxes due to EM, TM and SM and writing (20) quantitively from (2) yields:

$$\mathrm{MTF} \propto \frac{1}{D(\alpha j^2 + \beta j^3 + \gamma j^4)} \approx Aj^{-n}e^{\frac{E_a}{kT}} \tag{21}$$

where $\alpha$, $\beta$ and $\gamma$ are determined by the parameters in experiments or equivalently the ones in previous equations. The rightmost-hand side equation is the well-known Black's equation where $A$ is a pre-exponential constant factor and $n$ is an empirically found parameter. As it can be seen there is an intuitive agreement between flux divergence with Black's equation where the current density exponent $n$ and constant $A$ are traditionally determined empirically. In other words, flux divergence analysis can enrich Black's empirical equation by explaining the model parameters. Empirical extractions of $n$ usually set it to be between 2 to 4 – depending on which terms are more dominant.

## 5. EXPERIMENTS: VARIOUS THERMAL PROFILES

Extensive experiments have been performed to verify the validity of our findings and models. Table 1 shows the application of our model to intermediate-length interconnects in 10nm technology under various thermal profiles (due to Joule heating). The values for geometrical, electrical, mechanical and thermal properties of technology are obtained from [1-3][15-19].

**Table 1: Stress evolution and violation checking under different temperature distributions**

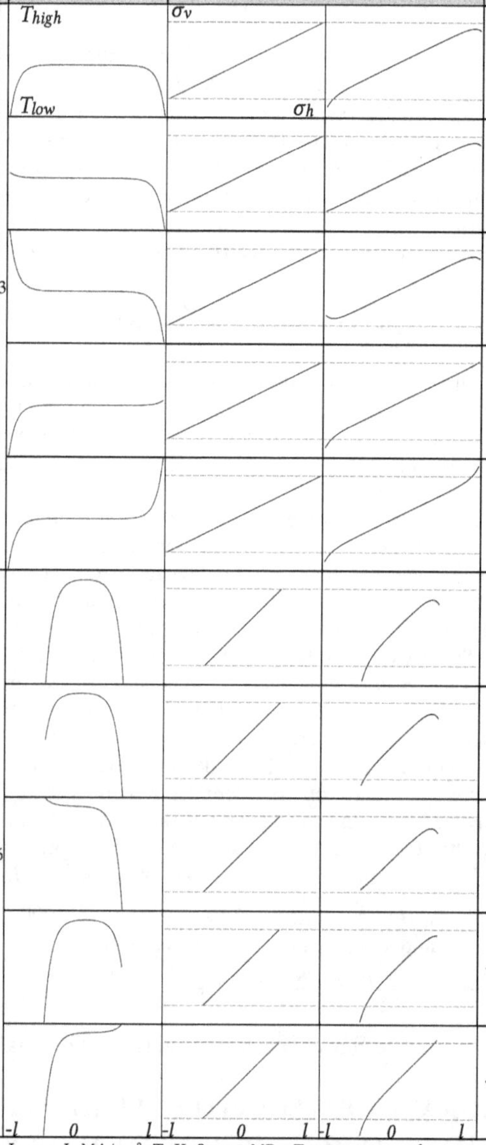


| L | J | Temperature | Stress: Finite Element Methods, Blech [3] | Stress: Finite Element Methods, New | Models, Extrusion: Blech | Models, Extrusion: New | Models, Voiding: Blech | Models, Voiding: New |
|---|---|---|---|---|---|---|---|---|
| 100 | 3 | | | | ✓ | ✓̲ | ✓ | × |
| | | | | | ✓ | ✓ | ✓ | × |
| | | | | | ✓ | × | ✓ | × |
| | | | | | ✓ | ✓̲ | ✓ | ✓ |
| | | | | | ✓ | ✓̲ | ✓ | ✓̲ |
| 50 | 6 | | | | ✓ | ✓̲ | ✓ | × |
| | | | | | ✓ | ✓̲ | ✓ | × |
| | | | | | ✓ | × | ✓ | × |
| | | | | | ✓ | ✓̲ | ✓ | × |
| | | | | | ✓ | ✓̲ | ✓ | ✓̲ |

Units: L: um, J: MA/cm², T: K, Stress: MPa. Temperature and stress ranges: $T_{low}$ = 374 to $T_{high}$ = 383 and -800 to 800MPa. Critical stresses=500MPa (dotted lines). Anode: $-l = -50$ , Cathode: $l = -50$ . ✓: violated, ×: not violated, ✓̲: aggravated

The experimental results in Table 1 present the experiments on two similar wires with lengths of 50um and 100um. Current density of 3x10¹⁰A/m² and 6x10¹⁰A/m² are applied with different boundary conditions to cover several nonuniform solutions of the heat equation. We use common structures which can be adjusted by any technology. Readers may note that the presented model is technology independent and universal. It can accommodate any wiring configuration and technology through different values for material, electrical and thermal properties of

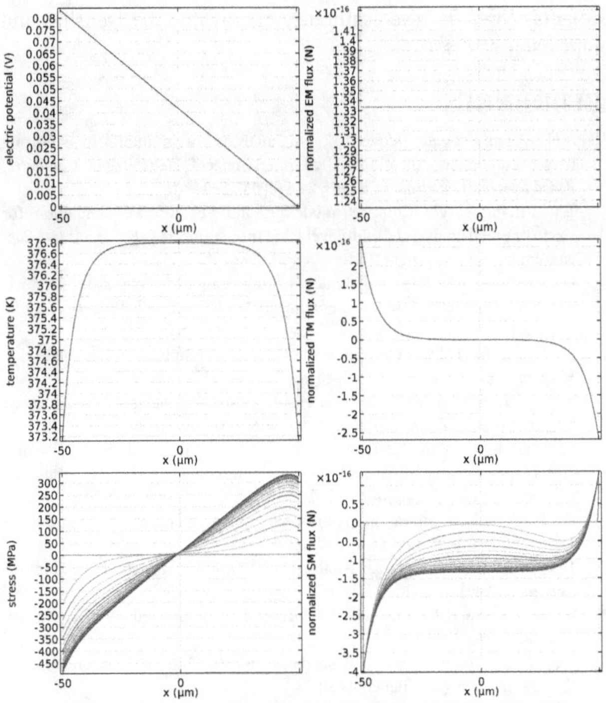

Figure 3: Left column: Applied electric potential, temperature rise (Joule heating) and evolving stress (top to bottom, respectively). Right column: normalized fluxes due to EM, TM and SM (top to bottom, respectively). The experiment shows stress evolution from a no-stress state ($t = 0$ s) to the steady state ($t = 7e7$ s $= 2.2$ years).

components. As it can be seen in Table 1 there are considerable differences in terms of violations predicted by the proposed model and the existing ones. They are caused by not considering TM in existing models.

In particular, when the temperature gradients are negative towards the cathode and from the anode, such gradients alleviate the tensile and compressive stresses. This can be exploited by designers to have a greater reliability margin in terms of the maximum length or current density as temperature, indeed, increases the resilience of interconnect. On the other hand, positive temperature gradients towards the cathode and from the anode, aggravate the tensile and compressive stress. Table 1 demonstrates a comprehensive scheme for the impact of different temperature distributions on immortality conditions. The conventional Blech based EM rules may assess the EM violations incorrectly (last columns in Table 1). Such effects are severer for larger current density (compare cases $3x10^{10}A/m^2$ vs $6x10^{10}A/m^2$.

In general, two situations may occur: (1) in some cases, the existing models may wrongly scrutinize reliability in unfailing parts and consequently impose unnecessary design tightening and (2) in some other cases, they may underestimate serious problems causing unpredicted behaviors or catastrophic failures to occur. The existing models for reliability evaluation are usually pessimistic in case of interconnect voiding and optimistic when extrusion occurs. Without loss of generality and for the sake of discussion, the absolute values of the corresponding critical stress are assumed to be 500MPa [3][21]. The wires therefore are assumed to just violate the critical threshold.

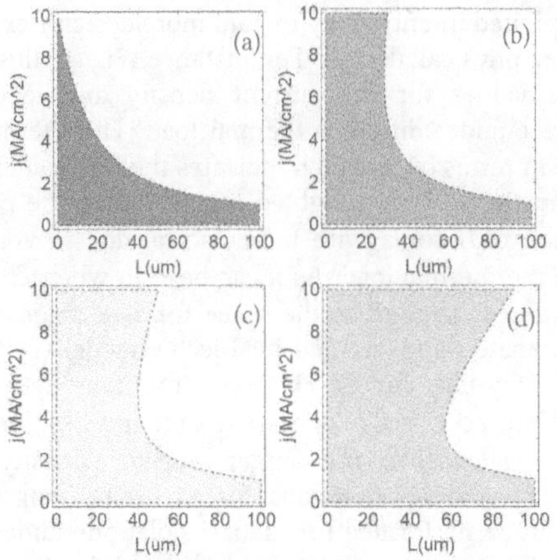

Figure 4: The permissible values for $j$ and $L$ under different thermal load. Contour lines correspond to different values of normalized thermal effect (Joule Heating) (a) $\mathcal{L}$=0, (b) $\mathcal{L}$=2, (c) $\mathcal{L}$=4 and (d) $\mathcal{L}$=8.

Table 1 demonstrates that Blech based models relying on $jL$ roduct can wrongly evaluate the health of interconnects. In all ases the products of current density and length are the same nd thus they are assessed to have the same reliability and fetime. However, the proposed model distinguishes these cases roperly. Indeed, the immortality of a wire should be evaluated y $jL - j^2\mathcal{L}^2$ rather than $jL$. The results are in a strong greement with detailed FEA experiments.

For a detailed discussion on how temperature evolution and :ress evolution are mutually related, case 1 in Table I is iscussed in detail using the stress evolution model. The results are presented in Fig 3. For ease of discussion, the flux values are normalized by their common factor (i.e. $BD/kT$). Application of current density results in EM. As a side effect, a temperature rise occurs through Joule heating process. The temperature gradient produces atomic flux and consequently causes TM. While current is applied and temperature raises, stress develops simultaneously. These three fluxes compete against each other and reconcile in a steady state.

The new model confirms that thermomigration usually (i.e. for the thermal profile of $\cap$) tends to aggravate compressive stress and potentially exacerbate the risk of extrusion or shorts. On the other hand, thermomigration mitigates tensile stress and possibly alleviates the risk of voiding or opens. Indeed, atoms tend to migrate from hot to cool areas. Since the hottest location is usually towards the center of the interconnect line, some atoms travel to anode and increase the compression, and some atoms move back to cathode and compensate depletion and consequently reduce the tensile stress. Intuitively, increasing temperature usually mitigates shrinkage and intensifies expansion. This may cause serious effects (i.e. stress aggravation Thermomigration interacts with electromigration and stress migration, it may result in (1) asymmetric stress distribution, (2) early hillock formation (shorter lifetime), (3) late voiding (longer lifetime) and (4) non-end failures. The experimental results indicate that due to such effects many expected failures may not occur or some new may occur.

The proposed model also explains several experimental observations that may have been inexplicable before such as some unexpected failure locations. For instance, our experiments reveal that having temperature effect included in aging process can be exploited intentionally to gain more design flexibility and freedom in physical design. For instance, Fig 4 illustrates the admissible values for the current density and length of an interconnect under different thermal load. The thermal load is presented in terms of $\mathcal{L}$ which indicates the heat generation due to Joule heating. The highlighted regions show the permissible combination of $jL$ for a wire to be mortal due to voiding with respect to the thermal load. As it can be seen when $\mathcal{L}$ is zero, i.e. Joule Heating is negligible, the space for safe values of $j$ and $L$ can be estimated and verified by Blech's model (i.e. the outer region of 1/xy-like curve). However, for non-negligible Joule heating effect, i.e. $\mathcal{L} \neq 0$ (e.g. cases (b), (c) and (d)), term $j^2\mathcal{L}^2$ in $jL \pm j^2\mathcal{L}^2$ , allows having larger current density without experiencing voiding violations for the same length. Similar analysis can be performed for hillock violations under different distributions. It implies increasing thermal load may loosen design rules in terms of max current density and increase design flexibility.

## 6. CONCLUSION

In summary, depending on the temperature evolution due to the Joule Heating and heat convection, the admissible space for values of $j$ and $L$ can no longer be explained by Blech's model yet our novel model captures it correctly.

The evolution of temperature within metallic interconnect due to Joule heating is studied in detail. A new model is presented to provide a steady state temperature profile under any arbitrary non-uniform conditions. The model is then incorporated in models for material migration. The stress development and aging process were investigated considering the Joule heating induced thermomigration. It was shown that neglecting such effects during reliability assessment of interconnects may lead to wrong evaluation for modern interconnect technologies. New criteria, as a result, are developed to check the immortality of wires under any thermal, electrical and mechanical conditions. These criteria do not suffer from common problems of Blech-based methods (i.e. pessimistic void predication and optimistic hillock estimation).

Various temperature profiles have been investigated in detail. It was shown, depending on the steady state profile of temperature, the voiding and hillock potential appearance will be affected, and therefore Blech based method cannot be trusted. The new models confirm that thermomigration usually (i.e. for the thermal profile of ∩) tends to aggravate compressive stress and potentially exacerbate the risk of extrusion or shorts. On the other hand, thermomigration mitigates tensile stress and possibly alleviates the risk of voiding or opens. In general cases, when the temperature gradients are negative towards the cathode, such gradients alleviate the tensile and compressive stresses. This can be exploited by designers to have a greater reliability margin in terms of the max length or current density as temperature. On the other hand, positive temperature gradients towards the cathode, aggravate the tensile and compressive stress.

## REFERENCES


[1] A.H. Ajami *et al.* "Modeling and analysis of nonuniform substrate temperature effects on global ULSI interconnects." *IEEE Trans. Computer-Aided Design of Integrated Circuits*, 24.6 (2005): 849-861.

[2] T.Y. Chiang *et al.* "Compact modeling and SPICE-based simulation for electrothermal analysis of multilevel ULSI interconnects." *IEEE/ACM Intl Conf on Computer-aided design*, 2001.

[3] K.-D. Lee *et al.* "Effect of Joule Heating on electromigration in dual-damascene copper low-k interconnects." *IEEE Int. Reliability Physics Symposium (IRPS)*, 2017.

[4] R. Brain, "Interconnect scaling: Challenges and opportunities." *IEEE Int. Electron Devices Meeting (IEDM)*, 2016.

[5] B. Li *et al.* "Thermal characterization and challenges of advanced interconnects." *IEEE Int. Reliability Physics Symp.* IRPS, 2016.

[6] M. Hauschildt *et al.* "Electromigration early failure void nucleation and growth phenomena in Cu and Cu (Mn) interconnects." *IEEE International Reliability Physics Symposium (IRPS)*, 2013.

[7] J.R. Black, "Electromigration—A brief survey and some recent results." *IEEE Trans. on Electron Devices* 16.4 (1969): 338-347.

[8] T.-Y. Chiang, Electrothermal Analysis of VLSI Interconnects. Diss. Stanford University, 2004.

[9] H.S. Carslaw and J. C. Jaeger. Conduction of heat in solids. Vol. 2. Oxford: Clarendon Press, 1959.

[10] S.R. Nassif, "Power grid analysis benchmarks." *IEEE Design Automation Conference*, 2008. (IBM Benchmark)

[11] Comsol Multiphysics (tool), available [online] https://www.comsol.com/

[12] J.S. Chawla et al. "Resistance and electromigration performance of 6 nm wires." IEEE Int. Interconnect Technology Conference/Advanced Metallization Conf. (IITC/AMC), 2016.

[13] B. Kaczer, "Present and Future of FEOL Reliability—from Dielectric Trap Properties to Reliable Circuit Operation." *IEEE Int. Electron Devices Meeting (IEDM)*, 2016.

[14] T. Standaert et al. "BEOL process integration for the 7 nm technology node." IEEE Int. Interconnect Technology Conf./Advanced Metallization Conf. (IITC/AMC), 2016.

[15] Short Course, "Technology Options at the 5 Nanometer Node. " *IEEE Int. Electron Devices Meeting* (IEDM), 2016.

[16] P. Raghavan *et al.* "Metal stack optimization for low-power and high-density for N7-N5." *SPIE Advanced Lithography*, 2016.

[17] A. Abbasinasab and M. Marek-Sadowska, "RAIN: A Tool for Reliability Assessment of Interconnect Networks—Physics to Software," *Proc. ACM Design Automation Conference (DAC), 2018.*

[18] M.A. Korhonen *et al.* "Stress evolution due to electromigration in confined metal lines." *J. of Appl. Physics* 73.8 (1993)

[19] A. Abbasinasab and M. Marek-Sadowska. "Blech effect in interconnects: Applications and design guidelines." *Proc. ACM Int. Symp. on Physical Design*, 2015.

[20] I.A. Blech, and C. Herring. "Stress generation by electromigration." *Applied Physics Letters* 29.3 (1976): 131-133.

[21] R.A.Oriani, "Thermomigration in solid metals." *J. of Physics and Chemistry of Solids* 30.2 (1969): 339-351.

[22] H.V. Nguyen *et al.* "Effect of thermal gradients on the electromigration life-time in power electronics." *Int. Reliability Physics Symp.*, 2004.

[23] H.B. Chen et al. "Analytical Modeling of Electromigration Failure for VLSI Interconnect Tree Considering Temperature and Segment Length Effects." *IEEE Trans on Device and Materials Reliability* (2017).

# Fault Classification and Coverage of Analog Circuits using DC Operating Point and Frequency Response Analysis

Sayandeep Sanyal [1], Shan Pavan Pani Krishna Garapati [2], Amit Patra [3], Pallab Dasgupta [1]
Mayukh Bhattacharya[4]
[1] Department of Computer Science and Engineering, Indian Institute of Technology Kharagpur
[2] Advanced Technology Development Centre, Indian Institute of Technology Kharagpur
[3] Department of Electrical Engineering, Indian Institute of Technology Kharagpur
[4] Synopsys Inc., USA
sayandeep.sanyal@iitkgp.ac.in,garapatiphanikrishna@gmail.com,amit.patra@ieee.org,
pallab@cse.iitkgp.ernet.in,mayukh@synopsys.com

## ABSTRACT

Detection of faults in a mixed-signal SOC at the pre-silicon stage is a challenge, especially when it has substantial analog components. Given the time taken for simulating analog circuits, designing tests to detect faults in them is not a straightforward task. Achieving a high fault coverage without doing extensive time-consuming transient simulation of the circuit under test (CUT) has remained elusive in the analog and mixed-signal (AMS) domain. Unlike test generation approach for digital designs which leverage logical equivalence between faults, in analog circuits, there does not exist any notion of logical equivalence, and therefore each fault needs to be treated independently. In this paper, we propose to use a combination of DC operating point analysis and AC analysis of the CUT to identify equivalent faults in analog circuits. We also put forward a methodology of synthesizing inputs which will be able to detect the faults during post-silicon testing. Our studies reveal the effectiveness of this approach in identifying equivalent faults and achieving high fault coverage with considerably reduced computations. By using proposed methodology of fault classification and input signal synthesis, we have been able to achieve a high fault coverage where most of the detectable faults are successfully covered.

## KEYWORDS

Fault Classification, Coverage, DC analysis, Frequency Response

**ACM Reference format:**
Sayandeep Sanyal [1], Shan Pavan Pani Krishna Garapati [2], Amit Patra [3], Pallab Dasgupta [1] and Mayukh Bhattacharya[4]. 2019. Fault Classification and Coverage of Analog Circuits using DC Operating Point and Frequency Response Analysis. In *Proceedings of Great Lakes Symposium on VLSI 2019, Tysons Corner, VA, USA, May 9–11, 2019 (GLSVLSI '19)*, 6 pages.
https://doi.org/10.1145/3299874.3317976


ACM ISBN 978-1-4503-6252-8/19/05…$15.00
https://doi.org/10.1145/3299874.3317976

## 1 INTRODUCTION

With the increasing number of transistors in the circuits, the complexity in properly testing them is also going up. The testing of modern System on Chip (SOC) has become so much resource consuming (both computational and time) that at one point it is not even practical to do comprehensive pre-silicon testing of the whole circuit. The primary reasons for that are the computational power and time needed by the analog simulators to simulate large transistor-level netlists, and also due to the infinite number of possible test input combinations existing due to the presence of real-valued signals. In the case of digital circuits, test designers take advantage of the well-defined logical equivalence to construct equivalent fault classes, such that if a test input can detect one fault, it will also detect all other faults present in the same equivalent class, resulting in substantial reduction in the number of simulations required for fault coverage. But no such definition of equivalence exists in the analog domain. As a result, extensive simulations have to be carried out in the pre-silicon phase, to come up with an optimal set of test vectors which can achieve the desired fault coverage.

At present, the standard method for detecting faults in a fabricated chip is as follows. The verification engineer simulates the circuit for each fault injected in the transistor level netlist and looks for detectable deviation in the outputs. Given the sizes of the analog circuit netlists, their possible input signal combinations, and the time taken for one simulation of the netlist, the time and effort needed for carrying out this task are substantial.

Initial approaches for post-silicon fault detection were based on analyzing the input current waveform of the circuit under fault-free and faulty conditions to infer about the presence of a fault, both catastrophic as well as parametric [10]. Analyzing techniques such as wavelet transform [1] and spectral analysis [4] were put forward. In [2] the authors proposed a methodology for detecting catastrophic faults by analyzing the current consumption waveform of the circuit. They have got promising results by testing the methodology on a Power-On-Reset circuit.

Another line of work has been to identify equivalent fault classes in the circuit so that testing for only one member of such class ensures the coverage of others. Authors in [5] have demonstrated an efficient way of testing AMS circuits which includes a fault clustering technique and running faster simulations at reduced accuracy. Their claim of a more efficient analog testing methodology is backed up by the results on an industrial DC-DC converter circuit.

The drawback is that it needs the user to identify certain commonly used analog cells (eg., a differential amplifier) which may not always be feasible while working with bigger circuits. This technique has been incorporated in a designing framework in [12]. But the authors have also mentioned the fact that for applying this technique there should be controllability and observability of individual cells in the CUT, which is not feasible on industry level circuits. A new fault clustering technique is also proposed in [9] where the circuit is simulated, and the output signal values at different time intervals are taken into consideration to build hierarchical clusters of the faults. But here also the circuit has to be simulated for every possible fault, which is not advisable for bigger circuits which take much more time to simulate. Also, no percentage fault coverage estimate was proposed here. [17] reports methodology to achieve accurate fault coverage estimate by relative likelihood weighted stratified random sampling. The relative likelihood of faults is estimated from the parasitic resistances and capacitances as well as from the sizes of mosfets in the circuit. Faults are sampled based on the relative likelihood, and the accuracy of fault coverage is computed. Though this methodology is promising, it lacks the scope for comprehensive coverage of faults, which is essential for circuits used in safety critical operations. All the techniques mentioned above aim at reducing the time taken in the testing of analog circuits, but some of them lack the potential to achieve high fault coverage rates, while others have scalability concerns for bigger circuits.

Frequency domain analysis was previously demonstrated in [8, 19]. In [14, 15] testability and observability of faults under different frequencies were studied by analyzing the sensitivities of different faults and parameters at those frequencies. Observability and controllability measures have also been utilized in automatically generating test vectors to detect analog faults [6, 7, 16]. This approach is computationally expensive as the observability and controllability of the nodes of the CUT have to be calculated separately for each class of circuits. [11] has applied Support Vector Machine (SVM) on the sampled output response to design effective tests for fault coverage, which again involves running considerable number of transient simulations.

In this paper, we propose 1) a computationally efficient methodology to identify equivalent fault classes without doing expensive transient simulations and 2) to design test inputs that ensure detection of faults in a circuit in the post-silicon stage. From our experimental results, we have observed that a well-formulated combination of DC operating point analysis and frequency domain analysis can not only be done in much less time than circuit simulation but can also reveal a lot of information about the presence of a fault in the circuit. The rest of the paper has been organized as follows: In Section 2 we explain our proposed methodology. Section 3 presents the results on some test circuits and analog benchmark circuits along with a comparison with one of the proposed approaches. Finally, in Section 4, we place our concluding remarks.

## 2 METHODOLOGY

This section describes our methodology for detecting faults present in an analog netlist. The backbone of our approach is the usage of DC operating point analysis along with AC analysis for analog circuits. We have divided our methodology into two parts, one dealing with the fault detection and classification techniques based on analyses of the circuit in pre-silicon stage, and the other with a procedure to synthesize input signals so that high fault coverage percentage can be achieved during post-silicon testing.

### 2.1 Fault Detection and Classification

*2.1.1 Applying the inputs to the circuit.* Before doing any analysis, the CUT is first properly biased by supplying rated voltage and current values to the input ports. Let $\mathcal{I} = \{(P_1, X_1), (P_2, X_2), \ldots, (P_Q, X_Q)\}$ denote the set of inputs such that $\forall i \in [1, Q]$, port $P_i$ is given a bias voltage or current of value $X_i$. This ensures that the circuit will stay in its operating region while further analyses are being done.

*2.1.2 Initial Clustering with DC Operating point Analysis.* Let $\mathcal{F}_0 = \{f_1, f_2, f_3, \ldots, f_n\}$ denote the fault set, where $n$ is the total number of faults to be checked for. With the proper biasing input $\mathcal{I}$, as mentioned in the previous paragraph, DC operating point analysis is done for the fault-free circuit and all faulty circuits corresponding to each element in $\mathcal{F}_0$. Depending on the DC operating point of the output, we divide $\mathcal{F}_0$ into two sets as follows.

- $\mathcal{F}^{dc}_{covered}$, set of faults which produce a detectable deviation ($\geq$ 10mV, say, a fair value to be considered as a deviation) of the output operating point voltage from the fault-free value
- set of faults which remain undetected (deviation < 10mV)

For the fault-free circuit and the faults which remain undetected, we define the state of the circuit as an $\mathcal{N}$-tuple consisting of the DC operating point $V_{DS}$ values of all the $\mathcal{N}$ transistors present in the circuit. Let $\mathcal{S}_{f_i}$ denote the state under fault $f_i$ and $\mathcal{S}_{f_0}$ is the state of the fault-free circuit. Let $\mathcal{D}_{f_i f_j}$ denote the Euclidean distance between states $\mathcal{S}_{f_i}$ and $\mathcal{S}_{f_j}$. The following decisions are made from the pair-wise Euclidean distances.

- Fault $f_i$ is said to be *undetectable* if $\mathcal{D}_{f_0 f_i} \approx 0$
- Fault $f_i$ is said to be *detectable* if $\mathcal{D}_{f_0 f_i} \neq 0$
- Out of the detectable faults, fault $f_i$ and $f_j$ are grouped under the same fault cluster if $\mathcal{D}_{f_i f_j} \approx 0$

Let us say, with the DC analysis data, we were able to form $k$ such clusters, represented as $C_1, C_2, \ldots, C_k$.

*2.1.3 Clustering Refinement with AC analysis.* Along with the same bias input $\mathcal{I}$, an AC voltage source with $1mV$ magnitude is placed at the input port ($P_I$) of the CUT and a frequency sweep analysis is done over an user-defined frequency range. On doing the frequency sweep, the magnitude gain and phase difference between the input port ($P_I$) and an output port ($P_O$) is obtained over the entire chosen frequency range. Such frequency responses are obtained by doing AC analysis for the following circuits.

- Fault-free circuit
- $k$ faulty circuits, taking one fault from each cluster $C_i$, $\forall i \in [1, k]$

To further distinguish a faulty circuit from the fault-free one, we compare their respective frequency responses, both magnitude and phase, obtained from AC analysis of the circuit. As the frequency response is obtained over a continuous frequency domain, a comparison between two plots is done by sampling them at certain discrete frequencies and comparing the magnitude and phase values of the two plots at those frequencies. Let the faults mentioned above for which AC analysis is done be denoted by $\mathcal{F}' = \{f'_1, f'_2, f'_3, \ldots, f'_k\}$ and let $\Omega = \{\omega_1, \omega_2, \omega_3, \ldots, \omega_N\}$ denote a set of frequencies at which the frequency response is sampled, where $N$ is the total number of samples.

We represent the acquired data in a 4-tuple defined as $\mathcal{D} = (\lambda, \phi, \mathcal{F}', \Omega)$, where :

- $\mathcal{F}'$ is the set of faults
- $\Omega$ is the set of sample frequencies
- $\lambda$ is the set containing magnitude values corresponding to each element in set $\mathcal{F}' \times \Omega$
- $\phi$ is the set containing phase values corresponding to each element in the set $\mathcal{F}' \times \Omega$

We have observed from our experiments on different circuits (given in Section 3) that the frequency response of all the faults in a given cluster are identical. Therefore, if a fault $f'_i \in C_i$ and $f'_j \in C_j$ produce identical frequency responses, the clusters $C_i$ and $C_j$ are merged to form a single cluster. Let after such refinement, $k' (\leq k)$ clusters are formed, denoted as $C_1^{new}, C_2^{new}, \ldots, C_{k'}^{new}$.

#### 2.1.4 *Final Fault Coverage.*

Let $\lambda_{ij}$ and $\phi_{ij}$ respectively denote the magnitude and phase of the circuit under fault $f_i$ and at $\omega_j$ sample frequency. Values of fault-free circuit are represented by $i = 0$, i.e., $\lambda_{0j}$ and $\phi_{0j}$ represent the magnitude and phase values respectively of the fault-free circuit at frequency $\omega_j$. We say that fault $f_i$ is covered at $\omega_j$ frequency if either $\lambda_{ij}$ or $\phi_{ij}$ differs from $\lambda_{0j}$ or $\phi_{0j}$ respectively beyond a tolerance, i.e., $|\lambda_{ij} - \lambda_{0j}| > \lambda_{tol}$ or $|\phi_{ij} - \phi_{0j}| > \phi_{tol}$, where $\lambda_{tol}$ and $\phi_{tol}$ are the magnitude and phase tolerances respectively. Since all the faults in a given fault cluster have the same frequency response, if a fault $f_i \in C_p^{new}$ is covered at frequency $\omega_j$, all the faults in $C_p^{new}$ will also be covered at $\omega_j$.

We start with the initial fault list $\mathcal{F} = \mathcal{F}_0 = \{f_1, f_2, f_3, \ldots, f_n\}$. All the faults present in $\mathcal{F}^{dc}_{covered}$ are said to be covered at 0 frequency and are dropped from the fault set $\mathcal{F}$. From the frequency response data, the fault coverage estimate is done by repeating the following steps at each frequency sample points $\omega_j, \forall j \in [1, N]$.

(1) A fault $f_i$ is dropped from the fault list $\mathcal{F}$ if it gets covered.
(2) If a fault, $f_i \in C_p^{new}$ gets covered, all the faults belonging to $C_p^{new}$ are also marked as covered and thus dropped from $\mathcal{F}$.
(3) Percentage Fault coverage at a frequency $\omega_j$ is given as follows.
Percentage Fault Coverage $= \frac{n-|\mathcal{F}|}{n} * 100$

The entire procedure of fault clustering and coverage is described in Algorithm 1.

## 2.2 Design of Test Input

With the data obtained by doing DC and AC analysis of the circuit in the pre-silicon phase, we now focus on designing an input signal that will be able to detect the faults during post-silicon testing. The faults present in $\mathcal{F}^{dc}_{covered}$ can be detected by supplying the DC input $\mathcal{I}$. For the rest of the faults, the basis is that if the magnitude and phase values obtained from the frequency response of the faulty circuit differ from their fault-free counterpart at certain frequencies, then an input signal whose Fourier series predominantly contains

**Algorithm 1:** Fault Clustering and Coverage with DC and AC analysis

**Input:** Fault list : $\mathcal{F}_0 = \{f_1, f_2, f_3, \ldots, f_n\}$;
$\Omega = \{\omega_1, \omega_2, \omega_3, \ldots, \omega_N\}$;
Magnitude tolerance : $\lambda_{tol}$ ;
Phase tolerance : $\phi_{tol}$ ;
**Output:** Progressive Percentage Fault Coverage

$\mathcal{F} = \mathcal{F}_0$
$\mathcal{F}^{dc}_{covered} = \varnothing$
**for** *each element* $f_i \in \mathcal{F}_0$ **do**
  carry out DC operating point analysis with fault $f_i$
  **if** *(deviation of output port from fault-free* $\geq$ *10mV)* **then**
    $\mathcal{F}^{dc}_{covered} = \mathcal{F}^{dc}_{covered} + \{f_i\}$
    $\mathcal{F}_0 = \mathcal{F}_0 - \{f_i\}$
  **else**
    compute Euclidean distance, $\mathcal{D}_{f_0 f_i}$, between circuit states $\mathcal{S}_{f_i}$, under fault $f_i$, and fault-free state $\mathcal{S}_{f_0}$
    **if** $(\mathcal{D}_{f_0 f_i} \approx 0)$ **then**
      $f_i$ is undetectable
      $\mathcal{F}_0 = \mathcal{F}_0 - \{f_i\}$
Cluster the remaining faults in $\mathcal{F}_0$, faults $f_i$ and $f_j$ are placed in the same cluster if $\mathcal{D}_{f_i f_j} \approx 0$
Clusters formed : $C_1, C_2, \ldots, C_k$
Construct the set $\mathcal{F}' = \{f'_1, f'_2, f'_3, \ldots, f'_k\}$ taking one element from each of the $k$ clusters
**for** *each element* $f'_i \in \mathcal{F}'$ **do**
  carry out AC analysis with fault $f'_i$
Construct the data set $\mathcal{D} = (\lambda, \phi, \mathcal{F}', \Omega)$
Refined Clusters based on frequency response obtained from AC analysis : $C_1^{new}, C_2^{new}, \ldots, C_{k'}^{new}$
$\mathcal{F} = \mathcal{F} - \mathcal{F}^{dc}_{covered}$
% Fault Coverage from DC analysis $= \frac{n-|\mathcal{F}|}{n} * 100$
**for** $(j = 1;\ j \leq N;\ j = j + 1)$ **do**
  **for** *each element* $f_i \in \mathcal{F}$ **do**
    **if** $(\lambda_{ij} \notin [\lambda_{0j} - \lambda_{tol}, \lambda_{0j} + \lambda_{tol}] \ || \ \phi_{ij} \notin [\phi_{0j} - \phi_{tol}, \phi_{0j} + \phi_{tol}])$ **then**
      $\mathcal{F} = \mathcal{F} - \{C_p^{new} | f_i \in C_p^{new}\}$
  % Fault coverage till $\omega_j$ frequency $= \frac{n-|\mathcal{F}|}{n} * 100$
Final Fault Coverage $= \frac{n-|\mathcal{F}|}{n} * 100$

those frequencies will also be able to detect the faults during a transient analysis. From the AC analysis of the faulty circuits we have their magnitude and phase values at each of the sample frequencies $\omega_i \in \Omega$. If a fault $f_i$ is covered by frequencies $\{\omega'_1, \omega'_2, \omega'_3, \ldots, \omega'_M\}$, our experimental results show that a multi-frequency sinusoidal input signal $x(t) = A_0 + \sum_{i=1}^{M} A_i sin(\frac{2\pi}{\omega'_i})t$, will be able to detect the fault during the transient analysis, where $A_0, A_1, A_2, \cdots, A_M$ are chosen such that the circuit stays in its operating region. As for example, if the circuit is known to operate within the input signal range of $[a : b]$ (say), then the following configuration will be used. $A_0 = \frac{a+b}{2}; A_1 = A_2 = \cdots = A_M = \frac{1}{M} * \frac{b-a}{2}$

This ensures that the input stays in its allowable range even at the time points where peaks or troughs of all sinusoidal signals coincide. Not only that, if an input signal $x(t)$ is able to detect a fault $f_i \in C_p^{new}$, it will also be able to detect all faults present in the cluster $C_p^{new}$. We have shown by multiple experimental results in the following section that such custom synthesized inputs are able to detect the faults.

## 3 RESULTS AND COMPARISON

This section presents the experimental results of the above-mentioned methodology on some test circuits and some analog benchmark circuits [18]. We have also compared our methodology with the one presented in [9]. We have taken the entanglement measure [3] to show the similarities between the clusters formed by our approach (as mentioned in 2.1.3) and the one proposed in [9]. In addition to that, we have also given a fault coverage metric.

### 3.1 Low Dropout Regulator

Our first test circuit is a Low Dropout Regulator (LDO). A total of 74 catastrophic faults (open and short faults) were injected in it and DC analysis was done for the 74 faulty circuits by giving the proper bias inputs to the circuit as described in Section 2.1.1. A total of 30 faults got detected in this phase, and the rest of the faults were clustered into 24 clusters based on their DC state ($S_{f_i}$ under fault $f_i$, as defined in Section 2.1.2). Thus, AC analysis was done for 24 faults (taking one from each cluster) with a frequency sweep range of 0.01Hz to 10GHz. The port $V_{in}$ and $V_{out}$ were chosen as the input and output port respectively for the AC analysis, while sample frequencies were selected in each decade ranging from 0.01Hz to 10GHz, i.e., $\Omega = \{0.01, 0.1, 1, 10, 100, \ldots, 1G, 10G\}$. Fault detection and clustering were done as explained in Section 2.1 by taking $\lambda_{tol} = 1dB$ and $\phi_{tol} = 15°$ (value kept same for all the testcases). Figure 3 shows the progressive increase in percentage fault coverage as more number of frequency samples are taken into consideration (frequency 0 corresponds the the fault coverage achieved by doing DC analysis). It shows that out of the 74 faults injected, 17 (≈23%) were not detected. Out of those 17 faults, 11 were marked as *undetectable* (as explained in Section 2.1.2). On doing transient analysis with 74 faulty circuits under normal working conditions, we found that 11 faults were actually giving fault-free output responses. The same was also verified during the DC operating point analysis where these faults came out to be *undetectable*. The reason for such behaviour was found to be that, those faults were not able to inject any faulty behaviour in the circuit. As for example, in transistor M108 (Figure 1a), a gate to source short fault results in connecting the gate, already at 0 volt (ENH is connected to 0 volt), to ground. Similarly, a gate to source short in M87 (Figure 1b) is meaningless. Transistors M91 and M89, in Figure 1c, are a pair of transistors which do not get turned on during normal operation, and thus have no effect on the output in normal operating conditions.

We have compared our approach with the one presented in [9]. For transient analysis, a square wave input (pulse width = $4\mu sec$, time period = $7\mu sec$, on value = 1.5V) was given at $V_{in}$, LDO circuit was simulated for $50\mu sec$, $V_{out}$ values at every $5\mu sec$ was taken. The total simulation time in both the cases are shown in Table 2. The

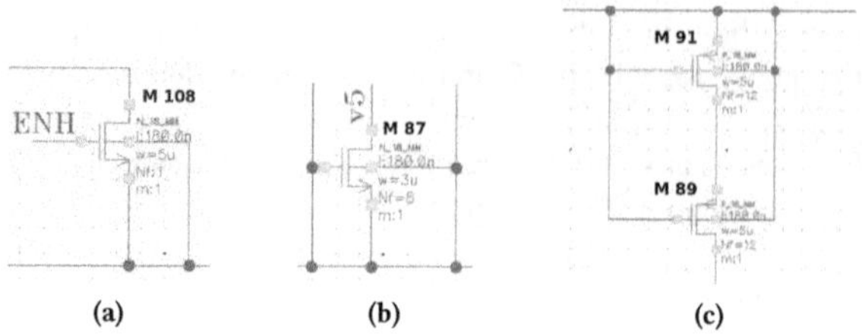


**Figure 1: Examples of *undetectable* Faults**

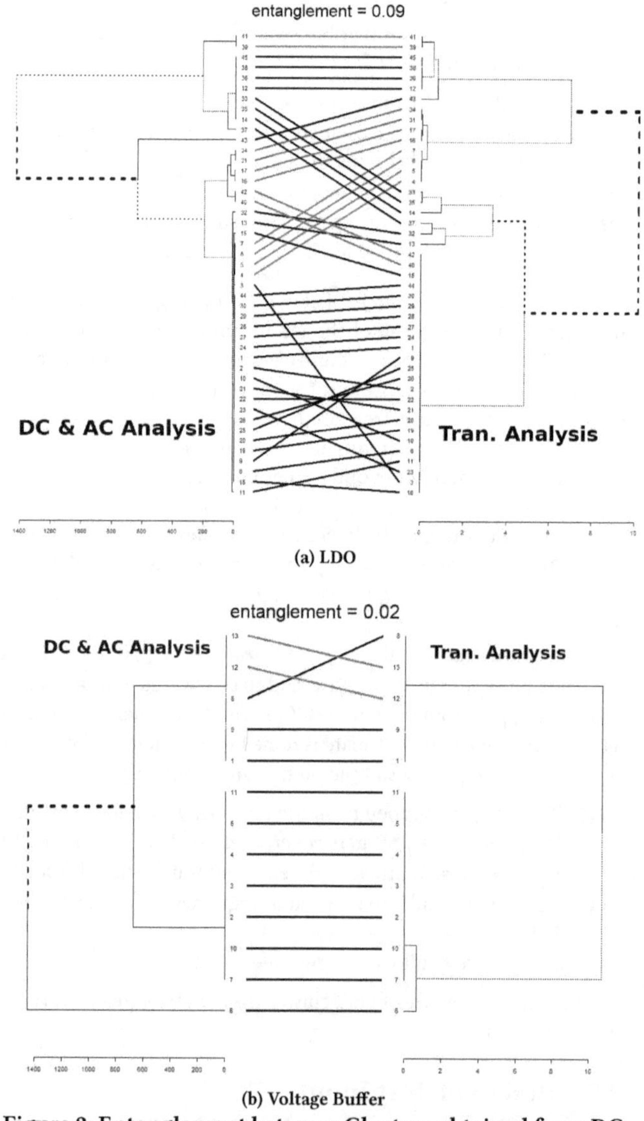


**Figure 2: Entanglement between Clusters obtained from DC and AC analysis and transient analysis**

fault clustering based on both analyses are shown by dendrograms along with their entanglement in Figure 2a. The left-hand side shows the hierarchical clustering of 45 elements (1 fault-free and 44 which are not detected by DC analysis) based on their frequency response data, while the right-hand side shows the hierarchical clusters of the same based on the sampled out $V_{out}$ values from

| Circuit | Entanglement |
|---|---|
| LDO | 0.09 |
| Voltage Buffer | 0.02 |
| Differential Amplifier | 0.16 |
| Voltage Regulator | 0.03 |
| OPAMP | 0.09 |
| Comparator | 0.12 |

**Table 1: Entanglement measures between clusters formed from DC and AC analysis and transient analysis**

the transient analysis. Each fault from the left cluster is joined with its corresponding fault in the right one with a straight line. Comparing the leaf level clusters on both sides, it can be seen that majority of the faults which form a single cluster in transient are also clustered into one cluster in case of AC analysis. This gives us an idea that the equivalent fault classes formed by frequency response (AC analysis) data are almost similar to the ones formed from transient analysis data. A similarity measure between the two hierarchical clusters, entanglement, is also shown. To compare the two hierarchical clusters, they are re-arranged in the best possible way to make the lines, joining same faults on both sides, as much horizontal as possible. Under this arrangement, the entanglement value is a measure of how similar the two hierarchical clusters are. If all the lines are horizontal, then the entanglement value is zero, i.e. the less the entanglement value, the more similar are the two hierarchical clusters.

### 3.2 Voltage Buffer

Our next test circuit consists of a voltage buffer consisting of 13 transistors. A total of 32 faults were injected in the circuit and DC operating point analysis was done where 20 faults got detected and 2 clusters were formed out of the remaining faults. By taking one fault from each of the two clusters, AC analysis was done (as explained in Section 2.1.3) for a frequency range of 0.01Hz to 10GHz and 8 more faults got detected. The fault coverage analysis was done (as explained in Section 2.1.4) and the results are shown in Figure 3. For comparison, we excited the circuit with a square wave (pulse width = $4\mu sec$, time period = $7\mu sec$, on value = 1.8V) did the transient analysis for $50\mu sec$, while taking samples of $V_{out}$ value at every $10\mu sec$. The hierarchical clustering derived from magnitude-phase values from AC analysis, and from sampled out voltage values from transient analysis are compared and their entanglement index is shown in Figure 2b and Table 1.

### 3.3 2-stage Differential Amplifier

We applied our proposed methodology on a two-stage single ended differential amplifier having 8 transistors. On giving proper inputs to the circuit (as mentioned in Section 2.1.1) DC operating point analysis was done by injecting 24 faults one by one following the methodology put forward in Section 2.1. Since all the faults got covered with the DC analysis only, the AC analysis was not required at all. The fault coverage statistics is presented in Figure 3.

While doing the transient analysis, a square wave voltage source (pulse width = $0.4msec$, time period = $0.7msec$, on value = 0.1mV) was placed at the non-inverting terminal, and the inverting terminal was grounded. The output voltage of the amplifier was sampled at every $0.5msec$ for a transient simulation run of $5msec$ which generated the hierarchical clusters. Table 1 shows the entanglement, as a measure of similarity between the clusters generated from our methodology and the one proposed in [9].

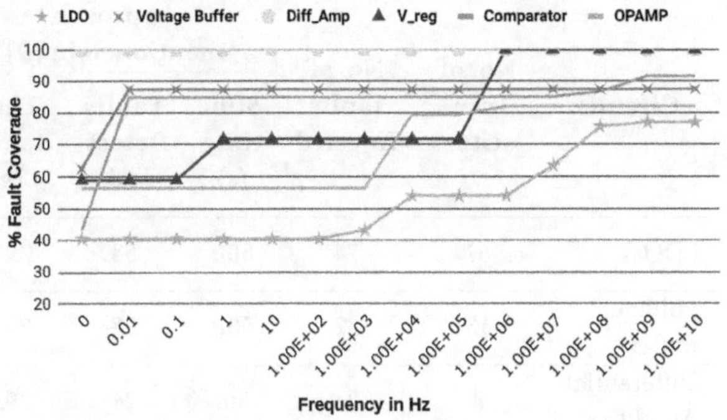


**Figure 3: Progressive Percentage Fault Coverage in Different test and benchmark circuits**

### 3.4 Analog Benchmark Circuits

We applied our methodology on three analog benchmark circuits proposed in [18], i.e., OPAMP, Voltage Regulator, and Comparator. Short circuit faults of 1 Ω between the transistor terminals were injected in the circuits one by one and the fault coverage was computed as described in Section 2.1. The results are shown in Figures 3 and summarized in Table 2. Equivalent fault clusters were formed using our proposed approach (as described in Section 2.1.3) and from transient analysis (as in [9]). Comparisons between the clusters are shown by the entanglement measures in Table 1.

### 3.5 Validation of the Results

To ensure that these faults can also be detected during the post-silicon phase, custom inputs were synthesized for each fault following the procedure mentioned in Section 2.2. To verify the credibility of these custom synthesized inputs in detecting faults, we carried out transient simulations for all the faults, with those inputs, for all the circuits mentioned in Section 3.1, 3.2, 3.3, and 3.4. In all the cases it also showed similar fault coverage results and thus validated our statement mentioned in Section 2.2 to a great extent. Thus by doing DC and AC analysis, we were able to design inputs that are able to detect faults in the post-silicon phase. Since we have not come across a fault in our test circuits for which the simulator fails to converge during DC or AC analysis, we advise extra caution to be taken during the post-silicon testing of such faults if any.

One major advantage in using the proposed combination of DC operating point analysis and AC analysis over transient analysis in estimating fault coverage is that simulation time is only dependent on the frequency sweep range. On the other hand, while doing a transient analysis of a circuit, there might be some faults which will only manifest themselves at the output after a certain amount of time has passed. So in the transient analysis we need to simulate the circuit for a minimum amount of time for a fault to be detected, which is costly. As shown in Table 2, our methodology is more time efficient in determining open or short faults in a circuit and the

| Circuits | No. of Tran-sistors | No. of faults Injected | Approach mentioned in [9] | | | Our approach | | | | | Time Taken (s) (DC+AC analysis) |
|---|---|---|---|---|---|---|---|---|---|---|---|
| | | | Sim. time (s) | Faults Detect-ed | Time taken (s) | DC Analysis | | AC Analysis | | Total Faults Detect-ed | |
| | | | | | | Det. by DC | No. of Clusters | No. of AC analysis | Det. by AC | | |
| LDO | 67 | 74 | $50\mu$ | 53 | 128.8 | 29 | 24 | 24 | 27 | 56 | 43.6 |
| Voltage Buffer | 13 | 32 | $50\mu$ | 28 | 25.1 | 20 | 2 | 2 | 8 | 28 | 11.7 |
| Differential Amplifier | 8 | 24 | $5m$ | 24 | 39.7 | 24 | 0 | 0 | 0 | 24 | 7.7 |
| Voltage Regulator | 14 | 39 | $50\mu$ | 39 | 20.2 | 20 | 11 | 11 | 19 | 39 | 14.7 |
| OPAMP | 14 | 39 | $50\mu$ | 31 | 19.8 | 22 | 10 | 10 | 10 | 32 | 14.1 |
| Comparator | 21 | 60 | $20\mu$ | 51 | 29.9 | 24 | 19 | 19 | 31 | 55 | 23.1 |

**Table 2: Comparison between combination of DC and AC analysis (our approach) and transient analysis (proposed in [9])**

computational advantage is more prominent as the complexity of the circuit increases. The transient simulation time was taken as small as possible, while the frequency range was kept quite wide to depict a pessimistic scenario. The reduction in computation would become more noticeable once we factor in that some circuits might have to be simulated for a longer amount of time for some faults to be detected.

## 4 CONCLUSION

We have presented a computationally efficient procedure for clustering of faults in an analog circuit in the pre-silicon phase and proposed a methodology to synthesize inputs to detect the faults during post-silicon testing. The same methodology of testing the circuit with test inputs synthesized from the frequency response data, can also be extended to circuits having no accessible analog ports by following the test structure as shown in [13]. Instead of using traditional transient analysis, we have taken the approach of exercising the power of DC and AC analyses in diagnosing analog circuits. We have taken six test cases (three are analog benchmark circuits) to illustrate the validity of proposed methodology. We have compared the proposed methodology with an existing one, to show the computational advantage achieved by us.

## 5 ACKNOWLEDGEMENT

We would like to acknowledge Synopsys Inc, USA for supporting the research through the grant entitled "Synopsys CAD Laboratory Project Phase II".

## REFERENCES

[1] Swarup Bhunia and Kaushik Roy. 2002. Dynamic Supply Current Testing of Analog Circuits Using Wavelet Transform. In *Proc. of 20th VLSI Test Symposium.*

[2] Anthony Coyette, Georges Gielen, Ronny Vanhooren, and Wim Dobbelaere. 2014. Optimization of Analog Fault Coverage by Exploiting Defect-Specific Masking. In *Proc. of 19th IEEE European Test Symposium.*

[3] Tal Galili. 2015. dendextend: an R package for visualizing, adjusting and comparing trees of hierarchical clustering. *Bioinformatics* 31, 22 (2015), 3718–3720. https://doi.org/10.1093/bioinformatics/btv428

[4] Georges Gielen, Zhihua Wang, and Willy Sansen. 1994. Fault Detection and Input Stimulus Determination for the Testing of Analog Integrated Circuits Based on Power-Supply Current Monitoring. In *Proc. of the IEEE/ACM International Conference on Computer-Aided Design.*

[5] Nuno Guerreiro, Marcelino Santos, and J.P. Teixeira. 2013. Analogue and Mixed-Signal Production Test Speed-Up by Means of Fault List Compression. 04 (2013), 407–421. http://dx.doi.org/10.4236/cs.2013.45054

[6] Sam Huynh, Jinyan Zhang, Seongwon Kim, Giri Devarayanadurg, and Mani Soma. 1999. Efficient Test Set Design for Analog and Mixed-Signal Circuits and Systems. In *Proc. of 8th Asian Test Symposium.*

[7] Sam D Huynh, Seongwon Kim, Mani Soma, and Jinyan Zhang. 1998. Testability Analysis and Multi-Frequency ATPG for Analog Circuits and Systems. In *Proc. of International Conference on Computer-Aided Design.*

[8] D Jurisic, N Mijat, and V Cosic. 1996. Frequency Domain Approach to Fault Diagnosis of Analog Filters. In *Proc. of 3rd International Conference on Electronics, Circuits, and Systems.*

[9] Oezlem Karaca, Jerome Kirscher, Arnaud Laroche, Andreas Tributsch, Linus Maurer, and Georg Pelz. 2016. Fault Grouping for Fault Injection Based Simulation of AMS Circuits in the Context of Functional Safety. In *Proc. of 13th International Conference on Synthesis, Modeling, Analysis and Simulation Methods and Applications to Circuit Design (SMACD).*

[10] Walter M Lindermeir, Thomas J Vogels, and Helmut E Graeb. 1998. Analog test design with I/sub DD/measurements for the detection of parametric and catastrophic faults. In *Proc. of Design, Automation and Test in Europe.*

[11] Ting Long, Houjun Wang, and Bing Long. 2011. Test generation algorithm for analog systems based on support vector machine. *Signal, Image and Video Processing* 5, 4 (2011), 527–533.

[12] Ricardo Martins, Nuno Lourenço, Nuno Horta, Nuno Guerreiro, and Marcelino Santos. 2015. Embedding Fault List Compression Techniques in a Design Automation Framework for Analog and Mixed-Signal Structural Testing. In *Proc. of Design of Circuits and Integrated Systems (DCIS).*

[13] Anuja Sehgal, Sule Ozev, and Krishnendu Chakrabarty. 2006. Test Infrastructure Design for Mixed-Signal SOCs with Wrapped Analog Cores. *IEEE Transactions on Very Large Scale Integration (VLSI) systems* 14, 3 (2006), 292–304.

[14] Mustapha Slamani and Kaminska Bozena. 1994. Multifrequency Testability Analysis for Analog Circuits. In *Proc. of 12th VLSI Test Symposium.*

[15] Mustapha Slamani and Kaminska Bozena. 1996. Fault Observability Analysis of Analog Circuits in Frequency Domain. *IEEE Transactions on Circuits and Systems II: Analog and Digital Signal Processing* 43, 2 (Feb 1996), 134–139.

[16] Mani Soma, Sam Huynh, Jinyan Zhang, Seongwon Kim, and Giri Devarayanadurg. 2001. Hierarchical ATPG for Analog Circuits and Systems. *IEEE Design & Test of Computers* 18, 1 (2001), 72–81.

[17] Stephen Sunter, Krzysztof Jurga, Peter Dingenen, and Ronny Vanhooren. 2014. Practical random sampling of potential defects for analog fault simulation. In *Proc. of IEEE International Test Conference.*

[18] Stephen Sunter and Peter Sarson. 2017. A/MS Benchmark Circuits for Comparing Fault Simulation, DFT, and Test Generation Methods. In *Proc. of International Test Conference.*

[19] Michael W Tian and C-J Richard Shi. 1997. Rapid Frequency-Domain Analog Fault Simulation Under Parameter Tolerances. In *Proc. of the 34th Design Automation Conference.*

# Crash Skipping: A Minimal-Cost Framework for Efficient Error Recovery in Approximate Computing Environments

Yan Verdeja Herms
Department of Computer Science
University of Chicago
Chicago, IL, USA
yanverdeja@uchicago.edu

Yanjing Li
Department of Computer Science
University of Chicago
Chicago, IL, USA
yanjingl@uchicago.edu

## ABSTRACT

We present a lightweight technique to minimize error recovery costs in approximate computing environments. We take advantage of the key observation that if an application crashes in a "non-critical" region of its execution, then skipping the crash and allowing the execution to continue oftentimes results in "acceptable" output, due to the inherent fault-tolerance of approximate applications. By skipping application crashes, the program is given a chance to recover from an error on its own, without expending computing power towards error recovery. The system-level support required to implement our Crash Skipping technique imposes negligible overhead. Experimental results from representative approximate applications demonstrate that our technique is effective, resulting in successful error recovery for 56% of application crash cases on average, with a maximum recovery rate of 81%. By combining our technique with application restart, we obtain ~33% improvement in performance/ energy consumption compared to recovering from crashes by restarting alone. This benefit is comparable to what can be gained using aggressive checkpointing techniques, but without the added system design and complexity that such techniques impose.

## CCS CONCEPTS

• Hardware → Fault tolerance • Hardware → Hardware reliability

## KEYWORDS

Approximate computing; Reliability; Robust systems

**ACM Reference format:**

Yan Verdeja Herms and Yanjing Li. 2019. Crash Skipping: A Minimal-Cost Framework for Efficient Error Recovery in Approximate Computing Environments. In *GLSVLSI '19: 2019 Great Lakes Symposium on VLSI. ACM, Tysons Corner, VA, USA.* https://doi.org/10.1145/3299874.3317986

## 1 Introduction

Due to critical challenges associated with traditional technology scaling, approximate computing has emerged as an active field of study that trades program accuracy for energy savings or performance improvements [1, 3, 9 10, 12, 16, 19, 21, 26-31, 33]. Taking advantage of the fact that some applications—referred to as *approximate applications* in this paper[1]—allow their results to fall within an acceptable range instead of demanding a single "golden" result, resilience requirements for the underlying hardware can be relaxed to minimize system power/energy usage (e.g., by minimizing error detection, correction, and recovery costs, or reducing supply voltage).

However, approximate applications cannot tolerate all errors. Errors often result in "visible" symptoms at the application or system levels – e.g., application crashes (due to out-of-bounds memory accesses, invalid opcodes, etc.), system crashes (such as kernel panics, machine check exceptions, etc.), or system hangs (due to deadlocks). Unlike silent data corruption (SDC), these errors can be easily detected; however, the cost associated with error recovery in response to a visible symptom can be very high.

Our goal is to enable ultra-efficient error recovery strategies in order to achieve greater system-level savings in the context of approximate computing. Application crashes account for a large percentage (>99%) of all visible error symptoms [7]. We make a key observation regarding this important type of errors: due to the inherent fault-tolerance of approximate applications, if the crash occurs in a "non-critical" program region, skipping it can allow the execution to continue normally and finally produce an "acceptable" output in many cases.

We leverage this key observation to present an extremely lightweight framework that minimizes the overhead associated with error recovery upon crashes in approximate applications. Our technique, called *Crash Skipping*, allows an application to continue execution by treating the instruction that caused an exception as a nop, while imposing minimal modifications to the OS and hardware. The high-level benefit of our technique is shown in Fig. 1: when *successful* (i.e., the program runs to completion with acceptable outputs upon skipping crashes), power/energy

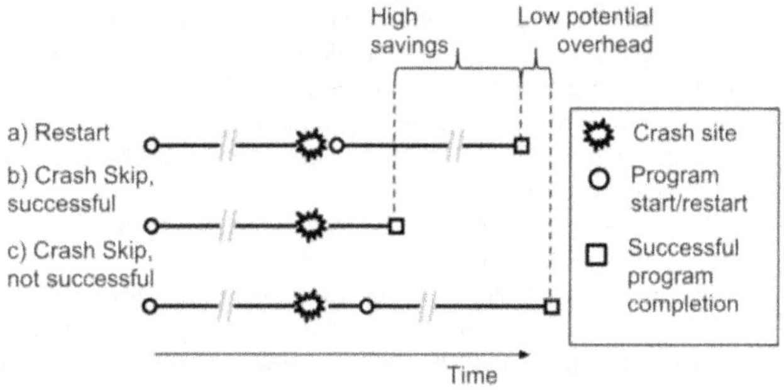


**Figure 1: Benefits of Crash Skipping.**

[1] Other terms such as probabilistic applications, RMS (Recognition, Mining, and Synthesis) applications, soft-computing applications, and applications with elastic outputs, etc., are also used in the literature.


ACM ISBN 978-1-4503-6252-8/19/05...$15.00
https://doi.org/10.1145/3299874.3317986

overhead associated with error recovery is eliminated. Even when *not successful* (i.e., the program continues to encounter application crashes after a certain number are skipped), at which point a program restart would need to take place, the additional overhead is small compared to the basic application restart technique.

Our results confirm that Crash Skipping is effective. We perform extensive fault injection experiments across representative approximate applications from the SPEC, PARSEC, and Rodinia benchmark suites and show that Crash Skipping successfully salvages 56% of application crashes. In cases where Crash Skipping is not successful, it only adds an average of ~3% execution time overhead before a restart takes place. Overall, the minimal-cost Crash Skipping technique achieves a 33% improvement in performance/energy, which is comparable to aggressive checkpoint-and-rollback recovery techniques without their significant system-level costs and complexity. The major contributions of this paper are:

1. The finding that crashes in approximate applications do not always require program restarts or rollbacks.
2. An introduction of the novel Crash Skipping technique.
3. The implementation and evaluation of the Crash Skipping technique to demonstrate its effectiveness.

The remainder of this paper is organized as follows. Section 2 provides relevant background and motivation. Section 3 describes the Crash Skipping technique. Section 4 details our methodology to evaluate the technique. Section 5 summarizes our results and is followed by related work in Sec. 6 and conclusions in Sec. 7.

## 2 Motivation and Background

In approximate computing, reliability requirements are relaxed to achieve improvements in system-level energy efficiency and performance. Though approximate applications possess an inherent resilience to errors, some protection is still required to mitigate system anomalies (application/system crashes, deadlock, etc.) and guarantee acceptable output quality. Traditional resilience techniques fail to utilize approximate applications' inherent error tolerance and impose high system-level costs. They are therefore not adequate in approximate computing environments, and light-weight methods are required.

In this work, we focus on application crashes in general-purpose approximate computing environments. Previous work, through accurate large-scale error injection experiments on hardware, reported that application crashes account for 5%-13% of all cases, and are also the majority (>90%) of all error cases for both transient errors (i.e. soft errors or variation-induced errors) [7] and permanent errors [23]. Application crashes can be readily detected by light-weight solutions [8, 11, 13, 22, 25, 35]; however, it can take an error a long time (e.g., billions of cycles) to show up as an application crash. Therefore, small error detection latency cannot be guaranteed.

This limitation has direct implications on two main classes of backward error recovery techniques: application restart and checkpoint-and-rollback. Without guarantees on error detection latency, fine-grained check-pointing is not adequate, as a small rollback may not undo the initial errored instruction. It thus follows that application restart or coarse-grained checkpoints with long checkpoint intervals should be used for error recovery in approximate applications, yet both of these recovery techniques introduce high overheads.

Restarting an application requires that the system re-computes all of the instructions that had been executed until the point of the crash, wasting much useful work, especially if the program had been running for a long time. Even in coarse-grained application or system checkpointing and rollback, the checkpoint intervals depend on error detection latency which may be quite long [18]. Moreover, the rollback or restore operation itself – which involves reloading architectural registers, reverting the physical memory and storage space, etc. – can still take a long time (800ms for a 100ms checkpoint interval and more for longer intervals [24]).

## 3 Crash Skipping

### 3.1 Opportunities for Efficient Error Recovery

Our goal is to improve error recovery efficiency in approximate computing environments. A critical observation in this work is that if crashes occur in "non-critical" regions of approximate applications, they do not always require program restarts or rollbacks. We demonstrate an example of such cases taken from the SPEC *vpr* benchmark, which calculates the optimal placement configurations for FPGA chips. The *try_swap* function is used to compare the difference in cost between two potential configurations, and swaps in the configuration with the lower cost. If a skipped crash in this function results in the generation of a sub-optimal configuration in the current iteration, it tends to be fixed by a later iteration because the algorithm iterates over many more potential configurations.

### 3.2 Key Idea

Our idea is to provide OS and hardware support for skipping application crashes in approximate computing environments. More formally, "Skipping Crashes" means that, upon an exception being raised during the execution of an instruction (referred to as the *faulting instruction*): (1) all instructions prior to it are guaranteed to be completed normally, (2) the faulting instruction itself is treated as a nop, and (3) the program continues execution at a later point chosen based on the *granularity* of the skip.

We investigate two granularities for Crash Skipping:

1. *Instruction:* the program continues execution starting from the faulting instruction's next *sequential* instruction.[2]
2. *Function:* upon nullifying the faulting instruction, the program jumps to the return address of the function it is currently in, effectively exiting the function.

We provide different skipping granularities because we observe that Crash Skipping at the instruction granularity sometimes results in new crashes occurring in the subsequent instances of the initial faulting instruction (e.g. if the execution is in a loop). In such a case, even though it is simpler to implement instruction-level skipping, it is beneficial to skip ahead to avoid dealing with many "similar" crashes and extending the runtime. Function granularity addresses this issue but requires slightly higher design complexity and is more aggressive. We compare the two granularities further in Sec. 5.

To eliminate the case where crashes continue to be generated after a number of skips, we also set a *threshold* to limit the number of times that skips are allowed to occur for each thread of an application. This parameter also plays an important role in controlling output quality, and can be systematically and automatically obtained, as discussed in the next section.

[2] In ISAs with variable length instructions such as x86, if an opcode invalid exception is raised, it would not be possible to determine the address of the next sequential instruction. In this case, we execute the opcode in the byte following the PC of the faulting instruction.

### 3.3 Output Quality Control

With aggressive configurations of Crash Skipping (e.g., setting a very large *threshold* value, especially if function granularity is used), the chances that an application could run till completion are expected to be high, but the generated output may not fall within the acceptable range, because a large amount of computation in the main algorithm may be skipped. Thus, it is important to determine the appropriate threshold values for different applications. Below, we present a systematic methodology for this purpose.

Our methodology, shown in Fig. 2, takes in the following inputs: (1) the application program along with a representative input dataset, (2) a quality evaluation function which is application-specific and supplied by the programmer/user, and (3) an error model. Based on the error model, we generate various fault sites at which to perform error injection experiments. For each experiment, our iterative approach determines *max_threshold*, which is the largest value of *threshold* for which Crash Skipping allows the application to finish while ensuring the output falls within an acceptable range. The output of this methodology is the minimum of the *max_threshold* values across a statistically significant sample of experiment runs, which can be used as the final threshold value for the application (a smaller value may also be used to be conservative).

### 3.4 OS Support

Systems with Crash Skipping support are configured to optionally skip crashes up to a certain threshold for each individual software thread. Such information must be tracked for each thread separately. Thus, the following modifications are made in the OS:

1. We include three additional fields in the context of each thread (the data structure called the *TCB* in Linux): *skip_type*, *skip_threshold*, and *skip_num*. *skip_type* can be set to SKIP_NONE (i.e., Crash Skipping is not allowed), SKIP_INST (Crash Skipping is enabled with instruction granularity), or SKIP_FN (Crash Skipping is enabled with function granularity). *skip_num* is the actual number of skips that have been performed on this thread, and *skip_threshold* is the total number of skips allowed before reverting to the original error recovery method available in the system (e.g., application restart).
2. A new system call to specify the desired *skip_type* and *skip_threshold*, and reset *skip_num*. By default, *skip_type* is initialized to SKIP_NONE unless it is specified otherwise by the application designer/user.
3. An updated context switch routine which saves/restores information about *skip_type*, *skip_threshold*, and *skip_num* in addition to the main states specified in the original TCB (program counter, stack pointer, etc.). This allows the requirements specific for each running thread to be conveyed to hardware correctly.

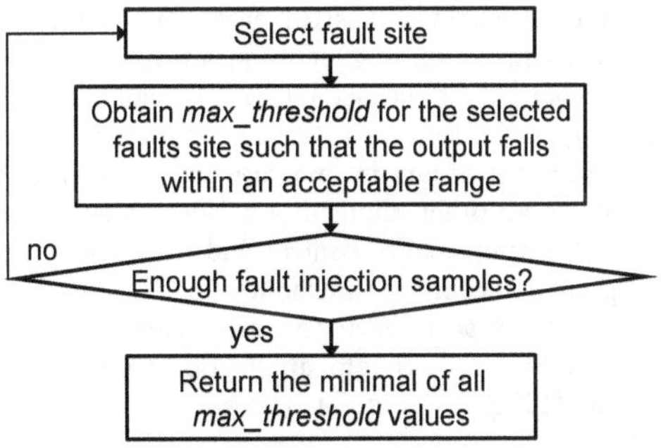


**Figure 2: Systematic Methodology to determine the threshold value for the Crashing Skipping technique.**

### 3.5 Hardware Support

Minimal hardware changes, primarily involving exception handling logic, are required to support Crash Skipping.

Typical exception handling mechanisms involve the following steps: (1) the processor detects an exception condition (e.g., opcode invalid, divide by 0, or memory access violations), and raises an exception signal; (2) upon receiving an exception condition, the exception handling logic outputs correct control signals to flush the pipeline in order to achieve precise exception; (3) the exception handler logic then updates the PC to start execution at the appropriate exception handling routine, which has a known PC (e.g., from the vectored interrupt table).

The modifications required to support Crash Skipping at instruction granularity include:

1. Three new architectural registers to hold the values of *skip_type*, *skip_threshold*, and *skip_num* for the current thread.
2. When an exception is raised, instead of always jumping to the exception handling routine, the processor first checks two conditions: (1) if skip_type is equal to SKIP_INST, and (2) if skip_num is less than skip_threshold. If both are true, the PC in the next cycle is set to the next sequential instruction.

For Crash Skipping at the function granularity, we also extend the return stack, which is prevalent in modern processors for the purpose of effective return address prediction [32], to include the value of the stack pointer prior to a call instruction. Then, when an exception is raised, the processor checks if *skip_type* is SKIP_FN and *skip_num* is less than *skip_threshold*. If so, it sets the PC to the return address of the current function, and also writes the correct value to stack pointer.[3] Although the return value is unlikely to be correct, the program's final output might still be acceptable. All hardware changes are summarized in Fig. 3.

## 4 Evaluation Setup

To demonstrate the efficacy and the efficiency of Crash Skipping, we implement the technique using Pin, Intel's dynamic instrumentation tool [20], which is widely used and also adopted in previous approximate computing studies (e.g., [5]). The tool was used to perform fault injections, both when determining the *threshold* value and when simulating the skipping of resulting application crashes. Furthermore, to evaluate the hardware modification cost, we apply the necessary hardware changes in the industrial open-sourced openSPARC T2 design that supports 8 cores and 64 hardware threads, and synthesize the RTL using Synopsys Design Compiler with the Synopsys EDK 32nm/28nm libraries.

### 4.1 Error Model and Fault Injection

We focus on transient errors (which include soft errors and dynamic variations) and general-purpose systems in our evaluation, due to their wide availability. However, the methodology can be extended to other system and error models as well. Our chosen error models are adopted from [35]: (1) performing a single bit flip in the instruction's destination register or memory write destination, (2) replacing an instruction's

[3] It would be more accurate to also restore the values of all callee-saved registers. However, this imposes higher hardware cost, and may not be critical in the context of approximate computing.

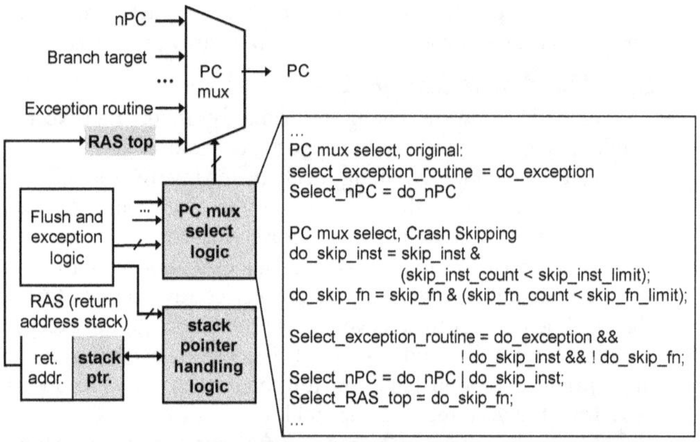


**Figure 3: Hardware implementation of Crash Skipping. New/modified components are shaded.**

destination register or memory write destination with random data, (3) performing a single bit flip in the instruction word.

Although it is more accurate to perform fault injection experiments at the hardware level [7], it is adequate to use architecture-level injections for our purpose because they increase the likelihood of inducing program crashes (which is the behavior our technique aims to resolve) and they enable our experiments to comprehensively measure the efficacy of Crash Skipping as a lightweight error-handling scheme.

For each experiment (per application and per fault model), we randomly select a statistically significant number of fault sites to yield a margin of error less than 3% at a 95% confidence interval.

## 4.2 Workloads

We selected compute- and memory-intensive applications from a broad range of disciplines, taken from the PARSEC [2], SPEC [14], and Rodinia [4] benchmark suites. These applications are commonly used in work on approximate computing. Similar to previous work, we use the following output quality metric [6, 34].

**blackscholes:** calculates prices for a set of options from the market (analytics). The output if considered to be acceptable if >90% of the prices match the golden output.

**hotspot:** estimates the temperature of a processor (physics simulation). The output is considered acceptable if >90% of the temperatures match the golden output.

**kmeans:** clustering algorithm (data mining). The output is considered acceptable if at least 90% of the elements match the golden output in the final clusters.

**parser:** parses sentences in English (linguistics). The output must exactly match the golden output without errors.

**vpr**: determines optimal placement of components in a FPGA chip (computer-aided design). The output must exactly match the golden output without errors.

Note that we are conservative in the output metrics for *parser* and *vpr,* since their algorithms are "approximate" (see Sec. 3.1).

# 5 Results

## 5.1 Hardware Overhead

OpenSparc T2 already supports precise exception. Therefore, the hardware changes discussed in Sec. 3.5 are applicable to this design. In each OpenSPARC T2 core, a module called the *Trap Logic Unit* is responsible for handling exceptions. It takes in exception and flush signals from the main pipeline and determines the appropriate action to handle the exceptions. We modified the exception and flush handling logic as discussed in Sec. 3.5 to support our Crash Skipping technique. We also implemented the return address stack, since it is not supported in the original design. Compared to the original design, the area and power of the modified openSPARC T2 core is increased by *no more than 0.0005%,* which is minimal.

## 5.2 Crash Skipping Threshold Values

We integrate the methodology outlined in Sec. 3.3 into a Pin tool to determine the *threshold* values for different applications along with their respective output quality metric, as described in Sec. 4.2. We use the small input datasets when determining the threshold values. The error model and fault injection trials are discussed in Sec. 4.1, and Table 1 shows the threshold values for both instruction granularity and function granularity (less than 73 and 5, respectively).

**Table 1: Crash Skipping Threshold Values.**

| Application | Instruction Granularity | Function Granularity |
|---|---|---|
| Blackscholes | 4 | 4 |
| hotspot | 10 | 3 |
| kmeans | 60 | 2 |
| parser | 73 | 5 |
| vpr | 4 | 2 |

## 5.3 Crash Skipping Success Rate

We use another Pin tool to perform fault injection experiments emulating the effects of Crash Skipping for various applications. The *threshold* values for each application are set based on the results shown in Table 1. However, we use the large input sets (instead of the small input sets used to obtain the threshold values) and new randomly selected fault sites for evaluation purposes.

Upon an application crash, there are three potential outcomes when Crash Skipping is applied:

1. "Crash Skipping Success": the program reaches the end of its execution and produces acceptable results.
2. "Unrecoverable error": the program requires a program restart to recover the crash (e.g., if the program continues to cause new exceptions past the programmed threshold).
3. "Unacceptable output": the program exits but the output is not within an acceptable range.

Our results show that, with our methodology to systematically determine the threshold values for each application, there is *no* case where the Crash Skipping techniques results in "unacceptable output." By contrast, if we set larger threshold values—100 for instruction granularity and 10 for function granularity—unacceptable output occurs in one case in *blackscholes,* and in 1-4.6% of cases in all other applications. These results confirm the importance of output quality control and the effectiveness of our methodology in determining threshold values for this purpose.

In Figure 4, we report the success rate, which is calculated as (# Crash Skipping Success) / (# total application crashes), for both the SKIP_INST and SKIP_FN granularities.

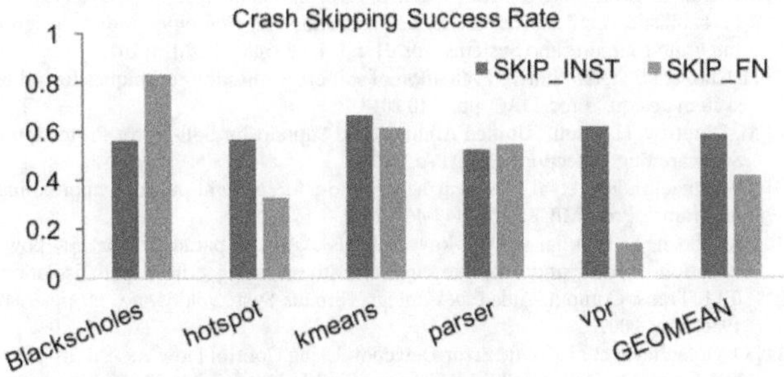


**Figure 4: Success rate of Crash Skipping.**

Overall, we observe that most of the time (>56% on average, and up to 66%), Crash Skipping with the instruction granularity (SKIP_INST) is successful. The average success rate for the function granularity (SKIP_FN) is 40%. Generally, SKIP_INST yields a better success rate than SKIP_FN, with the exception being *blackscholes*, where SKIP_FN yields a significantly higher success rate than SKIP_INST (81% vs. 56%). This is because *blackscholes* has a fairly high inherent fault tolerance that can withstand and benefit from aggressively skipping larger regions of code.

In practice, the best choice of skip granularity is specific to individual applications, and fault injection experiments such as the ones presented in this paper may be used to aid the selection. In the case of long-running applications that cannot be run with representative inputs, fault injection into their "proxy applications" may be used instead for profiling purposes [15].

## 5.4 Performance and Energy Efficiency

Figure 5 compares the overhead between application restart (*restart*), checkpoint-and-rollback (*cp*), and Crash Skipping with SKIP_INST, compared to the fault-free execution in all fault-injection runs of the *blackscholes* application. Application restart can result in large overhead (up to ~100%, because a crash can occur near the end of an application). For checkpoint-and-rollback, we optimistically assume that the overhead is fixed at 1 billion instructions (corresponding to 1sec execution time for a very modest system with CPI = 1 and clock speed = 1GHz) and that no extra overhead is required to capture each checkpoint. The optimistic, constant overhead associated with checkpoint-and-rollback is thus very small. Crash Skipping results in even lower overhead in the majority of the cases, given its high success rate.

Since application performance and energy is directly proportional to the number of instructions executed (given that the hardware power and area overhead associated with Crash Skipping is very small, as shown in Sec. 5.1), we calculate the expected improvements on performance and energy that can be obtained with Crash Skipping with both SKIP_INST and SKIP_FN, compared to the basic application restart approach. The results are shown in Fig. 6. On average, 33% performance/energy improvements are achieved for SKIP_INST. SKIP_FN performs similarly to SKIP_INST in all cases except for *vpr*, where the improvement is smaller mainly due to a higher number of "unrecoverable error" outcomes. The 33% improvement is similar to what can be achieved with an aggressive checkpoint-and-rollback technique such as [24] – the results are within 3% of each other—but it is achieved with much lower overhead.

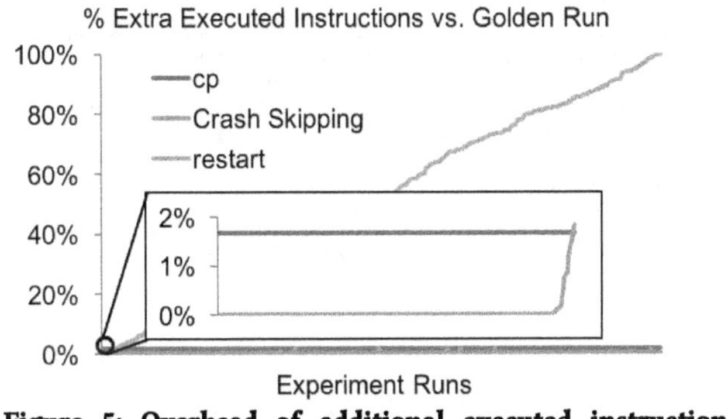


**Figure 5: Overhead of additional executed instruction compared to a golden run for three different recovery strategies for blackscholes from the PARSEC benchmark suite. SKIP_INST is used with Crash Skipping.**

# 6 Related Work

Although approximate computing is a very active research topic, there is very little work focusing on efficient error recovery upon application crash for approximate applications.

In [17], a lightweight checkpointing scheme is proposed for approximate applications, where a checkpoint consists of only the PC, program stack, and the architectural register file, in order to reduce design complexity and overhead associated with error recovery. However, the core idea of Crash Skipping is fundamentally different from checkpoint-and-rollback techniques in that it achieves a unique benefit by completely eliminating the overhead associated with taking a checkpoint, as well as the need for rolling back when Crash Skipping is successful.

Loop perforation is a technique which, like ours, makes use of the fact that not all intermediate instructions need to execute successfully for approximate programs to reach acceptable output. It transforms loops to execute a subset of their iterations only (i.e., skipping certain iterations) [33]. Nevertheless, loop perforation is an approximate computing technique in software and its goal is to obtain optimal tradeoffs in application performance/energy and output quality, which is an orthogonal concept to Crash Skipping.

ERSA [6] is a framework that aims to eliminate application crashes by partitioning the system into strictly reliable and relaxed reliable regions at both the hardware and software levels, and providing lightweight checks for the relaxed reliable region. While memory access related application crashes (e.g., memory access violations) can be eliminated with their lightweight bounds checks, other types of exceptions (e.g., opcode invalid, incorrect exception signals) can still occur. Our technique can be applied in the ERSA framework to improve its error recovery efficiency.

There also exists previous work that identifies critical vs. non-critical data using either the programmer's knowledge [19, 27] or

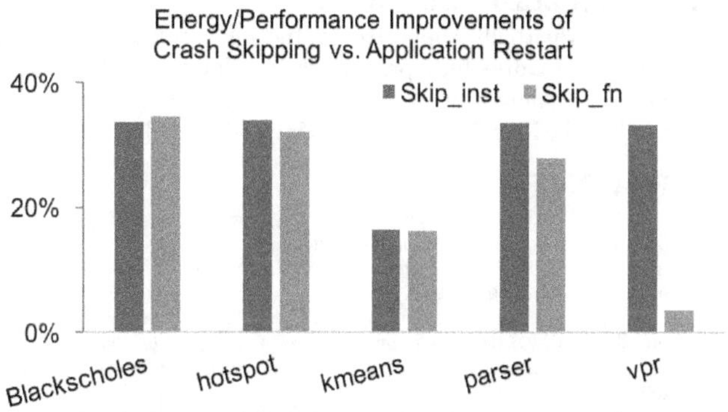


**Figure 6: Energy/performance improvement obtained from Crash Skipping.**

automated frameworks [5]. This shows that it is possible to separate an approximate application into "reliable" and "critical" regions (or kernels). Errors occurring in the reliable regions are not likely to affect the quality of the application output, while those in the critical regions are. Selective protections in approximate applications may then be applied so that errors are less likely to occur in regions which affect critical data. Our Crash Skipping technique can also benefit from these techniques: if errors are limited to non-critical regions, it is very likely that any crashes are a result of non-critical errors and can thus be skipped.

We perform a preliminary analysis on the potential benefit of combining our technique with this line of previous work by performing error injections solely into "noncritical" instructions for *vpr*. We identified any data which represented components of the FPGA in this application as critical. Memory regions are tagged as critical if they are allocated for critical data structures (identified as such by the programmer) and registers are marked as critical if data is loaded into them from critical memory regions. Finally, instructions are statically classified as "noncritical" if they do not operate on memory regions or architectural registers containing critical data. When injecting faults only into noncritical instructions, our Crash Skipping technique with instruction granularity yields ~85% success rate with a threshold value of only 10 (a significant improvement over the ~60% success rate shown in Fig. 4). We expect that the success rate can be further improved by investigating a more optimized way to determine critical regions (e.g., using the automated framework proposed in [5]). These are interesting future directions that are beyond the scope of this paper.

## 7 Conclusion

This paper explores an extremely lightweight error recovery framework for approximate applications. We observe that, due to their inherent fault-tolerance, approximate applications can produce acceptable output even if exceptions resulting from low-level errors are ignored. Based on this finding, we develop a technique to skip crashes up to a per-program defined threshold, significantly reducing the overhead typically associated with recovery techniques (e.g., application restart) while adding minimal design complexity and negligible system-level costs. In future work, we plan to further evaluate Crash Skipping with more comprehensive error models and higher error rates on a wider range of applications. We also plan to optimize the technique further by investigating ways to skip crashes only in "non-critical" regions of an application.

## ACKNOWLEDGMENTS

This work is partially supported by the undergraduate research fellowship and work-study program at the University of Chicago. Computing resources used to perform our experiments were provided by the RIVER system at the University of Chicago.

## REFERENCES

[1] W. Baek, T. M. Chilimbi, "Green: A framework for supporting energy-conscious programming using controlled approximation", Proc. PLDI, pp. 198-209, 2010.
[2] C. Bienia, et al., "The PARSEC benchmark suite: Characterization and architectural implications," Proc. PACT, 2008.
[3] L. Chakrapani, et al., "Ultraefficient (embedded) SoC architectures based on probabilistic CMOS (PCMOS) technology", Proc. DATE, pp. 1-6, 2006.
[4] S. Che et al., "Rodinia: A benchmark suite for heterogeneous computing," Proc. IISWC, pp. 44-54, 2009.
[5] V. K. Chippa, et al., "Analysis and characterization of inherent application resilience for approximate computing," Proc. DAC, pp. 1-9, 2013.
[6] H. Cho, L. Leem and S. Mitra, "ERSA: Error Resilient System Architecture for Probabilistic Applications," in IEEE Transactions on Computer-Aided Design of Integrated Circuits and Systems, vol. 31, no. 4, pp. 546-558, April 2012.
[7] H. Cho, et al., "Quantitative evaluation of soft error injection techniques for robust system design," Proc. DAC, pp. 1-10 2013.
[8] M. Dimitrov, H. Zhou, "Unified Architectural Support for Soft- Error Protection or Software Bug Detection", Proc. PACT, 2007.
[9] H. Esmaeilzadeh, et al., "Neural acceleration for general-purpose approximate programs", Proc. MICRO, pp. 449-460, 2012.
[10] S. Ghosh, S. Bhunia, and K. Roy, "CRISTA: A new paradigm for low-power variation-tolerant and adaptive circuit synthesis using critical path isolation", IEEE Trans. Comput.-Aided Des. Integr. Circuits Syst., vol. 26, no. 11, pp. 1947-1956, Nov. 2007.
[11] O. Goloubeva, et al., "Soft- Error Detection Using Control Flow Assertions", Proc. Intl. Symp. On Defect and Fault Tolerance in VLSI Systems, 2003.
[12] J. Han, M. Orshansky, "Approximate computing: An emerging paradigm for energy-efficient design", Proc. of IEEE European Test Symposium, 2013.
[13] S. K. S. Hari, et al., "mSWAT: Low-cost Hardware Fault Detection and Diagnosis for Multicore Systems", Proc. MICRO, 2009.
[14] J.L. Henning, "SPEC CPU2006 benchmark descriptions," 2006.
[15] T. Z. Islam, et al., "A Machine Learning Framework for Performance Coverage Analysis of Proxy Applications," SC16: Int'l Conference for High Performance Computing, Networking, Storage and Analysis, pp. 538-549, 2016.
[16] A. B. Kahng, et al., "Designing a processor from the ground up to allow voltage/reliability tradeoffs", Proc. HPCA, 2010.
[17] X. Li and D. Yeung, "Application-Level Correctness and its Impact on Fault Tolerance," Proc. HPCA, pp. 181-192, 2007.
[18] T. Li, R. Ragel and S. Parameswaran, "Reli: Hardware/software Checkpoint and Recovery scheme for embedded processors," Proc. DATE, pp. 875-880, 2012.
[19] S. Liu, et al., "Flikker: Saving dram refresh-power through critical data partitioning", SIGPLAN Not., vol. 46, no. 3, pp. 213-224, Mar. 2011.
[20] C.K. Luk et al., "PIN: Building customized program analysis tools with dynamic instrumentation," ACM SIGPLAN Notices, pp. 190-200, 2005.
[21] J. Meng, S. Chakradhar, A. Raghunathan, "Best-effort parallel execution framework for recognition and mining applications", Proc. IEEE Int. Symp. Parallel Distributed Process., pp. 1-12, 2009.
[22] K. Pattabiraman, et al., "Dynamic Derivation of Application-Specific Error Detectors and their Implementation in Hardware", Proc. European Dependable Computing Conference, 2006.
[23] A. Pellegrini, et al., "CrashTest: A fast high-fidelity FPGA-based resiliency analysis framework," Proc. ICCD, pp. 363-370, 2008.
[24] M. Prvulovic, Zheng Zhang and J. Torrellas, "ReVive: cost-effective architectural support for rollback recovery in shared-memory multiprocessors," Proc. ISCA, pp. 111-122, 2002.
[25] S. Sahoo, et al., "Using Likely Program Invariants to Detect Hardware Errors", Proc. DSN, 2008.
[26] M. Samadi, et al., "Sage: Self-tuning approximation for graphics engines", Proc. MICRO, pp. 13-24, 2013.
[27] A. Sampson, et al., "Enerj: Approximate data types for safe and general low-power computation", Proc. PLDI, pp. 164-174, 2011.
[28] J. San, et al., "Branch and data herding: Reducing control and memory divergence for error-tolerant gpu applications", Multimedia IEEE Transactions, vol. 15, no. 2, pp. 279-290, Feb 2013.
[29] J. San, et al., "Doppel-ganger: A cache for approximate computing", Proc. MICRO, 2015.
[30] J. Sartori, R. Kumar, "Architecting processors to allow voltage/reliability tradeoffs", Proc. Intl. Conf. on Compilers Architectures and Synthesis for Embedded Svstems, pp. 115-124, 2011.
[31] N. Shanbhag, "Reliable and energy-efficient digital signal processing", Proc. DAC, pp. 830-835, 2002.
[32] K. Skadron, et al., "Improving prediction for procedure returns with return-address-stack repair mechanisms," Proc. MICRO, pp. 259-271, 1998.
[33] S. Sidiroglou-Douskos, et al., "Managing performance vs. accuracy trade-offs with loop perforation", Proc. of the 19th ACM SIGSOFT Symposium and the 13th European Conference on Foundations of Software Engineering, 2011.
[34] R. Venkatagiri, et al., "Approxilyzer: Towards a systematic framework for instruction-level approximate computing and its application to hardware resiliency," Proc. MICRO, pp. 1-14, 2016.
[35] N. Wang, S. Patel, "ReStore: Symptom-Based Soft Error Detection in Microprocessors", IEEE Transactions on Dependable and Secure Computing, vol. 3, no. 3, July-Sept 2006.

# Voltage-Controlled Magnetoelectric Memory Bit-cell Design With Assisted Body-bias in FD-SOI

Hao Cai, Menglin Han, Weiwei Shan, Jun Yang
hao.cai@seu.edu.cn
National ASIC System Engineering Center, School of Electronic Science & Engineering, Southeast University
Nanjing, 210096, China

You Wang, Wang Kang, Weisheng Zhao
Fert Beijing Institute, BDBC and School of Electronic and Information Engineering, Beihang University
Beijing, 100191, China

## ABSTRACT

Voltage-controlled magnetic anisotropy (VCMA)-magnetic tunnel junction (MTJ) is incorporated into FD-SOI CMOS technology. The design space of 1 transistor-1 MTJ (1T-1M) bit-cell is explored through varied VCMA pulse duration/amplitude and scaling down transistor dimensions. The design point with 1.1 V VCMA pulse amplitude, 0.44 ns pulse duration and W/L = 400 nm/30 nm access transistor shows the ultra low write energy in VCMA-MTJ based bit-cell. It achieves a minimum 3.18 fJ/bit switching energy with 28-nm FD-SOI process. Access transistor sizing is studied, while the ultra low power implementation may lead to MTJ switching failure. Voltage assisted techniques for failure mitigation are proposed based on body-bias generator (BBG). The BBG not only provides VCMA pulse signal to control MTJ barrier, but also generates body-bias to boost the transistor performance. In the presence of forward body-bias (FBB) and increased VCMA pulse level, the proposed strategy is effective in switching failure compensation as well as writing delay improvement.

## CCS CONCEPTS

• **Hardware → Spintronics and magnetic technologies.**

## KEYWORDS

VCMA-MTJ, design boundary, voltage assisted techniques, ultra-low power, FD-SOI

**ACM Reference Format:**

Hao Cai, Menglin Han, Weiwei Shan, Jun Yang and You Wang, Wang Kang, Weisheng Zhao. 2019. Voltage-Controlled Magnetoelectric Memory Bit-cell Design With Assisted Body-bias in FD-SOI. In *Great Lakes Symposium on VLSI 2019(GLSVLSI'19), May 9–11, 2019, Tysons Corner, VA, USA.* ACM, New York, NY, USA, 6 pages. https://doi.org/10.1145/3299874.3317982

## 1 INTRODUCTION

As the scaling down of the semiconductor device geometries continuously goes on, the energy consumption has become a critical bottleneck in future memories [7, 17, 22]. Compared with conventional CMOS technology, spintronic devices feature high power efficiency because of zero standby and low dynamic power. As a promising candidate to replace SRAM, spin transfer torque magnetic random access memory (STT-MRAM) has not been commercialized due to high energy consumption and latency during write operation [9]. Instead of current induced switching method (e.g., STT), magnetic tunnel junction (MTJ) with voltage-controlled magnetic anisotropy (VCMA) effect provides flipping of the magnetization upon a voltage pulse, irrespective of the initial state [12, 21]. Compared to STT switching, this method achieves less energy consumption and higher density, as well as the improved switching latency thanks to very little charge flow required to operate, which drastically reduces the Ohmic losses and Joule heating.

VCMA is considered as an energy-efficient switching method for the next-generation MRAM [10, 12, 15, 18, 20, 21]. However, VCMA efficiency (denoted as the change of interfacial magnetic anisotropy energy per unit electric field [15]), must be improved along with decreased switching latency and lower supply voltage ($V_{dd}$). Previous work of VCMA based bit-cell mainly focused on performance optimization, e.g., scaling of MTJ oxide thickness, seeking optimal pulse duration and amplitude [5, 10, 18, 20]. Until now there is a lack of precision analysis for energy-efficiency as well as failure mitigation method in MRAM bit-cell using VCMA-MTJ.

Therefore, an exploration of the precessional VCMA switching with 1T-1M architecture is needed. In this work, a commercial 28-nm ultra-thin body and BOX fully-depleted silicon on insulator (FD-SOI) process is used to realize the hybrid MTJ-CMOS circuit. In summary, we make the following key contributions:

- To the knowledge of the authors, FD-SOI process is firstly integrated with VCMA-MTJ. Voltage assisted technique and body-bias generator (BBG) are proposed to enhance VCMA-MTJ writing latency, as well as to overcome process variation induced failure.
- Design space exploration in precessional VCMA-MTJ shows design boundary factors and realizes a 3.18 fJ/bit writing energy as the minimum energy point (MEP).
- Access transistor sizing strategy, VCMA pulse duration and amplitude scaling are investigated for high energy-speed efficiency target.

## 2 PRELIMINARY WORK

The VCMA mechanism can be explained as follows: an electric field induces an accumulation of electron charges, then brings about a change of occupation of atomic orbitals at the interface, which in conjunction with spin-orbit interaction, finally results in a change of magnetic anisotropy [1, 13]. Fig. 1(a) illustrates the VCMA-MTJ structure. Recent studies have shown that the interfacial PMA of


*GLSVLSI '19, May 9–11, 2019, Tysons Corner, VA, USA*

ACM ISBN 978-1-4503-6252-8/19/05...$15.00
https://doi.org/10.1145/3299874.3317982

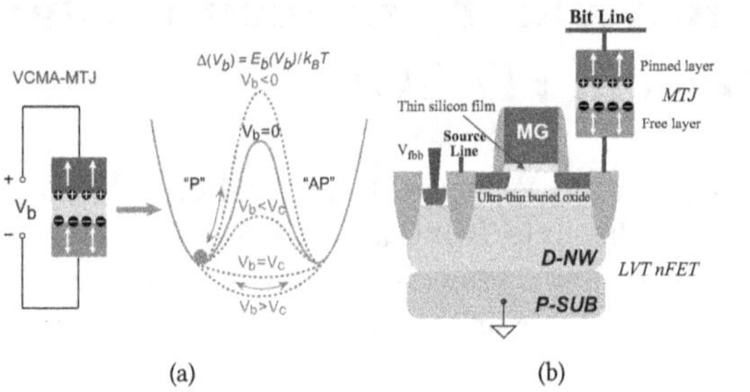


**Figure 1: (a) Typical structure of the VCMA-MTJ. The impact of voltage difference on the MTJ energy barrier ($E_b$) in the presence of VCMA effect. (b) FD-SOI LVT NMOS and its 1T-1M bit-cell.**

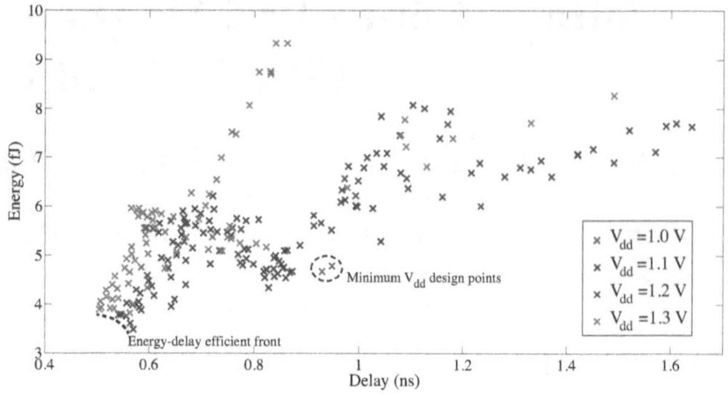


**Figure 2: VCMA-MTJ switching energy-delay efficient front&design space (P-to-AP switching). The design space is explored from 80-400 nm transistor width (80nm step-up). The range of studied pulse width is from 0.3 ns to 0.6 ns, with 0.02 ns step-up.**

ferromagnet/oxide stacks (e.g. CoFeB/MgO) can be modulated by an external voltage (or an electric field), which is called voltage-controlled magnetic anisotropy effect [6].

If a positive voltage is applied on the MTJ and the pulse amplitude is equal to or larger than $V_c$, the energy barrier will be entirely eliminated. Thus, the magnetization of the free layer can precessionally oscillate between the parallel (P) and anti-parallel (AP) states as precessional VCMA switching. An MTJ operated in this regime requires a precise control of the voltage pulse duration or additional write-verify algorithms to guarantee the successful switching [11].

FD-SOI device enlarges the physically-described range of back-plane polarizations. The buried-oxide under the thin silicon film enables transistor back-plane as a second gate allowing to form another channel at the poly-silicon/metal oxide interface [4, 8, 14]. A forward/reverse back-bias voltage (FBB/RBB) can be applied into performance adjustment of FD-SOI transistor, which changes the electrostatic control of the transistors and shifts their threshold voltage ($V_t$). More drive current can be obtained at the expense of increased leakage current (FBB), or reduced leakage with reduced performance (RBB).

## 3 DESIGN SPACE OF 1T-1M BIT-CELL

Fig. 1(b) shows the cross-sectional view of LVT (low power-low $V_t$) NMOS and the 1T-1M (one access transistor with one MTJ) writing circuit. A VCMA-MTJ compact model [10] and a 28-nm UTBB-FD-SOI design-kit are utilized to study the write performance under bit-cell sizing, VCMA pulse duration and pulse amplitude scaling. The energy-delay efficiency is studied with 500 MHz switching frequency. The average delay and energy consumption of P-AP and AP-P switching are used to study the 1T-1M bit-cell performance.

### 3.1 VCMA-MTJ design space exploration

VCMA-MTJ switching performance is dependent on transistor sizing ($W/L$), VCMA pulse duration ($t_b$) and amplitude. Compared to traditional STT-MTJ magnetization switching, electric field is used in VCMA effect to replace electric current, which significantly lowers the dynamic power consumption [10]. VCMA pulse is normally-off (with 0V pulse amplitude) during idle and MTJ sensing operation.

The tradeoffs between area and other design factors are simulated based on LVT FD-SOI transistor. Regarding to circuit bit-cell area, the dimension of access transistor in 1T-1M VCMA-MTJ writing circuit can be greatly reduced (e.g., W/L = 48 nm/32 nm with PTM 32-nm design kit [20]). We evaluate the 1T-1M layout area with 28-nm UTBB-FD-SOI design-kit: when $W$ = 80 nm, layout-area is reduced to 0.119 $\mu m^2$, whereas the $W$ = 400 nm design leads to 0.41 $\mu m^2$ (33.3% energy penalty as well). Fig. 2 illustrates switching energy-delay space considering transistor sizing ($W$ = 80 nm to 400 nm and minimum transistor length $L$ = 30 nm) and varied VCMA pulse duration (0.3 ns to 0.6 ns). A minimum 1.0 V VCMA pulse amplitude can be utilized to switch MTJ with optimal pulse duration (around 0.4 ns).

VCMA pulse amplitude scaling is executed for design space exploration. The lowest VCMA pulse amplitude ($V_{dd}$ = 1 V) is realized with 0.42 ns pulse durations, 400 nm width access transistor. However, this simple VCMA amplitude scaling may bring forth MTJ switching failure due to the requirement of optimal $t_b$. As shown in Fig. 2, the $V_{dd}$ = 1 V design points are with low energy-delay efficiency due to the large switching delay. The $V_{dd}$ scaling induced deterministic functional failure still exists when $V_{dd}$ = 1.1 V, the successful switching of VCMA-MTJ can only be guaranteed with 0.4 ns-0.46 ns $t_b$ when minimum width access transistor (80 nm) is used. Further voltage (above 1.3 V $V_{dd}$) boost leads to less significant latency improvement. The latency saturation and process variation induced failure will be discussed.

High performance, ultra-low power and energy-delay efficient VCMA-MTJ writing specification can be realized according to our design space exploration. As shown in Fig. 2, the high $V_{dd}$ design (e.g., 1.2 V and 1.3 V) leads to an increased power consumption with worse energy-delay efficiency. The lowest energy consumption (3.18fJ/bit) is realized with access transistor $W$ = 400 nm, $V_{dd}$ = 1.1 V with $t_b$ = 0.44 ns. Minimum delay is achieved with $W$ = 400 nm, $V_{dd}$ = 1.3 V with $t_b$ = 0.38 ns. The energy-delay efficient design front is illustrated in Fig. 2.

Transistor sizing is performed according to power-delay specification. When pulse duration is lower than 0.3 ns, or higher than 0.6 ns, the VCMA-MTJ writing efficiency is significantly reduced, which may lead to switching failure [10]. Fig. 3 shows the dependence of

**Table 1: Design points of 1T-1M bit-cell writing performance.**

| | W (nm) | $V_{dd}$ (V) | $t_b$ (ns) | Delay (ns) | Power ($\mu$W) | Failure(mos) | Failure(mos+mtj) |
|---|---|---|---|---|---|---|---|
| High-performance region | 400 | 1.3 | 0.38 | 0.474 | 7.717 | 0 | 0 |
| Minimum energy point | 400 | 1.1 | 0.44 | 0.52 | 6.109 | 2.4% | 11.9% |
| Power-delay efficiency | 160 | 1.1 | 0.42 | 0.787 | 5.241 | 4.7% | 14.1% |
| | 80 | 1.2 | 0.38 | 0.962 | 5.073 | 6.1% | 21.3% |
| Low-power region (increased writing latency) | 80 | 1.2 | 0.36 | 1.165 | 4.865 | 9.1% | 26% |
| | 160 | 1.1 | 0.34 | 1.38 | 4.63 | 39% | failure |
| | 160 | 1.1 | 0.32 | 1.47 | 4.51 | 82% | failure |

**Table 2: Precessional VCMA writing performance**

| | [20] | [10] | This work |
|---|---|---|---|
| Tech. node | 32nm Bulk | 40nm Bulk | 28nm FDSOI |
| Switch delay | 1.42 ns | 0.45 ns | 0.52 ns |
| Dyn. energy | 10.1 fJ/bit | 6.14 fJ/bit | 3.18 fJ/bit |

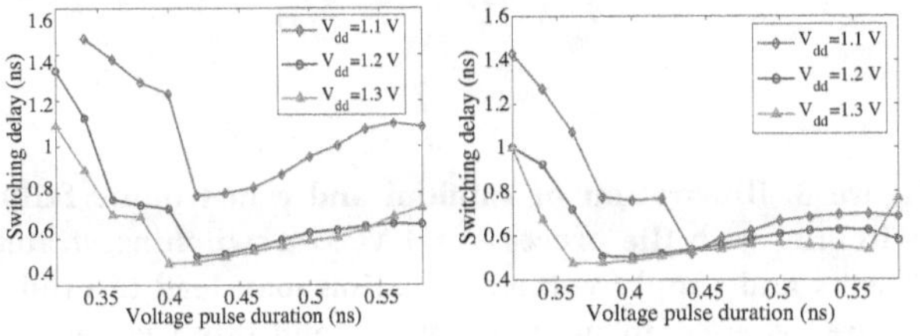


(a) $W$ = 80 nm (b) $W$ = 400 nm

**Figure 3: MTJ switching delay versus voltage pulse duration ($t_b$). The switch delay is dependent on VCMA pulse voltage and the dimension of access transistor. The optimal $t_b$ is varied from 0.36-0.46 ns.**

switching delay and VC pulse duration. The optimal $t_b$ is dependent on VC pulse voltage and transistor dimension, which is varied between 0.36-0.46ns. Table 1 summarizes VCMA-MTJ write design points for high-performance, minimum energy point, power-delay efficiency and low-power. Variability simulations show impact of process induced failure rate in the ultra low-power region. Failure rate can be alleviated by increasing VC pulse amplitude and access transistor width, as well as using optimal VC pulse duration. In summary, an energy-delay evaluation of the marginal boundaries of 1T-1M bit-cell feasible region is obtained through functional simulations. A minimum W/L=160 nm/30 nm access transistor dimension, 1.1 V VA pulse amplitude with optimal pulse duration is required for successful MTJ writing. Table 2 compares the achieved minimum energy point with 3.18 fJ/bit dynamic energy consumption. Comparing with the VCMA-MTJ reported in 32-nm PTM and 40-nm bulk-CMOS [10, 20], the minimum energy per 1-bit non-volatile data writing are improved by 68.5% and 48.2%, respectively.

## 3.2 Design boundary investigation

The design boundary of VCMA pulse duration has been well-studied in [10, 20]. Effective pulse duration range is 0.3 ns to 0.8 ns. The access transistor sizing and VCMA pulse amplitude scaling raise concerns as well. The MTJ writing performance depends on the energy-delay tradeoff that is chosen according to these design factors.

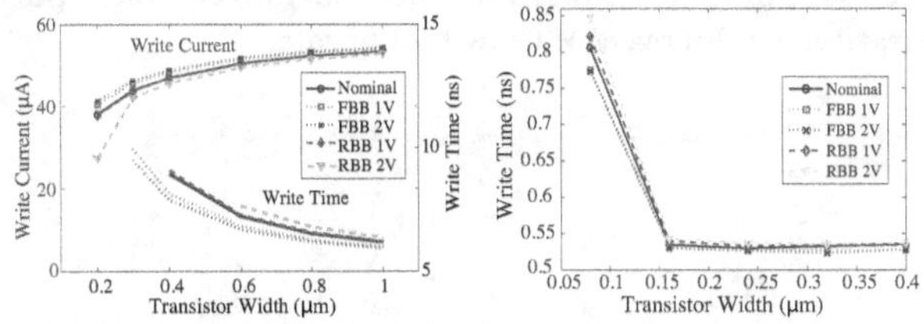


(a) STT-MTJ write (b) VCMA-MTJ write

**Figure 4: (a) STT-MTJ write performance with body-bias. The additional body-bias shows very limited impact to MTJ write due to large dimension transistors. (b) Precessional VCMA-MTJ performance with body-bias, $V_{dd}$=1.2 V, $t_b$=0.42 ns. The write time (switching delay) is sensitive to body-bias with minimum transistor dimension (80 nm/30 nm).**

*3.2.1 Transistor width.* STT-MRAM bit cell requires high electric current to change the magnetic state which normally relies on large width of writing access transistors. Fig. 4(a) presents the writing performance with different forward/reverse body-bias. Even if body-bias voltage is increased to 2 V, its impact on write current and minimum write duration is not evident. Minimum width/length of access transistor in precessional VCMA-MTJ write circuit has smaller layout area as well as better scalability in density [20]. Fig. 4(b) shows the switching delay versus transistor width under different transistor implementation in the VCMA-MTJ bit cell. Considering switching delay, large width ($W$ = 400 nm) case is less sensitive to body-bias than the minimum dimension.

The process variation induced writing failure probability is estimated based on the 1-bit 1T-1M cell. The impact of global process variation and local mismatch of FD-SOI transistor and VCMA-MTJ are studied with 1000 runs Monte-Carlo analysis in the analog design environment (ADE-XL). As shown in Fig. 5, the writing probability is highly dependent on VCMA pulse and access transistor dimension. Minimum dimension design points (W/L=80 nm/30 nm) show pessimistic switching rate. Longer VCMA pulse duration can increase MTJ switching rate (W>160 nm). Fig. 6 shows successful VCMA-MTJ switching rate versus VCMA pulse duration with incremental VCMA pulse amplitude. MTJ switching probability can be guaranteed with large access transistor dimension (e.g., $W$ = 400 nm), as well as optimal pulse duration (around 0.4 ns) and amplitude ($V_{dd}$ is higher than 1.2 V).

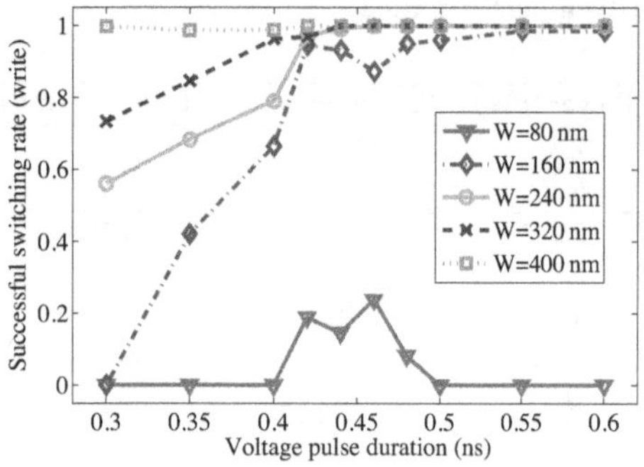


**Figure 5: Successful VCMA-MTJ switching rate versus VCMA pulse duration under 1.1 V VCMA pulse amplitude. The usage of larger transistor width and longer VCMA pulse duration can increase MTJ switching rate.**

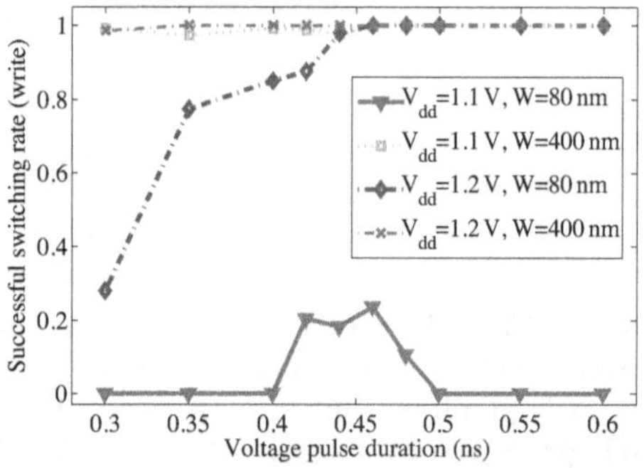


**Figure 6: An optimal VCMA pulse duration improves the writing probability ($V_{dd}$ = 1.2 V, $W$ = 80 nm). The probability is guaranteed with optimal pulse duration and amplitude, as well as large dimension of access transistor.**

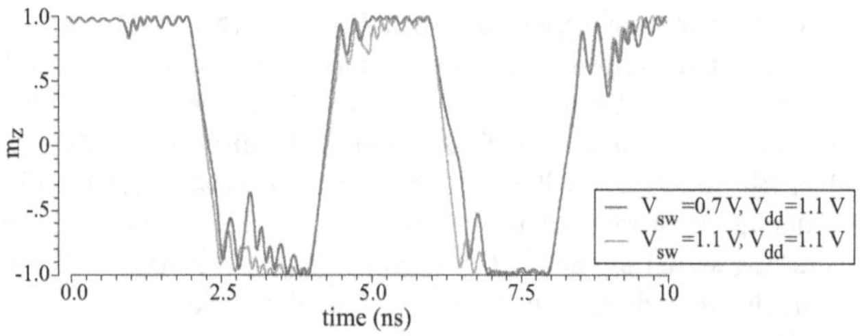


**Figure 7: Illustration of the magnetization dynamic of the free layer with the precessional VCMA switching strategy. A 700 mV $V_{sw}$ (whereas $V_{dd}$ = 1.1 V with optimal pulse duration) is realized in the write operation. Compared a $V_{dd}$ = $V_{sw}$ = 1.1 V case, we only obtain 2.1% improvement in the dynamic power consumption, with 21.8% delay penalty.**

*3.2.2 VCMA pulse voltage.* Further voltage scaling is evaluated at design boundary, e.g., $V_{dd}$ = 1.0 V. However, low VCMA effect leads to writing failure except for $W$ = 400 nm, $t_b$ = 0.44 ns/0.46 ns (see Fig. 2). The continuous scaling down will cause catastrophic switching failure (under 1 V). A tentative voltage scaling of transistor gate voltage ($V_{sw}$) is simulated. As shown in Fig. 7, functionality is confirmed with a 700 mV $V_{sw}$ (whereas $V_{dd}$ = 1.1 V with optimal pulse duration). Compared to the $V_{dd}$ = $V_{sw}$ = 1.1 V case, we only obtain 2.1% improvement in the dynamic power consumption, with 21.8% delay penalty. Thus, lower $V_{sw}$ implementation is not an efficient method to improve energy-delay tradeoff.

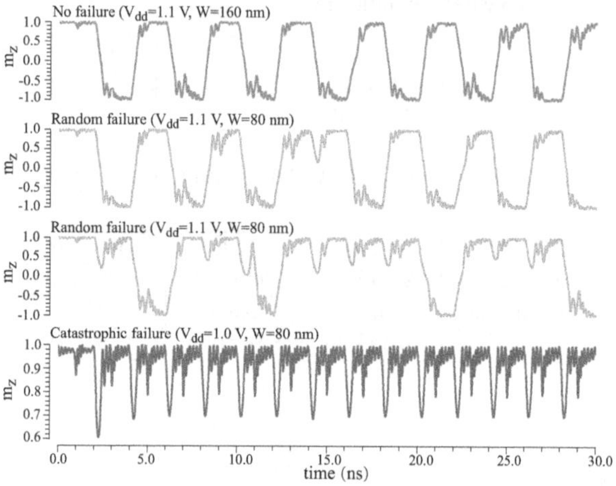


**Figure 8: Illustration of random and catastrophic failure switching with the precessional VCMA switching strategy. Process and supply voltage variation may lead to random failure, whereas insufficient supply and input voltage can cause catastrophic failure.**

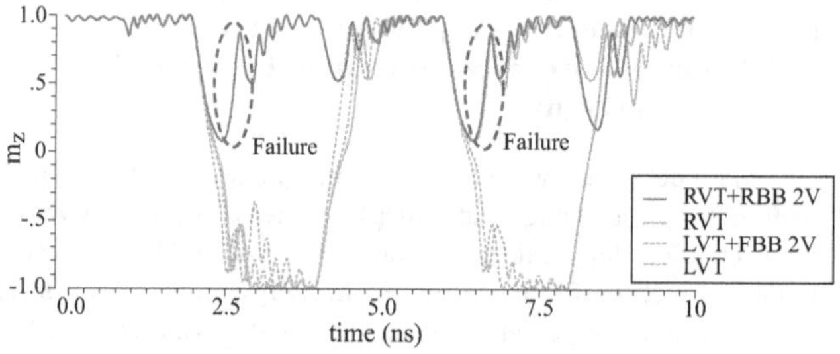


**Figure 9: Additional body bias ($V_{dd}$ = 1 V, $t_b$ = 0.44 ns). It induces random failure (with RVT) and catastrophic failure (RVT + 2V RBB) of MTJ switching. The LVT designs achieve the successful VCMA switching.**

Fig. 8 illustrates random/catastrophic failure with the precessional VCMA switching. Process and $V_{dd}$ variation may lead to random failure, whereas insufficient supply/input voltage can cause catastrophic failure. As shown in Fig. 9, it induces random failure (with RVT) and catastrophic failure (RVT transistor with 2 V RBB), whereas the LVT designs achieve successful VCMA switching.

# 4 VOLTAGE ASSISTED MTJ WRITING

## 4.1 Failure mitigation strategy

Design boundary raises concerns about reliability, since process variation may induce performance fluctuation and switching failure [3]. In SRAM bit-cell, voltage assisted techniques have been

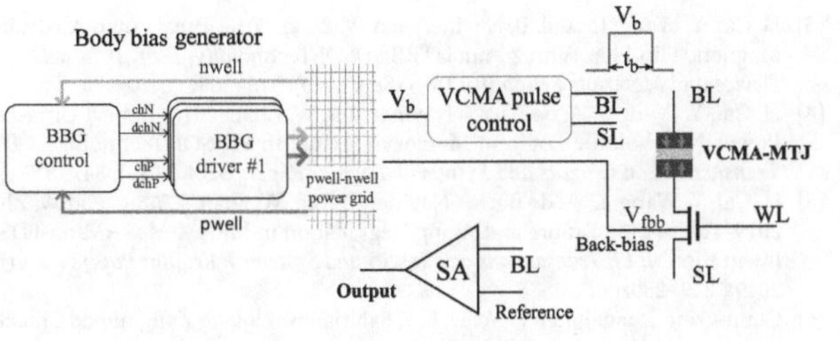

Figure 10: The programmable body-bias generator with a step-size of 100 mV is used to generate VCMA pulse and FBB voltage [2].

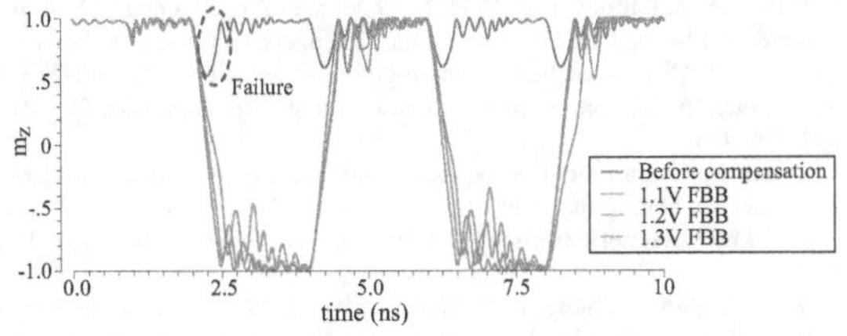

(a) $W$ = 80 nm, $t_b$ = 0.42 ns

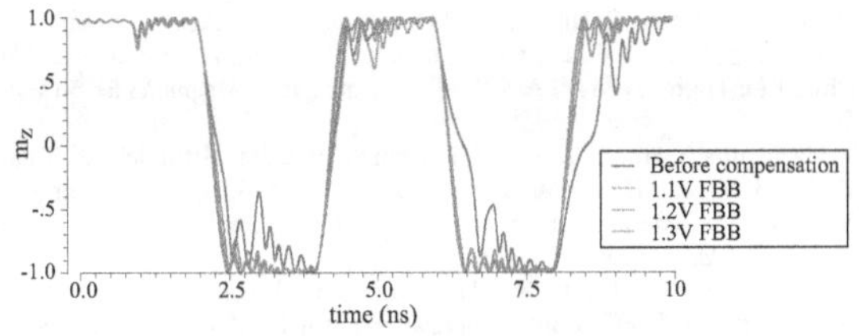

(b) $W$ = 400 nm, $t_b$ = 0.42 ns

**Figure 11: (a) VCMA-MTJ switching with $W$ = 80 nm, $t_b$ = 0.42 ns. Switching failure is realized before compensation (1.1 V, no body-bias implementation) (b) Switching with $W$ = 400 nm, $t_b$ = 0.42 ns. The detail power-delay tradeoff is presented in Table 3.**

well-developed by over or under-driving word line, bit line and body nodes [16, 19]. In this work, a performance enhancement strategy is proposed for VCMA-MTJ operation. Fig. 10 illustrates the block diagram of VCMA-MTJ writing circuit based on body-bias generator (BBG). A programmable BBG (specific IP in design kit) is utilized with a step-size of 100 mV [2], which provides both voltage pulse for VCMA-MTJ and FBB boost for FD-SOI nMOS transistor. As shown in Fig. 10, the transistor well bias is controlled by on chip BBG drive and BBG control. In this study, we consider a body-bias range from 1 V to 1.5 V, as the FBB for nMOS LVT transistor type. The amplitude of VCMA voltage is generated from BBG and then modulated by VCMA pulse control block.

The proposed strategy is used once the designed VCMA-MTJ writing circuit suffers performance degradation and process variation induced functional failure (e.g., magnetic device and transistor). The access transistor is implemented with FD-SOI LVT transistor so that body-bias modulation can be applied to writing circuit. The enhancement mechanism is initialized by sharing VCMA pulse signal to nMOS body node (normally nMOS LVT body connects to ground). The body voltage is modulated from 0V to the VCMA voltage level (higher than 1.0 V), so that VCMA-MTJ switching performance can be improved by FBB (especially benefits the boundary design points). The proposed strategy is therefore shown to provide delay improvement in the presence of additional body-bias, as well as increased VCMA pulse level.

Fig. 11 illustrates the magnetization dynamic of the free layer using precessional VCMA switching with 1.1 V pulse amplitude. Table 3 shows the simulation results of performance adjustment in VCMA-MTJ write operation, with 0.42 ns pulse duration. When $W$ = 80 nm, switching failure is realized with 1.0 V VCMA pulse. An incremental compensation voltage amplitude with a step-size of 100 mV is provided by a programmable BBG. The increasing of pulse amplitude leads to penalty in power consumption. For example, it can be seen that the tradeoff between delay improvement and power penalty is efficient with $W$ = 400 nm.

**Table 3: Performance adjustment of VCMA-MTJ switching step-up from $V_{dd}$ = 1.1 V.**

| Width | Compensation | Switch delay | Dyn. power |
|---|---|---|---|
| 80nm | No body-bias | Failure | Failure |
| | $V_{dd}$=$V_{fbb}$=1.1 V | 1.44 ns | 4.807$\mu$W |
| | $V_{dd}$=$V_{fbb}$=1.2 V | -45.9% | +20.4% |
| | $V_{dd}$=$V_{fbb}$=1.3 V | -64% | +43.5% |
| 400nm | No body-bias | 1.4 ns | 5.12 $\mu$W |
| | $V_{dd}$=$V_{fbb}$=1.1 V | -58.7% | +11.2% |
| | $V_{dd}$=$V_{fbb}$=1.2 V | -61.6% | +52.6% |
| | $V_{dd}$=$V_{fbb}$=1.3 V | -62.3% | +91% |

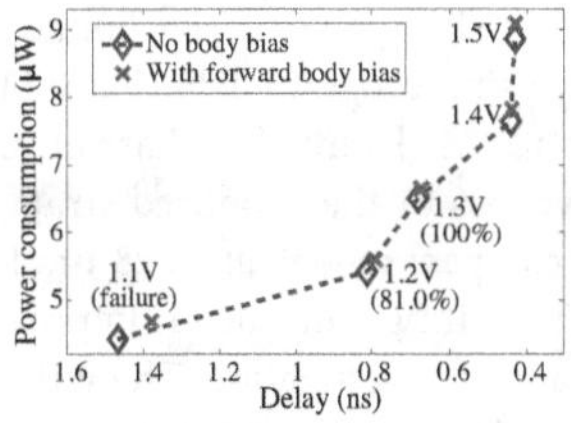

(a) $W$ = 80 nm, $t_b$ = 0.4 ns

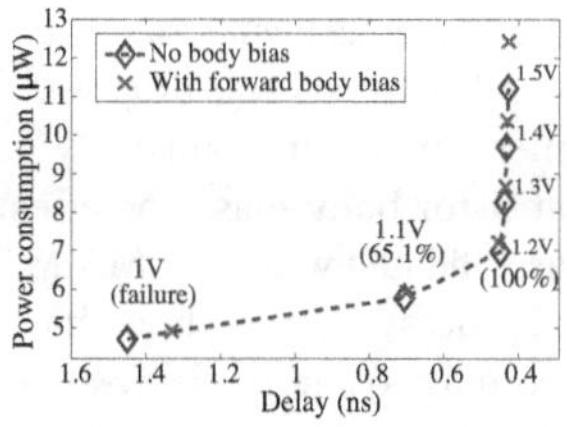

(b) $W$ = 400 nm, $t_b$ = 0.4 ns

**Figure 12: BBG assisted body-bias and incremental VCMA pulse amplitude overcome the writing failure. (a) Access transistor width $W$ = 80 nm, the fist step-up compensation achieves 81% successful writing rate with 1.2 V FBB and $V_{dd}$ (77.2% without FBB). (b) $W$ = 400 nm, the fist step-up compensation has 65.1% successful writing rate enhancement (61.7% without FBB).**

In order to validate the proposed voltage assisted technique, we perform a step-up enhancement process for two design points: $t_b$ = 0.4 ns, $V_{dd}$ step-up from 1.1 V ($W$ = 80 nm) and 1 V ($W$ = 400 nm). 1T-1M writing circuit with and without body-bias are simulated. As shown in Fig. 12, the proposed voltage-assisted method can mitigate failure design points to an improved yield with the power consumption tradeoff. Due to the VCMA-MTJ switching mechanism, the switching latency shows an improvement potential until $V_{dd}$ = 1.2 V ($W$ = 400 nm), or $V_{dd}$ = 1.3 V ($W$ = 80 nm).

## 4.2 Discussion

In this work, the analysis uses the experimental validated VCMA-MTJ compact model to perform design space exploration in 1T-1M MRAM bit-cell. Meanwhile, unlike STT-MTJ counterpart, robust 1T-1M bit-cell with VCMA switching can be realized with the minimum dimension of access transistor. Using FDSOI technology in 1T-1M MRAM bit-cell has proven to be an effective integration way for improved energy efficiency and failure resilience. The power and performance metrics are dependent on the applied bit-line voltage, the characteristic of access transistor and process variation. We propose a combined voltage adjustment strategy applied to bit-line and FD-SOI transistor body, by using the on-chip body-bias generator. This BBG solution can provide dynamic and step-up performance adjustment, yield compensation for memory cells, as well as other building blocks in FD-SOI based circuits and systems, with the design tradeoff in layout area and power consumption.

By using simple voltage scaling, we find that a minimum 1 V bit-line voltage is required for 1T-1M bit cell, whereas the efficient energy-delay front is composed by the step-up bit-line voltage (from 1.1 V to 1.3 V). In addition, voltage adjustment in word-line via access transistor shows less impact comparing the proposed bit-line strategy.

# 5 CONCLUSION

Precessional VCMA-MTJ switching and its FD-SOI integration were studied in this paper. An intensive design space exploration was executed in 1T-1M bit-cell by considering VCMA pulse amplitude, pulse duration, access transistor sizing and layout area. A performance enhancement strategy applies to low power design boundary in 1T-1M bit-cell was proposed, by using programmable body-bias generator to simultaneously control MTJ tunneling barrier and transistor body-bias. The effectiveness of the proposed strategy was validated with a VCMA-MTJ compact model and a 28-nm FD-SOI process. Results show that MTJ writing efficiency is improved according to energy-delay-area tradeoff investigation. The writing failure rate at design boundary was significantly reduced by using assisted body-bias boosting and incremental VCMA pulse amplitude. Various interesting properties were derived from VCMA-MTJ writing operation for further realistic optimization.

# ACKNOWLEDGMENT

This work was supported by the National Science and Technology Major Project of China under Grant 2017ZX01030101 and Pilot School Reform Funding Program in Southeast University (No.1106007132)

# REFERENCES

[1] Stewart E. Barnes, Jun'ichi Ieda, and Sadamichi Maekawa. 2014. Rashba Spin-Orbit Anisotropy and the Electric Field Control of Magnetism. *Scientific report* 4 (2014), 4105:1–5.
[2] M. Blagojevic, M. Cochet, B. Keller, P. Flatresse, A. Vladimirescu, and B. Nikolic. 2016. A fast, flexible, positive and negative adaptive body-bias generator in 28nm FDSOI. In *2016 IEEE Symposium on VLSI Circuits (VLSI-Circuits)*. 1–2.
[3] H. Cai, Y. Wang, L. A. d. B. Naviner, and W. Zhao. 2016. Breakdown Analysis of Magnetic Flip-Flop With 28-nm UTBB FDSOI Technology. *IEEE Transactions on Device and Materials Reliability* 16, 3 (Sep. 2016), 376–383.
[4] H. Cai, Y. Wang, L.A. de Barros Naviner, and W. Zhao. 2016. Robust Ultra-Low Power Non-Volatile Logic-in-Memory Circuits in FD-SOI Technology. *IEEE Transactions on Circuits and Systems I: Regular Papers* 64, 4 (2016), 847–857.
[5] H. Cai, Y. Wang, L. A. de Barros Naviner, X. Liu, W. Shan, J. Yang, and W. Zhao. 2019. Addressing Failure and Aging Degradation in MRAM/MeRAM-on-FDSOI Integration. *IEEE Transactions on Circuits and Systems I: Regular Papers* 66, 1 (Jan 2019), 239–250.
[6] Chun-Gang Duan, Julian P. Velev, R. F. Sabirianov, Ziqiang Zhu, Junhao Chu, S. S. Jaswal, and E. Y. Tsymbal. 2008. Surface Magnetoelectric Effect in Ferromagnetic Metal Films. *Phys. Rev. Lett.* 101 (Sep 2008), 137201.
[7] T. Endoh, H. Koike, S. Ikeda, T. Hanyu, and H. Ohno. 2016. An Overview of Nonvolatile Emerging MemoriesâĂŤ Spintronics for Working Memories. *IEEE Journal on Emerging and Selected Topics in Circuits and Systems* 6, 2 (June 2016), 109–119.
[8] P. Flatresse, B. Giraud, J. P. Noel, B. Pelloux-Prayer, F. Giner, D. K. Arora, F. Arnaud, N. Planes, J. Le Coz, O. Thomas, S. Engels, G. Cesana, R. Wilson, and P. Urard. 2013. Ultra-wide body-bias range LDPC decoder in 28nm UTBB FDSOI technology. In *Solid-State Circuits Conf. Digest of Tech. Papers (ISSCC), 2013 IEEE Intl.* 424–425.
[9] S. Kanai, M. Yamanouchi, S. Ikeda, Y. Nakatani, F. Matsukura, and H. Ohno. 2012. Electric field-induced magnetization reversal in a perpendicular-anisotropy CoFeB-MgO magnetic tunnel junction. *Applied Physics Letters* 101, 12 (2012), 122403.
[10] W. Kang, Y. Ran, Y. Zhang, W. Lv, and W. Zhao. 2017. Modeling and Exploration of the Voltage-Controlled Magnetic Anisotropy Effect for the Next-Generation Low-Power and High-Speed MRAM Applications. *IEEE Transactions on Nanotechnology* 16, 3 (2017), 387–395.
[11] H. Lee, J. G. Alzate, R. Dorrance, X. Q. Cai, D. MarkoviÄĞ, P. Khalili Amiri, and K. L. wang. 2015. Design of a Fast and Low-Power Sense Amplifier and Writing Circuit for High-Speed MRAM. *IEEE Transactions on Magnetics* 51, 5 (May 2015), 1–7.
[12] T. Maruyama, Y. Shiota, T. Nozaki, K. Ohta, N. Toda, M. Mizuguchi, A. Tulapurkar, T. Shinjo, M. Shiraishi, S. Mizukami, Y. Ando, and Y. Suzuki. 2009. Large voltage-induced magnetic anisotropy change in a few atomic layers of iron. *Nature Nanotechnology* 4 (2009), 158–161.
[13] Manish K. Niranjan, Chun-Gang Duan, Sitaram S. Jaswal, and Evgeny Y. Tsymbal. 2010. Electric field effect on magnetization at the Fe/MgO(001) interface. *Applied Physics Letters* 96, 22 (2010), 222504.
[14] J. P. Noel, O. Thomas, M. A. Jaud, O. Weber, T. Poiroux, C. Fenouillet-Beranger, P. Rivallin, P. Scheiblin, F. Andrieu, M. Vinet, O. Rozeau, F. Boeuf, O. Faynot, and A. Amara. 2011. Multi-$V_T$ UTBB FDSOI Device Architectures for Low-Power CMOS Circuit. *IEEE Transactions on Electron Devices* 58, 8 (2011), 2473–2482.
[15] P. Ong, N. Kioussis, P. Khalili Amiri, and K. Wang. 2016. Electric-field-driven magnetization switching and nonlinear magnetoelasticity in Au/FeCo/MgO heterostructures. *Scientific Reports* 6 (2016), 29815.
[16] A. Raychowdhury, B. Geuskens, J. Kulkarni, J. Tschanz, K. Bowman, T. Karnik, S. L. Lu, V. De, and M. M. Khellah. 2010. PVT-and-aging adaptive wordline boosting for 8T SRAM power reduction. In *2010 IEEE International Solid-State Circuits Conference-(ISSCC)*. 352–353.
[17] K. Roy, S. Mukhopadhyay, and H. Mahmoodi-Meimand. 2003. Leakage current mechanisms and leakage reduction techniques in deep-submicrometer CMOS circuits. *Proc. IEEE* 91, 2 (Feb 2003), 305–327.
[18] S. Sharmin, A. Jaiswal, and K. Roy. 2016. Modeling and Design Space Exploration for Bit-Cells Based on Voltage-Assisted Switching of Magnetic Tunnel Junctions. *IEEE Transactions on Electron Devices* 63, 9 (2016), 3493–3500.
[19] T. Song, W. Rim, S. Park, Y. Kim, J. Jung, G. Yang, S. Baek, J. Choi, B. Kwon, Y. Lee, S. Kim, G. Kim, H. S. Won, J. H. Ku, S. S. Paak, E. Jung, S. S. Park, and K. Kim. 2016. A 10nm FinFET 128Mb SRAM with assist adjustment system for power, performance, and area optimization. In *2016 IEEE International Solid-State Circuits Conference (ISSCC)*. 306–307.
[20] S. Wang, H. Lee, F. Ebrahimi, P. K. Amiri, K. L. Wang, and P. Gupta. 2016. Comparative Evaluation of Spin-Transfer-Torque and Magnetoelectric Random Access Memory. *IEEE Journal on Emerging and Selected Topics in Circuits and Systems* 6, 2 (2016), 134–145.
[21] Wei-Gang Wang, Mingen Li, Stephen Hageman, and C. L. Chien. 2012. Electric-field-assisted switching in magnetic tunnel junctions. *Nature Materials* 11 (2012), 64–68.
[22] S. Yu and P. Chen. 2016. Emerging Memory Technologies: Recent Trends and Prospects. *IEEE Solid-State Circuits Magazine* 8, 2 (Spring 2016), 43–56.

# Low Cost Hybrid Spin-CMOS Compressor for Stochastic Neural Networks

Bingzhe Li*
University of Minnesota, Twin Cities
Minneapolis, MN, USA
lixx1743@umn.edu

Jiaxi Hu*
University of Minnesota, Twin Cities
Minneapolis, MN, USA
huxxx499@umn.edu

M. Hassan Najafi
University of Louisiana at Lafayette
Lafayette, LA, USA
najafi@louisiana.edu

Steven Koester
University of Minnesota, Twin Cities
Minneapolis, MN, USA
skoester@umn.edu

David J. Lilja
University of Minnesota, Twin Cities
Minneapolis, MN, USA
lilja@umn.edu

## ABSTRACT

With expansion of neural network (NN) applications lowering their hardware implementation cost becomes an urgent task especially in back-end applications where the power-supply is limited. Stochastic computing (SC) is a promising solution to realize low-cost hardware designs. Implementation of matrix multiplication has been a bottleneck in previous stochastic neural networks (SC-NNs). In this paper, we introduce spintronic components into the design of SC-NNs. A novel spin-CMOS matrix multiplier is proposed in which the stochastic multiplications are performed by CMOS AND gates while the sum of products is implemented by spintronic compressor gates. The experimental results indicate that compared to the conventional binary implementations the proposed hybrid spin-CMOS architecture can achieve over 125×, 4.5× and 43× reduction in terms of power, energy and area consumptions, respectively. Moreover, compared to previous CMOS-based SC-NNs, our design saves the power by 3.1× - 7.3×, reduces energy consumption by 3.1× - 7.3× and decreases area by 1.4× - 7.6× while maintaining similar recognition rates.

## CCS CONCEPTS

• **Hardware** → *Spintronics and magnetic technologies*; *Logic circuits*;

## KEYWORDS

Stochastic computing; Neural network; Spintronic; Compressor

**ACM Reference Format:**

Bingzhe Li, Jiaxi Hu, M. Hassan Najafi, Steven Koester, and David J. Lilja. 2019. Low Cost Hybrid Spin-CMOS Compressor for, Stochastic Neural Networks. In *Great Lakes Symposium on VLSI 2019 (GLSVLSI '19), May 9–11, 2019, Tysons Corner, VA, USA.* ACM, New York, NY, USA, 6 pages. https://doi.org/10.1145/3299874.3317989

*Authors contributed equally


*GLSVLSI '19, May 9–11, 2019, Tysons Corner, VA, USA*

ACM ISBN 978-1-4503-6252-8/19/05...$15.00
https://doi.org/10.1145/3299874.3317989

## 1 INTRODUCTION

Neural networks (NNs) have become a popular technology in many fields. To solve complex problems designers need to add more and more neurons and layers into NNs which result in higher hardware cost in terms of power, energy and area. However, applications such as the Internet of Things (IoT) cannot tolerate high power or energy consumption due to insufficient power and energy supply. Therefore, reducing the hardware cost becomes a crucial issue for back-end NN-based applications.

Stochastic computing (SC) [1] as a promising technology can implement complex arithmetic operations using simple logic gates. For example, multiplication operations are implemented using simple standard AND gates in SC [2]; Additions can be achieved by OR gates as proposed in [3]. In terms of applications, previous works [4–12] have applied the SC technology to implementation of NNs to achieve energy-efficient and low-power hardware designs. For instance, Li *et al.* [5] proposed a NN implemented using stochastic components only, which successfully reduced the power consumption. Nevertheless, the implementations like [5] led to higher error rates compared to the conventional binary implementations due to the correlation and imprecision of bit-stream-based representation and inaccuracy of OR- and multiplexer-based additions. To solve this issue, hybrid stochastic-binary adders are introduced to sum up the products of matrix elements in the binary domain and so improve the accuracy [6–10]. However, such solutions are sub-optimal regarding the hardware cost due to the use of binary full adders.

Spintronic devices, which utilize electron spin instead of electron charge as the computation variable, provide new design opportunities to conventional VLSI circuits. In this paper, we present a hybrid spin-CMOS architecture to implement cost-efficient SC-based NNs. By taking advantage of the spin diffusion current, we design a novel compressor gate which can efficiently compress N sparse stochastic streams to M dense stochastic streams (N > M). The hierarchical compressor gates together with simple AND gates can realize stochastic matrix multiplication with very low hardware cost. The device functionalities and power/energy consumption are simulated and calculated by using the physics-based compact model [13]. Our experimental results show that, compared to the binary implementations of NNs and the previous SC-NNs implemented by CMOS circuits, the hybrid spin-CMOS architecture can significantly reduce the hardware cost of NNs in terms of power, energy, and area consumptions while achieving slightly higher

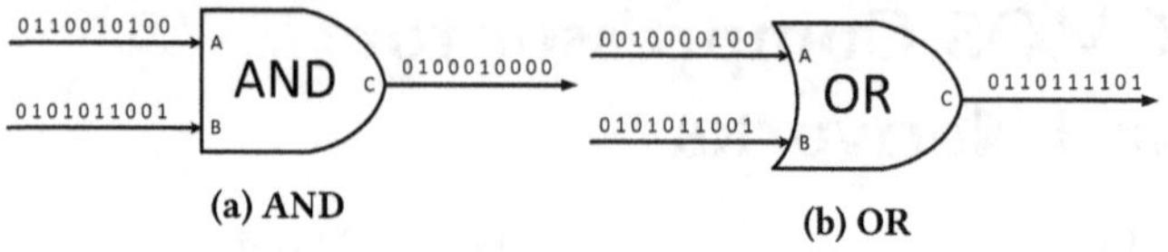


**Figure 1: Stochastic multiplication and addition for the unipolar format.**

recognition error rates compared to the conventional fixed-point binary implementations.

The remainder of this paper is organized as follows: Section 2 provides the background on SC and the motivation behind this work. Section 3 explains the functionality of the proposed compressor. Section 4 introduces the physical implementation of the spin-CMOS compressor. Section 5 shows the architecture of hybrid spin-CMOS SC-NNs, and the comparisons of recognition error rates and hardware cost. The conclusions are drawn in Section 6.

## 2 BACKGROUND AND MOTIVATION

### 2.1 Stochastic Computing

SC can achieve complex arithmetic operations with simple logic gates. A floating-point number in the [0,1] interval is expressed by a sequence of binary bits, called bit-stream, in which all bits have the same weight. The expressed value is based upon the probability of the bits being logic '1'. Unipolar and bipolar are the two common formats [14] to encode a floating-point number into a bit-stream representation. In this work, our proposed SC-NNs are implemented with the unipolar format.

Stochastic number generator (SNG) is used to generate bit-streams. The SNG is conventionally implemented using random number generators (RNGs) and comparators. A random number from an RNG is compared to a constant number (target value) in each cycle and the output of comparison generates one bit of the bit-stream. Linear feedback shifted registers (LFSRs) are widely used as the RNG in the SNGs. By exploiting spintronic devices, prior work [15, 16] reduced the hardware cost of the SNG and achieved promising performance in terms of both power consumption and hardware area cost.

For arithmetic operations, depending on the format of bit-streams, multiplication is implemented using an AND gate (Figure 1a) for the unipolar and an XNOR gate for the bipolar format. The addition can be implemented by OR gate (Figure 1b) for the unipolar format and the MUX gate can be used for both unipolar and bipolar formats.

### 2.2 Motivation

Matrix multiplication is the most compute-intensive operation in NNs. Previously, researchers used OR or MUX gates to implement the required stochastic additions for matrix multiplications [5]. However, due to the correlation and the non-scalable characteristics, the OR and MUX-based stochastic adders cause large error rates when the number of inputs is large. To decrease this error rate, authors in [6] and [16] proposed parallel counters and approximate parallel counters (APC), respectively. However, these binary adder-based implementations only achieve suboptimal hardware solutions because of the use of costly binary full adders particularly when

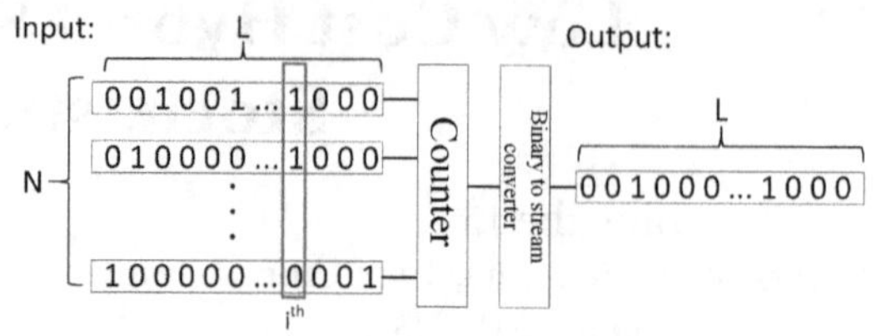


**Figure 2: A demo of N-input stochastic addition in neural networks with L bit-length [16].**

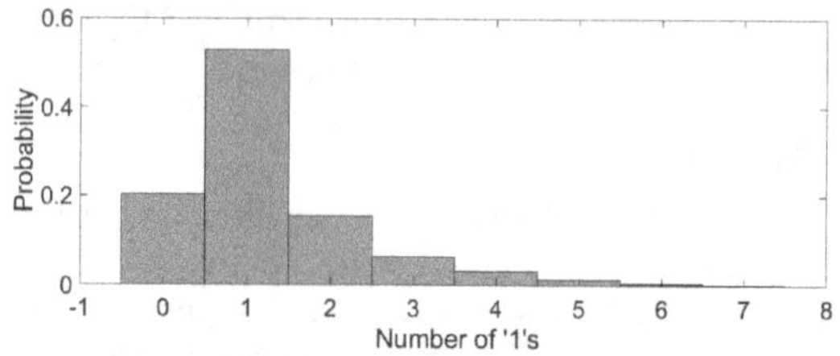


**Figure 3: The probability of the numbers of '1's per clock cycle at the inputs of the counter shown in Figure 2**

adding a large number of inputs. Efficient reduction of the hardware cost while providing similar recognition rates as the conventional binary designs is still a challenging task.

For matrix multiplications in stochastic NNs, most output values are located in the range of (-1, 1). The output values larger than 1 or smaller than -1 will be approximately assigned to 1 or -1 or be scaled to (-1, 1). As shown in Figure 2, assume that there are N bit-streams with L bit-length at the inputs. If we use a counter to compute the summation of N bit-streams and then convert it back to one bit-stream (the operation is equivalent to the N-input addition), the number of '1's in the input bit-streams should be equal to the number of '1's in the output bit-stream. Since the matrix multiplication results (intermediate results in NNs) are usually very small, it is highly possible that the number of '1's in one cycle (like $i^{th}$ cycle) at the input side is smaller than a small threshold value.

To investigate the above assumption, we studied the statistics of the number '1's in the stochastic matrix multiplication of NNs. Figure 3 plots the probability of the numbers of '1's per clock cycle at the inputs of the counter shown in Figure 2. For example, for the $i^{th}$ cycle in Figure 2 it has about 20% probability that all 500 inputs are '0' and about 55% probability that 500 inputs only have one '1'. Therefore, in the case of Figure 3, the 500 inputs have over 90% probability to contain less than four '1's per clock cycle, which means that the 500 bit-streams can be approximately compressed to three bit-streams. Therefore, if we develop a design that can efficiently compress $X$ bit-streams to $Y$ bit-streams ($X >> Y$), it will tremendously decrease the hardware cost of the parallel counters and hence the total hardware cost of the SC-based NNs.

## 3 FUNCTIONALITY OF COMPRESSOR

The compressor gates are designed to take N unipolar encoded stochastic bit-streams as input and compress them into M streams ($N$ and $M$ are the number of inputs and outputs of the compressor gate,

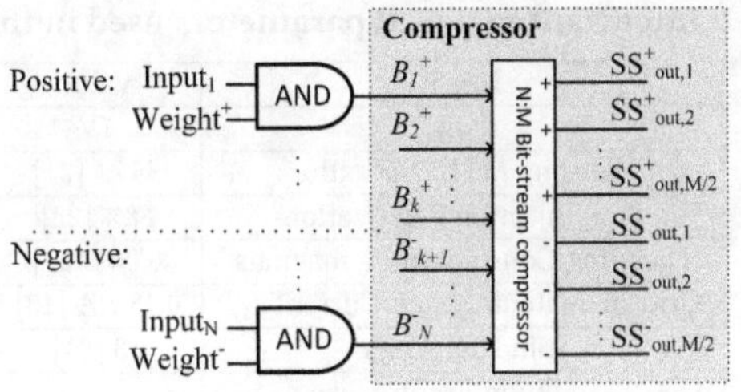


**Figure 4: Schematic design of an N-to-M compressor gate.**

respectively, and $N > M$). The proposed compressors combining with AND gates is used as the matrix multiplier in the stochastic NN. The inputs of the compressor gate are the products of bit-streams which are operated by using AND gates as shown in Figure 4. In the stochastic matrix multiplication, since we use the unipolar encoded bit-streams, the negative values are first regarded as positive values and later partitioned into positive and negative parts as shown in Figure 4. Since input images and outputs of each layer (assume activation function uses sigmoid function) are always positive, the signs of products depend only on the signs of the weights, which are deterministic after training of NNs. Therefore, the number of positive inputs, $K$, is deterministic in Figure 4. The function of the N-to-M compressor is to sum up the N input bits (the sum of bits in positive streams subtracts the sum of bits in negative streams) in every cycle. The compressor gate uses M output bits to express the summed value, in which half of the outputs stands for positive values and the other half expresses negative values. Assume $S$ is the summed value in one clock cycle:

$$S = \sum_{i=1}^{K} B_i^+ - \sum_{i=K+1}^{N} B_i^- \tag{1}$$

where $B_i^{+/-}$ is the $i^{th}$ input bit-stream value for the $+/-$ streams at a clock cycle. The M outputs are designed such that

$$\begin{cases} SS^+_{out,j} = 1, j = 1, 2, ..., M/2, & \text{if } M/2 \leq S \\ SS^+_{out,j} = 1, j = 1, 2, ..., S, & \text{if } 0 \leq S < M/2 \\ SS^-_{out,j} = 1, j = 1, 2, ..., |S|, & \text{if } -M/2 < S < 0 \\ SS^-_{out,j} = 1, j = 1, 2, ..., M/2, & \text{if } S \leq -M/2 \\ SS^{\pm}_{out,j} = 0, & \text{otherwise} \end{cases} \tag{2}$$

where $j = 1, 2, ..., M/2$ is the index of the output bit-streams.

Figure 5a shows a structure of a 6-to-4 compressor assuming K=3. In this case, the compressor can compute the range of the summation result, $S$, from -2 to +2. For example, in the $6^{th}$ cycle in Figure 5a the positive inputs are '111' while the negative inputs are '000'. As a result, $S = 3$, which is out of the range (-2, +2). The compressor gives the result as +2 rather than +3, of which the outputs have '11' at the positive and '00' at the negative side. As another example, in the $3^{rd}$ cycle in Figure 5a, the positive and negative inputs have three and two '1's, respectively. Two '1's at the positive and negative inputs cancel each other and only one '1' is left at the positive side. The summation result in this case is a single '1' and thus only the output $SS^+_{out,1}$ is set to '1'. For the cases that the total number of '1's of input bit-streams in one cycle is

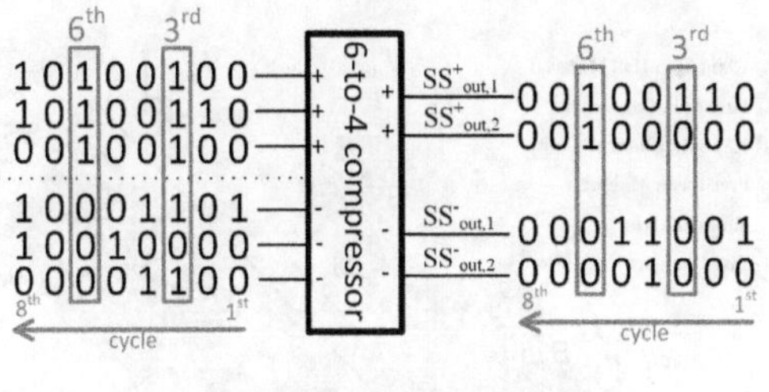


**(a) A 6-to-4 compressor gate**

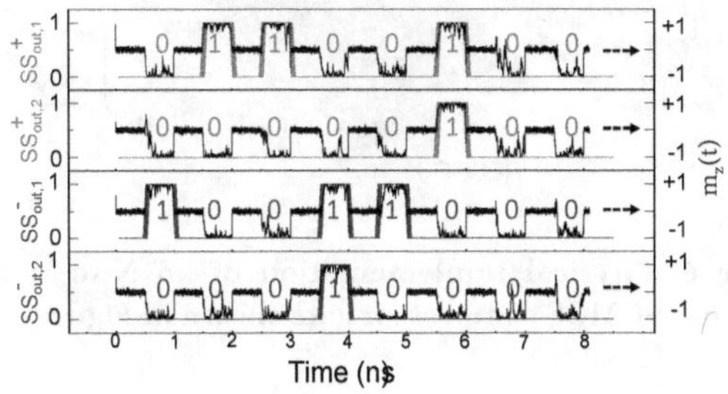


**(b) Transient simulation of the 6-to-4 compressor gate shown in (a).**

**Figure 5: An example of a 6-to-4 compressor gate with six inputs and four outputs (N=6, M=4, K=3 in Figure 4).**

zero or one, the outputs will have zero '1' and one '1', respectively, as seen in the $2^{nd}$ and $7^{th}$ cycles. As discussed in Section 2, it is very likely to see that the number of '1's in the inputs is less than a threshold value (M), in which the compressor gate accurately represents the summation of the N bit-streams using the M outputs bit-streams. As can be seen in Figure 5b, the proposed spin-CMOS compressor gate can successfully realize the functionality shown in Figure 5a. The implementation details are discussed in Section 4.

# 4 SPIN-CMOS BASED COMPRESSOR IMPLEMENTATION

In this section, we discuss the implementation of the proposed hybrid spin-CMOS based compressor. Figure 6 shows the structure of the proposed compressor gate which is based on a nonlocal spin valve with multiple inputs and outputs [17]. The nonlocal spin valve provides the ability to operate spin diffusion currents which are efficient in implementing analog summations [18]. The N inputs are connected to the N bit-streams. If an input bit is '1', the charge current injects non-equilibrium spin from the ferromagnetic (FM) spin injector into the nonmagnetic (NM) spin channel. The injected spin diffuses evenly to the M outputs. The polarity of one input stream is defined as the injected spin polarization which is determined by the magnetic states of the FM injector. If multiple '1s' arrives at the inputs, the injected spins will sum up at the merging point ('X' in the middle of Figure 6) of N·M channels in an analog manner. The control transistors at the input terminals cut out the charge current path to achieve low power performance if the input is '0'.

At the injector terminals, tunnel barriers are used to enhance the spin injection polarization, P, and prevent the cross-talk between

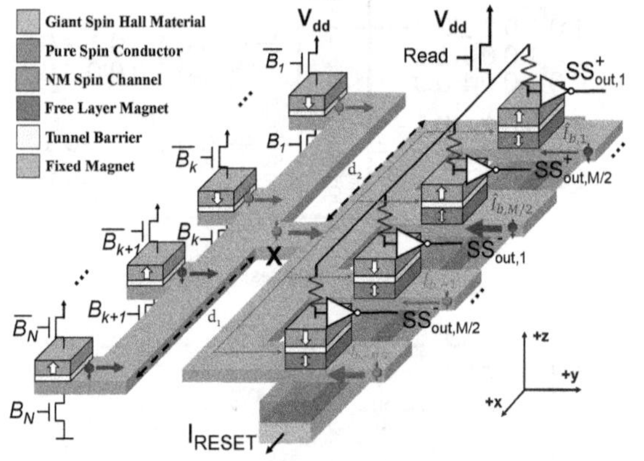


**Figure 6: Physical implementation of an N-to-M hybrid spintronic-CMOS compressor gate shown in Figure 4.**

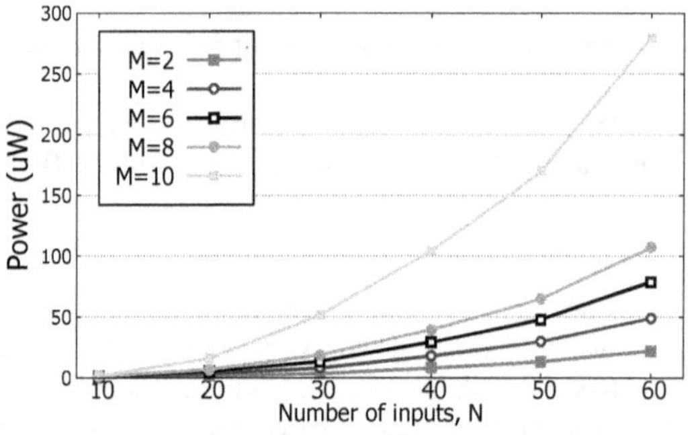


**Figure 7: Power consumption of one N-to-M compressor gate with only one '1' appearing at its inputs.**

inputs [18]. The analog summation of up/down spin current naturally emulates the arithmetic operation of positive and negative stochastic bits in Eq. 1. At the point 'X', the total output spin current can be written as:

$$\hat{I}_{s,tot} = I_0 \sum_{i=1}^{N} \hat{m}_{z,i} B_i = I_0 (\sum_{i=1}^{K} B_i - \sum_{i=K+1}^{N} B_i) = S \cdot I_0 \hat{z} \quad (3)$$

where $B_i$ is the incoming bit at the i-th input and $m_z$ is the z-magnetization of the corresponding FM injector. $I_0$ is the unit output current from single input which is defined by the diffusion equation: $I_0 = \eta \cdot PI_c \cdot e^{-d_1/\lambda_s}$. $I_c$ is the applied charge current and $\eta = 0.5$ is the output efficiency of spin current [13]. $d_1$ is the distance between the injectors to 'X' and $\lambda_s$ is the spin diffusion length. By programming the magnetic state of the FM injectors, the K value of each compressor gate can be individually programmed from 0 to N [17].

At the output terminals, Eq. 2 is implemented by a series of low-power spin current comparators, which are based on magnetic tunnel junctions (MTJs) built on NM spin channels. The switching of the free layer (FL) magnets are determined by the competition between the output spin currents and the bias spin currents. Beneath the NM layer, a stack of pure spin conductor and Giant Spin

**Table 1: Important material parameters used in this work**

| Name | Value |
|---|---|
| $V_{dd}$ | 1V |
| Sensing MTJ TMR ratio | 354% [21] |
| Spin Injection Polarization | 88% [22] |
| Damping Constant of FL magnets | 0.005 [23] |
| Critical Switching Spin Current $I_{sc}$ | 0.18 $\mu$A [13] |
| Spin Hall Angle | 18 [24] |
| Minimum Feature Size (Spintronic Components) | 15nm |

Hall Material [19] are introduced as the "reset clock." Because of the "Giant Spin Hall Effect," a charge current in the Giant Spin Hall Material (GSHM) generates $\hat{I}_{s,SHE}$ with in-plane spin polarization on its top surface. $\hat{I}_{s,SHE}$ switches the FL magnets to in-plane, which is the energy maximum state. Once the RESET signal is "OFF", a weak perturbation can determine the switching of FL magnets. Since in SC the operation frequency is high, the FL magnets can be designed with low thermal stabilities, $\Delta$ [20]. As shown in Figure 5b, with $\Delta = 4k_BT$, the FL magnet can still well maintain its state at 1 GHz.

The MTJ senses the state of FL magnets and transfer it into a voltage signal. To reduce the process-induced variation, in the voltage divider, the reference resistor should also be a neighboring MTJ but with its magnetic state always fixed. The resistance value of the reference MTJ is determined such that when the sensing MTJ is in the parallel state, the corresponding $SS_{out}$ will be '1', otherwise the output will be '0' [18]. The unit output spin current, $I_0$, and the critical switching current of FL magnets, $I_{sc}$, are designed as: $I_0 = 2MI_{sc}e^{d_2/\lambda_s}$ such that the spin currents that arrive the output equal to $2I_{sc}$ if there is only a single '1' at the inputs of the compressor gate. $d_2$ is the distance between 'X' and outputs. Correspondingly, the bias spin currents, which can also be generated by nonlocal spin valves, are designed as $|\hat{I}_{b,j}| = \mp(2 \cdot j - 1)I_{sc}$ for positive (or negative) outputs ($j = 1, ..., M/2$ is the index of output terminals). As a result, by measuring the analog level of the $\hat{I}_{s,tot}$, a compressor gate can count the net amount of the input bits. Figure 5b shows the simulation of a 6-to-4 compressor gate by using the modular approach for spintronic devices. The magnetic dynamics are simulated by solving the Landau-Lifshitz-Gilbert equation with the random thermal fluctuation and the spin torques [13]. In each cycle, the FL magnets are first reseted to in-plane by $\hat{I}_{SHE}$. Then, the RESET signal is "OFF" and the READ signal is "ON" by which the FL magnets complete switching. Based on the parameters in Table 1, the switching delay of FL magnets is shown to be less than $100ps$.

A physical limitation on fan-in and fan-out is also considered: the length of NM channels are assumed to increase linearly with N and M: $d_1 = N \cdot 2F$ and $d_2 = M \cdot 2F$, where $F$ is the minimum feature size. As a result, the applied charge current, $I_c$, exponentially increases with N+M if $d_1 + d_2 > \lambda_s$, which sets the trade-off between the energy consumption per gate and the fan-in and fan-out abilities. Figure 7 shows the power scaling trend of a compressor gate when only a single '1' appears at its inputs. Its strong dependence on the N and M suggests that the energy consumed for nonlocal spin torque switching is still dominating. Thus, increasing $\lambda_s$ or decreasing $I_{sc}$ can further improve the energy efficiency. In the rest of this

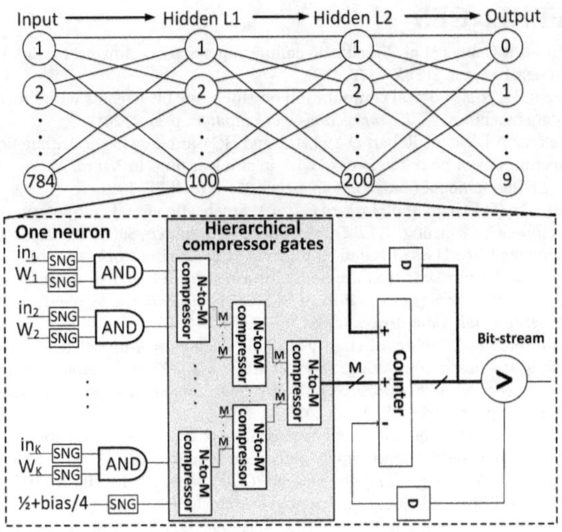


**Figure 8: Stochastic neural network implementation with a single neuron architecture**

paper, the N value of each compressor gate is kept under 50 and a hierarchical structure is utilized to implement the summation over a large number of inputs (Figure 8).

## 5 IMPLEMENTATION OF NEURAL NETWORKS

In this section, SC-based implementation of a restricted Boltzmann machine (RBM) classifier [25] with a 784-100-200-10 configuration is investigated. The stochastic implementation of the RBM classifier, the recognition error rates, and the hardware cost for different implementations are discussed in the following sections.

### 5.1 Implementation

First, we introduce the NN implementation using the hybrid spin-CMOS devices. The basic unit is a neuron formulated as $out = \sigma(X * W + bias)$ where $\sigma$ is the activation function; $X$ is the input of the neuron; $W$ and $bias$ are constant values in the classification which are obtained from training process.

The MTJ based SNG [26] is used to generate bit-streams in the neuron architecture of Figure 8. The inputs are ANDed with the weighted bit-streams to obtain the intermediate products of matrix multiplications. N-to-M bit-stream compressors are then used in a hierarchical structure to reduce the number of counter inputs to M. Finally, the output of the counter goes through a comparator to convert it back into bit-stream representation and feed the next layer of the NN. The activation function uses the stochastic approximate sigmoid function, $\frac{x+2}{4}$, proposed in [7] which is integrated in the neuron structure of Figure 8.

### 5.2 Recognition Error Rate

To evaluate the recognition error rates, the MNIST handwritten digit image dataset [27] is used which includes 60,000 training images and 10,000 testing images. For the classification process, the weights and biases of the RBM NN are trained and regarded as constant values for the classifier. Due to a long simulation time, we tested each 10,000 images classification process three times and averaged the error rates.

**Table 2: Comparison of recognition error rates of RBMs**

| Type | N-to-M | Bit-length: | | | |
|---|---|---|---|---|---|
| | | 32 | 64 | 128 | 256 |
| Binary | - | 2.05% | | | |
| Stochastic#1 [6][16] | - | >10% | 6.06% | 5.58% | 4.34% |
| Stochastic#2 [7][8] | - | 3.20% | 3.00% | 2.84% | 3.08% |
| This work | *N-to-2 | >15% | >15% | >15% | >15% |
| | 10-to-4 | 3.99% | 3.26% | 2.82% | 2.79% |
| | 10-to-6 | 3.79% | 3.20% | 2.68% | 2.88% |
| | 20-to-4 | 4.00% | 3.21% | 3.03% | 2.77% |
| | 20-to-6 | 3.62% | 2.97% | 2.77% | 2.69% |
| | 30-to-4 | 4.02% | 3.23% | 2.91% | 2.94% |
| | 30-to-6 | 3.81% | 2.97% | 2.77% | 2.71% |
| | 40-to-4 | 4.15% | 3.64% | 3.36% | 3.22% |
| | 40-to-6 | 3.85% | 3.13% | 2.96% | 2.89% |

Note: $^*N \geq 10$ might be 10, 20, 30, etc. and when M=2, the error rates are larger than 15% which are not acceptable.

Four different design methodologies are investigated in this paper. As reported in Table 2, the 8-bit fixed point implementation has the lowest recognition error rate. Both the CMOS stochastic and our hybrid spin-CMOS stochastic implementations obtain similar recognition error rates. By increasing the bit-length, the error rates of stochastic implementations become closer to the error rates of the fixed-point implementation. For our hybrid spin-CMOS implementations, we also investigate the impact of the ratio of inputs to outputs (N/M) on the error rate. As reported in Table 2, when M=2, the recognition error rates are larger than 15%. The reason behind this relatively higher error rates is that in this case the proposed spin-based compressor compresses the inputs to only one '+1' or only one '-1' which results in losing '±1's when one cycle contains more than one '±1'. For example, the case in Figure 3 shows that there is more than 20% probability to generate two or more '1's in each cycle. Consequently, when M=2, the output of the compressor cannot accurately express those 20% '1's resulting in such a high error rate. Therefore, we will not consider the case of M=2 for the implementations. For other cases, when decreasing the ratio N/M, the error rates are slightly decreased. This is because the spin-based compressors with lower ratios of N/M have a lower compression rate and thus introduce smaller errors into the addition operations. In summary, with decreasing the ratio N/M and increasing the bit-length, the recognition error rates are decreased.

### 5.3 Hardware Cost

To evaluate the hardware cost, the Synopsys Design Compiler is used to synthesize the RBM NN with the FreePDK 45nm library [28] for the CMOS designs including the proposed implementation, conventional binary, and previous stochastic implementations. The power consumption is reported at a constant frequency of 1GHz. The spintronic components are quantitatively simulated using the device and material parameters summarized in Table 1. To provide a fair comparison, we use the MTJ-based SNGs of [26] to generate the required random numbers in all stochastic implementations.

**Table 3: Hardware comparisons among different works (32 bits for stochastic works)**

| Method | N-to-M | Power (@1GHz) ($mW$) | Area ($mm^2$) | Energy ($nJ$) |
|---|---|---|---|---|
| #1 8-bit Fixed-Point | N/A | 39617 | 55.77 | 39.62 |
| #2 [6][16] | N/A | 1929.77 | 2.06 | 61.75 |
| #3 [7][8] | N/A | 1004.03 | 1.39 | 32.13 |
| #4 This work | 10-to-4 | 258.36 | 1.01 | 8.27 |
| | 10-to-6 | 270.00 | 1.28 | 8.64 |
| | 20-to-4 | 263.59 | 0.87 | 8.43 |
| | 20-to-6 | 273.89 | 0.93 | 8.76 |
| | 30-to-4 | 271.47 | 0.86 | 8.69 |
| | 30-to-6 | 289.27 | 0.88 | 9.26 |
| | 40-to-4 | 292.06 | 0.85 | 9.35 |
| | 40-to-6 | 315.97 | 0.87 | 10.11 |

Four implementations, (**#1**) the conventional fixed-point binary implementation, (**#2**) the CMOS stochastic implementation with the bipolar format [16][6], (**#3**) the CMOS implementation with the unipolar format [7][8], and (**#4**) the hybrid spin-CMOS implementation are compared in terms of power, area and energy consumption. As shown in Table 3, compared to the CMOS binary implementation, our designs can achieve over 125× power reduction, over 43× area reduction and 4.5× energy reduction. Compared to the previous CMOS stochastic implementations, our designs reduce about 3.1× - 7.3× power, 1.4× - 7.6× area and 3.1× - 7.3× energy consumption.

Moreover, we investigate the impact of different ratios of N/M on the hardware cost. When increasing the ratio of N/M, the total area of the NN is reduced because a larger ratio means a smaller number of compressor gates. Changing N and M has a direct impact on the power and energy numbers as discussed in Section 3. As shown in Table 3, by increasing N and M, the power and energy consumption are both increased. Thus, the design with the compressor ratio of 10-to-4 has the lowest power and energy consumption.

## 6 CONCLUSION

In this work, we proposed a hybrid spin-CMOS based stochastic neural network architecture targeting low-cost design. We proposed a spin-CMOS based compressor to compress the input bit-streams into a smaller number of output bit-streams which can significantly reduce the hardware cost of the entire neural network. Experimental results showed that our proposed design obtains similar recognition error rates compared to previous stochastic implementations while achieving slightly higher error rates compared to the conventional binary implementation. In terms of hardware cost, compared to the conventional CMOS-based fixed-point binary implementation, our designs achieve over 125× power reduction, over 43× area reduction and 4.5× energy reduction. Compared to the previous CMOS stochastic implementations our designs reduce about 3.1× - 7.3× power, 1.4× - 7.6× area and 3.1× - 7.3× energy.

## 7 ACKNOWLEDGMENTS

This work was supported in part by National Science Foundation grant no. CCF-1408123 and Seagate Technology.

## REFERENCES


[1] Brian R Gaines et al. Stochastic computing systems. *Advances in information systems science*, 2(2):37–172, 1969.

[2] Peng Li, et al. Logical computation on stochastic bit streams with linear finite state machines. *IEEE Transactions on Computers*, page 1, 2012.

[3] Jeffery A Dickson, Robert D McLeod, and HC Card. Stochastic arithmetic implementations of neural networks with in situ learning. In *Neural Networks, 1993., IEEE International Conference on*, pages 711–716. IEEE, 1993.

[4] Bradley D Brown and Howard C Card. Stochastic neural computation. ii. soft competitive learning. *IEEE Transactions on Computers*, 50(9):906–920, 2001.

[5] Bingzhe Li, M Hassan Najafi, and David J Lilja. Using stochastic computing to reduce the hardware requirements for a restricted boltzmann machine classifier. In *Proceedings of the 2016 ACM/SIGDA International Symposium on Field-Programmable Gate Arrays*, pages 36–41. ACM, 2016.

[6] Ao Ren, et al. Sc-dcnn: Highly-scalable deep convolutional neural network using stochastic computing. In *Proceedings of the Twenty-Second International Conference on Architectural Support for Programming Languages and Operating Systems*, pages 405–418. ACM, 2017.

[7] Bingzhe Li, et al. Neural network classifiers using stochastic computing with a hardware-oriented approximate activation function. In *2017 IEEE 35th International Conference on Computer Design (ICCD)*, pages 97–104. IEEE, 2017.

[8] Vincent T Lee, et al. Energy-efficient hybrid stochastic-binary neural networks for near-sensor computing. In *2017 Design, Automation & Test in Europe Conference & Exhibition (DATE)*, pages 13–18. IEEE, 2017.

[9] S Rasoul Faraji, et al. Energy-Efficient Convolutional Neural Networks with Deterministic Bit-Stream Processing. In *Design, Automation, and Test in Europe (DATE)*, 2019.

[10] Bingzhe Li, et al. Neural network classifiers using a hardware-based approximate activation function with a hybrid stochastic multiplier. *ACM Journal on Emerging Technologies in Computing Systems (JETC)*, 15(1):12, 2019.

[11] Reza Hojabr, et al. SkippyNN: An Embedded Stochastic-Computing Accelerator for Convolutional Neural Networks. In *Design Automation Conference (DAC)*, 2019.

[12] Bingzhe Li, M Hassan Najafi, and David J Lilja. Low-cost stochastic hybrid multiplier for quantized neural networks. *ACM Journal on Emerging Technologies in Computing Systems (JETC)*, 2019.

[13] Kerem Yunus Camsari, Samiran Ganguly, and Supriyo Datta. Modular approach to spintronics. *Scientific reports*, 5:10571, 2015.

[14] Bradley D Brown and Howard C Card. Stochastic neural computation. i. computational elements. *Computers, IEEE Transactions on*, 50(9):891–905, 2001.

[15] Rangharajan Venkatesan, et al. Spintastic: Spin-based stochastic logic for energy-efficient computing. In *Proceedings of the 2015 Design, Automation & Test in Europe Conference & Exhibition*, pages 1575–1578. EDA Consortium, 2015.

[16] Kyounghoon Kim, et al. Dynamic energy-accuracy trade-off using stochastic computing in deep neural networks. In *Proceedings of the 53rd Annual Design Automation Conference*, page 124. ACM, 2016.

[17] Behtash Behin-Aein, et al. Proposal for an all-spin logic device with built-in memory. *Nature nanotechnology*, 5(4):266, 2010.

[18] Jiaxi Hu, et al. Using programmable graphene channels as weights in spin-diffusive neuromorphic computing. *IEEE Journal on Exploratory Solid-State Computational Devices and Circuits*, 2018.

[19] Shehrin Sayed, et al. Spin funneling for enhanced spin injection into ferromagnets. *Scientific reports*, 6:28868, 2016.

[20] Kerem Yunus Camsari, et al. Stochastic p-bits for invertible logic. *Physical Review X*, 7(3):031014, 2017.

[21] Hong-xi Liu, et al. Giant tunneling magnetoresistance in epitaxial co2mnsi/mgo/co2mnsi magnetic tunnel junctions by half-metallicity of co2mnsi and coherent tunneling. *Applied Physics Letters*, 101(13):132418, 2012.

[22] Benjamin Balke, et al. Mn 3 ga, a compensated ferrimagnet with high curie temperature and low magnetic moment for spin torque transfer applications. *Applied physics letters*, 90(15), 2007.

[23] S Mizukami, et al. Long-lived ultrafast spin precession in manganese alloys films with a large perpendicular magnetic anisotropy. *Physical review letters*, 106(11):117201, 2011.

[24] DC Mahendra, et al. Room-temperature high spin–orbit torque due to quantum confinement in sputtered bi x se (1–x) films. *Nature materials*, page 1, 2018.

[25] Geoffrey E Hinton and Ruslan R Salakhutdinov. A better way to pretrain deep boltzmann machines. In *Advances in Neural Information Processing Systems*, pages 2447–2455, 2012.

[26] Ankit Mondal and Ankur Srivastava. Power optimizations in mtj-based neural networks through stochastic computing. In *Low Power Electronics and Design (ISLPED, 2017 IEEE/ACM International Symposium on*, pages 1–6. IEEE, 2017.

[27] Yann LeCun, Corinna Cortes, and CJ Burges. Mnist handwritten digit database. *AT&T Labs [Online]. Available: http://yann. lecun. com/exdb/mnist*, 2, 2010.

[28] James E Stine, et al. Freepdk: An open-source variation-aware design kit. In *Microelectronic Systems Education, 2007. MSE'07. IEEE International Conference on*, pages 173–174. IEEE, 2007.

# Functionally Complete Boolean Logic and Adder Design Based on 2T2R RRAMs for Post-CMOS In-Memory Computing

Zongxian Yang
Department of Electrical and Computer Engineering
University of Waterloo
Waterloo, ON, Canada
zongxian.yang@uwaterloo.ca

Yixiao Ma
Department of Electrical and Computer Engineering
University of Waterloo
Waterloo, ON, Canada
y287ma@edu.uwaterloo.ca

Lan Wei
Department of Electrical and Computer Engineering
University of Waterloo
Waterloo, ON, Canada
lan.wei@uwaterloo.ca

## ABSTRACT

In-memory computing (IMC) paradigm has attracted extensive attention for future electronics to overcome the bottleneck and memory wall problem in the von Neumann systems. Nonvolatile logic based on resistive random-access memory (RRAM) is a promising route to implement such architecture. This paper presents the circuits and computing methodology to implement functionally complete Boolean logic and arithmetic block co-design using the CMOS-compatible 2-transistor-2-RRAM (2T2R) structure with reversely connected bipolar RRAM pairs. Arbitrary logic functions for two and multiple operands could be implemented in one-step operation, after which the computation results are *in situ* stored as the nonvolatile resistive states of the RRAM. In this design, the logic functionality is achieved by simply applying external operational voltages and/or corresponding RRAM initial states to the proposed 2T2R units. Compared with the traditional CMOS designs where the circuit topologies change with logic functions, the proposed 2T2R chain has a universal design with repeated unit blocks, independent of the logic functions. The highly regular and symmetric circuit structure makes it easy for design, integration, and fabrication. The proposed computing scheme/structure is intrinsic, clean, and efficient for IMC applications and presents superior performance in speed and area. The result of the study could build a technology cell library that can be potentially used as input to a technology-mapping algorithm for processing in-memory applications.

## CCS CONCEPTS

• **Hardware**~Non-volatile memory; • **Hardware**~Logic families

## KEYWORDS

Non von Neumann; in-memory computing; resistive random access memory (RRAM); nonvolatile; 2T2R; Boolean logic; adder



GLSVLSI '19, May 9–11, 2019, Tysons Corner, VA, USA.

ACM ISBN 978-1-4503-6252-8/19/05...$15.00.
https://doi.org/10.1145/3299874.3317993

**ACM Reference format:**

Zongxian Yang, Yixiao Ma and Lan Wei. 2019. Functionally Complete Boolean Logic and Adder Design Based on 2T2R RRAMs for Post-CMOS In-Memory Computing. In *Proceedings of the Great Lakes Symposium on VLSI 2019, Washington, D.C., USA, May 9-11, 2019 (GLSVLSI '19), 6 pages.* https://doi.org/10.1145/3299874.3317993

## 1 Introduction

Moore's law has been driving the scaling of the CMOS technology for a few decades. The further scaling beyond the 5nm technology node is becoming extremely hard nowadays due to the challenges of the physical limits and increasing non-ideal effects (e.g. subthreshold leakage current, parasitics, variation, etc.) [1]. Meanwhile, the traditional von Neumann architecture is struggling in this big-data era caused by the bottleneck in data communication due to the separation of processing unit and memory storage. The concept of in-memory computing (IMC) has therefore been proposed in order to revitalize the further development of high-performance energy-efficient integrated circuits [2]. In this paradigm, the functions of CPU and memory are integrated together to eliminate the massive data transfer latency and energy consumption. The information is both processed and stored *in situ* in the nonvolatile memory cells.

Among the emerging nonvolatile memories such as phase change memory (PCM) [3], resistive random access memory (RRAM) [4], and magnetic random access memory (MRAM) [5], RRAM, has been intensively investigated thanks to its descent performance with regards to device structure, cell area, operation speed, power consumption, CMOS compatibility, scalability, endurance, and potential of high-density 3-D integration [6].

Various RRAM-based nonvolatile logic methodologies have been proposed to implement Boolean logics such as material-implication (IMP)-based logic [7], memristor-aided logic (MAGIC) [8], memristor ratioed logic (MRL) [9], and 1T1R logic [10]. The performance of one design methodology could be evaluated based on its computational complexity, more specifically, spatial complexity and temporal complexity. Here, in RRAM-based logic implementation, spatial complexity refers to area consumption (i.e., number of RRAM and transistor needed), while temporal complexity means speed (i.e., steps/cycles required). The computation methods presented so far have difficulties and limitations to realize complex functions efficiently with regular circuit structure (to achieve easy integration and fabrication) and

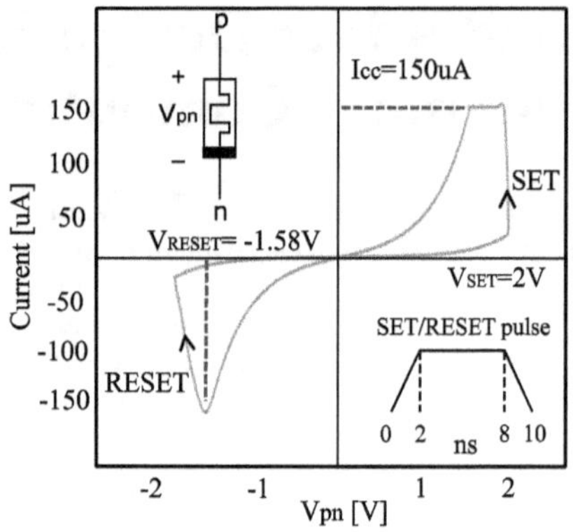

Figure 1: Current-voltage characteristics of the RRAM device used in this paper. The device is simulated with ASU RRAM model [6] calibrated to IMEC device [15]. (Insets show a RRAM device with two terminals (p as anode and n as cathode) and the SET/RESET pulses used in the simulation.)

low computation complexity. Thus, most of these designs only focus on the realization of fundamental logic functions, e.g., IMP, FALSE, and NAND.

Moreover, the RRAM-based full-adder is designed to demonstrate the basic arithmetic block in the IMC architecture using IMP [11], complementary resistive switches (CRS) [12], hybrid CMOS circuits [13], and the newly proposed 1T1R RRAMs [14]. However, up till now, the existing designs are only able to implement the adder with lengthy iteration process, complex circuit structure, and/or mandatory complicated peripheral circuits (current-voltage converter, sense amplifiers, block decoders, and register stack) to support IMC.

In this work, we propose functionally complete Boolean logic scheme in two-transistor-two-RRAM (2T2R) structure using two reversely connected RRAM devices as logic gates. Logic functions are performed by applying operational voltages to the 2T2R circuits. The operations are flexible and clean with functional reconfiguration and low computational complexity. All of the 16 Boolean logic functions for two operands and some common logics for multiple operands could be realized in one-step operation. Furthermore, the design of 4-bit ripple-carry adder (RCA) is realized to demonstrate the flexible and efficient implementation of arithmetic circuits.

## 2 2T2R Logic

A RRAM device is a two-terminal (p as anode and n as cathode) device (Fig. 1 inset), whose resistance switches between a high-resistance state (HRS) and a low-resistance state (LRS) depending on the bias between the two terminal ($V_{pn}$). Bipolar RRAMs switch from HRS to LRS (SET process) when $V_{pn}$ reaches $V_{SET}$ (>0) while from LRS to HRS (RESET process) when $V_{pn}$ goes below $V_{RESET}$ (<0). Fig. 1 shows the I-V characteristics of a $HfO_x$-based RRAM device. The simulated curves are generated by ASU RRAM model [6] in the 1T1R structure, calibrated to match the experimental RRAM behavior from IMEC [15] with a 20mV/s SET/RESET pulses. In this paper, fast pulses (Fig. 1 inset) are used for digital operations which result in $V_{SET}$ = 2V and $V_{RESET}$ = -1.58V.

In our 2T2R logic concept (shown in Fig. 2(a)), six inputs are encoded as two RRAM states before the operation (P and Q) and four voltage pulses applied to the four terminals ($V_U$, $V_L$, $G_P$, $G_Q$); two outputs are represented by the RRAM states after the operation (P' and Q'). For the RRAM state, LRS and HRS represents logic "0" and logic "1", respectively. For the voltage pulse, low voltage potential (0V or grounded) represents logic "0" and high voltage potential represents logic "1". At high voltage potential, $V_U$ and $V_L$ could be different for different computations. The choices of $V_U$ and $V_L$ are determined by the target logic operations as explained in 2.1-2.3. $G_P$ and $G_Q$ are overdrive gate voltages (=$V_G$) applied to transistors to reduce transistor resistance and avoid any threshold voltage drop between gate and source. Note that one challenge in fabricating the 2T2R logic structure in practical in-memory computing circuits is that integrating RRAM between interconnect layers and MOSFETs will require local interconnects between MOSFETs and RRAMs. Such complication can potentially be solved using RRAM with selectors. Similar circuit units were proposed in literature before. However, in those circuits, the inputs are either RRAM states [7], [19] or voltage potentials [12], but never both. Our proposal allows both the states of RRAM and the voltage potentials to be used as inputs, which significantly expands the flexibility and functionality of the proposed units. Multiple operand operations are now enabled, which could greatly improve the circuit efficiency and cascadability as shown in the adder example.

Based on the definition above, the logic computation (operation) is explained as following: first, prepare two of the logical input variables as RRAM states (P and Q); second, apply pulse signals to corresponding terminals ($V_U$, $V_L$, $G_P$, $G_Q$) simultaneously, serving as other four of the logical input variables. The outputs are then *in situ* stored in the RRAMs as P' and Q', achieving the so-called IMC. The logic values of the outputs (P' and Q': RRAM states after one-step operation) are determined by the logic values of the inputs including $V_U$, $V_L$, $G_P$, $G_Q$ (i.e. voltages at four terminals) and P and Q (i.e. initial RRAM states before computation). The electric voltage levels at $V_U$ and $V_L$ not only represent logic 0 or 1 as two of the inputs. The selection of the electric voltage values also defines the

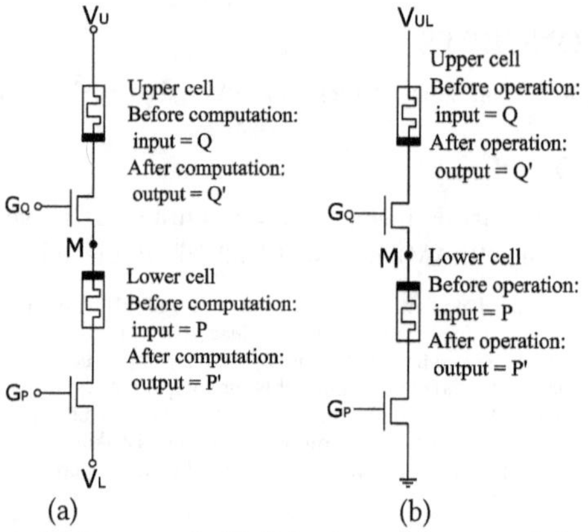

Figure 2: (a) Proposed 2T2R logic structure with back-to-back RRAM pair. (b) ($V_U$, $V_L$, $G_P$, $G_Q$) are fixed to be (1, 0, 1, 1).

**Table I: Truth table for P/Q and P'/Q' when ($V_U$, $V_L$, $G_P$, $G_Q$) = (1, 0, 1, 1): P'=P (bit hold), Q'=P·Q (AND). Q'=P·1 (bit transfer) operation is highlighted in green.**

| P | Q | P'=P | Q'=P·Q |
|---|---|---|---|
| 0 | 0 | 0 | 0 |
| 0 | 1 | 0 | 0 |
| 1 | 0 | 1 | 0 |
| 1 | 1 | 1 | 1 |

**Table II: Truth table for P/Q and P'/Q' when ($V_U$, $V_L$, $G_P$, $G_Q$) = (1, 0, 1, 1): P'=Q⟶P (IMP), Q'=0 (bit set). P'=Q⟶0 (NOT) operation is highlighted in blue.**

| P | Q | P'=Q⟶P | Q'=0 |
|---|---|---|---|
| 0 | 0 | 1 | 0 |
| 0 | 1 | 0 | 0 |
| 1 | 0 | 1 | 0 |
| 1 | 1 | 1 | 0 |

**Table III: Truth table for P/Q and P'/Q' when ($V_U$, $V_L$, $G_P$, $G_Q$) = (1, 0, 1, 1): P'=Q⟶P (IMP), Q'=P·Q (AND).**

| P | Q | P'=Q⟶P | Q'= P·Q |
|---|---|---|---|
| 0 | 0 | 1 | 0 |
| 0 | 1 | 0 | 0 |
| 1 | 0 | 1 | 0 |
| 1 | 1 | 1 | 1 |

operations/functionalities. Depending on the high voltage potential of $V_U$ and $V_L$ (as logic "1"), there are several functionally complete logic families (LFs), enabled by different ranges of high voltage potential of $V_U$ and $V_L$. Here, it is worth noting that due to the symmetric structure (two RRAMs connected in back-to-back (p-n-n-p) manner), exchanging the variables $V_U$ and $V_L$ is equivalent to exchanging positions of the lower and upper cells (P and Q). This is useful to flexibly assign variables in the 2T2R-based circuit design.

For different ratio of $V_{SET}$ and $|V_{RESET}|$ (different RRAM characteristic), the available LFs and the corresponding high voltage potential of $V_U$ and $V_L$ ranges are different. However, for any single logic family, the logic completeness is guaranteed. The LFs are discussed below using the examples of the IMEC's device ($V_{SET}/|V_{RESET}|$ = 1.27) shown in Fig. 1.

## 2.1 Logic Family 1 (LF1)

In LF1, the high voltage potentials of $V_U$ and $V_L$ are chosen to be $V_{LF1} \in (V_{SET}, 2|V_{RESET}|)$. The complete relation between inputs and outputs after one-step computation is given by the following Eq.:

$$P' = P \cdot (V_U + \overline{V_L} + \overline{G_P} + \overline{G_Q} + Q); \quad (1)$$

$$Q' = Q \cdot (\overline{V_U} + V_L + \overline{G_P} + \overline{G_Q} + P). \quad (2)$$

A simplified case is shown in Fig. 2(b) as an example, when ($V_U$, $V_L$, $G_P$, $G_Q$) are fixed to be (1, 0, 1, 1). In this case, Eq. (1) and (2) are simplified to P'=P (bit hold) and Q'=P·Q (AND). the truth table of P/Q and P'/Q' could be derived based on the principle of voltage divider. In cases of P=Q=0 or P=Q=1, $V_{LF1}$ will be equally divided between upper and lower cells since they have the same resistance (both in LRS or both in HRS). Since $V_{LF1} \in (V_{SET}, 2|V_{RESET}|)$, $V_{Upn} = -V_{Lpn} = 0.5V_{LF1}$ is insufficient to initiate any operations. Thus P'=P and Q'=Q. In case of (P=0, Q=1), $V_{LF1}$ is initially dropped mainly across the upper cell (in HRS) and a SET process is initiated ($V_{Upn} \approx V_{LF1}$, $V_{Lpn} \approx 0$). Eventually, Q'=0 (LRS). Lower cell stays at LRS (P'=0). In case of (P=1, Q=0), $V_{LF1}$ is mainly dropped across the lower cell. ($V_{Upn} \approx 0$, $V_{Lpn} \approx -V_{LF1}$), no operation happens, thus P'=1 and Q'=0.

## 2.2 Logic Family 2 (LF2)

In LF2, the high voltage potentials of $V_U$ and $V_L$ are chosen to be $V_{LF2}$ ($>2V_{SET}>2|V_{RESET}|$). Similarly, the complete functions of input and output variables after one-step computation are given by Eq. (3) and (4):

$$P' = P \cdot (V_U + \overline{V_L} + \overline{G_P} + \overline{G_Q}) + V_U \overline{V_L} G_P G_Q \bar{P} \bar{Q}; \quad (3)$$

$$Q' = Q \cdot (\overline{V_U} + V_L + \overline{G_P} + \overline{G_Q}) + \overline{V_U} V_L G_P G_Q \bar{P} \bar{Q}. \quad (4)$$

The truth table as in Table II indicates the Boolean functions of P' and Q' in the simplified case of ($V_U$, $V_L$, $G_P$, $G_Q$) = (1, 0, 1, 1), where Eq. (3) and (4) are simplified to P'=Q⟶P (IMP) and Q'=0 (bit set). Similar analysis applies for the cases of (P=1, Q=0) and (P=0, Q=1). For the case of P=Q=0, because $V_{LF2} > 2V_{SET} > 2|V_{RESET}|$, $V_{Upn} = -V_{Lpn} = 0.5V_{LF2}$ is now sufficient to initiate a RESET process for the lower cell. Thus P'=1. For P=Q=1, the same voltage is also sufficient to initiate a SET process for the upper cell.

## 2.3 Logic Family 3 (LF3)

In LF3, the high voltage potentials of $V_U$ and $V_L$ are chosen to be $V_{LF3} \in (2|V_{RESET}|, 2V_{SET})$. Eq. (5) and (6) give the full description of outputs as functions of input variables under LF3. Table III presents the state transition from P/Q to P'/Q' when ($V_U$, $V_L$, $G_P$, $G_Q$) = (1, 0, 1, 1), which could be obtained similarly.

$$P' = P \cdot (V_U + \overline{V_L} + \overline{G_P} + \overline{G_Q} + Q) + V_U \overline{V_L} G_P G_Q \bar{P} \bar{Q}; \quad (5)$$

$$Q' = Q \cdot (\overline{V_U} + V_L + \overline{G_P} + \overline{G_Q} + P) + \overline{V_U} V_L G_P G_Q \bar{P} \bar{Q}. \quad (6)$$

Each LF discussed above is functionally complete, which could be derived from corresponding Eq. (1)-(6). One major innovation of this proposed design is to allow both RRAM states and terminal voltages to be used as inputs, which significantly expands the flexibility and functionality of the circuit. Taking LF3 as an example, Table IV summarizes the variable assignments in LF3 to implement all the 16 Boolean logics (computation result stored in P') for 2 input operands. (The associated output Q' can be derived accordingly in each case, which is not given in the table.) Additionally, some common logics for multiple input operands (up to five) according to LF3 are shown in Table V. Similar tables can be generated for LF1 and LF2. Since each LF is functionally complete, usually one LF is sufficient for the entire circuit. (e.g. we only use LF3 for the adder design.) Thus, no more than two electric voltage levels are required to be generated, one as $V_{LF}$ and the other as $V_G$, if different from $V_{LF}$.

The variables for each logical computation are not unique and could be assigned flexibly in different ways, such as the two XOR/XNOR implementations in Table IV. This is particularly useful for cascadability, since the signals to be cascaded should be preferred to be stored as RRAM states.

# 3 Arithmetic Block Design

In order to demonstrate the proposed work's capability and advantages of designing complex arithmetic circuits, the design of to implement complex arithmetic circuit does not require complicated peripheral circuits for signal conversion and data transfer (such as sense amplifiers, block decoders, and register

**Table IV: Variable assignment for 16 Boolean logics of output P' in LF3 for two input operands. The highlighted computation will be used to calculate sum-output in the full-adder design.**

| Logic function $P'$ | P | Q | $V_U$ | $V_L$ | $G_P$ | $G_Q$ |
|---|---|---|---|---|---|---|
| 0 | 0 | X | 0 | X | A | B |
| 1 | 1 | X | 1 | X | A | B |
| A | A | X | 1 | 1 | X | B |
| B | B | X | 1 | 1 | X | A |
| $\bar{A}$ (not A) | 1 | 0 | 0 | A | 1 | 1 |
| $\bar{B}$ (not B) | 1 | 0 | 0 | B | 1 | 1 |
| A+B (OR2) | A | 0 | 1 | 0 | B | 1 |
| $\bar{A}+\bar{B}$ (NAND2) | 1 | 0 | 0 | 1 | A | B |
| AB (AND2) | A | B | 0 | 1 | 1 | 1 |
| $\bar{A}\bar{B}$ (NOR2) | 0 | B | 1 | A | 1 | 1 |
| $A+\bar{B}$ (RIMP) | 1 | 0 | A | B | 1 | 1 |
| $\bar{A}+B$ (IMP) | 1 | 0 | B | A | 1 | 1 |
| $\bar{A}B$ (NIMP) | B | 0 | 0 | A | 1 | 1 |
| $A\bar{B}$ (RNIMP) | A | 0 | 0 | B | 1 | 1 |
| $\bar{A}B+A\bar{B}$ (XOR) | A | 0 | $\bar{A}$ | A | B | 1 |
| | A | $\bar{B}$ | $\bar{A}$ | A | 1 | 1 |
| $AB+\bar{A}\bar{B}$ (XNOR) | A | 0 | $\bar{A}$ | A | $\bar{B}$ | 1 |
| | A | B | $\bar{A}$ | A | 1 | 1 |

**Table V: Variable assignment for some common logics of output P' in LF3 for multiple (three to five) input operands. The highlighted computation will be used to calculate carry-output in the full-adder design in 3.1.**

| Logic function $P'$ | $P$ | $Q$ | $V_U$ | $V_L$ | $G_P$ | $G_Q$ |
|---|---|---|---|---|---|---|
| $A+B+C$ (OR3) | 1 | 0 | A | $\bar{B}$ | $\bar{C}$ | 1 |
| $\bar{A}+\bar{B}+\bar{C}$ (NAND3) | 1 | 0 | 0 | A | B | C |
| $ABC$ (AND3) | 0 | 0 | A | 0 | B | C |
| $\bar{A}\bar{B}\bar{C}$ (NOR3) | 0 | A | 1 | B | $\bar{C}$ | 1 |
| $A+B+C+D$ (OR4) | 1 | 0 | A | $\bar{B}$ | $\bar{C}$ | $\bar{D}$ |
| $\bar{A}+\bar{B}+\bar{C}+\bar{D}$ (NAND4) | 1 | 0 | $\bar{D}$ | A | B | C |
| $ABCD$ (AND4) | 0 | 0 | A | $\bar{D}$ | B | C |
| $\bar{A}\bar{B}\bar{C}\bar{D}$ (NOR4) | 0 | 0 | $\bar{A}$ | B | $\bar{C}$ | $\bar{D}$ |
| $A+B+C+D+E$ (OR5) | 1 | E | A | $\bar{B}$ | $\bar{C}$ | $\bar{D}$ |
| $\bar{A}+\bar{B}+\bar{C}+\bar{D}+\bar{E}$ (NAND5) | 1 | $\bar{E}$ | $\bar{D}$ | A | B | C |
| $ABCDE$ (AND5) | 0 | $\bar{E}$ | A | $\bar{D}$ | B | C |
| $\bar{A}\bar{B}\bar{C}\bar{D}\bar{E}$ (NOR5) | 0 | E | $\bar{A}$ | B | $\bar{C}$ | $\bar{D}$ |
| $AB+AC+BC$ | C | 0 | A | $\bar{B}$ | 1 | 1 |

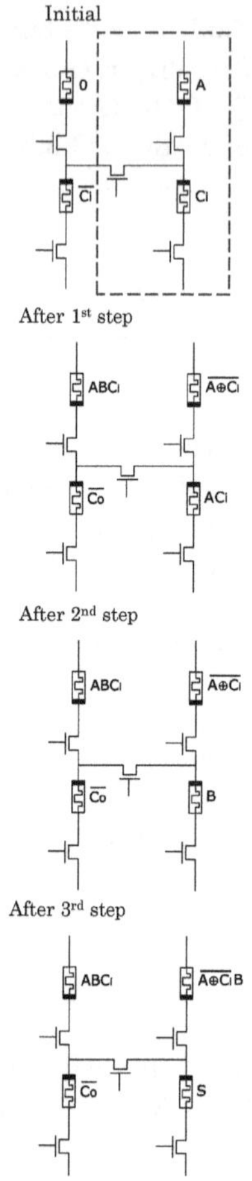


**Figure 3: The circuit structure (2x 2T2Rs) and three-step computation process of the proposed 1-bit full adder. The dashed box refers to one 3T2R unit. The four RRAM-state transitions after each step are labeled. Step 1 is to calculate $\overline{A \oplus C_\iota}$ and $\overline{C_o}$. Step two is to input $B$. Step three is to obtain $S$.**

stack) to support the in-memory operation, which is a major advantage over the previously proposed designs such as the 1T1R-based designs in [14]. The stored resistive state does not need to 4-bit RCA is presented in this section. The proposed 2T2R chain be converted into the voltage potential for the next-stage operations because the RRAM states stored in P'/Q' of the first stage can be directly used as inputs (P/Q) of the next stage. Thus, the cascade capability in the proposed 2T2R-based IMC system is efficiently enabled by the highly symmetric circuit structure and effective operations shown in Table I, II, and III, which could be also reflected by the following design methodologies of 4-bit adder.

## 3.1 1-bit Full Adder

The 1-bit full adder is firstly designed based on the proposed 2T2R RRAM to further build 4-bit RCA. The full adder adds three binary inputs $(A, B, C_i)$ and generates two binary outputs $(S, C_o)$, namely, sum and carry-out. The outputs could be calculated by inputs according to the following Eq.:

$$S = (A \oplus C_i) \oplus B; \tag{7}$$

$$\overline{C_o} = \bar{A}\bar{B} + \bar{A}\overline{C_\iota} + \bar{B}\overline{C_\iota}. \tag{8}$$

Since the inputs are either voltage levels or RRAM states while outputs are only in the form of RRAM states, it is important that the output to be cascaded to the next stages are mapped to the RRAM-state inputs of the next stages. This avoids the need to have assisting circuitry to convert resistive states into voltage levels. For example, in the adder design, we intentionally calculate $(A \oplus C_i)$ first and then perform another XOR operation with $B$.

We will use only LF3 for this design with $V_{LF3}$ = 3.5V. According to (5) and the highlighted rows in Table IV, the first XOR ( $A \oplus C_i$ ) logic could be performed by assigning $(A, \overline{C_\iota}, \bar{A}, A, 1, 1)$ to (P, Q, $V_U$, $V_L$, $G_P$, $G_Q$). For the second XOR logic with $B$ , to avoid the signal conversion, we assign $(B, \overline{A \oplus C_\iota}, \bar{B}, B, 1, 1)$ to (P, Q, $V_U$, $V_L$, $G_P$, $G_Q$) to calculate $S$. Note that during the second XOR computation, the result of the first XOR computation presents as input in the form of its complement ( $\overline{A \oplus C_\iota}$). Therefore, it is more efficient to calculate $\overline{A \oplus C_\iota}$ (XNOR, highlighted in Table IV) by applying $(A, C_\iota, \bar{A}, A, 1, 1)$ to (P, Q, $V_U$, $V_L$, $G_P$, $G_Q$) in the first step to save one NOT operation. As for the carry-out $C_o$, we calculate its complement $\overline{C_o}$ instead (similar to the inverted carry in CMOS design) to maximize the design efficiency and make the initial state of multiple-bit adder uniform. According to (5) and the highlighted row in Table V, $\overline{C_o}$ could be calculate by assigning $(\overline{C_\iota}, 0, \bar{A}, B, 1, 1)$ to (P, Q, $V_U$, $V_L$, $G_P$, $G_Q$).

Based on the discussion above, the 1-bit full adder could be implemented in three steps with two 2T2R structures, shown in Fig. 3. A 3-transistor-2-RRAM (3T2R) chain can be formed with 2T2R cells connected through one NMOS pass gate (1T). The back-to-back structures (p-n-n-p) ensure that any RRAM can form a pair with another RRAM in the chain to perform the proposed operations, regardless of whether the RRAMs are in the upper Position or lower. This eliminates the need to add additional routing or control gates to form the p-n-p-n pair when two RRAMs are both in upper or lower rows as in [19]. The 2T2R structure here ensures that any two of the RRAM cells can perform any operations listed in Table I-III, which makes cascade

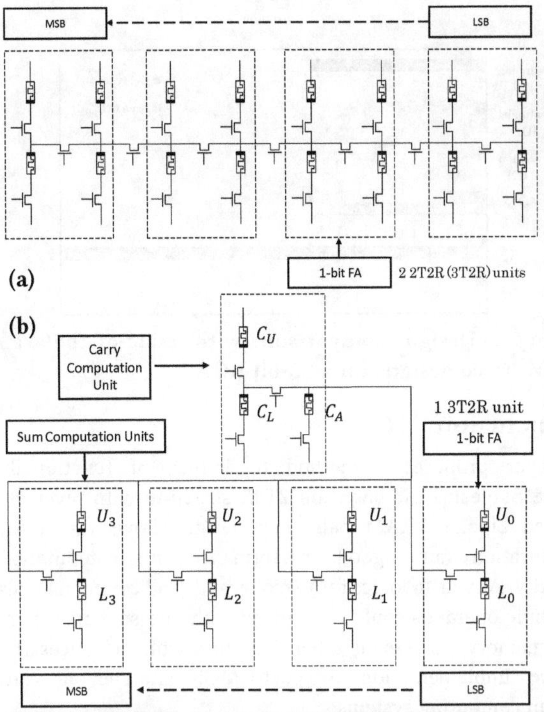


Figure 4: (a) Schematic of a 4-bit RCA with repeated structure (3T2R chain). Each two 3T2R units shown in the dashed box is a 1-bit full adder. (b) A more compact design of RCA to reduce area, with greater customization.

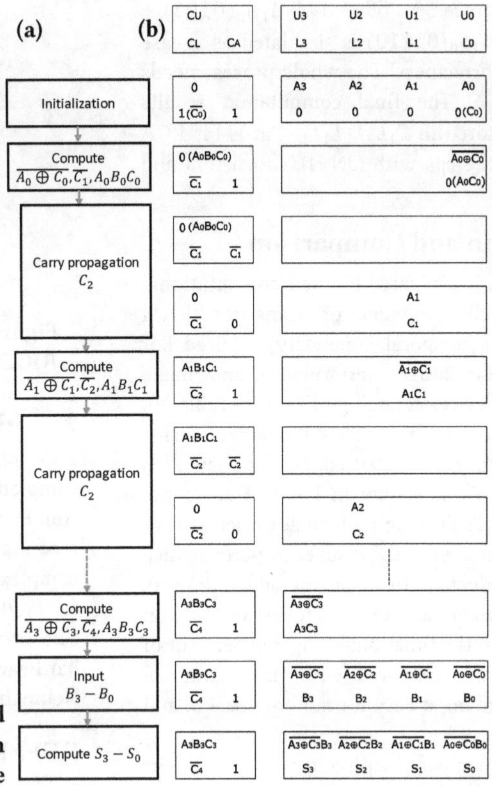


Figure 5: (a) Computation flow chart of the compact design of 4-bit RCA. The steps between computing $C_2$ and computing $\overline{A_3 \oplus C_3}$ and $\overline{C_4}$ are omitted for simplicity. (b) The corresponding RRAM state transition. The values in the left and right boxes represent the RRAM states of carry and sum computation units, respectively. For example, in the initialization step, the carry computation unit is programmed so $C_U = 0$ and $C_L = C_A = 0$, while the sum computation unit is programmed as $U_i = A_i$ and $L_i = 0$. Each bit is initialized in a uniform pattern.

(carry-propagation) easy to be realized without peripheral circuits.

For the adder implementation, the 1st step calculates $\overline{A \oplus C_i}$ aand $\overline{C_o}$ in the right and left 2T2R simultaneously. The input $B$ is programmed into the lower cell in the right 2T2R during the 2nd step. Finally, another XOR is performed to obtain $S$. The sum and carry-out are stored as RRAM states, enabling non-volatile storage for computation results.

## 3.2 4-bit Ripple-Carry Adder

To demonstrate more complex calculations in arithmetic block design, 4-bit RCA to compute $[A_3A_2A_1A_0] + [B_3B_2B_1B_0] = [C_4S_3\, S_2\, S_1\, S_0]$ is developed based on the 1-bit full-adder design to verify the feasibility and flexibility of the adder implementation. To design 4-bit RCA, we could use 1-bit full-adder as universal unit block (3T2R chain) as shown in Fig. 4(a) with repeated structure. A more compact design could be implemented by utilizing one shared 4T3R unit for carry computation and propagation (shown in Fig. 4(b)) to save about half of the area. The routing, however, has to be slighted customized, rather than the generic connection in Fig. 4(a). The upper carry computation unit is comprised of one 2T2R ($C_U$ and $C_L$) for carry calculation and one 1T1R ($C_A$) to assist carry propagation. The 3T2R units ($U_i$ and $L_i$) in the lower sum computation units are used for sum calculation.

The computation flow chart is illustrated as in Fig. 5(a). Fig. 5 (b) presents the corresponding RRAM state transitions in each

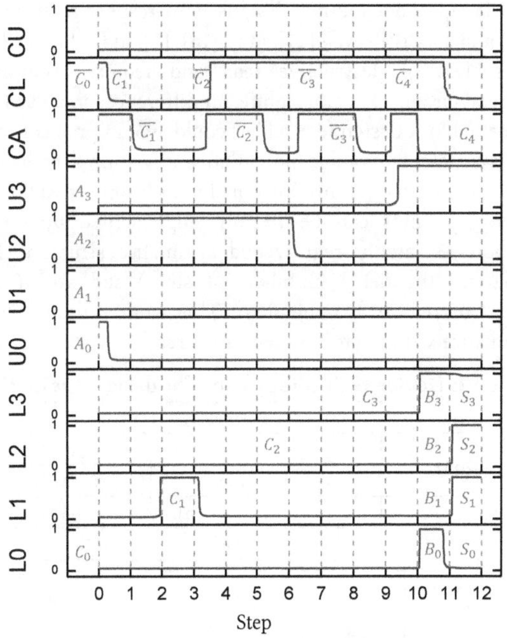


Figure 6: Simulation of $A_3A_2A_1A_0(0101) + B_3B_2B_1B_0(1001) = C_4S_3\, S_2\, S_1\, S_0(01110)$ as a case study to verify the design correctness (all the transistors are at minimum 60nm widths using TSMC 65nm library). The simulations are performed in Cadence Virtuoso. Three electric voltage levels are required for the adder operation including $V_{LF3}$= 3.5V, $V_{GP}$ = 2.5V, and $V_{GQ}$ = 3V.

step. The carry propagation is performed in two steps: bit transfer operation betw een $\overline{C_o}$ (of LSB) and 1 (of second LSB); NOT operation between $\overline{C_o}$ (of LSB) and 0 (of second LSB).

The computation process of $A_3A_2A_1A_0(0101) + B_3B_2B_1B_0(1001) = C_4S_3S_2S_1S_0(01110)$ is simulated as a case study to verify the design correctness. The whole process needs 12 steps, shown in Fig. 6. The final computation results $C_4S_3\ S_2\ S_1\ S_0(01110)$ are stored in $C_AL_3L_2L_1L_0$. An N-bit RCA could be implemented in 3N steps with (3N+4) Transistors and (2N+3) RRAMs.

## 3.3 Design Evaluation and Comparison

The compact design of RCA is evaluated by their computational complexity, more specifically, number of transistor/RRAM (spatial complexity) and steps (temporal complexity) required. For this work, we evaluate the design performance and make comparisons based on the device technology listed in Table VI. The design is firstly compared with CMOS static adder, mirror adder, and transmission-gate (TG) based adders for their area consumption of a 32-bit RCA, as shown in Fig. 7. Due to the efficient implementation of 2T2R logic and small device size of RRAM device, the design in this work show superior performance especially in area (~87% reduction from mirror adder design). Moreover, the design based on our 2T2R RRAM focuses mainly on the signal encoding, in which the functionality is independent of the circuit topology/structure compared with the traditional CMOS and ASIC designs, making it easy for not only design and integration but also fabrication.

Additionally, the work is compared with other state-of-the-art RRAM-based adder (32-bit) designs with respect to their delay (steps) and area (RRAMs) [11], [12], [16]-18]. In [12], the CRS has the problem of destructive read and requires complicated peripheral circuits. Several significant differences include: (1) our arithmetic block design (e.g. adder) could avoid signal conversion (resistive state to voltage potential) and requires no complex peripheral circuits, (2) any logic including complex XOR/XNOR for two operands can be flexibly implemented by one-step operation, (3) highly regular and symmetric structure. Fig. 8 summarizes the delay (numbers of steps) and area (RRAM) required to realize a 32-bit RCA. This work presents descent performance with regard to speed and area.

**Table VI: Device technology used for design evaluation.**

| Device Technology | | |
|---|---|---|
| RRAM | $e$ (nm) | 5 |
| | $A$ – Are (nm$^2$) | 100 ($4F_m^2$) |
| CMOS | $e$ (nm) | 65 |
| | $A$ – Area (nm$^2$) | 8450 ($2F_c^2$) |

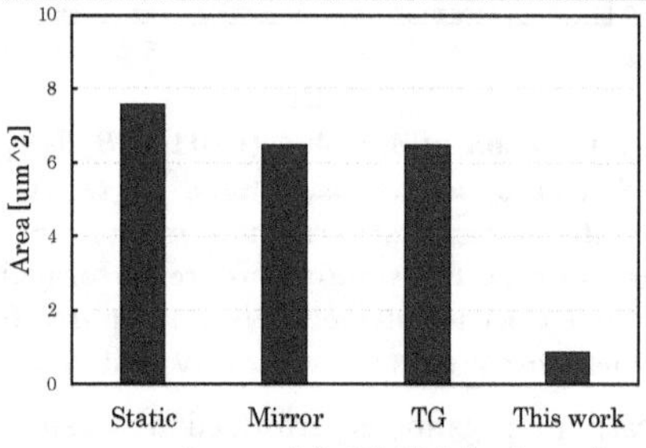


**Figure 7: Area comparison with CMOS designs for 32-bit RCA. The compact design saves ~87% area from CMOS mirror adder.**

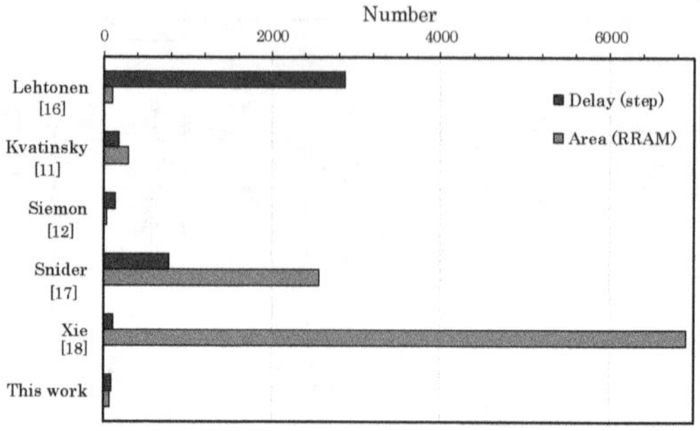


**Figure 8: Design comparison with state-of-the-art RRAM-based designs for a 32-bit RCA.**

## 4 Conclusion

This paper proposes a method to implement functionally complete Boolean logic based on 2T2R structure with reversely connected bipolar RRAM pair. The design shows functional reconfiguration and good performance in computation complexity. Any of 16 logics for two operands and common logics for multiple operands could be realized with one-step operation. The in-memory processing scheme in this work advances the hardware implementation of post-CMOS and beyond-von-Neumann computing systems.

## REFERENCES

[1] Loke, A. L. S., et al. Analog/mixed-signal design challenges in 7-nm CMOS and beyond. *2018 Ieee Custom Integrated Circuits Conference (Cicc) (2018)*, 1-8.

[2] Jeong, D. S., Kim, et al. Memristors for Energy-Efficient New Computing Paradigms. *Advanced Electronic Materials*, 2, 9 (Sep 2016).

[3] Cassinerio, M., et al. Logic Computation in Phase Change Materials by Threshold and Memory Switching. *Advanced Materials*, 25, 41 (Nov 2013), 5975-5980.

[4] Wong, H. S. P., et al. Metal-Oxide RRAM. *Proceedings of the Ieee*, 100, 6 (Jun 2012), 1951-1970.

[5] Ney, A., et al. Programmable computing with a single magnetoresistive element. *Nature*, 425, 6957 (Oct 2003), 485-487.

[6] Chen, P. Y. and Yu, S. M. Compact Modeling of RRAM Devices and Its Applications in 1T1R and 1S1R Array Design. *Ieee Transactions on Electron Devices*, 62, 12 (Dec 2015), 4022-4028.

[7] Borghetti, J., et al. 'Memristive' switches enable 'stateful' logic operations via material implication. *Nature*, 464, 7290 (Apr 2010), 873-876.

[8] Kvatinsky, S., et al. MAGIC-Memristor-Aided Logic. *Ieee Transactions on Circuits and Systems Ii-Express Briefs*, 61, 11 (Nov 2014), 895-899.

[9] Kvatinsky, S., et al. MRL - Memristor Ratioed Logic. *2012 13th International Workshop on Cellular Nanoscale Networks and Their Applications (Cnna)* (2012).

[10] Wang, Z. R., et al. Functionally Complete Boolean Logic in 1T1R Resistive Random Access Memory. *Ieee Electron Device Letters*, 38, 2 (Feb 2017), 179-182.

[11] Kvatinsky, S., et al. Memristor-Based Material Implication (IMPLY) Logic: Design Principles and Methodologies. *Ieee Transactions on Very Large Scale Integration (Vlsi) Systems*, 22, 10 (Oct 2014), 2054-2066.

[12] Siemon, A., et al. A Complementary Resistive Switch-Based Crossbar Array Adder. *Ieee Journal on Emerging and Selected Topics in Circuits and Systems*, 5, 1 (Mar 2015), 64-74.

[13] Xia, Q. F., et al. Memristor-CMOS Hybrid Integrated Circuits for Reconfigurable Logic. *Nano Letters*, 9, 10 (Oct 2009), 3640-3645.

[14] Wang, Z. R., et al. Efficient Implementation of Boolean and Full-Adder Functions With 1T1R RRAMs for Beyond Von Neumann In-Memory Computing. *Ieee Transactions on Electron Devices*, 65, 10 (Oct 2018), 4659-4666.

[15] Chen, Y. Y., et al. Balancing SET/RESET Pulse for > 10(10) Endurance in HfO2/Hf 1T1R Bipolar RRAM. *Ieee Transactions on Electron Devices*, 59, 12 (Dec 2012), 3243-3249.

[16] Lehtonen, E., et al. Stateful Implication Logic with Memristors. *2009 Ieee/Acm International Symposium on Nanoscale Architectures* (2009), 33-36.

[17] Snider, G. Computing with hysteretic resistor crossbars. *Applied Physics a-Materials Science & Processing*, 80, 6 (Mar 2005), 1165-1172.

[18] Xie, L., et al. Fast Boolean Logic Mapped on Memristor Crossbar. *2015 33rd Ieee International Conference on Computer Design (Iccd)* (2015), 335-342.

[19] Balatti, S., Ambrogio, S. and Ielmini, D. Normally-off Logic Based on Resistive Switches-Part I: Logic Gates. *Ieee Transactions on Electron Devices*, 62, 6 (Jun 2015), 1831-1838.

# Jump Search: A Fast Technique for the Synthesis of Approximate Circuits

Linus Witschen
Paderborn University, Germany
witschen@mail.upb.de

Hassan Ghasemzadeh Mohammadi
Paderborn University, Germany
hgm@mail.upb.de

Matthias Artmann
Paderborn University, Germany
martmann@mail.uni-paderborn.de

Marco Platzner
Paderborn University, Germany
platzner@mail.upb.de

## ABSTRACT

State-of-the-art frameworks for generating approximate circuits automatically explore the search space in an iterative process - often greedily. Synthesis and verification processes are invoked in each iteration to evaluate the found solutions and to guide the search algorithm. As a result, a large number of approximate circuits is subjected to analysis - leading to long runtimes - but only a few approximate circuits might form an acceptable solution.

In this paper, we present our *Jump Search* (JS) method which seeks to reduce the runtime of an approximation process by reducing the number of expensive synthesis and verification steps. To reduce the runtime, JS computes impact factors for each approximation candidate in the circuit to create a selection of approximate circuits without invoking synthesis or verification processes. We denote the selection as *path* from which JS determines the final solution. In our experimental results, JS achieved speed-ups of up to 57x while area savings remain comparable to the reference search method, Simulated Annealing.

## CCS CONCEPTS

• **Hardware → Logic synthesis**; **Methodologies for EDA**; **Software tools for EDA**; *Emerging technologies.*

## KEYWORDS

Approximate computing; design automation; parameter selection; circuit synthesis

**ACM Reference Format:**

Linus Witschen, Hassan Ghasemzadeh Mohammadi, Matthias Artmann, and Marco Platzner. 2019. Jump Search: A Fast Technique for the Synthesis of Approximate Circuits. In *Great Lakes Symposium on VLSI 2019 (GLSVLSI '19), May 9–11, 2019, Tysons Corner, VA, USA.* ACM, New York, NY, USA, 6 pages. https://doi.org/10.1145/3299874.3317998


*GLSVLSI '19, May 9–11, 2019, Tysons Corner, VA, USA*

ACM ISBN 978-1-4503-6252-8/19/05...$15.00
https://doi.org/10.1145/3299874.3317998

## 1 INTRODUCTION

Many applications in various domains either exhibit an inherent error resilience, e.g., multimedia processing, or do not provide a golden result, e.g., recommender systems. The design paradigm Approximate Computing utilizes this fact to trade off a circuit's output quality against a target metric, e.g., hardware area, delay, or energy consumption. Approximations can be applied at all levels of the computing stack, from the software level down to the logic and circuit level [7]. In this work, we are focusing on the circuit level and, more precisely, on the automatic as well as efficient generation of *Approximate Circuits* (AxCs).

Frameworks to automatize the process of generating AxCs have been presented in the past [6, 8, 9, 12, 13]. The approximation process states an optimization problem with various objectives such as hardware area, delay, or energy consumption. A major issue for the optimization problem is that only very few general assumptions can be made about the search space. Thus, to find an optimal solution (i.e., an optimal AxC), iterative heuristic-based search methods are employed and the search space is expanded step-by-step - often greedily. The solutions (i.e., AxCs) found are then evaluated and ranked. For the evaluation of the AxCs, current frameworks employ synthesis and verification steps. Since the search space is usually large, a large number of solutions is found and thus a large number of evaluation steps is invoked. However, the evaluation step generally shows a considerable runtime - especially the verification step. In fact, the evaluation dictates the runtime of the framework and, in general, it applies that the more synthesis and verification steps are invoked, the longer is the runtime of the approximation process. Many of the AxCs found, however, are not of interest, i.e., are beyond the acceptable quality.

In this paper, we seek to minimize the runtime of the approximation process with our novel approach *Jump Search* (JS). JS executes two phases to achieve this goal:

(1) Pre-select AxCs from the search space by using a heuristic function without invoking synthesis or verification steps.
(2) For evaluation, invoke synthesis and verification steps only for judiciously chosen AxCs to minimize the runtime.

In the first phase, JS utilizes a heuristic function to select the most promising AxCs from all AxCs in the search space. The selected AxCs are sorted by their depth in the search space, where a deep depth results in more approximations applied to the circuit. For each depth, JS selects only one AxC. We denote the set of selected AxCs as *path*, since the set represents a sequence of AxCs, from the original circuit towards the boundaries of the search space, i.e., towards AxCs with more approximations applied. The runtime of the first phase is short since no synthesis or verification steps are invoked. In the second phase, JS searches on the path for the AxC with the deepest depth, i.e., the AxC with the most aggressive approximations applied, which satisfies the user-defined quality constraints. The search in the second phase of JS is allowed to *jump* over AxCs to find the resulting AxC more efficiently. Since expensive synthesis and verification steps are only invoked in the second phase, JS is able to significantly reduce the runtime. A disadvantage of this approach is that the search might jump over an optimal solution. However, we anticipate two benefits from our approach: 1) we can quickly find an acceptable AxC and evaluate the potential of savings in a circuit; and 2) we find a *good* starting point in the search space for a subsequent, more thoroughly operating search method, fine-tuning the AxC found by JS.

The path selected in the first phase of JS is affecting the quality of the final outcome. Thus, the employed heuristic function is key. In our novel approach, JS uses parameter selection techniques to determine the impact of each *candidate* - a subcircuit subject to approximations - on the quality of the overall circuit. Furthermore, an impact factor for the area is determined for each candidate. Our experimental results show that JS can achieve speed-ups of up to 57x while area savings remain comparable to the reference algorithm.

The remainder of this paper is structured as follows. In Section 2, we discuss related work. In Section 3, we present the details of our parameter selection and of our JS approach. The effectiveness of JS is highlighted in our experimental results in Section 4. Finally, we conclude the paper and describe the future work in Section 5.

## 2 RELATED WORK

Various frameworks for the automated generation of AxCs have been presented in the past. Venkataramani et al. [13] presented SALSA that forms a so-called *quality constraint circuit*, comprising of the original circuit, the AxC, and the quality function. The primary inputs of the quality constraint circuit are fed into the original circuit and the AxC. The respective output of the original circuit and the AxC form the inputs of the quality function. The quality function has a single output bit, indicating whether the AxC violates the quality constraints. Initially, the AxC is identical to the original circuit. Rather than employing a search technique, SALSA first identifies the *approximate don't cares* of the quality function. Then, standard don't care optimization techniques are used to approximate the circuit while ensuring that the quality constraints are satisfied. In this way, SALSA generates combinational AxCs which adhere to the quality constraints by construction.

Venkataramani et al. also presented SASIMI [12], a framework which uses *substitute-and-simplify* as approximation technique. SASIMI identifies near-identical signals, i.e., signals that show a similar behavior, and substitutes one with the other to simplify the logic. The identified signals are ranked using a heuristic function which considers area and delay parameters. Hill climbing search selects the highest ranked signal pair for substitution until the quality constraints are violated and the search terminates. In each iteration of the search, SASIMI carries out synthesis and simulation processes to identify signal pairs and to evaluate the AxC's error.

Chandrasekharan et al. [4] proposed to transform the logic function of the combinational input circuit into an *AND-Inverter Graph* (AIG) representation and to identify the critical path in the AIG. Then, a search algorithm greedily selects the node on the critical path with the smallest cut size and replaces it with constant 0. After each replacement, a SAT solver formally verifies the quality of the AxC. The process terminates if the AxC violates the quality constraints or the maximum number of iterations is reached.

Nepal et al. [8] proposed the ABACUS methodology which operates on the behavioral description of the input circuit and transforms the circuit into an *Abstract Synthesis Tree* (AST). Starting from the original circuit, ABACUS iteratively applies transformations to the currently selected AST to create different AxCs. In each iteration of ABACUS, the AxCs are synthesized to determine area and power characteristics, and testing evaluates the accuracy of each circuit. The resulting three circuit parameters are combined into a fitness function. The circuit with the best fitness is greedily selected as the next current circuit. The process terminates after a user-defined number of iterations, and the Pareto frontier, trading off accuracy for power, is provided to the user.

The ASLAN framework by Ranjan et al. [9] approximates sequential input circuits and provides a guarantee that the resulting AxC never violates the quality constraints. In a pre-processing step, ASLAN identifies subcircuits in the input circuit amenable to approximations, so-called *candidates*. Then, different approximated variants of each candidate are generated by applying varying quality constraints to each candidate and different approximations. The resulting variants differ in their quality and energy consumption; the ensemble of all variants form ASLAN's search space. Finally, ASLAN performs hill climbing search to find the combination of approximated candidates that minimizes the energy consumption of the overall circuit. ASLAN pre-generates the entire search space, traverses it iteratively, and invokes verification in each iteration.

Liu and Zhang's SCALS framework [6] initially maps the input gate-level logic to a target technology. In an iterative process, various AxCs are generated by extracting subnetlists from the mapped netlist which are then subjected to randomly chosen approximations or optimizations. The AxCs generated in each iteration are then evaluated based on their error, determined via testing, and their area. A Metropolis-Hastings algorithm controls the selection of AxCs and terminates after a defined number of iterations.

Soeken et al. [10] represent the circuit description as a BDD and apply approximations to reduce the size of the BDD. Froehlich et al. [5] also utilize a BDD representation to determine an optimal BDD, i.e., a BDD with a minimum number of nodes, satisfying the quality constraints. Using BDDs allows the authors to make very precise statements about the resulting error. The major weakness of these approaches, however, is that BDDs are only applicable to small, combinational circuits. Thus, the approaches may be applied to small subcomponents of a design, which would then require a subsequent quality verification process for the overall design.

Barbareschi et al. [2] proposed IDEA as a high-level synthesis framework in which a branch-and-bound-based algorithm selects the appropriate approximation for the candidates from all possible ones. In each iteration, IDEA utilizes a depth-first search strategy and examines all approximation possibilities for a target candidate until no more possible approximations are available. Afterwards,

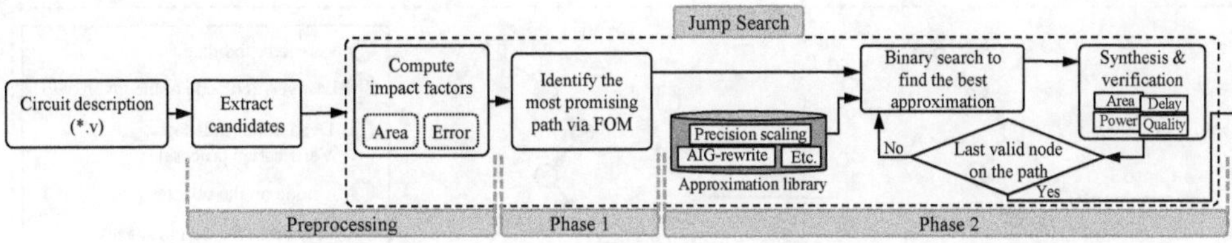


**Figure 1: Overview of the Jump Search synthesis framework**

IDEA backtracks. IDEA spends the largest amount of the search budget on identifying the best possible approximation of the early selected candidates in the design.

Awais et al. [1] presented a framework which utilizes a *Monte-Carlo Tree Search* (MCTS) algorithm in order to identify the target candidates for approximation as well as their appropriate approximations, given a specified search budget. MCTS selects a candidate and iteratively applies different types of approximations to it until the algorithm identifies other promising candidates in the design space through a number of heuristic functions. The new candidates are then iteratively subjected to different approximations. The process continues until the given search budget is exhausted. The employed heuristic functions limit the applicability of the framework, since the functions rely on several hyper-parameters, which have to be tuned for each circuit before the synthesis process.

The approximation techniques or frameworks presented in the past heavily rely on synthesis and verification results, either to guide the search, e.g., ASLAN, or to evaluate randomly generated AxCs, e.g., SCALS, leading to considerable runtimes.

Our JS method seeks to reduce the runtime of the approximation process with two novel approaches:

(1) Prior to the approximation process, JS determines the candidates' impacts on the overall output quality using parameter selection techniques and the candidates' impacts on the overall circuit area;
(2) JS pre-selects a set of AxCs based on a heuristic evaluation, and thus, avoids excessive invocations of synthesis and verification processes.

# 3 THE SYNTHESIS OF APPROXIMATE CIRCUITS USING JUMP SEARCH

In this section, we explain the concepts of JS, a fast synthesis method for AxCs. We first describe the workflow of the proposed synthesis framework. Then, we explain the details of impact factors and JS.

## 3.1 Overview

The goal of JS is to reduce the runtime of an approximation process while achieving area savings comparable to other, more exhaustive search techniques. JS achieves reductions in runtime mainly through the minimization in the number of synthesis and verification steps, as these are usually the most expensive tasks.

The proposed framework is illustrated in Figure 1. In the preprocessing step, JS identifies subcircuits in the input circuit amenable to approximations, usually arithmetic components. The subcircuits are denoted as *candidates*. In the next step, the candidates are analyzed in terms of their impact on the area and the precision of the design. The goal of the analysis is to start approximations from the candidates that have the highest impact on the circuit size and the lowest impact on the quality of the design. In fact, the costly search-based optimization process is strictly controlled to exclude unpromising candidates. For each candidate, two impact factors are determined: 1) the candidate's impact on the overall area of the circuit (denoted as $if_{area}$) and 2) the candidate's impact on the overall output quality or error, respectively, of the circuit (denoted as $if_{err}$).

To determine a candidate's $if_{area}$, the particular candidate's output is tied to constant 0 and the overall circuit is synthesized. The relative saving in area represents the candidate's $if_{area}$ and ranges from 0 (the candidate has no impact on the circuit area) to 1 (the candidate renders the overall circuit logic obsolete).

A candidate's $if_{err}$ is determined with a parameter ranking method described in more detail in the next section. Here, the basic idea is to sample the outputs of each candidate as well as of the primary output(s) of the input design. From the sampled output values a dataset is compiled, containing input and output parameters. The input parameters are represented by the outputs of the candidates. The output parameters are represented by the primary output(s) of the input design. In a testbench, uniformly distributed random values are assigned to the primary inputs of the input circuit to generate different input and output parameters. The sampled parameters are then compiled into the dataset which is processed by the ranking method to provide JS with the contribution of each candidate on the quality of the primary output(s).

Throughout the approximation process, various AxCs are produced, comprising of different approximated versions of the candidates. The impact factors guide JS towards the selection of AxCs which apply aggressive approximations on the most promising candidates, i.e., those candidates which have a high $if_{area}$ and a low $if_{err}$. From the selected AxCs, a modified binary search finds the AxC that satisfies the user-defined quality constraints and is subjected to the most aggressive approximations, and thus, potentially large savings in the target metric. To find such an AxC, synthesis and verification steps are invoked for a precise evaluation of the AxC. Due to the pre-selection of AxCs of interest, which only relies on pre-computed parameters, and the binary search, the number of expensive synthesis and verification steps is reduced in JS. Finally, the Verilog code of the most promising AxC is generated.

## 3.2 The Parameter Selection

The impact of a candidate on the error (i.e., $if_{err}$) is estimated via a parameter selection operator. For this purpose, *Least Absolute Shrinkage and Selection Operator* (LASSO) [11] is exploited to rank the candidates according to their contributions on the circuit

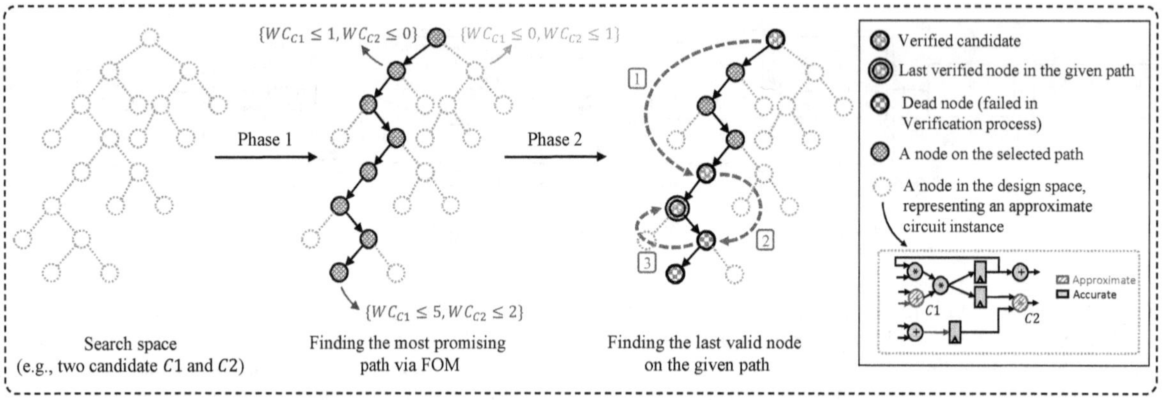


**Figure 2: Visualization of the Jump Search concept.**

output(s). LASSO, as a linear regression technique, uses $l_1$−norm regularization in its objective function and ranks the parameters subject to the following objective function:

$$min \sum_{i=1}^{n} \{\tfrac{1}{2}\left\|y_i - \mathbf{w}^T\mathbf{x}_i\right\|_2^2 + \lambda \left\|\mathbf{w}\right\|_1\} \quad (1)$$

where $y_i \in \mathbb{R}$ is the output sample of the circuit, $\mathbf{w} \in \mathbb{R}^n$ is the vector of regression coefficients, and $\mathbf{x}_i \in \mathbb{R}^n$ refers to a vector of input parameters. Moreover, $\lambda \in \mathbb{R}$ denotes the regularization hyper-parameter and controls the values of the regression coefficients. In case of a multiple-output circuit, we use an aggregation function, e.g., weighted arithmetic mean, to estimate the contribution of each input parameter. For multiple-fanout candidates, we take into account each output as a separate input parameter. Here, the maximum value of the corresponding coefficients is selected as the impact factor of the candidate.

The hyper-parameter $\lambda$ controls the values and the number of non-zero coefficients. A large value for $\lambda$ decreases the number of non-zero elements in $\mathbf{w}$ and hence keeps the value of the objective function small. It should be noted that a small value in Equation 1 does not necessarily mean a small modeling error and therefore a preferred ranking. The linear regression along with the penalty term implies a consistent parameter ranking. Thus, we just tune $\lambda$ in a way that the number of non-zero coefficients is maximized. The absolute values of the coefficients then represent the contribution of each candidate to the output and are used as $if_{err}$ in JS' heuristic function.

## 3.3 The Jump Search

Algorithm 1 shows the pseudocode of JS. JS takes the original circuit $i$ together with user-defined quality constraints $\epsilon$ as inputs. In a pre-processing step (lines 4-8), the candidates $C$, usually arithmetic components in the original circuit $i$, are identified. For each of the identified candidates, $if_{area}$ (line 6) and $if_{err}$ (line 8) are determined with the approaches described previously.

After the pre-processing, the first phase of JS is executed (lines 9-15). In this phase, JS iteratively plans a path $P$ through the search space in which each step on the path represents a different AxC. The candidates define the dimensions of the search space and each candidate is described by a *local error bound*, which comprises of an error metric (we consider the *Worst-Case Error* (WC)) and an error threshold. This approach enables JS to expand the search space in a controlled way and each solution or AxC is uniquely defined.

Figure 2 (left tree) visualizes this at the example of a circuit with two candidates, *C1* and *C2*. The original circuit *i*, for example, is described by $\{WC_{C1}{\leq}0,\ WC_{C2}{\leq}0\}$. Increasing the local error bounds of the candidates presumably leads to a reduced quality of the overall circuit but also to larger area savings. Starting from the original circuit $i$ ($\{WC_{C1}{\leq}0,\ WC_{C2}{\leq}0\}$), a possible next step on the path is defined by modifying the local error bound of one candidate (lines 9 and 14). For the exemplary circuit in Figure 2 (center tree), $\{WC_{C1}{\leq}1,\ WC_{C2}{\leq}0\}$ and $\{WC_{C1}{\leq}0,\ WC_{C2}{\leq}1\}$ are the possible next steps; blue circles highlight the planned path. JS plans the path by selecting the AxC with the highest *Figure of Merit* (FOM) (line 12). The FOM is computed by the heuristic function in Equation 2 (line 11).

```
Input: i= description of the circuit, ϵ= quality constraints
Output: a= approximate instance satisfying quality constraints
1  Function jumpSearch(i, ϵ):
2      C ← ∅; // Set of candidates
3      P ← {i}; // Path, each step represents an AxC
       /* Pre-processing                                          */
4      C ← identifyCandidates( i );
5      foreach c ∈ C do
6          c.if_area ← impactArea( c );
7      end
8      computeImpactError( i, C );
       /* Phase 1: path planning                                  */
9      next_steps ← getNextSteps( i )
10     while next_steps do
11         evaluateSteps( next_steps ); // Compute FOM of each step
12         n ← getBestStep( next_steps );
13         P.append( n );
14         next_steps ← getNextSteps( n );
15     end
       /* Phase 2: binary search                                  */
16     l ← 0; u ← len(P)-1;
17     while l ≠ u do
18         m= (u+l)/2 + 1; a ← P[m];
19         synthesizeAndVerify( i, a, ϵ );
20         if isValid( a ) then l ← m ;
21         else u ← m-1; a ← P[l] ;
22     end
23     return a;
```

**Algorithm 1:** Pseudocode of the Jump Search algorithm.

$$FOM(S) = \sum_{c} \sqrt{\frac{Err(c)}{MaxE(c)}} \times \frac{IF_{Area}(c)}{|IF_{Err}(c)|+1} \quad (2)$$

The heuristic estimates the FOM of each step $S$ for each given candidate $c$. For each candidate, the applied error threshold $Err$, the maximal possible error of the candidate $MaxErr$, as well as the $\mathrm{if}_{area}$ and $\mathrm{if}_{err}$ are taken into account. Note that each parameter is a pre-computed value; thus, the first phase does not invoke any synthesis or verification processes. The first phase plans a path that increases the depth, i.e., the level of approximation, with each step. The phase terminates when no more steps are available, i.e., the end of the search space is reached.

The heuristic function guides JS towards AxCs which reduce the quality of the candidates with a low impact on the overall circuit quality but a high impact on the circuit area. The term under the square root balances the quality reduction of the candidates to avoid only reducing the quality of certain candidates.

In the second phase, JS performs a binary search on path $P$ to find the AxC with the deepest depth which still satisfies the user-defined quality constraints $\epsilon$ (line 16-22). JS seeks to find the deepest AxC since we assume that this AxC was subjected to the most aggressive approximations, and thus, shows high area savings - which might not be optimal but significant. Figure 2 (right tree) visualizes the second phase. Path $P$ from the first phase is highlighted in blue, the valid AxCs are highlighted in green and invalid AxCs in red. The binary search maintains three indicies: a lower bound $l$, an upper bound $u$, and the middle index $m$. The search synthesizes and verifies the AxC at step $m$ on the path $P$ (line 18-19) and adjusts the lower bound $l$ and upper bound $u$ accordingly (line 20 and 21). In Figure 2 (right tree), the red arrows point to the middle index of the search, i.e., the AxC subjected to evaluation; the circled red numbers indicate the execution order. The search terminates when $l$ and $u$ are equal, i.e., the deepest AxC is found which satisfies the quality constraints (highlighted by the green circle with doubled outlines). In the second phase, JS invokes synthesis and verification process as this is inevitable to evaluate the AxCs (line 19-21). However, compared to related work, JS significantly reduces the number of invoked synthesis and verification process due to the pre-selection of AxCs in the first phase.

## 4 EXPERIMENTAL SETUP AND RESULTS

For the evaluation of our approach, we have used a subset of the approximate computing benchmark set, PaderBench[1], comprising of six circuits. Firstly, we simulated each circuit with a dataset of 10,000 random vectors and sampled the output values of the candidates as well as the circuit's output. From the sampled data, LASSO computes the $\mathrm{if}_{err}$ of each candidate. Secondly, for each candidate, the output is tied to constant 0 and ABC [3] is invoked to report on the circuit's FPGA 4-LUT usage to determine the candidate's $\mathrm{if}_{area}$.

The JS algorithm has been implemented and is available in our approximation framework, CIRCA[2] [14]. For each benchmark circuit, we have applied the worst-case error metric, varying the error bound from 0.50% to 5.00% of the maximal possible output value,

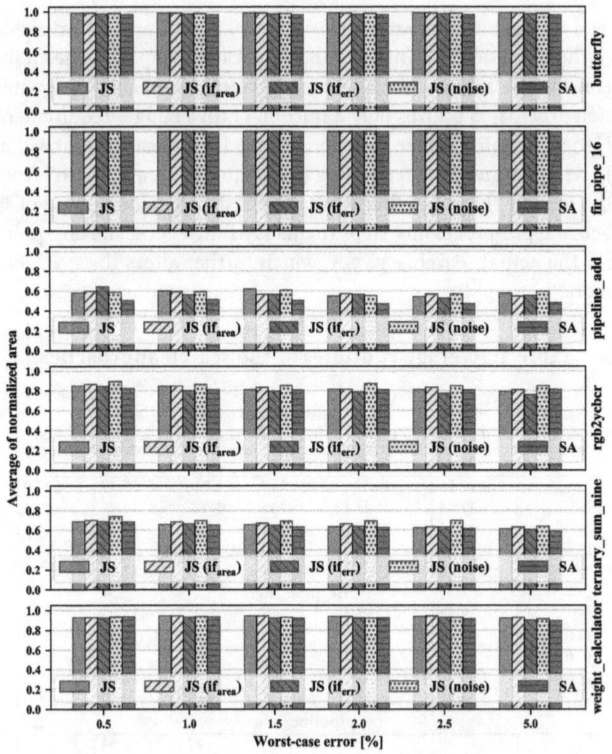


**Figure 3: Normalized area results.**

and performed four experiments to evaluate the influence of different impact factors on the results: JS performs (1) with the pre-computed impact factors, $\mathrm{if}_{area}$ and $\mathrm{if}_{err}$; (2) with noise added to the impact factors to emulate a random path; (3) with $\mathrm{if}_{area}$ as the only impact factor taken into account ($\mathrm{if}_{area}$ in the results); and (4) with $\mathrm{if}_{err}$ as the only impact factor taken into account ($\mathrm{if}_{err}$ in the results). *Simulated Annealing* (SA) has been used as a reference implementation, since previously performed experiments have shown that the algorithm achieves significant area savings.

We have run each experiment ten times and report the averaged normalized area as well as runtimes. The experiments have been performed on a compute cluster which runs Scientific Linux 7.2 (Nitrogen), provides 2 Gigabyte of main memory per job, and comprises nodes with an Intel® Xeon E5-2670@2.6GHz (16 cores).

Figure 3 shows the experimental results. Both JS and SA achieve area savings, and, for all benchmarks, JS achieves savings comparable to SA. *pipeline_add*, however, states an exception where the area savings of JS are significant, yet slightly worse than SA's. Furthermore, the results show that taking a random path already leads to notable area savings on average; taking into account the provided impact factors, however, leads to better results on average. Comparing the results of $\mathrm{if}_{area}$ and $\mathrm{if}_{err}$ shows that following only the guidance of $\mathrm{if}_{err}$ leads to slightly better results in the majority of the cases (sometimes even better than SA), suggesting that the impact of $\mathrm{if}_{err}$ on the path planning could be increased by a weight.

Table 1 shows the average runtimes of the experiments. The table reveals that JS achieves speed-ups of up to 57x and clearly outperforms SA in this regard. Overall, while the area savings on

[1]https://go.upb.de/paderbench
[2]https://go.upb.de/circa

average remain comparable, JS' runtime is significantly shorter due to the reduction of synthesis and verification steps. Furthermore, considering the runtime as a budget parameter of the approximation process, JS utilizes only a fraction of SA's budget requirement. Hence, to gain further area savings, we imagine a third phase in JS which utilizes the remaining budget to fine tune the AxC from the second phase. In other words, the first and second phase of JS become pre-processing steps to quickly find a good starting point for the actual search, e.g., SA, which further alters the AxC, but more thoroughly.

**Table 1: Average runtimes of the search approaches.**

| Search method | Worst-case error [%] 0.50 | 1.0 | 1.50 | 2.00 | 2.50 | 5.00 |
|---|---|---|---|---|---|---|
| **butterfly** | | | | | | |
| JS | 17:20 | 16:52 | 17:11 | 17:16 | 17:17 | 17:07 |
| JS ($if_{area}$) | 17:04 | 16:15 | 16:46 | 17:22 | 16:46 | 17:19 |
| JS ($if_{err}$) | 15:50 | 16:59 | 17:12 | 16:48 | 16:23 | 16:44 |
| JS (noise) | 17:22 | 17:26 | 17:30 | 17:00 | 17:01 | 16:43 |
| SA | 3:53:18 | 3:46:56 | 3:46:25 | 3:48:41 | 3:52:19 | 3:57:30 |
| **fir_pipe_16** | | | | | | |
| JS | 13:53 | 13:25 | 13:46 | 13:27 | 13:25 | 13:33 |
| JS ($if_{area}$) | 13:19 | 13:23 | 13:34 | 13:10 | 12:56 | 14:01 |
| JS ($if_{err}$) | 14:08 | 13:18 | 13:31 | 14:15 | 13:52 | 13:37 |
| JS (noise) | 13:06 | 13:10 | 12:35 | 13:12 | 12:24 | 13:33 |
| SA | 3:40:32 | 3:43:39 | 3:27:02 | 3:43:14 | 3:34:36 | 3:16:00 |
| **pipeline_add** | | | | | | |
| JS | 29 | 25 | 25 | 27 | 34 | 24 |
| JS ($if_{area}$) | 25 | 23 | 26 | 25 | 24 | 27 |
| JS ($if_{err}$) | 25 | 26 | 23 | 24 | 23 | 23 |
| JS (noise) | 28 | 25 | 26 | 24 | 23 | 35 |
| SA | 2:31 | 2:32 | 2:36 | 2:45 | 2:44 | 2:46 |
| **rgb2ycbcr** | | | | | | |
| JS | 7:11 | 7:07 | 7:31 | 7:47 | 7:40 | 8:04 |
| JS ($if_{area}$) | 7:13 | 7:23 | 7:31 | 7:46 | 7:31 | 7:40 |
| JS ($if_{err}$) | 7:22 | 7:42 | 8:09 | 8:09 | 8:05 | 8:06 |
| JS (noise) | 7:29 | 7:47 | 8:01 | 8:00 | 7:47 | 9:18 |
| SA | 4:27:34 | 4:47:00 | 4:46:55 | 5:58:23 | 5:36:35 | 7:16:34 |
| **ternary_sum_nine** | | | | | | |
| JS | 44 | 41 | 43 | 44 | 41 | 45 |
| JS ($if_{area}$) | 40 | 43 | 44 | 38 | 39 | 43 |
| JS ($if_{err}$) | 41 | 39 | 40 | 41 | 39 | 39 |
| JS (noise) | 47 | 41 | 40 | 41 | 44 | 43 |
| SA | 4:00 | 4:23 | 5:54 | 5:12 | 5:07 | 5:02 |
| **weight_calculator** | | | | | | |
| JS | 14:37:26 | 11:53:40 | 4:37:38 | 7:18:44 | 11:18:25 | 8:30:48 |
| JS ($if_{area}$) | 14:38:33 | 13:12:27 | 6:37:08 | 8:03:40 | 13:00:33 | 9:20:41 |
| JS ($if_{err}$) | 14:41:01 | 12:44:24 | 13:49:32 | 10:02:02 | 14:26:41 | 9:02:23 |
| JS (noise) | 11:14:21 | 13:47:01 | 6:59:13 | 8:46:52 | 4:24:13 | 6:47:21 |
| SA | 1:04:36:58 | 1:08:16:42 | 1:10:05:39 | 1:07:29:23 | 1:10:43:29 | 1:01:34:45 |

The runtimes are shown in the format days:hours:minutes:seconds.

## 5 CONCLUSION AND FUTURE WORK

In this work, we have presented our Jump Search method - an approach to reduce the runtime of approximation processes. JS utilizes parameter selection techniques to pre-compute impact factors for the approximation candidates of a circuit. The first phase of JS uses the impact factors to plan a path through the search space without invoking expensive synthesis or verification steps. The path, i.e., the resulting set of AxCs of interest, is evaluated in the second phase to determine the outcome of JS. In our experimental results, we have achieved significant reductions in the runtimes of the approximation processes while providing area savings comparable to a reference method, Simulated Annealing. Even though JS' area savings are slightly worse on average compared to SA, JS is beneficial for two reasons: 1) JS returns an AxC which improves the target metric, enabling the swift evaluation of potential for savings in a circuit and 2) JS can be employed as a pre-processing step to find a good starting point in the search space from where the found AxC can be fine tuned. JS achieves the reduction in runtime mainly because of its novel approach to utilize parameter selection techniques to pre-compute impact factors which allow for the evaluation of AxCs without invoking synthesis or verification.

In the future, we want to compare different parameter selection techniques and extend JS by a third phase, which uses the second phase's endpoint as a starting point, and fine tunes the found AxC. Finally, we envision JS to introduce checkpoints in the first phase. At such checkpoints, JS can update its heuristic and, if necessary, re-plan the path, i.e., backtrack in the search space.

## ACKNOWLEDGMENTS

The authors gratefully acknowledge the funding of this project by computing time provided by the Paderborn Center for Parallel Computing (PC2).

## REFERENCES

[1] Muhammad Awais, Hassan Ghasemzadeh Mohammadi, and Marco Platzner. 2018. An MCTS-based Framework for Synthesis of Approximate Circuits. In *Proceedings of the Conference on Very Large Scale Integration (VLSI-SoC '18)*. IEEE, 219–224.

[2] Mario Barbareschi, Federico Iannucci, and Antonino Mazzeo. 2016. Automatic design space exploration of approximate algorithms for big data applications. In *Proceedings of the 30th International Conference on Advanced Information Networking and Applications Workshops (WAINA '16)*. IEEE, 40–45.

[3] Robert Brayton and Alan Mishchenko. 2010. ABC: An Academic Industrial-Strength Verification Tool. In *Computer Aided Verification*, Tayssir Touili, Byron Cook, and Paul Jackson (Eds.). Springer Berlin Heidelberg, 24–40.

[4] Arun Chandrasekharan, Mathias Soeken, Daniel Groesse, and Rolf Drechsler. 2016. Approximation-aware Rewriting of AIGs for Error Tolerant Applications. In *Proceedings of the 35th International Conference on Computer-Aided Design (ICCAD '16)*. ACM, Article 83, 8 pages.

[5] Saman Froehlich, Daniel Große, and Rolf Drechsler. 2017. Error Bounded Exact BDD Minimization in Approximate Computing. In *Proceedings of the 47th International Symposium on Multiple-Valued Logic (ISMVL '17)*. IEEE, 254–259.

[6] Gai Liu and Zhiru Zhang. 2017. Statistically certified approximate logic synthesis. In *Proceedings of the 36th International Conference on Computer-Aided Design (ICCAD '17)*. IEEE, 344–351.

[7] Sparsh Mittal. 2016. A Survey of Techniques for Approximate Computing. *ACM Computing Surveys (CSUR)* 48, 4, Article 62 (March 2016), 33 pages.

[8] Kumud Nepal, Yueting Li, R. Iris Bahar, and Sherief Reda. 2014. ABACUS: A Technique for Automated Behavioral Synthesis of Approximate Computing Circuits. In *Proceedings of the Conference on Design, Automation & Test in Europe (DATE '14)*. IEEE, Article 361, 6 pages.

[9] Ashish Ranjan, Arnab Raha, Swagath Venkataramani, Kaushik Roy, and Anand Raghunathan. 2014. ASLAN: Synthesis of Approximate Sequential Circuits. In *Proceedings of the Conference on Design, Automation & Test in Europe (DATE '14)*. IEEE, Article 364, 6 pages.

[10] Mathias Soeken, Daniel Große, Arun Chandrasekharan, and Rolf Drechsler. 2016. BDD minimization for approximate computing. In *Proceedings of the 21st Asia and South Pacific Design Automation Conference (ASP-DAC '16)*. IEEE, 474–479.

[11] Robert Tibshirani. 1996. Regression shrinkage and selection via the lasso. *Journal of the Royal Statistical Society. Series B (Methodological)* (1996), 267–288.

[12] Swagath Venkataramani, Kaushik Roy, and Anand Raghunathan. 2013. Substitute-and-simplify: A Unified Design Paradigm for Approximate and Quality Configurable Circuits. In *Proceedings of the Conference on Design, Automation & Test in Europe (DATE '13)*. IEEE, 1367–1372.

[13] Swagath Venkataramani, Amit Sabne, Vivek Kozhikkottu, Kaushik Roy, and Anand Raghunathan. 2012. SALSA: Systematic Logic Synthesis of Approximate Circuits. In *Proceedings of the 49th Annual Design Automation Conference (DAC '12)*. ACM, 796–801.

[14] Linus Witschen, Tobias Wiersema, Hassan Ghasemzadeh Mohammadi, Muhammad Awais, and Marco Platzner. 2018. CIRCA: Towards a Modular and Extensible Framework for Approximate Circuit Generation. (2018), 6 pages. Presented at the 3rd Workshop on Approximate Computing (AxC '18).

# SAT-Based Placement Adjustment of FinFETs inside Unroutable Standard Cells Targeting Feasible DRC-Clean Routing

Anton Sorokin
Intel Corporation
Hillsboro, OR, USA
anton.a.sorokin@intel.com

Nikolay Ryzhenko
Intel Corporation
Hillsboro, OR, USA
nikolai.v.ryzhenko@intel.com

## ABSTRACT

In this paper, we present an algorithm of the transistor placement that takes unroutable standard cells and makes them routable by moving transistors in local windows. It converts the task of placement of gridded FinFETs into a Boolean problem and employs SAT, an accurate computing technology. The Boolean problem models possible moves of transistors as well as possible routes. Track assignment mimics an industrial router. Manufacturing rules are modeled using a special layout data model that is directly translated into SAT. A SAT solver finds legal transistor placement ensuring subsequent DRC-clean routing. The speed of SAT solvers makes the flow practical for most complex cells from a standard cell library.

## CCS CONCEPTS

• Hardware~Standard cell libraries • Hardware~Physical synthesis

## KEYWORDS

Standard cell libraries, placement, layout, FinFET, SAT, Boolean satisfiability, design rules

**ACM Reference format:**

Anton Sorokin, Nikolay Ryzhenko. 2019. SAT-Based Placement Adjustment of FinFETs inside Unroutable Standard Cells Targeting Feasible DRC-Clean Routing. *In Proceedings of ACM Great Lakes Symposium on VLSI (GLSVLSI'19). May 9–11, 2019, Washington, D.C., USA,* ACM, New York, NY, USA, *6 pages.* https://doi.org/10.1145/3299874.3317965

## 1. Introduction

### 1.1 Cell synthesis problem

For decades, since standard cells appeared, layout migration (also called compaction or shrinking) helped to build significant portions of libraries generating standard cells with reasonable quality [2, 3]. Since 22nm technology, shrinking becomes impractical because it leads to multiple design rule violations that cannot be fixed by simple local post-processing operations. Physical synthesis of standard cells from a transistor-level netlist description [1, 4, 5, 6, 7, 8, 9] is employed for modern technology nodes instead of compaction of existing layouts. Synthesis flow starts with the transistor folding. Every large field effect transistor (FET, or a device, or a transistor) is split into smaller ones connected in parallel (called legs) to fit P and N diffusion rows within the cell height. The optimal number of legs defines cell area and depends on design rules and transistor netlist [10]. Given the legged netlist, placement tools define the accurate position and orientation for every transistor determining the cell area. Detailed routers [11, 12, 13, 14, 15, 16] connect sources, gates, and drains of transistors by wires and vias according to the netlist description; router also connects pull-up and pull-down signals of the circuit with the corresponding power and ground rails. Post-routing layout compaction allows to achieve better quality of cells [17]. Modern manufacturing technologies also require insertion of dummy metal wires [18] and post-routing reduction of the manufacturing hot spots [19].

In this paper, we propose a solution for transistor placement at the standard cell level. The problem statement is as follows. Given a netlist of transistors, the task is to place already legged FETs into legal positions within the minimal area. The placement must comply with design rules for diffusion and polysilicon gates, it must be routable, and the subsequent routing should satisfy requirements on power, performance, reliability, and other specific constraints. By Design Rules we imply rules which can be expressed as relative constraints on layout objects in a limited size window.

### 1.2 Recent work and up-to-date challenges

The manufacturing cost of high-volume ICs is defined by many conflicting objectives of design quality, yield, and turnaround time. Die area has the greatest impact on the cost. Thus, Gupta and Hayes [8] reported in 2000 in a statement that remains relevant for the industry "just a 1% increase in the Pentium die size increases the annual manufacturing costs by $63.5 million; a 15% size increase costs $961 million more". Historically, most works on the transistor placement focus on the cell area minimization. Two primary optimizations, *diffusion sharing* and *gate alignment* are employed in all works differing in implementation details. The Euler search is used for stacking transistors minimizing the diffusion area [4, 6, 20]; a netlist is


GLSVLSI '19, May 9–11, 2019, Washington, D.C., USA

ACM ISBN 978-1-4503-6252-8/19/05...$15.00
https://doi.org/10.1145/3299874.3317965

converted into a graph where nets are vertices and transistors are edges. An Integer Linear Programming is used in [8] to maximize the number of vertically aligned gates connected directly by the polysilicon layer. A recursive enumeration [9] generates partial placement solutions filling the cell area starting from the left cell side and moving the right cell boundary until the finished placement of all transistors is obtained. The limited number of the best partial placements is used at every incremental stage of the algorithm to make new variants on the next iteration adding remaining transistors. The objective function maximizes both the diffusion sharing and the same-net gate alignment. All possible placements are enumerated and the algorithm backtracks if current partial solution cannot be a part of the best solution found so far. Ideas of [9] were extended in [5] to consider routability better and to perform simultaneous folding and placement of FETs. Later, [5] evolved to [15] to handle FinFETs on the fixed poly and diffusion grids (see Section 2.1). Partial placements are checked in [15] against 7nm design rules for diffusion and poly.

During enumeration, the number of partial placements on every iteration is multiplied in several times. Without a reasonable objective function, the number of placements (and, unfortunately, mostly unroutable) at the end becomes astronomical. Routability prediction is an important aspect. In [9], the perimeter of the bounding box is used to minimize the wire length; it implicitly models routability. [5] uses a weighted triple cost function modeling wire length and density. [15] considers several design rules and the width of the bounding box of all gate. In [4], transistors have an associated weight predicting probabilistic wire routing. The proof of routability is an open question. Cremer *et al.* [15] simply state that their approach produces solution "as small and as routable as possible". This common message is relevant for any placement algorithm since the solutions are routable only with some probability. In fact, any implementation has non-trivial settings those adjust the objective function for the given layout fabric, the number of available tracks, design rules, and even for the type of the cell. Thus, [5] uses custom user-defined numeric parameters for different types of cells and custom net weights.

Summarizing, we can highlight challenges and trends of the up-to-date transistor placement as follows:

- Requirements for the minimal-area, performance-aware, and reliable solutions remain actual and important.
- However, routability prediction dominates among other aspects of the transistor placement since the 22nm technology. It becomes a difficult problem because of the complex non-local design rules for poly, diffusion, metal wires, and contacts at the cell level.
- In such conditions, conventional objective functions based on congestion estimation and wire length do not work anymore. It is usual when two almost identical transistor placements with a little difference are actually routed and unrouted unpredictably. To deal with this, numerous placement solutions are generated rather than a few most promising candidates, hoping that at least one will be routed.

## 1.3 Proposed flow for transistor placing

To build routable transistor placements, we propose to use a Boolean satisfiability problem (SAT), an accurate computing technology. Modern SAT solvers provide solutions for large problems with millions of literals and clauses demonstrating affordable run time. However, SAT is an NP-complete problem. An unconstrained Boolean formulation easily can exceed the capacity of the solvers. To use advantages of accurate solving and to exclude unfeasible and unacceptable solutions, we propose a mixed two-stage placement approach. During the *first stage*, given a legged netlist, an enumerative approach builds an initial reasonable solution. A router [16] attempts to route this variant.

If this fails, during the *second stage* we employ a Boolean satisfiability problem that modifies the placement making it routable. Transistors are moved from their initial positions within a limited window. Feasible net routes are constructed to ensure routability and necessary design rules are modeled using an accurate Boolean layout data model [21]. The initial placement, allowed transistor moves, possible routes, and design rules are converted into a common SAT formulation. A SAT solver finds a new routable placement. Thus, by construction a new placement solution can be routed without DRVs. During the SAT solving stage, we do not allow cell area growth to retain the optimal cell area. If SAT fails, we increase the target cell area by one poly track and repeat the whole flow.

The rest of the paper is organized as follows. In Section 2, we start with the modeling of grids, layout and diffusion design rules, and formulate the problem of the transistor placement. Enumerative approach is highlighted in Section 3. In Section 4, we describe in detail a topology-driven SAT placement. Experimental results are presented in Section 5. We draw a conclusion in Section 6.

# 2. Preliminaries and Problem Formulation

Technical challenges of the optical lithography enforce various forms of layout regularity. Uniform polysilicon width, pitch, and orientation is a common example. Topaloglu [22] states that jogs in poly layer and irregular poly tracks are not printable anymore. FinFET design introduces another level of the layout regularity. FinFETs, originally invented to fix short channel effects and leakage currents of planar bulk MOSFETs [23], will determine and drive the industry for the next few technology nodes. A FinFET device has an essentially different structure compared to a conventional MOSFET. In FinFETS, a polysilicon gate surrounds a vertical diffusion fin are isolated by an oxide layer; two contacts form the source and the drain of the transistor (Fig. 1a). Diffusion fins are manufactured forming a uniform grid. Fig. 1b depicts a single-fin device; fig. 1c shows a device with 3 fins. It is important to note that legging, diffusion sharing, and gate alignment also make sense for FinFETs as well as for MOSFETs [15]. Gridded structure of FinFETs allows to use a discrete problem formulation and pattern-based DRC as we show in the next sections. Although FinFETs and MOSFETs have different structures, design tools draw FinFETs as traditional planar transistors (Fig. 1d), as we do in subsequent figures.

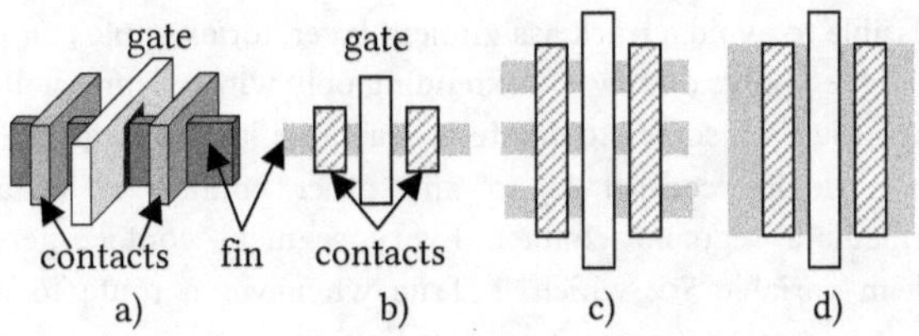


**Figure 1: Simplified view of a FinFET device with a single diffusion fin (a); the view from the top (b); a FinFET device with 3 fins (c); a design view (d).**

We use a uniform grid for the polysilicon layer. Wires have a fixed pitch $P_{poly}$ and an identical width $W_{poly}$. A common uniform grid with pitch $P_{diff}$ is used both for P and N FinFET diffusions. Width of every transistor device (in figures and in data models) equals to an integer of $P_{diff}$. Devices are placed at intersections of polysilicon and diffusion grid lines (Fig. 2).

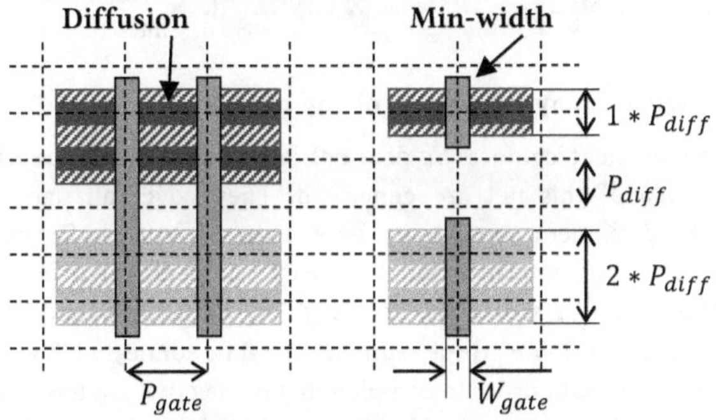


**Figure 2: Uniform polysilicon and diffusion grids.**

Manufacturing rules dictate the *layout style* of a standard cell. It includes layout of power and ground rails, cell height, width of *P* and *N* regions, extra rules for wire routing at cell boundaries, etc. Thus, minimal diffusion length $L_{diff}$ and minimal gaps between diffusions in horizontal direction $G_h$ and in vertical direction $G_v$ define a rectangular region inside a cell where devices can be placed. Allowed positions for transistors inside that region are enumerated and defined *a priori* by the layout style and polysilicon and diffusion grids (Fig. 3).

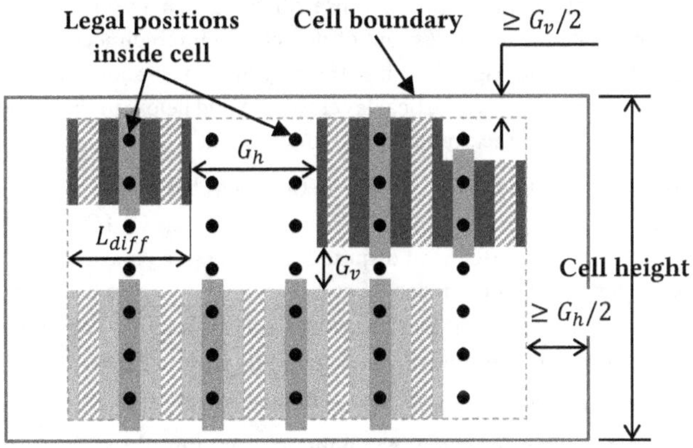


**Figure 3: Gridded layout of a 1-D cell.**

*Problem formulation:* Given a netlist of legged transistors and a designated rectangular region with fixed allowed sitting positions, fixed left, top, and bottom sides and open right side, we formulate the problem as follows: to assign location to every transistor leg so that they fit into the minimal region. There should exist a layout that implements electrical connection between transistor contacts through routing layers using wire segments and vias. The resulting placement and routing must not violate electrical and design rules. The quality of the placement is optimized by maximizing diffusion sharing, diffusion and gate alignment, and minimizing the wire length.

## 3. Enumerative Placement

We apply a two-stage placement flow. During the first stage, an enumerative approach builds an initial reasonable solution optimizing horizontal wire length, pin access, and maximal wire density in vertical cuts. To keep the paper size, we address the readers to [5, 9, 15]. In our enumerative placer we have similar implementation with an extension for unfeasible partial placement detection to handle *design rules for diffusion fins* such as *min length, spacing, clustering*. The result of this stage is a transistor placement without electrical shorts in all layers and without major DRVs in diffusion.

In this work, we cannot disclose actual design rules but can illustrate the approach. FinFETs are 3D structures, and etch variability is a problem for high-aspect ratio processes. Therefore, FinFETs have a significant number of restricted design rules. In our discrete formulation, geometrical design rules for diffusion are modeled via a finite number of forbidden transistor patterns. In [24], Kawa provides an example that "lonely" placed 1-fin P-type FinFET is no longer effective when the device is not part of a cluster. It enforces to use strict clustering rules for active P-devices to ensure proper functionality. Having such a rule, a procedure checks during enumeration presence or absence of a forbidden pattern on a regular grid: if there is an active 1-fin P-type device and there are no devices on all four of its sides – it is an illegal pattern (Fig. 4).

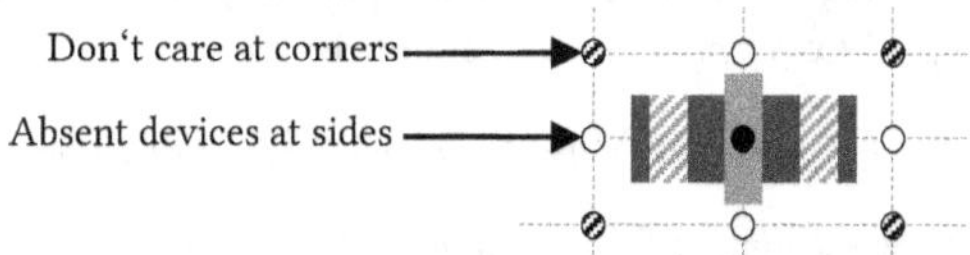


**Figure 4: "Lonely" placed 1-fin P-type FinFET.**

## 4. Routing-Driven SAT Placement

### 4.1 SAT formulation

In this section, we present an algorithm which performs device placement ensuring subsequent routability. The algorithm converts the following tasks into a concurrent SAT problem:

1. Find legal transistor placement;
2. Find feasible connections between transistor contacts;
3. Forbid any DRVs by using rule patterns on a gridded layout.

Given $N$ transistors $\{D\}$, we formulate the placement problem as follows. For every transistor $D_i$, location $(x, y)$ on a grid, and flip $f$ define a Boolean variable $D_{i,x,y,f}$. Flip $f$ defines whether the source of the transistor is placed on the left or on the right. If location $(x, y)$ is chosen for transistor, the appropriate variable is to be assigned to $True$. Transistor $D_i$ must have one and only one location and flip variable set to $True$. By adding expression (1) into the SAT problem, we ensure that transistor is placed. Expression (2) ensures that this transistor is created only once.

$$\bigvee_{i=1;\,\forall x,y,f}^{N} D_{i,x,y,f} = True \qquad (1)$$

$$\bigvee_{i=1;\forall(x1,y1,f1)\neq(x2,y2,f2)}^{N} D_{i,x1,y1,f1} \wedge D_{i,x2,y2,f2} = False \qquad (2)$$

Transistors $D_i$ and $D_j$ cannot occupy the same position and cannot share gates or diffusions if this sharing creates a short of different nets. Pair conflicts between different transistors are expressed similarly to (2). It completes the placement problem for the SAT.

Layout is composed of rectangular gridded objects. Such an object (i.e. a via or a piece of wire) has a fixed geometry, and location on a rectangular grid. Manufacturing rules are expressed via Boolean functions of these objects [21]. Some Boolean expressions for arbitrary design rules can be found in [21]. For example, (3) codes an illegal diffusion pattern from Fig. 4.

$$D_{x,y} \wedge \overline{D_{x-1,y}} \wedge \overline{D_{x+1,y}} \wedge \overline{D_{x,y-1}} \wedge \overline{D_{x,y+1}} = False \qquad (3)$$

Routing problem is solved by connecting transistors using a fixed routing grid. A transistor has two diffusion contacts and a poly contact which are assigned to appropriate nets. General routing task is split into: 1) creating connections from transistor contacts to routing track segments, and 2) providing connectivity between different segments of the same net (Fig. 5).

When transistor $D_i$ is placed at some position $(x, y)$, its contacts are assigned to corresponding nets (Fig. 5a). Corresponding Boolean variable $C_{n,j,k}$ represents a *device contact* at location $(j, k)$ and assigned to a net $n$. The contact grid $(j, k)$ and the diffusion grid $(x, y)$ have their own indices (4).

$$D_{i,x,y,0} = C_{j,k,source\_net} \wedge C_{j+1,k,gate\_net} \wedge C_{j+2,k,drain\_net}$$
$$D_{i,x,y,1} = C_{j,k,drain\_net} \wedge C_{j+1,k,gate\_net} \wedge C_{j+2,k,source\_net} \qquad (4)$$

$$\overline{C_c} \vee R_1 \vee \ldots \vee R_{num\_routes\_for\_this\_device\_contact} = True \qquad (5)$$

$$\overline{Sc_s} \vee R_1 \vee \ldots \vee R_{num\_routes\_to\_this\_segment\_contact} = True \qquad (6)$$

$$\overline{Sc_s} \vee S_1 \vee \ldots \vee S_{n\_segments\_over\_segment\_contact} = True \qquad (7)$$

If a *device contact* is used, it is to be connected to a track assignment *segment contact,* a seed metal wire at the given $Y$-track and $X$-coordinate. (Fig. 5b). We enumerate possible *routes* $\{R\}$ to segment contacts $\{S\}$ in a predefined window around the device. A route (Fig. 5c) is a candidate wire between a device contact and a segment contact. Every route gets a Boolean variable $R$. Extra routes between device contacts are created and added to $\{R\}$ if it is possible to avoid a track assignment layer, for example connect two aligned polys directly by extending poly wires. Expression (5) obliges the SAT solver to create at least one layout route of $\{R\}$ from a device contact $C_c$ to any other contact or to any intermediate segment contact. Every segment contact gets a Boolean variable $Sc$, which is True whenever a route to this contact is created. Segment contact $Sc$ cannot appear without at least one route $R$ connected to $Sc$ (6).

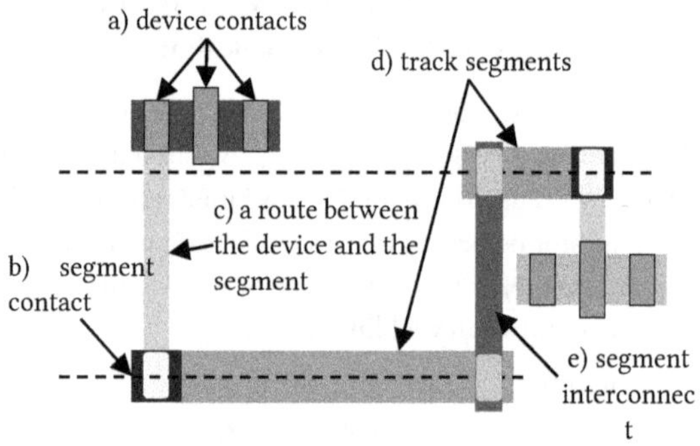


**Figure 5: Layout objects of the connectivity model.**

For all segment contacts $Sc$ of a net, all possible track routes $S$ (*segments*) of this net are generated. They cover all pairs of generated segment contacts in the same routing track. Segment contact cannot appear without at least one segment over that contact. If a SAT solver sets two segment variables $S_i$ and $S_k$ of the same net to $True$, these segments must be connected to avoid dangling wires. In order to complete net connectivity, a few extra interconnection rules are added into the SAT formulation:

1. There must be no gap between a segment contact $Sc_i$ and at least one another segment contact to the right $Sc_j$. This gap is filled by one or two added *segments* (Fig. 5d).
2. A vertical *interconnection segment* (Fig. 5e) must exist between every overlapping pairs of *segments.*
3. All rightmost segment contacts of the same net are to be connected with an *interconnect segment.*

Two horizontal segment contacts and vertical wire tracks are shown in Fig. 6a. These contacts are to be connected. Fig. 6b, 6c, and 6d depict three options those fill the gap between the seed segment contacts. Fig. 6e and 6f depict two interconnect options for the case in Fig. 8b using the routing layer above and the routing layer below. Vertical layers above and below in this figure have the same tracks and widths for simplicity.

Boolean variables $\{G\}$ and $\{I\}$ define possible fixed gaps and interconnects correspondingly. We omit formulas for $\{G\}$ and $\{I\}$. These are straightforward disjunction expressions like (5) and (6). One part of disjunction describes negation of a constrained layout situation (like $\overline{C_c}$ in (5)). The rest of the disjunction requires at least one of the solutions to be $True$ to fix this case (like $R_1 \vee \ldots \vee R_{num\_routes\_for\_this\_device\_contact}$ in (5)).

Thus, five types of layout components were introduced: a device contact, a segment contact, a route between contacts, a horizontal track *segment,* and a vertical *segment interconnect.* Summarizing, the SAT formulation is as follows:

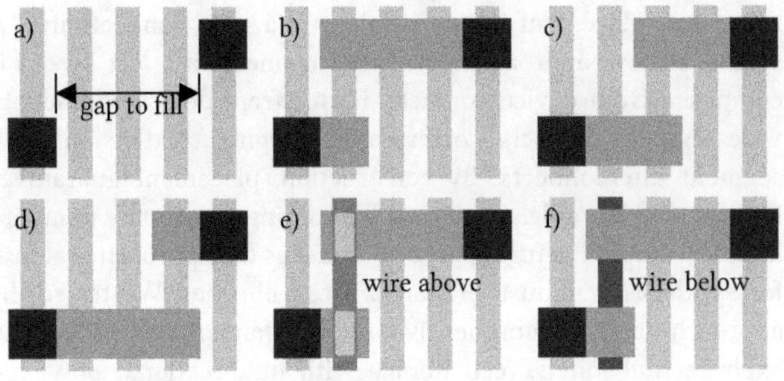


**Figure 6: Connectivity of two segment contacts.**

1. One and only one (1, 2) location/orientation variable $D_{i,x,y,f}$ is assigned to $True$ for every device $D_i$.
2. Device contact variables $\{C\}$ are set to $True$ (4).
3. At least one route $R$ must be set to $True$ for every used contact $C$ (5). The route connects either two device contacts directly or connects this contact $C$ with some segment contact $Sc$ at a designated track layer. Segment contact $Sc$ cannot appear without at least one route $R$ connected to $Sc$ (6).
4. Every segment contact must have at least one fixed gap $\{G\}$ with at least one segment contact on the right. Where a single fixed gap is a pair of overlapping *segments*.
5. Every overlapping pair of segments must have at least one created interconnect $\{I\}$.
6. Contacts, routes, segments consist of gridded layout objects.
7. Layout objects cannot form any forbidden layout patterns subject to formulas like (3). Design rules include lengths, spacing, offsets, and overlaps between wires, forbidden via configurations, minimal metal enclosures for vias, and many others. We refer to works [14] and [21] to show how various gridded design rules are converted into Boolean expressions.

As a result, the SAT solver produces DR-clean transistor placement. All nets get complete routing by construction, because every segment contact is connected to at least one other segment contact on the right. Segments must either overlap in one track or get a vertical interconnect. Routing is not optimized but the formulation guarantees that at least one routable solution exists. A router [16] creates a new optimized routing from scratch.

## 4.2 Using initial sub-optimal placement

In the above SAT formulation, we enumerate layout options in several places:

1. Any device can be placed at any legal location within the given cell area.
2. Routes between a device contact and segment contacts are enumerated in a window around the device contact (Fig. 5c).
3. Wires that fix gaps between segment contacts are enumerated for all possible pairs of contacts (Fig. 6b, 6c, 6d).
4. Every pair of overlapping segments has several interconnecting options (Fig. 6e and 6f).

The number of Boolean literals grows in a non-linear way with the problem size. It is defined by the cell area, the number of transistors, and the number of nets. To limit the solution space, we formulate a SAT task over the enumerative placer result by limiting possible transistor placement by 2-3 grid points from the original location. This combination of the preliminary enumerative approach and subsequent SAT solving was found efficient for the synthesis of the most complex and largest standard cells.

# 5. Experimental Results

## 5.1 Capacity studies

The target of the first experiment was to measure the capacity of the proposed placement approach: runtime, memory, and scalability. Representative cells were taken from an experimental FinFET cell library with unidirectional poly and metal layers.

**Table 1: Capacity studies.**

| Input | | | SAT variables | | | Run time, sec. or h:m | | |
|---|---|---|---|---|---|---|---|---|
| Cell index | #transistors | #nets | #trans. locations | #segments | #interconnects | SAT | Enumerative | Enumerative then SAT |
| 1 | 40 | 30 | 2K | 26K | 9M | inf | 0:04 | - |
| | | | 228 | 15K | 3M | - | - | 0:05 |
| 2 | 38 | 22 | 2K | 18K | 6M | inf | 0:03 | - |
| | | | 212 | 12K | 4M | - | - | 0:12 |
| 3 | 70 | 47 | 7K | 100K | 52M | inf | 0:33 | - |
| | | | 668 | 44K | 15M | - | - | 56:32 |
| 4 | 24 | 16 | 672 | 5K | 1M | 0:13 | 0:01 | - |
| | | | 196 | 4K | 1M | - | - | 0:01 |
| 5 | 28 | 15 | 1K | 6K | 2M | 0:02 | 0:01 | - |
| | | | 156 | 3K | 1M | - | - | 0:02 |
| 6 | 48 | 8 | 2K | 20K | 3M | 1:07 | 0:04 | - |
| | | | 436 | 5K | 1M | - | - | 0:06 |
| 7 | 32 | 12 | 1K | 5K | 500K | 14s | 8s | - |
| | | | 184 | 3K | 350K | - | - | 9s |
| 8 | 32 | 10 | 1K | 7K | 1M | 0:03 | 6s | - |
| | | | 184 | 3K | 357K | - | - | 8s |
| 9 | 14 | 12 | 280 | 3K | 200K | 40s | 13s | - |
| | | | 76 | 1K | 88K | - | - | 14s |
| 10 | 12 | 10 | 168 | 1K | 70K | 1s | 2s | - |
| | | | 64 | 786 | 45K | - | - | 2s |

Experiments were run using solver [25] on Intel 3.2GHZ CPU utilizing a single core. In Table 1, cells 1 to 5 represent 2-D (i.e. double-row-height) sequential cells. The largest cells 1 to 3 were routed using two different horizontal layers for track assignment segments. Others were routed using just one layer. Cells 6 to 10 are 1-D (i.e. single-row-height) sequential and combinational cells. In all experiments, only one vertical layer was used for segment interconnects. The second column of the table shows the number of transistors in a cell (#transistors). #nets shows the number of different nets which are to be routed in the cell. "SAT variables" represent the SAT problem size. "Transistor locations" is a total number of Boolean variables used to describe possible transistor placement. "#segments" shows the number of Boolean variables used to describe wire segments. "#interconnects" shows the number of Boolean variables used to describe interconnects between segments. K and M correspond to thousands and millions respectively. In the run time section of the table, the first field "SAT" corresponds to an unconstrained SAT task formulation: a device can be placed anywhere inside the cell. The second field shows the run time of enumerative placement algorithm. The "Enumerative then SAT" shows the run time of enumerative placement run with further SAT solver refinement of the result. In the SAT solver task formulation for this run, the transistor location was limited by 2 grid points offset from the enumerative run result. The run time "inf" shows that the task was not able to finish; "s" corresponds to seconds. The time is in hours:minutes otherwise. The peak memory consumption was below 10GB.

## 5.2 Routability studies

In the second experiment, 75 different cells were divided into two groups. The first group contained 41 simple combinational cells like INV, BUF, AND, OR, and AOI with 2 to 5 inputs. The second group contained 34 complex cells such as XOR, adders, sequential cells. The final routing was done as a separate task using a high quality industrial router. Routed solutions were DRC-clean and satisfied pin-access and other requirements.

We compared pure SAT approach, pure enumerative approach, and a mix "Enumerative then SAT". Table 2 represents the results. "Placed" is the number of placed cells. "R. of P." is the number of routed cells among placed cells. Both the absolute number and the percentage are presented for every run. Pure SAT-based placer failed to create any placement for 53% of complex cells due to runtime limit. Enumerative placer was able to finish all cells, but then the router was able to route only 88% of simple cells and 65% of complex cells. A combined approach "Enumerative then SAT" was able to place 100% of simple cells and 94% of complex cells. In this flow, all placed solutions were routed successfully.

**Table 2: Routability studies.**

| | SAT | | Enumerative | | Enum. then SAT | |
|---|---|---|---|---|---|---|
| | Placed | R. of P. | Placed | R. of P. | Placed | R. of P. |
| 41 simple cells | 41<br>100% | 41<br>100% | 41<br>100% | 36<br>88% | 41<br>100% | 41<br>100% |
| 34 complex cells | 16<br>47% | 16<br>100% | 34<br>100% | 22<br>65% | 32<br>94% | 32<br>100% |

## 6. Conclusion

In this paper, we presented an algorithm of transistor placement inside standard cells. The approach solves routability prediction problem that dominates in standard cell since 22nm. The impact of non-local design rules of 193nm optical lithography cannot be adequately modeled by conventional cost functions. Usually only sign-off routing can report whether a placement is routable or not. The proposed placement flow consists of two stages. A fast algorithm similar to [9] and [15] constructs an initial solution with minimal cell area, total wire length and its result to be very close to a routable state. Here, we use pattern-based checks for diffusion design rules to provide a DRC-clean placement ready for routing. If the router fails, a subsequent SAT-based approach resolves local routing conflicts by moving devices in local regions around the original positions. The SAT problem is solved concurrently for transistor placement, design rules, and net connectivity. A segment-based approach models net connectivity. Net layout is composed from device contacts, routes from device contacts to wire segment contacts, corresponding segment extensions, and segment interconnects. By construction, placement guarantees that there exists at least one feasible routing. Regularity of layout in modern manufacturing processes makes the approach practical for synthesis of industrial standard cell libraries. We tested the approach on a comprehensive set of standard cells from an experimental FinFET cell library with unidirectional poly and metal layers. The proposed approach synthesized, i.e. placed and then DRC-clean routed 73 of 75 input cells (97%), while the enumerative approach allowed to synthesize 58 of 75 cells (77%).

## References


[1] A. M. Ziesemer, R. Reis, Physical design automation of transistor networks, Microelectronic Engineering, Vol. 148, Issue C, December 2015, pp. 122-128.

[2] D. S. Fu et al., Topology-driven cell layout migration with collinear constraints, International Conference on Computer Design, Oct. 4-7, 2009, pp. 439-444.

[3] F. Fang, J. Zhu, Calligrapher: a new layout migration engine based on geometric closeness, IEEE Transactions on CAD of ICs and Systems, 2005, Vol. 24, Issue 9, pp. 1347-1361.

[4] C. Lazzari, C. Santos, R. Reis, A new transistor-level layout generation strategy for static CMOS circuits, 13th IEEE International Conference on Electronics, Circuits and Systems, 2006, pp. 660-663.

[5] S. Hougardy, T. Nieberg, J. Schneider, BonnCell: automatic layout of leaf cells, The 18th Asia and South Pacific Design Automation Conference, Jan 22-25, 2013, pp. 453-460.

[6] R. Karmazin, C. Otero, R. Manohar, cellTK: automated layout for asynchronous circuits with nonstandard cells, The 19th International Symposium on Asynchronous Circuits and Systems, May 19-22, 2013, pp. 58-66.

[7] M. Guruswamy et al., CELLERITY: a fully automatic layout synthesis system for standard cell libraries, The 34th Design Automation Conference, 1997, pp. 327-332.

[8] A. Gupta, J. Hayes, CLIP: integer-programming-based optimal layout synthesis of 2D CMOS cells, ACM Transactions on Design Automation of Electronic Systems, Vol. 5 Issue 3, July 2000, pp. 510-547.

[9] R. B.-Yehuda, J. A. Feldman, R. Y. Pinter, S. Wilmer, Depth-first-search and dynamic programming algorithms for efficient CMOS cell generation, IEEE Tran. on CAD, V. 8, N. 7, July 1989.

[10] J. Cortadella, Area-optimal transistor folding for 1-D gridded cell design, IEEE Transactions on Computer-Aided Design of ICs and Systems, 2013, Vol. 32, Issue 11, pp. 1708-1721.

[11] Hsueh-Ju Lu et al., Practical ILP-based routing of standard cells, Conference on Design, Automation and Test in Europe, 2016, pp. 245-248.

[12] N. Ryzhenko, S. Burns, Standard cell routing via Boolean satisfiability, The 49th Design Automation Conference, June 3-7, 2012, pp. 603-612.

[13] Wei Ye et al., Standard cell layout regularity and pin access optimization considering middle-of-line, Great Lakes Symposium on VLSI, 2015, pp. 289-294.

[14] J. Cortadella, J. Petit, S. Gomez, F. Moll, A Boolean rule-based approach for manufacturability-aware cell routing, IEEE Transactions on CAD of ICs and Systems, 2014, Vol. 33, Issue 3.

[15] P. Cremer, S. Hougardy, J. Schneider, J. Silvanus, Automatic cell layout in the 7nm era, ISPD'17 Proceedings of the 2017 ACM on International Symposium on Physical Design, pp. 99-106.

[16] N. Ryzhenko, S. Burns, A. Sorokin, M. Talalay. Pin Access-Driven Design Rule Clean and DFM Optimized Routing of Standard Cells under Boolean Constraints. In Proceedings of ACM International Symposium on Physical Design (ISPD'19). April 14–17, 2019, San Francisco, CA, USA.

[17] A. Ziesemer, R. Reis, Simultaneous two-dimensional cell layout compaction using MILP with ASTRAN, IEEE Computer Society Annual Symposium on VLSI, 2014, pp. 350-355.

[18] Y. Lin, B. Yu, D. Z. Pan, High performance dummy fill insertion with coupling and uniformity constraints, The 52nd Annual Design Automation Conference, June 7-11, 2015.

[19] F. Yang, Y. Cai, Q. Zhou, J. Hu, SAT based multi-net rip-up-and-reroute for manufacturing hotspot removal, Conference on Design, Automation and Test in Europe, 2010.

[20] B. Basaran, R. Rutenbar, An O(n) algorithm for transistor stacking with performance constraints, The 33rd Design Automation Conference, June 3-7, 1996, pp. 221-226.

[21] G. Suto, Rule agnostic routing by using design fabrics, The 49th Design Automation Conference, June 3-7, 2012.

[22] R. Topaloglu, Design with FinFETs: Design rules, patterns, and variability, IEEE/ACM International Conference on Computer-Aided Design, 2013, pp. 569-571.

[23] V. Subramanian et al., Planar bulk MOSFETs versus FinFETs: An analog/RF perspective, IEEE Transactions on Electron Devices, 2006, Vol. 53, Issue 12, pp. 3071-3079.

[24] J. Kawa, FinFET Design, Manufacturability, and Reliability, White Paper, https://www.synopsys.com/designware-ip/technical-bulletin/finfet-design.html

[25] http://www.labri.fr/perso/lsimon/glucose

# A Scalable and Process Variation Aware NVM-FPGA Placement Algorithm

Chengmo Yang
University of Delaware
chengmo@udel.edu

Yuan Xue
University of Delaware
xueyuan@udel.edu

## ABSTRACT

As non-volatile memory (NVM) based FPGAs gain increasing popularity, FPGA synthesis tools start to tune the synthesis flow to match NVM characteristics. State-of-the-art NVM FPGA placement algorithms tried to reduce the high reconfiguration cost induced by the costly NVM programming process. However, they are not only limited in scalability but also fail to consider process variation. This paper aims to overcome these limitations. Blocks in the NVM-FPGA are no longer uniform but classified into fast, slow, and dead blocks. Moreover, the proposed placement algorithm reduces computation complexity by not searching the entire design space for an optimal solution with minimum reconfiguration cost, but computing the reconfiguration cost just-in-time. Verilog-to-Routing (VTR)-based implementation confirms its effectiveness in reducing critical path length and speeding up the placement process, while still saving reconfiguration cost by up to 74.2%.

## CCS CONCEPTS

• **Hardware** → **Non-volatile memory**; **Placement**; *Emerging architectures.*

## KEYWORDS

FPGA, Non-volatile memories, Low power design, Placement

**ACM Reference Format:**
Chengmo Yang and Yuan Xue. 2019. A Scalable and Process Variation Aware NVM-FPGA Placement Algorithm. In *Great Lakes Symposium on VLSI 2019 (GLSVLSI '19), May 9–11, 2019, Tysons Corner, VA, USA.* ACM, New York, NY, USA, 6 pages. https://doi.org/10.1145/3299874.3317971

## 1 INTRODUCTION

FPGAs play an important role in IC design by offering high degrees of reconfigurability and self-adaptivity, a key request of many embedded and cyber-physical systems. However, traditional FPGAs cannot meet the rapidly growing needs of popular applications such as bioinformatics and neural networks, because their on-chip reconfigurable components are built with SRAMs which suffer from low cell density [1], high power dissipation [2], and low error resistance [3]. To overcome these limitations, researchers have proposed the use of Non-Volatile Memories (NVM) in FPGAs, and demonstrated the feasibility of building on-chip reconfigurable components with Spin-Transfer Torque Magnetic RAM (STT-RAM) [4], Resistive RAM (RRAM)[5], and Phase Change Memory (PCM) [6], to name a few. These NVM-FPGAs are expected to offer more reconfigurable resources, consume less power, and be more resilient to power supply interruptions.

Despite the aforementioned advantages, NVMs are also known for their shortcomings of slow write speed, high write energy, and limited endurance [7]. To mitigate the potential adverse impact on FPGA reconfiguration latency, energy, and programming cycles, a number of synthesis optimizations have been proposed for NVM-FPGAs. Specially, NVM-friendly placement techniques [8, 9] have been proposed to reduce the reconfiguration cost, represented as the number of NVM cells programmed during reconfiguration. While effective, these techniques search the entire design space for an optimal solution [8], thus tremendously increasing the execution time of the placement algorithm. Another limitation is that previous NVM-FPGA synthesis optimizations ignore process variation (PV) during fabrication. When technology scales below 65nm [10], PV causes high variations in the attributes of devices and wires, which in turn lead to significant variations in delay, power, and aging speed of different FPGA on-chip components. The PV influence on NVM-FPGAs is even more severe than SRAM-FPGAs, as the feature size of NVM is smaller and the technology is less mature [11].

This work aims to tackle the limitations of previous NVM-FPGA synthesis optimizations, by proposing a more scalable and process variation aware NVM-FPGA placement framework. First, on-chip reconfiguration components in the NVM-FPGA are no longer treated uniformly but classified into fast, slow, and dead blocks based on PV information. Such classification is performed repetitively throughout the whole FPGA lifetime to account for the impact of aging. A *block variation-aware placement region selection* approach is proposed for selecting a minimum-size region with sufficient number of fast blocks for a given design. Second, a *scalable NVM-FPGA placement* algorithm is proposed, which computes reconfiguration cost just-in-time and drastically speeds up the placement process, making it more suitable for large designs than the state-of-the-art NVM-FPGA placement algorithm [8]. Overall, this work makes the following contributions.

- Development of non-uniform block delay models and a corresponding placement region selection algorithm to account for PV and aging.
- Design of a scalable placement algorithm that balances reconfiguration cost and timing while reducing placement overhead.
- Incorporation of the proposed NVM-FPGA framework into the Verilog-to-Routing (VTR) CAD tool [12] for evaluation.


ACM ISBN 978-1-4503-6252-8/19/05...$15.00
https://doi.org/10.1145/3299874.3317971

In the rest of this paper, Section 2 reviews background knowledge of NVM-FPGAs and their synthesis optimizations, as well as process variation and aging issues. Section 3 describes the proposed placement region selection and scalable placement algorithm. Section 4 presents the experimental setup and results, while Section 5 concludes the paper.

## 2 BACKGROUND

**NVM-FPGAs**: FPGAs typically include three types of on-chip reconfigurable resources: configurable logic blocks (CLBs), connection blocks (CBs), and switch boxes (SBs). CLBs are used to implement logic functions. In each CLB there is a cluster of basic logic elements (BLEs), each of which is made of one look up table (LUT) and two flip-flops. SBs are used for routing, and CBs are used to connect CLBs and SBs locally.

Configuration of each CLB, SB, and CB is controlled by on-chip memory cells which can be implemented with NVM cells. Various NVM-FPGA architectures have been developed/proposed. Actel has taped out Flash-based FPGAs [13]. [6] proposed 3D architectures for PCM-based FPGAs. The NVM-FPGA proposed in [4] utilizes STT-RAM, a magnetic storage element, as the basic memory cell. RRAM based FPGAs are proposed in [5]. These efforts prove the feasibility of NVM-FPGAs.

**NVM-FPGA Synthesis**: Recently, researchers started to work on tuning the FPGA synthesis flow to fit NVM characteristics. In [14], a multi-context switching framework is proposed for Racetrack memory based FPGA, to speed up reconfiguration and save power. Placement algorithms are proposed in [8] to reduce the reconfiguration cost of CLBs for NVM-FPGAs. In [15], an algorithm to reuse paths during routing and minimize reconfiguration writes to SBs is proposed. In [9], a runtime and reconfiguration dual aware placement strategy is proposed for a SRAM-NVM hybrid FPGA architecture. In [16], a memory and logic co-placement is proposed for balancing the write distribution across memory and logic blocks in RRAM-FPGAs. However, none of these previous synthesis optimizations have considered process variation, which is one of the main focus of this work.

Technically, the proposed work is most closely related with [8] in that both of them aim to reduce CLB reconfiguration cost through placement optimizations. However, the algorithms in [8] explore the entire design space offline to find an optimization solution with minimum reconfiguration cost. As a result, they are unscalable and only suitable for relatively small designs. In contrast, this work computes CLB reconfiguration cost just-in-time during the placement stage, and hence is more scalable and supports larger designs.

**Process Variation Impact**: Process variation (PV) is the natural occurrence in deep sub-micron and nano-scale technologies. With PV, critical parameters such as channel length, width, and oxide thickness shift from designed values. Common PV includes random dopant fluctuation (RDF), line-edge and linewidth roughness (LER, LWR), oxide thickness variations, defects and traps, patterning proximity effect, to name a few [17].

NVM devices are more vulnerable to PV than SRAM as the feature size of NVM is expected to be smaller and the technology is less mature [11]. For example, thicker GST($Ge_2Sb_2Te_5$) layer in PCM will require higher programming current [18], which may in turn lead to higher power consumption and reduced programming cycles, while the over-aging element would have larger access delay and lower reliability. It is shown in [18] that PV could increase PCM programming power by 96% and shorten PCM endurance by 50X. Some recent works have considered process variation of NVM devices. For example, the work in [19] considers PV-induced reliability degradation for Flash-based storage systems and proposes a read improvement scheme. A wear-leveling technique for multi-level PCM is proposed in [20] with process variation considerations.

PV leads to significant variations in read and write speed, power, and aging speed of different reconfiguration components of an FPGA. In [21], a statistical simulation method is introduced to study PV's adverse effect on the stability of configuration memory. In [10], a degradation model considering PV is constructed and the corresponding evaluation method is given. In [22], a two-phase placement algorithm is proposed to maximize design reliability under PV when voltage scaling is applied. All these works target SRAM-based FPGAs and focus on the configuration memory. In contrast, the proposed work targets NVM-based FPGAs and considers PV's impact on CLBs during placement.

## 3 PROPOSED PLACEMENT FRAMEWORK

In a nutshell, this work targets the *placement* stage on the synthesis flow and hence focuses on *CLBs* which are the only type of blocks configured during placement. It introduces two steps to the conventional synthesis flow, namely, *process variation (PV) aware region selection* and *scalable NVM-FPGA placement*, to be applied after packing and before routing. The goals are reducing CLB reconfiguration cost as well as improving performance by reducing critical path delay.

### 3.1 PV-Aware Placement Region Selection

*3.1.1 Block classification.* Block variation comes from two factors: the *initial PV distribution* introduced during fabrication, as well as *aging*, reflected as the programming cycles of various CLBs.

Block delay and reliability can be measured with some existing approaches, such as the delay variation monitor approach in [23] and the fault detection method in [24]. CLBs with stuck-at faults (either worn out or due to fabrication flaws) are marked as "dead blocks" and will no longer be used. For the remaining fault-free CLBs, their access delays (i.e., read speed) will be measured and a user defined ratio $\alpha$ will be employed to differentiate fast and slow blocks on the FPGA. This proposed model is generic and can be extended to include other FPGA blocks (i.e., SBs and CBs) as well. Figure 1 presents an example of block classification.

$$\alpha = \frac{fast\ block\ count}{total\ block\ count} \tag{1}$$

To account for the impact of aging, the delay and reliability measurement takes place *repetitively* throughout the FPGA lifetime, e.g., upon placing $n$ designs. A new measurement can be performed during the gap period between configuring two designs to completely hide its overhead. In a new measurement, a fast block may become a slow block while a slow block may end up as a dead block.

*3.1.2 Placement region selection.* Traditionally, a placement region is a square (or near-square) region [12] located at one fixed corner of

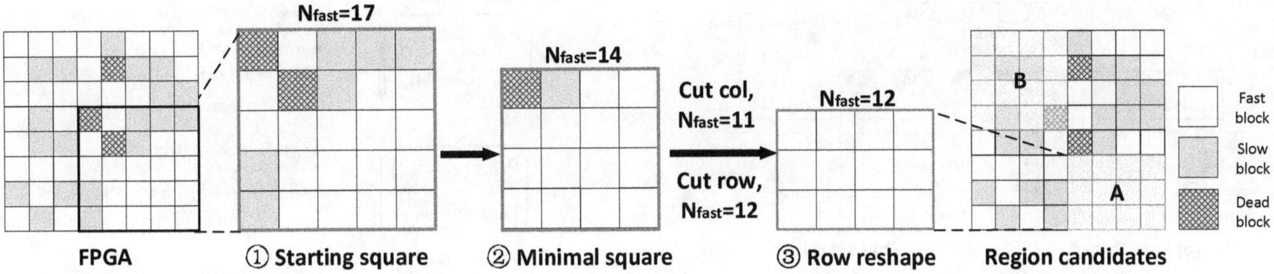


**Figure 1: A region selection example. Design block number $N$=11, fast block ratio $\alpha$=0.65. The bottom right corner region is selected in three steps. Region candidate A is better than B.**

---

**Algorithm 1** Process variation aware region selection

---

**Input:** Design logic block number $N$, FPGA block classification, and fast block ratio $\alpha$.
**Output:** Placement region $Region = \{L_H, L_V\}$.
1: **for** each FPGA corner **do**
2: Set initial square length $B_{init} = \lceil\sqrt{\frac{N}{\alpha}}\rceil$;
3: Compute $N_{fast}$;
4: Try to shrink to $B - 1$ while ensuring $N_{fast} \geq N$;
5: Try to reshape to $L_H - 1$ and $L_V - 1$, compute $N_{fast}$;
6: If both are valid, choose the one with higher $N_{fast}$;
7: Compute fast block ratio $N_{fast}/(L_H \times L_V)$;
8: **end for**
9: Choose the region with highest $N_{fast}/(L_H \times L_V)$.

---

the FPGA, as this shape and position tend to minimize critical path delay, improve routability, and reduces the distances to I/O pins. Instead of using a fixed location and shape, the proposed region selection scheme searches all four corners of the FPGA, finds four candidates, and chooses the best region among the four candidates, as sketched in Algorithm 1. It imposes an extra criterion, that is, the number of fast blocks in the selected region (denoted as $N_{fast}$) must be sufficient to hold the design which requires $N$ CLBs:

$$N_{fast} \geq N \tag{2}$$

To search for a minimum region that satisfies inequality (2), the algorithm first searches for the minimal square (lines 2-4). Assume a placement region has horizontal length $L_H$ and vertical length $L_V$. If $N_{fast}$ in the region satisfies inequality (2), the algorithm tries to shrink both $L_H$ and $L_V$ by one. The new $N_{fast}$ can be easily computed by subtracting the fast block count on the removed row and column. If the reduced region does not meet inequality (2), the minimum square length $B_{min}$ is obtained. In the next step, the algorithm tries to reshape the region to the minimal near-square, by removing one row or one column on the boundary and checking if the reshaped region still satisfies inequality (2). If both row removing and column removing satisfy the constraint, the solution with more remaining fast blocks will be used.

Figure 1 illustrates the region search process with an example. Assume the design requires $N$=11 CLBs, and the average ratio of fast blocks $\alpha$=0.65. The initial square length $L_V$=$L_H$=$\lceil\sqrt{11/0.65}\rceil$=5. Within this region $N_{fast}$=17>$N$. Then the square is shrinked to $L_V$=$L_H$=4, and $N_{fast}$=14>$N$. However, if the square is shrinked to $L_V$=$L_H$=3, we will have $N_{fast}$<$N$, thus $4 \times 4$ is the minimal square. Step 3 shows that both row reshape and colomn reshape are possible, but row reshape leads to more remaining fast blocks $N_{fast}$=12. Therefore the $3 \times 4$ region becomes the selected region candidate, shown as region A on the FPGA.

Although the region selection process works at any location on the FPGA, it is performed at each corner so as to minimize the distances to I/O pins. Four placement region candidates will be obtained, and the one with the smallest size and highest ratio of fast blocks $N_{fast}/(L_H \times L_V)$ will be chosen (line 9 of Algorithm 1). For example, in Figure 1, region A is selected as it is smaller than region B and has 100% fast blocks.

## 3.2 Scalable NVM-FPGA Placement

After selecting an appropriate region with a sufficient number of fast blocks for the given design, the *scalable NVM-FPGA placement* takes place within the selected region. This section first introduces the proposed NVM-FPGA placement algorithm and then compares it with the state-of-the-art NVM-FPGA placement [8] in terms of complexity to highlight its advantages.

*3.2.1 Scalable Placement Algorithm.* A generic FPGA placement flow is composed of *four* major steps. First, an initial placement is generated as the starting point. Then, the algorithm enters the iterative stage. At each iteration, two blocks are randomly selected to form a swapping trial, which is either accepted or rejected based on pre-defined acceptance conditions. Finally, the algorithm checks whether the current placement process meets the termination condition. The proposed placement algorithm differs from the state-of-the-art NVM-FPGA placement [8] in initial placement generation, swapping block selection, and swapping acceptance condition.

First, the initial placement in the state-of-the-art placement is a globally optimal min-bit-flip (MBF) placement with minimum reconfiguration cost [8]. Such cost is computed bit-by-bit as most NVM-FPGA optimizations employ a read-before-write strategy to reduce NVM writes at the bit level. However, it is unnecessary to start with a time-consuming optimal mapping because the later swapping trials which aim to balance timing, congestion, and reconfiguration cost will destroy the optimality in reconfiguration cost anyway. As a result, the proposed algorithm starts not with the MBF placement but with a random placement, generated by randomly placing all the CLBs on the fast blocks in the selected placement region. This change largely reduces the complexity of the placement algorithm without noticeably degrading its quality.

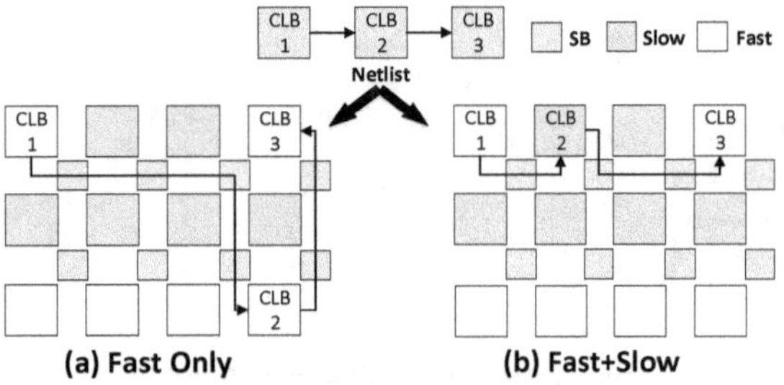


**Figure 2: Benefit of using slow blocks. Block delay becomes longer, but the path length is largely shortened.**

Second, the proposed placement differs from the state-of-the-art in that it considers process variation across different blocks. While the initial placement only uses fast blocks, at the block swapping stage the algorithm allows the use of slow blocks as it offers more placement flexibilities in terms of timing and routablility considerations. Figure 2 shows a sample design with three CLBs and two paths, CLB1→CLB2 and CLB2→CLB3. The placement region has six slow blocks and six fast blocks. Figure 2(a) shows a placement that uses only fast blocks, while in Figure 2(b) the position of CLB2 is swapped to a slow block. This swapping is beneficial because although the block delay of CLB2 becomes longer, the two paths are largely shortened. For this reason, the proposed algorithm allows fast to slow block swapping.

Regarding the swapping acceptance condition, the state-of-the-art uses a cost function to integrates timing, congestion, and reconfiguration cost, and accepts a swapping trial only if the cost becomes lower (i.e., $\Delta Cost < 0$), indicating that the swapping is beneficial. This greedy strategy may end up sticking at a local optimal point. To avoid this undesired case and explore globally for more possible solutions, the proposed algorithm adopts *simulated annealing* [25], which accepts a swapping trial not only when $\Delta Cost < 0$ but also if $e < r^{-\frac{\Delta Cost}{T}}$, wherein $r$ is a random value in $(0, 1)$ and $T$ is the temperature. $T$ decreases as the algorithm proceeds, allowing it to eventually converge to a near-optimal point.

*3.2.2 Placement complexity.* The design space of reconfiguration cost includes three types of flexibilities [8], as illustrated in Figure 3. Assume a design requires $m$ CLBs, the selected placement region includes $n$ CLBs, each CLB contains $v$ LUTs, and each LUT has $k$ inputs among which $l$ are used. The whole design space is:

$$Flex_{\text{Design}} = (2^{k-l} \times \frac{k!}{(k-l)!}) \times (v!) \times (\frac{n!}{(n-m)!}) \quad (3)$$

State-of-the-art NVM-FPGA placement algorithm [8] explores all the three types of flexibilities to generate a globally optimal MBF placement and use it as an initial placement. Its steps and complexity are illustrated in Figure 3. Specifically, it first computes a CLB level reconfiguration cost matrix $R_{CLB}[m][n]$, and then applies the KM algorithm [26] with $O(mn^2)$ complexity to solve the optimal mapping problem. However, computing $R_{CLB}$ is time consuming as each of the $mn$ elements in the matrix is the cost of an optimal mapping at the CLB level, shown as $C_{lut}$ in Figure 3. Generation of $C_{lut}$ consists of KM mapping cost $O(v^3)$ and matrix $R_{LUT}[v][v]$ construction cost. Similarly, each of the $v^2$ elements in $R_{LUT}$ is the cost of an optimal mapping at the input level, shown as $C_{input}$

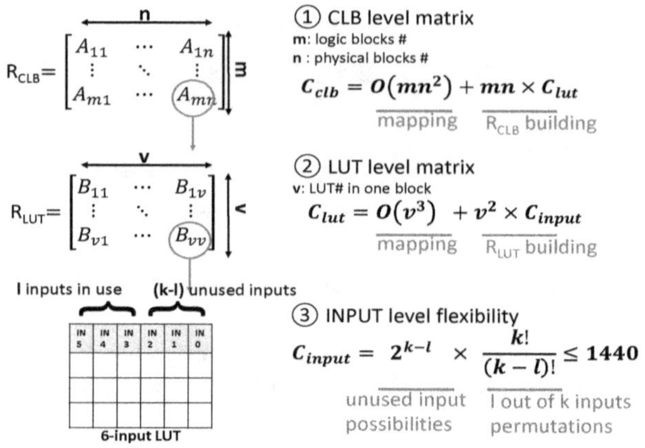


**Figure 3: State-of-the-art placement complexity**

in Figure 3. To compute $C_{input}$, the input level flexibility is fully explored by numerating all possibilities. Each of the $k - l$ unused inputs have two possible values (0 and 1), while the $l$ used inputs have full permutations. For the standard setting of 6-input LUT ($k$=6), the highest possible value of $C_{input}$ is 1440, reached when $l$ is 4 or 5. Considering these three levels of complexities, the overall complexity $C_{design}$ of the state-of-the-art MBF placement is:

$$\begin{aligned} C_{design} &= O(mn^2) + mn \times [O(v^3) + v^2 \times 1440] \\ &= O(mn^2) + O(mnv^3) + 1440 \times O(mnv^2) \quad (4) \end{aligned}$$

The proposed placement algorithm reduces the complexity from two perspectives. First, it starts not with a globally optimal MBF placement but with a random placement, thus completely eliminating the CLB-level overhead (term $O(mn^2)$ in Equation (4)). This also implies that the CLB-level reconfiguration cost matrix $R_{CLB}[m][n]$ does not need to be fully constructed *a priori* but can be computed just-in-time during swapping trials. Specifically, an element $R_{CLB}[i][j]$ is computed only if a swapping trial decides to map $CLB_i$ to $BLK_j$ and if $R_{CLB}[i][j]$ has not been computed yet. Assume $\delta$ is the sparsity of the matrix, the total number of calculated elements in $R_{CLB}[m][n]$ is $\delta \times mn$.

Second, as shown in Equation (4)), the most time consuming part of the placement procedure is the exploration of input-level flexibility ($1440 \times O(mnv^2)$). In the proposed algorithm, such flexibility is not explored in block swapping trials. Instead, direct input mapping is taken when computing $R_{LUT}$, and hence $C_{input} = 1$. Later upon finishing CLB-level and LUT-level mappings, input-level flexibility will be explored. The complexity is $1440 \times mv$ since $m \times v$ LUTs are used in total and each LUT requires up to 1440 trials to find the optimal input-level mapping. The overall complexity of the proposed placement is:

$$\begin{aligned} C'_{design} &= \delta \times mn \times [O(v^3) + v^2 \times 1] + mv \times 1440 \\ &= O(\delta mnv^3) + O(\delta mnv^2) + 1440 \times mv \quad (5) \end{aligned}$$

A comparison between Equations (4) and (5) shows that the proposed placement algorithm improves the state-of-the-art by completely eliminating CLB level-complexity, reducing LUT-level complexity by $1/\delta$ times, and reducing input-level complexity by $nv$ times.

**Table 1: Benchmark circuits**

| No | Benchmark | CLB# | LUT# |
|---|---|---|---|
| 1 | stereovision1 | 1365 | 13066 |
| 2 | stereovision0 | 1479 | 14622 |
| 3 | LU8PEEng | 2583 | 21954 |
| 4 | bgm | 3419 | 30089 |
| 5 | stereovision2 | 3635 | 36341 |
| 6 | LU32PEEng | 8861 | 88608 |
| 7 | mcml | 10436 | 104066 |

**Table 2: Experimental configurations in use**

| No | Schemes | PV | Region | Placement | Block types |
|---|---|---|---|---|---|
| 1 | VTR | - | - | VTR | Fast |
| 2 | VTR+PV | ✓ | - | VTR | Fast+Slow |
| 3 | VTR+PVRS+F | ✓ | ✓ | VTR | Fast |
| 4 | VTR+PVRS | ✓ | ✓ | VTR | Fast+Slow |
| 5 | R&T+PVRS | ✓ | ✓ | R&T | Fast+Slow |
| 6 | Proposed | ✓ | ✓ | Proposed | Fast+Slow |

# 4 EXPERIMENTAL EVALUATION

## 4.1 Experimental Methodology

The proposed placement framework is incorporated into the VTR 7.0 CAD flow [12] for evaluating its impact on placement complexity, design timing, and NVM-FPGA endurance. The experimental FPGA architecture is Stratix IV GX, with a 40nm fabrication library. Each CLB consists of 10 LUTs, and each LUT has 6 inputs. A simulator written in C is used to simulate PV on the FPGA. Normal distribution is applied. The overall fast block ratio $\alpha = 0.8$. The delay models in VTR 7.0 have been modified to reflect the differences in the three types of blocks. Fast blocks still use the standard delay model, while slow blocks are set to be 50% slower than the standard model based on the results of [9]. The delay of dead block is set to infinite.

The largest benchmarks offered by VTR (with 1000+ CLBs) are selected to evaluate the complexity of the proposed algorithm. Benchmark information is listed in Table 1, ranked by design size in ascending order. Six experimental configurations are evaluated, as listed in Table 2. Each configuration is defined by four metrics: process variation (PV), placement region selection, the placement algorithm, and the type of blocks used.

## 4.2 PV Aware Region Selection Evaluation

Our first set of experiments evaluates the proposed PV aware region selection in terms of timing. The first four configurations in Table 2 are compared. "VTR" is the original VTR placement without considering PV in the FPGA. "VTR+PV" considers PV but does not perform region selection. "VTR+PVRS+F" and "VTR+PVRS" perform PV-aware placement region selection. The former uses only fast blocks, while the latter uses both fast and slow blocks.

The results of critical path delay are shown in Table 3. "VTR" serves as the baseline and raw data are displayed, while ratios over the baseline are given for the other three configurations. "VTR+PV" demonstrates the necessity for considering PV in placement. If PV is ignored, the critical path delay is severely increased by 22.7% on average. "VTR+PVRS" and "VTR+PVRS+F" demonstrate the effectiveness of the proposed region selection algorithm in overcoming PV introduced block performance degradation in real chips. They only slightly increase the critical path delay by 4.1% and 6.2% on overage. "VTR+PVRS" outperforms "VTR+PVRS+F" with 2.1% timing improvement, which comes from the opportunities provided by slow blocks in shortening path delays, and is consistent in each benchmark. Accordingly, "VTR+PVRS" will be used as the baseline for the study of placement algorithms.

**Table 3: Critical path delay of three configurations**

| Benchmark | VTR (ns) | VTR+PV (ratio) | VTR+PVRS+F (ratio) | VTR+PVRS (ratio) |
|---|---|---|---|---|
| stereovision1 | 5.608 | 130.8% | 100.0% | 100.0% |
| stereovision0 | 4.438 | 132.0% | 100.0% | 100.0% |
| LU8 | 146.186 | 109.5% | 101.5% | 99.6% |
| bgm | 27.392 | 128.3% | 110.4% | 106.1% |
| stereovision2 | 15.281 | 129.5% | 118.4% | 110.8% |
| LU32 | 147.109 | 118.5% | 105.2% | 105.1% |
| mcml | 106.523 | 109.9% | 107.8% | 107.2% |
| AVE | - | 122.7% | 106.2% | 104.1% |

## 4.3 Scalable Placement Evaluation

Our second set of experiments evaluates the proposed placement algorithm in term of its complexity and its impact on NVM-FPGA endurance and design timing. It is compared with the baseline VTR placement and the state-of-the-art NVM-FPGA placement "R&T" [8]. For a fair comparison, all the placement algorithms are applied in the selected placement region and they all use both fast and slow blocks. To create the reconfiguration scenario similar with [8], six test pairs (TP) are constructed from the benchmarks in Table 1. TP*i* tries to configure benchmark *i* on the FPGA with benchmark *i*+1 being the existing content. For example, *TP*1 is to configure "stereovision1" on the FPGA by modifying existing design "stereovision0".

Table 4 shows a comprehensive comparison among different placement techniques. "VTR+PVRS" is used as the baseline for which raw data are presented, while ratios over the baseline are given for "R&T+PVRS" and "Proposed".

*4.3.1 Complexity evaluation.* The sparsity $\delta$ of the reconfiguration matrix $R_{CLB}[m][n]$ is evaluated to show the efficiency of just-in-time reconfiguration cost computation. As shown in Table 4, most of the test cases have less than 0.5 sparsity. TP6 has the lowest sparsity of 0.302. This confirms the complexity advantage of computing $R_{CLB}$ elements only when necessary.

The execution time of different algorithms is compared, also shown in Table 4. The execution time of "VTR+PVRS" is mainly spent on performing placement trials. It clearly shows an increasing trend as the design size increases. For "R&T+PVRS", its execution time is composed of two parts, the time in generating the initial MBF placement, and the time in performing placement trials. With a larger design size, the execution time of "R&T+PVRS" increases superlinearly; TP1 execution time is 1.38X of "VTR+PVRS", while TP6 execution time is 1.89X of "VTR+PVRS". This reflects the complexity of generating MBF placement, which increases by a factor of $O(n^3)$ theoretically. For large designs, the overhead for generating MBF would be overwhelming. In comparison, "Proposed" integrates reconfiguration cost computation into the placement trial process.

**Table 4: Execution time, reconfiguration cost, and critical path delay of three placements**

| | $\delta$ | Execution time | | | Reconfiguration cost | | | Critical path delay | | |
|---|---|---|---|---|---|---|---|---|---|---|
| | | VTR+PVRS (second) | R&T+PVRS (ratio) | Proposed (ratio) | VTR+PVRS (bit-flip count) | R&T+PVRS (ratio) | Proposed (ratio) | VTR+PVRS (ns) | R&T+PVRS (ratio) | Proposed (ratio) |
| TP1 | 0.666 | 210.8 | 138.0% | 105.3% | 2.91E+05 | 45.9% | 48.3% | 5.608 | 101.9% | 101.7% |
| TP2 | 0.423 | 219.2 | 142.0% | 90.0% | 4.04E+05 | 38.6% | 38.9% | 4.438 | 126.2% | 119.5% |
| TP3 | 0.514 | 755.4 | 144.0% | 100.0% | 7.86E+05 | 41.0% | 68.2% | 145.647 | 106.6% | 105.6% |
| TP4 | 0.403 | 1107.1 | 160.3% | 101.7% | 9.62E+05 | 72.3% | 82.8% | 29.053 | 103.8% | 106.5% |
| TP5 | 0.418 | 965.1 | 167.0% | 98.8% | 8.77E+05 | 25.7% | 25.8% | 16.934 | 107.5% | 107.6% |
| TP6 | 0.302 | 7737.9 | 189.6% | 99.2% | 2.30E+06 | 69.5% | 66.3% | 154.602 | 109.6% | 109.8% |
| AVE | 0.454 | - | 156.8% | 99.1% | - | 48.8% | 55.1% | - | 109.3% | 108.4% |

As the number of swapping trials is more-or-less stable, its execution time is close to "VTR+PVRS" even for large designs. The slight fluctuation is due to variations in swapping trial number and the difference in reconfiguration matrix sparsity.

Overall, this study confirms that the proposed placement is much more scalable than the state-of-the-art NVM-FPGA placement.

*4.3.2 Performance evaluation.* Table 4 also compares the performance of three placement schemes in terms of reconfiguration cost (i.e., the number of NVM writes) and timing. For reconfiguration cost, "R&T+PVRS" achieves the lowest reconfiguration cost of 48.8% on average. This is because the algorithm is based on minimal reconfiguration cost placement "MBF" and it controls the tradeoff process so that the final reconfiguration cost is bounded to MBF. In comparison, the reconfiguration cost of "Proposed" is not bounded to MBF because both the initial placement and swapping trials are randomly generated. While "Proposed" outperforms "R&T+PVRS" for some test cases such as TP6, its average reconfiguration cost is 6.3% more than "R&T+PVRS".

For critical path delay, "R&T+PVRS" shows a 9.3% overhead and "Proposed" only has 8.4% overhead on average. "Proposed" achieves slightly better timing because the weight of timing cost is constant in its cost model (which is used for evaluating swapping trials). However, "R&T" gradually reduces the weight of timing cost to prioritize reconfiguration cost towards the end of placement.

Overall, for the proposed NVM-FPGA algorithm, the small loss in reconfiguration cost is acceptable considering its better timing and significant advantage in complexity.

## 5 CONCLUSIONS

A scalable and process variation (PV) aware NVM-FPGA placement framework has been proposed in this paper. Blocks in the FPGA are classified into three types to model the impact of PV, and the proposed framework chooses a qualified placement region considering block variations. Furthermore, a scalable NVM-FPGA placement has been developed to balance reconfiguration cost and timing, with dramatically reduced complexity compared with state-of-the-art schemes. Experiments based on large VTR benchmarks show that the proposed scheme effectively balances reconfiguration cost and timing without introducing noticeable execution time overhead on top of VTR placement. This work potentially increases the popularity and practicality of NVM-FPGAs.

## ACKNOWLEDGMENT

This work is partially supported by NSF Award #1527464.

## REFERENCES


[1] G. Dai, Y. Chi, Y. Wang, and H. Yang, "FPGP: Graph processing framework on FPGA a case study of breadth-first search," in *FPGA*, pp. 105–110, 2016.
[2] C.-H. Chen, P.-C. Hsiu, T.-W. Kuo, C.-L. Yang, and C.-Y. M. Wang, "Age-based PCM wear leveling with nearly zero search cost," in *DAC*, pp. 453–458, 2012.
[3] Actel, *Understanding soft and firm errors in semiconductor devices*, 2002.
[4] W. Zhao, E. Belhaire, C. Chappert, and P. Mazoyer, "Spin transfer torque STT-MRAM–based runtime reconfiguration FPGA circuit," *TECS*, vol. 9, Oct. 2009.
[5] X. Tang, G. Kim, P.-E. Gaillardon, and G. D. Micheli, "A study on the programming structures for RRAM-based FPGA architectures," *TCS I*, vol. 63, Apr. 2016.
[6] Y. Chen, J. Zhao, and Y. Xie, "3D-nonfar: Three-dimensional non-volatile FPGA architecture using phase change memory," in *ISLPED*, pp. 55–60, 2010.
[7] http://www.itrs2.net/2013-itrs.html, *ITRS*, 2013.
[8] Y. Xue, P. Cronin, C. Yang, and J. Hu, "Fine-tuning CLB placement to speed up reconfigurations in NVM-based FPGAs," in *FPL*, pp. 1–8, 2015.
[9] Q. Lou, M. Zhao, L. Ju, C. J. Xue, J. Hu, and Z. Jia, "Runtime and reconfiguration dual-aware placement for SRAM-NVM hybrid FPGAs," in *NVMSA*, pp. 1–6, 2017.
[10] M. Yabuuchi and K. Kobayashi, "Evaluation of FPGA design guardband caused by inhomogeneous NBTI degradation considering process variations," in *FPT*, pp. 1–6, 2010.
[11] L. Shi, Y. Di, M. Zhao, C. J. Xue, K. Wu, and E. H.-M. Sha, "Exploiting process variation for write performance improvement on NAND flash memory storage systems," *TVLSI*, vol. 24, Feb. 2015.
[12] J. Luu, J. Goeders, M. Wainberg, A. Somerville, T. Yu, K. Nasartschuk, M. Nasr, S. Wang, T. Liu, N. Ahmed, K. B. Kent, J. Anderson, J. Rose, and V. Betz, "VTR 7.0: Next Generation Architecture and CAD System for FPGAs," *TRTS*, vol. 7, Jun. 2014.
[13] www.actel.com/documents/PA3HB.pdf, *Proasic3 flash family FPGAs handbook, Actel*, 2011.
[14] K. Huang, R. Zhao, and Y. Lian, "Racetrack memory-based nonvolatile storage elements for multicontext FPGAs," *TVLSI*, vol. 25, Sep. 2015.
[15] Y. Xue, P. Cronin, C. Yang, and J. Hu, "Routing path reuse maximization for efficient NV-FPGA reconfiguration," in *ASP-DAC*, pp. 360–365, 2016.
[16] Y. Xue, C. Yang, and J. Hu, "Age-aware logic and memory co-placement for RRAM-FPGAs," in *DAC*, pp. 1–6, 2017.
[17] K. Kuhn, "Managing process variation in Intel's 45nm CMOS technology," *Intel Technology Journal*, vol. 12, Jun. 2008.
[18] W. Zhang and T. Li, "Characterizing and mitigating the impact of process variations on phase change based memory systems," in *MICRO*, pp. 1–12, 2009.
[19] Q. Li, L. Shi, Y. Di, Y. Du, C. J. Xue, and E. H. Sha, "Exploiting process variation for read performance improvement on LDPC based flash memory storage systems," in *ICCD*, pp. 681–684, 2017.
[20] M. Zhao, L. Jiang, Y. Zhang, and C. J. Xue, "SLC-enabled wear leveling for MLC PCM considering process variation," in *DAC*, pp. 1–6, 2014.
[21] Y. Xu, L. Liu, M. Chan, and J. Watt, "Process variation impact on FPGA configuration memory," in *ISQED*, pp. 613–616, 2009.
[22] S. Golshan, A. Khajeh, H. Homayoun, E. Bozorgzadeh, A. Eltawil, and F. J. Kurdahi, "Reliability-aware placement in SRAM-based fpga for voltage scaling realization in the presence of process variations," in *CODES+ISSS*, pp. 257–266, 2011.
[23] A. Ghosh, R. M. Rao, C.-T. Chuang, and R. B. Brown, "On-chip process variation detection and compensation using delay and slew-rate monitoring circuits," in *ISQED*, pp. 815–820, 2008.
[24] C.-Y. Chen, H.-C. Shih, C.-W. Wu, C.-H. Lin, and P.-F. Chiu, "RRAM defect modeling and failure analysis based on march test and a novel squeeze-search scheme," *IEEE Transactions on Computers*, vol. 64, Jan. 2015.
[25] S. Kirkpatrick, C. D. Gelatt, Jr., and M. P. Vecchi, "Optimization by simulated annealing," *Science*, vol. 220, pp. 671–680, 1983.
[26] H. Kuhn, "The hungarian method for the assignment problem," in *NRLQ*, pp. 83–97, Mar. 1955.

# Functional Obfuscation of Hardware Accelerators through Selective Partial Design Extraction onto an Embedded FPGA

Bo Hu, Jingxiang Tian, Mustafa Shihab, Gaurav Rajavendra Reddy, William Swartz, Yiorgos Makris, Benjamin Carrion Schaefer, Carl Sechen
{bo.hu,jxt122130,mustafa.shihab,gaurav.reddy,bill-swartz,yiorgos.makris,schaferb,carl.sechen}@utdallas.edu
Department of Electrical Computer Engineering, The University of Texas at Dallas,Richardson, TX, U.S.A, 75080-3021

## ABSTRACT

The protection of Intellectual Property (IP) has emerged as one of the most serious areas of concern in the semiconductor industry. To address this issue, we present a method and architecture to map selective portions of a design, given as a behavioral description for High-Level Synthesis (HLS) to a high-security embedded Field-Programmable Gate Array (eFPGA). In this manner, only the end-user has access to the full functionality of the chip. Using six benchmark circuits, we show that our approach is effective. In all cases, the Time-To-Break (*TTB*) is so long (at least 8 million hours) that for all practical purposes the designs are secure, while incurring area overheads of around 5%. Further, latencies were only slightly increased, while the computation times are under one minute.

## CCS CONCEPTS

• **Security and privacy → Security in hardware**; **Hardware-based security protocols**;

## KEYWORDS

hardware security; obfuscation; high level synthesis; embedded FPGA

**ACM Reference format:**
Bo Hu, Jingxiang Tian, Mustafa Shihab, Gaurav Rajavendra Reddy, William Swartz, and Yiorgos Makris, Benjamin Carrion Schaefer, Carl Sechen. 2019. Functional Obfuscation of Hardware Accelerators through Selective Partial Design Extraction onto an Embedded FPGA. In *Proceedings of Great Lakes Symposium on VLSI 2019, Tysons Corner, VA, USA, May 9–11, 2019 (GLSVLSI '19)*, 6 pages. ACM, New York, NY, USA.
https://doi.org/10.1145/3299874.3317992

## 1 INTRODUCTION

Contemporary semiconductor manufacturing largely follows a fabless business model wherein third-party foundries are provided with the source files (i.e., in GDSII format) of an integrated circuit (IC) design and are contracted to fabricate it. Considering the geopolitical position of the majority of the semiconductor manufacturing industry, this fabless model incurs an inherent security and trustworthiness risk. More specifically, the entire intellectual property (IP) of an IC design is exposed to the-potentially untrusted-foundry or any rogue element therein and is, therefore, subject to malicious manipulation and/or theft. As a result, protecting sensitive parts of the design (*e.g.*, trade secrets, classified data/algorithms, competitive advantage circuits, etc.) and ensuring functional integrity of the received ICs becomes very challenging. Furthermore, such security and trust concerns continue to exist after an IC is deployed in the field of operation. Indeed, reverse engineering may still reveal the secret IP contained in an IC, while dormant malicious logic can be activated post-deployment in order to compromise its functional integrity. Accordingly, design obfuscation and hardware Trojan solutions are urgently required.

These fundamental development and supply chain changes have led to serious security and trustworthy concerns, as these companies now do not have control over the manufacturing process and hence do not control how many ICs the foundry has actually manufactured. To address this issue we propose to extract selectively parts of an ASIC design and map it into an embedded FPGA (eFPGA) with the objective of obfuscating the functionality of the design.

Intelligent attacks, such as the use of a Boolean Satisfiability (SAT) solver [14], have been developed and compromised most early obfuscation schemes. This, has resulted in an on-going race between new defenses and new attacks, reinforcing the need for further research in this area [4, 5, 16]. In this work, we utilize a design obfuscation approach that omits parts of it from the fabricated silicon and reinstates it via post-manufacturing programming. We will show that using FPGA-style lookup tables (LUTs) to implement the omitted portion of the function provides high security levels.

The main contribution of this work is an algorithm to extract a portion of a design to be mapped onto the eFPGA, such that there is a limited area and delay overhead while providing a very high security benefit.

## 2 RELATED WORK

The obfuscation based approach transforms a given circuit into a functionally equivalent circuit that is significantly more difficult (ideally impossible) to reverse engineer. Some examples include the dedicated obfuscation of DSP circuits by performing high-level transformations during the design stage and inserting multiplexers in the datapath controlled by a FSM [4].

Due to the significance of the targeted problem, the last decade has seen a flurry of research activity in a number of different directions. Concepts such as Active Metering [2, 11], Logic Encryption [10, 17], State Obfuscation [3], Design Camouflaging [9], Split Manufacturing [8], and many others have been introduced. Each such solution comes with each own strengths and limitations and, to date, no single solution has been successful in addressing the security


*GLSVLSI '19, May 9–11, 2019, Tysons Corner, VA, USA*

ACM ISBN 978-1-4503-6252-8/19/05.
https://doi.org/10.1145/3299874.3317992

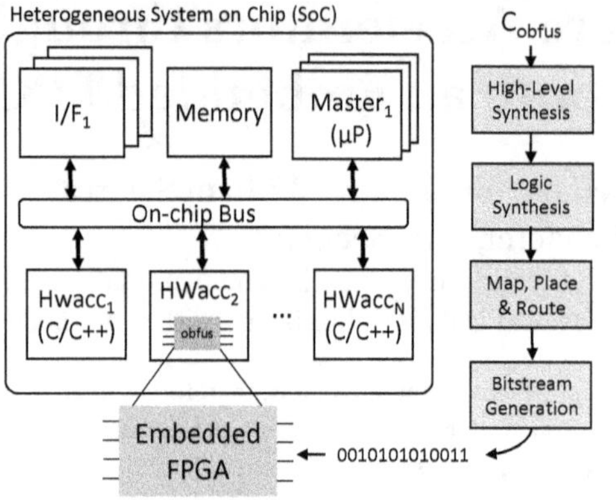


**Figure 1: Design obfuscation via post-fabrication programming of an embedded FPGA (eFPGA) of a portion of a dedicated hardware accelerator.**

and trust challenges in a cost-effective manner. Split manufacturing, for example, divides the design into front end of line (FEOL) and back end of line (BEOL) and uses different foundries for each part, so that the entire design is never exposed. Yet two foundries are required, along with additional logistics for completing the design. Design time and performance overhead is also potentially incurred. Similarly, design camouflaging through the use of library cells that contain decoy elements can make reverse engineering far more difficult (yet still not impossible) but it also incurs significant overhead and does not protect the GDSII file from an attacker at the foundry. Logic encryption and state obfuscation embed a design within a larger space, wherein only a correct key will yield the correct functionality. These solutions are very well studied and understood, yet when applied at scale they do incur significant overhead. Furthermore, an unlocked IC is still subject to reverse engineering, unless additional costly provisions are taken in order to hide the key or individualize it per fabricated IC.

Closer to our work, the authors in [14] proposed to implement dedicated functions using reconfigurable logic to obfuscate the design and show an example of obfuscating the instruction decode unit of a LEON2 open source SPARC V8 architecture processor. Their approach is nevertheless ad-hoc. In [16] the authors present a method to extract at the gate-netlist level different paths and map their gates to non-volatile spin transfer torque (STT) based reconfigurable LUTs. Although a promising approach, it is currently not feasible to fabricate these types of hybrid circuits. The authors in [13] also extract at the gate-netlist level and map the obfuscation part to the transistors in a fine-grained embedded FPGA.

Our work is different from the previous work in that we propose a design flow for mapping different design portions at the behavioral level and hence can understand the security vs. overhead trade-offs early on in the design flow.

## 3 EMBEDDED FPGA

The obfuscated portions of a system design, determined by the algorithms presented in this work, can be mapped to any embedded FPGA (eFPGA). There are multiple commercial eFPGAs on the market. The most notable vendors include Achronix [1] and Quicklogic [7]. These eFPGAs are based on traditional 4-input, 1-output LUTs and can contain multiple hard macros such as embedded DSP modules and memories.

The key issue is then how to find an ideal portion of a design, given as behavioral decription for high-level synthesis (HLS), to map onto an eFPGA [15] to enable effective design obfuscation.

**Problem Formulation:** Given a behavioral description $C$ to be synthesized as an ASIC, selectively extract different portions of $C$ to be mapped onto the eFPGA, such that $C = C_{ASIC} \cup C_{eFPGA}$, and such that by extracting different $C_{eFPGA}$, a unique list of obfuscated designs ($D_{obfusi}$) are obtained, $D_{obfus}List = \{D_{obfus1}, D_{obfus2}, \ldots, D_{obfusn}\}$, with unique area, latency and security trade-offs, with $D_{obfusi} = \{A_i, L_i, S_i\}$, where $A_i$ is the area, $L_i$ the latency and $S_i$ the security metric. Out of all $D_{obfus}List$, we are only interested in the pareto-optimal ($D_{obfus}(opt)$), where a Pareto-optimal design can be defined as a design in which it is impossible to improve one metric without making at least one of the other metrics worse.

The fundamental concept behind using an eFPGA for design obfuscation is shown in Fig. 1. Specifically, we propose to replace the sensitive parts of a design, which we wish to withhold from an untrusted foundry, with the eFPGA. After the chips are fabricated and received from the foundry, the withheld design portions are programmed into the eFPGA fabric to complete the IC functionality. This idea holds great potential in addressing both IP protection and design integrity concerns.

Without the programming bits in place, the functionality of the eFPGA cannot be determined. For example, when the layout of a design is in the untrusted foundry or when a chip is not programmed, the eFPGA block has no meaningful functionality and the required program cannot be extracted, as it does not exist. This work assumes that the bitstream is encrypted, similar to commercial FPGAs and hence cannot be reverse engineered nor copied.

## 4 SECURITY METRIC

In order to successfully map different portions of a circuit to the eFPGA, we need a security metric that quickly and effectively reveals how secure the resultant circuit is, in addition to the area and performance overheads associated with it. Approximate area and performance overheads can be obtained from the HLS tool once $C_{ASIC}$ and $C_{eFPGA}$ are synthesized into RTL. Thus, a security metric ($S$) is required such that after HLS our proposed method can determine the security level of each configuration.

For example, if only a single-line of $C$ code is mapped to an eFPGA block, such as a large multiplier, an attacker might reasonably try to guess that a single operator was being obfuscated. Therefore, in the context of HLS, a key aspect of obfuscation is the number of operators being assigned to an eFPGA block. Another important factor is the number of cells to be implemented in the eFPGA, as larger numbers of cells greatly impairs any possible SAT-based (or brute-force) attack. A SAT-based attack must enumerate all possible cells (each "cell" being implemented by one LUT) in the eFPGA. Thus, we use the product of the number of cells ($cell_i$) and the number of operators ($op_i$) as the security cost function ($S_i$) for each obfuscated design ($D_{obfusi}$):

$$S_i = cell_i \times op_i \quad (1)$$

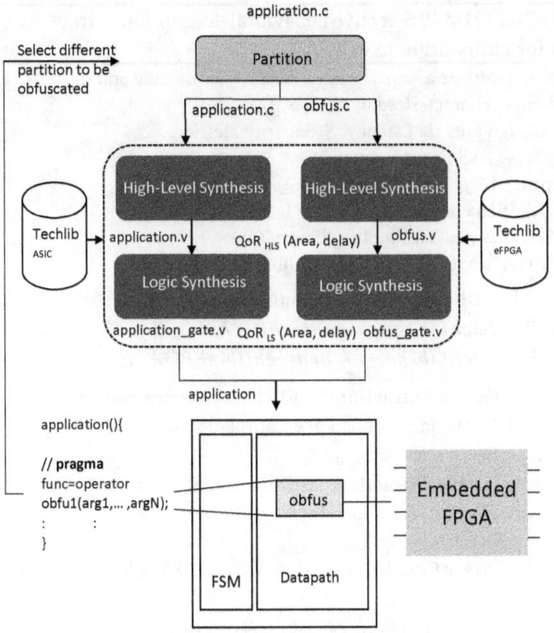


**Figure 2: Design obfuscation design methodology starting from a behavioral description for HLS.**

After we obtain the pareto-optimal designs ($D_{obfus}(opt)$) using the security metric in Eq. 1, we will select one of those designs with an acceptable area overhead and compute the time-to-break ($TTB$) for both a SAT-based and brute-force based attack. The $TTB$ for a SAT-based attack is given by:

$$TTB_{SBA} = 100^{cell_i} \times max(bitstreamload_i, executetime_i) \quad (2)$$

Here we conservatively assume that each LUT can only implement 100 different logic functions. We further conservatively ignore the substantial obfuscation due to the unknown (to the attacker) switch-box routing. $Bistreamload_i$ is the time it takes to load the new bitstream to the eFPGA, and $executetime_i$, the execution time of a single test vector. Here, $bitstreamload_i = Bitstream_i \times clockperiod$ and $executetime_i = latency_i \times clockperiod$, where the latency is in clock cycles and the clock period is the inverse of the operating frequency.

Besides a SAT-based attack, a brute-force attack is also possible. We assume that the attacker has knowledge of the eFPGA, and knows how to generate a bitstream but does not know which bitstream configurations lead to a valid circuit (a set of configured logic gates and their interconnections). In this type of attack, the following steps are iteratively applied: 1) a bitstream is generated, 2) the bitstream is loaded into the eFPGA block and 3) at least one test vector is executed to determine if the configuration is valid or not. This test is indispensable but not sufficient. In the case that a valid output is generated, then other test vectors would need to be applied to fully guarantee the correctness of the complete circuit. Assuming one circuit portion mapped to an eFPGA obtained from $C_eFPGA$, requiring a *bitstream* to be configured:

$$TTB_{BFA} = 2^{bitstream_i} \times max(bitstreamload_i, executetime_i) \quad (3)$$

**ALGORITHM 1:** Function encapsulation

$C_{obfus\_single}$: New generated Behavioral description
*sub_module*: obfuscated module to be mapped to eFPGA
*top_module*: top module to be mapped to ASIC
**input:** $C_{orig}$ *Behavioral description*
/* **Code Annotation** : annotate by pragma */
**while** *(line* $\in C_{orig}$*)* **do**
  annotate by /* pragma forloop */ or
  /* pragma if-else */ or
  /* pragma operation line */ ;
**end**
/* **FuncEncp:** Function encapsulation */
**for** *( each pragma* $\in C_{orig}$*)* **do**
  generate *sub_module*;
  generate *top_module*;
**end**
**output:** set of pairs $\{C_{obfus\_single}\}$ = { *sub_module*, *top_module*}

where $TTB_{BFA}$ is a function of the bitstream size (*bitstream*), which is in turn a function of $C_{eFPGA}$, since the larger the portion of the application mapped to the eFPGA, the larger the bitstream becomes.

## 5 OBFUSCATION DESIGN METHODOLOGY

This section describes the methodology used to find which portion or portions of a behavioral description for HLS should be mapped to an eFPGA block, trading off a limited amount of area/power overhead for a high level of security. The proposed obfuscation method starts with a library pre-characterization step for the ASIC and eFPGA, based on the technology that the design team is targeting. This is important to get accurate area and delay information right after HLS. The results of this pre-characterization step is a technology library, which is in turn used by our selective extraction method. It then proceeds, following a divide and conquer strategy, by selecting individual sections of the behavioral descriptions and mapping them onto the eFPGA block. Finally, it merges all the results to obtain the best solutions. The next subsections describe these main steps in detail, as explained in Algorithm 2.

### 5.1 Pre-characterization and Library Generate

HLS can be defined as the process of converting an untimed behavioral description into a Register Transfer Level (RTL) description that can efficiently execute it. HLS executes three main steps: Resource allocation, scheduling and binding. In the scheduling step, the synthesizer schedules the different operations in the code based on the data dependencies and delay information of each operator.

Thus, in order for the synthesizer to successfully schedule operations in a control step, the synthesizer needs to know the delay of each functional unit (FU). For this purpose, commercial HLS tools provide library characterizers which extract the area and delay information of every basic primitive for the target technology/eFPGA.

Therefore, the technology library of the ASIC and the eFPGA block are generated in this pre-characterization stage. This allows our method to use a commercial HLS tool and get accurate preliminary results of how mapping different portions of the code onto the eFPGA affects the overall area and performance. We call this $QoR_{HLS}$ (Quality of results).

This step only needs to be executed once, unless the target technology changes. Once the technology libraries for the ASIC and eFPGA are generated (lines 2-3 in Algorithm 2), our proposed method can continue by selectively extracting different portions of the behavioral description and quickly quantifying the effect of this extraction on the area, delay and security of the circuit.

## 5.2 Selective extraction

Selecting the portion to obfuscate at the behavioral level has the advantage of allowing the design team to know exactly which portion of the design is obfuscated, whereas this is not straightforward at the gate-netlist, where the design team might lose intuition on what exactly is obfuscated. Fig. 2 and lines 4-31 in Algorithm 2 highlights how the selective extraction method works, which is composed of three main steps.

**Step 1: Function encapsulation**

The first step, called function encapsulation, starts by selecting individual lines of code from the behavioral description and encapsulates them into a functional operator (lines 8-11 of Algorithm 1). HLS tools have great controllability mainly through the use of pragmas. This allows the designer to control how to synthesize arrays (*e.g.*, RAM or registers), loops (*e.g.*, unrolling, partially unrolled or pipelined) and functions (*e.g.*, inline, goto or function operator). This last option is used in the proposed method. Synthesizing functions as operators allows users to encapsulate functions as functional units. The original idea behind this is to allow the user to control the amount of parallelism in the resultant circuit, as *inlining* generates a hardware block for every function call, and *goto* creates a single hardware block for the function. Encapsulating a function into an operator allows users to control the number of instantiations for the given function and thus the amount of parallelism. This is typically done by specifying the instantiation number in a constraint file.

**Pragma annotation :** Pragma annotation seeks to discover all *mappable* lines that qualify for obfuscation, where *mappable* implies a line that can be isolated and mapped as functional operator. We annotate the pragma to all *mappable* lines by analyzing the code syntax as 4 types:

Type 1 is a single operation line which contains an assignment instruction. This is often a major part of C code examples and often is part of the other syntax types (examples are lines 9, 12 and 15 for $C_{orig}$ in Fig. 3).

Type 2 applies to $for\ loop$ syntax. The start and end of a $for\ loop$ must lie within one module, however, pragmas internal to a $for\ loop$ can be placed in a sub-module. An example is lines 2-13 for $C_{orig}$ in Fig. 3).

Type 3 is an $if or if-else$ condition. The start and end of an $if$ or $if - else$ condition must lie within one module, however, pragmas internal to $if$ or $if - else$ condition can be placed in a sub-module. An example is lines 5-10 for $C_{orig}$ in Fig. 3).

Type 4 represents all other syntax that is not qualified to be mapped to the eFPGA, for example, the main function, global or local variable declarations, and comments.

After each line is classified into one of the above 4 types, the three pragma types are annotated as shown in lines 3-5 in Algorithm 1.

---

**ALGORITHM 2:** Selective behavioral description extraction for obfuscation in eFPGA

Define $Dobfus$ as a partitioned design (sub-module and top module) characterized by $A$, $L$, $S$, $f_{target}$
$A$: Design area $L$: Latency $S$: Security metric
$f_{target}$: HLS target frequency
**input:** $\{C_{orig}, Lib_{ASIC}, Lib_{eFPGA}, f_{target}\}$
$C_{orig}$: Behavioral description to be obfuscated
$ASIC\_db$: ASIC technology library (db)
$eFPGA\_db$: eFPGA technology library (db)

1 /* **Pre-Characterization :** Initialization*/
2 $HLSTechLib_{ASIC} = gentechlib(ASIC\_db)$;
3 $HLSTechLib_{eFPGA} = gentechlib(eFPGA\_db)$;
4 /* **Selective Extraction:** Step1 Function encapsulation */
5 Call Algorithm 1 ( Function encapsulation )
6 /*produces a set $\{C_{obfus\_single}\}$ */
7 /* **Selective Extraction:** Step2 Individual Extraction*/
8 **for** *each* $C_{obfus\_single}$ **do**
9   $D_{eFPGA} = hls\_eFPGA(C_{eFPGA}, f_{target}, HLSTechLib_{eFPGA})$;
10   $D_{ASIC} = hls\_asic(C_{ASIC}, f_{target}, HLSTechLib_{ASIC})$;
11   $D_{obfus\_single} = \{D_{eFPGA}, D_{ASIC}\}$ ;
12   **if** $A_{total} > A_{max}$) **then**
13     discard $D_{obfus\_single}$;
14   **end**
15 **end**
16 /* **Selective Extraction:** Step3 Results Merging*/
17 **for** *each* $C_{obfus\_single}$ **do**
18   $C_{obfus\_merged} = C_{obfus\_single}$;
19   **for** *each subsequent* $C_{obfus\_single}$ **do**
20     /* Merging*/
21     $C_{obfus\_merged} = C_{obfus\_single} \cup C_{obfus\_merged}$;
22     $D_{eFPGA\_merged} = hls\_eFPGA(C_{eFPGA\_merged}, f_{target},$
23     $HLSTechLib_{eFPGA})$;
24     $D_{ASIC\_merged} = hls\_asic(C_{ASIC\_merged}, f_{target}, HLSTechLib_{ASIC})$;
25     **if** $A_{total} <= A_{max}$) **then**
26       $D_{obfus\_merged} = \{D_{eFPGA\_merged}, D_{ASIC\_merged}\}$ ;
27     **else**
28       $C_{obfus\_merged} -= C_{obfus\_single}$;
29     **end**
30   **end**
31 **end**
**output:** $Dobfus_{opt} = pareto-optimal\{D_{obfus\_merged}\}$;

---

These pragma annotated lines can be isolated and mapped as a functional operator.

**Function encapsulation:** We group the *mappable* lines with pragmas into a new function with the appropriate attributes and types (*e.g.*, lines 12-21 of $C_{obfus}$ in Fig. 3). Then, each *mappable* line is encapsulated using the functional operator option pragma (*e.g.*, line 12 in $C_{obfus}$ in Fig. 3). Also, local variables inside the

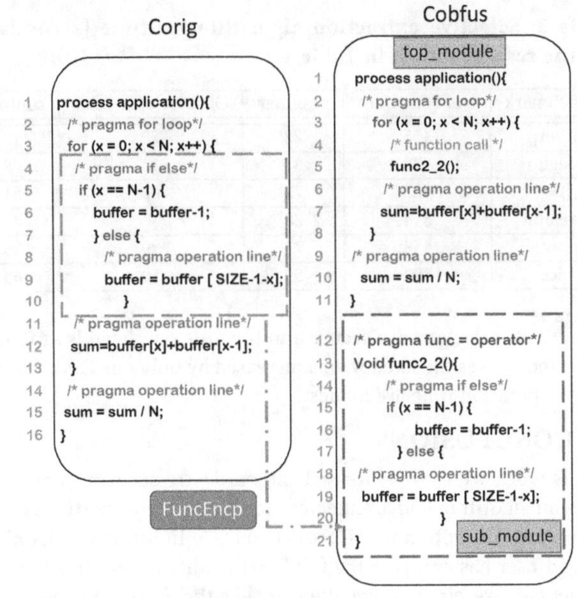


**Figure 3: Example of function encapsulation.**

new C function need to be declared as global variations in order to maintain the functionality. We call this step function encapsulation (FuncEncp).

**Step 2: Individual Obfuscation**

Since the functional operator option is used to encapsulate the portion of the behavioral description to be mapped to the eFPGA, as shown in Fig. 2, once the selected portion is automatically encapsulated into a function and the functional operator pragma specified, two separate files are generated when the behavioral description is parsed. One file with the main functionality of the application (application.c or *top_module*) and another with the part to be obfuscated (obfus.c or *sub_module*). These files can be in turn synthesized separately. The HLS proceeds with *top_module* (application.c) using the ASIC technology library ($HLSTechLib_{ASIC}$) and the encapsulated portion (obfus.c) using the eFPGA technology library ($HLSTechLib_{eFPGA}$), both generated in the library pre-characterization stage.

The result is two RTL descriptions; one for the top module (application.v) and one for the encapsulated module (obfus.v), and a report file with the quality of results ($QoR_{HLS}$) indicating the area of each module and latency. Our method also computes the security cost function $S_i$ (Eq. 1) of this configuration. This allows our method to determine the overhead of mapping specific portions of code to the eFPGA quickly as well as measuring the added security.

Experimental results have shown that the $QoR_{HLS}$ is good enough to guide our explorer in finding the best mappings, but that the actual area and delay information reported is often not too accurate (on average, we have observed differences of 20-30%). Thus, as shown in Fig. 2, the flow is extended to allow a full logic synthesis for the RTL code generated after HLS. The logic synthesis output is a gate netlist for the two modules and a new more accurate report ($QoR_{LS}$). This, allows us to more accurately characterize the obfuscated architecture.

Our proposed method iteratively considers each line of C code as the obfuscated portion and re-synthesizes it. If the area overhead

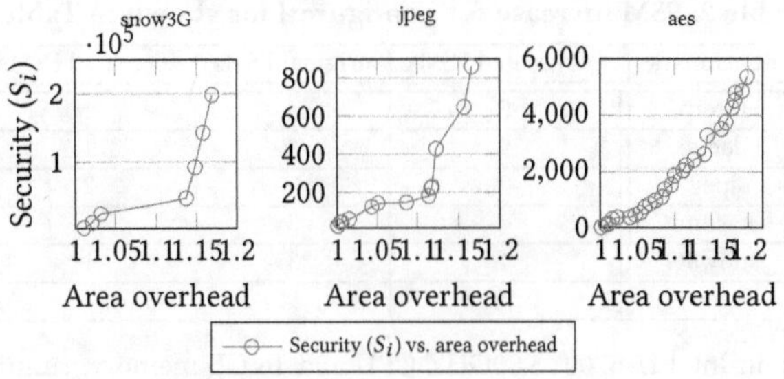


**Figure 4: Area overhead vs. security cost function (Eq. 1) for pareto-optimal designs.**

**Table 1: Area overhead vs. security metric (TTB) for both brute-force and SAT-based attack [hours]**

| Benchmark | area overhead [%] | $TTB_{bfa}[hrs]$ | $TTB_{sba}[hrs]$ |
|---|---|---|---|
| interp | 4 | $2^{65}$ | $2^{56}$ |
| decim | 7.8 | $2^{32}$ | $2^{23}$ |
| jpeg | 5.1 | $2^{1594}$ | $2^{134}$ |
| kasumi | 4.8 | $2^{1187}$ | $2^{169}$ |
| snow3G | 3.2 | $2^{201}$ | $2^{119}$ |
| aes | 4.7 | $2^{321}$ | $2^{70}$ |

exceeds a specified value (lines 13-15 and lines 25-29 in Algorithm 2), then this line will not be considered for inclusion in the obfuscated portion.

**Step 3: Merging of Results**

Our proposed method continues by merging the results obtained in step 1, whereby each result is due to the obfuscation of a single line of C code. In this step, multiple lines of C code are considered for possible concurrent obfuscation. To achieve this, the proposed method grabs each valid single obfuscated line, in turn, and iteratively seeks to merge additional subsequent obfuscated lines of C code. Once the area constraint would be violated, merging ceases and the merging process starts over with the next valid single line of obfuscated C code (lines 19-30 in Algorithm 2). Note that each single valid line of obfuscated C code is trial merged with subsequent lines of obfuscated C code until the area constraints are violated. This means that there may be considerable overlap, in terms of lines of obfuscated C code, between the various mergings. However, this design space will be significantly pruned, retaining only the Pareto-optimal points, after considering the area overhead, delay overhead and security of each merging.

## 6 EXPERIMENTAL RESULTS

Different computationally intensive applications, amiable to hardware acceleration, were selected in order to test our proposed method. For this purpose, six SystemC benchmarks from the freely available Synthesizable SystemC Benchmark suite S2CBench [12] were used. In particular, they are : 3-stage *interpolation* filter, 5-stage *decimation* filter, *jpeg* encoder, *snow3G* stream cipher, *kasumi* block cipher used in mobile communications and *aes*.

The HLS tool used is CyberWorkBench from NEC [6] and the target technology is Globalfoundries 65nm. The HLS target frequency is fixed in all cases to 200MHz and the logic synthesis tool used is Synopsys's Design Compiler. The experiments are conducted

**Table 2: FSM increase for configurations shown in Table 1**

| Benchmark | obfuscated FSMs | original FSMs | increased FSMs |
|---|---|---|---|
| interp | 5 | 4 | 1 |
| decim | 9 | 8 | 1 |
| jpeg | 48 | 46 | 2 |
| kasumi | 4 | 3 | 1 |
| snow3G | 4 | 3 | 1 |
| aes | 10 | 9 | 1 |

on an Intel i7-6700 3.50GHZ CPU and 16 GB memory, running CentOS 7.0. It should be noted that in order to get accurate results, the results presented are those reported after logic synthesis.

Fig. 4 shows the Pareto-optimal trade-off curve design space exploration results for benchmarks *snow3G, jpeg* and *aes* as an example of area overhead versus security cost function. The y-axis represents the security cost function (Eq. 1) when different portions of the behavioral description are mapped onto the eFPGA. The area overhead was restricted to 20 percent more than the original circuit size. It shows, as expected, a relationship between the size of the circuit mapped to the eFPGA block and the security. The larger the portions of the circuit mapped to the eFPGA block, the more secure the circuit becomes.

Table 1 lists area overhead versus the $TTB$ security metric for both brute-force and SAT-based attacks for the six benchmarks used. We select the obfuscated designs ($D_{obfus}$) with the area overhead fixed at around 5% from the Pareto-optimal configurations as an example to show the $TTB$ in hours. $TTB$ is obtained from Eq. 2 and Eq. 3 in Section 4 where bitstream size ($bitstream_i$), logic cell number ($cell_i$) and $latency_i$ are obtained from *QoR* of the logic synthesis step. In each case, for all practical purposes, it would not be possible for an attacker to reverse engineer the design.

One additional dimension that Fig. 4 does not cover is the performance overhead introduced by mapping a portion of the design to the eFPGA. In order to simplify the analysis, Table 2 summarizes the increase in FSMs for configurations shown in Table 1. In all cases, the target operating frequency of 200MHz could be met, as we provided the HLS tools with the detailed technology libraries of the ASIC and eFPGA, and hence the scheduling phase of the HLS process can insert more or less logic circuits in a single step so that the 5ns maximum delay (1/200MHz) is not violated. The performance degradation is thus observed as the number of FSMs required to produce a new output, as the extra delay introduced from the eFPGA block can force more scheduling steps. Table 2 shows the FSM increase of the six benchmarks. Only one additional state is needed after obfuscation for 5 of the 6 benchmarks.

In Table 3, the second column is the number of lines of C code in the benchmarks. The third column is the number of pragmas, or candidate code lines that could be obfuscated. The fourth column is the number of lines of code implemented in the eFPGA, for the results in Table 1. The last column shows the running time of our proposed design space exploration method for the results in Table 1, where in this case the run time of the HLS process accounts for 25% of the total runtime while the logic synthesis accounts for the remaining 75%. In all cases, the $TTB$ is so long that for all practical

**Table 3: Selective extraction algorithm runtime [seconds] for the results shown in Table 1**

| Benchmark | # of code lines | pragma# | Obf.# of code lines | runtime |
|---|---|---|---|---|
| interp | 155 | 28 | 22 | 18 |
| decim | 433 | 34 | 13 | 22 |
| jpeg | 482 | 72 | 62 | 51 |
| kasumi | 314 | 28 | 4 | 25 |
| snow3G | 458 | 73 | 6 | 26 |
| aes | 892 | 59 | 10 | 64 |

purposes the designs are secure and the area overhead is around 5%. In most cases the latency was increased by only one FSM, while the computation time are modest.

## 7 CONCLUSIONS

In this work we have addressed the hardware security problem using an algorithm and architecture to map selective portions of a behavioral description for HLS to an eFPGA. In this manner, only the end-user has access to the full functionality of the chip. Using six benchmark circuits, we showed that the $TTB$ is so long (at least 8 million hours) that for all practical purposes the designs are secure, while incurring area overheads of around 5%. Further, latencies were only slightly increased, while the computation times are under one minute.

## REFERENCES


[1] Achronix. 2018. Speedcore eFPGA. (2018).

[2] Yousra Alkabani et al. 2007. Active Hardware Metering for Intellectual Property Protection and Security. In *Proceedings of 16th USENIX Security Symposium on USENIX Security Symposium (SS'07)*. Article 20, 16 pages.

[3] R. S. Chakraborty and S. Bhunia. 2009. HARPOON: An Obfuscation-Based SoC Design Methodology for Hardware Protection. *IEEE TCAD* 28, 10 (Oct 2009), 1493–1502.

[4] Y. Lao et al. 2015. Obfuscating DSP Circuits via High-Level Transformations. *IEEE TVLSI* 23, 5 (May 2015), 819–830.

[5] Bao Liu et al. 2014. Embedded Reconfigurable Logic for ASIC Design Obfuscation Against Supply Chain Attacks. In *DATE*. 243:1–243:6.

[6] NEC. 2015. CyberWorkBench v.5.2. (2015).

[7] Quicklogic. 2018. ArticPro. (2018).

[8] J. Rajendran et al. 2013. Is split manufacturing secure?. In *2013 DATE*. 1259–1264.

[9] J. Rajendran et al. 2013. Security Analysis of Integrated Circuit Camouflaging. In *SIGSAC Conference on Computer & Communications Security (CCS '13)*. 709–720.

[10] J. Rajendran et al. 2015. Fault Analysis-Based Logic Encryption. *IEEE Trans. Comput.* 64, 2 (Feb 2015), 410–424.

[11] Jarrod A. Roy et al. 2008. EPIC: Ending Piracy of Integrated Circuits. In *DATE*. 1069–1074.

[12] Carrion Benjamin Schafer et al. 2014. S2CBench:Synthesizable SystemC Benchmark Suite. *IEEE Embedded Systems Letters* 6, 3 (2014), 53–56.

[13] Mustafa M. Shihab et al. 2019. Design Obfuscation through Selective Post-Fabrication Transistor-Level Programming. In *Design, Automation & Test in Europe Conference & Exhibition (DATE)*. IEEE.

[14] S.Liu et al. 2013. Achieving Energy Efficiency Through Runtime Partial Reconfiguration on Reconfigurable Systems. *ACM Trans. Embed. Comput. Syst.* 12, 3 (2013), 72:1–72:21.

[15] Jingxiang Tian et al. 2017. A field programmable transistor array featuring single-cycle partial/full dynamic reconfiguration. In *Design, Automation & Test in Europe Conference & Exhibition (DATE), 2017*. IEEE, 1336–1341.

[16] T. Winograd et al. 2016. Hybrid STT-CMOS designs for reverse-engineering prevention. In *DAC*. 1–6.

[17] M. Yasin et al. 2016. On Improving the Security of Logic Locking. *IEEE Transactions on Computer-Aided Design of Integrated Circuits and Systems* 35, 9 (Sept 2016), 1411–1424.

# HydraRoute: A Novel Approach to Circuit Routing

Mohammad Khasawneh
mkhasaw1@binghamton.edu
SUNY Binghamton Computer Science Department
Binghamton, New York

Patrick H. Madden
pmadden@binghamton.edu
SUNY Binghamton Computer Science Department
Binghamton, New York

## ABSTRACT

Routing for dense circuits is a major challenge for VLSI physical design. Most routing approaches rely at least partially on a "rip-up and reroute" scheme, where solution quality and run times can be impacted profoundly by the order in which nets are routed. Other routing tools rely on backtracking methods embedded in integer linear programming solvers. In this paper, we present a novel approach which avoids backtracking, and largely eliminates the routing order considerations, by constructing a large number of routings simultaneously. By keeping "options open," our approach sidesteps conflicts. Our approach is a factor of ten faster than other recent work, reduces via counts by 30% or more, and is competitive on both wire length and completion rates. The approach is simple, scalable, and adaptable to the complex constraints of modern circuit fabrication processes.

## CCS CONCEPTS

• **Hardware** → **Wire routing**; • **Mathematics of computing** → *Combinatorial optimization.*

## KEYWORDS

circuit routing, electronic design automation, combinatorial optimization

**ACM Reference Format:**

Mohammad Khasawneh and Patrick H. Madden. 2019. HydraRoute: A Novel Approach to Circuit Routing. In *Great Lakes Symposium on VLSI 2019(GLSVLSI'19), May 9–11, 2019, Tysons Corner, VA, USA.* ACM, New York, NY, USA, 6 pages. https://doi.org/10.1145/3299874.3317997

## 1 INTRODUCTION

With each year, Moore's Law brings more transistors, and more complex circuitry. The design and fabrication of these circuits has also grown dramatically in complexity. There is a strong preference for algorithms and techniques that scale nearly linearly in run time; higher complexity methods may perform well on small "toy" problems, but can be impractical for industrial applications.

The focus of this paper is on circuit routing, which is a particularly challenging step in the physical design process. With millions of interconnecting nets, each with a wide range of plausible topologies, finding a conflict-free design rule compliant set of routes is difficult.

The order in which nets are routed can have a significant impact on routing success. Each net that is routed consumes some of the limited available resources, and also creates new obstacles and barriers that subsequent nets must avoid. When a router fails to find a way to connect a net, a lengthy rip-up and reroute process is a common strategy: completed nets are removed, in the hope that by changing the routing order, or allocating routing resources differently, a legal solution can be found.

In this paper, we present HydraRoute, a novel approach to circuit routing. Our primary contribution is a new combinatorial optimization approach, which side-steps the problem of net ordering to a great degree, and which avoids the need for backtracking. Rather than constructing a single routing solution, we create a multitude of routings simultaneously. As with conventional routers, we perform the routing of nets one at a time – but consider multiple paths for each, generating multiple potential solutions. Like the mythical creature the hydra, routing conflicts eliminate some solutions from consideration – but as they are removed, new solutions spring forth.

On recently released routing benchmarks used by a number of different groups, we show that our approach can route to near completion quickly and easily, finding solutions that have low wire length, low numbers of vias, all while avoiding the twists and turns encountered with maze-routing based methods. Our approach is flexible and extensible; it can be adapted to consider a wide range of metrics, and the constraints imposed by modern fabrication processes.

## 2 PRIOR WORK

In the earliest days of integrated circuit design, relatively few layers of interconnecting wire were available; routing between cells was performed in routing channels[1], with occasional need for switchbox routing[2]. Spacing between rows of cells was variable, adjusting to the needs of the routing channels. With modern design, however, almost all routing is performed over-the-cell, with standard cell rows packed together to share power lines. When routing becomes overly congested, it may be impossible to make required connections; there is no simple way to shift circuit elements to make more space. Modern placement tools focus on white space allocation as a means to avoid routing congestion.

Traditional routing tools are heavily reliant on maze-search algorithms, with Dijkstra's shortest path algorithm[3] playing a prominent role. Signal nets are normally decomposed into either spanning or Steiner trees, and then each tree branch is routed independently.

Routing a single net can be a relatively simple matter when there is little congestion. Things quickly become more difficult when multiple routes compete for resources. When routing a net fails,


ACM ISBN 978-1-4503-6252-8/19/05...$15.00
https://doi.org/10.1145/3299874.3317997

previously routed nets can be removed[4]; "rip-up and reroute" is well known.

The Pathfinder[5] routing tool in particular has influenced much of the work in routing. When there is contention for routing resources, the "cost" of these resources is increased, so that when alternative paths are available, they are used instead. Iteratively adjusting routing costs, along with ripping up and rerouting connections, can address many congestion issues.

A perennial concern in circuit routing has been the impact of net routing order. If a net $n_i$ is routed first, it may consume some of the available resources – a routing track or via location – which could be essential for a subsequent net $n_j$. Net $n_j$ might also have impact on other nets. While many authors have explored shortest nets first, longest nets first, and strategies such as densest-area-first, none can guarantee an ideal ordering.

Once a routing region has become congested, subsequent routes may detour – further depleting routing resources. In some situations, a feedback situation exists, with routes becoming progressively more circuitous.

In our work, we view this problem not as one fundamentally of net order – but instead, that a net routed earlier consumes resources needed later.

Another difficulty with routing are rapidly evolving design rules. In the early $\lambda$-rule[6] era, spacing requirements, via sizes, and so on, were relatively simple, with each interconnect layer having a regular, uniform grid.

With modern fabrication technology, there are minimum and maximum wire lengths, complex via spacing constraints, and vastly different routing pitches across multiple layers. Much of the recent work in routing have pursued integer linear programming and Boolean satisfiability[7] methods; with these, conflicts are addressed by backtracking through the solution space.

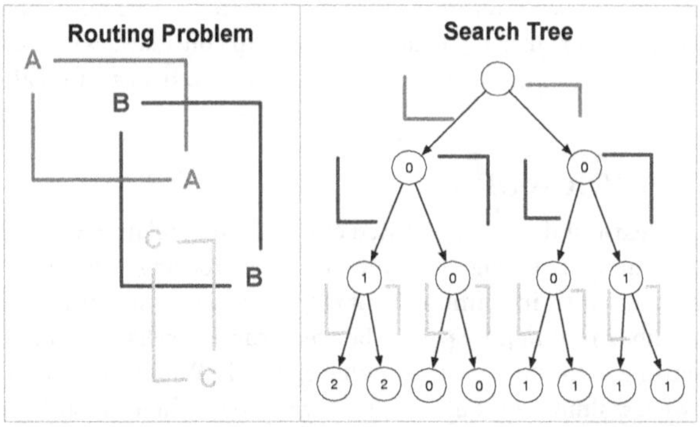


**Figure 1: A simple planar routing problem, and a sketch of our routing approach. Each of the nets to be connected has two potential routings, "lower left" and "upper right" variants. The routing solution space is explored in breadth-first manner, with each level of the tree branching out to encode the different possible routings. The number of design rule violations is computed for each tree vertex.**

## 3 THE HYDRAROUTE APPROACH

In this section, we describe our novel routing approach. We will use a relatively simple set of design rules, and focus on how we achieve a high degree of routing success without resorting to a lengthy rip-up and reroute process. A key advantage of our approach is that it is not as heavily dependent on net routing order as prior methods.

Instead of constructing a single routing solution, we construct a *set* of solutions – with nets in each of these solutions choosing different paths. If a critical routing resource has been used in one of the solutions, a conflict can be avoided – simply by selecting a different routing solution from the set.

We illustrate our approach in Figure 1. On the left, we present a simple planar routing problem consisting of three pairs of points to connect, *A*, *B*, and *C*. Individually, any pair of points could be connected with a simple one-bend route, which we'll refer to as either "upper right" or "lower left." This example uses planar routing to make the conflicts easier to see; the same principles extend to multiple layer routing (or the constraints introduced by more complex design rules).

With a conventional routing approach, routing one net at a time can potentially lead to a difficult situation. If net *A* is routed in the upper-right manner, net *B* is forced to select the lower-left option to avoid a conflict. When we consider net *C*, it is completely blocked by net *B*; it might be possible to detour net *C*, but this consumes more routing resources (making routing of subsequent nets even more difficult). A rip-up and reroute strategy might resolve the issues – but it would require ripping up not only net *B*, but net *A* as well.

Our approach operates as follows:

- The routing net for *A* results in two distinct routing solutions, one for the upper-right, and a second for the lower-left.
- We then take these two solutions, combine them with the potential routings for *B*, to arrive at four different routing solutions. When each path for each new net is considered, we trace back through the tree to identify routing conflicts and design rule violations.
- Considering net *C* next, we create eight different possible routing results.

Obviously, if we simply perform branching on each level of the tree, the solution space and run time grow exponentially. In mythology, the "hydra" was a monster with multiple heads; if one head was cut off, two more would grow in it's place. We adopt a "hydra" strategy, cutting off solutions that have created conflicts, while allowing tree branches with fewer violations to bifurcate into multiple new solutions.

For each route, potential conflicts are precomputed before tree construction begins, with each path having a list of other paths on prior nets that cause violations – checking to see if a new path conflicts with a prior choice can be done quickly.

The number of concurrent solutions, effectively the maximum number of heads that we allow for the "hydra," can be specified by the user. In practice, the number needed for high quality results is lower than might be expected, with experimental results illustrating this clearly. Pseudocode for our approach is shown in Algorithm 1.

### 3.1 Path Construction

In Figure 2, we show potential routing paths considered by our approach. We use simple I-, L-, and Z-shaped routes, and do not introduce detours. Paths $p1$ and $p2$ are straight line segments, which

**Algorithm 1** Multiple routing solution approach of HydraRoute.

```
for each net n_i do
    constructPaths(n_i);
end for
heap pq = newHeap();
heapInsert(pq, dummynode);
for each net n_i do
    heap layer = newHeap();
    for each node parent in pq do
        for each path p for net n_i do
            node child is created by combining p with the parent
            solution
            compute cost of child
            heapInsert(layer, child);
        end for
    end for
    pq = layer;
end for
```

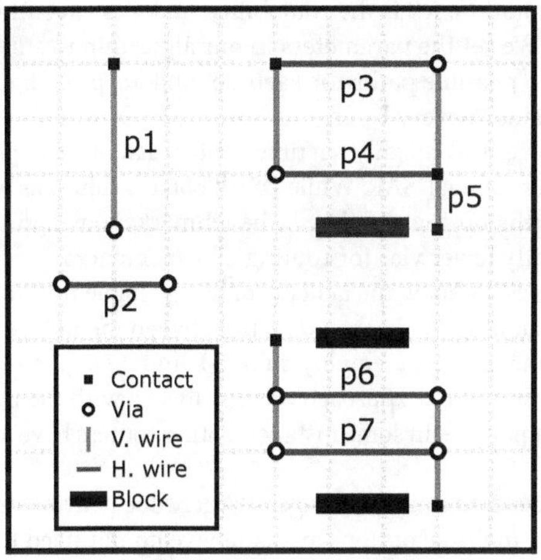


**Figure 2: Simple routing patterns considered by our approach. When pins are horizontally or vertically aligned, a direct connection is considered. Pins may have multiple contact points, increasing the number of possible paths. Obstacles and keep-out regions are honored, eliminating some paths from consideration.**

can either be vertical or horizontal. The choice to include vias on either end is determined by the starting point and the direction of the wire. For example, if the starting pin is on the vertical layer and the end pin is on the horizontal layer, a via should be added at that end point to complete the connection as is the case in *p*1.

An L-shaped segment is constructed between pins that lie on different X and Y coordinates, such that they form a rectangle. If both sides of the rectangle are unobstructed, two valid path choices exist between the two pins; these are shown as *p*3 and *p*4 in the figure. In the same figure, *p*5 is a valid upper right path formed singularly because the other potential, lower left, path is blocked. If both paths that would form a rectangle are blocked, and no other pin access points can be used to form paths, we build all valid Z-shaped paths between the two closest pins, shown as *p*6 and *p*7.

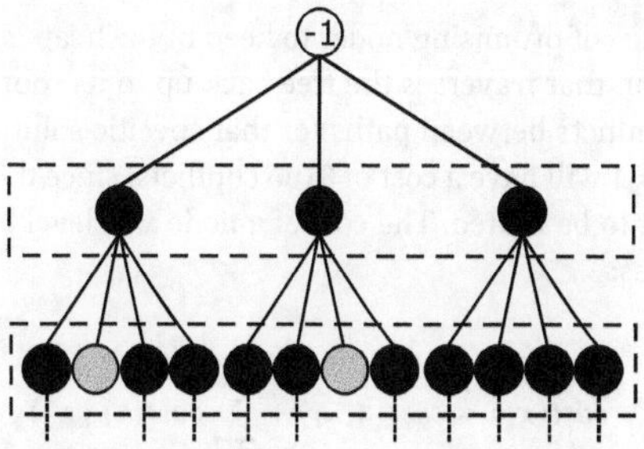


**Figure 3: The state of our algorithm two steps after it starts**

Precomputing potential conflicts between paths enables our routing approach to be exceptionally fast. We use the underlying grid structure to record which paths use different routing resources, sort this information to capture conflicts while filtering to eliminate duplication, and then build lists of conflicts for each path. Because each net is relatively "local" the number of conflicts is a near linear factor, rather than something that scales with problem sizes. Computational geometry techniques could be applied to make this process even more computationally efficient.

## 3.2 Search and Conflict Cost Ranking

The routing process considers one net at a time. We first sort the nets horizontally, based on the center of mass for each net. The nets are then ordered, one routing grid "column" at a time, in increasing *y* order. This ordering ensures that there is some locality in which the nets are considered – and that when conflicts are encountered, it is often with nets that were recently considered. In our experimental results, we have strong evidence that this approach can achieve a high degree of routing success; as part of our current work, we are exploring other routing order strategies.

Figure 3 shows the operation of our algorithm after two nets have been routed. At any point during execution, the height of the tree is equal to the number of nets that have been routed. The height of this tree after an entire run will be the number of nets in its input.

The white node at the top, denoted by -1, is a root node where branching starts. A unique routing solution is formed by using parent pointers to trace from a leaf node back towards the root of the tree, with each node along the path designating a specific path choice for a specific net. A node is identified by a tuple of the form *nid:pid*, where nid identifies which net path pid belongs to. Path IDs start from 0 for the leftmost path in a level up to *j-1*, where *j* is the number of valid paths in net *i*. For example, if we assume the first level in figure 3 is an expansion of net 319, which contains 3 valid paths, then nodes in that level will be identified as 319:0, 319:1, and 319:2 respectively.

We use a minimum heap data structure of maximum size *k* to keep track of the top *k* paths in the net under study; only the most promising paths are used for further expansion. Dashed boxes surrounding nodes in Figure 3 show candidate paths the heap might hold. Black nodes in the second level in Figure 3 show nodes that were found to be the most promising for that net, while gray nodes are those that were discarded as non-promising for further expansion. There can only be a maximum of *k* black nodes at each level.

The choice of promising nodes to keep in the heap is subject to a cost function that traverses the tree back up to its root looking for possible conflicts between paths for that specific solution. Initially, nodes at $i = 1$ will have a cost of 0 (no conflicts) since they represent the first net to be routed. The cost of a node $x$ at level $i$ can then be calculated as:

$$cost(x_i) = cost(x_{i-1}) + \sum_{j=0}^{i-1} cost(x_i \mid x_j)$$

When we start expanding a level all nodes are inserted into its heap while it still contains less than $k$ paths. Once filled, however, the cost function is used to determine which nodes are discarded and which are the most promising. If the calculated cost of a node is less than the minimum cost in the current level's heap, it replaces the current minimum; otherwise that node is discarded.

Our cost function allows expansion to include any combination of costs that a design might study. For the purpose of this study, we chose our cost as the presence of physical conflicts between paths, but it can be easily expanded to accommodate any combination of more complex metrics such as wire coupling capacitance.

## 4 EXPERIMENTAL RESULTS

Rapidly changing design rules have resulted in much of the published work on routing using benchmarks tailored for specific fabrication technologies. There are relatively few "stock" routing benchmarks, compared to what one might find with circuit placement. We utilize routing benchmarks provided by the authors of [8, 9], which are based on synthesized OpenSparc T1 designs, first used in [10]. These prior works focused on routing for directed self-assembly fabrication technologies, with double patterning lithography. As our focus is on general routing techniques, we use a classic Mead-and-Conway routing approach, with routing and vias occurring on the routing grid; we do not place additional constraints on via spacing, or require line extensions – thus, the routing problems considered are not equivalent.

The circuit benchmarks have multiple electrically equivalent pin positions for most cells, giving multiple contact points for each net endpoint. The nets have been decomposed by the authors of [8] into two-pin connections.

There are two layers of metal for routing, and a number of obstacles and barriers in each of the benchmark files. Table 1 presents a summary of benchmark statistics.

Our routing approach is effectively pattern-based, similar to what has been done in a number of other routing tools[11–13]. The first step of our routing tool is to enumerate possible connection paths – the L and Z shapes between contact points, which also avoid all fixed obstacles. The third column of Table1 shows the total number of all possible paths that make up the entire solution space for each benchmark; the routing solution is formed when one path is selected for each net. The average number of possible paths for each connection varies; on average, there are roughly sixty possible simple paths for each net.

Potential conflicts between pairs of paths from different nets are precomputed; each possible path has roughly seventy other paths that would create a design rule violation.

**Table 1: Benchmarks: #Paths is the total number of valid paths, #PpN is the average number of paths per net, and #CpP is the average number of conflicts per path.**

| Benchmark | #Nets | #Paths | #PpN | #CpP |
|---|---|---|---|---|
| ecc | 1,671 | 140,199 | 83 | 71 |
| efc | 2,219 | 108,331 | 48 | 63 |
| ctl | 2,706 | 125,395 | 64 | 54 |
| alu | 3,108 | 213,789 | 68 | 90 |
| div | 5,813 | 305,844 | 52 | 64 |
| top | 22,201 | 1,569,617 | 70 | 94 |

### 4.1 Routing Results

We implemented our router in C++ and ran all experiments on an Intel Xeon server with 64GBs of memory. Routing benchmark details are shown in Table 1; we obtained this set of benchmarks from the authors of [8].

We compare our results with previous work in table 2. In the table, *WL* stands for wire length, *VpN* is the number of vias per net in a solution, *R%* is the routability, and *T* is execution time in seconds. We set the parameters in our algorithm to study the top thirty two possible paths for each net and keep track of the best ten solutions at every layer.

Our solver was roughly ten times faster than the best-performing competitor router, DSAR. While DSAR obtains solutions with lower wire lengths on four of the six benchmarks, our approach uses significantly fewer vias for routing all benchmarks.

These results show the benefits of using simple routing patterns; rather than jumping back and forth between metal layers to complete connections, we employ simple L and Z shaped routes. The paths chosen by our approach are not always with the closest pair of contact points – in some instances, other routers have lower wire lengths.

The execution time advantage is largely due to avoiding conflicts by having multiple options available; we do not need to perform rip-up and reroute, or to backtrack through the solution space. The efficiency of the approach allows it to scale to industrial-sized designs.

Our routing approach is also extremely flexible. The constraints imposed on routes, and the "cost" of any given violation, are independent of the solution method.

### 4.2 Impact of the Hydra Approach

We wish to emphasize the impact of considering multiple routing solutions simultaneously. This is perhaps the most significant difference between the work presented here, and prior approaches.

First, Figure 5 shows the improvement in solution quality as we change the number of paths considered for each net of the *top* benchmark. In our preprocessing, we generate possible routing paths, and compute the potential conflicts between them – during routing, we only consider the paths which have the fewest potential conflicts. If we increase the number of paths considered, run time increases linearly – but the number of conflicts encountered drops dramatically, leveling off and then providing only limited gains. We show the results of varying the number of paths considered for all benchmarks in Table 3. The observation to make is that it is useful

**Table 2: Result Comparison With Competitive Routers. HydraRoute is configured to study the top 32 paths with a heap size of 10. The design rules used by different groups has varied; we use a simple Mead-and-Conway routing model.**

| | Liu2016[10] | | | | PARR[8] | | | | Conv 1D Router | | | |
|---|---|---|---|---|---|---|---|---|---|---|---|---|
| | WL | VpN | R% | T(s) | WL | VpN | R% | T(s) | WL | VpN | R% | T(s) |
| ecc | 41497 | 2.31 | 91.1 | 16.7 | 46588 | 2.66 | 96.4 | 19.9 | 37452 | 1.94 | 99.9 | 4.26 |
| efc | 54459 | 2.31 | 82.4 | 100.5 | 57834 | 2.40 | 94.9 | 34.5 | 48712 | 2.48 | 99.9 | 19.9 |
| ctl | 67470 | 2.24 | 87.2 | 93.8 | 72388 | 2.42 | 95.2 | 37.1 | 60059 | 2.14 | 99.9 | 22.02 |
| alu | 68491 | 2.26 | 79.4 | 143.4 | 75679 | 2.44 | 95.1 | 45.9 | 65139 | 2.35 | 99.7 | 20.19 |
| div | 139309 | 2.29 | 79.4 | 253.5 | 155704 | 2.51 | 94.6 | 106.0 | 124108 | 2.22 | 99.8 | 97.03 |
| top | N/A | N/A | N/A | N/A | 513366 | 2.47 | 95.3 | 763.2 | 424869 | 2.22 | 98.8 | 1558.32 |
| AVG | N/A | N/A | N/A | N/A | 1.20 | 1.48 | 0.95 | 2.17 | 0.99 | 1.32 | 1.00 | 3.71 |
| | DSAR[9] | | | | SPIE-14[14] | | | | Hydra-32 | | | |
| | WL | VpN | R% | T(s) | WL | VpN | R% | T(s) | WL | VpN | R% | T(s) |
| ecc | 37801 | 1.96 | 100 | 13.6 | 44193 | 2.43 | 100 | 10.56 | 38999 | 1.68 | 99.8 | 2.4 |
| efc | 49686 | 2.30 | 100 | 26.6 | 57024 | 2.78 | 99.9 | 27.5 | 50180 | 1.71 | 99.4 | 4.2 |
| ctl | 60574 | 2.14 | 100 | 56.9 | 69397 | 2.58 | 100 | 57.9 | 62575 | 1.66 | 99.7 | 5.9 |
| alu | 67140 | 2.41 | 100 | 45.8 | 77322 | 2.90 | 99.9 | 56.12 | 63172 | 1.75 | 99.8 | 9.4 |
| div | 125734 | 2.23 | 100 | 278.4 | 144316 | 2.70 | 99.9 | 246.09 | 131104 | 1.60 | 99.7 | 27.5 |
| top | 423194 | 2.16 | 100 | 4133.3 | 491182 | 2.60 | 99.9 | 4382.50 | 422058 | 1.69 | 99.8 | 414.3 |
| AVG | 0.99 | 1.31 | 1.00 | 9.82 | 1.15 | 1.59 | 1.00 | 10.31 | 1.00 | 1.00 | 1.00 | 1.00 |

for the router to have options, but an abundance of options is not necessary.

Figure 6 clearly illustrates the impact of our "hydra" approach. Rather than having a single routing solution, we have a multitude; routing conflicts cause some branches to be pruned, while others bifurcate. With only a single solution – in some ways comparable to a conventional routing approach – we obtain results with large numbers of routing conflicts, even when many different routing paths are considered. As we increase the number of simultaneous solutions up to fifty, we see almost immediate and dramatic gains, and then a leveling off of improvements. Because there are diminishing returns beyond ten simultaneous solutions (but increasing run times), our current implementation uses ten as the default value.

The routing solution the *ecc* benchmark is shown in Figure 4.

**Table 3: Number of conflicts when varying number of best paths studied. *TOP 1* shows the amount of conflicts arising when we look at the solution space from narrow angles provided by algorithms that are highly influenced by net ordering.**

| | TOP 1 | TOP 4 | TOP 16 | TOP 32 |
|---|---|---|---|---|
| ecc | 194 | 30 | 3 | 3 |
| efc | 389 | 74 | 14 | 12 |
| ctl | 403 | 66 | 12 | 7 |
| alu | 582 | 108 | 9 | 4 |
| div | 1123 | 186 | 25 | 16 |
| top | 4028 | 640 | 54 | 25 |

## 5 CONCLUSION AND FUTURE WORK

A fundamental challenge in circuit routing is the interplay between many individual nets. The routing of one can take resources away from another; when conflicts occur, it is seldom clear which net should be rerouted, and in what manner. In this work, we have explored a novel approach to circuit routing. By maintaining a large number of unique routing solutions, there is a chance that at least one of those solutions will be compatible when routing a new net. Pruning the solution space keeps the problem from growing exponentially. Routing solutions with conflicts are pruned in favor of solutions that have fewer challenges.

This is in stark contrast with "traditional" approaches in which there is considerable focus on only a single routing solution, where rip-up and reroute is an integral part of the overall strategy.

The increased compute demands from maintaining multiple routing solutions is more that paid for by an avoidance of rip-up and reroute. Our approach is also space efficient, sharing parts of routing solutions, with the tree used by our optimization approach only specifying a routing path index for each net, rather than a complete specification of all routing geometry.

The correct-by-construction path generation allows our method to be used with modern fabrication processes; line extensions, complex via patterns, and so on, can be supported easily.

As part of our current work, we are adapting HydraRoute to perform routing within arbitrarily sized windows – this allows better scalability, as well as the opportunity to reroute portions of a design where conflicts occur. We are adding support for commercial file formats, to integrate into a complete design automation flow, and making our route generation methods more modular.

## REFERENCES

[1] D. N. Deutsch. Compacted channel routing. In *Proc. Int. Conf. on Computer Aided Design*, pages 223–225, 1985.
[2] J. P. Cohoon and P. L. Heck. Beaver: a computational geometry based tool for switchbox routing. *IEEE Trans. on Computer-Aided Design of Integrated Circuits and Systems*, 7:684–697, 1988.
[3] E. Dijkstra. A note on two problems in connexion with graphs. *Numerische Mathematik*, 1:269–271, 1959.
[4] W. A. Dees and R. J. Smith. Performance of interconnection rip-up and reroute strategies. In *Proc. Design Automation Conference*, pages 382–390, 1981.

**Figure 4: Wiring (above) and via placement (below) results for the *ecc* benchmark.**

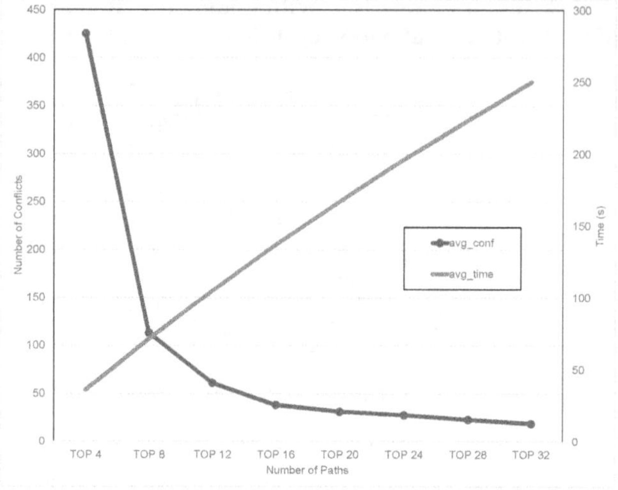


**Figure 5: A run time/quality trade-off can be achieved by varying the number of paths considered. Here, we show results for a heap size of 10, and adjust the number of paths considered for each net. These results are the weighted averages for routing all benchmarks.**

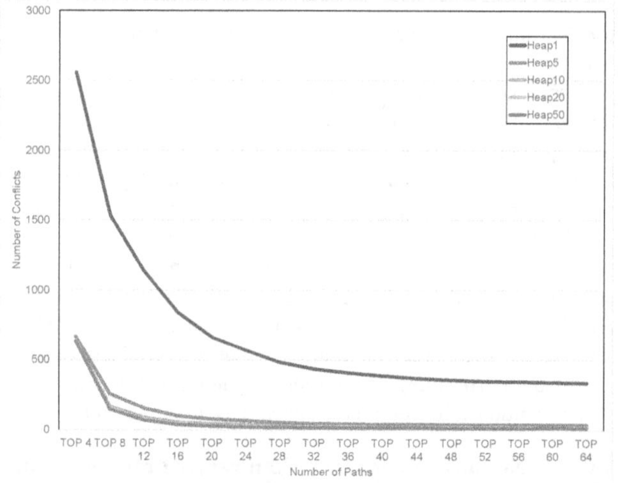


**Figure 6: The Hydra approach explores multiple routing solutions simultaneously, pruning low quality solutions. Preserving only a single solution is comparable to a traditional routing approach – this is by far the worst performing option. Expanding the number of solutions considered simultaneously improves results; this is the key advantage of our method. The results shown here are for the routing benchmark *top*.**


[5] L. McMurchie and C. Ebeling. Pathfinder: a negotiation-based performance-driven router for FPGAs. In *Proc. Int. Symp. on Field-Programmable Gate Arrays*, pages 111–117, 1995.

[6] C. Mead and L. Conway. *Introduction to VLSI Systems.* Addison-Wesley, 1993.

[7] Nikolai Ryzhenko and Steven Burns. Standard cell routing via boolean satisfiability. In *Proceedings of the 49th Annual Design Automation Conference*, pages 603–612. ACM, 2012.

[8] Xiaoqing Xu, Bei Yu, Jhih-Rong Gao, Che-Lun Hsu, and David Z Pan. PARR: Pin-Access Planning and Regular Routing for Self-Aligned Double Patterning. *ACM Trans. Design Automation of Electronic Systems*, 21(3):42:1—-42:21, 2016.

[9] Jiaojiao Ou, Bei Yu, Xiaoqing Xu, Joydeep Mitra, Yibo Lin, and David Z Pan. DSAR: DSA aware Routing with Simultaneous DSA Guiding Pattern and Double Patterning Assignment. In *Proceedings of the 2017 ACM on International Symposium on Physical Design*, pages 91–98. ACM, 2017.

[10] Iou Jen Liu, Shao Yun Fang, and Yao Wen Chang. Overlay-Aware Detailed Routing for Self-Aligned Double Patterning Lithography Using the Cut Process. *IEEE Transactions on Computer-Aided Design of Integrated Circuits and Systems*, 35(9):1519–1531, 2016.

[11] R. G. Wood and R. A. Rutenbar. FPGA routing and routability estimation via boolean satisfiability. In *FPGA*, pages 119–125, 1997.

[12] R. Kastner, E. Bozogzadeh, and M. Sarrafzadeh. Predictable routing. *Proc. Int. Conf. on Computer Aided Design*, pages 110–113, 2000.

[13] Y. Zhang and C. Chu. RegularRoute: An efficient detailed router applying regular routing patterns. *Trans. VLSI Systems*, 21(9):1655–1668, 2013.

[14] Yuelin Du, Zigang Xiao, Martin DF Wong, He Yi, and H-S Philip Wong. Dsa-aware detailed routing for via layer optimization. In *Alternative Lithographic Technologies VI*, volume 9049, page 90492J. International Society for Optics and Photonics, 2014.

# Balanced Factorization and Rewriting Algorithms for Synthesizing Single Flux Quantum Logic Circuits

Ghasem Pasandi
Department of Electrical and Computer Engineering
University of Southern California
Los Angeles, California, USA
pasandi@usc.edu

Massoud Pedram
Department of Electrical and Computer Engineering
University of Southern California
Los Angeles, California, USA
pedram@usc.edu

## ABSTRACT

Single Flux Quantum (SFQ) logic with switching energy of $100zJ$[1] and switching delay of *1ps* is a promising post-CMOS candidate. Logic synthesis of these magnetic-pulse-based circuits is a very important step in their design flow with a big impact on the total area, power consumption, and critical path delay. SFQ circuits has some properties different from CMOS which should be taken into consideration in the design and implementation flow of these circuits. One of these properties is requirement of path balancing in the standard SFQ circuit design. Standard CMOS-based rewriting and factorization algorithms fail to preserve the balancing property of SFQ circuits. Therefore, they end up generating circuits with huge path balancing overheads. Our proposed balanced factorization and rewriting algorithms are designed specifically to solve this problem. Experimental results show that a combination of balanced factorization and rewriting algorithms reduces the path balancing overhead by an average of 63% for 15 benchmark circuits, and area by up to 23% compared to state-of-the-art logic synthesis tools.

## CCS CONCEPTS

• **Computer systems organization**; • **Hardware** → **Logic synthesis**; **Combinational synthesis**;

## KEYWORDS

AIG, Factorization, Logic Synthesis, Refactoring, Rewriting, RSFQ, SFQ, Single Flux Quantum, SDE, Superconducting Digital Electronics, Technology Mapping

**ACM Reference Format:**

Ghasem Pasandi and Massoud Pedram. 2019. Balanced Factorization and Rewriting Algorithms for Synthesizing Single Flux Quantum Logic Circuits. In *Great Lakes Symposium on VLSI 2019 (GLSVLSI '19), May 9–11, 2019, Washington, D.C., USA.* ACM, New York, NY, USA, 6 pages. https://doi.org/10.1145/3299874.3317967

## 1 INTRODUCTION

Shrinking CMOS devices has provided a decades-long advances in computing. However, by increasing challenges to scaling of these devices and by slowing the Moore's law down (end of Moore's law), new device, circuit, architectural, and system level solutions are needed to keep up with ever increasing demand for energy efficient and high speed circuits and systems [1]. Superconducting Digital Electronics (SDE), especially the Single Flux Quantum (SFQ) family, is proven to be a good candidate to achieve energy efficient and high performance systems [2], hence, a potential replacement for CMOS technology. SFQ devices are made of Josephson junctions (JJs), which are superconducting devices working based on the Josephson effect [3]. The switching delay of these devices is as low as $1ps$ with consuming $100zJ$ energy per switching [4]. This switching energy is even less than what is predicted by International Technology Roadmap for Semiconductors (ITRS) for 2020 [1], which again shows the prominence of these devices as a replacement for CMOS technology.

The first family of the SFQ logic is called Resistive (later on Rapid) Single Flux Quantum (RSFQ) logic, which was developed in the 1980s and uses resistors (JJs in the latest version) to regulate the biasing current to JJs [5]. RSFQ gates can operate as fast as 370GHz at $T = 4.2K$ [4]. In [6], the maximum speed of 770GHz is also reported for an RSFQ T-Flip-Flop (TFF).

While superiority of SFQ circuits in achieving super fast and very low-power circuits has been proven, there is no optimum full design automation suite for these devices. On the other hand, due to some key differences between SFQ and CMOS logic, CMOS Computer Aided Design (CAD) tools cannot be directly used for SFQ circuits. Therefore, it is critical to develop appropriate CAD tools including synthesis, place-and-route, timing and power analysis, and verification tools to fully automate the design and test process of SFQ circuits.

In this paper, we present balanced factorization and rewriting algorithms, which are designed to synthesize SFQ circuits efficiently. Unlike the standard factorization and rewriting algorithms, our proposed algorithms preserve balance of the given circuit during the logic synthesis. As a result, a huge reduction in path balancing overheads of these circuits is achieved, which is translated into saving in the total area. Please note that the proposed algorithms would be of interest for any technology that requires path balancing or adheres to a clocked propagation of data (gate-level pipelined, see Section 2.1.1) through out a circuit.

## 2 PRELIMINARIES

### 2.1 Background on SFQ

SFQ logic uses a single quantum of magnetic flux ($\Phi_0 = h/2e = 2.07mV \times ps$) to represent binary information. In this representation, the presence of a pulse is considered as "logic-1", while the absence of a pulse means "logic-0". Operation of SFQ logic is based on over-damped Josephson junctions, and hence, it does not experience the problem of hysteric I-V characteristics (IVCs), which degrades the

[1] $1z$ is equal to $10^{-21}$.


*GLSVLSI '19, May 9–11, 2019, Washington, D.C., USA*

ACM ISBN 978-1-4503-6252-8/19/05...$15.00
https://doi.org/10.1145/3299874.3317967

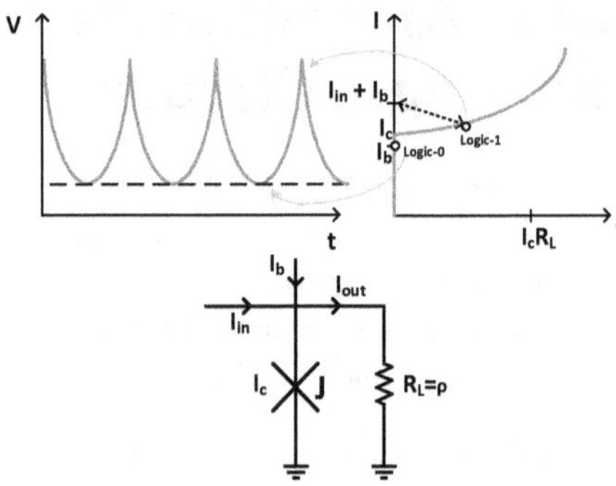


**Figure 1. Schematic of an SFQ buffer, its IVC and the pulse shape representation of data in SFQ (waveforms are adopted from [7]).**

operation speed of "1" to "0" switching [7]. Figure 1 shows the IVC and the pulse shape representation of data in an SFQ buffer.

Here is a couple of gate/circuit level properties of SFQ circuits. For more details please see [5, 8–10]:

*2.1.1 Gate-level pipeline.* In SFQ logic, most of gates (except for splitters, confluence buffers, IO cells, and TFFs) receive a clock signal. There are three main methods for clock distribution in SFQ circuits: (i) *clock-follow-data* where a clock signal arrives at a gate when its inputs have already been arrived and processed by the gate, (ii) *counter-flow clocking* where the clock flows in the opposite direction of the data, and (iii) *concurrent-flow clocking* in which the clock and data flow in the same direction.

*2.1.2 Path Balancing.* In standard SFQ circuit design, to guarantee the correct functionality, length of any path in terms of the gate count from any Primary Input (PI) to any Primary Output (PO) of the circuit should be the same. Otherwise, some path balancing D-Flip-Flops (DFFs) should be inserted into shorter paths to balance the whole circuit. If an SFQ circuit is not path balanced, there will be at least one gate with an early (late) input. This input will be consumed in a wrong clock cycle and causes generation of a potentially wrong output, which can propagate to the final outputs of the circuit.

## 2.2 Background on Logic Synthesis

Logic synthesis is divided into *technology-independent* and *technology-dependent* (*technology mapping*) phases. In the first phase, several transformations are performed to reduce the number of literals in the final form of a given Boolean expression. In the second phase, which is the final stage of the logic synthesis, suitable gates from a given library are assigned to nodes of the network in order to satisfy some constraints or to minimize some cost functions. Before technology mapping, the Boolean network is transformed into And Inverter Graphs (AIGs). This step is called *technology decomposition*, and such a network is called the *subject graph.*

A *k-feasible cone* at node $v$ of a network $N = (V, E)$, denoted by $C_v$, is defined as a sub-graph containing $v$ and its predecessors satisfying two conditions: (i) number of inputs of this sub-graph should be fewer than or equal to $k$, (ii) all paths connecting $v$ to a node in $C_v$ lies entirely in $C_v$. A cut $C$=$(X, X')$ with source $s$ and sink $t$ in a given network $N$ is defined as a partition of the set $V$ into two sets $X$ and $X' = V - X$ such that $s \in X$, and $t \in X'$. $C$=$(X, X')$ is a trivial cut, if set $X$ has only one member (source $s$). The *node cut-size* of a cut $C$=$(X, X')$ denoted by $n(X, X')$ or $n(C)$ is defined as the number of boundary nodes in $X'$ which are adjacent to some nodes in $X$. These boundary nodes are called the *leaf nodes* of the cut. A cut $C$=$(X, X')$ is called *k-feasible* if its node cut-size is at most $k$ (i.e. $n(C) \leq k$). A *k-feasible cut* of a node $v$ is defined as a valid *k-feasible* cut, in which node $v$ is the source node of the cut and the sink node is a PI. A *fanin (fanout) cone* of a node $v$ in a network $N = (V, E)$ is defined as the set of nodes in $V$ that can be reached through the fanin (fanout) edges of $v$.

A *literal* is a variable or its negation, e.g. $x$, $x'$. A *cube* is AND (conjunction) of a set of literals. An *algebraic expression* $F = \{C_i\}$, which consists of a set of cubes, is an expression in which no cube contains another one, i.e., $C_i \subsetneq C_j, i \neq j$. An expression that is not algebraic is called *Boolean.* The *support* of an expression $F$ is the set of variables that $F$ explicitly depends on. The *product of two cubes $C_i$ and $C_j$* is a cube defined by the following:

$$C_iC_j = \begin{cases} \emptyset \ : if\ \exists x \in C_i \cup C_j \ \&\ x' \in C_i \cup C_j \\ C_i \cup C_j \ : otherwise \end{cases}$$

The *product of two Sum-Of-Product (SOP) expressions* $F$ and $G$ is a SOP expression denoted by $FG$, defined by $FG = \{C_iC_j \mid C_i \in F \,\&\, C_j \in G \,\&\, C_iC_j \neq \emptyset\}$. The product $FG$ is an *algebraic product* if $F$ and $G$ are algebraic expressions and have disjoint variable support. The *sum of two SOP expressions* $F$ and $G$ denoted by $F + G$ is a set defined by $F + G = \{C_i \mid C_i \in F \ or\ C_i \in G\}$. The sum $F + G$ is an *algebraic sum* if $F$ and $G$ are algebraic expressions and no cube in $F$ contains a cube in $G$ and vice versa. A *factored form* is defined recursively as follows: a factored form is either a product or sum where a product (sum) is either a single literal or product (sum) of factored forms. Also, a factored form can be defined as a parenthesized algebraic expression. For example, *ab+c(a+b), a, acd'* are factored forms, but *b(c+d)'* is not a factored form.

## 3 RELATED WORK

Brayton [11] presented a few methods for obtaining different factored forms of a given logic expression. These methods range from fast purely algebraic methods to Boolean ones, which are slower but capable of providing more saving in the total literal count. Iman and Pedram [12] addressed the problem of reducing power consumption by extending algebraic procedures for node extraction and factorization targeting minimization of a cost function that measures the power cost of Boolean expressions. Roy *et. al* [13] introduced a unique cost function based on decomposed factored forms representation of a given Boolean expression to guide clustering and factorization methodologies for minimizing the power consumption.

Mishchenko *et. al* [14] presented the Directed Acyclic Graph (DAG)-aware AIG rewriting algorithm, by extending the DAG-aware circuit compression method in [15]. In DAG-aware AIG rewriting, 4-feasible cuts of nodes are computed and function of each cut together with its NPN-class[2] is determined using a hash-table lookup. According to [16], for 4-input expressions, there are

[2]Two expressions F and G are NPN-equivalent or belong to the same NPN-class, if F can be achieved from G by Negation, Permutation of its inputs or Negation of its output.

222 NPN-classes, among which around 100 are being used more frequently in most of the well-known benchmark circuits [14], which can be pre-computed and stored.

Soeken and Thomsen [17] showed that it is possible to use standard expression rewriting rules to derive fairly complex formulas which is beneficial in algebraic operations used in reversible logic circuits. Haaswijk *et. al* [18] showed that the use of exact synthesis for logic rewriting can be improved by a better sub-network selection strategy, avoiding useless enumerations, and employing XOR majority graphs. In this paper, we present balanced factorization and rewriting, which are the first structural factorization and rewriting approaches to the best of our knowledge.

# 4 BALANCED FACTORIZATION AND REWRITING

## 4.1 Balanced Factorization

In the standard method of computing algebraic factored forms, given $F = G_1G_2 + R$, a factorization value is calculated as follows:

$$\begin{aligned} fact\_val &= lits(F) - (lits(G_1) + lits(G_2) + lits(R)) \\ &= (|G_1| - 1) \times lits(G_2) + (|G_2| - 1) \times lits(G_1) \end{aligned} \quad (1)$$

in which, it is assumed that $G_1$, $G_2$, and $R$ are algebraic expressions, *lits(F)* returns literal count of $F$, and $|G_1|$ is the number of cubes in the SOP form of $G_1$. This value represents the number of literals that is saved by performing the corresponding factorization. The literal saving is translated into the node count reduction in the subject graph and it results in total area saving for CMOS circuits. Therefore, if a factored form gives the highest factorization value among all possible factored forms, it has a good chance to minimize the total area in CMOS circuits. However, in SFQ circuits, due to requirement of path balancing, the said standard method for selecting the best factored forms will not necessarily result in a circuit with the least area. It even can increase the total area compared with the case of not applying any factorization algorithms. This is because the standard factorization algorithm does not preserve the balance of the network being generated during the factorization process.

To solve the above problem, we propose a balance preserving factorization algorithm, and consider the cost of path balancing when calculating the factorization value. More precisely, we first generate a factoring tree for each factored form of a given expression. Factoring tree is a labeled tree in which each node is labeled with either × or + expressing a conjunctive, and disjunctive operations, respectively. Also, in a factoring tree, each leaf node is a literal. Next, we compute level[3] of each node in the said factoring tree. Then, we compute an imbalance factor (denoted by Λ) for this factoring tree. To define Λ, first we need to define the imbalance factor of a node in a factoring tree. If the maximum level of immediate fanin nodes of the node $v$ in a factoring tree is $L_{max}$, the imbalance factor of this node is calculated as follows:

$$\lambda_v = \sum_{v_i \in fanins(v)} (L_{max} - level(v_i)) \quad (2)$$

where *fanins(v)* is the set of immediate fanin nodes of node $v$, and $level(v_i)$ is the level of one of these fanins. The imbalance factors of leaf nodes are 0. The imbalance factor of a tree $t = (V_t, E_t)$ denoted by $\Lambda_t$ is calculated by summing up the imbalance factors of nodes of this tree:

$$\Lambda_t = \sum_{v \in V_t} \lambda_v \quad (3)$$

[3]Level of a node $v$ in a network $N = (V, E)$ which is modeled by a DAG, is defined as the length of the longest path in terms of the node count from any leaf node to $v$.

**Algorithm 1:** Balanced Factorization

```
Input: A Boolean network N = (V, E)
Output: Optimized network N_OPT = (V_OPT, E_OPT)
// pre-processing:
Convert the given network into AIG;
Sort nodes in V to be in topological order;
Compute k-feasible cuts of each node;
for each node v in V do
    for each cut C_j in k-feasible cuts of v do
        Extract function of v based on inputs of C_j;
        Generate factoring trees and compute their
          blnc_overhead_val (Eq (4));
    Select a factored form for node v with the least value for
      blnc_overhead_val;
// Generate a new network using the best factored forms
   for each node:
N_OPT = Generate_Ntk(N);
return N_OPT;
```

Finally, to consider the effect of both node (or literal) count and imbalance factor, a new factorization value is defined and computed as follows:

$$blnc\_overhead\_val = |V_t| + \Lambda_t \quad (4)$$

where $|V_t|$ is the total node count of the factoring tree $t$. Please note that unlike standard factorization method, in which a factored form with maximum value for $fact\_val$ is selected, in balanced factorization, we select a factored form which minimizes *blnc_overhead_val*. This is because a factored form with smaller value for *blnc_overhead_val* consumes fewer number of nodes and has smaller path balancing overhead (smaller value for imbalance factor).

*Example 1*: Suppose $F = age + agf + bge + bgf + cdge + cdgf$. One possible factoring tree for this expression is shown in Figure 2. Total node count of this tree is equal to six and its imbalance factor is $\Lambda = 0 + 0 + 1 + 1 + 2 + 1 = 5$. Therefore, the balanced factorization value of this factored form is equal to 11.

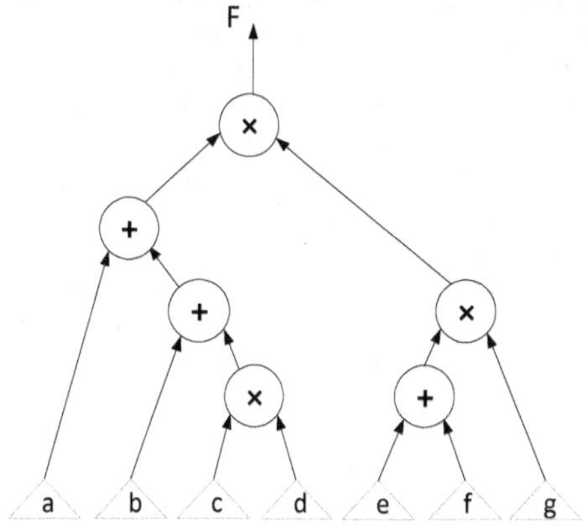


**Figure 2. A factoring tree for the expression given in the example 1.**

Algorithm 1 shows pseudo code of balanced factorization. As seen, after converting the given network into AIG representation (line 1), nodes are sorted to be in a topological order (a node will be visited only when all of its predecessors have been visited) in line 2, and k-feasible cuts (k=4) for each node is computed (line 3). Then, a factored form which gives the least balanced factorization value is selected for each node (lines 4-8), and finally, the optimized network is generated in line 9.

## 4.2 Balanced Rewriting

Balanced rewriting is a step in the technology-independent combinational logic synthesis flow of SFQ circuits which uses fast local transformation of AIG nodes. Input to this algorithm is an AIG representation of the given network. In the balanced rewriting algorithm similar to the DAG-aware AIG rewriting in [14], the given AIG is traversed in a topological order starting from leaf nodes of the graph. For each node $v$ in this graph, *4-feasible* cuts are computed as in [19]. For each computed cut of node $v$, all pre-computed 4-variable Boolean expressions that can implement the function of this node is tried. Different from the DAG-aware AIG rewriting algorithm presented in [14], in balanced rewriting algorithm, in addition to extracting the node count of the new rewritten expression, we calculate an imbalance factor for the corresponding sub-graph (similar to Section 4.1). To calculate the saving that is achieved from the rewritten version of the Boolean function of node $v$, we keep track of the sum of the current number of nodes and imbalance factors in the current sub-graph ($m_1$) and the new value for this sum after substituting a candidate sub-graph ($m_2$). If $m_2 < m_1$, there is a positive gain and the new rewritten version will be accepted. After visiting all nodes of the network and trying the rewritten version of their Boolean function, the final optimized AIG is constructed by tracing back the best solutions for nodes connected to POs (reverse topological ordering traversal).

# 5 EXPERIMENTAL RESULTS

The balanced rewriting and factorization algorithms are implemented inside an open source logic synthesis and verification tool called ABC [20]. Two sets of experimental results are extracted. The first set is node count, imbalance factor and sum of them before performing technology mapping, and the second set is total area and logical depth after finishing the technology mapping. The baseline for comparing our technology-independent optimizations is ABC's built-in optimization scripts including resyn, resyn2, resyn2a. For mapping, the standard cut-based technology mapping command (*map*) of ABC is employed, and an SFQ library of gates as in [21], consisting of *and2, or2, xor2, DFF, splitter,* and *inverter* gates are used, and several ISCAS [22], EPFL [23], MCNC [24], and arithmetic benchmark circuits are considered.

Notice that similar to the definition of imbalance factor for a factoring tree in Section 4.1, we can define an imbalance factor for a DAG too. Also, to compare different technology-independent optimization algorithms, we assign a total cost to a subject graph. The total cost of a subject graph is defined as sum of its imbalance factor and total number of nodes in its AIG representation.

Interleaving balanced rewriting and factorization commands together with *balance* command of ABC[4], provides higher reduction in total node count and imbalance factor of a given subject graph. Moreover, our experiments show that the order of applying

[4]This command performs algebraic AND-balancing [25].

**Table 1. Different technology-independent optimization scripts.**

| script | Corresponding sequences of commands |
|---|---|
| ABC's resyn | b; rw; rwz; b; rwz; b |
| ABC's resyn2 | b; rw; rf; b; rw; rwz; b; rfz; rwz; b |
| ABC's resyn2a | b; rw; b; rw; rwz; b; rwz; b |
| Our blnc_syn1 | brw; brf; b |
| Our blnc_syn2 | brf; b; brw; brwz; b; brfz; brwz; b |

these optimization commands can make a huge difference for some benchmark circuits. In the following, we provide an example from [26] to demonstrate this.

*Example 2*: Suppose $F = abg + acg + adf + aef + afg + bd + be + cd + ce$[5]. Applying standard rewriting, balance, and refactoring commands with this order will generate an optimized AIG as shown in Figure 3a with eight nodes, imbalance factor of four and total cost of 12. Applying ABC's resyn2 script (see Table 1) will generate the subject tree shown in Figure 3b with nine AIG nodes, imbalance factor of three and total cost of 12. However, if balanced rewriting, balanced factorization, and balance command of ABC are applied with this order, the resulting subject tree will be as shown in Figure 3c which is perfectly balanced, has seven AIG nodes, imbalance factor of 0, and total cost of seven.

We introduce two sets of optimization scripts called *blnc_syn1* and *blnc_syn2*, and also considered three optimization scripts of ABC. Table 1 shows these scripts and their corresponding sequence of commands. In these scripts, *b* is an alias for *balance command* of ABC, *rw* is an alias for standard rewriting, and *rf* is an alias for standard refactoring. Also, *rwz* and *rfz* are aliases for standard rewriting and refactoring, respectively with accepting zero gains. In our scripts, *brf* stands for balanced factorization and *brw* stands for balanced rewriting. Also, *brwz* and *brfz* are *brw* and *brf*, respectively with accepting zero gains.

Figure 4 shows values of imbalance factors for graphs generated by each set of optimization scripts listed in Table 1 together with the case when no optimization is employed. On average for 15 benchmark circuits, our blnc_syn1 and blnc_syn2 optimization scripts reduce the imbalance factor by 1.06×, and 1.38×, respectively compared with the case of applying no optimizations, and 41%, and 63%, respectively compared with resyn2 (the best among resyn, resyn2, resyn2a). Table 2 lists the graph cost function of different benchmark circuits generated by various optimization scripts. On average for 15 benchmark circuits, our blnc_syn1 and blnc_syn2 reduces this parameter by 68%, and 83%, respectively compared with the case of not applying any optimizations, and 19%, and 30%, respectively compared with resyn2.

Figure 5 shows the logical depth (critical path length) of different circuits optimized by employing different optimization scripts and mapped by ABC's cut-based technology mapper (plus splitter insertion and path balancing [8]). On average for 15 benchmark circuits, our blnc_syn1 and blnc_syn2 optimization scripts reduce the logical depth by 26% and 36%, respectively compared with the case of not applying any technology-independent optimizations. When it is compared with resyn2, the average improvements are 10% and 18%, respectively for blnc_syn1 and blnc_syn2. Table 3 lists total area of these circuits. The total area includes area of gates, path

[5]This expression is mentioned in page 434 of [26] for comparing literal saving that different factorization algorithms can provide.

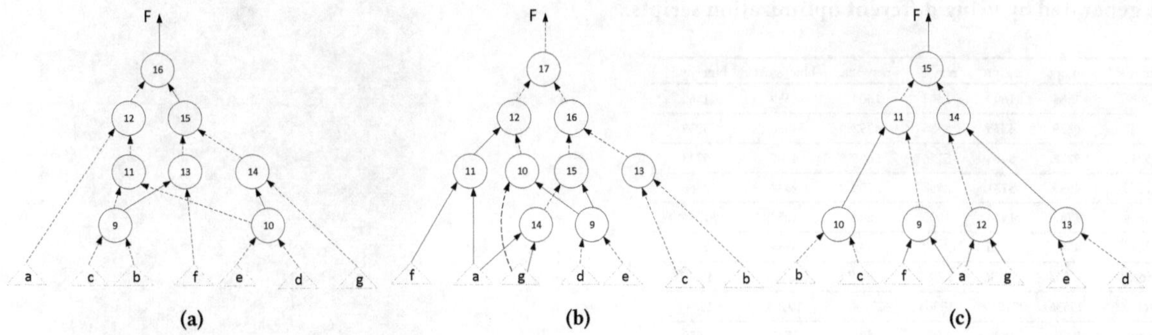

Figure 3. Three AIGs obtained for Boolean expression mentioned in the example 2. Nodes are 2-input AND gates, and dashed lines are inverted edges. (a) generated by applying standard rewriting, balance, and refactoring commands of ABC [20], (b) generated by applying resyn2 optimization script of ABC, and, (c) a perfectly balanced tree generated by our blnc_syn1 optimization script (see Table 1).

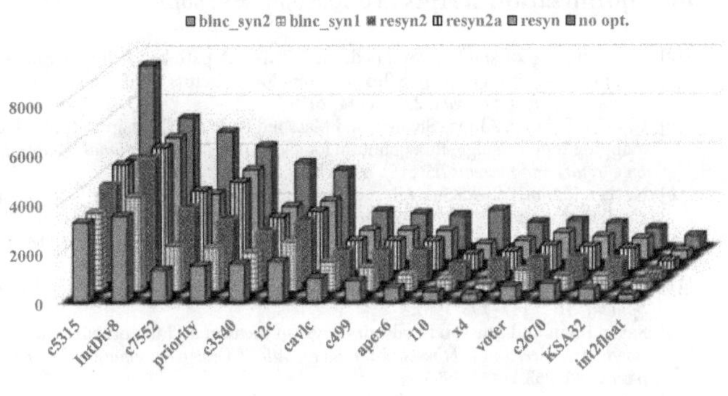

**Figure 4. Comparing imbalance factors of original graphs (no opt.) and those generated by different optimization scripts. For better exhibition purposes, the data for *priority*, *i10*, and *voter* circuits are scaled down by a factor of 10.**

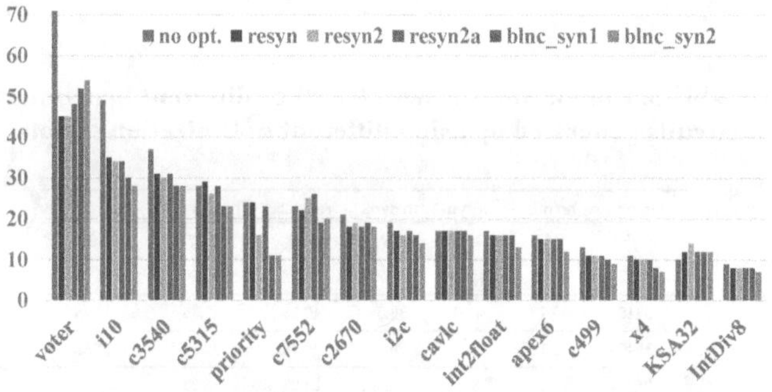

**Figure 5. Comparing logical depth of the mapped circuits optimized by using different optimization scripts and the original one (no opt.). For better exhibition purposes, the data for *priority*, and *IntDiv8* circuits are scaled down by a factor of 10.**

balancing DFFs, and splitters. On average for 15 benchmark circuits, blnc_syn1 reduces area by 21% compared with the case when no technology-independent optimizations are employed. Also, it has almost the same average area as resyn2. blnc_syn2 reduces area by 28% when compared to not using any technology-independent optimizations, and by 4% when compared to resyn2. blnc_syn2 reduces area for *x4* circuit by 23% when it is compared to resyn2.

Figure 6 shows the post place-and-route of the ISCAS c7552 benchmark circuit which is optimized using the blnc_syn2 script. The dimensions are $8440\mu m \times 8420\mu m$, which shows around 38% less chip area compared with the case of not applying blnc_syn2 (dimensions: $10090\mu m \times 9750\mu m$). Smaller chip has usually shorter critical interconnect, hence, it results in increasing the frequency of the local clock. For this reason, the chip generated by applying our blnc_syn2 enjoys increase in the local clock frequency from 13GHz to 14GHz.

## 6 CONCLUSION

In this paper, balanced factorization and rewriting algorithms are presented. Unlike standard rewriting and refactoring algorithms, our technology-independent optimization algorithms preserve balance of the given graph while optimizing it. Experimental results show that our optimization scripts reduce imbalance factor by an average of 1.38×. Using an SFQ library of gates, our optimization scripts reduce total area and logical depth after technology mapping by an average of 28%, and 36%, respectively for 15 benchmark circuits.

## ACKNOWLEDGEMENT

The research is based upon work supported by the Office of the Director of National Intelligence (ODNI), Intelligence Advanced Research Projects Activity (IARPA), via the U.S. Army Research Office grant W911NF-17-1-0120. The U.S. Government is authorized to reproduce and distribute reprints for Governmental purposes notwithstanding any copyright notation herein. This project is also supported in part by a grant from the Software and Hardware Foundations program of the National Science Foundation.

The presented place-and-route results are generated by using software tools provided by S. N. Shahsavani and T. Lin from the University of Southern California.

**Table 2. Comparing the graph cost of different benchmark circuits generated by using different optimization scripts.**

| circuit | no opt. | resyn | resyn2 | resyn2a | blnc_syn1 | blnc_syn2 |
|---|---|---|---|---|---|---|
| c499 | 1884 | 1604 | 1604 | 1604 | 1389 | 1362 |
| c7552 | 6879 | 4275 | 4438 | 4792 | 3638 | 3039 |
| c5315 | 9275 | 5428 | 5176 | 5609 | 4665 | 4743 |
| c3540 | 4569 | 3131 | 2958 | 3108 | 2642 | 2560 |
| c2670 | 1785 | 1544 | 1503 | 1545 | 1257 | 1345 |
| i2c | 4567 | 3596 | 3608 | 3587 | 3334 | 2932 |
| priority | 43083 | 37486 | 25772 | 36652 | 18505 | 15371 |
| voter | 25536 | 21519 | 18565 | 20350 | 19104 | 15544 |
| cavlc | 2271 | 1893 | 1882 | 1891 | 1867 | 1659 |
| int2float | 825 | 580 | 590 | 580 | 573 | 507 |
| KSA32 | 1477 | 1437 | 1340 | 1436 | 1180 | 1156 |
| IntDiv8 | 5677 | 5296 | 5295 | 5296 | 4175 | 3854 |
| i10 | 18851 | 8580 | 8415 | 8489 | 6937 | 6191 |
| x4 | 1555 | 1082 | 1093 | 1082 | 683 | 661 |
| apex6 | 2069 | 1817 | 1825 | 1819 | 1405 | 1307 |

**Table 3. Comparing the area ($mm^2$) of different benchmark circuits generated by using different optimization scripts.**

| circuit | no opt. | resyn | resyn2 | resyn2a | blnc_syn1 | blnc_syn2 |
|---|---|---|---|---|---|---|
| c499 | 5.37 | 4.91 | 4.91 | 4.91 | 4.85 | 4.59 |
| c7552 | 41.11 | 35.95 | 36.76 | 39.23 | 34.55 | 34.92 |
| c5315 | 45.73 | 41.4 | 38.54 | 40.15 | 35.35 | 39.26 |
| c3540 | 22.11 | 21.52 | 20.99 | 20.78 | 22.06 | 21.82 |
| c2670 | 28.12 | 23.93 | 25.8 | 24.28 | 25.22 | 25.39 |
| i2c | 35.91 | 31.72 | 30.7 | 31.72 | 32.2 | 29.72 |
| priority | 171.22 | 158.11 | 91.41 | 154.73 | 107.38 | 93.06 |
| voter | 258.93 | 168.15 | 138.24 | 169.78 | 162.65 | 132.45 |
| cavlc | 12.15 | 11.79 | 11.93 | 11.75 | 11.85 | 12.09 |
| int2float | 4.95 | 4.6 | 4.55 | 4.6 | 4.64 | 4.34 |
| KSA32 | 9.16 | 8.38 | 9.32 | 8.42 | 9.61 | 10.17 |
| IntDiv8 | 21.24 | 20.38 | 20.42 | 20.38 | 20.95 | 20.13 |
| i10 | 118.71 | 82.6 | 80.97 | 80.57 | 78.12 | 72.27 |
| x4 | 11.1 | 8.6 | 8.8 | 8.85 | 7.71 | 7.13 |
| apex6 | 20.85 | 19.22 | 19.24 | 19.08 | 19.48 | 17.2 |

**Figure 6. Post place-and-route of ISCAS c7552 benchmark circuit synthesized by applying our technology-independent optimization script, *blnc_syn2*. Dimensions are $8440\mu m \times 8420\mu m$. Dimensions of the chip without applying our optimization scripts are $10090\mu m \times 9750\mu m$.**

# REFERENCES


[1] T. N. Theis and H. S. P. Wong. The end of moore's law: A new beginning for information technology. *Computing in Science Engineering*, 19(2):41–50, Mar 2017.

[2] D Scott Holmes, Andrew L Ripple, and Marc A Manheimer. Energy-efficient superconducting computing-power budgets and requirements. *IEEE Transactions on Applied Superconductivity*, 23(3), 2013.

[3] Brian David Josephson. Possible new effects in superconductive tunnelling. *Physics letters*, 1(7):251–253, 1962.

[4] PI Bunyk, A Oliva, VK Semenov, M Bhushan, KK Likharev, JE Lukens, MB Ketchen, and WH Mallison. High-speed single-flux-quantum circuit using planarized niobium-trilayer josephson junction technology. *Applied physics letters*, 66(5):646–648, 1995.

[5] KK Likharev and VK Semenov. Rsfq logic/memory family: A new josephson-junction technology for sub-terahertz-clock-frequency digital systems. *IEEE Transactions on Applied Superconductivity*, 50(1), 1991.

[6] W Chen, AV Rylyakov, Vijay Patel, JE Lukens, and KK Likharev. Rapid single flux quantum t-flip flop operating up to 770 ghz. *IEEE Transactions on Applied Superconductivity*, 9(2):3212–3215, 1999.

[7] Rudolf Gross, Achim Marx, and Frank Deppe. *Applied superconductivity: Josephson effect and superconducting electronics.* De Gruyter, 2015.

[8] Ghasem Pasandi and Massoud Pedram. PBMap: A path balancing technology mapping algorithm for single flux quantum logic circuits. *IEEE Transactions on Applied Superconductivity*, 29(4):1–14, 2019.

[9] Ghasem Pasandi, Alireza Shafaei, and Massoud Pedram. SFQmap: A technology mapping tool for single flux quantum logic circuits. In *International Symposium on Circuits and Systems (ISCAS)*. IEEE, May 27, 2018.

[10] Naveen Katam, Alireza Shafaei, and Massoud Pedram. Design of multiple fanout clock distribution network for rapid single flux quantum technology. In *22nd Asia and South Pacific Design Automation Conference (ASP-DAC)*, pages 384–389. IEEE, 2017.

[11] Robert K Brayton. Factoring logic functions. *IBM Journal of research and development*, 31(2):187–198, 1987.

[12] Sasan Iman and Massoud Pedram. Logic extraction and factorization for low power. In *Proceedings of the 32nd annual ACM/IEEE Design Automation Conference*, pages 248–253. ACM, 1995.

[13] Sumit Roy, Harm Arts, and Prithviraj Banerjee. Powershake: A low power driven clustering and factoring methodology for boolean expressions. In *Proceedings of the conference on Design, automation and test in Europe*, pages 967–968. IEEE Computer Society, 1998.

[14] Alan Mishchenko, Satrajit Chatterjee, and Robert Brayton. DAG-aware AIG rewriting a fresh look at combinational logic synthesis. In *Proceedings of the 43rd annual Design Automation Conference*, pages 532–535. ACM, 2006.

[15] Per Bjesse and Arne Boralv. DAG-aware circuit compression for formal verification. In *Proceedings of the 2004 IEEE/ACM International conference on Computer-aided design*, pages 42–49. IEEE Computer Society, 2004.

[16] Saburo Muroga. Logic design and switching theory. *John Wiley & Sons*, 1979.

[17] Mathias Soeken and Michael Kirkedal Thomsen. White dots do matter: rewriting reversible logic circuits. In *International Conference on Reversible Computation*, pages 196–208. Springer, 2013.

[18] Winston Haaswijk, Mathias Soeken, Luca Amarú, Pierre-Emmanuel Gaillardon, and Giovanni De Micheli. A novel basis for logic rewriting. In *2017 22nd Asia and South Pacific Design Automation Conference (ASP-DAC)*, pages 151–156. Ieee, 2017.

[19] Jason Cong and Yuzheng Ding. Flowmap: An optimal technology mapping algorithm for delay optimization in lookup-table based fpga designs. *IEEE Transactions on Computer-Aided Design of Integrated Circuits and Systems*, 13(1):1–12, 1994.

[20] Mishchenko et. al. ABC : A system for sequential synthesis and verification. *Berkeley Logic Synthesis and Verification Group*, 2018.

[21] C. Fourie. Rsfq cell library, 2018.

[22] Mark C Hansen, Hakan Yalcin, and John P Hayes. Unveiling the iscas-85 benchmarks: A case study in reverse engineering. *IEEE Design & Test of Computers*, 16(3):72–80, 1999.

[23] Amaru et. al. The epfl combinational benchmark suite, 2017.

[24] Saeyang Yang. *Logic synthesis and optimization benchmarks user guide: version 3.0.* Microelectronics Center of North Carolina (MCNC), 1991.

[25] Alan Mishchenko, Robert Brayton, Stephen Jang, and Victor Kravets. Delay optimization using sop balancing. In *Computer-Aided Design (ICCAD), 2011 IEEE/ACM International Conference on*, pages 375–382. IEEE, 2011.

[26] Gary D Hachtel and Fabio Somenzi. *Logic synthesis and verification algorithms.* Springer Science & Business Media, 2006.

# A Majority Logic Synthesis Framework for Adiabatic Quantum-Flux-Parametron Superconducting Circuits

Ruizhe Cai
Northeastern University
USA
cai.ruiz@husky.neu.edu

Olivia Chen
Yokohama National University
Japan
olivia.chen@ieee.org

Ao Ren
Ning Liu
Caiwen Ding
Northeastern University
USA

Nobuyuki Yoshikawa
Yokohama National University
Japan
nyoshi@ynu.ac.jp

Yanzhi Wang
Northeastern University
USA
yanz.wang@northeastern.edu

## ABSTRACT

Adiabatic Quantum-Flux-Parametron (AQFP) logic is an adiabatic superconductor logic that has been proposed as alternative to CMOS logic with extremely high energy efficiency. In AQFP technology, majority-based gates have the same area as two-input AND/OR gates while offering more complex logic. Therefore, majority-based logic (MAJ) is more preferred than and-or-inverter-based logic (AOI) to implement logic functions in AQFP for higher energy efficiency. In this paper, we propose a majority gates synthesis framework for AQFP circuits that is capable of converting any AOI netlist to its corresponding MAJ netlist by mapping all feasible three-input sub-netlists to corresponding MAJ based implementations. In addition, the proposed tool can insert the optimal amount of buffers and splitters for equivalent delay as required in the AQFP technology. Experimental results suggest that the proposed method can reduce delay and area by up to 60.00% and 60.98%, respectively.

## KEYWORDS

Superconducting electronics, AQFP, majority gates, logic synthesis

**ACM Reference Format:**

Ruizhe Cai, Olivia Chen, Ao Ren, Ning Liu, Caiwen Ding, Nobuyuki Yoshikawa, and Yanzhi Wang. 2019. A Majority Logic Synthesis Framework for Adiabatic Quantum-Flux-Parametron Superconducting Circuits. In *Great Lakes Symposium on VLSI 2019 (GLSVLSI '19), May 9–11, 2019, Tysons Corner, VA, USA.* ACM, New York, NY, USA, 6 pages. https://doi.org/10.1145/3299874.3317980

## 1 INTRODUCTION

Constructed by resistance-less wires and ultrafast switches, superconductor based circuits using Josephson junctions (JJ) can perform at clock frequencies of several tens of gigahertz and even hundreds or thousands of times as energy efficient as their CMOS cousins. For its superior potential in operation speed and energy efficiency, it has been perceived to be an important candidate to replace state-of-the-art CMOS, as recognized by the U.S. IARPA C3 and SuperTools Programs and Japan MEXT-JSPS Project. The design and fabrication of superconducting circuits have been already established [6, 7, 21]. A prototype superconducting microprocessor "Core 1" has been demonstrated in 2004 [21], which is able to execute instructions at a high clock frequency of several tens of gigahertz, and with extremely low-power dissipation. These achievements make superconducting electronics highly promising for future high-performance computing and deep space applications.

The Rapid-Single-Flux-Quantum (RSFQ) technology, proposed by K. Likharev, O. Mukhanoc, V. Semenov in 1985 [12], is the most matured technology and can operate at an ultra-high speed of hundreds of GHz while maintaining extremely low switching energy ($10^{-19}$J). However, it suffers from an increasing static power as on-chip resistors are needed to supply constant DC bias current to the main RSFQ circuit. Numerous methods have been proposed to resolve the static power dissipation problem of RSFQ, including low-voltage RSFQ (LV-RSFQ) [20], reciprocal quantum logic (RQL) [8], LR-biased RSFQ [26] and energy-efficient single-flux quantum (eSFQ) [14].

The *Adiabatic Quantum-Flux-Parametron* (AQFP) technology uses AC bias/excitation currents as both multi-phase clock signal and power supply [18] to mitigate the power consumption overhead of DC bias while operating at a frequency of few GHz. Despite operating at a lower frequency compared to RSFQ, AQFP is remarkably energy efficient, given the fact that the AQFP technology is the only technology that is capable of achieving energy dissipation near quantum limits using practical circuit parameters and fabrication processes including the AIST standard process and the MIT-LL sfq process [15, 22]. Physical testing results of an AQFP 8-bit carry-look-ahead adder and large scale circuits consisting up-to 10,000 AQFP logic gates have demonstrated the AQFP being a promising technology that is robust against circuit parameter variations [19].

Despite the high application potential of AQFP in VLSI circuits, a systematic, automatic synthesis framework for AQFP is lacking. Unlike CMOS logic that relies on And-Or-Inverter-based (AOI) representation, AQFP logic prefers majority-based (MAJ) gates (majority gates and variations with negations at input/output) as three-input


*GLSVLSI '19, May 9–11, 2019, Tysons Corner, VA, USA*

ACM ISBN 978-1-4503-6252-8/19/05...$15.00
https://doi.org/10.1145/3299874.3317980

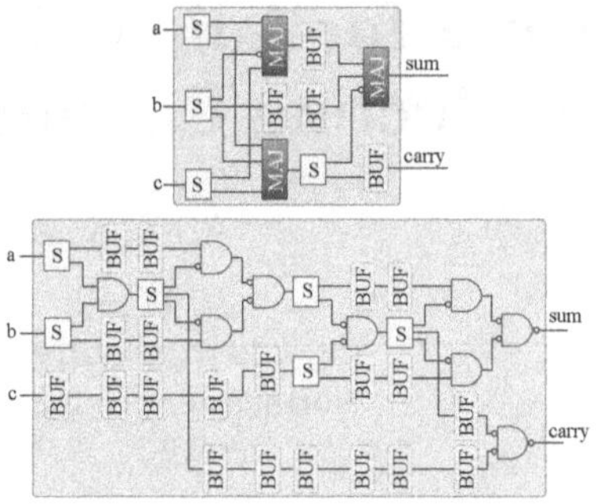


**Figure 1: Comparison between the MAJ-based implementation and the AOI-based implementation of a 1-bit full-adder using the AQFP technology.**

majority-based gates utilize the same JJ resources as two-input AND/OR gates. As shown in Fig. 1, in AQFP technology, the MAJ-based implementation of a 1-bit full-adder is much smaller and faster compared to the AOI counterpart. In addition, the AQFP technology requires all data-paths to any gate having equal delay (clock phases) due to its clock-synchronized data propagation nature. This path balancing scheme relies on splitters and buffers. The above features restrict conventional CMOS synthesis methods being directly applied on AQFP to achieve the optimal results. While methods for majority synthesis exist in literature, a systematic synthesis framework for AQFP capable of converting from existing AOI designs is still imminent. Such framework can provide a faster design flow as existing CMOS based designs can be converted from their AOI netlists and integration with existing open-source AOI synthesis tools can offer higher maturity and reliability.

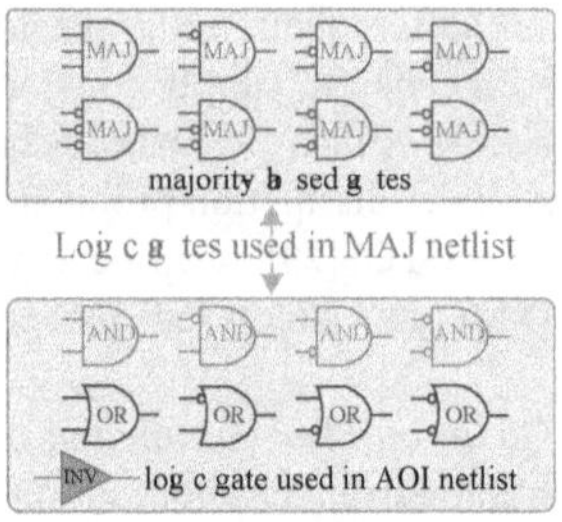

**Figure 2: Logic gates in the MAJ netlist.**

In this paper, we propose a complete framework producing MAJ netlists for AQFP from AOI netlists. As illustrated in Fig. 2, MAJ netlist utilizes majority-based gates as well as logic gates used in AOI netlist, when majority-based gates will not bring benefit on JJ count/delay. The input AOI netlist is first converted to a MAJ netlist by mapping all feasible three-input net to their corresponding two-level MAJ-based implementation. The converted netlist is then inserted with buffers and splitters for equal delay (clock phase), which is required by the AQFP technology. The proposed method has been applied on AOI netlists of multiple logic circuits to test its efficiency. Experimental results show that the proposed method can reduce delay and area by up-to 60.00% and 60.98% respectively. Overall, the proposed framework can convert AOI netlists to AQFP compatible MAJ netlist for excellent resource and timing efficiency.

## 1.1 AQFP Superconducting Logic

As shown in Fig. 3, the basic logic structure of AQFP circuits is buffers consisting of a double-Josephson-Junction SQUID [4]. An AQFP logic gate is mainly driven by AC-power, as mentioned above, serves as both excitation current and power supply. By applying excitation current $I_x$, typically in the order of hundreds of micro-amperes, excitation fluxes are applied to the superconducting loops via inductors $L_1$, $L_2$, $L_{x1}$ and $L_{x2}$. Depending on the small input current $I_{in}$, either the left or the right loop stores one single flux quantum. Consequently, the device is capable of acting as a buffer cell as the logic state can be represented by the direction of the output current $I_{out}$. Accordingly, the storage position of the quantum flux in the left or the right loop can be encoded as logic '1' or '0' as the directions of current are opposite.

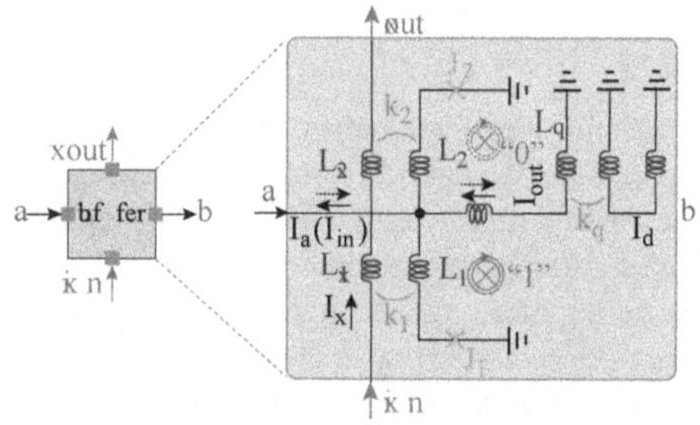

**Figure 3: Symbol of an AQFP buffer gate and its junction level schematic.**

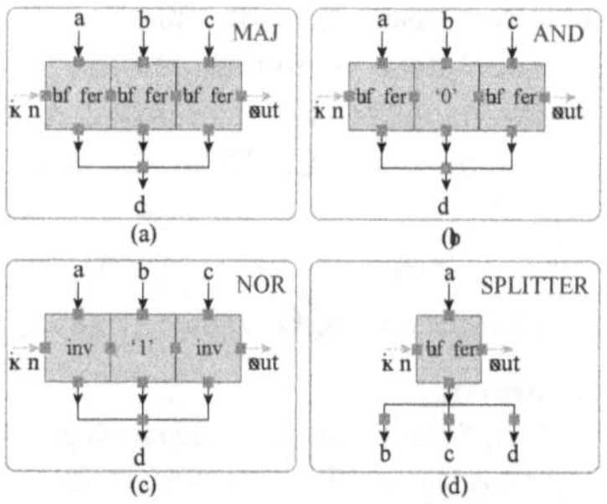


**Figure 4: (a). An AQFP majority gate, which consists of 3 buffers; (b). An AQFP AND gate, which consists of 2 buffers and a constant '0' gate; (c). An AQFP NOR gate, which consists of 2 inverters and a constant '1' gate; (d). An AQFP 1-to-3 splitter, which consists of a buffer.**

The AQFP inverter and constant cell are designed from AQFP buffer. The AQFP inverter is implemented by negating the coupling coefficient of the output transformer in the AQFP buffer, while the constant gate in AQFP is designed using asymmetry excitation flux inductance in the AQFP buffer. The AQFP splitter is also implemented based on the AQFP buffer as shown in Fig. 4. Please note that, unlike CMOS gates, which are connected to fan-out gates directly, all AQFP gates need to be connected to splitters for fan-out more than one.

The AQFP standard cell library is built via the *minimalist design approach* [19], in other words, designing more complicated gates using a bottom-up manner. Logic gate shown in Fig. 4 (a) is a majority gate as the output, 'd', depends on the number of '1's at inputs, 'a' to 'c'. Replacing any buffer with inverter can produce a variation of the majority gate (such as the minority gate). We call these variations *majority-based gates*, with a total of 8 types of gates shown in Fig. 2. AND/OR gates in AQFP are designed from majority-based gate by replacing one of the buffers or inverters with a constant gate. As illustrated in Fig. 4 (b)-(c), an AQFP AND gate is implemented by two buffers and one constant '0' while an AQFP NOR gate is implemented by two inverters and one constant '1'. In AQFP technology, three-input majority-based gates and two-input AND/OR based gates have the same area and delay, which makes majority-based gates a desirable choice.

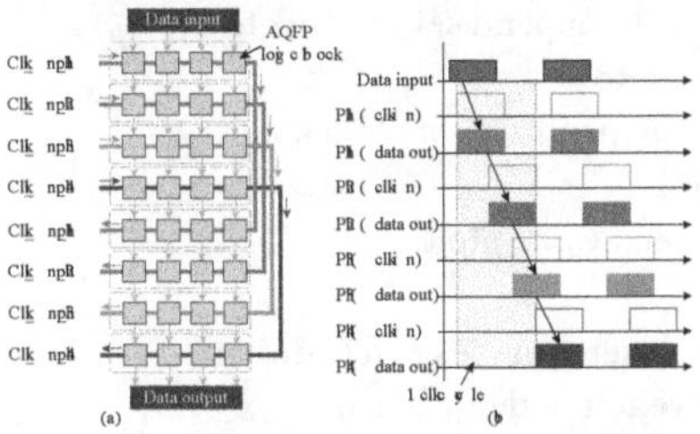


**Figure 5: (a). 4-phase clocking scheme for AQFP circuits; (b). Data propagation between neighbouring clock phases.**

Unlike the conventional CMOS technology, both combinational and sequential AQFP logic cells are driven by AC-power. In addition, the AC power serves as clock signal to synchronize the outputs of all gates in the same clock phase. Consequently, data propagation in AQFP circuits requires overlapping of clock signals from neighbouring phases. Fig. 5 presents an example of typical clocking scheme of AQFP circuits and data flow between neighbouring clock phases. Such clock-based synchronization characteristic also requires that all inputs for each gate should have the same delay (clock phases) from the primary inputs.

### 1.2 Majority Synthesis

The majority synthesis is beneficial for a number of nanotechnologies, such as Quantum Cellular Automata (QCA) [11], Single Electron Tunnelling (SET) [16] and Tunnelling Phase Logic (TPL) [5]. Many of these technologies utilize majority-based gates as basic logic units. In conventional synthesis flow for CMOS logic, Boolean logic functions are simplified and expressed in two standard forms: sum of products (SOP) and product of sums (POS). Both two forms, which cannot be efficiently expressed using MAJ network given the complexity of multi-level MAJ network, are represented in terms of AOI network.

The very first majority synthesis approaches include Karnaugh-map method [13], reduced-unitised table [2]. These methods target simple logic [3]. Other early majority synthesis methods were introduced based on a cubic representation of three-variable Boolean functions [23, 27]. These methods can convert up-to three-variable Boolean functions to the optimal MAJ network. Most comprehensive majority synthesis methods [3, 9, 10, 24] that are capable of performing multi-level and multi-output synthesis firstly decompose Boolean functions into three-feasible or four-feasible networks. The decomposed networks are then converted to corresponding majority compositions using different primary-set based mapping methods. One of the most commonly adopted mapping method [10] introduces a primary-set consisting of 40 primitive functions. Each three-feasible network is mapped to either one majority-based gate or a two-level majority-based structure based on the primary set. The Majority Expression Lookup Table (MLUT)-based method adopted 90 primitive functions set for conversion after decomposition [24]. Another approach performs exact synthesis for Majority-Inverter Graphs (MIGs) from logic expression with size and depth optimum based on satisfiability modulo theories (SMT) solver [17]. This method converts a logic expression into a decision problem and decomposes it into multiple SMT solvers using majority Boolean algebra.

In this work, instead of synthesizing from Boolean function, we focus on a different approach that converts an existing AOI network to a MAJ network. Unlike existing majority synthesis methods that decompose Boolean functions into three-feasible sub-networks for further mapping, the proposed method finds three-feasible networks from an AOI network, then maps them to corresponding MAJ structures. Converting from AOI network could allow faster workflow for synthesizing AQFP circuits based on existing design. In addition, it enables integration with existing open-source synthesis tools (e.g., YoSys), which allows mature and reliable workflow.

## 2 MAJORITY SYNTHESIS FOR AQFP LOGIC

The proposed framework contains two main tasks: majority-based mapping and buffer/splitter insertions (levelling). The mapping task converts any AOI netlist to its MAJ counterpart. The levelling part modifies any netlist for equal delay (clock phase) at the outputs, which is required by AQFP technology. This is achieved by inserting splitters for fan-outs and buffers for balancing the path delay (clock phase) to each gate.

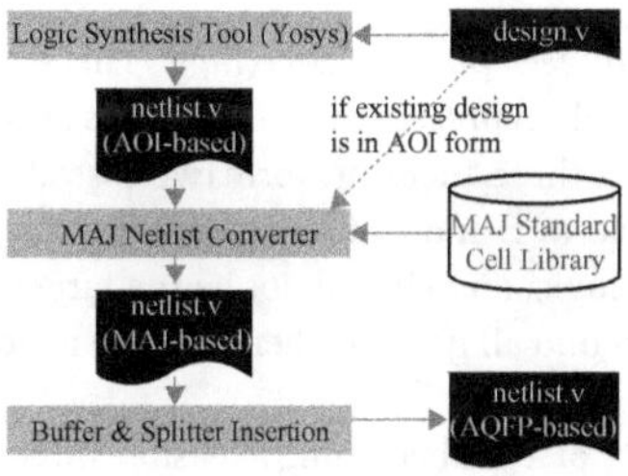


**Figure 6: Workflow of the proposed AQFP synthesis framework**

The top-down workflow used in the proposed framework is shown in Fig. 6. The high-level description of the design is firstly synthesized to its AOI netlist using a CMOS-based open-source synthesis tool 'Yosys' [25]. The AOI netlist is then converted to its MAJ netlist counterpart. Finally, all paths in the MAJ netlist are levelled with buffers and splitters to generate the AQFP-compatible netlist.

### 2.1 Majority Conversion

The proposed mapping method can convert an AOI netlist to a MAJ netlist. As shown in Fig. 7, a netlist can be considered as a directed graph. Each node represents a net and stores corresponding logic using Karnaugh map. For further simplification, all negations (inverters) are integrated to the node's output. Therefore, an AOI netlist can be represented using a directed graph where each node has two parents, while a MAJ netlist can be represented using a directed graph where each node has two or three parents.

Using this representation scheme, the proposed method can be summarised in three key steps: The first step is to find all feasible three-input nets in an AOI netlist that can be efficiently represented using majority-based gates, with gain in JJ count. Except for the case that the three inputs form two cascaded AOI gates, all nodes that can be represented using three ancestors can be converted to a majority-based representation with less JJ count. The second step uses a table-based majority mapping method [10], which maps each three-input representation to two-level majority-based logic schemes. The last step determines the final mapping for each three-input net from their mapping candidates while maintaining the minimum total resource.

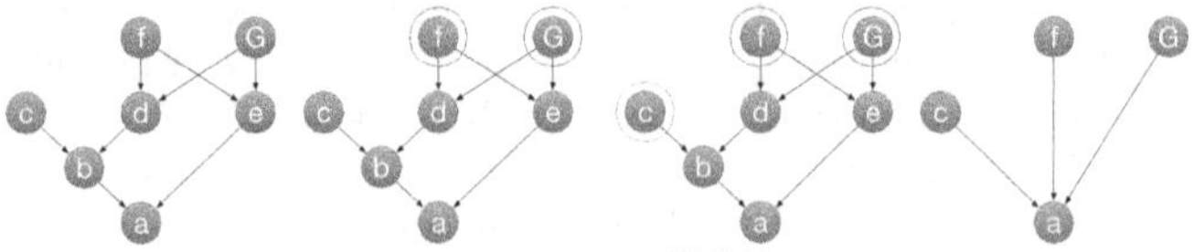

(a) Input graph (b) Find mutual ancestors (c) Add spouse (d) Merge net

**Figure 7: Example of feasible three-input net searching: (a) Step 1: input AOI net as a directed graph; (b) Step 2: Find mutual ancestors of the parents (node *b* and node *c*) of the target output (node *a*), which are node *f* and node *g*; (c). Step 3: Add spouses of the nodes that are on the path to the mutual ancestors but not on the path to the group (node *e* is the spouse to node *d*, and node *e* is not on any path to the mutual ancestors); (d). Step 4: Merge net from nodes *e, f, g* to *a*.**

*2.1.1 Feasible three-input Nets Searching.* This step finds all nodes that can be logically represented by three of its ancestors, except for the case when the three ancestors form two cascaded AND/OR gates. These nets (A and/or B and/or C) cannot be further optimized using majority-based logic, and should not be the target for replacement. This step should find all nets that benefit from majority-based gates representation.

The feasibility of a net becoming a feasible three-input net can be determined by Algorithm 1. This proposed method first determines the intersection of its two branches, each branch containing one of its parents and corresponding ancestors. The mutual ancestors are then partitioned into several sets. Nodes in the same set are independent, i.e., each node cannot be decedents of any other nodes in the same set. Finally, for each node in a set, find all spouses of its decedents above the target net that are not decedents to any other nodes in the same set, then add the qualified nodes to the set.

All sets from the previous step are the ancestors that are capable of representing the target net. As the main objective is to determine three-input feasibility, only the sets that contain three nodes need to be taken into further consideration. If no set qualifies, the target net is not three-input feasible. If more than one set containing three nodes exist, the set that is furthest from the target should be chosen as the ancestors to merge. As indicated in the *level* function in

**Algorithm 1:** Feasible Three-Input Nets Searching Algorithm

```
input  : target node N
output : new parent nodes of N
if number of parents of N is 2 then
    A_L = set(Ancestors of the left parent of N);
    A_R = set(Ancestors of the right parent of N);
    M = A_R ∩ A_L;
    Create C as an empty list, each item in C is a set of nodes;
    foreach node m in M do
        Create C_temp as an empty list, each item in C_temp is a
          set of nodes;
        foreach set of nodes c in C do
            if m ∉ decedents(n), ∀n ∈ c then
                append set c ∪ {m} to C_temp
            end
            append set {m} to C_temp
        end
        extend C_temp to C
    end
    foreach set of nodes c in C do
        foreach node c_n in c do
            foreach decedent c_n^d of c_n do
                if spouse(c_n^d) ∉ decedents(n), ∀n ∈ c then
                    add spouse(c_n^d) to c
                end
            end
        end
    end
    s = ∅;
    foreach set of nodes c in C do
        if number of nodes is c is 3 then
            if s == ∅ or level(c) > level(s) then
                s ← c
            end
        end
    end
    if s ≠ ∅ then
        return s
    end
end
return parent(N)
```

Algorithm 1, the distance between a set of nodes and the target net can be evaluated by the summation of level difference from each ancestor to the target net. For finding three-input nets, no more than four levels of ancestors need to be searched. The merge step operates in a depth-first order, which can be implemented using a stack data structure as the result returned from the target node will be the next target nodes. A detailed example is shown in Fig. 7.

*2.1.2 Majority Mapping.* All three-input feasible nets found in the previous step can be mapped to corresponding majority-based gates representation based on their Karnaugh map using the method proposed in [10]. This method uses a primary gate set to map a three-input net. Regardless of its logic, every three-input net can be mapped to an up-to two level majority-based structure [10].

As introduced in [10], the primary set contains 40 logic for up to three inputs, and can be categorised as follows: 1) static logic (0 and 1); 2) primary input or inverse (6 combinations); 3) AND/OR-based logic (AND gate and OR gate from two of three inputs, and their variations by negating one or both inputs, 24 combinations in total); 4) MAJ-based logic (8 combinations). Each mapping scheme returns a two-level MAJ structure whose first level comprises three gates in primary set and second level is either a MAJ gate or an AND/OR-based gate (if level 1 contains static logic). In other words, for a given three-input function $d = F(a, b, c)$, $d$ is mapped as $d = M(P_x(a, b, c), P_y(a, b, c), P_z(a, b, c))$ where $M$ denotes majority function and $P_x$, $P_y$ and $P_z$ stand for three primitive functions chosen from the primary set. Each three-input logic can correspond to multiple MAJ mappings.

To determine if a primitive gate can be selected for a qualified MAJ mapping scheme for a three-input net, a Karnaugh map checking method is applied [10]. This method iterates all combinations of three primitive gates to check if it is equivalent in function with the target net by comparing their Karnaugh maps. If the Karnaugh map of the net to be mapped matches one in the primary gates, it is mapped accordingly. Otherwise, the net is mapped to the aforementioned two-level majority-based logic.

*2.1.3 Majority Logic Sharing.* For all three-input nets that share the same logic, certain mapping scheme can further reduce resources as some of the level-1 primary gates can be shared among three-input nets. The optimal results can only be achieved by iterating through all combinations of three-input net mapping. However, it is possible to achieve a near-optimal solution with a less complex approach, especially when the number of involved nets is very large. This greedy approach first determines the popularity of each primary gate among all mapping schemes of involved nets, i.e., how many nets can be mapped using each specific primary gate, then selects the mapping combination with the most popular primary gates for each net.

For the optimal solution, a full iteration is still required. To further reduce the iteration size, we first select the mapping scheme for each three-input net with the minimum resource (i.e., the mapping scheme with more static logic or primary logic is preferred). Finally, all combinations of mapping schemes of involved nets are iterated to obtain mapping for each three-input net that consumes the least total resources.

## 2.2 Buffers and Splitters Insertion

AQFP requires all inputs to each gate having the same delay (clock phases). Therefore, any "bare-bone" netlist needs further modification to satisfy such requirement: all fan-outs more than 2 need splitter to duplicate data and faster data-paths need buffers for delay levelling. The first step determines splitter insertions. Splitters are inserted for each fan-out more than 2. The number of splitters to be inserted is determined by the AQFP library (the maximum fan-out for splitter). Once all fan-outs have been processed, the delay for each net needs to be re-calculated. With new delay for each net calculated, buffers are inserted in each data-path to every gate accordingly to produce equal delay. Since the logical structure of the netlist is fixed, buffer insertion can be accomplished with any order, without restriction by the critical path. In addition, to

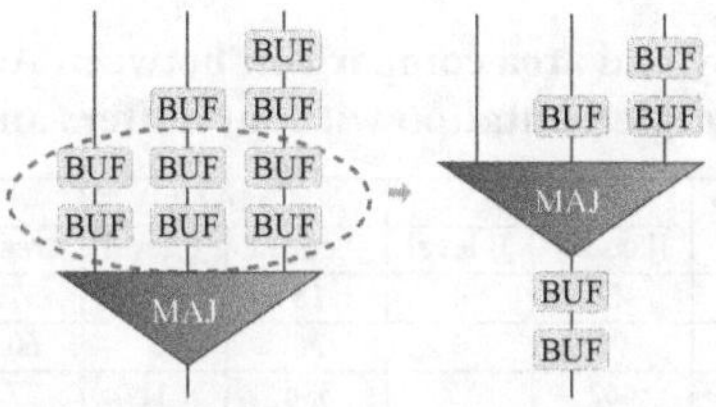


**Figure 8: Buffer merging example for a majority gate whose inputs are connected to 2, 3, 4 buffers, respectively. Buffer merging can reduce buffer amount by nearly 50% in this specific case.**

further reduce buffer consumption, a buffer merging step is applied. For each gate, if all of its inputs have buffer inserted, the shared number of buffers is moved to its output without logic change. As shown in Fig. 8, three inputs to the target gate have 2, 3, 4 buffers, respectively. This structure can be simplified by moving two buffers to the output of the target gate, and the number of buffers at inputs are reduced to 0, 1, 2, respectively. This step can guarantee the least total buffer count. Unlike splitters and buffers insertion that can be processed in a random order regardless of delay, buffer merging must be checked from the node with minimum delay to the output. This is because the delay (clock phase) within the internal nodes will change through this buffer merging step.

# 3 EXPERIMENTS AND ANALYSIS

## 3.1 Experiments Setup

To validate the effectiveness of the proposed method, several AOI netlists are used to produce corresponding MAJ netlists and delay and area are compared. Comparison between base netlists without buffer and splitter is also taken into account to test the efficiency of the proposed conversion method. The input AOI netlists are produced using the open-source synthesis tool Yosys [25]. Adders, multipliers and some of the ISCAS85 benchmark circuits [1] are tested. AOI netlists for adders and multipliers are synthesized using Yosys from their corresponding arithmetic expression. Netlists for circuits from ISCAS85 benchmark are synthesized from their source HDL codes [1].

## 3.2 Results and Analysis

Comparison results of delay and area are presented in Table 2 and Table 1. Results with buffer/splitter and without buffer/splitter are both presented. As shown in Table 1, the proposed conversion method is very effective as both delay and area can be largely reduced by up to 50.00% and 57.14%, respectively. Huge reduction in area suggests that the proposed conversion method can effectively locate feasible three-input nets and convert them to corresponding MAJ structure while maintaining the minimum overall resource consumption.

With buffers and splitters inserted, as shown in Table 2, the proposed method can reduce up to 60.00% and 60.98% in delay and area, respectively. It can be observed that the proposed framework achieves the highest gains in adders and multipliers. For the ISCAS85 benchmark circuits, optimization results depend on the design. For instance, the 'c17' circuit does not benefit from majority-based gates at all while the 'c6288' circuit can be implemented with

**Table 1: delay and area comparison between AOI-based and MAJ-based implementation without buffers and splitters**

| Device | AOI | | MAJ | | Reduction | |
|---|---|---|---|---|---|---|
| | JJ count | JJ level | JJ count | JJ level | area (%) | delay (%) |
| 1-bit adder | 42 | 4 | 18 | 2 | 57.14 | 50.00 |
| 2-bit adder | 90 | 4 | 36 | 3 | 60.00 | 25.00 |
| 8-bit adder | 462 | 17 | 336 | 11 | 27.27 | 35.29 |
| 3-bit multiplier | 222 | 11 | 174 | 7 | 21.62 | 36.36 |
| 4-bit multiplier | 498 | 17 | 360 | 11 | 27.71 | 35.29 |
| 8-bit multiplier | 2634 | 35 | 1980 | 23 | 24.82 | 34.28 |
| c17 | 36 | 3 | 36 | 3 | 0.00 | 0.00 |
| c432 | 732 | 26 | 726 | 26 | 0.01 | 0.00 |
| c880 | 1838 | 27 | 1646 | 18 | 10.44 | 33.33 |
| c1908 | 1776 | 21 | 1578 | 21 | 11.15 | 0.00 |
| c5315 | 7952 | 26 | 7490 | 23 | 5.80 | 11.54 |
| c6288 | 11220 | 89 | 5904 | 48 | 47.38 | 46.07 |

**Table 2: delay and area comparison between AOI-based and MAJ-based implementation with buffers and splitters**

| Device | AOI | | MAJ | | Reduction | |
|---|---|---|---|---|---|---|
| | JJ count | JJ level | JJ count | JJ level | area (%) | delay (%) |
| 1-bit adder | 82 | 10 | 32 | 4 | 60.98 | 60.00 |
| 2-bit adder | 182 | 11 | 80 | 6 | 56.04 | 45.45 |
| 8-bit adder | 1278 | 33 | 1176 | 23 | 7.98 | 30.30 |
| 3-bit multiplier | 542 | 22 | 346 | 14 | 36.16 | 36.36 |
| 4-bit multiplier | 1252 | 33 | 888 | 21 | 29.07 | 36.36 |
| 8-bit multiplier | 6824 | 71 | 5448 | 42 | 20.16 | 40.85 |
| c17 | 60 | 5 | 60 | 5 | 0 | 0 |
| c432 | 3134 | 39 | 3072 | 39 | 1.98 | 0.00 |
| c880 | 6676 | 40 | 5914 | 30 | 11.41 | 25.00 |
| c1908 | 7126 | 38 | 6818 | 38 | 4.32 | 0.00 |
| c5315 | 32068 | 42 | 30910 | 40 | 3.61 | 4.76 |
| c6288 | 55248 | 180 | 25870 | 94 | 53.17 | 47.78 |

53.17% less resource for 47.78% less latency. Overall, the proposed framework can produce very promising results in terms of area and timing efficiency as suggested by the experimental results.

# 4 CONCLUSION

In this paper, we propose a complete framework that is capable of converting a base AOI netlist to its MAJ netlist counterpart with buffers and splitters that is compatible with the AQFP technology. The proposed framework contains two-main parts: converting an AOI netlist to its corresponding MAJ netlist and inserting buffer/splitter for equal delay as required by the AQFP technology. Experimental results by comparing multiple logic circuits suggest that the proposed method can produce promising results as up-to 60.00% and 60.98% in delay and area can be reduced, respectively.

# ACKNOWLEDGEMENTS

This research is based upon work supported by the Office of the Director of National Intelligence (ODNI), Intelligence Advanced Research Projects Activity (IARPA), via the U.S. Army Research Office grant W911NF-17-1-0120.

# REFERENCES

[1] [n. d.]. http://www.pld.ttu.ee/~maksim/benchmarks/iscas85/verilog/.

[2] Sheldon B Akers. 1962. Synthesis of combinational logic using three-input majority gates. In *Proceedings of the Third Annual Symposium on Switching Circuit Theory and Logical Design*. IEEE, 149–158.

[3] Amjad Almatrood and Harpreet Singh. 2017. A comparative study of majority/minority logic circuit synthesis methods for post-CMOS nanotechnologies. *Engineering* 9, 10 (2017), 890.

[4] John Clarke and Alex I Braginski. 2006. *The SQUID handbook: Applications of SQUIDs and SQUID systems*. John Wiley & Sons.

[5] Hossam AH Fahmy and Richard A Kiehl. 1999. Complete logic family using tunneling-phase-logic devices. In *Microelectronics, 1999. ICM'99. The Eleventh International Conference on*. IEEE, 153–156.

[6] Timur V Filippov, Anubhav Sahu, Alex F Kirichenko, Igor V Vernik, Mikhail Dorojevets, Christopher L Ayala, and Oleg A Mukhanov. 2012. 20 GHz operation of an asynchronous wave-pipelined RSFQ arithmetic-logic unit. *Physics Procedia* 36 (2012), 59–65.

[7] Hisao Hayakawa, Nobuyuki Yoshikawa, Shinichi Yorozu, and Akira Fujimaki. 2004. Superconducting digital electronics. *Proc. IEEE* 92, 10 (2004), 1549–1563.

[8] Quentin P Herr, Anna Y Herr, Oliver T Oberg, and Alexander G Ioannidis. 2011. Ultra-low-power superconductor logic. *Journal of applied physics* 109, 10 (2011), 103903.

[9] Zhi Huo, Qishan Zhang, Sansiri Haruehanroengra, and Wei Wang. 2006. Logic optimization for majority gate-based nanoelectronic circuits. In *Circuits and Systems, 2006. ISCAS 2006. Proceedings. 2006 IEEE International Symposium on*. IEEE, 4–pp.

[10] Kun Kong, Yun Shang, and Ruqian Lu. 2010. An optimized majority logic synthesis methodology for quantum-dot cellular automata. *IEEE Transactions on Nanotechnology* 9, 2 (2010), 170–183.

[11] Craig S Lent and P Douglas Tougaw. 1997. A device architecture for computing with quantum dots. *Proc. IEEE* 85, 4 (1997), 541–557.

[12] K. K. Likharev and V. K. Semenov. 1991. RSFQ logic/memory family: a new Josephson-junction technology for sub-terahertz-clock-frequency digital systems. *IEEE Transactions on Applied Superconductivity* 1, 1 (March 1991), 3–28. https://doi.org/10.1109/77.80745

[13] HS Miller and Richard O Winder. 1962. Majority-logic synthesis by geometric methods. *IRE Transactions on Electronic Computers* 1 (1962), 89–90.

[14] Oleg A Mukhanov. 2011. Energy-efficient single flux quantum technology. *IEEE Transactions on Applied Superconductivity* 21, 3 (2011), 760–769.

[15] Shuichi Nagasawa, Yoshihito Hashimoto, Hideaki Numata, and Shuichi Tahara. 1995. A 380 ps, 9.5 mW Josephson 4-Kbit RAM operated at a high bit yield. *IEEE Transactions on Applied Superconductivity* 5, 2 (1995), 2447–2452.

[16] Takahide Oya, Tetsuya Asai, Takashi Fukui, and Yoshihito Amemiya. 2002. A majority-logic nanodevice using a balanced pair of single-electron boxes. *Journal of nanoscience and nanotechnology* 2, 3-4 (2002), 333–342.

[17] Mathias Soeken, Luca Gaetano Amarù, Pierre-Emmanuel Gaillardon, and Giovanni De Micheli. 2017. Exact synthesis of majority-inverter graphs and its applications. *IEEE Transactions on Computer-Aided Design of Integrated Circuits and Systems* 36, 11 (2017), 1842–1855.

[18] Naoki Takeuchi, Dan Ozawa, Yuki Yamanashi, and Nobuyuki Yoshikawa. 2013. An adiabatic quantum flux parametron as an ultra-low-power logic device. *Superconductor Science and Technology* 26, 3 (2013), 035010.

[19] Naoki Takeuchi, Yuki Yamanashi, and Nobuyuki Yoshikawa. 2015. Adiabatic quantum-flux-parametron cell library adopting minimalist design. *Journal of Applied Physics* 117, 17 (2015), 173912.

[20] Masamitsu Tanaka, Masato Ito, Atsushi Kitayama, Tomohito Kouketsu, and Akira Fujimaki. 2012. 18-GHz, 4.0-aJ/bit Operation of Ultra-Low-Energy Rapid Single-Flux-Quantum Shift Registers. *Japanese Journal of Applied Physics* 51, 5R (2012), 053102. http://stacks.iop.org/1347-4065/51/i=5R/a=053102

[21] Masamitsu Tanaka, Futabako Matsuzaki, Toshiaki Kondo, Naoki Nakajima, Yuki Yamanashi, Akira Fujimaki, Hisao Hayakawa, Nobuyuki Yoshikawa, Hirotaka Terai, and Shinichi Yorozu. 2004. A single-flux-quantum logic prototype microprocessor. In *Solid-State Circuits Conference, 2004. Digest of Technical Papers. ISSCC. 2004 IEEE International*. IEEE, 298–529.

[22] Sergey K Tolpygo, Vladimir Bolkhovsky, Terence J Weir, Alex Wynn, Daniel E Oates, Leonard M Johnson, and Mark A Gouker. 2016. Advanced fabrication processes for superconducting very large-scale integrated circuits. *IEEE Transactions on Applied Superconductivity* 26, 3 (2016), 1–10.

[23] K Walus, G Schulhof, and GA Jullien. 2004. High level exploration of quantum-dot cellular automata (QCA). In *Signals, Systems and Computers, 2004. Conference Record of the Thirty-Eighth Asilomar Conference on*, Vol. 1. IEEE, 30–33.

[24] Peng Wang, Mohammed Y Niamat, Srinivasa R Vemuru, Mansoor Alam, and Taylor Killian. 2015. Synthesis of majority/minority logic networks. *IEEE Transactions on Nanotechnology* 14, 3 (2015), 473–483.

[25] C Wolf. [n. d.]. yosys. http://www.clifford.at/yosys/.

[26] Nobuyuki Yoshikawa and Y Kato. 1999. Reduction of power consumption of RSFQ circuits by inductance-load biasing. *Superconductor Science and Technology* 12, 11 (1999), 918.

[27] Rumi Zhang, Konrad Walus, Wei Wang, and Graham A Jullien. 2004. A method of majority logic reduction for quantum cellular automata. *IEEE Transactions on Nanotechnology* 3, 4 (2004), 443–450.

# A Processing-In-Memory Implementation of SHA-3 Using a Voltage-Gated Spin Hall-Effect Driven MTJ-based Crossbar

Chengmo Yang
University of Delaware
chengmo@udel.edu

Zeyu Chen
University of Delaware
zeyuchen@udel.edu

## ABSTRACT

Processing-In-Memory (PIM), which implements logic operations within memory cells, opens up a new direction on organizing data and computation. Leveraging resistive or magnetic characteristics of nonvolatile memory (NVM) devices, platforms such as PLiM and ReVAMP have been proposed. This paper presents a PIM implementation of SHA-3, a state-of-the-art secure hash algorithm using a Voltage-Gated Spin Hall-Effect (SHE) Driven magnetic tunnel junction (MTJ) based crossbar, which is able to achieve a complete set of Boolean operations. The work includes the design of the crossbar circuit, the instruction set, and both unpipelined and pipelined implementations of SHA-3. Experimental results show that the proposed SHE MTJ-based implementation is able to achieve 2.16X higher throughput than a state-of-the-art Resistive RAM based SHA-3 implementation. Further throughput improvement can be achieved with multiple message hash (MMH) pipelining.

## CCS CONCEPTS

• **Hardware → Non-volatile memory; Hardware accelerators; Emerging architectures.**

## KEYWORDS

Processing-in-Memory; Non-volatile memories

**ACM Reference Format:**

Chengmo Yang and Zeyu Chen. 2019. A Processing-In-Memory Implementation of SHA-3 Using a Voltage-Gated Spin Hall-Effect Driven MTJ-based Crossbar. In *Great Lakes Symposium on VLSI 2019 (GLSVLSI '19), May 9–11, 2019, Tysons Corner, VA, USA.* ACM, New York, NY, USA, 6 pages. https://doi.org/10.1145/3299874.3317972

## 1 INTRODUCTION

Today's applications entail more data storage and computing power than ever before. However, when executed on a traditional von Neumann architecture that separates computation and data storage, the time and energy taken to commute the inputs from the memory to the processor and then write the results back to the memory is hundreds or even thousands of times longer than the computation operation itself. The existing solution to this well known "memory wall" problem relies on multiple levels of caches. Unfortunately, the limited memory bandwidth still imposes a crucial limitation for data-intensive applications.

One promising solution to overcome the bottleneck of von Neumann architecture is *processing-in-memory (PIM)*, which integrates logic and memory on the same device. PIM can be achieved with emerging non-volatile memory (NVM) devices, which leverage physical characteristics such as resistance or magnetic field to store data and are able to perform logic operations as well. A number of NVM-based PIM designs have been proposed. Among them, IMPLY [1], majority function [2], and Boolean [3] are three representative designs based on Resistive RAM (RRAM) memory.

Compared with RRAM, spintronic magnetic memory (MRAM) shows its advantages of longer endurance and lower power consumption. Different MRAM-based logic implementations have been shown in [4–6]. Recently, Kang *et al.* reported a realization of stateful reconfigurable logic functions via a single three-terminal magnetic tunnel junction (MTJ) device, which exploits a novel voltage-gated Spin Hall Effect (VG-SHE) driven magnetization-switching mechanism [7]. This device is a promising candidate for future PIM architecture implementations. To demonstrate its potential, this work presents an implementation of SHA-3 [8], the latest secure hash algorithm standard released by NIST, on a VG-SHE driven MTJ crossbar. A secure hash function is an important component of data confidentiality used for data authentication. The basic operations of SHA-3 are XOR, rotation, and AND, which can be efficiently implemented on a VG-SHE driven MTJ crossbar. This work develops a comprehensive PIM implementation of SHA-3, including the design of the crossbar circuit, the instruction set, an unpipelined single message hash (SMH) implementation, and a pipelined multiple message hash (MMH) implementation. Compared with the most related previous work, i.e., a SHA-3 implementation on a RRAM crossbar [9], the proposed SMH and MMH designs improve throughput by 216% and 851%, respectively.

The rest of this paper is organized as follows. Section 2 introduces the fundamental structure of VG-SHE driven MTJ and its reconfigurable logic implementation, followed by a brief description of SHA-3. Section 3 presents the implementation details of SHA-3 on a VG-SHE driven MTJ crossbar. Section 4 experimentally compares the proposed MTJ crossbar with state-of-the-art SHA-3 implementations. At the end, conclusions are given in Section 5.

## 2 PRELIMINARIES

### 2.1 VG-SHE Driven MTJ Device

The VG-SHE driven MTJ structure was proposed in [7]. Figure 1(a) shows the schematic of this three-terminal device. The voltage

This work is partially supported by NSF Award #1527464.


*GLSVLSI '19, May 9–11, 2019, Tysons Corner, VA, USA*

ACM ISBN 978-1-4503-6252-8/19/05...$15.00
https://doi.org/10.1145/3299874.3317972

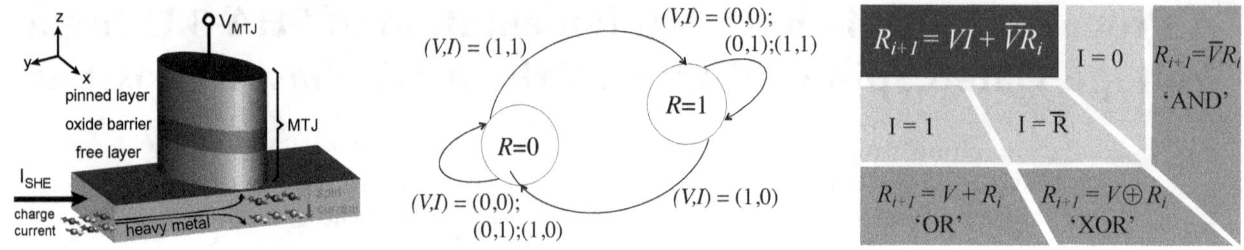


(a) Device schematic (b) State transition diagram (c) Boolean logic

**Figure 1: Three-terminal VG-SHE driven MTJ device and its stateful reconfigurable logic.**

$V_{MTJ}$ and the current $I_{SHE}$ are the two inputs, represented as $V$ and $I$, respectively. The resistance of the MTJ is the state and output, denoted as $R$, which can be read out by measuring the tunnel magnetoresistance of the MTJ. The key property of this device is that the current for switching the SHE-driven MTJ can be modulated by a voltage applied across the MTJ via the voltage-controlled magnetic anisotropy (VCMA) mechanism. Further details can be found in [7].

This work makes the following assumptions regarding inputs and output: (1) a high/low resistance state represents logic state and output $R$=1/0; (2) a positive bias voltage (600 mV) corresponds to input $V$=1, while a zero bias voltage represents $V$=0; (3) a positive/negative SHE current $\pm I_{SHE}$ denotes input $I$=1/0.

Functionality of this three-terminal MTJ device can be summarized by a state machine, shown in Figure 1(b). Once the MTJ is applied with a positive voltage (i.e., $V$=1), the next state $R_{i+1}$ depends on the polarity of the SHE current (i.e., $R_{i+1}$=$I$); If a zero bias voltage is applied (i.e., $V$=0), the next state will not change (i.e., $R_{i+1}$=$R_i$). Combining the two cases, the stateful Boolean logic function can be expressed as:

$$R_{i+1} = VI + \bar{V}R_i \tag{1}$$

Equation (1) indicates that the MTJ can be viewed as a *memory* cell when input $V$ is used as a control signal. On the other hand, when input $I$ is used as a control signal, the MTJ can be viewed as a *logic* cell. As illustrated in Figure 1(c), $I$ can be used to select among AND, OR, and XOR operations between $V$ (or $\bar{V}$) and $R$. This is the key to the proposed crossbar design.

## 2.2 VG-SHE Driven MTJ Crossbar

A high density cross-point array built with the VG-SHE driven MTJ device was proposed in [7]. The crossbar structure is composed of multiple strings of MTJ devices located on a heavy metal strip. The wordline (WL) and sourceline (SL) switches are row-wise, while the bitline (BL) switches are column-wise. They together control the memory and logic operations. Status of these switches as well as values of the two inputs $V$ and $I$ are summarized in Table 1 for each memory and logic operation.

Figure 2 illustrates the read and write operations in VG-SHE crossbar, which require one and two cycles, respectively. To perform read (Figure 2(a)), the SL switch of the selected row is activated, a small negative voltage is applied on all the columns, and all the BL switches are activated. Data can be read out via measuring the tunnel resistance state. As shown in Figure 2(a), a 'low/high' on

**Table 1: Signal values in memory/logic operations**

| | WL | SL | BL | V | I |
|---|---|---|---|---|---|
| **Read** | OFF | ON | ON | $-V$ | |
| **Write** | ON<br>ON | ON<br>ON | $\overline{D_{DMR}}$<br>$D_{DMR}$ | 1 | $-I_{SHE}$<br>$+I_{SHE}$ |
| **AND** | ON | ON | $D_{DMR}$ | 1 | $-I_{SHE}$ |
| **OR** | ON | ON | $D_{DMR}$ | 1 | $+I_{SHE}$ |
| **XOR** | OFF<br>ON<br>ON | ON<br>ON<br>ON | ON<br>$D_{DMR}$<br>$\overline{D_{DMR}}$ | $-V$<br>$D_{XR}$<br>$D_{XR}$ | <br>$-I_{SHE}$<br>$+I_{SHE}$ |

the bitline represents data '1/0'. After passing through the sense amplifier (SA) and comparator, the readout data is stored in the data memory register (DMR).

Write operations take two cycles because currents of different polarities need to be flowed through the heavy metal. This process is shown in Figure 2(b). Both SL and WL switches of the selected row are activated. All the columns are applied with a positive voltage, while the BL switches are controlled by the data in DMR and a control signal $S$. In step 1, $S$=1 which connects the columns corresponding to 0's in the DMR. MTJs on those columns are written with 0's, by flowing $-I_{SHE}$ through the heavy metal. In step 2, $S$=0 and columns corresponding to 1's in the DMR are connected. MTJs on those columns are written with 1's, by flowing $+I_{SHE}$ through the heavy metal.

Logic operations AND and OR are highly similar to the write operation. As shown in Table 1, status of WL and SL switches are the same in these three operations. AND and OR differ from write in that they require only one cycle and the control signal $S$ is always set to 0. Moreover, AND and OR use different values of $I$. As shown in Figure 1(c), OR is performed when $I$=1, while AND is performed when $I$=0. This difference is reflected in the last column of Table 1.

## 2.3 Introduction to SHA-3

SHA-3 is a subset of the cryptographic primitive family *Keccak* [8]. It is based on sponge construction, which operates on a state of $b$=$r$+$c$ bits; $r$ is the *rate* or *blocksize* which comes directly from the message, $c$ is the *capacity* and determines the security level, and $b$ is the state which is $5 \times 5 \times w$ bits long, with $w$ denoting the word size. In the most commonly used case of SHA3-256, $w$=64, $b$=1600, $r$=1088, and $c$=512.

Sponge construction uses the block permutation function Keccak-$f$, which consists of 24 rounds. In each round, the message block is operated in 5 steps: $\theta$, $\rho$, $\pi$, $\chi$, and $\iota$, as shown in Algorithm 1. Each

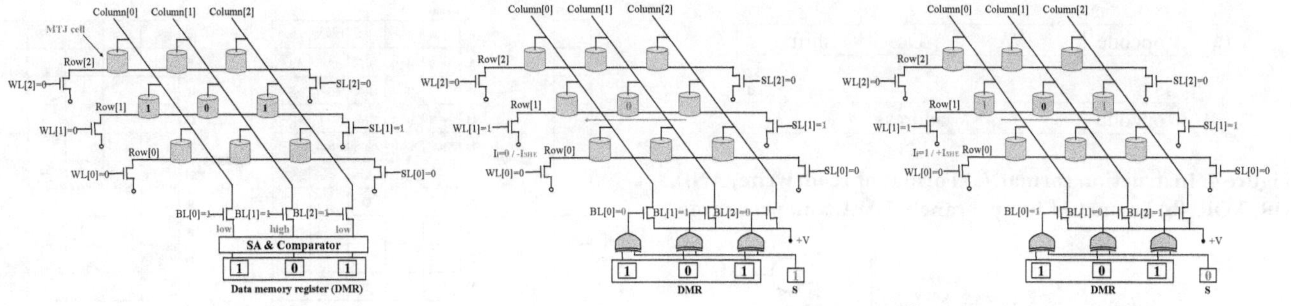


(a) (b)

**Figure 2: Illustration of (a) read; (b) 2-step write in VG-SHE crossbar. Step 1 writes 0's and step 2 writes 1's.**

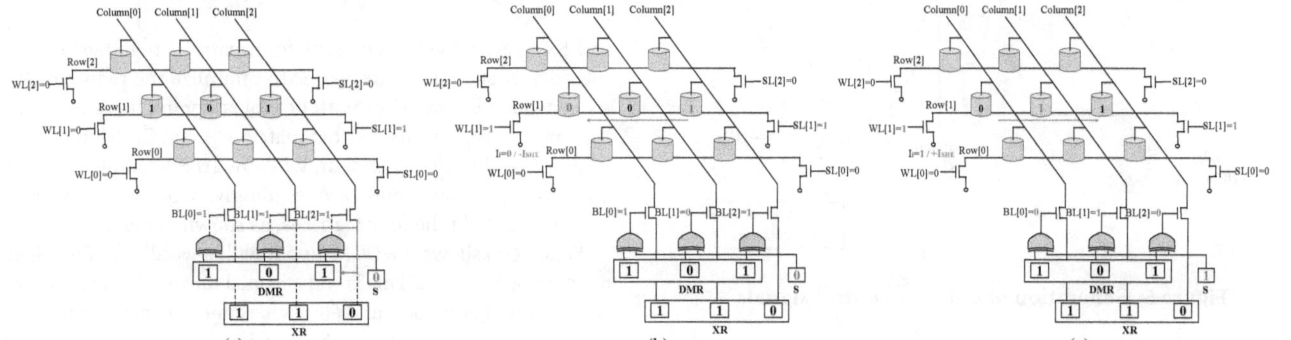


(a) (b) (c)

**Figure 3: Implement XOR on a VG-SHE crossbar in 3 steps; (a) Data $R_i$=101 on the second row is read into DMR; (b) MTJs with $R_i$=1 and $V$=1 are programed to $R_{i+1}$=0; (c) MTJs with $R_i$=0 and $V$=1 are programed to $R_{i+1}$=1.**

**Algorithm 1** Keccak-$f$ round function

**Require:** $A$: message block matrix; $RC$: round constant;
**Ensure:** Hashed message block $A$

\# $\theta$ step
1: C[x] = A[x,0]⊕A[x,1]⊕A[x,2]⊕A[x,3]⊕A[x,4] ∀x in 0...4
2: D[x] = C[x-1]⊕(C[x+1]≪1) ∀x in 0...4
3: A[x,y] = A[x,y]⊕D[x] ∀(x,y) in (0...4,0...4)
\# $\rho$ and $\pi$ step
4: B[y,2x+3y] = A[x,y]≪r[x,y] ∀(x,y) in (0...4,0...4)
\# $\chi$ step
5: A[x,y] = ($\overline{B[x+1,y]}$∧B[x+2,y]) ∀(x,y) in (0...4,0...4)
6: A[x,y] = A[x,y]⊕B[x,y] ∀(x,y) in (0...4,0...4)
\# $\iota$ step
7: A[0,0] = A[0,0]⊕RC

round takes two inputs: $A$ is a $5 \times 5$ matrix with 64-bit elements, while $RC$ is the round constant that varies across rounds. At line 4, $r[x, y]$ is the rotation matrix. Both $RC$ and $r[x, y]$ are known and given in [8]. As the algorithm shows, the basic operations of SHA-3 are XOR, rotation, and AND, which can be efficiently implemented in a VG-SHE driven MTJ crossbar.

# 3 PROPOSED SHA-3 IMPLEMENTATION

This section presents the details on implementing SHA-3 on a VG-SHE driven MTJ crossbar, from circuit level all the way up to instruction level.

## 3.1 XOR and Write Implementations

While Figure 1(c) shows that XOR in a single MTJ can be achieved by setting $I=\overline{R_i}$, this is not the case for XORing a whole word line in the crossbar since $+I_{SHE}$ and $-I_{SHE}$ cannot co-exist on the same row at the same time.

To implement XOR, we introduce another register, i.e., the XOR register (XR). More importantly, since the BL switches need to be controlled by the data read from the crossbar, such data will be placed in DMR while the other input will be placed in XR. Figure 3 shows the steps for XORing $R_i$=101 and $V$=110 and getting $R_{i+1}$=011, which takes three cycles. In cycle 1, $R_i$ is read into DMR, shown in the red path in Figure 3(a). In cycle 2, the MTJs with $R_i$=1 and $V$=1 are programed to $R_{i+1}$=0. This is achieved by setting $S$=0 which applies $R_i$=101 on the BL switches and hence conducts Column [0] and [2]. Meanwhile, 110 is applied on the bit lines, and $-I_{SHE}$ is flowed through the heavy metal. As a result, 0' is written to the MTJ on Column[0], while the MTJ on Column[2] remains unchanged. Finally, in cycle 3, the MTJs with $R_i$=0 and $V$=1 are programed to $R_{i+1}$=1. This is achieved by setting $S$=1 which applies $\overline{R_i}$=010 on the BL switches and hence conducts Column[1]. By applying 110 on the bit lines and flowing $+I_{SHE}$ through the heavy metal, 1' is written to the MTJ on Column[1].

Write operations in the VG-SHE driven MTJ crossbar can be optimized as well. While the original write operations introduced in [7] take two cycles for writing 0's and 1's, write in the proposed design is reduced to one cycle with the help of a precharge' operation. Specifically, by activating all the BL switches, applying positive

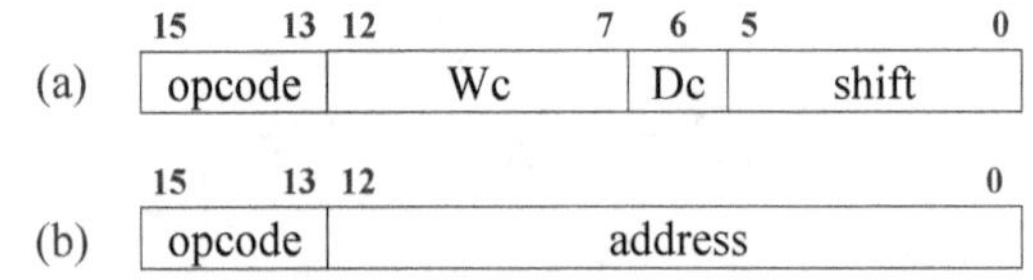


**Figure 4: Instruction format. (a) Format of read, write, AND, OR, XOR. (b) Format of jump, branch, DMA, and precharge.**

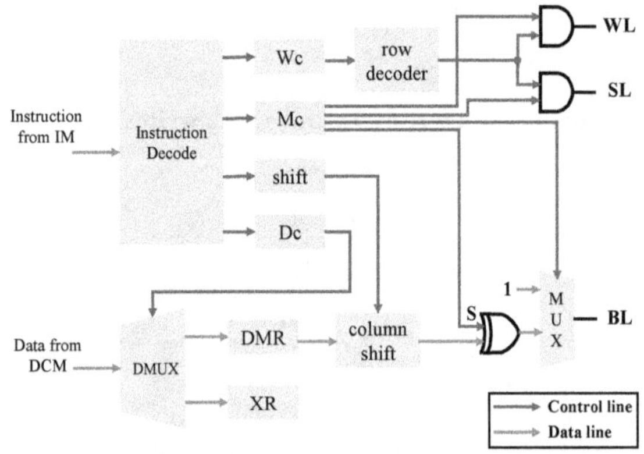


**Figure 5: Generation of crossbar control signals**

voltage on all the columns, and flowing $+I_{SHE}$ through multiple rows, all these rows are written with 1's simultaneously in one step. Later when writing data on these precharged rows, only 0's need to be programed which can be completed in one cycle.

## 3.2 Generation of Crossbar Control Signals

To realize both memory (read, write) and logic (XOR, AND, rotation) operations, we develop a PIM architecture similar to the ReVAMP platform [10]. The architecture uses a data and computation memory (DCM) which stores data and performs computation directly on data, as well as an instruction memory (IM) which stores the instructions for controlling the DCM. Both IM and DCM are VG-SHE driven MTJ cross-point arrays.

The proposed PIM architecture uses a fix-length instruction set. Two instruction formats are supported, shown in Figure 4. Most of instructions, including read, write, AND, OR, and XOR, are in the first format. It has four fields: a 3-bit opcode, a 6-bit wordline address $W_c$, a 1-bit signal $D_c$ determining the read destination (1' for DMR and 0' for XR), and a 6-bit shift offset for implementing bitwise shift and rotation. Figure 5 shows the circuit for generating the signals for controlling the WL, SL and BL switches, selecting read destination, and implementing shift based on instruction decoding results. The second format is used for branch, jump, as well as direct memory access (DMA) instructions that can be used to load A[x,y] to DCM before starting the Keccak-$f$ function. It is also used for implementing the aforementioned precharge instruction which requires a 6-bit starting address and a 6-bit ending address that can be held together in the 'address' field of the instruction.

## 3.3 Data Layout

As shown in Algorithm 1, each round of the Keccak-$f$ function operates on four matrices A, B, C and D with sizes of 5×5, 5×5, 5×1,

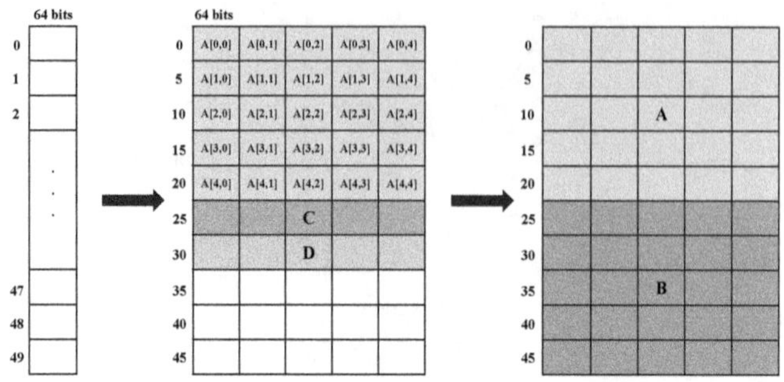


**Figure 6: DCM state transition. (a) DCM layout; (b) DCM state in step $\theta$; (c) DCM state in step $\rho$, $\pi$ and $\chi$**

and 5×1, respectively. While the four matrices together require a memory of 60 words, our goal is to minimize the required DCM size, by allowing matrices with non-overlapping lifetime to share the same space. It turns out that matrices A and C, C and D, D and A, and A and B are dependent, while matrix B can overwrite the space occupied by C and D. Accordingly, a DCM of 50 words is sufficient to hold the four matrices, as shown in Figure 6.

Figure 6(a) shows the DCM layout with a word size of 64-bit and a length of 50 words. This is transformed into a 10×5 matrix representation in Figure 6(b) and 6(c), wherein each entry corresponds to 64 bits. Figure 6(b) shows the data layout in step $\theta$. Words 0-24, 25-29 and 30-35 are respectively allocated to matrices A, C and D. Updates to matrix A[x,y] at line 3 of Algorithm 1 is performed in-place. Figure 6(c) shows the data layout in steps $\rho$, $\pi$, and $\chi$. Words 25-49 are allocated to matrix B, which overwrites matrices C and D.

In the rest of this paper, all the logic and memory operations are assumed to operate on a word with all the 64 bits being processed simultaneously. It is also assumed that $A[x, y]$ is loaded into DCM before the Keccak-$f$ function starts.

## 3.4 Keccak-$f$ Implementation

Table 2 presents the implementation of the Keccak-$f$ function step by step. This part describes each step in detail and computes the number of cycles and instructions needed, which are summarized in Table 3.

*3.4.1 step $\theta$.* Line 1 in Algorithm 1 is a five-input XOR operation. Before starting it, one cycle will be spent on precharging words 25-34 (i.e., the locations of C[x] and D[x]) in DCM to 1. Then, A[x,0] is read into DMR and written to DCM on the address of C[x]. This is shown in Table 2. After that, A[x,1] is read into XR and XORed with the data at the location of C[x]. The second step is repeated 4 times with inputs A[x,1] to A[x,4]. Overall, it takes $(N_{read}+N_{write})+4\times(N_{read}+N_{xor})=18$ cycles and 2+4×2=10 instructions to update one element of C[x]. $N_{read}$, $N_{write}$, and $N_{xor}$ denote the latencies of read, write, and XOR operations, which equal 1, 1, and 3, respectively. Since C[x] has 5 elements, line 1 of Algorithm 1 requires 5×18+1 (for precharging)=91 cycles and 50 instructions in total.

Line 2 in Algorithm 1 takes one read and one write to write C[x+1] and then one read and one XOR for XORing C[x-1] and C[x+1]. Data rotation ($C[x + 1] \ll 1$) is achieved with a column

**Table 2: Step-by-step implementation of Keccak-$f$. (* indicates bit shift during write)**

| Step | Op | Input | Output | Repeat |
|---|---|---|---|---|
| $\theta 1$ | read | DCM (A[x,0]) | DMR | |
| | write | DMR | DCM (C[x]) | |
| | read | DCM (A[x,i]) | XR | i=1 to 4 |
| | XOR | XR, DCM (C[x]) | DCM (C[x]) | |
| $\theta 2$ | read | DCM (C[x+1]) | DMR | |
| | write* | DMR | DCM (D[x]) | |
| | read | DCM (C[x-1]) | XR | |
| | XOR | XR, DCM (D[x]) | DCM (D[x]) | |
| $\theta 3$ | read | DCM (D[x]) | XR | |
| | XOR | XR, DCM (A[x,i]) | DCM (A[x,i]) | i=0 to 4 |
| $\rho$ & $\pi$ | read | DCM (A[x,y]) | DMR | x=1 to 4 |
| | write* | DMR | DCM (A[x,y]) | y=1 to 4 |
| $\chi 1$ | read | DCM (B[x+2,y]) | DMR | |
| | write | DMR | DCM (A[x,y]) | x=1 to 4 |
| | read | DCM (B[x+1,y]) | DMR | y=1 to 4 |
| | AND | DMR, DCM (A[x,y]) | DCM (A[x,y]) | |
| $\chi 2$ | read | DCM (B[x,y]) | XR | x=1 to 4 |
| | XOR | XR, DCM (A[x,y]) | DCM (A[x,y]) | y=1 to 4 |

shifter and does not bring any extra cycle, as shown in Figure 5. Overall, this line requires $5\times(N_{read}+N_{write}+N_{read}+N_{xor}) = 30$ cycles and 5×4=20 instructions in total.

Line 3 of Algorithm 1 updates the 5×5 state matrix A[x,y]. For each row, D[x] is read into the XR register once and used as the input for the entire row. Therefore, each row takes $N_{read}+5\times N_{xor} = 16$ cycles and 6 instructions. The entire state takes 80 cycles and 30 instructions to update.

*3.4.2 steps $\rho$ and $\pi$.* This step reads from matrix A and writes to matrix B. Same as before, this step requires one cycle for precharging words 25-49 (i.e., the locations of B[x,y]) so as to save write latency. Then, A[x,y] is read into DMR and written into B[y,2x+3y]. Overall, this step requires $1{+}25\times(N_{read} + N_{write}){=}51$ cycles and 50 instructions.

*3.4.3 step $\chi$.* This step computes matrix A based on matrix B. First, words 0-24 (i.e., the locations of A[x,y])) are precharged. Then, B[x+2,y] is read into DMR and then written into the location of A[x,y]. Next, B[x+1,y] is read into DMR and then ANDed with the data at the location of A[x,y]. Note that as Figure 1(c) shows, when $I{=}0$, $R_{i+1}{=}\overline{V}R_i$. In other words, by flowing $-I_{SHE}$ through the heavy medal, we directly get A[x,y]= $\overline{B[x+1,y]} \wedge B[x+2,y]$. This line requires $1{+}25\times(N_{read}{+}N_{write}{+}N_{read}{+}N_{and}){=}101$ cycles and 100 instructions to complete.

In line 6 of Algorithm 1, B[x,y] is readout and then XORed with A[x,y]. It requires $25\times(N_{read}{+}N_{xor}){=}100$ cycles and 50 instructions in total.

*3.4.4 step $\iota$.* This step (line 7 of Algorithm 1) involves a single XOR of the round constant $RC$ and the element $A[0,0]$. It takes $(N_{read}{+}N_{xor}){=}4$ cycles and 2 instructions to complete.

**Table 3: Implementation details of SHA-3 round function**

| Step | Cycle # | Instruction # |
|---|---|---|
| $\theta 1$ | 91 | 50 |
| $\theta 2$ | 30 | 20 |
| $\theta 3$ | 80 | 30 |
| $\rho$ and $\pi$ | 51 | 50 |
| $\chi 1$ | 101 | 100 |
| $\chi 2$ | 100 | 50 |
| $\iota$ | 4 | 2 |
| **Total** | 457 | 302 |

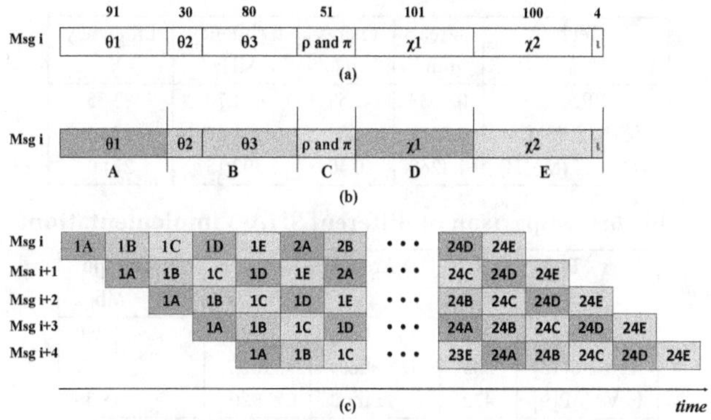

**Figure 7: Different implementations of the Keccak function. (a) Unpipelined implementation. Each round takes 457cycles. (b) A 5-stage pipeline with a longest stage (B) of 110 cycles. Each round takes 550 cycles. (c) Steps for processing 5 messages for 24 rounds. '1A' indicates stage A of round 1.**

## 3.5 Unpipelined vs. Pipelined Implementations

The proposed VG-SHE driven MTJ implementation of SHA-3 can be done in both unpipelined and pipelined forms. For single message hash (SMH), the input of each round function relies on the output of the previous round. As a result, an unpipelined implementation such as the one in Figure 7(a) is used. As each round takes $N_{round}{=}457$ cycles and loading the initial state A[x,y] takes 25 cycles, the overall latency of the unpipelined implementation is $24\times N_{round}{+}25$ = 10993 cycles.

While the different rounds of a single message cannot be pipelined because of data dependency, a pipelined implementation can be used for multiple message hash (MMH). Figure 7(b) shows a 5-stage pipeline which merges $\theta 2$ and $\theta 3$ as well as $\chi 2$ and $\iota$. The pipeline length is constrained by the longest stage ($\theta 2$ and $\theta 3$) which takes 110 cycles. This implementation requires a larger DCM to hold 5 messages simultaneously (i.e., 250 words). as well as 5 individual ports so that different messages can be processed in parallel at different pipeline stages, as shown in Figure 7(c). It takes 110×(24×5+4)=13640 cycles to process 5 messages and 5 cycles to load the first message (since there are 5 ports), while the latency for loading the other messages is completely hidden. Therefore the overall latency of the pipelined implementation is 13645 cycles.

# 4 EXPERIMENTAL RESULTS

The proposed VG-SHE driven MTJ based crossbar memory is simulated with NVSim [14]. Both SMH and MMH implementations are

**Table 4: Key parameters of NVSim**

| VG-MTJ [7] | RRAM [11] |
|---|---|
| feasure size = 80 nm | feasure size = 10 nm |
| read time = 0.5 ns | set time = 1 ns |
| switching time = 2.3 ns | reset time = 1 ns |
| read energy = 5 fJ | read energy = 0.6 pJ |
| write energy = 12 fJ | write energy = 0.6 pJ |
| low resistance = 50 $k\Omega$ | low resistance = 100 $k\Omega$ |
| high resistance = 100 $k\Omega$ | high resistance = 1000 $k\Omega$ |
| DCM size = 400 bytes | DCM size = 344 bytes |

**Table 5: Results of NVSim**

| Tech. | area $mm^2$ | energy $\mu J$ | frequency MHz | Efficiency |
|---|---|---|---|---|
| RRAM | 0.1438 | 1.53 | 471.70 | 83.55 |
| VG-MTJ (SMH) | 0.3608 | 0.39 | 401.61 | 282.5 |
| VG-MTJ (MMH) | 1.4263 | 0.40 | 392.15 | 274.0 |

**Table 6: Comparison of different SHA-3 implementations**

| Tech. | f MHz | Area | Latency cycles | Throughput Mbps |
|---|---|---|---|---|
| Virtex5[12] | 248 | 134 slices | 1730 | 250 |
| Virtex6[13] | 285 | 188 slices | 466 | 77 |
| ReVAMP[9] | 472 | 0.144 $mm^2$ | 27920 | 18.38 |
| Pro.(SMH) | 402 | 0.361 $mm^2$ | 10993 | 39.75 |
| Pro.(MMH) | 392 | 1.426 $mm^2$ | 13645 | 156.34 |

simulated. Meanwhile, the RRAM-based SHA-3 implementation introduced in [9] is also simulated. The key device parameters are listed in Table 4, while the simulation results are shown in Table 5.

Compared with RRAM, the proposed VG-SHE driven MTJ-based crossbar consumes much lower energy per round, as a result of the fewer cycles and lower read/write energy of the device. On the other hand, it requires more area due to the larger feature size of the device. Note that the area of MMH is more than 5 times of the area of SMH due to the need of extra I/O ports as well as registers between pipeline stages. Finally, cycle time is computed as the longest read/write latency, and frequency is determined accordingly. The cycle times of VG-SHE driven MTJ-based crossbar is about 18%–20% slower than RRAM. However, this does not necessarily implies performance degradation since the proposed PIM impelementation requires fewer cycles to process each round of the message hash.

Table 6 compares the proposed SMH and MMH implementations with existing FPGA-based (first two rows) and RRAM-based (3rd row) SHA-3 implementations. Data of frequency, area, latency, and throughput are reported. Moreover, the efficiency of the PIM implementations is reported in Table 5. Throughput and efficiency are computed with the following equations:

$$Throughput = \frac{Blocksize \times \#MH}{Latency} \times Frequency \quad (2)$$

$$Efficiency = \frac{Throughput}{Area \times Energy} \quad (3)$$

Blocksize is the length of the message block processed by the hash function at a given time, and #MH equals 1 and 5 in SMH and MMH, repestively. Each slice of Vertex 5 and 6 family is comprised of 450 and 256 bits, respectively. The proposed PIM design, in comparison to the FPGA-based implementations, implements a lightweight controller and requires far less hardware. In terms of latency, the proposed SMH and MMH implementations outperform the RRAM implementation by 2.54 and 2.05 times, respectively. Such latency improvement directly leads to 2.16 and 8.51 times throughput improvement, thus confirming the performance advantage of the proposed designs. Finally, in terms of design efficiency, the proposed VG-SHE driven MTJ implementations are more than 3 times of ReVAMP, making it a suitable candidate for resource constrained systems.

## 5 CONCLUSIONS

NVM-based Processing-In-Memory (PIM) architectures open up a new direction to break through the bottleneck in traditional von Neumann architectures. This paper presented a PIM architecture built with VG-SHE driven MTJ devices and showed a comprehensive implementation of SHA-3, including the design of the crossbar circuit, the instruction set, the step-by-step implementation of Keccak-$f$ function, and both unpipelined single message hash (SMH) and pipelined multiple message hash (MMH) implementations. Our design outperforms FPGA-based and RRAM-based implementations in terms of throughput and efficiency, making it a suitable candidate for resource constrained systems.

## REFERENCES

[1] J. Borghetti, G. S. Snider, P. J. Kuekes, J. J. Yang, D. R. Stewart, and R. S. Williams, "'Memristive' switches enable 'stateful' logic operations via material implication," *Nature*, vol. 464, no. 7290, p. 873, 2010.
[2] P.-E. Gaillardon, L. Amarú, A. Siemon, E. Linn, R. Waser, A. Chattopadhyay, and G. De Micheli, "The programmable logic-in-memory (PLiM) computer," in *Design, Automation & Test in Europe Conference & Exhibition (DATE)*, 2016, pp. 427–432.
[3] S. Kvatinsky, D. Belousov, S. Liman, G. Satat, N. Wald, E. G. Friedman, A. Kolodny, and U. C. Weiser, "Magic-Memristor-Aided Logic," *IEEE Transactions on Circuits and Systems II: Express Briefs*, vol. 61, no. 11, pp. 895–899, 2014.
[4] S. Gao, G. Yang, B. Cui, S. Wang, F. Zeng, C. Song, and F. Pan, "Realisation of all 16 Boolean logic functions in a single magnetoresistance memory cell," *Nanoscale*, vol. 8, no. 25, pp. 12 819–12 825, 2016.
[5] C. Wan, X. Zhang, Z. Yuan, C. Fang, W. Kong, Q. Zhang, H. Wu, U. Khan, and X. Han, "Programmable spin logic based on spin hall effect in a single device," *Advanced Electronic Materials*, vol. 3, no. 3, 2017.
[6] J. Lee, D. I. Suh, and W. Park, "The universal magnetic tunnel junction logic gates representing 16 binary Boolean logic operations," *Journal of Applied Physics*, vol. 117, no. 17, 2015.
[7] H. Zhang, W. Kang, L. Wang, K. L. Wang, and W. Zhao, "Stateful reconfigurable logic via a single-voltage-gated spin hall-effect driven magnetic tunnel junction in a spintronic memory," *IEEE Transactions on Electron Devices*, vol. 64, no. 10, pp. 4295–4301, 2017.
[8] P. Pritzker and P. Gallagher, "SHA-3 standard: Permutation-based hash and extendable-output functions," *Information Tech Laboratory National Institute of Standards and Technology*, pp. 1–35, 2014.
[9] D. Bhattacharjee, V. Pudi, and A. Chattopadhyay, "SHA-3 implementation using ReRAM based in-memory computing architecture," in *18th International Symposium on Quality Electronic Design (ISQED)*, 2017, pp. 325–330.
[10] D. Bhattacharjee, R. Devadoss, and A. Chattopadhyay, "ReVAMP: ReRAM based VLIW architecture for in-memory computing," in *Design, Automation & Test in Europe Conference & Exhibition (DATE)*, 2017, pp. 782–787.
[11] H.-S. P. Wong, H.-Y. Lee, S. Yu, Y.-S. Chen, Y. Wu, P.-S. Chen, B. Lee, F. T. Chen, and M.-J. Tsai, "Metal–oxide RRAM," *Proceedings of the IEEE*, vol. 100, no. 6, pp. 1951–1970, 2012.
[12] J. Winderickx, J. Daemen, and N. Mentens, "Exploring the use of shift register lookup tables for Keccak implementations on Xilinx FPGAs," in *26th International Conference on Field Programmable Logic and Applications (FPL)*, 2016, pp. 1–4.
[13] S. Kerckhof, F. Durvaux, N. Veyrat-Charvillon, F. Regazzoni, G. M. de Dormale, and F.-X. Standaert, "Compact FPGA implementations of the five SHA-3 finalists," in *International Conference on Smart Card Research and Advanced Applications*. Springer, 2011, pp. 217–233.
[14] X. Dong, C. Xu, N. Jouppi, and Y. Xie, "NVSim: A circuit-level performance, energy, and area model for emerging non-volatile memory," in *Emerging Memory Technologies*. Springer, 2014, pp. 15–50.

# Exploring Processing In-Memory for Different Technologies

Saransh Gupta, Mohsen Imani, and Tajana Rosing
CSE Department, UC San Diego, La Jolla, CA 92093, USA
{sgupta, moimani, tajana}@ucsd.edu

## ABSTRACT

The recent emergence of IoT has led to a substantial increase in the amount of data processed. Today, a large number of applications are data intensive, involving massive data transfers between processing core and memory. These transfers act as a bottleneck mainly due to the limited data bandwidth between memory and the processing core. Processing in memory (PIM) avoids this latency problem by doing computations at the source of data.

In this paper, we propose designs which enable PIM in the three major memory technologies, i.e. SRAM, DRAM, and the newly emerging non-volatile memories (NVMs). We exploit the analog properties of different memories to implement simple logic functions, namely OR, AND, and majority inside memory. We then extend them further to implement in-memory addition and multiplication. We compare the three memory technologies with GPU by running general applications on them. Our evaluations show that SRAM, NVM, and DRAM are 29.8× (36.3×), 17.6× (20.3×) and 1.7× (2.7×) better in performance (energy consumption) as compared to AMD GPU.

## CCS CONCEPTS

• **Hardware** → **Emerging technologies**; *Integrated circuits*;

## KEYWORDS

Processing in Memory; Non-volatile memories; SRAM; DRAM; Memristors; Energy efficiency; Analog computing

**ACM Reference Format:**

Saransh Gupta, Mohsen Imani, and Tajana Rosing. 2019. Exploring Processing In-Memory for Different Technologies. In *Great Lakes Symposium on VLSI 2019 (GLSVLSI '19), May 9–11, 2019, Tysons Corner, VA, USA.* ACM, New York, NY, USA, 6 pages. https://doi.org/10.1145/3299874.3317977

## 1 INTRODUCTION

In this era of the internet of things (IoT), billions of devices are connected together to form a network. These devices generate a huge amount of data leading to the concept of big data. Many applications run several machine learning, neural network, and other emerging algorithms on this raw data to draw meaningful results [1–3]. In the current computing systems, all processing tasks are done on CPU/GPU cores while the data to be processed is stored in memory [4]. The process of bringing the entire data to the processing core becomes a bottleneck owing to the limited data bandwidth. The cache hierarchy in these systems tries to accelerate this process but it fails when the size of the data becomes too large to fit into various cache levels.

Processing in memory present possible solutions to this data transfer bottleneck [5–8]. It processes data inside memory, *i.e.* the source of the data, without using any power hungry cores [9–11]. Although many PIM techniques have been proposed recently, the majority of them are application specific. For example, [5, 12–14] accelerate neural networks in memory. Similarly, work in [15] and [16, 17] designed a PIM architecture for acceleration of brain-inspired computing and graph processing applications. There are some works like [18] which support limited basic functions in memory but fail to implement complex functions like addition and multiplication. However, some work implemented basic logic functions in memory and extended them to implement advanced functions like addition and multiplication [12, 19–22]. These techniques can be extended to implement several functionalities in memory but they suffer from huge latency bottleneck mainly due to the slow switching speeds of NVMs.

The PIM techniques discussed above, as well as most of the other proposed techniques, are targeted towards NVMs and use the programmable resistance provided by them to implement logic. Since the current computing systems majorly use SRAMs and DRAMs, these techniques do not provide readily implementable solutions for the data transfer bottleneck that these systems face. The work in [23] tried to implement PIM in DRAM by decoupling logic and memory circuits in different dies using 3D-stacking. However, the designing and manufacturing challenges involved with such approaches have limited their use.

In this paper, we propose GPIM (general processing in-memory) to enable PIM in three major memory technologies, namely SRAM, DRAM, and the emerging NVM technologies. The major contributions of this paper are as follows:

- We propose novel circuits for SRAM, DRAM, and NVM to enable PIM. These circuits are configurable and the same circuit can implement multiple fundamental operations, including OR, MAJ, and AND. We also implement in-memory addition and multiplication in GPIM-enabled SRAM, DRAM, and NVM.
- For NVM and SRAM, GPIM exploits the differential effective resistance of logic states to generate data dependent current. In the case of DRAM, GPIM uses data-controlled capacitive charging to execute logic. Unlike the previous PIM approaches, neither does our implementation destroy the stored data, nor does it require creating temporary copies for processing.
- GPIM significantly reduces the number of memory device switches involved in PIM operations, thereby increasing the lifetime of the memory. Moreover, it also minimizes the number of memory cells required for performing PIM operations. It increases the effective memory utilization.

## 2 RELATED WORK

Processing in memory has recently gained interest owing to the emergence of new memory technologies with the capability to both store data as well as process it. Several PIM techniques have been proposed to accelerate emerging applications. For example, [13] accelerates neural networks by storing weights in memory and applying inputs directly to them in the form of current. The work in [5]


*GLSVLSI '19, May 9–11, 2019, Tysons Corner, VA, USA*

ACM ISBN 978-1-4503-6252-8/19/05...$15.00
https://doi.org/10.1145/3299874.3317977

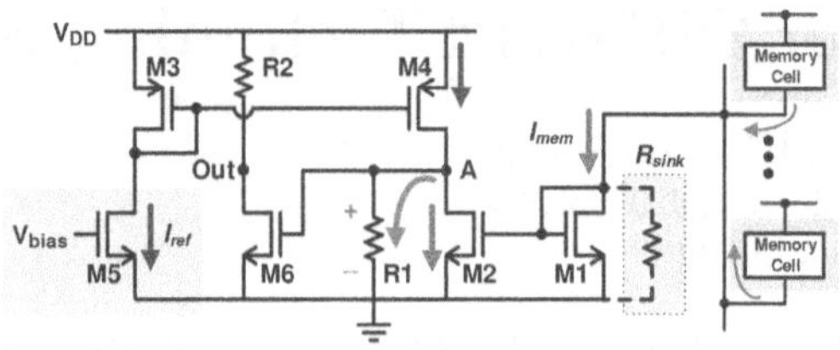

**Figure 1: Current-based implementation of logic functions.**

uses spiking-based neuromorphic computing to multiply inputs, applied at bitlines, with the weights, stored in the memory, to implement neural networks in memory. Such techniques do accelerate the process but depend upon utilizing multi-leveled RRAM devices. These multi-leveled devices suffer from severely low endurance issues. Moreover, some of these also use power-hungry ADCs and DACs, which contribute significantly to the power requirements of the system.

There are many PIM techniques which deal with general implementations [20, 22, 24]. The work in [18] implements the basic operations like bitwise OR, AND. However, it does not support functions like addition and multiplication, limiting the use of such technique for most of the applications. The work in [20, 25] introduces schemes to implement addition in crossbar memory. This is further extended in [22] to improve the efficiency of addition and implement multiplication in memory. These techniques are general but suffer from the high latency involved in a large number of device switches. Moreover, [22] uses configurable interconnects which add area overhead to the memory block.

Some researches also present PIM like techniques for SRAMs and DRAMs. For example, [26] presents approaches to improve the performance and energy efficiency of compute caches. Such caches are able to execute only simple bitwise functions on the data stored in SRAM cells using sense amplifiers. The work in [27] accelerates machine learning by doing computations in SRAM cell. However, it uses large DACs to implement it, introducing significant power and area overheads. The work in [23] exploits the concept of 3D stacking to separate the logic and memory circuits into different dies, overcoming the cost challenges involved in integrating memory and logic. These work do propose PIM techniques for SRAM and DRAM but they have limited functionality and are not directly applicable to more general systems running various kinds of applications.

On the other hand, we propose GPIM which implements basic logic functions by modifying the sense amplifiers for SRAM, DRAM, and emerging memory technologies. We further extend it to implement addition and multiplication in memory.

## 3 GENERAL PROCESSING-IN MEMORY

The dissimilarity in the behavior of different memory technologies calls for different types of circuits to enable PIM in memory. We propose two types of circuits, a current-based circuit for NVMs and SRAM and voltage-based circuit for DRAM.

### 3.1 Current-based Implementation

In this section, we design an analog circuit which exploits the difference in current flowing through the NVM and SRAM memory cells in different states. This reduces the number of transistors needed to implement logic. Also, it is faster than the slow purely in-memory implementations which rely on multiple data-driven device switches to implement various functions [20, 25]. Moreover, the proposed circuits do not affect the read/write characteristics of the memories.

*3.1.1 Analog Properties of SRAM and NVM.* **NVM:** Emerging NVM technologies, like Resistive Random Access Memory (RRAM), Phase Change Memory (PCM), save data in form of their resistance/matter state. In all the cases, a data readout occurs by applying a voltage across the memory cells and measuring the current through it. The sense amplifiers at the periphery of the memory blocks sense this current to output the stored data. Our design modifies this sense amplifier to enable the execution of logic.

The total current through the memory cells, say d1, d2, and d3, depends upon the resistance of the devices, hence the stored data. In our setup, we consider a low (high) resistive state as logic '1' ('0'). For example, in the case of memristors (ReRAM), we represent logic '1' and '0' with resistive states of $10k\Omega$ ($R_{on}$) and $10M\Omega$ ($R_{off}$) respectively. So, the current is maximum when all the three bits are logic '1' and minimum when they are all logic '0'.

**SRAM:** Unlike NVM, SRAM is volatile in nature. The data in SRAM is stored in the form of logic state maintained by two cross-coupled inverters as shown in Figure 2a. In a memory cell, one of the inverters stores logic '1' at the output node while the other stores logic '0.' The inverter with logic '0' at the output node has the NMOS transistor in on state. A transistor in on state has a much lower resistance than that in off state. We exploit this property to implement basic functions in SRAM.

*3.1.2 Circuit Design.* The memory cells in a column of the memory block share the same sense amplifier. So, the data bits to be processed are required to be present in the same column of the block. The memory cells are selected by activating the corresponding wordlines (which select the memory row) and bitlines (which select the required column sense amplifier). The voltage applied at wordlines makes the current flow through the memory cells. The total current through the selected memory cells is passed through the sense amplifier.

**Proposed Circuit:** Figure 1 shows the proposed circuit. It compares the current through memory cells with a reference current. For now, we ignore the resistor $R_{sink}$ in the circuit. The transistor pairs M1-M2 and M3-M4 form current mirrors. M5 acts as reference current generator while M6 and R2 form the output stage. The total current from the memory cells is passed through M1. This current is copied to the M2 by the current mirror. The bias voltage, $V_{bias}$ applied to the gate of M5 directly controls the current through it, making it a voltage controlled current source. We use this current source to generate the reference current. This same current flows through M3 as well which is copied by M4. In other words, the current through M4 is directly proportional to the bias voltage.

Since, M2 and M4 try to drive different currents, the resistor connected to the drains of both the transistors acts as the path to drain the excess current. This also develops a voltage difference across the resistor, R1. This voltage is dependent upon the amount of current flowing through R1. As the current through R1 increases, the voltage at node 'A' increases as well. Node 'A' controls the output transistor, M6. As the voltage at node 'A' increases beyond the threshold of M6, it turns on and pulls the output node to ground. While the output node remains at a higher voltage when M6 is off.

**Implementing `MAJ`, `OR`, and `AND`:** The current through a memory cell changes with data. This allows us to use the total current through multiple cells to directly implement logic functions. To implement a function like `MAJ`, the reference current is set close to the current that is generated when two of the memory cells store data '1'. Hence, in the case when two out of three data bits are '1,' the current through M2 is close to the current through M4. Hence, very little current flows through R1 and voltage generated at node A is less than the threshold voltage of M6. M6 remains off,

**Table 1: Circuit parameters for RRAM and SRAM**

| | RRAM | | | RRAM ($R_{on}$ <$1k\Omega$) | | | SRAM | | |
|---|---|---|---|---|---|---|---|---|---|
| | OR | MAJ | AND | OR | MAJ | AND | OR | MAJ | AND |
| $V_{bias}$ (V) | 0.5 | 0.7 | 0.9 | 0.5 | 0.7 | 0.9 | 0.3 | 0.45 | 0.6 |
| $I_{ref}$ (uA) | 10 | 30 | 50 | 10 | 30 | 50 | 30 | 15 | 5 |
| Latency (ps) | 50 | 50 | 50 | 50 | 50 | 50 | 150 | 150 | 150 |
| Energy (fJ) | 5.3 | 8.1 | 9.1 | 374.9 | 377.0 | 378.4 | 10.2 | 7.9 | 5.9 |

maintaining the output node high. When one or none of the bits are '1' the current through M2 reduces and the voltage at node A rises. This switches M6 on which pulls the output node low. In the case when all the three bits are high, the current through M2 is limited by the current that can be supplied by M4. However the difference between the two currents is very low and the M6 remains off, keeping output node high. The same technique is extended to implement OR and AND. The only required change is the bias voltage controlling M5. For implementing OR (AND), the bias voltage is reduced till the reference current becomes equal to the current through the memory cells when one (three) of the data bits is '1'.

Table 1 shows the required bias voltages, generated currents, latency, and energy consumption for different functions. Ideally, the current varies linearly with the change in data stored in the memory cells. However, the current sensing transistor of sense amplifier has an on resistance of its own which is comparable to $R_{on}$ of the memory, which introduces non-linearity in the behavior of current. The current comparison technique still works since the change in current is significant and detectable by the proposed circuit.

*3.1.3 Technology Dependent Variations.* **NVM:** NVM characteristics depend upon the material used for making the device. Hence, the effective resistance of device as well as the performance vary with the process. While the proposed method works well for devices with $R_{on}$ greater $1k\Omega$, other NVM devices require slight modifications in the circuit.

In such situation, the large ON resistance of the current mirroring NMOS transistor results in a huge resistance drop across the transistor. Since there is a very little drop across memory cells, the change in voltage across the cells and hence the current through them is not detectable. In order to overcome this issue, we introduce a resistor, $R_{sink}$, in parallel to the current mirroring transistor. The resistance of this resistor is equal to $R_{on}$ of the memory cell. It acts as a current sink for the current through the memory cells. The voltage at the common node is now dependent upon the data stored in the memory. Majority of the current now flows through the sink resistor. However, the current into the current mirror is now determined by the voltage at the common node. Since the voltage is dependent upon data, the current becomes data dependent as well. The remaining circuit works as before. However, using a sink resistor introduces a low resistive path for the current to flow, resulting in a direct increase in the total power consumption of the circuit.

**SRAM:** In the case of SRAMs, we do not have access to the terminal which drains the current out of the memory cell like in case of RRAM. Hence, we connect a gated voltage source to the bitline. Whenever the logic is to be executed, the voltage source is activated and the current through it is copied to the logic circuit using PMOS current mirror. The original read/write mechanism remains the same, wherein the voltage source is deactivated and the conventional conditioning circuit is used. At the time of logic execution, the conditioning circuits are disabled with only the auxiliary circuit being activated. This circuit is similar to the one proposed previously with roles of NMOS and PMOS interchanged. The voltage source feeds current to the memory cells directly through bitlines.

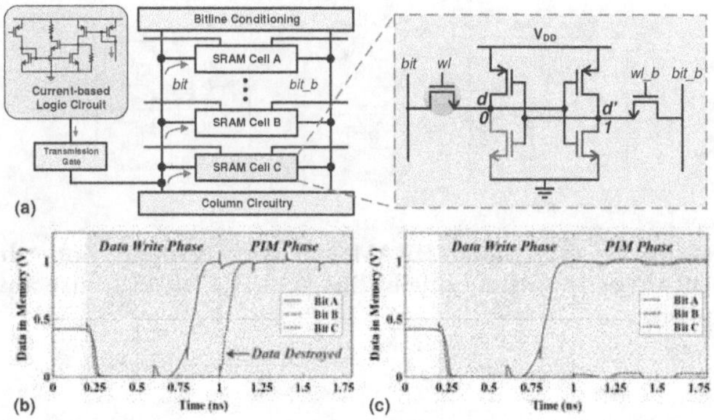


**Figure 2: (a) Overview of GPIM in SRAM; (b) effect of GPIM circuitry on stored data; (c) SRAM data while using the data preserving techniques.**

The amount of current discharging through a memory cell depends upon the data it stores. The node of the cross-coupled inverter storing '1' presents a higher resistance to the ground due to the NMOS transistor being switched off. On the contrary, the node with '0' has a lower resistance to ground. The data to be processed should be present in the memory cells connected to the same bitline. To execute logic in SRAM, we activate the wordlines corresponding to the concerned memory cells.

*Preserving data in SRAM* — The major difference between SRAM and NVM is the way that data is stored. In the case of SRAM, it is possible that logic execution destroys the data stored in a cell as shown in Figure 2b. For example, the node *d* in the SRAM cell C (storing '0') in Figure 2a can be charged due to the constant voltage applied during the GPIM execution phase, destroying the initial data. Our design adopts techniques to preserve data in SRAM while enabling easy logic execution [28]. We reduce the voltage for the access transistor encircled in Figure 2a in the execution phase to prevent the circuit from having a strong effect on the data stored in SRAM. This decreases the effective amount of current that flows through the memory cell and hence diminishes the possibility of data bits getting flipped. However, long and repeated access to the same memory cell can still lead to a situation where the data is destroyed. In order to prevent this, we split the wordline access. Here, only the access transistor directly connected to the GPIM circuit is activated while the other remains off during the execution stage. This ensures the presence of a strong logic state in the other half of the cell, hence preserving the data. The effectiveness of the techniques can be observed in Figure 2c, where the stored data remains intact throughout the execution phase.

## 3.2 Voltage-based Implementation

In this section, we introduce a circuit which uses the DRAM bitline voltage to selectively charge the output capacitor. The total charge developed at the capacitor is used to implement different functions in-memory.

*3.2.1 Analog Properties of DRAM.* DRAM cells are generally used in the folded bitline subarray arrangement as shown in Figure 3a. Figure 3b shows a DRAM cell. DRAM stores data in the form of charge on a capacitor, accessible via a transistor. A read operation on a DRAM cell is destructive in nature. Hence, a read is followed by a write operation to preserve data in memory. Moreover, the charge on the storage capacitor leaks out over time and requires a periodic refresh of data. Hence, unlike the previously discussed memories, the effective resistance of a DRAM cell is independent

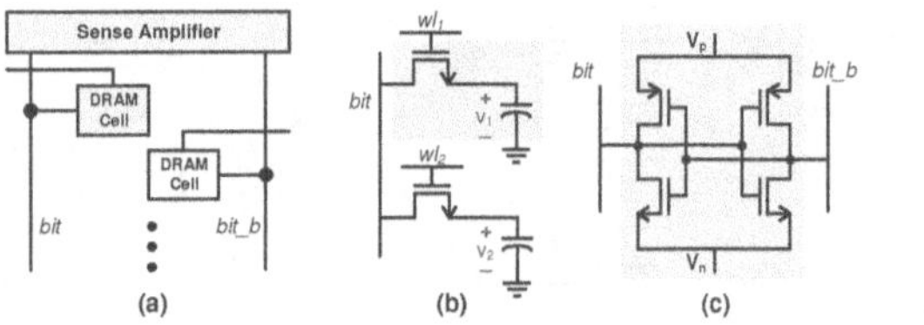


**Figure 3: (a) Folded DRAM subarray configuration; (b) DRAM cells on the same bitline; (c) basic DRAM sense amplifier.**

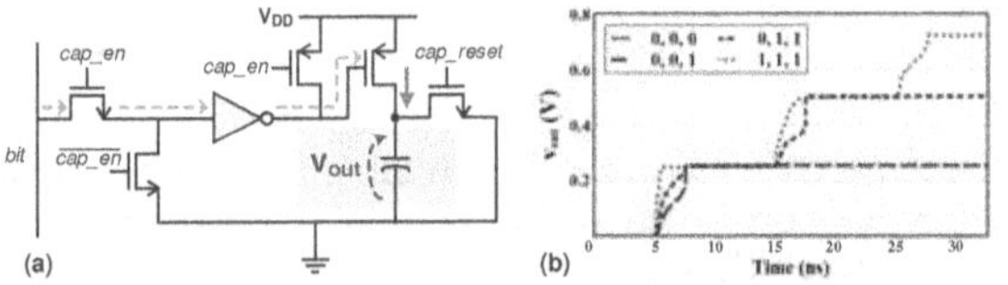


**Figure 4: (a)** GPIM **circuit for DRAM; (b) data-dependent voltage at the output capacitor.**

of the data stored. Hence, the usual current sensing circuit won't work for DRAM.

*3.2.2 Circuit Design.* **Differential Sense Amplifier:** Figure 3c shows the basic sense amplifier used in DRAM. It is made up of two cross-coupled inverters. The voltage across the inverters is controlled by signals $V_p$ and $V_n$. Of the two bitlines, only one bitline reads in a cycle while the other acts as the reference. While reading, the access transistor of a DRAM cell is activated. The cell either pulls down or pushes up one of the bitlines by a small amount, depending upon the stored data. This difference generated between the two bitlines is amplified by pulling down $V_n$ to 0 and then pulling up $V_p$ to $V_{DD}$. This amplification results in rewriting the cell with the value that was just read. Hence, such a read operation is non-destructive in nature in contrast to the traditional DRAM read operation.

**Proposed Circuit:** We propose controlled capacitor charging based circuit to implement logic in DRAM. Figure 4a shows the proposed circuit. The circuit consists of a capacitor whose charging is regulated by the voltage at bitline. A signal, *cap_en*, activates the logic circuit once the bitline has read the data. Whenever the logic circuit is active and the voltage at bitline is above the threshold of the high $V_T$ inverter, the capacitor is charged by the power supply. The three memory cells are read one at a time and the capacitor is activated after every read operation. The capacitor is charged whenever the stored bit is '1' while its charge does not change if the stored bit is '0.' In addition to the control switches and inverter, the circuit uses some transistors to pull up or down certain nodes to ensure correct functioning. The *cap_reset* signal discharges the capacitor completely at the beginning of every logic execution phase.

**Implementing `MAJ`, `OR`, and `AND`:** The total voltage developed at the capacitor at the end determines the number of bits which are '1,' as shown in Figure 4b. In our experimental setup for 3-bit logic operations, the voltage levels 0.25V, 0.50V, and 0.72V correspond to the presence of one, two, and three logic high ('1') bits. So, a final voltage greater than or equal to 0.25V corresponds to `OR` being true. Similarly, a voltage greater than or equal to 0.50V and 0.72V translates to `MAJ` and `AND` being high respectively.

## 3.3 GPIM Architecture

Figure 5 shows the overview of the proposed GPIM. It consists of an array of memory cells. Each memory cell is connected to a wordline and a bitline, except a SRAM cell which is connected to 2 wordlines and 2 bitlines. The controller handles the column and row circuitry which control the bitline and wordline voltages, respectively. The sense amplifier is responsible for reading the data and processing it. Depending upon the memory technology, the sense amplifier will be one of the circuits proposed in the previous sections. Figure 5 shows the structure of these possible sense amplifiers. Each bitline has a GPIM circuit which outputs `OR`, `MAJ`, or `AND` depending upon the bias voltage. The output of the sense amplifier is supplied to a gate array, as shown in Figure 5, which is required to perform other operations like addition. This gate array just relies on the output of the GPIM sense amplifiers and not directly on the actual data. In some cases, intermediate results are written back to the memory for each bit and used to calculate the results for next bit. N-bit addition, implemented similar to [22], is a simple example of such a case where $C_{out}$ of each 1-bit addition is written back to memory.

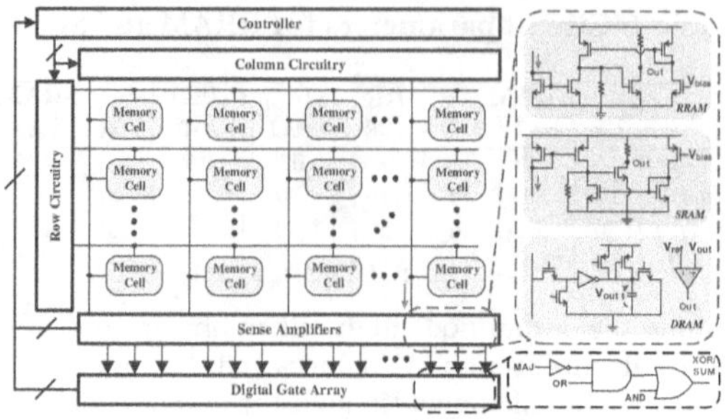


**Figure 5:** GPIM **Overall Architecture**

**Advantages of** GPIM: GPIM provides the following benefits:
*Latency* — The latency of implementing bitwise functions (`OR`, `MAJ` or `AND`) using the proposed amplifiers involves a read and logic execution. Both data read and logic execution being fast, are done together in a single cycle for SRAM and RRAM. For DRAM, the logic execution is slower than the DRAM write operation and has a latency approximately equal to 3 write cycles. Effectively, the circuit takes 2 or 4 cycles to execute 1-bit addition which is quite less than the time taken by previous PIM techniques to implement the same functionality.
*Energy Consumption* — GPIM benefits in energy consumption due to two major factors, (i) less dependency on device write operations and (ii) reduced number of memory operations required for implementing logic.
*Device Switches in NVMs* — PIM in NVMs is challenged by low endurance issues. Implementing logic using sense amplifiers reduces the number of read/write operations in memory, helping with the issue. For example, 32-bit addition in [22] involves around 400 device switches while GPIM uses only 31 device switches.
*Memory Utilization* — The proposed technique does not require a separate processing area in the memory block as in the case of previously proposed PIM designs. Previous designs require the use of a memory size much larger than the storage capacity to accommodate for processing memory cells. This is not required by our design since the processing happens in the sense amplifiers, increasing the effective utilization of the memory.

# 4 EXPERIMENTAL RESULTS

## 4.1 Experimental Setup

Performance and energy consumption of proposed hardware are obtained from circuit level simulations for a 45nm CMOS process technology using Cadence Virtuoso. We use VTEAM memristor

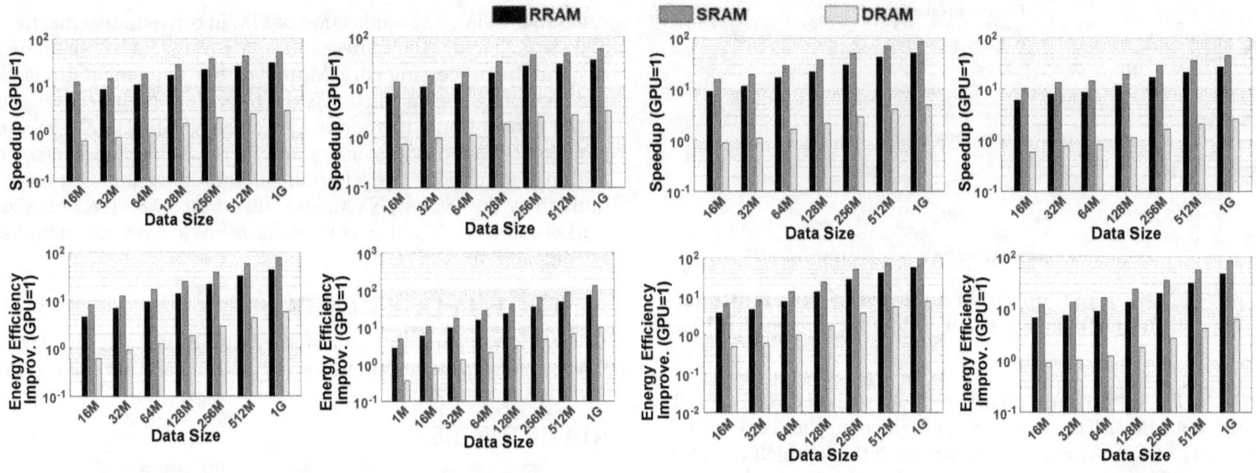


(a) Sobel (b) Robert (c) FFT (d) HAAR

**Figure 6: Speedup and energy efficiency improvement of preforming PIM operation over different applications.**

**Table 2: Comparison of 3-bit bitwise operations and 32-bit addition and multiplication in RRAM with prior work**

| Design | Metric | OR | MAJ | AND | XOR | 32b ADD | 32b MUL |
|---|---|---|---|---|---|---|---|
| GPIM | Latency (ns) | 0.05 | 0.05 | 0.05 | 0.18 | 33.7 | 80.1 |
| | Energy (fJ) | 5.31 | 8.07 | 9.11 | 24.5 | $1.16 \times 10^3$ | $29.6 \times 10^3$ |
| | Device Switches | 0 | 0 | 0 | 0 | 31 | $\sim 1.2 \times 10^3$ |
| MAGIC [20, 22] | Latency (ns) | 3.3 | 5.5 | 5.5 | 9.9 | 457.6 | 1090.3 |
| | Energy (fJ) | 48.1 | 96.4 | 96.2 | 192.6 | $9.2 \times 10^3$ | $181 \times 10^3$ |
| | Device Switches | 3 | 6 | 6 | 12 | ~400 | $\sim 7.5 \times 10^3$ |

model [29] for our memory design simulation with $R_{ON}$ and $R_{OFF}$ of $10k\Omega$ and $10M\Omega$ respectively. We design the conventional 6T SRAM cell with standard transistor sizing using 45nm technology library with normal $V_{TH}$ cells. In case of DRAM, the cell is designed in the same technology using the 1T-1C configuration with a storage capacitor of 30fF.

We compare the efficiency of the proposed GPIM with AMD Radeon R9 390 GPU, a recent GPU architecture, with 8GB memory. In order to avoid the disk communication in the comparison, all the data used in the experiments is preloaded into 64GB, 2.1GHz DDR4 DIMMs. We used Hioki 3334 power meter to measure the power consumption of GPU. We tested both GPIM and GPU over four OpenCL applications: *Sobel, Robert, Fast Fourier transform (FFT)* and *DwHaar1D*. For image processing applications, we used random images from *Caltech 101* [30] library, while for non-image processing applications inputs are generated randomly. Majority of these applications consists of additions and multiplications. The other common operations such as square root have been approximated by these two functions in OpenCL code.

## 4.2 Energy and Performance Comparison

We compare GPIM with the state-of-the-art prior work [20, 22]. The work in [20] is based on MAGIC logic family. It uses NOR computations to implement different functions in memory. The work in [22] used it to implement data-intensive additions and multiplications in memory. Table 2 compares the implementation of a 32-bit adder using GPIM for RRAM devices with those in [20, 22]. It shows that GPIM outperforms all the previous implementations. It performs at least 2.4× times better than the fastest adder. A major part of this improvement comes from the fact that GPIM avoids the huge latency associated with RRAM device switches by implementing logic using sense amplifiers. We evaluate GPIM for 32-bit multiplication. We compare it with [22] since it is the only switching based PIM supporting multiplication in memory. Our results show that in the case of RRAM, GPIM is 15× faster and consumes 6× less energy. This improvement can be credited to the lower latency and energy consumption of the MOSFETs as compared to RRAM devices.

## 4.3 GPIM Exploration over Technologies

We compare the three memory technologies, SRAM, DRAM, and RRAM, with traditional GPU core on the basis of performance and energy consumption. The comparison was done by running four different applications on all technologies. The experiments were conducted assuming that the memories were big enough to store the required data. Figure 6 shows that SRAM performs better than all other technologies, being on an average 29.8× faster than GPU while having 36.3× lower energy consumption. Here, while comparing performance, we take into consideration the absolute latency of execution. RRAM has latency and power consumption close to those of SRAM, on an average 17.6× and 20.3× respectively as compared to GPU. It also follows trends similar to SRAM over different applications. However, DRAM performs worse than even GPU in some cases. It also has the least performance and energy efficiency among the three memory technologies, being on an average 1.7× faster and 2.7× more energy efficient as compared to GPU.

**SRAM:** The results indicate that SRAM is the best solution for in-memory processing. However, this may not be a feasible option. The major drawback of SRAM is its cell area which goes as high as $140F^2$ in commercial SRAMs. Hence, having really huge SRAM blocks becomes too expensive. However, SRAMs can be utilized as PIM when the data size is small which still gives a significant improvement as compared to traditional GPU cores. The fast in-memory processing opportunities provided by SRAMs can also be exploited by compute caches [26] to reduce the data transfers across cache hierarchy.

**RRAM:** RRAM has performance and energy consumption metrics close to SRAM. Unlike SRAM, RRAMs are dense with a cell size of $4F^2$ when used in a crossbar configuration. Processing in RRAM devices is bottlenecked by the slower device switching speed as compared to SRAM. Moreover, RRAM is challenged by endurance issues. However, GPIM reduces the number of device switches required while processing data, which partially reduces these issues.

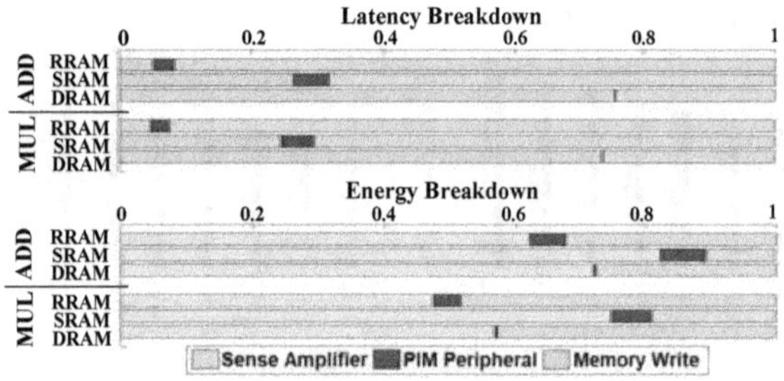


**Figure 7: Latency and energy breakdown of different technologies while performing 32-bits addition and multiplication.**

**DRAM:** DRAM performs poorly, even worse than GPU for small data sizes (< 64MB). This is due to the high latency and energy requirements of DRAM read and write operations which directly impact the efficiency of PIM in DRAM. However, as the data size increases, beyond 64MB in our experimental setup, the data transfer costs associated with the traditional GPU cores start dominating. Since PIM reduces these data transfers, GPIM for DRAM starts performing better than GPU with lower energy consumption. Hence, PIM is suitable for DRAM when the data size gets huge.

## 4.4 Performance and Energy Breakdown

Figure 7 shows the distribution of total latency and energy consumption among different stages of GPIM. The breakdown of latency for RRAM reveals that in the case of both addition and multiplication, the majority of the time (>90%) is spent in writing back the intermediate results to the memory. This is due to the high device switching latency of RRAM, which GPIM avoids as much as possible in logic execution. The latency for SRAM is distributed between the auxiliary circuit and memory write back in the ratio of about 2:5. This can be attributed to the reduced write latency of SRAM as compared to RRAM, while the logic execution latency for SRAM is more than that of RRAM. In the case of a DRAM, the distribution is quite different with logic execution taking the majority of the time. This happens because GPIM performs sequential reads of the data to be processed, which happens in parallel in RRAM and SRAM.

The breakdown of energy for addition reveals that the energy consumed by the logic circuit is greater than the device write energy for all the three memories. A major factor behind this behavior is the use of multiple copies of the logic circuit for different functions. In case of multiplication, the number of device writes is high, resulting in a greater contribution by the device write operations to the total energy consumption. The energy consumption for SRAM are highly skewed towards logic circuits because the device writes in SRAM are very efficient.

## 4.5 GPIM Area Overhead

The area overhead of GPIM depends upon the size of a memory bank. Our evaluations for a 4*M*b memory bank indicate that GPIM introduces overheads of 0.83%, 3.5%, and 4.1% for SRAM, DRAM, and RRAM respectively. This result follows the densities of different memories, with overhead being lesser for a memory with larger cell area. Moreover, for a fixed memory bank size, the overhead reduces with an increase in the number of rows in the bank.

# 5 CONCLUSION

In this paper, we proposed GPIM which enabled PIM in SRAM, NVMs, and DRAM. The circuits exploit the analog properties of the respective memories to implement a fast and energy efficient solution for PIM. The application of PIM in conventional memories allows us to avoid the unnecessary data transfers between memory and the processing core. Moreover, our implementations use fast switching speeds of transistors to achieve high performance in the conventional memories as well as NVMs. GPIM executes basic logic functions in memory and then uses them to implement arithmetic functions like addition and multiplication. Our evaluations show that SRAM, NVM, and DRAM are 29.8× (36.3×), 17.6× (20.3×) and 1.7× (2.7×) better in performance (energy consumption) as compared to AMD GPU.

# ACKNOWLEDGEMENTS

This work was partially supported by CRISP, one of six centers in JUMP, an SRC program sponsored by DARPA, and also NSF grants #1730158 and #1527034.

# REFERENCES


[1] C. Perera *et al.*, "Context aware computing for the internet of things: A survey," *IEEE Communications Surveys & Tutorials*, vol. 16, no. 1, pp. 414–454, 2014.
[2] J. Gubbi *et al.*, "Internet of things (iot): A vision, architectural elements, and future directions," *Future generation computer systems*, vol. 29, no. 7, pp. 1645–1660, 2013.
[3] M. Imani *et al.*, "A framework for collaborative learning in secure high-dimensional space," in *Cloud Computing (CLOUD)*, IEEE, 2019.
[4] H. Zhang *et al.*, "In-memory big data management and processing: A survey," *IEEE TKDE*, vol. 27, no. 7, pp. 1920–1948, 2015.
[5] A. Shafiee *et al.*, "Isaac: A convolutional neural network accelerator with in-situ analog arithmetic in crossbars," in *IEEE ISCA*, pp. 14–26, IEEE Press, 2016.
[6] M. Soltiz *et al.*, "Memristor-based neural logic blocks for nonlinearly separable functions," *IEEE TC*, vol. 62, no. 8, pp. 1597–1606, 2013.
[7] M. Imani *et al.*, "Rapidnn: In-memory deep neural network acceleration framework," *arXiv preprint arXiv:1806.05794*, 2018.
[8] N. Talati *et al.*, "Concept: A column oriented memory controller for efficient memory and pim operations in rram," *IEEE Micro*, 2019.
[9] S. Shirinzadeh *et al.*, "Fast logic synthesis for rram-based in-memory computing using majority-inverter graphs," in *IEEE/ACM DATE*, EDA Consortium, 2016.
[10] M. Soeken *et al.*, "An mig-based compiler for programmable logic-in-memory architectures," in *IEEE/ACM DAC*, pp. 1–6, Ieee, 2016.
[11] G. Piccolboni *et al.*, "Investigation of the potentialities of vertical resistive ram (vrram) for neuromorphic applications," in *IEEE IEDM*, pp. 17–2, IEEE, 2015.
[12] M. Imani *et al.*, "Floatpim: In-memory acceleration of deep neural network training with high precision," in *ISCA*, ACM, 2019.
[13] C. Merkel *et al.*, "Neuromemristive systems: Boosting efficiency through brain-inspired computing," *Computer*, vol. 49, no. 10, pp. 56–64, 2016.
[14] S. Gupta *et al.*, "Nnpim: A processing in-memory architecture for neural network acceleration," *IEEE Transactions on Computers*, pp. 1–1, 2019.
[15] M. Imani *et al.*, "Exploring hyperdimensional associative memory," in *HPCA*, pp. 445–456, IEEE, 2017.
[16] M. Zhou *et al.*, "Gas: A heterogeneous memory architecture for graph processing," in *ISLPED*, p. 27, ACM, 2018.
[17] M. Zhou *et al.*, "Gram: graph processing in a reram-based computational memory," in *ASP-DAC*, pp. 591–596, ACM, 2019.
[18] M. Imani *et al.*, "Mpim: Multi-purpose in-memory processing using configurable resistive memory," in *ASP-DAC*, pp. 757–763, IEEE, 2017.
[19] A. Siemon *et al.*, "A complementary resistive switch-based crossbar array adder," *IEEE JETCAS*, vol. 5, no. 1, pp. 64–74, 2015.
[20] N. Talati *et al.*, "Logic design within memristive memories using memristor-aided logic (magic)," *IEEE TNANO*, vol. 15, no. 4, pp. 635–650, 2016.
[21] S. Gupta *et al.*, "Felix: Fast and energy-efficient logic in memory," in *ICCAD*, pp. 1–7, IEEE, 2018.
[22] M. Imani *et al.*, "Ultra-efficient processing in-memory for data intensive applications," in *ACM/IEEE DAC*, p. 6, ACM, 2017.
[23] R. Nair *et al.*, "Active memory cube: A processing-in-memory architecture for exascale systems," *IBM Journal of Research and Development*, vol. 59, no. 2/3, pp. 17–1, 2015.
[24] Y. Kim *et al.*, "Orchard: Visual object recognition accelerator based on approximate in-memory processing," in *ICCAD*, pp. 25–32, IEEE, 2017.
[25] S. Kvatinsky *et al.*, "MAGIC–Memristor-aided logic," *IEEE TCAS II*, vol. 61, no. 11, pp. 895–899, 2014.
[26] S. Aga *et al.*, "Compute caches," in *IEEE HPCA*, pp. 481–492, IEEE, 2017.
[27] J. Zhang *et al.*, "In-memory computation of a machine-learning classifier in a standard 6t sram array," *IEEE JSSC*, vol. 52, no. 4, pp. 915–924, 2017.
[28] S. Jeloka *et al.*, "A 28 nm configurable memory (tcam/bcam/sram) using push-rule 6t bit cell enabling logic-in-memory," *IEEE JSSC*, vol. 51, no. 4, 2016.
[29] S. Kvatinsky *et al.*, "Vteam: a general model for voltage-controlled memristors," *IEEE TCAS II*, vol. 62, no. 8, pp. 786–790, 2015.
[30] "Caltech Library." http://www.vision.caltech.edu/Image_Datasets/Caltech101/.

# BLADE: A BitLine Accelerator for Devices on the Edge

William Andrew Simon, Yasir Mahmood Qureshi
Alexandre Levisse, Marina Zapater, David Atienza
Embedded Systems Lab (ESL), Swiss Institute of Technology Lausanne (EPFL)
Lausanne, Switzerland
{william.simon,yasir.qureshi,alexandre.levisse,marina.zapater,david.atienza}@epfl.ch

## ABSTRACT

The increasing ubiquity of edge devices in the consumer market, along with their ever more computationally expensive workloads, necessitate corresponding increases in computing power to support such workloads. In-memory computing is attractive in edge devices as it reuses preexisting memory elements, thus limiting area overhead. Additionally, in-SRAM Computing (iSC) efficiently performs computations on spatially local data found in a variety of emerging edge device workloads. We therefore propose, implement, and benchmark BLADE, a BitLine Accelerator for Devices on the Edge. BLADE is an iSC architecture that can perform massive SIMD-like complex operations on hundreds to thousands of operands simultaneously. We implement BLADE in 28nm CMOS and demonstrate its functionality down to 0.6V, lower than any conventional state-of-the-art iSC architecture. We also benchmark BLADE in conjunction with a full Linux software stack in the gem5 architectural simulator, providing a robust demonstration of its performance gain in comparison to an equivalent embedded processor equipped with a NEON SIMD co-processor. We benchmark BLADE with three emerging edge device workloads, namely cryptography, high efficiency video coding, and convolutional neural networks, and demonstrate 4x, 6x, and 3x performance improvement, respectively, in comparison to a baseline CPU/NEON processor at an equivalent power budget.

## KEYWORDS

In-memory processing, In-SRAM processing, Bitline computing, Edge computing.

**ACM Reference Format:**
William Andrew Simon, Yasir Mahmood Qureshi and Alexandre Levisse, Marina Zapater, David Atienza. 2019. BLADE: A BitLine Accelerator for Devices on the Edge . In *Great Lakes Symposium on VLSI 2019 (GLSVLSI '19), May 9–11, 2019, Tysons Corner, VA, USA.* ACM, New York, NY, USA, 6 pages. https://doi.org/10.1145/3299874.3317979

## 1 INTRODUCTION

As of 2018, 41% of Americans owned a digital home assistant, e.g. Amazon's Alexa or Google's Home, and over 25% owned more than three smart home devices [16]. In the same year, 77% of Americans owned a smartphone, for the first time overtaking PC ownership at just 75% [1]. As edge device adoption accelerates, their compute power must increase correspondingly to meet application demands.

As edge devices are naturally limited in physical size and power, innovations must be developed that boost performance while maintaining low area and power overheads. In this context, in-memory computing presents an attractive solution as it boosts compute power through preexisting hardware elements, while also reducing power consumption due to data movement [3]. Much research in this field focuses on in-DRAM computing to reduce data movement and take advantage of the logic layer available in 3D DRAM stacks [12, 17, 25]. However, the emerging field of in-SRAM Computing (iSC) also shows promise as it takes advantage of SRAM array bitline/wordline structure and the contained data's inherent locality to perform SIMD-like operations without involving the processor [3]. Different iSC architectures have been explored, from simple bitwise logic caches [3] to transposing caches that perform complex operations [14] and large, complex 10T-based arrays that can fully pipeline many operations [4]. However, each of these architectures have drawbacks in terms of computational complexity, size, and performance. Currently there are no iSC architectures designed specifically to address the unique requirements of edge device physical design and workloads.

To fulfill this need, we propose BLADE, a BitLine Accelerator for Devices on the Edge. Its physical and architectural characteristics are ideal for small edge device caches. In particular, BLADE performs complex operations such as `add`, `multiply`, and `greater/less than`, in a massive (i.e. 1024 bitwise/128 8bit) SIMD-like fashion, necessary for increasingly complex workloads. By utilizing conventional 6T bitcells and standard bitline multiplexing, BLADE maintains a low (8%) area overhead. Finally, utilizing local bitlines gives BLADE the most efficient voltage/frequency Pareto curve down to 0.6V of any state-of-the-art iSC architecture.

We validate BLADE at the electrical and system level to demonstrate its correct functionality as well as applicability to emerging edge device workloads. From an electrical standpoint, we implement BLADE in 28nm bulk CMOS technology and validate its reliable operation from 0.6V (415Mhz) to 1V (2.2Ghz) , taking into account process variations and post-layout parasitics and extracting timing and energy characteristics. To demonstrate system-level functionality, we extend the gem5 [8] architectural simulator with BLADE, integrating the previously acquired timing values to create a timing accurate simulator capable of running any workload on a full Linux stack. Our robust electrical simulations combined with a realistic, full software stack allows us to benchmark BLADE acceleration on emerging edge device workloads such as cryptography, video processing, and neural networks, while taking into account system level events such as cache misses, system calls, and architecture specific bottlenecks. BLADE is in fact the first complex operation iSC architecture to be profiled on a full software stack.


*GLSVLSI '19, May 9–11, 2019, Tysons Corner, VA, USA*

ACM ISBN 978-1-4503-6252-8/19/05...$15.00
https://doi.org/10.1145/3299874.3317979

Thus, the contributions of this paper are as follows:

- We propose BLADE, the first iSC architecture designed specifically for edge devices.
- We implement BLADE in 28nm bulk CMOS, demonstrating reliable operation down to 0.6V without performance degradation (416Mhz) - a first for iSC architectures.
- We design a timing-accurate gem5 extension for BLADE, allowing workload profiling on a full software stack.
- We profile BLADE with the primary kernels of three edge device workloads, namely cryptography, image processing, and neural networks, demonstrating 4x, 6x, and 3x performance improvements, respectively, against an identical embedded processor equipped with a NEON SIMD co-processor.

The rest of the paper is structured as follows. Section 2 discusses state-of-the-art iSC architectures. Section 3 describes the edge device workloads we use to profile BLADE. Section 4 explains BLADE's bitline architecture and its optimization to edge devices. Section 5 describes our benchmarking methodology in gem5, and finally Section 6 presents and analyzes benchmark results.

## 2 RELATED WORK - BITLINE COMPUTING

BitLine (BL) computing utilizes SRAM structures, cache or otherwise, to perform computations at a much lower transistor count than a standard logic circuit. Jeloka *et al.* [21] demonstrate that sensing the BL and BL bar of simultaneously activated bitcells results in an `and` or `nor` operation of the bitcell values, respectively. Compute Caches [3] extend the number of operations with the addition of extra logic to support a `xor` operation, as illustrated in Figure 1. With this base BL logic architecture, complex operations can be achieved through various means. Neural Cache [14] performs bit serial complex operations by transposing operands to occupy a single BL and performing series of bitwise operations on them. DRC$^2$ [4] implements carry logic across BLs to facilitate complex operations. Finally, Dong *et al.* [11] rely on deeply depleted channel technology and an unconventional 4T bitcell design to achieve an ultra-low voltage iSC architecture.

While these proposals highlight the potential of iSC, each has drawbacks, both in general and in the context of edge device computing. In particular, DRC$^2$'s architecture deviates significantly from typical cache structure as it utilizes 10T SRAM cells and complex periphery for maximum performance, resulting in what is more an accelerator than a cache. Alternatively, the ultra low voltage (0.3V) iSC architecture presented in [11] relies on unconventional CMOS technology (deeply depleted channel) and modified 4T bitcells, known to suffer from stability issues [9] and disturb risks, as well as showing poor performance with voltage scaling (100Mhz@0.6V).

While such architectures may be beneficial to edge devices, they are in veins of research parallel to this work. Compute Caches and Neural Cache, on the other hand, are reliant on the 6T bitcell architecture presented in [21], which has been demonstrated to function in a frequency/voltage range of 800MHz/1V to 70MHz/0.7V. Neural Cache assumes iSC frequency can be improved up to 2.5GHz, however the cache upon which Neural Cache's profiling is based cannot achieve such frequencies at <0.85V [20], well above the 0.66V wordline voltage limitation presented in the work. Neural Cache also relies on bit serial computation to perform complex operations.

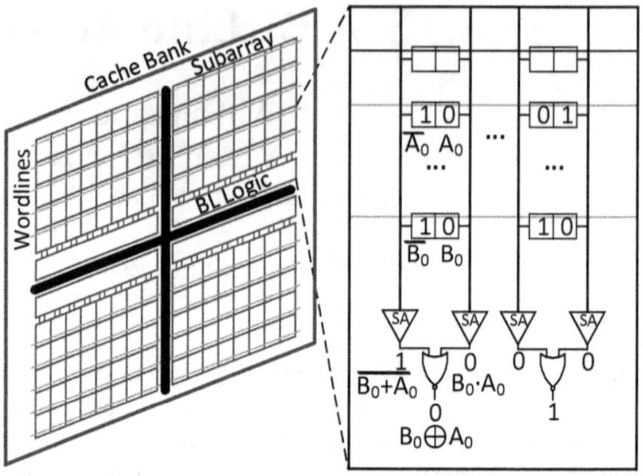


**Figure 1: Cache subarray with AND/NOR/XOR BL computing.**

While this increases the number of parallel operations, the resultant latency from bit serial computation reduces the throughput such that it is comparable to more standard approaches utilizing carry logic, as demonstrated in DRC$^2$ and in this work. Lastly, Neural Cache's reliance on operand transposition reduces the operation granularity at which such an architecture can improve performance; in other words, mingling iSC and CPU operations results in a significant transposition overhead, mitigating performance gains.

In contrast to the above mentioned approaches, BLADE specifically targets edge devices by utilizing a conventional 6T SRAM bitcell design with shared read ports to avoid data corruption, limit area overhead, and avoid frequency reduction while being compatible with any CMOS technology. Further, BLADE uses a conventional carry chain that allows interspersion of iSC and CPU operations at no performance loss, and we have robustly simulated it down to 0.6V to guarantee its operation in conditions typical of edge devices.

## 3 EDGE DEVICE WORKLOADS

As the adoption of edge devices increasingly supplant traditional compute environments such as servers, emerging workloads will increasingly resemble those of traditional servers in function and complexity. While designing BLADE, we focused specifically on designing an architecture optimized for such workloads, and hence chose applications representative of three such fields for profiling.

### 3.1 Cryptography

As the IoT continues to expand, more and more sensitive data will be being transferred between edge level devices and servers [28]. The need for data security and privacy in the midst of this data explosion is such that many processors now include hardware support for common cryptographic functions [6]. Given the ongoing and increasing need for data privacy, as well as emerging technologies such as blockchain, we have included the Secure Hash Algorithm 3 (SHA-3) [13] in our BLADE benchmarks, an integrity algorithm used in data encryption and to detect data tampering.

### 3.2 HEVC Video Processing

Multimedia creation and consumption makes up the largest portion of total mobile app usage, with Youtube being the second most downloaded mobile application at 52.1%, behind Facebook [23].

**Table 1: BLADE operation support and cycle count.**

| Operation | Cycle Count |
|---|---|
| Bitwise (and, nor, xor, not) | 2 |
| Shift | 2*(# shifts) |
| Add | 2 |
| Subtract | 4 |
| Multiplication | 1 + 2*(operand bit width) + 2*3 |
| Greater/Less Than | 10 |
| Copy | 2 |

Video streaming, music, and mobile games all require significant and increasing processing capabilities. Specifically, with the advent of 4K cameras in phones, the ability to efficiently compress video data will become a necessity for video streaming apps such as Twitch and Facebook Live [15]. As such, we choose the HEVC video encoding program Kvazaar [30] as one of our BLADE benchmarks.

## 3.3 Convolutional Neural Networks

Since Alexnet [22] was unveiled in 2012, Convolutional Neural Networks (CNNs) have become the premier neural net for tasks such as image and language processing [10, 26] and object detection [24]. Given their extreme utility, hardware support on mobile platforms for neural network inference and specifically CNNs has become increasingly attractive [18, 19]. We therefore choose to benchmark CNNs on BLADE. Specifically, we implement our testbench on the Arm Compute Library framework (ACL) [2], a suite of functions designed by ARM to optimally utilize its NEON SIMD co-processor.

# 4 EDGE DEVICE OPTIMIZATION

In targeting edge devices, several design choices in terms of architecture design and integration into the cache hierarchy were made to optimize BLADE for the previously presented workloads.

## 4.1 Supporting Edge Level Applications

BLADE performs simple bitwise operations and, nor, and xor in a manner similar to [3] and demonstrated in Figure 1, namely, by activating two wordlines and sensing the resulting discharge at the output of a single ended sense amplifier. However, in order to support emerging edge device workloads, support for complex operations such as addition and multiplication is also necessary. Hence, we extend the simple BL logic with the addition of a xor and two nor gates, as illustrated in Figure 2-b. The output of the xor gate is in fact an addition between the bits of the two activated wordlines, while the output of the nor gates is a carry bit that can be fed to the following BL logic, resulting in a carry ripple adder. The carry line also doubles as a shift if only one wordline is activated.

With the implementation of addition and shift logic, many more complex operations become possible through a series of simple operations. For example, multiplication can be accomplished through a series of additions and shifts. In this work, we accelerate these complex operations through the inclusion of latches after the sense amplifiers and before the writeback logic, allowing pipelining of add+shift stages, as well as an add write-forward line, allowing 2 cycle add+shifts. Alternatively, in a highly area constrained environment, these latches and write-forward lines could be omitted at

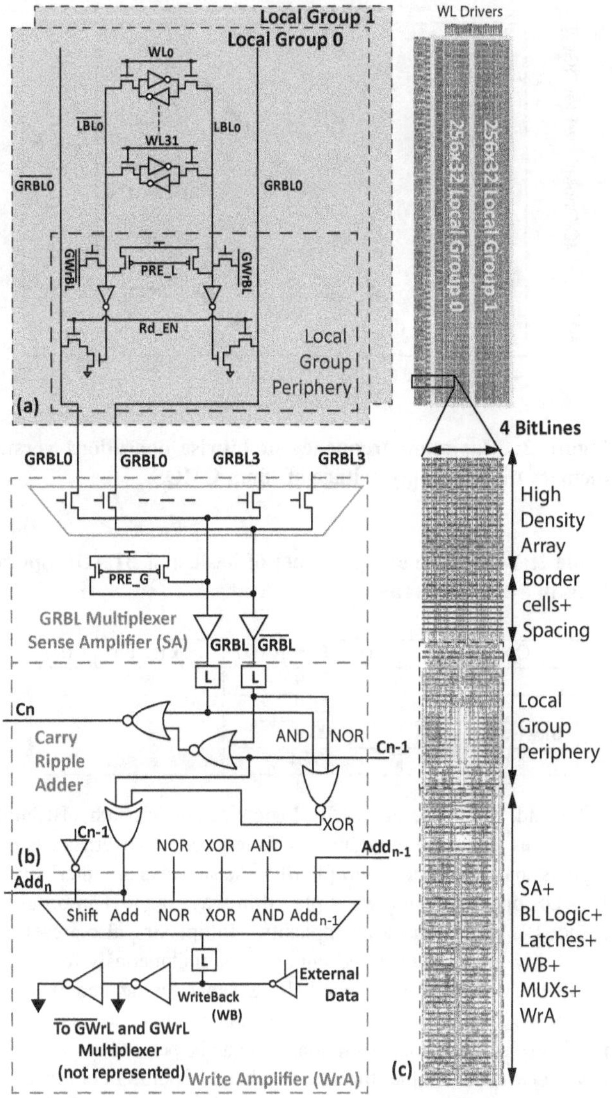


**Figure 2: Layout view of a 256×64 BLADE memory with detailed layout and schematic diagram of the memory periphery.**

the cost of higher cycle counts for complex operations. Table 1 lists all currently supported operations and their respective cycle counts, assuming the cache design detailed in Section 4.3. This cache design utilizes a typical 64 byte wordline length, meaning that a minimum of 512/64 bitwise/8bit operations can be performed per in-cache operation, with this number dependent on cache size and geometry.

## 4.2 Optimized for Small Caches

Several architectural decisions were made in order to optimize BLADE particularly for the small caches found in edge devices. First, we choose to integrate BLADE into the L1 cache in order to simplify cache coherency. Any data requests by the BLADE controller are serviced as standard reads by the cache controller, and similarly, any evictions from the CPU or due to snoop protocol are serviced by the cache controller, with the BLADE controller being notified if relevant data has been evicted.

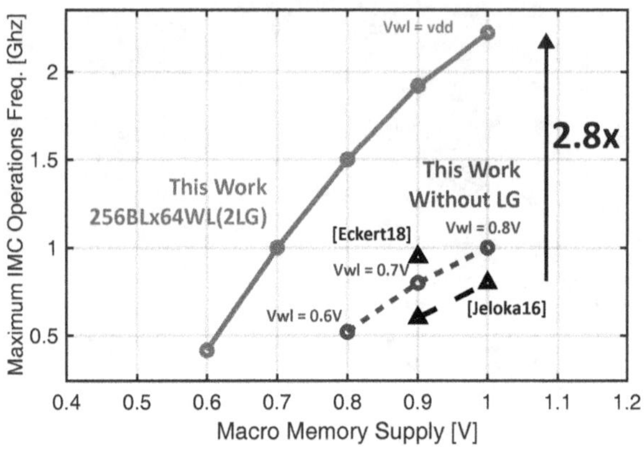


**Figure 3: Maximum frequency of bitwise operations versus memory macro supply voltage at 28nm CMOS.**

**Table 2: Worst case energy values of basic and BLADE operations in a 256×64 array.**

| Operation | Active Energy (fJ) | Leakage Energy (fJ) |
|---|---|---|
| Rd | 23.9 | 88.9 |
| Wr | 25.9 | |
| Bitwise Operation | 23.8 | |
| 8 bit add | 207.4 | |

Second, we implement the BL logic block underneath a BL multiplexer, as illustrated in Figure 2. This reduces area overhead as BL logic is shared between multiple BLs. As set ways are interleaved, BLADE operands are always placed in ways 0 and 1 in order to reduce BLADE controller complexity. Multiplexing also preserves the ability to read cache and tag arrays simultaneously for faster read/write times, known as parallel-tag data access and common in L1 caches. Implementation under the BL multiplexer reduces the number of simultaneous operations that can be performed per cycle, however we believe that the area overhead of putting complex BL logic underneath every BL would make such a design infeasible.

## 4.3 BLADE at Low Voltage

The ability to operate at low voltage is important in power-constrained edge level devices. Unfortunately, cache voltage scaling in iSC architectures is extremely limited due to the risk of data corruption [21]. Data corruption results from the fact that activating two wordlines simultaneously shorts the wordlines' bitcells along their BLs, leading to the possibility of bitcell flipping. The architectures presented in [3, 14] overcome this issue by reducing wordline voltage (underdrive). However, this solution comes at a cost of significantly reduced compute frequency and precludes low voltage operation.

In order to meet the wide voltage range requirements of edge devices while maintaining high frequency, BLADE reuses Local BitLines (LBLs), already reported in many cache architectures [27], to perform reliable, high frequency iSC operations. Each wordline is contained inside a Local Group (LG), which contains a variable number of wordlines and dedicated read/write periphery. All LGs in a subarray are connected in parallel to global read/write BLs(GRBL/GWrL), and are isolated from other LGs, preventing

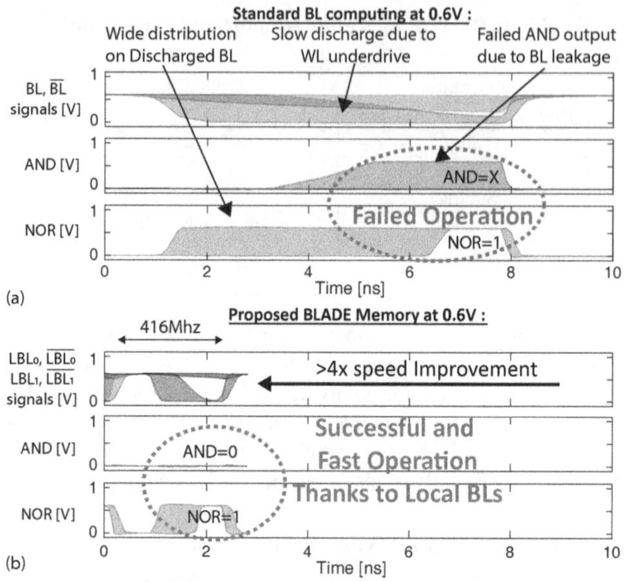


**Figure 4: Transient simulations of bitwise AND, NOR operations at 0.6V on (a) previously published architectures and (b) the proposed BLADE architecture. Thanks to its Local BL organization, BLADE does not require WL underdrive and can achieve fast operation at low voltage while standard architectures are not operational due to BL leakage.**

bitcell shorting or flipping. Figure 3 plots voltage/frequency points for BLADE, both with and without LGs, as well as those of other works. BLADE's voltage/frequency Pareto curve is the most efficient of any conventional state-of-the-art iSC architecture, with a voltage/frequency range between 0.6V/416MHz-1V/2.2GHz.

We implement BLADE in 28nm high performance CMOS technology PDK from TSMC and simulate BLADE's critical paths, considering post-layout parasitics and CMOS variations (10,000 monte-carlo runs at 300K). In this work, we simulate a 256 BL ×64WL memory array with 2 LGs (32WL per LG). This array has an area efficiency of 55.7%, of which the BL logic accounts for 8%. Figure 4 compares the operation of the BLADE memory operating at 0.6V with the same architecture while not using LGs. Beyond showing over 4× speed improvement, it illustrates how BL leakage due to underdriven wordlines preclude correct iSC functionality for standard iSC architectures at 0.6V. We also measure the energy consumption of basic cache operations at a cache frequency of 2.2GHz, as seen in Table 2.

It should be noted that the use of LGs results in a small area overhead [27] and an additional data placement constraint, namely that operands cannot share the same local BL in order to achieve frequencies shown on the red curve in Figure 3. Other placement constraints are discussed in [3], and can be overcome via various architecture-specific solutions. We believe that the nearly 3x frequency gain provided by local BLs outweighs its costs in area and programming complexity. Further, as local BLs are already present in many cache architectures, primarily to improve speed and read stability [27], BLADE in fact improves area efficiency by providing a secondary usage of existing hardware.

**Table 3: Simulator Parameters**

| | |
|---|---|
| Processor | 2GHz, 4 stage pipeline, ARMv8 ISA in-order core, 7 entry LSQ |
| NEON Co-processor | 128 bit registers 16 parallel 8-bit operations |
| L1-I Cache | 32kB, 4-way, 1 cycle access |
| L1-D Cache | 32kB, 4-way, 1 cycle access, BLADE extension |
| L2 Cache | mostly-exclusive, 1MB, 4-way, 6 cycle access |
| Memory | DDR3 2133MHz, 4GB |
| BLADE | Max 1024/128 bitwise/8bit simultaneous operations |

# 5 BENCHMARK SETUP

## 5.1 Benchmarking BLADE in gem5

In order to validate the performance gain of this work at a system level, we implement a timing accurate model of BLADE in the architectural simulator gem5 [8]. This is accomplished by first laying out a BLADE SRAM array as discussed in Section 4.3 and extracting critical path timing values. We then extend gem5's L1 cache with a BLADE controller and BL logic, integrating the previously extracted timing values to guarantee cycle accurate simulation. The simulator is calibrated with the parameters outlined in Table 3, which emulates the ARMv8 A53 in-order core found on the ARM Juno development board [7], and running an Ubuntu 18.04 LTS software environment that demonstrates less than 4% timing inaccuracy on profiling tests compared to physical hardware. The simulator also supports operations utilizing a NEON SIMD co-processor [5]. NEON is a well-established and documented SIMD accelerator present on many edge devices, therefore we choose to evaluate the performance of BLADE against NEON. gem5 does not provide reliable system level energy or power estimations, so we do not include such estimations in our performance results beyond individual instruction energy consumption presented in Section 4.3. However, previously presented work demonstrates how iSC architectures reliably reduce energy consumption by reducing instruction processing and eliminating data movement [3]. Such a claim can be grasped intuitively by considering that performing an equivalent number of operations on an array of operands via BLADE, which can perform 128 simultaneous operations, vs NEON, which can perform 16 8 bit operations simultaneously, will result in significantly reduced memory access and data movement, and hence reduced energy consumption.

## 5.2 Benchmarking Methodology

In order to benchmark BLADE's performance on the target applications, we profile each application and identify its most compute intensive kernel. Each kernel has been highly optimized for use on the NEON, providing a robust comparison for BLADE. The kernels in question are the block permutation kernel of SHA-3, the FIR filter of Kvazaar, and the convolutional layer of an ACL CNN; these kernels consume 94%, 35%, and 90% of total application runtimes, respectively. We therefore extract each kernel and run a series of benchmarks, sweeping size parameters related to each kernel. For the FIR filter and convolutional kernels, we also vary cache associativity and cache size, respectively, to demonstrate interesting trends that apply to iSC architectures in general, as detailed in Section 6.

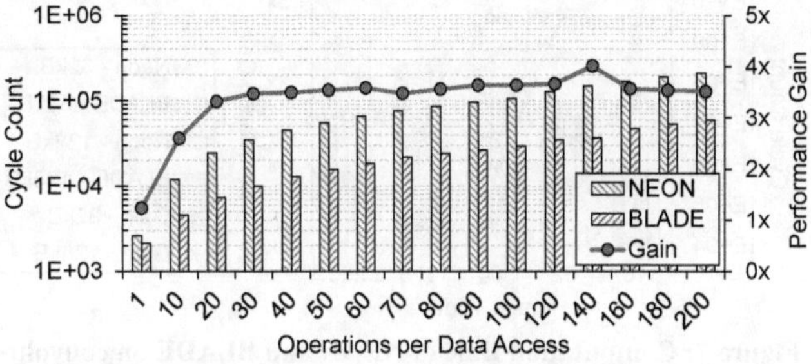


**Figure 5: Computation time of NEON and BLADE on bitwise operations.**

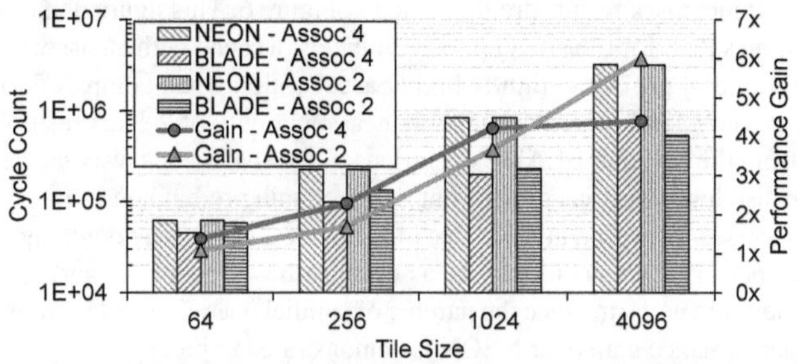


**Figure 6: Computation time of NEON and BLADE on FIR operations.**

# 6 BENCHMARK RESULTS

## 6.1 Bitwise Operations

The block permutation kernel of SHA-3 involves performing a large number of bitwise operations, namely `xor`, `shift`, and and, on each byte of information in a series of up to 24 rounds to permute it to an encrypted character sequence. Such a kernel allows us to explore the performance of BLADE with respect to the number of operations performed on data per data access. We therefore design a kernel in which varying amounts of bitwise computations are performed on data per access from memory.

Figure 5 illustrates the performance gains of BLADE over NEON for operation counts between 1 and 200 per data access for 4096 bytes of data. At lower numbers of operations, function time is dominated by memory access, resulting in ~1x acceleration for BLADE. However, as the number of bitwise operations per data access increases, BLADE acceleration improves correspondingly, saturating at ~3.5x speed-up. This saturation is reached at 30 operations per access, well under the >400 operations per byte that SHA3-256 performs, indicating that at this point compute time becomes dominant over access time. Overall, the maximum performance gain over a NEON co-processor is demonstrated to be 4x.

## 6.2 FIR Filter

In order to benchmark Kvazaar's FIR filter function, we extract and run the function in isolation on the available sub-image tile sizes according the HEVC standards [29]. The function utilizes 4 separate 8-tap FIR filters by which the input image is filtered in a horizontal and then vertical manner, resulting in 16 filtered outputs. We also vary cache geometry, specifically associativity, for this benchmark in order to illustrate a general trend relating to iSC architectures, namely that of operation efficiency in relation to cache geometry.

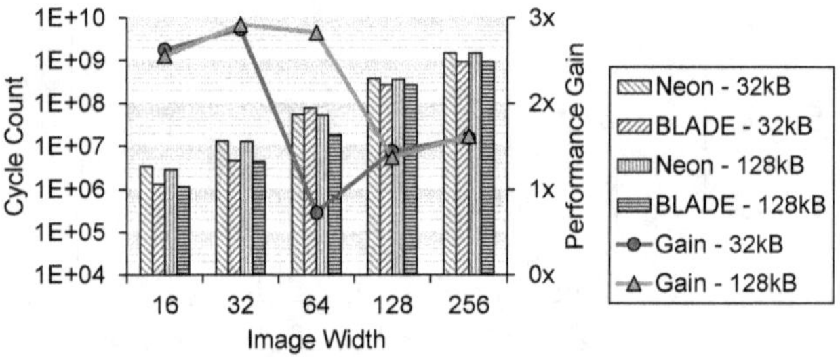


**Figure 7: Computation time of NEON and BLADE on convolution operations.**

Benchmark results are illustrated in Figure 6. This figure demonstrates that, for tile sizes up to 1024 pixels, a cache with an associativity of 4 provides slightly higher acceleration when compared to an equivalently sized cache with an associativity of 2. This results from the fact that BLADE operations in the shallower 4-way cache cause less evictions of relevant data, reducing redundant memory accesses. However, at a tile size of 4096, the 2-way cache dominates in performance, as it is twice as deep as the 4-way cache and can therefore perform twice the number of parallel operations. Maximum performance gain over NEON is demonstrated to be 6x.

## 6.3 Convolution

Finally, we also benchmark the convolutional layer of a CNN implemented in ACL. Our convolutional layer benchmark has 32 input planes and 32 output planes, and performs 3x3 convolution at stride 1 with a padding of 1 to maintain equivalent dimensions. Input/output data is stored in 32 bit fixed point notation, while weights are stored in 8 bit fixed point notation. We convolve input layers with widths varying from 16 to 256 pixels at 2 different cache sizes, 32kB and 128kB, demonstrating a trend relating cache size to iSC efficiency.

Figure 7 illustrates benchmark results for the convolutional layer. As can be seen, each cache size provides similar acceleration over the NEON processor. However, there are sharp performance drop offs at tile widths of 64 and 128 for the 32kB and 128kB caches, respectively. This is a result of the fact that with an output width of 32, the resultant output planes fit entirely within the L1 cache, simplifying the kernel loop design and substantially reducing data movement overhead. At an output width of 64 however, output planes no longer fit within the cache, necessitating a more complex kernel loop to meet operand locality constraints as discussed in Section 4.3, and resulting in a high data movement overhead. By increasing L1 cache size to 128kB, larger layer sizes can be supported at higher speeds. Similar results could be obtained by moving BLADE to lower cache hierarchies; however, this would come at a trade-off of increased coherency complexity if the lower level caches were shared. Overall, a maximum performance gain of 3x over NEON is demonstrated for the convolutional layer of a CNN.

# 7 CONCLUSION

As edge device workloads become more computationally complex, innovative architectures will be necessary to maintain high performance in area and energy constrained environments. In this work we have presented BLADE, an iSC architecture that reuses the preexisting L1 cache with a small (8%) area overhead to perform massively parallel computation at the best voltage/frequency ratios (0.6V/415MHz-1V/2.2GHz) of any conventional iSC architecture. BLADE is demonstrated to outperform an equivalent CPU/NEON processor by significant margins (4x, 6x, 3x) across a variety of cache geometries for a variety of emerging workloads while maintaining or reducing energy consumption. Our results demonstrate that iSC architectures are a promising avenue of research to meet the increasing computational needs of edge device workloads.

# ACKNOWLEDGMENTS

This work has been partially supported by the EC H2020 RECIPE (GA No. 801137) project, and the ERC Consolidator Grant COMPUSAPIEN (GA No. 725657).

# REFERENCES

[1] 2018. http://www.pewinternet.org/fact-sheet/mobile/
[2] 2018. https://developer.arm.com/technologies/compute-library
[3] Shaizeen Aga, S. Jeloka, et al. 2017. Compute Caches. In *HPCA*. 481–492.
[4] Kaya Can Akyel, H. P. Charles, et al. 2016. DRC2: Dynamically Reconfigurable Computing Circuit based on memory architecture. In *ICRC*. 1–8.
[5] ARM. 2009. Introducing NEON.
[6] ARM. 2014. ARM Cortex-A53 MPCore Processor Cryptography Extension.
[7] ARM. 2015. ARM Versatile Express Juno r2 Development Platform.
[8] Nathan Binkert, B. Beckmann, et al. 2011. The Gem5 Simulator. *SIGARCH Comput. Archit. News* 39, 2 (Aug. 2011), 1–7.
[9] Reda Boumchedda, J. Noel, et al. 2017. High-Density 4T SRAM Bitcell in 14-nm 3-D CoolCube Technology Exploiting Assist Techniques. *VLSI* (2017), 2296–2306.
[10] Ronan Collobert and J. Weston. 2008. A Unified Architecture for Natural Language Processing: Deep Neural Networks with Multitask Learning. In *ICML*. 160–167.
[11] Qing Dong, S. Jeloka, et al. 2018. A 4 + 2T SRAM for Searching and In-Memory Computing With 0.3-V $V_{DDmin}$. *JSSC* 53, 4 (April 2018), 1006–1015.
[12] Mario Drumond, A. Daglis, et al. 2017. The Mondrian Data Engine. In *ISCA 44*. 639–651.
[13] Morris J. Dworkin. 2015. SHA-3 Standard: Permutation-Based Hash and Extendable-Output Functions. *FIPS* (2015).
[14] Charles Eckert, X. Wang, et al. 2018. Neural Cache: Bit-Serial In-Cache Acceleration of Deep Neural Networks. *CoRR* abs/1805.03718 (2018).
[15] Chang Ge, N. Wang, et al. 2018. QoE-Assured 4K HTTP Live Streaming via Transient Segment Holding at Mobile Edge. *J-SAC* 36, 8 (Aug 2018), 1816–1830.
[16] GfK. 2018. GfK Smart Home study 2018.
[17] Saugata Ghose, K. Hsieh, et al. 2018. Enabling the Adoption of Processing-in-Memory: Challenges, Mechanisms, Future Research Directions. *CoRR* (2018).
[18] Vinayak Gokhale, J. Jin, et al. 2014. A 240 G-ops/s Mobile Coprocessor for Deep Neural Networks. In *CVPR*.
[19] Song Han, X. Liu, et al. 2016. EIE: Efficient Inference Engine on Compressed Deep Neural Network. In *ISCA 43*. 243–254.
[20] Min Huang, M. Mehalel, et al. 2013. An Energy Efficient 32-nm 20-MB Shared On-Die L3 Cache for Intel Xeon Processor E5 Family. *JSSC* (2013), 1954–1962.
[21] Supreet Jeloka, N.B. Akesh, et al. 2016. A 28 nm Configurable Memory (TCAM/BCAM/SRAM) Using Push-Rule 6T Bit Cell Enabling Logic-in-Memory. *JSSC* 51, 4 (2016), 1009–1021.
[22] Alex Krizhevsky, I. Sutskever, et al. 2017. ImageNet Classification with Deep Convolutional Neural Networks. *Commun. ACM* 60, 6 (May 2017), 84–90.
[23] Adam Lella. 2014. Comscore Reports June 2014 U.S. Smartphone Subscriber Market Share.
[24] Shaoqing Ren, K. He, et al. 2015. Faster R-CNN: Towards Real-Time Object Detection with Region Proposal Networks. In *NIPS 28*. 91–99.
[25] Vivek Seshadri, D. Lee, et al. 2017. Ambit: In-memory Accelerator for Bulk Bitwise Operations Using Commodity DRAM Technology. In *MICRO*. 273–287.
[26] Karen Simonyan and A. Zisserman. 2015. Very Deep Convolutional Networks for Large-Scale Image Recognition. *CoRR* abs/1409.1556 (2015).
[27] Mahmut Sinangil, H. Mair, et al. 2011. A 28nm high-density 6T SRAM with optimized peripheral-assist circuits for operation down to 0.6V. *ISSCC* (2011).
[28] Saurabh Singh, P. Sharma, et al. 2017. Advanced lightweight encryption algorithms for IoT devices: survey, challenges and solutions. *JAIHC* (2017), 1–18.
[29] Gary J. Sullivan, J. Ohm, et al. 2012. Overview of the High Efficiency Video Coding (HEVC) Standard. *TCSVT* 22, 12 (Dec 2012), 1649–1668.
[30] Marko Viitanen, A. Koivula, et al. 2016. Kvazaar: Open-Source HEVC/H.265 Encoder. In *ACMMM 24 (MM '16)*. 1179–1182.

# Enhancing the Lifetime of Non-Volatile Caches by Exploiting Module-Wise Write Restriction

Sukarn Agarwal and Hemangee K. Kapoor
Department of CSE, IIT Guwahati, Guwahati, Assam 781039, India
{sukarn, hemangee}@iitg.ac.in

## ABSTRACT

The emerging Non-Volatile Memory (NVM) technologies offer a good combination of high density and near-zero leakage power, becoming the strongest candidate in the memory hierarchy including caches. However, the weak write endurance of these memories creates a bottleneck towards their employment in the cache hierarchy. This weak endurance shows its effects due to the write variations introduced by the applications and the existing cache management policies. Such variations result in early breakdown of the NVM cells reducing the effective lifetime of the NVM memory component.

This paper proposes a technique to mitigate intra-set write variation, i.e. write variations occurring within the cache set. Our policy divides the cache logically into multiple equal-sized modules. During execution, the writes are distributed uniformly across different ways of the different modules within the set. Experimental results using full system simulation show that the proposed technique reduces the intra-set write variation significantly over the baseline and the existing techniques.

## CCS CONCEPTS

• **Computer systems organization** → *Multicore architectures*; • **Hardware** → Spintronics and magnetic technologies.

## KEYWORDS

Non-volatile Memories; Lifetime; Write variation; STT-RAM

**ACM Reference Format:**
Sukarn Agarwal and Hemangee K. Kapoor. 2019. Enhancing the Lifetime of Non-Volatile Caches by Exploiting Module-Wise Write Restriction. In *Great Lakes Symposium on VLSI 2019 (GLSVLSI '19), May 9–11, 2019, Tysons Corner, VA, USA.* ACM, New York, NY, USA, 6 pages. https://doi.org/10.1145/3299874.3317987

## 1 INTRODUCTION

The development of semiconductor technology has led to the large integration of the cores on a chip. As a result, the number of memory requests is increasing rapidly. Large-sized Last Level Cache (LLC) plays a crucial role here to avoid off-chip memory access and improving application performance. Traditional caches made up of SRAM provide high endurance and performance. However, SRAM has very low density, low scalability, and large leakage energy. Recently, the emergence of Non-Volatile Memory (NVM) technologies diverted the attention of memory architects to think about the memory hierarchy made up of alternative technologies other than the charge based volatile technologies. These NVM technologies include Spin Transfer Torque Random Access Memory (STT-RAM), Resistive Random Access Memory (ReRAM), Phase Change Random Access Memory (PCRAM) etc. These NVM technologies rely on resistance as an information carrier and provide attractive features such as read latency and energy comparable to SRAM, in addition to high density, near-zero leakage power, and good scalability.

However, due to weak write endurance of NVMs, the possibilities for the replacement in place of traditional memory technologies within the cache hierarchy reduces. The write endurance values for the different NVM technologies are: $10^{11}$ writes for ReRAM [8], $10^{8}$ writes for PCRAM [12] and the approximate value for STT-RAM is $10^{15}$ writes but the value tested so far is $4 * 10^{12}$ writes [11]. In contrast, the write endurance values for traditional charge-based memory technologies are more than $10^{15}$ writes. With the weak write endurance, the lifetime of the non-volatile caches is further affected by the write variations introduced by the running applications. In caches, the write variations are categorized into two categories: *Inter-set* and *Intra-set.* The inter-set write variation actually takes place due to non-uniform write distribution across the cache sets. On the other hand, the intra-set write variation is due to distinct write counts of the blocks within the cache set.

This paper presents an efficient technique to mitigate the intra-set write variation present in the cache. To measure the impact of

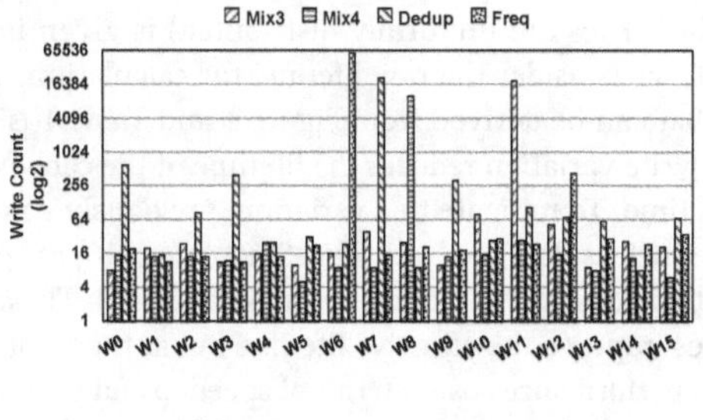


**Figure 1: Write Counts among the ways (W0 to W15) for the four different workloads in the baseline STT-RAM.**

**Table 1: Lifetime (in years) Comparison Analysis for the ideal STT-RAM and the actual STT-RAM based cache**

| | PARSEC v2.1 | | | | | SPEC CPU 2006 | | | |
|---|---|---|---|---|---|---|---|---|---|
| Workload | Body | Cann | Dedup | Freq | X264 | Mix1 | Mix2 | Mix3 | Mix4 |
| Ideal | 41.8K | 3.8K | 4.8K | 43.4K | 8.7K | 3.21K | 7.44K | 14.9K | 25.5K |
| Baseline | 38 | 19.3 | 30.9 | 25.1 | 8.65 | 47.3 | 6.33 | 25.8 | 45.7 |


ACM ISBN 978-1-4503-6252-8/19/05...$15.00
https://doi.org/10.1145/3299874.3317987

intra-set write variation, we conducted an experiments with 16MB 16-way associative L2 cache in quad-core system (Details about the experimental setup are reported in Section 4) and results are presented in the Figure 1 and Table 1 (Note that the write endurance value taken for the calculation is $4*10^{12}$ from [11]). Figure 1 shows a non-uniform write distribution among the ways ($W0$ to $W15$) inside the cache set and its impact on the lifetime of the non-volatile STT-RAM-based cache compared to the ideal STT-RAM-based cache (where the writes are uniformly distributed) is given in table 1. In table 1, we consider the raw lifetime for calculation. The conclusion that can be derived from Figure 1 and Table 1 is that the intra-set write variation reduces the lifetime of the cache over the period of time. To mitigate this variation, previously some of the technique such as PoLF [14] and WriteSmoothing [10] are proposed (we briefly discuss these techniques in Section 2.2). These former techniques improve the effective lifetime but at the same time incurs extra performance cost in terms of speedup and energy. In this paper, to control intra-set write variation with less performance and energy overheads, we make some ways of a set write-restricted, i.e. read-only over an interval. Firstly, our policy divides the cache into multiple equal-sized parts called modules in such a way that each module contains an equal number of sets. During the execution, for a certain predefined interval, $m$ ways are chosen from a module and made write-restricted. At the end of the interval, the next $m$ ways are chosen and treated as a write-restricted for the next interval and the process continues until the end of execution. Note that each module of the cache can have different $m$ ways selected. In this paper, we applied our proposed technique on STT-RAM based LLC (i.e. L2 cache). This is because, the two most recent fabricated STT-MRAM LLCs by Intel and Samsung reports the $10^6$ endurance in [5, 13]. The main contributions of this paper are as follows:

- The paper presents a technique to mitigate the intra-set write variation and improve the lifetime of non-volatile based cache. It divides the cache into multiple modules and controls write variation within each module.
- Experimental evaluation is performed over the full system simulator GEM5 [3] and results are compared with two existing techniques: Polf [14], WriteSmoothing [10] and the baseline STT-RAM with no wear-leveling associated.
- In-depth analysis with different configurations of L2 cache as LLC and, with the different parameters of the method are also presented.

The rest of the paper is organized as follows: Background and Related works are presented in Section 2. Proposed Wear Leveling technique is reported in Section 3. Section 4 illustrates the experimental methodology. Results and analysis are discussed in Section 5. The paper is concluded in Section 6.

## 2 BACKGROUND AND RELATED WORKS

### 2.1 Background

*2.1.1 Coefficient of Intra-set Write Variation and Lifetime.* The paper proposes a wear-leveling policy to mitigate the intra-set write variation present in the cache. The write variation inside the cache is measured with the help of coefficient [14]. Equation (1) represents the coefficient of intra-set write variation: $IntraV$ that measures the average coefficient of write variation inside the cache set.

$$IntraV = \frac{1}{S.Write_{avg}} \sum_{k=1}^{S} \sqrt{\frac{\sum_{l=1}^{A} \left( W_{k,l} - \sum_{m=1}^{A} \frac{W_{k,m}}{A} \right)^2}{A-1}} \tag{1}$$

In the eq. (1), $A$ is the cache associativity, $S$ is the number of cache sets, $W_{k,l}$ is write count in set $k$ and way $l$ and $Write_{avg}$ is the average number of writes in a cache bank. Following equation represent the average write count:

$$Write_{avg} = \frac{\sum_{k=1}^{S} \sum_{l=1}^{A} W_{k,l}}{S.A} \tag{2}$$

### 2.2 Related Works

In the existing literature, many intra-set wear level techniques have been proposed. This section briefly illustrates all such policies. In addition, we also discuss some of the inter-set wear leveling policies.

$i^2$wap proposed by Wang et al. [14] reduces both inter-set and intra-set write variation present inside the cache. The first technique to reduce the intra-set write variation is PoLF where the data block is invalidated after a fixed number of writes (represented by the variable called flush threshold or FT). The second technique to mitigate the inter-set write variation is Swap Shift where two sets interchange their mapping by invalidating the data after a fixed number of writes. The technique WriteSmoothing reported by Mittal et al. [10] partitions the cache into multiple equal-sized modules and reduces the write variation of each module by shutting down one of the hot sub-way and transfer their data to the cold sub-way inside the module. Another technique EqualChance proposed by Mittal et al. [9] reduces the write variation inside the set by transfer or swap of the hot blocks with the invalid or clean location inside the cache set. Different inter-set wear leveling policies that change the set mapping and redirect the writes are reported in [1, 7].

In this paper, we compared our proposed technique with the state of art technique: PoLF and, the WriteSmoothing. We compare with WriteSmoothing because it divides the cache into multiple modules similar to the proposed approach.

## 3 PROPOSED WEAR LEVELING TECHNIQUE

### 3.1 Architecture

Here we discuss our proposed wear leveling technique called Module Wise Write Restriction (MWWR). The key idea of the proposed methodology is to logically divide the cache into multiple equal-sized modules or parts (in such a way that each module contains an equal number of sets) and use $m$ different ways in each module at the regular intervals of the application execution. We call these ways inside the module as sub-ways. During an interval, the selected sub-ways in a module are treated as a write-restricted (or read-only) sub-ways. In particular, all the write requests from the L1 cache to the selected sub-ways of the module are redirected to other ways (other than the selected sub-ways) of the module within the same cache set. In each interval, the selection of sub-ways in the module is based upon a counter associated with each sub-way of the module. The use of the counter is to track the number of L1 write accesses that the particular sub-way entertained in the past interval(s). In each interval and for each module, the $m$ sub-ways with maximum counter values are chosen and treated as a write-restricted sub-ways. At the end of the interval, the next $m$ sub-ways

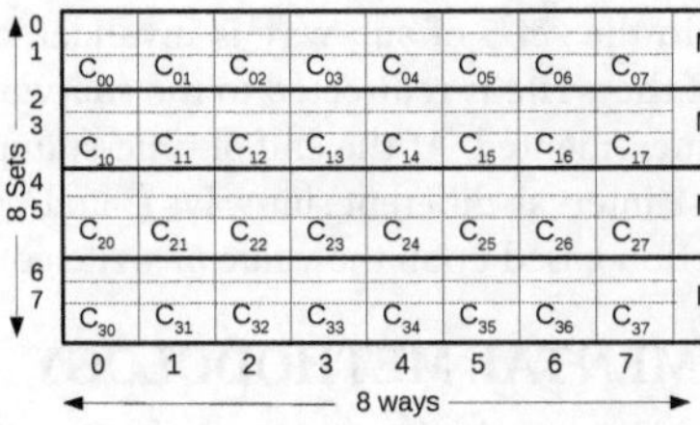


**Figure 2: Example of the proposed L2 cache architecture**

of each module are chosen and the process continues till the end of the execution. Note that, in order to remove the possibility of choosing the same sub-way(s) within the module in the successive intervals, the sub-way counter of each selected sub-way is reset to zero. Note that other inferior sub-ways counters are remained to be intact. Initializing the counter with zero ensure that all the other lightly written sub-ways counters get the chance for the write restriction over the intervals by accumulating the writes in the past intervals. Also, note that these $m$ sub-ways may not be contiguous.

Consider a set associative cache with $S$ number of cache sets and associativity $A$. Let the total number of modules in the cache is $M$ then each module in the cache has following sets of attributes:

- Total number of sets in the module ($S_{mod}$): $S/M$.
- All the sub-ways-j of sets in a module share the same counter. Hence, the total number of counters in a module: $A$.
- Total number of counters in a cache bank: $A * M$.
- Module label for a given set-id ($C_{set}$) of a cache bank: $\lfloor C_{set}/S_{mod} \rfloor$.

The example of our architecture is presented in Figure 2. As shown in the figure, an 8-way set associative L2 cache ($A$ = 8) having 8 sets ($S$ = 8) and 4 modules ($M$ = 4) is considered. The four modules of the cache are labeled with $M_0$, $M_1$, $M_2$ and $M_3$. With the given values, the $S_{mod} = S/M = 2$ cache sets are present inside the module and a total of $A * M = 32$ counters are needed to tracks the write accesses of each sub-ways of the modules inside a cache bank in the current interval or in the past intervals until it is reset to zero. In the figure, these sub-way counters are represented by variable $C_{ij}$ where $i$ represents the module-id and $j$ denotes the sub-way id. For example, $C_{04}$ is counter for module-$M_0$ and sub-way 4 of all sets in $M_0$. Similarly, the counters $C_{00}$ to $C_{07}$ represent the counter for each sub-way in the module $M_0$.

## 3.2 Operation

The operation of proposed wear leveling technique is elaborated through Algorithm 1. In the algorithm, the parameter $I$ acts as a tunable value for the regular interval (line 1). The total number of sub-ways that are treated as a write-restricted in each module is represented by the variable $m$ (line 2). The variable $M$ represents the total number of modules inside a cache bank (line 3). *ModulewaysList* is a list of lists of size $M * m$. It contains the $m$ sub-ways id of all the $M$ modules which are treated as write-restricted in that particular period of the regular interval $I$ (line 4). The *ModulewaysList* is populated in each interval. The counter associated with each sub-way of the module is represented by the variable $C_{ij}$ (line 5).

For the initial $I$ cycles of process execution, the cache bank is treated as a normally available bank (line 6). Once the process

**Algorithm 1** Wear Leveling Algorithm - MWWR

1: $I$ : Predefined interval.
2: $m$ : Number of sub-ways in each module that are treated as read only or write restricted.
3: $M$: Number of modules in the cache.
4: List < *integer*, List < *integer* >> *ModulewaysList* : List of write restricted sub-ways in each module. Size of list is $M * m$.
5: $C_{ij}$ : Sub-way counter with respect to $i^{th}$ module and $j^{th}$ sub-way that records the number of write accesses from L1 cache to that particular sub-way. $0 \leq i < M, 0 \leq j < cache\_assoc$.

6: Run application for $I$ cycles treating the whole cache as normally available cache.
7: After the $I$ cycles treat $m$ ways of each module as read-only or write restricted.
8: **repeat**
9:   **for** every interval $I$ **do**
10:     **for** $k \leftarrow 0$ to $M$ **do**
11:       **for** $l \leftarrow 0$ to $m$ **do**
12:         Let $C_{ij}$ be the maximum counter among all the counters in the module i of cache. $0 \leq j < cache\_assoc$
13:         $ModulewaysList[k][l] = j$ {**create module list of heavily written ways**}
14:         $C_{ij} = 0$
15:       **end for**
16:     **end for**
17:     **for** each request $R$ from L1 cache to the block $B$ in L2 cache during $I$ cycles **do**
18:       **if** $R == ReadHit$ **then**
19:         Perform the read operation as in the conventional cache.
20:       **else if** $R == WriteHit$ **then**
21:         **if** the request R is for the block B that belongs to the current *ModulewaysList* **then**
22:           The write request for the block $B$ is redirected to the other location $L$ in the same cache set. Note that $L \notin ModulewaysList$.
23:           The corresponding sub-way counter $C_{ij}$ of the location $L$ is incremented.
24:         **else**
25:           Write operation is performed on $B$ as in conventional cache. Increment the counter $C_{ij}$ of the way where the block $B$ is present.
26:         **end if**
27:       **else**
28:         Forward the Request $R$ to main memory to fetch the block. Keep the newly arrived block in a location $L$ such that $L \notin ModulewaysList$. {**cache miss**}
29:       **end if**
30:     **end for**
31:   **end for**
32: **until** the end of the execution

executes the $I$ cycles, different sub-ways of the different modules are treated as a write-restricted for the next $I$ cycles (line 7). The selection of sub-ways in each module is based upon the counter $C_{ij}$ associated with the sub-ways of the modules. In particular, from each module, maximum $m$ sub-way counters are chosen and placed into the *ModulewaysList* of that particular module (line 12 and 13). By this way, the proposed technique restricts the chances of heavily written sub-ways of the modules to get further more writes in the next interval. Once the $m$ sub-ways of the module are selected for write restriction, the respective counters associated with them are reset to zero (line 14). When the interval $I$ ends, the write restricted sub-way list is prepared again for each module and the process continues until the end of execution.

In the meanwhile, between the intervals, for each request $R$ coming from L1 cache to the L2 cache, the tag lookup operation is performed for that particular request in the L2 cache. Based upon the result of lookup operation and the type of request, different operations are performed in the L2 cache which is as follows (Note that the PUTX used in the following cases represents the writeback of dirty data from the L1 cache to L2 cache):

- **Read Hit:** The read operation is performed for the requested block $B$ as same as in the conventional cache (line 18 and 19).
- **Write Hit (Write-back or PUTX) and block $B$ not in** *ModulewaysList*: The write request $R$ is served from the original

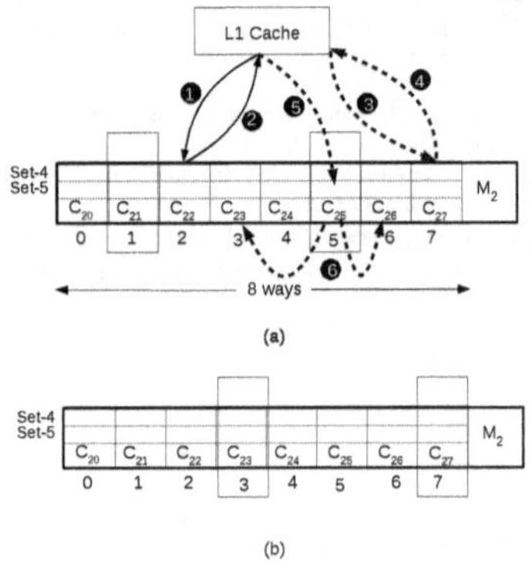


**Figure 3: Working example of the proposed wear leveling technique. (a) Status of module-2 at time-stamp t1 (b) Status of module-2 at time-stamp t2**

location of block $B$. Once request is served, the sub-way counter of the module where block $B$ is located is incremented (line 24 to 26).

- **Write Hit (Write-back or PUTX) and block $B$ in** *ModulewaysList*: If the requested block $B$ is present in the cache at location $T$ that belongs to the *ModulewaysList*, then the write request $R$ (from L1 cache) is redirected to the first invalid way of the same cache set other than the ways belonging to *ModulewaysList*. In case, if there is no invalid entry present in the other ways of same cache set, one Least Recently Used (LRU) victim block is picked, say $v$ from the location $L$. Note that the location L is the location other than the *ModulewaysList* for that particular module. Once the victim entry $v$ is selected, the write-back operation is scheduled for $v$ according to the status of its dirty bit. Subsequently, the request $R$ is redirected to the location $L$ and the block is written in that location. Once the request is served, the block $B$ is invalidated from its location $T$. The counter for the sub-way where the write was redirected, $L$ in this case, is incremented (line 20 to 23).
- **Cache Miss:** The request $R$ from the L1 cache is forwarded to next level of memory. When the requested block has arrived, it is placed in a location other than those belonging to *ModulewaysList* for that particular module (line 27 to 29).

The working example of the proposed wear leveling technique is depicted in Figure 3. As shown in the figure (a) at time-stamp t1, in module-2 ($M_2$), the sub-way 1 and 5 are treated as write-restricted for the current interval (*ModulewaysList*[2] = {1, 5}). Three cases are considered in part(a) to demonstrate the method with respect to $M_2$ i.e. set-4 and set-5 of a cache bank. In the first case, a read request (shown by arrow-1) to the sub-way 2 of set-4 is served normally by the cache (arrow-2). In the second case, the write request (shown by dotted arrow-3) from the L1 cache to set-4 and sub-way 7 is served (arrow-4) normally by the L2 cache. Once the write operation is completed, the respective counter $C_{27}$ is incremented. For the last case, the write request (arrow-5) from the L1 cache to the set-5 and sub-way 5 (sub-way treated as write restricted in the current interval) is redirected (arrow-6) to the one of the other ways (3 and 6 in our case) based upon the availability and the victim entry location in the same cache set. Depending upon where the write is redirected, the respective sub-way counter is incremented and the data block in the set 5 of sub-way is invalidated because of its relocation. If the write is redirected to the sub-way 3 then the counter $C_{23}$ is incremented. At the end of time-stamp t1 interval, for time-stamp t2 interval, different sub-ways (3 and 7) are selected for write restriction based upon the value of write counters.

## 4 EXPERIMENTAL METHODOLOGY

We implemented our proposed wear leveling policy: MWWR on a full system simulator GEM-5 [3]. In the simulator, we used MESI CMP based cache controller with Ruby memory module. Table 2 shows the system parameters used in the simulations. Table 3 shows the timing and energy parameters for the L2 configurations obtained by NVSIM [4] at 32 nm technology node. To evaluate our simulated system, we use both multi-threaded: PARSEC [2] and multi-programmed: SPEC CPU 2006 [6] benchmark suites, Table 4. We simulate each multi-programmed workload for one billion instruction after warming up to 250 million instructions.

We evaluate our technique: MWWR against two existing techniques: PoLF and WriteSmoothing (termed as Wsmooth) and the baseline STT-RAM (STT) that uses LRU as a replacement policy with no support of wear leveling. In PoLF, the value of FT is set to 10. Whereas in Wsmooth, the limit of the maximum sub-ways to be turned off in each module is set to 3, and the parameter $\lambda$=15%, the interval value is set to 5M cycles and the number of modules to 128. All computation and selection of the modules with transfer and storage overhead are modeled in the same way as similar to [10].

In MWWR, during the write redirection, the tag needs to be transferred from the current write-restricted sub-way to the new location within the cache set. The transfer of tags requires 128 additional 42-bit swap buffers and extra three cycles (1 cycle to transfer the tag from the sub-way to swap buffer, 1 cycle for writing the data into the swap buffer and 1 cycle for transferring the data from the swap buffer to the new location). The size of the counters ($C_{ij}$) associated with each module of the sub-way is set to 10 bit[1]. We assume that the computation or selection of the *ModulewaysList* is not on the critical path as it can be computed in the background just before the end of the current interval.

## 5 RESULTS AND ANALYSIS

Out of the different configurations, MWWR examined on 16 MB 16-way set-associative L2 cache with $I$=5M cycles, $M$=128 and, $m$=4.

**Coefficient of Intra-set Write Variation:** Figure 4 shows the coefficient of intra-set write variation. Our proposed technique: MWWR reduces the intra set write variation from 154.4% (STT), 114.6% (Polf), 88.8% (Wsmooth) to 61.4% (MWWR). The reduction in intra-set write variation over STT is basically due to uniform-write distribution by MWWR inside each module. However, the further reduction in coefficient by MWWR against Polf and Wsmooth is due to two reasons: (i) Polf invalidates the data randomly without concerning its write behavior. (ii) The MWWR selects the $m$ hot sub-ways for the write restriction in each interval and with Wsmooth, the hot-sub-way are turned off only when the module's intra-set write variation increases beyond $\lambda$. Note that hot-sub-way(s) represent the sub-way(s) having maximum write count(s) among the other sub-ways.

[1]Based on the experimental results, we selected the most stable sized $C_{ij}$

**Table 2: System Parameters**

| Components | Parameters |
|---|---|
| Processor | 2Ghz, Quad Core, X86 |
| L1 Cache | Private, 32 KB SRAM Split I/D caches, 4-way set associative cache, 64B block, 1-cycle latency, LRU, write-back policy |
| L2 Cache | Shared, 64B block, LRU, write-back policy |
| Main Memory | 2GB, 160 cycle Latency |
| Protocol | MESI CMP Directory |

**Table 3: Timing and Energy Parameters for STT-RAM L2 cache**

| L2 Configuration | Leakage Power (mW) | Hit Energy (nJ) | Miss Energy (nJ) | Write Energy (nJ) | Hit Latency (ns) | Miss Latency (ns) | Write Latency (ns) |
|---|---|---|---|---|---|---|---|
| 32MB, 16way | 454.35 | 0.486 | 0.094 | 4.215 | 5.047 | 1.616 | 12.425 |
| 16MB, 32way | 423.03 | 0.534 | 0.193 | 6.296 | 4.19 | 1.522 | 11.974 |
| 16MB, 16way | 406.22 | 0.432 | 0.092 | 4.162 | 4.227 | 1.560 | 11.974 |
| 16MB, 8way | 405.40 | 0.387 | 0.047 | 3.189 | 4.225 | 1.558 | 11.974 |
| 8MB, 16way | 136.2 | 0.329 | 0.096 | 4.164 | 3.605 | 1.479 | 11.81 |

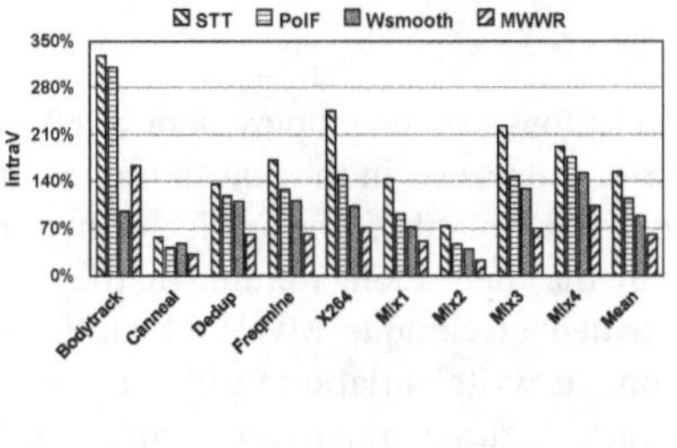


**Figure 4: Intra Set write variation (Lesser is better).**

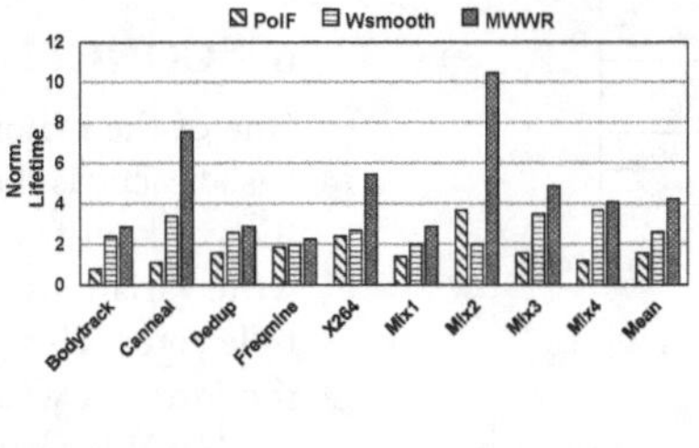


**Figure 5: Normalized Lifetime with respect to STT (More is better).**

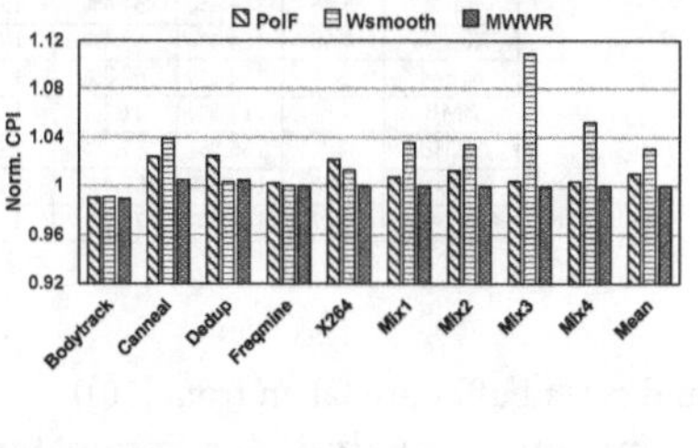


**Figure 6: Normalized CPI with respect to STT (Lesser is better).**

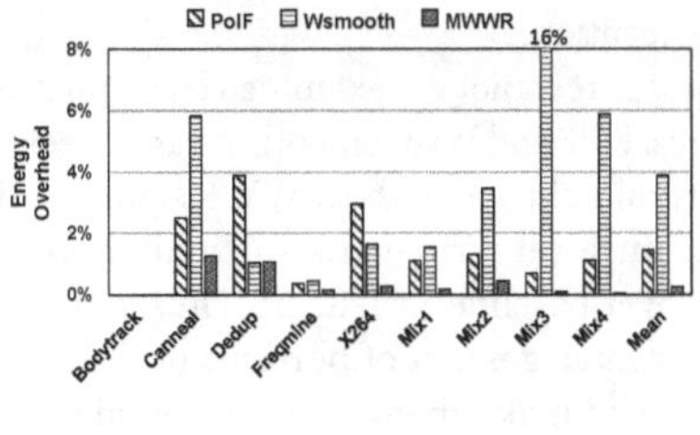


**Figure 7: Energy overhead with respect to STT (Lesser is better).**

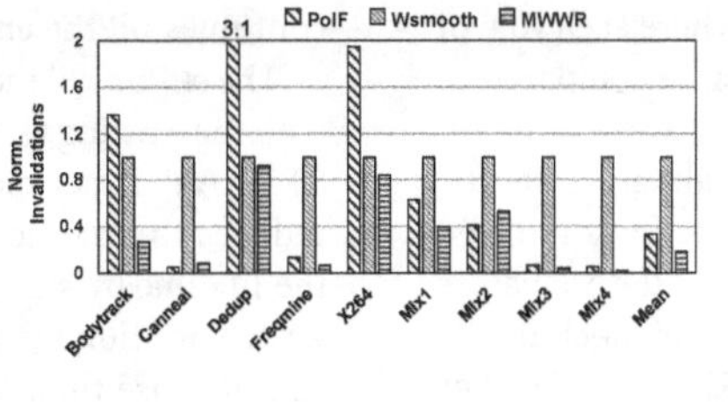


**Figure 8: Normalized Invalidation with respect to Wsmooth (Lesser is better).**

**TABLE 4:** BENCHMARKS USED FOR EVALUATION

| Benchmark suite | Benchmarks |
|---|---|
| PARSEC v2.1 | Bodytrack (Body), Canneal (Cann), Dedup, Freqmine (Freq) X264 |
| SPEC CPU2006 | **Mix1:** perlbench, gcc, milc, hmmer<br>**Mix2:** soplex, omnetpp, bzip2, libquantum<br>**Mix3:** gobmk, tonto, sjeng, namd<br>**Mix4:** calculix, astar, dealII, h264ref |

**Relative Lifetime Improvement:** Figure 5 shows the normalized lifetime w.r.t STT and is presented against the STT, Polf, and Wsmooth. Our proposed technique MWWR improves the lifetime by 4.25 times against the STT, 2.71 times against the Polf and, 1.63 times against the Wsmooth. These respective improvements are basically due to the reduction in the write variation coefficient values by the proposed technique MWWR.

**Effect on Performance:** Figure 6 presents the normalized speedup (against the STT). MWWR maintains the same performance with the baseline STT. This is because MWWR evicts only LRU block from the other sub-ways which in turn increase the miss rate only by 2.4%. The respective values in the increase of miss rate by PoLF and WSmooth are 12.8% and 29.3%. We observe 1% degradation in CPI w.r.t STT by Polf due to increased allocation and eviction of MRU blocks in the cache. WSmooth shows performance degradation with respect to STT by 3.32%. This degradation is due to turning off the sub-ways in each module of the cache increasing the miss rate, and the extra cycles taken for the write operations due to block transfer from hot sub-way to cold sub-way inside module.

**Effect on Energy:** Due to write redirections and the transfer of tags, MWWR consumes slightly more energy compared to baseline STT as shown in Figure 7. The energy overhead percentage against the baseline STT is merely 0.27%. However, with respect to PolF and, Wsmooth, there is an improvement in the energy overhead by 1.14% and, 3.3%. This gain in the energy by MWWR over Polf and Wsmooth is due to: (i) Polf invalidates MRU which in turn increases the allocations (writes) in the cache. (ii) Wsmooth moves the block from the hot sub-way to the cold sub-way which incurs extra writes.

**Effect on Invalidation:** Figure 8 shows normalized invalidations w.r.t Wsmooth by the MWWR and Polf. MWWR reduces the invalidations by 45.3% and, 81.6% with respect to Polf and, Wsmooth. Compared to Polf, the reduction is because of the selective invalidations by MWWR. The reduction compared to Wsmooth is mainly due to the difference between the write redirection policy of MWWR (transfer to any position of cache set) and block-transferring policy with Wsmooth (transfers from hot to one cold sub-way).

**Storage Overhead:** In our technique, we use $A$ number of 10-bit $C_{ij}$ counters with each module of the cache in order to record the write accesses of each sub-way. In addition, 128 42-bit swap buffers are used to transfer the tags. Also, the list *ModulewayList* of size m*M is composed by the entry of size $\log_2 A$. Thus, the percentage overhead implementation of MWWR compared to baseline STT-RAM is merely 0.02% for the selected values. On the other hand, the percentage savings in storage overhead of MWWR compared to Wsmooth is 81.1% (Note that the storage bits required for counters

**Table 5: Comparative Analysis for different parameters of L2 cache and Algorithm (Lft.= Life Time, Base = Baseline STT-RAM, EDP = Energy-Delay Product) Ref = 16MB, 16 way, m = 4, M = 128, I = 5M**

| Param. | Norm. Lft. | IntraV Base | IntraV MWWR | Norm. EDP | Invalidations (k) |
|---|---|---|---|---|---|
| Reference | 4.25 | 154.4% | 61.4% | 1.02 | 645k |
| I=2M | 4.83 | 154.4% | 57.6% | 1.03 | 680k |
| I=10M | 3.85 | 154.4% | 64.5% | 1.02 | 573k |
| m=8 | 4.94 | 154.4% | 60.3% | 1.04 | 786k |
| m=2 | 3.86 | 154.4% | 67.4% | 1.01 | 458k |
| M=256 | 4.68 | 154.4% | 59.4% | 1.03 | 658k |
| M=64 | 3.9 | 154.4% | 62.8% | 1.02 | 612k |
| 8MB | 4.92 | 119.3% | 41.2% | 1.02 | 751k |
| 32MB | 4.1 | 186.5% | 85.7% | 1.02 | 504k |
| A=8way | 3.70 | 120.9% | 57.4% | 1.04 | 714k |
| A=32way | 5.47 | 189.4% | 79.7% | 1.02 | 480k |

and swap buffer are taken from [10]).

**Comparative Analysis for Parameters:** In addition to the results presented in the previous text, we also conducted experiments with different values of the parameters using different configurations of cache. Note that the value given in the table is given w.r.t STT. Table 5 presents the comparative analysis where each row of the table shows the one change in parameter value compared to the reference values.

**Change in Interval (*I*):** With the large interval value, the frequency of write-restricted sub-way selection process is reduced compared to the reference case. This, in turn, reduces the premature invalidation process from the L2 cache because the block invalidated from the write redirection are mostly the LRU blocks. Further, with large interval value, the coefficient of intra-set write variation is larger with lesser improvement in a lifetime compared to the reference case. The opposite is seen in the case of the small interval.

**Change in Write-Restricted Sub-Ways (*m*):** On increasing the write restricted sub-ways, more writes are redirected which in turn improves the lifetime and reduce the coefficient of intra-set write variation more than the reference case, and vice-versa, in case of a smaller number of write-restricted sub-ways.

**Change in number of Modules (*M*):** On increasing the number of modules, the granularity of wear-leveling is increased as it includes the smaller number of sets in the module. This, in turn, improves the lifetime and reduces the intra-set write variation more than the reference case. Opposite is seen with a smaller number of modules.

**Change in Capacity:** Cache with larger size experiences lesser capacity misses as compared to cache with a smaller size. This leads to the longer residency of the block and higher write-variation compared to the reference case. In both cases: large and small-sized cache, our technique effectively reduces the write variation and improves the lifetime.

**Change in Associativity (*A*):** Higher associative cache experiences less conflict misses compared to lower associative cache. This, in turn, increases the residency of a block and intra-set write variation inside the cache. In both cases, higher and lower associativity, MWWR significantly reduces the intra-set write variation and improves the lifetime.

Based on the above analyses, we present the best optimal trends of the proposed technique for the different configurations of caches in Table 6. Note that the recommended values are with respect to reference values (mentioned in Section 5) and = given in the table refers to the same value as the reference.

**Table 6: Recommended Values of *m*, *M* and *I***

| Cache Configuration | m | M | I |
|---|---|---|---|
| Small Size, Small Assoc. | ↓ | ↓ | = /↓ |
| Small Size, Large Assoc. | ↑ | ↓ | ↑ |
| Large Size, Small Assoc. | ↓ | ↑ | ↓ |
| Large Size, Large Assoc. | ↑ | ↑ | ↓ |

## 6 CONCLUSION

One of the major bottlenecks towards the employment of NVM based cache is the weak write endurance. In the real environment, the weak write endurance of non-volatile cache is affected by the write variations generated by the applications running on the multiple cores. This paper presented a technique: MWWR to mitigate the intra-set write variation: i.e. write variation inside the cache set. MWWR partitions the cache logically into multiple equal-sized modules and treats different sub-ways of each module for the certain predefined interval as write-restricted. Once the interval ends, the next set of sub-ways are chosen from the module and the process continues till the end of execution.

The efficacy of the proposed technique is examined by comparing with the existing techniques: PoIF and WriteSmoothing and baseline STT-RAM. Experimental results show that the MWWR significantly reduces the coefficient of intra-set write variation and improves the lifetime by 4.25 times over baseline STT-RAM. Thus, reducing write variation by modular management of portions of the cache can increase their lifetime and make them capable candidates in the memory hierarchy.

## REFERENCES


[1] S. Agarwal and H. K. Kapoor. 2017. Targeting inter set write variation to improve the lifetime of non-volatile cache using fellow sets. In *2017 IFIP/IEEE International Conference on Very Large Scale Integration (VLSI-SoC)*. 1–6.

[2] C. Bienia et al. 2008. *The PARSEC benchmark suite: Characterization and architectural implications.* Technical Report. in princeton university.

[3] N. Binkert et al. 2011. The Gem5 Simulator. *SIGARCH Comput. Archit. News* 39, 2 (Aug. 2011), 1–7.

[4] X. Dong et al. 2012. NVSim: A Circuit-Level Performance, Energy, and Area Model for Emerging Nonvolatile Memory. *Trans. Comp.-Aided Des. Integ. Cir. Sys.* 31, 7 (2012), 994–1007.

[5] O. Golonzka et al. 2018. MRAM as Embedded Non-Volatile Memory Solution for 22FFL FinFET Technology. In *Electron Devices Meeting (IEDM)*. IEEE.

[6] J. L. Henning. 2006. SPEC CPU2006 Benchmark Descriptions. *SIGARCH Comput. Archit. News* 34, 4 (Sept. 2006), 1–17.

[7] M. R. Jokar et al. 2016. Sequoia: A High-Endurance NVM-Based Cache Architecture. *IEEE Transactions on Very Large Scale Integration (VLSI) Systems* 24, 3 (March 2016), 954–967.

[8] Y. B. Kim et al. 2011. Bi-layered RRAM with unlimited endurance and extremely uniform switching. In *VLSIT*. 52–53.

[9] S. Mittal and J. S. Vetter. 2014. EqualChance: Addressing Intra-set Write Variation to Increase Lifetime of Non-volatile Caches. In *INFLOW*.

[10] S. Mittal et al. 2014. WriteSmoothing: Improving Lifetime of Non-volatile Caches Using Intra-set Wear-leveling. In *2016 International Great Lakes Symposium on VLSI (GLSVLSI)*. ACM, 139–144.

[11] S. Mittal et al. 2015. A Survey Of Architectural Approaches for Managing Embedded DRAM and Non-Volatile On-Chip Caches. *IEEE Transactions on Parallel and Distributed Systems* 26, 6 (June 2015), 1524–1537.

[12] M. K Qureshi et al. 2011. Phase change memory: From devices to systems. *Synthesis Lectures on Computer Architecture* 6, 4 (2011), 1–134.

[13] Y. J. Song et al. 2018. Demonstration of Highly Manufacturable STT-MRAM Embedded in 28nm Logic. In *Electron Devices Meeting (IEDM)*. IEEE.

[14] J. Wang et al. 2013. i2WAP: Improving non-volatile cache lifetime by reducing inter- and intra-set write variations. In *HPCA*. 234–245.

# Mitigating the Performance and Quality of Parallelized Compressive Sensing Reconstruction Using Image Stitching

Mahmoud Namazi
mnamazi@ucsb.edu
University of California, Santa Barbara

Hosein Mohammadi Makrani
hmohamm8@gmu.edu
George Mason University

Zhi Tian
ztian1@gmu.edu
George Mason University

Setareh Rafatirad
srafatir@gmu.edu
George Mason University

Mohamad Hosein Akbari
mohammad.akbari@student.sharif.ir
Sharif University of Technology

Avesta Sasan
asasan@gmu.edu
George Mason University

Houman Homayoun
hhomayou@gmu.edu
George Mason University

## ABSTRACT

Orthogonal Matching Pursuit is an iterative greedy algorithm used to find a sparse approximation for high-dimensional signals. The algorithm is most popularly used in Compressive Sensing, which allows for the reconstruction of sparse signals at rates lower than the Shannon-Nyquist frequency, which has traditionally been used in a number of applications such as MRI and computer vision and is increasingly finding its way into Big Data and data center analytics. OMP traditionally suffers from being computationally intensive and time-consuming, this is particularly a problem in the area of Big Data where the demand for computational resources continues to grow. In this paper, the data-level parallelization of OMP through blocking is examined. Traditionally blocking has been used to accelerate the performance of OMP reconstruction for big data image analytics. However, as we show in this work, blocking, particularly in the form of vectorizing, introduces significant error in terms of PSNR and SSIM index in the reconstruction quality. In response, we deploy the concept of stitching to recover the lost accuracy. We further examine the influence of the level of blocking and amount of stitching (overlap between each block) with regard to reconstruction time and reconstructed image quality. While stitching boosts up the image reconstruction accuracy significantly, the object detection count results show anywhere from 11.84% to 140.54% improvement, depending on the cases being compared, it introduces significant overhead with regard to reconstruction time. To address the overhead, we deploy hardware accelerated base solutions. Given the emergence of hardware accelerators in data centers and for big data analytics in form of FPGAs, our solution effectively utilizes this resource to enhance the performance overhead of stitching by 25%. We show the minimum block size required for an FPGA speed-up.


*GLSVLSI '19, May 9–11, 2019, Tysons Corner, VA, USA*

ACM ISBN 978-1-4503-6252-8/19/05...$15.00
https://doi.org/10.1145/3299874.3317991

## KEYWORDS

OMP; Compressive Sensing; Acceleration; Big Data; Cloud Computing; Data Centers

**ACM Reference Format:**

Mahmoud Namazi, Hosein Mohammadi Makrani, Zhi Tian, Setareh Rafatirad, Mohamad Hosein Akbari, Avesta Sasan, and Houman Homayoun. 2019. Mitigating the Performance and Quality of Parallelized Compressive Sensing Reconstruction Using Image Stitching. In *Great Lakes Symposium on VLSI 2019 (GLSVLSI '19), May 9–11, 2019, Tysons Corner, VA, USA.* ACM, New York, NY, USA, 6 pages. https://doi.org/10.1145/3299874.3317991

## 1 INTRODUCTION

In recent years, Orthogonal Matching Pursuit (OMP) has emerged as one of several methods used to reconstruct sparse signals from random measurements [1]. OMP is one of several methods utilized in Compressive Sensing (CS), a novel set of techniques which enable the reconstruction of sparse signals sampled at sub-Nyquist rates [2]. By requiring fewer samples, CS requires sensors to run for the less time and use less energy, a great benefit in applications such as MRI imaging [3], radar, and 360° cameras. OMP serves as one of many reconstruction algorithms in CS, others include basis pursuit and total-variation minimization.

CS is used in a wide variety of applications where signals need to be processed with as few samples as possible. By projecting the captured signal to a lower dimensional space, chosen by the measurement matrix, it allows one to sample the signal at a lower rate than what the Shannon-Nyquist Theorem would predict. Additionally, it allows the signal to be compressed to larger degree. The trade-off is that decompressing the signal takes a significant amount of time and computational power. One such application is in 3D 360° cameras [4]. In this application, signals need to be high resolution and hence require a wide bandwidth. Both higher compressibility and faster imaging times are needed. By requiring fewer samples and doing both the compression and sampling in a single step, compressive sensing fulfills two highly sought-after criterion in this application. Current issues that exist are that reconstruction can be time-consuming and require large amounts of memory. Currently, however, faster imaging times can be acquired through the parallelization of compressive sensing.

In cloud computing and big data analytics, CS has been used to reduce active memory and speedup analytics algorithms in a scalable fashion [5]. In many types of big data queries, particularly high-value statistics, approximate results can suffice. CS can be used to query high-dimensional sparse data, essentially providing a compressed snapshot of the data. Since CS can go below the Shannon-Nyquist frequency with regard to sampling rates, this leads to less active memory, IO, and traffic volume. However, faster sampling times are needed as data center volumes continue to grow. Additionally, as data center memory volumes continue to grow, this also places pressure on CS from the aspect of memory usage, as the dictionary, a matrix which is used to compress the original data, grows with the size of the data.

Although OMP, in the CS context, has the advantage of requiring fewer samples, the drawback is that CS reconstruction is time-consuming and computationally expensive. There are trade-offs between OMP and other CS reconstruction techniques. Another algorithm, $l_1$-minimization, which OMP serves as an approximation for, is better in terms of accuracy, but is even more time-consuming and difficult to implement.

To address the challenge of slow reconstruction time, this paper first examines the blocking method for OMP. In blocking, an image signal is split into approximately equal-sized block. Each block is then sampled and reconstructed separately. Once reconstruction is complete, the blocks are then put back together in order to recreate the original image. One form of blocking is called vectorizing, this is where vertical columns of pixels are used as the block instead of square-like sections of the image. One unique contribution of this paper is in clarifying the relationship between block size and reconstruction time, as well as reconstruction quality. We show that while blocking improves performance with regard to reconstruction time, it introduces reconstruction quality loss, in response to which we introduce stitching. In stitching, an image is blocked such that there is overlap between blocks, in order to create redundancy and, in theory, improve image quality after reconstruction. The differences between blocking, vectorizing, and stitching are further clarified in Figure 1.

In our analysis, we examine the trade-off between reconstruction quality and reconstruction time when stitching and blocking are implemented. Last, we implement a parallelized version of the OMP algorithm [6] on an FPGA and examine the minimum block size where an FPGA would be faster than a CPU. To the best of our knowledge, this is the first paper that thoroughly analyzes blocking, including vectorizing, and deploys stitching as a response to the reduction of reconstruction quality incurred by blocking. By clarifying the impact of blocking and stitching, we hope to clear the way for faster and better-quality CS-based OMP image reconstruction.

## 2 BACKGROUND AND RELATED WORK

Orthogonal Matching Pursuit (OMP) is an iterative greedy algorithm, which allows for the sparse approximation of a function, given an over-complete dictionary [7]. OMP can be used to perform signal recovery from random measurements [1]. The basic theory that lies behind compressive sensing and the one OMP is focused on solving is Equation 1.

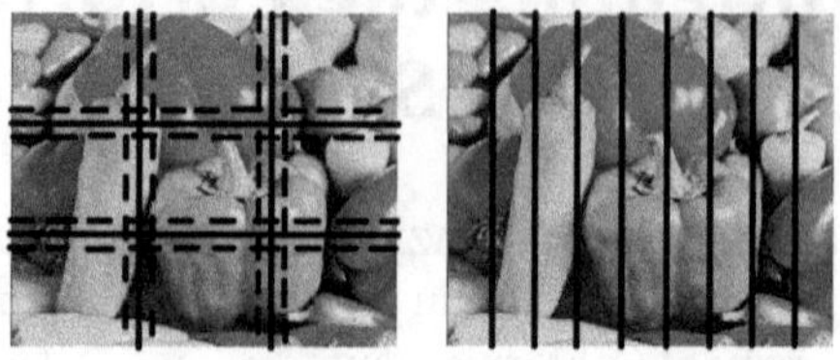

**Figure 1: The concept of blocking is illustrated on the left where the the image is divided into blocks which can be processed separately. Stitching is illustrated by extending each solid line into the dotted lines, creating overlap with the adjacent block. Vectorizing is illustrated on the right, the blocks become rectangular rather than square.**

$$y = \phi x \tag{1}$$

In this equation, $\phi$ is a matrix of dimension M x N, where M < N is the number of measurements and N is the size of the signal, $x$. Multiplying $\phi$ and $x$ yields $y$ which is referred to as the measured signal and is of length M. It is the projection of $\phi$ onto $x$. The goal of compressive sensing is to recover $x$, given $y$ and $\phi$. According to compressive sensing, if $y$ has a sparse representation recovery of the original signal is possible, even if the sampling rate is lower than that called for by the Shannon-Nyquist Theorem. Reconstruction involves finding the best solution to the undetermined system of linear equations created by $y = \phi x$. The computational complexity of this problem comes most significantly from solving the least square problem. Previous works, as described below, have tried to solve this problem through a variety of methods and can be divided into algorithm improvements [8, 9], parallel architecture implementations [10, 11], and hardware/software co-design [6, 12, 13, 9].

Kulkarni et.al. [6] present a parallelization where the OMP algorithm is split into three kernels: dot product, sort, and least squares. Each of these kernels is then parallelized on an FPGA in order to reduce execution time. The design is implemented on a Xilinix Virtex 7 FPGA. It is shown that for a 128x128 image, the proposed reconfigurable architecture gives a 1.8x to 2.67 speedup. Alternative parallelization methods, such as blocking, are not proposed in this paper, although vectorizing (processing each column of the image separately) is used. In [14], Kulkarni and Mohsenin carry out an analysis of OMP on 7 different implementations. They design and implement a custom 61-core solution which gives a 24x speedup when compared to CPU implementations.

In [10], OMP is implemented on an Application Specific Instruction-set Processor (ASIP). This implementation targets portable devices where operation is expected to be over an extended period of time with limited energy resources. The paper shows trade-offs in power and performance. The CS processor, which has sub-$V_t$ latch-based memories, operates at 0.37 V with a clock frequency of 100 KHz and total power of 288nW. A 62x speedup is achieved versus OMP running on a baseline low-power processor.

In [12], OMP is implemented on a GPU. Fujimoto's matrix-vector multiplication algorithm is adopted for the projection module and the matrix-inverse-update algorithm is adopted for the least-squares module. It was shown that a 40x speedup can be obtained with a GTX480 GPU on an Intel Core i7 CPU. This paper does not explore blocking or stitching as alternative parallelization methods.

Sermwuthisarn et.al. [8] present an analysis of the parallelization of OMP with blocking. They complete reconstruction in MATLAB using blocking and stitching (where the blocks overlap) on 64 x 64 size images. This implementation only includes 8 x 8 blocks, so no analysis is done on differing block size and differing amounts of overlap between blocks in stitching. A total of 3 images are analyzed, making it difficult to draw any conclusive results. Additionally, no hardware alternatives are presented in this work.

In [13], OMP is implemented using Q-R decomposition for the matrix inverse kernel. A new algorithm is implemented for finding the inverse square root of fixed-point numbers. The entire OMP algorithm is implemented on a Xilinix FPGA Virtex-5 and used to reconstruct a 256-length signal. At the time of publication, this implementation was 2.4-times faster than the state-of-the-art implementation. This implementation includes advances in the algorithm, as well as a hardware implementation in order to best optimize the reconstruction time. Similarly, Yang et al. [9], present an optimized OMP algorithm where Cholesky decomposition is used to solve the LS problem in a highly parallel-friendly manner. Furthermore, they implement their algorithm on a GPU implementation and achieve a 38x speedup as compared to using a CPU with LAPACK for solving the LS problem.

Rabah et al. [11] present an algorithm where Cholesky decomposition and a modified Newton-Raphson method are used to solve the linear problem, which although not novel, is then optimized for hardware implementation through Simulink. The design is implemented on a Virtex-6 FPGA and achieves the best seen results with a reconstruction time of 0.34 $\mu s$ and PSNR of 38.9 dB with a signal length of 1024, all while having a reconfigurable architecture.

In this work, we primarily analyze the consequences of changes in the OMP algorithm, through blocking and stitching. Examining varying block sizes, varying levels of overlap between blocks, and their effect on the reconstruction time and image quality has not been previously examined and is the primary contribution of this article. This paper also presents the minimum block size required in order for an FPGA to provide an improvement in time over a CPU.

## 3 ALGORITHM

The OMP algorithm requires two inputs, a measurement matrix ($\phi$) and a measured signal ($y$). At each iteration (t), the dot product of the transpose of $\phi$ and $y$ is taken in order to find the column in $\phi$ most correlated with $y$. The set of most correlated columns form a matrix which is used to obtain a new estimate for the signal $x_t$. After k iterations, we arrive at a final approximation for the signal. The algorithm is explained step-by-step in Algorithm 1. In the context of compressive sensing, $\phi$ is formed by the matrix multiplication of a sensing matrix and a representation matrix, which are used to sample the image and transform the sampled matrix to a sparse domain.

**Algorithm 1** OMP Reconstruction Algorithm

1: Initialize $R_0 = y$, $\phi_0 = \emptyset$, $\Lambda_0 = \emptyset$, $\Phi_0 = \emptyset$ and $t = 0$
2: Find Index $\lambda_t = max_{j=1...n}$ subject to $| < \phi_j R_{t-1} > |$
3: Update $\Lambda_t = \Lambda_{t-1} \bigcup \lambda_t$
4: Update $\Phi_t = [\Phi_{t-1} \ \phi_{\Lambda_t}]$
5: Solve the Least Squares Problem
$x_t = \min_x || y - \Phi_y \ x||^2$
6: Calculate new approximation: $\alpha_t = \Phi_t \ x_t$
7: Calculate new residual: $R_t = y - \alpha_t$
8: Increment t, and repeat from step 2 if t<k
After all the iterations, we can find correct sparse signals.

## 4 PROPOSED WORK

n this work, we seek to explore the data-level parallelization of OMP in order to assuage problems with high reconstruction time and large memory requirements, due to the size of the dictionary when attempting to reconstruct the entirety of an image at once. Rather than exploring the speeding up of subroutines and instruction-level parallelism, which has been previously explored on a variety of hardware [6, 10, 12], we explore the blocking of the input image (before sampling), i.e. data-level parallelism. First, we explore blocking. In blocking, the image is split into m non-overlapping blocks. Depending on m, the blocks may be square or rectangular. The case where the blocks are adjacent vertical columns is called vectorizing. The individual blocks are sampled separately, using a random Gaussian matrix as the measurement matrix. For the representation basis, we use discrete cosine wavelets. The blocks are then reconstructed sequentially, and the original image is rebuilt, with each block being placed in its original location. With stitching, overlap is introduced between blocks. We examine stitching with overlaps of 2 and 5 pixels between adjacent blocks. We then average over overlapping sections. After reconstruction of the individual blocks, the entire image is made by averaging over the overlapping sections between blocks. In theory, this should improve the reconstructed image quality by creating a level of redundancy which can be exploited to improve what may be a poor reconstruction in one of the blocks.

By blocking the image, we are creating a series of local $l_1$-minimization problems as opposed to a larger global one. There are no guarantees that solving the $l_1$-minimization problem for a small subsection of an image will give the same solution if we solved the global problem and then referred to the same subsection.

We investigate image quality through two measures. First, we examine the Peak Signal-to-Noise Ratio (PSNR) which is a measure of the ratio of maximum signal power to noise power, in decibels. In a sense, the PSNR is a local measurement since it measures how the highest intensity regions of the image compare to the amount of noise. Finally, we examine the SSIM index which is a method for measuring the similarity between two images. Since the SSIM index is calculated over the entire image, it gives a more blanket metric for the entirety of the image. This gives a more global metric for comparison of the reconstructed image to the original.

In order to further analyze the quality of each reconstruction, we count the number of objects in each image through region boundary tracing. We then carry out the same analysis on each reconstructed image and compare the number of objects in the original image to the number of objects in the reconstructed image. We examine the percent difference of images in the reconstructed image versus the original and make comparisons between blocking and stitching.

Finally, we implement OMP on a Xilinix Zynq-7000 SoC and derive an equation for the number of cycles required to process an input vector with N components (in bytes). We find the number of blocks required to achieve a speedup for hardware acceleration compared to software.

# 5 IMPLEMENTATION RESULTS

## 5.1 Quality and Time Results

The experiments were carried out on a server-class Xeon E5-2670 (2.60Ghz) processor. Due to large RAM constraints, brought on by the measurement matrix and the reconstruction process, we constrained our biggest block size to 32 x 32 with 256 x 256 images. The OMP algorithm was implemented in C. We acquired a large image database from [15]. The quality and time and results were averaged over 10 trials of each of the images. The reconstruction time and quality metric results can be seen in Tables 1 and 2, respectively. Figure 2 plots both the time and PSNR results for each blocking configuration.

**Table 1: Time Results**

| Number of blocks | Reconstruction Time (seconds) |
|---|---|
| 64 | 120.280 |
| 256 | 9.508 |
| 1024 | 6.563 |
| 4096 | 4.492 |
| 64 (vectorized) | 120.262 |
| 256 (vectorized) | 9.472 |
| 1024 (vectorized) | 6.532 |
| 4096 (vectorized) | 4.471 |
| 64, 2 pixel overlap | 197.25 |
| 256, 2 pixel overlap | 23.14 |
| 256, 5 pixel overlap | 79.32 |
| 1024, 2 pixel overlap | 11.86 |

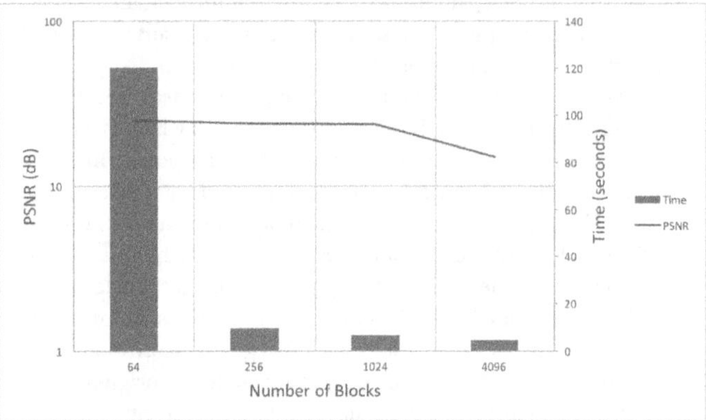


**Figure 2: PSNR and Time vs. Number of Blocks**

**Table 2: Quality Results**

| Number of blocks | PSNR | SSIM Index |
|---|---|---|
| 64 | 24.991 | 0.628 |
| 256 | 23.871 | 0.629 |
| 1024 | 23.591 | 0.660 |
| 4096 | 14.943 | 0.368 |
| 64 (vectorized) | 22.792 | 0.462 |
| 256 (vectorized) | 24.113 | 0.578 |
| 1024 (vectorized) | 21.368 | 0.486 |
| 4096 (vectorized) | 14.573 | 0.263 |
| 64, 2 pixel overlap | 26.990 | 0.628 |
| 256, 2 pixel overlap | 25.111 | 0.669 |
| 256, 5 pixel overlap | 26.850 | 0.726 |
| 1024, 2 pixel overlap | 25.904 | 0.629 |

Several trends are observed in the figure. It can be seen that as the number of blocks increases, the reconstruction time per block decreases exponentially. This is as expected, since less iterations of the OMP algorithm are needed to finish reconstruction. Additionally, $\Lambda$ contains less columns, and so, steps 6 and 7, as outlined in Algorithm 1, require less computation. With larger block sizes, each step of the OMP algorithm takes progressively longer time as the size of $\Lambda$ increases and more computation is required at each step.

Next, we observe interesting trends in the PSNR. It can be seen that as the block size decreases, the PSNR generally decreases. Although the changes are not as drastic as the change in reconstruction time per block, it can be seen that at 4096 blocks there is a large drop in the PSNR. We can observe that at these block sizes, a large amount of noise appears to be generated in the process of reconstruction. However, there is a very gradual drop going from a single block to greater block sizes. Vectorizing appears, in most of the cases, appears to give poor PSNR results. The only vectorizing case that has competitive results is the 256 case, this may be due to the fact that since the image itself is 256 x 256, features are scaled to the height of the image and therefore are more amenable to compression and reconstruction in this case.

The SSIM index trend follows the PSNR. In general, it appears that larger blocks give slightly better reconstruction results, with respect to quality. Although the SSIM index of 1024 blocks is the best, this can likely be attributed to it being particularly amenable to this dataset. Nonetheless, the general trend holds that less, larger blocks give better quality results.

Next, we examine the results from having overlap between blocks and averaging over these overlapping sections, referred to as stitching. The results can again be seen in Tables 1 and 2.

We observe that the reconstruction times increase significantly, which would be expected since each block is larger. Additionally, there is an averaging process which was not present before with blocking.

With regard to quality, it is clear that even a small amount of stitching increases the quality of the image reconstruction. This can be seen when comparing the stitching results to their blocking counterparts. This increase in quality is seen across both the PSNR and SSIM index results.

## 5.2 Object Detection Analysis

The experiments with regard to object detection were carried out separately from the quality and time experiment. These experiments were carried out on a Xeon E5-2670 processor, as well. Matlab was used to count the number of objects in each image. The results were averaged over 10 trials for each image in the database. The object detection count of the reconstructed image was compared to that of the original image and the percent difference was found. The percent difference was averaged over the image database. These results can be seen in Table 3 and Figure 3.

**Table 3: Object Detection Results**

| Number of blocks, overlap | Percent Difference Object Count (%) |
|---|---|
| 64 | 68.66 |
| 256 | 68.53 |
| 1024 | 59.83 |
| 4096 | 181.71 |
| 64 (vectorizing) | 95.94 |
| 256 (vectorizing) | 140.61 |
| 1024 (vectorizing) | 160.84 |
| 4096 (vectorizing) | 555.23 |
| 64, 2 pixel overlap | 41.59 |
| 256, 2 pixel overlap | 47.99 |
| 256, 5 pixel overlap | 41.17 |
| 1024, 5 pixel overlap | 42.26 |

It can be seen in Table 3, similar to the quality results, that a greater number of blocks leads to poorer reconstruction results when the reconstruction is compared to the original image. It is likely that the large number of blocks causes artifacts to be created between blocks when they are put in their proper position. These results further elucidate the relationship between the number of blocks and image quality. Vectorizing again has poor results, similar to the SSIM index results shown in Table 2. The stitching results appear to be much better. This is due to the averaging effect that occurs between blocks in stitching. The averaging improves bad reconstruction results in any one particular block and smooths over the artificially created objects and artifacts.

## 5.3 FPGA Implementation Results

There are three possible solutions for reducing the time overhead incurred by stitching in a cloud computing environment. These solutions include more CPU nodes, which is not cost effective, introducing GPUs, which can be power hungry in cloud usage, and finally FPGAs which have been shown to be most effective in the cloud computing domain, including use in Microsoft's Project Catapult. Here, we show a proof of concept using a particular Zynq platform, however, the analysis and methods shown can be applied to other FPGAs. The proposed FPGA implementation was carried out on a Zedboard development kit, using the Xilinx Zynq-7000 SoC. The measured signal input is the constricting factor in the algorithm, so this analysis is based on the number of bytes in this particular input. A variety of image sizes were reconstructed, with a maximum measured signal input of 40 bytes, which corresponds to a vector size of 10 components when each component is 32 bits.

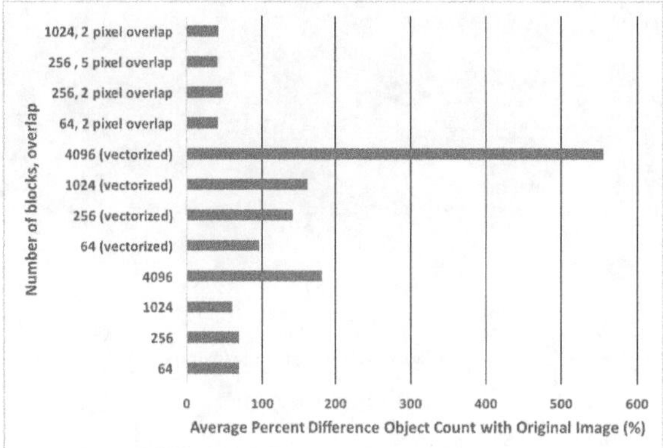


**Figure 3: Impact of differing number of blocks and overlap on the percent difference in number of objects detected when compared to the original image**

Through experiment, we observed that the DMA time is 500 - 530 cycles. The transfer time for each byte from the ARM processor to the FPGA, on this particular board, is 2 cycles. By adding together the DMA time, the transfer time, and the time it takes for the FPGA to do the relevant matrix multiplication operations, we get equation 2, where N is the total number of samples multiplied by the number of bytes it takes to represent each component in the input vector.

$$\text{Time (in cycles)} = \text{DMA Time} + 2N + (N/8) + N \qquad (2)$$

Due to the limited amount of memory on the Zedboard (89.15% of LUT used when the measured signal was 40 bytes, as shown in Table 6), we can use this equation to extrapolate the reconstruction time of a larger measured signal.

**Table 4: Resource utilization of HW+SW acceleration**

| Resources | Available | Utilization (%) |
|---|---|---|
| BRAM | 280 | 77.35 |
| DSP48 | 220 | 34.86 |
| FF | 106400 | 8.54 |
| LUT | 53200 | 89.15 |

By comparing this extrapolation to measured reconstruction times from running the algorithm solely on the ARM processor, we are able to approximate the measured signal size at which the hardware implementation outperforms the software implementation, with regard to reconstruction time. This can be seen in Figure 4.

Based on Figure 4, it can be seen that the break-even point occurs at approximately a measured signal size of 350 bytes for the Zynq platform, when the software implementation outperforms the hardware implementation with regard to reconstruction time. If we make assumptions on the size of each component in the measured dataset, we can derive the minimum size with regard to block size that would be required for a hardware speedup. For example, if we assume each component in the measured dataset has a size of 4 bytes, that they are sampled at a rate of 50%, then we would gain a hardware speedup at a granularity of 256 blocks or less for a 256 x 256 image. This speedup is restricted only to the algorithm-level

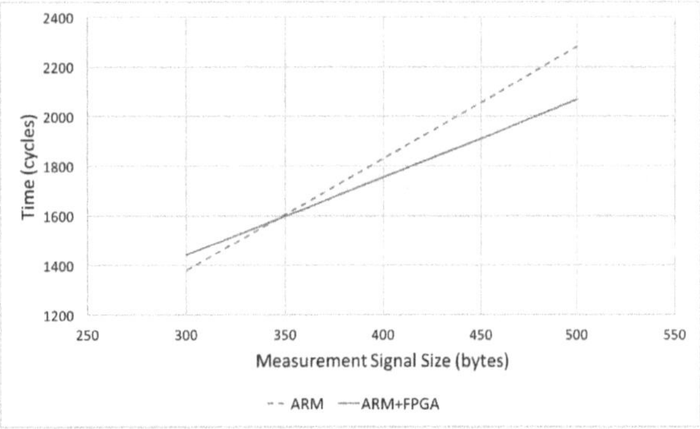


**Figure 4: Impact of the size of the measurement signal input on time it takes for algorithm to complete**

parallelization. At the data-level, there would also be a speedup proportional to the number of parallel instances involved as each block could be processed separately.

## 6 CONCLUSION

This paper presents the first thorough examination of blocking and stitching data-level parallelization methods for the OMP compressive sensing reconstruction algorithm, including varying block sizes and degrees of overlap. The accuracy and reconstruction time of the images are examined across different block sizes, as well as across different amounts of overlap between adjacent blocks in the case of stitching. The results indicate that while blocking reduces computational time when compared to reconstructing an entire image at once, it incurs a modest reduction in image quality. Vectorizing, a commonly used method for parallelization of OMP is shown to give poor global image quality results when compared to square blocking. It is shown that stitching improves PSNR by up to several decibels and the SSIM index by up to 15% when compared to blocking. Similarly, in the object count analysis, there is a 11.84% to 140.54% improvement, based on the cases that are compared. Finally, it is shown that parallel architectures can be utilized in order to reduce the overhead of stitching. While blocking gives large benefits with regard to reconstruction time and reduction in needed RAM, stitching is better from an image quality perspective. We show that this overhead can be reduced by up to 25% using FPGAs for blocks past a particular block size.

## 7 ACKNOWLEDGMENTS

This work was supported in parts by the National Science Foundation under grant CSR-1526913.

## REFERENCES


[1] Joel A. Tropp and Anna C. Gilbert. 2007. Signal recovery from random measurements via orthogonal matching pursuit. *IEEE Transactions on Information Theory*, 53, 12, 4655–4666. DOI: 10.1109/tit.2007.909108. https://doi.org/10.1109/tit.2007.909108.

[2] E.J. Candes, J. Romberg, and T. Tao. 2006. Robust uncertainty principles: exact signal reconstruction from highly incomplete frequency information. *IEEE Transactions on Information Theory*, 52, 2, 489–509. DOI: 10.1109/tit.2005.862083. https://doi.org/10.1109/tit.2005.862083.

[3] Michael Lustig, David Donoho, and John M. Pauly. 2007. Sparse mri: the application of compressed sensing for rapid mr imaging. *Magnetic Resonance in Medicine*, 58, 6, 1182–1195. DOI: 10.1002/mrm.21391. https://doi.org/10.1002/mrm.21391.

[4] Ahmed Nabil Belbachir, Stephan Schraml, Manfred Mayerhofer, and Michael Hofstatter. 2014. A novel hdr depth camera for real-time 3d 360 degree panoramic vision. In *2014 IEEE Conference on Computer Vision and Pattern Recognition Workshops*. IEEE. DOI: 10.1109/cvprw.2014.69. https://doi.org/10.1109/cvprw.2014.69.

[5] Jiaxing Zhang, Ying Yan, Liang Jeff Chen, Minjie Wang, Thomas Moscibroda, and Zheng Zhang. 2014. Impression store: compressive sensing-based storage for big data analytics. In *HotCloud*.

[6] Amey M. Kulkarni, Houman Homayoun, and Tinoosh Mohsenin. 2014. A parallel and reconfigurable architecture for efficient omp compressive sensing reconstruction. In *Proceedings of the 24th edition of the great lakes symposium on VLSI - GLSVLSI 14*. ACM Press. DOI: 10.1145/2591513.2591598. https://doi.org/10.1145/2591513.2591598.

[7] Y.C. Pati, R. Rezaiifar, and P.S. Krishnaprasad. 1993. Orthogonal matching pursuit: recursive function approximation with applications to wavelet decomposition. In *Proceedings of 27th Asilomar Conference on Signals, Systems and Computers*. IEEE Comput. Soc. Press. DOI: 10.1109/acssc.1993.342465. https://doi.org/10.1109/acssc.1993.342465.

[8] Parichat Sermwuthisarn, Supatana Auethavekiat, and Vorapoj Patanavijit. 2009. A fast image recovery using compressive sensing technique with block based orthogonal matching pursuit. In *2009 International Symposium on Intelligent Signal Processing and Communication Systems (ISPACS)*. IEEE. DOI: 10.1109/ispacs.2009.5383863. https://doi.org/10.1109/ispacs.2009.5383863.

[9] Depeng Yang, Gregory. D. Peterson, and Husheng Li. 2012. Compressed sensing and cholesky decomposition on fpgas and gpus. *Parallel Computing*, 38, 8, 421–437.

[10] Jeremy Constantin, Ahmed Dogan, Oskar Andersson, Pascal Meinerzhagen, Joachim Rodrigues, David Atienza, and Andreas Burg. 2013. An ultra-low-power application-specific processor with sub-vt memories for compressed sensing. In *VLSI-SoC: From Algorithms to Circuits and System-on-Chip Design*. Springer Berlin Heidelberg, 88–106. DOI: 10.1007/978-3-642-45073-0_5. https://doi.org/10.1007/978-3-642-45073-05.

[11] Hassan Rabah, Abbes Amira, Basant Kumar Mohanty, Somaya Almaadeed, and Pramod Kumar Meher. 2015. Fpga implementation of orthogonal matching pursuit for compressive sensing reconstruction. *IEEE Transactions on Very Large Scale Integration (VLSI) Systems*, 23, 10, 2209–2220.

[12] Yong Fang, Liang Chen, Jiaji Wu, and Bormin Huang. 2011. Gpu implementation of orthogonal matching pursuit for compressive sensing. In *2011 IEEE 17th International Conference on Parallel and Distributed Systems*. IEEE. DOI: 10.1109/icpads.2011.158. https://doi.org/10.1109/icpads.2011.158.

[13] Jerome L.V.M. Stanislaus and Tinoosh Mohsenin. 2012. High performance compressive sensing reconstruction hardware with qrd process. In *2012 IEEE International Symposium on Circuits and Systems*. IEEE. DOI: 10.1109/iscas.2012.6271921. https://doi.org/10.1109/iscas.2012.6271921.

[14] Amey Kulkarni and Tinoosh Mohsenin. 2015. Accelerating compressive sensing reconstruction omp algorithm with cpu, gpu, fpga and domain specific many-core. In *2015 IEEE International Symposium on Circuits and Systems (ISCAS)*. IEEE. DOI: 10.1109/iscas.2015.7168797. https://doi.org/10.1109/iscas.2015.7168797.

[15] [n. d.] In http://decsai.ugr.es/cvg/dbimagenes/g256.php.

# Towards Optimizing Refresh Energy in embedded-DRAM Caches using Private Blocks

Sheel Sindhu Manohar, Sukarn Agarwal and Hemangee K. Kapoor
Indian Institute of Technology Guwahati, Assam 781039, India
{sheel.manohar,sukarn,hemangee}@iitg.ac.in


## ABSTRACT

In recent years, the increased working set size of applications craves for more memory demand in terms of large size Last Level Caches (LLC). To fulfill this, embedded DRAM (eDRAM) caches have been considered as one of the best alternatives over conventional SRAM caches. eDRAM has a property of low leakage and provides more capacity in the same area footprint of SRAM. However, its retention period consumes significant refresh energy in the periodic refresh. In this paper, we present an approach to minimize the total energy spent on refreshes by considering the presence of private blocks in the LLC. Our approach restricts refreshing of those blocks that are loaded exclusively from the main memory on an LLC miss. Experimental result using full system simulation show 55% reduction in the total number of refreshes compared to baseline policy; and 62% reduction in total power consumption over SRAM.


## CCS CONCEPTS

• **Computer systems organization → Multicore architectures;**


## KEYWORDS

embedded DRAM; Last Level Cache; Refresh Energy; Private Blocks

**ACM Reference Format:**
Sheel Sindhu Manohar, Sukarn Agarwal and Hemangee K. Kapoor . 2019. Towards Optimizing Refresh Energy in embedded-DRAM Caches using Private Blocks. In *Great Lakes Symposium on VLSI 2019 (GLSVLSI '19), May 9–11, 2019, Tysons Corner, VA, USA.* ACM, New York, NY, USA, 6 pages. https://doi.org/10.1145/3299874.3317995


## 1 INTRODUCTION

Recent trends in the scaling of process technology require one to meet various challenges in the context of performance and power of multicore systems. Nowadays, with many cores present in the system, there is a high demand for more cache capacity. Current cache technologies made up of SRAM needs improvement in terms of power, performance, and scalability. To mitigate the challenges of SRAM, nowadays alternative emerging volatile/non-volatile memory technologies such as embedded DRAM (eDRAM), Spin Transfer Torque Random Access Memory (STT-RAM), Resistive Random Access Memory (ReRAM) etc are considered as a viable option for the Last Level Cache (LLC). These technologies provide many benefits over the conventional SRAM counterparts. These benefits include high scalability, lesser leakage power and more capacity in the same area footprint of SRAM. However, the costly write operation and weak write endurance of emerging Non-volatile memory technologies make eDRAM as a feasible option for LLC.

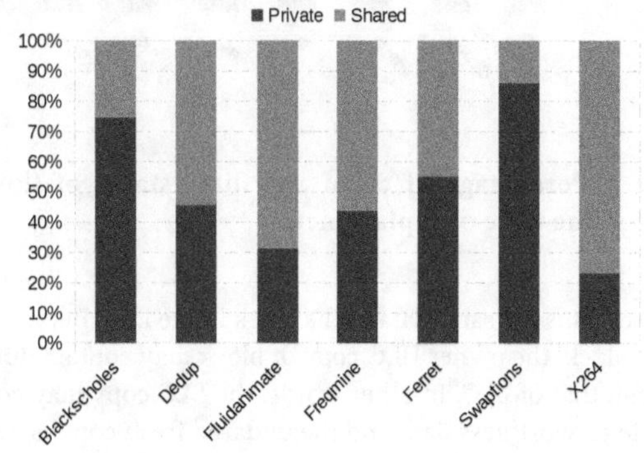


**Figure 1: Percentage of private and shared blocks for various benchmarks**

The eDRAM technology is based on Dynamic RAM (DRAM) & has the disadvantage of charge loss on the capacitors. eDRAM has a small retention time (the time interval over which one can retain the valid value of stored data) in terms of micro-second and requires a periodic refresh before the charge leaks away after each interval called refresh period. Compared to normal DRAM, the refresh period of eDRAM is $10^3$ times lesser. For instance, Barth,[4] reported the refresh period of eDRAM to be $40\mu s$, in comparison to the $64ms$ retention time of the conventional DRAM. In other words, one would need to refresh more often than the conventional DRAM. Also for the large LLC capacity, these frequent refresh operations consume a significant amount of energy and block the normal cache access requests when the cache banks are busy with the refresh process. In some of the cases, these refresh operations consume up to 70% of the total power consumption and degrade the system performance significantly[7]. Thus, reducing refresh overhead in eDRAM could save a lot of chip power and improve the performance[16].

In the existing literature, several policies to optimize refresh operations in eDRAM have been proposed. But as per our knowledge, no previous technique uses the concept of private blocks to minimize the refresh operations. Private blocks are those blocks that are cached by a single core with exclusive access permission [8][13]. On the other hand, blocks cached by the multiple cores with read-only permission are called shared blocks. With shared block, throughout the lifetime, the block in Upper-Level Cache


*GLSVLSI '19, May 9–11, 2019, Tysons Corner, VA, USA*

ACM ISBN 978-1-4503-6252-8/19/05...$15.00
https://doi.org/10.1145/3299874.3317995

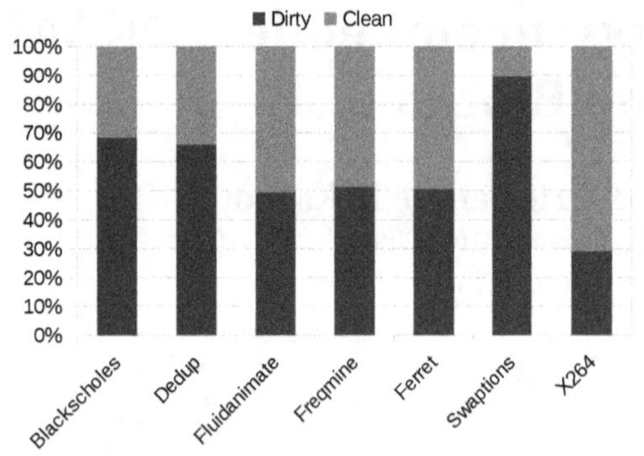


**Figure 2: Percentage of clean and dirty status of the LLC blocks at the time of replacement**

(ULC) contains the same data as the block in the LLC. But in case of private block, the owner ULC copy of block may contain different data than that of LLC. In other words, the LLC copy may contain the stale or worthless data and the updated fresh copy is present with the ULC. In such cases, the stale data at LLC is updated when there is a write-back from ULC or when the block is replaced exclusively from the ULC. To measure the impact of private block and its content, we presented an analysis in Figures 1 and 2(Please refer to the experimetal setup in section 4.1). Figure 1 shows the percentage of private and shared blocks in the LLC and figure 2 shows the percentage of the private blocks containing dirty data at the time of replacement. The conclusion that can be derived from these figures is that on an average, 51% of the blocks are private blocks and among these blocks 58% of the time this exclusive data was dirty at the time of replacement. Both these facts motivate us to identify the private blocks and propose a technique that avoids the refreshing these blocks in eDRAM based LLC.

The main contributions of this paper are as follows:

- We identified the blocks privately cached by the higher level cache and avoid refreshing of these blocks in the eDRAM based LLC.
- To identify private block and to minimize the refreshes, we make some changes in the conventional MESI protocol.
- Experimental evaluation is done on a full system simulator Gem5[8] which is integrated with modules to support eDRAM caches. Results show significant improvement in refresh energy savings and the overall performance.

The rest of the paper is organized as follows. Section II discusses the related work in eDRAM and its energy optimization. Section III discusses our proposed Technique. Section IV discusses the experimental setup and results. Finally, we draw conclusions in Section V.

## 2 BACKGROUND AND RELATED WORK

### 2.1 Embedded DRAM

An embedded DRAM cell consists of an access transistor and a storage capacitor. The capacitor used for eDRAM is either a deep-trench capacitor or stacked capacitor, where the access is controlled by a transistor [14]. Over the time the capacitor losses charge and hence an eDRAM cell requires a periodic refresh operation. As capacitor losses charge, the refresh process consists of sensing the cell data from the cell to the sense amplifier and replenishing the partially lost charge[12][6]. This capacitor leakage increases with technology scaling. As shown in Fig. 3, data is represented by the charge on the capacitor. The Access transistor connects the capacitor to the bit lines which transfers the data bits to the sense amplifier. The row to be selected is controlled by the word line connected to the transistor.

### 2.2 All Bank Periodic Refresh

The very naive and basic technique for refreshing the eDRAM is the burst mode. In a Simple periodic refresh technique, all the banks are refreshed simultaneously as shown in the figure 4. All the banks would be busy while refreshing and cache will not be available while the refresh is going on. No normal access would be served for a fixed interval of time when LLC is unavailable.

### 2.3 Periodic Round Robin Refresh (PRR) - Baseline

In this subsection, we explain our baseline refreshing technique e.g. periodic round robin refresh and how it is different from the basic periodic refresh(all-bank refresh scheme). Our baseline is a modified version of all bank refresh scheme, which staggers refreshes across the interval in a round robin fashion [5]. In particular, it is formulated as follows. From the given retention time, compute the global refresh interval, which is nothing but the number of cycles after which each bank needs to be refreshed.

$$Global\ ref.\ interval = retention\ time \times clockfreq$$

Depending on the number of cache banks, divide this global refresh interval such that the banks trigger a refresh in a staggered fashion, as shown in figure. 5. As seen from the fig, the gap between refreshes of two banks allows the next bank to serve normal cache accesses. This reduces the one time stall for all banks, as faced by the all bank refresh scheme. Formally,

$$Bank\ ref.\ interval = global\ ref.\ interval \div num\_banks$$

Note that depending on the refresh interval and the size of the bank, some banks may get refreshed in parallel for a small duration. Whenever a bank is getting refreshed it causes contention with the normal cache access. Here we have to handle two cases: (i) normal cache access comes when a bank is being refreshed; and (ii) bank refresh trigger comes when normal access has come. For the former, the normal cache access is stalled and will be served only after the bank refresh operation has completed. In case the bank refresh trigger comes when normal cache access is pending, we give priority to bank refresh and hence stall the normal cache access. This access can resume once the refresh operation has completed. As can be noted, the quicker the refresh completes, the faster the stalled requests can be processed.

### 2.4 Related Work

Many researchers proposed works regarding reducing energy consumption by saving the number of refresh counts. Zoran[15] proposed a coherency based refresh saving technique in DRAM. It

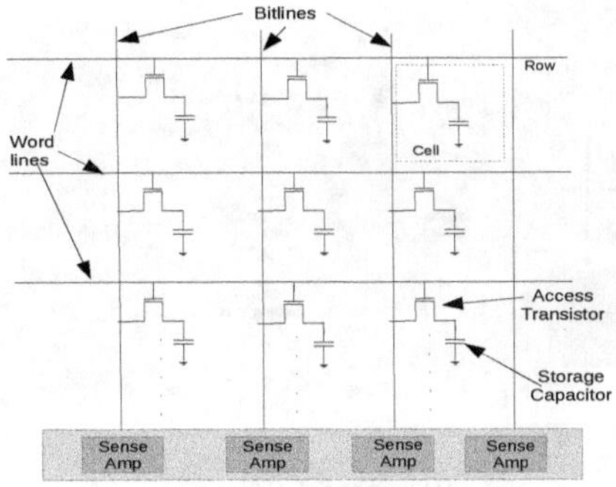


Figure 3: Diagram of eDRAM bank

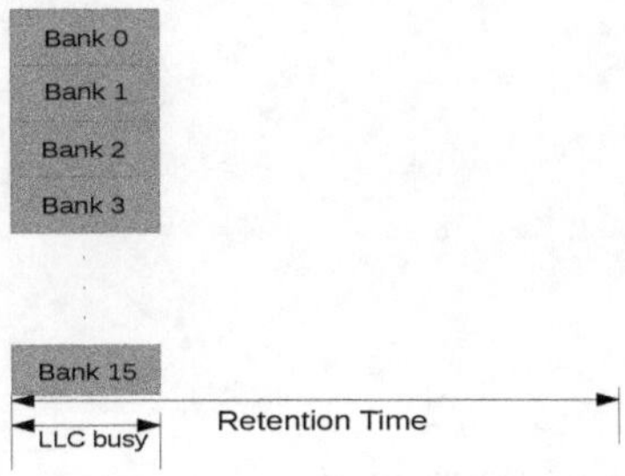


Figure 4: Conceptual Diagram of Basic Periodic Refresh Technique called the all bank refresh

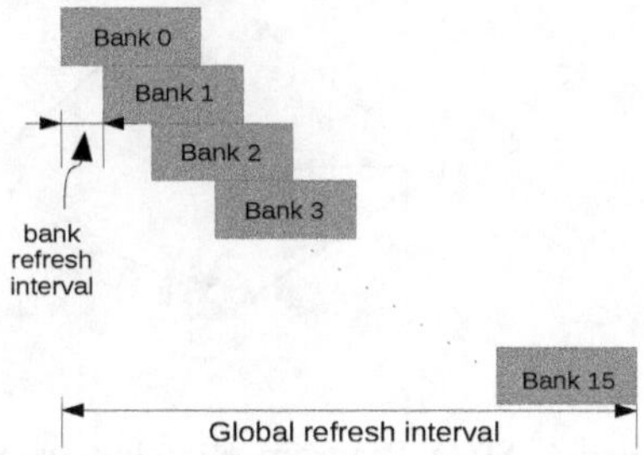


Figure 5: Conceptual Diagram of Periodic Round Robin Refresh(PRR) Technique

reduces energy on an average up to 57% with a performance loss of 8%. Mittal[16], proposed a cache reconfiguration approach for saving leakage and refresh energy by cache coloring. They provide colors to specific regions and turn-off eDRAM cache dynamically for saving cache energy. This technique also includes limitation due to cache coloring, whereas cache reconfiguration flushes the cache and further increases access time to main memory due to increased misses.

Kong et al.[5] proposed an idea of selective fine-grain round robin refresh scheme. They experiment on a multi-banked cache for refresh operation optimization and reported a reduction of 13.3% energy per instruction for their proposed technique from basic all-bank refresh scheme. Agrawal [1] proposed different techniques for refresh reduction. One of the proposed techniques uses poly-phase refreshing. It divides retention time interval into multiple phases. Refresh for cache line is done accordingly at the beginning of phase rather than at the beginning of the retention period. They also proposed time based and data-based refresh savings policies for different type of hot and cold cache lines. Chang[9] provided a detailed technology comparison between SRAM, STT-RAM and refresh optimized eDRAM. It Proposes an effective idea of deadline prediction to reduce refresh operation in eDRAM.

Reohr[17] discusses various approaches for reducing refreshes for eDRAM caches like no refresh policy, periodic refresh policy and line-level refresh. These policies reduce refresh overheads but increase cache misses. Agrawal[2] proposed a mathematical model of eDRAM retention time and reported the existence of spatial correlation in-between the cells. Accordingly, they divided the cache into tiles(logical regions) and refresh each tile using different refresh rates. As per our knowledge, none of the above policies exploit the use of private blocks to save refreshes in eDRAM based LLCs.

# 3 PROPOSED METHODOLOGY-PBOR

This section describes the proposed policy, Private Block based Optimised Refresh (PBOR), that reduces the number of refreshes based on the concept of private blocks. In particular, the paper proposes that the cache blocks that are privately cached by higher level caches will not be refreshed in the eDRAM based LLC. When the block is loaded from the main memory for the first time, depending on its category it will be identified as a private block or a prospective shared block. If the block is identified as private an additional bit associated with the cache entry will indicate the status. In particular, this bit tells whether the block has to be refresh or not; and is termed as *to-refresh*. By default for each block this bit is set to 1 and whenever a block is declared as private, this bit is reset to 0.

At the end of retention time, the cache bank is refreshed. During this, the to-refresh bit of each block is checked, and in case it is reset, the refresh to that block is skipped. Note that this saves a lot of refreshes, thus leading to lesser stall time for normal cache accesses, improving performance and saving refresh energy. This facility comes at the cost of some additional consideration during normal cache access.

Consider the situation when the bit=0 and a new request comes for this block to the LLC. In this case, the block in LLC might have invalid data as it was not refreshed regularly. Therefore the data for this block has to be fetched from the higher level cache. The entry in the directory is used to identify the owner of the block and it is used subsequently to provide the data to the requester. This requires changes to the MESI protocol.

Table 1: Table of request and responses

| L2 Request or Response | Description |
|---|---|
| GETS | Read Request |
| GETX | Write Request |
| GET_INSTR | Instruction Request |
| PUTS | Clean block Replacement |
| DATA | Data from Main memory |

## 3.1 Changes to the MESI protocol

Figure 6 shows the state diagram of the new states added to the protocol to handle the situations arising from the non-refreshed private blocks. The remaining states of MESI (not covered by the figure) behave as in a normal MESI protocol. Below we describe each state and actions associated with them. A request/response reaching to the LLC can belong to the categories mentioned in table 1.

On an LLC miss, the block is brought from the next level before sending it to the higher level (L2 in our case). According to our proposal, we have to identify private blocks and manage the to-refresh bit accordingly. Subsequent requests to such blocks and actions taken are discussed in this subsection. First, we list all the relevant states of the state diagram.

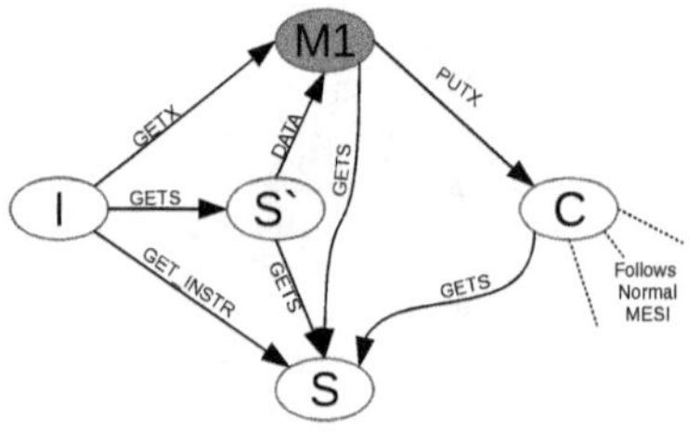


**Figure 6: State Diagram showing transitions of states in eDRAM according to the MESI protocol**

- I: Invalid block entry of L3 Cache.
- S′: This state acts as an intermediate state in the state diagram. The transition from this state happens when data block is loaded from main memory on GETS. If in between loading of the block into the cache another request meddles for the same block, it will be served as a shared block. Otherwise, if no other request issued by L2 for this block it will be served with exclusive permission to L2
- S: Block is in the shared state in L3 with read permission. This state is considered for the refresh operation
- M1: Block is held in exclusive permission by the L2 cache. The copy present in the L3 cache is stale
- C: Data block written back from L2. L3 has a fresh copy of data block. Considered for the refresh operation.

*3.1.1 Handling response from the main memory on a miss.* The description of transitions of states according to L2 request or main memory response are given below:

- Initially all blocks are in invalid state in the cache. A block also becomes invalid after a valid data item is evicted from it. In this case the to-refresh bit is 0.
- If the LLC receives a request to load an instruction, GET_INSTR, it loads the block from the main memory, sends the block to the requesting L2 cache and makes the state of the block as S. Blocks having state S have the to-refresh bit set to 1.
- Consider the request GETS, which indicates that the requester wants the block in read-only mode. Here, the block is likely to be loaded in private mode if there are no sharers. We therefore change the state to an intermediate state S′. While the block is loaded from the memory, in case there is an intervening GETS request from another L2, the next state becomes S, as we have more than one sharer for the block. However, if there is no intervening request, then the block is given to the requester with exclusive permission. Here the state changes to the new state M1. This state indicates a block in a private/exclusive mode. Such a block is likely to have stale data in the LLC and hence need not be refreshed. The to-refresh bit for this block in state M1 is set to 0.
- Consider the request GETX, which indicates that the requester wants the block with exclusive permission to modify the content. Here the block is clearly a private block and hence the state of the block becomes M1, having to-refresh bit=0.

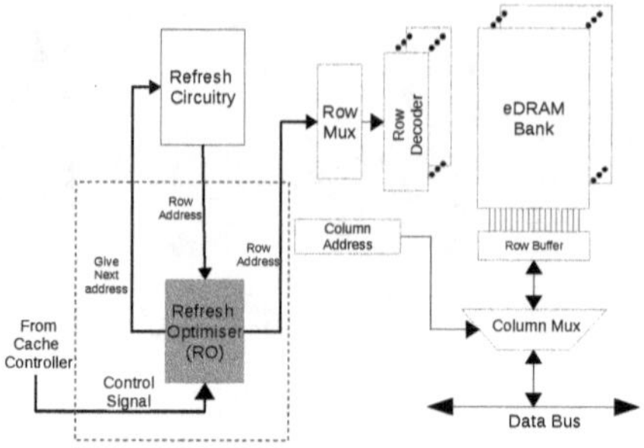


**Figure 7: Proposed eDRAM Architecture**

*3.1.2 Changes in the states of the block when the block is either replaced from L2 cache or if there is a new request or response from L2 cache.* The description of transitions of states are given below:

- Consider the case when the block is in state M1 and another L2 cache requests access to this block by issuing a GETS. When the LLC receives the request from the new L2 cache, the LLC fetches the block from the owner and forwards it to the requesting L2. The block is now shared by multiple caches and the state becomes S. This state has the to-refresh bit equal to 1.
- Consider the case when the block is in state M1 in the L2 cache and the cache evicts the block. The owner issues a PUTX request and sends the block to the LLC. LLC updates its copy and the directory entry of the owner for the cache block is also deleted. The block is now present only in the LLC and its state becomes C. Note that, as this is the only copy of the block, we have to keep it valid by refreshing it. Therefore the to-refresh bit is 1. When the block is in state C, it handles all the future requests as per the original MESI protocol.

## 3.2 LLC Architecture

Figure 7 shows the high-level diagram of the proposed eDRAM architecture. The eDRAM banks are shown along with the row and column addresses, the row decoders, the row buffer that contains the data of the enabled row and the column MUX that selects the appropriate block from the row buffer in order to transfer the data on to the data bus. The dotted rectangle shows the new components added to the architecture. It mainly consists of a logic block *Refresh Optimiser (RO)* that receives inputs from the cache controller. The cache controller detects private blocks based on the states as per the changes in the MESI protocol and communicates the information to the RO unit. The RO unit maintains the information of addresses and the associated to-refresh bit for every address. During the periodic refresh, the refresh circuitry generates the address to be refreshed and sends it to RO. As we need to avoid refreshes of the private blocks the address generated by the refresh circuitry is controlled by the RO-unit. The RO unit gets the address from the refresh circuitry and checks the corresponding to-refresh bit. The following cases are considered:

- If to-refresh=1, then the row address is forwarded to the row decoder so that the address gets refreshed.

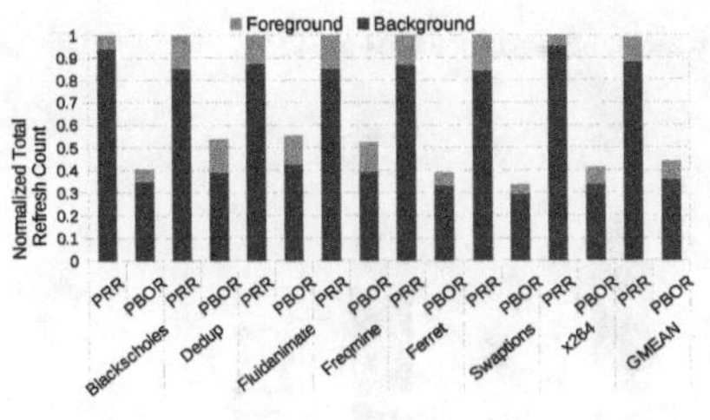

**Figure 8: Normalized Total no. of refreshes incurred in PBOR w.r.t PRR**

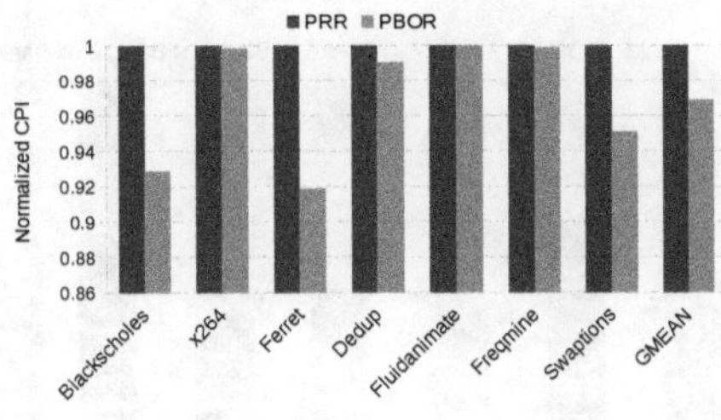

**Figure 9: Normalized CPI for PRR and PBOR**

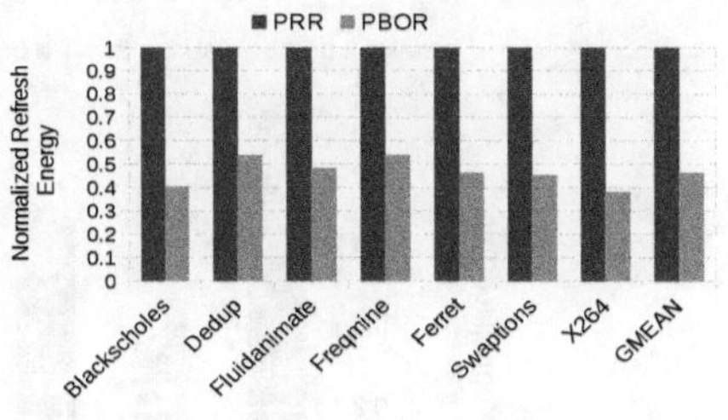

**Figure 10: Normalized Refresh Energy of proposed PBOR over PRR**

**Table 2: Architectural Parameters**

| Components | Parameters |
|---|---|
| Processor | 3Ghz, Quad-core, X86 |
| L1 Cache | Private SRAM based 32KB 8 way set-associative, split I/D caches, 64B block, 1 cycle access latency, LRU, write back policy |
| L2 Cache | Private SRAM based 256KB 8 way set-associative, 64B block, 8 cycle access latency, LRU, write back policy |
| L3 Cache | Shared, eDRAM based 4MB, 16 banks( each bank of 256KB) 16 way associative, 64 Byte line size, LRU, 15 cycle access latency, 15 cycle refresh latency(one cache line), $40\mu s$ retention time |

- If to-refresh=0, then the address is skipped and a signal '*get next address*' is sent to the refresh circuitry to get the next address to be refreshed.

## 3.3 Hardware Overhead

The additional hardware blocks required for the proposed architecture is the Refresh optimizer. Refresh Optimiser consists of a to-refresh bit for each particular cache block. In particular, for a 4MB 16way set associative cache, 65,536 bits are required which is only 0.19% of total eDRAM cache size. Fault tolerance and reliablity aspects over the to-refresh bits are not considered in the design.

# 4 EXPERIMENTAL EVALUATION

## 4.1 Experimental Setup

We evaluate our proposal on a full system simulator GEM5[10]. The memory module is simulated using the Ruby module inside GEM5. The MESI CMP based cache coherence protocol is used and modified to implement the proposed refresh optimization proposal. Table 2 shows the architecture parameters used in our setup. We use L1 and L2 as private caches and an eDRAM based L3 as the last level cache.

The LLC has 16 banks and we perform a block level refresh at each bank. The proposal uses a time staggered refresh timing for all 16 banks so that all the banks are not stalled at the same time. The retention time is taken as $40\mu s$ [4]. CACTI [11] is used to model the wire delays, cache area, energy and power values for SRAM based cache. The inter-bank refresh trigger value is computed such that within the retention time all banks are refreshed in a staggered fashion. PARSEC [3] benchmarks with medium size input are used to evaluate our proposed policy. These benchmarks include a large variety of multi-threaded applications such as mining, multimedia, animation, computer vision, etc. All the design overheads and effects of protocol changes are taken into consideration during simulations. We compare the proposed policy (PBOR) with baseline refresh scheme (PRR) that refreshes each and every cache line.

## 4.2 Results and Analysis

**Number of refreshes:** All eDRAM banks get periodically refreshed. As refresh is a high priority task, it gets preference over normal cache access. In par- ticular, when a request comes to access the LLC and the bank is currently undergoing a refresh, the request is stalled. We categorise the refreshes into two types: (i) foreground refresh occur when the current cache accesses are stalled due to bank getting refreshed; (ii) background refresh occur when the bank is not accessed while it gets refreshed. In case of foreground refreshes the accesses are stalled and it affects the performance of the system, whereas background refreshes do not affect performance.

As we avoid refreshing private blocks, we save on several unnecessary refreshes. Figure 8 shows the reduction in refreshes achieved by our proposed methodology against the baseline which refreshes every cache line. We get a reduction in the range of 47-63% in total refreshes with an average reduction of 55%. The blocks which are held privately by the higher level caches are not refreshed. Such blocks will incur a refresh only after they are written back to the LLC.

The data blocks get distributed across the LLC banks depending upon the application behavior and working set size. Some banks get more accesses whereas some other banks get fewer accesses. Also, some banks have more blocks cached privately by higher level caches compared to other cache banks. Figure 11 shows the bank-wise reduction in the number of refreshes for all benchmarks with respect to baseline PRR policy. One can see that some banks benefit more from the private blocks compared to others. Such banks get released from refreshing overhead much earlier giving quicker opportunity to start normal cache accesses.

**Performance:** While the cache is getting refreshed, the normal cache accesses have to be stalled. The reduction in the number of refreshes implies that the cache is not blocked for a long time. This implies performance improvement due to faster access latency of the LLC. Figure 9 shows the normalized Cycles Per Instruction (CPI) for the baseline and proposed approach. We get an improvement in CPI in the range of 1-9% with an average of 4%. We get this reduction, as background refreshes are more than foreground refreshes.

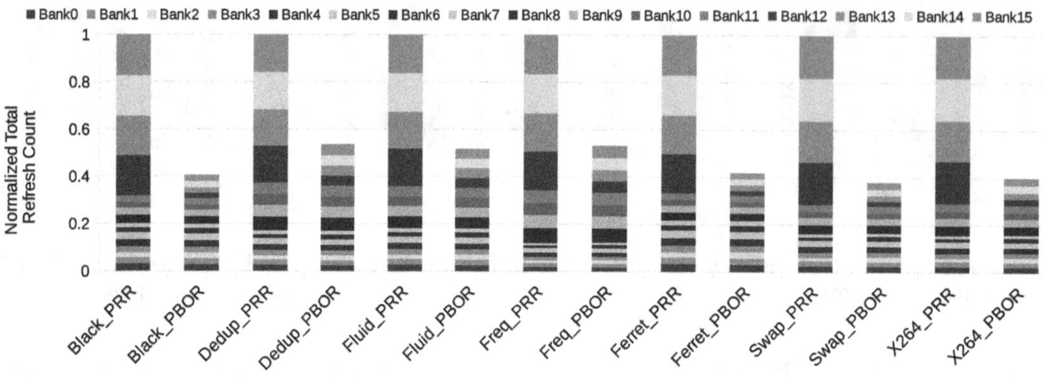


**Figure 11: Bankwise Normalized Refresh Counts of PBOR and PRR**

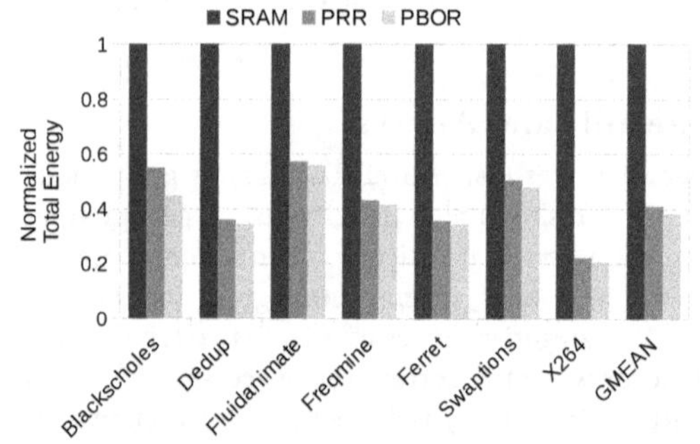


**Figure 12: Normalized Total Energy Consumption for PRR and proposed technique w.r.t SRAM**

**LLC Energy Consumption:** LLC consumes energy for normal accesses as well as for refreshing the cache lines. Even in the cases when the refreshes do not stall the normal cache access, they still incur energy. Reduction in the number of refreshes thus also leads to a reduction in energy consumption. Figure 10 shows the normalized reduction in refresh energy. We get a reduction in the range of 46-63% with an average of 54%.

Replacing SRAM with eDRAM based LLC gives savings in leakage energy. The read and write energy required by eDRAM is also less compared to SRAM. Hence we get a considerable reduction in the access energy for eDRAM over SRAM. The effect of refreshes on the total energy is shown in figure 12. Here the values include the static, dynamic as well as the refresh energy. We get an average reduction in total energy by 60% and 62% respectively in PRR and PBOR over baseline SRAM.

## 5 CONCLUSION

This paper proposed the use of eDRAM as a replacement for SRAM in the last level cache. Low leakage of eDRAM comes at the cost of less retention time, and thus requires periodic refreshes. The paper proposed to identify blocks that are privately cached by higher level caches and avoid refreshing them in the LLC. This saves considerable number of refreshes as well as refresh energy. The MESI cache coherence protocol is modified to identify the private blocks. An additional logic block is proposed that coordinates with the refresh circuitry and controls which addresses get refreshed.

From experiments, it was observed that the number of refreshes was reduced by 55% over basic refresh scheme. As the cache banks are stalled for lesser duration compared to the basic scheme we get improvement in performance by 4% on average. Compared to SRAM based cache we save overall total energy by 62%.

Thus, if one can manage refreshes carefully, eDRAM based LLC can become a valid replacement of SRAM.

## REFERENCES


[1] A. Agrawal et al. 2013. Refrint: Intelligent refresh to minimize power in on-chip multiprocessor cache hierarchies. In *HPCA-2013*. 400–411.

[2] A. Agrawal et al. 2014. Mosaic: Exploiting the spatial locality of process variation to reduce refresh energy in on-chip eDRAM modules. In *HPCA-2014*. 84–95.

[3] C. Bienia et al. 2008. The PARSEC benchmark suite: Characterization and architectural implications. In *PACT-2008*. 72–81.

[4] J. Barth et al. 2008. A 500 MHz Random Cycle, 1.5 ns Latency, SOI Embedded DRAM Macro Featuring a Three-Transistor Micro Sense Amplifier. *IEEE Journal of Solid-State Circuits* 43, 1 (Jan 2008), 86–95.

[5] J. Kong et al. 2017. Towards refresh-optimized EDRAM-based caches with a selective fine-grain round-robin refresh scheme. *Microprocessors and Microsystems* 49 (2017), 95 – 104.

[6] J. Liu et al. 2012. RAIDR: Retention-aware intelligent DRAM refresh. In *ISCA-2012*.

[7] Mohammad Alizadeh et al. 2012. Versatile refresh: low complexity refresh scheduling for high-throughput multi-banked eDRAM. In *ACM SIGMETRICS '12*.

[8] M. Lodde et al. 2012. Dynamic Last-Level Cache Allocation to Reduce Area and Power Overhead in Directory Coherence Protocols. In *Euro-Par 2012 Parallel Processing*. Springer Berlin Heidelberg, Berlin, Heidelberg, 206–218.

[9] M. T. Chang et al. 2013. Technology comparison for large last-level caches (L3Cs): Low-leakage SRAM, low write-energy STT-RAM, and refresh-optimized eDRAM. In *HPCA-2013*. 143–154.

[10] N. Binkert et al. 2011. The gem5 simulator. *ACM SIGARCH Computer Architecture News* 39, 2 (2011), 1–7.

[11] N. Muralimanohar et al. 2009. CACTI 6.0: A tool to model large caches. *HP laboratories* (2009), 22–31.

[12] P. G. Emma et al. 2008. Rethinking Refresh: Increasing Availability and Reducing Power in DRAM for Cache Applications. *IEEE Micro* 28, 6 (Nov 2008), 47–56.

[13] S. Agarwal et al. 2018. Reuse-Distance-Aware Write-Intensity Prediction of Dataless Entries for Energy-Efficient Hybrid Caches. *IEEE T-VLSI) Systems* 26, 10 (Oct 2018), 1881–1894.

[14] S. Mittal et al. 2017. DESTINY: A Comprehensive Tool with 3D and Multi-Level Cell Memory Modeling Capability. *JoLPE* 7, 3 (2017).

[15] Z. Jaksic and R. Canal. 2014. DRAM-based coherent caches and how to take advantage of the coherence protocol to reduce the refresh energy. In *DATE-2014*.

[16] S. Mittal. 2013. A Cache Reconfiguration Approach for Saving Leakage and Refresh Energy in Embedded DRAM Caches. *CoRR* abs/1309.7082 (2013).

[17] W.R. Reohr. 2006. Memories: Exploiting Them and Developing Them. , 303 - 310 pages.

# Extending Student Labs with SMT Circuit Implementation

Erik Brunvand
School of Computing
University of Utah
elb@cs.utah.edu

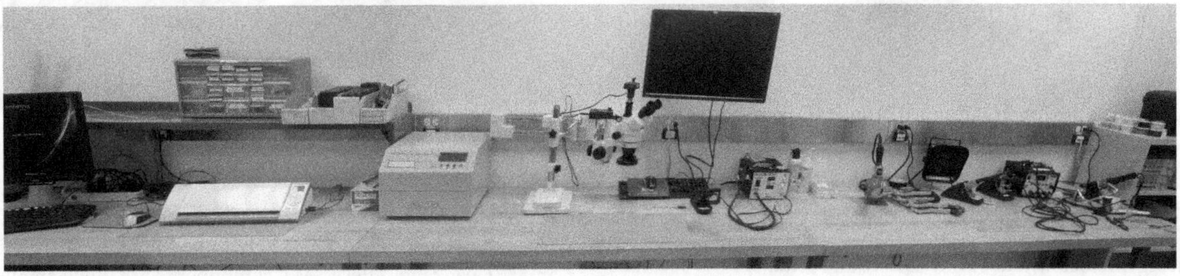

**Figure 1: Our student lab with SMT equipment. From left to right: CAMEO mylar cutter (with host PC), SMTmax reflow oven, inspection microscope, hot-air rework station, heat gun for shrink-tubing, hot-tweezers and fine-pitch soldering station.**

## ABSTRACT

Computer Science and Computer Engineering classes related to digital circuits, embedded systems, Human Computer Interaction (HCI), and a wide variety of "maker" subjects, would often like to include *physical computing* projects. Extending these physical computing ideas to *physical realization* of circuits is the next logical step, and has traditionally happened with low-cost non-soldered prototyping such as breadboards. However, many modern circuit components are now available only in tiny surface-mount technology (SMT) packages. Using these components essentially requires that students are able to design printed circuit boards (PCBs) specifically for their module. In this paper we describe an experience report of how we enhanced a student lab in a cost-effective way to enable students to develop, assemble, and solder custom PCBs that contain SMT components. This allows modern circuit components to be used, offers an enriched hands-on experience, and enables an expansion of the scope and complexity of student projects.

## CCS CONCEPTS

**• Social and professional topics → Computing education programs; • Hardware → PCB design and layout.**

## KEYWORDS

Maker Space, Physical Computing, Printed Circuit Boards


*GLSVLSI '19, May 9–11, 2019, Tysons Corner, VA, USA*

ACM ISBN 978-1-4503-6252-8/19/05...$15.00
https://doi.org/10.1145/3299874.3317968

**ACM Reference Format:**
Erik Brunvand. 2019. Extending Student Labs with SMT Circuit Implementation. In *Great Lakes Symposium on VLSI 2019 (GLSVLSI '19), May 9–11, 2019, Tysons Corner, VA, USA.* ACM, New York, NY, USA, 6 pages. https://doi.org/10.1145/3299874.3317968

## 1 INTRODUCTION

In this paper we describe how we enhanced a student lab at our University to support SMT assembly and reflow soldering of student-designed PCBs in a cost-effective way. This has greatly expanded the scope of projects that students can attempt during a semester. We will include a list of the specific equipment used and prices from when we installed the equipment as but one example of how this can be done. This information, especially prices, will quickly become out of date, but we hope that providing specific examples and prices will ground the information somewhat. We will also describe the procedure we use with that equipment that has achieved good results with student projects, and note when a step is only necessary for the most complex projects. The specific example is from our Computer Engineering Senior Capstone course as these are the most complex circuits designed by students in our program, and put the most stress on the procedure. Simpler projects can be done with a subset of the equipment/procedures in other courses in our CS curriculum from maker workshops and CS1 to sophomore courses to senior electives. Our hope is that the description will be detailed enough so that others can use this as a model for enhancing their own labs, and enable a new generation of students to include hands-on design, prototyping, and assembly of custom electronics back into their curricula.

Digital fabrication and makerspaces have a fascinating bidirectional relationship with computing: "making" can be an entry point to programming [4, 28] and programming can be an entry point to making [38, 39] Makerspaces and fablabs are becoming common in K-12 schools [5, 9], community centers [29, 43], and university settings [7, 31]. Along with the physical aspects of makerspaces (3D printing, laser cutters, etc.), physical computing that involves

**Figure 2: An example breadboard circuit implemented using DIP packages and through-hole parts such as resistors and LEDs.** (Photo by Windell Oskay, CC BY-SA 2.0)

interfacing microcontrollers with sensors and actuators has become a natural extension to maker activities [3, 36]. Especially with rise of user-friendly embedded platforms such as Arduino and Raspberry Pi, the ability to quickly develop and deploy circuits along side physical constructions has become an intriguing extension to other maker activities.

A variety of approaches have been used to gently introduce circuits to computing students including e-textiles where circuits are constructed with conductive thread [13, 24], printing circuits using conductive inks or computer printers [10, 15], and constructing circuits using stickers and other conductive materials [19, 37]. These approaches are generally related to casting electronics as a crafting activity [14, 23, 30].

At the university level, Computer Science [22] and Computer Engineering [21] curricula can include substantial coursework that involves digital logic and computer hardware. A wide variety of computer science courses including digital logic, computer design, embedded systems, Human Computer Interaction (HCI), and physical computing courses may want to extend their labs to include circuit implementation [27, 36]. As these circuit implementations move past the prototyping or crafting stages, printed circuit boards (PCBs) will be the natural next step to make a more robust and permanent implementation. Designing PCBs is also an essential enabling technology that allows the use of modern integrated circuits, many of which are only available in surface-mount technology (SMT) packages.

## 1.1 Background

Since the mid 1960's the standard format for integrated circuits has been the Dual Inline Package (DIP) with pins on 0.1 inch (2.54mm) centers. Because of this standardization hardware prototyping infrastructure (breadboards, wire-wrap boards, proto-boards), have been standardized to use that 0.1 inch pitch, including components such as resistors and capacitors that can also use that spacing. This form factor is instantly recognizable for previous generation students and instructors. See Figure 2 for an example of a small system from a maker workshop using a solderless breadboard.

In a more modern setting, components that both professionals and students are more likely to encounter are packaged in tiny surface-mount technology (SMT) packages intended primarily for automatic (robotic) assembly and reflow soldering. In fact, many modern components are unlikely to be available in anything but an SMT package. These SMT components are much smaller than through-hole components and result in higher density on a circuit board, but are essentially impossible to use on their own without designing a custom printed circuit board (PCB). There are a variety of SMT-DIP adapters and breakout boards available for some components, but at a much higher cost and much more limited selection than the native SMT components. Figure 3 shows another workshop circuit, this one featuring a transistor that drives a solenoid. The circuit is prototyped on the left with soldered 0.1 inch-pitch components, and on the right on a PCB using a mix of components including SMT packages.

**Figure 3: Soldered prototype circuit for controlling a solenoid on the left, and PCB version on the right**

A typical SMT package for an integrated circuit is designed to sit on the surface of a PCB, not to have leads go through holes in the board, and the leads are likely to be on 1mm to 0.5mm centers (or smaller). Passive devices (resistors, capacitors, etc.) are also designed to sit on the PCB's surface and come in standard sizes that are based on the rectangle size of the package in hundredths of an inch. A 1206 package, for example, is roughly 0.12in by 0.06in. This means that devices range from roughly the size of a grain of rice (1206 and 0805) to a sesame seed (0603) to something close to a fleck of pepper (01005 components are roughly twice the size of the period in this sentence). See Figure 4 for examples of SMT components. On the left are 0603, 0805, 1206, and 1210 sized passive components. The integrated circuits shown have pin pitches from 1.2mm to 0.5mm. This figure is sized so that the components are shown in actual sizes. Note that a possible source of confusion is that while I am using imperial-measured parts for passive components in this paper (more common in the USA), SMT parts may also be measured in metric sizes where the numbers are dimensions in millimeters. A good overview of SMT packages can be found on Wikipedia [47].

SMT components are designed to be soldered to the PCB using reflow soldering [46]. This is a technique where a viscous solder paste consisting of a mix of solder and flux is applied to the solder pads on the PCB or is squeegeed onto the board through a stencil, applying solder to all pads in one pass. The components are assembled onto the board by nestling them into the small puddles of solder. The board, thus assembled, is put into a reflow oven where the temperature is carefully raised and lowered according to a schedule that matches the characteristics of the solder paste.

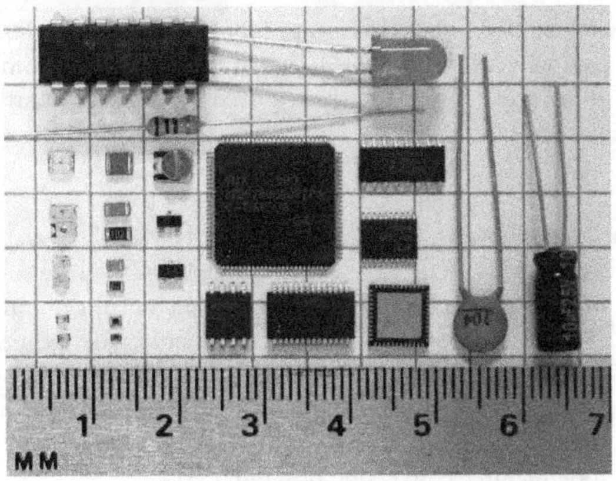


**Figure 4: Actual size SMT chips and passive components (LEDs, resistors, and capacitors). Classic through-hole components are also shown for scale.**

**Figure 5: PCB for DC motor control circuit designed by a student in our CS embedded systems course. This board features a mix of through-hole and SMT components.**

However, with a little care, most SMT packages can also be soldered using traditional hand-soldering techniques.

To get around the problem of using SMT components, there have been a variety of "toolkit" approaches where circuits, including SMT components, are pre-assembled onto small PCBs (sometimes called "breakout boards") so that they can be more easily connected to other components, such as embedded controllers like Arduino. Examples of these toolkit approaches include LittleBits [8], Phidgets [18], and Gadgeteer [44]. While these toolkits make assembly of prototype circuits easy, they are also quite a bit more expensive than the raw components, and limit students to the set of components available in the toolkit. To add flexibility in terms of component choice, and to reduce the size of the resulting prototype, custom PCBs are the answer. One example of introducing PCB design to a novice workshop on physical computing is reported by Mellis et. al. [32]. In this work they are exploring how participants in a workshop with no prior experience adjust to the use of custom PCBs. Other groups have built on those ideas to consider PCB design in maker workshops with novices [4, 38, 45]

**Figure 6: A PCB designed, assembled and soldered in the student lab by Nathan Hansen and Phillip Bradbury. The processor is an ARM Cortex M3 in an LQFP 48 package with 0.5mm pitch pins.**

## 2 COURSES

In our department there are a number of classes that make use of our lab's SMT PCB capabilities. These range from a cross-disciplinary class where CS and Art students design and build kinetic/electronic sculptures in interdisciplinary groups [11, 12], to an embedded systems course for CS students. Figure 5 shows a DC motor controller board designed by students in that class. We also have an "embedded" section of CS1 that includes simple circuit design along with physical computing as an introduction to Computer Science and programming.

Another course where SMT capabilities have had a huge impact is our Computer Engineering Senior Project course. This is the capstone team project course for our Computer Engineering program taken by senior undergraduates. Projects in the Computer Engineering capstone are required to have a mix of both hardware and software designed and implemented by the students. With the addition of PCB design skills and SMT assembly and soldering to the lab, six out of seven teams in a recent offering of the course included a student-designed PCB with SMT parts as part of their project. An example of a student-designed board from this class is seen in Figure 6. It is difficult to directly compare the quality and complexity of projects from year to year, and difficult to attempt some sort of controlled study of a class without the lab enhancements because these projects would simply not be possible without SMT PCB capabilities. The components that the students used are not available in other package types. In our maker workshops and lower-division CS courses the SMT components are valuable to keep the curricula current with modern components, but in the senior Computer Engineering capstone they are essential.

## 3 LAB ENHANCEMENTS

The first requirement for working with custom PCBs and SMT components is to introduce PCB design tools to the students. These tools typically start with a schematic view of a circuit, and then allow the designer to produce a layout of a PCB that implements that schematic. We have had good success introducing these tools to non-electronics students, and others have had similar success (e.g. [32]). We have used three different PCB tools in different contexts, and there are many others out there to choose from.

- **Fritzing:** Popular with makers and K-12 programs, Fritzing [26] is a tool that allows circuits to be described not as an abstract schematic, but as a direct connection of wires on a breadboard or a platforms such as Arduino, with an option to generate a PCB as an alternative implementation style.
- **Eagle CAD [6]:** Eagle is widely used by hobbyists and is supported by hobbyist web sites such as Sparkfun and Adafruit who publish Eagle footprint libraries for most parts that they sell. Eagle has a freeware version that restricts designs to two signal layers and a 4x3.2 inch board area that may be completely sufficient for student lab needs.
- **KiCad [25]:** This is an open-source community-supported tool that runs on a wide variety of platforms. Around half of the student teams used KiCad because of the open-source nature, but the support, especially in terms of footprints for non-common parts, is less than with Eagle.

Even with the ability to make SMT-capable PCBs, some restrictions on what types of SMT components are used can increase the success rate. For example, in two-terminal components (resistors, capacitors, LED's, etc.) we recommend using nothing smaller than 0603, and to prefer 1206 and 0805 if possible. Smaller components are certainly possible, but dramatically increase the soldering difficulty. For larger components, we recommend that students to not go below a 0.5mm lead pitch, and to not mess with ball grid array (BGA) or QFN/DFN packages that have a set of issues all their own, especially for rework. Packages that have been used with good success include SOIC, SSOP, TSSOP, QFP, LQFP, and TQFP.

Once the PCBs are designed, they must be fabricated. Partly because of the small SMT parts, the circuit traces are typically too fine for easy fabrication in-house. Also, with denser designs using many small components, at least a two-layer board is usually required. Fortunately, with the rise of "maker" interest in PCBs, there are many cost-effective ways to get high-quality small-volume PCBs fabricated. These typically have minimum trace widths/spacing of 6-8 mils in 1oz copper. Some fabrication houses that our students have used include:

- **OSH Park [35]:** This is a popular fabrication service for hobbyists. The cost is $5.00/in$^2$ for a two-layer board and $10.00/in$^2$ for a four-layer board with 6mil minimum width traces and three copies of the board included in that price. Turnaround is around 12-14 days.
- **Advanced Circuits [1]:** This fabrication facility has an option for a single larger two-layer board of up to 60in$^2$ for $33 (four-layer boards are $66). Boards can have 6mil traces, and there is a five-day turnaround.
- **JLC PCB [20]:** This service is based in China, uses 5mil traces on 2-layer boards, and 3.5mil traces on multi-layer boards. The service is very inexpensive and can have very swift turnaround on the order of a week. Without paying for expedited shipping, however, there may be additional shipping delays. A recent deal included 10 copies of a 100x100mm 2-layer board for $2.

## 3.1 Equipment List

A photo of the side of the student lab devoted to SMT assembly and soldering is shown in Figure 1. The following is the list of equipment that we installed in our lab to support assembly and soldering of SMT components on student-designed PCBs (equipment marked with an asterisk is not strictly required for simpler boards and simpler circuits):

- ***Stencil definition:** In order to apply the solder paste only to the pads on the board where components will be soldered, a solder stencil can be cut. This is a stencil, generated by PCB CAD programs, that has holes only where the solder paste should be applied. To convert this Gerber solder-mask description to something that can be cut out of mylar and be used as a stencil we use "gerber2graphtec," a free and open-source conversion program [33].
- ***Stencil cutting:** To actually cut the mylar for the stencil, we use a hobbyist vinyl cutter that is geared to scrapbooking and other crafts. Specifically we have installed a Silhouette CAMEO cutting machine [40]. This consumer-grade cutter costs approximately $270 and easily cuts the 4mil mylar that we use for stencils [42]. These in-house stencils work reasonably well, but most PCB fabrication houses can also provide a thin stainless steel stencil for a modest cost that is even more accurate.
- **Assembly:** To assemble the components onto the board (after the application of solder paste), and for hand-soldering and rework as needed, it is extremely helpful to have an inspection microscope. An inspection scope is a relatively low-powered binocular microscope with a ring light around the lens. There are many microscopes that would work - we chose a "Circuit Zoom Stereo Microscope" from Amscope [2]. Prices depend on features - our scope was around $570.
- ***Soldering Oven:** The reflow soldering action takes place in a reflow oven. While hand soldering is certainly possible, a reflow oven can make the soldering a one-step process. Dwwe have found that small inexpensive bench-top "mini reflow ovens" work well for our lab. We have had good success with small ovens from SMTmax that cost from $550-$900 depending on size [34].
- **Rework:** Even with the most careful schematic design, first-spin PCBs often have issues, and components can also sometimes be damaged in the assembly process or over time and need to be replaced. It's also possible that for some parts of a design hand-soldering is needed for some reason. Because of this, good soldering stations with fine-pitch soldering tips and drag-soldering tips are desirable both for hand-soldering and for rework. We have also found that soldering tweezers - essentially a tweezer with a soldering iron in each arm of the tweezer - are useful for grabbing SMT components for rework. There are many hot tweezers to choose from, and nearly all high-end soldering stations have a hot tweezer option. We have found that the inexpensive tweezers from Circuit Specialists work well at only $90 [17]. Also, For point-specific reflow, it is possible to use a hot-air soldering system. This is essentially a high-temperature small-tipped heat gun. We have used a station from X-tronic that includes both a hot-air system and a fine-pitch traditional soldering iron and starts at around $150 [48].

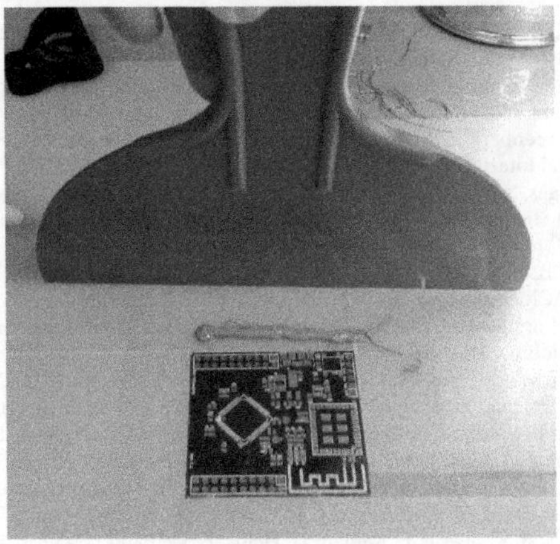

**Figure 7: Plastic putty knife being used to apply solder paste through the stencil.**

- **Other supplies:** Other consumable supplies include solder paste (we like the water washable type [16]), flux pen for hand-soldering and rework [41], blank mylar for stencils [42], and other miscellaneous lab supplies.

# 4 EXAMPLE AND PROCEDURE

This example uses a board that was designed and assembled by undergraduate students Dan Willoughby and Zach Toolson. This is a fairly complex board that is more representative of a senior project board than a maker-workshop board. A simpler board would likely not bother with the solder stencil. The procedure starts with a fabricated PCB. In this case Dan and Zach used KiCad, but any PCB tool will work if it produces Gerber output files. Once the board has been fabricated and the components been acquired, the procedure is as follows:

(1) Either place solder carefully on every solder pad on the PCB, and go to step 8, or create a solder mask (following steps).
(2) Convert the Gerber solder mask layer in your PCB description to a "graphtec" format using gerber2graphitec [33].
(3) Cut a stencil of the converted solder mask on 4mil mylar using an automated cutter such as the Silhouette CAMEO.
(4) Carefully tape the stencil onto the board, lining up the openings over the pads on the board. The inspection scope is very useful in this step to make sure that the openings in the stencil are aligned with the solder pads on the board.
(5) Apply the solder paste near one edge of the board, ready to be deposited on the PCB through the stencil with the squeegee. See Figure 7.
(6) Use a plastic putty knife to squeegee the solder paste across the stencil to apply the paste to the board. We have found that it is best to apply the solder in one steady pass rather than try to move back and forth across the stencil (see Figure 7).
(7) Carefully lift the stencil leaving the solder only on the solder pads of the PCB.
(8) Verify with the scope that each copper pad actually has solder on it. You may need to place a small amount of solder paste on some pads using a toothpick or tweezers. You may also need to remove extra solder paste that is bridging multiple pads. You don't actually have to be perfect here, especially for fine-pitch pads. The reflow process will draw solder to the pads and away from the coated parts of the board.

**Figure 8: Components being placed on the circuit board after the solder paste has been applied.**

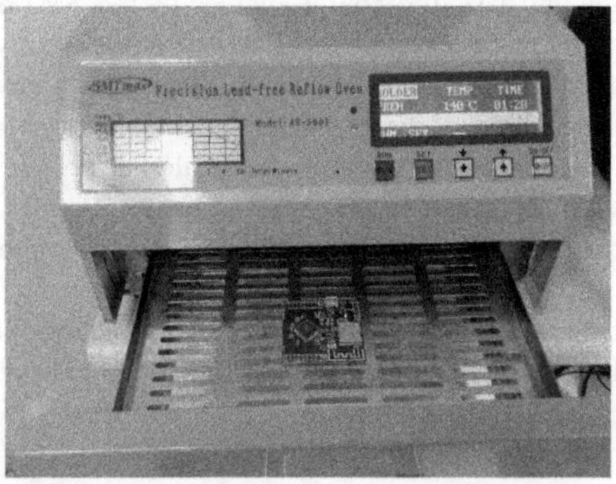

**Figure 9: Board with placed components about to be soldered in the reflow soldering oven.**

(9) Now use regular fine-point tweezers to carefully place the components onto the board, nestling them into the solder paste (Figure 8). The paste is sticky and will hold the components into position. Components should be placed as carefully as possible, but it's all right if they're slightly crooked. When the solder flows during the reflow process surface tension will tend to pull the components into place. The inspection scope is very useful in this step, especially for components with a large number of pins.
(10) Once the components are placed, carefully transfer the board to the reflow oven. Figure 9 shows this board on the oven tray ready to be slid into the oven.
(11) Fire up the oven to go through the reflow process. If your oven is not vented to the outside (ours is not), place a filter fan such as you would use for soldering behind the oven to draw the fumes through the filter. Let the oven cool before removing the soldered board.
(12) Inspect the resulting soldered board using the scope to see if there are any issues before applying power. If there are, use the soldering equipment to rework and fix the issues.
(13) Apply power and enjoy your completed, working board.

## 5 CONCLUSIONS

Prototyping with modern integrated circuits and circuit components essentially requires the ability to deal with SMT components. Fortunately, using these parts with a reflow soldering setup is not all that difficult, or expensive. Certainly care must be taken when using parts with fine pitch leads, or that are physically tiny, but our experience is that this is very feasible in an undergraduate CS lab, and even with non-major or maker-workshop students. A production setup for SMT and reflow would be extremely expensive, but a student lab setup such as described here can be installed for under $2000 Even with a few added extras and upgraded equipment from the basic suggestions in this paper, the cost is unlikely to exceed $3000 for the capital equipment.

We have found that the re-introduction of hands-on system prototyping and assembly that is enabled by this SMT and reflow equipment has made a noticeable difference in the quality and complexity of the projects our students pursue. This allows student projects to develop exactly the board/system they need rather than settle for the board they can buy. It also flexes their design skills to imagine the complete system with all the required components to make the board work. Finally, there is a hard-to-quantify sense of ownership and accomplishment that the students get from deploying their own board in their projects that has seemed to really raise the level of excitement in the lab. This seems to be an essential "maker" capability for modern physical computing.

## ACKNOWLEDGMENTS

Many thanks to our students who have helped develop and debug this flow: Anh Luong, Phillip Bradbury, Nathan Hansen, Brent Mellor, Zach Toolson, Dan Willoughby, and Chase Wilson.

## REFERENCES

[1] Advanced Circuits. 2018. Printed circuit board (PCB) fabrication. (2018). http://www.4pcb.com/.
[2] AmScope. 2018. 3.5X-90X Circuit Zoom Stereo Microscope (SM-4TZ-144). (2018). http://www.amscope.com/.
[3] Chris Anderson. 2012. *Makers: The New Industrial Revolution.* Random House.
[4] F. Anderson, T. Grossman, and G. Fitzmaurice. 2017. Trigger-Action-Circuits: Leveraging Generative Design to Enable Novices to Design and Build Circuitry. In *UIST '17*. ACM.
[5] G. Angello, S. L. Chu, O. Okundaye, N. Zarei, and F. Quek. 2016. Making As the New Colored Pencil: Translating Elementary Curricula into Maker Activities. In *IDC '16*. ACM.
[6] Autodesk. 2018. EAGLE PCB Design Software. (2018). https://knowledge.autodesk.com/support/eagle/learn-explore/caas/sfdcarticles/sfdcarticles/Eagle-Education.html.
[7] T. Barrett, M. Pizzico, B. Levy, R. R Nagel, J. Linsey, K Talley, C. Forest, and W. Newstetter. 2015. A Review of University Maker Spaces. In *ASEE Annual Conference*. Seattle, Washington.
[8] A. Bdeir and T. Ullrich. 2011. Electronics As Material: LittleBits. In *TEI '11*. ACM.
[9] Paulo Blikstein and Dennis Krannich. 2013. The Makers' Movement and FabLabs in Education: Experiences, Technologies, and Research. In *IDC '13*. ACM.
[10] Erik Brunvand. 2013. Electrified Printmaking: Using Conductive Ink to Create Active Images. In *Impact8 conference*. Dundee, Scotland.
[11] E. Brunvand and P. Stout. 2011. Kinetic Art and Embedded Systems: A Natural Collaboration. In *SIGCSE '11*. ACM.
[12] E. Brunvand and P. Stout. 2012. Collaborative Design Experience with Kinetic Sculpture. In *College Art Association (CAA) conference*. Los Angeles, CA.
[13] Leah Buechley and Michael Eisenberg. 2008. The LilyPad Arduino: Toward Wearable Engineering for Everyone. *IEEE Pervasive Computing* 7, 2 (2008).
[14] Leah Buechley and Hannah Perner-Wilson. 2012. Crafting Technology: Reimagining the Processes, Materials, and Cultures of Electronics. *ACM Trans. Comput.-Hum. Interact.* 19, 3 (Oct. 2012).
[15] Varun Perumal C and Daniel Wigdor. 2015. Printem: Instant Printed Circuit Boards with Standard Office Printers & Inks *(UIST '15)*. ACM.
[16] Chip Quik inc. 2017. Solder Paste, no clean, water washable. (2017). http://www.chipquik.com.
[17] Circuit Specialists. 2018. BlackJack SolderWerks 60 Watt Solder Station with Hot Tweezers. (2018). http://www.circuitspecialists.com.
[18] Saul Greenberg and Chester Fitchett. 2001. Phidgets: Easy Development of Physical Interfaces Through Physical Widgets. In *UIST '01*. ACM.
[19] S. Hodges, N. Villar, N. Chen, T. Chugh, J. Qi, D. Nowacka, and Y. Kawahara. 2014. Circuit Stickers: Peel-and-stick Construction of Interactive Electronic Prototypes. In *CHI '14*. ACM.
[20] JLC PCB. 2018. Shenzhen JLC Electronics Co, Ltd. (2018). https://jlcpcb.com.
[21] Joint ACM/IEEE Task Group on Computer Engineering Curricula. 2016. Computer Engineering Curricula. http://www.acm.org/binaries/content/assets/education/ce2016-final-report.pdf. (2016).
[22] Joint ACM/IEEE Task Group on Computer Science Curricula. 2013. Computer Science Curricula. http://www.acm.org/education/CS2013-final-report.pdf. (2013).
[23] Yasmin B. Kafai, Eunkyoung Lee, Kristin Searle, Deborah Fields, Eliot Kaplan, and Debora Lui. 2014. A Crafts-Oriented Approach to Computing in High School: Introducing Computational Concepts, Practices, and Perspectives with Electronic Textiles. *Trans. Comput. Educ.* 14, 1 (March 2014).
[24] Y. B. Kafai, K. Searle, E. Kaplan, D. Fields, E. Lee, and D. Lui. 2013. Cupcake Cushions, Scooby Doo Shirts, and Soft Boomboxes: E-Textiles in High School to Promote Computational Concepts, Practices, and Perceptions. In *SIGCSE '13*.
[25] KiCad. 2018. An open source software suite for Electronic Design Automation (EDA). (2018). http://www.kicad-pcb.org.
[26] André Knörig, Reto Wettach, and Jonathan Cohen. 2009. Fritzing: A Tool for Advancing Electronic Prototyping for Designers. In *TEI '09*. ACM.
[27] P. Koopman, H. Choset, and R. Gandhi et. al. 2005. Undergraduate Embedded System Education at Carnegie Mellon. *ACM Trans. Embed. Comput. Syst.* 4, 3 (Aug. 2005).
[28] Winnie W.Y. Lau, Grace Ngai, Stephen C.F. Chan, and Joey C.Y. Cheung. 2009. Learning programming through fashion and design: a pilot summer course in wearable computing for middle school students. In *SIGCSE '09*. ACM.
[29] Silvia Lindtner, Garnet D. Hertz, and Paul Dourish. 2014. Emerging Sites of HCI Innovation: Hackerspaces, Hardware Startups and Incubators. In *CHI '14*. ACM.
[30] J. Lo, C. Torres, I. Yang, J. O'Leary, D. Kaufman, W. Li, M. Dontcheva, and E. Paulos. 2016. Aesthetic Electronics: Designing, Sketching, and Fabricating Circuits Through Digital Exploration. In *UIST '16*. ACM.
[31] Owen G. McGrath. 2016. Making a Makerspace: Designing User Services to Serve Designing Users. In *SIGUCCS '16*.
[32] David A. Mellis, Leah Buechley, Mitchel Resnick, and Björn Hartmann. 2016. Engaging Amateurs in the Design, Fabrication, and Assembly of Electronic Devices. In *ACM Conference on Designing Interactive Systems (DIS '16)*. ACM.
[33] Peter Monta. 2018. Gerber2graphtec: Cut SMT stencils from gerber files using a Graphtec cutter. Source on GitHub. (2018). https://github.com/pmonta/gerber2graphtec.
[34] Omxie Corp. 2018. Mini automatic reflow ovens (Models AS-5060 and AS-5001). (2018). http://www.smtmax.com/.
[35] OSH Park. 2018. A community printed circuit board (PCB) ecosystem. (2018). https://oshpark.com/.
[36] Dan O'Sullivan and Tom Igoe. 2004. *Physical Computing, Sensing and Controlling the Physical World with Computers.* Course Technology Press.
[37] Jie Qi, Andrew "bunnie" Huang, and Joseph Paradiso. 2015. Crafting Technology with Circuit Stickers. In *IDC '15*. ACM.
[38] Rohit Ramesh, Richard Lin, Antonio Iannopollo, Alberto Sangiovanni-Vincentelli, Björn Hartmann, and Prabal Dutta. 2017. Turning Coders into Makers: The Promise of Embedded Design Generation. In *SCF '17*. ACM.
[39] Jennifer A. Rode, Anne Weibert, Andrea Marshall, Konstantin Aal, Thomas von Rekowski, Houda El Mimouni, and Jennifer Booker. 2015. From Computational Thinking to Computational Making. In *UbiComp '15*. ACM.
[40] Silhouette America, inc. 2018. The Silhouette CAMEO. (2018). https://www.silhouetteamerica.com/shop/machines.
[41] SRA Soldering Products. 2017. SRA #80 Water Soluable Flux Pen. (2017). http://sra-solder.com.
[42] Stencil Ease International, LLC. 2018. 4 mil Blank Mylar Stencil Sheets. (2018). http://www.stencilease.com.
[43] Nick Taylor, Ursula Hurley, and Philip Connolly. 2016. Making Community: The Wider Role of Makerspaces in Public Life. In *CHI '16*. ACM.
[44] N. Villar, J. Scott, S. Hodges, K. Hammil, and C. Miller. 2012. .NET Gadgeteer: A Platform for Custom Devices. In *Pervasive 2012*. Lecture Notes in CS.
[45] C. Wang, H. Yeh, B. Wang, T. Wu, H. Tsai, R. Liang, Y. Hung, and M. Y. Chen. 2016. CircuitStack: Supporting Rapid Prototyping and Evolution of Electronic Circuits. In *UIST '16*. ACM.
[46] Wikipedia. 2017. Reflow Soldering. (2017). http://en.wikipedia.org/wiki/Reflow_soldering.
[47] Wikipedia. 2017. surface-Mount Technology. (2017). http://en.wikipedia.org/wiki/Surface-mount_technology.
[48] X-Tronic International Inc. 2018. X-Tronic Model #4040-XTS Hot Air Rework Station. (2018). http://www.xtronicusa.com/.

# Teaching the Next Generation of Cryptographic Hardware Design to the Next Generation of Engineers

Aydin Aysu
Department of Electrical and Computer Engineering
North Carolina State University, Raleigh, NC, U.S.A
aaysu@ncsu.edu

## ABSTRACT

Evolving threats against cryptographic systems and the increasing diversity of computing platforms enforce teaching cryptographic engineering to a wider audience. This paper describes the development of a new graduate course on hardware security taught at North Carolina State University during Fall 2018. The course targets an audience with no background on cryptography or hardware vulnerabilities. The course focuses especially on *post-quantum cryptosystems*—the next-generation cryptosystems mitigating quantum computer attacks—and evolves into designing specialized hardware accelerators for post-quantum cryptography, executing sophisticated implementation attacks (e.g., side-channel and fault attacks), and building countermeasures on such hardware designs. We discuss the curriculum design, hands-on assignment's development, final research project outcome, and the results obtained from the course together with the associated challenges. Our experience shows that such a course is feasible, can achieve its goals, and liked by the students, but there is room for improvement.

## KEYWORDS

education, hardware security, post-quantum cryptography, FPGA

**ACM Reference Format:**

Aydin Aysu. 2019. Teaching the Next Generation of Cryptographic Hardware Design to the Next Generation of Engineers. In *Great Lakes Symposium on VLSI 2019 (GLSVLSI '19), May 9–11, 2019, Tysons Corner, VA, USA.* ACM, New York, NY, USA, 6 pages. https://doi.org/10.1145/3299874.3317994

## 1 INTRODUCTION

The supply for cybersecurity specialists does not scale with the demand, causing what is known as the *cybersecurity talent gap* [12]. Indeed, the unfilled cybersecurity job openings will triple by 2021 reaching to 3.5 million [6]. There are two main causes for this gap. First, capabilities of adversaries are disproportionately increasing—cybersecurity failures are expected to double in five years causing \$6 trillion annually [6]. Each new vulnerability adds a layer of complexity to the defense framework, which has to mitigate all attacks in the threat model. Second, especially with the rise of the Internet-of-Things (IoT), more computing devices surround us and they are all connected, widening the surface of exploits.

Among cybersecurity exploits, hardware attacks are of growing concern because trusted computing in hardware is fundamental for all information security practices. The basis of security guarantees in digital systems boils down to a set of cryptographic operations executing in a hardware root-of-trust. When this root is compromised, security enforcement mechanisms at higher abstraction levels will inevitably fail. Driven by political or economic agendas, motivated entities are thus targeting the hardware layer with ever-advancing attacks [16]. Meanwhile, such systems are deployed in mobile and IoT context that have limited resources to enforce security.

To take on the daunting task of securing cyberinfrastructure under such circumstances, we need to train a large number of hardware security specialists. This paper describes the development of a new graduate course on hardware security with an emphasis on next-generation cryptosystems. The objective of the course is to provide a breadth of understanding of hardware security and an in-depth comprehension of the implementations of cryptographic hardware, potential exploits, and associated defenses. The challenge of such a course is to cover related concepts in hardware design, applied cryptography, computer architectures, and statistics, among others, while balancing the breadth and depth of relevant subjects.

The method we used was to first introduce the basics of applied cryptography and interleave the teaching of implementation attacks in between as they fit. We design a set of assignments for students to analyze implementation attacks and apply them on real cryptosystems through hands-on experiments. This is accompanied with presenting and discussing key papers on related topics. The course gradually evolves into a self-proposed final research project that tackles an open-ended problem. The breadth is covered towards the second half of the course through instructor-led lectures.

We argue that every electrical and computer engineering department should include a hardware security course. Although such courses have been taught in some universities [8, 9, 11, 13, 15, 17, 20] in US, none have (based on public information) our focus on next-generation cryptographic systems. We share our experience in developing this course and provide useful feedback for future adopters.

## 2 PRELIMINARIES

The title and hence the subject of our course is Cryptographic Engineering and Hardware Security. Hardware security is a broader concept that goes beyond crypto-engineering and studies various ways the hardware can lose trust. While we do recognize such issues, e.g., in hardware Trojans, phyiscal unclonable functions, logic locking, etc., and teach them to provide a breadth of knowledge, the course has a certain focus on efficient and secure implementation of cryptography and specifically post-quantum cryptography. This section provides a background on related subjects.

### 2.1 Implementation Attacks

The standard model of cryptography assumes that the adversaries are limited by the amount of time and computational power available. Under this model, ciphers are build with the premise of making theoretical cryptanalysis computationally infeasible. The standard model, however, does not capture implementation attacks. Such attacks can indeed extract secret information by exploiting hardware behaviors of the computing device while it processes cryptographic functions. These attacks are not necessarily the result of *bad* implementations per se, but they naturally occur due to the way hardware


*GLSVLSI '19, May 9–11, 2019, Tysons Corner, VA, USA*

ACM ISBN 978-1-4503-6252-8/19/05...\$15.00
https://doi.org/10.1145/3299874.3317994

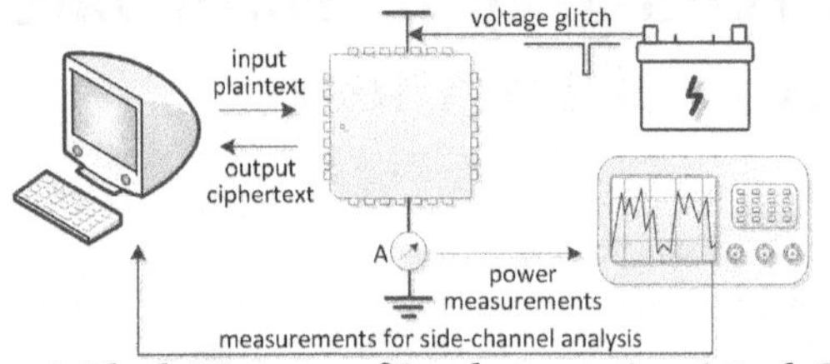


**Figure 1: Block Diagram of Implementation Attack Setup**

fundamentally operates. Straightforward realizations will thus be vulnerable to such attacks unless there is a specific defense.

Implementation attacks are broadly categorized into invasive and non-invasive attacks. While invasive attacks change execution behaviors to achieve its goal, non-invasive attacks simply rely on observing/analyzing execution-related side-effects.

*2.1.1 Non-Invasive Attacks: Side-Channel Analysis.* Side-channel analysis extracts secret information from a physical platform by observing unintentional implementation effects of computations. These attacks break cryptosystems without breaking the mathematical structure of the encryption but instead by analyzing leaks that are correlated with secret key values. Power consumption is major source of hardware vulnerability because CMOS power is data dependent—when a secret key is processed, there is an inherent dependency of the key values and the resulting switching activity.

*Simple Power Analysis* (SPA) is commonly referred to the types of attacks that abuse control-flow variations generated from key-dependent branches. These attacks observe large differences in power characteristics that distinguish a certain sequence of operations from another [10]. *Differential Power Analysis* (DPA), by contrast, can extract small data-flow variations by analyzing many power measurements obtained under the same secret key [10].

*2.1.2 Invasive Attacks: Fault Attacks.* Fault attacks perturb the device behavior and deduce the secret key from faulty executions. The classic example is the attack on RSA signatures where a single fault inserted during modular exponentiation can cause a faulty output that leaks private keys [3]. There are various ways to inject faults into computing devices and exploiting faulty behavior [21].

*2.1.3 Experimental Setup.* Figure 1 outlines a typical experimental setup for side-channel and fault attacks. In side-channel scenario, the target device storing the secret key executes cryptographic operations and the oscilloscope captures the power consumption during these computations. Measurements are then returned with the associated input/output to apply the side-channel attack. In fault attack scenario, the supply voltage is glitched for a short period causing a faulty output, which is analyzed to extract the secret key. Figure 2 depicts the board used in the course to apply side-channel and fault attacks. This setup uses the SAKURA-G evaluation board [7], which includes (circled in white) a Xilinx Spartan-6 FPGA for cryptographic processing, an SMA connection to measure FPGA power consumption, and an external voltage supply pin for voltage glitching.

## 2.2 Post-Quantum Cryptography

Existing public-key cryptosystems like Diffie-Hellman, RSA, DSA, and ECDSA, rely on the difficulty of solving integer factorization or discrete logarithm problems, which are *not* conjectured to be NP-hard and which have polynomial-time quantum solutions [14, 18]. Post-quantum cryptography seeks alternative cryptosystems that are secure against quantum cryptanalysis. These are still classical algorithms that operate on classical computers but they rely on different problems. Among such proposals, *lattice-based cryptography* is a major candidate in which the security can be reduced to NP-hard lattice problems such as the shortest and closest vector problem [1, 5]. These problems, like other NP-hard problems, cannot be exponentially accelerated by quantum or classical computers.

**Figure 2: The SAKURA-G Hardware Security Platform**

# 3 COURSE STRUCTURE AND OVERVIEW

This section gives an overview of the course and describes its structure and schedule. The course targets students with hardware/software coding background—since graduate students typically know how to design software, setting an HDL course as a prerequisite is sufficient. The course does not expect prior knowledge of cryptography or related hardware security issues.

## 3.1 Course Objectives

The primary objective of the course is to develop an understanding of the various issues related to cryptographic engineering and hardware security. We set the learning objectives as follows.

- Develop cryptographic implementations from a given algorithmic/mathematical description and apply prevalent optimization techniques for embedded deployment
- Demonstrate major implementation attacks on cryptographic hardware, and design efficient and effective countermeasures
- Identify state-of-the-art cryptographic primitives and evaluate their use for novel applications
- Analyze key components of trusted computing platforms and vulnerabilities of modern computer architectures

## 3.2 Course Structure

We structure the course with 5 components. We intend to cover both the depth and the breadth of topics through different components—while **regular lectures** provide the breadth, the rest explore the depth. This structure is very similar to a course taught at Virginia Tech [17]. Our main difference is the focus on post-quantum cryptography. The five course components are summarized as follows.

**(1) Regular Lectures** are taught by the instructor or a guest lecturer from academia or industry and cover various topics on hardware security (details in 1). **(2) Course Assignments** are hands-on experiments to design cryptographic hardware and to demonstrate implementation attacks/defenses. **(3) Paper Presentations** allow students to study and present important related concepts not covered during lectures—selection of papers is completed early in the course. **(4) Paper & Presentation Reviews** motivate students to read the papers prior to their presentation; several students are randomly selected at the beginning of the course to review the presenter and the paper. **(5) Final Projects** are self-defined, open-ended research projects testing the usability of student's developed expertise for the future. At the end of the course, students present their final projects and prepare a report in a publication format.

**Table 1: Course Schedule for Fall 2018**

| Week | Days | Topics | Deadline |
|---|---|---|---|
| 1 | 23 Aug | Introduction & Course Overview | |
| 2 | 28/30 Aug | Symmetric-Key Cryptosystems | |
| 3 | 4/6 Sep | Side-Channel Analysis (SCA) – Part I | Paper Select |
| 4 | 11/13 Sep | No lecture: Inclement Weather | |
| 5 | 18 Sep | Public-Key Cryptosystems | Assignment |
| 5 | 20 Sep | Side-Channel Analysis – Part II | I |
| 6 | 25 Sep | Hash Functions | |
| 6 | 27 Sep | Paper Presentations (SCA Attacks) | |
| 7 | 2 Oct | Post-Quantum Encryption – Part I | |
| 7 | 4 Oct | No lecture – Fall Break | |
| 8 | 9 Oct | Paper Presentations (SCA Defenses) | Assignment |
| 8 | 11 Oct | Random Number Generators (RNGs) | II |
| 9 | 16 Oct | Paper Presentations (RNGs + Bit-Slice) | |
| 9 | 18 Oct | Post-Quantum Encryption – Part II | |
| 10 | 23 Oct | Physical Unclonable Functions (PUFs) | |
| 10 | 25 Oct | Paper Presentations (PUFs) | |
| 11 | 30 Oct | Fault Attacks and Countermeasures | Assignment |
| 11 | 1 Nov | Lightweight Cryptography | III-A |
| 12 | 6 Nov | Paper Presentations (Faults + Lightweight) | Assignment |
| 12 | 8 Nov | Hardware Trojans (HT) and Backdoors | III-B |
| 13 | 13 Nov | Project Phase I Presentations | Project |
| 13 | 15 Nov | Trusted Computing Bases (TCBs) | Phase-I |
| 14 | 20/22 Nov | No lecture – Thanksgiving | |
| 15 | 27 Nov | Paper Presentations (HT + TCBs) | |
| 15 | 29 Nov | Micro-Architectural Attacks/Defenses | |
| 16 | 4 Dec | No lecture – Instructor Unavailable | |
| 16 | 6 Dec | Paper Presentations (Micro-Arch. Attacks) | |
| 17 | 18 Dec | Finals: Project Phase II Presentations | Phase-II |

## 3.3 Course Schedule

Table 1 shows the course schedule and the timing of course activities. The course is designed for the 17-week academic semester of the university. The final's week are allocated for the presentation of the final project's results. Paper presentations, which cover an important concept related to the lectures, take place as close as possible to the associated lecture. One challenge with this tight schedule is to leave some redundant time in between to cover instructor unavailability and inclement weather.

## 3.4 Student Background

In the first lecture, we conducted a short survey to assess the background and interests of course participants. The survey consisted of 5 written questions, some asking for a brief description of their background on hardware and cryptography. The class returned 29 filled responses and the majority were anonymous. The mean scores for hardware and cryptography background was respectively 3.1 and 1.4, which meet our expectations. All but 6 students reported that they took at least one course on hardware design; 8 reported that they have industry experience. By contrast, only 5 students have reported a prior knowledge of cryptography. To further probe student's hardware background, we conducted another survey in the second lecture that consisted of 5 basic questions on digital design and HDL. The results align with the self-evaluations: out of the 30 completed reports, 5 students showed a lack of fundamental understanding. Unfortunately, the anonymity of the survey responses does not allow correlating course outcome to prior background.

# 4 ASSIGNMENT DEVELOPMENT & RESULTS

Cybersecurity education should not be purely theoretical. Assignments play a major role in this course as they test the understanding of the core concepts and their real-world applicability. All assignments are hands-on experiments that require building and/or breaking cryptosystems. Assignments prepare students for the final project, where they will use such skills on an open-ended problem.

## 4.1 Assignment I: Differential Power Analysis

The purpose of the first assignment is to provide a practical introduction to power-based side-channel analysis. The assignment asks to apply DPA on the Advanced Encryption Standard (AES). The students are given 10000 power measurements (i.e. time plots, traces) taken during AES Electronic Codebook (ECB) executions running on SAKURA-G with the associated input/output values of AES, and are asked to extract the 128-bit unknown secret key via DPA. Note that the theoretical security of this AES is $2^{128}$ yet the student's goal is to break it in 10000 tests. The students are also not given the AES hardware design but instead require to reverse-engineer the design parallelism from the power profile. Prior to this assignment, DPA and AES are covered in class. The assignment walks students step-by-step through the attack procedure.

We believe that this assignment is a good introduction to cryptographic engineering because it shows how a real implementation using the current encryption standard can truly be vulnerable to implementation attacks in practice. Figure 3 shows the attack results from a submission. All 128-bits (16 bytes) of the secret key are indeed vulnerable to DPA—in all cases, the correlation trace for the correct key byte guess reveals a distinguishable relation with power compared to incorrect guesses. The submissions show that 24 out of 28 students were able to successfully conduct the attack.

## 4.2 Assignment II: Hardware Design of Post-Quantum Public-Key Encryption

The purpose of the second assignment is to let students study a cryptographic algorithm in detail and develop its hardware implementation with proper optimizations. The assignment requires designing an FPGA implementation of the lattice-based Ring-Learning-with-Errors (R-LWE) post-quantum public-key scheme with binary errors. Prior to the assignment, public-key encryption and lattice cryptography (but not the specific algorithm) is covered in the lectures. The students, however, are given very little guidance this time. The assignment simply points to the reference paper [4] and provides a testbench for hardware output verification. The testbench I/O is strictly enforced in the assignment. To impose design-space exploration, half of the groups are forced to design for maximum throughput and the other half to minimum area.

Figure 4 illustrates the outcome of Assignment II. 8 out of 11 groups (of two students) were able to design a stable and functionally correct hardware. The figure summarizes the area-cost (in LUT

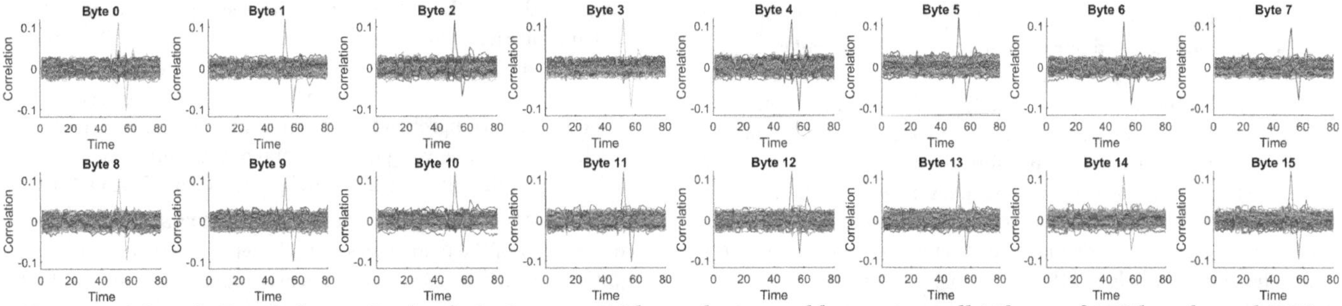


**Figure 3: A Sample Result from a Student's Assignment I. The student was able to extract all 16 bytes of AES key through DPA**

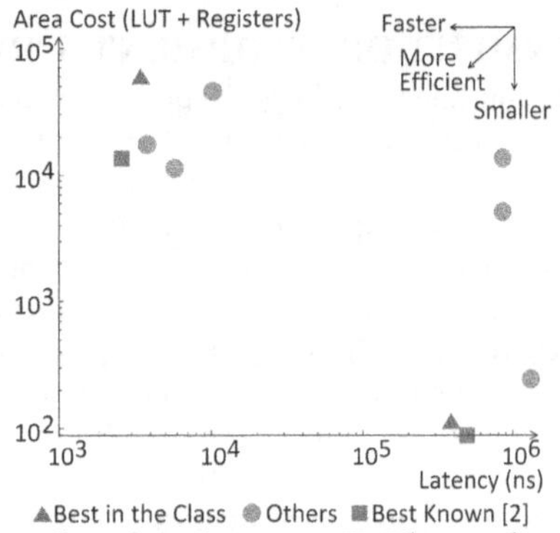


**Figure 4: Results of Assignment II. The quality of the best implementations are close to the published work.**

+ Registers) and the throughput (in Seconds per operation) of those designs and compares it with the best published prior work [2]. The student's designs vary in quality but yield a sufficient coverage of the design space. The results show that some graduate students can achieve almost an expert-level design that is close to the published work—the fastest design is only 25% slower than the previous best and the smallest design is only 27% larger. Given more design time, these designs can arguably reach the same level of optimality.

## 4.3 Assignment III: Implementation Attacks on Post-Quantum Encryption

The purpose of the last assignment is to critically analyze a cryptographic hardware and devise novel implementation attacks. This assignment asks to deploy the post-quantum encryption developed during Assignment II into a real FPGA (on SAKURA-G) and apply implementation attacks to recover the secret key. We want to spark the creativity of the students and let them explore different attacks. Prior to the assignment, the instructor and paper presentations extensively covered fault attacks and such attacks are further incentivized through bonus points. This assignment is organized with groups of 4 and is further broken down into two steps.

*4.3.1 III-A: SAKURA-G Integration and Verification.* During the first step, the students are asked to verify their design running on the FPGA platform. We deliberately design the testbench of Assignment II to match it with the I/O system interface of SAKURA-G. Despite this enforced compatibility and verified simulations, several groups had difficulty integrating their hardware mainly due to wrong interface assumptions and Synthesis/P&R issues. Having groups of 4 allowed students to have two options regarding which design to pursue. We also provided a GUI to control the hardware execution through software: to set or randomly generate inputs and keys, control the number of inputs/measurements, and verify the result in real-time by comparing it to a software emulation.

*4.3.2 III-B: Attacks on the Developed Hardware.* All four groups eventually have gone after SPA vulnerabilities because they are indeed simple to carry out. One group explored applying fault attacks but later pivoted due to fault automation challenges. Figure 5 demonstrate the vulnerability: when the secret key bit is 1, there is considerably more actions during lattice polynomial multiplication (partial product calculation and intermediate sum update) resulting in higher switching activity. Therefore, the secret key can simply be read on the power trace—a post-quantum secure encryption scheme turns out to be surprisingly vulnerable to implementation attacks and this attack can be deduced/conducted by graduate students who had no knowledge of the field two months ago!

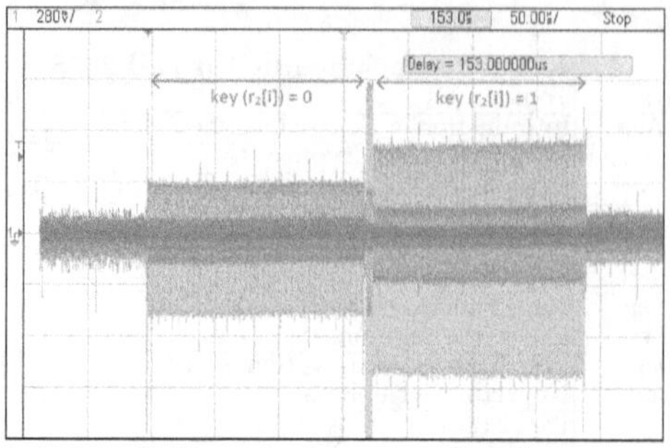

**Figure 5: A Result from Assignment III. The group was able to break the post-quantum cryptosystem through SPA.**

An interesting modification to this assignment could be organizing it in a capture-the-flag style where groups work on breaking each other's implementations—this can be further augmented by making students develop side-channel defenses. We can also request carrying out more attacks to exhaust the SPA option and to inspire groups to investigate other side-channel and fault attacks.

## 4.4 Calibrating Assignment Difficulty

The time requirement for each assignment will be a distribution as there will always be some that will progress faster than the others. During the last lecture, we conducted a written survey and ask students the time they spend on course components. We obtained 15 completed, anonymous responses. The average time spent on Assignment I, II, and III were respectively 13.5, 22.7, and 19.2 hours. Meanwhile, it was 13.3 and 3.8 hours respectively on paper presentation and review. Due to the gap between the last lecture and the final project (see Table 1), we could not get this number for final projects. These numbers may be biased because students that spend more time may already have dropped or withdrawn from the course, but they are consistent: we asked the time spent on Assignment II reports to cross-validate, which revealed an average of 22.9 hours, which is very close to the 22.7 hours obtained in the survey. A result we derive from these numbers is to extend or add another assignment after the first one to balance assignment load.

# 5 COURSE OUTCOME AND ANALYSIS

## 5.1 Final Research Projects

Table 2 presents the final projects pursued by the students ranked in terms of success. 3 projects have accomplished the proposed work, 5 had partial success completing pieces of the project, and 3 have failed to produce any reasonable deliverable. An interesting result of this course component is that all groups, with some guidance, were able to come up with a novel project that can improve the state-of-the-art. The three successful projects can clearly be turned into a research paper with some effort—the first one is a solid work on its own and the other two can be combined to this end. It is not surprising that the best project is done by the same student that achieved the best result in Assignment II. This student used his background on GPU architectures with the topics learned in the class to realize a low overhead side-channel defense for GPU timing side-channels. We emphasize again that these are students had little to no experience on hardware security yet they can be raised to a level not just to comprehend the existing work but to contribute to it. Indeed, we are following up on several of these projects with the goal of submitting them as a research paper during Spring 2019.

## 5.2 Course Participation and Interest

The capacity of the course was initially set to 30 students but this limit was raised to 45 due to increased demand. After the first

**Table 3: Course Evaluation Results**

| # | Question | Grades Given 5 | 4 | 3 | 2 | 1 | Course Statistics Mean | Std | SEM | Nr | Department Statistics Mean | Std | SEM | Nr |
|---|---|---|---|---|---|---|---|---|---|---|---|---|---|---|
| 1 | The instructors teaching aligned with the courses learning objectives/outcomes | 8 | 3 | 0 | 2 | 0 | **4.3** | 1.1 | 0.31 | 13 | **4.3** | 0.9 | 0.03 | 663 |
| 2 | The instructor was receptive to students outside the classroom | 10 | 3 | 0 | 0 | 0 | **4.8** | 0.4 | 0.12 | 13 | **4.4** | 1 | 0.04 | 656 |
| 3 | The instructor explained material well | 4 | 6 | 1 | 2 | 0 | **3.9** | 1 | 0.29 | 13 | **4.1** | 1.1 | 0.04 | 660 |
| 4 | The instructor was enthusiastic about teaching the course | 10 | 3 | 0 | 0 | 0 | **4.8** | 0.4 | 0.12 | 13 | **4.4** | 0.9 | 0.03 | 664 |
| 5 | The instructor was prepared for class | 8 | 4 | 1 | 0 | 0 | **4.5** | 0.7 | 0.18 | 13 | **4.4** | 0.9 | 0.03 | 665 |
| 6 | The instructor gave useful feedback. | 7 | 5 | 1 | 0 | 0 | **4.5** | 0.7 | 0.18 | 13 | **4.2** | 1.1 | 0.04 | 658 |
| 7 | The instructor consistently treated students with respect | 10 | 3 | 0 | 0 | 0 | **4.8** | 0.4 | 0.12 | 13 | **4.5** | 0.9 | 0.03 | 668 |
| 8 | Overall, the instructor was an effective teacher | 6 | 3 | 2 | 2 | 0 | **4** | 1.2 | 0.32 | 13 | **4.2** | 1.1 | 0.04 | 660 |
| 9 | The course materials were valuable aids to learning | 6 | 4 | 1 | 2 | 0 | **4.1** | 1.1 | 0.31 | 13 | **4.2** | 1 | 0.04 | 666 |
| 10 | The course assignments were valuable aids to learning | 8 | 3 | 1 | 1 | 0 | **4.4** | 1 | 0.27 | 13 | **4.2** | 1.1 | 0.04 | 656 |
| 11 | This course improved my knowledge of the subject | 8 | 3 | 0 | 1 | 1 | **4.2** | 1.3 | 0.36 | 13 | **4.3** | 1 | 0.04 | 664 |
| 12 | Overall, this course was excellent | 8 | 3 | 0 | 1 | 1 | **4.2** | 1.3 | 0.36 | 13 | **4.1** | 1.1 | 0.04 | 663 |

Std=Standard Deviation, SEM=Standard Error of Mean, Nr=Number of Responses

**Table 2: Final Research Projects Ranked in Terms of Success**

| # | Final Project Topic | Size | Results |
|---|---|---|---|
| 1 | Masking-inspired side-channel defenses for GPUs | 1 | Success |
| 2 | High-level synthesis of R-LWE decryption | 2 | Success |
| 3 | High-level synthesis of SIMON block cipher | 2 | Success |
| 4 | Enhanced power monitors for remote side-channel attack | 2 | Partial |
| 5 | Novel side-channel attacks on R-LWE encryption | 1 | Partial |
| 6 | Side-channel driven design-space exploration | 2 | Partial |
| 7 | High-level synthesis of PRESENT block cipher | 2 | Partial |
| 8 | Hardware realization of BIKE post-quantum scheme | 2 | Partial |
| 9 | Accelerating memory-hard functions on FPGAs | 2 | Failure |
| 10 | Hardware realization of LOTUS post-quantum scheme | 1 | Failure |
| 11 | Compiler optimizations for lightweight cryptography | 1 | Failure |

week, 42 students were enrolled in the class. This number, however, gradually reduced to 23 after the drop period and withdrawals. 18 out of the 23 enrollments were taking the course with full credits. The average number of enrollment for special topics courses in the department is 13 and our course is ranked 4th out of 14 courses offered during the semester in terms of graduate enrollment—this clearly shows the interest of students to the topic. 5 out of this 23 participants were taking the course as an audit with pass/fail option. This number is significantly high compared to 4 other audits (out of 180) in other special topic courses, which further implies student interest but inability to take the course due to the other coursework.

## 5.3 Course Evaluations

Table 3 summarizes course evaluation scores. Overall, the course is on par and even slightly above average compared to department's statistics. The students rated instructor's feedback, availability, and enthusiasm relatively higher, while grading the teaching effectiveness lower—being instructor's first course, this score is expected to increase in the future iterations. The written comments (reducted for anonymity) can be accessed using the following link: https://www.dropbox.com/s/v8ixbgyws9xlb63/written-comments_Redacted.pdf?dl=0. We further discuss the feedback in Section 6 as they relate to future changes of the course. In addition to the formal evaluations, we also asked students to comment on their likes/dislikes about the course during the last lecture's survey. As the main trend, out of the 15 reported, 9 commented they liked hands-on assignments and 5 stated they disliked (the lack of) the level of depth.

## 5.4 Course Grade Distribution

Table 4 summarizes student's course component scores and the final letter grades. The majority of the participants have succeeded in the assignments, presentations and evaluations thus the deciding factor in the grades has been the final research projects—those who succeeded (or partially succeeded) got significantly better grades. The median letter grade of the class is A-, while the mean is B+ due to a few very low scores. The distribution of A, B, and C grades are respectively 56%, 28%, 16%, which is comparable to the department's Fall 2017 special topics course distribution of 66%, 29%, 5%.

# 6 COURSE CHALLENGES

To help adoption of a similar course, this section discusses the major challenges, potential resolutions, and our future plans.

## 6.1 Participant Demographics

The department's Master of Science in Electrical and Computer Engineering attracts a large number graduate students. This program has a non-thesis option, which is an intensive, three-semester program with a heavy course load. The majority of the course participants belonged to this profile: 16 out of 18 (22 out of 25 counting audits) were in this category, whereas the other 3 students were 1 senior undergrad and 2 PhD candidates. While the students performed competently when given clear tasks with step-by-step instructions, the challenge has been to enforce out-of-the-box thinking with the assignments (which is arguably necessary for cybersecurity) and to impose a research-oriented mindset for the final project. This is reflected in assignment results, where they spent considerably less time in the first assignment, in final projects that failed, and in course evaluations where several students raised concerns about research aspects. The heavy coursework also limits the amount of time this group of students can spend on each course. It would be an interesting study to teach this course exclusively to PhD students *with* master's thesis (i.e., students with some research background and relatively lower course load) and compare their results/reactions with the current group.

## 6.2 First-Time and One-Time Challenges

A major challenge of the course has been finding the right infrastructure and preparing the basic setup to teach hardware security. We have used the SAKURA-G board [7], which is a platform designed especially for side-channel attacks, fault injection attacks, physical unclonable functions and dynamic reconfiguration. This selection enabled us to prepare the assignments with relatively less effort. We did not provide a full automation for the side-channel and fault attacks that can integrate the PC, oscilloscope, voltage supply source, and SAKURA-G, but instead asked students to prepare it for Assignment III-B. Although the automation was successfully developed for the scope of that assignment, it was not sufficient for one final project and caused its failure.

One particular challenge was to obtain a sufficient number of boards from the SAKURA-G providers in Japan in short notice—we were able to initially get 3 boards in three months and 2 more boards afterwards, which led Assignment III to be organized in groups of 4 due to its heavy reliance on measurements. Performing this assignment with groups of 2 (with 12 boards) would have been a better option but would cost an extra $10,500 USD given the $1500 board price. Another option is using the Hardware Hacking Security Education Platform (HaHa) [19] once it becomes commercially available. There is a clear need for cheap, easily-accessible boards sold in US with more extensive hardware/software infrastructure.

**Table 4: Score and Letter Grade Statistics of Participants**

| Component | Max. | Min. | Median | Mean | Std | SEM |
|---|---|---|---|---|---|---|
| Assignment I | 10 | 0 | 10 | 9.04 | 2.86 | 0.12 |
| Assignment II | 10 | 0 | 10 | 8.57 | 2.88 | 0.13 |
| Assignment III-A | 5 | 0 | 5 | 4.78 | 1.04 | 0.05 |
| Assignment III-B | 5 | 0 | 5 | 4.65 | 1.04 | 0.05 |
| Paper Presentations | 20 | 16 | 18 | 18.26 | 1.28 | 0.07 |
| Paper & Presentation Review | 10 | 0 | 9.75 | 8.81 | 2.37 | 0.13 |
| Project Proposal | 15 | 11 | 15 | 13.11 | 1.32 | 0.07 |
| Project Results | 25 | 5 | 20 | 18.28 | 5.84 | 0.32 |
| **Total Socre** | **100** | **71.8** | **90.15** | **87.39** | **8** | **0.44** |
| **Letter Grade** | A+ | C+ | A- | B+ | | |

Std=Standard Deviation, SEM=Standard Error of Mean

## 6.3 Breadth vs. Depth

It is particularly challenging to balance the breadth vs. depth of course topics. On the one hand, introducing new concepts is crucial to make the future system designers aware of common hardware security issues. On the other hand, the depth of knowledge enables working on related concepts after the course. The current emphasis seems to be too much on the breadth—6 out of 8 written evaluation responses comment focusing more on depth rather than breadth. This trend is also visible in our last lecture's survey. One option to resolve this issue is to separate this course into two courses or to set a cryptography course as prerequisite. We do not intend to follow this direction. Another option is to remove some content, e.g., architectural aspects to cover more depth—this may have drawbacks because some students may exclusively be interested in those concepts. If course enrollment grows, it may not be possible to have the paper presentation component so they can be replaced for a more efficient coverage of depth through regular lectures.

## 6.4 Drop/Withdraw/Audit Related Issues

The course's reliance on group work generates a layer of complexity when students drop, withdraw, or change course participation to audit, which may happen without instructor's approval or notice. As a result, group sizes may change, papers may not be presented at the last minute, and the course schedule may alter accordingly. These cases have to be handled in an ad-hoc manner as there currently seems to be no systematic solution. This issue can be due to extended drop/withdraw periods, irregular audit procedures, and having tuition cap that leads students to take more courses early on and drop one later in the semester based on course load.

## 6.5 Planned Future Changes

Based on the lessons learned from the first iteration of this course, we plan to implement the following changes in the next edition.

- To improve it's understanding, we plan to add an assignment on fault attacks towards lattice-based post-quantum (R-LWE) cryptosystems. This can be done after Assignment II.
- We plan to extend Assignment III by asking a defense implementation and more advanced attacks beyond SPA.
- We will reconsider paper presentation component of the course. Due to scheduling challenges and scalability issues, we may replace it with regular lectures on paper's topics.
- We aim to start final projects earlier in the semester and ask for 1 or 2 progress reports. The caveat of this approach is that earlier project proposals can limit the scope since the students have not yet been exposed to several topics.
- We will explore alternatives for the development platform.
- We plan to include several short quizzes to motivate students to further study the course contents in detail.

# 7 CONCLUSIONS AND FUTURE DIRECTIONS

There is a critical need to raise the next-generation of hardware engineers with the awareness of hardware security. To that end, we discussed the curriculum design, assignment development, course organization, and associated challenges of a new course with specific focus on cryptographic engineering for post-quantum systems. We provide a basis for improvement and give recommendations for others who wish to offer a similar course. We strongly emphasize the importance of public/formal discussions, peer-reviewed publications, and collaborations on better establishing such courses. Although we do not discuss it in the scope of this work, a more scalable approach is an online course on hardware security [13], which would definitely have its own unique challenges. Another issue is the lack of a textbook to teach the course.

# 8 ACKNOWLEDGEMENTS

This work was supported in part by the NSF under Grants No. 1850373. Titan Xp GPU used is donated by Nvidia Corporation.

# REFERENCES

[1] Miklós Ajtai. 1996. Generating hard instances of lattice problems. In *Proceedings of the twenty-eighth annual ACM symposium on Theory of computing*. ACM, 99–108.

[2] A. Aysu, M. Orshansky, and M. Tiwari. 2018. Binary Ring-LWE hardware with power side-channel countermeasures. In *2018 Design, Automation Test in Europe Conference Exhibition (DATE)*. 1253–1258.

[3] Dan Boneh, Richard A. DeMillo, and Richard J. Lipton. 2001. On the Importance of Eliminating Errors in Cryptographic Computations. *Journal of Cryptology* 14, 2 (01 Mar 2001), 101–119. https://doi.org/10.1007/s001450010016

[4] Johannes Buchmann, Florian Göpfert, Tim Güneysu, Tobias Oder, and Thomas Pöppelmann. 2016. High-Performance and Lightweight Lattice-Based Public-Key Encryption. In *Proceedings of the 2Nd ACM International Workshop on IoT Privacy, Trust, and Security (IoTPTS '16)*. ACM, New York, NY, USA, 2–9.

[5] O. Goldreich, D. Micciancio, S. Safra, and J.-P. Seifert. 1999. Approximating shortest lattice vectors is not harder than approximating closest lattice vectors. *Inform. Process. Lett.* 71, 2 (1999), 55 – 61.

[6] "Herjavec Group". 2017. *Cybersecurity Jobs Report – 2017 Edition*. Technical Report.

[7] H. Guntur, J. Ishii, and A. Satoh. 2014. Side-channel AttacK User Reference Architecture board SAKURA-G. In *2014 IEEE 3rd Global Conference on Consumer Electronics (GCCE)*. 271–274. https://doi.org/10.1109/GCCE.2014.7031104

[8] Yier Jin. visited on 2018-12-27. http://www.eecs.ucf.edu/~jinyier/courses/EEE4932/

[9] Jens-Peter Kaps. visited on 2018-12-27. https://ece.gmu.edu/~jkaps/teaching.html

[10] Paul Kocher, Joshua Jaffe, and Benjamin Jun. 1999. Differential Power Analysis. In *Advances in Cryptology — CRYPTO' 99*, Michael Wiener (Ed.). Springer Berlin Heidelberg, Berlin, Heidelberg, 388–397.

[11] Farinaz Koushanfar. visited on 2018-12-27. http://eceweb.ucsd.edu/~fkoushanfar/teaching/teaching.html

[12] Brian NeSmith. 2017. The Cybersecurity Talent Gap Is An Industry Crisis. https://www.forbes.com/sites/forbestechcouncil/2018/08/09/the-cybersecurity-talent-gap-is-an-industry-crisis/#3da7cbfca6b3

[13] Jim Plusquellic. visited on 2018-12-27. http://ece-research.unm.edu/jimp/HOST/index.html

[14] John Proos and Christof Zalka. 2003. Shor's Discrete Logarithm Quantum Algorithm for Elliptic Curves. *Quantum Info. Comput.* 3, 4 (July 2003), 317–344. http://dl.acm.org/citation.cfm?id=2011528.2011531

[15] Jeyavijayan Rajendran. visited on 2018-12-27. https://cesg.tamu.edu/all-courses/

[16] Jordan Robertson and Michael Riley. 2018. The Big Hack: How China Used a Tiny Chip to Infiltrate U.S. Companies.

[17] Patrick Schaumont. 2017. Secure Hardware Design - ECE 5520. http://rijndael.ece.vt.edu/schaum//teaching/5520/

[18] P. Shor. 1999. Polynomial-Time Algorithms for Prime Factorization and Discrete Logarithms on a Quantum Computer. *SIAM Rev.* 41, 2 (1999), 303–332. https://doi.org/10.1137/S0036144598347011

[19] Jason Vosatka Shuo Yang and Swarup Bhunia. 2018. Hardware Hacking Security Education Platform (HaHa SEP v2). In *2018 IEEE International Symposium on Hardware Oriented Security and Trust (HOST) – Hardware Demo*. http://www.hostsymposium.org/host2018/hwdemo/HOST_2017_hwdemo_8.pdf

[20] Mark Tehranipoor. visited on 2018-12-27. http://tehranipoor.ece.ufl.edu/hst.html

[21] I. Verbauwhede, D. Karaklajic, and J. Schmidt. 2011. The Fault Attack Jungle - A Classification Model to Guide You. In *2011 Workshop on Fault Diagnosis and Tolerance in Cryptography*. 3–8. https://doi.org/10.1109/FDTC.2011.13

# A Web-based Remote FPGA Laboratory for Computer Organization Course

Han Wan
School of Computer Science and Engineering
Beihang University, Beijing, China
wanhan@buaa.edu.cn

Kangxu Liu
School of Computer Science and Engineering
Beihang University, Beijing, China
liukangxu@buaa.edu.cn

Jiazhen Lin
School of Computer Science and Engineering
Beihang University, Beijing, China
16061018@buaa.edu.cn

Xiaopeng Gao
School of Computer Science and Engineering
Beihang University, Beijing, China
gxp@buaa.edu.cn

## ABSTRACT

Learning in digital systems could be enhanced by applying a learn-by-doing mechanism. In this paper the implementation of a web-based remote FPGA laboratory for Computer Organization course is proposed. The projects created for this course are designed towards entry-level users thus producing a trouble-free virtualization of experimental equipment that in turn maximizes educational gain. The network laboratory had made learners complete all the experimental activities through the Internet without the limitation of time, space and resources. We show also some preliminary results compared between Fall 2016 and Fall 2017 semester, which highlight improved student engagement, learning and achievement.

## CCS CONCEPTS

• **Social and professional topics → Computer engineering education;** • **Hardware → Programmable logic elements.**

## KEYWORDS

Remote FPGA Laboratory; Web-based Laboratory; Digital Systems Education

**ACM Reference Format:**
Han Wan, Kangxu Liu, Jiazhen Lin, and Xiaopeng Gao. 2019. A Web-based Remote FPGA Laboratory for Computer Organization Course. In *Great Lakes Symposium on VLSI 2019 (GLSVLSI '19), May 9–11, 2019, Tysons Corner, VA, USA.* ACM, New York, NY, USA, 6 pages. https://doi.org/10.1145/3299874.3317999

## 1 INTRODUCTION

The Massive Open Online Course (MOOC) had offered rich educational opportunities to millions of learners. Students can learn at their own pace; they could identify and break through misconceptions before moving on to more advanced material.


*GLSVLSI '19, May 9–11, 2019, Tysons Corner, VA, USA*

ACM ISBN 978-1-4503-6252-8/19/05...$15.00
https://doi.org/10.1145/3299874.3317999

MITx's 6.002x on edX [1] had found mechanisms for integrating circuit design problems into online learning platform by using circuit simulation tools, but learners cannot access to physical laboratory equipment due to scaling and physical support issues.

There are a few available examples of remote laboratories like LabVIEW [2] virtual instrumentation, could enable web control and monitoring of the laboratory equipment. Furthermore, engineering students could perform the experiments in real time, from anywhere and whenever is suitable for them and at a reduced cost.

iLab [3] whose architecture provides services for user authentication, authorization, experiment storage, and scheduling. The implementation has been tested successfully by deploying the MIT Microelectronics WebLab in a large undergraduate course involving over 100 students.

The computer system played an important role in the curriculum for computer science major students. In order to understand of computer system more comprehensive and in the systematic view, the knowledge units introduced in the Computer Organization Course should be covered in the experiments. Especially, training the learners to establish a simple processor is a good way to deepen learners' understanding of computer architecture. This work could be broken down into several learning phases, from design the digital circuit basics, to implement a processor which is compatible to a given simplified ISA, and a micro-system that supports the interrupt mechanism and peripheral devices.

American university [4] presented a GUI-based hardware simulator for teaching CPU design. The datapath builder allows microarchitecture building blocks (registers, ALUs, and multiplexors) to be laid out and wired together. And the control builder used a control state machine. Building the online digital circuit laboratory based on simulation has a major shortcoming is that, the performance of cycle accurate simulator could not support a complicated design, such as a pipelined MIPS CPU.

Gabriel [5] integrated the remote laboratory VISIR (Virtual Instrument Systems in Reality) of electronic circuits' practices into their course. The virtual workbench that replicates physical circuit breadboards help in wiring and measuring the electronic circuits remotely. Zhang [6] presented a remote FPGA lab platform designed for computer system curriculum experiments. Both of these practices focus on enabling MOOC students to conduct course experiments with real hardware online.

The structure of the article is as follows: Section 2 reviews our course design and highlights the remote laboratory architecture. Section 3 describes the implementation of the local device cluster. Section 4 elaborates the design of the cloud-based management server. Section 5 presents one laboratory case and show how to complete the experiment with the remote laboratory. Section 6 concludes work.

# 2 BACKGROUND

## 2.1 Course Design

The Computer Organization is a second-year course offered in School of Computer Science and Engineering at Beihang University. In this course, students learn how to design a pipelined MIPS CPU using Verilog-HDL to deepen their understanding of the computer structure. As shown in Fig. 1, we conducted our SPOC (small private online course) based on Open edX platform, where learners could help each other interpret the material and share their interpretations in the discussion forum. Through this distributed learning, participants gain a better understanding of the materials which were published online by the instructors.

Furthermore, students could get immediate evaluation feedback from the platform where we built an external grader to evaluate the digital design automatically. In addition, learners need to modify their homework design to meet the new requirement which is published during the in-class session. For example, they may need to modify their CPU design to support a larger scale MIPS instruction set. If their design passed the automatic online evaluation, learners would have a face to face discussion with the teacher or TA. In addition, we also run the similarity detection to guarantee the learning quality.

Open edX platform helped to record all the activities that learners triggered both at home and in-class, our data processing engine could extract learning related features and store into the database. On the other hand, instructors could analysis the discussion posts and common errors that emerged in the evaluation system, and then improve the online instructional resources. Furthermore, the Q & A process during the in-class session also feedback the weakness in the online tutorial.

As shown in Fig. 2, we adopted Kung-Fu style project-based competency mechanism, before learners move on to do the next project, they must pass the test of current one during the in-class session [7]. There were 9 different projects in each semester, P0-P7 were designed in the simulation environment and learners will operate the FPGA board in P8:

- The first 3 projects help learners to grasp the elementary concepts, including digital components/state machine design, and MIPS assembly language programming. To achieve the above objectives, the graphical tool (Logisim [8]) for logic circuits design and simulation was introduced. In addition, a MIPS simulator (MARS [9]) is used to help in learning assembly language programming. The online instructional materials covered the topics of digital design methodologies and design flows, the Verilog-HDL syntax and its use for digital system specification. The structure of the assignments is composed of the simpler structures of combinatorial logic, sequential circuits, and Finite State Machines(FSMs).

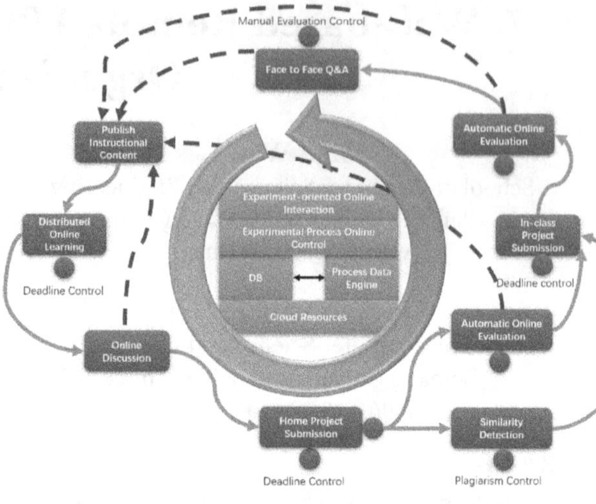


**Figure 1: Blended learning mode based on the Open edX platform.**

- From Project 3 to Project 6, students learn the intermediate concepts about the datapath and control unit design for single-cycle CPU (supporting 8 MIPS instructions) and pipelined CPU (supporting 50 MIPS instructions).
- Learners need to design a micro-system that support interrupt mechanism in P7, and in the final project, they need to implement a micro-system with peripheral devices based on their P7's design. The assignments guided students first to simulate the system behavior using HDL simulators like the ISE simulator [10] accompanied with the waveform viewer. Having verified the correctness of the simulation behavior, learners could download and verify the design on the remote board.

## 2.2 Remote Laboratory Architecture

As shown in Fig. 3, the main components of the proposed remote laboratory system include the local device cluster, the cloud-based management server, and the web interface that could be accessed by learners. First, the local device cluster deployed in the campus network which is composed of several device units. And each unit consists of a host computer and a PCB with two FPGA chips (the Experiment FPGA and the Monitor FPGA). The device cluster is connected with the management server via the Internet. Then, the cloud-based management server undertakes tasks such as user authentication, device monitoring, resource scheduling, and signaling exchange. The web application enables users from external networks to operate the hardware that is located in the campus without a VPN.

# 3 LOCAL DEVICE CLUSTER

As mentioned in Section 2.2, a horizontally expandable cluster is proposed to support the remote laboratory, and each device unit has a unique serial number. It takes advantage of the classic Client-Server (C/S) model to easily scale the laboratory devices. Furthermore, the

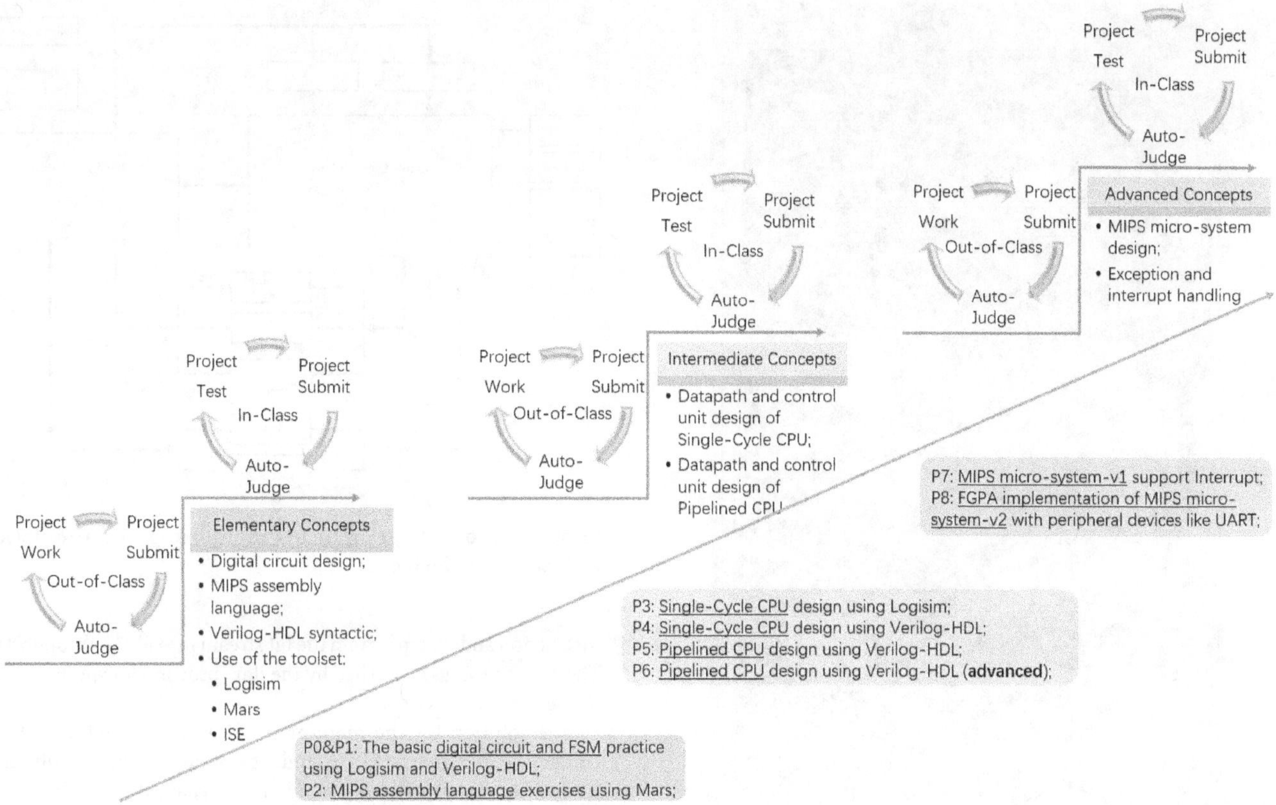


**Figure 2: Kung-Fu style project-based course syllabus.**

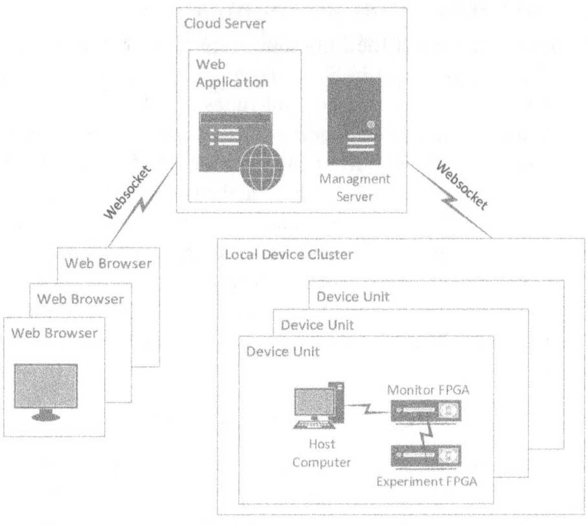


**Figure 3: System architecture of the web-based remote FPGA laboratory.**

system can continue operating without interruption when one or more of device units fail.

As shown in Fig. 4, a device unit consists of an FPGA board, an x86 industrial computer (as a host computer) and a USB serial connector. In our practice, we use a Mini-ITX motherboard, which integrates an Intel Atom D525 (Pineview-D) Dual-Core 1.8GHz (13W) processor along with built-in graphics card and network, to play the role of the host computer. The entire unit is powered by a 12V DC power supply that connected to the host computer, and then a 4-pin connector transfers DC power to the FPGA board. In addition, the motherboard has industrial-grade reliability and can operate stably for a long time in a high-temperature environment.

To support digital system design courses, two FPGA chips are placed on the customized FPGA board, one is the Xilinx Spartan-6 XC6SLX100 and the other one is the Xilinx Spartan-6 XC6SLX16. The XC6SLX100 works as the experiment FPGA for learners to explore their designs. And the XC6SLX16 acts as the monitor FPGA, which is in charge of programming the experiment FPGA, simulating inputs, and sampling peripheral signals. As can be seen from the photography, there are empty pads on the FPGA board which are reserved for peripherals such as LEDs, digital tubes, DIP switches, and buttons. In earlier versions, we installed these peripherals on the PCB to verify that if their physical state is consistent with the data collected by the monitor FPGA. And we leave those pads empty to reduce cost and increase yield.

Communication between the FPGA board and the host computer is handled by the connector in Fig. 4. We uses a single-channel

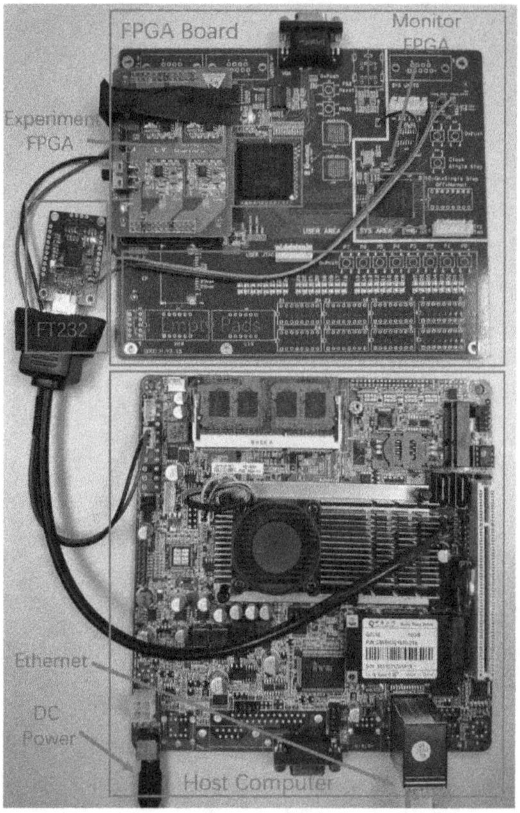


Figure 4: A set of laboratory hardware, including an FPGA board, a host computer and the FT232 connector between them.

FT232 module to allow the host computer to transmit data frames over the USB port to the UART interface of the monitor FPGA.

## 3.1 Remote Programming

The usual way to program an FPGA in the laboratory is to use a Xilinx Platform Cable USB. Under the guidance of Xilinx iMPACT tool, it's easy for college students to complete the FPGA configuration process. We came up with two solutions to achieve low-cost programming of FPGAs.

First of all, we show our solution for the experiment FPGA, which needs to be programmed at the beginning of each experiment. As far as we know, the iMPACT is using standard JTAG (Joint Test Action Group) protocol to program and debug FPGAs. Every fully compliant JTAG device includes a shift register composed of boundary scan cells, a 5-pin (TCK, TMS, TDI, TDO, and TRST) Test Access Port (TAP), and a state machine controller. For programming the experiment FPGA without iMPACT, when we drive the TMS pin low and toggle the TCK pin, the state machine will go to "Run-Test/Idle" state. Then, we use a similar way to drive the state machine to "SHIFT-IR" state and send the instruction OPCODEs through TDI pin. After that, the state machine is turned into "SHIFT-DR" state and TCK pin is toggled to receive the device IDCODE. After inquiring the Device ID, we can send CFG_IN (configuration input)

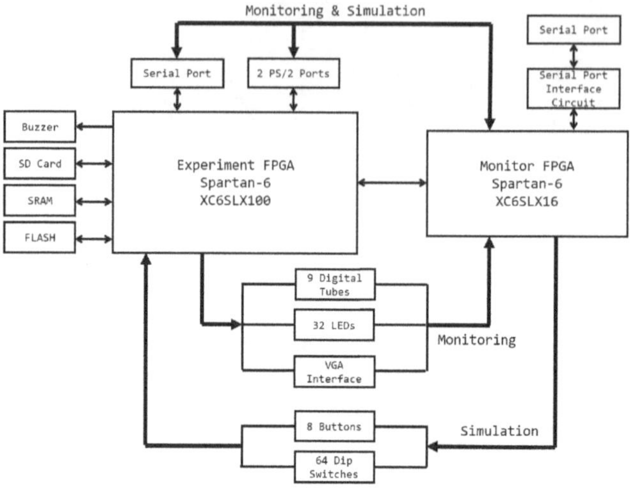


Figure 5: Block diagram of I/O monitoring and simulation in laboratory device.

instruction and then program the bit stream into FPGA through TDI. The above process is finished by the jtag_proc module programmed in the monitor FPGA.

The solution for the monitor FPGA is elaborated as follows. Unlike the experiment FPGA, it does not need to be reconfigured frequently. Therefore, we placed an external SPI chip (Winbond 25Q80BVSIG, an 8Mb SPI Flash) to configure the monitor FPGA. The loading time of this programming method is longer than using JTAG.

## 3.2 I/O Monitoring and Simulation

The block diagram of the I/O monitoring and simulation of the FPGA board is depicted in Fig. 5. For peripherals that only have output capabilities, such as digital tubes and LEDs, we sample their status at a certain frequency. The message is sent to the host computer by the serial port of the monitor FPGA only when the acquired state changes. The peripheral devices used for input, like buttons and DIP switches, we map the learners' operations on Web interface to pull-ups or pull-downs of the corresponding pins of the experiment FPGA. Furthermore, for two-way interactive peripherals, such as PS/2 and UART, we map the students' input to the experiment FPGA and pass the feedback to the learners through the Web interface.

# 4 CLOUD-BASED MANAGEMENT SERVER

To support the remote laboratory, we conducted a management server on the public cloud platform. The management server supports following functions: user authentication, device monitoring, resource scheduling, and signaling exchange. Fig. 6 illustrates the basic workflow of the management server.

## 4.1 User Authentication

The first step in processing an incoming user request is to verify its identity. In our practice, we integrated the user account of the Open edX platform via OAuth2 protocol. To be specific, we first added

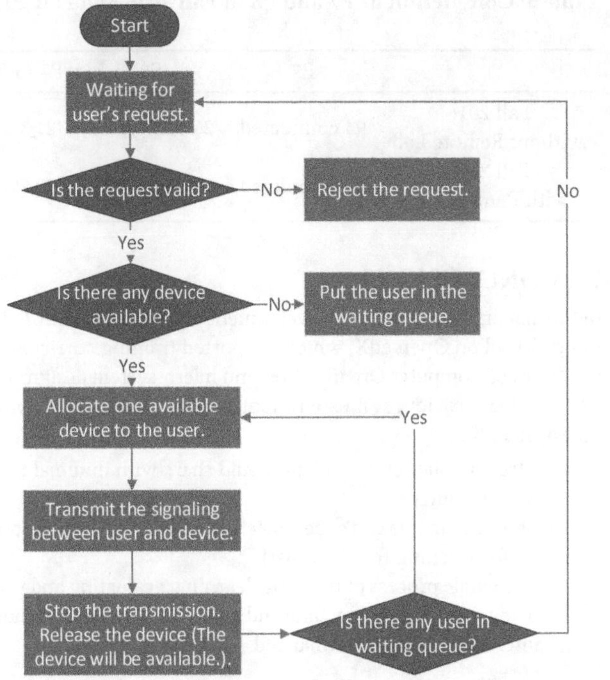


**Figure 6: A flow chart that describing the basic functions of the management server.**

an OAuth2 client in the Open edX admin panel and configured it as a Confidential Client. Second, we redirected unauthorized requests to the OAuth2 authentication page on the Open edX server with a one-time token. Third, if the user successfully logged in to the Open edX platform and granted the laboratory access to his account information, then the user would be redirected back to the management server with his identity, including username, real name, student id, and enrolled courses. Finally, the management server would verify the identity and issue a cookie for the remainder of the session.

## 4.2 Resource Scheduling

Efficiently scheduling the users' demand for devices is one of the core issues of the remote laboratory. Since the number of devices is limited, waiting is inevitable when lots of learners apply for devices at the same time. The key is to ensure the fairness of scheduling and balance the wear of the devices. In our practice, we set up two queues on the management server, one is for the available devices and the other one is for the waiting users. When a device allocation request arrives, if the idle devices' queue is not empty, then the device at the head of the queue will be removed and assigned to the user; otherwise, the request will be pushed into the waiting users' queue. And when a device release event triggered, if there is a request in the waiting users' queue, the device will be assigned to the user at the head of the queue and the request will be removed; otherwise, the device will be pushed into the idle devices' queue. In this way, the load balancing of devices is achieved.

## 4.3 Web Interface

Considering efficiency and browser compatibility, we choose Vue.js to build the front-end of the web interface. In addition, we also use the websocket protocol to connect the browser with the management server. Websocket provides full-duplex communication channels over a single TCP connection. And it has been supported by most major browsers. With the advantage of websocket protocol, data can be sent from server to client at any time, without the client's requesting. As in the remote laboratory, the management server often need to push the status changes of peripherals to browser. Furthermore, it is easy to perform protocol level "ping" to check if the client still alive. It greatly reduces the idle waiting caused by unexpected TCP connection breaks.

# 5 DEMONSTRATION

In this section, we present a laboratory case and show how to use the remote lab to complete the experiment.

## 5.1 Experiment Requirements

*5.1.1 Basic System Environment Implemented in P7.*

- A five-stage pipeline CPU which supports 53 MIPS instructions.
- A bridge which is a kind of address resolution device connects external devices with the CPU, so that the interrupt signal can be sent to CPU and programmers can access the device by using memory accessing instructions.
- A System Control Coprocessor (CP0) is needed to manage exceptions (including interrupt).

*5.1.2 Tasks to Be Completed.*

- Implement a timer that can count upwards from 0 to a specified time interval set by users through the switch group. When the timer reaches the time interval, the timer will be reset and count upwards again. and display counting information using the digital tubes.
- **Input**: Use Switch Group A to set the time interval. From left to right, each switch present one bit of a 32-bit number from high bit to low bit (If one switch is in the high position, it presents one, zero otherwise.).
- **Output**: Display the counting state through 8 8-segment digital tubes. Each tube can present a single-bit hexadecimal number.

## 5.2 Implementation

*5.2.1 External Device.* Implement the following devices using Verilog and connect them to the bridge outside the CPU:

- Digital tubes
- DIP switches and buttons

*5.2.2 MIPS Code.* Develop a MIPS assembly program that can set the timer and jump into a loop waiting for interrupt with an exception handler at 0x00004180 which can handle the interrupt from the timer (counting and set the digital tube state).

The expected result of the remote laboratory is shown in Fig. 7.

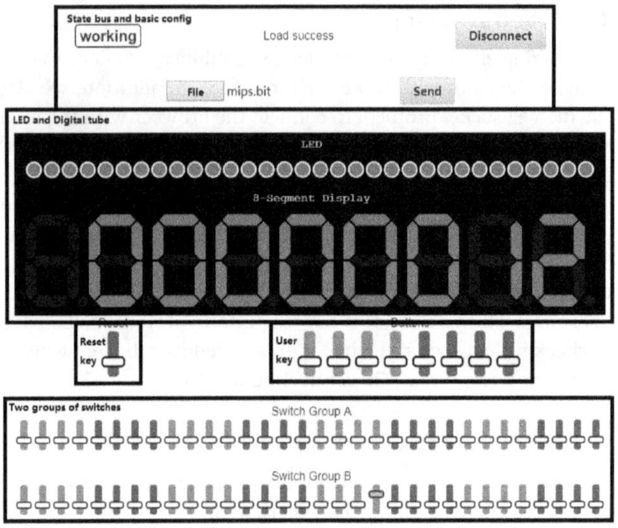


**Figure 7: Expected result of the remote laboratory during the experiment.**

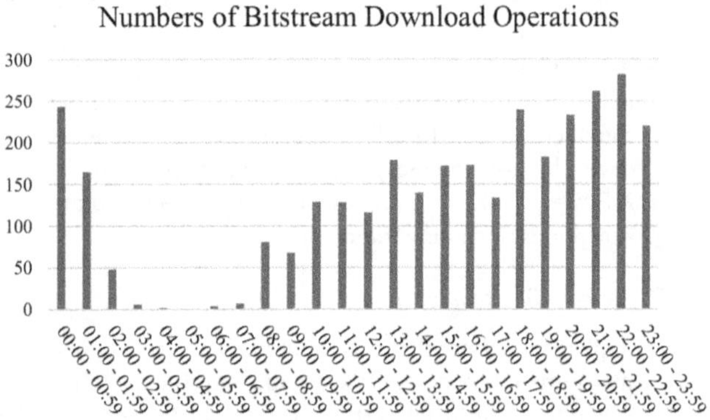


**Figure 8: Distribution of bitstream download operations in two weeks.**

## 6 RESULT AND DISCUSSION

In this section, we discuss the learning behavior observed in teaching practice, and the impact of the remote FPGA laboratory on learning performance.

Fig. 8 shows the distribution of learners' bitstream download operations. Since the first step in conducting FPGA based experiments is to download the bitstream, we use the statistics of this operation to analyze learners' behavior. From Fig. 8, we can see that more students preferred to verify and improve their designs from 18:00 to 01:00. The possible reasons for this phenomenon are that there are more course schedules during the day, or it is easier to find continuous time for project work at night. The remote laboratory allows students to conduct experiments with the FPGA at any time, from anywhere, through the Internet.

And it can be concluded from Table 1 that the enthusiasm of completing P8 was significantly improved in the semester with the remote laboratory.

**Table 1: Completion of P7 and P8 in Fall 2016 and Fall 2017**

| | P7 | P8 | P7 / P8 |
|---|---|---|---|
| Fall 2016 without Remote Lab | 94 completed | 20 completed | 21.3% |
| Fall 2017 with Remote Lab | 55 completed | 28 completed | 50.9% |

## 7 CONCLUSIONS

In this paper, we present the development of a remote FPGA Laboratory based on Open edX, which supported training curricula on the topics of Computer Organization and micro-system design. The advantage of providing an experimental facility with open remote access including:

- Large number of individuals could share with minimal hardware resources;
- The participants can experience real system behavior instead of just learning from simulation;
- The whole process of teaching, learning, evaluating and practicing, is not limited by time and space, and the asynchronous interaction could be enhanced.

## ACKNOWLEDGMENTS

This work was partially supported by the Computer Education Research Association of Chinese Universities (CERACU2019R12) and by the Research & Practice Program of New Engineering Disciplines (Beihang-Tencent Cooperation).

## REFERENCES

[1] P. F. Mitros, K. K. Affidi, G. J. Sussman, C. J. Terman, J. K. White, L. Fischer, and A. Agarwal. Teaching electronic circuits online: Lessons from mitx's 6.002x on edx. In *IEEE International Symposium on Circuits and Systems*, pages 2763–2766, 2013.

[2] S. Chatterji, S. L. Shimi, Amit Kumar Singh, and Anshul Gaur. Web laboratory in instrumentation engineering for distance education using labview. In *Innovation and Technology in Education*, pages 240–244, 2013.

[3] J. Harward, J. Del-Alamo, V. Choudhary, K. DeLong, J. Hardison, S. Lerman, and et al. ilab: A scalable architecture for sharing online experiments. In *International Conference on Engineering Education*, 2004.

[4] M. Black. A hardware simulator for teaching cpu design. In *Proceedings of the 17th ACM annual conference on Innovation and technology in computer science education*, pages 380–380. ACM, 2012.

[5] G. Diaz, F. G. Loro, M. Castro, M. Tawfik, E. Sancristobal, and S. Monteso. Remote electronics lab within a mooc: Design and preliminary results. In *Experiment@ International Conference (exp. at'13), 2013 2nd*, pages 89–93. IEEE, 2013.

[6] Y. Zhang, Y. Chen, X. Ma, Y. Tang, Y. Niu, S. Li, and W. Liu. Remote fpga lab platform for computer system curriculum. In *Proceedings of the ACM Turing 50th Celebration Conference-China*, page 3. ACM, 2017.

[7] H. Wan, X. Gao, and Q. Liu. Hybrid teaching mode for laboratory-based remote education of computer structure course. In *2016 IEEE Frontiers in Education Conference (FIE)*, pages 1–8, Oct 2016.

[8] Logisim a graphical tool for designing and simulating logic circuits. http://www.cburch.com/logisim/.

[9] S. Pete and V. Ken. Tutorial on mars at ccsc-cp. https://courses.missouristate.edu/KenVollmar/mars/tutorial.html. Drury University, Apr. 13-14, 2007.

[10] Ise design suite. https://www.xilinx.com/products/design-tools/ise-design-suite.html.

# System-on-a-Chip Design as a Platform for Teaching Design and Design Flow Integration

Jacob Covey
School of Electrical and Computer Engineering
Purdue University
West Lafayette, Indiana, USA
jcovey@purdue.edu

Mark C. Johnson
School of Electrical and Computer Engineering
Purdue University
West Lafayette, Indiana, USA
mcjohnso@purdue.edu

## ABSTRACT

The design of microelectronic systems requires integration and cooperation across multiple disciplines, but most curriculum is taught in unconnected pieces. This makes the creation of manageable projects that reflect the design experience very difficult. The System-on-a-Chip Extension Technologies (SoCET) group is an undergraduate design group modelled after industry. SoCET is a multi-semester project of primarily undergraduate students in the process of iteratively improving, prototyping, fabricating, and testing an SoC. The group recently taped out its fourth iteration of the SoC and submitted it for fabrication. Students on the SoCET team are divided into smaller groups which focus on specific SoC design tasks. These tasks are connected by a near industry grade design flow forcing students to address system and design flow integration issues. This framework enables students to approach engineering as an integrative process and learn relationships between seemingly separate disciplines.

## KEYWORDS

Design Flow, Engineering Education, Integration, Industry, System-on-Chip, VLSI

**ACM Reference Format:**

Jacob Covey, and Mark C. Johnson. 2019. System-on-a-Chip Design as a Platform for Teaching Design and Design Flow Integration. In *Great Lakes Symposium on VLSI 2019 (GLSVLSI '19), May 9–11, 2019, Tysons Corner, VA, USA.* ACM, New York, NY, USA, 5 pages. https://doi.org/10.1145/3299874.3318000

## 1. INTRODUCTION

A core concept in engineering is the process of integrating knowledge from separate disciplines and combining them in a way that creates something new. But the current approach to engineering education in academia is that education becomes more specific as you progress - this is especially true of a bachelor's degree. Engineering education follows a bottom up procedure in that a student first learns general tools for approaching engineering problems (like math and physics) and then moves on to progressively more specialized "topic-based" courses. This view of education focuses on depth of knowledge and ignores the importance of integration and leaves students with little understanding of how disparate topics within a discipline relate to each other. This important schism in our approach to engineering education is addressed by Bordogna [1] in his keynote speech at the NSF Engineering Education Innovator's Conference:

*"Most curricula require students to learn in unconnected pieces—separate courses whose relationship to each other and to the engineering process are not explained until late in a baccalaureate education, if ever. The content of the courses may be valuable, but this view of engineering education appears to ignore the need for connections and for integration—which should be at the core of an engineering education."*

The SoCET group addresses this issue by providing students a platform to use the depth of information learned in topic-based courses (example: software or analog design) and apply it to a project where it needs to be used in the context of the larger system. Students are separated into subteams that focus on subsystems within the SoC and these subsystems reflect a student's topic-based coursework. Coupled with the design flow students are forced to consider not only how their subsystem will work but how it will work with all other subsystems.

The most recent SoC tapeout was a large design consisting of 338,836 logic gates. A design of this size driven by students is complex and requires a thoughtful process of integration of both the design and design flow. The design flow implemented by SoCET enables the transformation of requirements to a fabricated SoC. It is the connective element that establishes the relationship between separate topics and guides integration.

## 2. OVERVIEW OF SoCET

SoCET is a system-on-a-chip design group consisting of undergraduate and graduate students working together with two supervisory staff and a research assistant. The group is funded by IN3 (Indiana Innovation Institute) and collaborates with Naval Surface Warfare Center – Crane, on the ASSURE (Achieving Scientifically Secured User Reassurance in Electronics) project.


*GLSVLSI '19, May 9–11, 2019, Tysons Corner, VA, USA*

ACM ISBN 978-1-4503-6252-8/19/05…$15.00
https://doi.org/10.1145/3299874.3318000

Students on the team participate for credit, on a volunteer basis or as an intern. The EDA software and IP are hosted on a single server for better control of access to restricted IP.

SoCET in of itself is not a course but is enabled by existing course structures at Purdue University. Students can interact with SoCET through several different avenues.

1. ECE 279, 379 & 479, Vertically Integrated Projects [2] (2 Credit Hours)
2. ECE 479 Vertically Integrated Projects Senior Design (2 Credit Hours x 2 semesters)
3. ECE 496, Electrical and Computer Engineering Projects (1-3 Credit Hours)
4. ECE 49022, Electrical Engineering Senior Design Projects (4 Credit Hours)
5. Volunteer participation
6. Paid undergraduate internship

These options allow students to engage with SoCET continuously over the course of their education. SoCET is a long-term project so this is an important feature for the group. The design, verification, fabrication and testing of a single chip iteration is done over the course of a year or more. Consequently, having students participate for multiple semesters is beneficial to introduce continuity to the project and reduce time-delay due to the setup/training of incoming students.

Students join subteams which are led by either a graduate student or an experienced undergraduate SoCET member. A team leader establishes realistic semester goals and gives students tasks for the semester. In general, it is preferred if a student selects a subteam that reflects their experience but there are no enforced prerequisites. The subteams are divided accordingly:

*Digital Design:* The digital design team is responsible for creating the System Verilog source code which describes the hardware of the SoC.

*Software Design:* The software team is responsible for developing methods and code that test and demonstrate the functionality of the SoC.

*Physical Design*: The physical design team is responsible for the physical implementation of the digital and analog design.

*Verification*: The verification team is responsible for developing the UVM (Universal Verification Methodology) framework to functionally verify the SoC.

*Post Silicon*: The post silicon team handles the packaging, PCB test platform design and fabricated SoC testing.

The students can choose several different kinds of tasks depending on their level of experience and interest. Since this is a long-term project one of these tasks is to continue an already established project that takes longer than one semester to complete. This is generally where inexperienced students start because it builds off an existing knowledge base. A second task would be to start work that we would like to incorporate into SoCET but have not yet begun. The final option would be to propose something new which reflects your interests and can be incorporated into SoCET.

The criteria for which members of SoCET are assessed need to be flexible since tasks are likely to change on a semester basis and different members will be completing entirely different tasks. Another important factor derives from the fact that the project and tasks are open ended. Like industry, students may run into unexpected challenges and the scope of the task may change. For example, a student was trying to integrate an internally designed FPU into the SoC but was unable to complete the task because of changes in the RISC-V ISA standard that still need to be incorporated into the processor core. Ultimately, students are assessed by feedback provided by team leaders on how effectively they are working towards their goal, how well a student documents work and provides evidence of progress, attendance and participation at meetings and a final paper summarizing their completed work and experience.

The project objective of SoCET so far has been to design an SoC that functions as a general-purpose microcontroller and can be customized for more targeted applications. For example, one senior design team is implementing modifications to the RISC-V core, exploiting sparsity to execute light weight machine learning code more efficiently. The flexible architecture of our chip mimics most industrial SoC platforms by incorporating the following elements:

1. External IP
2. Internal IP
3. One or more general programmable processing units
4. A bus system for internal communication
5. Mixed Signal Components

So far, the team has taped out and fabricated four chips, AFT (ASIC Fab & Test) x01 - x04 and is currently developing AFT x05. The architecture of AFT x04 is shown in Figure 1 and the physical layout is shown in Figure 2. The AFTx04 chip included the following features:

1. RISC-V based core, RISC-V Business [3]
2. AHB / APB bus system
3. Debug Unit
4. GPIO module
5. ROM/RAM & memory controller
6. Ring Oscillator

## 3. EVOLUTION OF THE DESIGN FLOW

SoCET students can engage with a project starting from requirements to testing a fabricated part. A high-level structure of the design flow is as follows:

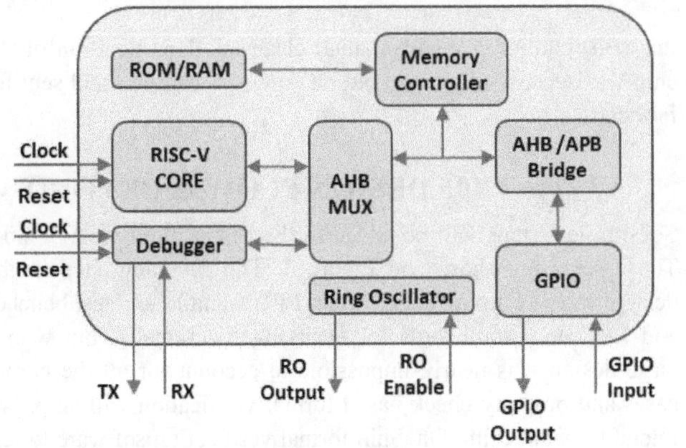


**Figure 1:** *AFT x04 block level architecture*

1. Creation of Requirements
2. IP negotiation and licensing
3. Quality review and identification of existing intellectual property (IP) and external IP for reuse
4. Module Design: HDL, full custom analog, external IP, verification IP, test software
5. Chip Assembly and verification
6. Tapeout
7. Fabrication
8. Packaging and support PCB design
9. Chip bring up on PCB support
10. Evaluation of success

The design flow has evolved over time for two reasons. The first reason is there have been changes in our fabrication facility which required us to switch EDA tools to be compatible with the new design kit. Secondly, as the chip has become more complicated and the group has gained more experience, we have increased how thoroughly our design flow verifies our SoC and enables post-manufacturing test.

## 3.1 AFTX01 – AFTX03 DESIGN FLOW

AFT x01 – x03 used the design flow shown in Figure 3. The first three tapeouts were a process of refining the basic design flow and working out kinks in both the steps and chip design itself.

AFT x01 began as an FPGA project written largely in VHDL. This first iteration of the chip consisted of a Cortex-M0 32-bit CPU, Debug unit, 2D GPU, SRAM memory controller, GPIO, SPI master/slave, full custom bidirectional IO pads and an ARM® AMBA® AHBLite bus matrix.

The source code was verified in two ways – through FPGA emulation and testbenches. The Altera software Quartus II was used to synthesize our source code to an FPGA and verify functionality. Mentor Graphics ModelSim/Questa, an HDL simulator and a core simulation engine respectively, were used with testbenches to verify expected functionality and timing. Next, logic synthesis was performed on the source code to generate a mapped netlist of gates using Synopsys Design Compiler. Again, ModelSim/Questa was used to verify the functionality of the netlist. It is a common issue to see the source

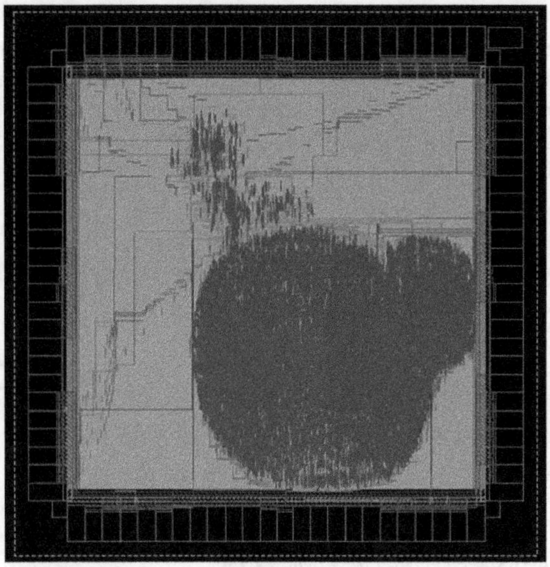

**Figure 2:** *AFT x04 physical layout*

code and the mapped netlist not generating the same output. Once the functionality of the netlist was verified Place & Route (P&R) was performed using Cadence SoC Encounter. For this iteration of the chip P&R was only used on the core. Because the target cell library did not include complete I/O pads, the I/O pad frame was handled separately. Once P&R was successfully performed on the core the new netlist was again verified with testbenches to make sure the output matched the previous netlists. Layout Versus Schematic (LVS), Design Rule Check (DRC), and Parasitic Extraction (PEX) were performed next using a mix of Cadence Assura/Chameleon. For this iteration of the chip full custom I/O pads were created with Cadence Virtuoso. With these pads the pad frame was created manually, and hand connected to the core. With the chip being fully assembled the GDS-II file was created and the chip was sent out for fabrication. The PCB team selected a package for the chip and developed a board for testing.

Chip bring up began and it was immediately obvious that there was an issue with the chip. When power was applied there was a very high current draw. A voltage of 1.2V was only achieved with a current of 2A which induced chip failure. Inspection with a microscope revealed that the high current melted the bonding wires. Continued investigations revealed a catastrophic failure in the DRC of the full custom pads which caused a short between power and ground pads.

AFT x02 was a second attempt at AFT x01 and consequently had the same feature set. The design flow for this iteration of the chip remained the same as AFT x01 except more focus was directed at the manual connection of the pad frame to the core. A more thorough manual inspection of the wiring was used to avoid a short circuit.

Chip bring up began and this time there was no short between power and ground pads. There was also activity on the output pin when using an input clock of (chip frequency)/2. This result was proof that logic formation occurred. Next a serial connection with the debugger was established, and code execution began. There was a delay due to errors on the PCB that ended up being correctable. The final design ended up running at 16.5MHz instead of the designed speed of 50MHz. This was a result of inappropriate timing constraints on the memory interface.

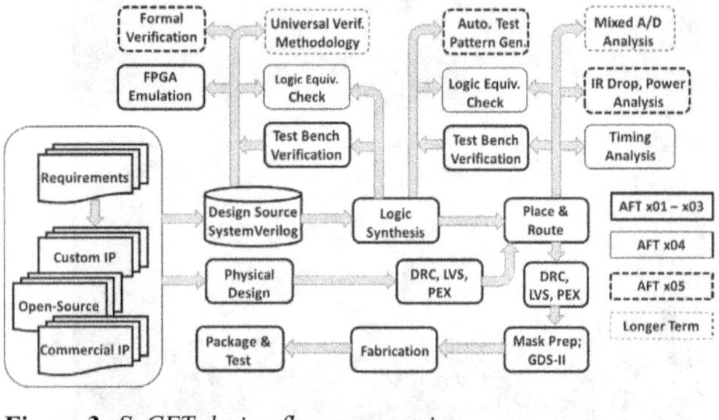


**Figure 3:** *SoCET design flow progression*

AFT x03 also used the same design flow as the prior two tapeouts. This iteration of the chip was more focused on architectural changes. The chip was successfully taped out and fabricated. But only a minimal chip bring up was performed. The choice of package used on this iteration of the chip proved to be especially difficult to mount to a PCB and testing was never completed. Later attempts at testing the chip were also a failure due to new students taking on the task with improper documentation of the package pinout.

## 3.2 AFTX04 DESIGN FLOW

AFT x04 saw a change in design kit and large increase in architectural complexity. Consequently, there needed to be revisions in the design flow to improve verification of the design and switch to EDA tools compatible with the new design kit. The base design flow used in AFT x01 – x03 remained the same except for some changes in EDA tools:

1. Logic Synthesis uses Cadence RTL Compiler
2. Place & Route uses Cadence Innovus
3. LVS, DRC & PEX uses Mentor Graphics Calibre
4. Testbenches use both Cadence NCSim and Mentor Graphics Questa

Figure 3 shows the design flow steps added to AFT x04. The first change in the design flow is the introduction of Logic Equivalency Checking (LEC) using Cadence Conformal. We use LEC to prove that each netlist performs the same function. The next change was that P&R was executed on the entire chip instead of just the core. This was done running a .tcl scrip with Innovus. This script also generated a timing report for the now routed design. This step of the design proved to be very challenging. Innovus was unable to handle a design rule that specified if a wire was longer than a certain length it needed a larger via. This initially resulted in hundreds of thousands of DRC errors. We were able to reduce this to hundreds of errors by setting a parameter that inserted buffers into wires of a certain length. But this still required a lot of manual clean up. This iteration of the chip was successfully taped out on August 19th, 2018 and sent for fabrication.

## 3.3 AFTX05 DESIGN FLOW & BEYOND

Several new steps will be added to the design flow on AFT x05. These steps are shown on Figure 3. The first new step in the design flow is Formal Verification. FPGA emulation, test benches and LEC are useful tools for verifying functionality but with a large design it is nearly impossible to account for all the corner cases and property check based formal verification will help. We intend to begin using OneSpin formal verification software to test our chip. We also would like to include Automatic Test Pattern Generation (ATPG) to create a more exhaustive post-silicon test plan. For this Cadence Modus DFT Software will be used to perform ATPG. Universal Verification Methodology (UVM) will also be integrated into our design. UVM is an industry standard method of functional verification and the scale of our design warrants its usage. Finally, we would like to include IR Drop and Power Analysis using a combination of Cadence Innovus and Voltus.

Figure 3 also shows design flow steps that will be added on to iterations of the chip beyond AFT x05. UVM is time consuming to implement due to a lack of exposure in course work and the scale of the task. So, the process of integrating UVM into the entire SoC will require more tapeouts than AFT x05. Mixed signal simulation will also be needed as we are working to incorporate mixed signal components such as digital to analog and analog to digital converters. In the future we intend to test cloud-based Cadence tools for the backend of our design flow. We also anticipate a shift to a more advanced processing node which would require an even more thorough verification process than we currently use.

## 3.4 DESIGN FLOW CURRICULUM

Prior to working with SoCET students at Purdue are likely to have dealt with some aspect of our design flow in their coursework but nothing to this scale. For example, in ECE 559 MOS VLSI Design (a senior/graduate level design course), students' final projects require transistor level design, layout, and verification of a digital subsystem such as a multiplier. This task involves using Cadence Virtuoso to develop circuit schematics, create layouts, perform LVS, DRC, PEX and test their design with an HSPICE simulator. These steps resemble the physical design steps of our design flow but are only a small portion of our design flow and lack the additional complexity of system level integration.

Another course ECE 337, ASIC Design Laboratory, covers standard cell design of digital circuits using Verilog. Students write source code in Verilog, perform Logic Synthesis using Synopsys Design Compiler and Place & Route using Cadence Innovus. Testbenches are used with Mentor Graphics Questa to verify circuit functionality at different stages of the design flow. This design flow is more extensive than what is seen in a typical course but lacks the complexity, rigorous functional verification, physical verification, and post silicon elements.

## 4. CHALLENGES

This structure of SoCET presents unique integration challenges a student is not likely to experience in a topic-based course. These challenges come in two forms: design integration and design flow integration.

Since SoCET is a multidisciplinary, multi-semester effort with a design flow that guides a project from requirements to testing a fabricated SoC students engage with system integration in a much more unabridged way. The chip designed by SoCET students is larger and more complex than can be completed in a single semester. It integrates analog, digital, software, post-silicon testing, and complex verification. In the bottom up engineering education format each of these topics warrants a single course and consequently are unlikely to be dealt with in the same project. Or at least not to the extent completed here. This type of experience is much more representative of the diverse nature of engineering.

The integration of the design flow is also a unique educational challenge presented by SoCET. Since this design is so large there is a need for a well-established procedure to transform requirements to a fabricated part. It also creates a strong need for a well thought out plan for design verification. This has required students to progressively learn and integrate new EDA tools and verification techniques into our design flow to ensure the function of our fabricated chips as complexity has increased. Courses generally opt to use less complicated forms of verification like testbenches. SoCET enables students to learn and integrate industry standard methods of verification which otherwise might not be experienced until after graduation. Also, unlike other courses this design flow is not a prepackaged part of the course its creation and ongoing development is the work of students.

## 5. STUDENT IMPACT

The original SoC team formed in August 2012. In the seven academic years that have nearly transpired, a total of 100 students have participated in the team either for academic credit, on a volunteer basis, or as part time employment. Many of these students have chosen to participate for multiple semesters, usually initially for academic credit, and later a volunteer basis. On average, students are active in the team for two semesters, but 13 students were active for 3 or more semesters. In fact, two students, now Ph.D. students doing SoC related research, have been on the team for 6 years each. In units of student-semesters, students have participated for a total of 193 student-semesters. The team for spring 2019 has 24 members of which 8 are receiving academic credit, 3 are paid undergraduate interns, and one is a paid research assistant. The remainder are volunteer members.

While it is true that most students on the team will not engage in all aspects of a full EDA flow, students learn how their work contributes to the overall project by virtue of weekly meetings in which the entire team reviews progress, discusses a variety of design/test/verification topics, welcomes guest speakers, and members give presentations and design reviews one to another.

Another indicator of the impact of the SoC team is employment in closely related work. Of the 100 students who have been part of the SoC team, 52 have completed their education. We were able to determine the employment status of 37, primarily by means of LinkedIn profiles. From those 37, 22 are engaged in SoC/VLSI related work, 10 are in software engineering positions, and 5 are in other kinds of engineering positions. Employers of those in SoC/VLSI related positions include Intel (7), IBM (2), Broadcom (2) , Apple (2), Bosch Australia, Cadence, Micron, NXP Semiconductor, Nokia, Northrop-Grumman, Qualcomm, and Texas instruments. One is a professor at the Universidad Industrial de Santandar, Columbia, with a research focus on analog and mixed signal VLSI design.

## 6. CONCLUSION

The multi-semester structure of the SoCET group paired with its integration heavy focus provides a unique solution to integration education. SoCET provides a platform for students to apply knowledge gained from specialized courses and experience a near industry quality microelectronic system design project. The value of this project to students is demonstrated by the extensive volunteer involvement in the project and by the extent to which team alumni continue with SoC related work in industry and academia.

## ACKNOWLEDGEMENTS

This work was supported by IN3 (Indiana Innovation Institute) as a part of the ASSURE (Achieving Scientifically Secured User Reassurance in Electronics) project, contract #17002. Special thanks to Naval Surface Warfare Center – Crane for offering continual guidance and support.

## REFERENCES

[1] Joseph Bordogna, "Next generation Engineering: Innovation through integration," in Proc. NSF Eng. Educ. Innovator's Conf., April 8, 1997, Keynote address.

[2] Coyle, E.J., Allebach, J.P., and Garton-Krueger, J. (2006). The Vertically-Integrated Projects (VIP) Program in ECE at Purdue: Fully Integrating Undergraduate Education and Graduate Research. Proceedings of the 2006 ASEE Annual Conference and Exposition, Chicago, IL.

[3] John Skubic, Jacob R. Stevens, Chuan Tan Yean, Dr. Mark Johnson, and Dr. Matthew Swabey. Riscvbusiness: A configurable, extensible core. Technical report, Purdue University-West Lafayette, 2017.

# UPIM : Unipolar Switching Logic for High Density Processing-in-Memory Applications

Joonseop Sim*, Saransh Gupta*, Mohsen Imani, Yeseong Kim, and Tajana Rosing
University of California San Diego
{j7sim,sgupta,moimani,yek048,tajana}@ucsd.edu

## ABSTRACT

Internet of Things (IoT) has built a network with billions of connected devices which generate massive volumes of data. Processing large data on existing systems requires significant costs for data movements between processors and memory due to limited cache capacity and memory bandwidth. Processing-In-Memory (PIM) is a promising solution to address the issue. Prior techniques that enable the computation in non-volatile memory (NVM) are designed on a bipolar switching mode, which suffers from a high sneak current in a crossbar array (CBA) structure. In this paper, we propose a unipolar-switching logic for high-density PIM applications, called UPIM. Our design exploits a unipolar-switching mode of memristor devices which can be operated in 1D1R structure hence suppresses the sneak current that exists in prior PIM technologies. Moreover, UPIM takes advantages of a 3D vertical crossbar array (CBA) structure to increase memory utilization per unit area for high-density applications. Our evaluation on a wide range of applications shows that the UPIM achieves up to 31.3× energy saving and 113.8× energy-delay product (EDP) improvement as compared to a recent GPGPU architecture. As compared to the state-of-the-art PIM design based on the bipolar switching mode, our design achieves 3.1× lower energy consumption.

## KEYWORDS

PIM; Memristor; Sneak current; Unipolar switching; 3D CBA

**ACM Reference Format:**

Joonseop Sim*, Saransh Gupta*, Mohsen Imani, Yeseong Kim, and Tajana Rosing. 2019. UPIM : Unipolar Switching Logic for High Density Processing-in-Memory Applications. In *Great Lakes Symposium on VLSI 2019 (GLSVLSI '19), May 9–11, 2019, Tysons Corner, VA, USA.* ACM, New York, NY, USA, 4 pages. https://doi.org/10.1145/3299874.3318011

## 1 INTRODUCTION

Many of today's applications face huge challenges to improve their performance, since the amount of data to be processed significantly increases with the emergence of the Internet of Things [1]. Although electronic circuit integration and scaling of semiconductor devices have significantly increased the number of processing units and memory sizes, the limited on-chip memory capacity and memory bandwidth hinder further efficiency improvement on the conventional computing systems [2–4]. Processing-in-memory (PIM) is a promising technique to address the issue of data movement congestion between processing cores and memory by performing essential operations inside the memory, instead of sending all the data to processing cores [5–11]. It can significantly reduce the amount of data transferred between the memory and processing cores, thus accelerating big data applications.

Prior studies show that non-volatile memories (NVMs) have great potential to enable the PIM functionalities by exploiting analog characteristics of the memory devices. High density, lower energy consumption, and scalability of NVMs make them suitable candidates to replace the memories in conventional architectures [12]. For example, the work in [13, 14] proposed a modified sense amplifier to enable bitwise operations. The work in [15–18] support in-memory bitwise operations or arithmetic operations with a few Boolean functions. The existing NVM-based PIM designs enable essential logic functions in a crossbar array (CBA) structure which is suitable for memristor devices due to its small cell size ($4F^2$). However, when applying their techniques to a large CBA structure, there are two main drawbacks. First, most of these designs work with a bipolar switching mode, which is vulnerable to sneak current paths during read and write operations [19]. The sneak current becomes more serious when the array size increases because it increases the number of unselected cells which form undesired sneak current paths. Second, to execute arithmetic operations, e.g., addition and multiplication, they require extra cells to store intermediate computation results with multiple cycles of bitwise operations [6, 18, 20]. This hinders area efficiency for the high-density applications.

In this paper, we propose *UPIM*, a novel processing-in-memory architecture, which enables PIM functions using unipolar-switching mode with 3D-layered structure. The main contributions of this paper include:

- To the best of our knowledge, this is the first work that supports PIM logic with unipolar-switching memristors for the 1D1R cell structure. This design offers a sneak current reduction compared to the existing bipolar-based 1R structure for a high-density CBA.
- We show our proposed design that supports fundamental Boolean operations in the memory, including NOR, NAND, and NOT. They enable PIM-based arithmetic operations, e.g., addition and multiplication.
- We also propose a PIM-enabled 3D vertical crossbar structure to further increase the area efficiency by overlapping the intermediate cells.

Our experimental results show that the proposed design achieves up to 31.3× energy saving and 113.8× EDP improvement, as compared to a recent GPGPU architecture.

## 2 DESIGN OVERVIEW

### 2.1 Memristor Switching Modes

There are two classes of ReRAM switching mode depending on the applied bias polarity. One is 'unipolar', where the switching between high resistance state (HRS) and low resistance state (LRS) is not relevant to the polarity of the operating voltage and the other is 'bipolar', where the reset switching (LRS ⟶ HRS) and set

*Joonseop Sim and Saransh Gupta contributed equally to this research.


ACM ISBN 978-1-4503-6252-8/19/05...$15.00
https://doi.org/10.1145/3299874.3318011

switching (HRS → LRS) take place with the opposite of the bias polarity [21]. Unipolar switching has the following advantages: (i) the symmetric property in polarity which provides an easier implementation in the memory arrays and (ii) reducing the sneak current and write disturb by adding a selector device such as a diode [22]. Consider an M×N array, there are $(N-1)(M-1)$ sneak current paths when a single cell on the black line is intended to be read. Therefore, the total current includes the summation of sneak current with original cell current. The overall sneak current can be represented by Eq. (1) [19].

$$I_{SNEAK} = V_R \times \left( \frac{R_F}{N-1} + \frac{R_R}{NM-M-N+1} + \frac{R_F}{M-1} \right)^{-1} \quad (1)$$

where $V_R$ is the applied voltage, and $R_F$ and $R_R$ are the corresponding resistance when *forward* and *reverse* current flow, respectively. Eq. (1) has a significant implication that since majority of cells have sneak current paths in reverse direction, increasing $R_R$ to rectify the reverse current is a critical requirement to suppress sneak current dissipation. In contrast to most prior work which enables PIM functions in bipolar devices [6, 15, 16, 18], in this paper we propose a unipolar-based logic family which can reduce the sneak current and results in static energy saving. In the following subsections, we explain how the design enables logic functions using unipolar devices.

## 2.2 Unipolar-based logic within NVM

Fig. 1(a) shows the basic structure of the proposed UPIM. To simplify the explanation, we show a logic that supports two-input NOR operation, but it can be extended to multi-input logics in a straight-forward way. Each unipolar device consists of a memristor device and a diode. The input values are stored in two memristors, $R_{IN1}$ and $R_{IN2}$, while the other memresistor, $R_{OUT}$ stores the computation result. The logical values are stored in each memresistor as resistance states in the input/output memristors. HRS in either $R_{IN1,2}$ or $R_{OUT}$ indicates the logical value of 0, while LRS represents 1. In our experiment, we exploit the memristor model in [23], whose $R_{LRS}$ and $R_{HRS}$ are 10KΩ and 10MΩ, respectively. Our logic also has one additional resistor, $R_G$, whose resistance is configurable. In this work, we select $R_G = 300K\Omega$, a value between $R_{LRS}$ and $R_{HRS}$ based on the consideration of process variation. We explain the detailed configuration in Section 3.3. All four resistors are connected to the BL. Fig. 1(b) shows how to set the operation voltage, $V_{IN}$ and $V_{OUT}$, considering $V_{SET}$. In our design, $V_{IN}$ has a lower voltage than $V_{SET}$, and a $V_{OUT}$ is higher than $V_{SET}$.

To perform the NOR operation, our design first initializes the $R_{OUT}$ to $R_{HRS}$. We then apply the $V_{IN1}$ and $V_{IN2}$ voltages to the input memristors and $V_{OUT}$ to the output memristor. Fig. 1(c) shows how the proposed logic performs the NOR operation. In the two-input case, the stored values in the input memristors have four combinations: 00, 01, 10 and 11. When both inputs have high resistance, i.e., '00', the voltage on the BL ($V_{BL}$) is almost pulled into ground, while the voltage across $R_{OUT}$ ($V_{OUT}$-$V_{BL}$) is close to $V_{OUT}$. Since $V_{OUT}$-$V_{BL}$ is larger than $V_{SET}$, it incurs the SET switching of the $R_{OUT}$ to $R_{LRS}$. Note that the applied voltage across the diode is negligible as compared to the voltage applied to $R_{OUT}$ since $R_{OUT}$ is previously initialized as HRS. In all other cases (i.e., 01, 10, and 11), at least one of the input memristors has a low resistance state. Therefore, the $V_{BL}$ voltage has a higher voltage close to $V_{IN}$. For instance, if the case of '10', where $R_{IN1}$ and $R_{IN2}$ have LRS and HRS, respectively, the net resistance is close to $R_{IN1}$. Since the voltage ratio of $R_{IN1}$ to $R_G$ is close to zero, (≈ 0.03 in our experiment), $V_{BL}$ is almost $V_{IN}$. Thus, the $R_{OUT}$

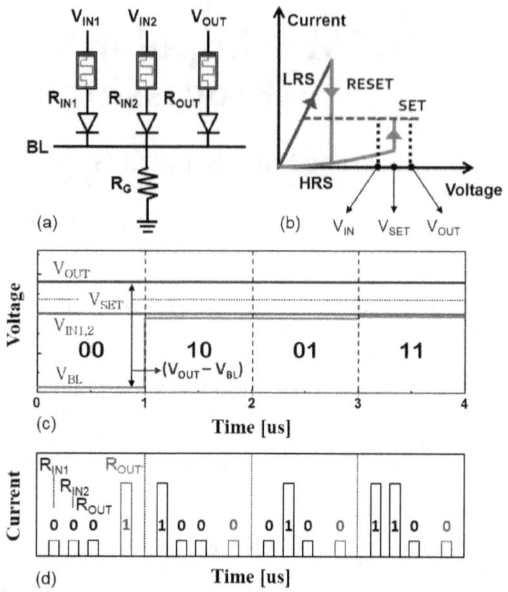


**Figure 1: Proposed unipolar-based NOR logic: (a) Schematic of the NOR gate (b) Voltage conditions (c) NOR gate simulation result (d) Resistance behaviors depending on input states**

keeps the high resistance state representing the logical 0. Fig. 1(d) shows the resistance behavior of the UPIM NOR gate. $R_{OUT}$ and $R_{OUT'}$ indicate resistance states from the output resistor prior to operation and after applying $V_{IN}$, respectively. Except for the case of '00' which the SET switching occurs in $R_{OUT}$, all the other cases keep the $R_{OUT}$ as high resistance state, presenting NOR operation.

## 2.3 Integration to 3D CBA structure

The proposed design executes arithmetic functions using NOR operations. Existing NOR-based approaches require additional cells to store intermediate results. The area overhead due to the generated intermediate states is not suitable for high-density applications. In this work, we utilize a 3D structure to minimize the area cost. Fig. 2(a) shows the conventional 2D logic implemented in a memory array. In this structure, the intermediate operation results are stored in the same plane while consuming an extra cell area. In contrast, as shown in Fig. 2(b), the 3D structure can store the intermediate results in a different layer. Therefore, the intermediate cell is hidden under/over the memory cells, increasing chip density as compared to the 2D case.

Fig. 3 presents the comparison diagram of 2D and 3D cases. We denote the area of memory cells, which is used to store data, by $A_{memory}$. $A_{logic}$ and $A_{shift}$ are the areas of intermediate cells for storing logic results and of the interconnects, respectively. We define *cell efficiency* as the ratio of the memory area over the total area. In the 2D design, since the intermediate cells take chip area, the cell efficiency is represented by $A_{memory}/(A_{memory}+A_{logic}+A_{shift})$. In contrast, for the 3D case, the intermediate cells for all arithmetic logic can be completely stacked on the top of the memory cells. If the number of layers is $n$, the cell efficiency of 3D design is given by $(n \times A_{memory})/(A_{memory}+A_{shift})$. This means that, with the 3D logic stacking, it can achieve high area efficiency.

Fig. 4 shows our integration design of 3D logic-in-memory. The $V_{IN}$ and $V_{OUT}$ are applied to wordlines connected to memory cells and intermediate cells, respectively. For example, if the $V_{IN}$ is applied to 'A' and 'B' cell, the result of NOR operation is stored at a cell where the $V_{OUT}$ is applied. As appeared in the figure, the

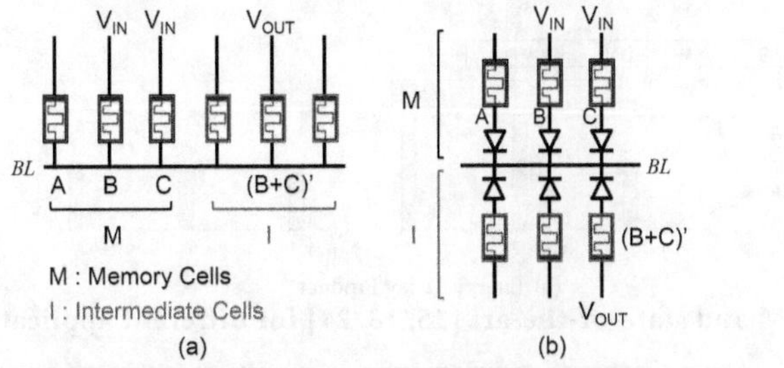


**Figure 2: Schematic of (a) Prior 2D and (b) Proposed 3D logic in memory**

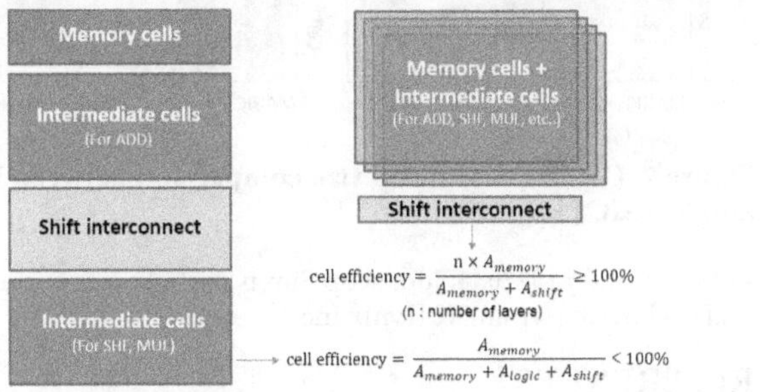


**Figure 3: Diagram of prior 2D (left) and proposed 3D (right) PIM structures**

proposed 3D structure can improve the chip density by storing the intermediate results in a different layer compared to the 2D structure. Moreover, a memory layer and a computation layer are paired and they can be stacked with multiple layers. Therefore, our design enables parallel operation with a single input signal. In the case of Fig. 4, the UPIM NOR operations of A and B, D and E can be executed in parallel with a single PIM operation. Table. 1 summarizes the comparison of the proposed UPIM to existing technologies.

## 3 EXPERIMENTAL RESULTS

### 3.1 Experimental Setup

Performance and energy consumption have been obtained by Cadence Virtuoso and Spectre simulators with 45nm CMOS process technology. We use *VTEAM* memristor model [23] with $R_{LRS}$ and $R_{HRS}$ of 10KΩ and 10MΩ respectively. We implement the diode model with saturation current (*IS*), ohmic resistance (*RS*) and emission coefficient (*N*) for 1.8e-5*A*, 1.43Ω and 1.22, respectively. We compare the efficiency of the proposed UPIM design with AMD R390 GPU and state-of-the-art PIM designs, [15, 18, 24].

### 3.2 Energy and Performance

As discussed in Section 2.1 and 2.2, our unipolar-based logic is operated in the 1D1R structure, which shows lower static power consumption by reducing sneak current dissipation. Fig. 5 shows the energy and energy-delay product (EDP) improvements of running applications on proposed UPIM and state-of-the-art PIM designs [15, 18, 24], which use 1D1R and 1R cell structures, respectively. All results are normalized to energy and EDP of AMD GPU. For each application, the size of the input dataset is fixed to 512MB. In traditional cores, the energy and performance of computation consist of two terms: computation and data movement. In conventional cores, the data movement is restricted by a small cache size of a transitional core which increases the number of cache miss. Consecutively, this degrades the energy consumption and performance of data movement between the memory and caches. In contrast, in PIM architecture the dataset is already stored in the memory and computation is a major cost. Although the memory-based computation is slower than transitional CMOS-based computation (*i.e.* floating point units in GPU), in processing the large dataset, the

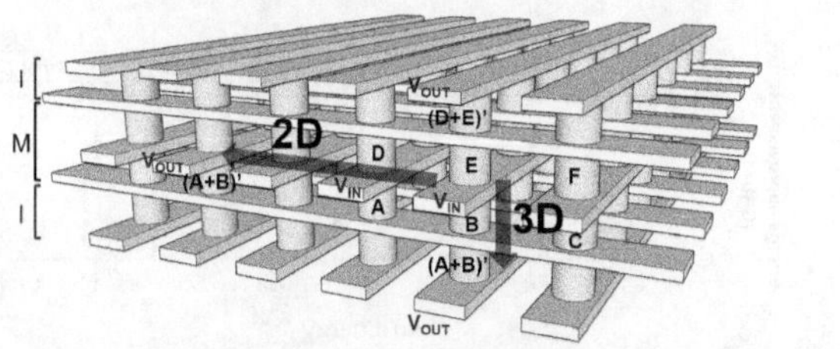


**Figure 4: The integrated structure of 3D UPIM**

**Table 1: performance of proposed UPIM and other technologies**

| | IMPLY [18] | MAGIC [15] | 2D-UPIM | 3D-UPIM |
|---|---|---|---|---|
| Cell Structure | 1R | 1R | 1D1R | 1D1R |
| Condition | $2(V_{cond}, V_{set})$ | $1(V_0)$ | $2(V_{in}, V_{out})$ | $2(V_{in}, V_{out})$ |
| Functions | IMPLY (False) | OR, NOR, NOT, AND, NAND | | |
| Power | High leakage | High leakage | Low | Low |
| Density | Low | Low | Low | High |

PIM works significantly faster than GPU. Our evaluation shows that UPIM achieves 31.3× energy efficiency, and 113.8× EDP improvement as compared to GPU. As compared to the state-of-the-art PIM design based on the bipolar switching mode, UPIM achieves 3.1× lower energy consumption. The higher efficiency of the UPIM comes from its more efficient approach in calculating a single NOR operation as explained in Sec. 2.2.

### 3.3 Process Variation

The UPIM design uses a configurable resistor, $R_G$. To make our design robust, we determine the resistor value with consideration of process variation, which most of today's technology suffers. In our experiment, there are two major factors that induce process variation, memristor dimension, and near-far cell difference. The dimension variation comes from a diameter deviation during lithograph and etching process in the formation of pillar memristors, which results in the resistance variation on UPIM [25]. The resistance variation also occurs between near and far cells in a memory array. We consider the *near-far effect* on the UPIM operations in a mat array with the size of 1Mb as shown in Fig. 6(a). When $R_G$ and $R_{OUT}$ are located on an edge of the mat, the resistance recognized from either $R_G$ or $R_{OUT}$ are different over near and far cells. For example, in the case of the far cells, the BL resistance are added to a memristor resistance. Since $V_{BL}$ is the electrical potential of the point at which $R_G$ meets the BL, $R_{IN}[1023]$ additionally includes the resistance of the BL connected to 1024 cells, while $R_{IN}[0]$ does not have such an effect.

Fig. 6(b) shows $V_{BL}$ characteristic as a function of $R_G$, when input values are 00 and 01, considering the factors of the process variation. All $V_{BL}$ transfer curves are presented with dimension variation of 10%, denoted as (H). As $R_G$ increases, the electrical potential in the BL increases due to an escalation of the voltage applied to $R_G$. $V_{OUT} - V_{BL}$ has to be higher than $V_{SET}$ for the case of 00 and lower than $V_{SET}$ for other cases, i.e., 10,01,11. Thus, the gap between $V_{OUT} - V_{BL}$@10 and $V_{OUT} - V_{BL}$@00 needs to be enough wide for operation stability. The voltage gap, denoted as $V_{BL}$ margin, is tunable by adjusting $R_G$ value. Fig. 6(c) shows the simulation results of the $V_{BL}$ margin for different $R_G$. We extract an optimized $R_G$ point from the graph of $V_{BL}$ margin with an $R_G$. Based on this analysis, we choose the optimal $R_G$ value, $R_{G,OPT}$, by 300KΩ to guarantee computation accuracy, despite existing process instability.

### 3.4 Evaluation for Area Efficiency

We evaluated the area efficiency of our design as compared to the MAGIC [15], a state-of-the-art PIM design. The area efficiency of the PIM techniques is mainly dependent on two factors, i.e., the

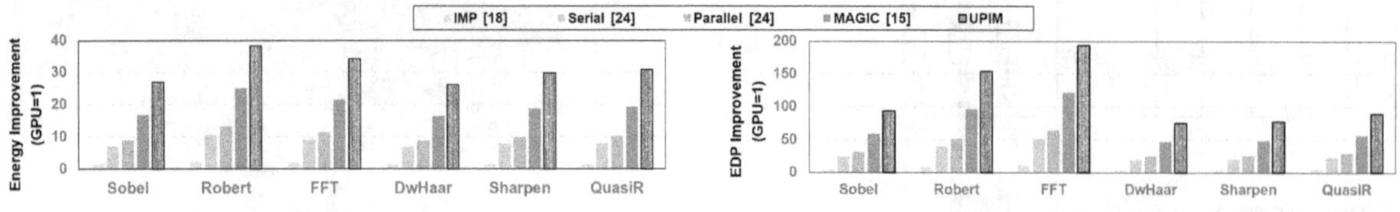


(a) Energy (b) Energy-Delay Product

**Figure 5: Energy and Energy-delay product improvement of UPIM and state-of-the-art [15, 18, 24] for different applications.**

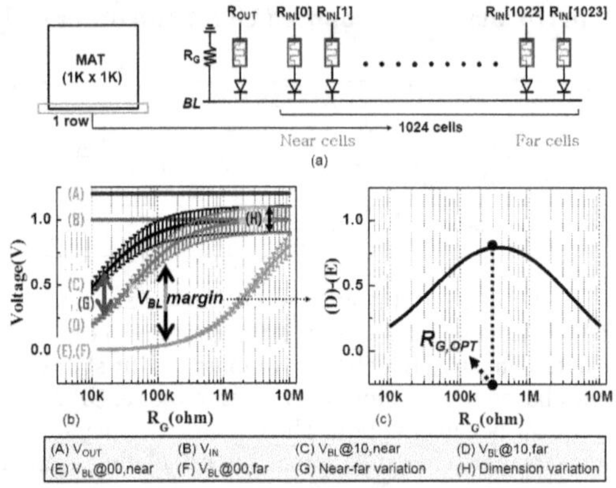


**Figure 6: $V_{BL}$ margin and $R_G$ optimization**

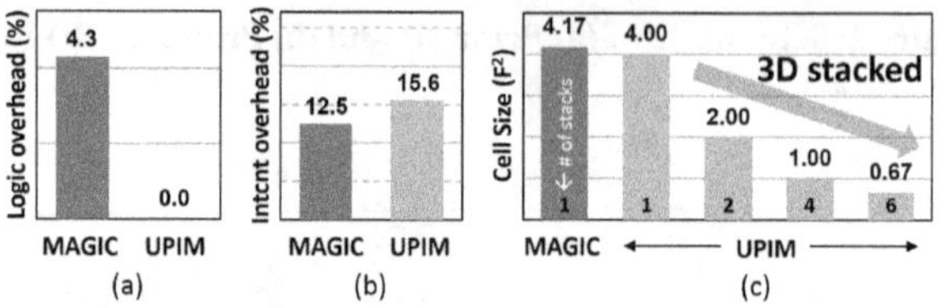


**Figure 7: Overhead and cell size comparison between UPIM and MAGIC [15]**

area overhead for intermediate cells and for interconnects. The two overheads were defined by $A_{LOGIC}$ / $A_{MEM}$ and $A_{INT}$ / $A_{MEM}$ where $A_{LOGIC}$ and $A_{INT}$ are the area of additional cells for logic functions and interconnect design, and $A_{MEM}$ is the area of original memory cells. As shown in Fig 7(a), the UPIM outperforms the MAGIC in terms of the logic overhead. Since the UPIM design stacks the intermediate cells on different layers, it can implement the arithmetic operations, i.e., addition and multiplications, without area penalty for the logic. On the other hand, Fig. 7(b) shows the effect of 3D-stacked structure on integration density for the interconnects. The result shows that the interconnects in the 3D-stacked design require additional overhead for vertical shifts. However, since the UPIM design exploits the vertical transistors for the interconnects, it occupies less area over the conventional planar transistor. This makes the interconnect overhead minimal, i.e., only 3.1% compared to the MAGIC design. Fig. 7(c) shows the area efficiency comparison in terms of the cell size for different 3D stack decisions. Although the cell size difference between UPIM and MAGIC is less than 5% in a single layer, the efficiency increases as more stacks are exploited. For the six-layered structure, the cell size of UPIM reaches $0.67F^2$, which is much less than $4F^2$, considered as the minimum cell size of 2D-based memristor design.

## 4 CONCLUSION

We present an energy efficient and high-density PIM architecture which enables logic-in-memory based on unipolar-switching memristors. The proposed design resolves the static power issue due to the sneak current by implementing the logic in the 1D1R cell structure. Our design also addresses the low cell-density of other PIM technologies due to extra area consumption for storing computation results by implementing them in 3D CBA. The experimental results show that our design presents 3.1× and 31.3× improvement in energy consumption compared to the state-of-the-art PIM designs and the GPU architecture, respectively.

## ACKNOWLEDGMENTS

This work was partially supported by CRISP, one of six centers in JUMP, an SRC program sponsored by DARPA, and also NSF grants #1730158 and #1527034. Joonseop Sim is partially supported by a Ph.D. fellowship from SK Hynix Inc.

## REFERENCES


[1] C. Yang *et al.*, "Big data and cloud computing: innovation opportunities and challenges," *International Journal of Digital Earth*, 2017.

[2] M. Ieong *et al.*, "Silicon device scaling to the sub-10-nm regime," *Science*, 2004.

[3] M. Imani *et al.*, "A framework for collaborative learning in secure high-dimensional space," in *Cloud Computing (CLOUD)*, IEEE, 2019.

[4] G. Dimitroulakos *et al.*, "Alleviating the data memory bandwidth bottleneck in coarse-grained reconfigurable arrays," in *Application-Specific Systems, Architecture Processors, 2005. 16th IEEE International Conference on*, IEEE, 2005.

[5] J. Sim *et al.*, "Lupis: latch-up based ultra efficient processing in-memory system," in *19th International Symposium on Quality Electronic Design (ISQED)*, IEEE, 2018.

[6] S. Gupta *et al.*, "Felix: Fast and energy-efficient logic in memory," in *ICCAD*, pp. 1–7, IEEE, 2018.

[7] M. Imani *et al.*, "Rapidnn: In-memory deep neural network acceleration framework," *arXiv preprint arXiv:1806.05794*, 2018.

[8] M. Zhou *et al.*, "Gas: A heterogeneous memory architecture for graph processing," in *ISLPED*, p. 27, ACM, 2018.

[9] M. Imani *et al.*, "Exploring hyperdimensional associative memory," in *HPCA*, pp. 445–456, IEEE, 2017.

[10] S. Gupta *et al.*, "Nnpim: A processing in-memory architecture for neural network acceleration," *IEEE Transactions on Computers*, pp. 1–1, 2019.

[11] Y. Kim *et al.*, "Orchard: Visual object recognition accelerator based on approximate in-memory processing," in *ICCAD*, pp. 25–32, IEEE, 2017.

[12] L. Chang *et al.*, "Reconfigurable processing in memory architecture based on spin orbit torque," in *2017 IEEE/ACM International Symposium on Nanoscale Architectures (NANOARCH)*, IEEE, 2017.

[13] S. Li *et al.*, "Pinatubo: A processing-in-memory architecture for bulk bitwise operations in emerging non-volatile memories," in *Design Automation Conference (DAC), 2016 53nd ACM/EDAC/IEEE*, IEEE, 2016.

[14] M. Imani *et al.*, "Mpim: Multi-purpose in-memory processing using configurable resistive memory," in *Design Automation Conference (ASP-DAC), 2017 22nd Asia and South Pacific*, pp. 757–763, IEEE, 2017.

[15] S. Kvatinsky *et al.*, "Magic: Memristor-aided logic," *IEEE Transactions on Circuits and Systems II: Express Briefs*, 2014.

[16] M. Imani *et al.*, "Ultra-efficient processing in-memory for data intensive applications," in *the 54th Annual Design Automation Conference 2017*, ACM, 2017.

[17] M. Imani *et al.*, "Floatpim: In-memory acceleration of deep neural network training with high precision," in *ISCA*, ACM, 2019.

[18] E. Lehtonen *et al.*, "Stateful implication logic with memristors," in *Proceedings of the 2009 IEEE/ACM International Symposium on Nanoscale Architectures*, IEEE Computer Society, 2009.

[19] J. Y. Seok *et al.*, "A review of three-dimensional resistive switching cross-bar array memories from the integration and materials property points of view," *Advanced Functional Materials*, 2014.

[20] N. Talati *et al.*, "Logic design within memristive memories using memristor-aided logic (magic)," *IEEE Transactions on Nanotechnology*, 2016.

[21] T.-C. Chang *et al.*, "Resistance random access memory," *Materials Today*, 2016.

[22] E. Amrani *et al.*, "Logic design with unipolar memristors," in *Very Large Scale Integration (VLSI-SoC), 2016 IFIP/IEEE International Conference on*, IEEE, 2016.

[23] S. Kvatinsky *et al.*, "Vteam: A general model for voltage-controlled memristors," *IEEE Transactions on Circuits and Systems II: Express Briefs*, 2015.

[24] A. Siemon, S. Menzel, R. Waser, and E. Linn, "A complementary resistive switch-based crossbar array adder," *IEEE journal on emerging and selected topics in circuits and systems*, vol. 5, no. 1, pp. 64–74, 2015.

[25] F. W. Sears *et al.*, *College physics*. Addison Wesley Publishing Company, 1974.

# Fence-Region-Aware Mixed-Height Standard Cell Legalization

SangGi Do
Design Enablement Team
Samsung Electronics
Hwaseong, Korea
sanggi.do@samsung.com

Mingyu Woo
Electrical & Computer Engineering
UCSD
California, U.S.
mwoo@eng.ucsd.edu

Seokhyeong Kang
Electrical Engineering
POSTECH
Pohang, Korea
shkang@postech.ac.kr

## ABSTRACT

We propose a fence-region-aware mixed-height standard cell legalization that can optimize the placement of standard cells that have more than a two row height in various shapes of the fence region. The algorithm consists of pre-legalization and mixed-height standard cell legalization steps to prioritize cell legalization; then a quality refinement step that uses simulated annealing reduces the displacement. Our proposed method achieved 63% improvement in the average quality score and 72% improvement in average runtime, compared to the winners of the ICCAD-2017 contest.

## CCS CONCEPTS

• **Hardware → Physical design (EDA); Placement;**

## KEYWORDS

Mixed-Height Standard Cell; Detailed Placement; Legalization

**ACM Reference Format:**

SangGi Do, Mingyu Woo, and Seokhyeong Kang. 2019. Fence-Region-Aware Mixed-Height Standard Cell Legalization . In *Great Lakes Symposium on VLSI 2019 (GLSVLSI '19), May 9–11, 2019, Tysons Corner, VA, USA.* ACM, New York, NY, USA, 4 pages. https://doi.org/10.1145/3299874.3318012

## 1 INTRODUCTION

The standard cell method is an efficient and effective approach to integrated circuit design. This method encapsulates the large-scale integration (transistor level) into an abstract logic representation (gate level). This encapsulation decreases the physical design complexity for electronic design automation (EDA). However, in advanced technology nodes, the designs are so complex that conventional standard cells have reached a limit of routability. Thus, a multi-deck standard cell that occupies multiple rows has been proposed for the new technology nodes. This technique can reduce internal wire congestion, shrink the standard cell area, reduce power consumption, and increase optimality of cell assignment compared with the conventional single-deck design. However, this multi-deck design is not yet widely used because it impairs cell legalization.

Cell legalization is the process of ensuring that the circuit design emplaces cells appropriately and in the allotted space. In the standard cell design flow, cell legalization has become difficult because of complicated design rules and design utilization at advanced technology nodes [1]. Furthermore, multi-deck standard cell structure increases the physical design complexity of legalization exponentially.


*GLSVLSI '19, May 9–11, 2019, Tysons Corner, VA, USA*

ACM ISBN 978-1-4503-6252-8/19/05...$15.00
https://doi.org/10.1145/3299874.3318012

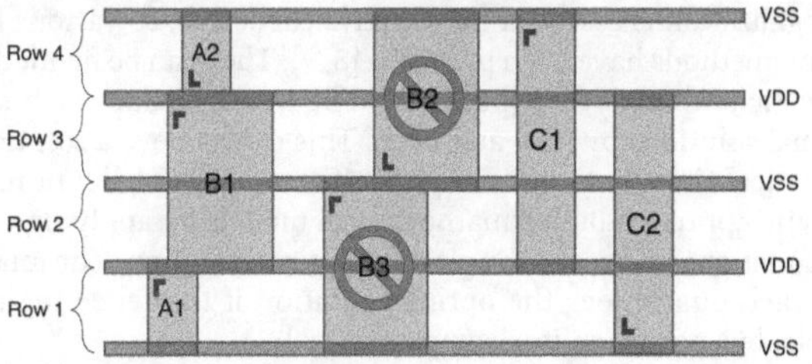


**Figure 1: An example of multi-deck standard cell power alignment. Red bars: Power (VDD); blue: ground (VSS); A1, A2: single row height cells; B1, B2, B3: double row height cells; C1, C2: triple row height cells. B2 and B3 violate power alignment.**

The most important characteristic of the conventional standard cell is that every standard cell has the same height; this strategy greatly simplifies design a chip by EDA methods. However, the multi-deck standard cell has various cell heights and causes problems with power alignment and vertical overlap. The power alignment problem (Fig. 1) for multi-deck standard cells occurs because multi-deck standard cells cannot be flipped to align power.

Vertical overlap is also a problem. The multi-deck standard cells occupy several rows, and therefore can overlap both horizontally and vertically. The fence region further aggravates the legalization problem. In advanced System-on-Chip technology obstacles, such as 3D-IC with Through Silicon Via(TSV), complicate the area in which standard cells can be placed [2]. Thus, the importance of the fence region-aware legalization increases.

Several multi-deck standard cell legalization methods have been proposed recently; they can be categorized as (i) heuristic and (ii) analytic approaches. Heuristic approaches [3, 4] can solve the legalization problem quickly, but cannot guarantee an optimal solution. Analytic methods [5, 6] convert the legalization problem into other well-known problems which can be solved using existing solvers.

In this paper, we propose a multi-deck standard cell legalization method that is aware of fence regions and uses metaheuristic optimization. The proposed method uses multi-stage legalization to achieve a near-optimal solution while maintaining a global placement result. To preserve the global placement result, our proposed method minimizes both maximum cell displacement and total cell displacement. The main contributions of this work are:

- Our proposed method can legalize mixed-height standard cells on a complex fence region.
- Our method achieves a higher quality score and a lower runtime than the top ranked results under the ICCAD-2017 contest benchmarks.
- Our binary has compatibility with *Innovus* and the source code is published as an open source through the *GitHub* [7].

The rest of this paper is organized as follows. Section II briefly explains previous cell legalization studies and their limitations. Section III introduces our proposed method, fence-region-aware multi-deck standard cell legalization. Section IV provides experimental results, evaluation metric and analysis. Section V summarizes the results and concludes the paper.

## 2 RELATED WORKS

Standard cell legalization is an important problem in the placement procedure of physical circuit design. The placement procedure is divided into global placement and detailed placement. Global placement optimizes wire-length, routability, power and other factors, but ignores legalization. Detailed placement legalizes the results of global placement. The objective of standard cell legalization is to align the standard cells and remove overlaps to fit the design rules, while maintaining the global placement result.

Legalization is essential for the physical design, so various legalization methods have been proposed [8, 9]. They can be divided into heuristic and analytic approaches. The heuristic approach seeks optimal solutions by trial-and-error. This can achieve a solution in a practical time, but does not guarantee an optimal solution. The analytic approach builds mathematical models by applying objective functions and seeks the globally-optimal solution. The analytic approach guarantees the optimal solution if the fence region is simple, but not when it is complex (Fig. 2).

**Figure 2: Examples of LCP based multi-deck standard cell legalization. (a) global placement result with a fence region. (b) faulty legalization result obtained using a Linear Complementary Problem with a fence region.**

### 2.1 Single-deck Standard Cell Legalization

Single-deck standard cell legalization considers the case in which every standard cell has the same height. This problem is much easier than multi-deck standard cell legalization. Because of the high complexity of solving analytical models, heuristic approaches are common for standard cell legalization problems. Tetris [8] and Abacus [9] have been widely utilized for single-deck standard cell legalization.

### 2.2 Multi-deck Standard Cell Legalization

Multi-deck standard cell legalization problem is much more complex than single-deck standard cell legalization, because moving a multi-deck cell affects several placement rows concurrently. Thus, heuristic approaches were tried first: Wang et al. [4] extends Abacus, and Lin et al. [10] uses dynamic programming.

However, recent studies use analytic approaches. Hung et al. [6] uses dynamic programming with refinement based on Linear Programming (LP). Chen et al. [5] converts the legalization problem to a Linear Complementarity Problem (LCP). The state-of-the-art is LCP-based legalization. However, this approach is not an effective solution when the fence region exists (Fig. 2b). LCP-based legalization does not consider vertical cell movement, so a significant number of standard cells can violate the fence region. This limitation is exacerbated when space utilization is high.

## 3 PROPOSED ALGORITHM

For the multi-deck legalization, we propose a multi-stage algorithm that consists of three procedures (Fig. 3): pre-legalization, multi-deck standard cell legalization, and quality refinement. The pre-legalization and multi-deck legalization steps prioritize cell legalization; the quality refinement focuses on reducing displacement. First, the pre-legalization step arranges region violation cells

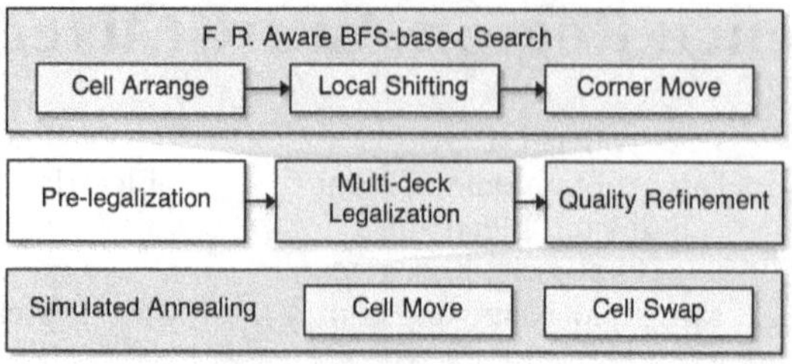


**Figure 3: Overall flow of our proposed algorithm.**

that global placement has put outside of the fence region. Then the multi-deck standard cell legalization step legalizes remaining cells in three small steps; cell arrangement, local cell shifting, and corner weight move. Finally, the quality refinement step uses simulated annealing to reduce the displacement.

### 3.1 Pre-legalization

During the placement stage, hierarchical design has sub-modules; their physical regions can be assigned using EDA tools. Benchmarks from the ICCAD-2017 contest contain various numbers of fence regions [1]. The pre-legalization step (Fig. 4) only legalizes cells that violate a fence region. Displacement of these cells can cause the maximum cell displacement, so we consider them first to minimize the maximum cell displacement. The positions of pre-legalized cells are fixed to preserve the maximum cell displacement quality during the subsequent multi-stage legalization process. The cells that violate regions shrink into or stretch out to the fence region.

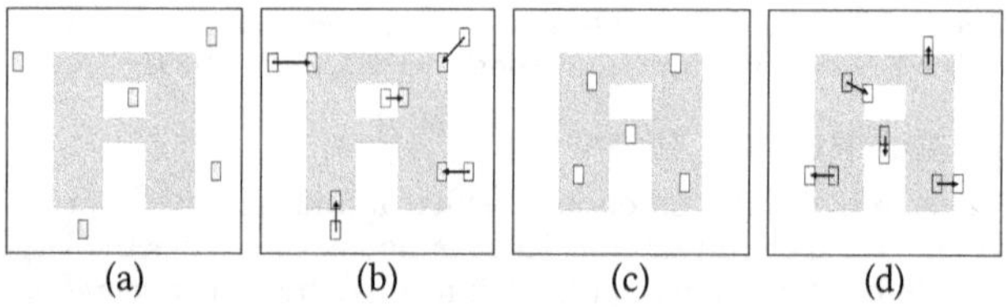


**Figure 4: Examples of pre-legalization. (a) Region-violation cells that are outside the fence region. (b) shrink into the region. (c) Region-violation cells that are inside the fence region. (d) stretch out to the region. Gray cells must be within the A-shaped fence region, and white cells must be placed outside of it.**

### 3.2 Multi-deck Standard Cell Legalization

Multi-deck standard cell legalization consists of three steps: cell arrangement, local cell shifting, and corner weight move. This algorithm finds a nearest available position for the multi-deck standard cell. When the search algorithm cannot find an available position, the local cell shifting algorithm tries to insert the multi-deck standard cell by shifting peripheral cells. When this local cell shifting cannot find an available position, the corner weight move algorithm is required. Legalization complexity of large cells is higher than small cells, so the algorithm sort all cells in descending order of size. Using the sorted result, cell arrangement, local cell shifting, and corner weight move strategies are conducted sequentially.

*3.2.1 Fence-Region-Aware BFS.* Fence-region-aware BFS (FRA-BFS; Algorithm 1) is a core algorithm of the proposed multi-deck standard cell legalization method, and is used in all steps of multi-deck legalization. The concept of the search algorithm comes from previous detailed placement algorithm [11]. Our search algorithm can find a nearest available position by considering moves in both the x- and y directions by using a 2-D grid structure; this ability is an improvement of previous methods, which can only consider movement in the x direction [4–6, 10].

**ALGORITHM 1:** Fence-Region-Aware BFS

```
input  : C ← Target cell, P(x,y) ← Search point coordinates
output : T(x,y) ← Nearest Available Position
1  Define A as available position array.
2  Define G as 2-D grid of circuit by rows and sites.
3  Define G'(s) as a set of encapsulated square region which distance is s from P(x,y).
   (Initial s is zero.)
4  while A is empty do
5      if s is larger than L or out of boundary then
6          return false.
7      end
8      Construct G'(s).
9      for each square region in G'(s) do
10         if square region has an available position for C then
11             Push the available position into A.
12         end
13     end
14     if A is not empty then
15         Find nearest available point T(x,y) from A.
16         return T(x,y).
17     end
18     Increase the search distance s.
19 end
```

FRA-BFS takes target cell $C$ as an input, generates coordinates $P_{(x,y)}$ of the search point, and find the nearest available position $T_{(x,y)}$. For the physical layout, the row height is larger than the site width. Thus, we have constructed the encapsulated square grid $G_0$ which consists of multiple sites (Lines 2-3). For each square in $G_0$, we select a single available position and put it into an available position array (Lines 10-12). $G_0$ has fewer available positions compared to a 2-D grid $G$, so the runtime of FRA-BFS can be reduced. The procedure searches the surrounding area from center to the boundary of $G_0$ until the nearest available position is found (Lines 4-19). In the loop, the search distance is increased when no position is available (Line 18). If the search boundary exceeds the search limit $L$, the procedure stops searching (Lines 5-7). The search limit $L$ is empirically defined by a displacement constraint. If this constraint is not specified, $L$ is the larger of die width and die height.

*3.2.2 Cell Arrangement.* Cell arrangement is the first strategy that moves a cell into the nearest available position from the global placement result. The displacement is the distance between the initial and legalized position, so we should minimize the cell displacement. With the global placement result, we perform FRA-BFS during the cell-arrangement procedure. FRA-BFS has search limits, so it may not find an available position; in that case, the local cell shifting procedure is required.

*3.2.3 Local Cell Shifting.* Shifting a single cell can cause significant cell movements. To solve this problem, the local-cell-shifting algorithm sets a region and rearranges peripheral cells by using the FRA-BFS algorithm. First, a region clip is generated by the size of target cell P (Fig. 5a). The region clip defines the peripheral cells and disallowed area, which is generated from a cell that is partially within the region clip (Fig. 5b). After overlapping cells are collected, peripheral cells are ready for local cell shifting (Fig. 5c). Next, target cell A is placed appropriately and peripheral cells are placed (Fig. 5d). We sort the peripheral cells in descending order of size.

*3.2.4 Corner Weight Move.* This is the final legalization strategy. The failure of cell arrangement and local cell shifting means that the area is densely occupied, so the possible legalization strategy is to minimize the distance between peripheral cells. The corner weight move divides the fence region into four sub-regions, and then in each sub-region the corner weight move shift the cells toward the corner. Cells are moved in ascending order of their distance from the corner. This strategy is effective when the fence regions are densely occupied.

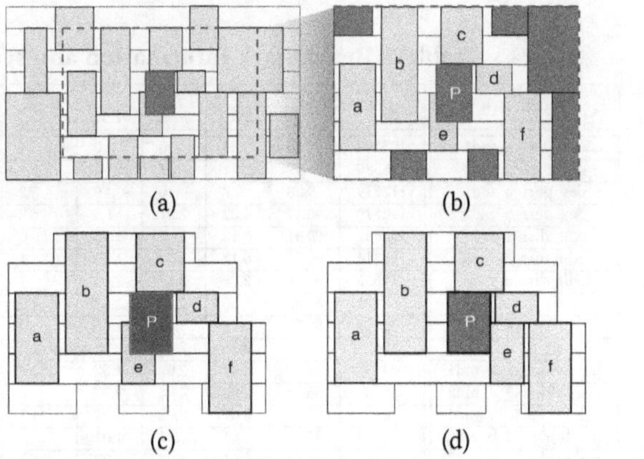


**Figure 5: Example local cell shifting. (a) Region clip is defined by selected cell P. (b) Cell area that is cut off by the region clip is treated as a disallowed area (dark grey), and cells (a to f) within the selected region are treated as movable cells. (c) The initial state is generated by region selection. (d) The peripheral cells are rearranged.**

## 3.3 Quality Refinement

After the multi-deck standard cell legalization step, we optimize the results further in a quality-refinement stage. We optimize the results by applying a simulated annealing technique. Cell moving and cell swapping optimize maximum and total displacements during the simulated annealing iterations. These movements and swaps do not affect the legality of results.

*3.3.1 Cell Move.* Cell movement can improve the displacement quality. If the displacement penalty of target cell is less than the threshold value, we move the target cell. This movement might increase the cell displacement. From the previous cell move, another cell movement decreases the cell displacement. These two cell movements combine to decrease both the total displacement and the maximum displacement. The displacement threshold is proportional to the width of core site and inverse proportional to the number of iteration steps.

*3.3.2 Cell Swap.* Cell swap can also improve the displacement quality. The principle of cell swap is the same as the previous cell move. However, to ensure that the maintaining legalized result is retained, we can only swap same-sized cells. By swapping two identically-sized cells, both the total and the maximum displacement are decreased. This cell swapping is effective when the utilization is high, because cell swapping can optimize the displacement quality without changing the layout placement.

*3.3.3 Simulated Annealing.* The simulated annealing is a probabilistic technique to approach the global optimum of a given objective function. In this work, we use total displacement as the objective function. For temperature scheduling, an escape condition is considered as the cell swap and cell move ratio per the total number of cells. For effective legalization between quality and runtime, we set the escape constant k as 0.004 empirically. The optimization process proceeds for each fence region, and the simulated annealing is iterated until the escape function stops it. At each iteration step, the moving cell and swapping cell pairs are selected randomly.

# 4 EXPERIMENTAL RESULTS

Our experiments and evaluations are based on the ICCAD-2017 contest [1] environment. We built our binary by using C++, and executed it on a 2.2 GHz Intel Xeon workstation with 64 GB of memory, which are similar to the ICCAD-2017 contest environment. We consider 15 benchmarks from the ICCAD-2017 contest (Table 1). We neglect one benchmark that only contains single-deck standard cells and lacks a fence region.

**Table 1: Benchmark Information and score comparison with the ICCAD-2017 Contest Winners.**

| Benchmark | # Cells | Cell type | | | | # F.R. | Max F-Util. | Util. | Team ranked #1 | | Team ranked #2 | | Team ranked #3 | | Ours | |
|---|---|---|---|---|---|---|---|---|---|---|---|---|---|---|---|---|
| | | 1xH | 2xH | 3xH | 4xH | | | | $S_{total}$ | Time | $S_{total}$ | Time | $S_{total}$ | Time | $S_{total}$ | Time |
| des_perf_a_md1 | 103589 | 95.66 | 4.34 | 0 | 0 | 4 | 72.64 | 55.11 | 22.15 | 14.39 | 459.27 | 9.35 | 10948.43 | 35.62 | 9.52 | 3.85 |
| des_perf_a_md2 | 103589 | 96.99 | 1 | 1 | 1 | 4 | 75.99 | 55.92 | 192.59 | 17.42 | 952.05 | 11.93 | 283.3 | 38.19 | 57.69 | 3.55 |
| des_perf_b_md1 | 112679 | 94.8 | 5.2 | 0 | 0 | 12 | 96.2 | 54.98 | 0.39 | 6.59 | 1.14 | 10.85 | ***0.69** | 12.08 | 0.63 | 3.43 |
| des_perf_b_md2 | 112679 | 90.47 | 6.02 | 2.01 | 1.5 | 12 | 71.74 | 64.69 | 0.81 | 6.26 | 1.2 | 18.01 | 1.09 | 12.65 | 0.82 | 2.72 |
| edit_dist_1_md1 | 130661 | 90.31 | 6.12 | 2.04 | 1.53 | 0 | N/A | 67.47 | 0.88 | 8.58 | 1.03 | 20.6 | 2.88 | 14.14 | 1.9 | 1.9 |
| edit_dist_a_md2 | 127414 | 90.31 | 6.12 | 2.04 | 1.53 | 1 | 9.73 | 59.42 | 0.76 | 7.59 | 1.2 | 31.5 | 1.37 | 14.36 | 1.03 | 2.31 |
| edit_dist_a_md3 | 119626 | 93.88 | 2.04 | 2.04 | 2.04 | 1 | 9.3 | 57.22 | 1.18 | 21.02 | 30.48 | 12.1 | 5.95 | 39.84 | 1.18 | 2.43 |
| fft_2_md2 | 32281 | 89.62 | 6.56 | 2.18 | 1.64 | 0 | N/A | 83.12 | 0.78 | 1.6 | 1.31 | 30.64 | 1.09 | 4.35 | 0.9 | 0.51 |
| fft_a_md2 | 30625 | 89.57 | 6.59 | 2.19 | 1.65 | 0 | N/A | 32.41 | 0.77 | 1.41 | 0.9 | 2.5 | 1.14 | 3.16 | 0.78 | 0.84 |
| fft_a_md3 | 30625 | 93.42 | 2.19 | 2.19 | 2.19 | 0 | N/A | 31.24 | 0.6 | 1.36 | 0.67 | 2.45 | 0.92 | 2.95 | 0.62 | 0.86 |
| pci_bridge32_a_md1 | 29533 | 90.39 | 6.07 | 2.02 | 1.52 | 3 | 38.67 | 49.57 | 1.03 | 1.43 | 1.51 | 2.51 | 1.66 | 2.75 | 1.07 | 1.28 |
| pci_bridge32_a_md2 | 29533 | 85.51 | 7.08 | 4.04 | 3.37 | 3 | 62.44 | 57.72 | 1.22 | 4.02 | 22.78 | 2.47 | 4.63 | 7.21 | 1.45 | 1.12 |
| pci_bridge32_b_md1 | 26134 | 90.38 | 6.07 | 2.02 | 1.52 | 3 | 35.98 | 28.68 | 2.07 | 6.42 | 1.71 | 1.83 | 1.54 | 8.49 | 1.18 | 1.59 |
| pci_bridge32_b_md2 | 26134 | 97.97 | 1.01 | 1.01 | 1.01 | 3 | 41.67 | 19.72 | 14.27 | 6.35 | 8.82 | 1.79 | 4.48 | 8.5 | 3.61 | 1.68 |
| pci_bridge32_b_md3 | 26134 | 94.94 | 1.01 | 2.02 | 2.02 | 3 | 62.09 | 23.98 | 32.62 | 3.9 | 17.95 | 1.58 | 40.94 | 8.39 | 19.22 | 2.17 |
| | | | | | | | Avg. | | 18.14 | 7.22 | 100.14 | 10.67 | 753.34 | 14.18 | 6.77 | 2.01 |
| | | | | | | | N. Avg. | | 1 | 1 | 5.44 | 1.48 | 40.92 | 1.96 | 0.37 | 0.28 |

#F.R.: number of and fence regions; Cell types. 1xH, 2xH, 3xH and 4xH of cell type are the proportions portion of single-deck, double-deck, triple-deck, and quadruple-deck standard cells, respectively;. Max F-Util:. are maximum utilization of fence regions; Util.: utilization of entire benchmark. ***Bold** means given solution is illegal.

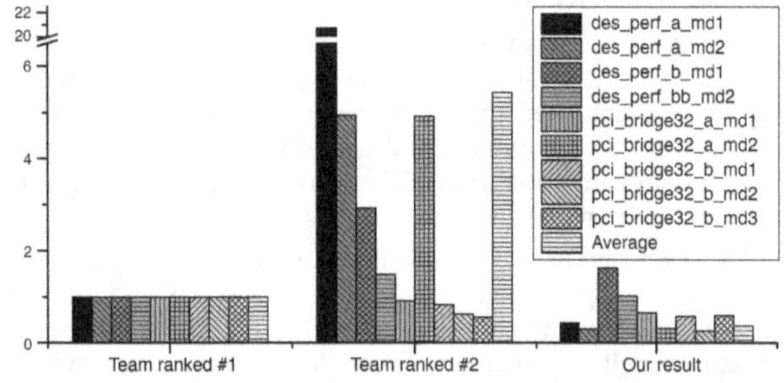


**Figure 6: Normalized $S_{total}$ comparison in multiple fence region benchmarks.**

## 4.1 Evaluation

The concept of our evaluation metric is inspired by the ICCAD-2017 contest. Evaluation scoring considered the maximum displacement score($S_{md}$), the average displacement score($S_{ad}$), and HalfPerimeter Wire Length (HPWL) score($S_{hpwl}$). The total score($S_{total}$) is the product of these three partial scores. Evaluation scores for top contestants in the ICCAD-2017 contest are calculated from published DEF results on the contest website.

## 4.2 Results

Our proposed fence region-aware legalization method achieved 63% and 72% improvement in average quality score and average runtime, respectively. We compared our $S_{total}$ and runtime results and those of the ICCAD-2017 contest winners (Table 1, Figs. 6). Runtime analysis of each step of our proposed method demonstrates that File I/O consumed 65.6% of runtime; legalization consumed only 10.9%, and optimization consumed only 23.5%.

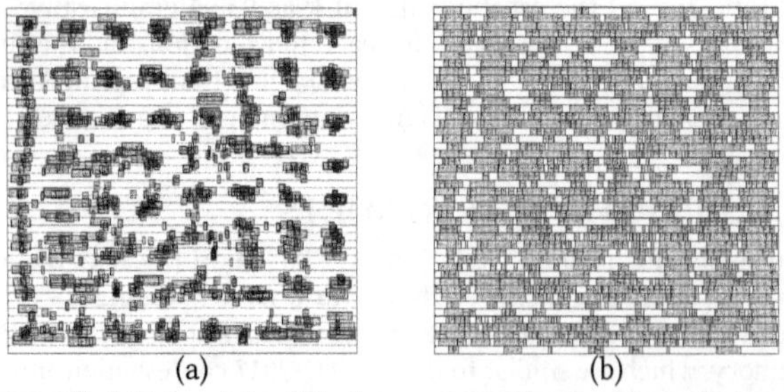

(a) (b)

**Figure 7: Initial and detailed placement result using spi_top design and TSMC 65*nm* PDK. (a) initial placement result using *Innovus*, and (b) is legalized result using our binary.**

## 4.3 Innovus Compatibility

We check compatibility of our binary [7] with *Cadence Innovus Implementation System.* We use TSMC 65*nm* and ASAP 7*nm*[12] PDK and various open source RTL design such as aes_cipher_top, spi_top, and pci_bridge32. We use *Synopsys Design Compiler* to synthesize netlist and generate initial placement DEF file using *Innovus.* Our binary generates legalized DEF file using initial placement DEF file and LEF file from PDK. Legalized DEF files are verified using *Innovus.* Fig. 7a shows initial placement result of spi_top using TSMC65*nm* PDK and Fig. 7b shows legalized placement result.

# 5 CONCLUSIONS

We have proposed a fence-region-aware multi-deck standard cell legalization method that uses a multi-stage and metaheuristic optimization. Our work can handle various heights of the multi-deck standard cell, and consider various shapes of fence regions. Our proposed method achieves an effective solution for the multi-deck standard cell legalization. Furthermore, we realize that our simulation binary supports other design and PDK which is out of the ICCAD-2017 contest environment.

# REFERENCES


[1] N. K. Darav, I. S. Bustany, A. Kennings, and R. Mamidi, "ICCAD-2017 CAD Contest in Multi-Deck Standard Cell Legalization and Benshmarks", *Proc. ICCAD*, 2017.

[2] K. Athikulwongse, A. Chakraborty, J. Yang, D. Z. Pan, S. K. Lim, "Stress-Driven 3D-IC Placement with TSV Keep-Out Zone and Regularity Study" *Proc. ICCAD*, 2010, pp. 669-674.

[3] W. -K. Chow, C. -W. Pui, and E. F. Y. Young, "Legalization Algorithm for Multiple-Row Height Standard Cell Design", *Proc. DAC*, 2016, pp. 83:1-83:6.

[4] C. -H. Wang, Y. -Y Wu, J. Chen, Y. -W. Chang, S. -Y. Kuo, W. Zhu, and G. Fan, "An Effective Legalization Algorithm for Mixed-Cell-Height Standard Cells", *Proc. ASP-DAC*, 2017, pp. 450-455.

[5] J. Chen, Z. Zhu, W. Zhu, and Y. -W. Chang, "Toward Optimal Legalization for Mixed-Cell-Height Circuit Designs", *Proc. DAC*, 2017, pp. 52:1-52:6.

[6] C. -Y. Hung, P. -Y. Chou, and W. -K. Mak, "Mixed-Cell-Height Standard Cell Placement Legalization", *Proc. GLSVLSI*, 2017, pp. 149-154.

[7] "Open Source Detailed Placement engine" *https://github.com/sanggido/OpenDP*

[8] D. Hill, "Method and System for High Speed Detailed Placement of Cells within an Integrated Circuit Design", *US Patent* No. 6370673, 2002.

[9] P. Spindler, U. Schlichtmann and F. M. Johannes "Abacus: Fast Legalization of Standard Cell Circuits with Minimal Movement", *Proc. ISPD*, 2008, pp. 47-53.

[10] Y. Lin, B. Yu, X. Xu, J. -R. Gao, N. Viswanathan, and W. -H. Liu, "MrDP: Multiple-row Detailed Placement of Heterogeneous-sized Cells for Advanced Nodes", *Proc. ICCAD*, 2016, pp. 7:1-7:8.

[11] S. Kim, S. Do, and S. Kang, "Fast Predictive Useful Skew Methodology for Timing-Driven Placement Optimization", *Proc. DAC*, 2017, pp. 55:1-55:6.

[12] LT. Clark, V. Vashishtha, L. Shifren, A. Gujja, S. Sinha, B. Cline, "ASAP7: A 7-nm finFET predictive process design kit", *Microelectronics Journal*, 53(2016), pp. 105-115.

# A Case for Heterogeneous Network-on-Chip Based H.264 Video Decoders

Milad Ghorbani Moghaddam
Dept. of Electrical and Computer Engr., Marquette Univ.
Milwaukee, Wisconsin
milad.ghorbanimoghaddam@marquette.edu

Cristinel Ababei
Dept. of Electrical and Computer Engr., Marquette Univ.
Milwaukee, Wisconsin
cristinel.ababei@marquette.edu

## ABSTRACT

The design of a heterogeneous network-on-chip (NoC) based H.264 video decoder is proposed. A thorough investigation using a system simulator developed as the combination of a cycle accurate NoC simulator together with complete implementations of all the video decoder modules is presented. The target hardware platform is a multicore system-on-chip, where the cores were designed for specific functions that correspond to the modules of the video decoder. Because such cores have different sizes and aspect ratios, a heterogeneous NoC is employed to facilitate the communication between modules. This is different from the reference case of a homogeneous NoC based hardware platform, where all cores are general purpose processors with the same area and where the NoC is a regular mesh NoC. The investigation looks at the impact of core sizes and floorplan for a given technology node as well as at the performance variation across several technology nodes.

## CCS CONCEPTS

• **Hardware** → **Network on chip**; • **Computer systems organization** → *Data flow architectures*; *System on a chip*; • **Computing methodologies** → Image compression.

## KEYWORDS

H.264 video decoder; heterogeneous network-on-chip; homogeneous network-on-chip

**ACM Reference Format:**
Milad Ghorbani Moghaddam and Cristinel Ababei. 2019. A Case for Heterogeneous Network-on-Chip Based H.264 Video Decoders. In *Great Lakes Symposium on VLSI 2019 (GLSVLSI '19), May 9–11, 2019, Tysons Corner, VA, USA.* ACM, New York, NY, USA, 4 pages. https://doi.org/10.1145/3299874.3318013

## 1 INTRODUCTION

The network-on-chip (NoC) has gained in popularity as a scalable communication mechanism between an increasingly large number of cores in integrated multicore chips [1]. NoCs can be classified into two major types, homogeneous and heterogeneous. In a homogeneous NoC, the routers are identical and arranged in a 2D regular array with the assumption that processing elements (PEs) are also identical or have the same area and aspect ratio. This naturally leads to identical tiles (tile = NoC router + PE), which in turn enhances the design predictability and simplifies the IC fabrication. We have studied a homogeneous NoC based H.264 video decoder design in our previous work in [2]. In contrast, a heterogeneous NoC is irregular; the routers are not arranged anymore in a regular array. Locations and distances between routers can vary, generally dictated by the size and placement of the heterogeneous cores that make-up the hardware platform. In addition, routers are not restricted to be identical and their number of input/output ports can vary, based on how many different PEs are connected to a given router. All these make the design of heterogeneous NoCs to be more difficult; as a result they have been studied less. In previous work, we introduced a complete design flow for the design and optimization of heterogeneous NoCs and its complete implementation is publicly available [3].

The simulation tool developed in this paper combines the complete video decoder algorithm simulator from [2] with the heterogeneous NoCs synthesis and optimization tool from [3] to investigate the proposed heterogeneous NoC based H.264 video decoder. Thus, the full system simulator developed here is capable of simulating both the heterogeneous NoC and the H.264 modules as a whole system, where the evaluation is done on real video streams, which exercise the NoC with truly realistic traffic.

## 2 PROPOSED HETEROGENEOUS NOC BASED H.264 VIDEO DECODER

Video coding is a basic algorithm that is used virtually in all video applications including digital TV, mobile TV, and online video streaming. Due to lack of space, we kindly refer the reader to [4] for background information on the H.264 video decoder algorithm.

The main idea of the design presented in this paper is that the modules of the H.264 video decoder are to be implemented and executed as specialized or specific PEs in order to achieve the highest performance. This approach is different from the reference case, where the H.264 modules were assumed to be executed on general purpose CPUs of a regular tiled multicore processor with regular mesh homogeneous NoC based communication, as it was the case in previous work [2]. Because when the modules are implemented as specific PEs their size and aspect ratio can be different, we must use a heterogeneous NoC for communication among modules.

The steps in the design approach proposed in this paper are illustrated in Fig. 1. The first portion of this design flow is adapted from the previous work on synthesis of heterogeneous NoCs [3]. The input to this design flow is the application communication task graph (CTG). The file with the CTG information also includes information about the specific PEs (sizes and aspect ratios) that execute the corresponding H.264 modules. Furthermore, information about


*GLSVLSI '19, May 9–11, 2019, Tysons Corner, VA, USA*

ACM ISBN 978-1-4503-6252-8/19/05...$15.00
https://doi.org/10.1145/3299874.3318013

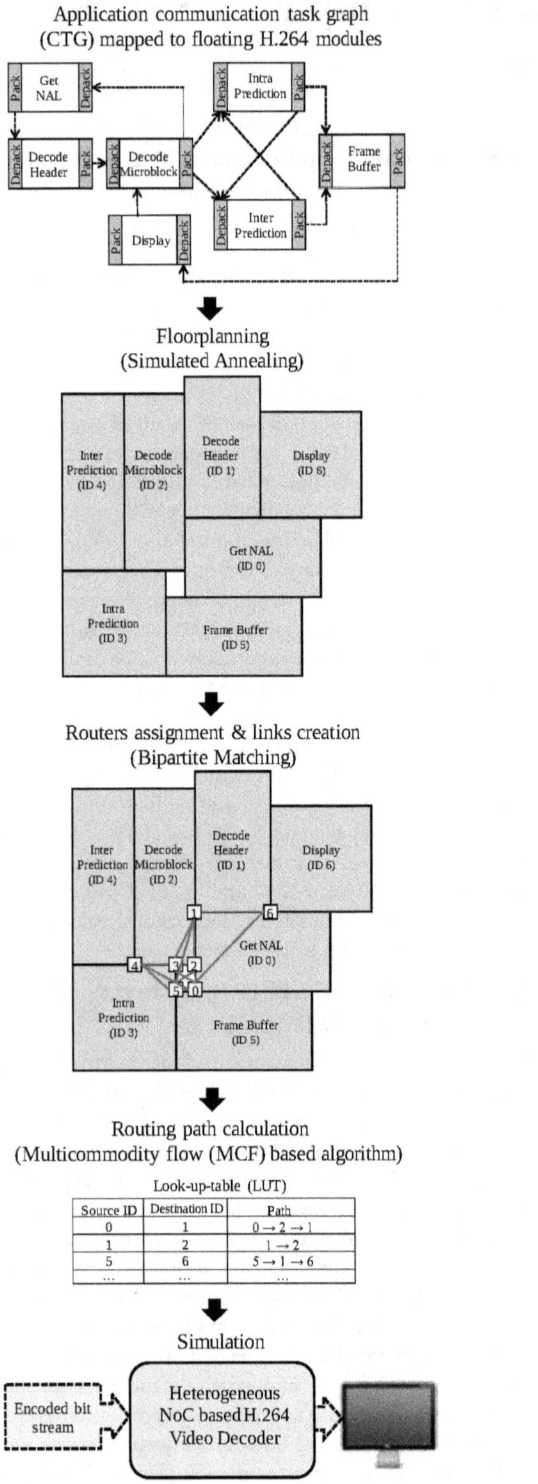


**Figure 1: Overview of the proposed design flow to synthesize the heterogeneous NoC for the H.264 video decoder design and to simulate the whole system.**

the communication volume between these modules is included as well. This information will be used by the floorplanning algorithm, which will attempt to place PEs that communicate heavily as close as possible to each other. The floorplanning algorithm is based on the popular B*-tree model and it employs a simulated annealing (SA) technique to find the best placement of the PEs. The cost function of the SA algorithm is a weighted combination of the total area and the total wirelength of the design [3].

After the floorplanning is done, in the next step, each PE is assigned to an NoC router. NoC routers are assumed to be located in the corners of the PEs. This router assignment step is implemented through an efficient bipartite matching algorithm, which finds the best matching of PEs to routers such that connectivity between PEs will be implemeneted via minimal routing paths through the network. Once the routers are assigned, the step of routing paths calculation follows. In this step, the best routing paths between PEs are found using a multicommodity flow (MCF) algorithm. The result of this step is the information that captures the exact routes for all packets between any source and destination PEs. This information is effectively stored in the so-called routing look-up-tables (LUTs) inside each router of the heterogeneous NoC. At the end of this step, we have information on the synthesized heterogeneous NoC, the exact routing paths, in addition to the C++ routines that implement the functions of all the H.264 video decoder modules.

All this information is then used in the second portion of the design flow from Fig. 1. In this portion, we develop a full system simulation framework similar to that in the previous work from [2]. The difference here is that we use a heterogeneous NoC and that we assume the H.264 modules implemented as specific PEs and not as general purpose CPUs. This full system simulation framework is capable of simulating the whole H.264 design in realtime (with video stream files are supplied as input) as a combination of the heterogeneous NoC and of the video decoder function modules. In this way, truly realistic traffic exercises the NoC and the average network latency and power consumption are as accurate as we can get via simulations. The output of the simulation framework includes average network latency and power consumption numbers, reported at the end of the simulation of a given video stream testcase, in addition to rendering in realtime the decoded video on the monitor of the computer used for simulations, as indicated at the bottom of Fig. 1.

## 3 SIMULATION RESULTS

The complete design flow from Fig. 1 was implemented in C++ as a computer program that automates all steps. The implementation of the first portion of Fig. 1 is adapted from the previous work on heterogeneous NoC synthesis [3] while the second portion that does (heterogeneous NoC + H.264) simulation is a modified version of the simulator from the previous work in [2], which uses C++ complete descriptions of each H.264 module from [5]. We report simulation results for ten different video stream benchmarks. These benchmarks are listed in Table 1, where their resolution is given in numbers of pixels horizontally (i.e., on a row) x number of pixels vertically (i.e., on a column). The files of these benchmarks were downloaded from [6, 7].

The investigation looks at the impact of core sizes and floorplan within a given technology node as well as at the performance

Table 1: Summary of the ten video benchmarks.

| Benchmark | Resolution (width x height) | Benchmark | Resolution (width x height) |
|---|---|---|---|
| Girl | 352x288 | Stefan | 352x240 |
| Freeway | 352x288 | Bigbuckbunny | 352x240 |
| Golf | 352x288 | Coastguard | 352x240 |
| Plane | 352x288 | Flower | 352x240 |
| Shore | 352x288 | Foreman | 352x240 |

variation across several technology nodes. Simulation results are reported as the average network latency, power consumption, and power-delay-product (PDP) for each video benchmark. The average network latency numbers are directly reported by the heterogeneous NoC simulator. To estimate the power consumption, the NoC simulator is integrated with the Orion 2.0 power model for NoCs for a default 65 nm technology node [8], validated with real data from the Intel's 80 core chip [9]. This is the most accurate NoC power model to date, that considers the switching activities inside each NoC router as resulted from the handling of real data carried as packets through the network.

## 3.1 Heterogeneous NoC based H.264 Video Decoder vs. Homogeneous NoC based H.264 Video Decoder

In the first set of simulations, we look at how the performance of the heterogeneous NoC based H.264 video decoder changes for different video testcases in comparison with the homogeneous NoC based H.264 video decoder from [2]. For the heterogeneous NoC based design, we assume different levels of optimization of the specific PEs that implement the various decoder modules. These levels of optimization translate into different areas of the PEs, which can result into different floorplans of the heterogeneous chip. Therefore, better PE optimization assumes a smaller area for the PE. Specifically, we considered four different levels of such optimization, which were translated into four different assumed areas for the PEs.

All area scaling experiments used as a reference the larger area of the general purpose CPU that was used in the homogeneous NoC based decoder design from [2]. The heterogeneous NoC + H.264 design used in all simulations used the best floorplan (see Fig. 2) identified during the floorplanning step from the design flow in Fig. 1, where for each PE we assumed available three different aspect ratios, as illustrated in Fig. 3. The simulation results for the default 65 nm technology node are reported in Table 2. We note that the heterogeneous NoC based H.264 video decoder design offers consistently predictable performance.

The results from the comparison between the reference homogeneous NoC based decoder design and the proposed heterogeneous NoC based decoder design are reported in Fig. 4. Aside from the four different levels of assumed heterogeneous PE optimization indicated as 90%, 70%, 50% and 30% smaller PE area, we also include the case when no optimization of the heterogeneous PE is done at all. That is indicated as the 100% in Fig. 4. This case is essentially a design with heterogeneous PEs with the same size as the homogeneous general purpose CPUs but with communication done via a heterogeneous NoC. These results are calculated under the assumption that the global interconnect delay varies linearly with the wire length, which is possible when wires are integrated

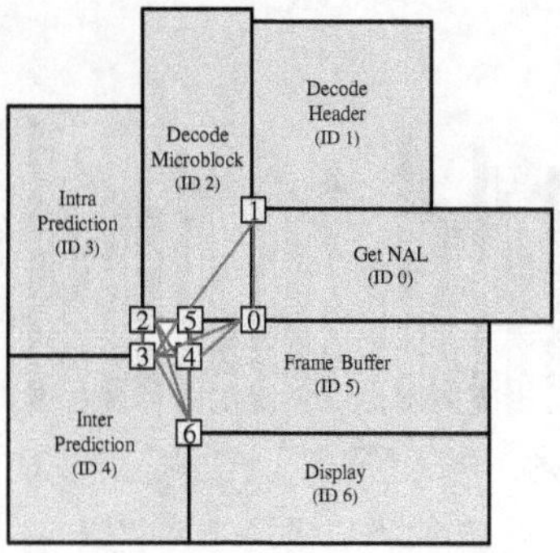


Figure 2: The best floorplan identified and used in all simulations. The heterogeneous NoC is formed by seven routers numbered from 0 to 6.

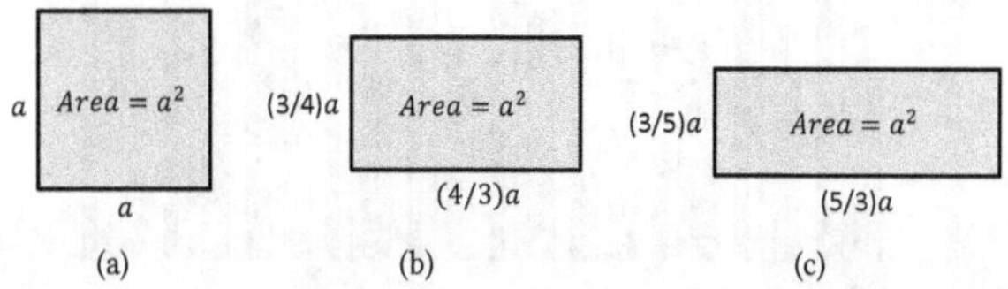


Figure 3: Three different aspect ratios assumed for each PE.

Table 2: Hetero NoC + H.264 modules simulation, 65 nm.

| Benchmark | Power consumption (W) | Average latency (cycles) | Power Delay Product, (PDP) |
|---|---|---|---|
| Girl | 0.1028 | 7.5740 | 0.7786 |
| Freeway | 0.1032 | 7.5751 | 0.7817 |
| Golf | 0.103 | 7.5800 | 0.7807 |
| Plane | 0.1033 | 7.5724 | 0.7822 |
| Shore | 0.1027 | 7.5778 | 0.7782 |
| Stefan | 0.1034 | 7.5819 | 0.7839 |
| Bigbuckbunny | 0.1029 | 7.5886 | 0.7808 |
| Coastguard | 0.103 | 7.5783 | 0.7805 |
| Flower | 0.1034 | 7.5827 | 0.7840 |
| Foreman | 0.1029 | 7.5822 | 0.7802 |

with repeaters according to the ITRS interconnect roadmap [10]. Note that if we assumed a quadratic dependency of wire delay with length, the comparison would be significantly more in favor of the heterogeneous NoC based decoder design. We observe that the heterogeneous NoC based decoder significantly outperforms the homogeneous NoC based decoder, with more than 20% in terms of power consumption and with more than 40% in terms of average network latency.

## 3.2 Impact of Technology Downscaling

In this section, we used the technology downscaling models from [11, 12] and the information on technology trends reported in the ITRS roadmap from [10] to investigate the variation of the performance of the proposed heterogeneous NoC based H.264 video decoder across different technology nodes. The result of this investigation is reported in Fig. 5 for the *Plane* benchmark only. Similar plots were obtained for all other simulated video benchmarks. This graph shows on the left y-axis the actual power-delay-product (PDP) numbers, with the delay being used as the average number

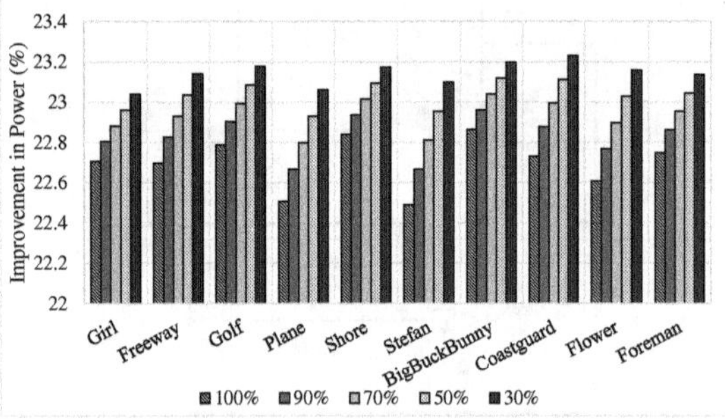


(a)

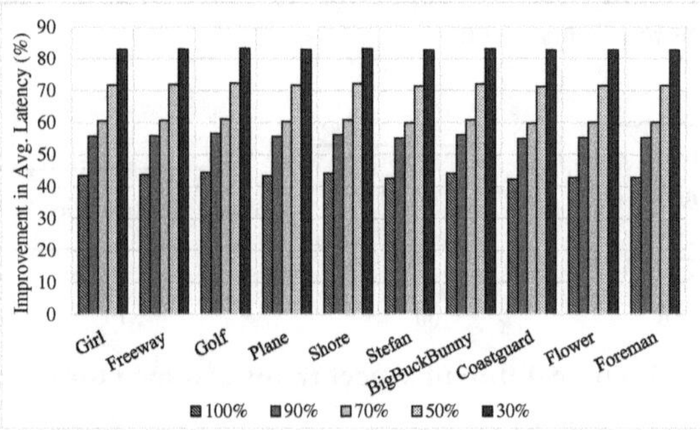


(b)

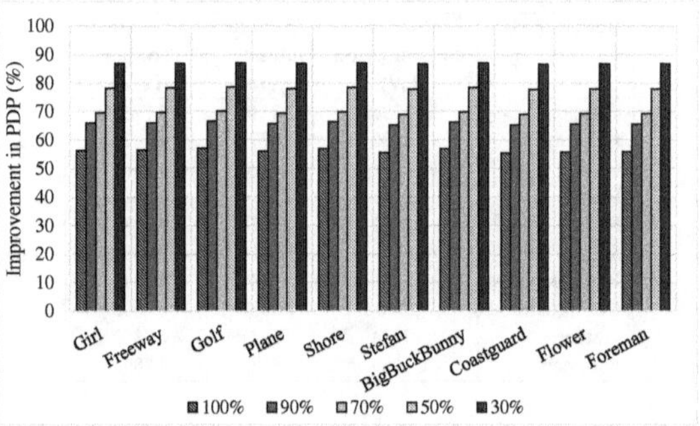


(c)

**Figure 4: Improvement of the heterogeneous NoC based decoder over the homogeneous NoC based decoder for heterogeneous PE sizes not-scaled (100%) and scaled to 90%, 70%, 50% and 30% of the reference homogeneous CPU sizes. (a) NoC power improvement, (b) average NoC latency improvement, and (c) NoC PDP improvement.**

of cycles, as reported by the NoC simulator. The right y-axis shows the ratio between the PDP values of each of the heterogeneous cases and the PDP value of the reference homogeneous case. This figure provides interesting insights into the effect of technology downscaling from 65 nm down to 7 nm on the PDP performance metric. We note that while the PDP numbers go down with technology downscaling in all cases, the heterogeneous NoC based decoder maintains a performance advantage over the homogeneous NoC based decoder. However, this performance advantage decreases

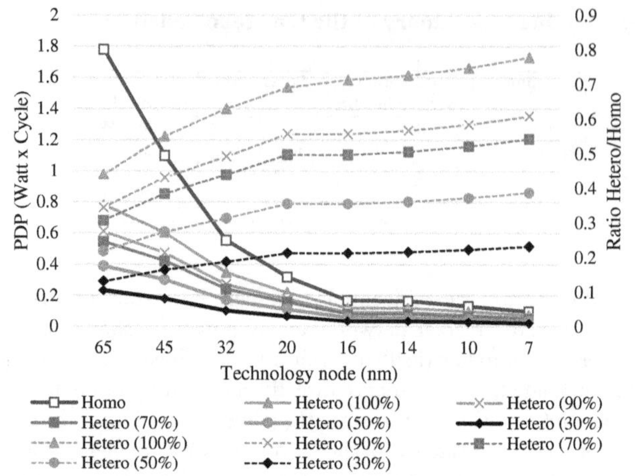


**Figure 5: Impact of technology downscaling impact on the power-delay-product for the *Plane* benchmark.**

slightly as we move from 65 nm towards 20 nm, after which it remains almost the same as we move towards 7 nm. In addition, the differences between different optimized versions of the heterogeneous NoC based decoder are not as significant at deeper technology nodes.

# 4 CONCLUSION

The design of a heterogeneous NoC based H.264 video decoder was presented and compared with the reference case of a homogeneous NoC based H.264 video decoder via full system simulations. The impact of heterogeneous core sizes and floorplan within a given technology node as well as the performance difference variation across technology nodes from 65 nm down to 7 nm were investigated. Simulation results indicated that the heterogeneous design offered consistently better performance compared to the reference homogeneous case across all technology nodes, although, at deeper technology nodes the performance gap shrinks slightly.

# REFERENCES

[1] R. Marculescu, U.Y. Ogras, L.-S. Peh, N.E. Jerger, and Y. Hoskote, "Outstanding research problems in NoC design: system, microarchitecture, and circuit perspectives," *IEEE TCAD*, vol. 28, no. 1, pp. 3-21, 2009.

[2] M.G. Moghaddam and C. Ababei "Performance evaluation of network-on-chip based H.264 video decoders via full system simulation," *IEEE Embedded Systems Letters*, vol. 9, no. 2, pp. 49-52, 2017.

[3] C. Ababei, "Efficient congestion-oriented custom Network-on-Chip topology synthesis," *IEEE Int. Conf. on Reconfigurable Computing and FPGAs (ReConFig)*, 2010.

[4] ITU-T H.264, Advanced video coding for generic audiovisual services, 2012. [Online]. Available: http://www.itu.int/ITU-T/recommendations/rec.aspx?rec=11466

[5] Martin Fiedler, Implementation of a basic H.264/AVC Decoder, 2016. [Online]. Available: http://keyj.emphy.de/files/projects/h264-src.tar.gz

[6] FastVDO: H.264 Video streams, 2018. [Online]. Available: http://www.fastvdo.com/H.264.html

[7] YUV Video Sequences, 2018. [Online]. Available: http://trace.eas.asu.edu/yuv

[8] A.B. Kahng et al., "ORION 2.0: A power-area simulator for interconnection networks," *IEEE TVLSI*, vol. 20, no. 1, pp. 191-196, 2012.

[9] S.R. Vangal et al., "An 80-tile sub-100-W TeraFLOPS processor in 65-nm CMOS," *IEEE Journal of Solid-state Circuits*, vol. 43, no. 1, pp. 29-41, 2008.

[10] The International Technology Roadmap for Semiconductors (ITRS), 2013. [Online]. Available: https://www.semiconductors.org/clientuploads/Research_Technology/ITRS/2013/2013Interconnect.pdf

[11] A. Stillmaker and B. Bevan, "Scaling equations for the accurate prediction of CMOS device performance from 180 nm to 7 nm," *Integration, the VLSI Journal*, vol. 58, pp. 74-81, 2017.

[12] H. Ron, K.W. Mai, and M.A. Horowitz, "The future of wires," *Proceedings of the IEEE*, vol. 89, no. 4, pp. 490-504, 2001.

# A 16b Clockless Digital-to-Analog Converter with Ultra-Low-Cost Poly Resistors Supporting Wide-Temperature Range from -40℃ to 85℃

Xuedi Wang, Xueqing Li, Longqiang Lai, Huazhong Yang
Tsinghua University
Beijing, China
wangxd16@mails.tsinghua.edu.cn,XueqingLi@tsinghua.edu.cn,llq14@mails.tsinghua.edu.cn,yanghz@tsinghu.edu.cn

## ABSTRACT

High-precision digital-to-analog converter (DAC) is a critical component in process control, data acquisition, and testing instruments. In order to achieve high resolution and a wide-temperature range, conventional designs have been adopting high-cost thin-film resistors with laser-trimming to improve the matching property and thus the DAC resolution. In this work, targeting at lowering the cost, we propose an analog resistor redundancy, full code, and piecewise-linear calibration scheme to enable the use of low-cost poly resistors in a standard CMOS process. In order to overcome the drift over a wide temperature range, a feedback circuit is proposed to guarantee that the resistance of the switch can track the resistor with temperature changes. Therefore, the DAC can be calibrated under a specific temperature and tested under an arbitrary temperature from -40℃ to 85℃ using the same calibration codes. The 16b DAC was implemented in a $0.25\mu m$ $5V$ CMOS process with $5V$ CMOS devices and poly resistors rather than thin film resistor. The test result shows that it can achieve the INL≤0.5LSB, INL≤4LSB, and INL≤4LSB at 25℃, -40℃ and 85℃ respectively, using the same calibration code. It settles in $1\mu s$ and it has below $5nV \cdot s$ glitch. The current consumption is $1.7mA$ from $5V$ voltage supplies.

## CCS CONCEPTS

• **Hardware → Data conversion.**

## KEYWORDS

digital to analog converter; calibration; resistor mismatch; INL

**ACM Reference Format:**
Xuedi Wang, Xueqing Li, Longqiang Lai, Huazhong Yang. 2019. A 16b Clockless Digital-to-Analog Converter with Ultra-Low-Cost Poly Resistors Supporting Wide-Temperature Range from -40℃ to 85℃. In *Great Lakes Symposium on VLSI 2019 (GLSVLSI '19), May 9–11, 2019, Tysons Corner, VA, USA.* ACM, New York, NY, USA, 4 pages. https://doi.org/10.1145/3299874.3318014


*GLSVLSI '19, May 9–11, 2019, Tysons Corner, VA, USA*

ACM ISBN 978-1-4503-6252-8/19/05...$15.00
https://doi.org/10.1145/3299874.3318014

## 1 INTRODUCTION

With the pervasiveness of digital applications, digital-to-analog converters have become essential building blocks for the interface between the digital and analog domains. And the DAC should have a good balance between high precision, low power consumption, small area, and a wide output amplitude range. In the meantime, the drift over temperature should be insignificant.

At present, general-purpose DACs are usually based on classic DAC architectures. For example, resistor DACs are used in the high- accuracy field[6], current-steering DACs are used in the high-speed field such as wideband wireless communication[3], and delta-sigma DACs are widely used in the high-quality digital audio signal processing[11]. Nowadays, for a DAC with a precision of more than 12 bits, a commonly used structure is the thermometer decoding structure followed by an R2R structure, which can make a good trade-off between the number of resistors and the linearity. But this architecture also suffers from the non-ideal factors. Base on this architecture, this work designs an effective calibration circuit to guarantee high DAC precision.

In addition to the high accuracy, in order to overcome the drift over the temperature, one conventional technique is to adopt the temperature-insensitive thin film resistor. However, the thin film resistor is costly. In this work, we use the poly resistor in the standard CMOS process rather than the thin film resistor to reduce the costs.

The major contributions of this work can be summarized as follows:

- In this work, targeting at lowering the cost, an analog redundancy full code calibration scheme is proposed to enable the use of low-cost poly resistors in a standard CMOS process. The 16b DAC has been fabricated and the measured INL is 0.5LSB with the proposed calibration scheme.
- A feedback switch circuit is proposed to adaptively control the gate voltage of the switch over different temperatures and thus keep the resistance matching between the poly resistor and the switch.
- The number of segments in piecewise linearity is optimized to not only reduce the on-chip memory area but also ensure the performance of the DAC at wide-range temperatures.

In the rest of this paper, Section II describes the non-ideal factors in detail. Section III introduces the 16b DAC architecture. Section IV describes the circuit details, and Section V presents the result of the experiment.

## 2 BACKGROUND AND RELATED WORK

The first INL degradation arises from the resistor mismatch. One conventional technique to reduce the resistor mismatch is wafer-level laser trimming[9][10]. However, mechanical stress during plastic packing can cause serious matching problems. The architecture proposed in this work uses the poly resistor to reduce the costs and adopts the analog redundancy full code calibration scheme to achieve excellent DC accuracy.

The second source of INL is the temperature dependence of the poly resistor. One conventional technique to solve this problem is to adopt the thin film resistor[6]. However, the thin film resistor is expensive. In this work, we use the poly resistor and the analog redundancy full code calibration scheme to ensure that the calibration codes can cover the resistance variation over a wide temperature range.

The third source of INL in this type of DACs occurs as a result of voltage drops across CMOS switches. The classic solution to this problem is a technique in[7] which equalizes the NMOS and PMOS switch resistance. However, the temperature dependency of the switch resistance is different from that of the poly resistors. In this work, a feedback circuit is proposed to guarantee that the resistance of the switch can track the resistor as temperature changes.

## 3 THE 16B DAC ARCHITECTURE

The DAC is fabricated in an ultra-low-cost $0.25\mu m$ standard CMOS process with the poly resistor, eliminating the need for laser trimming and thin film resistors. The proposed calibration codes are obtained at the room temperature and the DAC can be used under an arbitrary temperature from -40℃ to 85℃ using the same calibration codes.

The architecture of the 16b DAC is shown in Fig.1. The DAC includes a main DAC and a calibration DAC. In order to ensure the calibration accuracy, the calibration step size should be as small as possible. In order to ensure the calibration range, the number of adjustable steps should be as many as possible. We can choose the number of the calibration bits and exploit the proportional relationship between the main DAC and the calibration DAC to make a trade-off between the calibration accuracy and the calibration range.

During the test, the calibration codes for each main DAC are obtained to guarantee the high calibration accuracy. Since our calibration DAC has a 12b resolution, the calibration codes should be 1/16 of the main codes theoretically. However, due to various non-ideal factors, the actual value deviates from the theoretical value. In this scenario, it can be compensated by changing the calibration codes. If the actual output value of the DAC is higher than the theoretical value, the calibration code can be adjusted to a value smaller than the ideal calibration code to reduce the output of the entire DAC. Similarly, if the actual output value of the DAC is lower than the theoretical value, the calibration code can be adjusted to a value larger than the ideal calibration code to increase the output of the entire DAC.

For more convenient calculations, the circuit of the structure can be modeled and analyzed[4].

$V_{out}$ can be represented corresponding to the digital input $V_b$ as:

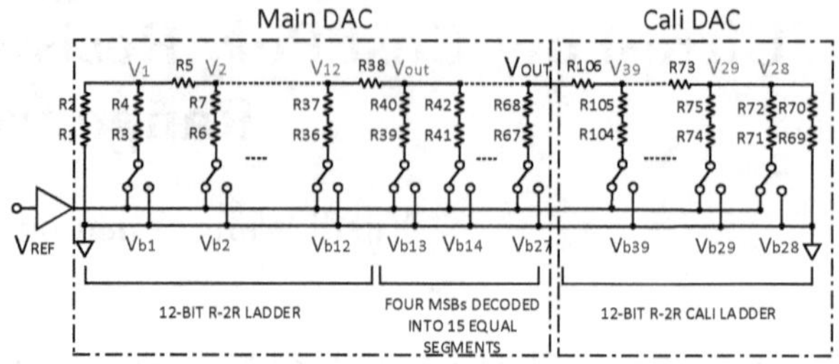


**Figure 1: 16b DAC architecture with the calibration circuit**

$$\mathbf{V} = \mathbf{A}^{-1} \cdot \mathbf{B} \cdot \mathbf{V}_b \tag{1}$$

where $\mathbf{V} = \{V_1, V_2, ..., V_{out}, ..., V_{38}\}^T, \mathbf{V}_b = \{V_{b1}, V_{b2}, ..., V_{b39}\}^T$, $\mathbf{A}$ and $\mathbf{B}$ are related to the $R_1$ to $R_{106}$.

This proposed architecture overcomes the mismatch of the poly resistor and the drift over temperature. As long as the number of the calibration bits and the proportional relationship between the main DAC and the calibration DAC is selected appropriately, the calibration range could be sufficiently wide, so that the DAC could be calibrated under the room temperature and maintain the accuracy under an arbitrary temperature from -40℃ to 85℃. It can greatly reduce the on-chip memory area and improve the performance of the chip in extreme environments.

## 4 CIRCUIT IMPLEMENTATION DETAILS

This section focuses on the analysis and processing of various non-ideal factors in the design process, including resistor mismatch, resistance voltage modulation factor, and voltage drops across the switch.

### 4.1 Resistance Mismatch

Resistance mismatch refers to the deviation between the actual value and the ideal value. This bias has a different impact on each device, resulting in a non-ideal case where the same device exhibits different performance in practice.

For resistance DACs with a resolution more than 12b, the resistor matching degree is an essential factor to their performance[1]. For a 16b resolution, using only the segmentation method without any calibration techniques, the required resistance mismatch tolerance is below $10^{-5}$ to achieve the performance requirement of 0.5LSB, which is very difficult to achieve using the existing common process.

After adopting the calibration circuit, the resistance mismatch tolerance of the 16b DAC is reduced from $10^{-5}$ to $10^{-3}$ by choosing the number of the calibration bits and the proportional relationship between the main DAC and the calibration DAC, which is more preferable in applications with requirements of limited area and cost, as shown in Fig.2(a).

### 4.2 Voltage Modulation Factor

For poly resistors, the resistance may vary as the voltage across the resistor changes, resulting in serious linearity reduction. The

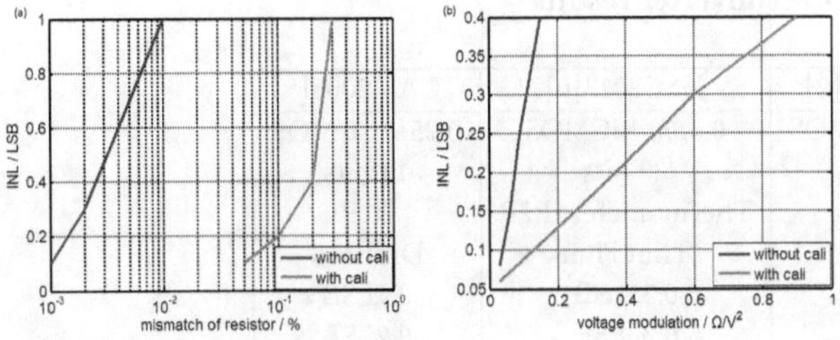


**Figure 2: (a)INL under different resistor mismatch with calibration and without calibration(b)INL under different voltage modulate factor with calibration and without calibration**

analog redundancy full code calibration scheme can effectively mitigate the effects of the voltage modulate factor by choosing the number of the calibration bits and the proportional relationship between the main DAC and the calibration DAC appropriately. In the case of considering only the resistance voltage modulation factor, the tolerance of the resistance voltage modulation effect can be relaxed by 7 times with the proposed method compared to the non-calibration technique, as shown in Fig.2(b).

## 4.3 Feedback Switch Circuit

The INL of the conventional R2R DAC is related to the resistance of the switch. Besides, the resistance drift of the MOS switch and that of the poly resistor over temperature is also different.

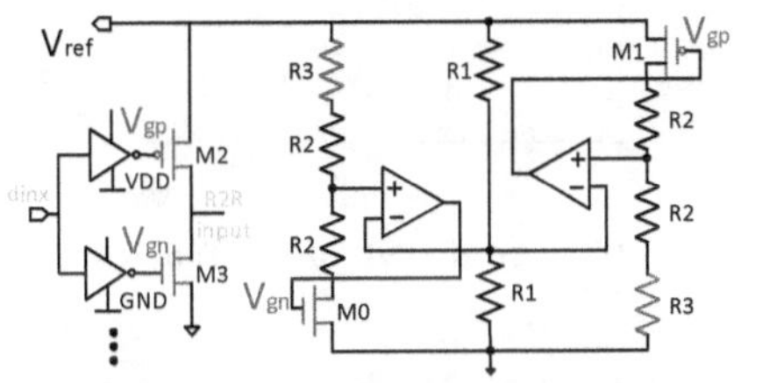


**Figure 3: switch circuit to guarantee the resistance of the switch can track the resister with temperature changes**

The proposed circuit is shown in Fig.3. It guarantees that the resistance of the P switch equals that of the N switch. The feedback circuit can adjust the $V_{gp}$ and $V_{gn}$ to make the resistance theoretically equal even if the temperature is changed. The resistance of R3 should be the same as the equivalent resistance of M1, which ensures that the equivalent resistance of the P switch and the N switch are the same. On the other hand, as long as the operating states of M1 and M2 are the same, their equivalent resistance can be guaranteed to be the same as R3.

## 4.4 Piecewise Linear Arithmetic

The piecewise linear method is applied to the 16b DAC to achieve an optimized trade-off between the accuracy and the on-chip memory area. Using more segments in piecewise linearity increases the on-chip memory area, and using more complex interpolation method increases the digital circuit area. We only store the calibration code word corresponding to a part of the main codeword and the remaining codes are obtained by linear interpolation. By optimizing the number of segments, the on-chip memory area is successfully reduced, and the performance of the DAC at wide-range temperatures is ensured.

# 5 MEASUREMENT RESULT AND DISCUSSION

The 16b DAC was implemented in a $0.25\mu m$ standard CMOS process with $5V$ CMOS devices. A microphotograph of the chip is shown in Fig.4. It has 3-channel 16b DACs. The total area of the prototype including pads is $3mm \times 2.8mm$. Measurement results show $1.5mA$ from the power supplies of one channel DAC and the total power consumption of one channel is $7.5mW$ under a $5V$ voltage supply.

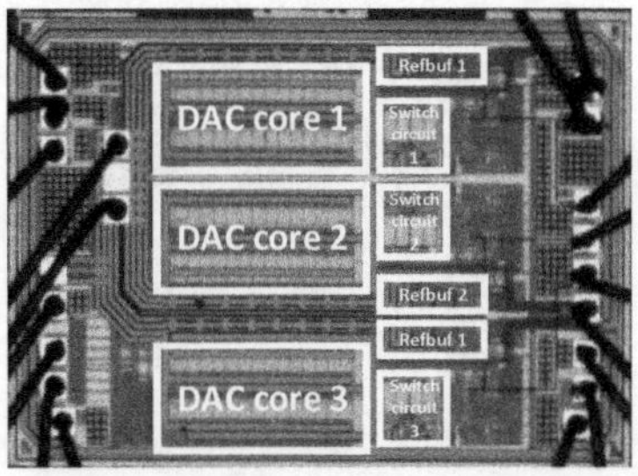


**Figure 4: Chip microphotograph**

Unless otherwise specified, all the following results were measured with reference voltages of $4.096V$. The DAC was just calibrated at 25℃ and measured at an arbitrary temperature from -40℃ to 85℃ , using the same calibration codes obtained at 25℃. Testing the accurate INL and DNL of the 16b DAC with 65,536 codes of data takes approximately 5 hours. Fig.5(a) depicts the measured results at the room temperature. The maximum INL is 0.6LSB. Fig.5(d) shows the DNL of the DAC at the room temperature. The DNL is 0.5LSB.

Fig.5(b) shows the measured results at -40℃ using the same calibration codes obtained at 25℃. The maximum INL is 4LSB. And Fig.5(e) shows the DNL at -40℃. The maximum DNL is 4LSB.

We also measure the INL and DNL at 85℃ using the same calibration codes obtained at 25℃. Fig.5(c) shows the INL of the DAC. The maximum INL is 4LSB. Fig.5(f) shows the DNL of the DAC at 85℃. The maximum DNL is 4LSB.

The DAC output settles within $1\mu s$ when the code is changed from 0x4000 (1/4 full sale) to 0xC000 (3/4 full scale). It has below $5nV \cdot s$ glitches when the code is changed from 0x8000 to 0x7FFF.

Some similar DACs are compared with the fabricated DAC as shown in TABLE.1. Our DAC test result is superior to [2], [5], [8]. [6] reported a 20b DAC with 0.35LSB INL, better than this DAC, but it is processed in $0.6\mu m$ BiCMOS with the thin film resistor, which is more expensive than our process. In addition, [6] needs a power voltage supply of $\pm 10V$ , and consumes much higher power consumption of $84mW$.

**Table 1: comparison of the D/A converter results**

| | This work | TCASI2018[2] | JSSC2013[6] | TCASI2008[5] |
|---|---|---|---|---|
| Process node | $0.25\mu m$ COMS | $0.25\mu m$ BiCMOS | $0.6\mu m$ BiCMOS | $0.25\mu m$ CMOS |
| Resolution | 16bits | 12 bits | 20 bits | 14 bits |
| Architecture | Thermometer+R2R | R2R | Thermometer+R2R | R2R |
| Resister Type | Poly | Poly | Thin Film | Diffused |
| INL | 0.5LSB | 0.67LSB | 0.35LSB | 0.7LSB |
| DNL | 0.5LSB | 0.23LSB | 0.30LSB | 0.2LSB |
| Settle time | $1.5\mu s$ | - | $1\mu s$ | $1\mu s$ |
| Glitch | $5nV \cdot s$ | - | $3.1nV \cdot s$ | - |
| Power | $7.5mW$ | $131mW$ | $84mW$ | $1.7mW$ |
| Area | $0.935mm^2$ | $12mm^2$ | $9.6mm^2$ | $0.47mm^2$ |

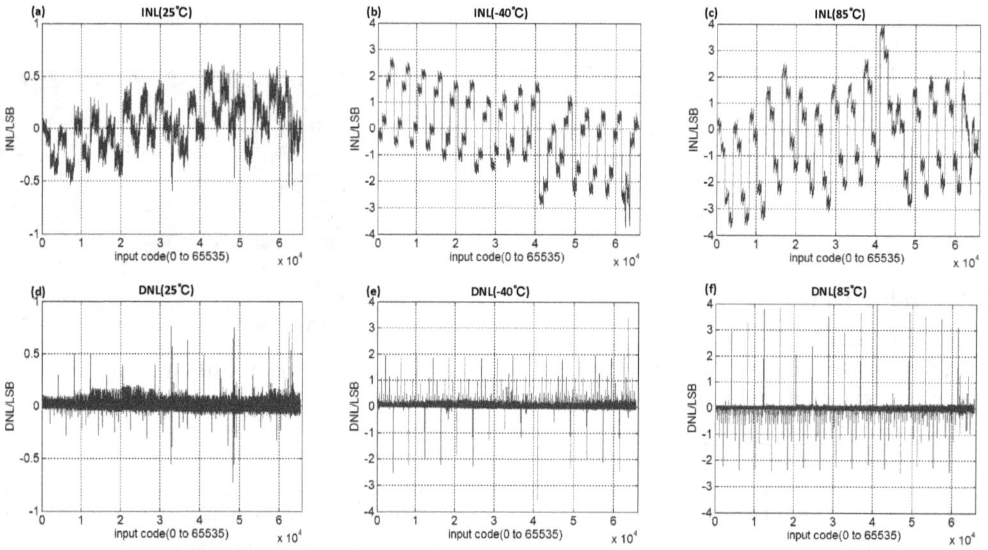


**Figure 5: Measured INL of the fabricated 16 bit DAC at (a) 25℃ (b) -40℃ (c) 85℃. Measured DNL of the fabricated 16 bit DAC at (d) 25℃ (e) -40℃ (f) 85℃.**

# 6 CONCLUSION

This paper demonstrates a 16b DAC is fabricated in an ultra-low-cost $0.25\mu m$ standard CMOS process with the poly resistor, eliminating the need for laser-trimming and exotic thin film processes. The calibration codes can be obtained under the room temperature and work successfully at any temperature from -40℃ to 85℃ using the same calibration codes. The test result shows that the presented DAC can achieve INL≤0.5LSB, INL≤4LSB, and INL≤4LSB at 25℃ -40℃ and 85℃, respectively, using the same calibration code. The DAC output settles within $1\mu s$ and has below $5nV \cdot s$ glitches. The current consumption is $1.7mA$ from a $5V$ voltage supply.

# REFERENCES

[1] Chun-Chieh Chen and Nan-Ku Lu. 2013. Nonlinearity analysis of R-2R ladder-based current-steering digital to analog converter. In *Circuits and Systems (ISCAS), 2013 IEEE International Symposium on.* IEEE, 833–836.

[2] Hua Fan, Dagang Li, Kelin Zhang, Yuanjun Cen, Quanyuan Feng, Fei Qiao, and Hadi Heidari. 2018. A 4-Channel 12-Bit High-Voltage Radiation-Hardened Digital-to-Analog Converter for Low Orbit Satellite Applications. *IEEE Transactions on Circuits and Systems I: Regular Papers* 99 (2018), 1–9.

[3] Chi-Hung Lin, F Van Der Goes, J Westra, Jan Mulder, Yu Lin, Erol Arslan, Emre Ayranci, Xiaodong Liu, and Klaas Bult. 2009. A 12b 2.9 GS/s DAC with IM3âĹł-60dBc beyond 1GHz in 65nm CMOS. In *Solid-State Circuits Conference-Digest of Technical Papers, 2009. ISSCC 2009. IEEE International.* IEEE, 74–75.

[4] David Marche and Yvon Savaria. 2010. Modeling R-2R segmented-ladder DACs. *IEEE Transactions on Circuits and Systems I: Regular Papers* 57, 1 (2010), 31–43.

[5] David Marche, Yvon Savaria, and Yves Gagnon. 2008. Laser fine-tuneable deep sub-micron CMOS 14 bit DAC. *IEEE Trans. Circuits Syst. I, Reg. Papers* 55, 8 (2008), 2157–2165.

[6] Roddy C McLachlan, Alan Gillespie, Michael CW Coln, Douglas Chisholm, and Denise T Lee. 2013. A 20b clockless DAC with sub-ppm-inl 7.5 nv/âĹŽ Hz-noise and 0.05 ppm/âŮę c-stability. *IEEE J. Solid-State Circuits* 48, 12 (2013), 3028–3037.

[7] Richard A Meaney and Raymond J Speer. 1991. Voltage-switching d/a converter using p-And n-channel mosfets. US Patent 5,075,677.

[8] Douglas A Mercer. 2007. Low-Power Approaches to High-Speed Current-Steering Digital-to-Analog Converters in $0.18\mu m$ CMOS. *IEEE Journal of Solid-State Circuits* 42, 8 (2007), 1688–1698.

[9] J Ramirez-Angulo and Randall L Geiger. 1988. New laser-trimmed film resistor structures for very high stability requirements. *IEEE Transactions on Electron Devices* 35, 4 (1988), 516–518.

[10] Bruce J Tesch and Juan C Garcia. 1997. A low glitch 14-b 100-MHz D/A converter. *IEEE Journal of Solid-State Circuits* 32, 9 (1997), 1465–1469.

[11] Xiaoliang Yao, Liyuan Liu, Dongmei Li, Liangdong Chen, and Zhihua Wang. 2010. A 90dB DR audio delta-sigma DAC with headphone driver for hearing aid. In *Image and Signal Processing (CISP), 2010 3rd International Congress on*, Vol. 6. IEEE, 2890–2893.

# A Skyrmion Racetrack Memory based Computing In-memory Architecture for Binary Neural Convolutional Network

Yu Pan[1] , Peng Ouyang[1,3] , Yinglin Zhao[1] , Shouyi Yin[2] , Youguang Zhang[1] , Shaojun Wei[2] and Weisheng Zhao[1,3]

[1] Fert Beijing Institute, BDBC, Beihang University, Beijing, China

[2] Institute of Microelectronics, Tsinghua University, Beijing, Chian

[3] Hefei Innovation Research Institute, School of Microelectronics, Beihang University, Hefei, China

## ABSTRACT

A Skyrmion Racetrack Memory (SRM) based Computing In-Memory Architecture (SRM-CIM) was proposed in this paper. Both data and computing operation can be achieved in SRM-CIM. SRM-CIM is used to support convolutional computing in Binary Convolutional Neural Network (BCNN). Experimental results show that SRM-CIM achieves 98.7% and 82% energy reduction when compared with RRAM and SOT-MRAM based counterparts.

## KEYWORDS

Skyrmion; Computing in memory; BCNN; Low Power.

**ACM Reference format:**

Yu Pan, Peng Ouyang, Yinglin Zhao, Shouyi Yin, Youguang Zhang, Shaojun Wei, and Weisheng Zhao. 2019. A Skyrmion Racetrack Memory based Computing In-memory Architecture for Binary Neural Convolutional Network. In Proceedings of 2019 Great Lakes Symposium on VLSI (GLSVLSI'19). ACM, New York, NY, USA, 4 pages. https://doi.org/10.1145/3299874.3318015

## 1 Introduction

CNN is widely used in face recognition and speech recognition, etc. However, it is characterized by vast amounts of data to perform energy consuming operation like multiplication, which is contradict with the ultra-low power demand in artificial intelligence devices. BCNN has been proposed to reduce power consumption by converting inputs and weights to binary value, which reduces the operation data greatly with small precision loss [1]. Meanwhile, the complex multiplication operations are replaced by *AND* operation in binary convolutional operations. That is easier to be achieved in circuit level and needs less energy.

Data transfer between memory unit and processing unit still consumes a large part of computing resource, because transferring data consumes more resource than computing it. The works of [2] solve the data transfer bottleneck issue in a computing in-memory way. All these designs are based on volatile memory SRAM, which still has the problems as the performance is limited by the constraints of SRAM itself, like large cell area and high leakage current [3]. Non-volatile memory (NVM), like resistive random-access memory (RRAM) [4], Spin Toque Transfer Magnetic Random Access Memory (SOT-MRAM) [5], Domain Wall Memory (DWM) [6], are promising candidates to replace SRAM for their unique properties such as near-zero standby energy consumption. Among these NVMs, DWM is widely researched for its outstanding features like higher density, lower power consumption. Recently, Skyrmion Racetrack Memory (SRM) [7] is of great interest. Skyrmion has great stability, very small size (~nm) and it needs lower shift current ($10^6$ A/m$^2$) compared with DWM ($10^{11}$-$10^{12}$ A/m$^2$). So it is appealing as information carrier for future nanoelectronics [8][9][10].

In this work, we propose SRM-CIM to achieve both data and computing operation in memory. This design efficiently supports binary convolutional computing shown in Figure 1. The binary convolutional computing is converted to the Bit-count of the AND results of input and weight tensors here. Inputs and weights of BCNN show sparsity which makes the computing inefficient. However, the designs in [4] and [5] did not consider the sparsity and have memory access redundancy. SRM needs near-zero energy to write logic "0", this can be used to solve the sparsity issue to reduce computational burden. We perform the convolutional process basically by fully making use of the shift characteristic of SRM, which reduces data memory access redundancy. We applied our design in typical BCNN Xnor-net, simulation results show that this work achieves 98%, 82% and 77% energy reduction when compared with RRAM, SOT-MRAM and SRAM based counterparts.

## 2 SRM-CIM Architecture

### 2.1 Skyrmion Racetrack Memory

Figure 2 is a Skyrmion Racetrack Memory. The whole circuit is a nano racetrack that consisted of ferromagnetic layer, heavy metal layer, and substrate. Skyrmions (blue solid circles) are induced by interfacial Dzyaloshinskii-Moriya interaction (DMI) between ferromagnetic layer and heavy metal layer. A binary data "1" ("0") can be represented by the presence (absence) of the skyrmion on the racetrack, which exhibit different resistance values on MTJ read head. Multiple ports (read ports, write ports and shift ports) are distributed on the racetrack to control the generation, movement, and detection of skyrmions. Write word line (WWL), shift word line (SWL) and read word line (RWL) can be enabled to support write, shift and read operation.

### 2.2 SRM-CIM Architecture and application

Figure 3(a) is the overall architecture of SRM-CIM. The memory array consists of Vertical and Horizontal Racetrack Group (VRG and HRG) which stores Inputs data and weights data respectively.

† Corresponding author: Peng Ouyang (e-mail: oyp2017@buaa.edu.cn). Yu pan and Peng Ouyang contributed equally to this work.



*GLSVLSI '19, May 9–11, 2019, Tysons Corner, VA, USA*



ACM ISBN 978-1-4503-6252-8/19/05…$15.00

https://doi.org/10.1145/3299874.3318015

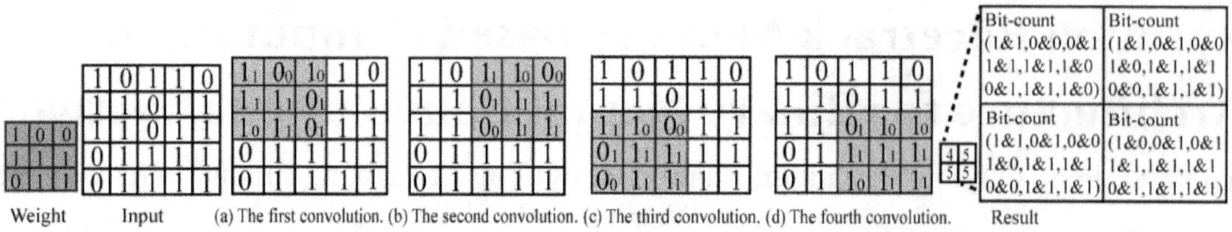

Figure 1: Convolutional process of 3×3 weight tensors scan in 5×5 input tensors with a 2 step size.

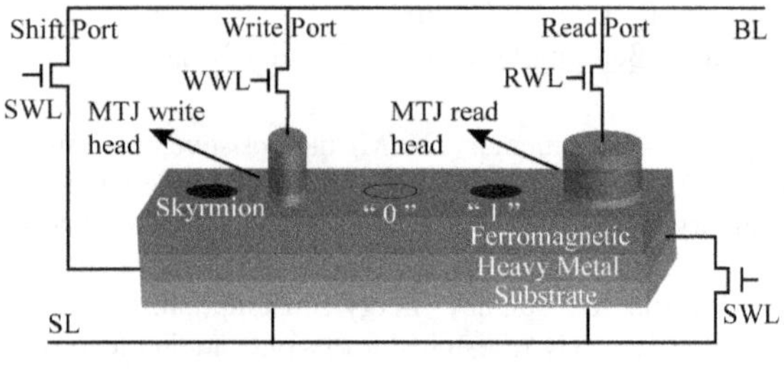

Figure 2: Skyrmion Racetrack Memory.

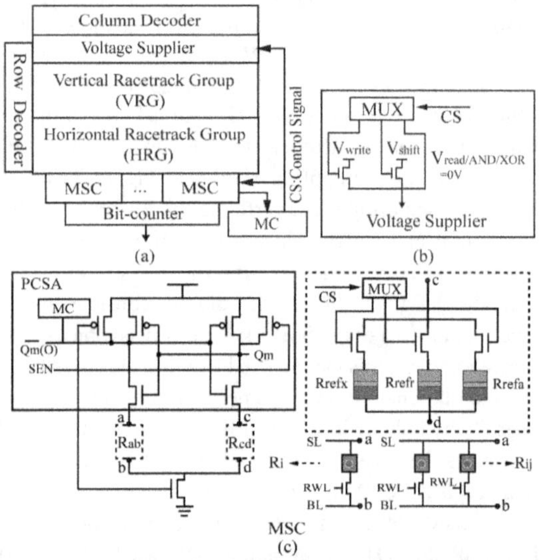

Figure 3: (a) Overall architecture of SRM-CIM. (b) Voltage Driver. (c) Modified Sensing Circuit.

Figure 4 shows their internal structure and corresponding binary data stored in. Solid blue circles (black hollow circle) mean the present (absent) of skyrmions. Modified Sensing Circuit (MSC) shown in Figure 3(c) based on pre-charged sense amplifier (PCSA) proposed in [11] is designed for *Read, AND* and *XOR* operations. Bit-counter is used to achieve *Bit-count* operation. Based on these structures above and controlled by the Mode Controller (MC), SRM-CIM can achieve the following main operations. Voltage Supplier shown in Figure 3(b) supplies corresponding voltage according to different operation demand.

***Write operation***: As shown in Figure 2, when the WWL is enabled, a spin polarization current will be produced by adding a positive voltage between bit line (BL) and source line (SL). If the current is larger than the critical current, there will generate a skyrmion representing logic data "1" after a certain time. On the contrary, if there is not a skyrmion, it represents a logic data "0".

***Shift operation***: When SWLs on both sides of the racetrack are enabled, shift current will be produced by adding a positive voltage between BL and SL. If shift current is greater than the critical current of shifting, skyrmions move at a certain speed to the right based on the current density.

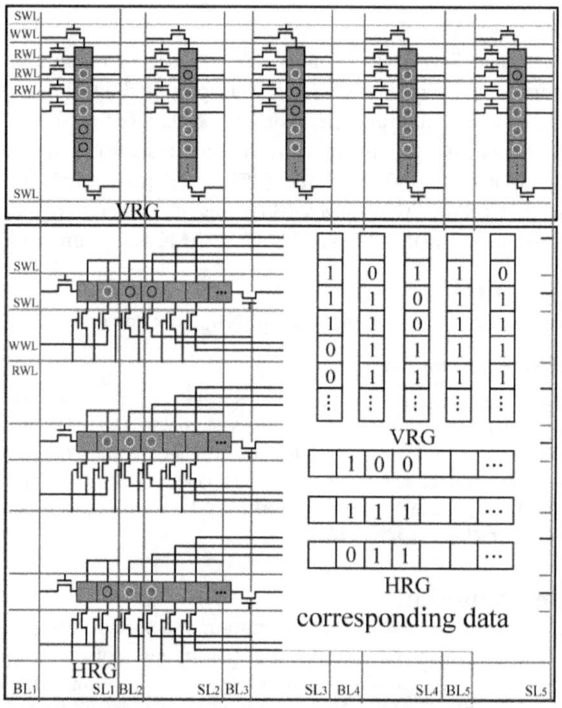

Figure 4: The internal structure of VRG and HRG and corresponding data stored in VRG and HRG

***Read operation***: MSC connects BL to node a and SL to node b so that the resistance state of accessed cell (cells) can be sensed by connecting a reference resistance to node c and d. Table 1 shows parameters of *Read, AND and XOR operation*. "pre" and "abs" mean the present and absent of skyrmion at racetrack. The structure of the cell to be read is shown in Figure 3(c) presented by $R_i$ (i is logic data "1" or "0"). $R_1$ and $R_0$ are the corresponding resistances value at read heads. Rref is reference resistance between node c and d. $R_1$ > Rrefr > $R_0$. When WL is enabled and $V_{read}$ is 0 V, the data will be read from $\overline{Qm}$(O) based on MSC.

***AND operation***: The structure of the cells to do *AND* and *XOR operation* is shown in Figure 3(c) presented by $R_{ij}$ (i and j can be "1" or "0"). $R_{ij}$ is the resistance value of $R_i$ in parallel with $R_j$. Rrefa is reference resistance, $R_{11}$ > Rrefa > $R_{10}$ = $R_{01}$ > $R_{00}$. When WLs of the two accessed cells are enabled and $V_{and}$ is 0 V, the *AND* result will be output from $\overline{Qm}$(O) based on MSC.

***XOR operation***: In *XOR operation*, Rrefx is reference resistance, and $R_{11}$ > $R_{10}$ = $R_{01}$ > Rrefx > $R_{00}$. It needs two steps to get *XOR* result: *step 1* MSC excludes *AND operation* and transmits the output signal $\overline{Qm}$(O) to MC. *step 2* Based on the signal from $\overline{Qm}$(O).

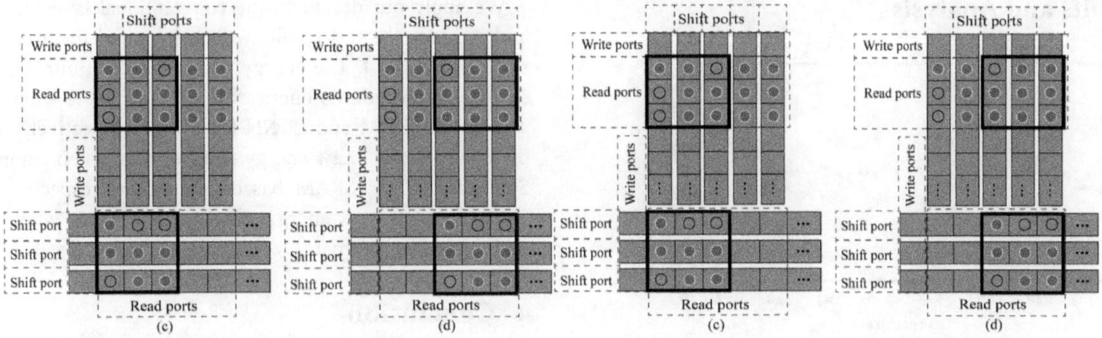


**Figure 5: Data storage and shift process of the scan convolutional process shown in Figure 1**

MC output control signal CS to decide if enable Rrefx and then using PCSA to get *XOR* result. If $\overline{Qm}$(O) output "1" at *step 1.* It means the data to be accessed are "1, 1". MC dosen't enable any reference resistor so that $\overline{Qm}$(O) will output "0" in *step 2.* If $\overline{Qm}$(O) output "0" at *step 1,* MC will enable reference resistor Rrefx. Then $\overline{Qm}$(O) can output *XOR* result of other cases.

**Table 1 Parameters in *Read, AND and XOR* operations**

| | Skyrmion | Logic data | $R_i$/ $R_{ij}$ ($R_{ab}$) | Rref ($R_{cd}$) | $\overline{Qm}$ (O) |
|---|---|---|---|---|---|
| *Read* operation | pre | 1 | $R_1$ | Rrefr= | 1 |
| | abs | 0 | $R_0$ | $(R_1+R_0)/2$ | 0 |
| *AND/ XOR*(step 2) operation | (pre,pre) | (1, 1) | $R_{11}$ | Rrefa= | 1/0 |
| | (pre,abs) | (1, 0) | $R_{10}$ | $(R_{11}+R_{10})/2$ | 0/1 |
| | (abs,pre) | (0, 1) | $R_{01}$ | Rrefx= | 0/1 |
| | (abs,abs) | (0, 0) | $R_{00}$ | $(R_{00}+R_{10})/2$ | 0/0 |

**TABLE 2 SRM-CIM MAIN PARAMETERS.**

| Parameter | Value |
|---|---|
| Racetrack dimension | 1000 nm×80 nm×0.4 nm |
| Mesh size | 1nm×1nm×0.4 nm |
| Perpendicular magnetic anisotropy Ku | 8e5J/m3 |
| DMI constant D | 3 mJ/m3 |
| Exchange stiffness A | 15 pJ/m |
| MTJ read/write head diameter | 40nm/20nm |

## 2.3 Mapping Strategy for Convolutional Process

Figure 5 shows the data storage and shifting process of the process shown in Figure 1. There is a write port on the left unit and a read port on each unit of each horizontal racetracks in HRG. We write all the inputs and weights to the VRG and HRG before executing the scan convolutional process. As shown in Figure 5 (a), inputs data and weights data that are circled by the black solid lines are the data to be accessed. *AND operations* are done between inputs and weights of the three rows of HRG and VRG respectively. Then the three *AND* results are transmitted to Bit-counter. Finally, the result of convolutional computing (a) will be output from Bit-counter. In Figure 5(b), weights are moved right two-unit length to support the second convolutional computing (b). In Figure 5(c), inputs are moved up two-unit lengths so that the inputs that to be accessed in the last two convolutional computing are moved to the read heads. Meanwhile, weights are moved back to the left to execute the third convolutional computing (c). Then in Figure 5(d), move weights to the right as shown in Figure 5(b), we will achieve the last convolutional computing (d). Thus, this design and mapping strategy, can perform the convolutional process in Figure 1 and achieve the scan convolutional process without any memory access redundancy, which greatly reduces the computing energy.

# 3 Experiments

## 3.1 Methodology

We tested the work in the MNIST dataset and evaluated it using Xnor-Net [1]. Table 2 shows the main material parameters of SRM-CIM that are extracted from [8]. OOMMF micromagnetic simulation are used to obtain current density, access time of generating and moving skyrmion and skyrmion shift velocity parameters. The SRM/CMOS devices hybrid SRM-CIM architecture is evaluated by Cadence Virtuoso. Figure 6(a) shows the process of producing a skyrmion with a current density J=1e13A/m$^2$. It needs only 0.04ns. Figure 6(b) shows the moving process of skyrmion when current density is 5e10A/m$^2$. Skyrmion has a transverse velocity except a longitudinal velocity initialy and then the transverse motion stops at a certain distance and moves along the nanotrack at a steady rate. For a skyrmion chain, all the skyrmions moves along the same trajectory with almost equal space because of the repulsions between the skyrmions. Figure 6(c) is a continuous process that produces and moves multiple skyrmions. If we produce a skyrmion and move the skyrmion chain for 1ns like 2.08ns to 3.12ns, all the skyrmions move 65nm. If we move the skyrmion chain for 1ns only like 4.16ns to 5.16ns, all the skyrmions on the racetrack move 57nm with a speed of 57m/s. Here a 65nm bit cell length is adopted and the data takes 1.14ns to move one bit because of the 57m/s shift velocity in Figure 3.

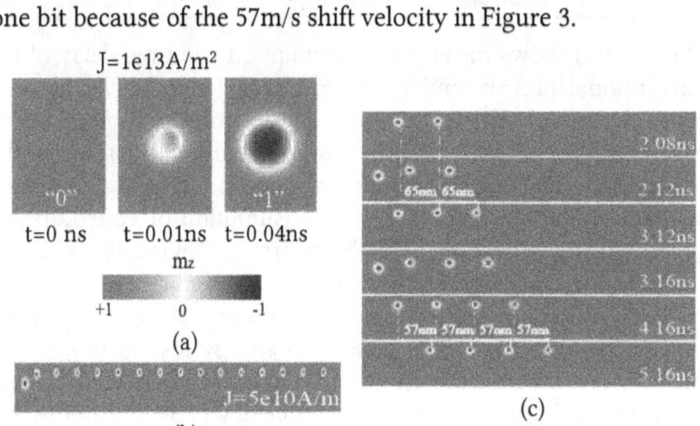


**Figure 6: (a) The process of producing a skyrmion. (b) The moving process of skyrmion. (c) The continuous process that produces and moves multiple skyrmions.**

### 3.2 Results and Analysis

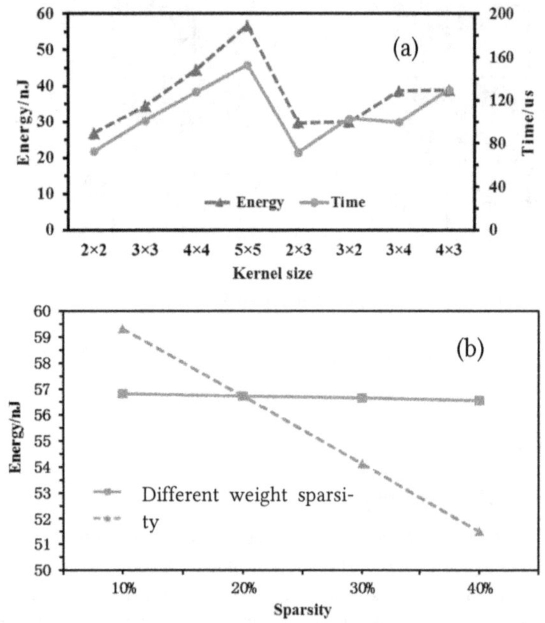


**Figure 7: (a) Energy consumption and time delay of the scanning process under different kernel size for 64 × 64 input (step length is 1, weight and input sparsity are 20%). (b) Energy consumption with different input sparsity.**

TABLE 3 ENERGY AND DELAY COMPARISON OF DIFFERENT IMAGE SIZE.

| Image size | 64×64 | 128×128 | 256×256 | 512×512 |
|---|---|---|---|---|
| Energy(nJ) | 26.8 | 107.2 | 429.4 | 1718.6 |
| Delay(us) | 72.6 | 259.0 | 1200 | 4800 |

TABLE 4 COMPARISON WITH THE STATE-OF-THE-ARTS

| Network | Memory | Energy | Delay | Energy efficiency |
|---|---|---|---|---|
| CNN | RRAM[4] | 18.39uJ | / | / |
| BCNN | RRAM[4] | 13.55uJ | / | / |
| | SRAM[2] | 0.745 uJ | 23.38us | 17.4181 |
| | SOT-MRAM[5] | 0.92 uJ | / | / |
| | SRM-CIM | 0.17 uJ | 37.81us | 6.4277 |

Figure 7(a) shows the energy consumption and time delay of the convolutional process under different kernel size. It can be seen that as the kernel size increases, the energy consumption and time delay increase, which is the inevitable result of increasing the writing data and operation number with the increase of kernel size. Figure 7(b) shows the energy consumption of convolutional process varies with input (weight) sparsity. Obviously, with the increase of the sparsity, energy consumption reduces almost linearly. This is because writing logic data "0" does not need any operation of SRM, which means almost no energy loss to write logic data "0". We take advantage of the feature of SRM to solve the sparsity issue in BCNN, the energy efficiency is further improved. When the input sparsity is 20%, energy consumption is reduced from 59.43nJ to 56.74nJ, which improves energy efficiency by 8.7%. Table 3 shows the energy and time delay comparison of different image size. The kernel size is 2×2, and the sparsity of both weight and input are 20%. It need only ~uJ to process a 512×512 image.

We apply our design to the convolutional layer of XNOR-Net and compare the test results with the state-of-the-arts [2], [4], [5] shown in Table 4. The energy consumption of our design is only 0.17uJ, which reduces energy by 99% and 98.7% when compared with CNN-RRAM and BCNN-RRAM [4] respectively. And it reduces 81.5% and 77.1% energy consumption when compared with SOT-MRAM and SRAM based counterpart respectively [2] [5]. SRM-CIM improves energy efficiency by 63.1% when compared with SRAM counterpart.

## 4 Conclusion

In this paper, we propose a Skyrmion Racetrack Memory based computing in-memory architecture for binary neural network, which can execute both memory operation and in-memory computing operation (*AND* operation and *XOR* operation). When executing convolutional scan process of 2×2 kernel size in 64×64 inputs, it can achieve 26.751nJ energy consumption with execution time of 72.641us. SRM-CIM achieves 98.7% energy reduction when compared with RRAM based counterpart when applied to convolutional layer in the typical case of BCNN: Xnor-Net.

## ACKNOWLEDGMENTS

This work was supported in part by the National Science Foundation for Young Scientists of China under Grant KZ73030401, in part by Beihang hefei science city project under Grant 01-0004-01 from Beihang University Hefei Innovation Research Institute. Special Foundation of Beijing Municipal Science & Technology Commission under Grant No. Z161100000216149.

## REFERENCES

[1] Rastegari, M., Ordonez, V., Redmon, J., & Farhadi, A. (2016, October). Xnor-net: Imagenet classification using binary convolutional neural networks. In European Conference on Computer Vision (pp. 525-542). Springer, Cham.

[2] Khwa, W. S., Chen, J. J., Li, J. F., Si, X., Yang, E. Y., Sun, X., ... & Chang, M. F. (2018, February). A 65nm 4Kb algorithm-dependent computing-in-memory SRAM unit-macro with 2.3 ns and 55.8 TOPS/W fully parallel product-sum operation for binary DNN edge processors. In Solid-State Circuits Conference-(ISSCC), 2018 IEEE International (pp. 496-498). IEEE.

[3] Choi, Y. G., Yoo, S., Lee, S., & Ahn, J. H. (2011, June). Matching cache access behavior and bit error pattern for high performance low Vcc L1 cache. In Design Automation Conference (DAC), 2011 48th ACM/EDAC/IEEE (pp. 978-983). IEEE.

[4] Tang, T., Xia, L., Li, B., Wang, Y., & Yang, H. (2017, January). Binary convolutional neural network on rram. In Design Automation Conference (ASP-DAC), 2017 22nd Asia and South Pacific (pp. 782-787). IEEE.

[5] Angizi, S., He, Z., Parveen, F., & Fan, D. (2018, January). IMCE: Energy-efficient bit-wise in-memory convolution engine for deep neural network. In Proceedings of the 23rd Asia and South Pacific Design Automation Conference (pp. 111-116). IEEE Press.

[6] Sun, Z., Wu, W., & Li, H. (2013, May). Cross-layer racetrack memory design for ultra high density and low power consumption. In Design Automation Conference (DAC), 2013 50th ACM/EDAC/IEEE (pp. 1-6). IEEE.

[7] Fert, A., Cros, V., & Sampaio, J. (2013). Skyrmions on the track. Nature nanotechnology, 8(3), 152.

[8] Kang, W., Huang, Y., Zheng, C., Lv, W., Lei, N., Zhang, Y., ... & Zhao, W. (2016). Voltage controlled magnetic skyrmion motion for racetrack memory. Scientific reports, 6, 23164.

[9] Huang, Y., Kang, W., Zhang, X., Zhou, Y., & Zhao, W. (2017). Magnetic skyrmion-based synaptic devices. Nanotechnology, 28(8), 08LT02.

[10] Li, S., Kang, W., Huang, Y., Zhang, X., Zhou, Y., & Zhao, W. (2017). Magnetic skyrmion-based artificial neuron device. Nanotechnology, 28(31), 31LT01.

[11] Zhao, W., Chappert, C., Javerliac, V., & Noziere, J. P. (2009). High speed, high stability and low power sensing amplifier for MTJ/CMOS hybrid logic circuits. IEEE Transactions on Magnetics, 45(10), 3784-3787.

# TASecure: Temperature-Aware Secure Deletion Scheme for Solid State Drives

Bingzhe Li
University of Minnesota, Twin Cities
Minneapolis, MN, USA
lixx1743@umn.edu

David H.C. Du
University of Minnesota, Twin Cities
Minneapolis, MN, USA
du@umn.edu

## ABSTRACT

With the increasing concerns of security, the secure deletion for SSDs becomes very costly due to its out-of-place update (i.e., an update is performed in a new location leaving the old data un-touched). Some previous studies used a combined erase-based and cryptography-based method to find a heuristic deletion scheme. However, the deletion overhead is still large since a key may be associated with too many pages. Therefore, how to reduce the secure deletion overhead further is becoming an interesting research issue. In this paper, a temperature-aware secure deletion scheme (TASecure) is proposed. Data with the same temperature are stored in the same region in order to reduce the overhead of secure deletion. The temperature of a data is referred to the frequency of the data is updated. Moreover, the regions based on their temperature are associated with different numbers of keys and are applied with different secure deletion schemes. Finally, the experimental results indicate that our proposed secure deletion scheme can reduce the secure deletion cost about 1.2x to 19x compared to previous studies.

## CCS CONCEPTS

• **Security and privacy** → *Database and storage security*; • **Computer systems organization** → *Architectures*;

## KEYWORDS

Solid state drive; Secure deletion; Invalid data; Temperature

**ACM Reference Format:**
Bingzhe Li and David H.C. Du. 2019. TASecure: Temperature-Aware Secure Deletion Scheme for Solid State Drives. In *Great Lakes Symposium on VLSI 2019 (GLSVLSI '19), May 9–11, 2019, Tysons Corner, VA, USA.* ACM, New York, NY, USA, 4 pages. https://doi.org/10.1145/3299874.3318016

## 1 INTRODUCTION

With the rapid development of the electrical devices and Internet, various types of information are stored as digital in storage media. How to keep data privacy and security has becoming more and more important. One important security issue is how to securely delete invalid data in the storage media [1]. Due to the high performance of solid state drives (SSDs), SSDs currently have been becoming prevailing across many computing environments from the mobile devices to the cloud systems. People expect the SSDs having the same security features as the traditional hard disks. However, due to the different granularity of write and erase operations, SSDs use out-of-place updates with the log-structure [2]. As a result, the updated data will not directly overwrite its original value and need to be written to free space (new location). The out-of-place updates keep the invalid data still in the SSDs until they are garbage collected. This provides an opportunity for adversaries or attackers to recover these invalid but probably sensitive data.

To overcome the secure issue of invalid data in SSDs, two basic methods were proposed. One is called erase-based deletion. The idea is to erase all invalid data for secure deletion. The other method is called cryptography-based scheme [3], which first encrypts data before writing them to the flash. Meanwhile, the keys used in the encryption are also stored in the flash. However, the above methods confront large overhead of migration when securely deleting invalid data. To reduce the migration overhead, some other works combined these two methods to lower erase and migration overhead. For example, ErasuCrypto [4] used either erase-based or cryptography-based method to delete blocks. The greedy heuristic algorithm is used to determine whether a block uses the erase-based or the cryptography-based deletion. However, above works did not consider the effect of the workload access patterns. According to the access patterns, the efficient I/O allocation in SSDs may help significantly reduce the migration and erase overhead during secure deletion.

In this paper, a new Temperature Aware Secure deletion scheme called TASecure is proposed to reduce overhead of the secure deletion. First, according to the historical accumulated update frequency (called temperature), the pages/data are classified to several regions and the data in the same region have similar update frequency (the same temperature). After that, chunks in the same region contain the same number of blocks and the pages/data across different blocks in the same chunk are encrypted by the same key. As a result, the TASecure scheme is capable of lowering the overhead of secure deletion with dynamic data allocation and different chunk configurations for different real workloads. Finally, the experimental results indicate that our proposed secure


*GLSVLSI '19, May 9–11, 2019, Tysons Corner, VA, USA*

ACM ISBN 978-1-4503-6252-8/19/05...$15.00
https://doi.org/10.1145/3299874.3318016

deletion scheme can out-perform existing schemes in terms of the secure deletion cost.

## 2 BACKGROUND AND MOTIVATION

Due to the out-of-place update as discussed above, the invalid data are kept in the SSD after updates and before erased. The purpose of secure deletion is to destroy invalid data permanently in order that adversaries cannot recover those invalid data. Two basic schemes, an erase-based and a cryptography-based, were proposed as discussed in the introduction section. For the erase-based scheme, during deletion process the blocks containing invalid pages will be erased. Meanwhile, all valid pages in the block must be migrated to free pages. The cryptography-based scheme encrypts data with security keys. The encrypted data and keys are stored in the flash memory. To securely delete the invalid data pages, the SSD only needs to delete the keys of the invalid data pages. The encryption algorithm normally uses the advanced encryption standard (AES) [5]. To save space, pages across multiple blocks can share the same key. These multiple blocks with shared keys comprise one **chunk**. The number of blocks in the chunk is called **chunk size** ($C_z$). Thus, if there are valid data pages sharing a key with invalid data pages, the valid pages must be migrated to free space before deleting the key. Therefore, the above two deletion schemes face large overhead of erase, decryption, migration, and re-encryption.

To overcome the high overhead, Liu *et al.* [4] proposed a secure deletion scheme called ErasuCrypto, which combines both erase-based and cryptography-based schemes together. The basic idea is that in one chunk ErasuCrypto uses a heuristic algorithm to find the minimum secure deletion cost (as seen in Eq. (1)) by applying either cryptography-based or erase-based scheme to each block.

$$cost = \#Mgr + k \times \#Era \tag{1}$$

where, $\#Mgr$ and $\#Era$ indicate the number of migrations and the number of erases separately for secure deletion. $k$ is the coefficient to indicate the ratio of the cost between erase and migration operations.

Some other works [4][6][7][8] also focused on reducing the overhead of secure deletion. In [6], they partitioned the secure and insecure data in order to get rid of unnecessary migrations. However, the scenario of insecure and secure is not common. People always want to protect the data on the whole drive. Another technique called 'scrubbing' [9][7][10][11] is a page-level secure deletion scheme, which generally reprograms invalid pages in order to make those valid pages un-accessible. However, the scrubbing method may introduce unpredictable disturbs to the valid pages within the same blocks. Wang *et al.* [8] proposed a new encryption and secure deletion for mobile devices. The mobile host generates the keys for storage devices and saves the key block space. However, the drawback of this scheme is that the storage device is permanently attached to the host and cannot be used by other systems.

Overall, previous works [4][6][7][8] passively address the secure deletion issue without any intent to optimize data scheduling and management. Therefore, there is an opportunity to further reduce the overhead of secure deletion by actively scheduling and managing incoming data.

**Algorithm 1** TASecure Data Classification and Allocation

```
1: procedure DATA CLASSIFICATION AND ALLOCATION
2:     while t < T do // Collecting access frequency in T
3:         Compute slice number S_i of Req_t
4:         Acc_TBL[S_i] +=1
5:     Compute max and min values in Acc_TBL
6:     Compute N centroids for N regions, centroid_j = max − min * jN
7:     New request coming (Req)
8:     Compute the slice number (S) of Req
9:     Compute Euclidean distance dS, centroid_j.
10:    if dS, centroid_j is the minimum for all j from 0 to N-1 then
11:        Region#j ← Req
```

**Algorithm 2** TASecure Deletion

```
procedure SECURE DELETION
    if Region#0 then
        Erase-based deletion for the region#0
        ...
    else
        Do greedy heuristic algorithm [4]
```

## 3 TASECURE SCHEME

In this section, we mainly introduce the temperature-aware secure (TASecure) scheme. The basic idea is to separate potentially valid and invalid data in order to reduce the secure deletion overhead. There are two major steps in the TASecure scheme. The first step is to classify requests according to their historical access patterns and to assign them to the regions with the same temperature. The second step is to apply proper deletion schemes to different temperature regions. In Section 4, the configuration of the SSDs are provided with the constant key block overhead.

For the first step of the TASecure scheme, it is the data classification and allocation as seen in Algorithm 1. First, the SSD logical space is split into **slices**, which are consecutive logical spaces (the default size of a slice is 20MB), to record the historical access patterns. We do not use the page-level recording since it needs much larger space to store the historical information. During a period $T$, the number of writes are recorded in **Acc_TBL** as seen at Lines 2-4 of Algorithm 1. Then, the centroid values are computed, which are representative values for each region/classification category (Lines 5-6). For example, suppose that there are two regions (N=2, **N** indicates the number of regions), the maximum and minimum values in the Acc_TBL are the two representative values for these two groups. Once obtaining the centroids, a new coming request in the next period can be classified based on those centroids. The euclidean distances are compute between the slice number (**S**) of the request and each centroid value. Then, the request should be stored into the region of which centroid and its $S$ value achieve the minimum euclidean distance. By

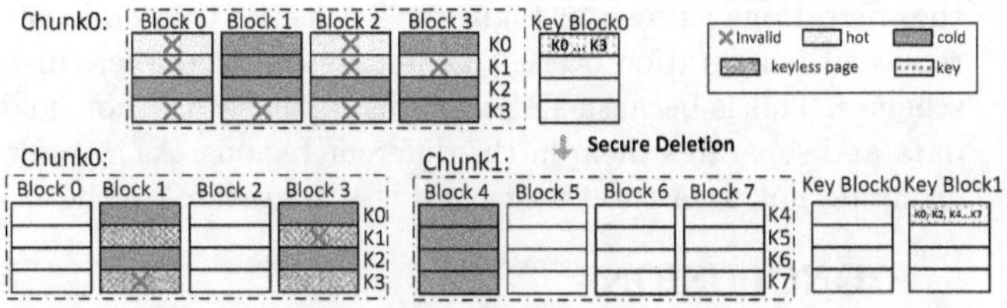


**Figure 1: An example of the ErasuCrypto scheme for secure deletion with the chunk size of 4. Secure deletion causes 4 migrations and 3 erases.**

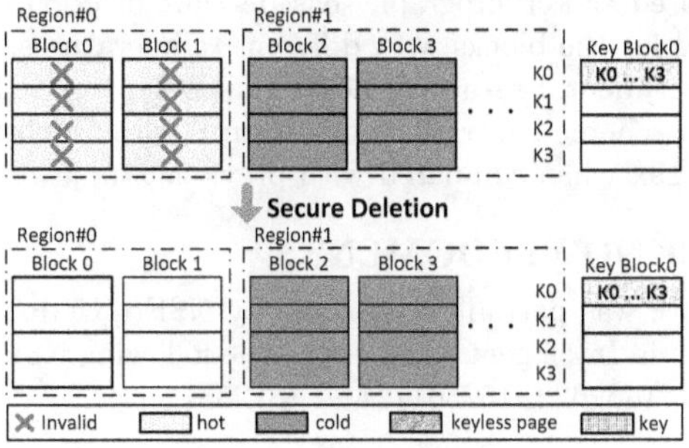


**Figure 2: An example of the TASecure scheme for secure deletion chunk size = 4. Secure deletion causes no migration and 3 erases.**

doing that, data will be stored in the region which contains the same temperature data.

The second step is the TASecure deletion process as shown in Algorithm 2. As discussed above, data have been partitioned into different regions based on their temperature. In the hottest region (access frequencies of requests are high), the blocks contain the largest staleness value (number of invalid pages/total block size). Thus, we can only use the erase-based scheme with little migration overhead for the hottest region as seen at Lines 2-3 of Algorithm 2 and no encryption is needed in this region. There are two advantages. The first one is that without encryption and decryption processes data access latency will be reduced. The other is that no key block is needed and thus it saves space. For the other regions, they use the heuristic algorithm [4] to determine which deletion scheme is used for their blocks (Lines 5-6).

Figure 1 and Figure 2 are two examples to indicate the overhead of ErasuCrypto and TASecure schemes. Two schemes have the same key block overhead (data blocks : key blocks = 4:1). As seen in Figure 1, for the ErasuCrypto scheme the hot and cold data are mixed in the blocks. Since the hot data have the higher probabilities to be updated, most of hot data become invalid. Therefore, during the secure deletion process, ErasuCrypto scheme erases Block0 and Block2 due to its high staleness (erase-based) and deletes the keys of block1 and block3 (cryptography-based). Compared to ErasuCrypto, as seen in Figure 2, the proposed TASecure groups the data with the same temperature in the same blocks. As

**Table 1: SSD configuration**

| Parameter | Value | Parameter | Value |
|---|---|---|---|
| SSD capacity | 250GB | # of pages/block | 128 |
| Page Size | 4KB | Read latency | 25us [14] |
| Slice size | 20MB | Erase latency | 1.5ms [14] |
| # of key blocks | 250 | Program Latency | 200us [14] |

**Table 2: MSR Cambridge trace configuration [12]**

| | Duration (hrs) | Number of IOs (Millions) | | Total request size (GB) | |
|---|---|---|---|---|---|
| | | Write | Read | Write | Read |
| prn_0 | 168 | 4.98 | 0.602 | 45.96 | 13.12 |
| prn_1 | 168 | 2.77 | 8.46 | 30.78 | 181.35 |
| proj_1 | 168 | 2.50 | 21.14 | 25.58 | 750.36 |
| usr_1 | 168 | 3.86 | 41.43 | 56.13 | 2079.23 |
| usr_2 | 168 | 1.99 | 8.58 | 26.47 | 415.28 |
| hm_0 | 168 | 2.58 | 1.42 | 20.47 | 9.96 |
| rsrch_0 | 168 | 1.30 | 0.13 | 10.82 | 1.39 |
| stg_1 | 168 | 0.80 | 1.40 | 5.99 | 79.52 |
| prxy_0 | 168 | 12.14 | 0.38 | 53.80 | 3.05 |
| ts_0 | 194 | 1.49 | 0.32 | 11.34 | 4.13 |

a result, the pages with updates are grouped in the same block. Therefore, the TASecure scheme only needs 3 block erases without any migration. Moreover, after secure deletion, TASecure contains less number of invalid and keyless pages than ErasuCrypto which might cause large garbage collection overhead in future.

# 4 EXPERIMENTAL RESULTS

In this section, the performance of different secure deletion schemes are compared based on the simulation results.

## 4.1 Environment Setup

The SSD configuration is listed in Table 1. The SSD capacity is 250GB. The migration and erase latencies are 225us and 1.5ms, respectively. Thus, we set $k$ value in Eq. (1) to 7. The number of key blocks is set to 250. It means that the chunk size is 8 for the ErasuCrypto scheme. The encryption algorithm uses the AES algorithm with 128 bits (AES-128). The real trace Cambridge MSR traces [12] is used. The experimental results are obtained based on the DiskSim simulator [13] with the SSD model extension. We assume that the secure deletion command is triggered after replaying each 168-hour trace.

## 4.2 Performance Comparison

In this subsection, the deletion performance comparison between TASecure, ErasuCrypto, Erase-based scheme and cryptography-based scheme is provided. Three metrics, the secure deletion cost in Eq. (1), number of migrations and number of erases, are used to indicate the secure deletion overhead. The chunks size is set to 8. It means that 8 pages are encrypted by the same key. Therefore, the total number of key blocks for TASecure, ErasuCrypto and Cryptography-based scheme is 250.

Figure 3, Figure 4 and Figure 5 indicate the normalized secure deletion cost, number of migrations and number of erases between TASecure, ErasuCrypto, Erase-based scheme and cryptography-based scheme, respectively. For the secure

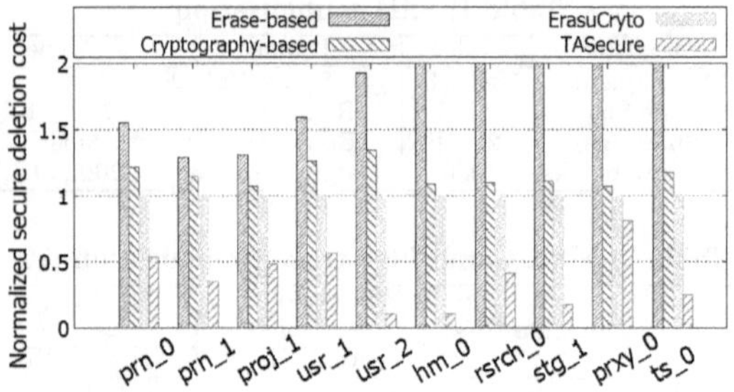


**Figure 3: Normalized secure deletion cost comparison between TASecure, ErasuCrypto, erase-based scheme and cryptography-based schemes.**

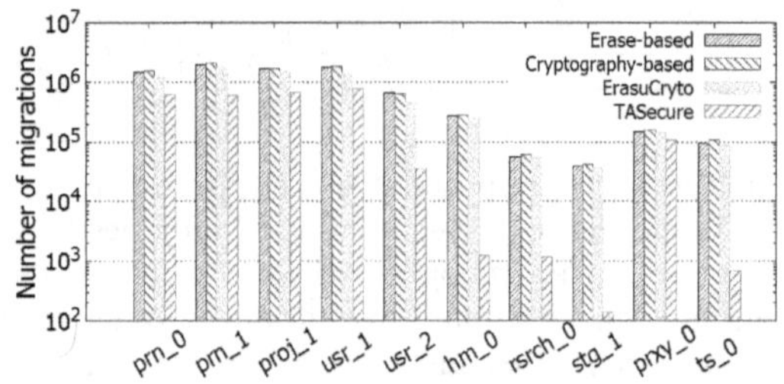


**Figure 4: Number of migrations between TASecure, ErasuCrypto, erase-based scheme and cryptography-based schemes. (y-axis is log-scale)**

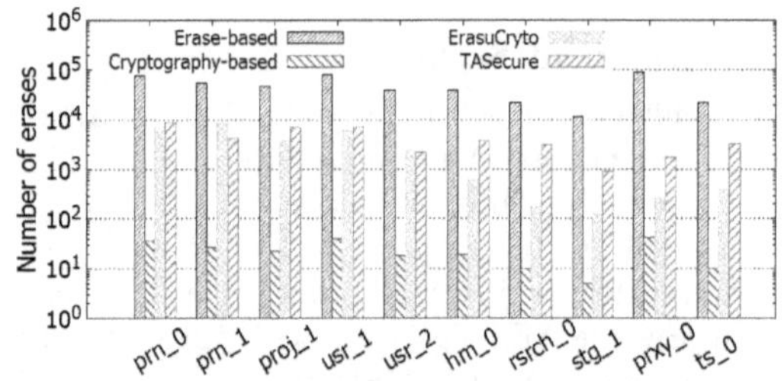


**Figure 5: Number of erases between TASecure, ErasuCrypto, erase-based scheme and cryptography-based schemes. (y-axis is log-scale)**

deletion cost, the cost of ErasuCrypto is normalized to one. As seen in Figure 3, the erase-based scheme obtains the worse secure deletion cost and the cryptography-based scheme is the second worse secure deletion scheme. The proposed TASecure achieves the lowest secure deletion cost. Compared to the erase-based scheme, TASecure achieves about 2.7x - 19.8x cost reduction. Compared to the cryptography-based scheme, TASecure obtains 1.3x - 12.7x secure deletion cost reduction. Also, TASecure gets 1.2x to 9.4x less cost than ErasuCrypto. In summary, the proposed TASecure obtains on average about 9.5x, 4.8x and 4.1x cost reduction compared to erase-based, cryptography-based and ErasuCrypto schemes, respectively.

The details of the secure deletion cost are provided based on the number of page migrations and block erases in Eq. (1). For the migrations as seen in Figure 4, TASecure tremendously reduces the migration overhead compared to the other three schemes. This is because TASecure distinguishes the hot/cold data and separates them in the different regions. As a result, grouping hot data together causes less migration overhead.

# 5 CONCLUSION

In this paper, the temperature-aware secure deletion scheme is proposed. According to the temperature of the data pages in SSDs, the pages with the same or similar temperature are stored in the same block in order to reducing the migration overhead during deletion period. Meanwhile, both the erase-based and cryptography-based secure deletion methods are used for the blocks with different temperatures. Finally, the experimental results indicate that our proposed secure deletion scheme can reduce the secure deletion cost about 20% to 19x when compared with previous studies.

# 6 ACKNOWLEDGMENTS

This work was partially supported by NSF I/UCRC Center Research in Intelligent Storage and the following NSF awards 1421913, 1439622, 1525617, and 1812537.

# REFERENCES

[1] Cyril Guyot, et al. Implementing secure erase for solid state drives, August 21 2012. US Patent 8,250,380.
[2] Peter Desnoyers. Analytic modeling of ssd write performance. In *Proceedings of the 5th Annual International Systems and Storage Conference*, page 12. ACM, 2012.
[3] Joel Reardon, et al. Data node encrypted file system: Efficient secure deletion for flash memory. In *Proceedings of the 21st USENIX conference on Security symposium*, pages 17–17. USENIX Association, 2012.
[4] Chen Liu, et al. Erasucrypto: A light-weight secure data deletion scheme for solid state drives. *Proceedings on Privacy Enhancing Technologies*, 2017(1):132–148, 2017.
[5] Royal Canadian Mounted Police. G2-003 hard drive secure information removal and destruction standards, 2003.
[6] Hoda Aghaei Khouzani, et al. Architecting data placement in ssds for efficient secure deletion implementation. In *Proceedings of the International Conference on Computer-Aided Design*, page 42. ACM, 2018.
[7] Wei-Chen Wang, et al. Scrubbing-aware secure deletion for 3-d nand flash. *IEEE Transactions on Computer-Aided Design of Integrated Circuits and Systems*, 37(11):2790–2801, 2018.
[8] Minshen Wang, et al. A novel data secure deletion scheme for mobile devices. In *2018 27th International Conference on Computer Communication and Networks (ICCCN)*, pages 1–8. IEEE, 2018.
[9] Ping-Hsien Lin, et al. Achieving fast sanitization with zero live data copy for mlc flash memory. In *Proceedings of the International Conference on Computer-Aided Design*, page 41. ACM, 2018.
[10] Michael Yung Chung Wei, et al. Reliably erasing data from flash-based solid state drives. In *Fast*, volume 11, pages 8–8, 2011.
[11] Kyoungmoon Sun, et al. Models and design of an adaptive hybrid scheme for secure deletion of data in consumer electronics. *IEEE Transactions on Consumer Electronics*, 54(1), 2008.
[12] Dushyanth Narayanan, et al. Write off-loading: Practical power management for enterprise storage. *ACM Transactions on Storage (TOS)*, 4(3):10, 2008.
[13] Greg Ganger, et al. The disksim simulation environment (v4. 0). *Parallel Data Lab, http://www. pdl. cmu. edu/DiskSim/Online-document*, 2009.
[14] Ping Huang, et al. Shiftflash: Make flash-based storage more resilient and robust. *Performance Evaluation*, 68(11):1193–1206, 2011.

# An Asymmetric Dual Output On-Chip DC-DC Converter for Dynamic Workloads

Xingye Liu
ECE Department
Virginia Tech
Blacksburg, Virginia, US
xingye15@vt.edu

Paul Ampadu
ECE Department
Virginia Tech
Blacksburg, Virginia, US
ampadu@vt.edu

## ABSTRACT

We propose a novel two-stage hybrid on-chip DC-DC converter targeting low power applications with multiple supply voltage domains and dynamic workloads. The converter has a nominal input voltage of 1.2V and generates two asymmetrically regulated output voltages simultaneously. The high-power output channel provides voltages ranging from 0.3V to 1.1V and up to 12mA load current; on the other hand, the low-power output channel delivers voltages varying from 0.3V to 0.5V with up to 1mA load current. The high-power output is able to respond to load transition requests with a peak voltage slew rate of 16V/μs and maximum voltage ripple of 49mV. During load transitions at the high-power channel, the low-power output voltage with fixed load remains stable with less than 7.6% ripples and a worst-case droop of 45 mV. In addition, when load transitions are requested at both output channels simultaneously, there are no observable voltage droops/spikes at the outputs; thus, cross regulations are significantly reduced. Even with input voltage glitches, additional voltage spikes/droops at each output are less than 5%. Peak power efficiency achieved is 73%.

## CCS CONCEPTS

• **Hardware** → **Power conversion**; • **Hardware** → Chip-level power issues;

## KEYWORDS

Dual-Output, DC-DC converter, low power, load transient response, fast response, reliable, hybrid converter

**ACM Reference format:**
Xingye Liu and Paul Ampadu. 2019. An Asymmetric Dual Output On-Chip DC-DC Converter for Dynamic Workloads. In *GLSVLSI '19: 2019 Great Lakes Symposium on VLSI, May 9–11, 2019, Washington, D.C., USA.* ACM, New York, NY, USA, 4 pages. https://doi.org/10.1145/3299874.3318017


*GLSVLSI '19, May 9–11, 2019, Tysons Corner, VA, USA*

*ACM ISBN 978-1-4503-6252-8/19/05...$15.00*
*https://doi.org/10.1145/3299874.3318017*

## 1 INTRODUCTION

Power management is one of the major issues in low-power systems-on-chip (SoCs) as workloads demand flexible and time-variant operations. For power consumption in the order of 10mW, on-chip power supplies are usually preferred, considering response time, efficiency and footprint, to meet dynamic load operation and transition requests. In commercial SoCs such as Blackghost family [14] and ARM-Cortex subsystems [10], processors need adjustable supply voltages to enable various operation modes. Meanwhile, on-chip sensors and digital modules, such as body-bias control circuits [11], usually operate under low supply voltages and require independent tunable power supplies. These bring challenges to conventional on-chip powering systems where each load has dedicated power supply. It suffers from area overhead and a larger number of passives components are required for more on-chip workloads [6].

Single-inductor-multiple-output (SIMO) topology is an alternative where different outputs channels have shared inductors for energy-storage [2], [4]. However, DC offset errors and voltage droops during load transitions are remaining problems. Another inductor-based buck converter [12] provides 5 outputs with improved cross regulations by using charge control and assigning accurate amount of power to each output as desired. But high-quality off-chip inductors are usually required.

Compared to inductor-based solutions, a SC-based topology is proposed in [3] that generates two output voltages (0.8V and 1.6V) each supporting 600mA load. Both transient response and cross regulation are improved by applying continuous gate-drive modulations. A 123-phase SC converter based on a ring structure is proposed in [9] for wearable devices. The converter provides up to 2.5 V/μs output voltage slew rate and limits ripples to 30mV. However, capacitor-based topologies suffer from discrete output voltages, complicated control and inherent losses [7].

Considering limitations of using only capacitors or inductors, hybrid DC-DC converters provide alternate solutions [8], [13]. A multilevel multistage hybrid converter is proposed in [1] to generate an output ranging from 0.1V to 1.0V by dynamically reconfiguring the SC circuits while the inductor only serves as a low-pass filter. In this paper we follow this approach and propose a novel hybrid on-chip DC-DC converter with dual asymmetrical outputs targeting different power levels and voltages. With a simplified digital control mechanism, load transient response is improved compared to the state-of-the-art. Section 2 introduces the converter architecture, control mechanism and related optimization methods. Section 3 shows load transient responses results of the converter and power efficiencies. Section 4 discusses the advantages and limitations and compare with other works. Section 5 concludes the work with some future directions.

# 2 PROPOSED DC-DC CONVERTER

## 2.1 Proposed Converter Topology

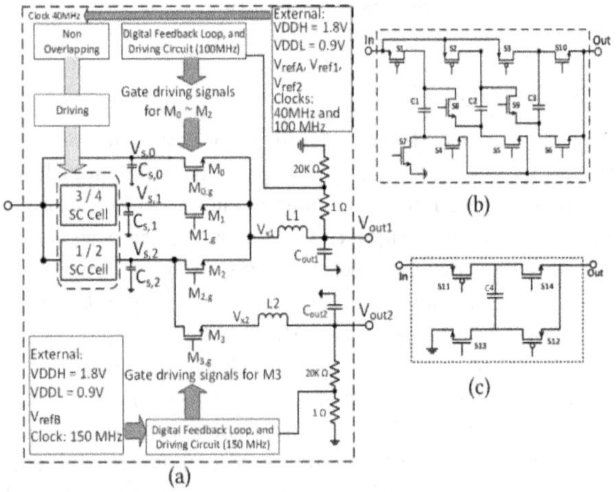



**Figure 1: (a) Proposed two-stage hybrid DC-DC converter with two independent output channels for different voltage domains and controlled by separate digital feedback loops; Topologies of the two SC cells used at the first stage of the proposed converter with conversion ratios (b) ¾; (c) ½.**

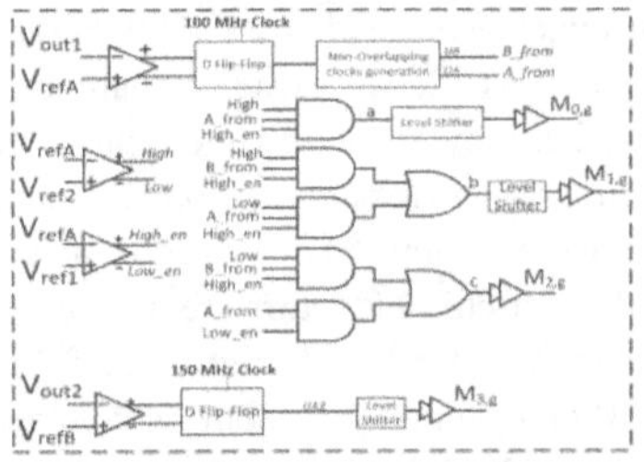

**Figure 2: Structure of two digital feedback loops that control the switched-inductors of the proposed converter with external clocks and references of $V_{refA}$, $V_{refB}$, $V_{ref1}$ = 0.4$V_{in}$ and $V_{ref2}$ = 0.67$V_{in}$.**

The proposed converter is shown in Figure 1 with control scheme. The converter consists of two stages which are responsible respectively for generating pre-regulated inner voltages and fully regulated output voltages. Two switched capacitor cells with different conversion ratios are used as the first stage with fixed configurations. Two separate digital feedback loops compare $V_{refA}$ and $V_{refB}$ with output voltages and control switches $M_0$ – $M_3$. $V_{out1}$ delivers 300mV to 1.1V with up to 12 mA load while $V_{out2}$ provides 300mV to 500mV with up to 1mA load current. Considering voltage division of each stage, we set external references $V_{ref1}$ as 0.4$V_{in}$ and $V_{ref2}$ = 0.67$V_{in}$ so different output voltages can be provided from proper SC cells. We assume two clock signals are available from off-chip sources. Two VDDs (VDDL = 0.9V and VDDH = 1.8V) are needed as well.

## 2.2 Converter Size and Loss Optimizations

Power efficiency $\eta$ of the converter is calculated in equation (1).

$$\eta = \frac{V_{out\,1}I_{out\,1} + V_{out\,2}I_{out\,2}}{V_{out1}I_{out1} + V_{out2}I_{out2} + P_{loss} + V_{drive}I_{drive}} \quad (1)$$

The overall efficiency calculation includes power at all output channels. Detailed loss calculations can be found in [7]. $C_{fly}$ (flying capacitor), $f_{sw}$ (switching frequency) and $W_{sw}$ (total width of transistors) are design variables to be optimized based on load resistance $R_L$ and each output voltage $V_o$. It shows that:

$$f_{sw\text{-}opt} \propto \frac{1}{C_{fly}R_L} \quad (2)$$

$$W_{sw\text{-}opt} \propto \sqrt{\frac{V_o^2}{V_{sw}}\frac{R_{on}C_{fly}}{R_L C_{gate}}} \quad (3)$$

In the proposed converter, equivalent load resistance for SC cells include all components (switches $M_0$ to $M_3$, inductors and the loads) at the second stage. The second step of the optimization is for switches $M_0$ to $M_3$ and the inductor, and it is similar to optimization process of traditional buck converters shown in [2].

# 3 RESULTS

The converter is simulated in 32nm SOI CMOS technology in Cadence. The components sizes and values are listed in Table 1. $C_{s,0}$ is designed as an off-chip 10nF capacitor.

**Table 1: Components Details**

| Components | Size |
|---|---|
| S1~ S3, S11, S12 | $W_{sw}$ =160 μm |
| S4 ~ S10, S13, S14 | $W_{sw}$ = 80 μm |
| C1 ~ C4, $C_{s,1}$, $C_{s,2}$ | 1nF deep trench |
| $C_{out1}$ | 8nF deep trench |
| $C_{out2}$ | 5nF deep trench |
| Inductor L1, L2 | 1.25 nH on-chip |
| $M_0$ ~ $M_2$ | $W_{sw}$ = 400 μm |
| $M_3$ | $W_{sw}$ = 50 μm |

As shown in Figure 3, when two outputs are responding to load transition requests simultaneously, there is no observable cross regulations and voltage ripples are less than 5.5%.

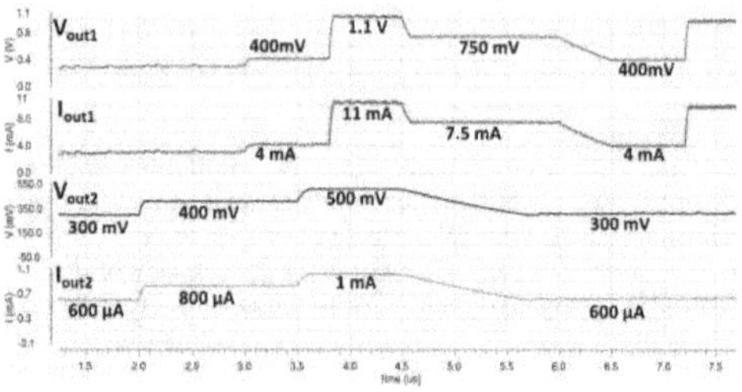



**Figure 3: Transient responses of both outputs of the converter with load resistors of 100 Ohms and 500 Ohms when each output voltage switches between different levels independently.**

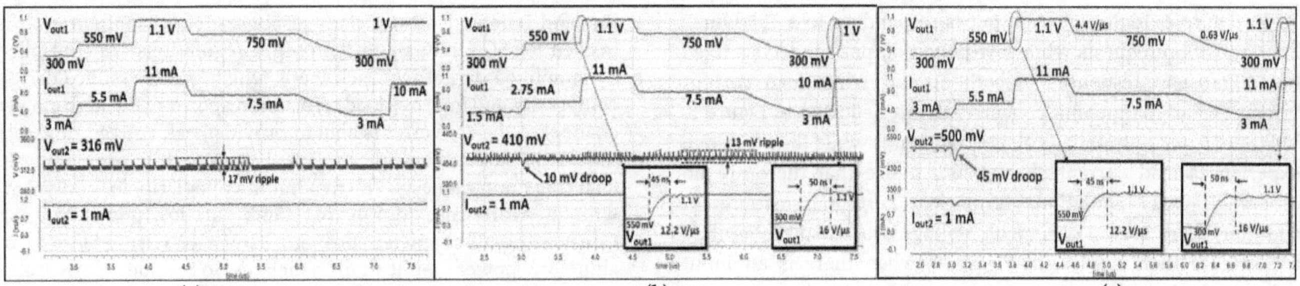


(a) (b) (c)

**Figure 4: Transient responses of both outputs when high-power output $V_{out1}$ switches between different levels with a load resistor of 100 Ohms and low-power output supplies 1mA at (a) 316 mV; (b) 410 mV; and (c) 500 mV.**

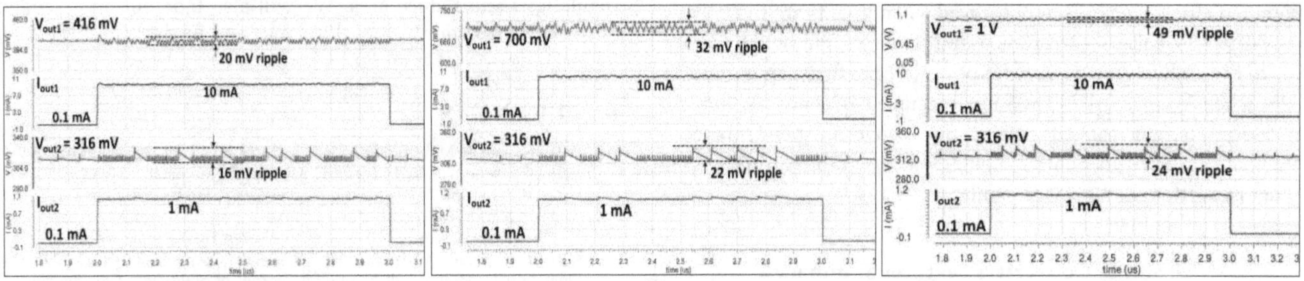


(a) (b) (c)

**Figure 5: Transient responses of both outputs when low-power output has 10x current transitions at 316mV while high-power output has 100x load current transitions with (a) $V_{out1}$ = 416 mV; (b) $V_{out1}$ = 700 mV and (c) $V_{out1}$ = 316mV showing no cross regulations and max 49 mV and 24 mV ripples at high-power and low-power outputs respectively.**

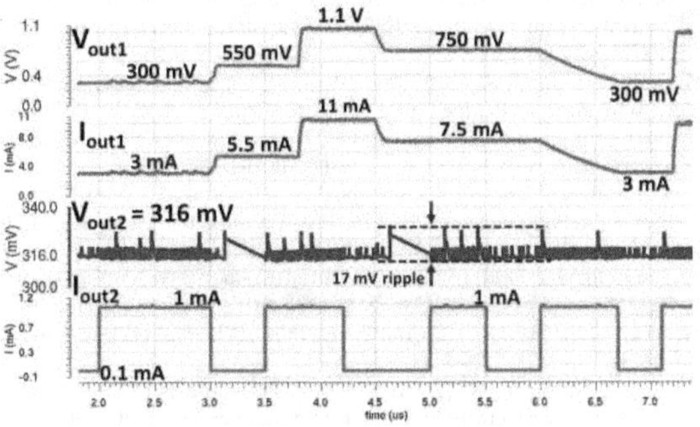


**Figure 6: Transient responses of both outputs of the converter when high-power output $V_{out1}$ switches between different levels while low-power output is fixed at 316mV with intermittent 10x load current transitions showing a peak 17mV ripple.**

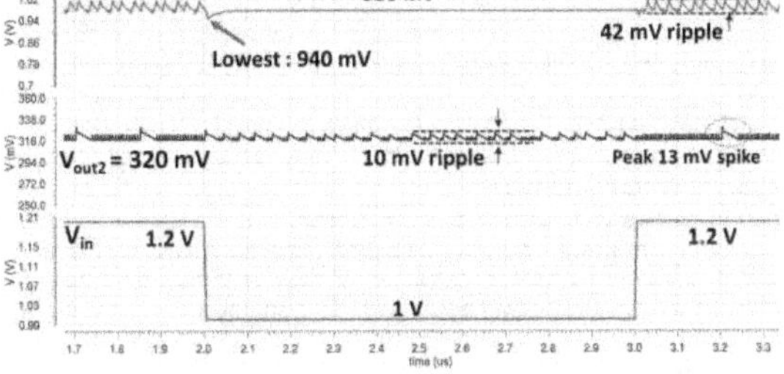


**Figure 7: Transient responses of both outputs with an input voltage glitch of 200 mV while $V_{out1}$ = 1 V and $V_{out2}$ = 320 mV showing 40 mV droop and 42 mV ripple at high-power output.**

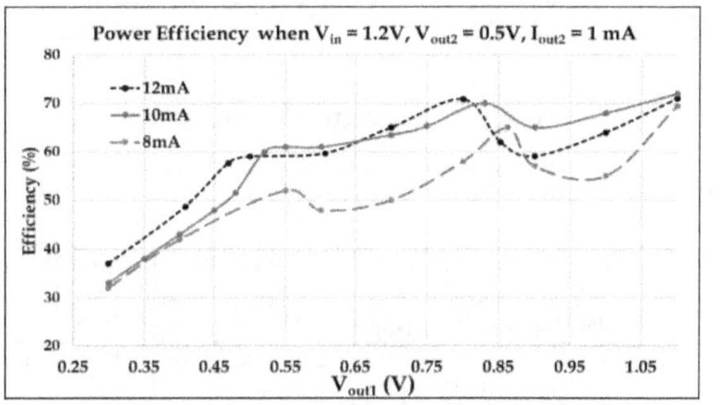


**Figure 8: Power efficiency of the proposed converter versus high-power output voltage with load current of 8, 10 and 12 mA while low-power output is fixed at 500 mV with 1mA load current.**

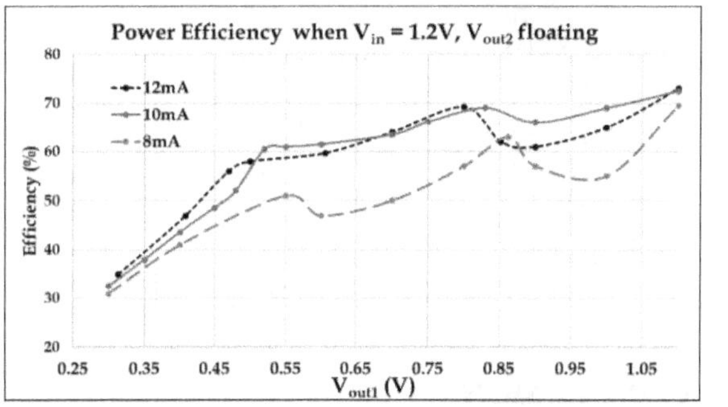


**Figure 9: Power efficiency of the proposed converter based on high-power output voltage with load current of 8, 10 and 12 mA separately while low-power output is floating.**

In Figure 4, high-power output is responding to a 100 Ohms load transition requests while low-power output connects a fixed load. Transient responses of both outputs when load current transitions are happening concurrently are reported in Figure 5. In Figure 6 one output has voltage transitions while the other one experiences load current change. We notice that there are no observable cross regulations during load current transitions. In addition, there are no observable voltage droops/spikes as they are smaller than ripples. In Figure 7, when there is an input voltage glitch, both outputs remain stable with less than 5% voltage droops or spikes. In Figure 8 and 9, power efficiencies of our converter for different cases are shown and the high-power output dominates the loss. For different loads, three common efficiency peaks are observed when $V_{out1}$ is around 0.5V, 0.8V and 1.1V because at certain output voltages one switch from $M_0$ to $M_2$ is always-on to transfer power. Peak efficiency is about 73% when $V_{out1}$ is 1.1V. Total area occupied is about 0.6 mm$^2$, including output capacitors and our converter performance summary is listed in Table 2. Table 3 shows comparisons with other converters that provide similar functions.

**Table 2: Converters Features Summary**

| | |
|---|---|
| **$V_{in}$ and $V_{out}$** | Vin 1.2V, $V_{out1}$ 0.3 – 1.1V, $V_{out2}$ 0.3 – 0.5V |
| **Slew rate** | 16 V/μs step- up, 4.4V/μs step-down |
| **Efficiency** | Peak 73% |
| **Ripple and Droop** | 49mV max ripple, 45 mV worst-case droop |
| **Technology and Area** | 32nm, 0.6 mm$^2$ |

**Table 3: Converters Comparisons**

| Paper year | Specifics | Efficiency | Implementation |
|---|---|---|---|
| [1] 2018 | $V_{in}$ 1.2V, $V_{out}$ 0.1 - 1.1V<br>0.4V/μs $V_{out}$ transition<br>50mV max voltage ripple | 14% - 93% | 65nm, 2.34 mm$^2$ |
| [3] 2017 | $V_{in}$ 2.7 - 4.2V, $V_{out}$ 0.8V & 1.6V, max 20mV ripples | 66% - 87% | 130nm, 3.3 mm$^2$ |
| [5] 2017 | $V_{in}$ 1.2V, $V_{out}$ 0.45 - 1.05V<br>2.9V/μs step-up<br>84mV max ripple | 28% - 71% | 130nm, 1.2 mm$^2$ |
| [9] 2017 | $V_{in}$ 1.6 - 2.2V, $V_{out}$ 0.6 - 1.2V<br>2.5V/μs step-up<br>0.9/μs step-down<br>30mV max ripple | 60% - 80% | 65nm, 0.84 mm$^2$ |
| [12] 2018 | $V_{in}$ 3.3 - 4V, five outputs:<br>0.9V, 1.2V, 1.5V, 1.8V, 2.2V<br>Max 25mV ripple | 52% - 86% | 180nm, 5.5 mm$^2$ |
| Our work | $V_{in}$ 1.2V, $V_{out1}$ 0.3 - 1.1V<br>$V_{out2}$ 0.3V - 0.5V<br>16V/μs step-up<br>4.4V/μs step down<br>Max 49mV voltage ripple | 32% - 73% | 32nm, 0.6 mm$^2$ |

## 4 CONCLUSION

We presented a novel hybrid DC-DC converter that has two asymmetrical output channels for different on-chip workloads with limited cross regulations. Meanwhile, both outputs provide fast and reliable load transient responses. No reconfiguration is needed for SC circuits and the output regulations are controlled by simplified digital feedback loops which greatly reduce design complexity and improve load transient responses. The high-power channel of the converter is able to provide peak voltage slew rate at least 2x faster than other relevant works while responding to load transition requests. The maximum voltage ripple is only 7.6% with a worst-case droop of 45mV at low-power output. Considering all characteristics, our converter is suitable for on-chip low power applications (such as IoT node or wearable devices) that demand at least two supply voltage domains, and fits dynamic workloads that require fast and reliable voltage/current transitions. In future works, we will explore and boost the converter efficiency for various power levels, improve cross regulations and reduce area. We will also tape out an extended prototype with improved performance and further optimizations.

## REFERENCES


[1] A. Abdulslam, B. Mohammad, M. Ismail, P. P. Mercier and Y. Ismail. 2018. A 93% Peak Efficiency Fully-Integrated Multilevel Multistate Hybrid DC–DC Converter. In *IEEE Transactions on Circuits and Systems I: Regular Papers*, vol. 65, no. 8 (2018), 2617-2630.

[2] C. Chen and A. Fayed. 2015. A Low-Power Dual-Frequency SIMO Buck Converter Topology With Fully-Integrated Outputs and Fast Dynamic Operation in 45 nm CMOS. In *IEEE Journal of Solid-State Circuits*, vol. 50, no. 9 (2015), 2161-2173.

[3] Z. Hua and H. Lee. 2017. A 1.2A auto-configurable dual-output switched-capacitor DC-DC regulator with continuous gate-drive modulation achieving <0.01mV/mA cross regulation. *2017 IEEE Custom Integrated Circuits Conference (CICC)*, Austin, TX, 1-4.

[4] Y. Jiang and A. Fayed. 2016. A 1 A, Dual-Inductor 4-Output Buck Converter With 20 MHz/100 MHz Dual-Frequency Switching and Integrated Output Filters in 65 nm CMOS. In *IEEE Journal of Solid-State Circuits*, vol. 51, no. 10 (2016), 2485-2500.

[5] M. Kar, A. Singh, A. Rajan, V. De and S. Mukhopadhyay. 2017. An All-Digital Fully Integrated Inductive Buck Regulator with A 250-MHz Multi-Sampled Compensator and a Lightweight Auto-Tuner in 130-nm CMOS. In *IEEE Journal of Solid-State Circuits*, vol. 52, no. 7 (2017), 1825-1835.

[6] D. Kilani, B. Mohammad, M. Alhawari, H. Saleh and M. Ismail. 2018. A Dual-Output Switched Capacitor DC–DC Buck Converter Using Adaptive Time Multiplexing Technique in 65-nm CMOS. In *IEEE Transactions on Circuits and Systems I: Regular Papers*, vol. 65, no. 11 (2018), 4007-4016.

[7] H. Le, S. R. Sanders and E. Alon. 2011. Design Techniques for Fully Integrated Switched-Capacitor DC-DC Converters. In *IEEE Journal of Solid-State Circuits*, vol. 46, no. 9 (2011), 2120-2131.

[8] S. Lim, J. Ranson, D. M. Otten and D. J. Perreault. 2015. Two-Stage Power Conversion Architecture Suitable for Wide Range Input Voltage. In *IEEE Transactions on Power Electronics*, vol. 30, no. 2 (2015). 805-816.

[9] Y. Lu, J. Jiang and W. Ki. 2017. A Multiphase Switched-Capacitor DC–DC Converter Ring With Fast Transient Response and Small Ripple. In *IEEE Journal of Solid-State Circuits*, vol. 52, no. 2 (2017), 579-591.

[10] J. Myers, A. Savanth, R. Gaddh, D. Howard, P. Prabhat and D. Flynn. 2016. A Subthreshold ARM Cortex-M0+ Subsystem in 65 nm CMOS for WSN Applications with 14 Power Domains, 10T SRAM, and Integrated Voltage Regulator. In *IEEE Journal of Solid-State Circuits*, vol. 51, no. 1 (2016), 31-44.

[11] H. Okuhara, A. B. Ahmed and H. Amano. 2018. Digitally Assisted On-Chip Body Bias Tuning Scheme for Ultra Low-Power VLSI Systems. In *IEEE Transactions on Circuits and Systems I: Regular Papers*, vol. 65, no. 10 (2018), 3241-3254.

[12] N. Pham, T. Yoo, T. T. Kim, C. Lee and K. Baek. 2018. A 0.016 mV/mA Cross-Regulation 5-Output SIMO DC-DC Buck Converter Using Output-Voltage-Aware Charge Control Scheme. In *IEEE Transactions on Power Electronics*, vol. 33, no. 11 (2018), 9619-9630.

[13] R. C. N. Pilawa-Podgurski and D. J. Perreault. 2012. Merged Two-Stage Power Converter With Soft Charging Switched-Capacitor Stage in 180 nm CMOS. In *IEEE Journal of Solid-State Circuits*, vol. 47, no. 7 (2012). 1557-1567.

[14] Y. Pu *et al.* 2018. A 9-mm² Ultra-Low-Power Highly Integrated 28-nm CMOS SoC for Internet of Things. In *IEEE Journal of Solid-State Circuits*, vol. 53, no. 3 (2018), 936-948.

# CNNWire: Boosting Convolutional Neural Network with Winograd on ReRAM based Accelerators

Jilan Lin, Shuangchen Li, Xing Hu, Lei Deng, Yuan Xie
{jilan,shuangchenli,xinghu,leideng,yuanxie}@ucsb.edu
University of California, Santa Barbara

## ABSTRACT

Resistive random access memory (ReRAM) demonstrates the great potential of in-memory processing for neural network (NN) acceleration. However, since the convolutional neural network (CNN) is widely known as compute-bound, current ReRAM-based accelerators are not able to support CNN efficiently. In this paper, we for the first time propose the **CNN** accelerator with **Wi**nograd's convolution on **Re**RAM (CNNWire), which minimizes the multiplications to enable fast and efficient CNN inference. We realize the convolution with Winograd Processing Element (WPE) based on convolutional tiles. Interconnections between WPEs are designed aiming to improve the data reuse. Finally, we introduce the full mapping flow to implement the Winograd convolution The results show that CNMWire gains 3.85× energy efficiency boosting and 3.24× speedup on average among different CNN benchmarks, compared with traditional GEMM based mapping.

## CCS CONCEPTS

• **Computing methodologies** → **Machine learning**; • **Hardware** → **Application specific integrated circuits**;

## KEYWORDS

CNN, ReRAM, Winograd Convolution

**ACM Reference format:**

Jilan Lin, Shuangchen Li, Xing Hu, Lei Deng, Yuan Xie. 2019. CNNWire: Boosting Convolutional Neural Network with Winograd on ReRAM based Accelerators. In *Proceedings of Great Lakes Symposium on VLSI 2019, Tysons Corner, VA, USA, May 9–11, 2019 (GLSVLSI '19)*, 4 pages. https://doi.org/10.1145/3299874.3318018

## 1 INTRODUCTION

The inference for neural network (NN) is both time- and energy-consuming. Recently, the Resisitive Random Access Memory (ReRAM) becomes attractive to researchers by showing the ability to perform matrix-vector multiplication (MVM) within memory arrays.

ReRAM demonstrates two main advantages when conducting NN acceleration. First, ReRAM conducts very fast MVM. When the data are stored in the ReRAM crossbar array, we can get the results within a single cycle. Second, ReRAM provides a promising non von-Neumann architecture. Since the matrix data are stored in the memory array, the data movement for weights is not needed any more, and thus we archive the in-situ computation and save the time and energy cost for data fetching.

However, as the most common used NNs in computer vision, CNNs are compute-bound and not friendly to ReRAM devices. The reason is that convolution requires much of the execution time and frequent input reusing for every weight kernel, but currently it is difficult to leverage the data reusing in analog field with analog caching. As studies have shown digital/analog interfaces occupy the majority of the energy consumption in ReRAM based analog computing [5], this limits the ReRAM-based CNN accelerators.

In this paper, we for the first time propose Winograd convolution based CNNs acceleration on ReRAM. Winograd convolution is a fast algorithm [8], which has already been applied in the cuDNN [1]. Leveraging the transforming for inputs and filters, Winograd algorithm turns the convolution into matrix operation and makes the least times of multiplication. We analyze the data flow for the algorithm and design the full architecture with mapping scheme. As dealing with tiled convolution, we realize Winograd Processing Element (WPE) for every tile, which conducts the transform in digital field and leverages the channelized accumulating in ReRAM crossbars. Further, to make better use of the data locality and reusing, interconnections are designed for fast data transfer between WPEs. The main contributions of this work are as follows:

- We boost the CNN with a novel architecture enabling **Wi**nograd algorithm on **Re**RAM devices (CNNWire). We design Winograd Processing Elements (WPEs) for tiles in convolution. We propose buffer organization and interconnections between WPEs to enhance the data reusing in Winograd tiles.
- We proposed a full mapping scheme to implement convolutional layers in CNNWire with transforming the element-wise multiplication into channelized matrix multiplication.
- We evaluate our architecture by comparison with traditional GEMM mapping and overlapped mapping, which shows about 3.85× energy boosting and 3.24× speedup.

## 2 PRELIMINARY AND MOTIVATION

In this section, we will introduce ReRAM, CNN and Winograd algorithm. Then we present our motivation in detail.

### 2.1 RRAM and RRAM Computing System

ReRAM stores information with resistive cells. The ReRAM crossbar structure performs analog MVM with complexity of $O(1)$. Equ. 1 expresses the relationship between input voltage vector ($V_{in}$) and the output voltage vector ($V_{out}$) among cell conductance $g$.

$$v_{out}^{j} = \sum_{i=1}^{N} v_{in}^{i} g_{i,j} \tag{1}$$


ACM ISBN 978-1-4503-6252-8/19/05...$15.00
https://doi.org/10.1145/3299874.3318018

## 2.2 CNN and Winograd Convolution

A convolution layer can be expressed with Eq. 2:

$$d^{l+1}_{x,y,c_{l+1}} = f\Big(\sum_{c_l=0}^{C_l-1}\sum_{r=0}^{R-1}\sum_{s_l=0}^{S-1} d^{l}_{x+r,y+s,c_l} \times w^{l}_{r,s,c_l,c_{l+1}}\Big) \tag{2}$$

Here $C$ is the number of feature maps with size $H^l \times W^l$, and $l$ denotes the current layer. The size of a kernel is $R \times S$. $w^l$ is the weight and $d^l$ is the input data. $f$ is a non-linear function.

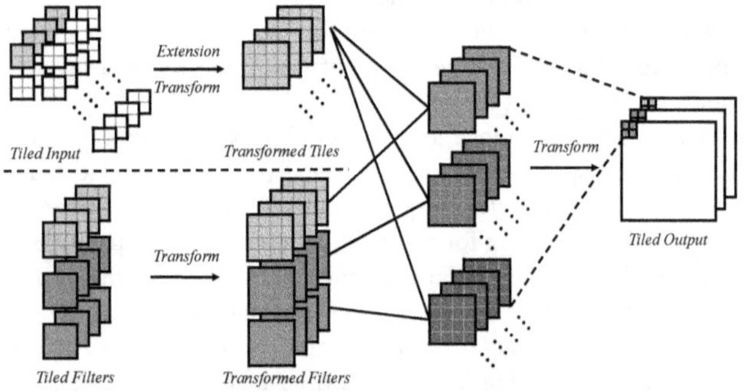


**Figure 1: An illustration of Winograd convolution.**

Fig. 1 gives an illustration of Winograd convolution. It first tiles the input feature maps (IFMs) into $2 \times 2$ pieces. Second, both the tiles and kernels are transformed into the same dimension. Third, we conduct element-wise multiplication, and then transform back to the convolution results. The process can be formulated as Eq. 3:

$$y = A^T[(Gw_lG^T) \odot (B^T d_l B)]A \tag{3}$$

The $A, G, B$ are three transform matrices. With $4 \times 4$ tiles and convolutional kernel of $3 \times 3$, the transform matrix A and B for input/output can be as simple as shown in Eq. 4:

$$A = \begin{bmatrix} 1 & 0 \\ 1 & 1 \\ 1 & -1 \\ 0 & -1 \end{bmatrix}, B^T = \begin{bmatrix} 1 & 0 & -1 & 0 \\ 0 & 1 & 1 & 0 \\ 0 & -1 & 1 & 0 \\ 0 & 1 & 0 & -1 \end{bmatrix} \tag{4}$$

## 2.3 Motivation

Previous work presented two mappings for convolution. The first one is GEneral Matrix Multiplication (GEMM) based mapping [7]. As shown in Fig. 2(a), it unfolds the 3-D convolution and computes as matrix multiplication. An alternative is to directly do the convolution with overlapped weights mapping scheme [10], as shown in

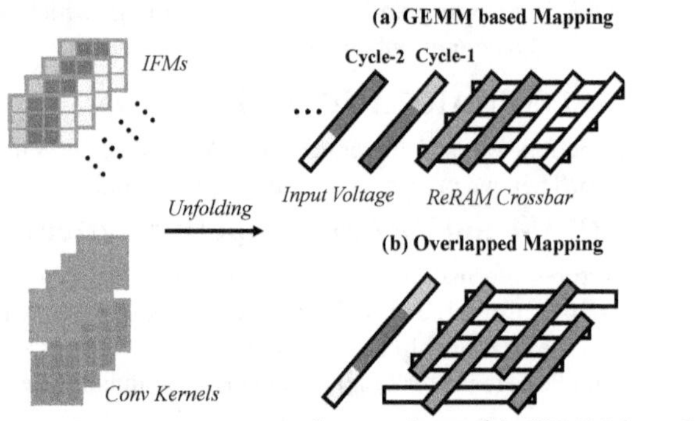


**Figure 2: Two common used mappings. (a) GEMM based mapping. (b) Overlapped mapping.**

Fig. 2(b). Kernels get duplicated in the crossbar array, and a longer vector of input pixels can directly does the convolution in 1 cycle.

GEMM based convolution requires iterative computing to traverse the IFM, which makes CNN quite compute-intensive. Besides, we need two cycles of DA converting and the data reuse cannot be fully exploited. Fig. ref{fig:moti gives the comparison between the energy/time consumption and parameter amount. We find that the convolutional layers dominate the execution time and energy for CNNs. For VGG-16, about 10% convolution parameters occupy more than 90% execution time and energy for the total network.

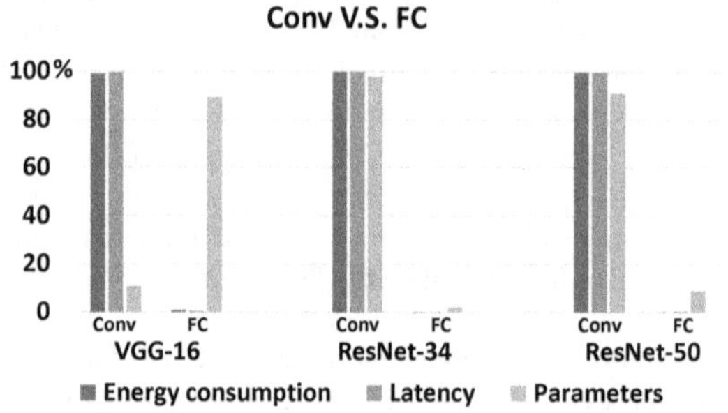


**Figure 3: The energy/time consumption of convolutional and FC layers. The data are shown in percentage.**

Overlapped mapping reduces the DA interfaces and is able to increase the throughput arbitrarily by duplicating more kernels. However, this obviously requires more memory capacity. Also, it introduces redundancy in crossbar as we see some ReRAM cell not used. Fig. 4 demonstrates the trend of memory utilization rate when increasing the duplication times, with mapping the conv3-128 layer in VGG-16. For the crossbars with size $64 \times 64$, the utilization rate keeps going down, and with only 3 times of duplication, more than 40% of the memory is idle.

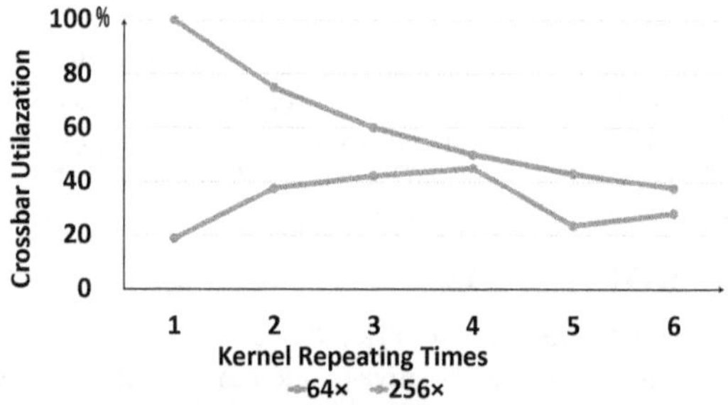


**Figure 4: The ReRAM utilization degrading curve.**

# 3 CNNWIRE ARCHITECTURE

In this section, we first introduce the full architectures of CNNWire, and then the mapping for Winograd algorithm.

## 3.1 Overview of the architecture

Fig. 5 shows the overview of CNNWire. Within a bank, the key components are Winograd Processing Elements (WPEs). WPE aims to process a channelized tile in Winograd algorithm. The transformed convolutional kernels are stored in the ReRAM array. The input/output bank buffers are composed with SRAM. A controller mainly decides the compute modes (Winograd based convolution, GEMM based convolution, FC, etc.) in WPEs. Finally, we enable the interconnections between WPEs to make use of the data reuse.

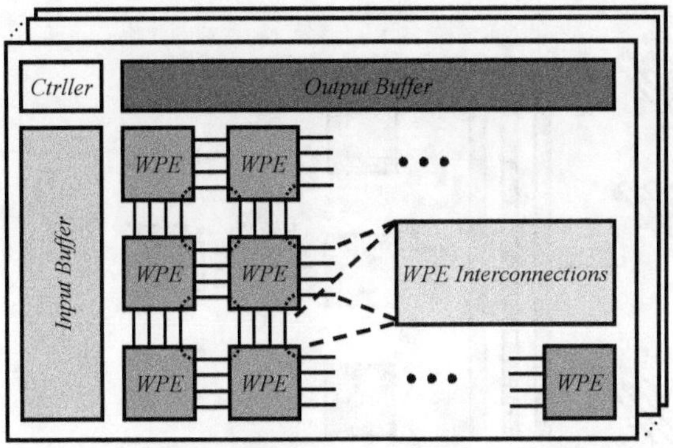


**Figure 5: The overview of the whole architecture.**

## 3.2 Winograd Processing Element

As shown in Fig. 7, WPE processes tiled IFMs (shown in orange) and gets the convolution results (shown as colored tiles). WPE consists of Winograd transform modules in Equ. 4, Matrix Vector (MV) multipliers, functional units, and input/output buffers. The tiled IFMs are buffered with registers, which will get transformed with WTM_B array and sent to the ReRAM based MV multiplier. WTM_A array deals with outputs transform.

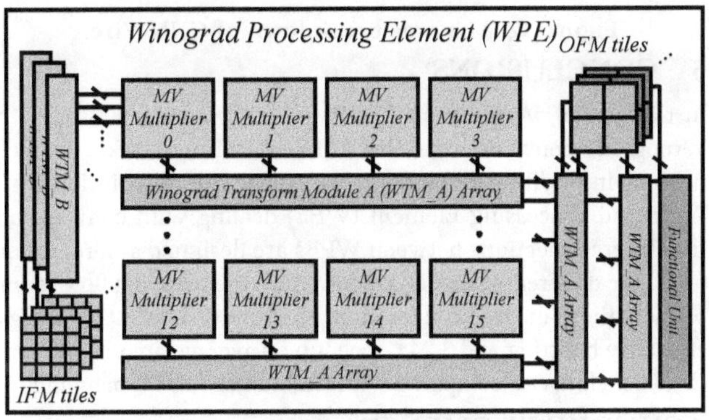


**Figure 6: A illustration of WPE design.**

***Winograd Transform Module (WTM)*** are designed to complete the transform process for input and output tiles. According to Eq. 4, only 2/4 adders and NOT gates are needed for a 4-input vector. Besides, several modules are organized into arrays, which is for better leveraging the data locality.

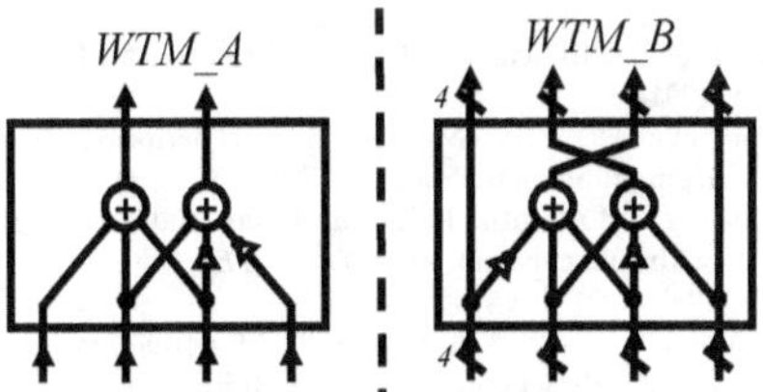


**Figure 7: The designs for Winograd transform.**

***MV multipliers*** are realized by ReRAM crossbars along with shifting and adding trees, with complement format storing in ReRAM. We decide single-bit ReRAM for a higher reliability. No two pieces of crossbars are required anymore for positive and negative values. After the computations complete in crossbars, the results will shift certain number of bits according to the slice index and add together.

***Functional unit*** is for activation and pooling operations.We only enable ReLU in the module.

## 3.3 Buffer and Communication Optimization

ReRAM devices are known for the energy-efficient reading but not writing [9]. Therefore, it is not suitable for activation buffer needing frequent data update. In CNNWire, we use SRAM for global bank buffer. On the other hand, regesiter files compose the buffer within WPE. We design interconnections between WPEs to reduce the data reloading from the global buffer. As shown in the Fig. 8, the input buffer in WPE is partitioned in 4 blocks, with 1 directly reading from global buffer, and 3 sharing with adjacent WPEs. This is because 1/4 of the extended tile is unique but 3/4 is shared.

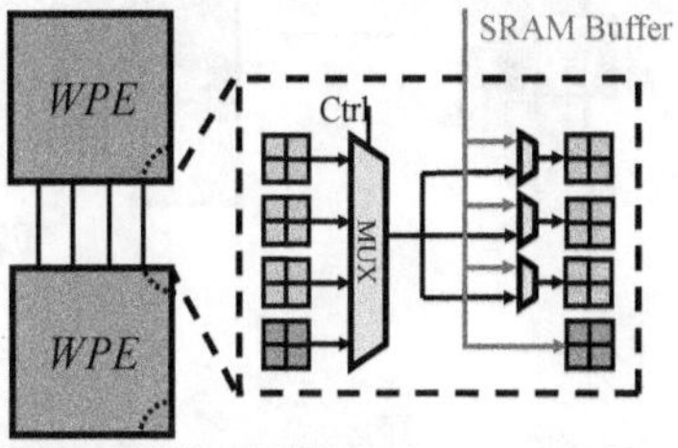


**Figure 8: The WPE interconnections.**

## 3.4 Winograd Mapping

Fig. 9 illustrates the mapping for Winograd convolution. First, IFMs are partitioned into $2 \times 2 \times C_l$ tiles as shown in orange. Then they are extended into $4 \times 4 \times C_l$ with adjacent pixels. Second, within the WPE, the data get transformed with WTM_B into $4 \times 4 \times C_l$. Third, the $3 \times 3 \times C_l$ filters, as shown in three colors, already get pre-transformed and stored in the crossbars. The element-wise matrix multiplication are accumulated across channels. As shown in the Fig. 9, deeper colors represent the first vector mapped to crossbar column, while lighter ones represent the 16th vector. In total 16 sets of ReRAM crossbars are needed. Finally, the MVM results are three vectors with length of 16. We fold them into $4 \times 4$ tiles and transform them back to $2 \times 2$, which are convolutional results.

# 4 EVALUATION

In this section, we evaluate the performance, energy results and area overhead of CNNWire.

## 4.1 Experiment Setup

We evaluate CNNWire with simulation. ReRAM and SRAM are simulated with NVSim [2] and CACTI 6.0 [6], and digital designs are synthesized with Synopsys DC with 45nm technology. DA/AD are referred to [3, 4]. ReRAM capacity has been fixed at 64MB per bank with 8 banks. We set 1KB registers for WPE buffer, and 4MB SRAM buffer per bank. System clock is 200MHz. We compare with GEMM based mapping and overlapped mapping The benchmarks are VGG-16 and ResNet serie. For $1 \times 1$ convolution and fully-connected layers, all the three mappings get to be the same.

## 4.2 Performance

As shown in Fig. 10, CNNWire improves the inference by 3.24× on average compared with GEMM based mapping, and outperforms the overlapped mapping (OM) by 1.22× on average - the reason for a relatively small speedup is that the overlapped mapping could maximize the throughput with arbitrary duplication.

For ResNet-50 and VGG-16, the speedups are lower than ResNet-18/34. The reason for ResNet-50 traces back to the huge amount of $1 \times 1$ convolutions, since there are 2 of 3 $1 \times 1$ convolutional layers within every residual block. For VGG-16, the convolution layer 1

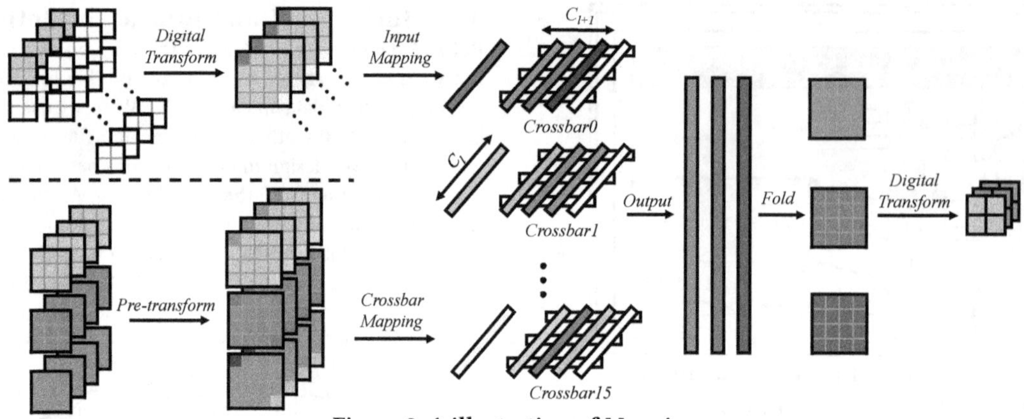


Figure 9: A illustration of Mapping.

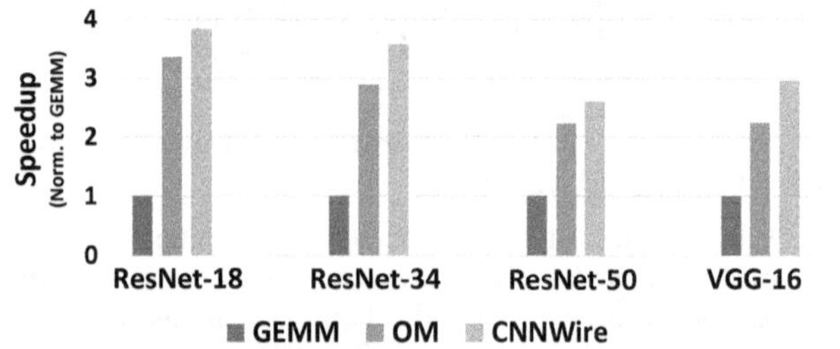


**Figure 10: The speedup among three mappings, which have been normalized to GEMM based mapping.**

needs kernel size of 7 × 7 by GEMM with the largest IFMs, leading to huge amount of inefficiency.

## 4.3 Energy

Fig. 11 gives energy results of CNNWire. On average 3.85× energy efficiency boosting is observed compared with GEMM, while 1.88× on everage compared with overlapped mapping. It is still found that 1 × 1 convolutions degrades the energy performance in ResNet-50.

As shown in the energy breakdown, AD/DA interfaces occupy most of the energy consumption for ReRAM computing. CNNWire reduces a considerable amount of AD/DA energy with efficient Winograd convolution. Besides, the cost of buffering has also been reduced notably with the implementation of WPE interconnections.

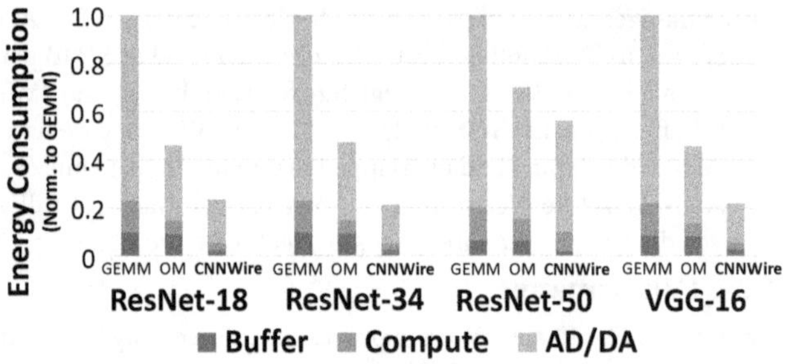


**Figure 11: The energy consumption among three mappings with normalization to GEMM based mapping.**

## 4.4 Area

The area breakdown of CNNWire is shown in Fig. 12. The AD/DA take over 80% area, with the ReRAM crossbar array being a really small part. The digital part occupies the second largest area. Our introduced Winograd transform circuits bring 6% area overhead, which is relatively small.

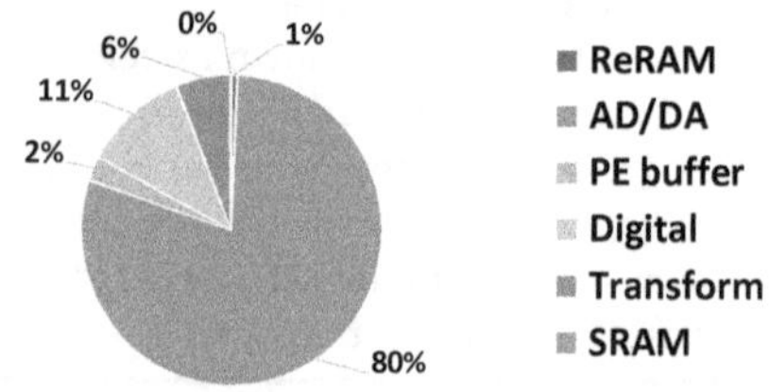


**Figure 12: The area breakdown of CNNWire.**

## 5 CONCLUSIONS

In this paper, we prensent CNNWire, a **CNN** accelerator with **Wi**nograd's convolution on **Re**RAM (CNNWire) to tackle the inefficiency in traditional mapping. We realize the convolution with Winograd Processing Element (WPE) dealing with convolution tiles.Interconnections between WPEs are designed aiming to improve the data reuse. Finally, we introduce the mapping flow to implement the Winograd convolution. The results show 3.85× energy efficiency boosting and 3.24× speedup on average among different CNN benchmarks, compared with traditional GEMM mapping.

## ACKNOWLEDGMENTS

This work was supported in part by CRISP, one of six centers in JUMP, a SRC program sponsored by DARPA, NSF grant CCF 1740352 and SRC nCORE NC-2766-A, and NSF 1500848, 1719160, 1725447, and 1730309.

## REFERENCES

[1] Sharan Chetlur et al. 2014. cuDNN: Efficient Primitives for Deep Learning. *CoRR* abs/1410.0759 (2014).
[2] Xiangyu Dong et al. 2012. NVSIM: A circuit-level performance, energy, and area model for emerging nonvolatile memory. *IEEE TCAD* 31, 7 (2012), 994–1007.
[3] Brian P Ginsburg and Anantha P Chandrakasan. 2007. 500-MS/s 5-bit ADC in 65-nm CMOS with split capacitor array DAC. *IEEE Journal of Solid-State Circuits* 42, 4 (2007), 739–747.
[4] Hyeok-Ki Hong et al. 2012. A 7b 1GS/s 7.2 mW nonbinary 2b/cycle SAR ADC with register-to-DAC direct control. In *CICC*. IEEE, 1–4.
[5] Boxun Li et al. 2015. Merging the interface: Power, area and accuracy co-optimization for rram crossbar-based mixed-signal computing system. In *DAC*. IEEE, 1–6.
[6] Naveen Muralimanohar, Rajeev Balasubramonian, and Norman P Jouppi. 2009. CACTI 6.0: A tool to model large caches. *HP laboratories* (2009), 22–31.
[7] Linghao Song et al. 2017. PipeLayer: A pipelined ReRAM-based accelerator for deep learning. In *HPCA*. 541–552.
[8] Shmuel Winograd. 1980. *Arithmetic complexity of computations*. Vol. 33. Siam.
[9] H-S Philip Wong et al. 2012. Metal–oxide RRAM. *Proc. IEEE* 100, 6 (2012), 1951–1970.
[10] Zhenhua Zhu et al. 2018. Mixed Size Crossbar based RRAM CNN Accelerator with Overlapped Mapping Method. In *ICCAD*.

# Feed-Forward XOR PUFs: Reliability and Attack-Resistance Analysis

S. V. Sandeep Avvaru and Keshab K. Parhi
Department of Electrical and Computer Engineering, University of Minnesota, Minneapolis, MN 55455 USA
avvar002@umn.edu,parhi@umn.edu

## ABSTRACT

Physical unclonable functions (PUFs) can be used to generate unique signatures of integrated circuit (IC) chips. XOR arbiter PUFs (XOR PUFs), that typically contain multiple standard arbiter PUFs as their components, are more secure than standard arbiter PUFs. This paper proposes design of feed-forward XOR PUFs (FFXOR PUFs) where each component PUF is a feed-forward arbiter PUF (FF PUF). Arbiter PUFs suffer from two main drawbacks: vulnerability to modeling attacks and degraded reliability. It is shown that FFXOR PUFs cannot be accurately modeled if the number of component PUFs is more than 5 or 6. We also state that the number of machine learning runs required to learn a model using evolutionary strategies increases by a factor of $N^2/2$ if $N$-stage FF PUFs with one loop are used as components instead of standard arbiter PUFs. In general, for FF PUFs with $k$ loops (one intermediate arbiter), it would increase by a factor of $\binom{N}{k+1}$. We also show that the use of a *thresholding strategy* can increase the reliability of FFXOR PUFs by about 30% for a 15% noise level.

## KEYWORDS

Hardware Security; XOR PUF; Feed-Forward PUF; Feed-Forward XOR PUF; Artificial Neural Network; Reliability; Security

**ACM Reference Format:**

S. V. Sandeep Avvaru and Keshab K. Parhi. 2019. Feed-Forward XOR PUFs: Reliability and Attack-Resistance Analysis. In *Proceedings of Great Lakes Symposium on VLSI 2019 (GLSVLSI '19).* ACM, New York, NY, USA, 4 pages. https://doi.org/10.1145/3299874.3318019

## 1 INTRODUCTION

Physical unclonable functions (PUFs) are integrated circuits used to securely authenticate devices or generate cryptographic keys without the involvement of non-volatile memories. PUFs harvest natural randomness in manufacturing process variations to create unique signatures for every integrated circuit (IC) chip. Ever since they were first introduced in the early 2000s, numerous PUF structures have been proposed [5]. Arbiter PUFs have been shown to be vulnerable to modeling attacks [2, 10]. Despite this limitation, they are used as building blocks in variants like XOR arbiter PUFs, lightweight secure PUFs, and composite PUFs because of their low area overhead and availability of a large set of *challenge-response pairs* (CRPs). Two of the biggest issues in this context are low reliability [7] and vulnerability to attacks [10]. Reliability is a measure of the variation of the response signature, for a set of challenges, as the noise is varied. FF PUFs and XOR PUFs [11] have been suggested as more secure alternatives to arbiter PUFs. But the added security comes at the cost of reduced reliability. One of the goals of this paper is to evaluate XOR PUFs in terms of their resilience against attacks (security) and against noise (reliability).

Authors in [3, 6, 10, 12] have presented methods to attack XOR PUFs using machine learning. One major issue with XOR PUFs is that their models can be expressed as linear decision boundaries [10] which makes it easier to learn an accurate model. In this paper, we assume a black-box approach to modeling XOR PUFs. Additionally, the existing studies [3, 4, 6, 10, 12] are only limited to XOR PUFs with standard arbiter PUFs as elements, called *standard XOR PUFs*. We simulate and analyze XOR PUFs with FF PUFs as elements, called *feed-forward XOR PUFs* (FFXOR PUFs), and assess their security and reliability. Since FF PUFs are inherently nonlinear, a linear approximation similar to the cases of standard XOR PUFs or Interpose PUFs is not applicable. Artificial neural networks (ANNs) are used to learn the models and the amount of data an attacker requires to learn an accurate predictive model is estimated. It is important to note that our work is limited to modeling attacks and does not focus on side-channel attacks. To the best of the authors' knowledge, no prior paper has either proposed or analyzed the security and reliability aspects of FFXOR PUFs.

The rest of the paper is organized as follows. The results of security analysis are presented and discussed in Section II. Reliability analysis is presented in Section III. Section IV concludes the paper.

## 2 SECURITY ANALYSIS

In this work, Standard arbiter PUFs and FF PUFs, used as components for XOR PUFs, are simulated using additive linear delay model. For each stage, the delay difference is sampled from an independent identical Gaussian distribution with zero mean and unit variance ($\mathcal{N}(0, 1)$) [3, 9, 10]. The intermediate and final bias values are sampled from $\mathcal{N}(0.1, 1)$. The non-zero mean of the bias accounts for the skew in total path delay due to the arbiter and other factors like the cumulative effect of noise and bias at each stage [2].

For security analysis, XOR PUFs and FFXOR PUFs with number of levels $l = 2$ to $l = 8$ are simulated and their neural network models are trained. 32-stage MUX PUFs were used as the components for each XOR PUF. FF PUFs containing a feed-forward loop whose intermediate response is computed at the 15th stage ($N_1$) and is fed into the 25th stage ($N_2$) were used as components of


*GLSVLSI '19, May 9–11, 2019, Tysons Corner, VA, USA*

ACM ISBN 978-1-4503-6252-8/19/05...$15.00
https://doi.org/10.1145/3299874.3318019

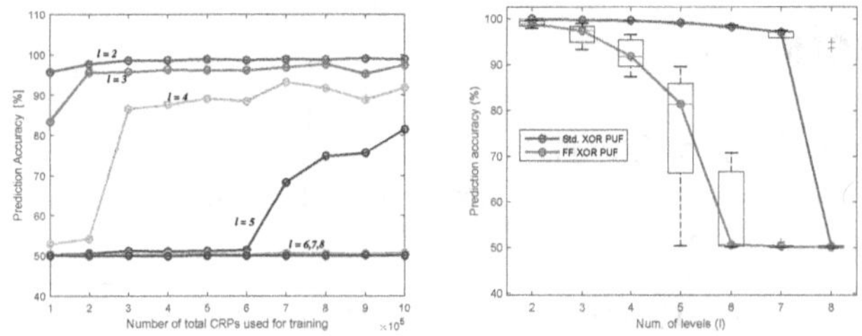


(a) Acc. *vs.* training size (FFXOR). (b) Acc. *vs.* num. of levels ($l$).

**Figure 1: Prediction accuracy as function of training data size and number of XOR levels. The number levels is varied from $l = 2$ to $l = 8$. The FF PUFs contain one loop from $N_1 = 15$ to $N_2 = 25$. The number of stages ($N$) is 32.**

FFXOR PUFs. XOR PUFs with $l \geq 8$ were found to be attack resistant. For each of these configurations, data for 10 PUF instances were generated. For each instance, 1.2 million challenge-response pairs (CRPs) are extracted. 1 million CRPs are used to train the model and 100,000 CRPs are used for testing and validation each. For every PUF instance, several models were trained by increasing the size of the training set from 100k to 1M and the prediction accuracy on an independent test-set is reported. The randomly chosen test challenges are kept consistent across all the models to have an unbiased comparison. For configurations with standard arbiter PUFs as components, mutlilayer perceptrons with 2 hidden layers were implemented with 60 and 30 neurons in each hidden layer, respectively. Since ANNs with 2 hidden layers were unable to accurately model FFXOR PUFs, 3 hidden layer structures with 120, 30 and 15 neurons, respectively, were trained. The training and testing errors are compared for each model to make sure that there is no over-training.

## 2.1 Results and Discussion

Prediction accuracies of standard arbiter XOR PUFs were evaluated by increasing the size of the training set from 100,000 CRPs to 1 million CRPs. Figure 1(a) shows how prediction accuracies of attack models vary with respect to training size for FFXOR PUFs. The number of levels is varied from $l = 2$ to $l = 8$. As expected, the prediction accuracy increases with increase in the training size and smaller XOR PUFs are easier to model as compared to higher number of XOR inputs (say $l = 7, 8$). Each accuracy value is the median of 10 PUF instances. PUFs with $l = 2, 3, 4$ achieve more than 90% accuracy while the models for PUFs with $l \geq 5$ are not as accurate. The maximum accuracy values attained using 1 million CRPs as a function of number of component PUFs in the circuit are presented in Figure 1(b). The model accuracies of standard and feed-forward XOR PUFs can be observed. Each value is presented in the form of a box-plot of 10 instances. It can be observed that FFXOR PUFs require significantly more resources to attack as compared to standard XOR PUFs. This follows from the fact that the number of ANN parameters required to train standard arbiter PUFs is $33 \times 60 \times 30 \times 1 = 59,400$ and for FF PUFs, it is $33 \times 120 \times 30 \times 15 \times 1 = 1,782,000$. Note that the input layer has 33 parameters, including the bias, since the input size is 32 bits. This costs more computational resources and processing time for the attacker. This difference is expected to be more significant when dealing with XOR PUFs with more than 128 or 256 bit-challenges. The results in Figure 1(b) also show that the standard XOR PUFs studied in this paper can be trained with more than 95% prediction accuracy up to 7 levels while FFXOR PUFs with 5 levels only attain a maximum prediction accuracy of 80% and the models for more than 5 levels are just as good as random guessing (50% accuracy). These observations offer an important insight that more secure XOR PUFs can be designed with much less area overhead by replacing standard arbiter PUFs with FF PUFs as elements.

Logistic regression based attack strategies as shown in [10] are not valid for FFXOR PUFs since the component PUFs are not linear. Even though we know that alternatives such as evolutionary strategies or multi-layer perceptrons can be used to train FF PUFs, it has been shown that training FF PUFs is much harder compared to training standard arbiter PUFs [1, 10]. For example, a 128-bit standard arbiter PUF requires 2.10 seconds while a FF PUF requires 3:15 hours using evolutionary strategy[10]. In recent work by Becker, it has been shown that XOR PUFs can be attacked by using evolutionary strategies [3]. However, this method may not be applicable to attack FFXOR PUFs unless the internal arbiter output locations are known to the attacker. The attacker could potentially examine all possible FF loop positions and identify the design via trial and error. But this requires a significant increase in the attack time. For FFXOR PUFs composed of N-stage FF PUFs as components, there are $\frac{N(N-1)}{2}$ possible FF loop placements for *one* loop. Therefore, the number of machine learning runs increases by 496 times for 32 bits and 2016 times for 64 bits. In general, for FF PUFs with one intermediate arbiter and $K$ loops, it would increase by a factor of $\binom{N}{k+1}$. For a 6-loop FF PUF, this number increases to 621 million.

# 3 RELIABILITY ANALYSIS

## 3.1 Definition of Reliability

Depending on the challenge bits, the path delays of the two paths of an arbiter PUF can be comparable thereby causing the arbiter to enter a meta-stable state. Under these circumstances, small variations in source voltage, ambient temperature or other environmental and measurement noise can affect the response. The *reliability* of a PUF under noise is mathematically defined in terms of its intra-chip variation (or intra-chip Hamming distance) [9]. Assume that $R$ is an $n$-bit response vector used as a reference and the noisy response-vectors are denoted by $R'$. An empirical estimate of intra-chip variation $P_{intra}$ is given by,

$$P_{intra} = \frac{1}{m} \sum_{i=1}^{m} \frac{HD(R, R'_i)}{n} \tag{1}$$

where $m$ is the number of noisy responses. Reliability can be computed as $(1 - P_{intra}) \times 100\%$.

For reliability analysis, noisy responses were generated by adding Gaussian noise with varying standard deviation to the delay difference at each stage. As a result, the distribution is modified to $\Delta_i \sim \mathcal{N}(0, 1) + \mathcal{N}(0, (\sigma_n)^2)$. Here, $\sigma_n$ denotes the standard deviation of the noise. Once again, XOR PUFs with 2 levels to 8 levels were evaluated for the reliability analysis. To emulate the effect of

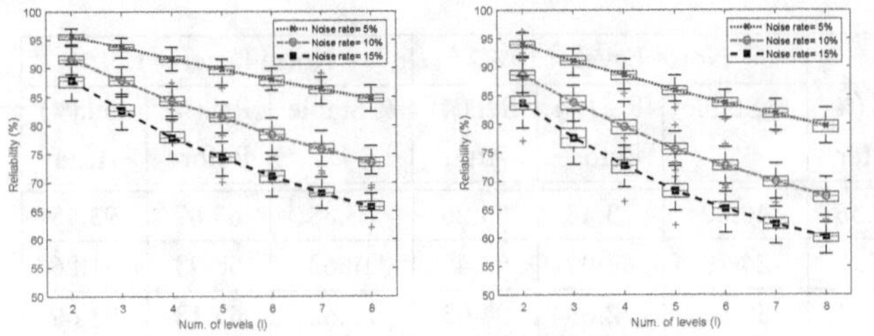

(a) Standard XOR PUFs (b) Feed-Forward XOR PUFs

**Figure 2: Reliability *vs.* number of levels for 32-stage standard and FFXOR PUFs.**

environmental and measurement noise, Gaussian noise with zero mean and a standard deviation corresponding to 5%, 10% and 15% noise levels is added to the delay difference at each stage and to the arbiter delay [9]. *Noise level* is defined as the ratio of the standard deviation of the noise to the standard deviation of delay differences at each stage. For a given design configuration, 100 PUF instances were generated. 1000 randomly chosen unique challenges are used to extract a 1000-bit response-vector for each instance. 100 noisy response vectors are generated for each of the 100 PUF instances for the purpose of computing reliability.

## 3.2 FFXOR PUFs with Single-Loop FF PUFs

FF PUFs that were used as the components for the XOR PUFs consist of a FF loop placed between stages $N_1 = 10$ and $N_2 = 20$. XOR PUFs with number of XORs ($l$) varying from 2 to 8 are studied. The change in reliability with increase in the number of XOR levels is shown in Figure 2. It can be observed that the reliability decreases as the number of levels increases and that FFXOR PUFs have less reliability compared to standard XOR PUFs of the same size. Moreover, the reliability values of FFXOR PUFs drop at a slightly higher rate with respect to the value of $l$. These values can be used to extrapolate the trend to estimate how reliability scales with the increase in the number of arbiter PUFs used. This demonstrates that reliability of XOR PUFs can be as low as 60% (for $l = 8$). We considered 64-bit feed-forward PUFs (N = 64) with the intermediate output measured at the 10th stage ($N_1 = 10$) and feeding into the 40th stage ($N_2 = 40$) and verified that they have similar reliability to 32-stage PUFs shown in Figure 2 . It has been shown in [9] that reliability of an $N$-stage FF PUF depends on $\arctan(\sqrt{\frac{N_2-1}{N-N_2+1}})$ which is equal to 0.88 and 0.895 for the 32-bit and the 64-bit FF PUFs, respectively.

## 3.3 Soft-Response Thresholding

For a given challenge, *soft-response* is defined as the probability that the response is 1 ($Pr(R = 1)$) under environmental variations [13]. The soft-responses were computed by applying the same challenge 100 times under the presence of noise. As a convention, we use a 90% threshold to measure the consistency of a response. That is, if the response is 0 or 1 in 90% of the cases, it is considered a *stable response*. Otherwise, it is referred to as an *unstable response*. A fundamental limitation of XOR PUFs is that a large portion of the responses could be unstable, resulting in low reliability as illustrated in Figure 2. For a FFXOR PUF with 8 levels, it was observed that 25.9% of the responses are stable.

We know that soft-responses can be computed by repetitive measurement of responses. Soft-responses of the 8-level FFXOR PUF were computed by assigning each challenge 100 times. A subset of challenges were then chosen by thresholding the soft-responses using 90-10 thresholding. The challenges that generate stable responses are referred to as *stable challenges*. Instead of using a set of 1000 randomly chosen challenges, 1000 stable challenges were used to compute the reliability. Table 1 shows that reliability of XOR PUFs during authentication can be significantly increased by thresholding the soft-responses and identifying stable challenges. For example, the reliability of an 8-level FFXOR PUF (with one loop) can be increased from 58.9% to 91.3% (assuming 15% noise).

## 3.4 FFXOR PUFs with Multi-Loop FF PUFs

As a counter-measure to the lower reliability of FF PUFs compared to standard arbiter PUFs, a *modified FF PUF* (MFF PUF) structure was proposed in [9]. The idea is to have the intermediate arbiter output feeding into two consecutive stages instead of one. FFXOR PUFs with MFF PUFs as the components were simulated and their reliability was computed. Furthermore, we extend the analysis to FFXOR PUFs consisting of FF PUFs with multiple loops. Results of the reliability analysis of 8-level FFXOR PUFs up to 8 loops is presented in Table 1. The proportion of stable challenges and the reliability values computed before and after thresholding are shown for different noise levels. These values were computed using 90% threshold and each value is the median of 100 PUF instances. The results show that MFF PUFs can be used to attain reliability close to standard XOR PUFs. In case of PUFs with one intermediate arbiter, having 1,3 or 5 loops results in less reliability compared to having even number of loops. The reliability and the proportion of stable challenges can be substantially low, 53% (approx.) and 1-3%, respectively, when multiple intermediate arbiters are used. Two such examples can be noticed in the Table. However, having MFF loops leads to better reliability. The results confirm that the soft-response thresholding strategy can be employed to significantly increase the reliability of response signatures to at least 89%. It is also important to note that XOR PUFs have a huge set of challenges to choose from, i.e., $2^N$ challenges for N-bit PUFs. For 64-bit XOR PUFs, if we assume that a mere 1% of the challenges are stable, the server still has $1.8 \times 10^5$ trillion (1% of $2^{64}$) stable challenges.

# 4 CONCLUSION

This paper shows that FFXOR PUFs are better alternatives to standard XOR PUFs, in terms of their attack-resistance. Standard XOR PUF and FF XOR PUFs with 32-bit challenges, up to 8 XOR levels are evaluated using multi-layer perceptrons and the results are compared. It is worth noting that reliability based machine learning attacks have been shown to outperform other machine learning attacks on XOR PUFs. This is because they utilize a *divide-and-conquer approach* which reduces the number of model parameters from $l(N+1)$ to $N+1$ for XOR PUFs with $l$ components of $N$-stages each. But, the divide-and-conquer approach used in reliability based attacks is dependent on the fact that reliability of a response bit depends equally on each of the component PUFs [3]. However, this

**Table 1: Percentage of Stable Challenges and Reliability Before and After Thresholding. Threshold = 90%.**

| No. of Arbs/ Loops | FF Loops Locations | Noise Level = 5% | | | Noise Level = 10% | | | Noise Level = 15% | | |
|---|---|---|---|---|---|---|---|---|---|---|
| | | % Stable | Rel.(%) Before | Rel.(%) After | % Stable | Rel.(%) Before | Rel.(%) After | % Stable | Rel.(%) Before | Rel.(%) After |
| 0/0 | - | 65.5 | 84.63 | 97.36 | 40.69 | 73.48 | 95.26 | 23.88 | 65.67 | 93.45 |
| 1/1 | $10 \rightarrow 40$ | 52.1 | 78.65 | 96.2 | 24.73 | 66.09 | 93.45 | 10.63 | 58.93 | 91.26 |
| 1/2 | $10 \rightarrow 40, 41$ (MFF) | 63.78 | 83.98 | 97.21 | 38.94 | 72.63 | 94.95 | 22.62 | 65.18 | 93.09 |
| 1/2 | $10 \rightarrow 30, 40$ | 58.45 | 81.35 | 96.75 | 32.07 | 69.67 | 94.25 | 16.54 | 62.4 | 92.41 |
| 1/3 | $10 \rightarrow 30, 40, 50$ | 52.14 | 78.66 | 96.26 | 24.65 | 65.99 | 93.41 | 10.5 | 59.07 | 91.34 |
| 1/4 | $10 \rightarrow 30, 31, 40, 41$ | 62.74 | 83.27 | 97.18 | 37.70 | 72.21 | 94.82 | 21.45 | 64.58 | 92.86 |
| 1/4 | $10 \rightarrow 20, 30, 40, 50$ | 54.81 | 79.92 | 96.43 | 27.73 | 67.61 | 93.76 | 12.85 | 60.16 | 91.75 |
| 1/5 | $10 \rightarrow 20, 30, 40, 50, 60$ | 52.34 | 78.74 | 96.15 | 24.61 | 66.37 | 93.37 | 10.6 | 59.03 | 91.28 |
| 1/6 | $10 \rightarrow 30, 31, 40, 41, 50, 51$ | 61.81 | 83.12 | 97.1 | 36.64 | 71.73 | 94.75 | 20.61 | 64.26 | 92.7 |
| 1/6 | $10 \rightarrow 30, 35, 40, 45, 50, 55$ | 56.52 | 80.49 | 96.52 | 29.44 | 68.44 | 94 | 14.35 | 61.11 | 91.96 |
| 1/8 | $10 \rightarrow 20, 21, 30, 31, 40, 41, 50, 51$ | 61.43 | 82.72 | 96.96 | 35.76 | 71.52 | 94.59 | 19.74 | 63.93 | 92.72 |
| 1/8 | $10 \rightarrow 20, 25, 30, 35, 40, 45, 50, 55$ | 54.82 | 79.67 | 96.51 | 27.55 | 67.48 | 93.79 | 20.73 | 60.39 | 91.68 |
| 4/4 | $10 \rightarrow 20; 15 \rightarrow 30; 25 \rightarrow 40$ $35 \rightarrow 50$ | 33.47 | 70.40 | 94.66 | 9.98 | 58.74 | 91.44 | 2.72 | 53.42 | 89.5 |
| 4*/8 | $10 \rightarrow 20, 21; 15 \rightarrow 30, 31;$ $25 \rightarrow 40, 41; 35 \rightarrow 50, 51;$ | 57.73 | 81.14 | 96.75 | 33.09 | 70.04 | 94.30 | 18.18 | 63.02 | 92.56 |
| 4/4 | $15 \rightarrow 55; 20 \rightarrow 50; 25 \rightarrow 45;$ $30 \rightarrow 40$ | 26.17 | 66.92 | 94.01 | 6.16 | 56.21 | 90.89 | 1.45 | 52.48 | 88.80 |
| 4*/8 | $15 \rightarrow 55, 56; 20 \rightarrow 50, 51;$ $25 \rightarrow 45, 46; 30 \rightarrow 40, 41;$ | 58.01 | 81.26 | 96.85 | 33.36 | 70.18 | 94.52 | 18.36 | 63.32 | 92.58 |

* The intermediate arbiters are connected to modified FF loops.

would not be the case if *heterogeneous* FFXOR PUFs are used, making them more attack resistant. In a heterogeneous FFXOR PUF, the component PUFs are non-identical, i.e., these components could be different FF PUF structures with different number of arbiters and loops. Therefore, future work should investigate heterogeneous FFXOR PUFs. The effect of number of XOR levels and the number of FF loops on the reliability of FFXOR PUFs under different noise levels is presented and a soft-response thresholding strategy is demonstrated as an effective countermeasure to degraded reliability. Reliability values as low as 52% were increased to 89%. Future efforts will be directed towards studying the aging effects of FFXOR PUFs [8].

## ACKNOWLEDGMENTS

This research has been supported by the National Science Foundation under grant number CNS-1441639 and the Semiconductor Research Corporation under contract number 2014-TS-2560.

## REFERENCES

[1] S. V. S. Avvaru, C. Zhou, C. H. Kim, and K. K. Parhi. 2017. Predicting hard and soft-responses and identifying stable challenges of MUX PUFs using ANNs. In *Midwest Symposium on Circuits and Systems (MWSCAS)*. 934–937.

[2] S. V. S. Avvaru, C. Zhou, S. Satapathy, Y. Lao, C. H. Kim, and K. K. Parhi. 2016. Estimating Delay Differences of Arbiter PUFs Using Silicon Data. In *Proceedings of Design, Automation and Test in Europe (DATE)*. 543–546.

[3] G. T. Becker. 2015. The gap between promise and reality: On the insecurity of XOR arbiter PUFs. In *Int. Workshop on Cryptographic Hardware and Embedded Systems*. 235–255.

[4] F. Ganji, S. Tajik, and J. Seifert. 2015. Why Attackers Win: On the Learnability of XOR Arbiter PUFs. In *Trust and Trustworthy Computing*, Mauro Conti, Matthias Schunter, and Ioannis Askoxylakis (Eds.). Springer Int. Publishing, Cham, 22–39.

[5] C. Herder, M. Yu, F. Koushanfar, and S. Devadas. 2014. Physical Unclonable Functions and Applications: A Tutorial. In *Proc. of the IEEE*, Vol. 102. 1126–1141.

[6] G. Hospodar, R. Maes, and I. Verbauwhede. 2012. Machine learning attacks on 65nm Arbiter PUFs: Accurate modeling poses strict bounds on usability. In *IEEE International Workshop on Information Forensics and Security (WIFS)*. 37–42.

[7] S. Katzenbeisser, Ü.l Kocabaş, V. Rožić, A. R. Sadeghi, I. Verbauwhede, and C. Wachsmann. 2012. PUFs: Myth, Fact or Busted? A Security Evaluation of Physically Unclonable Functions (PUFs) Cast in Silicon. In *Proceedings of 14th Int. Workshop on Cryptographic Hardware and Embedded Systems (CHES)*. 283–301.

[8] A. Koyily, S. V. S. Avvaru, C. Zhou, C. H. Kim, and K. K. Parhi. 2018. Effect of aging on linear and nonlinear MUX PUFs by statistical modeling. In *Asia and South Pacific Design Automation Conference (ASP-DAC)*. 76–83.

[9] Y. Lao and K. K. Parhi. 2014. Statistical Analysis of MUX-Based Physical Unclonable Functions. *IEEE Trans. on Computer-Aided Design of Integrated Circuits and Systems* 33, 5 (May 2014), 649–662.

[10] U. Rührmair, J. Sölter, F. Sehnke, Xiaolin Xu, A. Mahmoud, V. Stoyanova, G. Dror, J. Schmidhuber, W. Burleson, and S. Devadas. 2013. PUF Modeling Attacks on Simulated and Silicon Data. *IEEE Trans. on Information Forensics and Security* 8, 11 (Nov 2013), 1876–1891.

[11] G. E. Suh and S. Devadas. 2007. Physical Unclonable Functions for Device Authentication and Secret Key Generation. In *44th ACM/IEEE DAC*.

[12] C. Zhou, K. K. Parhi, and C. H. Kim. 2017. Secure and reliable XOR arbiter PUF design: An experimental study based on 1 trillion challenge response pair measurements. In *54th ACM/IEEE DAC*. 1–6.

[13] C. Zhou, S. Satapathy, Y. Lao, K. K. Parhi, and C. H. Kim. 2016. Soft Response Generation and Thresholding Strategies for Linear and Feed-Forward MUX PUFs. In *Proc. of Int. Symposium on Low Power Electronics and Design (ISLPED)*.

# Exploring Design Trade-offs in Fault-Tolerant Behavioral Hardware Accelerators

Zhiqi Zhu, Farah Naz Taher and Benjamin Carrion Schafer
Department of Electrical and Computer Engineering
The University of Texas at Dallas
zhiqi.zhu@utdallas.edu,farah.taher@utdallas.edu,schaferb@utdallas.edu

## ABSTRACT

High-Level Synthesis (HLS) allows the automatic generation of hardware accelerators with unique design metrics. This work leverages this unique feature and presents a method to increase the search space of fault-tolerant hardware accelerators. The proposed method is based on a two-stage approach that automatically generates Pareto-optimal configurations for the hardware accelerators with different area, performance and reliability to mitigate the effect of soft errors. The first stage performs a source-to-source transformation on the behavioral description to annotate the $N$-modular redundancy directly at the source code including the voter, while the second stage then performs a HLS design space exploration (DSE) on this newly obtained behavioral description. Compared to performing the exploration on a single module and then replicating the accelerator $N$ times, the proposed exploration strategy leads to a much richer search space. Experiments show that our proposed method leads to better results compared to the state-of-the-art by expanding the search space considerably.

## CCS CONCEPTS

• **Hardware → Datapath optimization**; **Fault tolerance**; *Hardware accelerators*;

## KEYWORDS

Fault Tolerance; High-Level Synthesis; Design Space Exploration

**ACM Reference Format:**
Zhiqi Zhu, Farah Naz Taher and Benjamin Carrion Schafer . 2019. Exploring Design Trade-offs in Fault-Tolerant Behavioral Hardware Accelerators . In *Great Lakes Symposium on VLSI 2019 (GLSVLSI '19), May 9–11, 2019, Tysons Corner, VA, USA.* ACM, New York, NY, USA, 4 pages. https://doi.org/10.1145/3299874.3318020

## 1 INTRODUCTION

Redundancy has demonstrated its effectiveness in detecting and/or masking faults: either transient errors due to radiation single event upsets (SEU) or permanent faults caused by electro-migration or time-dependent dielectric breakdown (TDDB). Although much work has been proposed in the past in terms of fault-tolerant HLS, most of them propose to modify the synthesis process to achieve systems with higher fault-tolerance by automatically adding the $N$-modular redundancy during the process and then making use of different levels of resource sharing [7] [8]. In resource sharing, a single Functional Unit (FU) is shared among different operations in the source code by inserting multiplexers at its inputs and outputs. In order to steer the data through the datapath containing the shared FUs, the HLS process typically generates a Finite State Machine (FSM) that produces the control signals for these multiplexers. Thus, different levels of resource sharing can be achieved by instantiating more or less FUs during the HLS process.

However, there is one major practical limitation with this approach. Hardware designers do not have control over the internal synthesis process, thus, making previous work impractical. In addition, modern HLS tools enable the generation of unique micro-architectures by using a more powerful synthesis *knob.* In particular synthesis directives in the form of pragmas. These pragmas are comments inserted directly at the behavioral description that allow the designer to control, how to synthesize arrays (*e.g.* RAM or registers), loops (*e.g.* fully unroll, partially unroll or pipeline) and functions (*e.g.* inline or not). This implies that when setting a unique combination of these synthesis directives, a micro-architecture of the accelerator with unique area, performance, power and reliability is generated.

Based on this, this work presents a novel approach based on a source-to-source transformation stage that, given a behavioral description, automatically annotates on the description the $N$-modular redundancy including the voter. Our proposed method then continues by performing a design space exploration (DSE) on this new behavioral description in order to find a set of Pareto-optimal implementations of the $N$-modular redundant system with unique area vs. performance vs. reliability trade-offs. As shown in the experimental results section, this approach leads to a much wider search space than previous work. In summary, this paper makes the following contributions:

- Introduce an $N$-modular redundancy method that takes a single behavioral description as input for HLS and performs a source-to-source transformation to directly annotate the $N$-modular redundancy on the behavioral descriptions.
- Modifies a HLS design space explorer to include reliability in the cost function leading to Pareto-optimal micro-architectures of unique area vs. performance and reliability trade-offs.

## 2 RELATED WORK

Much work is being done in the fault-tolerance domain to improve the reliability of VLSI circuits. This section only highlights the


*GLSVLSI '19, May 9–11, 2019, Tysons Corner, VA, USA*

ACM ISBN 978-1-4503-6252-8/19/05...$15.00
https://doi.org/10.1145/3299874.3318020

most important works relevant to this work. Karri and Orailoglu developed the first methodology to maximize performance in the presence of fault-tolerance constraints for ASICs using HLS [7] [8]. The main approach relied on sharing functional units (FUs) to minimize the area overhead. Wu et al. [14] extended this work by proposing a hybrid time and hardware redundancy system. In [13], the authors more recently proposed a reliability-centric HLS approach that maximizes reliability by characterizing each hardware component, particularly adders and multipliers. Glass et al. [4] expanded this idea by developing a genetic algorithm to explore the design space of functional units with different reliabilities.

Recently, the authors in [11] introduced a scheduling and binding heuristic for HLS that explores tradeoffs between resource usage, latency, and the amount of redundancy. The authors in [5] followed a similar approach. Finally, in [2] the authors introduce a compiler pass called StitchUp, which identifies the control critical parts of the design, then automatically replicates only those parts.

The main idea of previous works is to enable different degrees of resource sharing in HLS to obtain micro-architectures of a unique area, performance and reliability trade-offs or to selectively replicate some portions of the synthesized accelerator. These previous work are mainly achieved by modifying in the HLS process to enable design optimization. Our proposed approach has two main advantages compared to previous works: First, it leads to better results by extending the search space because it generates micro-architectures with different trade-offs by applying synthesis directives as well as FU resource sharing. Secondly, it is practical as it can be implemented without the modification of synthesis process and thus, it can be used with any commercial HLS tool. In this work, we assume that the HLS tool is a standard commercial tool that performs basic HLS without any fault-tolerance information. Based on the this, we can formulate the problem to be solved in this work as follows:

**Problem Formulation:** Given a behavioral description for HLS ($C_{in}$) and the amount of redundancy required (*e.g.* DWC or TMR), find a set of Pareto-optimal designs $PO = \{D_1, D_2, \ldots, D_n\}$, such that every design $D_i$ has a unique area ($A_i$), latency ($L_i$) and reliability ($R_i$) $\{A_i, L_i, R_i\}$ by setting different synthesis directives (attributes) in the form of pragmas and maximum number of different type of FUs, $D_i \leftarrow \{Atrr_1, Attr_2, \ldots, Attr_x, FU_1(max), \ldots, FU_k(max)\}$, where the attributes $Attr_i$ control the synthesis of *arrays*, *loops* and *functions*, and $FU_i$ include adders, multipliers and dividers.

# 3 PROPOSED METHOD

Fig. 1 shows an overview of the proposed method based on two main stages. The first stage does a source-to-source transformation on the behavioral input description for HLS ($C_{in}$) and automatically annotates the $N$-modular redundancy into a new behavioral description ($C_{NMR}$), while the second stage performs a HLS design space exploration on the newly generated behavioral description $C_{NMR}$, resulting in a list of Pareto-optimal ($PO$) configurations with the unique area ($A$) vs. performance (given in latency $L$) vs. reliability ($R$) trade-offs, $PO = \{D_1(A_1, L_1, R_1), \ldots, D_n(A_n, L_n, R_n)\}$. The stages are described in detailed as follows:

***Stage 1: Source-to-Source Transformations:*** This first stage takes as input the behavioral description that needs to be *hardened* ($C_{in}$) and the required redundancy amount (either DWC or TMR). Based

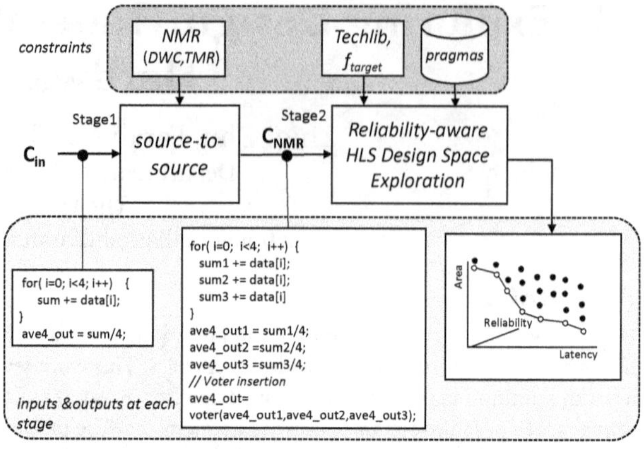


**Figure 1: Proposed method overview.**

on this, it continues by parsing the entire description and generating a new behavioral description with the desired redundancy by declaring all variables $N$ times and replicating each statement in the code ($C_{NMR}$). This implies that this new behavioral description can be synthesized to a fully spatial redundant system by allowing the number of resource to be increased (doubled for the DWC cased and tripled in the TMR case), while if the number of resources is kept identical to the number of resources used when synthesizing the original behavioral description ($C_{in}$), then a fully time $N$-redundant system is created. Finally, this stage inserts the voter into the behavioral description that compares the $N$ outputs and selects the one with the one with the largest number of identical values. This ensures that when computing the reliability of the resultant micro-architecture, the voter is also taken into account and makes the micro-architecture self-contained as the voter is also synthesized (HLS) with the rest of the behavioral description.

***Stage 2: Reliability-aware HLS Design Space Exploration (DSE):*** Commercial High-Level Synthesis (HLS) tools only report area and performance (*i.e. delay and latency*) metrics as part of their synthesis outputs. However, in this work, we have to assess the reliability of every newly generated micro-architecture, as the main goal is to explore the trade-offs in terms of area vs. performance and reliability. Thus, we need to be able to evaluate the reliability of every design when we modify the synthesis attributes and/or the amount of resource sharing.

*Reliability Calculation:* To address this, we calculate the reliability as the negative exponential of failure rate multiplied by total execution time as suggested by [3] and shown in (1). In this work, we consider soft-errors caused by high-energy neutrons. The failure rate is obtained by multiplying the Soft Error Rate (SER) with the Architectural Vulnerability Factor (AVF). This leads to the reliability calculation as follows:

$$R = e^{-(SER \times AVF) \times Time} \tag{1}$$

(1) *Architectural Vulnerability Factor (AVF)*: The probability that an error (such as soft-error) results in failure, i.e., changes the output of the circuit [6]. In this work, we consider $AVF$ as 1, which implies that an error will always be lead to a failure.
(2) *Soft-Error Rate*: $SER$ for combinational logic, latches, and SRAMs are obtained from the model discussed in [12] as

$3 \times 10^{-5}$, $1 \times 10^{-5}$ and $9 \times 10^{-6}$ respectively. To obtain the total *SER* of a specific design, we consider the accumulation of SER by multiplying the SER by area of the circuit.

(3) *Design Execution Time (Time)*: *Time* is obtained as the multiplication of latency, critical path delay and number of execution cycles. Here, latency is the number of clock cycles required to generate a new output. The critical path delay is the longest combinational delay of design reported by the HLS tool, which limits the maximum operating frequency of the accelerator. Finally, in this work we consider $1 \times 10^7$ runs as the number of execution cycles.

*High-Level Synthesis DSE:* The problem to be solved in this work can be classified as a multi-objective optimization problem. In this work, we make use of a Genetic algorithm (GA), which has been shown to produce good results within a *reasonable* amount of time for these type of multi-objective optimization problems. The use of GA in this context is often referred to as Multi-objective Genetic Algorithm (*MO-GA*)[1]. In this particular work, the objectives of the GA-based explorer is to find the Pareto-optimal designs that minimize area (*A*), maximize reliability (*R*) and minimize the latency(*L*) (maximize performance). Thus, in this work, we define the *MO-GA* cost function as $C_{MO-GA} = \alpha A - \beta R + \gamma L$, where the sign of the reliability is negative because this terms should be maximized, while the signs of the area and latency are positive as these terms need to be minimized. Based on this, the goal of the search heuristic is to minimize the total cost function. Because the output is a 3-dimensional trade-off curve, the weights of this cost function ($\alpha$, $\beta$ and $\gamma$) have to be updated adaptively to reflect the importance of either minimizing area or latency or maximizing reliability.

The *MO-GA* based explorer developed in this work is based on two main phases. The first phase explores the synthesis directives in the form or pragmas, while the second phase explores the effect of functional unit constraints (amount of resource sharing) for that particular set of directives. This order is important because it has been shown that the synthesis directives have a higher impact on the different design metrics as they fix the resultant micro-architecture, *e.g.* deciding if arrays should be synthesized as memories or not, while the FUs constraints simply search the design space *nearby* by controlling the amount of resource sharing for that particular micro-architecture [9].

*Phase-1: Synthesis Directives Exploration.* The first phase generates unique combinations of synthesis directives and inserts them automatically in the input behavioral description. The synthesis directives used by the *MO-GA* explorer control how to synthesize *arrays* (*e.g.* registers, ROM, or RAM), *loops* (*e.g.* pipelined with different Data Initiation Intervals (DIIs), unrolled, partially unrolled or not unrolled) and *functions* (inlined or not). Thus, every array, loop and function in the behavioral description to be explored is considered as a gene and each iteration of the exploration generates a unique sequence of these genes, which build a chromosome *CM*. In this work, *CM*={loops, func, arrays}, which *arrays*={*ROM,LOGIC, RAM, REG, EXPAND*}, *loop*={*pipeline, unroll_all, unroll_0, unroll_partial*}, and *func*={*inline, goto*}.

The explorer starts by generating *M* unique chromosomes (*CM*). Two chromosomes $CM_1$ and $CM_2$ are selected randomly as parents, and a cross-over operator is then applied on them, with specified

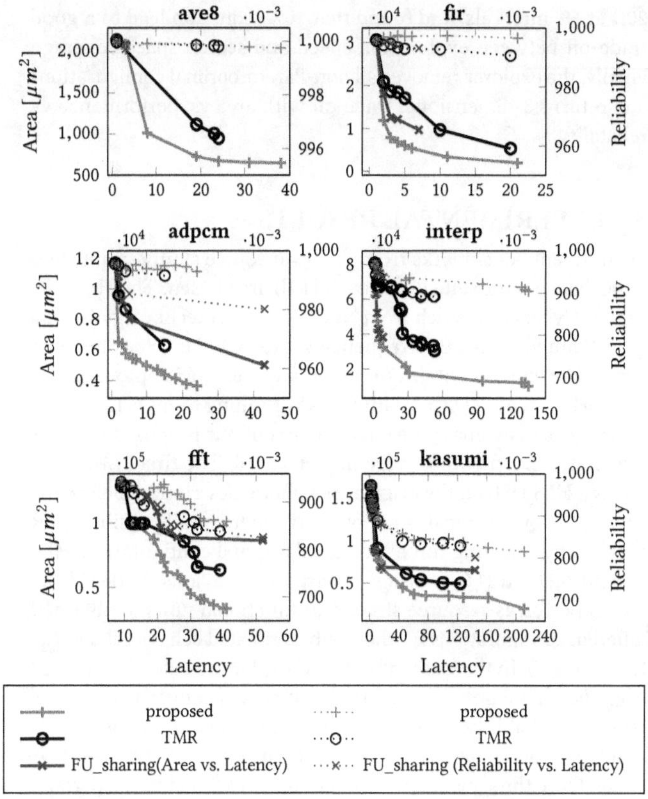


**Figure 2: Pareto-optimal trade-off curve between area and latency as well as reliability.**

probabilities $r\_crs$(=80%), by choosing a random cut-off point in their gene list that exchange partial chromosome to create a new chromosome ($CM_{1\_2}$). These new offspring are then mutated by random selection of one of its genes and substituting it by another synthesis directive. The mutation rate $r\_mut$ is also defined as an input parameter to our *MO-GA* explorer, which in this case is set to be 10%.

The explorer continues by synthesizing the offspring to extract the area and latency results, and calculating reliability based on the equation presented in the previous section. Finally, one of the parents is substituted with the offspring in case that its cost is smaller. The *MO-GA* process repeats until a certain exit condition is reached. In this work, if no new offspring with a lower cost is found after *n* iterations (*e.g.* n = 10), the exploration stops. Once the explorer stop, the weight parameters ($\alpha$, $\beta$ and $\gamma$) of cost function is updated to the processes re-initialized.

*Phase-2: Functional Unit Count (FCNT) Exploration. Phase*-1 fixes the micro-architecture and uses as many *FUs* as needed to maximize parallelism. In this phase, we investigate the effect on area, latency and reliability by exploring the number of functional units (*FUs*) for each Pareto-optimal design found after Phase-1. Therefore, once *Phase-1* finishes, the explorer retrieves the function units constraint file generated by the HLS tools, which indicates the number and types of different FUs been used for that particular set of synthesis directives, and then reduces the number of *FUs* by a constant percentages. We tried different reduction rates, ranging from 5% to

20% at 5% intervals, and found that 10% reduction lead to a good trade-off between exploration speed and search space coverage. Finally, the explorer removes all non-Pareto-optimal configurations and returns 3-dimensional trade-off with area vs. performance vs. reliability.

## 4 EXPERIMENTAL RESULTS

Six different benchmarks from the open source synthesizable SystemC benchmark suite (S2CBench [10]) are chosen. The HLS tool used is CyberWorkBench from NEC. The target technology is *Nangate* 45nm and the HLS frequency set to 100MHz (clock cycle of 10ns). The experiments were run on an Intel i5-6500 processor of 3.20 GHz machine with 16GByte RAM running CentOS Linux.

In order to evaluate the effectiveness of our proposed method, two additional methods were implemented: The first (*TMR*) performs a HLS DSE on the original behavioral description (before the source-to-source transformation) and generates all possible TMR systems by selecting three individual optimal configurations; the second method (*FU_sharing*) is based on previous work [7] [8], which performs resource sharing of functional units to obtained different configurations for the newly annotated behavioral description ($C_{NMR}$). In this case only the FU exploration step is executed (e.g. *Phase-2*). Pareto-optimal trade-off curves between area vs. latency vs. reliability are shown in Fig. 2. Because a 3-dimensional graph does not allow to easily interpret the results, the trade-off between these three parameters are plotted on a 2-dimensional graph with area on one y-axis, reliability on the other y-axis vs. latency on the x-axis (solid lines denote the area vs. latency trade-offs and dotted lines the reliability vs. latency tradeoffs).

In order to qualitatively and quantitatively compare the results of the three methods, we use *ADRS* and *Pareto Dominance*, which are well-known metrics to evaluate Pareto-optimal solutions in multi-objective optimization problems. The value of ADRS is inversely proportional to the degree of similarity between the two Pareto sets. A high ADRS value indicates that a significant part of the reference Pareto-front is missing in the approximate Pareto set.

The results reported were computed by comparing the Pareto-front of each method compared to the reference Pareto-front. As these methods are probabilistic, they were executed 5 times using different random seeds and the best overall results reported for each method. Moreover, due to the extremely large design space, it is not feasible to obtain the optimal solution. Thus, the reference Pareto-front is obtained by combining all the results of all the methods over all the different runs. This is a standard way of comparing different multi-objective optimization methods.

Table-1 shows the *ADRS* and *Pareto-Dominance* results for the *TMR* and *FU_sharing* methods because our proposed method always leads to best results that *ADRS_proposed* = 0% and *Dominance_proposed* = 100%. *TMR* method and *FU_sharing* method lead to *ADRS* and *Pareto-Dominance* as 27.1%, 11.3% and 74.9%, 14.6% on average that compared to our proposed method respectively.

In terms of runtime our proposed method is 2.13× slower than the *TMR* method because the search space is extended considerably. The *FU sharing* method is the fastest one as it only explores the design space by changing the number of FUs. Considering of the importance of fault-tolerance, we believe that the run-time overhead is more than acceptable, also considering that the design space exploration only needs to be performed once.

**Table 1: Design Space Exploration Quality of Results (QoR).**

| | TMR | | FU_sharing [7] | |
|---|---|---|---|---|
| Bench | ADRS [%] | Dom. [%] | ADRS [%] | Dom. [%] |
| ave8 | 24.3 | 14.3 | 135.9 | 28.6 |
| fir | 39.1 | 12.5 | 98.4 | 12.5 |
| adpcm | 19.2 | 8.3 | 13.1 | 8.3 |
| interp | 19.2 | 8.3 | 91.4 | 8.3 |
| fft | 32.1 | 12.5 | 68.6 | 6.25 |
| kasumi | 28.4 | 11.8 | 42.1 | 23.5 |
| Avg. | 27.1 | 11.3 | 74.9 | 14.6 |

## 5 CONCLUSION

In this paper, we have introduced a practical method to create a large variety of triple-modular fault-tolerant systems with different area vs. performance vs. reliability trade-offs from a single untimed behavioral description. This method allows hardware designers using commercial HLS tools to generate efficient TMR system automatically without requiring any modification in the underlying HLS process and thus, proving the practicality of this technique. Experimental results corroborate that our method works well.

## REFERENCES

[1] Agoston E Eiben, P-E Raue, and Zs Ruttkay. 1994. Genetic Algorithms with Multi-parent Recombination. In *International Conference on Parallel Problem Solving from Nature.*

[2] S. T. Fleming and D. B. Thomas. 2016. StitchUp: Automatic control flow protection for high level synthesis circuits. In *DAC*. 1–6.

[3] Michael J Flynn and Wayne Luk. 2011. *Computer System Design: System-on-Chip.* John Wiley & Sons.

[4] M. Glass, M. Lukasiewycz, T. Streichert, C. Haubelt, and J. Teich. 2007. Reliability-Aware System Synthesis. In *2007 Design, Automation Test in Europe Conference Exhibition*. 1–6.

[5] G. Lee, D. Agiakatsikas, T. Wu, E. Cetin, and O. Diessel. 2017. TLegUp: A TMR Code Generation Tool for SRAM-Based FPGA Applications Using HLS. In *FCCM*. 129–132.

[6] Shubhendu S Mukherjee et al. 2003. A Systematic Methodology to Compute the Architectural Vulnerability Factors for a High-performance Microprocessor. In *Symposium on Microarchitecture (MICRO).*

[7] A. Orailoglu and R. Karri. 1992. A Design Methodology For The High-level Synthesis Of Fault-tolerant ASICs. In *VLSI Signal Processing, V, 1992., [Workshop on]*. 417–426.

[8] A. Orailoglu and R. Karri. 1996. Automatic synthesis of self-recovering VLSI systems. *IEEE Trans. Comput.* 45, 2 (Feb 1996), 131–142.

[9] B. Carrion Schafer. 2016. Probabilistic Multiknob High-Level Synthesis Design Space Exploration Acceleration. *IEEE Transactions on Computer-Aided Design of Integrated Circuits and Systems* 35, 3 (March 2016), 394–406.

[10] B. C. Schafer and A. Mahapatra. 2014. S2CBench: Synthesizable SystemC Benchmark Suite for High-Level Synthesis. *IEEE Embedded Systems Letters* 6, 3 (2014), 53–56.

[11] A. Shastri, G. Stitt, and E. Riccio. 2015. A scheduling and binding heuristic for high-level synthesis of fault-tolerant FPGA applications. In *ASAP*. 202–209.

[12] Premkishore Shivakumar et al. 2002. Modeling the Effect of Technology trends on the Soft Error Rate of Combinational Logic. In *Dependable Systems and Networks (DSN).*

[13] S. Tosun et al. 2005. Reliability-centric high-level synthesis. In *Design, Automation and Test in Europe*. 1258–1263 Vol. 2.

[14] Kaijie Wu and R. Karri. 2004. Fault secure datapath synthesis using hybrid time and hardware redundancy. *IEEE Transactions on Computer-Aided Design of Integrated Circuits and Systems* 23, 10 (Oct 2004), 1476–1485.

# Automatic Extraction of Requirements from State-based Hardware Designs for Runtime Verification

Minjun Seo and Roman Lysecky
Department of Electrical and Computer Engineering, University of Arizona, Tucson, AZ, USA
mjseo@email.arizona.edu, rlysecky@ece.arizona.edu

## ABSTRACT

Runtime monitoring and verification enables a system to monitor itself and ensure system requirements are met even in the presence of dynamic environments. For hardware, state-based models are widely used, but verifying the correctness between the state-based model and hardware implementation is time-consuming and difficult. This paper presents a novel method for extracting hardware verification requirements from state-based hardware models to construct a hierarchical runtime monitoring graph that can be efficiently used at runtime to verify correctness.

## CCS CONCEPTS

• Hardware~Model checking • Computing methodologies~Model verification and validation

## KEYWORDS

Runtime verification, formal requirements models, periodic statement machines, hardware-based observations.

### ACM Reference format:

Minjun Seo and Roman Lysecky. 2019. Automatic Extraction of Requirements from State-based Hardware Designs for Runtime Verification. In ***GLSVLSI '19: 2019 Great Lakes Symposium on VLSI, May 9-11, 2019, Washington, D.C., USA. ACM, New York, NY.*** 4 pages. DOI: https://doi.org/10.1145/3299874.3318021

## 1 INTRODUCTION

Defining and verifying system requirements is a challenging task in embedded systems. Test-based verification and formal verification comprise a considerable effort that accounts for 75% of the total system design effort [4]. However, despite existing efforts, complete system verification at design time is considered to be almost impossible due to system complexity, dynamic execution behaviors, and unpredictable system inputs.

Runtime monitoring and verification enables a system to monitor its own execution to support rapid in-situ failure detection and enables tracing a failure's root cause, especially root causes that arise due to unknown environmental, physical, and operating conditions. However, cost, size, area, and energy constraints often limit which monitoring and verification approaches can be employed. A key concern is the need to ensure the monitoring method does not change the observable system state and to avoid any timing changes. Such intrusive interactions could lead to synchronization and scheduling problems that then lead to catastrophic system failures. Thus, runtime monitoring and verification methods should be non-intrusive, especially for safety-critical and life-critical embedded systems.

Embedded systems typically require tight interactions and interfacing between software and hardware components. Many embedded systems are implemented as systems-on-a-chip (SOC) that have a large number of hardware components. Verifying embedded systems at runtime not only includes verifying software execution, but also verifying the correct execution of hardware components, and interactions thereof. Thus, runtime monitoring and verification methods must also be able to monitor and verify the execution of hardware components.

In this paper, we present an extension of our runtime software requirements monitoring framework [10] to incorporate non-intrusive in-situ requirements monitoring for state-based hardware designs (NIRM-H) in embedded systems. We present a methodology for extracting hardware verification requirements from state-based hardware models to construct a hierarchical runtime monitoring graph (HRMG). To support automated synthesis of requirements for state-based hardware description, a formal model that extends the concept of periodic state machines with explicitly defined data transfer/synchronization is employed. The synthesized HRMG is a compact model of the system requirements that can be monitored at runtime using on-chip hardware, which can efficiently monitor the system execution with no performance overhead.

## 2 RELATED WORK

Runtime monitoring for hardware can be utilized to dynamically verify that behaviors of a system's hardware components adhere to the required system properties. However, most monitoring methods for hardware are not specifically targeted at system-level in-situ and runtime verification, but rather target the monitoring of specific operations or target verification/testing before system deployment. Trace-based methods for runtime monitoring (e.g., ChipScope [2], MED [6]) use large volumes of real-time trace data for analysis, which allow only a very simple level of verification, such as specifying a trigger with a simple condition. Event-based methods (e.g., ARBD [8], BusMOP [7], Heffernan et al. [5]) use hardware to detect events. Thus, event-based monitoring requires analyzing less data and results in simpler implementations that enable on-chip verification. Formal models, such as timed automata (TA) [1] and linear temporal logic (LTL) [9], are useful

This research was partially supported by the National Science Foundation under Grant CNS-1563652.



*GLSVLSI '19*, May 9–11, 2019, Tysons Corner, V A, USA

ACM ISBN 978-1-4503-6252-8/19/05...$15.00
https://doi.org/10.1145/3299874.3318021

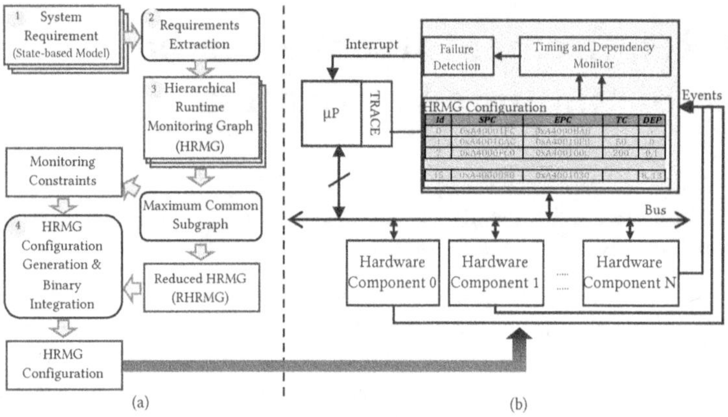


Figure 1: Non-Intrusive In-situ Requirements Monitoring methodology.

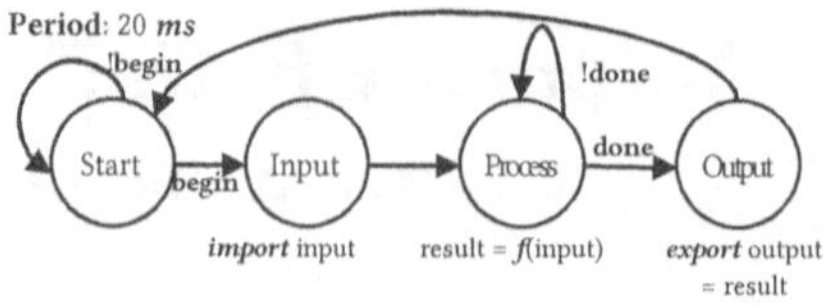


Figure 2: Example periodic state machine.

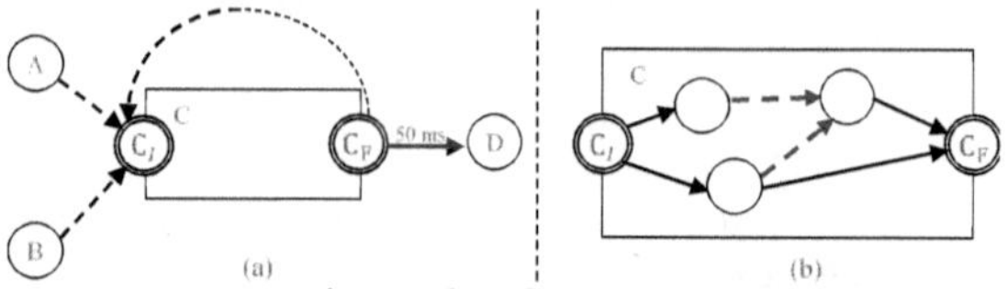


Figure 3: a) Top-level HRMG including hierarchical event C, and b) internal events and dependencies for hierarchical event C.

for verification, but these approaches require that system designers specify requirements in a separate model that is conceptually disjoint from the hardware design itself.

## 3 NIRM METHODOLOGY

Figure 1 (a) presents an overview of the non-intrusive requirements monitoring (NIRM) methodology consisting of: 1) initial hardware development with state-based models, 2) automated synthesis of requirements from the state-based model, 3) construction of a hierarchical runtime monitoring graph (HRMG) for each state machine, integration and simplification of the HRMGs using maximum common subgraph algorithm, and 4) generation of the configuration that will be programmed within the NIRM hardware. Figure 1 (b) presents an overview of the integration of the in-situ, non-intrusive monitoring hardware that verifies requirements at runtime within the deployed system.

### 3.1 Periodic State Machine (PSMs)

For verifying state-based hardware components, we assume a formal definition of the hardware model exists, or the hardware description itself enables the automatic extraction to create the hardware model. In our approach, we integrate concepts of periodic finite state machines with explicit definitions of data communication and synchronization between state machines in hardware and between hardware and software components.

**Definition 1.** ***A periodic state machine (PSM) is a tuple*** $G = \langle P, S, S_0, \delta, IM, EX \rangle$ ***where:***

- P is the period at which the state machine executes. The period P is defined as an explicit time unit, e.g. 200 ns
- S is a finite and non-empty set of vertices, where each vertex represents a state. A state is fired at multiple of P time units.
- $S_0$ is an initial state, an element of S
- $\delta$ is the state-transition function: $\delta: S \times \Sigma \rightarrow S$ where $\Sigma$ is a transition condition.
- IM is a set of shared variables from other PSMS that are imported into this PSM
- EX is a set of shared variables that are exported from this PSM that can be imported to other PSMs

**Definition 2.** ***A state S in a PSM G is a tuple*** $S = \langle V_i, A, Ve \rangle$ where:

- $V_i$ is a shared variable in a state, $V_i \in I$
- $V_e$ is a shared variable in a state, $V_e \in E$
- A is a set of actions (statements) executed in state S

If a state needs to access data exports from another PSM, the PSM model requires the explicit access of that data using an ***import*** statement. Similarly, if the PSM needs to output data to be communicated to another PSM, an explicit ***export*** is required.

Figure 2 shows a graphical representation of a periodic state machine (PSM) that has a 20 ms period, 4 states, 3 statements, 1 ***import*** variable, and 1 ***export*** variable.

### 3.2 Runtime Monitoring Model

We define a hierarchical runtime monitoring graph (HRMG) that is constructed from the state-based PSM models, which captures all requirements that can be monitored. The HRMG defines the set of events that is observable at runtime, the execution orders of those events, and timing constraints between events. All communication (i.e., ***import*** and ***export***) in the state-based models are considered system events.

**Definition 3.** ***An HRMG is a tuple*** $G = \langle V_G, E_G \rangle$ where:

- $V_G$ is a finite set of vertices, where each vertex represents a system event.
- $E_G$ is a set of edges representing dependencies between vertices. Each edge $E \in E_G$, defined as $E = V_G \rightarrow V_G'$, represents a dependency between two events $V_G$ and $V_G'$. $V_G$ is the source event, and $V_G'$ is the sink event.
- If a deterministic time constraint exists between $V_G$ and $V_G'$, an edge E may specify a worst-case execution time (WCET) constraint, defined as $V_G \xrightarrow{time} V_G'$. Note that the WCET can be obtained by period or probabilistic analysis.
- An edge has a type $\in$ {strong, weak} that specifies if the dependency is mandatory or optional. strong (solid arrow) represents a mandatory dependency. weak (dashed arrow) represents an optional dependency.
- A hierarchical event $H \in V_G$ is defined by a tuple $H = \langle V_H, E_H, H_I, H_F \rangle$. $H_I \in V_H$ is the initial vertex for H. External edges to H connect only to $H_I$. $H_F \in V_H$ is the final vertex for H. External edges from H only originate from $H_F$.
- For a hierarchical event H, all incoming edges to $H_I$ must have the same edge type (i.e., incoming edges must all be strong or weak dependencies).

Figure 3 presents an illustrative example of the HRMG model. Figure 3 (a) shows the top-level view of a graph consisting of 5 events, one of which is a hierarchical event, 3 weak dependencies, and 1 strong dependency. The hierarchical event C graphically depicts the initial ($C_I$) and final ($C_F$) events. $C_I$ has three incoming edges from A, B, and $C_F$ , all of which represent weak dependencies. Figure 3 (b) shows the events and dependencies within hierarchical event C, which consists of a total of 5 events, including the initial ($C_I$) and final ($C_F$) events. The edge $C_F \xrightarrow{50\,ms} D$

indicates that event D should occur no more than 50 ms after $C_F$.

### 3.3 Model Transform (PSM to HRMG)

The PSM represents the state-based hardware model, whereas the HRMG defines the requirements to be monitored at runtime. To create the HRMG, a PSMs-to-HRMG algorithm is utilized to extract requirements from each PSM, which are then combined into a single HRMG for the system-level hardware verification.

To extract the essential data communication, the algorithm first determines the subsets of ***import*** states and ***export*** states. For each pair of ***import*** states and ***export*** states, the algorithm analyzes the execution paths between the ***import***-to-***export*** and ***export***-to-***export*** state to determine both execution sequence dependencies and timing constraints. The algorithm traverses the PSM to count the number of intermediate states between the ***import*** and ***export*** state. If a finite number of states are encountered, a time constraint can be defined by the length of state sequence and PSM period. If the intermediate states have a cyclic path, the timing constraints will be infinite (∞). The algorithm constructs the corresponding events, and timing constraint if non-infinite, in the HRMG. When constructing the dependencies between events the HRMG, if the in-degree of any node is greater than 1, it needs to change all incoming edges to weak dependency. Finally, the algorithm uses a maximum common subgraph (MCS) algorithm [3] to identify common operation sequences in the RMGs to create hierarchal events. The MCS algorithm finds the largest completely connected subgraph starting with an event and ending with an event, creating a hierarchical event for the subgraph [10]. The MCS is iteratively applied to until no new hierarchical events can be found. When converting subgraphs to hierarchical events, edges to the hierarchical events are converted to weak dependencies as multiple executions may now occur before the hierarchical event, but not all events must occur.

## 4 NIRM HARDWARE

We developed a Xilinx Artix-7 FPGA (XC7A200T)-based prototype of a typical embedded system architecture incorporating the NIRM-H implementation. The NIRM hardware supports monitoring hardware components and verifying the requirements defined within an HRMG.

Multiple events from multiple hardware components must be observed at each hardware component, but those observed events are analyzed at the single NIRM component. As such, an event trace framework is used to efficiently communicate the observed events from each hardware component to the NIRM core. To support this, events detected at each hardware core are encoded using a 5-bit ***ComponentId***, 5-bit ***EventId***, and 32-bit ***Timestamp***. A ***NIRM Core Wrapper*** is integrated with each hardware component and uses an internal timer to determine the instance at which a local hardware event is observed. The ***NIRM Core Wrapper*** then transmits the timestamp of the local timer with the event's ***EventId*** and the component's ***ComponentId***. A ***NIRM-H Controller*** receives events from all ***NIRM Core Wrappers*** and implements a priority queue that forwards the incoming event with the smallest timestamp to the NIRM hardware each clock cycle. This ensures the NIRM component processes observed events in the correct execution order, even though the events will arrive at different times.

**Table 1: Area, power consumption, and percentage overhead for NIRM-H compared to a base system.**

| Monitored Components | Power (% overhead) | Area | |
|---|---|---|---|
| | | LUTs (% overhead) | FF (% overhead) |
| 4 | 0.145 W (4.04%) | 168 (1.5%) | 48 (0.5%) |
| 8 | 0.146 W (4.07%) | 410 (3.5%) | 136 (1.3%) |
| 16 | 0.148 W (4.12%) | 778 (6.4%) | 312 (2.9%) |
| 32 | 0.150 W (4.18%) | 1640 (12.6%) | 692 (6.2%) |
| 64 | 0.157 W (4.36%) | 3385 (22.9%) | 1486 (12.4%) |

Our methodology uses a hardware-based, on-chip monitor to ensure the system will not suffer any performance degradation. System designers must determine the maximum number of events to monitor when integrating the NIRM hardware. Table 1 presents the hardware area (LUTs and FFs), power consumption, and percentage area and power overhead (compared to a base system) for increasing number of monitored hardware components. Table 1 also shows the area and the power consumption scales linearly.

## 5 EXPERIMENTAL RESULTS

### 5.1 Representative PSM Models

To evaluate the PSM to HRMG synthesis, we developed 7 representative PSM models with increasing complexity. Table 2 summarizes the number of imports, exports, and states for each of PSMs, reporting the number of events, the number of strong and weak dependencies, and the number of timing requirements extracted. While the full specification of the representative PSMs is not shown for brevity, the following notes key features of each and their effect on the HRMG synthesis.

In PSM1, an ***export***-to-***export*** path exists. But due to 2 cyclic paths, the PSM to HRMG synthesis cannot determine a precise time constraint for the ***export***-to-***export*** path, so only a sequence dependency is generated. In PSM2, three ***import***-to-***export*** pairs and one ***export***-to-***export*** pair exists. The PSM to HRMG synthesis is able to determine time constraints for those paths, which are integrated into the resulting HRMG. PSM3 is similar to PSM2 but contains a cyclic path between states, so a precise timing constraint cannot be determined because of the cyclic path. PSM 4 – PSM 7 include multiple PSMs that communicate with each other. In PSM4, a state exports a shared variable that is imported by the other PSM in another state. This implies that the latter state should execute after the former state, the requirement of which is synthesized in the HRMG. In the resulting HRMG, an event has two weak dependencies to itself and to the event related to ***import*** according to the principle of handling OR relationships in HRMG. PSM5 contains two independent PSMs. When

**Table 2: HRMG requirements synthesis results.**

| ID | Import | Export | State | # Events | Dependencies | | Timing Constraints |
|---|---|---|---|---|---|---|---|
| | | | | | Strong | Weak | |
| PSM1 | 0 | 1 | 3 | 1 | 1 | - | - |
| PSM2 | 3 | 1 | 5 | 4 | - | 3 | 2 |
| PSM3 | 3 | 1 | 6 | 3 | - | 2 | - |
| PSM4 | 3 | 2 | 9 | 4 | 2 | 2 | 1 |
| PSM5 | 4 | 2 | 9 | 8 | 4 | 7 | 2 |
| PSM6 | 2 | 3 | 10 | 7 | 1 | 8 | 1 |
| PSM7 | 4 | 4 | 17 | 10 | 4 | 14 | 1 |
| CA | 9 | 8 | 20 | 13 | 1 | 19 | 11 |

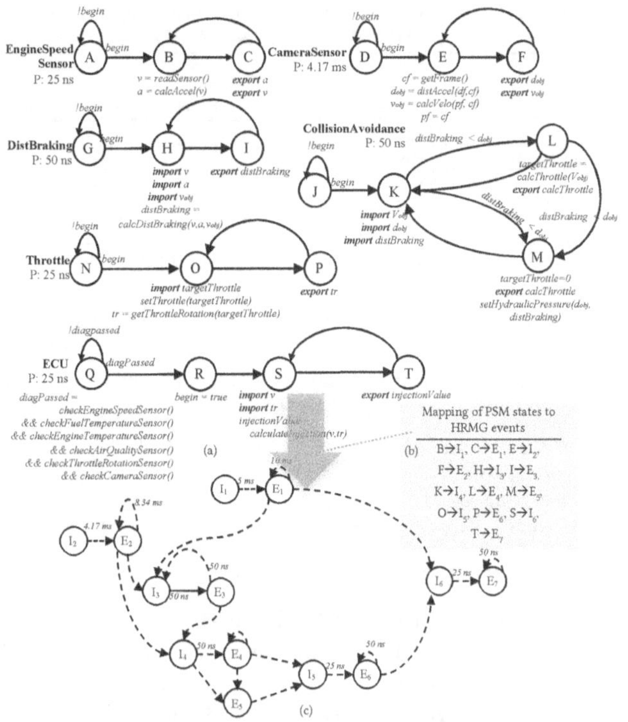


**Figure 4: (a) PSM model for collision avoidance system, (b) mapping information, and (c) corresponding HRMG. Note: These diagrams are intended to highlight the characteristic and complexity of the system, so details may not be visible.**

independent HRMG are combined, a source and sink node are added to merge the HRMG into a single HRMG, but no other dependencies exist. In PSM6, two of the PSMs have a shared variable, and the third PSM is independent of the other two. PSM7 has two PSMs, in which the second PSM has an ***import***-to-***export*** pair, and the time between the two is deterministic. Thus, a timing constraint is constructed for the event in the HRMG.

## 5.2 Case Study: Collision Avoidance

We further evaluate a case study of a safety-critical embedded system. Figure 4 (a) presents the PSMs for a video-based collision avoidance (CA) system. This implementation uses a single front-mounted camera to detect the location, distance, and speed of cars traveling in the same lane as the vehicle. The CA system calculates the minimum safe following distance and applies the brakes (and reduces throttle) automatically if the distance is less than the minimum safe distance.

The CA system consists of six PSMs. The ***EngineSpeedSensor*** PSM has a 25 ns period, which is the half the period at which the vehicle speed sensor is sampled. The ***EngineSpeedSensor*** PSM determines the velocity, $v$, computes the vehicles acceleration, $a$, and exports both to other PSMs. The ***CameraSensor*** PSM records video at 120 frames per second, which results in a period of 4.17 ms, and calculates the values $d_{obj}$ and $v_{obj}$, which are the distance to and speed of the vehicle in front of the current vehicle, respectively, using the current (***cf***) and previous frames (***pf***), which are exported in the next state, F. The ***DistBraking*** PSM determines the safe braking distance. In state H, the PSM imports the current vehicle speed ($v$), current vehicle acceleration ($a$), and speed of the vehicle in front ($v_{obj}$) and calculates the minimum safe traveling distance using the ***calcDistBraking*** function. The resulting distance, ***distBraking***, is exported in state I. The ***CollisionAvoidance*** PSM determines the throttle or braking required to maintain the minimum safe distance based on the distance to the vehicle in front ($V_{obj}$), speed of the vehicle ($d_{obj}$), and safe braking distance (***distBraking***). The Throttle PSM adjusts the actual throttle based on the current throttle position, ***throttleRotation***, and the imported target throttle, ***targetThrottle***. Lastly, the ECU is an integrated controller operating at 40 MHz that imports velocity and throttle positions to control engine operations. Note the ECU model has been simplified for demonstration.

Figure 4 (c) presents the resulting HRMG for the CA system and (b) lists the mapping between PSM states and HRMG events for the case study, the resulting HRMG consists of 13 events, 1 strong dependency, 19 weak dependencies, and 11 timing constraints. In addition, the case study shows a tendency to have more weak dependencies in the result than strong dependencies, which implies that the relationship between the component PSMs is tightly coupled.

# 6 CONCLUSIONS

We presented a non-intrusive in-situ requirements monitoring methodology for hardware designs for automatically extracting requirements and constructing HRMG from state-based hardware designs. Using both a set of representative state models of increasing complexity and a case study of a video-based collision avoidance system, we demonstrated the automated PSM to HRMG requirements synthesis process. Using efficient on-chip hardware, the NIRM approach can then monitor the execution of numerous interacting hardware components at runtime to ensure system requirements are not violated, and automatically reporting any such violations.

# REFERENCES


[1] Alur, R. 1999. Timed Automata. ***Computer Aided Verification***. Springer, Berlin, Heidelberg. 8–22.

[2] ChipScope Pro Software and Cores: 2012. ***https://www.xilinx.com/support/documentation/sw_manuals/xilinx14_7/chipscope_pro_sw_cores_ug029.pdf***.

[3] Durand, P.J., Pasari, R., Baker, J.W. and Tsai, C. 1999. An efficient algorithm for similarity analysis of molecules. ***Internet Journal of Chemistry***. 2, 17 (1999), 1–16.

[4] Hailpern, B. and Santhanam, P. 2002. Software debugging, testing, and verification. ***IBM Systems Journal***. 41, 1 (2002), 4–12.

[5] Heffernan, D. and Macnamee, C. 2016. Runtime observation of functional safety properties in an automotive control network. ***Journal of Systems Architecture***. 68, (2016), 38–50. DOI:https://doi.org/10.1016/j.sysarc.2016.05.001.

[6] Leatherman, R. and Stollon, N. 2005. An embedding debugging architecture for SOCs. ***IEEE Potentials***. 24, 1 (Feb. 2005), 12–16. DOI:https://doi.org/10.1109/MP.2005.1405795.

[7] Pellizzoni, R., Meredith, P., Caccamo, M. and Roşu, G. 2008. Hardware runtime monitoring for dependable COTS-based real-time embedded systems. ***Proceedings - Real-Time Systems Symposium***. (2008), 481–491. DOI:https://doi.org/10.1109/RTSS.2008.43.

[8] Peterson, K. and Savaria, Y. Assertion-based on-line verification and debug environment for complex hardware systems. ***2004 IEEE International Symposium on Circuits and Systems (IEEE Cat. No.04CH37512)*** II-685-8.

[9] Pnueli, A. 1977. The temporal logic of programs. ***18th Annual Symposium on Foundations of Computer Science (sfcs 1977)*** (Sep. 1977), 46–57.

[10] Seo, M. and Lysecky, R. 2017. Hierarchical non-intrusive in-situ requirements monitoring for embedded systems. (2017), 259–276.

# MirrorCache: An Energy-Efficient Relaxed Retention L1 STTRAM Cache

Kyle Kuan and Tosiron Adegbija
{ckkuan,tosiron}@email.arizona.edu
Department of Electrical & Computer Engineering
University of Arizona, Tucson, AZ, USA

## ABSTRACT

Spin-Transfer Torque RAM (STTRAM) is a promising alternative to SRAMs in on-chip caches, due to several advantages, including non-volatility, low leakage, high integration density, and CMOS compatibility. However, STTRAMs' wide adoption in resource-constrained systems is impeded, in part, by high write energy and latency. A popular approach to mitigating these overheads involves relaxing the STTRAM's retention time, in order to reduce the write latency and energy. However, this approach usually requires a dynamic refresh scheme to maintain cache blocks' data integrity beyond the retention time, and typically requires an external refresh buffer. In this paper, we propose *mirrorCache*—an energy-efficient, buffer-free refresh scheme. MirrorCache leverages the STTRAM cell's compact feature size, and uses an auxiliary segment with the same size as the logical cache size to handle the refresh operations without the overheads of an external refresh buffer. Our experiments show that, compared to prior work, mirrorCache can reduce the average cache energy by at least 39.7% for a variety of systems.

## CCS CONCEPTS

• **Computer systems organization → Processors and memory architectures**;

## KEYWORDS

Spin-Transfer Torque RAM (STTRAM); cache; retention time; non-volatile memory; energy efficient systems; write energy; write latency; emerging memory technologies.

**ACM Reference format:**
Kyle Kuan and Tosiron Adegbija. 2019. MirrorCache: An Energy-Efficient Relaxed Retention L1 STTRAM Cache. In *Proceedings of ACM Great Lakes Symposium on VLSI, Tysons Corner, VA, USA, May 9–11, 2019 (GLSVLSI '19)*, 4 pages.
https://doi.org/10.1145/3299874.3318022

## 1 INTRODUCTION

The Spin-Transfer Torque RAM (STTRAM) has emerged as a promising alternative for replacing traditional SRAMs in future on-chip caches. STTRAMs offer several attractive characteristics, such as non-volatility, low leakage, high integration density, and CMOS compatibility. However, some of STTRAM's most important challenges include its long write latency and high write energy [1, 2]. These challenges are attributed, in part, to the STTRAM's long *retention time*, which refers to how long data is retained in the memory in the absence of power [3]. Intrinsically, the retention time can be as long as 10 years. However, long retention time is typically over-provisioned for most cache data blocks [3]. Data blocks typically only need to remain in the cache for less than 1s before they are either replaced or invalidated. Thus, a viable STTRAM optimization is to substantially relax its retention time, thereby reducing the STTRAM's write latency and energy [3].

Even though relaxed retention time enables substantial energy and latency savings, several blocks may still need to remain in the cache beyond the retention time. To maintain the data correctness beyond the retention time, different techniques [1, 2] have been proposed to dynamically refresh the data block after the retention time has elapsed. Without loss of generality, we collectively refer to these techniques as the *dynamic refresh scheme (DRS)*. DRS typically writes a data block to a refresh buffer and back into the STTRAM cache to restart its retention clock in the cache. DRS also imposes overheads as a result of the buffer (leakage and area overheads) and the refresh operations (dynamic energy and time overheads). Our goal in this work is to mitigate these overheads.

We propose and explore the idea of *mirrorCache* as an energy-efficient relaxed retention L1 STTRAM cache that substantially mitigates the refresh buffer overheads. MirrorCache leverages STTRAM's density to enable an in-cache refresh function that eliminates the need for an external buffer. MirrorCache features a *main segment* and an equal-sized *auxiliary segment*. The cache's effective capacity is the size of the main segment. Rather than writing/reading refreshed data blocks to/from an external buffer as in prior work, mirrorCache writes to its auxiliary segment, and cache blocks can be fetched from either the main or auxiliary segments. Thus, mirrorCache eliminates the overheads concomitant to the external buffer (including its peripheral circuitry), and also substantially reduces the energy accrued during each refresh operation.

Using experiments with STTRAM caches designed with different retention times, our results reveal that mirrorCache reduces the overall cache energy by at least 39.7% on average, compared to prior work, without introducing substantial overhead. Our results also show that mirrorCache reduces the energy as compared to SRAM by at least 19.8%, on average, while trading off the latency for energy savings.


*GLSVLSI '19, May 9–11, 2019, Tysons Corner, VA, USA*

ACM ISBN 978-1-4503-6252-8/19/05...$15.00
https://doi.org/10.1145/3299874.3318022

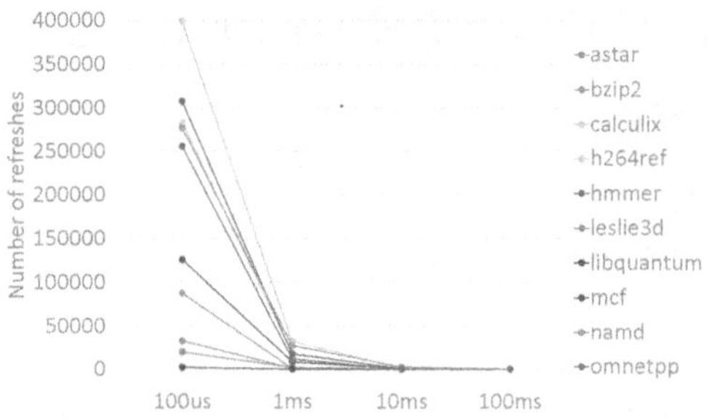


**Figure 1: Number of cache block refreshes for SPEC CPU2006 benchmarks**

## 2 BACKGROUND AND RELATED WORK

STTRAM uses a magnetic tunnel junction (MTJ) cell as the binary storage cell. MTJ contains two ferromagnetic layers separated by an oxide barrier/tunnel layer [4, 5]. Updating the MTJ cell's data bits relies on the magnetization switching of MTJ's free layer [4]. As a result, it takes more time and energy than conventional SRAM to change the free layer's magnetization state [5].

An approach for reducing the write energy and latency is to substantially relax STTRAM's data retention time, since it directly impacts the write energy and latency. The retention time can be relaxed by decreasing the MTJ cell's thermal stability or reducing the planar area [3]. Given a relaxed retention time STTRAM cache, *dynamic refresh schemes (DRS)* have been proposed to refresh data blocks that must remain beyond the retention time [1–3].

DRS incurs energy overheads due to the large number of refreshes and the need for a refresh buffer. Several techniques have been proposed to reduce the number of refreshes. For example, Jog et al. [1] refreshed only the first eight most recently used (MRU) blocks, and used a write buffer to bridge the surge of refresh requests and long STTRAM write time. Other techniques used compiler-assisted techniques to make refresh more efficient (e.g., [6]). However, DRS still requires a buffer to temporarily hold data blocks during refresh. Our work aims to minimize the overheads of DRS by leveraging the STTRAM's high density to eliminate the refresh buffer and its overheads. In effect, mirrorCache substantially reduces the leakage power and overall cache energy compared to DRS.

## 3 MIRRORCACHE

### 3.1 Cache block refresh analysis

To demonstrate the significance of the number of refreshed blocks and interplay with cache retention time, we analyzed the number of cache block refreshes required to maintain data correctness in different SPEC CPU2006 benchmarks. Figure 1 depicts the number of refreshes for different SPEC CPU2006 benchmarks running on 32KB L1 caches with retention times: 100$\mu s$, 1ms, 10ms, and 100ms.

As expected, smaller retention times, which consume less write energy and write latency, require substantially more refreshes. However, even though a longer retention time reduces the number of refreshes (e.g., the 100ms cache reduces the number of refreshes by 15x, on average), this comes at the expense of higher write energy and latency. Thus, it is important to minimize the overheads associated with the refresh operations.

### 3.2 Overview of mirrorCache

Figure 2 illustrates mirrorCache's operation. MirrorCache comprises of two equal-sized segments with identical organizations: the *main* and *auxiliary* (or *mirror*) segments. When a block must be refreshed, it is written to the auxiliary segment, and future references to the block are serviced from the auxiliary segment. If a block in the auxiliary segment needs to be refreshed, it is written back to the main segment and referenced from there. Block replacements are performed using normal replacement policies, e.g., least-recently used (LRU) or pseudo-LRU [7].

MirrorCache trades off physical area in favor of refresh efficiency, and offers a few advantages compared to DRS. First, mirrorCache eliminates the need for a refresh buffer, thereby eliminating the buffer's leakage power. Second, since the auxiliary segment is of equal size to the main segment, mirrorCache eliminates any chances of an oversubscribed buffer when several blocks must be refreshed simultaneously [8]. Third, since data can be directly fetched from the auxiliary segment, pipeline stalls are unnecessary when accessing data that is being refreshed. To prevent the overheads of tag comparisons for a larger cache, the tag array remains in 32KB setting, wherein a single status bit determines whether a block request is serviced from the main or auxiliary segment. Finally, mirrorCache reduces the dynamic energy incurred by each refresh operation since the writes to and reads from the external buffer are eliminated.

### 3.3 Identifying blocks to refresh

For simplicity, we opted to simply refresh all the blocks with longer lifetimes than the retention time (details in Section 4.2). To determine if and when blocks must be refreshed, we employ a *refresh counter* for each block, similar to prior work [2]. We implement the counter as a four-state finite state machine (FSM), resulting in a 2-bit per block overhead. The counter has a clock period $C = \frac{1}{P} * R$, where $R$ is the retention time, $P = S - 1$, and $S$ is the number of counter states (four in our case). When a block is written into the cache, the cache controller initializes the counter to zero, enables it, and then writes the block to the mirror segment when the counter's state reaches $P$.

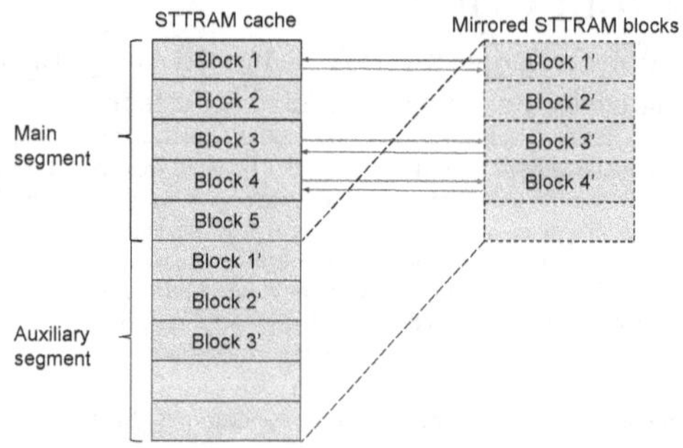


**Figure 2: Illustration of mirrorCache**

**Table 1: Cache parameters of SRAM and STTRAM with different retention times**

| Cache Configuration | SRAM: 32KB, STTRAM: 64KB physical size, 64B line size, 4-way; Buffer: 1KB | | | | | |
|---|---|---|---|---|---|---|
| Memory device | SRAM | STTRAM-100$\mu s$ | STTRAM-1ms | STTRAM-10ms | STTRAM-100ms | STTRAM-buffer |
| Write energy (per access) | 0.125nJ | 0.095nJ | 0.107nJ | 0.122nJ | 0.141nJ | 0.156nJ |
| Hit energy (per access) | 0.494nJ | 0.3nJ | 0.3nJ | 0.3nJ | 0.3nJ | 1.089nJ |
| Leakage power | 186.264mW | 154.686mW | | | | 285.666mW |
| Hit latency (cycles) | 2 | 1 | 1 | 1 | 1 | 1 |
| Write latency (cycles) | 2 | 3 | 4 | 5 | 7 | 1 |

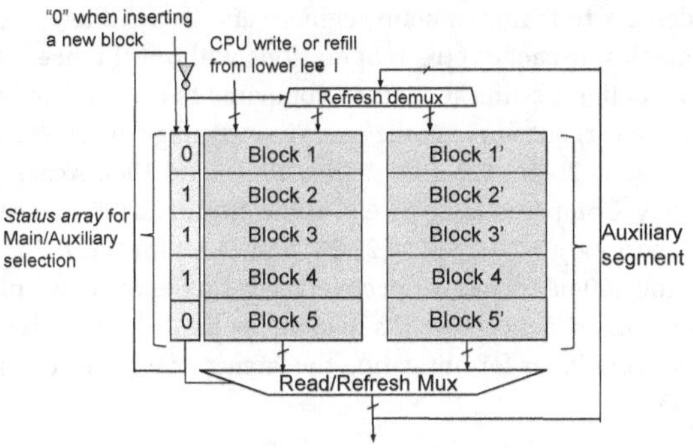


**Figure 3: mirrorCache architecture**

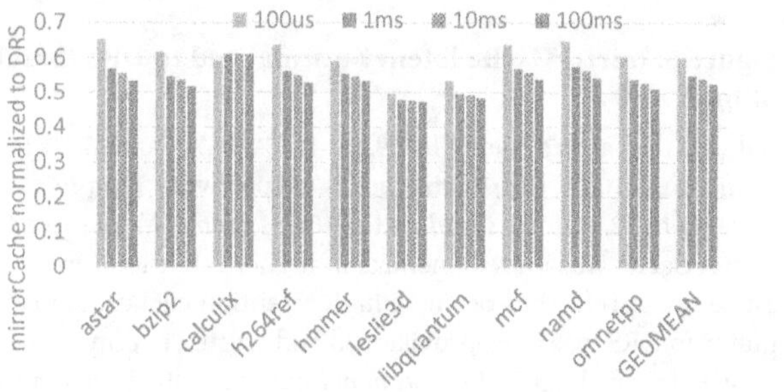


**Figure 4: mirrorCache energy normalized to DRS (baseline of one)**

## 3.4 MirrorCache architecture and overhead

Figure 3 illustrates mirrorCache's architecture and datapath for the main and auxiliary segments. To indicate the segment holding a cache block, we use a *status array* comprising of a status bit per block. Thus, the array size is equal to the number of logical cache blocks. For example, a 32KB cache would have a 512-element array, with one bit per element. When a block is inserted by CPU or refilled from lower level memory, the block would be allocated to the main segment, and the status bit is set to 0. When the counter FSM triggers a refresh, the status bit is read and inverted, indicating that the block is in the auxiliary segment; the datapath is then established for the block to be written to the auxiliary segment. Similarly, a refresh from the auxiliary segment writes the block into the main segment, and the status bit is set back to 0. For a fetch request, the status array indicates the active segment for the block; tag comparison is then performed as usual. The status array can be implemented in relaxed retention time STTRAM in order to easily integrate into the STTRAM cache. Overall, the overheads of implementing mirrorCache are from the status array and the muxes, as shown in Figure 3.

# 4 SIMULATION RESULTS

## 4.1 Experimental Setup

We modified GEM5 [9] to model both mirrorCache and DRS, for comparison to prior work. We used configurations similar to the ARM Cortex A15 [10], featuring a 2GHz clock frequency, and a private L1 cache with separate instruction and data caches. We focused on the data cache, since our analysis revealed that the target refresh problem was predominant in the data cache.

To explore the benefits of mirrorCache in various retention time scenarios, in comparison to prior work (DRS) and SRAM, we used a 32KB cache with 64B line size and 4-way set associativity. For a rigorous comparison, we implemented DRS as a best-case amalgam of prior methods assuming an ideal refresh scenario. That is, blocks are only refreshed if they are reused, no blocks expire because of insufficient refresh buffer space, and buffer bandwidth does not constitute a bottleneck. DRS featured a fully-associative 1KB STTRAM buffer, which is appropriately scaled from prior work [1]. The buffer's dynamic energy was 1.245nJ per refresh and 285.67mW leakage power from the buffer's peripherals and high associativity.

We considered four retention times: 100$\mu s$, 1ms, 10ms, and 100ms, which we empirically found to be sufficient for the range of considered benchmarks. We modeled the retention times using MTJ modeling techniques proposed in [11] and used NVSim [12] to construct the STTRAM cache for the different retention times. Table 1 depicts the STTRAM and SRAM cache parameters used in our experiments as obtained from the modeling tools and techniques. We used ten SPEC CPU2006 benchmarks [13], compiled for the ARM instruction set architecture. Each benchmark was run using the *reference* input sets for 100M instructions after fast-forwarding for 100M instructions.

## 4.2 Results

In this section, we present the results of our experiments to illustrate the benefits of mirrorCache as compared to DRS. Throughout this section, we refer to our proposed work as mirrorCache, and a cache featuring the dynamic refresh scheme simply as DRS.

*4.2.1 Energy Savings.* Overall, mirrorCache substantially reduced the refresh energy compared to DRS. Unlike DRS, where the average refresh energy for each application was approximately 47% of the total energy, mirrorCache reduced the refresh energy to an infinitesimal portion (< 1%) of the total energy, thereby resulting in substantial cache energy savings.

Figure 4 depicts the overall cache energy of mirrorCache normalized to DRS. On average across all the benchmarks, mirrorCache

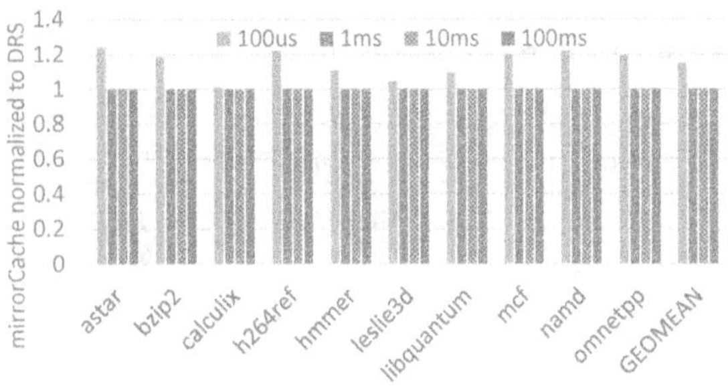


**Figure 5: mirrorCache latency normalized to DRS (baseline of one)**

reduced the cache's energy by 39.7%, 44.9%, 45.7%, and 47.2% for the 100$\mu s$, 1ms, 10ms, and 100ms caches, respectively. Energy savings were up to 52.8% for *leslie3d* on the 100*ms* cache. We observed that mirrorCache was more beneficial in higher retention time caches. Since fewer refreshes occur in high retention caches, the refresh buffer in DRS was over-provisioned and wasted energy.

We observed that *astar* and *namd* improved the least over DRS by 34.7% and 35.3% in the 100$\mu s$ cache. These two benchmarks' data blocks were frequently updated, had high dynamic read and write activities, and low refresh activity. Thus, the energy consumption of these benchmarks was dominated by the dynamic energy. However, by eliminating the refresh buffer, mirrorCache still achieved substantial energy savings for these benchmarks despite their low refresh activity.

*4.2.2 Latency.* We also evaluated mirrorCache's access latency benefits compared to DRS. In general, mirrorCache only achieved marginal latency benefits compared to DRS due to the additional write latency of the larger physical cache (Table 1) and the circuits to check the status bits.

Figure 5 depicts mirrorCache's latency normalized to DRS. For the 1*ms*, 10*ms*, and 100*ms* caches, mirrorCache achieved similar latency to DRS. For the 100$\mu s$ cache, however, mirrorCache degraded the latency for majority of the benchmarks by 14.93% on average, and by up to 24.29% for *astar*. We observed that in the 100$\mu s$ retention time, the latency overhead was dominated by the additional decoding circuits due to mirrorCache's increase in physical size. For the longer retention times, however, the overhead was dominated by the STT-RAM cell's write latency, which was equivalent for both DRS and mirrorCache, despite mirrorCache's increase in size. Across all benchmarks, *calculix* and *leslie3d* suffered the least latency degradation of 1.25% and 4.57%, respectively, in the 100$\mu s$ cache. We observed that *calculix* had few writes compared to other benchmarks and *leslie3d*'s latency was dominated by the miss latency. As such, neither benchmark was significantly affected by mirrorCache's increase in write latency.

*4.2.3 Comparison to SRAM.* We summarize the results of mirrorCache's comparison to SRAM, but omit graphs due to space constraints. On average, mirrorCache reduced the overall cache energy by 34.7%, 31.2%, 27.2%, and 19.8% for the 100$\mu s$, 1ms, 10ms, and 100ms caches, respectively, as compared to SRAM. MirrorCache reduced the overall cache latency by 17.5% and 6.8% for the 100$\mu s$ and 1ms, respectively, as compared to SRAM. For higher retention times (10ms and 100ms), however, mirrorCache *increased* the latency by 3.8% and 25.2%, respectively, with the most substantial increases occurring for write-intensive benchmarks like *omnetpp* and *h264ref*. We attribute these observations to STTRAM's long write latency (Table 1). We observed similar trends for DRS, so this was not a deficiency unique to mirrorCache.

# 5 CONCLUSIONS AND FUTURE WORK

In this paper, we proposed *mirrorCache* as an energy efficient design for mitigating the overheads of utilizing a refresh buffer in relaxed retention STTRAM caches. MirrorCache leverages the STTRAM's high density to feature a main segment and an auxiliary segment that enables in-cache refresh operations without the need for an external buffer. Results show that, compared to prior related work, mirrorCache reduced the cache energy, on average, by 39.7%, 44.9%, 45.7%, and 47.2% for the 100$\mu s$, 1ms, 10ms, and 100ms caches, respectively. Compared to an SRAM cache, mirrorCache reduced the cache energy by 34.7%, 31.2%, 27.2%, and 19.8% for the 100$\mu s$, 1ms, 10ms, and 100ms caches, respectively. For future work, we plan to explore mirrorCache's benefits in complex multi-level caches, and develop techniques for mitigating the latency overheads compared to SRAM.

# REFERENCES


[1] A. Jog, A. K. Mishra, C. Xu, Y. Xie, V. Narayanan, R. Iyer, and C. R. Das, "Cache revive: Architecting volatile stt-ram caches for enhanced performance in cmps," in *DAC Design Automation Conference 2012*, June 2012, pp. 243–252.

[2] Z. Sun, X. Bi, H. Li, W. F. Wong, Z. L. Ong, X. Zhu, and W. Wu, "Multi retention level stt-ram cache designs with a dynamic refresh scheme," in *2011 44th Annual IEEE/ACM International Symposium on Microarchitecture (MICRO)*, Dec 2011, pp. 329–338.

[3] C. W. Smullen, V. Mohan, A. Nigam, S. Gurumurthi, and M. R. Stan, "Relaxing non-volatility for fast and energy-efficient stt-ram caches," in *2011 IEEE 17th International Symposium on High Performance Computer Architecture*, Feb 2011, pp. 50–61.

[4] Z. Diao, Z. Li, S. Wang, Y. Ding, A. Panchula, E. Chen, L.-C. Wang, and Y. Huai, "Spin-transfer torque switching in magnetic tunnel junctions and spin-transfer torque random access memory," *Journal of Physics: Condensed Matter*, vol. 19, no. 16, p. 165209, 2007.

[5] C. Xu, D. Niu, X. Zhu, S. H. Kang, M. Nowak, and Y. Xie, "Device-architecture co-optimization of stt-ram based memory for low power embedded systems," in *2011 IEEE/ACM International Conference on Computer-Aided Design (ICCAD)*, Nov 2011, pp. 463–470.

[6] K. Qiu, J. Luo, Z. Gong, W. Zhang, J. Wang, Y. Xu, T. Li, and C. J. Xue, "Refresh-aware loop scheduling for high performance low power volatile stt-ram," in *2016 IEEE 34th International Conference on Computer Design (ICCD)*, Oct 2016, pp. 209–216.

[7] H. Ghasemzadeh, S. Mazrouee, and M. R. Kakoee, "Modified pseudo lru replacement algorithm," in *13th Annual IEEE International Symposium and Workshop on Engineering of Computer-Based Systems (ECBS'06)*. IEEE, 2006, pp. 6–pp.

[8] J. Ahn, S. Yoo, and K. Choi, "Dasca: Dead write prediction assisted stt-ram cache architecture," in *2014 IEEE 20th International Symposium on High Performance Computer Architecture (HPCA)*, Feb 2014, pp. 25–36.

[9] N. Binkert, B. Beckmann, G. Black, S. K. Reinhardt, A. Saidi, A. Basu, J. Hestness, D. R. Hower, T. Krishna, S. Sardashti, R. Sen, K. Sewell, M. Shoaib, N. Vaish, M. D. Hill, and D. A. Wood, "The gem5 simulator," *SIGARCH Comput. Archit. News*, vol. 39, no. 2, pp. 1–7, Aug. 2011.

[10] "Cortex-A15 Processor." [Online]. Available: https://www.arm.com/products/processors/cortex-a/cortex-a15.php

[11] K. C. Chun, H. Zhao, J. D. Harms, T. H. Kim, J. P. Wang, and C. H. Kim, "A scaling roadmap and performance evaluation of in-plane and perpendicular mtj based stt-mrams for high-density cache memory," *IEEE Journal of Solid-State Circuits*, vol. 48, no. 2, pp. 598–610, Feb 2013.

[12] X. Dong, C. Xu, Y. Xie, and N. P. Jouppi, "Nvsim: A circuit-level performance, energy, and area model for emerging nonvolatile memory," *Trans. Comp.-Aided Des. Integ. Cir. Sys.*, vol. 31, no. 7, pp. 994–1007, Jul. 2012.

[13] J. L. Henning, "Spec cpu2006 benchmark descriptions," *SIGARCH Comput. Archit. News*, vol. 34, no. 4, pp. 1–17, Sep. 2006.

# Design and Evaluation of DNU-Tolerant Registers for Resilient Architectural State Storage

Faris S. Alghareb[1,2] and Ronald F. DeMara[1]
[1]Department of Electrical and Computer Engineering, University of Central Florida, Orlando, FL 32816-2362 USA
[2]Department of Computer and Informatics Engineering, Ninevah University, Mosul 41001, Iraq

## Abstract

In this work, we aim to maintain the correct execution of instructions in the pipeline stages. To achieve that, the integrity for the data computed in registers during execution should be maintained via protecting the susceptible registers. Thus, we present a Double Node Upset Resilient Flip-Flop (DNUR-FF) circuit that can tolerate double errors while incurring low area and power overheads. We deploy the proposed soft-error resilient register at higher level to replace the most vulnerable registers in large-scale pipeline processors. The experimental results validate the robustness of our design by delivering superior fault coverage masking (100%) for both SEU and DNU errors. In addition, the proposed design utilizes partial spatial redundancy, and therefore, incurs reduced area overhead (31%) and realizes 58% of PDP improvement compared to Triple Module Redundancy (TMR) approach while delivering high-performance with low complexity and power consumption.

## CCS Concepts

• **Hardware → Circuit hardening; Transient errors and upsets; System-level fault tolerance**; *Sequential circuits; Error detection and error correction; Redundancy.*

## Keywords

Datapath resilience; pipeline registers; reliability; soft errors

**ACM Reference Format:**

Faris S. Alghareb and Ronald F. DeMara. 2019. Design and Evaluation of DNU-Tolerant Registers for Resilient Architectural State Storage. In *Great Lakes Symposium on VLSI 2019 (GLSVLSI '19), May 9–11, 2019, Tysons Corner, VA, USA.* ACM, New York, NY, USA, 4 pages. https://doi.org/10.1145/3299874.3318023

## 1 INTRODUCTION

In recent sub-micron CMOS electronics, the critical charge, $Q_{crit}$, needed to cause a transient fault decreases as $V_{DD}$ is scaled, and the Soft Error Rate (SER) has an exponential dependence on critical charge. Such trends are consistent with decreasing feature sizes due to technology scaling [4]. Therefore, random bit flips, caused by transient faults, are becoming a concern for reliable systems. These errors can corrupt data bits computed in registers or states stored in memory cells. At the architecture-level, the effect of these soft errors can be identified into two categories including: Silent Data Corruption (SDC) and Detected Unrecoverable Error (DUE). SDC errors occur when a transient fault propagates and corrupts the data, and then becomes a visible error. DUE, on the other hand, is detected by the system; however, it causes the system to freeze or crash without corrupting the user's data thereby rebooting the system is required [9]. Unlike DUE that makes the system unavailable, SDC errors result in unnoticed corrupted data. Thus, they are considered more significant in terms of reliability challenges as they might harm the system's functionality and/or user's data. This is because SDC can corrupt several components, such as registers, cache, arithmetic logic unit (ALU), multiplexer, memory, etc. [5].

At the chip level, memory protection techniques, or Error Correcting Code (ECC), are not sufficient for designs fabricated with advanced technology generations due to the logic soft-error, i.e., errors in latches/flip-flops and combinational logic, has become significant contributors to increase SER at the system-level [4, 6]. One solution to ensure data integrity of the registered states is by separating the bits of the same word. However, this scheme becomes a complicated process and might not be feasible for deeply-scaled register sets, as it impacts area and power consumption [4]. Developing Soft-Error (SE) resilient latches to budget or compensate for these transient faults is essential for resilient systems. This is because a glitch at the circuit-level can propagate to the system-level and eventually may become a user-visible error. Achieving soft-error resilience for these resources at the circuit-level is the starting point to design reliable computing architectures. Consequently, SER of any component has to be adequately low to satisfy the system-level reliability requirement.

In response to these aforementioned challenges, herein we developed energy-efficient and superior-performing soft-error resilient flip-flop circuits that significantly reduce the potential Single-Event Double Node Upset (SEDNU) occurring at susceptible nodes. The soft-error resilient flip-flop developed can be deployed in a pipeline processor or a mission-critical system to replace the most important and vulnerable registers, therefore, efficiently improving the system reliability by ensuring the integrity of states stored in the temporary registers. Thus, the contribution of this work includes: 1) designing a novel DNU-Resilient Flip-Flop (DNUR-FF) circuit. The DNUR-FF is developed at the circuit-level to achieve minimized area and power overheads while delivering superior fault masking coverage, 2) evaluating the deployment of the proposed DNUR-FF in a MIPS pipeline processor at the architecture-level to harden the pipeline registers, and 3) assessing a selective protection method to only harden the most susceptible registers in the pipeline stages.

Section 2 reviews the design and limitations of the prior work latching designs at the circuit-level and system-level. Section 3


*GLSVLSI '19, May 9–11, 2019, Tysons Corner, VA, USA*

ACM ISBN 978-1-4503-6252-8/19/05...$15.00
https://doi.org/10.1145/3299874.3318023

covers the proposed SE-resilient register. Experiments and results are presented in Section 4. Finally, Section 5 concludes the work.

## 2 Redundancy-based SE-Robust Designs

Here we discuss selected state-of-the-art radiation-hardening latching circuit designs, at both the circuit-level and system-level. Notice that the condition of a transient pulse (SET) to upset a latch or flip-flop circuit is that its duration has to be larger than the feedback loop delay of the latching circuit.

### 2.1 Soft-Error Resilience at the Circuit-Level

In the literature, numerous mitigation techniques have been introduced to increase the resilience of latches and flip-flops so that they become resistant to soft errors. For instance, Dual Interlocked-storage Cell (DICE) [3] is one prevalent design for hardening SEU inside latches due to its superior resilience of fault masking coverage and modest performance penalties. However, it still does not provide complete immunity to multiple nodes.

Spatial redundancy techniques such as TMR can be utilized for achieving single-fault masking-based reliability at the architecture-level. However, this method requires triplicating the protected datapath, and thus imposing significant area and power consumption overheads [1]. To minimize the overhead of the protection logic, an SEU-resilient latch design was introduced in [12] that triplicates the most sensitive paths along with redundant feedback loops. Although this design reduces area and power consumption overheads, it incurs significant delay since the redundant output comparison circuits are located on the critical delay path. Similarly, in [6], a DICE-base Double Node Charge Sharing SEU (DNCS-SEU) tolerant latch that is able to tolerate double errors (upsets) simultaneously was introduced. The design uses double DICE cells operating in parallel instead of double conventional latches. It achieves an effective masking coverage for both SEU and DNU, however, this is at the expense of high area overhead and power consumption.

### 2.2 Soft-Error Resilience at the System-Level

Similar to the circuit-level designs, the architecture-level soft-error mitigation approaches are mostly employing redundancy-based methods, which duplicate or triplicate the vulnerable components/circuits in the targeted system. On the other hand, error detection for arithmetic units, i.e., ALU, is achieved via information-based approaches such as Error-Correcting Codes (ECCs) [5]. Thus, the other susceptible components are the pipeline stages. They can be protected by employing Dual Module Redundancy (DMR) to fully duplicate the pipelines, a partial redundancy using Reduced Precision Redundancy (RPR), or checkpoint recovery. Both fully and partial duplication can detect and recover soft errors, whereas the latter can only be incorporated to perform recovery operations.

It is observed that incorporating redundancy by running duplicated or triplicated systems to achieve resilient fault tolerance in critical computing systems has impacted the system performance by incurring high energy consumption [2]. Investigating trade-offs between fault resilience and energy consumption has become urgent to realize a balance between fault resilience and energy-efficiency. In [7], it was reported that roughly 50% of the SDC errors result from the sequential circuits, i.e., latches and flip-flops, in Intel processors. Similarly, in [10], the authors projected that the majority of the system failures were found due to the vulnerability of some important registers in the targeted LEON3 processor core. Furthermore, in [5], it was concluded that an important reliability improvement (masking more than 70% of soft errors) can be achieved when hardening only 10% of the sequential logic, i.e., the most susceptible registers, in an ARM Cortex-R5 CPU core. Thus, even though numerous papers in the literature discuss recent innovations for SE-mitigation in memory devices, the focus herein is on protecting the registered states in datapaths due to its increasing importance.

## 3 PROPOSED SE RESILIENT DESIGNS

To achieve favorable tradeoffs between the protection cost (area overhead, power consumption, and delay) and resilience of fault masking coverage, we first identify the most vulnerable nodes, which are most prone to particle strikes, in large-scale latching circuits. The feedback and output nodes of a latching circuit are the most vulnerable nodes to cause an upset (SEU) [8]. Thus, the presented circuit considers hardening for these susceptible nodes, which maximize resilience of soft errors masking while minimizing the hardening cost.

### 3.1 Proposed Soft-Error Resiliency at Circuit-Level

The principle of the presented circuit is based on duplicating the susceptible nodes and employing an output feedback loop to construct protected internal interlocked nodes. Moreover, to protect the vulnerable nodes driving the output stage of the latch, we duplicate/triplicate these nodes to prevent the output bit from being flipped when a transient fault strikes an internal node. In this regard, the output changes according to the majority logic of internal nodes.

Figure 1 shows the design structure of the DNUR-FF circuitry. It is a master/slave design, and each latch composes of dual redundant interlocked loop, an ordinary latch, and clock-gating output comparator circuitry. While TG4/TG11 is added to transfer data to the output (Q) during the transparent mode of operation, and thus it achieves high speed via optimized propagation delay time (CLK-to-Q). Unlike the TMR latch design, here we employ a C-element circuit in the datapath logic of the upper and lower latch to protect the vulnerable nodes and improve the robustness of the latch at a cost of minimized area overhead and power consumption of redundant logic. Thus, to minimize area overhead and power consumption of protection logic, we replace the inverter in the upper and lower latch by a C-element circuitry that performs comparison and inversion on coming data bit instead of performing only inversion. Therefore, a masked output is produced at each internal node. In this regard, if a transient pulse is incident which causes a flip of the logic state of a vulnerable internal node, then the output remains unchanged until the next clock phase when the latch becomes transparent. This is achieved at an area overhead of utilizing two extra transistors (one PMOS and one NMOS transistor) in each redundant interlocked loop. Below, we discuss and evaluate the functionality and robustness of the proposed DNUR-FF design, we consider the slave latch shown in Figure 1.

Default operation mode: We consider first the DNU-free case. When the clock signal (CLK) is high and the complement clock signal (CLKB) is low, i.e., transfer mode, the data bit at the input is

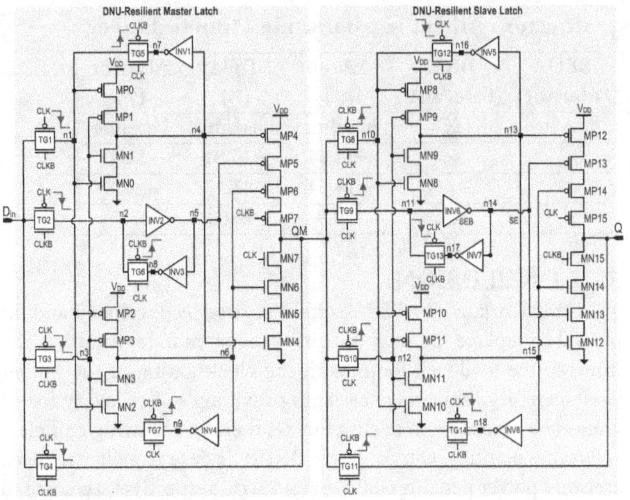

**Figure 1: Circuit schematic of the DNU-resilient flip-flop (DNUR-FF) proposed herein.**

transferred to the output (Q) through TG11 and stored into the ordinary latch configured by (INV6, INV7) through TG9 and also locked into the upper interlocked feedback loop constructed by (MP8-MP9 and MN8-MN9) and lower loop configured by (MP10-MP11 and MN10-MN11) through TG8 and TG10, respectively. In this way, the datapath delay (CLK-to-Q) is the propagation delay of TG11, thus the proposed circuit achieves significantly high throughput. When the CLK signal is low and CLKB is high, latching phase, both the upper and lower loop is driven through the C-element circuitry, thereby preventing transient faults striking on node n16 or n18 from being propagated to node n13 or n15, respectively. Thus, during the latching phase the feedback from the upper and lower loop is compared to ensure the integrity of data bit at the internal nodes. Thereafter, the logic state of nodes n13, n14, and n15 are compared via a clock-gating C-element circuit constructed by (MP12-MP15 and MN12-MN15) to produce the final masked output. Hence, the integrity of node n10, n12, n16, and n18 is ensured via the upper and lower comparison (C-element) circuit, whereas nodes n13, n14, and n15 are protected via the output comparator. Therefore, a particle strike induced DNU at single or even double vulnerable node(s) will be masked by means of the internal comparators and/or the output comparator.

## 3.2 Proposed Soft-Error Resiliency at System-Level

In this section, we incorporate the proposed circuit to improve reliability of a single core MIPS processor via hardening only the most vulnerable components in the targeted system. The proposed flip-flop replaces the pipeline registers (IF/ID, ID/EX, EX/MEM, and MEM/WB register) so that transient fault detection and correction storing circuitry is deployed only in the pipeline registers while the computations through the datapath can be protected using ECC methods. Thus, the proposed SE-resilient FF introduces a compromise solution to achieve more modest performance penalties. It incurs a small amount of redundancy for each register, redundant interlocked feedback loops with comparators, instead of triplicated datapaths and registers as in a TMR arrangement or a single datapath and triplicated registers as in the temporal redundancy. In addition to its high speed and low power consumption, the proposed register offers complete protection against both transient and upset errors. For the 32-bit pipeline MIPS processor, we replaced the four registers (32-bit each) in the pipeline stages, thus 128 circuits were deployed to protect the logic states. As a result, the robustness of the pipeline registers in the datapath are completely protected (100% rejection rate) against both SEUs and DNUs with 11.42% incurred area and roughly 8.56% of power consumption compared to area and power of total registers. While the speed degradation is considered negligible, the protection method of the proposed register does not impact the datapath delay.

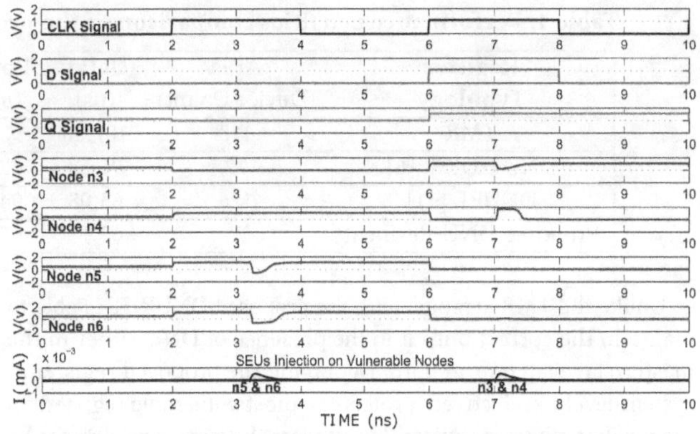

**Figure 2: Timing waveforms for the proposed DNU resilient flip-flop design when transient faults hit double vulnerable nodes.**

# 4 EXPERIMENTS AND RESULTS

Experiments are carried out to quantify and evaluate overheads of the above-mentioned proposed SE-resilient FF in terms of area, power consumption, propagation delay, and robustness of soft fault masking coverage. The proposed circuit is synthesized and simulated using HSPICE simulations based on 45nm HK-MG bulk CMOS PTM-based NanGate open source library [13] while the benchmark circuits/systems were synthesized via Synopsys Design Compiler.

## 4.1 SEU and DNU Immunity Evaluation

Here, a transient current source was connected to each vulnerable node, identified in Figure 1, with a maximum pulse amplitude of 577.35 $\mu$A and duration of 800 ps. This current source was injected into a single node to emulate SEUs, whereas double current sources were connected to double nodes, i.e., node pair, concurrently to mimic the effect of DNUs. These HSPICE simulations were carried out to determine the vulnerable node pairs, i.e., most susceptible to particle hits, so that if they suffered a hit and flipped the logic state, then the selected pair is considered unprotected. As shown in Figure 2, the injected SEUs temporarily alter the logic state of the struck nodes, and the impacted nodes (n3–n6) restore the correct logic values through the interlocked feedback loops. Therefore, the final output ($Q$) is not affected. Likewise, transient faults that occur at the output of TG11 are not a concern and will not affect the final output. This is due to the fact that the latch is transparent and its data is not valid during this time interval. Consequently, whether single or double vulnerable node(s) becomes upset concurrently, the proposed hardened design always ensures the correct bit state for the final output, $Q$.

**Table 1: Performance penalties comparison of the proposed soft-error resilient register using 45nm technology.**

| Register Typology | Area (Device Count) | Delay (ps) | Power ($\mu W$) | SEU Tolerant | DNU Tolerant | ΔArea (%) | ΔDelay (%) | ΔPower (%) |
|---|---|---|---|---|---|---|---|---|
| TMR | 110 | 107.16 | 92.72 | ✓ | X | baseline | baseline | baseline |
| DNUT-DICE [6] | 72 | 95.57 | 62.61 | ✓ | ✓ | −34.54 | −10.81 | −32.47 |
| DNURL [11] | 126 | 63.08 | 94.56 | ✓ | ✓ | +14.54 | −41.13 | +1.98 |
| Proposed DNU-Resilient | 76 | 62.12 | 67.03 | ✓ | ✓ | -30.9 | -42.03 | -27.70 |

Unlike the TMR arrangement, the proposed DNUR-FF is able to maintain the correct output in the presence of DNU either in the master/slave latch or in both. Deploying the proposed register at system-level to selectively protect the most vulnerable registers in the pipeline stages significantly increases the system robustness by ensuring the correct logic values for the stored states. As a result, since all the vulnerable registers become protected, the processor realizes complete fault masking coverage (SEU and DNU) of logic states temporary stored in the pipeline registers. Whereas incorporating the partial spatial redundancy using TMR approach achieves complete fault masking coverage only for SEU in single module.

## 4.2 Evaluation of Area, Power, and Delay

Here, the relative overheads in terms of occupied area (ΔArea), power consumption (ΔPower), and datapath delay (ΔDelay) of the proposed soft-error resilient circuit compared to the conventional TMR arrangement are listed in Table 1. The relative variations were determined as: $\Delta = [(Robust_{latch} - TMR_{latch}) / TMR_{latch}] \times 100\%$. At the system-level, the integrity of the computation of all functional units in the targeted processor assumed to be ensured using a coding-based technique, while the pipeline registers of the processor can be hardened via the proposed DNUR-FF.

To demonstrate the relative benefit of our proposed DNUR-FF circuitry, we compare it to the conventional TMR arrangement as baseline and with some recently presented prior work, as listed in Table 1. The evaluation results indicate that the proposed design reduces area and power overheads by roughly 30.9% and 27.7%, respectively, while improving circuit performance by 42.03%. This is because the datapath includes only the propagation delay of TG4/TG11 to transfer the coming data from input to output. Whereas in the TMR arrangement, the voting circuit is located in the critical path, and thus impacts the speed. On the other hand, although the FF design presented in [6] realizes higher reduction of area overhead and power consumption compared to the proposed DNUR-FF, it incurs higher delay due to the redundant output comparison circuits are also located in the critical path. Among the FF designs listed in Table 1, the proposed DNUR-FF circuit achieves the highest Power Delay Product (PDP) improvement. This makes the SE-resilient flip-flop developed herein suitable latching circuit to be used within energy-efficient systems in harsh environments.

Overall, the proposed design achieves favorable reduction (58%) for the PDP compared to the TMR arrangement, which represents the highest PDP improvement compared to the previously presented approaches listed in Table 1. Furthermore, each latch circuit in the proposed register is able to tolerate DNU simultaneously, which makes the presented circuit an attractive soft-error resilience storage element for nanoscale device technology.

# 5 CONCLUSION

In this work, a novel SE-resilient register is developed and deployed to replace the most sensitive registers in logic paths. The interceptive feedback loops with the clock-gating of the Muller C-element at output stage assist in providing self-recovery for all vulnerable nodes in an event of upset thereby achieving complete soft errors masking. Our proposed DNUR-FF design realizes reduced area and power penalties (30.9% and 27.7%, respectively) compared to TMR, while delivering a 42% speed performance improvement. In addition, it achieves complete DNU masking to prevent any potential transient faults from corrupting the computed architectural states in the targeted processor pipeline stages. Thus, the proposed design can be utilized to harden the critical or vulnerable registers against transient errors, including both SEU and DNU.

# References

[1] F. S. Alghareb, R. A. Ashraf, A. Alzahrani, and R. F. DeMara. 2017. Energy and Delay Tradeoffs of Soft-Error Masking for 16-nm FinFET Logic Paths: Survey and Impact of Process Variation in the Near-Threshold Region. *IEEE Transactions on Circuits and Systems II: Express Briefs* 64, 6 (June 2017), 695–699. https://doi.org/10.1109/TCSII.2016.2587763

[2] F. S. Alghareb, R. A. Ashraf, and R. F. DeMara. 2018. Designing and Evaluating Redundancy-Based Soft-Error Masking on a Continuum of Energy versus Robustness. *IEEE Transactions on Sustainable Computing* 3, 3 (July 2018), 139–152. https://doi.org/10.1109/TSUSC.2017.2764857

[3] T. Calin, M. Nicolaidis, and R. Velazco. 1996. Upset hardened memory design for submicron CMOS technology. *Nuclear Science, IEEE Transactions on* 43, 6 (Dec 1996), 2874–2878. https://doi.org/10.1109/23.556880

[4] A. Dixit and Alan Wood. 2011. The impact of new technology on soft error rates. In *IEEE International Reliability Physics Symposium (IRPS)*. 5B.4.1–5B.4.7. https://doi.org/10.1109/IRPS.2011.5784522

[5] X. Iturbe, B. Venu, and E. Ozer. 2016. Soft error vulnerability assessment of the real-time safety-related ARM Cortex-R5 CPU. In *2016 IEEE International Symposium on Defect and Fault Tolerance in VLSI and Nanotechnology Systems (DFT)*. 91–96. https://doi.org/10.1109/DFT.2016.7684076

[6] K. Katsarou and Y. Tsiatouhas. 2014. Double node charge sharing SEU tolerant latch design. In *2014 IEEE 20th International On-Line Testing Symposium (IOLTS)*. 122–127. https://doi.org/10.1109/IOLTS.2014.6873683

[7] S. Mitra, N. Seifert, M. Zhang, Q. Shi, and K. S. Kim. 2005. Robust system design with built-in soft-error resilience. *Computer* 38, 2 (Feb 2005), 43–52. https://doi.org/10.1109/MC.2005.70

[8] Martin Omana, D.Rossi, and C. Metra. 2007. Latch Susceptibility to Transient Faults and New Hardening Approach. *IEEE Trans. Comput.* 56, 9 (Sept 2007), 1255–1268. https://doi.org/10.1109/TC.2007.1070

[9] Marco Ottavi, Dimitris Gizopoulos, and Salvatore Pontarelli. 2018. *Dependable Multicore Architectures at Nanoscale.* Springer International Publishing.

[10] R. Travessini, P. R. C. Villa, F. L. Vargas, and E. A. Bezerra. 2018. Processor core profiling for SEU effect analysis. In *2018 IEEE 19th Latin-American Test Symposium (LATS)*. 1–6. https://doi.org/10.1109/LATW.2018.8347235

[11] A. Yan, Z. Huang, M. Yi, X. Xu, Y. Ouyang, and H. Liang. 2017. Double-Node-Upset-Resilient Latch Design for Nanoscale CMOS Technology. *IEEE Transactions on Very Large Scale Integration (VLSI) Systems* 25, 6 (June 2017), 1978–1982. https://doi.org/10.1109/TVLSI.2017.2655079

[12] Aibin Yan, Huaguo Liang, Zhengfeng Huang, Cuiyun Jiang, Yiming Ouyang, and Xuejun Li. 2016. An SEU resilient, SET filterable and cost effective latch in presence of PVT variations. *Microelectronics Reliability* 63, Supplement C (2016), 239 – 250. https://doi.org/10.1016/j.microrel.2016.06.004

[13] Wei Zhao and Yu Cao. 2006. New generation of Predictive Technology Model for sub-45nm design exploration. In *Quality Electronic Design, 2006. ISQED '06. 7th International Symposium on.* https://doi.org/10.1109/ISQED.2006.91

# Automated Analysis of Virtual Prototypes at Electronic System Level

Mehran Goli, Muhammad Hassan, Daniel Große, Rolf Drechsler
Cyber-Physical Systems, DFKI GmbH, 28359 Bremen, Germany
Institute of Computer Science, University of Bremen, 28359 Bremen, Germany

{mehran.goli,muhammad.hassan}@dfki.de,{grosse,drechsle}@cs.uni-bremen.de

## ABSTRACT

The exponential increase in functionality of *System-on-Chips* (SoCs) and reduced *Time-to-Market* (TTM) requirements have significantly altered the typical design and verification flow. *Virtual Prototyping* (VP) at the *Electronic System Level* (ESL) using SystemC and its *Transaction Level Modeling* (TLM) framework is an industry-accepted solution. VP design exploration, review, debugging, and integration of ever changing functional requirements can be made faster with the help of design understanding and visualization methods. Hence, in this paper, we propose a fully automated structural, and behavioral analysis approach for visualization of ESL VPs including TLM-2.0 VPs. At the heart of the analysis is a hybrid approach which uses static and dynamic methods to extract structural and behavioral information of the VP. Afterwards, the extracted information is translated into structural and graphical representations such as UML diagrams (specifying TLM-2.0 transactions' protocols), and XML format (describing designs' structure). Experimental results including a real-world VP shows the effectiveness of our approach.

**ACM Reference Format:**

Mehran Goli, Muhammad Hassan, Daniel Große, Rolf Drechsler. 2019. Automated Analysis of Virtual Prototypes at Electronic System Level. In *Great Lakes Symposium on VLSI 2019 (GLSVLSI '19), May 9–11, 2019, Tysons Corner, VA, USA.* ACM, New York, NY, USA, 4 pages. https://doi.org/10.1145/3299874.3318024

## 1 INTRODUCTION

The increasing functionality of *System-on-Chips* (SoCs) and reduced *Time-to-Market* (TTM) constraints have significantly altered the design and verification flow to meet the high market demand. This has led to the rapidly-growing adoption of *Virtual Prototypes* (VPs) at *Electronic System Level* (ESL) abstraction in the last decade. Essentially, a VP is an abstract, and executable software model written in SystemC [1] using its *Transaction Level Modeling* (TLM) [2] framework. The much earlier availability as well as the significantly faster simulation speed in comparison to the *Register Transfer Level* (RTL) models are among the main benefits of VPs. These enable hardware/software co-design and verification very early in the development flow. As a consequence, VPs are heavily used for early architecture exploration for the next generation of SoCs. This allows the systems architects to test new features and validate the capabilities of the SoC, i.e. to decide where to reuse existing *Intellectual Properties* (IPs) and where to create new hardware blocks. However, this decision making requires design understanding of the SoC, which includes both, structural as well as behavioral insight. For a complex SoC with hundreds of IPs it is very hard and time consuming to understand the interfacing, and communication patterns of the VP. Therefore, the first logical step is to consult the available documentation, but, there may be scenarios, e.g., third party IPs, or legacy models, where the documentation is poorly written, or not available at all [14]. Thus, the development team members spend significant time to reverse engineer the design, hence, increasing time-to-market. This has raised the need for design understanding and visualization methods which enhance the design experience, debugging facilities, and integrated development environments. However, one major challenge specific to behavioral understanding of the TLM-2.0 models is the communication interface. The VP models communicate through thousands of TLM-2.0 transactions which are difficult to follow, redundant, and unnecessary from the perspective of design understanding. A concise visualization of the underlying VP transactions flow can accelerate the revisions and additions, while helping significantly in design understanding. While several approaches exist; static [5, 9, 10, 14], and hybrid [4, 6–8, 11, 13, 16], for information extraction, analysis, and visualization of SystemC VPs, they have the following drawbacks: 1) no support for TLM-2.0 constructs [4, 6, 7, 13], 2) lack of precise behavior extraction (the extracted information mostly describes the designs' structure and do not trace their transactions or variable's state) [4, 6, 13, 14, 16], 3) low degree of automation [11], and 4) scalability [7, 8].

In this paper, we propose an automated hybrid data extraction and analysis approach for visualization of ESL VPs. Our approach extracts the structural, and behavioral information of the VP using static and dynamic methods. The analysis reduces the amount of redundant transactions generated by VPs to a small amount of unique transactions. This gives the designer a concise view of the complete VP model. Our approach consists of two phases, and focuses on TLM-2.0 constructs in particular. In phase one, static analysis is performed on the given VP to extract the structural information, and VP instrumentation is done for dynamic run-time behavioral information extraction. In phase two, the instrumented VP is executed, and run-time information is analyzed. For design understanding intention, the retrieved structural information is presented in an XML format. The extracted behavioral information is translated into a set of *Unified Modeling Language* (UML) diagrams. The UML diagrams defined in this paper reflect the behavioral information in a big scale view to empower designers to easily trace both transactions' data and flow at the same time. Moreover, the retrieved intermediate structured logs allow designers to use them for tasks of debugging, validation and verification off-the-shelf or with minimum translation effort into their desired forms. The approach is applied to several case studies including a real-world VP to show its precision, scalability, and advantages.

## 2 MOTIVATION

Consider the third Party *AT_BUS* VP (inspired from [3]) shown in Fig. 1 where the documentation is not available (or poorly written).


*GLSVLSI '19, May 9–11, 2019, Tysons Corner, VA, USA*

ACM ISBN 978-1-4503-6252-8/19/05...$15.00
https://doi.org/10.1145/3299874.3318024

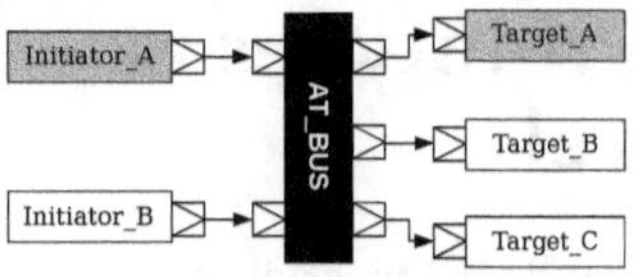


**Figure 1: The architecture of the *AT_BUS* VP.**

The VP includes six modules which differentiate on the basis of underlying base protocol transactions: two initiators (*Initiator_A*, *Initiator_B*), one interconnect (*AT_BUS*), and three targets (*Target_A*, *Target_B*, *Target_C*). *Initiator_A* communicates with target modules through *AT_BUS* by generating four types of *Approximately-timed* (AT) transactions. Two types $T_1$ and $T_2$ to access *Target_A* which is a memory (each type for different memory address ranges), and types $T_3$ and $T_4$ to access *Target_B* and *Target_C*, respectively. *Initiator_B* only generates transactions of type $T_4$ to communicate with all target modules. For example, consider the communication between *Initiator_A* and *Target_A* (the gray components in Fig. 1). The *Initiator_A* module generates transaction types $T_1$ and $T_2$ to access memory address range ($0x00$ to $0x0A$) and ($0x0B$ to $0xFF$) of the *Target_A* module based on the function calls and timing phases described in Table 1, respectively. Now consider a possible scenario that can happen during the design process.

**Scenario:** designers decide to reuse or revise some modules of the VP. For example, they want to modify the AT base protocol transaction type $T_1$ of the *Initiator_A* module and change it to $T_4$ including less transition phases to gain performance. This modification also needs to be applied to the *AT_BUS* and *Target_A* to properly build a communication path between the initiator and target modules through the interconnect. Before any changes can be applied to the VP, it needs to be properly understood. However, lacking a (good) documentation makes the understanding process very complex.

The first and common solution to handle the aforementioned scenarios is to use reverse engineering such as analyzing and instrumenting the existing source code and SystemC library (if required). This usually results in incomplete logs, work overhead, and waste of time in case of complex designs. In order to help designers in understanding the complexity of a given SystemC VP (especially for the third party or legacy designs), a SystemC analyzer tool is required that can properly extract and analyze both structure and behavior of the VP. The former refers to the modules' names, types (initiator, interconnect or target) and, instances and, binding information of modules' sockets. The latter refers to the three essential elements: transactions' *flow*, *data*, and *type*. The transaction's flow represents the order of TLM modules taking part in the transaction's lifetime (i.e. the period of time between transaction construction and destruction). For example the transaction's flow for both transaction types $T_1$ and $T_2$ generated by *Initiator_A* to access data in *Target_A* is based on the sequence order (1)→(2)→(3)→(2)→(1)→(2)→(3)→(2)→(1) where: (1) *Initiator_A*, (2) *AT_BUS* and, (3) *Target_A*. The transaction data denotes the transaction attributes such as data, address, length etc. The transaction's type refers to the transaction's timing model (Loosely-timed (LT) or AT) and in case of the AT model, it also specifies which type of the base protocol transactions is used. However, this element has not been considered by the existing SystemC analysis

**Table 1: Transactions timing models of the *AT-BUS* VP**

| Type | Communication Interface Call | Return Status | Phase Transition |
|---|---|---|---|
| $T_1$ | nb_transport_fw/nb_transport_bw | TA→TU | BRQ→BRP→ERP |
| $T_2$ | nb_transport_fw/nb_transport_bw | TA→TC | BRQ→BRP |
| $T_3$ | nb_transport_fw | TU→TC | BRQ→BRP→ERP |
| $T_4$ | nb_transport_fw | TC | BRQ |

**TC:** TLM_COMPLETED **TA:** TLM_ACCEPTED **TU:** TLM_UPDATED **BRQ:** BEGIN_REQUEST **BRP:** BEGIN_RESPONSE **ERP:** END_RESPONSE

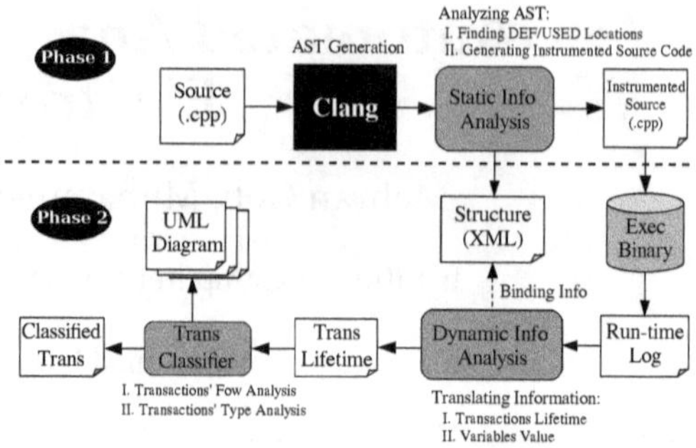


**Figure 2: The architecture of the proposed approach.**

approaches [11, 14] as they only extract the transactions' flow (but not their type). The two transaction types $T_1$ and $T_2$ have the same communication pattern (flow) but their timing phases are different, these methods fail to distinguish between them. Therefore, the proposed method must be able to extract all the aforementioned elements, distinguish the transactions' unique type and flow and finally present them in a proper graphical format (e.g. UML diagrams), thus, designers can quickly grasp the VP behavior.

# 3 METHODOLOGY

## 3.1 Overall Workflow

Fig. 2 provides an overview of the proposed approach including:

(1) analyzing the AST of a given VP to obtain two goals:
   (a) extracting the static information of the model which is required to describe design's structure and
   (b) using this information as the foundation for retrieving run-time information (i.e. behavior) by generating an instrumented version of the source code.

(2) retrieving the run-time information of the design by executing the instrumented binary model and translating it into structural formats.

## 3.2 Phase 1: Extracting Static Information

The extraction process is performed by visiting relevant nodes in the AST. As the top level entities of a VP are modules and global functions, the first entry point of extracting design's structure is to find the node including the information of the aforementioned entities. The information of modules' sockets (or signal ports), transaction (or variable) and member functions is also retrieved in the same way by visiting the corresponding nodes in the AST. This information is used to retrieve part of the design's structure (which is not available statically) and behavior (i.e. tracing transactions or variables values) at run-time. To do this, an instrumented version of the existing source code is automatically generated from the AST including *retrieving* statements. The statements are defined based on hierarchical structure where for tracing e.g. a transaction, the value of transaction's attributes and its related parameters such as timing annotation, phase (e.g. BEGIN_REQ) and functions' return status (e.g. TLM_COMPLETED) – for the AT model – are retrieved during execution. Moreover, the simulation time is extracted to notify the exact time of transaction or variable value changes. To trace a transaction after any possible change, we define two locations DEF and USED. The DEF location refers to the line of code where the transaction is defined (e.g. as a function arguments or a local variables within the function's body). In case of TLM-2.0 designs, the USED location refers to function calls (e.g. transport interfaces *b_transport* or *nb_transport*) where the transaction object is used as an input argument. Thus, the *retrieving* statements are inserted to the source code after the aforementioned locations.

```
1   struct Initiator_A: sc_module{
2   tlm_utils::simple_initiator_socket<Initiator_A, 32> init_socket;
3   ...
4   void thread_process(){
5   tlm::tlm_generic_payload* trans;
6   tlm::tlm_phase phase;
7   sc_time delay;
8   ...
9   status = init_socket->nb_transport_fw(*trans, phase, delay);
10  Fout<<"Initiator_A::thread_process::trans.ID="<<trans<<"DATA="<<trans->
        get_data_ptr()<<"CMD="<<trans->get_command()<<"ADR="<<trans->
        get_address()<<"RSP="<<trans->get_response_status()<<"DL="<<trans->
        get_data_length()<<"delay="<<delay<<"phase="<<phase<<"
        instance_name_module="<<this->name()<<"ST="<<sc_time_stamp()<<endl;
11  ...}
```

**Figure 3: A part of the instrumented source code of module *Initiator_A* of the *AT_BUS* VP.**

For example, consider a part of the source code related to the module `Initiator_A` of the *AT_BUS* VP (Fig. 3). Line 10 is not initially available. Assume that we want to trace all transactions generated by the `thread_process` function of the `Initiator_A` module. To do this, the VP's AST is analyzed by *Static Info Analysis* module (Fig. 2, Phase 1) to find DEF and USED locations in the source code. For example, consider a USED location (Line 9, in Fig. 3) where transaction `trans` is used as a function argument of the `nb_transport_fw` interface. To properly trace the transactions, all information related to the transactions' flow, data, and type must be extracted. This includes: 1) the module name (`Initiator_A`) and the parent function (`thread_process`) to which this transaction belongs and the transactions' reference address, 2) all attributes of the transactions which are data, address, response status, data length, and 3) transactions'related parameters which are the `phase` and `delay` arguments of the `nb_transport_fw` interface and its return status stored in the `status` variable. From the extracted information, the *retrieving* statement `Fout` (Line 10, Fig. 3) is automatically generated and inserted after the USED location in the new source code. The instructions `this->name()` and `sc_time_stamp()` are also added to the *retrieving* statement to identify that the transaction `trans` belongs to which instance of the `Initiator_A` module and the simulation time when the transaction is sent through the initiator socket `init_socket`, respectively.

## 3.3 Phase 2: Extracting Run-time Information

After generation of the instrumented source code, it is then automatically compiled with a standard C++ compiler (e.g. GCC or Clang) and executed to log the run-time information. The extracted information is translated into two formats XML (to reflect designs' structure) and UML (TLM-2.0 designs' behavior).

*3.3.1 Structure Presentation.* Major part of the designs' structure is extracted during the static analysis in the first phase. This information includes:

- the root name and type (for TLM modules can be initiator, interconnect or target which is identified by analyzing modules' sockets type) of each module,
- the name and type of each function,
- the variables (or signals) of each module and
- local variables of each function

The structural data that cannot be extracted during the static analysis is retrieved at run-time. This information (e.g. the instance name of modules and binding information of modules' ports and sockets) is extracted by *Dynamic Info Analysis* module from the *Run-time Log* and bounded to the static data. The final result is presented as an XML formatted file.

*3.3.2 Behavior Presentation.* Since the extracted information of each transaction is scattered over the *Run-time Log* file, an information analysis approach is required to reduce the complexity of understanding the extracted information.

The first step of this analysis is to describe each extracted transaction based on its flow, data, and type within its lifetime. This requires to isolate for each single transaction its corresponding information from other transactions. As a transaction object is passed as a function argument to a communication interface (*b_transport* or *nb_transport*) by reference, this address can be used to trace the transaction in the *Run-time Log*. However, the reference address may be re-used for new transactions as soon as an old one is discarded (i.e. no two transactions can share the same address simultaneously). Thus, the type of modules and transaction's related parameters (for AT model) are used to detect its start and end points. By this, detailed information of each transaction's lifetime is stored in the *Trans lifetime* (Fig. 2, Phase 2).

Since it is possible that many of the extracted transactions in *Trans lifetime* have the same flow and type (only their data is different), a further analysis step is required to only visualize those which present a unique behavior. This effectively reduces the number of generated UML diagrams, allowing designers to quickly understand the behavior of a given TLM-2.0 design.

**Classifying Transactions**: The transactions' classification is performed in two levels: first based on the transactions' flow (providing designers with an abstract view) and then type (an accurate analysis). In order to classify the transactions based on their flows, the *Trans Lifetime* file is analyzed by the *Trans Classifier* module. This analysis is performed by generating a *Communication Pattern String* (CPS) for each transaction's lifetime stored in the *Trans lifetime*. For a given transaction, the CPS is a string of characters generated by concatenating the root and instance names of all modules taking part in the transaction's lifetime. For example, the CPS for the transactions generated by the *Initiator_A* (Fig. 1) to access *Target_A* through *AT_BUS* is "`Initiator_A:init_0+AT_BUS:bus_0+Target_A:target_0`". By this, transactions in the *Trans lifetime* are categorized into several sub groups considered as *Unique Flow Group* (UFG) where each group presents a unique flow (communication pattern).

The next step of the transactions' classification is to perform a transaction type analysis in each UFG. For each transaction of a UFG, first the type of timing model is identified (LT or AT) based on the type of communication interface (*b_transport* or *nb_transport*). While the LT model can only be implemented in one way due to the TLM-2.0 base protocol, the AT model requires further analysis as it can be implemented in 13 unique ways. In case of the AT model, we take advantage of the transactions' related parameters to distinguish different types of the base protocol transactions in each group. To do this, a *Transaction Type String* (TTS) is generated for each AT model transaction's lifetime in a unique communication group. The TTS includes a concatenation of the communication interface(s), return status(es) and transition phase(s) of an AT model transaction. For example, the TTS of the $T_1$ transaction type (Table 1) generated by the *Initiator_A* module (Fig. 1) is "`fw/bw+TA/TU+BRQ/BRP/ERP`". Therefore, each UFG is divided into several sub groups where in each group the transactions have the same TTS. The UML diagram is generated for a transaction in each UFG that has a unique type. The final classified results are stored in the *classified Trans* by the *Trans Classifier* module (Fig. 2, Phase 2).

# 4 EXPERIMENTAL RESULTS

The *Static Info Analysis* module is implemented using the LibTooling library of Clang compiler [12]. The *Dynamic Info Analysis* and *Trans classifier* modules are implemented using C++ language. The proposed approach is applied to several standard VPs provided by Doulos [3] and [15]. All the experiments have been carried out on a PC equipped with 8 GB RAM and an Intel core i7 CPU running at 2.4 GHz. The experimental results of applying the proposed

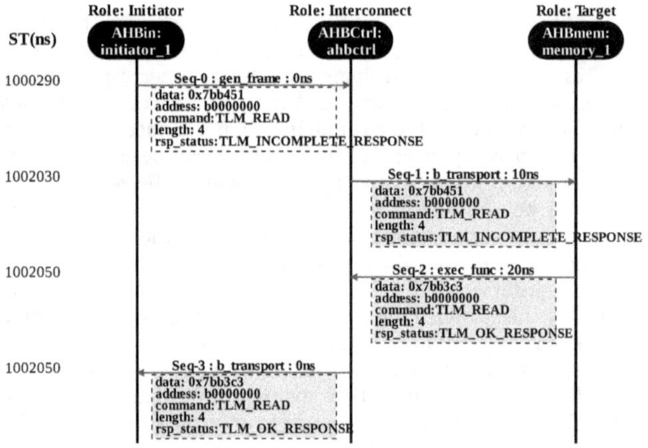


**Figure 4: UML diagram of SoCRocket-VP's LT transaction.**

approach to different types of SystemC VPs are shown in Table 2. The first two columns list names and lines of code for each VP, respectively. Column *TM* presents the timing model (LT or AT) of each VP. Column *#Trans* illustrates the number of each TLM-2.0 design's extracted transactions. Column *#UTrans* shows the number of unique transactions categorized by the number of unique flows (*F*), types (*T*) and generated UML diagrams (*UML*). Column *ET* list the execution time of the proposed approach followed by the required time for static (*P1*) and dynamic (*P2*) analysis. Column *CET* shows the pure compilation (*C*) and execution time (*E*) of each VP by GCC without any instrumentation. In the following we evaluate the quality of the proposed approach using a real-world case study.

**SoCRocket:** The proposed approach is utilized to extract both structure and behavior of the VP and generate UML sequence diagrams of the VP's unique transactions from the extracted run-time traces. As illustrated in Table 2, the proposed approach retrieved 7k transactions (5k LT and 2k AT model) from the VP. The results (column *#UTrans*) of the transactions' classification analysis (using *Trans Classifier* module) on the extracted transactions' lifetime (*Trans Lifetime* file) shows that, the VP includes 19 unique flows (communication patterns) and overall eight (one LT model and seven AT model) different types of base protocol transactions. Our method generated 21 UML diagrams for design understanding goal in less than a minute. Therefore, instead of reading the 50k lines of code of the VP distributed over more than 45 files, a simple glance over the quickly generated UML diagrams can significantly facilitate the design understanding and analysis process. The classified presentation of transactions' lifetime is stored in the *Classified Trans* to help designers for further possible analysis (e.g. debugging or validation) in the design process.

Fig. 4 shows the UML diagram of a single LT transaction's type of the SoCRocket VP in detail. The black shapes present root and instance name of modules within the design. The role (type) of each module is shown on top of the modules' name. The information on each arrow demonstrates interaction between two modules that is drawn from the caller to the callee w.r.t the simulation time. In particular, for a call from an instance of a TLM module, it presents the number of sequence, the name of the caller function, the timing phase (for AT model), timing annotation, and the return value of the callee (if available). Moreover, the generated UML model includes detailed transaction data. The box under each arrow shows the transaction's attributes which is passed as an argument from caller to callee. The white box illustrates a local transaction object while the blue boxes demonstrate a transaction object reached the callee through a function call. E.g. `seq-2` in Fig. 4 contains the

**Table 2: Experimental Results for all Virtual Prototypes**

| VP Name | LoC | TM | #Trans | #UTrans F | T | UML | ET (s) P1 | P2 | Tot | CET (s) C | E | Tot |
|---|---|---|---|---|---|---|---|---|---|---|---|---|
| LT-example[1] | 175 | LT | 500 | 1 | 1 | 1 | 1.4 | 0.53 | 1.93 | 1.3 | 0.1 | 1.4 |
| Example-4[1] | 547 | AT | 1000 | 2 | 4 | 5 | 2.5 | 0.2 | 2.7 | 1.8 | 0.1 | 1.9 |
| Example-5[1] | 650 | AT | 1000 | 8 | 2 | 9 | 3.2 | 0.3 | 3.5 | 2.1 | 0.2 | 2.2 |
| AT-example[1] | 2942 | AT | 1000 | 12 | 8 | 14 | 27.5 | 1.25 | 28.75 | 21 | 0.2 | 21.2 |
| Locking-two[1] | 3831 | LT/AT | 1000 | 14 | 10 | 16 | 29.2 | 1.85 | 31.05 | 24 | 0.3 | 24.3 |
| SoCRocket[2] | > 50000 | LT/AT | 7000 | 19 | 8 | 21 | 53.8 | 4.79 | 58.59 | 27.6 | 2.29 | 29.89 |

[1] Provided by [3] [2] Provided by [15] **LoC**: Lines of Code **TM**: Timing Model **LT**: Loosely-timed model **AT**: Approximately-timed model **#Trans**: number of Transaction **#UTrans**: number of Unique Transaction **ET**: Execution Time **CET**: Compilation and Execution Time by GCC without any instrumentation

information related to the response of the target module `AHBmem`. This information is the name of the called function (`exec_func`) and timing annotation (`20 ns`). It also includes the transaction data passed to the callee module (`AHBCtrl`) including the reference address of the transaction (`0x7bb3c3`), address (`b0000000`), command (`tlm::TLM_READ`), length (4), and response status (`tlm::TLM_OK_RESPONSE`).

# 5 CONCLUSION

The proposed approach provides designers with a fast solution to retrieve a significant amount of information describing the structure and behavior of a given VP. The approach is based on analyzing the AST of the design to extract static information and generate instrumented source code for run-time data extraction. The extracted information is translated into a structural and graphical representation, allowing designers to quickly understand the intricacies of VPs. We showed the effectiveness of the approach on several standard VPs including a real-world system. In future, we plan to extend the suggested information extraction and analysis approach for tasks of validation and verification at ESL.

*Acknowledgments:* This work was supported by the German Federal Ministry of Education and Research (BMBF) within the projects SATiSFy under grant no. 16KIS0821K, SecRec under grant no. 16K1S0606K, CONVERS under grant no. 16ES0656, and by the University of Bremen's graduate school SyDe, funded by the German Excellence Initiative.

# REFERENCES

[1] 2006. IEEE Standard SystemC Language Reference Manual. *IEEE Std 1666-2005*, 1–423.
[2] John Aynsley (Ed.). 2009. *OSCI TLM-2.0 Language Reference Manual*. Open SystemC Initiative (OSCI).
[3] John Aynsley. Accessed: 2018-06-30. TLM-2.0 Base Protocol Checker. https://www.doulos.com/knowhow/systemc/tlm2.
[4] Harry Broeders and René Van Leuken. 2011. Extracting behavior and dynamically generated hierarchy from SystemC models. In *DAC*. 357–362.
[5] Görschwin Fey, Daniel Große, Tim Cassens, Christian Genz, Tim Warode, and Rolf Drechsler. 2004. ParSyC: An Efficient SystemC Parser. In *SASIMI*. 148–154.
[6] Christian Genz and Rolf Drechsler. 2009. Overcoming limitations of the SystemC data introspection. In *DATE*. 590–593.
[7] Mehran Goli, Jannis Stoppe, and Rolf Drechsler. 2016. AIBA: an Automated Intra-Cycle Behavioral Analysis for SystemC-based Design Exploration. In *ICCD*. 360–363.
[8] Mehran Goli, Jannis Stoppe, and Rolf Drechsler. accepted 2018. Automated Non-intrusive Analysis of Electronic System Level Designs. *TCAD* (accepted 2018).
[9] Daniel Große, Rolf Drechsler, Lothar Linhard, and Gerhard Angst. 2003. Efficient Automatic Visualization of SystemC Designs.. In *FDL*. 646–658.
[10] Anirudh Kaushik and Hiren D. Patel. 2013. SystemC-clang: An open-source framework for analyzing mixed-abstraction SystemC models. In *FDL*. 1–8.
[11] Wolfgang Klingauf and Manuel Geffken. 2006. Design structure analysis and transaction recording in SystemC designs: A minimal-intrusive approach. In *FDL*.
[12] Chris Lattner. 2008. LLVM and Clang: Next generation compiler technology. In *BSD*. 1–2.
[13] Kevin Marquet and Matthieu Moy. 2010. PinaVM: a SystemC front-end based on an executable intermediate representation. In *EMSOFT*. 79–88.
[14] Tim Schmidt, Guantao Liu, and Rainer Dömer. 2016. Automatic Generation of Thread Communication Graphs from SystemC Source Code. In *SCOPES*. 108–115.
[15] Thomas Schuster, Rolf Meyer, Rainer Buchty, Luca Fossati, and Mladen Berekovic. 2014. SoCRocket - A virtual platform for the European Space Agency's SoC development. In *ReCoSoC*. 1–7, http://github.com/socrocket.
[16] Jannis Stoppe, Robert Wille, and Rolf Drechsler. 2013. Data extraction from SystemC designs using debug symbols and the SystemC API. In *ISVLSI*. 26–31.

# Dynamic Physically Unclonable Functions

Wenjie Xiong†, André Schaller‡, Stefan Katzenbeisser‡, and Jakub Szefer†
†Yale University, New Haven, CT, USA ‡Technische Universität Darmstadt, Darmstadt, Germany
wenjie.xiong@yale.edu,{schaller,katzenbeisser}@seceng.informatik.tu-darmstadt.de,jakub.szefer@yale.edu

## ABSTRACT

Physical variations in the manufacturing processes of electronic devices have been widely leveraged to design Physically Unclonable Functions (PUFs), which can be used for authentication and key storage. Existing PUFs are static, as their PUF responses remain the same regardless when the PUF is queried. Meanwhile, this paper presents the new concept of *Dynamic PUFs*, where the responses depend not only on the physical properties of the device but also on the timing of the PUF queries. One application of Dynamic PUFs is in dynamic software-hardware binding, where the control flow of the software can be tied to both the timing of the software and the physical properties of the hardware, in order to protect software execution. This paper presents a realization of Dynamic PUFs using DRAM modules. The evaluation is based on the decay-based DRAM PUFs, which can be realized today and were implemented on commodity devices for testing.

**ACM Reference Format:**
Wenjie Xiong, André Schaller, Stefan Katzenbeisser, and Jakub Szefer. 2019. Dynamic Physically Unclonable Functions. In *Great Lakes Symposium on VLSI 2019 (GLSVLSI '19), May 9–11, 2019, Tysons Corner, VA, USA.* ACM, New York, NY, USA, 4 pages. https://doi.org/10.1145/3299874.3318025

## 1 INTRODUCTION

The number of low-end embedded computing devices is continuously growing, and this growth is expected to accelerate further due to the interest in the Internet-of-Things (IoT). These low-end devices are being deployed in a variety of settings from healthcare to industrial environments, where the integrity and tamper resistance of the software is critical. Meanwhile, hardware support in the form of Physically Unclonable Functions (PUFs) can readily be used in low-end devices [1] and can be used to protect software from modification or from running on unauthorized devices [4]. PUFs extract unique and stable physical features emerging from fabrication variations of the underlying hardware modules. All existing PUFs are *static*, meaning a PUF response for a given challenge is stable and independent of the timing of the query.

This work proposes the new concept of *Dynamic PUFs*. A Dynamic PUF generates responses at device runtime, and the PUF responses depend on both the challenges and the timing of the PUF queries. Compared to the existing PUFs that give responses independently of the query times, Dynamic PUFs will give different responses even if the same PUF is queried with the same challenge, but at different times relative the most recent PUF reset. Dynamic PUFs can be realized with PUFs in DRAM, which can be accessed at system runtime and which have time-dependent responses [2, 12].

Dynamic PUFs can interact with software at runtime. With the new Dynamic PUFs, we also propose dynamic software-hardware binding, where the software can be designed to run only on authorized devices and only with correct timing. If the timing is wrong, the software will fail.

The contributions of this work are as follows:

- We introduce the concept of Dynamic PUFs, which have time-dependent responses.
- We show an application of Dynamic PUFs: the dynamic software-hardware binding.
- We develop a practical instance of a Dynamic PUF using a decay-based Dynamic DRAM PUF on Intel Galileo Gen 2 platform. We also evaluate the characteristics of the decay-based DRAM PUFs for their suitability as a Dynamic PUF.

## 2 DYNAMIC PUFS

PUFs extract unique and stable physical features from physical objects [1]. Given a challenge (also called a PUF query), a PUF can generate a response, which is a function of both the challenge and the physical features of the PUF. This is known as a challenge-response pair (CRP). Ideally, each physical object used as a PUF will generate a unique PUF response for each challenge (i.e., the uniqueness property of PUFs). Repeated queries with the same challenge on the same PUF should give the same response (i.e., the robustness property of PUFs), but in practice, they may vary a little due to noise. All of the existing PUF designs do not consider the timing of the PUF query in generating the response, and we call these Static PUFs.

Meanwhile, this work presents the notion of a *Dynamic PUF*. Different from the usual Static PUFs, Dynamic PUFs provide time-dependent PUF responses, i.e., the responses depend not only on the challenges but also on the timing of the PUF queries, relative to the most recent PUF reset.

### 2.1 Operation of Dynamic PUFs

Besides the usual PUF query operation, a Dynamic PUF has an extra operation called *Dynamic PUF Reset*, which resets the state of the PUF. A *Dynamic PUF Query* is akin to the PUF query for Static PUFs: given a PUF challenge, a PUF response will be returned. However, a Dynamic PUF will give different responses even if queried with the same challenge, but at a different time since the most recent *Dynamic PUF Reset*.


*GLSVLSI '19, May 9–11, 2019, Tysons Corner, VA, USA*

ACM ISBN 978-1-4503-6252-8/19/05...$15.00
https://doi.org/10.1145/3299874.3318025

### 2.2 Metrics for Dynamic PUFs

Ideal Dynamic PUF responses should have two features. First, responses at different times should be independent of each other, i.e., the response obtained at time $T_x$ is independent of the response at time $T_y$ when $|T_y - T_x| > \delta_{t0}$, where $\delta_{t0}$ is the time resolution of the Dynamic PUF. Second, the responses should be stable. The following metrics can be used to evaluate a Dynamic PUF.

***Time Resolution:*** Denoted by $\delta_{t0}$, time resolution indicates how sensitive the PUF responses are to the query time (since the last reset of the PUF). Each realization of a Dynamic PUF has a physical limit of the time resolution.

***Robustness and Uniquess:*** The *intra distance* is the distance between PUF responses of the same challenge and query time on the same PUF device. Here, distance is a measure of how different two PUF responses are, and it can be measured typically by the Hamming Distance or the Jaccard Index. The intra distance evaluates the robustness of the PUF. Ideally, the intra distance should be small. The *inter-challenge distance* is the distance between PUF responses from different PUF devices or the same PUF device but different challenges. It evaluates the uniqueness of PUF responses across different challenges and different PUF devices. Ideally, the inter-challenge distance should be large. The *inter-time distance* is the distance between PUF responses with the same challenge but with the different query times on the same PUF device, where the time difference between query times is greater than $\delta_{t0}$. It evaluates the uniqueness of the PUF responses across different query times.

### 2.3 Helper Data System for Dynamic PUFs

Usually, the inter-time distance is not ideal, and the PUF responses at different times are not independent. Thus, a Helper Data System (HDS) is needed to amplify the entropy from the raw PUF response and to extract the final PUF response corresponding to each query time. This requires a different HDS entry for each query time $T_x$. Also, noise exists in raw Dynamic PUF responses (the intra distance is not ideal) and error correction needs to be performed as well.

To retrieve the PUF response at a specific query time, the *Dynamic PUF Query* should indicate which helper data to use, by specifying an index to the entry in the HDS. To generate the HDS, a trusted party needs to measure the desired PUF CRPs with different query times in an *enrollment* phase.

## 3 DRAM PUFS AS DYNAMIC PUFS

DRAM, which is found in many commodity IoT and embedded platforms, has been shown to exhibit PUF behavior. There are three types of DRAM PUFs: decay-based DRAM PUFs [5–8, 10, 12], latency-based DRAM PUFs [2], and startup-based DRAM PUFs [11]. Here, we show that decay-based DRAM PUFs can be used as Dynamic PUFs.

In Dynamic DRAM PUFs, the PUF challenge is the address range of a *DRAM PUF region* from which the PUF will be extracted, and an *initial value* written to the cells at Dynamic PUF reset.

### 3.1 Decay-based DRAM PUFs

The decay-based DRAM PUF leverages the fact that DRAM cells lose data over time, which is also known as *DRAM decay.* Without refresh, each DRAM cell can only retain the data for a certain time, called *retention time.* Decay-based DRAM PUF responses are based on the variation of the retention times of the DRAM cells. A decay-based DRAM PUF is composed of a set of cells within a DRAM region. The retention time of each DRAM cell is believed to be random and related to fabrication variations [10, 12]. As illustrated in Figure 1, querying the decay-based DRAM at different times (e.g., at $T_1$ and $T_2$) will result in different bit flips in the DRAM region, which is the PUF response. We use the *decay time* to denote the time between the *Dynamic PUF Reset* and the *Dynamic PUF Query.* The time resolution $\delta_{t0}$ of the dynamic decay-based DRAM PUF is on the order of seconds. Latency-based DRAM PUF [2] can be an alternative implementation of Dynamic PUF, which has time resolution $\delta_{t0}$ on the order of nanoseconds, but cannot be easily realized in commodity devices today.

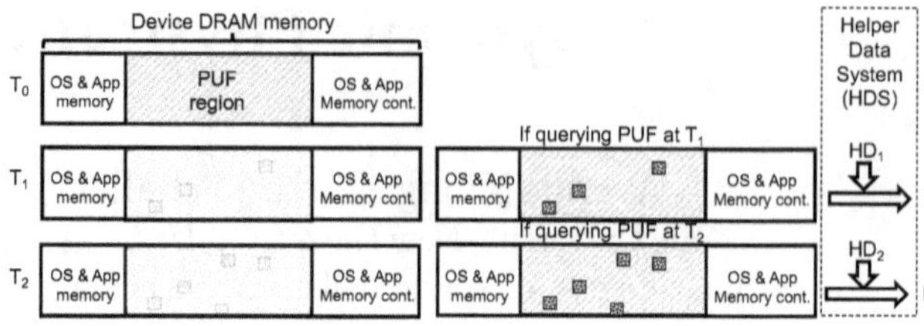


**Figure 1: The responses of a decay-based DRAM PUF depend on the query time since the PUF reset at $T_0$.**

DRAM has the additional property that each access to a DRAM cell (e.g., on a PUF query) implicitly refreshes all the DRAM cells in that row, which resets the Dynamic PUF. When one wants to query the PUF region several times after each reset, the PUF region should be subdivided into sub-regions. Each sub-region consists of a set of DRAM rows, and these DRAM rows do not have to be adjacent to each other. Upon a *Dynamic PUF Reset* request, all DRAM PUF sub-regions have their initial values set and refresh is disabled. To query the Dynamic PUF, an index to the HDS entry is provided as part of the *Dynamic PUF Query.* The index will also determine which sub-regions should be used for that query. On a query, only that sub-region will be accessed (and implicitly refreshed) while other sub-regions continue to decay.

### 3.2 Accessing the Decay-based Dynamic DRAM PUF at System Runtime

A decay-based Dynamic DRAM PUF can be implemented on a commercial, off-the-shelf device by selectively refreshing DRAM as shown in Figure 1, following [12]. First, on a Dynamic PUF Reset ($T_0$), the DRAM PUF region is reserved, so that neither OS nor applications use it, its cells are initialized with the initial value (e.g., all zeros), and the refresh of the DRAM module is disabled. To allow the OS and other applications use DRAM without decay, a customized kernel module can selectively access and thus refresh the DRAM rows [1], as in [12]. Upon a PUF query, the content of the DRAM PUF region is read as the raw PUF response.

[1]The refresh can be controlled by the kernel module and done at the same rate as in the DRAM standard, but this may use up significant CPU resources. If the system and application memory is refreshed at a reduced rate to save CPU resources, the system will be more vulnerable to Rowhammer attacks [3].

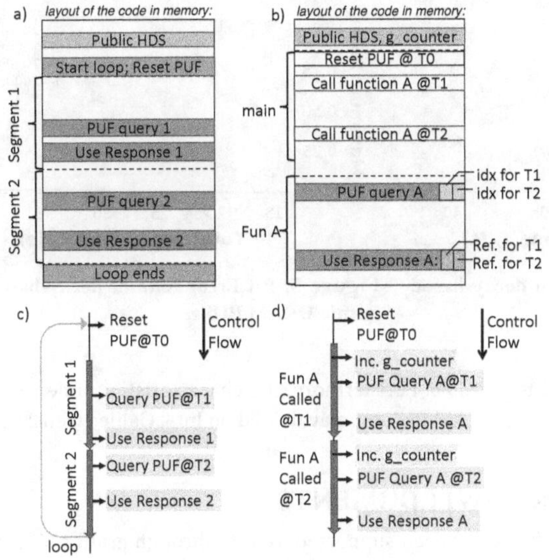


**Figure 2: Example code layout of software-hardware binding for a) straight-line code in a loop and b) repeated function calls. Parts c-d) show the control flow of each protection example of a-b).**

# 4 APPLICATIONS OF DYNAMIC PUFS

Software-hardware binding ties the software execution to a hardware token [4]. With software-hardware binding, the software can only be executed on authorized devices, and thus, it prevents illegal software distribution. In the context of software obfuscation, software-hardware binding has been used to strengthen the obfuscation [9]. When software-hardware binding is used, analyzing the binary will not reveal all the information of the software (e.g., targets of indirect jumps), and the attacker will not be able to reverse engineer the software completely. With a Dynamic PUF, this obfuscation can be even stronger, because an attacker needs to obtain all Dynamic PUF responses at different query times in order to reverse engineer the software.

One of the software-hardware binding approaches is to change all function calls to indirect jumps. Now, we show how to bind all such jumps to the Dynamic PUF responses. This can be achieved by inserting code to make a PUF query and replacing the indirect jump destination address with an exclusive-OR result of the Dynamic PUF response and a reference value. Below, we give examples of software-hardware binding with different software structures.

***Straight-Line Code:*** As shown in Figure 2 (a,c), at the beginning of the program, the Dynamic PUF will be reset. The Dynamic PUF is queried in each segment. The PUF response then depends on the execution time elapsed between the last PUF reset (at the beginning of the program) and the PUF query time. The destination address of the function call at *Use Response* 1 depends on the PUF response, and the program will continue the execute to segment 2.

***Programs with Repeated Function Calls:*** In this scenario, some code will be executed more than once, but in a deterministic way, as in Figure 2 (b, d). This could happen when a function is called several times repeatedly, e.g., *func A* is called twice from the main function. However, since a Dynamic PUF is used, the PUF will return different responses each time the PUF query code in the function is executed (assuming the time between the two PUF queries are larger than $\delta_{t0}$), and the PUF queries need to use different *idx* to the HDS entries at different times.

To make sure the functions will execute as designed if the PUF is queried several times, several *idx* are needed for PUF queries at different times and several reference values are needed when using the PUF responses. To achieve this, a global counter *g_counter* is inserted for each function to point to the correct *idx* and reference value to be used at runtime. Every time a function is called, the global counter will be increased by one. The PUF query code and response code will fetch the corresponding *idx* and reference value based on the value of the global counter and continue the correct execution only with a correct PUF value. For example, in Figure 2 (b), the $Use\ Response\ A$ has two reference values, one for each call.

***Programs with Loops:*** Within a loop, the PUF query will be executed several times. The same method as in repeated function calls can be applied if the number of loop iterations is fixed. Another solution is to reset the Dynamic PUF at the beginning of each loop, as shown with the loop in Figure 2 (a, c). Every time the code block in the loop is executed, the PUF response will be the same (relative to when the PUF was reset). Thus, no reference counter value in the code is needed.

# 5 EVALUATION

## 5.1 Dynamic PUF Characteristics

We evaluate the decay-based Dynamic DRAM PUF that can be deployed on commodity hardware today, in particular on Intel Galileo Gen 2 platforms with two 128 MiB DDR3. A heater and thermocouple are used with a control system to stabilize DRAM temperature at 40°C. We evaluated 8 MiB DRAM regions for PUF with decay times $\mathcal{T}_x$ ranging from 15s to 40s. To evaluate the time resolution $\delta_{t0}$, we denote $\delta_t$ as the smallest time difference between different query times, and evaluated different $\delta_t$.

Figure 3 shows the distribution of the intra, inter-challenge, and inter-time distance as discussed in Section 2.2. Here, we use the Jaccard index to measure the distance between different responses. The bit flips in each response are treated as a set of indices. The Jaccard index of the two sets ($A$ and $B$) from two responses are calculated by $J(A, B) \stackrel{\text{def}}{=} \frac{|A \cap B|}{|A \cup B|}$. When the two responses are identical, $J = 1$. When the two responses do not share any bit flips, $J = 0$. As shown in Figure 3, the intra Jaccard index is very close to 1, indicating that the PUF response is robust. The inter-challenge Jaccard index from two devices is very close to zero, meaning the PUF responses from different DRAM regions are very different. The inter-time Jaccard indices for time differences $\delta_t = \{5s, 2s, 1s\}$ are also shown in Figure 3. For all the three time differences, the inter-time Jaccard indices are smaller than the intra Jaccard index, indicating the responses from different decay times are different enough to be distinguished. Thus, the time resolution is better than 1s. And a bigger $\delta_t$ makes the responses between different decay times more distinguishable.

We use the HDS proposed in [8]. For each $T_x$, one enrollment measurement was taken at $T_x - 2\delta_t$, $T_x - \delta_t$, $T_x + \delta_t$ and $T_x + 2\delta_t$ separately, and cells that flip in the time interval $[T_x - 2\delta_t, T_x - \delta_t]$ and $[T_x + \delta_t, T_x + 2\delta_t]$ are enrolled in the HDS for $T_x$. The

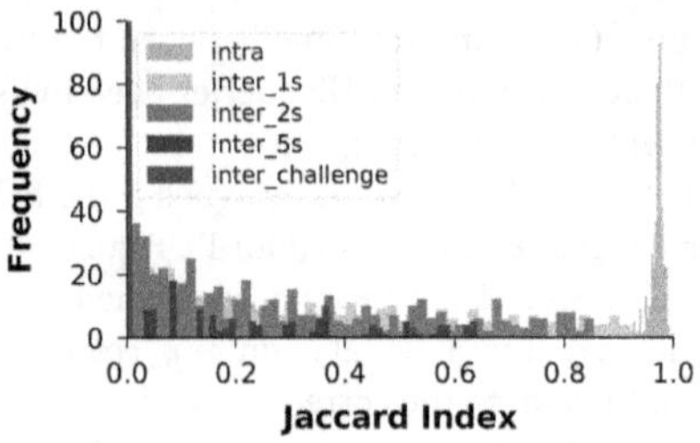

Figure 3: Distribution of inter and intra Jaccard indices.

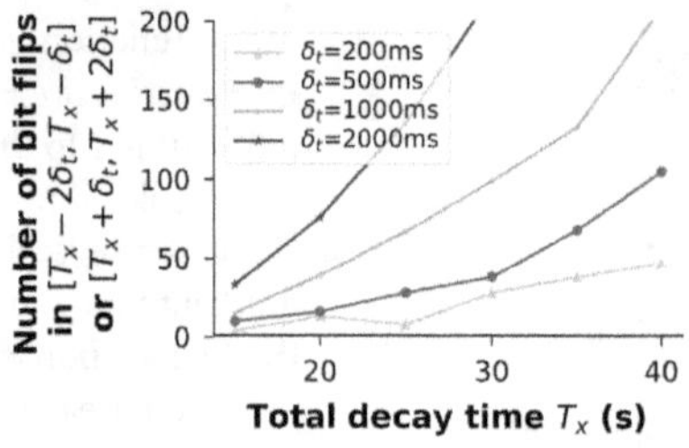

Figure 4: Available bit flips in decay-based Dynamic DRAM PUFs.

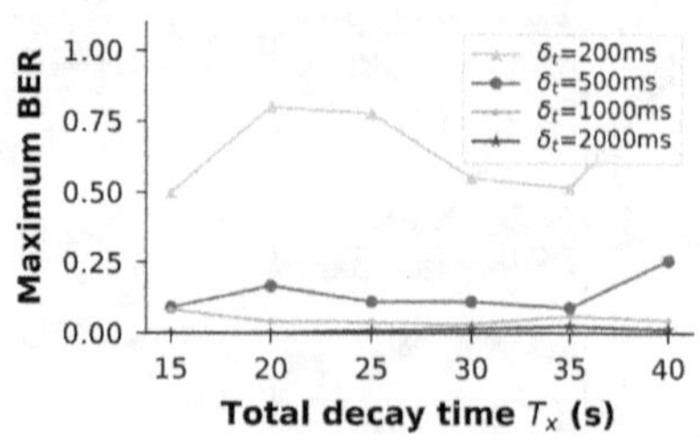

Figure 5: Bit Error Rate of decay-based Dynamic DRAM PUFs.

cells that flip in $[T_x - 2\delta_t, T_x - \delta_t]$ during enrollment should flip in response at $T_x$ and become logical 1, and the cells that flip in $[T_x + \delta_t, T_x + 2\delta_t]$ during enrollment should not yet flip in the response at $T_x$ and become logical 0. Then, ten measurements are taken at $T_x$ to evaluate the bit error rate (BER) of the enrolled cells. We evaluated total decay times $\mathcal{T}_x$={15s, 20s, 25s, 30s, 35s, 40s} and time differences $\delta_t$={2s, 1s, 500ms, 200ms}.

Figure 4 shows the average number of bit flips in the time interval $[T_x - 2\delta_t, T_x - \delta_t]$ or $[T_x + \delta_t, T_x + 2\delta_t]$ in the two boards measured. Figure 4 shows that longer $T_x$ or larger $\delta_t$ give more bits that can be used. To generate the HDS for time $T_x$, $32 \times 3 = 96$ bit flips are needed in time range $[T_x - 2\delta_t, T_x - \delta_t]$ and $[T_x + \delta_t, T_x + 2\delta_t]$, considering the case 32 bits are needed for each response and 3-repetition code are used for error correction code (ECC). With 8 MiB DRAM PUF size, when the total decay time is larger than 25s for $\delta_t = 2$s, it can provide more than 96 bits. To achieve a smaller $\delta_t$, a larger DRAM size should be used. To compute the average BER of the PUF reconstructions, with the generated HDS from the enrollment, we divide the number of cells that do not flip to their desired logical value by the total number of cells enrolled for each $T_x$. Figure 5 shows the maximum BER in all reconstructions for both evaluated devices. When the time difference $\delta_t$ is larger than 500 ms, the BER is smaller than 25%, which can be corrected by 3-repetition code. Figure 5 also shows that the minimum time resolution of the dynamic decay-based DRAM PUF is about 500 ms.

### 5.2 Applications and Dynamic PUF Overhead

To test dynamic software-hardware binding, we bind the Dynamic PUF response to a program which contains AES-128 encryption and decryption, as well as a program which contains SHA-512. Both programs contain repeated function calls and loops to show that the scheme can support programs with non-trivial structures. HDS is inserted into the program binary. For each PUF query, the HDS requires 384 Bytes (4 Bytes for each pointer, and with 3-repetition code, $3 \times 32$ cells are needed). The AES-128 application, for example, contains 9 PUF queries, the HDS takes up 3.4 KiB, and the total binary size is increased by 32.5%. The implementation is in software and no hardware overhead is required.

## 6 CONCLUSION

This paper presented the new concept of *Dynamic PUFs*, as well as their possible implementations and applications. Different from the usual static PUFs, Dynamic PUFs have time-dependent responses. With Dynamic PUFs, the software execution (timing) can affect the PUF response dynamically, making dynamic software-hardware binding possible. Furthermore, the characteristics of decay-based Dynamic DRAM PUF were evaluated on Intel Galileo Gen 2 boards.

## ACKNOWLEDGMENTS

This work has been supported by NSF through grant #1651945.

## REFERENCES

[1] Stefan Katzenbeisser, Ünal Kocabaş, Vladimir Rožić, Ahmad-Reza Sadeghi, Ingrid Verbauwhede, and Christian Wachsmann. 2012. PUFs: Myth, fact or busted? A security evaluation of physically unclonable functions (PUFs) cast in silicon. In *Cryptographic Hardware and Embedded Systems (CHES)*. Springer, 283–301.

[2] Jeremie S Kim, Minesh Patel, Hasan Hassan, and Onur Mutlu. 2018. The DRAM Latency PUF: Quickly Evaluating Physical Unclonable Functions by Exploiting the Latency-Reliability Tradeoff in Modern Commodity DRAM Devices. In *IEEE International Symposium on High Performance Computer Architecture (HPCA)*. IEEE, 194–207.

[3] Yoongu Kim, Ross Daly, Jeremie Kim, Chris Fallin, Ji Hye Lee, Donghyuk Lee, Chris Wilkerson, Konrad Lai, and Onur Mutlu. 2014. Flipping Bits in Memory Without Accessing Them: An Experimental Study of DRAM Disturbance Errors. In *Proceeding of the 41st Annual International Symposium on Computer Architecuture (ISCA)*. IEEE, 361–372.

[4] Florian Kohnhäuser, André Schaller, and Stefan Katzenbeisser. 2015. PUF-based software protection for low-end embedded devices. In *International Conference on Trust and Trustworthy Computing (TRUST)*. Springer, 3–21.

[5] Amir Rahmati, Matthew Hicks, Daniel E. Holcomb, and Kevin Fu. 2015. Probable Cause: The Deanonymizing Effects of Approximate DRAM. In *Proceedings of the 42nd Annual International Symposium on Computer Architecture (ISCA)*. ACM, 604–615.

[6] Sami Rosenblatt, Srivatsan Chellappa, Albert Cestero, Norman Robson, Toshiaki Kirihata, and Srikanth S Iyer. 2013. A Self-Authenticating Chip Architecture Using an Intrinsic Fingerprint of Embedded DRAM. *IEEE Journal of Solid-State Circuits* (2013), 2934–2943.

[7] André Schaller, Wenjie Xiong, Nikolaos Athanasios Anagnostopoulos, Muhammad Umair Saleem, Sebastian Gabmeyer, Stefan Katzenbeisser, and Jakub Szefer. 2017. Intrinsic rowhammer PUFs: Leveraging the rowhammer effect for improved security. In *IEEE International Symposium on Hardware Oriented Security and Trust (HOST)*. IEEE, 1–7.

[8] André Schaller, Wenjie Xiong, Nikolaos Athanasios Anagnostopoulos, Muhammad Umair Saleem, Sebastian Gabmeyer, Boris Skoric, Stefan Katzenbeisser, and Jakub Szefer. 2018. Decay-Based DRAM PUFs in Commodity Devices. *IEEE Transactions on Dependable and Secure Computing* (2018).

[9] Sebastian Schrittwieser, Stefan Katzenbeisser, Johannes Kinder, Georg Merzdovnik, and Edgar Weippl. 2016. Protecting software through obfuscation: Can it keep pace with progress in code analysis? *ACM Computing Surveys (CSUR)* 49, 1 (2016), 4.

[10] Soubhagya Sutar, Arnab Raha, and Vijay Raghunathan. 2016. D-PUF: An intrinsically reconfigurable DRAM PUF for device authentication in embedded systems. In *International Conference on Compliers, Architectures, and Sythesis of Embedded Systems (CASES)*. IEEE, 1–10.

[11] Fatemeh Tehranipoor, Nima Karimian, Kan Xiao, and John Chandy. 2015. DRAM based intrinsic physical unclonable functions for system level security. In *Proceedings of the 25th edition on Great Lakes Symposium on VLSI (GLSVLSI)*. ACM, 15–20.

[12] Wenjie Xiong, André Schaller, Nikolaos A Anagnostopoulos, Muhammad Umair Saleem, Sebastian Gabmeyer, Stefan Katzenbeisser, and Jakub Szefer. 2016. Runtime accessible DRAM PUFs in commodity devices. In *International Conference on Cryptographic Hardware and Embedded Systems (CHES)*. Springer, 432–453.

# RDTA: An Efficient Routability-Driven Track Assignment Algorithm

Genggeng Liu
Fuzhou University, Fuzhou, Fujian, China
liugenggeng@fzu.edu.cn

Zhen Zhuang
Fuzhou University, Fuzhou, Fujian, China
zhuang_zhen@126.com

Wenzhong Guo
Fuzhou University, Fuzhou, Fujian, China
guowenzhong@fzu.edu.cn

Ting-Chi Wang
National Tsing Hua University, Hsinchu, Taiwan
tcwang@cs.nthu.edu.tw

## ABSTRACT

This paper presents a routability-driven track assignment algorithm (RDTA) to efficiently estimate routability. Routability has become a very challenging issue in modern IC design and it can be effectively estimated by routing congestion. Track assignment is a stage towards bridging the gap between global routing and detailed routing. And track assignment can also analyze routing congestion more accurate than other routing stages like global routing. Some works have used track assignment to estimate routability. In this work, wire segments extracted from a global routing solution are assigned to proper tracks considering local nets, via locations and pin access. The overlap between wire segments extracted from a global routing solution can be effectively reduced by the algorithm so that the solution of RDTA can effectively estimate the routability.

**ACM Reference Format:**

Genggeng Liu, Zhen Zhuang, Wenzhong Guo, and Ting-Chi Wang. 2019. RDTA: An Efficient Routability-Driven Track Assignment Algorithm . In *Great Lakes Symposium on VLSI 2019 (GLSVLSI '19), May 9–11, 2019, Tysons Corner, VA, USA.* ACM, New York, NY, USA, 4 pages. https://doi.org/10.1145/3299874.3318026

## 1 INTRODUCTION

Routing is an important phase in VLSI physical design. It is divided into two stages, global routing and detailed routing. In the global routing stage, the routing area is divided into an array of g-cells. Global routing solution is a routing area with multiple g-cells. All the pins of a local net are in one g-cell, and they are ignored in the global routing stage. In the detailed routing stage, the pins of the same net are connected within the routing guide produced by global routing. As technology node advances, some issues like spacing rules between parallel wires should be considered during the routing phase [1]. The design complexity and the time complexity of routing algorithms greatly increase. Therefore, scholars introduce track assignment stage into physical design as a bridge between global routing and detailed routing.

Each straight wire which passes through one or more complete g-cells is treated as an iroute. Then track assignment assigns each iroute to a routing track within its corresponding g-cells. Some scholars have already carried out extensive and intensive researches on track assignment. Most work [2–9] is done to get a draft that can be used to guide detailed routing. These track assignment algorithms are all designed to maximize the number of assigned iroutes. Therefore, routing congestion is difficult to analyze.

The track assignment algorithm [10, 11] is used to estimate routability by providing routing congestion which can help early physical design phases fix the routability problems. The work [10] presents a negotiation-based track assignment algorithm (NTA), and NTA can get the track assignment solutions in a very short time for routability estimation. However, the problem of via locations and pin access is not considered. Therefore, the solutions are imprecise.

The work [11] presents a track assignment framework TraPL. The solution of TraPL considers all combinations of the tracks selected by the iroutes. TraPL considers local nets, via locations and pin access. Therefore, the solutions of TraPL are more accurate than NTA. But the iroute assignment order of TraPL is fixed, and TraPL has no rip-up and reassignment strategies. It makes TraPL fall into the local optimal solution. Moreover, for TraPL, it takes too much time to find the local optimal solution. Consequently, TraPL is not ideal for reducing the overlap.

To overcome the disadvantages of [10] and [11], we present a routability-driven track assignment algorithm (RDTA). RDTA assigns each iroute to a track while allowing the existence of iroute overlaps. And it can get pin-to-pin on-track routing solutions.

This paper makes the following contributions: RDTA takes local nets, via locations and pin access into account to get completely connected solutions. For via locations, we present a complete via location model. And we present a fast and effective method to connect pins. RDTA can effectively reduce the iroute overlaps between iroutes and the iroute overlaps between iroutes and blockages. Routability can be estimated effectively by reducing iroute overlaps. RDTA can reduce iroute overlaps in a short period of time. Compared with a prior work [11], RDTA achieves about 40% lower overlap cost than [11] on average. And RDTA is averagely about 9.22X faster than [11].

The remainder of this paper is organized as follows. In Section 2, we present the problem formulation. Section 3 presents RDTA in detail. Section 4 reports our experimental results. Finally, the conclusion is drawn in Section 5.

## 2 PROBLEM FORMULATION

Iroutes are extracted from both global and local nets. Given a global routing solution of a global net, a segment from a g-cell's center to another g-cell's center is treated as an iroute. In Figure 1, the global net $n_1$ is highlighted by a red box, and the two pins of $n_1$ are represented by two green squares. The blue segments $ir_1$ and


*GLSVLSI '19, May 9–11, 2019, Tysons Corner, VA, USA*

ACM ISBN 978-1-4503-6252-8/19/05...$15.00
https://doi.org/10.1145/3299874.3318026

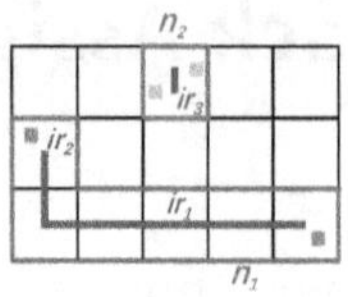

Figure 1: Illustration of the iroute.

$ir_2$ are the iroutes extracted from $n_1$. The iroute of a local net is a vertical trunk or a horizontal trunk. The trunk with a smaller length is chosen. The range of the trunk covers the span of the local net based on the locations of its pins. In Figure 1, the local net $n_2$ is highlighted by a red box in a g-cell, and the two pins of $n_2$ are represented by two yellow squares. The blue segment $ir_3$ is the iroute extracted from $n_2$.

Let $N$ denote the set of all nets including local nets and global nets. In one layer, each panel consists of a set of g-cells, and all g-cells are in a row or column of a routing layer. Let $P$ denote the set of all panels. For each panel $p$, $T_p$ denotes the set of tracks in the panel, and $I_p$ denotes the set of iroutes assigned to the panel. For each track $t$, $I_t$ denotes the set of iroutes assigned to the track, and $B_t$ denotes the set of blockages in the track. Let $ir_k$ denote the $k$-th iroute in $I_t$. Let $bl_k$ denote the $k$-th blockage in the $B_t$. RDTA assigns each iroute in $I_p$ to a track in $T_p$ instead of just assigning a subset of iroutes.

The overlap cost of iroutes in a track is defined below.

$$TOL_t = \sum_{i=1}^{l} OL_{i,t} \quad (1)$$

In Eq.(1), $OL_{i,t}$ denotes the number of assigned iroutes in the $i$-th unit length on the track $t$. And $l$ denotes the length of the track $t$.

The blockage cost between iroutes and blockages of a track is defined below.

$$TBOL_t = \begin{cases} \sum_{i=1}^{n}\sum_{j=1}^{m} BOL_{i,j,t} & , n > 0, m > 0 \\ 0 & , otherwise \end{cases} \quad (2)$$

In Eq.(2), $BOL_{i,j,t}$ denotes the overlap length between $ir_i \in I_t$ and $bl_j \in B_t$ on the track $t$. $TBOL_t$ denotes the blockage cost between iroutes and blockages in this track. In addition, $n$ and $m$ denote the number of assigned iroutes in the $I_t$ and the number of blockages in the $B_t$ respectively.

The optimization objective of RDTA is to minimize the total overlap cost as shown below.

$$Minimize : \sum_{p \in P} \sum_{t \in T_p} (TOL_t + TBOL_t) \quad (3)$$

# 3 RDTA

## 3.1 Track Assignment Framework

RDTA is divided into five stages. The five stages are as follows: the initial assignment stage, the iroute connection stage, the overlap reduction stage, the iroute connection stage and the pin connection stage. The initial assignment stage and the overlap reduction stage are introduced into our algorithm from NTA [10]. In both stages, NTA adopts a panel-by-panel processing. The first iroute connection stage can provide a track assignment solution, and the iroutes of the solution are connected by vias. Based on this more accurate solution, the overlap reduction stage can better reduce iroute overlaps. The second iroute connection stage determines the final location of each via. The last stage is the pin connection stage. When this stage is completed, RDTA can get a completely connected solution, and the solution can be used to estimate routability effectively.

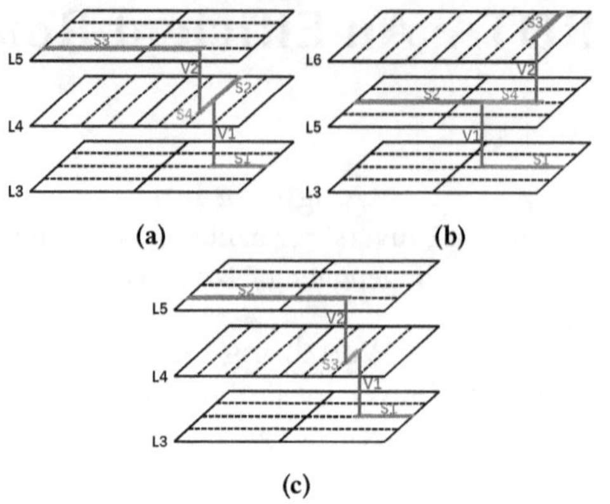

Figure 2: Illustration of the via location model in the iroute connection stage.

## 3.2 Initial Assignment Stage

In the initial assignment stage, RDTA uses a greedy algorithm of NTA to assign each iroute to a track, and it can get an initial assignment solution. The quality of this greedy algorithm depends on the order of assignment. Experiments prove that the best solution can be obtained by assigning iroutes from long to short. There are some metrics to evaluate the quality of a track assignment solution. The cost of assigning an iroute to one track is defined as below.

$$wlCost + \alpha \times overlapCost + \beta \times blkCost \quad (4)$$

In Eq.(4), $wlCost$, $overlapCost$ and $blkCost$ denote the wirelength cost, overlap cost and blockage cost respectively. The definition of the wirelength cost is the same as that of [10]. $\alpha$ and $\beta$ are user-defined parameters. And $\alpha$ and $\beta$ are respectively set to be 0.1 and 1000000 in our implementation.

For each iroute, the costs of the iroute assigned to each track are calculated. Then the track with the minimum cost is selected to assign the iroute.

## 3.3 Iroute Connection Stage

*3.3.1 Via Location Model.* In the industrial design, each layer has a preferred routing direction which is vertical or horizontal. In Figure 2, the preferred routing direction of the layer L3 and the layer L5 is horizontal, and the preferred routing direction of the layer L4 and the layer L6 is vertical. The black squares in Figure 2 represent g-cells. The iroutes and the g-cells are truncated to be shown in Figure 2.

We define three sub-models of our via location model. In orthogonal connection sub-model, a via location is determined by two orthogonal iroutes. In parallel direct connection sub-model, a via location is determined by two parallel iroutes connected directly. In parallel indirect connection sub-model, a via location is determined by two parallel iroutes, and the two parallel iroutes are connected by a new iroute.

In the via location model, the location of each via is determined by two iroutes. Because of the existence of three sub-models, our via location model contains all situations in which the location of

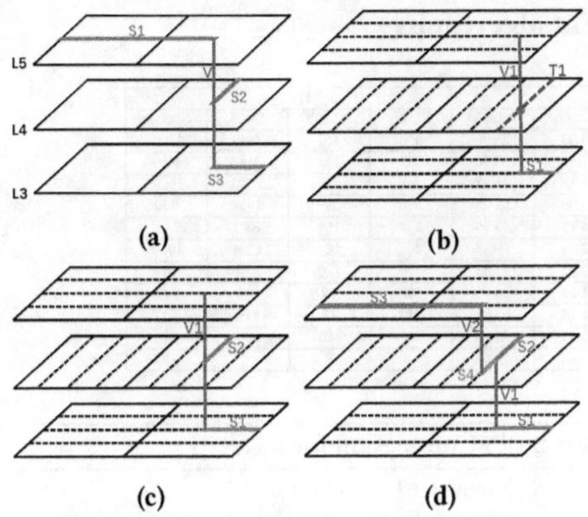


**Figure 3: Illustration of iroute connection.**

each via is determined by two iroutes. In the global routing solutions, the number of iroutes connected to the same via may exceed two. Therefore, for other iroutes that are not used to determine the locations of vias, if they cannot directly be connected to vias, they are connected to vias by adding new iroutes in the tracks with minimum increased overlap cost which is chosen from corresponding panels of all layers. The increased overlap cost of the new iroute assigned to one track is defined as below.

$$overlapCostInc + \beta \times blkCostInc \quad (5)$$

In Eq.(5), *overlapCostInc* and *blkCostInc* denote increased overlap cost and increased blockage cost respectively. $\beta$ is user-defined parameter. And $\beta$ is set to be 5 in our implementation. It is selected from a number of parameters through experiments so that the increased overlap cost and the increased blockage overlap cost of a solution can be well optimized for equalization.

Figure 2(a) shows the implementation of the orthogonal connection sub-model. It is assumed that the location of the via is determined by S1 and S2. Therefore, the location of the via is the intersection V1 of the tracks.

In the parallel direct connection sub-model, the location of the via need to have a track in the iroute orthogonal direction. The iroute orthogonal direction is the direction which is orthogonal with the iroute. The coordinate of the via in the iroute orthogonal direction is determined to be the coordinate of the track with the minimum iroute number in the panel of the via. Figure 2(b) shows the implementation of this sub-model. It is assumed that the location of the via is determined by S1 and S2. Since the horizontal coordinates of S1 and S2 are the same, the two iroutes can be directly connected without adding a new iroute.

In the parallel indirect connection sub-model, the new iroute is assigned to the track with minimum increased overlap cost calculated by Eq.(5). Figure 2(c) shows the implementation of this sub-model. It is assumed that the location of the via is determined by S1 and S2. Since the horizontal coordinates of S1 and S2 are not the same, they need to be connected by adding the new iroute S3. S3 is assigned to the track with minimum increased overlap cost calculated by Eq.(5) in the panel of the via.

*3.3.2 Iroute Connection Algorithm.* In the iroute connection stage, all nets are sorted by the length of the longest iroute in the net from long to short. Then RDTA connects all nets one by one. Algorithm 1 shows the pseudo code of the iroute connection stage for processing an iroute set $I_N$ of a net $N$. The inputs of the algorithm are the iroute set $I_N$ and a via set $V_N$ of the net $N$.

**Algorithm 1** Iroute Connection for a Net

```
Input: iroute set I_N, via set V_N
1: Sort I_N by layer from low to high
2: for each via v in V_N do
3:     assignNumber ← 0
4:     for each iroute ir connected to v in I_N do
5:         assignNumber ← assignNumber + 1
6:         if assignNumber = 1 then
7:             update v and the endpoint of ir
8:         else if assignNumber = 2 then
9:             use via location model to connect two iroutes
10:            if two iroutes are connected by a new iroute then
11:                add new iroute to I_N and new via to V_N
12:            end if
13:            update v and the endpoints of two iroutes
14:        else
15:            connect ir to v
16:            if ir is connected to v by a new iroute then
17:                add new iroute to I_N and new via to V_N
18:            end if
19:            update v and the endpoint of ir
20:        end if
21:    end for
22: end for
```

First, line 1 sorts all iroutes by their layer from low to high. Then, lines 5 to 20 connect the iroutes of each via by the layer from low to high. Figure 3 shows the illustration of Algorithm 1. Figure 3(a) gives a global routing solution.

When the first iroute should be connected, the algorithm updates the endpoint coordinates of the iroute *ir* and the via *v* to make that *v* is the intersection of *ir* and the track with the minimum iroute number in the panel of *v* (line 7). As shown in Figure 3(b), S1 is the first iroute. The location of V1 is the intersection of S1 and the track T1. T1 has the minimum iroute number.

When the second iroute should be connected, the algorithm uses the via location model to connect two iroutes (lines 9-13). As shown in Figure 3(c), S1 and S2 are connected together. The location of V1 is the intersection of S1 and S2. Finally, line 13 updates the two iroutes and the via.

When the iroute which is not used to determine the location of the via should be connected, the iroute is connected to the via (lines 15-19). As shown in Figure 3(d), S1 and S2 determine the location of V1. S3 should be connected. S3 is connected to V1 by adding a new iroute S4. S4 is assigned to the track with the minimum increased overlap cost calculated by Eq.(5). Finally, line 19 updates the via and the iroute.

## 3.4 Overlap Reduction Stage

In the overlap reduction stage, RDTA uses a negotiation scheme of NTA to rip up and re-assign iroutes iteratively. The iroute *ir* is selected to rip up, and the cost of it is defined as below.

$$overlapCost\,(ir, t) + historyCost\,(ir, t) \quad (6)$$

In Eq.(6), $overlapCost\,(ir, t)$ and $historyCost\,(ir, t)$ are the overlap cost and the history cost respectively when the iroute *ir* is on the track *t*. The definition of history cost is the same as that of NTA, and the history cost is needed by the negotiation scheme.

The costs of all iroutes are calculated based on Eq.(6). Then iroutes are ripped up iteratively in descending order of costs.

When the iroute *ir* is ripped up and it should be assigned to the track *t*, the cost of it is defined as below.

$$0.1 \times wlCost\,(ir, t) + \alpha_1 \times overlapCost\,(ir, t) + \beta \times blkCost\,(ir, t) + historyCost\,(ir, t) \quad (7)$$

**Table 1: Comparison between different algorithms**

| Circuit | OC(e6) | | | | | BC(e6) | | | | | Time(s) | | | |
|---|---|---|---|---|---|---|---|---|---|---|---|---|---|---|
| | RDTA | NTAPP | Imp(%) | TraPL | Imp(%) | RDTA | NTAPP | Imp(%) | TraPL | Imp(%) | RDTA | NTAPP | TraPL | Speedup |
| sb2 | 50.82 | 53.33 | 4.71 | 103.64 | 50.96 | 1.30 | 1.51 | 13.91 | 2.03 | 35.96 | 306 | 163 | 4649 | 15.19 |
| sb3 | 46.30 | 48.91 | 5.34 | 77.67 | 40.39 | 0.97 | 1.09 | 11.01 | 1.46 | 33.56 | 252 | 158 | 2442 | 9.69 |
| sb6 | 49.28 | 51.25 | 3.84 | 78.02 | 36.84 | 0.91 | 1.02 | 10.78 | 1.48 | 38.51 | 249 | 153 | 2580 | 10.36 |
| sb7 | 71.22 | 74.09 | 3.87 | 114.33 | 37.71 | 0.78 | 0.92 | 15.22 | 1.60 | 51.25 | 398 | 239 | 3668 | 9.22 |
| sb9 | 39.19 | 40.83 | 4.02 | 62.61 | 37.41 | 0.64 | 0.76 | 15.79 | 1.13 | 43.36 | 237 | 159 | 1681 | 7.09 |
| sb11 | 37.62 | 39.52 | 4.81 | 64.21 | 41.41 | 0.61 | 0.66 | 7.58 | 1.53 | 60.13 | 202 | 121 | 2204 | 10.91 |
| sb12 | 67.27 | 70.91 | 5.13 | 97.97 | 31.34 | 0.31 | 0.34 | 8.82 | 0.35 | 11.43 | 379 | 270 | 2954 | 7.79 |
| sb14 | 27.30 | 28.54 | 4.34 | 46.56 | 41.37 | 0.76 | 0.88 | 13.64 | 1.24 | 38.71 | 128 | 89 | 980 | 7.66 |
| sb16 | 30.29 | 32.07 | 5.55 | 54.20 | 44.11 | 0.44 | 0.50 | 12.00 | 1.17 | 62.39 | 113 | 79 | 810 | 7.17 |
| sb19 | 22.96 | 23.90 | 3.93 | 36.29 | 36.73 | 0.42 | 0.45 | 6.67 | 0.86 | 51.16 | 166 | 126 | 1178 | 7.10 |
| AVG | - | - | 4.55 | - | 39.83 | - | - | 11.54 | - | 42.65 | - | - | - | 9.22 |

In Eq.(7), $wlCost\,(ir,t)$, $overlapCost\,(ir,t)$ and $blkCost\,(ir,t)$ are the wirelength cost, overlap cost and blockage cost respectively when the iroute $ir$ is assigned to the track $t$. $historyCost\,(ir,t)$ is history cost. $\alpha_1$ and $\beta$ are set by users. And $\alpha_1$ is set to 0.1 at the beginning of the overlap reduction stage, and its value is increased by 0.1 after every $|I_p|/k$ iterations, where $|I_p|$ is the number of iroutes in the panel $p$ and $k$ is set to 10 in our implementation. $\beta$ is a very large constant and set to 100000 in our implementation.

The iroute $ir$ is assigned to the track with the minimum cost, and the cost is calculated by Eq.(7). The history costs of relative tracks are updated after assignment.

### 3.5 Pin Connection Stage

Algorithm 2 shows the pseudo code of the pin connection stage for processing the net $N$. The inputs of the algorithm are a set of pins $S_N$, a set of iroutes $I_N$ and a set of vias $V_N$ in the same net $N$. Lines 2 to 6 are used to connect local nets, and lines 8 to 13 are used to connect global nets. Since many pins are off tracks in the benchmarks, the pins should be connected to tracks.

When connecting a local net, each pin is connected to the trunk from lines 2 to 6. Line 3 connects the pin $s$ to the nearest track. Then line 4 connects the pin $s$ to the trunk. Finally, line 5 updates the endpoint coordinates of the trunk.

When connecting a global net, each pin is connected to the nearest connection component from lines 8 to 13. Connection components include vias, iroutes and pins. Line 9 connects the pin $s$ to the nearest track. Lines 10 to 11 connect the pin $s$ to the nearest connection component $c$.

**Algorithm 2** Pin Connection for a Net

**Input:** pin set $S_N$, iroute set $I_N$, via set $V_N$

```
1: if N is a local net then
2:     for each pin s in S_N do
3:         st = PinToNearestTrack(s, t_s)
4:         PinConnection(st, trunk)
5:         update trunk
6:     end for
7: else
8:     for each s in S_N do
9:         st = PinToNearestTrack(s, t_s)
10:        c = NearestComponent(st, S_N, V_N, I_N)
11:        PinConnection(st, c)
12:        update c
13:    end for
14: end if
```

## 4 EXPERIMENTAL RESULTS

RDTA is implemented in C/C++ language on a 3.5GHz Intel Xeon-based linux server with a 128G memory. The placement solutions of NTUplace4 [12] that were released by the DAC12 placement contest [13] are routed by a global router NCTUgr [14]. Then we adopt the global routing solutions to be the test cases of RDTA.

Table 1 compares the track assignment solutions produced by RDTA, TraPL [11] and NTA [10] with post-processing stage, and the placement solutions of the table are produced from NTUplace4 [12]. OC denotes the iroute overlaps between iroutes, and BC denotes the iroute overlaps between iroutes and blockages. The NTAPP is NTA with post-processing stage, and the post-processing stage includes the iroute connection stage using the via location model and the pin connection stage of RDTA. It can be found that RDTA achieves 4.55% lower OC and 11.54% lower BC respectively on average compared to NTAPP as shown in Table 1. Because the benchmarks and the source code of TraPL are not available, we implement TraPL by ourselves. By comparison, it can be found that RDTA achieves 39.83% lower OC and 42.65% lower BC respectively on average compared to TraPL. Therefore, RDTA can optimize OC and BC effectively. And RDTA can greatly improve the runtime compared to TraPL. It can be found from the experimental results that RDTA can get 9.22X speedup on average. In conclusion, RDTA can effectively reduce iroute overlaps. It means that RDTA can more accurately estimate the routability of the placer.

## 5 CONCLUSION

In order to more accurately estimate the routability, we propose a routability-driven track assignment algorithm. RDTA considers local nets, via locations and pin access to get completely connected track assignment solutions. It can effectively reduce the iroute overlaps to make its solutions more closer to detailed routing. Consequently, RDTA can be effectively used to find where routing congestion happen and how to solve them by the track assignment solutions.

## ACKNOWLEDGMENTS

This work was supported by the National Natural Science Foundation of China (Grand No. 61877010, 11501114).

## REFERENCES

[1] S. Mantik et al., ISPD 2018 initial detailed routing contest and benchmarks, in *Proc. of ISPD*, pp. 140-143, 2018.
[2] S. Batterywala et al., Track assignment: a desirable intermediate step between global routing and detailed routing, in *Proc. ICCAD*, pp. 59-66, 2002.
[3] R. Kay and R. A. Rutenbar, Wire packing - a strong formulation of crosstalk-aware chip-level track/layer assignment with an efficient integer programming solution, in *Proc. ISPD*, pp. 61-68, 2000.
[4] D. Wu et al., Timing driven track routing considering coupling capacitance, in *Proc. ASP-DAC*, pp. 1156-1159, 2005.
[5] Y. N. Chang et al., Non-slicing floorplanning based crosstalk reduction on gridless track assignment for a gridless routing system with fast pseudo-tile extraction, in *Proc. ISPD*, pp. 134-141, 2008.
[6] M. Cho et al., Track routing and optimization for yield, *IEEE TCAD*, 27(5), pp. 872-882, 2008.
[7] X. Gao and L. Macchiarulo, Track routing optimizing timing and yield, in *Proc. ASP-DAC*, pp. 627-632, 2011.
[8] Y.-W. Lee et al., Minimizing critical area on gridless wire ordering, sizing and spacing, *Journal of Information Science and Engineering*, pp. 157-177, 2014.
[9] B.-T. Lai et al., Native-conflict-avoiding track routing for double patterning technology, in *Proc. SOCC*, pp. 381-386, 2012.
[10] M.-P. Wong et al., Negotiation-based track assignment considering local nets, in *Proc. ASP-DAC*, pp. 378-383, 2016.
[11] D. Shi et al., TraPL: Track Planning of Local Congestion for Global Routing, in *Proc. DAC*, 2017.
[12] M.-K. Hsu et al., Routability-driven placement for hierarchical mixed-size circuit designs, in *Proc. DAC*, 2013.
[13] N. Viswanathan et al., The DAC 2012 routability-driven placement contest and benchmark suite, in *Proc. DAC*, pp. 774-782, 2012.
[14] W.-H. Liu et al., NCTU-GR 2.0: multithreaded collision-aware global routing with bounded-length maze routing, *IEEE TCAD*, 32(5), pp. 709-722, 2013.

# EraseMe: A Defense Mechanism against Information Leakage exploiting GPU Memory

Hongyu Fang, Miloš Doroslovački, Guru Venkataramani
{hongyufang_ee,doroslov,guruv}@gwu.edu
The George Washington University
Washington, DC, United States

## ABSTRACT

Graphics Processing Units (GPU) play a major role in speeding up computational tasks of the users, especially in applications such as high volume text and image processing. Recent works have demonstrated the security problems associated with GPU that do not erase the remnant data left behind by previous applications prior to OS context switching. In these attacks, adversaries are able to allocate their memory region on the same memory region used by previous applications and are able to steal their secrets. To overcome this problem, one needs to erase every modified memory page, and this process incurs very high latencies (order of several seconds to even minutes). In this work, we propose EraseMe, a lightweight, content-aware memory-cleansing framework that identifies and erases the sensitive memory pages left behind by victim applications. Our preliminary evaluation shows that EraseMe is able to increase the difficulty of image reconstruction by over 10× for the attacker.

## KEYWORDS

Data Remanence attacks, Memory Security, Cyber-Defense

**ACM Reference Format:**

Hongyu Fang, Miloš Doroslovački, Guru Venkataramani. 2019. EraseMe: A Defense Mechanism against Information Leakage exploiting GPU Memory. In *Great Lakes Symposium on VLSI 2019 (GLSVLSI '19), May 9–11, 2019, Tysons Corner, VA, USA.* ACM, New York, NY, USA, 4 pages. https://doi.org/10.1145/3299874.3318027

## 1 INTRODUCTION

Graphics Processing Units (GPU) are widely used in computer systems for acceleration of text processing and image rendering, machine learning and other computationally intensive applications. Recent work [2, 10, 13, 26] demonstrate that the GPU does not zero out physical memory pages in GPU global memory during page allocation owing to high performance overheads. Such remnant data contain rich information about the last application context such as websites browsed [10], or rendered images [26].

A straightforward solution to avoiding theft of remnant data in GPU memory is to blindly erase every memory page before it is allocated to the next context. However, as demonstrated by Pietro et al. [13], zeroing-out of 512MB GPU memory takes around 20 seconds which may negate the usefulness of GPUs meant to accelerate workload performance.

Prior work, such as Silent Shredder [1], was proposed to shred remnant data efficiently) without actually writing out zeroes in non-volatile memories and address their inherent write endurance issue. However, this mechanism requires use of specialized hardware for counter mode encryption that encrypt/decrypt memory pages, along with tracking page-level (major) counters and resetting of corresponding minor counters within the page to zero.

We note that, not all remnant data in GPU memory is vulnerable to giving away sensitive information about the users. Hence, one could potentially modify just secret-crunching regions of GPU-based applications and add extra functions to erase secrets at the end of executing the GPU kernel. However, this solution requires reprogramming several existing applications and relying on third party software developers to provide higher security to user data. Also, in many scenarios, the secrets of victim applications are not uniformly located in all memory pages. For instance, the information content in a PDF document is primarily concentrated in the text portion, and the white background region has no content. Through cleverly leveraging such information, we could aim for more targeted erasure of contents from GPU memory.

In this paper, we propose EraseMe, that uses simple histogram counter based information to target memory pages. The Operating System would erase these *targeted* memory pages with secrets before allocating them to a new context. With this design, the information leakage through GPU memory could be avoided for user-desired content while having low-cost implementation.

The main contributions of our work are:

- We propose EraseMe, a new security framework that guards against information leakage attacks by identifying GPU pages with high information content, and selectively erasing such pages before allocating them to the next context.
- We demonstrate the efficacy of our design in avoiding information leakage through data remanence using Tesseract report rendering benchmarks [16]. Our experimental results demonstrate that the difficulty of attackers to reconstruct information is increased by over 10×.

## 2 BACKGROUND

In this section, we study background on GPU and memory security.

### 2.1 GPU Execution Model

Execution of OpenCL-based [17] GPU programs typically involve two part: kernels and host. The host executes on the host device. The


ACM ISBN 978-1-4503-6252-8/19/05...$15.00
https://doi.org/10.1145/3299874.3318027

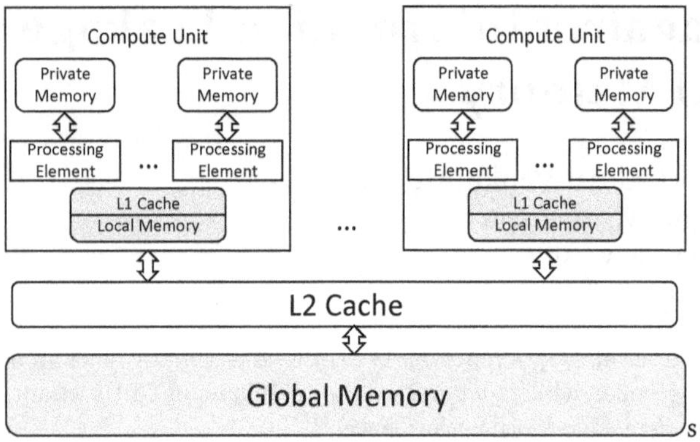


**Figure 1: GPU memory hierarchy (Note that the gray memory blocks are not cleaned at the end of kernel execution.)**

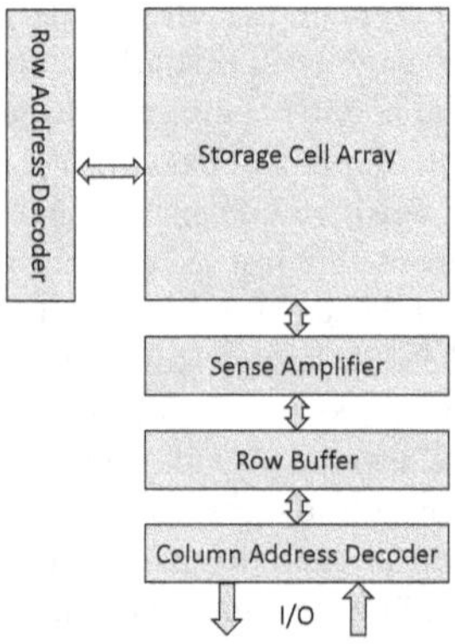


**Figure 2: The organization of DRAM**

kernels are configured by the host and execute on one or multiple OpenCL machine. In this work, the kernel is executed on GPU. The structure of GPU is shown in Figure 1. The instances of kernel are executed on processing elements, also known as GPU cores. Multiple processing elements form one compute unit. The GPU runs multiple kernels at the same time to accelerate the workloads.

## 2.2 GPU Memory Hierarchy

The memory hierarchy of GPU is shown in Figure 1. There are four types of memory in GPU: private memory, local memory, global memory and constant memory. Each private memory is attached to one processing element. Private memory is invisible to other processing elements in the same compute unit. Local memory is shared among all processing elements within one compute unit. We note that, in some GPUs, the L1 cache and local memory share the physical hardware and their sizes are configurable by users. The local memory and L1 cache implement coherence protocols among processing elements within one compute unit. The global memory is accessible to every compute unit. The constant memory is a read-only memory region within global memory. The size of constant memory is configured and initialized by the host. The coherence of memory blocks in global memory is not guaranteed.

| Memory Type | Vulnerability Window | Size | Reset Latency |
|---|---|---|---|
| Shared Memory | Before End of Context | 6MB | 0.22ms |
| Global Memory | After End of Context | 2GB | 20s |

**Table 1: GPU memory properties in Nvidia GeForce GT640. Vulnerability window shows when the attacker kernel can directly read the victim kernel's remnant data.**

## 2.3 DRAM Organization

The global memory of GPU is Dynamic Random Access Memory (DRAM) with 2GB to 8GB capacity. The organization of modern DRAM is shown in Figure 2. The stored bits can be located by its row address and column address. The row address firstly arrives to the DRAM. All bits within the row are read to row buffer. Then the column address arrives to row buffer and the content of accessed memory address is sent to memory bus (memory read) or written with the incoming data from memory bus (memory write). After the memory access, there are two policies to handle the data in row buffer: open page policy and close page policy. The open page policy does not precharge the row buffer until a different row in the same memory bank is accessed. The open page policy reduces the access latency for the same row (memory page) but increase the access latency of the row buffer miss. The close page policy recharge the row buffer right after the memory access. The close page policy makes the access latency of row buffer hit and row buffer miss equal which is slower than row buffer hit in open page policy and faster than row buffer miss in open page policy. The commercial DRAM may use both policies.

## 2.4 Remnant Data in GPU Memory

Prior work have demonstrated the security vulnerabilities arising from non-initilization in modern GPU memory during page allocation [10]. The local memory and private memory would not be erased at the end of context execution. The data in local and private memory are accessible for the host of next executing kernels before the host of last kernel ends its context. The remnant data in global memory are not erased during the page deallocation which makes the next context capable to access data from last context directly.

The attack on GPU memory can be categorized into two classes based on the different attack targets: local/private memory attack and global memory attack. The properties of these two level of GPU memories are shown in Table 1. To lastone2010openclunch local/private memory attack, the attacker kernel keeps dumping memory from local/private memory after the end of victim kernel and before the end of victim context. To launch global memory attack, the attacker keeps requesting a memory chunk equal to the size of free global memory. Once some parts of global memory are released by victim, the data contents are visible to the attacker.

A straightforward solution to solve the remnant memory problem in GPU is to erase memory pages after the end of kernels or context. As shown in Table 1, for private/local memory, the solution incurs lower overhead because the size of private and local memory is usually 16KB or 64KB per core. It takes less than 20ms to erase entire private/local memory after the end of kernel. However, the global memory of modern GPU is usually at gigabyte level. The

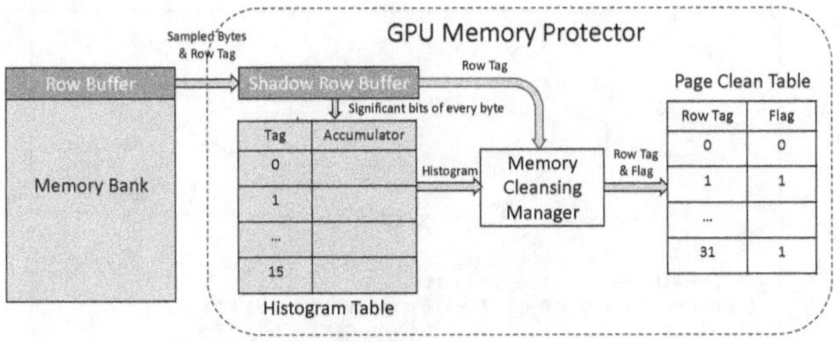


**Figure 3: EraseMe design overview (The shaded components are implemented through hardware while the white components are implemented in software.)**

zero-out of entire global memory takes from 20 seconds to 80 seconds for different machines [13]. Considering the fact that GPU is a performance-oriented machine, the high latency during context switch is undesirable.

### 2.5 Prior Studies in Memory Security

Security problem in CPU memory hierarchy is widely studied. Prior works demonstrated the information leakage problem through side and covert channels in memory and CPU caches [22, 25]. Previous studies have proposed hardware designs to defend main memory [14] and caches [3, 7–9, 18, 23] against information leakage attacks. Other works that profile software, detect memory bugs and increase software robustness [4, 6, 11, 12, 15, 19–21, 24] can be used in tandem to improve overall system security.

## 3 THREAT MODEL

After getting the remnant data of victim kernel, the attacker needs to reconstruct user-intelligible, useful information. Usually this step would happen through computer recognition algorithms because the remnant data is large and is in byte format, which leaves no pattern for human eyes to recognize. In this paper, the attacker first locates the position of the secret from all remnant data using Fast Fourier Transform. Then the attacker recognizes the text in the image using Optical Character Recognition (OCR) or identify the images using pre-trained machine learning models.

## 4 DESIGN

In this section, we propose the design of EraseMe, a low-overhead and user-configurable solution to information leakage exploiting GPU memory. EraseMe adds a hardware-performance-counter-like component to GPU memory, and collects statistics about information inside every memory page. The user can configure the system to identify valuable information inside pages, and can request the OS to erase some targeted memory pages with valuable content.

The structure of EraseMe is shown in Figure 3. A shadow row buffer is attached to each row buffer of memory bank in GPU global memory. The shadow row buffer samples and copies the bits stored in row buffer for histogramming. The memory cleansing manager implements user-configurable rules to analyze histogram data, and decide whether the memory page needs to be cleaned after deallocation. The memory cleansing manager updates the decision in the *page-clean* table which contains the memory page addresses and a flag indicating whether the page was deemed sensitive (using user-configured rules). Among all components in EraseMe, the shadow row buffer and histogrammer are implemented in hardware and added to every row buffer in GPU global memory. The memory cleansing manager is an application which reads histograms periodically and decides whether to clean the page after deallocation. The page-clean table is implemented in software as a protected data structure by the Operating System, which will access it upon page deallocation. The memory page with sensitive information would be cleaned before being allocated to the next process.

## 5 EXPERIMENTAL SETUP

We run experiments on AMD Radeon RX 470 GPU and analyze the remnant data in GPU global memory. We run Document Viewer as the victim. It renders reports from Tesseract Benchmarks [16] in gray scale.

### 5.1 Attacker and Information Extraction

The goal of attacker is to reconstruct the texts in rendered reports from remnant data in GPU as shown in prior work [26]. The attacker converts reconstructed images to texts using Tesseract OCR Engine [16]. The result of attack is evaluated by the accuracy of reconstruction. The reconstruction score is computed using FuzzyWuzzy [5], a robust string matching algorithm by comparing the reconstructed text and the original text. The goal of EraseMe is to stop the attacker from reconstructing the texts in reports by removing the memory pages containing the texts. To identify texts among all remnant data, we note that the entropy of memory pages should be high because memory pages with just plain white or black pixels do not contain any reconstructable information.

## 6 EVALUATION

Figure 4 shows the text image before and after the initialization by EraseMe. The EraseMe removes 20% of memory pages with highest entropy where each memory page contains 4096 pixels. Before being erased, the text in image is clear and could be accurately identified by Optical Character Recognition (OCR). After the cleansing of EraseMe, the text in image is not recognizable for human eye. Besides, an automated OCR cannot reconstruct the original text either. The output of OCR engine is full of meaningless characters.

Figure 5 shows the relationship between percentage of high entropy pages removed by EraseMe and scores obtained from reconstruction results. The score evaluates the information reconstructed by the attacker by comparing the output of OCR engine and the original texts using FuzzyWuzzy [5] algorithm. The highest output of the algorithm is 100, which indicates that the two compared strings are identical. Our results show that, by removing only 20% memory pages with highest entropy, EraseMe can reduce the reconstruction score of attacker from 80 to less than 10 where the attacker can barely get any useful information. In other words, EraseMe increases the difficulty of page reconstruction by over 10× for the attacker. With 40% memory pages being removed, the EraseMe can make 99% of information not recognizable to the attacker.

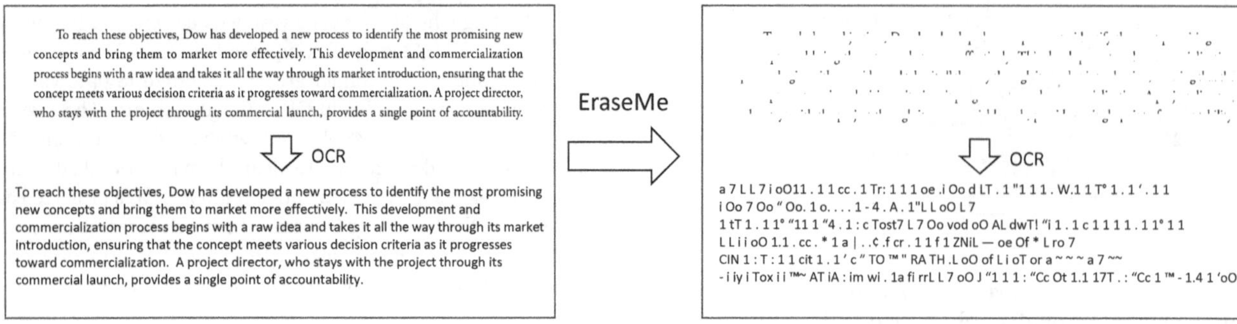


**Figure 4: Erasure efficacy of EraseMe. The upper left is the original image containing 3300 x 500 pixels. The upper right is the image cleaned by EraseMe. The bottom parts show the result of Optical Character Recognition Engine.**

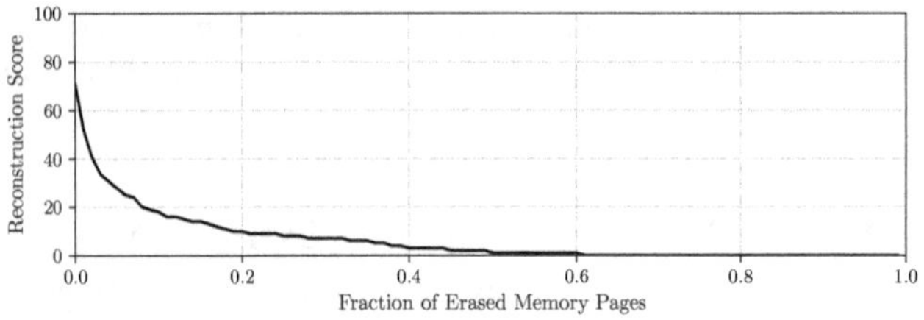


**Figure 5: The fraction of initialized memory page and the attacker's reconstruction score.**

## 7 CONCLUSION

In this paper, we proposed EraseMe, a light-weight framework to identify and remove the sensitive data in GPU global memory to prevent potential attacker to reconstruct the remnant data from previous applications.

## 8 ACKNOWLEDGEMENT

This manuscript is based on work supported by the US National Science Foundation under grant CNS-1618786, and Semiconductor Research Corp. (SRC) contract 2016-TS-2684.

## REFERENCES

[1] Amro Awad, Pratyusa Manadhata, Stuart Haber, Yan Solihin, and William Horne. Silent shredder: Zero-cost shredding for secure non-volatile main memory controllers. In *ACM SIGARCH Computer Architecture News*, volume 44, 2016.

[2] Xavier Bellekens, Greig Paul, James M Irvine, Christos Tachtatzis, Robert C Atkinson, Tony Kirkham, and Craig Renfrew. Data remanence and digital forensic investigation for cuda graphics processing units. In *FIP/IEEE International Symposium on Integrated Network Management*, 2015.

[3] Jie Chen and Guru Venkataramani. Cc-hunter: Uncovering covert timing channels on shared processor hardware. In *2014 47th Annual IEEE/ACM International Symposium on Microarchitecture*, pages 216–228. IEEE, 2014.

[4] Jie Chen, Guru Venkataramani, and H Howie Huang. Repram: Re-cycling pram faulty blocks for extended lifetime. In *IEEE/IFIP International Conference on Dependable Systems and Networks (DSN 2012)*, pages 1–12. IEEE, 2012.

[5] A Cohen. Fuzzywuzzy: Fuzzy string matching in python, 2011.

[6] Ioannis Doudalis, James Clause, Guru Venkataramani, Milos Prvulovic, and Alessandro Orso. Effective and efficient memory protection using dynamic tainting. *IEEE Transactions on Computers*, 61(1):87–100, 2012.

[7] Hongyu Fang, Sai Santosh Dayapule, Fan Yao, Miloš Doroslovački, and Guru Venkataramani. A noise-resilient detection method against advanced cache timing channel attack. In *2018 52nd Asilomar Conference on Signals, Systems, and Computers*, pages 237–241. IEEE, 2018.

[8] Hongyu Fang, Sai Santosh Dayapule, Fan Yao, Miloš Doroslovački, and Guru Venkataramani. Prefetch-guard: Leveraging hardware prefetches to defend against cache timing channels. In *2018 IEEE International Symposium on Hardware Oriented Security and Trust (HOST)*, pages 187–190. IEEE, 2018.

[9] Hongyu Fang, Sai Santosh Dayapule, Fan Yao, Miloš Doroslovački, and Guru Venkataramani. Prodact: Prefetch-obfuscator to defend against cache timing channels. *International Journal of Parallel Programming*, pages 1–24, 2018.

[10] Sangho Lee, Youngsok Kim, Jangwoo Kim, and Jong Kim. Stealing webpages rendered on your browser by exploiting gpu vulnerabilities. In *2014 IEEE Symposium on Security and Privacy (SP)*, pages 19–33. IEEE, 2014.

[11] Yongbo Li, Fan Yao, Tian Lan, and Guru Venkataramani. Sarre: semantics-aware rule recommendation and enforcement for event paths on android. *IEEE Transactions on Information Forensics and Security*, 11(12):2748–2762, 2016.

[12] Jungju Oh, Christopher J Hughes, Guru Venkataramani, and Milos Prvulovic. Lime: A framework for debugging load imbalance in multi-threaded execution. In *Proceedings of the 33rd International Conference on Software Engineering*, pages 201–210. ACM, 2011.

[13] Roberto Di Pietro, Flavio Lombardi, and Antonio Villani. Cuda leaks: a detailed hack for cuda and a (partial) fix. *ACM Transactions on Embedded Computing Systems (TECS)*, 15(1):15, 2016.

[14] Ali Shafiee, Rajeev Balasubramonian, Mohit Tiwari, and Feifei Li. Secure dimm: Moving oram primitives closer to memory. In *2018 IEEE International Symposium on High Performance Computer Architecture (HPCA)*, pages 428–440. IEEE, 2018.

[15] Jianli Shen, Guru Venkataramani, and Milos Prvulovic. Tradeoffs in fine-grained heap memory protection. In *Proceedings of the 1st workshop on Architectural and system support for improving software dependability*, pages 52–57. ACM, 2006.

[16] Ray Smith. An overview of the tesseract ocr engine. In *Document Analysis and Recognition, 2007. ICDAR 2007. Ninth International Conference on*, volume 2, pages 629–633. IEEE, 2007.

[17] John E Stone, David Gohara, and Guochun Shi. Opencl: A parallel programming standard for heterogeneous computing systems. *Computing in science & engineering*, 12(3):66, 2010.

[18] Guru Venkataramani, Jie Chen, and Milos Doroslovacki. Detecting hardware covert timing channels. *IEEE Micro*, 36(5):17–27, 2016.

[19] Guru Venkataramani, Ioannis Doudalis, Yan Solihin, and Milos Prvulovic. Memtracker: An accelerator for memory debugging and monitoring. *ACM Trans. Archit. Code Optim.*, 6(2):5:1–5:33, July 2009.

[20] Guru Venkataramani, Christopher J Hughes, Sanjeev Kumar, and Milos Prvulovic. Deft: Design space exploration for on-the-fly detection of coherence misses. *ACM Transactions on Architecture and Code Optimization (TACO)*, 8(2):8, 2011.

[21] Hongfa Xue, Yurong Chen, Fan Yao, Yongbo Li, Tian Lan, and Guru Venkataramani. Simber: Eliminating redundant memory bound checks via statistical inference. In *IFIP International Conference on ICT Systems Security and Privacy Protection*, pages 413–426. Springer, 2017.

[22] Fan Yao, Milos Doroslovacki, and Guru Venkataramani. Are coherence protocol states vulnerable to information leakage? In *2018 IEEE International Symposium on High Performance Computer Architecture (HPCA)*, pages 168–179. IEEE, 2018.

[23] Fan Yao, Hongyu Fang, Milos Doroslovacki, and Guru Venkataramani. Towards a better indicator for cache timing channels. *arXiv preprint arXiv:1902.04711*, 2019.

[24] Fan Yao, Yongbo Li, Yurong Chen, Hongfa Xue, Tian Lan, and Guru Venkataramani. Statsym: vulnerable path discovery through statistics-guided symbolic execution. In *2017 47th Annual IEEE/IFIP International Conference on Dependable Systems and Networks (DSN)*, pages 109–120. IEEE, 2017.

[25] Fan Yao, Guru Venkataramani, and Miloš Doroslovački. Covert timing channels exploiting non-uniform memory access based architectures. In *Proceedings of the on Great Lakes Symposium on VLSI 2017*, pages 155–160. ACM, 2017.

[26] Zhe Zhou, Wenrui Diao, Xiangyu Liu, Zhou Li, Kehuan Zhang, and Rui Liu. Vulnerable gpu memory management: towards recovering raw data from gpu. *Proceedings on Privacy Enhancing Technologies*, 2017(2):57–73, 2017.

# A Statistical Current and Delay Model Based on Log-Skew-Normal Distribution for Low Voltage Region

Peng Cao, Jiangping Wu, Zhiyuan Liu, Jingjing Guo, Jun Yang and Longxing Shi
National ASIC System Engineering Research Center, School of Electronic Science and Engineering
Southeast University
Nanjing, China
{caopeng, wujiangping, zyliuasic, guojingjing, dragon, lxshi}@seu.edu.cn

## ABSTRACT

The increasing performance variation and non-Gaussian distribution pose remarkable challenges to timing analysis for circuits operating in low voltage region. Accurate modeling of the statistical characteristics is urgently required with process variation consideration. In this paper, the statistical models for drain current and gate delay in low voltage region are established in analytical form based on the log-skew-normal (LSN) distribution via moment matching technique. Experimental results show that the probability distribution function (PDF) curves obtained from the proposed models for drain current and gate delay are highly fitted with Monte Carlo (MC) simulation results in sub/near-threshold regions. Moreover, owing to the proposed LSN-based statistical model, less than 8% error is introduced in the predicted sensitivity of gate delay and the maximum/minimum delay indicated by $\pm 3\sigma$ percentile points can be calculated more precisely than the LN-based method with up to 3× accuracy improvement for low supply voltage.

## CCS CONCEPTS

• Hardware→Statistical timing analysis

## KEYWORDS

Subthreshold voltage region; Near-threshold voltage region; Log-skew-normal distribution; Statistical model; $\pm 3\sigma$ percentile points

### ACM Reference format:

Peng Cao, Jiangping Wu, Zhiyuan Liu, Jingjing Guo, Jun Yang and Longxing Shi.2019. A Statistical Current and Delay Model Based on Log-Skew-Normal Distribution for Low Voltage Region.In *Proceedings of ACM Great Lakes Symposium on VLSI, Tysons Corner, VA, USA, May 2019(GLSVLSI'19).ACM, New York, NY, USA, 4 pages.*
https://doi.org/10.1145/3299874.3318028


*GLSVLSI '19, May 9–11, 2019, Tysons Corner, VA, USA*

ACM ISBN 978-1-4503-6252-8/19/05...$15.00
https://doi.org/10.1145/3299874.3318028

## 1 Introduction

Voltage scaling has been a well-known major strategy for reducing the power consumption [1]. However, despite the remarkable energy saving in low voltage domain, process variation imposes substantial cycle time design margin, which requires to be evaluated to meet the yield target [2] [3]. Moreover, the circuit parameters are severely non-Gaussian distributed in low voltage domain [4]. Hence, the design flow of circuits should utilize statistical models to predict the asymmetrical circuit performance parameters, which poses a major challenge to timing analysis.

Existing non-Gaussian distributed current and delay modeling approaches for circuits operating with low supply voltages can be roughly divided into two categories, namely fitting-based methods and analytical methods. Literatures [5-7] determine the statistical characteristics of the circuit delay by fitting inverse-Gaussian distribution, Weibull distribution, log-skew-normal (LSN) distribution from the Monte Carlo (MC) samples, respectively. Experimental results of these literature show a high accuracy by fitting-based methods to model the statistical behavior of circuit delay. However, they cannot reveal the relation with the process parameters and the environment parameters including supply voltage and load capacitance even at the cost of numerous MC simulations. Different from the fitting-based approaches, other works derive the distribution of current and delay analytically. In [8, 9], considering the logarithm form of current or delay in subthreshold region changes linearly with the normal distributed threshold voltage, a log-normal (LN) based models are derived analytically to reveal the effect of threshold voltage variation to the current and delay distribution. Similarly, LN-based distribution is employed to model the delay distribution of near-threshold region in [10, 11], where the derivation starts from a compact current model whose logarithmic form is the quadric relation with the threshold voltage. These aforementioned works derive the distribution of current and delay based on specific current models. However, an obvious drawback exists that the assumed LN distribution is not applicable to model the distribution across the low voltage domain, especially for near-threshold region.

In this paper, an LSN-based model for drain current and gate delay for low voltage region is proposed in analytical form with process variation consideration. The probability density function (PDF) and cumulative distribution function (CDF) of LSN distribution for drain current and gate delay are derived analytically via moment matching technique based on a compact transregional current equation. The statistical relation between the delay and the threshold voltage is revealed to achieve an accurate estimation of the sensitivity ($\sigma/\mu$) and the maximum/minimum delay at $\pm 3\sigma$ percentile point.

The rest of paper is organized as follows. Following the introduction, the predominant factor of process variation is identified and the analytical models for drain current and gate delay in sub/near-threshold region are reviewed in Section 2. In Section 3, the statistical models for current and delay are derived based on LSN distribution in low voltage region via moment matching technique, which are utilized to estimate delay sensitivity and the $\pm 3\sigma$ delay. Experiments and comparisons are made in Section 4. Finally, Section 5 draws the conclusion.

## 2 Preliminaries

### 2.1 Critical Factor of Process Variation

The process variations can be divided into the global and the local ones. As many prior publications have re-iterated, the main cause of local variation in modern technology is the threshold voltage ($V_{th}$) variation [12][13], which leads to asymmetric current and delay distribution at low voltage.

In this paper, $V_{th}$ is specified as the critical process variation in Gaussian distribution with the mean $\mu_0$ and the variance $\sigma_0^2$ ($V_{th} \sim N(\mu_0, \sigma_0^2)$), which determines the statistical characteristics of drain current and gate delay.

### 2.2 Threshold Voltage Dependent Drain Current and Delay Model in Low Voltage Region

In subthreshold voltage region, the drain current ($I_{on}$) is determined by

$$I_{on} = I_0 e^{\frac{V_{DD}-V_{th}}{n\phi_t}} \tag{1}$$

Where $V_{DD}$ is the supply voltage, $V_{th}$ denotes the threshold voltage, $\Phi_t$ is the thermal voltage, $n$ is the sub-threshold slope factor. In addition, $I_0$ is determined by

$$I_0 = \mu C_{ox}(n-1)\frac{W}{L}\phi_t^2 \tag{2}$$

where $\mu$ is the effective electron mobility, $C_{ox}$ is the oxide capacitance per unit, $W$ is the channel width, $L$ is the channel length.

Compared with (1), a transregional equation of $I_{on}$ is expressed as following for sub/near-threshold voltage [10]

$$I_{on} = I_0 K_0 e^{K_1\frac{V_{DD}-V_{th}}{n\phi_t}+K_2\left(\frac{V_{DD}-V_{th}}{n\phi_t}\right)^2} \tag{3}$$

where $K_0$, $K_1$, $K_2$ are the process-independent parameters.

Equation (3) can be represented as the following form

$$I_{on} = I_0 K_0 e^X \tag{4}$$

where $X$ is

$$X = J_1(V_{DD}-V_{th}) + J_2(V_{DD}-V_{th})^2 \tag{5}$$

and $J_1$ and $J_2$ are the scaled $K_1$ and $K_2$,

$$\begin{cases} J_1 = \dfrac{K_1}{n\phi_t} \\ J_2 = \dfrac{K_2}{(n\phi_t)^2} \end{cases} \tag{6}$$

The gate delay ($T_d$) can be calculated with a linear RC-delay model [10] as follows

$$T_d = K_f \frac{V_{DD}C_{load}}{I_{on}} \tag{7}$$

where $K_f$ is a fitting constant, $C_{load}$ is value of the load capacitance.

By substituting (4) into (7), the gate delay can be denoted as

$$T_d = K_f \frac{V_{DD}C_{load}}{I_0 K_0} e^{-X} \tag{8}$$

## 3 Statistical Current/Delay Model Based on Log-Skew-Normal Distribution

### 3.1 Derivation of Distribution Parameters with Moment Matching Technique

According to the content mentioned in [7], the drain current and gate delay can be assumed to follow LSN distribution. Literature [14] has demonstrated that for a LSN distributed random variable, its logarithmic form follows SN distribution. Thus, the term $X$ in (4) and (8) is SN distributed.

The property of SN distribution reveals that the mean ($\mu$), variance ($\sigma^2$), and skewness ($\gamma_1$) of the random variable $X$ used in (4) and (8) can be written as functions of its distribution parameters $\varepsilon$, $\omega$, and $\lambda$.

$$\begin{cases} \mu = \varepsilon + \omega\beta\sqrt{\dfrac{2}{\pi}} \\ \sigma^2 = \omega^2\left(1-\dfrac{2}{\pi}\beta^2\right) \\ \gamma_1 = \dfrac{4-\pi}{2}\dfrac{\left(\dfrac{2}{\pi}\beta^2\right)^{\frac{3}{2}}}{\left(1-\dfrac{2}{\pi}\beta^2\right)^{\frac{3}{2}}} \end{cases} \tag{9}$$

where $\beta$ can be written as

$$\beta = \frac{\lambda}{\sqrt{1+\lambda^2}} \tag{10}$$

$$\begin{cases} \mu = J_1V_{DD} - J_1\mu_0 + J_2V_{DD}^2 - 2J_2V_{DD}\mu_0 + J_2(\mu_0^2+\sigma_0^2) \\ \sigma^2 - J_2^2[2\sigma_0^4 + 4\sigma_0^2(V_{DD}-\mu_0+\dfrac{J_1}{2J_2})^2] \\ \gamma_1 = \dfrac{\left(J_2^3E\left[V_{DT'}^6\right] - \dfrac{3}{4}J_1^2J_2E\left[V_{DT'}^4\right] + \dfrac{3}{16}\dfrac{J_1^4}{J_2}E\left[V_{DT'}^2\right] - \dfrac{J_1^6}{64J_2^3}\right)}{\sigma^3} \\ \quad + \dfrac{-3\mu\sigma^2-\mu^3}{\sigma^3} \end{cases} \tag{11}$$

Since the random variable $X$ is a quadratic function of normally distributed threshold voltage $V_{th}$, the mean ($\mu$), variance ($\sigma^2$), and skewness ($\gamma_1$) of $X$ can also be calculated as (11) according to (5), where several terms in equation (15) for $\gamma_1$ can be expressed by

$$\begin{cases} E\left[V_{DT'}^6\right]=15\sigma_0^6+45\sigma_0^4\left(V_{DD}^{'}\right)^2+15\sigma_0^2\left(V_{DD}^{'}\right)^4+\left(V_{DD}^{'}\right)^6 \\ E\left[V_{DT'}^4\right]=3\sigma_0^4+6\sigma_0^2\left(V_{DD}^{'}\right)^2+\left(V_{DD}^{'}\right)^4 \\ E\left[V_{DT'}^2\right]=\sigma_0^2+\left(V_{DD}^{'}\right)^2 \\ V_{DD}^{'}=V_{DD}-\mu_0+\frac{J_1}{2J_2} \end{cases} \tag{12}$$

By employing moment matching technique, the LSN distribution parameters ($\varepsilon$, $\omega$, $\lambda$) of $X$ can be easily solved by joining (9) and (11), which are expressed as the mean ($\mu_0$) and standard deviation ($\sigma_0$) of threshold voltage and the supply voltage.

## 3.2 Deviation of Drain Current and Gate Delay Models

The analytical models for LSN-distributed drain current and gate delay are derived via the distribution parameters of $X$. From (4) and (8), the drain current ($I_{on}$) and gate delay ($T_d$) can be denoted as $Y$, which can be transformed from $X$ as

$$\begin{cases} Y=e^Z \\ Z=pX+q \end{cases} \tag{13}$$

where $p$ and $q$ are the coefficients for $I_{on}$ or $T_d$, which can be determined by (14) or (15).

$$\begin{cases} p=1 \\ q=\ln\left(I_0K_0\right) \end{cases} \quad for \;\; I_{on} \tag{14}$$

$$\begin{cases} p=-1 \\ q=\ln\left(\dfrac{K_fV_{DD}C_{load}}{I_0K_0}\right) \end{cases} \quad for \;\; T_d \tag{15}$$

The newly defined random variable $Z$ in (13) is the linear expression of $X$, whose distribution parameters ($\varepsilon_Z$, $\omega_Z$, $\lambda_Z$) are

$$\begin{cases} \varepsilon_Z=p\varepsilon+q \\ \omega_Z=p\omega \\ \lambda_Z=\lambda \end{cases} \tag{16}$$

Subsequently, the probability distribution function (PDF) and cumulative distribution function (CDF) for $Y$ with LSN distribution are then formulated as

$$f_{LSN}(Y)=\frac{2}{\omega_ZY}\phi\left(\frac{\ln(Y)-\varepsilon_Z}{\omega_Z}\right)\Phi\left(\lambda\frac{\ln(Y)-\varepsilon_Z}{\omega_Z}\right) \tag{17}$$

$$F_{LSN}(Y)=\Phi\left(\frac{\ln(Y)-\varepsilon_Z}{\omega_Z}\right)-2T\left(\frac{\ln(Y)-\varepsilon_Z}{\omega_Z},\lambda_Z\right) \tag{18}$$

where $T(H, A)$ is the Owen's $T$ function and can be given by

$$T(H,A)=\frac{1}{2\pi}\int_0^A\frac{e^{\frac{-H^2}{2}(1+t^2)}}{1+t^2}dt \tag{19}$$

As for $T_d$, the maximum/minimum delay can be derived as the $\pm3\sigma$ percentile points by letting the CDF to be $\Phi(\pm3)$, which is

$$\Phi\left(\frac{\ln\left(T_d\right)-\varepsilon_{T_d}}{\omega_{T_d}}\right)-2T\left(\frac{\ln\left(T_d\right)-\varepsilon_{T_d}}{\omega_{T_d}},\lambda_{T_d}\right)=\Phi\left(\pm3\right) \tag{20}$$

# 4 Experiment and Comparison

## 4.1 Experimental Setup

The proposed models have been evaluated in a commercial 40nm technology with a subthreshold voltage (0.3V) and a near-threshold voltage (0.5V) for inverters. The transistor sizes were set as fixed length of 40nm and varied widths ranging from 0.12um to 1.08um. The LSN-based analytical models for $I_{on}$ and $T_d$ are derived to obtain the corresponding PDFs and CDFs, which are compared with 10K Monte Carlo simulation results and prior LN-based models in low voltage region.

## 4.2 Model Validation and Comparison

Fig. 1 and Fig. 2 depict the PDFs of the proposed analytical model for the drain current and the gate delay for subthreshold (0.3V) and near-threshold (0.5V) domain with various transistor widths. It can be demonstrated that the proposed models show an excellent agreement with Monte Carlo simulation results.

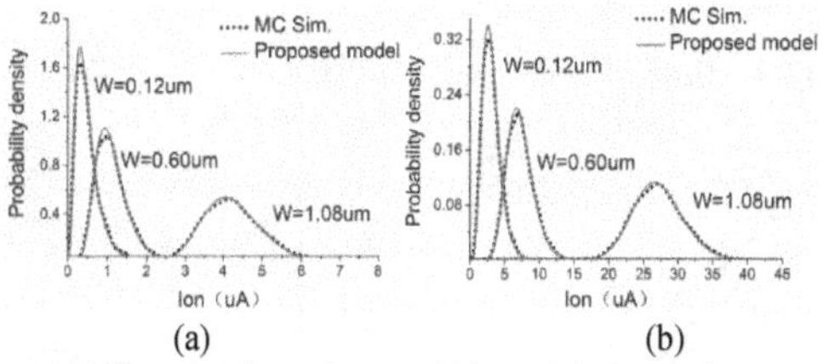


Fig. 1. Probability density of proposed model for drain current with supply voltage at (a) 0.3V; (b) 0.5V.

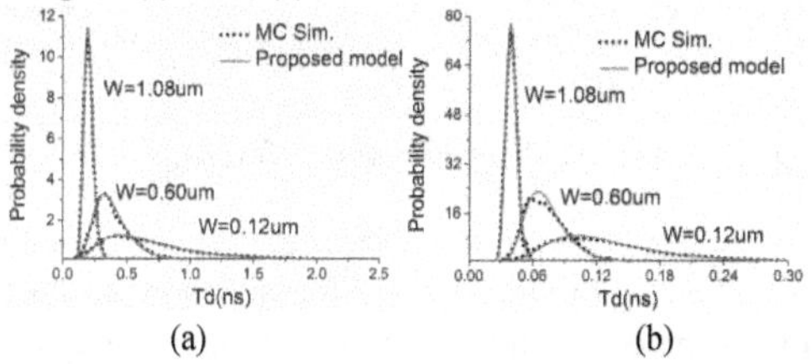


Fig. 2. Probability density of proposed model for inverter delay with supply voltage at (a) 0.3V; (b) 0.5V.

Comparisons with the prior LN-based models proposed in [8] and [10] in terms of the errors of the delay sensitivity ($\sigma/\mu$) and the maximum/minimum delay ($\pm3\sigma$) are illustrated in Fig.3, Fig. 4 and Fig.5, respectively. The delay models in [8] and [10] are analyzed based on the expression of the drain current as in (1) and (3), respectively, in which the delay variation was both derived under the assumption of LN distribution.

Fig. 3 shows that the proposed statistical model predicts the delay sensitivity with less than 8% error for all sizes, which is comparable with the model in [10] because both are derived based on the transregional drain current equation. Our work shows significant advantage over the model in [8] especially in near-threshold region where our model has a 1.92~3.22x accuracy improvement increased. The reason is that the analytical model for delay variation in [8] is based on the current equation for subthreshold region which leads to nonnegligible mismatch as the supply voltage rises to the near-threshold domain.

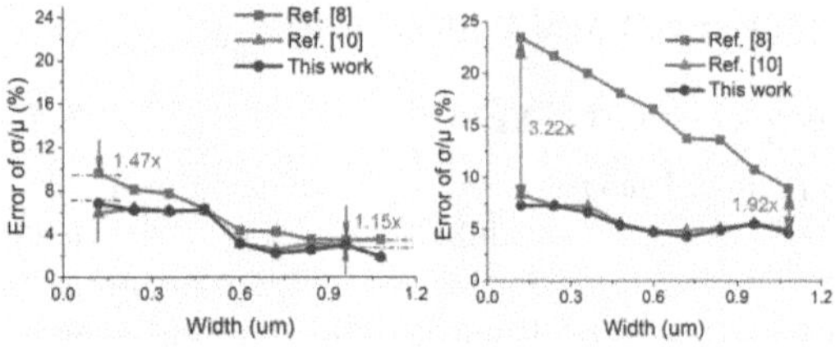


(a) (b)

Fig. 3. Error comparison of delay sensitivity at (a) 0.3V; (b) 0.5V.

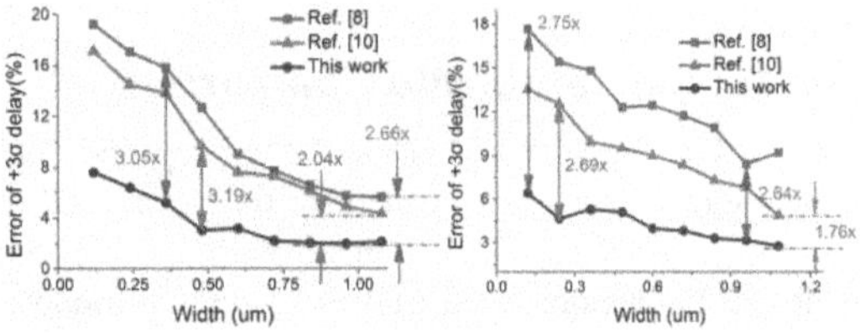


(a) (b)

Fig. 4. Error comparison of $+3\sigma$ delay at (a) 0.3V; (b) 0.5V.

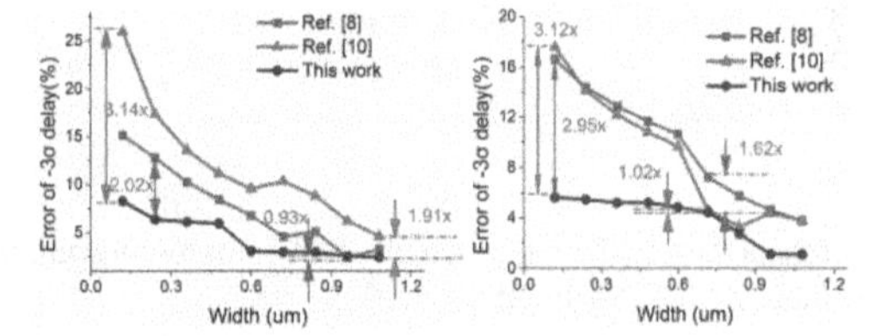


(a) (b)

Fig. 5. Error comparison of $-3\sigma$ delay at (a) 0.3V; (b) 0.5V.

Fig. 4 and Fig. 5 illustrate the error of $\pm 3\sigma$ percentile points of delay distribution predicted by different models. Our model outperforms the competitive models with the error reduction by 2.04~3.19x and 1.76~2.75x in subthreshold and near-threshold region respectively for the prediction of the $+3\sigma$ quantile point as shown in Fig. 4. It is worth noting that even though the model in [10] achieves a comparable accuracy with ours in terms of the delay sensitivity, the delay prediction in extreme condition ($3\sigma$ delay) reveals the demerit of the LN distribution for low voltage region, which is consistent with the experimental results demonstrated in [7] for 99% percentile points. For the prediction of $-3\sigma$ percentile point of delay distribution, it can be seen in Fig. 5 that this work shows the advantage of accuracy with less than 8% error at low voltage with up to over 3× accuracy improvement compared with the models in [8][10] for the minimum-sized inverter.

## 5 Conclusion

This paper proposes a LSN distributed model for the statistical drain current and gate delay in low voltage region. Through moment matching technique, related distribution parameters can be determined. Subsequently, the corresponding CDF is employed to calculate the $\pm 3\sigma$ percentile points. The propose model shows considerable fitness for analyzing the statistical characters in low voltage ranges.

## ACKNOWLEDGMENTS

This work was supported by the National Science and Technology Major Project (Grant No.2017ZX01030101).

## REFERENCES


[1] B. H. Chen, P. Y. Chou, Y. B. Fang, et al. "Design of ultra-low-leakage near-threshold dynamic circuits in nano CMOS for IoT applications,"International Conference on Nanotechnology, pp. 537-540, November 2016.

[2] H. Kaul, M. Anders, S. Hsu, et al. "Near-threshold voltage (NTV) design: opportunities and challenges," Proceedings of the 49th Annual Design Automation Conference, pp. 1153-1158, June 2012.

[3] U, Schlichtmann, "Frontiers of timing," System Level Interconnect Prediction (SLIP), 2017 ACM/IEEE International Workshop on. IEEE, pp. 1-4, 2017.

[4] P.Corsonello, F. Frustaci, M. Lanuzza, andS. Perri,"Over/undershooting effects in accurate buffer delay model for sub-threshold domain," IEEE Transactions on Circuits and Systems I: Regular Papers, vol. 61, no. 5, pp. 1456-1464, 2014

[5] J.Chen, S.Cotofana, S.Grandhi, et al."Inverse Gaussian distribution based timing analysis of Sub-threshold CMOS circuits,"Microelectronics Reliability, vol.55, no. 12,pp. 2754-2761, 2015.

[6] L. Zhang, J. Shao, C. C. P. Chen, "Non-gaussian statistical parameter modeling for ssta with confidence interval analysis," Proceedings of the 2006 international symposium on Physical design, ACM, pp. 33-38,April 2006

[7] H. A. Balef, M. Kamal, A. Afzali-Kusha, et al. "All-Region Statistical Model for Delay Variation Based on Log-Skew-Normal Distribution," IEEE Transactions on Computer-Aided Design of Integrated Circuits and Systems, vol. 35, no. 9, pp. 1503-1508, 2016

[8] F. Frustaci, P. Corsonello, and S. Perri,"Analytical delay model considering variability effects in subthreshold domain," IEEE Transactions on Circuits and Systems II: Express Briefs, vol. 59, no.3, pp. 168-172, February 2012.

[9] Y. Zhang, and B. H. Calhoun, "Fast, accurate variation-aware path timing computation for sub-threshold circuits," International Symposium on Quality Electronic Design, pp. 243-248, April 2014.

[10] S. Keller, D. M. Harris, and A. J. Martin, "A compact transregional model for digital CMOS circuits operating near threshold," IEEE Transactions on Very Large Scale Integration (VLSI) Systems, vol. 22, no. 10, pp. 2041-2053, November 2014.

[11] J. Shiomi, T. Ishihara, H. Onodera, "Microarchitectural-level statistical timing models for near-threshold circuit design," Design Automation Conference (ASP-DAC), 2015 20th Asia and South Pacific, IEEE, pp. 87-93, 2015.

[12] A. Mutlu, J. Le, R. Molina, and M. Celik, "A parametric approach for handling local variation effects in timing analysis," Proceedings of the 46th Annual Design Automation Conference, pp. 126–129, Jul. 2009

[13] B. Zhai, S.Hanson,D. Blaauw, et al. "Analysis and mitigation of variability in subthreshold design," Proceedings of the 2005 international symposium on Low power electronics and design, ACM, 2005.

[14] X. Li, Z. J. Wu, V. D. Chakravarthy, and Z. Q. Wu, "A Low-Complexity Approximation to Lognormal SumDistributions via Transformed Log SkewNormal Distribution," IEEE Transactions on Vehicular Technology, vol. 60, no. 8, pp. 4040-4045, 2011.

# Enabling Approximate Storage through Lossy Media Data Compression

Brian Worek
Dept. of Electrical & Computer Engineering
Virginia Tech
Blacksburg, VA, USA
briandw@vt.edu

Paul Ampadu
Dept. of Electrical & Computer Engineering
Virginia Tech
Blacksburg, VA, USA
ampadu@vt.edu

## ABSTRACT

As compute capabilities continue to scale, memory capacity and bandwidth continue to lag behind. Data compression is an effective approach to improving memory capacity and bandwidth; but prior works have focused primarily on lossless compression and retrieval for data-critical applications. While data integrity is critical to many applications, a growing number of memory-bound applications contain non-critical program data; this property can be exploited to improve memory performance and capacity. In this work, we enable approximate storage to exploit the inherent error resilience of multimedia and other applications, through lossy compression, to improve storage without adversely affecting application functionality. We realize an incidence of approximate storage through modification of the Base-Delta-Immediate algorithm to create a lossy memory compression algorithm. We conclude that approximate storage is an effective and promising technique for improving effective memory capacity and decreasing the energy cost of memory access; results show that memory capacity can be increased by 15% with only 3% loss in image recognition application quality.

## KEYWORDS

Approximate storage, lossy compression, inherent error resilience

**ACM Reference format:**

Brian Worek and Paul Ampadu. 2019. Enabling Approximate Storage through Lossy Media Data Compression. In *Proceedings of ACM Great Lakes Symposium on VLSI (GLSVLSI'19). ACM, Tysons Corner, Virginia USA, May 2019, 4 pages.* DOI: 10.1145/3299874.3318029

## 1 Introduction

Approximate storage mitigates the memory bottleneck by trading off storage accuracy for energy and performance. By exploiting the inherent error resilience (IER) of recognition, mining, and synthesis (RMS) applications, acceptable application-level quality can be maintained even when storage accuracy degrades [1-3]. A variety of approximate storage techniques exist at the circuit [4-8], architecture [9-12], and algorithmic [13-16] levels. In this work, we propose a general purpose approximate storage technique by invoking lossless compression at the cache, link, and main memory levels [13, 17, 18] to improve effective memory capacity. We realize approximate storage by applying dynamic precision scaling to the Base-Delta-Immediate (BΔI) lossless compression scheme [17].


ACM ISBN 978-1-4503-6252-8/19/05$15.00
https://doi.org/10.1145/3299874.3318029

## 2 BΔI Lossless Compression

Pekhimenko et. al [17] proposed Base-Delta-Immediate (BΔI), a value-based lossless cache compression scheme, which we choose to exploit for approximate storage due to its extremely low latency and dictionary-free operation. The major drawback to BΔI is its high area overhead. BΔI encodes a block of words as a base value followed by an array of delta values. Compression is achieved when the deltas require less space than the original words. Compressibility is dependent on the existence of low dynamic range among neighboring words, meaning they hold similar values. If consecutive words in a block have similar values, then the differences between those values will be small relative to the word size. A given uncompressed block and its corresponding compressed block are respectively defined by:

$$\textit{uncompressed block} = \{V_0, V_1, \ldots, V_{n-1}\}$$

$$\textit{compressed block} = \{\textit{base}, \Delta_0, \Delta_1, \ldots, \Delta_{n-1}\}, \text{ where } \Delta_i = V_i - \textit{base}$$

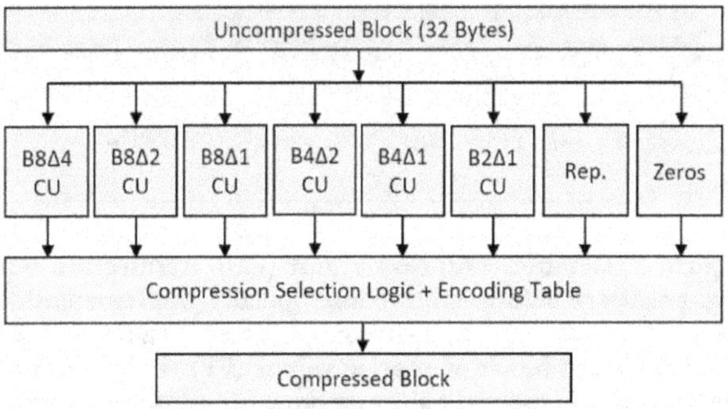


**Figure 1: The uncompressed block feeds into BΔI compressor units (CU) of different sizes. The most efficient valid encoding is then output as the compressed block.**

BΔI compression takes place over two major steps: BΔI arithmetic and encoding selection. During BΔI arithmetic, the uncompressed cache line feeds into several compressor units (CU) in parallel. Each CU operates on a specific base-delta, ($B$, Δ), byte width combination from the set of pairs:

$$(B, \Delta) = \{(8,1), (8,2), (8,4), (4,1), (4,2), (2,1)\}$$

The BΔI architecture is shown in Figure 1. Within each CU, a word in the cache-line is selected as a base of size B, and the differences between every word and the base are calculated. Differences are checked for a sign-extension beginning from its lower Δ bytes to determine if the they are small enough to be stored in the specified delta size. A given CU's output encoding is only valid if all of its differences are sign-extended from their lower Δ bytes. In addition to these base-delta CUs, there are units which check for and compress for zero or repeated values. Once all CUs have computed BΔI arithmetic, encoding selection is made based on a "compressible or not" signal output from every CU and a static encoding table. Of the valid CU encodings, the most space efficient one is selected and output as the compressed block.

## 3 Data Approximation

We introduce loss to BΔI by applying dynamic precision scaling to the subtraction operands of each CU. This improves data compressibility by increasing the probability of a more efficient compression encoding being valid for a given block at the cost of data integrity in the least significant bits (LSBs). We approximate the operands by right-shifting them so that their LSBs are shifted out and shift the value of the sign bit into the MSBs. This causes their sign bits to extend further, which causes the differences' sign bits to further extend too. A given base-delta's compression encoding is only valid if all of its differences are sign-extended from its lower Δ bytes. This means that extending the differences' sign bits increases the probability of that compression encoding being valid. If a more efficient compression encoding is valid, then more space is saved and the overall compression ratio improves.

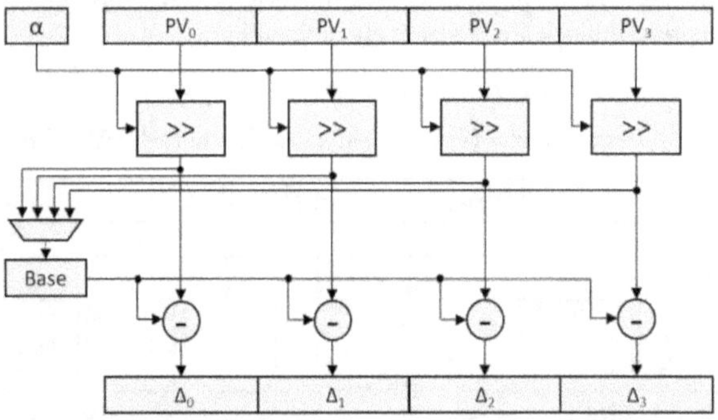


**Figure 2: Generic compressor unit (CU) architecture with right-shifters before subtraction. Specific implementations exist for all (B, Δ) encodings from Table 1. The uncompressed block of precise values (PV) is shown at the top. α controls the right shift amount for all input operands.**

Figure 2 shows our approximate CU. Following the precision scaling approach, we shift out the lower α bits of the subtraction operands by inserting right-shifters before the subtraction units' inputs. The shift amount is controlled by the approximation degree, α, which reduces the precision of each delta by α bits each. Rather than producing a difference accurate over the bit range [width-1: 0], each subtraction unit produces a difference accurate only over the range [width-1: α]. This quantizes the value of each delta by a factor of $1/2\alpha$. The lower α bits are implicitly set to the value of the sign bit and are later shifted back in during decompression. Since α is necessary for decompression, it is stored in the compressed block's meta data. The meta data overhead is shown in Table 1. The size of α stored in meta data varies from 3-5 bits depending on the (B, Δ) compression encoding. This enables max scaling of 7, 15, and 31 bits for bases 2, 4, and 8 respectively. α can be set to zero to enable lossless compression.

**Table 1: Approximated BΔI encoding table for 32-byte blocks. Sizes are in bytes.**

| Encoding Name | Base Size | Δ Size | Meta Size | Total Size |
|---|---|---|---|---|
| Zeros | 1 | 0 | 0 | 1 |
| Repeated Values | 8 | 0 | 1 | 9 |
| B8Δ1 | 8 | 1 | 2 | 14 |
| B8Δ2 | 8 | 2 | 2 | 18 |
| B8Δ4 | 8 | 4 | 2 | 26 |
| B4Δ1 | 4 | 1 | 2 | 15 |
| B4Δ2 | 4 | 2 | 2 | 23 |
| B2Δ1 | 2 | 1 | 1 | 21 |
| No Compression | N/A | N/A | 1 | 33 |

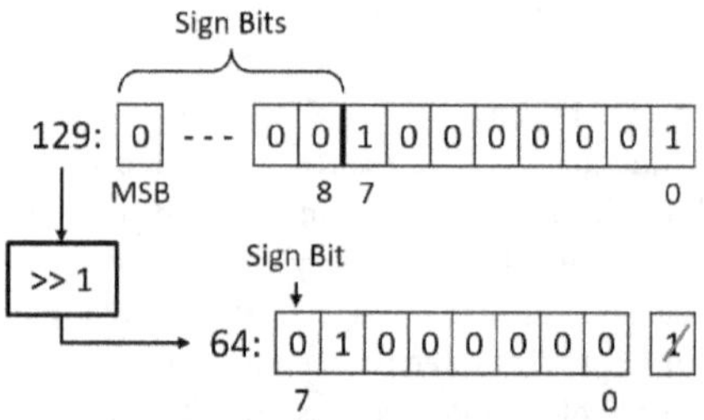


**Figure 3: The value 129 cannot be represented by a 1-byte signed word, but after right shifting by 1 bit, it can be stored as 64. Upon decompression, the bits would be left shifted and the approximate value 128 would be returned.**

This shifting is advantageous because each difference's sign is now extended by an extra α bits. Take for example a 1-byte delta, which holds a signed value range of -128 to 127. In lossless BΔI, a 1-byte delta would not be wide enough to hold a subtraction result of 129, as shown in Figure 3. This means a (B, Δ) pair with a 2-byte wide delta (less efficient encoding) is needed to hold it. If the subtraction operands were approximated with α=1, then each difference produced would be right-shifted by one bit. The difference value of 129 is now represented as 64 (not 65 because the LSB was dropped). A 1-byte delta is now wide enough to hold the difference value, but at the cost of the LSB of precision. A (B, Δ) encoding with a 1-byte wide delta can now be selected over a 2-byte wide delta encoding. According to Table 1, this saves 4 extra bytes in the case of an 8-byte base.

## 4 Evaluation Methodology

We evaluate our approximate storage technique's impact on data compressibility and quality by testing it on images from the Caltech 101 dataset [20]. This image dataset features common objects that are used for recognition algorithm training and testing (i.e. RMS). First, we explore the effectiveness of our technique in MATLAB. Next, we evaluate the impact of our technique on application quality using an image recognition API from Clarifai [21]. Clarifai's general recognition model uses convolutional neural networks (CNNs), a popular technique in RMS, to recognize common objects in images. We evaluate Clarifai's object prediction probability on the image dataset across degrading quality levels in order to determine our technique's impact on RMS application quality. We use the highest quality version of each image (α=0) as a baseline for measuring prediction probability degradation on lower quality versions (α>0). Finally, we synthesize the design into a gate level netlist using Cadence Encounter RTL compiler with a TSMC 65nm standard cell library.

# 5 Results

Here we present data on compression ratios, error metrics, image prediction, energy consumption, and hardware overhead. Our results show approximate storage of media data can significantly improve effective memory capacity and energy consumption for a small drop in media quality. In Figure 4, we present the decompressed approximate versions of a sample image for α = {0, 4, 8}. The quality loss in these images is similar to that for all approximated images in the dataset for the same value of α.

α = 0 (lossless) α = 4 α = 8

**Figure 4: Sample lossless and approximated images.**

MATLAB results show that our lossy extension of BΔI can achieve significantly higher compression ratios than lossless BΔI. We assume that internal memory fragmentation is avoided through the work of a compressed memory management scheme (also assumed in [17]). In Figure 5, we present the average compression ratio with and without meta data across all image categories for each of the seven tested quality levels (induced by α). Pekhimenko et al [17] do not include this meta data in their compression ratio evaluations of BΔI. It also shows that all compression ratios for α ≥ 4 are greater than that of lossless BΔI. Note that the remainder of our results do account for meta data.

Next we evaluate the errors induced by approximation using PSNR. Figure 6 shows the average compression ratio of all images versus average PSNR. For lossy compressed images, 28dB is considered an acceptable level of quality [15]. Our PSNR results show that acceptable image quality is maintained for α ≤ 6.

While PSNR is useful for evaluating error for lossy compressed images, it does not show the potential impact on application quality. Here we evaluate the impact of image quality loss on the accuracy of the Clarifai API [21]. Figure 7 shows average image compression ratio and concept prediction probability for every simulated level of α. Figure 8 shows the relative improvement and degradation of compression ratio and concept prediction probability respectively. For α ≤ 4, there is negligible loss in prediction probability, but compression ratios are low (< 1.1). This indicates that low levels of approximation on image data will not affect application output quality, but offers no practical increase in effective memory capacity. For α ≥ 8, compression ratio increases to nearly 1.6, but the prediction probability falls to less than 50%, an unacceptable amount of quality loss. When α=6, there is a slight drop in prediction probability and the compression ratio improves to nearly 1.2. Relative to the baseline lossless compression (α=0), prediction probability degrades by 3% and the compression ratio improves by over 15%.

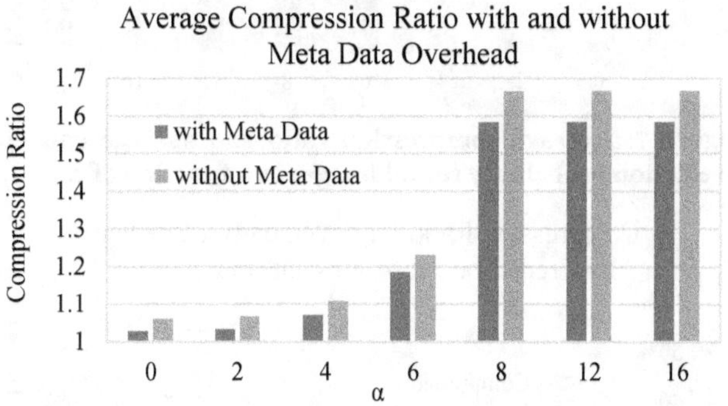


**Figure 5: Average image compression ratio with and without meta data for each level of approximation, α. Lossless BΔI is represented by α=0 without meta data.**

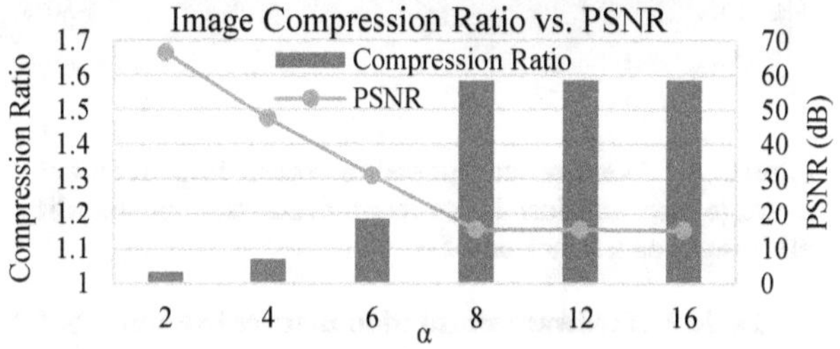


**Figure 6: Average compression ratio and average peak signal-to-noise (PSNR) for all images as a function of α.**

The simulated compression and decompression metrics of our work are presented in Table 2. Note that this model is capable of implementing α for all values in the range {0, 31}. In Table 3 we present the area and power overheads respectively of the shifters added to the BΔI compression technique. These tables show the major drawback to our technique is the significant increase in area and power relative to lossless BΔI. To evaluate the energy overhead of our technique, we compare its energy cost with the average energy cost of performing the DRAM accesses necessary to store an image using access operation data from [19]. Table 4 shows the average energy cost of performing enough DRAM accesses to store an image from our test dataset for the uncompressed size, BΔI compressed size, and approximated sizes. We compare this data with the energy cost of performing compression/decompression for an image, shown in Table 5, and find that total overhead energy cost is less than 0.1%. This shows that while the added shifters increase power and area relative to lossless BΔI, the total energy overhead is negligible.

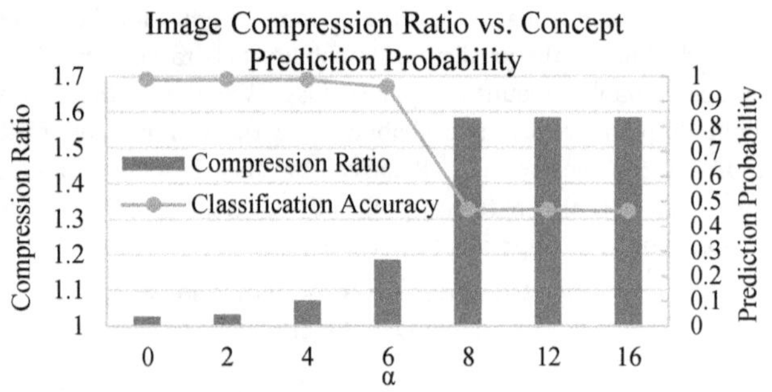


**Figure 7: Average compression ratio and average concept prediction probability for all images as a function of α.**

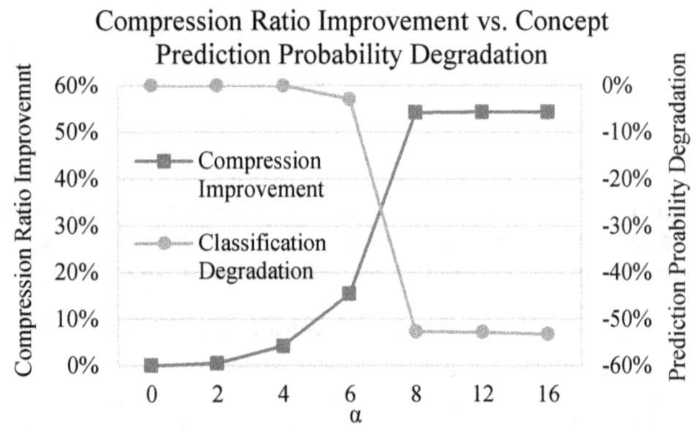


**Figure 8: Average compression ratio improvement and average degradation in concept prediction probability for all images as a function of α.**

**Table 2: Hardware simulation metrics in 65nm TSMC.**

| Module | Comp. | Decomp. | Total |
|---|---|---|---|
| Avg. Power (mW) | 1.506 | 0.467 | 1.974 |
| Latency (Cycles) | 1 | 1 | 2 |
| $F_{max}$ (MHz) | 210 | 360 | 360 |
| Area (mm$^2$) | 0.06245 | 0.03478 | 0.09723 |
| Area (kGE) | 53.39 | 29.74 | 83.13 |
| Throughput (Bytes/Cycle) | 32 | 32 | 64 |

**Table 3: Lossy compression and decompression shifters area (mm$^2$) and power (uW) overhead in 65nm TSMC.**

| Module | Comp. | Decomp. | Total |
|---|---|---|---|
| Total Area (mm$^2$) | 0.0624 | 0.0348 | 0.0972 |
| Shifters Area (mm$^2$) | 0.0203 | 0.0149 | 0.0351 |
| Shifters Area Overhead | 48.0% | 74.7% | 56.6% |
| Total Power (uW) | 1.506 | 0.467 | 1.974 |
| Shifters Power (uW) | 0.614 | 0.133 | 0.747 |
| Shifters Power Overhead | 68.8% | 39.7% | 60.9% |

**Table 4: Average DRAM access energy cost of storing images. Access energy data from Pedram et al. [19].**

| Image Version | Original | α=0 | α=2 | α=4 | α=6 | α=8 | α=12 |
|---|---|---|---|---|---|---|---|
| Avg. Access Energy Cost (uJ) | 67.3 | 65.6 | 65.3 | 63.0 | 56.9 | 42.5 | 42.5 |

**Table 5: Average compression and decompression energy costs relative to DRAM access energy cost.**

| Operation | Compression | Decompression | Total |
|---|---|---|---|
| Avg. Energy Cost per Image (uJ) | 0.0471 | 0.00852 | 0.0556 |
| Energy $Cost_{Op}$ / Energy $Cost_{Access}$ | 0.070% | 0.013% | 0.083% |

## 6 Conclusions

We presented a novel lossy compression technique using dynamic precision scaling to enable approximate storage for media data. Whereas small degrees of approximation bring marginal performance benefits and high degrees lead to unacceptable quality degradation, there exists an optimal point (α=6) that can yield significant performance improvements with low quality loss and low overhead costs. We find an increase in effective memory capacity of 15% for only 3% loss in image recognition accuracy and less than 0.1% total energy overhead. We conclude that approximate storage is an effective technique for increasing memory capacity of and decreasing access costs of media data.

## REFERENCES

[1] V. K. Chippa, S. T. Chakradhar, K. Roy and A. Raghunathan. Analysis and characterization of inherent application resilience for approximate computing. In DAC, 2013.
[2] X. Li and D. Yeung. Application-Level Correctness and its Impact on Fault Tolerance. In HPCA, 2007.
[3] P. Dubey. Recognition, Mining and Synthesis Moves Computers to the Era of Tera. Technology@Intel Magazine, February 2005.
[4] Song Liu, Karthik Pattabiraman, Thomas Moscibroda, and Benjamin G. Zorn. Flikker: saving DRAM refresh-power through critical data partitioning. SIGARCH Comput. Archit. News, March 2011.
[5] A. Sampson, J. Nelson, K. Strauss and L. Ceze. Approximate storage in solid-state memories. In MICRO, 2013.
[6] Hadi Esmaeilzadeh, Adrian Sampson, Luis Ceze, and Doug Burger. Architecture support for disciplined approximate programming. In ASPLOS, 2012.
[7] M. Cho, J. Schlessman, W. Wolf and S. Mukhopadhyay, "Reconfigurable SRAM Architecture with Spatial Voltage Scaling for Low Power Mobile Multimedia Applications," in IEEE Trans. on VLSI Systems, Jan. 2011.
[8] A. Ranjan, S. Venkataramani, X. Fong, K. Roy and A. Raghunathan, Approximate storage for energy efficient spintronic memories. In DAC, 2015.
[9] Bradley Thwaites, Gennady Pekhimenko, Hadi Esmaeilzadeh, Amir Yazdanbakhsh, Onur Mutlu, Jongse Park, Girish Mururu, and Todd Mowry. Rollback-free value prediction with approximate loads. In PACT, 2014.
[10] J. S. Miguel, M. Badr and N. E. Jerger. Load Value Approximation. In MICRO, 2014.
[11] J. S. Miguel, J. Albericio, A. Moshovos and N. E. Jerger. Doppelgänger: A cache for approximate computing. In MICRO, 2015.
[12] J. S. Miguel, J. Albericio, N. E. Jerger and A. Jaleel. The Bunker Cache for spatio-value approximation. In MICRO, 2016.
[13] A. Ranjan, A. Raha, V. Raghunathan and A. Raghunathan. Approximate memory compression for energy-efficiency. In ISLPED, 2017.
[14] Ye Tian, Qian Zhang, Ting Wang, Feng Yuan, and Qiang Xu. ApproxMA: Approximate Memory Access for Dynamic Precision Scaling. In GLSVLSI, 2015.
[15] C. Alvarez, J. Corbal and M. Valero. Fuzzy memoization for floating-point multimedia applications. In IEEE Trans. on Computers, July 2005.
[16] Y. Tian, T. Wang, Q. Zhang and Q. Xu. ApproxLUT: A novel approximate lookup table-based accelerator. In ICCAD, 2017.
[17] Gennady Pekhimenko, Vivek Seshadri, Onur Mutlu, Phillip B. Gibbons, Michael A. Kozuch, and Todd C. Mowry. Base-delta-immediate compression: practical data compression for on-chip caches. In PACT, 2012.
[18] Mittal, S. and Vetter, J. S., "A Survey of Architectural Approaches for Data Compression in Cache and Main Memory Systems," in IEEE Trans. on Parallel Distrib. Syst., 2016.
[19] A. Pedram, S. Richardson, M. Horowitz, S. Galal and S. Kvatinsky, "Dark Memory and Accelerator-Rich System Optimization in the Dark Silicon Era," in IEEE Design & Test, April 2017.
[20] L. Fei-Fei, R. Fergus and Perona, P. Learning generative visual models from few training examples: an incremental Bayesian approach tested on 101 object categories. In CVPR, 2004.
[21] https://clarifai.com/

# Thermal Fingerprinting of FPGA Designs through High-Level Synthesis

Jianqi Chen and Benjamin Carrion Schafer
Department of Electrical and Computer Engineering
The University of Texas at Dallas
jianqi.chen@utdallas.edu,schaferb@utdallas.edu

## ABSTRACT

This work investigates if temperature can be used to fingerprint FPGA designs and presents a method to generate a large number of functionally equivalent FPGA designs such that each design has a unique distinguishable thermal signature. The main methodology behind this work is based on the design space exploration of each hardware accelerator in the design specified as a behavioral description (*e.g.* ANSI-C, C++ or SystemC) to obtain a trade-off curve of designs with unique area vs. performance trade-offs as well as a third dimension that consists of the difference in their thermal profile. Experimental results, prototyping different hardware accelerators on a FPGA, and using a high resolution infrared camera, show the usability of our proposed method, which is able to distinguish between the different design versions and hence can serve to detect if an FPGA design is unlawfully being used.

## CCS CONCEPTS

**• Security and privacy → Hardware reverse engineering; • Hardware → Reconfigurable logic applications; Temperature optimization; Datapath optimization;**

## KEYWORDS

High-Level Synthesis; Design Space Exploration; Temperature; Fingerprinting; FPGAs

**ACM Reference Format:**

Jianqi Chen and Benjamin Carrion Schafer . 2019. Thermal Fingerprinting of FPGA Designs through High-Level Synthesis. In *Great Lakes Symposium on VLSI 2019 (GLSVLSI '19), May 9–11, 2019, Tysons Corner, VA, USA.* ACM, New York, NY, USA, 4 pages. https://doi.org/10.1145/3299874.3318030

## 1 INTRODUCTION

Semiconductor companies were in the past vertically integrated and had therefore tight control over the entire design, manufacturing and distribution chain. However, this trend has shifted due to the large costs of setting up their own production facilities. Many semiconductor companies are now fabless and mainly focus on the architectural development of the Hardware (HW) and contract silicon foundries for the manufacturing process. Second, due to increasingly tight time-to-market deadlines, semiconductor companies now heavily rely on third party IPs (3PIPs).


ACM ISBN 978-1-4503-6252-8/19/05...$15.00
https://doi.org/10.1145/3299874.3318030

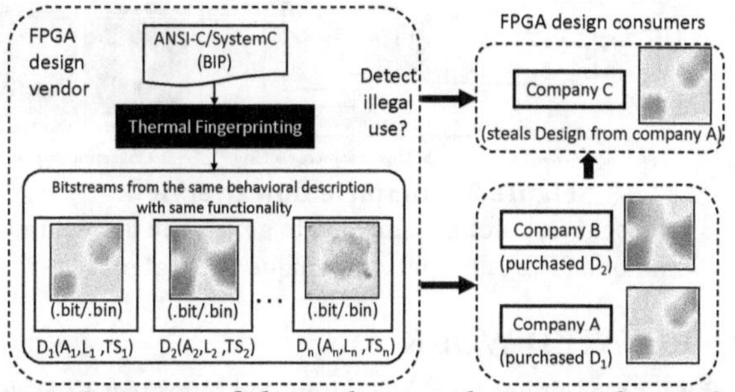


**Figure 1: Overview of thermal-aware detection of unauthorized hardware accelerators.**

In parallel to this, a fundamental paradigm shift in computer architecture is taking place. With the breakdown of Dennards scaling not all the transistors in the IC can be powered for a given thermal design constraint. One solution that is being proposed is to customize the computing platforms to the application domain, also known as domain specific computing.

The main problem when adapting these computing systems to different domains is that it is driving IC design to complexities never seen before, making their design extremely challenging. To address these issues, companies are relying on third party design houses to meet their schedules. These have in turn started to rely on High-Level Synthesis (HLS) to increase their design productivity. HLS has one particular advantage that this work exploits to create unique identifiable designs: The ability to generate different functional equivalent hardware accelerators from the behavioral description.

This distinct advantage of C-based VLSI design will be exploited in this work to automatically generate functional equivalent FPGA designs with similar area and performance but with unique intrinsic signatures, where in this work we use temperature as unique signature. This will allow FPGA design houses to deliver different design versions to different customers and then identify in the field if their designs are being lawfully used. Fig. 1 shows this graphically, where the FPGA design vendor generates a variety of different designs as bitstreams to configure the FPGA. Each design has a unique area ($A$), latency ($L$) and thermal signature ($TS$). These designs are licensed/sold to different companies (A and B in this case). It should be noted that in this work we assumes that the design consumer can encrypt the bitstream and hence the design provider cannot simply compare bitstreams. In summary, the main contributions of this work can be summarized as follows:

- Investigate if thermal profiles of hardware accelerators mapped on FPGAs can be used as fingerprints.

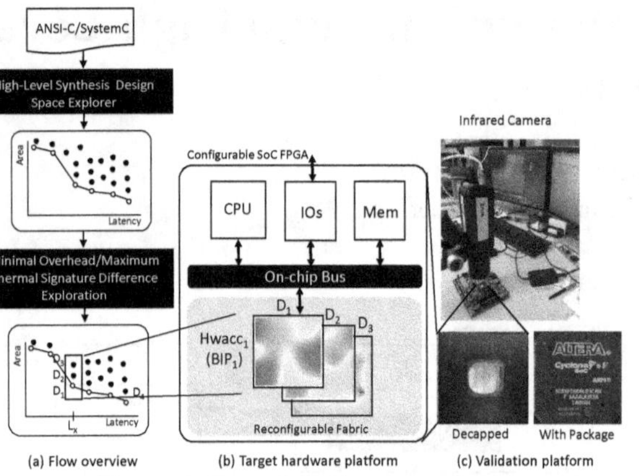


**Figure 2: Complete flow overview.**

- Present an automatic method to generate a large number of unique FPGA designs with unique thermal profiles.

## 2 RELATED WORK

Different techniques have been proposed to protect VLSI design companies from the unlawful use and/or reverse engineering of their designs.

The authors in [1] makes use of the electromagnetic emanations (EME) of ICs as fingerprints. In this case, EME are used to detect malicious alteration of the IC (*a.k.a* Hardware Trojan). Other work, uses the same principle to detect counterfeited ICs [2]. In [3] a tag circuit is inserted into an IC as a heat source, and the IC temperature variation over time can be extracted as the watermark. This thermal watermark is designed to identify falsely labeled chips, but it is not effective for preventing illegal use of IPs. This method is also not suitable for small and low power IPs because the area and power overhead is not acceptable. Also in [4] the authors use dynamic power analysis to detect the existence of malicious executions of a program running on a microcontroller. Based on this, the problem addressed in this work can be formulated as follows:

**Problem Formulation:** Given a behavioral description $C$ to be mapped as a hardware accelerator onto a FPGA, find $N$ number of unique micro-architectures obtained automatically from $C$ that lead to the most different thermal signatures ($TS$), $TS_{diff}(max)$, such that these micro-architectures can be easily distinguished apart when mapped onto the FPGA using thermal measurement equipment, *e.g.* an infrared camera. In addition, these micro-architectures should lead to the smallest possible area and performance overhead compared the closest Pareto-optimal equivalent micro-architectures obtained from $C$, that do not take into consideration $TS_{diff}$.

## 3 FINGERPRINTING BEHAVIORAL IPS

Fig. 2 shows an overview of the complete flow, the target platform, and the measurement equipment used to retrieve the thermal map. The main idea behind this work is to generate a pool of hardware accelerators mapped onto a FPGA with unique thermal signatures and sell these to different companies. These thermal signatures are registered in a database that can then be retrieved and compared against commercial products where the FPGA design vendor suspects the unlawful use of their design. Because the package of IC diffuses the temperature, this comparison will have to be done by decapping the package of the suspected IC and comparing it with the thermal profile stored in the database. This nevertheless only has to be done on the product obtained from the open market once.

Our proposed method takes as input a behavioral description ($C$) for HLS (*e.g.* in ANSI-C or SystemC) and generates $N$ designs with largest thermal signature difference ($TS_{diff}$). The user can specify any constrain regarding the designs, although the most favorable scenario is the case in which no constraints are specified, as any designs from the entire search space can be used.

The most common method of use, should generate multiple designs with the smallest area and latency overhead compare to the Pareto-optimal designs generated from the behavioral description when only area and performance are considered. These Pareto-optimal designs can be obtained by performing a HLS design space exploration (DSE), *e.g.* [5]. The result of a traditional HLS DSE is a trade-off curve with Pareto-optimal micro-architectures (HLS is a single process synthesis method), also called dominating designs ($POptList$), such that $POptList = \{D_1(A_1, L_1), \ldots, D_n(A_n, L_n)\}$, where each design $D_i$ is characterized by its area (A) and latency (L). This step is important because the objective of this work is to find designs with maximum thermal signature difference, but with smallest area and latency overheads with respect to the Pareto-optimal designs. An design consumer will most probably not acquire the design if the area and performance of the design is much worse than the same design that does not take into consideration the thermal signature, especially considering that the overhead does only benefit the FPGA design vendor and not the design consumer.

Thus, our proposed method, by default, includes a first phase that performs an HLS DSE for the given behavioral description in order to find the Pareto-optimal designs. It then continues by generating designs with the highest thermal signature difference and lowest area and performance overheads compared to them.

To validate the proposed method, designs with highest $TS_{diff}$ are prototyped on a FPGA and a high resolution infrared camera used to retrieve the thermal map, which is in turn compared with the golden pre-characterized thermal map. The main thermal-aware HLS DSE flow is sub-divided into 3 main phases as follows:

**Phase I : HLS Design Space Exploration:** This first phase is executed by default, but is only required if the objective is to maximize thermal signature difference and reduce the area and performance overheads compared to the temperature un-aware Pareto-optimal designs. The HLS explorer proposed in this work is based on a previously developed genetic algorithm (GA) [6]. In this case, the two objectives that need to be minimized are area and latency, where the latency is given in clock cycles as HLS tools do not predict well delays (*e.g.* they cannot account for the wire delay). Thus, the explorer uses the following cost function. $C = \alpha A + \beta L$, that is adaptively modified during the exploration process in order to explore the complete trade-off plane, where $A$ and $L$ are normalized to account for the size difference.

**Phase II : Thermal Signature (TS) Difference Maximization Exploration:** The goal of this phase is to find micro-architectures that have the highest thermal-signature difference ($TS_{diff}$) with minimum area and latency overheads compared to the Pareto-optimal designs found in phase 1 or any other constraint imposed, if any. Fig. 3 shows an overview of this complete phase, where the

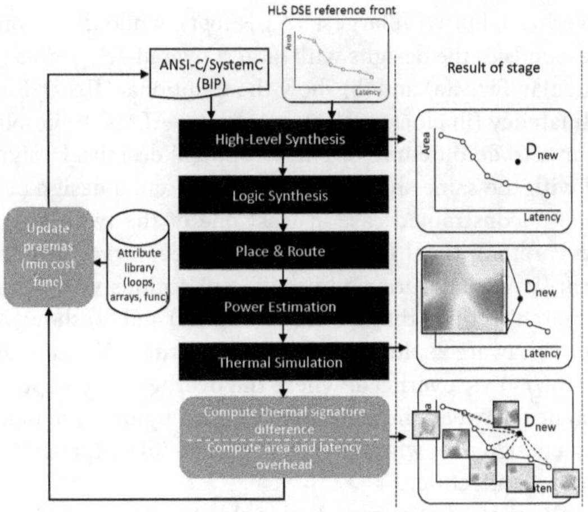


**Figure 3: Thermal signature difference exploration flow.**

black rectangles indicate third party tools and the gray ones our own method. This phase can be further sub-divided into three steps as follows:

**Thermal Map Generation:** A thermal map is generated for every newly synthesized design in this phase. This thermal map is used to generate a unique thermal signature and to guide the thermal-aware explorer in generating new designs that maximize the thermal signature difference with the already existing designs.

The thermal map is generated by feeding the results of the logic synthesis, placement & routing and power estimation to an open source thermal simulator. In this case Hotspot [7] is used.

**Thermal Signature Difference Computation:** In this step, the differences between the different thermal maps of the hardware accelerators generated are determined. For this, it has to be remembered that the final goal is to be able to recognize the thermal map when mapped onto a FPGA. Because the resolution of the infrared equipment is relatively low and considering the small die size of the FPGA, the exact location where the accelerator is placed cannot be retrieved. Thus, to be able to compare two thermal maps, our proposed method aligns the hottest cells of the two thermal maps and extracts two windows of equal sizes around the hottest cells. It then obtains a unique thermal signature ($TS$) for each extracted window. To generate the $TS$, we use perceptual hashing [8], which is an algorithm commonly used in finding online copyright infringements as well as digital forensics. The advantage of perceptual hashing is that it is robust enough to take into account dissimilarities, but flexible enough to distinguish between different thermal maps. Traditional cryptographic hashing methods, *e.g.* SHA and MD5 result in completely different hashes if a single bit changes, thus, making them not useful for this application. Perceptual hashing, in contrast, can be used to compare two images by calculating the Hamming distance. These dissimilarities include rotation and skew. This hash value is considered the thermal signature of a unique micro-architecture, which enables our work to compute the $TS_{diff}$ between pairs of $TS$ from different micro-architectures by computing the hamming distances between the $TS$, *e.g.* $TS_i$ and $TS_j$, $TS_{diff}(i, j) = \{H(TS_i, TS_j)\}$, where a large $H$ represents the hamming distance between the two perceptual hashes.

**Thermal-aware Exploration:** The thermal-aware explorer has the goal of finding micro-architectures from the behavioral description which have the largest thermal-signature difference. This explorer is based around the genetic algorithm used to generate the reference trade-off curve in phase I, but makes use of a different cost function. Initially a pool of random new designs is generated. It can also be executed in two modes: Mode I is unconstrained or mode II constrained. Mode I implies that phase 1 of our method is not required as the goal is simply to find the micro-architectures within the complete search space that have the largest thermal-signature difference without considering the area and latency differences between these two. The cost function that the genetic algorithm uses is $C = -TS_{diff}(i, j)$, where $TS_{diff}(i, j)$ is the thermal signature difference between micro-architectures $M_i$ and $M_j$. The negative sign implies that objective is to maximize $TS$ between different micro-architecture pairs.

In a more realistic case, the goal is not only to find the micro-architectures with highest $TS_{diff}$, but also with minimum overhead (area and latency) compared to the Pareto-optimal designs generated in phase I, as the FPGA design consumer, will most likely not acquire the design from the vendor if the overhead is too large compared to any competing offerings, especially considering that the design consumer does not benefit at all from the thermal fingerprinting. In this case, the explorer's cost function is $C = -\alpha TS_{diff}(i, j) + \beta DistPO$, where $DistPO$ is the smallest distance in terms of area and latency of the newly generated design with any of the Pareto-optimal designs on the trade-off curve found in phase I. In particular, $DistPO = \sqrt{((A_i - A_j)/A_{max})^2 + ((L_i - L_j)/L_{max})^2}$, where each term is normalized with the maximum value ($A_{max}$ and $L_{max}$). $\alpha$ and $\beta$ allow the search to either find designs with larger thermal difference ($\alpha$=0.9,$\beta$=0.1), smaller overheads ($\alpha$=0.1,$\beta$=0.9)or a balance of both ($\alpha$=0.5,$\beta$=0.5), thus allowing the explorer to sweep the entire search space. Based on this, the explorer follows the exact same mechanism as described in phase I, but with any of these two cost functions based on the preference set by the user. In addition, the explorer performs a logic synthesis and a thermal simulation for every new micro-architecture generated.

**Phase III : In-situ FPGA characterization:** The thermal simulation results are used to quickly find micro-architectures with largest thermal difference, but due to practical considerations like contribution of wires on power consumption, mismatches in the thermal model and actual FPGA. These thermal simulations will inevitably differ from the measured thermal map. Thus, a final step in the proposed method is to map the most promising micro-architectures (largest $TS_{diff}$) onto the target FPGA and characterize the thermal map (extract the $TS$) in-situ.

For this, Fig. 2 shows the experimental setup. To get more accurate measurement results, the FPGA is decapsulated (decapped) to make the die visible through laser ablation (performed by a specialized company). 90% of the die was exposed through this procedure and the FPGA was still fully functioning. Although costly and time consuming, this invasive method is only required once to characterize each of the micro-architectures being sold. It is also only required once to test the suspicious products line, not every product. The thermal signature extracted is then added to the thermal design database. To account for process variations, we repeated

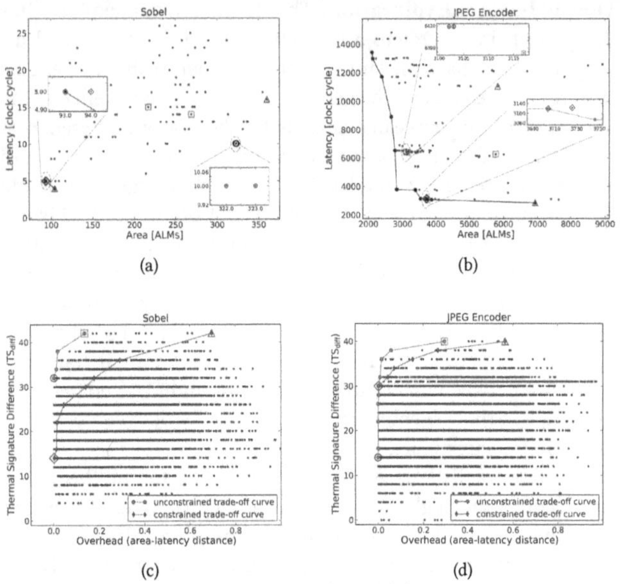


**Figure 4: Exploration Results (a) and (b) Area vs. Latency Exploration Results, (c) and (d) $TS_{diff}$ vs. overhead trade-off for sobel and jpeg encoder respectively**

this for three different FPGAs of the same family. We observed no differences in the thermal profile and hence all three measurements led to the same $TS$.

The same thermal signature difference computation is based again on perceptual hashing. In particular, we extract a thermal window from the measured thermal image with the same size as the simulation window with the hottest cell being at the center. Because the measurement from the camera is *noisy*, a pre-processing step is applied to create an even thermal map by applying a gaussian filter. Then perceptual hashing is applied onto this window to generate the thermal signature. This measured thermal signature is the actual golden signature ($TS_{golden}$) used as reference when comparing suspicious unlawful FPGA design.

# 4 EXPERIMENTAL RESULTS

Two computational intensive applications, amenable to hardware acceleration were selected in order to test our proposed method. For this purpose, two SystemC benchmarks of different complexities from the freely available Synthesizable SystemC Benchmark suite S2CBench [9] were used. In particular sobel (edge detection algorithm) and JPEG (jpeg encoder).

The HLS tool used is CyberWorkBench from NEC and the FPGA an Intel Cyclone V SoC FPGA mounted on a Terasic DE1-SoC board. The thermal measurement equipment used is a FLIR A655sc infrared camera with 640x480 LWIR resolution with 17 micro pixels .

The micro-architectures found during the exploration were mapped onto the FPGA. Two sets of experimental results are presented in this section. The first shows the results of the thermal-signature aware exploration flow while the second studies the robustness of the method.

Fig. 4 shows the results of the constrained and unconstrained exploration flow resulting in two trade-off curves of Pareto-optimal designs pairs, where we highlight two Pareto-optimal design pairs from each flow. The first pair corresponds to the designs with lowest overall overhead, but with largest $TS_{diff}(opt)$, while the second pair corresponds to the designs with largest overall $TS_{diff}(max)$.

In particular, Fig. 4(a) and (b) show the traditional HLS DSE results with latency (in clock cycles) vs. area (in ALMs) trade-offs, resulting in a trade-off curve of Pareto-optimal designs. Designs encircled with the same shape and color represent a design pair, where for the constrained case at least one of the two designs has to be Pareto-optimal (lay on the reference curve). For the sake of clarity, we have zoomed in different regions which contain micro-architectures that are close . Fig. 4(c) and (d) show the actual thermal-aware exploration results as thermal signature difference ($TS_{Diff}$) vs. overhead, where the overhead is computed as the distance between the two design. In this figure, each point represents a design pair, whereas in Fig. 4(a) and (b) each point is a single micro-architecture.

The results show that our method is able to return a trade-off curve or design pairs with unique $TS_{Diff}$ vs. overhead. Intuitively, the larger the overhead is, the larger the $TS_{Diff}$ is as the micro-architectures have very different internal structure. E.g. an array is synthesized as register and loops unrolled, while in the second micro-architecture the array is synthesized as RAM and the loops not unrolled. The results also show that the unconstrained method finds more design pairs with large $TS_{Diff}$, but larger overheads vs Pareto-optimal designs. This again is expected, as design pairs from the complete design space can be chosen as opposed to the constrained case, where one design has to be Pareto-optimal, thus reducing the search space considerably.

These results indicate that our proposed method works well in finding design candidates with high thermal signature difference.

# 5 CONCLUSION

In this work we have presented a method to generate hardware accelerators with unique thermal signatures from a single behavioral description. We perform detailed measurements using a state of the art infrared camera and conclude that the proposed approach can be used to fingerprint these designs.

# REFERENCES

[1] J. Balasch, B. Gierlichs, and I. Verbauwhede, "Electromagnetic circuit fingerprints for hardware trojan detection," in *2015 IEEE International Symposium on Electromagnetic Compatibility (EMC)*, pp. 246–251, Aug 2015.
[2] U. Guin, K. Huang, and D. DiMase, "Counterfeit integrated circuits: A rising threat in the global semiconductor supply chain," *Proceedings of the IEEE*, vol. 102, no. 8, pp. 1207–1228, 2014.
[3] T. Kean, D. McLaren, and C. Marsh, "Verifying the authenticity of chip designs with the designtag system," in *2008 IEEE International Workshop on Hardware-Oriented Security and Trust*, pp. 59–64, June 2008.
[4] K. Hasegawa, Y. M., and T. N., "Detecting the existence of malfunctions in microcontrollers utilizing power analysis," in *2018 IOLTS*, pp. 1–6, 2018.
[5] H.-Y. Liu and L. P. Carloni, "On learning-based methods for design-space exploration with high-level synthesis," in *2013 50th ACM/EDAC/IEEE Design Automation Conference (DAC)*, pp. 1–7, 2013.
[6] B. C. Schäfer and K. Wakabayashi, "Machine learning predictive modelling high-level synthesis design space exploration," *IET Computers & Digital Techniques*, vol. 6, no. 3, pp. 153–159, 2012.
[7] W. Huang, S. Ghosh, S. Velusamy, K. Sankaranarayanan, K. Skadron, and M. R. Stan, "Hotspot: a compact thermal modeling methodology for early-stage vlsi design," *IEEE Transactions on Very Large Scale Integration (VLSI) Systems*, vol. 14, pp. 501–513, May 2006.
[8] J. Fridrich and M. Goljan, "Robust hash functions for digital watermarking," in *Proceedings International Conference on Information Technology: Coding and Computing (Cat. No.PR00540)*, pp. 178–183, 2000.
[9] B. Carrion Schafer and A. Mahapatra, "S2CBench:Synthesizable SystemC Benchmark Suite," *IEEE Embedded Systems Letters*, vol. 6, no. 3, pp. 53–56, 2014.

# Deep RNN-Oriented Paradigm Shift through BOCANet: Broken Obfuscated Circuit Attack

Fatemeh Tehranipoor
San Francisco State University
tehranipoor@sfsu.edu

Nima Karimian
San Jose State University
nima.karimian@sjsu.edu

Mehran Mozaffari Kermani
University of South Florida
mehran2@usf.edu

Hamid Mahmoodi
San Francisco State University
mahmoodi@sfsu.edu

## ABSTRACT

Logic encryption obfuscation has been used for thwarting counterfeiting, overproduction, and reverse engineering but vulnerable to attacks. However, it was recently shown that *satisfiability − checking* (SAT) can potentially compromise hardware obfuscation circuits. In this paper, we develop a novel attack called *BOCANet* that can be beneficial from deep learning architecture to compromise hardware obfuscation circuits's key. Our approach involves exploiting deep recurrent neural network (D-RNN) model, and developing attack model to compromise the obfuscated hardware at least an order-of magnitude more efficiently and under resource-constrained scenarios. In our experiments, the *BOCANet* approach achieves an average success rate of 100% for 32 bit key size, 93.4% for 64 bit key size, 92.2% and 91.7% for 128 and 256 bit key size, respectively.

## KEYWORDS

Deep recurrent neural network, Hardware obfuscation, Logic encryption.

**ACM Reference Format:**

Fatemeh Tehranipoor, Nima Karimian, Mehran Mozaffari Kermani, and Hamid Mahmoodi. 2019. Deep RNN-Oriented Paradigm Shift through BOCANet: Broken Obfuscated Circuit Attack. In *Great Lakes Symposium on VLSI 2019 (GLSVLSI '19), May 9–11, 2019, Tysons Corner, VA, USA.* ACM, New York, NY, USA, 4 pages. https://doi.org/10.1145/3299874.3318031

## 1 INTRODUCTION

Hardware obfuscation technique is the process of transforming a function *F* to another function *F(O)*, which has the same functionality as *F*, e.g., input/output nature, and conceals (locks) the functionality of *F* (as shown in Fig. 1(a)) and/or the structure of an IC from attackers. Through logic encryption, a variant of hardware obfuscation techniques, a given combinational circuit is modified with newly-added inputs, denoted as key inputs, to ensure that the encrypted/locked circuit operates correctly, i.e., produces correct outputs, under a specific key value assertion (valid key). Fig. 1(b) shows a general schematic of logic locking obfuscation technique which contains functional input (input patterns to the circuit), key input (secret key that is stored in tamper resistant memory), locked circuit (including normal gates and added gates for key gates), and outputs from the locked circuit. An original circuit design and the its obfuscated circuit using extra gates are shown in Fig. 1(c) and (d). In logic encryption obfuscation, the correct key must not be accessible to the untrusted foundry. Otherwise, the foundry can use it to activate overproduction of ICs and sell them improperly and illegally [16]. Unfortunately, logic encryption has been recently proven to be compromised by a number of research groups, leaving it potentially vulnerable to various attacks in order to learn the correct key (secret key). Examples of such attacks include satisfiability-checking (SAT) based attack in [11] proposed recently by Subramayan *et al.*, a fault analysis attack that directly propagates the key bits to the circuit outputs proposed in [7], and a randomized, local key-searching algorithm to search the key that can satisfy a subset of correct input/output patterns proposed in [6]. Recent research has also focused on attacks/countermeasures for logic locking [9, 17, 19]. Nevertheless, we note that although SAT attack can successfully break several existing logic locking techniques, not only there exist countermeasures against such attacks in the state-of-the-art (including the recent delay+logic locking (DLL) scheme in [16]), but the sheer amount of time/resources to mount the attack could hinder its efficacy. Note that SAT attack takes few hours to effectively predict the secret key [11].

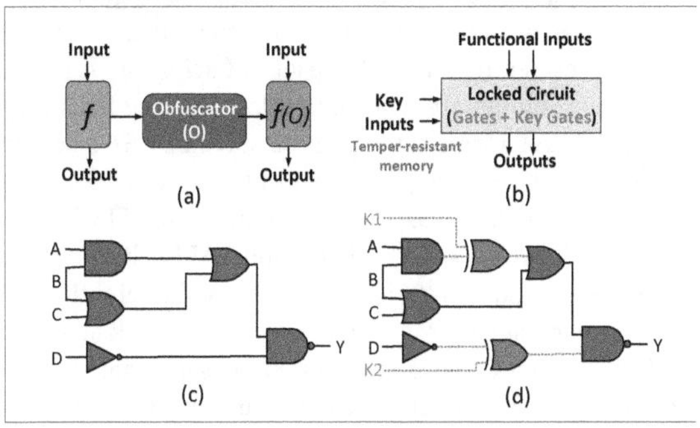


**Figure 1: Schematic of (a) a general obfuscation scheme, (b) a general logic locking obfuscation, (c) an original circuit without key gates and key inputs, and (d) an encrypted circuit with key gates and key inputs.**


*GLSVLSI '19, May 9–11, 2019, Tysons Corner, VA, USA*

ACM ISBN 978-1-4503-6252-8/19/05...$15.00
https://doi.org/10.1145/3299874.3318031

In this paper, we propose a new attack model against logic encryption obfuscation using deep recurrent neural network (D-RNN) denoted as BOCANet: Broken obfuscated circuit attack (see [3] for background). Given a very small number of input/output patterns (< 0.5%) from the logic encryption obfuscated circuit, this attack enables not only to reconstruct the secret key but also predict the unknown outputs by giving the input patterns of the circuit (without the need of secret key) and vice versa.
Specifically, the major contributions of the proposed work are as follows. **i). Broken obfuscated circuit attack, BOCANet:** We introduce BOCANet, a novel attack framework scheme. BOCANet incorporates D-RNN to compromise the secret key from obfuscated hardware (logic locking) an order-of-magnitude more efficiently (> $20X$ faster with relatively high success rate) compared to existing SAT attacks. **ii). BOCANet strength properties:** In order to objectively measure the success of the proposed attack, we test our BOCANet scheme to break a number of experimented $ISCAS-85$ benchmarks (16 different) successfully. In order to demonstrate the effectiveness of our proposed framework, we evaluated the benchmarks with varying secret key sizes (32-bit, 64-bit, 128-bit, and 256-bit). **iii). BOCANet obliviousness of secret keys and unknown I/O pairs:** We consider two attack frameworks, Attack1 (Key Reconstruction) and Attack2 (Output Guessing).

The rest of the paper is organized as follows. We first describe SAT attack in Section 2. In Section 3, we present the BOCANet in details. Section 4 shows the results. The literature review is presented in Section 5. We finally conclude the paper in Section 6.

## 2 SAT ATTACKS

Satisfiability-checking (SAT) based attack is a newly-proposed attack [11], threatening the security of logic encryption circuits by deciphering a functionality-correct key (w.r.t. combinational logic) of most locking techniques within a few hours [16]. The main step in the SAT-based attack is to use two copies of the encryption logic circuit with the same input but different keys (lock-keys), under a given constraint, to check whether it is still possible to generate different outputs from the locked circuit. Such small number of input/output pairs are denoted as differentiating input patterns (DIPs) that can be used to eliminate incorrectly-guessed keys. Each DIP is then used to query the original circuit blackbox to get the correct output. The DIP with output is then used to further constrain the keys under consideration. In fact, the idea of using DIP is to exclude at least one wrong key from consideration. Finding DIPs requires a sequence of SAT formula that can be solved by SAT solvers. In order to defeat SAT attacks, a number of research works have proposed inserting additional SAT attack resistant logic blocks, e.g., the Anti-SAT block by Xie *et al.* [14] [15] and SARLock by Yasin *et al.* [18]. However, authors in [20] presented the vulnerabilities of Anti-SAT and propose signal probability skew (SPS) attack against Anti-SAT block. In general, there are several issues associated with SAT attacks in which we have resolved them in our BOCANet scheme. SAT attacks require a large amount of time and resources (area, power consumption, and delay). Also, extremely poor or fail performance is seen from SAT attack to find the solution for benchmarks with large secret key size; making them computationally infeasible. Furthermore and more importantly, there exist countermeasures against them in recent years that illustrates SAT attacks impracticality [14], [15],[18], etc. To speed this up, we propose a lightweight architecture based on LSTM. Our model is not only more efficient compared to existing SAT base attack in terms of computationally complexity, but also works on resource-constrained scenarios.

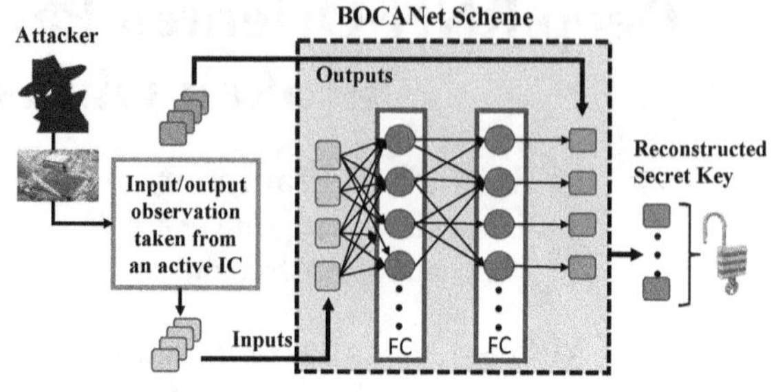


**Figure 2: Block diagram of our proposed BOCANet scheme.**

## 3 BOCANET SCHEME

### 3.1 Data Acquisition

For the purpose of data acquisition to test the vulnerability of logic locking obfuscated circuit, we consider open source obfuscation benchmarks [1] for our deep learning-based attack experiments. These benchmarks are combinational logic circuits with complexities ranging from less than a thousand to more than five thousand gates. These benchmarks utilize the logic-based obfuscation technique using random key gate insertion with secret key sizes ranging from 32 bits to 256 bits. We note that these keys are typically programmed in an on-chip non-volatile memory in a trusted environment after manufacturing. The size of the key is known information as it is visible form the circuit interface, but the key value is unknown. To generate input/output stimulus/response, we setup a SystemVerilog testbench [10] for each benchmark to simulate its gate level Netlist with randomly-generated input stimuli and obtain corresponding output responses. For large number of inputs, it would be prohibitive to simulate all possible input combinations as we would run out of either time and/or computer memory space to generate and store all combinations. Hence, we generate as many random stimuli as sufficient for the deep learning algorithm to come to a reasonable estimate of the key.

### 3.2 Attack Scheme

In this work, we introduce a new framework attack called BOCANet in which we use deep learning through recurrent neural network, i.e., D-RNN, to predict the key. The D-RNN is a deep learning-based algorithm that can perform the same task for every element of a sequence (data), with the output being dependent on the previous computations. In the BOCANet attack, our assumption is that there exist some input/output patterns from an obfuscated circuit available for an attacker in order to predict the keys. For these experiments, we have considered several benchmark circuits [1] with different key sizes (32-bit, 64-bit, 128-bit, and 256-bit) to evaluate the vulnerabilities and susceptibilities of this logic locking circuits to reconstruct keys. Here, we also assume that an attacker has access to only less than 0.5% of the total I/O pairs available

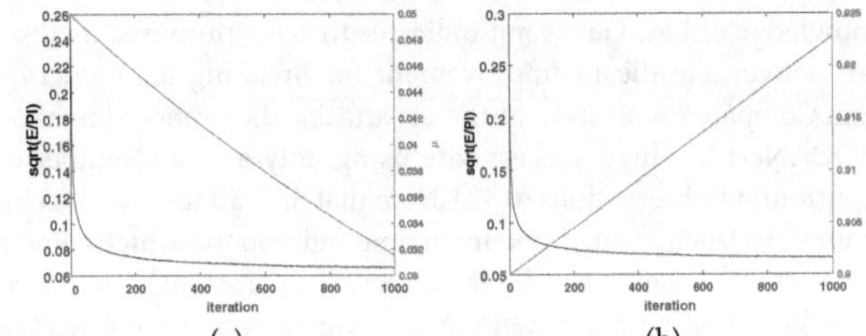

Figure 3: The MSE error (blue curve) *vs.* (a) training step (red line) and (b) momentum (red line).

from the obfuscated circuit to reduce the complexity of the attack framework. Note that in our pilot study, the goal is to see whether deep learning is able to generate the key of logic locking circuit using input/output stimulus. For the purpose of this experiment, since we do not have access to an activated IC, using ISCAS-85 obfuscated benchmarks, we had to manually set a key for the design under test, and check to see whether our proposed scheme can reconstruct the same key or not. In order to train our BOCANet scheme, we have implemented D-RNN [4] with long short-term memory (LSTM) [12].

## 3.3 Deep RNN Implementation

Recurrent neural networks have recently attracted prominent attention for modeling variable length sequences [5]. A D-RNN is a deep structure of a neural network that operates in time. At each time step, it accepts an input vector, updates its hidden layer through non-linear activation functions, and uses it to predict its output. Since D-RNN's hidden layer can store high-dimensional information, and its nonlinear dynamics can implement a powerful computation, it forms D-RNN to form a strong model to perform modeling and prediction functions with a high complex structure. In this paper, we explore deep extension of basic RNN to model our BOCANet for reconstructing key from obfuscated circuits. Given a sequence of inputs $x_1, x_2, x_3, ..., x_p$ and outputs $y_1, y_2, y_3, ..., y_q$, we want to predict the key $k_1, k_2, x_3, ..., k_n$. In order to do that, we train I/O pairs with LSTM RNN architecture.

In order to evaluate the performance of our attack model (BOCANet), one potential metric is mean-square-error (MSE). MSE is a cost function that measures the average of the squares of the errors; the difference between the estimator, i.e., obfuscated circuit output, and what is estimated, i.e., predicted output. Fig. 3(a) illustrates the impact of training step *vs.* momentum coefficient on MSE. As can be seen in Fig. 3(a), by decreasing the training step in each epoch, the D-RNN weight can be adjusted more efficiently than constant training. Fig. 3(b) represents how an increase in momentum has impact on the error rate of trained weights.

# 4 EXPERIMENTAL RESULTS

**(i) Training BOCANet**: To train our BOCANet scheme, we consider a small number of input/output observations taken from obfuscated circuit and from a huge pool of all possible I/O patterns. For instance, if a benchmark has $N$ inputs, $2^N$ different input stimuli are possible. We assume that the attacker has access to a limited

Table 1: Experimented obfuscated ISCAS-85 benchmarks, their characteristics, the required compromise time, and attack success rate

| | # Inputs/Outputs | # Gates | Key-Size | Time (s) | Success-Rate |
|---|---|---|---|---|---|
| **c432-SL320** | 36/7 | 209 | 32 Bits | **348** | 100% |
| **c880-SL320** | 60/26 | 404 | 32 Bits | **553** | 100% |
| **c1355-SL320** | 41/32 | 593 | 32 Bits | **461** | 100% |
| **c3540-SL320** | 50/22 | 1492 | 32 Bits | **490** | 100% |
| **c1355-SL640** | 41/32 | 641 | 64 Bits | **802** | 95.31% |
| **c880-SL640** | 60/26 | 447 | 64 Bits | **1035** | 89.23% |
| **c1908-SL640** | 33/25 | 822 | 64 Bits | **673** | 96.87% |
| **c3540-SL640** | 50/22 | 1546 | 64 Bits | **948** | 92.18% |
| **c1908-SL1280** | 33/25 | 918 | 128 Bits | **1121** | 92.96% |
| **c432-SL1280** | 36/7 | 345 | 128 Bits | **1019** | 94.53% |
| **c3540-SL1280** | 50/22 | 1640 | 128 Bits | **1250** | 91.40% |
| **c880-SL1280** | 60/26 | 540 | 128 Bits | **1385** | 89.84% |
| **c7552-SL2560** | 207/108 | 3365 | 256 Bits | **2033** | 88.67% |
| **c5315-SL2560** | 178/123 | 2373 | 256 Bits | **1941** | 91.01% |
| **c880-SL2560** | 60/26 | 739 | 256 Bits | **1634** | 92.96% |
| **c3540-SL2560** | 50/22 | 1834 | 256 Bits | **1577** | 94.14% |

and insignificant number of I/Os (less than 0.5% of the data). DD-RNN is trained by *load profile batches* randomly fetched from the load profile pool so that D-RNN is not only learning individual load patterns but also the common sharing load features and uncertainties. All layers of the networks, except for the last ones which contain linear neurons, are made of sigmoid type neurons and have a neuron for bias. We adjust the weights of the neural network to minimize the MSE on training set. In order to prevent local minimum and overfitting, recursive weight coefficients within a layer of back-propagation are chosen as appropriate batch size.

**(ii) Attack1-Key Reconstruction**: In this attack model, the attacker's objective is to reconstruct the key from logic encryption obfuscation circuit. As indicated earlier, using D-RNN, two phases are needed for this attack model. In the training phase, we train input and output pairs without providing any key to neural network. Once D-RNN's parameters and weights are trained, we apply a random key as an input. Next, during the test phase, the initial random key value will be later updated based on the MSE of the trained outputs and the newly-generated outputs due to the presence of key in the neural network. We have evaluated this attack on 16 different ISCAS-85 benchmarks with different size of keys (32-bit, 64-bit, 128-bit, and 256-bit). The information regarding the benchmarks are shown in Table 1. The second and the third column shows the number of input/outputs of each circuit; the number of gates associated to each benchmark is shown in the fourth column; The fifth column indicates the size of the keys; The required attack time (in seconds) for each of the 16 ISCAS-85 benchmarks and attack success rate are shown in the remaining column of the Table. Based on the results in Table 1, we were able to reconstruct the key (32 bits) from the benchmark ISCAS-85 c423 in less than 6 minutes (348 seconds) from BOCANet. Among the 4 benchmarks with 32 bits key size, the maximum and minimum time required to attack the logic locking circuits is between 6 to 9 minutes. For the second sets of benchmarks with 64 bits key size, prediction duration for the key took at least 11 minutes and at most 17 minutes. The third sets of benchmarks (128 bits key size), our BOCANet scheme needed a minimum of 17 minutes and a maximum of 23 minutes to reconstruct the keys. Finally, the last sets of benchmarks that have the key size of 256 which are very large and complicated circuits. Our proposed attack using D-RNN could break the keys in less than 35 minutes (2033 seconds - maximum time) and at least in 27 minutes. **Note that these results are conducted based on the assumption that an attacker has access to a very limited data (less than 0.5% of I/O values.** As seen in Table 1, the success rate of guessing keys (using two hidden layers) for logic encryption obfuscation benchmark is varying from 100% to at least 88.67% depending on the number of I/O numbers and secret key sizes. As shown in this Table, our BOCANet approach achieves an average success rate of 100% for 32 bit key size, 93.4% for 64 bit key size, 92.2% and 91.7% for 128 and 256 bit key size, respectively.

**(iii) Attack2-Output Guessing:** This attack scenario has two phases: **i) Training phase:** During the training phase, the D-RNN is supervised to learn from the data by presenting the training data at the input layer and dynamically adjusting the parameters of the D-RNN to achieve the desired output value from the input set. Basically, an attacker use I/O pairs to train D-RNN parameters. Once the parameters are trained, by giving new input patterns, D-RNN will be able to predict the corresponding output stimulus. In this scenario, we train only less than half a percent (< 0.5%) of the total available I/O patterns. **ii) Testing phase:** In order to evaluate our attack model, we test the D-RNN with one million new untrained input patterns to predict the outputs. Next, we compare the predicted outputs with the desired ones to ensure the success of our attack model. This scenario is applied to several ISCAS-85 benchmarks with various number of inputs and outputs.

## 5 LITERATURE REVIEW

AppSAT is another attack to logic locking which has been presented in HOST 2017. AppSAT [8] is a technique for approximate de-obfuscation based on the active learning with random querying and intermediate error estimation. The main goal in active-learning is to find a querying strategy that minimizing the number of queries required to learn the target function. While active learning is sample-efficient, it can be computationally expensive since it requires iterative retraining. In [13], a new parallelizing approach is proposed in order to resolve the scalability problem of SAT-based attacks which is due to the complexity of the underlying SAT solvers. Basically, an independent module partitioning and k-medoids clustering are applied to reduce the scale of SAT formulas; followed by a conflict avoidance strategy is proposed to enable parallelization. This will then reduce the SAT scale and results in a large speed up over the state-of-the-art fastest de-camouflaging tool. In [2]. authors propose a logic encryption method for resisting the SAT attack. Their method encrypts a circuit by primarily inserting XOR/XNOR key gates with the objective of simultaneously increasing the SAT solving iterations and complicating the SAT solving problems.

## 6 CONCLUSIONS AND FUTURE WORKS

This paper, for the first time, explores the potential of employing the state-of-the-art deep learning technique that allows an attacker to derive the key inputs from logic encryption hardware obfuscation techniques. We have also presented "output-guessing" attack in which an attacker can predict output values without having the knowledge of key. Our result indicates that the proposed method can deliver significant improvement for breaking logic encryption. Compared with state-of-the-art attacks, the proposed method (BOCANet) has high success rate using only a small number of input/output observations (0.5%). Note that SAT attacks has several limitations (such as huge amount of time and resources, high computationally and complexity for large secret key size, etc.). Therefore, we believe that with augmenting hardware attacks on obfuscated architectures by incorporating deep learning in our scheme not only a practical paradigm shift to attack such obscured circuits is proposed but also it can be utilized as a step forward towards finding the vulnerabilities of other hardware security approaches.

## REFERENCES


[1] 2017. Trust-Hub. https:/trust-hub.org/OBFbenchmarks.html.

[2] Yung-Chih Chen. 2017. Tree-Based Logic Encryption for Resisting SAT Attack. In *Asian Test Symposium (ATS), 2017 IEEE 26th*. IEEE, 46–51.

[3] Ian Goodfellow, Yoshua Bengio, Aaron Courville, and Yoshua Bengio. 2016. *Deep learning*. Vol. 1. MIT press Cambridge.

[4] Alex Graves, Abdel-rahman Mohamed, and Geoffrey Hinton. 2013. Speech recognition with deep recurrent neural networks. In *Acoustics, speech and signal processing (icassp), 2013 ieee international conference on*. IEEE, 6645–6649.

[5] Yann LeCun, Yoshua Bengio, and Geoffrey Hinton. 2015. Deep learning. *nature* 521, 7553 (2015), 436.

[6] Stephen M Plaza and Igor L Markov. 2015. Solving the third-shift problem in IC piracy with test-aware logic locking. *IEEE Transactions on Computer-Aided Design of Integrated Circuits and Systems* 34, 6 (2015), 961–971.

[7] Jeyavijayan Rajendran, Youngok Pino, Ozgur Sinanoglu, and Ramesh Karri. 2012. Logic encryption: A fault analysis perspective. In *Proceedings of the Conference on Design, Automation and Test in Europe*. EDA Consortium, 953–958.

[8] Kaveh Shamsi, Meng Li, Travis Meade, Zheng Zhao, David Z Pan, and Yier Jin. 2017. AppSAT: Approximately deobfuscating integrated circuits. In *Hardware Oriented Security and Trust, 2017 IEEE International Symposium on*. 95–100.

[9] Kaveh Shamsi, Meng Li, Travis Meade, Zheng Zhao, David Z Pan, and Yier Jin. 2017. Cyclic obfuscation for creating sat-unresolvable circuits. In *Proceedings of the on Great Lakes Symposium on VLSI 2017*. ACM, 173–178.

[10] C Spear. 2008. A Guide to Learning the Testbench Language Features. *System Verilog for verification, 2nd ed., Springer Publishing Company, Incorporated* (2008), 11–18.

[11] Pramod Subramanyan, Sayak Ray, and Sharad Malik. 2015. Evaluating the security of logic encryption algorithms. In *Hardware Oriented Security and Trust (HOST), 2015 IEEE International Symposium on*. IEEE, 137–143.

[12] Ilya Sutskever, Oriol Vinyals, and Quoc V Le. 2014. Sequence to sequence learning with neural networks. In *Advances in neural information processing systems*. 3104–3112.

[13] Xueyan Wang, Qiang Zhou, Yici Cai, and Gang Qu. 2018. A conflict-free approach for parallelizing SAT-based de-camouflaging attacks. In *Proceedings of the 23rd Asia and South Pacific Design Automation Conference*. IEEE Press, 259–264.

[14] Yang Xie and Ankur Srivastava. 2016. Mitigating sat attack on logic locking. In *International Conference on Cryptographic Hardware and Embedded Systems*. Springer, 127–146.

[15] Yang Xie and Ankur Srivastava. 2016. Mitigating sat attack on logic locking. In *International Conference on Cryptographic Hardware and Embedded Systems*. Springer, 127–146.

[16] Yang Xie and Ankur Srivastava. 2017. Delay locking: Security enhancement of logic locking against ic counterfeiting and overproduction. In *Proceedings of the 54th Annual Design Automation Conference 2017*. ACM, 9.

[17] Xiaolin Xu, Bicky Shakya, Mark M Tehranipoor, and Domenic Forte. 2017. Novel bypass attack and BDD-based tradeoff analysis against all known logic locking attacks. In *International Conference on Cryptographic Hardware and Embedded Systems*. Springer, 189–210.

[18] Muhammad Yasin, Bodhisatwa Mazumdar, Jeyavijayan JV Rajendran, and Ozgur Sinanoglu. 2016. Sarlock: Sat attack resistant logic locking. In *Hardware Oriented Security and Trust (HOST), 2016 IEEE International Symposium on*. IEEE, 236–241.

[19] Muhammad Yasin, Bodhisatwa Mazumdar, Ozgur Sinanoglu, and Jeyavijayan Rajendran. 2017. Removal attacks on logic locking and camouflaging techniques. *IEEE Transactions on Emerging Topics in Computing* (2017).

[20] Muhammad Yasin, Bodhisatwa Mazumdar, Ozgur Sinanoglu, and Jeyavijayan Rajendran. 2017. Security analysis of anti-sat. In *Design Automation Conference (ASP-DAC), 2017 22nd Asia and South Pacific*. IEEE, 342–347.

# STAT: Mean and Variance Characterization for Robust Inference of DNNs on Memristor-based Platforms

Baogang Zhang, Necati Uysal, and Rickard Ewetz
University of Central Florida, Orlando, FL 32816, USA
{baogang.zhang,necati}@knights.ucf.edu,{rickard.ewetz}@ucf.edu

## ABSTRACT

An emerging solution to accelerate the inference phase of deep neural networks (DNNs) is to utilize memristor crossbar arrays (MCAs) to perform highly efficient matrix-vector multiplication in the analog domain. An adverse challenge is that memristor devices may suffer stuck-at-fault defects, which may compromise the classification accuracy. Stuck-at-fault defects have previously been handled by neuron permutation or by retraining neural networks. In this paper, we propose the STAT framework that utilizes statistics to guide optimization techniques that provide robustness to stuck-at-fault defects. In particular, bias weights are modified to minimize the input error to each neuron with respect to an input vector. The input vector is selected to be equal to the mean from a statistical characterization. Variance statistics are used to define a weight significance metric, which is used to prioritize assigning weights connected to neurons with large (small) variance to non-defective (defective) memristors using neuron permutation, as errors introduced by neurons with small variance can be eliminated by modifying the bias weights. The experimental results demonstrate that the STAT framework improves the normalized classification accuracy from 62.1% to 96.1% without any hardware overhead.

**ACM Reference Format:**
Baogang Zhang, Necati Uysal, and Rickard Ewetz. 2019. STAT: Mean and Variance Characterization for Robust Inference of DNNs on Memristor-based Platforms. In *Great Lakes Symposium on VLSI 2019 (GLSVLSI '19), May 9–11, 2019, Tysons Corner, VA, USA.* ACM, New York, NY, USA, 4 pages. https://doi.org/10.1145/3299874.3318032

## 1 INTRODUCTION

Deep neural networks (DNNs) have achieved breakthrough results within image, audio and video recognition [6]. Matrix-vector multiplication is the dominating computation in the inference phase of DNNs. An emerging solution is to utilize memristor crossbar arrays (MCAs) to efficiently perform matrix-vector multiplication in the analog domain [5, 10]. The main challenge of performing inference of DNNs trained in software on memristor-based platforms is that the mapping to the platform must be robust to both defects and variations. Variations in the form of random telegraph


*GLSVLSI '19, May 9–11, 2019, Tysons Corner, VA, USA*

ACM ISBN 978-1-4503-6252-8/19/05…$15.00
https://doi.org/10.1145/3299874.3318032

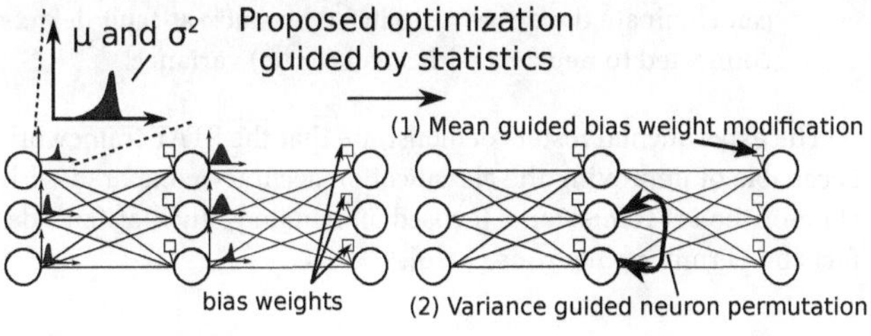


**Figure 1: (a) Mean ($\mu$) and variance ($\sigma^2$) statistics of the output from each neuron. (b) Proposed techniques of handling stuck-at-fault defects: (1) Mean guided bias weight modification and (2) Variance guided neuron permutation.**

noise (RTN), short noise, temperature variations, and non-ideal device characteristics were analyzed in [5]. Techniques to handle resistance drift were proposed in [9, 15]. A stuck-at-fault defect is the phenomena when the conductance of a memristor becomes stuck-on or stuck-off and cannot be further programmed [1, 11]. In [7], it was observed that stuck-at-fault defects may greatly degrade the classification accuracy of neural networks.

Stuck-at-fault defects in MCAs can be identified using the techniques in [1, 11, 13]. Methods to mitigate the negative impact of stuck-at-fault defects are concentrated on retraining, redundant hardware, or neuron permutation [2, 7, 8, 13, 16]. Retraining is based on training neural networks in software to have weights that mimic the defects in the hardware. The utilization of redundant hardware is based on using multiple parallel rows in an MCA to represent a single row in a weight matrix [14]. Neuron permutation is based on permuting the order of the neurons in each layer to assign large weights to memristors that are stuck-on and small weights to memristors that are stuck-off [2, 7, 16], i.e., to mask the errors in the memristor-based hardware. Most of these optimization techniques consider the representation of each weight equally important [2, 7, 13, 14]. However, it is well known that certain weights may have a high (or low) impact on the overall classification accuracy [4, 8, 12].

In this paper, we propose the STAT framework to facilitate robust inference of DNNs on memristor-based platforms. The main contributions of this paper are, as follows:

- **Characterization using mean and variance:** The STAT framework is based on recording the mean and variance of the output from each neuron and utilizing these statistics to guide optimization techniques focused on handling stuck-at-fault defects, as shown in Figure 1.
- **Mean guided bias weight modification:** This technique is involves modifying bias weights to minimize the input error to each neuron with respect to an input vector, as

shown in the top of Figure 1(b). Specifically, the bias weights are modified such that there are no input errors when the input vector to each layer is equal to the mean input vector.
- **Variance guided neuron permutation:** This technique aims to assign weights connected to neurons with high (low) output variance to non-defective (defective) memristors using neuron permutation [13, 16]. The motivation is that the proposed mean guided bias weight modification technique can eliminate the errors introduced by stuck-at-fault defects connected to neurons with small (or no) variance.

The experimental results demonstrate that the STAT framework is capable of improving the classification accuracy compared with state-of-the-art frameworks focused on handling stuck-at-fault defects by permuting neurons [7, 16].

## 2 PRELIMINARIES

**Model of stuck-at-fault defects:** In this paper, we model stuck-at-faults in similar to previous studies [2, 7, 13]. Let $W^r$ be the weight matrix realized when a weight matrix $W$ is mapped to an MCA. Let $w_k^r$ in $W^r$ be equal to $w_k$ in $W$ when the weight $w_k$ is mapped to a memristor without a defect. Moreover, $w_k^r$ is equal to $w_{min}$ or $w_{max}$ when $w_k$ is mapped to a memristor with a stuck-on defect or a stuck-off defect, respectively. $w_{min}$ and $w_{max}$ are the minimum and maximum value in $W$, respectively. Lastly, let $G^d$ be a matrix capturing the type and location of the stuck-at-fault defects in an MCA.

**Neural network fundamentals:** Each neural network consists of $L$ layers of neurons connected by synapses with associated weights, which is illustrated in Figure 2. Neural networks classify inputs into one of multiple output categories, which are each represented with a neuron in the final layer of the network. The classification of an input is performed by passing an input vector to the first layer and recording the output from the last layer. An input vector is passed through layer $l$ of a neural network by multiplying the input vector ($x_l$) with a weight matrix ($W_l$) and adding the bias weights ($b_l$) in order to obtain the input vector to the neurons of the layer ($y_l$), i.e., $y_l = W_l \cdot x_l + b_l$. Next, vector $y_l$ is passed through the activation function ($f$) of the neurons to compute the inputs to the next layer $x_{l+1} = f(y_l)$. The ideal classification accuracy of a neural network is obtained by evaluating the network using the weight matrices $W_l$ with $l$ in 2 to $L$.

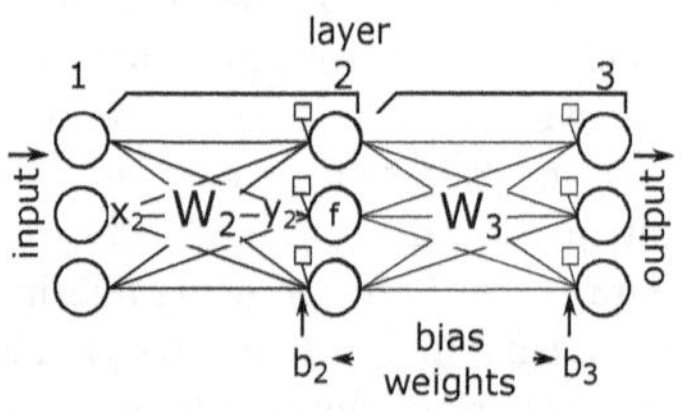


**Figure 2: Neural network notation in the paper.**

**Problem formulation:** This paper considers the problem of maximizing the classification accuracy when performing inference of DNNs using memristor-based platforms with stuck-at-fault defects. Consequently, the classification accuracy in the presence of defects is obtained by evaluating the neural network with the weight matrices $W_l^r$ instead of $W_l$ for $l$ in 2 to $L$. This is the model used in the experimental evaluation in Section 6.

## 3 PREVIOUS WORK

In this section, we review utilization of redundant hardware, neuron and weight significance, neuron permutation, and limitations of previous studies.

**Utilization of Redundant Hardware:** The technique of utilizing redundant hardware to provide robustness to stuck-at-fault defects is based on using two parallel (or multiple parallel rows) in an MCA to represent a single row in a weight matrix [14]. When two parallel memristors are used to represent a single weight, the weight is decomposed into a positive and negative component, i.e., $w_k = w_k^+ - w_k^-$. Next, the two memristors are programmed in tandem to compensate for each others errors [14]. Substantial robustness improvements at the expense of power and hardware overhead were demonstrated [14].

**Significant neurons and weights:** It is known that different neurons and weights have different impact (or significance) on the overall classification accuracy of DNNs [4, 8, 12]. Neuron and weight significance have been used to reduce the size of neural networks [4, 12] and to improve the robustness to stuck-at-fault defects [8].

**Neuron permutation:** The order of the neurons in each layer of a neural network can be permuted without changing the functionality of the network [13], which is illustrated in Figure 3(a). In particular, permuting two neurons in layer $l$ involves permuting the corresponding rows and columns in $W_l$ and $W_{l+1}$, which is shown in Figure 3(b). The permutation of neurons results in that different weights are mapped to different memristors in the MCAs.

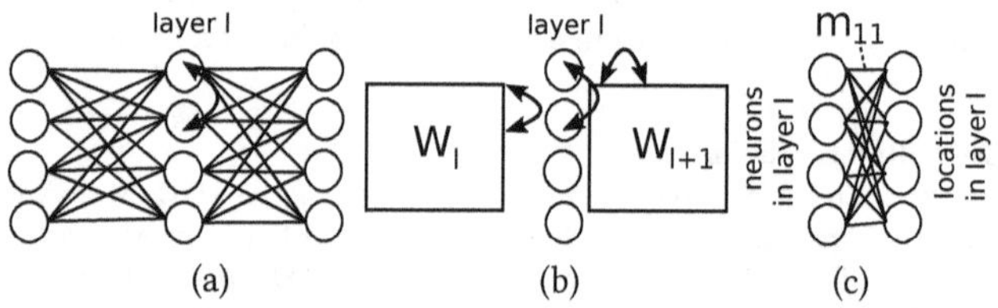


**Figure 3: (a) Neuron permutation [13]. (b) Corresponding row and column permutation in $W_l$ and $W_{l+1}$. (c) Minimum weight bipartite matching [2, 16]. The figure is adapted from [13, 16]**

It is difficult to directly optimize classification accuracy by permuting neurons. In [7], a sum weight variation (SWV) metric that captures the difference between $W$ and $W^r$ was proposed, as follows:

$$SWV(W) = \sum_{k \in W} |w_k^r - w_k|. \tag{1}$$

Clearly, SWV can be improved by permuting the neurons such that small (large) weights are assigned to memristors that are stuck-off (stuck-on) [7].

## 4 PROPOSED TECHNIQUES

In this section, we explain the characterization technique used in the STAT framework. Next, mean guided bias weight modification technique and the variance guided neuron permutation technique are explained. The techniques are integrated into the flow of the STAT framework in Section 5.

## 4.1 Mean and variance characterization

The characterization in the STAT framework consists of computing the mean and variance of the output from each neuron. The mean and variance statistics are straightforward to obtained by propagating the training dataset through a neural network and recording the output from each neuron for each input vector. Next, the mean and the variance of the output from each neuron are computed, respectively. The mean and variance of the inputs to layer $l$ are denoted $\mu_l$ and $\sigma_l^2$, respectively. The computed statistics are used in the two subsequent optimization techniques.

## 4.2 Mean guided bias weight modification

The objective of the mean guided bias weight modification technique is to adjust the bias weights such that there are no input errors to the neurons in a layer with respect to a specific input vector. In this paper, we modify the bias weights such that there are no input errors (to the neurons in each layer) when the input vector (to each layer) is equal to the mean input vector obtained from the statistical characterization. Consequently, the bias weights are modified as, follows:

$$b_l^u = b_l - (W_l^r - W_l) \cdot \mu_l. \tag{2}$$

where $b_l$ and $b_l^m$ are the original and modified bias weights, respectively. $\mu_l$ is the mean input vector to layer $l$ from the statistical characterization. $W_l$ and $W_l^r$ are the weight matrix and the realized weight matrix for layer $l$, respectively.

## 4.3 Variance guided neuron permutation

The objective of variance guided neuron permutation is to prioritize mapping weights connected to neurons with high variance to non-defective memristors using neuron permutation, as the modified bias weights technique can effectively compensate for errors from neurons with small variance.

To enable the neuron permutation techniques in earlier studies to facilitate such mappings, a *weight significance factor* $c_k$ is introduced for each weight $w_k$ to guide the neuron permutation in [13, 16]. Next, neuron permutation is performed with respect to a significance error (SE) metric, which is defined, as follows:

$$SE(W) = \sum_{k \in W} c_k \cdot (w_k^r - w_k)^2, \tag{3}$$

where $c_k$ is the weight significance factor for weight $w_k$. We also choose to minimize the square error instead of the linear error $|w_k^r - w_k|$, to avoid introducing large errors for certain weights in order to represent other weights more accurately.

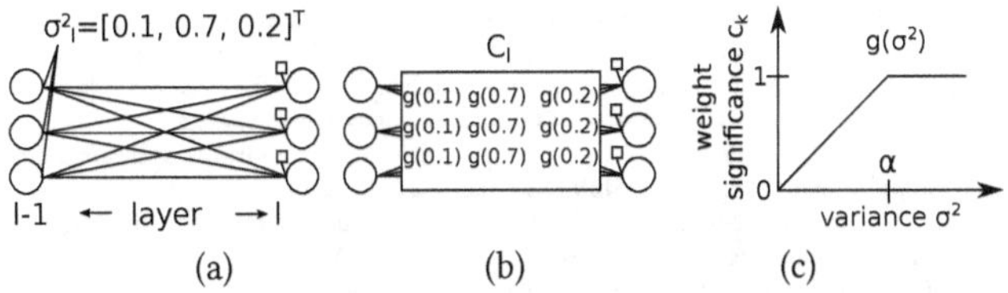


**Figure 4: (a) Variance of input to layer $l$. (b) Weight significance factors set based on the variance statistics. (c) The function $g$ used to defined the weight significance factors $c_k$.**

To prioritize that weights connected to neurons with high variance are assigned to non-defective memristors, the weight significance factors $c_k$ are specified, as follows:

$$c_k = g(\sigma_{lk}^2), \tag{4}$$

where $\sigma_{lk}^2$ is the recorded variance from the output of neuron $k$ in layer $l-1$. $\sigma_l^2$ denotes the vector of input variances to layer $l$, which is illustrated in Figure 4(a). The weight significance factors for $W_l$ with respect to the inputs to layer $l$ are shown in Figure 4(b). $g$ is the function shown in Figure 4(c). The purpose of the function $g$ is to prioritize all neurons with a variance above a threshold $\alpha$ equally. The parameter $\alpha$ is a user defined parameter determined based on Monte Carlo simulations.

# 5 FLOW OF THE STAT FRAMEWORK

The flow of the STAT framework is shown in Figure 5. The input to the framework is a neural network, an MCA for each weight matrix, and the redundancy factor $R$. The objective is to map the neural network to the memristor-based platform while minimizing the SE metric, which is expected to maximize the classification accuracy.

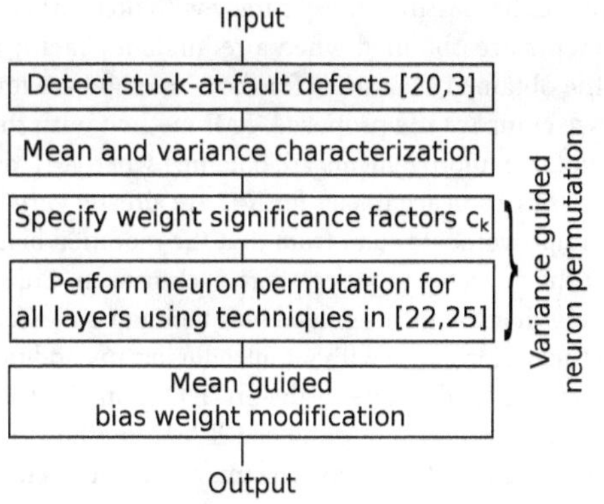


**Figure 5: Proposed flow of the STAT framework.**

The first step is *detect stuck-at-fault defects*, which consists of identifying the location and the type (stuck-on or stuck-off) of each defect in the MCAs using the methods in [1, 11]. The second step is *mean and variance characterization*, which involves propagating the training set through the network to obtain the mean and variance of each neuron. Using the variance statistics for the neurons, the weight significance factors are specified for each weight in the network . Next, the neuron permutation in [13, 16] is performed using the introduced weight significance factors. The combination of the weight significance factors and the neuron permutation forms the proposed *variance guided neuron permutation* step. Lastly, the *mean guided bias weight modification* step is applied.

# 6 EXPERIMENTAL EVALUATION

The proposed framework is implemented in C++. The experiments are performed on a 3.4 GHz machine with 32GB of memory. The neural networks are trained using Keras and TensorFlow. The proposed techniques are evaluated using two feed-forward neural networks trained on the MNIST dataset [3]. The dimensions of the neural networks are 784x500x10 and 784x500x300x10, with the software classification accuracy of 98.25% and 98.35%, respectively.

## 6.1 Effectiveness of STAT framework

The STAT framework is evaluated in Table 1. '$p$' is the percentage of defects and '$R$' is the redundancy factor. We evaluate several different methods in the table to demonstrate the effectiveness of the STAT framework. The baseline with no optimization is denoted '-'. The baseline with $R$=2 is equivalent to the method used in [14]. The technique of permuting neurons in [16] is called 'P [16]', which is obtained by only using the first and the fourth step in Figure 5. The 'PM' method is the 'P' method extended with the mean guided bias weight modification technique proposed in the STAT framework. The 'PMV' method denotes the 'PM' technique extended with the proposed variance guided neuron permutation. The run-time for all methods and both networks is less than five minutes.

In Table 1, it can be observed that stuck-at-fault defects greatly degrade the classification accuracy of both the three and four layer neural network. The classification accuracy can be greatly improved when a redundancy factor $R$=2 is used, as in [14]. However, the improved robustness comes at the expense of doubling the hardware utilization and power consumption.

Compared with the baseline '-', the 'P [16]' method can substantially improve the classification accuracy with no overhead. Drastic improvements are obtained when a redundancy factor of $R$=1 is used, as the obtained accuracies for the '-' method are low.

Next, we compare the proposed 'PM' method with the 'P [16]' method. Notable improvements are obtained when $R$=1, as the normalized classification accuracies for $R$=2 are already very high. The accuracy improvements stem from that the modified bias weights cancel out the expected input errors to each neuron. Consequently, we conclude that the mean guided bias technique is effective and improves the performance without introducing any additional overhead with respect to the state-of-the-art 'P [16]' method. Compared with the 'PM' method, the proposed 'PMV' method further improves the robustness to defects. The improvements stem from that

**Table 1: Evaluation of various methods in terms of normalized classification accuracy.**

| p | Tech-niques | $R$ | Normalized Accuracy(%) | | | |
|---|---|---|---|---|---|---|
| | | | Three-layer | | Four-layer | |
| % | P/M/V | | [min, max] | mean | [min, max] | mean |
| 10 | - | 1 | [39.3,76.0] | 62.1 | [33.7,48.3] | 39.8 |
| | P [16] | 1 | [59.3,90.5] | 78.5 | [33.7,51.9] | 43.3 |
| | PM | 1 | [91.5,97.2] | 94.9 | [39.0,69.1] | 54.5 |
| | PMV | 1 | [92.5,97.3] | 96.1 | [41.7,71.3] | 55.8 |
| | - [14] | 2 | [99.0,99.7] | 99.5 | [99.2,99.6] | 99.4 |
| | P [16] | 2 | [99.3,99.9] | 99.6 | [99.4,99.8] | 99.6 |
| | PM | 2 | [99.6,99.9] | 99.7 | [99.5,99.7] | 99.6 |
| | PMV | 2 | [99.7,100.0] | 99.8 | [99.5,99.8] | 99.6 |
| 20 | - | 1 | [13.3,37.6] | 25.6 | [10.5,19.7] | 13.8 |
| | P [16] | 1 | [26.4,63,8] | 43.4 | [9.2,37.5] | 19.2 |
| | PM | 1 | [68.9,82.0] | 75.3 | [10.5,26.1] | 19.4 |
| | PMV | 1 | [74.8,89.2] | 84.0 | [9.6,30.1] | 19.6 |
| | - [14] | 2 | [94.7,98.1] | 97.0 | [61.1,78.1] | 70.0 |
| | P [16] | 2 | [96.7,98.7] | 98.1 | [86.6,95.6] | 92.2 |
| | PM | 2 | [98.3,99.3] | 98.8 | [85.5,96.0] | 93.0 |
| | PMV | 2 | [97.8,99.3] | 98.8 | [89.1,96.1] | 93.5 |

weights connected to neurons with small variance are mapped to memristors with stuck-at-faults. The parameter $\alpha$ is obtained using a parameter sweep. Based on the results reported, we conclude that variance guided neuron permutation method further improves the performance without introducing additional overhead.

In conclusion, the STAT framework improves the robustness significantly over the previous state-of-the-art neuron permutation technique 'P [16]' without introducing any overhead. This is a steeping stone to our objective of executing DNNs on any memristor-based platform without any performance degradation and with $R$=1. Nevertheless, the experimental results demonstrate that there is a need for even better techniques to handle the four-layer (or large) neural network in the presence of many defects.

We note that high normalized classification accuracies can be obtained using retraining as demonstrated in [8] and [13]. However, these techniques require each neural network to be retrained for each memristor-based platform, which is not very practical as the training process is time consuming.

# 7 SUMMARY AND FUTURE WORK

Handling stuck-at-fault defects is one of the key challenges when accelerating DNNs using a memristor-based platforms. In this paper, we have demonstrated that statistics can be used to guide optimization techniques aimed at handling stuck-at-fault defect. In particular, the statistics were used in a proposed mean guided bias weight modification technique and a variance guided neuron permutation technique, which resulted in substantial improvements compared with the state-of-the-art framework in [16]. In the future, we will explore applying these techniques to convolutional neural networks on the CIFAR dataset.

# REFERENCES


[1] K. Beckmann et al. Nanoscale hafnium oxide rram devices exhibit pulse dependent behavior and multi-level resistance capability. *MRS Advances*, 1(49):3355–3360, 2016.

[2] L. Chen et al. Accelerator-friendly neural-network training: Learning variations and defects in rram crossbar. DATE'17, pages 19–24, 2017.

[3] Y. L. et al. The mnist database of handwritten digits. In *http://yann.lecun.com/exdb/mnist/*.

[4] S. Han et al. Deep compression: Compressing deep neural network with pruning, trained quantization and huffman coding. *CoRR*, abs/1510.00149, 2015.

[5] M. Hu et al. Dot-product engine for neuromorphic computing: Programming 1T1M crossbar to accelerate matrix-vector multiplication. DAC'16, pages 1–6, 2016.

[6] Y. LeCun et al. Deep learning. In *Nature*, pages 436–444, 2015.

[7] B. Liu et al. Vortex: Variation-aware training for memristor x-bar. DAC'15, pages 1–6, 2015.

[8] C. Liu et al. Rescuing memristor-based neuromorphic design with high defects. DAC'17, pages 87:1–87:6, 2017.

[9] X. Liu et al. Harmonica: A framework of heterogeneous computing systems with memristor-based neuromorphic computing accelerators. *IEEE TCAS-I*, 63(5):617–628, 2016.

[10] H. Miao et al. Memristor-based analog computation and neural network classification with a dot product engine. *Advanced Materials*, 30(9):1705914.

[11] A. van de Goor and Y. Zorian. Effective march algorithms for testing single-order addressed memories. EDAC-EUROASIC'93, pages 499–505, 1993.

[12] S. Venkataramani et al. Axnn: Energy-efficient neuromorphic systems using approximate computing. ISLPED'14, pages 27–32, 2014.

[13] L. Xia et al. Fault-tolerant training with on-line fault detection for RRAM-based neural computing systems. DAC'17, pages 1–6, 2017.

[14] L. Xia et al. Stuck-at fault tolerance in RRAM computing systems. *IEEE JETCAS*, 8(1):102–115, 2018.

[15] B. Yan et al. A closed-loop design to enhance weight stability of memristor based neural network chips. ICCAD'17, pages 541–548, 2017.

[16] B. Zhang et al. Handling stuck-at-faults in memristor crossbar arrays using matrix transformations. ASP-DAC'19, pages 438–443, 2019.

# LSM: Novel Low-Complexity Unified Systolic Multiplier over Binary Extension Field

Jiafeng Xie
Department of Electrical and Computer Engineering
Villanova University
Villanova, PA 19085
jiafeng.xie@villanova.edu

Chiou-Yng Lee
Computer Information & Network Engineering
Lunghwa University of Science and Technology
Taoyuan, Taiwan
pp010@gm.lhu.edu.tw

## ABSTRACT

Unified (hybrid field-size) systolic multiplier over $GF(2^m)$ (binary extension field) has attracted significant attentions from research communities recently as it can be used in reconfigurable cryptographic processors. In this paper, we present a novel **L**ow-complexity unified **S**ystolic **M**ultiplier (LSM) design strategy to address the above mentioned challenge. First, a novel multiplication algorithm for unified implementation is proposed first with detailed mathematical derivation. Then, an efficient systolic structure is then presented based on the proposed algorithm (with the help of several mapping techniques). Finally, a thorough complexity analysis is given to verify the superior performance of the proposed design (the proposed structure involves better complexities than the newly reported design).

## CCS CONCEPTS

• **Hardware** → **Very large scale integration design**; *Application-specific VLSI designs*; • **Computer systems organization** → Architectures; Systolic arrays.

## KEYWORDS

Binary extension field; fast algorithm; finite field multiplier; systolic structure; unified implementation

**ACM Reference Format:**
Jiafeng Xie and Chiou-Yng Lee. 2019. LSM: Novel Low-Complexity Unified Systolic Multiplier over Binary Extension Field. In *Great Lakes Symposium on VLSI 2019 (GLSVLSI '19), May 9–11, 2019, Tysons Corner, VA, USA.* ACM, New York, NY, USA, 4 pages. https://doi.org/10.1145/3299874.3318033

## 1 INTRODUCTION

Systolic finite field multiplier over $GF(2^m)$ (binary extension field) has drawn significant attentions recently due to its efficient performance in high-throughput and regularity and modularity of the design [3, 6, 7]. One of the recent trend is on the efficient implementation of high-performance reconfigurable cryptographic processor, which requires unified implementation of systolic multiplier (hybrid field-size) [3, 4, 7]. As the conventional designing of finite field multiplier typically lies in the single field-size, i.e., one multiplier for one specific one field-size, the unified multiplier is thus regarded as a bottleneck for the reconfigurable crypto-processor [4].

The National Institute of Standards and Technology (NIST) has recommended five polynomials for elliptic curve cryptography (ECC) applications [2]. Very recently [4], an efficient unified systolic multiplier based on NIST pentanomials and trinomials is presented. The design of [4], however, still suffers large area-occupation as the shared computation core is relatively small when compared to the original individual multipliers. Based on this consideration, in this paper, we propose to use a novel **l**ow-complexity unified **s**ystolic **m**ultiplier (LSM) design strategy to reduce the complexity further. The main contributions of this paper are summarized as:

- We have proposed a novel unified multiplication algorithm. Fast algorithm (Toeplitz Matrix-Vector Product (TMVP) approach [1]) has been employed to further reduce the involved complexity.
- We have proposed optimized techniques to efficiently map the proposed algorithm into desired structure.
- We have presented complexity analysis and comparison to confirm the efficiency of the proposed structure.

The rest of this paper is organized as follows. Section 2 gives the proposed unified multiplication algorithm. Section 3 presents the detailed designing process of the corresponding systolic structure. Complexity and comparison are presented in Section 4. The conclusions are finally given in Section 5.

## 2 LSM: MATHEMATICAL FORMULATION

**General multiplication.** In general, for three elements $A = \sum_{i=0}^{m} a_i x^i$, $B = \sum_{i=0}^{m} b_i x^i$, and $C = \sum_{i=0}^{m} c_i x^i$ ($a_i, b_i, c_i \in GF(2)$), we can have the finite field multiplication over $GF(2^m)$ as [2, 6] $C = AB \bmod f(x)$, where $f(x)$ is the polynomial determines the field. Then, one can further have

$$C = \sum_{i=0}^{m-1} Ab_i x^i \bmod f(x) = \sum_{i=0}^{m-1} A^{(i)} b_i, \tag{1}$$

where we define $A^{(i)} = A \cdot x^i \bmod f(x)$ and it can be further derived to have $A^{(i+1)} = A^{(i)} x \bmod f(x)$. Let $A^{(i+1)} =$


*GLSVLSI '19, May 9–11, 2019, Tysons Corner, VA, USA*

ACM ISBN 978-1-4503-6252-8/19/05...$15.00
https://doi.org/10.1145/3299874.3318033

$\sum_{j=0}^{m-1} a_j^{(i+1)} x^j \bmod f(x)$, we can have

$$\sum_{j=0}^{m-1} a_j^{(i+1)} x^j = \sum_{j=0}^{m-1} a_j^{(i)} x^{j+1} \bmod f(x). \tag{2}$$

For a general pentanomial $f(x) = x^m + x^{s_1} + x^{s_2} + x^{s_3} + 1$, one can have $x^m = x^{s_1} + x^{s_2} + x^{s_3} + 1$ such that (2) becomes

$$\begin{aligned} a_0^{(i+1)} &= a_{m-1}^{(i)}, a_{s_1}^{(i+1)} = a_{s_1-1}^{(i)} + a_{m-1}^{(i)}, \\ a_{s_2}^{(i+1)} &= a_{s_2-1}^{(i)} + a_{m-1}^{(i)}, a_{s_3}^{(i+1)} = a_{s_3-1}^{(i)} + a_{m-1}^{(i)}, \\ a_j^{(i+1)} &= a_{j-1}^{(i)}, \text{ for } 1 \le j \le m-1 \text{ and } j \ne s_1, s_2, s_3. \end{aligned} \tag{3}$$

While for a trinomial of $f(x) = x^m + x^s + 1$, one can have $x^m = x^s + 1$ such that (2) becomes

$$\begin{aligned} a_0^{(i+1)} &= a_{m-1}^{(i)}, a_s^{(i+1)} = a_{s-1}^{i} + a_{m-1}^{(i)}, \\ a_j^{(i+1)} &= a_{j-1}^{(i)}, \text{ for } 1 \le j \le m-1 \text{ and } j \ne s. \end{aligned} \tag{4}$$

**Proposed multiplication algorithm.** Let $m_1$ for pentanomial and $m_2$ for trinomial (assume $m_1 < m_2$). Then, let $m_1 = p \cdot q$ ($p$ and $q$ are integers) and $m_2 = p \cdot t$ ($t$ is also an integer and $t > q$). We also assume $A_1 = \sum_{i=0}^{m_1-1} a_i x^i$, $B_1 = \sum_{i=0}^{m_1-1} b_i x^i$, and $C_1 = \sum_{i=0}^{m_1-1} c_i x^i$ are for pentanomial-based multiplication, while $A_2 = \sum_{i=0}^{m_1-1} a_i x^i$, $B_2 = \sum_{i=0}^{m_1-1} b_i x^i$, and $C_2 = \sum_{i=0}^{m_1-1} c_i x^i$ are for trinomial-based multiplication (for $0 \le i \le m_1 - 1$, $a_i$ of $A_1$ and $A_2$ are the same, the same rule applies to $b_i$ and $c_i$). Finally, we can define $f_1(x) = x^{m_1} + x^{s_1} + x^{s_2} + x^{s_3} + 1$ and $f_2(x) = x^{m_2} + x^s + 1$ are the two polynomials.

For pentanoimal, we can have

$$\begin{aligned} C_1 =& A_1^{(0)} b_0 + A_1^{(1)} b_1 + \cdots + A_1^{(p-1)} b_{p-1} \to C_{1-1} \\ &+ \cdots \cdots \cdots \\ &+ A_1^{(m_1-p)} b_{m_1-p} + \cdots + A_1^{(m_1-1)} b_{m_1-1} \to C_{1-q}, \end{aligned} \tag{5}$$

where each $C_{1-i}$ ($1 \le i \le q$) can be expressed in a matrix-vector form of ($[\cdot]^T$ is the transposed function)

$$C_{1-i} = [A_1^{(pi-p)} \cdots A_1^{(pi-1)}][b_{pi-p} \cdots b_{pi-1}]^T, \tag{6}$$

Similarly, we can have

$$C_2 = \sum_{k=1}^{t} C_{2-k} = C_{2-1} + C_{2-2} + \cdots + C_{2-t}, \tag{7}$$

where $C_{2-k} = A_2^{(pk-p)} b_{pk-p} + \cdots + A_2^{(pk-1)} b_{pk-1}$, and can be expressed into the matrix-vector multiplication form of

$$C_{2-k} = [A_2^{(pk-p)} \cdots A_2^{(pk-1)}][b_{pk-p} \cdots b_{pk-1}]^T. \tag{8}$$

For simplicity of discussion, let us focus on the unified implementation of $C_{1-1}$ and $C_{2-1}$ first, which can be extended to other terms of (5) and (7). One can have the detailed matrix-vector form of (6) as

$$C_{1-1} = \begin{bmatrix} a_0 & a_{m_1-1} & \cdots \\ \vdots & \vdots & \vdots \\ a_{s_3} & a_{s_3-1} + a_{m_1-1} & \cdots \\ \vdots & \vdots & \ddots \end{bmatrix} \begin{bmatrix} b_0 \\ \vdots \\ b_{p-1} \end{bmatrix} = [A_{1-1}][B_{1-1}]^T, \tag{9}$$

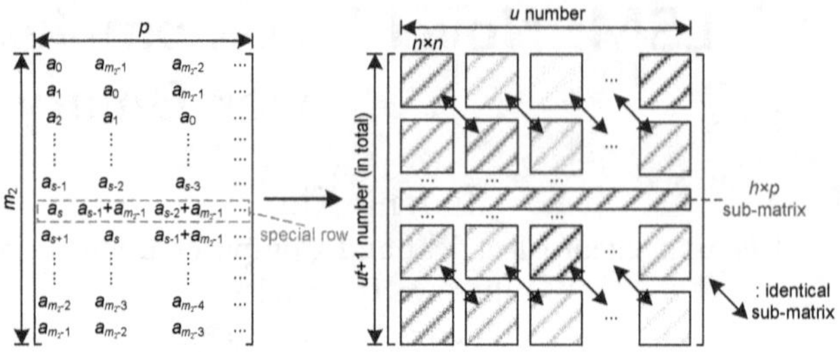


**Figure 1: Strategy of employing fast algorithm (TMVP approach) to the matrix $[A_{2-1}]$.**

where $[B_{1-1}]^T = [b_0 \cdots b_{p-1}]^T$.

Similarly, we can have $C_{2-1}$ of (7) as

$$C_{2-1} = \begin{bmatrix} a_0 & a_{m_2-1} & \cdots \\ \vdots & \vdots & \vdots \\ a_s & a_{s-1} + a_{m_2-1} & \cdots \\ \vdots & \vdots & \ddots \end{bmatrix} \begin{bmatrix} b_0 \\ \vdots \\ b_{p-1} \end{bmatrix} = [A_{2-1}][B_{2-1}]^T. \tag{10}$$

It is clear that $[A_{1-1}]$ of (9) is an $m_1 \times p$ matrix, while $[A_{2-1}]$ of (10) is an $m_2 \times p$ matrix. One can further split $[A_{2-1}]$ into two sub-matrices, i.e., $m_1 \times p$ and $(m_2 - m_1) \times p$

$$[A_{2-1}] = \begin{bmatrix} A'_{2-1} \\ A''_{2-1} \end{bmatrix}, \tag{11}$$

where

$$[A'_{2-1}] = \begin{bmatrix} a_0 & a_{m_2-1} & \cdots \\ \vdots & \vdots & \vdots \\ a_{m_1-1} & a_{m_1-2} & \cdots \end{bmatrix}, [A''_{2-1}] = \begin{bmatrix} a_{m_1} & \cdots \\ \vdots & \vdots \\ a_{m_2-1} & \cdots \end{bmatrix}, \tag{12}$$

We here propose to use $[A'_{2-1}]$ of (12) as the basic computation core, and $[A_{1-1}]$ of (9) can be obtained through the addition of computation core with an extra matrix as (note that $[B_{1-1}]^T$ and $[B_{2-1}]^T$ are the same)

$$[A_{1-1}] = [A'_{2-1}] + [E_1], \tag{13}$$

where $E_1$ is the mentioned extra matrix as (note that in field $GF(2^m)$, the addition of two identical elements is zero)

$$[E_1] = \begin{bmatrix} 0 & a_{m_1-1} + a_{m_2-1} & a_{m_1-2} + a_{m_2-2} & \cdots \\ 0 & 0 & a_{m_1-1} + a_{m_2-1} & \cdots \\ \vdots & \vdots & \vdots & \vdots \\ 0 & a_{m_1-1} & a_{m_1-2} & \cdots \\ \vdots & \vdots & \vdots & \vdots \\ 0 & 0 & 0 & \cdots \end{bmatrix}. \tag{14}$$

Thus, we can obtain $C_{1-1}$ and $C_{2-1}$ in a unified manner based on the following parallel processing as

$$\begin{aligned} C_{1-1} =& ([A'_{2-1}] + [E_1])[B_{1-1}]^T, \\ C_{2-1} =& \begin{bmatrix} A'_{2-1} \\ A''_{2-1} \end{bmatrix} [B_{2-1}]^T. \end{aligned} \tag{15}$$

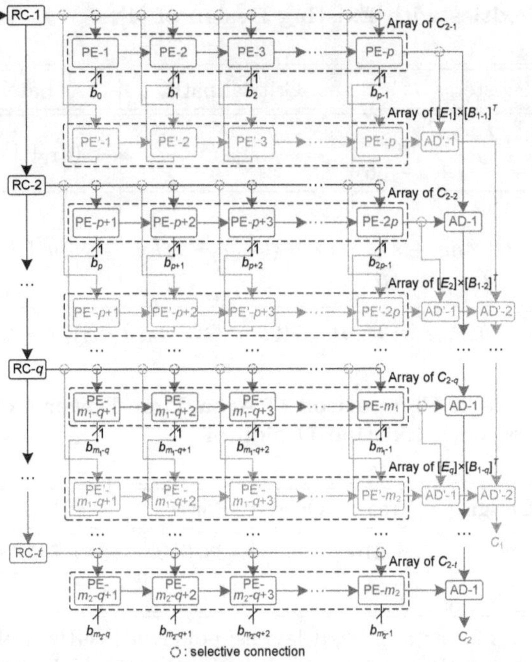

Figure 2: Proposed systolic structure mapped from Algorithm 1. RC: reduction cell. AD: addition cell.

Likewise, one can rewrite (7) as

$$C_2 = C_{2-1} + \cdots + C_{2-q} + C_{2-(q+1)} + \cdots + C_{2-t}, \quad (16)$$

where one can pair $C_{2-2}$, ..., and $C_{2-q}$, respectively, with $C_{1-2}, \ldots,$ and $C_{1-q}$ of (5) such that these paired sub-products can be processed in the unified format following the above proposed strategy ((9) to (15)). While the rest $(t-q)$ sub-products of (16) can be calculated individually. Note that due to the complexity differences exist in $C_{2-i}$ and $C_{1-i}$ (see (3) and (4)), each paired sub-products require "different" computation core matrix yet following the same resource-sharing principle. The above operations ((5) to (16)) can be summarized as the proposed algorithm.

**Fast algorithm employing.** To further reduce the involved computational complexity, one can employ the fast algorithm, i.e., TMVP method [1], where we can have four components, i.e., component matrix point (CMP), component vector point (CVP), point-wise multiply (PWM), and reconstruction (R).

*Proposed strategy to employ TMVP approach.* One can find that $[A_{2-1}]$ can be seen as a "Toeplitz"-like matrix and has the potential to be optimized further based on TMVP approach. Assume $p = nu$ and $m_2 = pt = nut$ ($u$ is an integer), such that we can decompose the original matrix $[A_{2-1}]$ into $u \times ut$ number of sub-matrices of size $n \times n$, where most of them can be realized through the above mentioned TMVP approach except those involved with the special row (i.e., contains the row of $[a_s \; a_{s-1} + a_{m-1} \; a_{s-2} + a_{m-2} \; \cdots]$, which can be realized by the regular calculation method, as shown in Fig. 1).

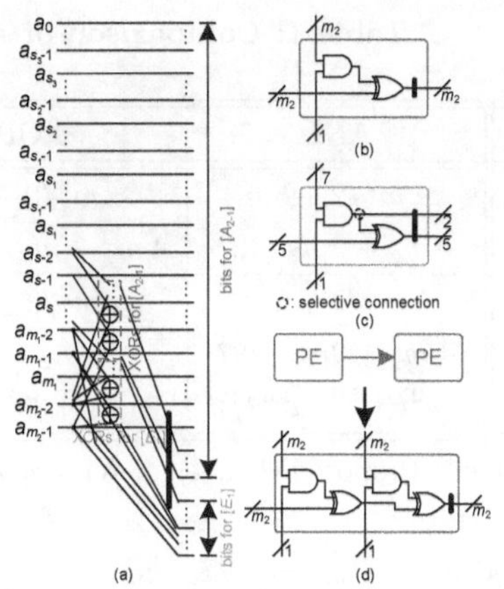

Figure 3: Internal structure of the RC-1. (b) Internal structure of the PE in the blue array. (c) PE'-3 in the green array. (d) Example of PE combination.

For efficient mapping into an optimized structure, one can also utilize the property of shifting elements in the matrix $[A_{2-1}]$ to have resource-sharing, i.e., the diagonal sub-matrices are the same and can be shared to save the area occupation (the CMP operations of these matrices are the same). Fig. 1 gives the detailed illustration of the proposed strategy of employing fast algorithm in $A_{2-1}$.

# 3 PROPOSED SYSTOLIC STRUCTURE

**Proposed systolic structure.** The proposed algorithm can be mapped into the systolic structure as shown in Fig. 2. We have used an "array-broadcasting" technique to pre-calculate a general input operand contains all the possible bits required for both blue and green systolic arrays (the last $t-q$ arrays are only blue arrays). Note that for the sake of registers saving, only those bits involved with XORs need to be latched through registers, as shown in Fig. 3(a). The internal structures of the two types of PEs are shown in Fig. 3(b) and (c), respectively (Fig. 3(c) is the internal structure of PE'-3).

After the processing of last PE in each paired arrays, there is an extra addition (AD') based on (15). One can also combine the neighboring PEs into one PE to reduce the register-complexity at the cost of slight increase in critical-path, as shown by the example shown in Fig. 3(d).

**TMVP-based implementation.** According to the strategy presented in Fig. 1, the computations of $C_{2-k}$ $(1 \leq k \leq t)$ can be realized by the TMVP approach to reduce the area-complexity. The blue array of Fig. 2 (the array of $C_{2-1}$, for example) can thus be realized by the structure shown in Fig. 4 (meanwhile the green arrays need to have the PE combination following the example of Fig. 3(d)).

As shown in Fig. 4, we have firstly decomposed each column of $[A_{2-1}]$ into $ut+1$ groups (based on the block decomposition strategy of Fig. 1), where we have split $A_2^{(0)}$ into $ut$ number of $n$-size groups and one special group (corresponds to the special $h$-size row in Fig. 1). Fig. 4(b) has shown the detailed internal structure of the new blue systolic array for $C_{2-1}$

**Table 1: Comparison of Area-Time Complexities with Existing Design of [4]**

| Design | AND | XOR | Register | Critical-path | Latency |
|---|---|---|---|---|---|
| [4][1] | $\simeq m_1^2/2+6m_1$ $+m_2^2+2m_2-27$ | $\approx m_1^2/2+9m_1$ $+m_2^2-m_2+s-26$ | $\approx m_1^2/2+m_2^2$ $+11m_1/2+4m_2+s-36$ | $T_A+T_X$ | $\approx (d_1+\log_2 l+8)$ |
| Proposed[2] | $\simeq m_1^2/2+6m_1$ $+m_2^2+2m_2-27$ $-u^2t(n^2-n^{\log_2 3})t$ | $\approx m_1^2/2+9m_1$ $+m_2^2-m_2$ $+s-26-K_1^*$ | $\approx m_1^2/2+m_2^2$ $+11m_1/2+4m_2+s$ $-36-u^2t(n^2-n^{\log_2 3})t$ | $T_A+(\log_2 n+1)T_X$ | $u+t+1$ |

[1]: Low-latency. [2]: Proposed (Fig. 4). *: $K_1=u^2n^2t^2-[n^{\log_2 3}(u+2ut+u^2t)-nu-2nut-(2.5n^{\log_2 3}-3n+0.5)(ut+2u-2)]t$.

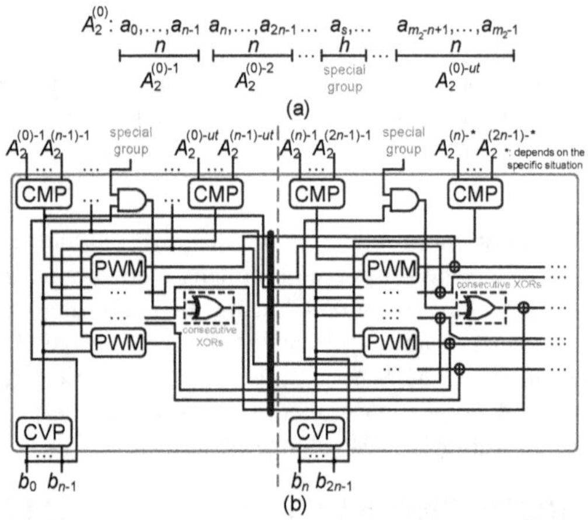


**Figure 4: (a) Illustration of the proposed grouping method for each operand within $A_{2-1}$. (b) Internal structure of the PEs within the blue array for $C_{2-1}$, where the dotted blue line represents the PE splitting line.**

based on TMVP approach, where the dotted blue line is used to represent the PE splitting line. Besides that, the resource-sharing strategy of these identical blocks shown in Fig. 1 is also employed in Fig. 4(b) to reduce the resource usage. As shown in Fig. 4(b), $ut$ number of $n$-size grouped sub-operands for $n$ columns of $[A_{2-1}]$ are fed to the CMP cells, respectively, according to the block positions of Fig. 1, to be processed with shared output of the CVP cell. After the AND operations in the PWM cells, all the output bits will be latched to the next PE through registers. The special group is processed in the regular format (similar to that shown in Fig. 3(d)) that AND operations are processed in parallel followed by consecutive XOR-based additions.

## 4 COMPLEXITY AND COMPARISON

To further estimate the efficiency of the proposed design, we have used the NanGate's Library Creator and the 45-nm FreePDK Base Kit from North Carolina State University (NCSU) [5]. We have used $m_1 = 163$ and $m_2 = 233$ ($f_1(x) = x^{163}+x^7+x^6+x^3+1$ and $f_2(x) = x^{233}+x^{74}+1$) to obtain the complexities of Table 2 ($n = 8$, $u = 4$, $t = 7$, and $h = 9$ for the proposed structure).

**Table 2: Comparison of Area-Time-Power Complexities with Existing Design of [4]**

| Design | Area | Delay | Power | ADP | PDP |
|---|---|---|---|---|---|
| [4][1] | 535,610 | 2.52 | 728,629 | 1,349,737 | 1,836,145 |
| Pro.[3] | 367,856 | 3.12 | 535,106 | 1,147,711 | 1,669,531 |

Units for area: $\mu m^2$; delay: ns; power: $\mu W$/GHz. Delay: Latency time=latency cycle×critical-path. ADP: area-delay product. PDP: power-delay product. [1]: $d_1 = 4$. [3]: where $n = 8$, $u = 4$, $t = 7$, and $h = 9$.

One can see that the proposed design significantly outperforms the existing design of [4], i.e., it has at least 15.0% less area-delay product (ADP) and 9.1% less power-delay product (PDP) than the existing low-latency design of [4] (optimized already), respectively. Besides that, the proposed design also has at least 30.9% less area-complexity and 24.9% less power-complexity than those of [4], respectively.

## 5 CONCLUSION

A new LSM design strategy is proposed in this paper to obtain efficient implementation of unified finite field multiplier over $GF(2^m)$. The detailed complexity analysis and comparison have shown that the proposed design outperforms the competing one of [4].

## REFERENCES


[1] Haining et al. Fan. 2007. A new approach to subquadratic space complexity parallel multipliers for extended binary fields. *IEEE Trans. Computers* 56, 2 (2007), 224–233.

[2] FIPS. 2000. 186-2. Digital Signature Standard. US Department of Commerce/National Institute of Standards and Technology.

[3] Kwiat G and Gauthier J. 2017. Reconfigurable Free-Space Quantum Cryptography System. US Patent App. 15/434,313.

[4] Qiliang et al. Shao. 2018. Low Complexity Implementation of Unified Systolic Multipliers for NIST Pentanomials and Trinomials Over GF(2m). *IEEE TCASI* 65, 8 (2018), 2455–2465.

[5] Nangate standard cell library. [n. d.]. [Online]. Available: http://www.si2.org/openeda.si2.org/projects/nangatelib.

[6] Jiafeng et al. Xie. 2013. Low latency systolic Montgomery multiplier for finite field GF(2m) based on pentanomials. *IEEE Trans. VLSI Systems* 21, 2 (2013), 385–389.

[7] Yiqun et al. Zhang. 2017. Recryptor: A reconfigurable in-memory cryptographic Cortex-M0 processor for IoT. In *VLSI Circuits, 2017 Symposium on*. IEEE, C264–C265.

# Binarized Depthwise Separable Neural Network for Object Tracking in FPGA

Li Yang, Zhezhi He, Deliang Fan
Department of ECE, University of Central Florida, Orlando, FL
{liyang,elliot.he}@knights.ucf,dfan@ucf.edu

## ABSTRACT

Object tracking has achieved great advances in the past few years and has been widely applied in vision-based application. Nowadays, deep convolutional neural network has taken an important role in object tracking tasks. However, its enormous model size and massive computation cost have became the main obstacle for deployment of such powerful algorithm in low power and resource limited embedded system, such as FPGA. Due to the popularization of the power-sensitive mobile platform, low power real-time tracking solution is strongly required. In order to address these challenges, we propose a low power and energy-efficient object tracking FPGA implementation based on a newly proposed binarized depthwise separable deep convolutional neural network. It can significantly reduce the model size and computation complexity simultaneously utilizing binarized (i.e., +1 and -1) depthwise separable convolution kernel and our proposed trainable threshold group binarization activation function. It can completely converts the dot product and accumulation based convolution operations into bit-wise XNOR and bit-count operations, while achieving state-of-the-art accuracy. Our proposed binarized depthwise separable model achieves ~57% Intersection over Union (IOU) on DJI object tracking dataset with only ~143.9Kb model parameter size. We then deploy our proposed model into the Xilinx PYNQ Z1 board with only 4.9Mb on-chip RAM. The experiment results show that our FPGA implementation achieves 11.1 frames per second for object tracking with only 2.61W.

**ACM Reference Format:**
Li Yang, Zhezhi He, Deliang Fan. 2019. Binarized Depthwise Separable Neural Network for Object Tracking in FPGA. In *Great Lakes Symposium on VLSI 2019(GLSVLSI'19), June 30–July 5, 2019, Tysons Corner, VA, USA.* ACM, New York, NY, USA, 4 pages. https://doi.org/10.1145//3299874.3318034

## 1 INTRODUCTION

In the last couple years, the climate of Artificial Intelligence, especially deep learning, has swept the various domains owing to its prominent performance over traditional methods [7]. As of our interest, object tracking is a intriguing topic which is the core function of many real-world applications. In virtue of deep learning technique, a trained deep neural network (DNN) can achieve up to 100 frames per second [5]. Comparing with traditional object tracking algorithm, deep learning has more powerful ability to extract feature from data. However, it relies on massive operations and model size, which makes the mobile device deployment encounter great challenges in terms of both computation and storage capability. Recently, in DAC Design Contest 2018 [3], many low power FPGA object tracking designs have been proposed to address such high computation cost and memory usage.

The contributions of this work mainly consist of two folds: 1) In the algorithm perspective, we propose a new method to optimize YOLO based object tracking deep neural network simultaneously using approximate weight binarization, trainable threshold group binarization activation function and depthwise separable convolution methods, to greatly reduce computation complexity and model size; 2) In the hardware part, we propose a new corresponding deep neural network accelerator architecture in FPGA to reduce latency, communication between off-chip and on-chip memory, and to maximize throughput according to hardware resources.

## 2 BINARIZED DEPTHWISE SEPARABLE DEEP NEURAL NETWORK FOR OBJECT TRACKING

### 2.1 Depthwise Separable Convolution

Recently, the depthwise separable convolution [10] has been proven it's efficiency in many state-of-the-art deep neural networks, such as MobileNet [6] and BD-NET [4], which factorize a conventional convolution layer into a depthwise convolution and a convolution with 1x1 convolution called pointwise convolution.

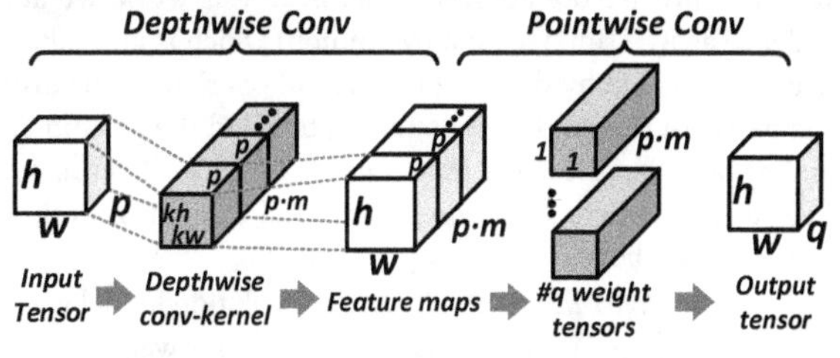


**Figure 1: Data-flow for depthwise separable convolution layer. Normally, the channel expansion $m$ is 1.[4]**

The data flow of depthwise separable convolution is shown in fig. 1. In the depthwise convolution layer, each channel of input tensor performs convolution with $p \cdot m$ kernels in the size of $kh \times kw$ (i.e. kernel-height and width) correspondingly, which produces $p \cdot m$ feature maps. $m$ is defined as *channel expansion*. Those generated feature maps are concatenated along its depth dimension as tensor in size of $h \times w \times (p \cdot m)$ which is taken as the input of pointwise convolution layer. The operation of such depthwise convolution


*GLSVLSI '19, June 30–July 5, 2019, Tysons Corner, VA, USA*

ACM ISBN 978-1-4503-6252-8/19/05...$15.00
https://doi.org/10.1145//3299874.3318034

can be mathematically described as:

$$F_{j \cdot p+i} = X_i * W_{j \cdot p+i},\ j \in [0, m-1] \tag{1}$$

where $i \in [1, p]$ is the index of depth of input tensor $X \in \mathbb{R}^{h \times w \times p}$. On the contrary to the distinctive depthwise convolution, pointwise layer is just normal spatial-convolution layer with $1 \times 1$ convolution kernel size. The ratio of computational cost between depthwise separable convolution and conventional convolution can be calculated as:

$$\frac{h \cdot w \cdot kh \cdot kw \cdot p \cdot m + h \cdot w \cdot p \cdot m \cdot q}{h \cdot w \cdot kh \cdot kw \cdot p \cdot q} = \frac{m(kh \cdot kw + q)}{kh \cdot kw \cdot q} \tag{2}$$

such ratio is approximated to $m/(kh \cdot kw)$ when the number of output channels $q >> kh \cdot kw$. In our work, we set the channel expansion m to 1 and the kernel size $kh \times kw$ is $3 \times 3$. In this case, the computation cost is only $1/9$ of the normal spatial-convolution.

**Table 1: Architecture of Our Model**

| Layer | Filter Shape | Input Shape | Kbits |
|---|---|---|---|
| Conv1 dw | 3x3x3 | 160x320 | 0.864 |
| BinConv2 | 64x3x1x1 | 160x320 | 0.1875 |
| MaxPool | | 80x160 | |
| BinConv3 dw | 3x3x64 dw | 80x160 | 0.5625 |
| BinConv4 | 128x64x1x1 dw | 80x160 | 8 |
| MaxPool | | 40x80 | |
| BinConv5 dw | 3x3x128 dw | 40x80 | 1.125 |
| BinConv6 | 128x128x1x1 | 40x80 | 16 |
| MaxPool | | 20x40 | |
| BinConv7 dw | 3x3x128 dw | 20x40 | 1.125 |
| BinConv8 | 128x128x1x1 | 20x40 | 16 |
| Conv9 | 25x128x1x1 | 20x40 | 100 |
| Total | | | 143.864 |
| IOU (DJI) | | | 57% |

## 2.2 Our Model

*2.2.1 Neural Network Structure.* In this section, we first present our binarized depthwise separable convolution neural network for object tracking. Except that the first and last layers are real-value tensors, all the rest layers are binarized in both weight and activation. Conv9 shown in the table 1 is fully-connected layer for prediction. Inspired by YOLOv2[9], we use the anchor boxes method to predict bounding box location and confidence score to reflect how precise the bounding box is. In this work, we define confidence as IOU (Intersection over union) which is an evaluation metric that yielded by dividing the area of overlap by the area of union between the predicted bounding box and the ground-truth bounding box. We divide the input images into a 20x40 grid, where each grid cell predicts 5 bounding boxes and computes confidence values for those boxes.

*2.2.2 Weight Binarization.* To binarize convolution kernel weights, we employ the popular approximation strategy for weight binarization first proposed in [8], which estimates the real-value weight kernel using a binary weight filter (i.e. -1 and +1) and a scaling factor $E$. The scaling factor should equal to the mean of absolute values of whole weight filters in current layer.

*2.2.3 Trainable Threshold Group Binarization Activation Function and XNOR Convolution.* In order to improve the accuracy while maintaining binary activation and XNOR based convolution operation (i.e. requiring both activation and weight in binary state), we propose a trainable threshold group binarization activation function, as shown in fig. 2, to replace original BinActive-XNORConv combination to a group of parallel BinActive-XNORConv modules, where each BinActive function has different trainable threshold $v_k$ to generate binary $x'_k$ from $x$.

$$x'_k = Sign(x - v_k) \tag{3}$$

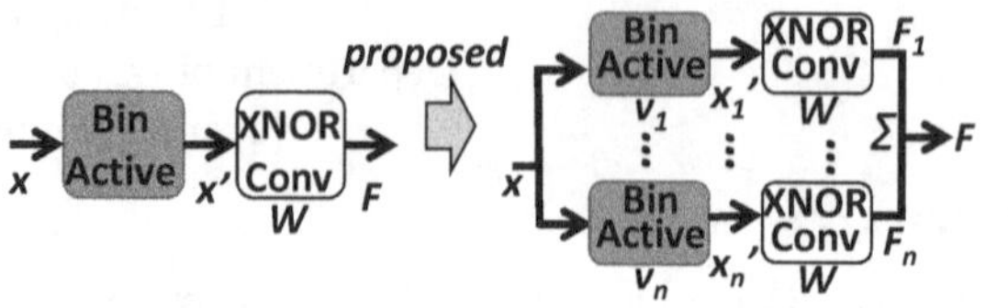


**Figure 2: Proposed trainable threshold group binarization activation function**

where trainable threshold $v$ is indexed by $k$, and $k$ is a integer ranging from 1 to n, where n=5 in this work. During the training of deep neural network, such threshold $v_k$ is also considered as a trainable parameter similar kernel weight. However, during the training, the sign function in eq. (3) owns zero derivatives almost everywhere, which makes it impossible to calculate the gradient using chain rule in backward path (i.e. training phase). Thus, the Straight-Through Estimator (STE) [1, 2] is applied to calculate gradient in this work. In the backward path, the input gradient of binarization activation function clones the gradient at output, if it is in the range from -1 to +1. Otherwise, the gradient is cancelled to preserve training performance:

$$\text{Backward}: \frac{\partial g}{\partial x} = \begin{cases} \frac{\partial g}{\partial x'} & if\ |x| \leq 1 \\ 0 & otherwise \end{cases} \tag{4}$$

During training, to keep the distribution of activation relatively stable, batch-normalization layer is inserted before binarization activation, which can normalize the feature maps to zero mean and unit variance. Moreover, to properly initialize $v_k$ during training phase, we use a input sample to obtain the distribution of interlayer tensor then manually setup the initial values. It is worth to note that all the parallel XNORConv layer in each module share the same binary weights for XNOR based convolution computation. Therefore, our method doesn't increase the overall model size.

*2.2.4 Binarized Depthwise Separable Convolution.* In this subsection, we apply previously discussed approximation weight binarization and our proposed trainable threshold group binarization activation for both depthwise convolution and pointwise convolution. In this case, except the first and last layer, the weights of all layers are binarized with a scaling factor as well as activations.

The weight and activation binarization function can be replaced by *XNOR* operation.The computation of depthwise convolution can be reformatted as:

$$BinF_{j \cdot p+i} = E_p * \sum_{k=1}^{n} 2*XNOR(X_i - v_{i,k}, W_{j \cdot p+i}) - nN,\ j \in [0, m-1] \tag{5}$$

where N is the number of corresponding weight filters to create one output value which equals to $kh * kw$ in depthwise convolution.

*2.2.5 Converting ReLU-BatchNorm-Binarization Activation-Weight Scaling Factor to Threshold Function.* In this work, we propose to integrate weight scaling factor with ReLu-BatchNorm-Binarization activation, which could totally eliminate multiplication in our binarized depthwise separable convolution.

Batch Normalization layer can be considered an affine function $\boldsymbol{y} = k\boldsymbol{x} + b$. Therefore, the cascaded BatchNorm-Binarization Activation-Weight scaling factor can be described as:

$$y = \begin{cases} E * Sign(kx + b) & if\ \boldsymbol{x} \geq 0 \\ b & otherwise \end{cases} \tag{6}$$

In the eq. (6), $x$ means the output tensor $BinF$ from previous convolution layer according to eq. (5). $E$ presents the weight scaling factor. In order to avoid multiplication and subtraction in eq. (5). We use $x''$ to represent $n$ sum of the $XNOR(X, W)$, so the $x$ can be described as:$\boldsymbol{x} = 2 * \boldsymbol{x''} - \boldsymbol{nN}$.

The eq. (6) can be realized through sign function ($Sign_\Delta()$) with adjusted threshold $\Delta$, where $Sign_\Delta(x) = +1$ when $x \geq \Delta$ and $Sign_\Delta(x) = 0$ when $x < \Delta$. Therefore, eq. (6) can be rewritten as:

$$y = \begin{cases} Sign_\Delta(x'') & if\ \boldsymbol{x''} \geq \boldsymbol{nN}/2 \\ b & otherwise \end{cases} \tag{7}$$

where $\Delta = -b/(Ek)$.

# 3 FPGA IMPLEMENTATION

## 3.1 Overall Architecture

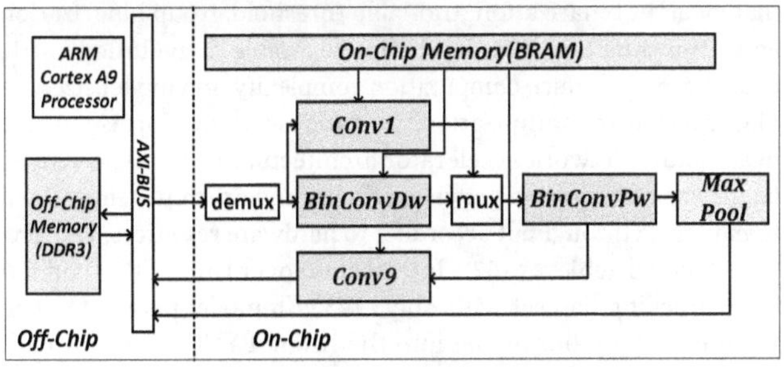


**Figure 3: Overall Architecture**

The overall architecture of our mapped model in FPGA is shown in fig. 3. There are totally four processing elements (PE) corresponding to four types of convolution layer respectively, namely Conv1, BinDw, BinPw and Conv9. Except first and last layer, all the rest binarized depthwise convolution layers reuse BinDw kernel which implement bitwise *XNOR* and *bitcount* operations. In order to further reduce communication between on-chip and off-chip, and maximize the usage of on-chip resources, BinDw and BinPw are allocated different hardware resources. In addition, it is worth to note that, benefiting from our deeply compressed model size (144Kbits), all of the network parameters can be stored in FPGA on-chip RAM. As widely known, communication between on-chip and off-chip memory is power hungry and time consuming. Our fully on-chip BNN could greatly reduce such communication and leaves more memory bandwidth for input images.

## 3.2 Hardware Optimization

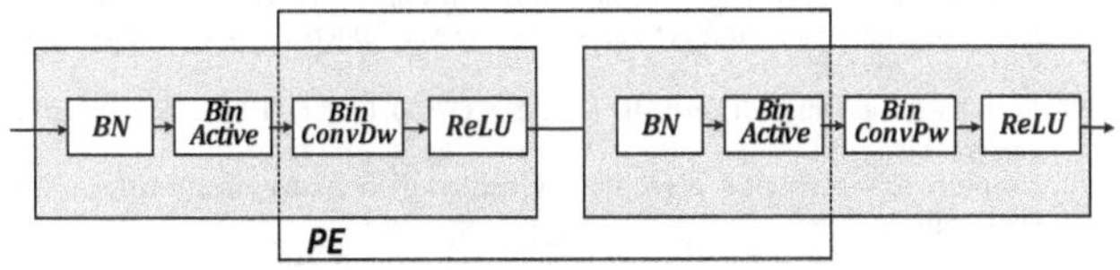


**Figure 4: Hardware Block Architecture**

*3.2.1 Block Optimization.* In order to more efficiently map model to FPGA, we further redefine the block architecture which makes it more hardware friendly without changing the whole pipeline architecture. fig. 4 shows the new processing element (PE) consisting of different computation components. Our optimized new PE consists of BinConv-ReLU and BatchNorm-BinActive. By redesigning PE in this way, it could be found that the outputs of each PE are in binary format since they are the direct outputs from binarized activation function (i.e. BinActive). Therefore, such optimization method guarantees inputs and outputs of each processing elements are both binary data, which greatly reduces the inter-layer communication data size. Moreover, such design is also necessary since we convert integrated ReLU-BarchNorm-BinActive into a more hardware friendly threshold function as described in eq. (7).

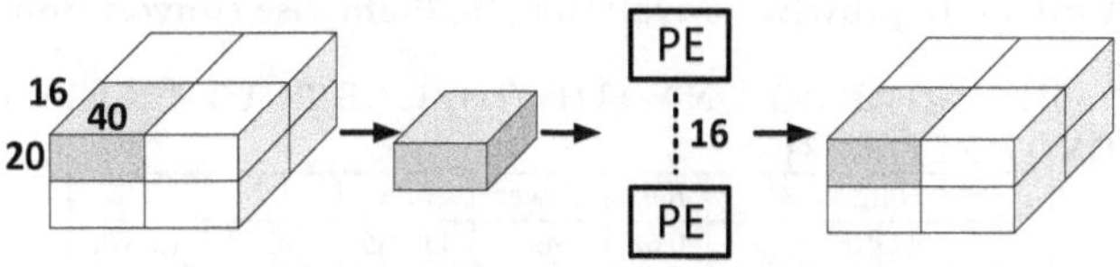


**Figure 5: Feature Maps Group**

*3.2.2 Feature Map Group.* Since the feature maps of different layers have different dimension, which means the computation pattern varies betwen layers. It is impossible for the whole feature maps to reuse *ConvDw* and *ConvPw* processing element. In order to solve this problem, we divide every feature map into the same size of groups as shown in fig. 5. Feature map groups are loaded into processing element for both depthwise and pointwise convolution, which will then create one corresponding output feature map group, one by one in pipeline.table 1 gives an example which using $20 \times 40 \times 16$ as the dimension of feature map groups.

*3.2.3 Processing Element.* The detailed processing element architecture is shown in fig. 6, which mainly consists of XNOR units, popcount units and following threshold units. As discussed in section 2.1, depthwise convolution and pointwise convolution have different computation cost, therefore the input buffer and XNOR unit contain different computation capacity. Processing elements are core computing unit to implement convolution operation. It can be seen that *XNOR-popcount-threshold* could compute in a parallel manner, which will load different weights(i.e. kernels) at the same clock cycle. Therefore, the number of parallel *XNOR* units, which is 16 in our work, corresponds to the output feature maps. As shown in fig. 7, depthwise and pointwise processing element can achieve $16 \times 5$ and $16 \times 16 \times 5$ computation in parallel respectively. Such operations could be easily implemented using LUTs in FPGA and are much more energy efficient compared to conventional dot-product, accumulation and Batch-Norm operations.

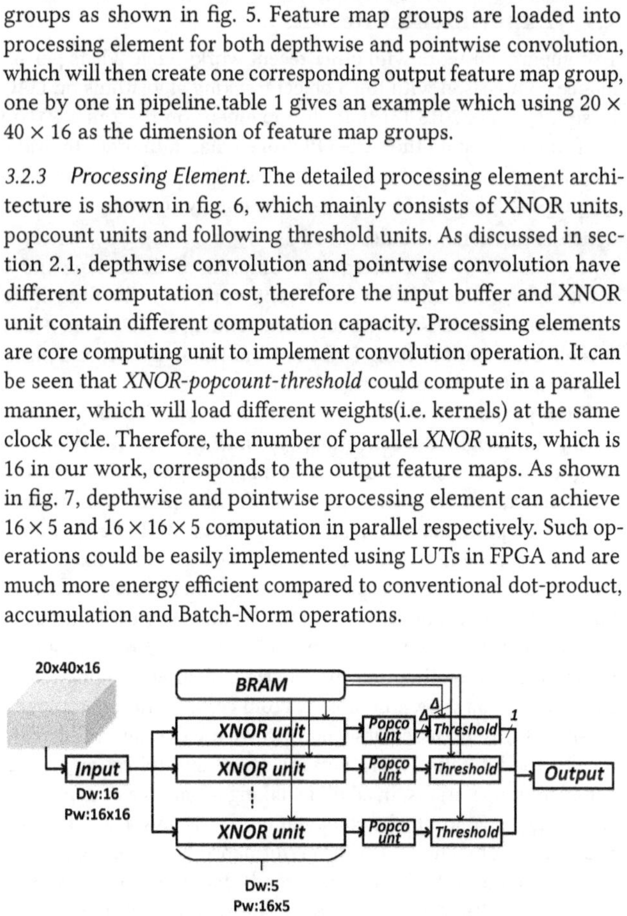


**Figure 6: Processing Element Architecture**

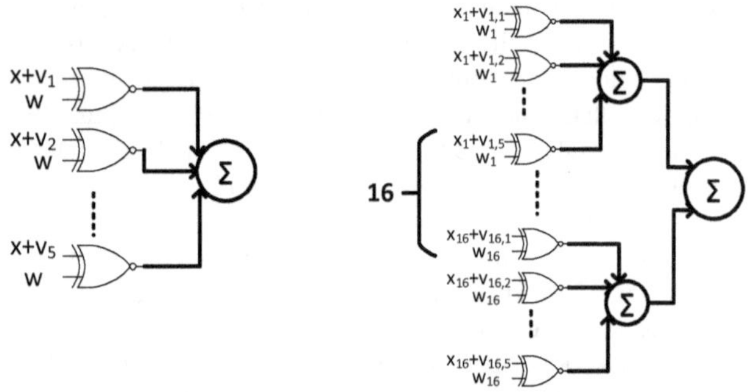


Figure 7: Multiple Shift XNOR for one input data in XNOR Unit, (a) Depthwise convolution, (b) Pointwise convolution

Table 2: COMPARISON WITH OTHER OBJECT TRACKING ON THE FPGA[3]

| Name | IOU | Power | FPS | ES | TS |
|---|---|---|---|---|---|
| TGIIF | 0.62 | 4.2 | 11.955 | 1.0318 | 1.2674 |
| SystemsETHZ | 0.49 | 2.45 | 25.968 | 1.3976 | 1.1794 |
| iSmart2 | 0.57 | 2.59 | 7.349 | 1.0297 | 1.1636 |
| traix | 0.61 | 3.11 | 5.445 | 0.8869 | 1.1523 |
| hwac-object-tracker | 0.52 | 3.66 | 4.935 | 0.8155 | 0.932 |
| **Ours** | 0.57 | 2.61 | 11.1 | 1.1477 | **1.224** |

# 4 EXPERIMENTAL RESULTS

## 4.1 Experimental Results

To compare our work with other recent works. table 2 lists performance comparison with top 5 object tracking algorithms on DAC Design Contest 2018 [3] that all implement on the same PYNQ platform and test on the same DJI drone dataset. In order to evaluate the performance of different trackers, two evaluation metrics are proposed, *ES* and *TS*. *ES* means the energy consumption score which is mathematical described as: $1 + 0.2 \times \log_2(\frac{\bar{E}}{E})$, where $\bar{E}$ represents the average energy consumption of all trackers and $E$ is the energy consumption for current work. *TS* is the final score which combines *IOU* and *ES* together, defining as: $IOU \times (1 + ES)$. It is obvious that our final TS score is ranked in the second place, which is only 0.04 smaller than TGIIF.

From pespective of model size and data type, TGIIF uses 8bit fixed point weight and activation. SystemsETHZ has full precision weights for the first and last layer, binary weights and 5 bit fixed point activation for the rest layers. 8bit fixed point weights and 16 bit fixed point activation are used in iSmart2. However, in our work, except the first and last layer use 32bit and 16bit fixed point weights and activations respectively, all the intermediate layers are binarized weights and activations (i.e. +1 and -1). Benefiting from depthwise separable convolution and trainable threshold group binarization activation, our model size is further compressed to $143.864Kbits$ as shown in table 1. From computation complexity perspective, as discussed in section 3.2. We use five parallel bit-wise $XNOR$ and bit-count operations instead of multiplication and accumulation operations. In addition, taking advantage of depthwise separable convolution, the computation cost is only 1/9 of the normal spatial-convolution. On the performance side, The top 2 trackers have higher FPS (frame per second) than our work as shown in table 2. TGIIF divides whole workflow into multiple threads which can process multiple images in pipeline in the system level perspective. SystemsETHZ utilizes mini-batch images as the input of the hardware accelerator which also achieves multiple images processing in pipeline. In our future work, we will keep optimizing our speed in latency or FPS.

Figure 8: PYNQ Power Measurement

# 5 CONCLUSION

In this paper, we propose a new method to optimize YOLO based object tracking deep neural network simultaneously using approximate weight binarization, trainable threshold group binarization activation function and depthwise separable convolution methods, to greatly reduce computation complexity and model size. For FPGA hardware optimization, we propose a new corresponding deep neural network accelerator architecture in FPGA to reduce latency,communication between off-chip and on-chip memory, and to maximize throughput according to hardware resources. Our proposed model achieves~57% Intersection over Union (IOU) on DJI objecttracking dataset with only~143.9Kb model parameter size. We then deploy our model into the Xilinx PYNQ Z1 board with only 4.9Mb on-chip RAM. The experiment results show it achieves 11.1 frames per second for object tracking with only 2.61W.

# ACKNOWLEDGEMENTS

This work is supported in part by the National Science Foundation under Grant No. 1740126 and Semiconductor Research Corporation nCORE.

# REFERENCES

[1] Yoshua Bengio et al. 2013. Estimating or propagating gradients through stochastic neurons for conditional computation. *arXiv preprint arXiv:1308.3432* (2013).
[2] Matthieu Courbariaux et al. 2016. Binarized neural networks: Training deep neural networks with weights and activations constrained to+ 1 or-1. *arXiv preprint arXiv:1602.02830* (2016).
[3] DAC. 2018. DAC Design Contest 2018. https://dac.com/content/2018-system-design-contest-1.
[4] Zhezhi He et al. 2018. BD-NET: A Multiplication-Less DNN with Binarized Depthwise Separable Convolution. In *2018 IEEE Computer Society Annual Symposium on VLSI (ISVLSI)*. IEEE, 130–135.
[5] David Held et al. 2016. Learning to track at 100 fps with deep regression networks. In *European Conference on Computer Vision*. Springer, 749–765.
[6] Andrew G Howard et al. 2017. Mobilenets: Efficient convolutional neural networks for mobile vision applications. *arXiv preprint arXiv:1704.04861* (2017).
[7] Yann LeCun et al. 2015. Deep learning. *nature* 521, 7553 (2015), 436.
[8] Mohammad Rastegari et al. 2016. Xnor-net: Imagenet classification using binary convolutional neural networks. In *European Conference on Computer Vision*. Springer, 525–542.
[9] Joseph Redmon and Ali Farhadi. 2017. YOLO9000: better, faster, stronger. *arXiv preprint* (2017).
[10] Laurent Sifre et al. 2014. *Rigid-motion scattering for image classification*. Ph.D. Dissertation. Citeseer.

# An Analytical-based Hybrid Algorithm for FPGA Placement

Chengyu Hu[1], Qinghua Duan[2], Liran Hu[1], Peng Lu[1],
Zhengjie Li[1], Meng Yang[1], Jian Wang[1], and Jinmei Lai[1] *
[1]Fudan University, [2]Chengdu Sino Microelectronic Technology Co., Ltd
[1]{15110720009, 17212020078,13110720020, 18112020031, mengyang, wjian, jmlai }@fudan.edu.cn,
[2]qh_duan@csmsc.com

## ABSTRACT

As the capacity of FPGA increases, FPGA placers that adopt Simulated Annealing (SA) algorithm take more and more runtime. To solve this problem, this paper presents HCAS, a Hybrid algorithm Combining Analytical method and SA. There are three modifications in HCAS: (1) In global placement, faster and better result is realized by modified analytical algorithm. (2) In detailed placement, proper tradeoff is made between quality and runtime through improvement of SA. (3) Optimization workload of timing and wirelength is reasonably assigned between global and detailed placement according to algorithm features. HCAS is implemented in the newest VPR. Compared to VPR placer, it obtains a speedup of 11.1x, with 3% shorter wirelength and 5% smaller critical path delay. Compared to other analytical-based hybrid placers, HCAS achieves greater speedup and enhancement of placement quality is similar or better.

## KEYWORDS

FPGA; Placement; Analytical; Simulated annealing; Hybrid algorithm;

**ACM Reference format:**

Chengyu Hu, Qinghua Duan, Liran Hu, Peng Lu, Zhengjie Li, Meng Yang, Jian Wang and Jinmei Lai. 2019. An Analytical-based Hybrid Algorithm for FPGA Placement. In Proceedings of 2019 Great Lakes Symposium on VLSI (GLSVLSI '19). *Tysons Corner, VA, USA*, 4 pages. https://doi.org/10.1145/3299874.3318035

## 1 INTRODUCTION

Simulated annealing is popular in the domain of FPGA placement, academic tool VPR [1] and commercial tool Quartus II [2] both adopt this algorithm. However, rapid growth of FPGA capacity makes SA placers take more and more runtime. Placement for some large benchmarks even takes several hours [3]. In order to reduce placement runtime without degrading placement quality, analytical-based hybrid algorithm is widely studied. It mainly includes two stages: global placement and detailed placement. In global placement, analytical algorithm is used to obtain a high-quality result in a short time. In detailed placement, algorithms of greedy or heuristic kind are applied to improve quality further.

In paper [4], hybrid placement algorithm includes three stages: building and solving analytical equation many times; legalizing analytical placement; low-temperature SA. Compared to VPR 4.3, a speedup of 5.8x is achieved and wirelength increase is 1.9%; In paper [5], global placement performs multiple analytical iterations and different types of blocks are solved and legalized separately. Then greedy algorithm is used in detailed placement. Compared to non-timing placer of Quartus II, a speedup of 4.1x is got at the cost of 5% longer wirelength. In paper [6], timing optimization is supported in global placement. During detailed stage, different algorithms are applied in different optimization targets. Compared to VPR 5.0, a speedup of 6.91x is achieved with 1% shorter wirelength and 7% smaller critical path delay. In paper [7], global placement aims at wirelength optimization. In detailed placement, cell swapping and cell matching are applied. Compared to VPR 7.0, a speedup of 3.07x is obtained with 6% shorter wirelength.

Although significant acceleration has been achieved in above researches, there is still some space for modifications: (1) global placement can be more efficient. On the one hand, it is not worth putting too much effort in solving analytical system [4] [5] [6] [7], because the analytical result will be broken by legalization. On the other hand, more considerations are needed for heterogeneous blocks, during building analytical system and legalizing analytical results [4] [5] [6] [7]. (2) Proper tradeoff between quality and runtime is required in detailed placement. Greedy-like algorithms are applied in [5] [7]. Solution space of them is small, leading to poor quality improvement. SA algorithm is used in [4] [6]. Its solution space is large, leading to much runtime. (3) Optimization workload should be assigned reasonably between global and detailed placement [4] [5] [6] [7]. Different Algorithms are used in these two stages, so optimization workload should be assigned according to algorithm features.

In order to overcome these shortcomings in previous work [4] [5] [6] [7] and achieve better speedup without quality degrading, this paper presents a modified hybrid placement algorithm, named HCAS. It adopts analytical algorithm in global placement and applies improved SA algorithm in detail placement.


ACM ISBN 978-1-4503-6252-8/19/05...$15.00
https://doi.org/10.1145/3299874.3318035

# 2 OVERVIEW OF HCAS ALGORITHM

HCAS has been incorporated in the newest version of VPR [8]. As shown in Fig.1, process of HCAS placer can be divided into three stages: (1) random initial placement; (2) analytical global placement. (3) SA detailed placement.

Some strategies are adopted in global placement to get faster and better result. In building step, connections of heterogeneous blocks will get unbalanced weight. In solving step, runtime is reduced by gradient descent with momentum [9]; in legalization step, two-step method is used for heterogeneous blocks.

Some strategies are used in detailed placement to realize proper tradeoff between runtime and quality. Before inner loops of SA start, temperature is initialized by formulated method and move distance is initialized by self-adaptive method, in order to reduce solution space of SA. During inner loops, directed moves are applied to accelerate SA convergence.

In addition, analytic algorithm is connection-based and good at optimizing critical path delay, while SA is net-based and prefers reducing wirelength. Thus, global placement is assigned more timing optimization by dynamic weight factor of timing, while detailed placement is assigned more wirelength optimization by dynamic tradeoff factor of wirelength.

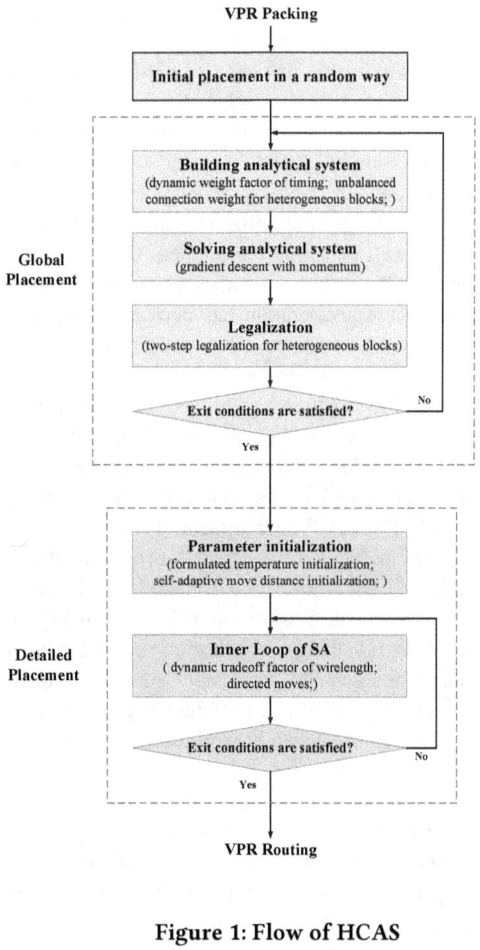


**Figure 1: Flow of HCAS**

# 3 GLOBAL PLACEMENT

During global placement, analytical algorithm is modified to be more efficient and obtain more timing optimization.

## 3.1 Building Analytical System

Here, wirelength and timing cost are computed. Besides, each block is expected to move to its legal position of the last iteration, so legalization cost needs to be included. Directions of x and y can be solved separately in the same way. Cost function of "x" direction is described as formula (1).

$$COST(x) = \sum_{ij \in C_{bb}} w_{bb}(i,j)\left(x_i - x_j\right)^2 + \sum_{ij \in C_{timing}} w_{timing}(i,j)\left(x_i - x_j\right)^2 \sum_{i,i0 \in C_{legal}} w_{legal}(i)\left(x_i - x_{i0}\right)^2 \quad (1)$$

$C_{bb}$, $C_{timing}$, $C_{legal}$ are sets of connections for wirelength, timing and legalization; $w_{bb}(i,j)$, $w_{timing}(i,j)$, $w_{legal}(i,j)$ are corresponding weights of connection between block i and block j; $x_i$ and $x_j$ are x coordinates of block i and block j; $x_{i0}$ is legal coordinate of block i in the last iteration.

Bound2Bound net module [10] is used to compute wirelength cost. About Timing cost, connections on critical paths should be considered; timing weight of a connection is related to timing criticality [6]. About legal cost, it is taken into account after the second analytical iteration. Pseudo connection is built between the placement block and its legal position of the last iteration [5].

### 3.1.1 Unbalanced connection weight for heterogeneous blocks

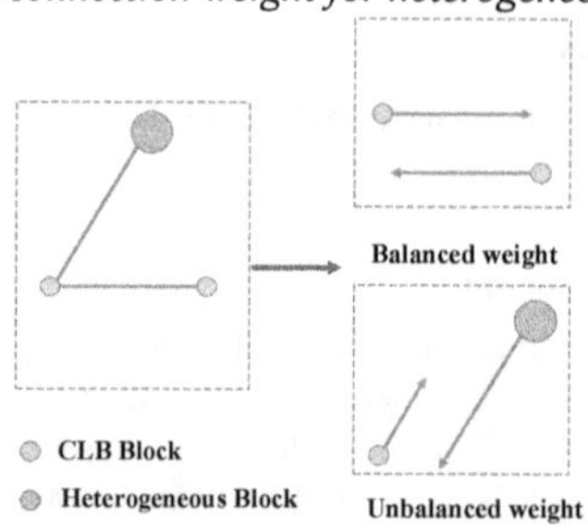


**Figure2: Unbalanced connection weight for heterogeneous blocks**

Heterogeneous blocks may deviate far from original analytical positions after legalization. This can result in increasing cost of connected CLB blocks. Therefore, unbalanced weight is designed for connections of a heterogeneous block and a CLB block. As shown in Fig.2, for a connection between two CLB blocks, we hope they will approach each other in solving step, so same weight will be added for the two blocks. However, for connection between a CLB block and a heterogeneous block, we hope a CLB block will approach other connected CLB blocks, rather than the connected heterogeneous block. Therefore, a smaller weight is added for the CLB block.

### 3.1.2 Dynamic weight factor of timing.

In global placement, timing optimization is favored by tuning timing weight factor. As shown in formula (2), timing weight factor is designed to increase dynamically with the number of iterations, so solutions of better timing can be found out when analytical algorithm is close to convergence.

$$\alpha = \alpha_0 + \mathrm{Min}(\alpha_{max}, \ \mathrm{delta}_\alpha * (\mathrm{iter\_num} + 1)) \quad (2)$$

## 3.2 Solving Analytical System

Gradient descent with momentum is used for solving analytical system. Its property of fast solving has been verified in [11]. The momentum is added to help stepping out of local optimal solution. Solving process can be formulized as formula (3) (4), where **x** is position vector and **v** is momentum.

$$\mathbf{x}_{iter\_num} = \mathbf{x}_{iter\_num-1} + \beta * \mathbf{v}_{iter\_num-1} \quad (3)$$

$$\mathbf{v}_{iter\_num} = \mathbf{v}_{iter\_num-1} - \gamma * \nabla COST(\mathbf{x}_{iter\_num}) \quad (4)$$

## 3.3 Legalization

At the beginning, a closest legal position is found for movable blocks and overlap is allowed. For "CLB" blocks, partition-based method [10] is adopted to eliminate overlap. For heterogeneous blocks, two-step method is applied separately for different block types: (1) all blocks of the same type are ranked according to their current cost. Then each block finds its best position in priority order. Overlap is forbidden here; (2) SA algorithm is used to further optimize positions of heterogeneous blocks.

# 4 DETAILED PLACEMENT

The target of detailed placement is improving global placement within acceptable time. This can be achieved by reducing solution space and accelerating search speed of SA process. Besides, more effort should be put in wirelength optimization.

## 4.1 Parameter Initialization

Temperature and move distance are critical parameters of SA. The former decides the probability that a block move of worse quality is accepted. The latter determines movable range of a block [1].

### *4.1.1 Formulated temperature initialization*

$$T_0 = \frac{T_{vpr\_sa}}{\beta_0 * (1 + Num_{Blocks})} \quad (5)$$

In detailed placement, initial temperature ($T_0$) should be smaller than normal SA algorithm. It decides the starting point of solution search. On the one hand, $T_0$ needs to be small enough to reject block moves that degrade global results seriously. On the other hand, $T_0$ cannot be too small to turn SA into greedy-like algorithm. Therefore, $T_0$ is designed as formula (5), where $T_{vpr\_sa}$ indicates initial temperature of VPR placer and $\beta_0$ is a factor.

### *4.1.2 Self-adaptive move distance initialization*

Initial move distance ($\mathrm{Rlim}_0$) decides size of solution space. Small $\mathrm{Rlim}_0$ leads to small solution space and poor optimization, while large $\mathrm{Rlim}_0$ results in great change of cost functions and low acceptance rate of block moves. Therefore, $\mathrm{Rlim}_0$ should take a proper value. In experiments, if $\mathrm{Rlim}_0$ makes move acceptance rate be 10%~15%, good quality is obtained. According to this clue, a self-adaptive method is proposed for $\mathrm{Rlim}_0$ initialization: The detail is shown in Fig.3, where grid_height and grid_width indicate device size, inner_num means number of block move of one SA inner loop, $a$ takes value about 10%~15%.

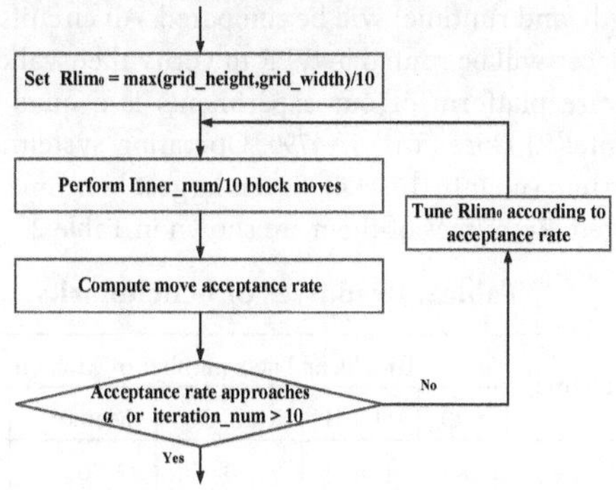


**Figure 3: Self-adaptive initialization of move distance**

## 4.2 Inner loop of SA

Compared to VPR SA, HCAS made two modifications in inner loops. First, dynamic tradeoff factor of wirelength is used to achieve more wirelength optimization. Second, directed moves are applied to speed up search of solution space.

### *4.2.1 Dynamic tradeoff factor of wirelength*

$$\Phi_{bb} = \Phi_0 + \frac{\mathrm{delta}\_\Phi}{1 + \beta * \mathrm{iter\_num}} \quad (6)$$

Tradeoff factor of wirelength means proportion of wirelength cost to total placement cost. It will influence optimization bias. As shown in formula (6), it is designed to decrease with iteration number. $\Phi_0$ is usually take the value of 0.5, delta_$\Phi$ can take the value of 0.1~0.2. This formula makes wirelength have more chances to be optimized in the early phase of detailed placement. In the final phase of detailed placement, timing will get same optimization as wirelength.

### *4.2.3 Directed Moves*

As number of inner loops increases, acceptance rate of block moves becomes lower and lower. At this time, strategy of directed move is used to accelerate convergence. As shown in Table 1, there are two types of directed moves existing in inner loops. About directed move of timing, blocks of critical paths will be put into a set. One block will be randomly selected from the set, and then the block will be moved to a random position. As for directed moves of wirelength, after a block is randomly selected, a position will be randomly selected from its median region [12].

**Table1: Two types of directed moves**

| | From block | To Position |
|---|---|---|
| Directed move of timing | Timing-critical | Random |
| Directed move of wirelength | Random | Median [12] |

# 5 EXPERIMENTAL RESULTS

HCAS is implemented in the newest VPR [8]. Benchmark circuits are packed by VPR packer and placed by different placers (VPR Placer, HCAS Placer). Placement results (critical path delay, wirelength, and runtime) will be compared. All circuits placed by HCAS placer will be routed by VPR to verity their validity.

Hardware platform of our experiments is a quad-core CPU, named Intel(R) Core (TM) i7-4790. Operating system is a 64-bit Linux system (ubuntu-16.04.4). Seven largest benchmarks of VPR are selected. Resources of them are shown in Table 2.

**Table2: Resources of benchmarks**

| Circuit name | Blocks and nets number of each circuit | | | | |
|---|---|---|---|---|---|
| | #IO | #CLB | Mult_36 | Memory | #Nets |
| bgm | 289 | 16613 | 0 | 0 | 49032 |
| LU32PEEng | 216 | 7252 | 32 | 168 | 57053 |
| LU64PEEng | 216 | 14005 | 64 | 340 | 109854 |
| LU8PEEng | 216 | 30685 | 0 | 0 | 71378 |
| mcml | 69 | 6472 | 27 | 159 | 65271 |
| stereovision1 | 278 | 9339 | 0 | 0 | 28968 |
| stereovision2 | 331 | 16791 | 0 | 0 | 55545 |

## 5.1 Compared to VPR

In order to test performance, we run VPR placer in timing-driven mode (timing tradeoff factor is set to 0.5) and compared HCAS with VPR placer in three aspects: wirelength, critical path delay and runtime. As shown in Table 3, HCAS gets a speedup of 11.1x, with 3% short wirelength and 5% smaller critical path delay.

**Table3: Comparison between VPR placer and HCAS placer**

| Circuit name | VPR Placer | | | HCAS placer | | |
|---|---|---|---|---|---|---|
| | WL | CPD | RT | WL | CPD | RT |
| bgm | 910 | 41.2 | 561 | 869 | 42.1 | 56 |
| LU32PEEng | 1519 | 74.8 | 694 | 1592 | 73.5 | 49 |
| LU64PEEng | 3775 | 77.9 | 1983 | 3765 | 72.8 | 162 |
| LU8PEEng | 1788 | 174.7 | 1616 | 1827 | 167.5 | 113 |
| mcml | 1056 | 45.2 | 647 | 950 | 46.3 | 44 |
| stereovision1 | 404 | 15.6 | 210 | 378 | 13.9 | 26 |
| stereovision2 | 769 | 32.1 | 583 | 726 | 28.0 | 70 |
| ***Ratio Geomean*** | **1.03** | **1.05** | **11.1** | | | |

(WL indicates wirelength and it has been divided by 1000, CPD and RT means critical path delay and run time, their measure unit is second)

## 5.2 Compared to Other Hybrid Placers

Here, HCAS placer is compared with other analytical-based hybrid placers in [4] [5] [6] [7]. Data of [4] [5] [6] [7] is got from comparison to SA placer. As shown in Table 4, HCAS placer outperforms all listed placers in speedup. Placement quality enhancement of HCAS is better than [4] [5] and similar to [6] [7]. This proves that strategies adopted in HCAS are effective.

**Table4: Comparison HCAS placer with other hybrid placers**

| | [4] | [5] | [6] | [7] | HCAS |
|---|---|---|---|---|---|
| Speedup | 5.8x | 4.1x | 6.91x | 3.07 x | 11.1x |
| Quality | WL: +1.9%; | WL: +5% | WL: -1% CPD: -7% | WL: -6% | WL: -3% CPD: -5% |

(WL: wirelength, CPD: critical path delay, +: worse, - : better)

# 6 CONCLUSIONS

In this paper, an analytical-based hybrid algorithm named HCAS is presented for FPGA placement. HCAS improves performance in three aspects: (1) Global placement is sped by faster analytical solving method and better result is achieved by two heterogeneous strategies. (2) Detailed placement realizes quality refinement in acceptable runtime by decreasing solution space and accelerating search during SA. (3) Optimization workload is reasonably assigned according to algorithm features. Finally, HCAS obtains a speed up of 11.1x with 3% short wirelength and 5% smaller critical path delay, compared to placer of VPR. This verifies that HCAS outperforms previous hybrid placers [4] [5] [6] [7].

# REFERENCES


[1] J. Luu, J. Goeders, M. Wainberg, A. Somerville, T. Yu, K. Nasartschuk, M. Nasr, S. Wang, T. Liu, N. Ahmed, K. B. Kent, J. Anderson, J. Rose and V. Betz "VTR 7.0: Next Generation Architecture and CAD System for FPGAs," ACM TRETS, Vol. 7, No. 2, June 2014, pp. 6:1 - 6:30.

[2] Adrian Ludwin and Vaughn Betz. 2011. Efficient and Deterministic Parallel Placement for FPGAs. ACM Trans. Des. Autom. Electron. Syst. 16, 3, Article 22 (June 2011), 23 pages. DOI=http://dx.doi.org/10.1145/1970353.1970355

[3] K. E. Murray, S. Whitty, S. Liu, J. Luu and V. Betz, "Titan: Enabling large and complex benchmarks in academic CAD," 2013 23rd International Conference on Field programmable Logic and Applications, Porto, 2013, pp. 1-8. doi: 10.1109/FPL.2013.6645503

[4] Yonghong Xu and M. A. S. Khalid, "QPF: efficient quadratic placement for FPGAs," International Conference on Field Programmable Logic and Applications, 2005., Tampere, 2005, pp. 555-558. doi: 10.1109/FPL.2005.1515784

[5] M. Gort and J. H. Anderson, "Analytical placement for heterogeneous FPGAs," 22nd International Conference on Field Programmable Logic and Applications (FPL), Oslo, 2012, pp. 143-150. doi: 10.1109/FPL.2012.6339278

[6] Tzu-Hen Lin, P. Banerjee and Y. Chang, "An efficient and effective analytical placer for FPGAs," 2013 50th ACM/EDAC/IEEE Design Automation Conference (DAC), Austin, TX, 2013, pp. 1-6.

[7] Y. Chen, S. Chen and Y. Chang, "Efficient and effective packing and analytical placement for large-scale heterogeneous FPGAs," 2014 IEEE/ACM International Conference on Computer-Aided Design (ICCAD), San Jose, CA, 2014, pp. 647-654. doi: 10.1109/ICCAD.2014.7001421

[8] VTR: https://github.com/verilog-to-routing/vtr-verilog-to-routing

[9] G. Liu, Z. Zhou, H. Zhong and S. Xie, "Gradient descent with adaptive momentum for active contour models," in IET Computer Vision, vol. 8, no. 4, pp. 287-298, August 2014. doi: 10.1049/iet-cvi.2013.0089

[10] M. Kim, D. Lee and I. L. Markov, "SimPL: An Effective Placement Algorithm," in IEEE Transactions on Computer-Aided Design of Integrated Circuits and Systems, vol. 31, no. 1, pp. 50-60, Jan. 2012. doi: 10.1109/TCAD.2011.2170567

[11] E. Vansteenkiste, S. Lenders and D. Stroobandt, "Liquid: Fast placement prototyping through steepest gradient descent movement," 2016 26th International Conference on Field Programmable Logic and Applications (FPL), Lausanne, 2016, pp. 1-4. doi: 10.1109/FPL.2016.7577303

[12] K. Vorwerk, A. Kennings and J. W. Greene, "Improving Simulated Annealing-Based FPGA Placement With Directed Moves," in IEEE Transactions on Computer-Aided Design of Integrated Circuits and Systems, vol. 28, no. 2, pp. 179-192, Feb. 2009. doi: 10.1109/TCAD.2008.2009167

# Approximate Memory with Approximate DCT

Shenghou Ma
ECE Department
Virginia Tech
Blacksburg, VA, USA
minux@vt.edu

Paul Ampadu
ECE Department
Virginia Tech
Blacksburg, VA, USA
ampadu@vt.edu

## ABSTRACT

Approximate Computing is an emerging computing paradigm where one exploits inherent error resilience of certain applications (e.g., digital signal processing, multimedia and artificial intelligence) and trades off absolute computation precisions for performance, power, area, and/or efficiency gains. Approximate memory is a sub-branch of general approximate computing focusing on memory systems that trade off perfect data fidelity for increased storage density and reduced energy consumption for both memory and IO. This paper presents a new way to achieve approximate memory for natural sampled data (sound, sensor data, image and video frames) by applying the well known discrete cosine transformation (DCT) in one dimension between the last level cache and main memory to reduce memory traffic while maintaining acceptable quality degradations. By using state-of-the-art approximate DCT transformations, the proposed scheme achieves 20.3% of storage area at 37dB PSNR and SSIM = 0.99. If further quality degradation up to SSIM ≈ 0.9 is allowed, the storage saving can be up to 40%. The critical path of the circuit is comparable to state of the art approximate memory schemes, with only 3 levels of 8-bit adders (14 adders per 8-byte data block).

## CCS CONCEPTS

• **Computer systems organization** → *System on a chip*; *Embedded hardware*.

## KEYWORDS

Approximate Computing; Approximate Memory; Discrete Cosine Transformation; Approximate DCT

**ACM Reference Format:**

Shenghou Ma and Paul Ampadu. 2019. Approximate Memory with Approximate DCT. In *Great Lakes Symposium on VLSI 2019 (GLSVLSI '19), May 9–11, 2019, Tysons Corner, VA, USA.* ACM, New York, NY, USA, 4 pages. https://doi.org/10.1145/3299874.3318036


ACM ISBN 978-1-4503-6252-8/19/05...$15.00
https://doi.org/10.1145/3299874.3318036

## 1 INTRODUCTION

Approximate computing is a promising technique to address the current power wall problem that plagues VLSI research. By exploiting the inherent error resilience nature of certain applications, like machine learning, data mining and signal processing, approximate computing explicitly trades off accuracy for reduced circuit complexity, and energy consumption. Approximate memory is a sub-branch of approximate computing, where the retrieved data might contain acceptable level of errors.

With the push to a more immersive computing experience, more and more data processed by computer will be sound, image and video. Most of those applications are memory-bound and has a large working set that cannot be stored fully onchip, which means frequent off-chip DRAM accesses are necessary, and that incurs up to 60X the energy consumption of a onchip access [7]. However, due to inherent limitation of the human perception system, human cannot discern tiny variations in the data, and this motivates the use of approximate computing techniques to reduce memory IO energy by reducing memory IO volume.

In this paper, we present a novel approximation memory technique by applying approximate DCT to lossy memory compression to exploit the high correlation between adjacent data bytes (which occurs naturally in sampled data like audio, image and video frames), and show its potential in increasing storage density and reducing energy consumption, while preserving perceived quality.

## 2 BACKGROUND & RELATED WORK

### 2.1 Approximate Memory

Approximate computing is not a new concept. In fact, even since digital signal processing is invented, we have been using approximation like converting floating point model to fixed point implementation and reducing bit widths to reduce hardware complexity for DSP algorithms. It is also used by lossy audio, image and video compression algorithms to drastically reduce storage requirements of media files. However, not until recently, there has been no motivation to apply the accuracy versus complexity tradeoff in more generic settings and more consciously.

Approximate memory is a sub-branch of approximate computing where memory does not store the data in full fidelity. Some also call this field approximate storage, but in this paper, we focus on non-permanent volatile storage medium like the main memory, instead of permanent non-volatile storage mediums like magnetic disks and flash, therefore approximate memory is more appropriate.

Over the last few years, researchers have proposed various techniques to achieve approximate memory and storage, for example, lossy memory compression [9], SRAM $V_{dd}$ scaling [10], reducing DRAM refresh rate [6], using unreliable multi-level cells [11] for less critical data, and tuning device specific parameters for data of different significance.

## 2.2 Approximate Memory Compression

In [9], the author proposes to extract the similar most significant bits and drop least significant bits of a group of words in a cache line to achieve lossy memory compression. This does not exploit the spatial feature of images and treat all data of equal importance. However, a common scheme in approximate memory research is that we first classify the data into multiple importance classes, and then apply different approximation to different classes.

Due to its energy compaction properties, discrete cosine transformation (DCT) has been widely used in image and video compression schemes but it has not been applied in approximate memory systems. We think the reasons are the following reasons. First, standard DCT has huge resource usage: the Chen DCT[1] as used by H.265 requires 16 multiplications and 26 additions for the 8-point transformation. Secondly, because images are two dimensional objects, in order to remove correlations from both dimensions, images need to transformed with two-dimension DCT. Not only this adds significant hardware complexity, its use of 2D sub-blocks of images also does not match the image organization in memory, which is usually row by row, or column by column.

# 3 PROPOSED DESIGN

There are two ways to address the dimensionality mismatch of images and image storage: store the image block-by-block, or just applying one dimensional DCT. The latter approach is more appealing because it does not require modification of the existing one dimension cache subsystem. Also, 2D DCT is much more expensive than 1D. For $N$-point DCT, 2D $n \times n$ DCT will require $2n$-fold computation increase compared to 1D DCT.

Because the larger the size of DCT, the better resolution in frequency domain it is beneficial to have larger DCT to better exploit the correlations between adjacent data items. However, as the complexity of DCT grows faster than linear for increasing point sizes, we must strike a balance between frequency resolution and implementation complexity. As the cache line for embedded applications is generally 32 bytes, due to complexity constraints, we will compare 8 and 16-point approximate DCT as a tradeoff between complexity and frequency resolution. To avoid making the decoding circuit a performance bottleneck, we will store the data in cache uncompressed and only compress the traffic between last level cache (LLC) and external memory, and this also removes the need to handle partial cache line updates. Additionally, most the energy is used by off-chip IO, so this approach still effectively addresses the power consumption.

## 3.1 Approximate 8 and 16-point DCT

To address the complexity of standard DCT, we also propose to use approximate DCT. In [8], the author proposed an approximate 8-point DCT using only 14 additions. Its structure follows a three stage with an FFT butterfly like structure, and with 4, 2 and 1 butterfly operators in each stage respectively, see Figure 1.

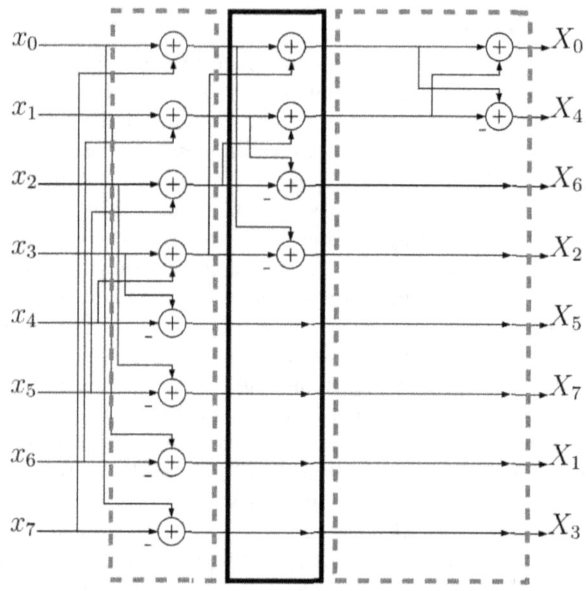


**Figure 1: Data flow graph for approximate 8-point DCT in [8] that only uses 14 adders.**

For the 16-point approximate DCT, We selected the one from [2] which builds on the 8-point one, based on its ease of lightweight hardware implementation.

According to [5], $N$-point DCT $y_k$ of input $x_i$ is defined as:

$$y_n = C_n \sum_{k=0}^{N-1} \cos \frac{2\pi n(2k+1)}{4N} x_k \tag{1}$$

where $C_0 = \sqrt{\frac{1}{N}}$ and $C_n = \sqrt{\frac{2}{N}}$ when $n \neq 0$.

DCT is an energy preserving orthogonal transformation, and its transformation matrix is orthonormal. If we use $\hat{\mathbf{M}}$ to denote the matrix for the approximate DCT, we can write the approximate DCT matrix as:

$$\hat{\mathbf{M}} = \hat{\mathbf{C}}\hat{\mathbf{T}} \tag{2}$$

where $\hat{\mathbf{C}}$ is a diagonal normalization matrix to make $\hat{\mathbf{M}}$ orthonormal. And the orthonormal conditions becomes:

$$\begin{aligned} \mathbf{I} = \hat{\mathbf{M}}\hat{\mathbf{M}}^T &= \hat{\mathbf{T}}\hat{\mathbf{C}}\hat{\mathbf{C}}^T\hat{\mathbf{T}} = \hat{\mathbf{T}}\hat{\mathbf{C}}^2\hat{\mathbf{T}} = \hat{\mathbf{C}}^2\hat{\mathbf{T}}\hat{\mathbf{T}} \\ \hat{\mathbf{C}}^{-2} &= \hat{\mathbf{T}}\hat{\mathbf{T}}^T \end{aligned} \tag{3}$$

Therefore, we just need to make sure $\hat{\mathbf{T}}$ has orthogonal columns, and then we can set the normalization matrix $\hat{\mathbf{C}} = \sqrt{\hat{\mathbf{T}}\hat{\mathbf{T}}^T}$ (the diagonal matrix $\hat{\mathbf{T}}\hat{\mathbf{T}}^T$ will have strictly positive diagonal, so the square root makes sense.)

Another constraint for us is that, unlike image compression, the normalization coefficients cannot be absorbed into the quantization matrix, so we require the normalization coefficients $\hat{\mathbf{C}}$ to be power of two only.

### 3.2 Approximate Memory with Approximate DCT

To make use of orthogonal approximate DCT for lossy memory compression based approximate memory, we first transform each contiguous 8 or 16-byte block of memory through the forward approximate DCT, then chop a configurable number of least significant bits from each components, depending on accuracy versus storage requirement tradeoff. When reading, the chopped bits will be filled with zeros.

Mathematically, the stored data $\hat{\mathbf{y}}$ is:

$$\hat{\mathbf{y}} = \text{drop}_m(\hat{\mathbf{M}}x) = \text{drop}_m(\hat{\mathbf{C}}\hat{\mathbf{T}}x) \quad (4)$$

where $\text{drop}_m(\cdot)$ implements the bit chopping, and the subscript $m$ indicates the application-specific quantization setting. The restored data $\hat{\mathbf{x}}$ becomes:

$$\hat{\mathbf{x}} = \hat{\mathbf{M}}^T \text{fill}_m(\hat{\mathbf{y}}) = \hat{\mathbf{T}}^T \hat{\mathbf{C}}^T \text{fill}_m(\hat{\mathbf{y}}) \quad (5)$$

and the $\text{fill}_m(\cdot)$ implements the filling of zeros for chopped bits.

However, due to the construction of the diagonal matrix $\hat{\mathbf{C}}$, its diagonal elements might be irrational square roots. We have two solutions: (1) we can move the multiplication of $\hat{\mathbf{C}}^T$ to the compression step so that it becomes $\hat{\mathbf{C}}^2$, whose diagonal elements are all of the form $2^{-n}$. (2) we can split the $\hat{\mathbf{C}}^2$ differently as the compression and decompression are separate circuits, and can use different normalization matrices.

After applying these transformations to eliminate irrational square roots, the final encoding becomes:

$$\hat{\mathbf{y}} = \hat{\mathbf{C}}^T \text{drop}_m(\hat{\mathbf{M}}\mathbf{x}) = \text{drop}_m(\hat{\mathbf{C}}^T \hat{\mathbf{C}}\hat{\mathbf{T}}\mathbf{x}) \quad (6)$$

and the decoding path is even simpler, just one matrix vector multiplication:

$$\hat{\mathbf{x}} = \hat{\mathbf{T}}^T \text{fill}_m(\hat{\mathbf{y}}) \quad (7)$$

To reduce the dynamic range of intermediate results, we will bias the data by -128 to make them signed rather than unsigned. And each stage has the same dynamic range as a result.

*3.2.1 Decoding and Encoding Circuit.* The circuit data flow diagram is straightforward after the preceding analysis, see Figure 2. Data from LLC comes in from left to the encoding circuit. After inverting the most significant bits to apply the $-128$ bias, the data is treated as signed 8-bit integer and the forward approximate DCT transformation is applied. Then the quantization setting determines how many bits to chop for each components, and then data is packed into main memory. The decoder just reverses the step, and use different quantization settings to fill in the chopped bits. It should note that the quantization setting is a global shared setting determined by the application based on acceptable quality degradation, so it is not stored along with the compressed data.

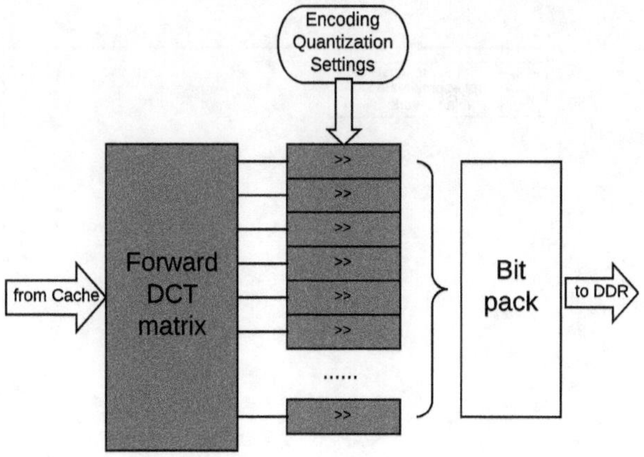


**Figure 2: data flow graph for encoding, and decoding circuit follows from it.**

## 4 RESULTS

### 4.1 Evaluation Methodology

We selected the 9144 300×200 images Caltech101 data set [4] and also bigger 3000 × 4000 natural images from the Image Compression Benchmark [3] to evaluate our approach for the target application of multimedia, DSP and AI. We used the PSNR (peak signal to noise ratio) and SSIM (Structural Similarity Index) to compare different approximate memory techniques. The compression ratio is defined as the ratio of compressed size to uncompressed size, so it is always in $[0, 1]$ range.

### 4.2 Results

Figure 3 and Figure 4 show the compression ratio versus PSNR and SSIM plots for the 8-point [8], 16-point [2] approximate DCT and also the result from state of the art approximate memory compression scheme from [9].

For better performances, we performed an exhaustive search on the best quantization setting, and the result is reported in Table 1.

| Bit shifts | Compression | PSNR (dB) | SSIM |
|---|---|---|---|
| $[0, 0, 0, 0, 0, 0, 0, 0]$[1] | 00.0% | 52.2 | 1.000 |
| $[1, 1, 1, 1, 1, 1, 1, 1]$ | 12.5% | 44.4 | 0.998 |
| $[1, 1, 1, 1, 1, 2, 2, 3]$ | 18.7% | 38.8 | 0.992 |
| $[1, 1, 1, 1, 1, 3, 2, 3]$ | 20.3% | 37.5 | 0.990 |
| $[0, 1, 2, 2, 2, 3, 2, 3]$ | 23.4% | 36.1 | 0.986 |

**Table 1: Optimal nonuniform quantization settings, which are much better than uniform setting of Figure 3 and Figure 4.**

As follow up work, we plan to design a hardware platform to complete a more realistic evaluation of energy consumption savings and hardware costs.

[1] This does not achieve any compression, and indicates a baseline quality loss incurred by fixed point implementation dropping fraction bits after multiplying $\mathbf{C}^2$.

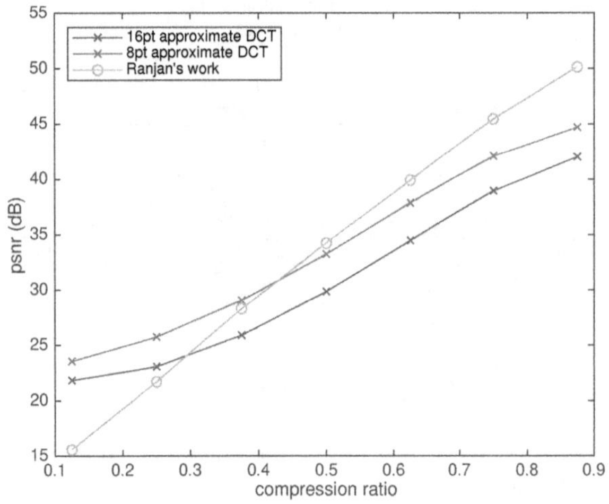


**Figure 3: PSNR vs compression ratio graph for uniform quantization setting between 8[8]/16[2]-point approximate DCT and [9]. Note the 8-point DCT outperforms the 16-point one consistently.**

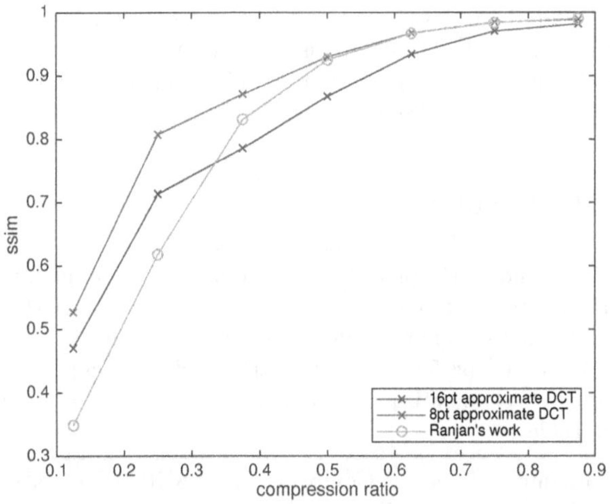


**Figure 4: SSIM vs compression ratio graph for uniform quantization setting between 8[8]/16[2]-point approximate DCT and [9]. Note our DCT-based solution maintain good SSIM even at higher compression ratios and is better than [9] when CR $< 0.5$.**

## 4.3 Discussion

From the measurement, it is clear that the 8-point approximate DCT has superior approximation memory compression performance than the 16-point one, which is counter-intuitive because larger point sizes should provide better energy compaction. But this is good news for us, because the 8-point one requires only 14 adders, as compared to 44 adders in 16-point case. Comparing to existing approximate memory techniques, orthogonal transformation based techniques can achieve better compression ratio with much less image quality degradation. Even though this work only considers 8-bit data items, for the specific application domain, we do not consider it a problem because most image data is still stored in 8-bit formats. We might need to consider 10-bit or even 12-bit when HDR imaging becomes more commonplace.

# 5 CONCLUSION

We proposed an approximate memory compression scheme based on 1D approximate DCT, and found that even when applying only to one dimension, it could reduce space by 20.3% while still having acceptable image quality. This approximate memory approach is fully transparent to the application, but in the future, we would like to explore whether making the application aware of the data reorganization could further increase the effectiveness of orthogonal transformation based technique by lifting it to exploit data correlations in both dimensions.

# REFERENCES


[1] Wen-Hsiung Chen, C. Smith, and S. Fralick. 1977. A Fast Computational Algorithm for the Discrete Cosine Transform. *IEEE Transactions on Communications* 25, 9 (September 1977), 1004–1009. https://doi.org/10.1109/TCOM.1977.1093941

[2] Thiago L. T. da Silveira, Raíza S. Oliveira, Fábio M. Bayer, Renato J. Cintra, and Arjuna Madanayake. 2017. Multiplierless 16-point DCT Approximation for Low-complexity Image and Video Coding. *Signal, Image and Video Processing* 11, 2 (01 Feb 2017), 227–233. https://doi.org/10.1007/s11760-016-0923-4

[3] Pete Fraser et. al. [n. d.]. The New Test Images: Image Compression Benchmark. http://imagecompression.info/test_images/. Accessed: 2018-12-13.

[4] Fei-Fei, R. Fergus and P. Perona. 2004. Learning Generative Visual Models from few Training Examples: an Incremental Bayesian Approach Tested on 101 Object Categories. In *Proceedings of the 2004 Conference on Computer Vision and Pattern Recognition (CVPR '04)*.

[5] E. Feig and S. Winograd. 1992. Fast Algorithms for the Discrete Cosine Transform. *IEEE Transactions on Signal Processing* 40, 9 (Sept 1992), 2174–2193. https://doi.org/10.1109/78.157218

[6] D. T. Nguyen, H. Kim, H. Lee, and I. Chang. 2018. An Approximate Memory Architecture for a Reduction of Refresh Power Consumption in Deep Learning Applications. In *2018 IEEE International Symposium on Circuits and Systems (ISCAS)*. 1–5. https://doi.org/10.1109/ISCAS.2018.8351021

[7] A. Pedram, S. Richardson, M. Horowitz, S. Galal, and S. Kvatinsky. 2017. Dark Memory and Accelerator-Rich System Optimization in the Dark Silicon Era. *IEEE Design Test* 34, 2 (April 2017), 39–50. https://doi.org/10.1109/MDAT.2016.2573586

[8] U. S. Potluri, A. Madanayake, R. J. Cintra, F. M. Bayer, S. Kulasekera, and A. Edirisuriya. 2014. Improved 8-Point Approximate DCT for Image and Video Compression Requiring Only 14 Additions. *IEEE Transactions on Circuits and Systems I: Regular Papers* 61, 6 (June 2014), 1727–1740. https://doi.org/10.1109/TCSI.2013.2295022

[9] A. Ranjan, A. Raha, V. Raghunathan, and A. Raghunathan. 2017. Approximate Memory Compression for Energy-Efficiency. In *2017 IEEE/ACM International Symposium on Low Power Electronics and Design (ISLPED)*. 1–6. https://doi.org/10.1109/ISLPED.2017.8009173

[10] L. Yang and B. Murmann. 2017. Approximate SRAM for Energy-Efficient, Privacy-Preserving Convolutional Neural Networks. In *2017 IEEE Computer Society Annual Symposium on VLSI (ISVLSI)*. 689–694. https://doi.org/10.1109/ISVLSI.2017.117

[11] H. Zhao, L. Xue, P. Chi, and J. Zhao. 2017. Approximate Image Storage with Multi-level Cell STT-MRAM Main Memory. In *2017 IEEE/ACM International Conference on Computer-Aided Design (ICCAD)*. 268–275. https://doi.org/10.1109/ICCAD.2017.8203788

# AQuRate: MRAM-based Stochastic Oscillator for Adaptive Quantization Rate Sampling of Sparse Signals

Soheil Salehi, Ramtin Zand, Alireza Zaeemzadeh, Nazanin Rahnavard, Ronald F. DeMara
Department of Electrical and Computer Engineering, University of Central Florida, Orlando, FL, 32816 USA

## ABSTRACT

Recently, the promising aspects of compressive sensing have inspired new circuit-level approaches for their efficient realization within the literature. However, most of these recent advances involving novel sampling techniques have been proposed without considering hardware and signal constraints. Additionally, traditional hardware designs for generating non-uniform sampling clock incur large area overhead and power dissipation. Herein, we propose a novel non-uniform clock generator called Adaptive Quantization Rate (AQR) generator using Magnetic Random Access Memory (MRAM)-based stochastic oscillator devices. Our proposed AQR generator provides ~ 25-fold reduction in area, on average, while offering ~ 6-fold reduced power dissipation, on average, compared to the state-of-the-art non-uniform clock generators.

## CCS CONCEPTS

• **Hardware → Data conversion; Spintronics and magnetic technologies; Emerging architectures;**

## KEYWORDS

Analog to Digital Converter, Adaptive Sampling Rate, Non-uniform Clock Generator, MRAM-based Stochastic Oscillator, Compressive Sensing.

**ACM Reference Format:**

Soheil Salehi, Ramtin Zand, Alireza Zaeemzadeh, Nazanin Rahnavard, Ronald F. DeMara. 2019. AQuRate: MRAM-based Stochastic Oscillator for Adaptive Quantization Rate Sampling of Sparse Signals.

In *Great Lakes Symposium on VLSI 2019 (GLSVLSI '19), May 9–11, 2019, Tysons Corner, VA, USA.* ACM, Washington, DC, USA, 4 pages. https://doi.org/10.1145/3299874.3318037

## 1 INTRODUCTION

Recently, non-uniform sampling approaches such as Compressive Sensing (CS) have been proposed to reduce the energy consumption of sampling operation by reducing number of samples in each frame, reduce required storage to save the sampled data, and reduce the data transmission due to lower number of samples taken [15, 19, 20]. Additionally, event-driven sampling, such as level-crossing sampling, has been widely adopted as a promising CS technique to maximize the performance of sampling operation while reducing energy consumption [18]. Furthermore, CS techniques are utilized to sample spectrally sparse wide-band signals close to their information rate rather than their Nyquist rate, which can be a challenge using conventional uniform sampling techniques due to the high cost of the hardware that is capable of performing the sampling operation at a high Nyquist rate.

Despite all the benefits that CS techniques offer, they are typically realized oblivious to the hardware limitations such as energy, bandwidth, and battery capacity. Additionally, signal-dependent constraints such as sparsity and noise level are ignored while studying the quantization rate and resolution trade-off. The aforementioned hardware-dependent and signal-dependent constraints alter during the sampling operation. Thus, an adaptive quantization rate and resolution optimization circuitry is required to maximize sampling performance while minimizing the number of samples to reduce energy consumption, data transmission, and storage. Adaptive quantization rate and resolution sampling might be readily achieved from the algorithm perspective, however it requires a hardware platform that is capable of real-time adaptation according to certain signal behavior such as sparsity rate. Recently, an adaptive optimization of the quantization rate and resolution during signal acquisition has been investigated in [14].

Previous works on adaptive quantization rate and resolution ADCs have been implemented using Complementary Metal Oxide Semiconductor (CMOS) technology and considering a low-pass signal model [3, 18]. Herein, we propose an spin-based Adaptive quantization rate (AQR) generator circuit that considers the signal dependent constraint as well as hardware limitations. The proposed AQR generator circuit utilized Magnetic Random Access Memory (MRAM)-based stochastic oscillator devices, which offer miniaturization and significant energy savings [6].

## 2 BACKGROUND AND RELATED WORK

Recently researchers have achieved significant performance improvements using sparse signal recovery techniques. Spectrally sparse signals are utilized in many applications such as frequency hopping communications, musical audio signals, cognitive radio networks, and radar/sonar imaging systems [14]. Additionally, a major challenge in spectrum sensing is that in most cases, the sparse components of the signal are spread over a wide-band spectrum and need to be acquired without prior knowledge of their frequencies. Moreover, spectrum-aware communication networks require Radio Frequency and mixed-signal hardware architectures that can achieve very wide-band but energy-efficient spectrum sensing [14].

The cornerstone to achieving CS approaches and non-uniform sampling techniques is the utilization of an asynchronous pseudo-random clock generator, usually referred to as non-uniform clock generator, which is consisted of a Linear Feedback Shift Register (LFSR) that selects a clock signal at random from a series of ring oscillators with different frequency and phases [3, 4, 10, 11, 13]. In


*GLSVLSI '19, May 9–11, 2019, Tysons Corner, VA, USA*

ACM ISBN 978-1-4503-6252-8/19/05....$15.00.
https://doi.org/10.1145/3299874.3318037

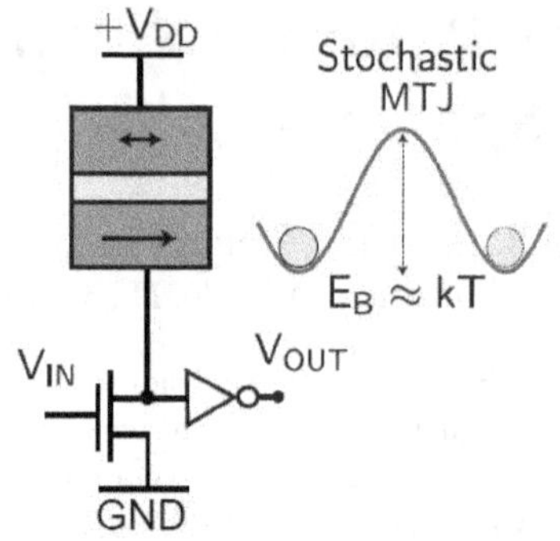


**Figure 1: The building block of the proposed spin-based AQR generator [6].**

most cases, these circuits require a large number of CMOS transistors and incur significant area overhead and power dissipation. Recently, a novel approach for generating the non-uniform clock using VCMA-MTJ devices is proposed in [11] and the authors have shown that their proposed design can achieve significant area and power dissipation reduction compared to the previous CMOS-based pseudo-random clock generators. However, the authors in [11] considered the frequency of the signal in order to generate the sampling clock, which limits the bandwidth and in case of spectrally sparse signals, where no prior knowledge of frequency is available, their proposed approach will face challenges. Herein, we consider the sparsity rate of the signal to generate the sampling clock. This will minimize the number of samples and results in more energy savings. Furthermore, our proposed design has reduced complexity compared to other designs proposed in the literature due to significant reduction in the CMOS circuit elements.

## 3 ADAPTIVE QUANTIZATION RATE GENERATOR

### 3.1 MRAM-based Stochastic Device as a Building Block for AQR generator

In this section, we show that a recently proposed building block with embedded MRAM technology can enable the hardware realization of an AQR generator. The structure of the MRAM-based stochastic device is shown in Fig. 1, which includes a magnetic tunnel junction (MTJ) that is a 2-terminal device with two different resistive levels depending on the orientation of its ferromagnetic (FM) layers, called *fixed layer* and *free layer.* The fixed layer is designed to have a fixed magnetic orientation, while the magnetization orientation of the free layer can be switched. In MRAM-based memory devices, a thermally-stable nanomagnet with a large energy barrier with respect to the thermal energy (kT) is utilized for free layer so that the fixed layer can function as a non-volatile memory. In recent years the use of superparamagnetic MTJs that are not thermally stable have been experimentally and theoretically investigated in search of functional spintronic devices [5, 7–9, 12, 17, 21, 22].

In this paper, we use an MRAM device with a low energy-barrier nanomagnet ($E_B \ll 40kT$), which is thermally unstable [6]. The resistance of an MTJ with such a low energy barrier nanomagnet randomly fluctuates between high ($R_{AP}$) and low resistance states ($R_P$). This creates a fluctuating output voltage at the drain of the NMOS transistor, which can be amplified by an inverter circuit to produce a stochastic output that can be modulated by the input voltage. In particular, the output voltage at the drain of the NMOS transistor can be shorted to the ground by reducing its drain-source resistance ($r_{ds}$) through increasing the input voltage ($V_{IN}$), or it can be near $V_{DD}$ by increasing the $r_{ds}$ through decreasing $V_{IN}$. The device operation can be comprehended by considering the MTJ conductance [6]:

$$G_{MTJ} = G_0 \left[ 1 + m_z \frac{TMR}{(2 + TMR)} \right] \quad (1)$$

where $m_z$ is the free layer magnetization that is stochastically fluctuating due to the thermal noise, $G_0$ is the average MTJ conductance, $(G_P + G_{AP})/2$, and $TMR$ is the tunneling magnetoresistance ratio. The drain voltage can be expressed as:

$$V_{DRAIN}/V_{DD} = \frac{(2 + TMR) + TMR\, m_z}{(2 + TMR)(1 + \alpha) + TMR\, m_z} \quad (2)$$

where $\alpha$ is the ratio of the transistor conductance ($G_T$) to the average MTJ conductance ($G_0$). The maximum fluctuations at the drain occurs when $\alpha \approx 1$, thus the MTJ resistance is approximately equal to the NMOS resistance when $V_{IN} = 0.5V_{DD}$. Since the drain voltage fluctuations are in the order of hundreds of mV for typical TMR values, an additional inverter is used to amplify the noise to produce output voltages ranging from 0 to $V_{DD}$.

### 3.2 AQR Generator Circuit

To realize an effective hybrid emerging device and CMOS circuit, one useful approach can be to consider stochastic and deterministic attributes separately. For instance, Fig. 2 depicts the proposed AQR generator circuit wherein a 2-terminal MTJ realizes stochastic behavior to provide the non-uniform clock generation capability.

The quantized Sparsity Rate Estimator (SRE) module shown in Fig. 2 estimates the sparsity rate of the digital output bit-stream by estimating the sparse spectral components of the digital output using an iterative algorithm. Recently, rapid and optimized sparse component estimation method is proposed in [14]. In the approach proposed in [14] in order to minimize the computational complexity of the sparse component estimation, an sliding window approach is utilized and the algorithm operates only one iteration on each frame of the input by utilizing the previous estimate as an initial value. This will result in gradual convergence of the sparse components to the actual values across iterations. These algorithms can be employed to find the sparsity rate of the signal. In most cases, sparsity rate of analog signals, which can be described as the number of non-zero elements in divided by the total number of elements the sparse representation of the signal, is between 5% to 15% in many applications including those targeted herein.

When the SRE module estimates the sparsity rate of the signal based on the digital output of the previous frame, it will then generate a voltage level according to that sparsity rate of the input analog signal. This voltage, referred to as $V_{SR}$, will be applied to the gate of the NMOS transistor shown in Fig. 2 and results in an stochastic bit-stream generated by the MRAM-based stochastic oscillator device. The stochastic bit-stream output generated by the MRAM-based stochastic oscillator device will be forwarded to the

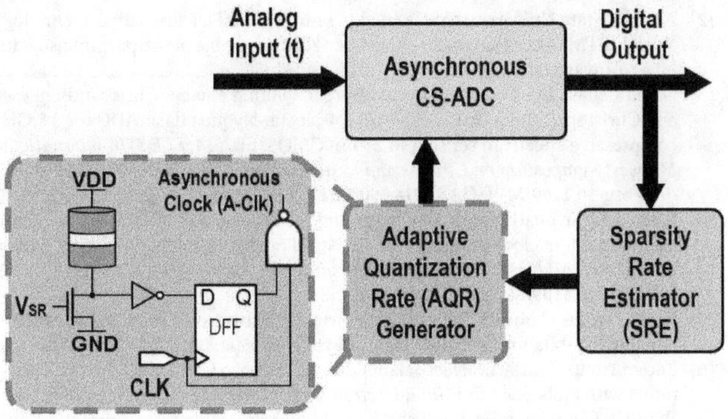


**Figure 2: Integration of AQR generator circuit within the Compressive Sensing ADC (CS-ADC) system design.**

D-Flip-Flop (D-FF) as shown in Fig. 2 and the result of the 2-input NAND gate between the output of the D-FF and the actual clock of the circuit will generate the required quantization rate to be used for the following frame of the signal acquisition, referred to as Asynchronous Clock (A-Clk) in Fig. 2. Additionally, the SRE module can also used by the recovery algorithms to efficiently recover the sampled signal [14]. Additionally, the A-Clk will be forwarded to the sparse recovery algorithm to provide necessary information about the samples taken from the signal to assist with the signal reconstruction.

To obtain the relation between the output probability of the stochastic MRAM-based AQR generator and its input voltage, we have applied an input pulse that its amplitude starts from $GND$ and is increased by 200mV every 100ns until it reaches $V_{DD}$. The output of the building block is sampled with a 1GHz clock frequency using a D-FF circuit, as shown in Fig. 3.

## 4 SIMULATION RESULTS

In order to evaluate and validate the behavior and functionality of the proposed AQR generator circuit, SPICE and MATLAB simulations were performed. We have utilized the 14nm High Performance FinFET Predictive Technology Model (PTM) [2] as well as the MRAM-based stochastic oscillator device model and parameters represented in [6] to implement and evaluate the proposed AQR generator circuit.

According to our results, AQR provides significant power dissipation and area reductions compared to the state-of-the-art nonuniform clock generators listed in Table 1 [3, 4, 11, 13]. According to our simulation results, power dissipation of the proposed AQR generator circuit is 22.64$\mu$W on average. With respect to area utilization, our proposed AQR design requires only 23 FinFET transistors, which attains a significant reduction in the transistor count and complexity of the non-uniform clock generator circuit present in state-of-the-art designs [3, 4, 11, 13]. Thus, AQR avoids high transistor counts while making it unnecessary to use of large LFSR circuits that contain numerous D-FFs as well as several logic gates and multiplexers. For a more equitable comparison in terms of area and power dissipation, we have derived (3) and (4) considering General Scaling method [16] to normalize the power dissipation and area of the designs listed in Table 1. Based on the General

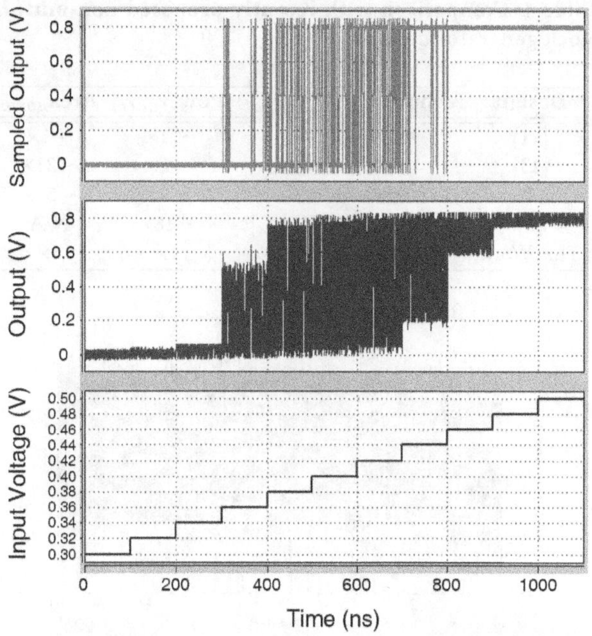


**Figure 3: The sampled output of the stochastic MRAM-based building block for AQR generator for various input voltages.**

Scaling method, voltage and area scale at different rate of $U$ and $S$, respectively. Thus, the power dissipation is scaled with respect to $1/U^2$ and area per device is scaled according to $1/S^2$ [16].

$$\begin{aligned} Power_{norm} &= \frac{Power_x}{Power_{AQR}} \times (\frac{1}{U})^2 \\ &= \frac{Power_x}{Power_{AQR}} \times (\frac{0.8V}{V_{nominal}})^2 \end{aligned} \tag{3}$$

$$\begin{aligned} Area_{norm} &= \frac{Area_x}{Area_{AQR}} \times (\frac{1}{S})^2 \\ &= \frac{Area_x}{Area_{AQR}} \times (\frac{14nm}{Technology})^2 \end{aligned} \tag{4}$$

where, $V_{nominal}$ is the nominal voltage of the technology model, $Technology$ refers to the technology node in nanometers, and subscript $x$ refers to the design that we want to scale its power dissipation and area according to the technology models. According to (3) and (4), AQR provides power dissipation reduction up to one-order-of-magnitude compared to the state-of-the-art nonuniform clock generators as listed in Table 1. Additionally, AQR offers up to one-orders-of-magnitude area reduction compared to the designs provided in Table 1 using the scaling comparison trends accepted in the literature.

As described in Section 3.2, sparsity rate of analog signals is usually within the range of 5%−15%. Fig. 4 depicts an example output of the AQR generator for sampling of a sparse signal with 5% sparsity rate. Moreover, we have embedded our proposed AQR generator within CS recovery algorithms called Orthogonal Matching Pursuit (OMP) and Compressive Sampling Matching Pursuit (CoSaMP) [1] in order to evaluate the architectural simulation results and in

**Table 1: Comparison with recently proposed non-uniform clock generator designs**

| Design | Technology ($V_{nominal}$) | $Power_{norm}$ | $Area_{norm}$ |
|---|---|---|---|
| [11] | 65nm (1.1V) | ~ 1× | ~ 1× |
| [13] | 65nm (1.1V) | ~ 2× | ~ 21× |
| [4] | 90nm (1.2V) | ~ 2× | ~ 51× |
| [3] | 28nm (1.0V) | ~ 18× | N/A |
| This Work | 14nm (0.8V) | 1× | 1× |

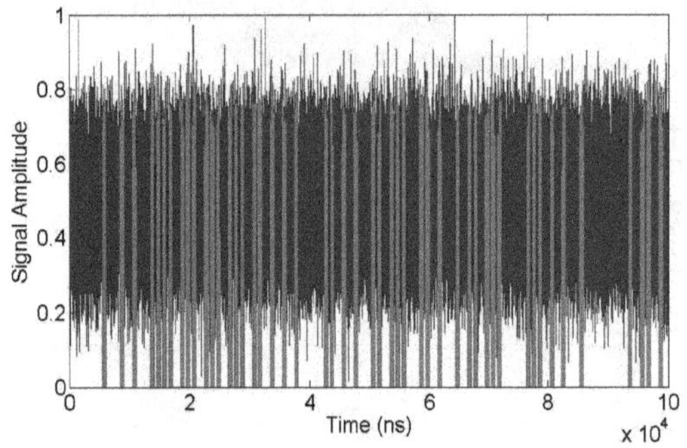


**Figure 4: Sampling an analog signal with sparsity rate of** 5% **using AQR generator. Blue represents the signal and Red represents the samples taken using the AQR generator.**

order to recover the signal from the samples taken using the AQR generator. According to the results, the mean normalized errors of the reconstruction of the signals with 5%, 10%, and 15% sparsity rates using OMP are 0.0504, 0.0446, and 0.0252, respectively. Moreoever, the mean normalized errors of the reconstruction of the signals with 5%, 10%, and 15% sparsity rates using CoSaMP are 0.0487, 0.0304, and 0.0245, respectively.

## 5 CONCLUSIONS

We have devised a novel non-uniform clock generator called Adaptive quantization rate (AQR) generator using MRAM-based stochastic oscillator devices. Our proposed AQR generator considers signal constraints, such as sparsity rate, as well as hardware constraints, such as area and power dissipation, in order to generate the non-uniform clock for the asynchronous CS-ADC. Compared to similar non-uniform clock generators presented in the literature, AQR generator provides significant area reduction of ~ 25-fold on average, while achieving power dissipation reduction of ~ 6-fold, on average.

## ACKNOWLEDGEMENT

This work was supported in part by the Center for Probabilistic Spin Logic for Low-Energy Boolean and Non-Boolean Computing (CAPSL), one of the Nanoelectronic Computing Research (nCORE) Centers as task 2759.006, a Semiconductor Research Corporation (SRC) program sponsored by the NSF through CCF 1739635, and by NSF through ECCS 1810256.

## REFERENCES

[1] 2009. CoSaMP: Iterative signal recovery from incomplete and inaccurate samples. *Applied and Computational Harmonic Analysis* 26, 3 (2009), 301–321.

[2] Arizona State University (ASU). [n. d.]. 14nm HP-FinFET Predictive Technology Model (PTM), accessed on 26 November 2018, available at: http://ptm.asu.edu/. http://ptm.asu.edu/. ([n. d.]). http://ptm.asu.edu/

[3] David Bellasi, Luca Bettini, Thomas Burger, Qiuting Huang, Christian Benkeser, and Christoph Studer. 2014. A 1.9 GS/s 4-bit sub-Nyquist flash ADC for 3.8 GHz compressive spectrum sensing in 28 nm CMOS. In *2014 IEEE 57th International Midwest Symposium on Circuits and Systems (MWSCAS)*. IEEE, 101–104. https://doi.org/10.1109/MWSCAS.2014.6908362

[4] Rashed Zafar Bhatti, Keith M. Chugg, and Jeff Draper. 2007. Standard cell based pseudo-random clock generator for statistical random sampling of digital signals. In *2007 50th Midwest Symposium on Circuits and Systems*. IEEE, 1110–1113. https://doi.org/10.1109/MWSCAS.2007.4488752

[5] Kerem Yunus Camsari, Rafatul Faria, Brian M Sutton, and Supriyo Datta. 2017. Stochastic p-bits for invertible logic. *Physical Review X* 7, 3 (2017), 031014.

[6] Kerem Yunus Camsari, Sayeef Salahuddin, and Supriyo Datta. 2017. Implementing p-bits with embedded mtj. *IEEE Electron Device Letters* 38, 12 (2017), 1767–1770.

[7] Won Ho Choi, Yang Lv, Jongyeon Kim, Abhishek Deshpande, Gyuseong Kang, Jian-Ping Wang, and Chris H Kim. 2014. A magnetic tunnel junction based true random number generator with conditional perturb and real-time output probability tracking. In *Electron Devices Meeting (IEDM), 2014 IEEE International*. IEEE, 12–5.

[8] Punyashloka Debashis, Rafatul Faria, Kerem Y Camsari, Joerg Appenzeller, Supriyo Datta, and Zhihong Chen. 2016. Experimental demonstration of nanomagnet networks as hardware for ising computing. In *Electron Devices Meeting (IEDM), 2016 IEEE International*. IEEE, 34–3.

[9] Akio Fukushima, Takayuki Seki, Kay Yakushiji, Hitoshi Kubota, Hiroshi Imamura, Shinji Yuasa, and Koji Ando. 2014. Spin dice: A scalable truly random number generator based on spintronics. *Applied Physics Express* 7, 8 (2014), 083001.

[10] Selcuk Kose, Emre Salman, Zeljko Ignjatovic, and Eby G. Friedman. 2008. Pseudo-random clocking to enhance signal integrity. In *2008 IEEE International SOC Conference*. IEEE, 47–50. https://doi.org/10.1109/SOCC.2008.4641477

[11] H Lee, C Grezes, A Lee, F Ebrahimi, P Khalili Amiri, and K L Wang. 2017. A Spintronic Voltage-Controlled Stochastic Oscillator for Event-Driven Random Sampling. *IEEE Electron Device Letters* 38, 2 (2017), 281–284. https://doi.org/10.1109/LED.2016.2642818

[12] Nicolas Locatelli, Alice Mizrahi, A Accioly, Rie Matsumoto, Akio Fukushima, Hitoshi Kubota, Shinji Yuasa, Vincent Cros, Luis Gustavo Pereira, Damien Querlioz, et al. 2014. Noise-enhanced synchronization of stochastic magnetic oscillators. *Physical Review Applied* 2, 3 (2014), 034009.

[13] Muhammad Osama, Lamya Gaber, and Aziza Hussein. 2016. Design of high performance Pseudorandom Clock Generator for compressive sampling applications. In *2016 33rd National Radio Science Conference (NRSC)*. IEEE, 257–265. https://doi.org/10.1109/NRSC.2016.7450836

[14] Soheil Salehi, Mahdi Boloursaz Mashhadi, Alireza Zaeemzadeh, Nazanin Rahnavard, and Ronald F. De Mara. 2018. Energy-Aware Adaptive Rate and Resolution Sampling of Spectrally Sparse Signals Leveraging VCMA-MTJ Devices. *IEEE Journal on Emerging and Selected Topics in Circuits and Systems* (2018), 1–1. https://doi.org/10.1109/JETCAS.2018.2857998

[15] Shriram Sarvotham, Dror Baron, Richard G. Baraniuk, Shriram Sarvotham, Dror Baron, and Richard G. Baraniuk. 2006. Measurements vs. Bits: Compressed Sensing meets Information Theory. *Allerton Conference on Communication, Control and Computing* (9 2006). https://scholarship.rice.edu/handle/1911/20323

[16] Aaron Stillmaker and Bevan Baas. 2017. Scaling equations for the accurate prediction of CMOS device performance from 180Âănm to 7Âănm. *Integration* 58 (6 2017), 74–81. https://doi.org/10.1016/J.VLSI.2017.02.002

[17] Brian Sutton, Kerem Yunus Camsari, Behtash Behin-Aein, and Supriyo Datta. 2017. Intrinsic optimization using stochastic nanomagnets. *Scientific reports* 7 (2017), 44370.

[18] Tzu-Fan Wu, Cheng-Ru Ho, and Mike Shuo-Wei Chen. 2017. A Flash-Based Non-Uniform Sampling ADC With Hybrid Quantization Enabling Digital Anti-Aliasing Filter. *IEEE Journal of Solid-State Circuits* 52, 9 (2017), 2335–2349. https://doi.org/10.1109/JSSC.2017.2718671

[19] Alireza Zaeemzadeh, Jamie Haddock, Nazanin Rahnavard, and Deanna Needell. 2018. A Bayesian Approach for Asynchronous Parallel Sparse Recovery. In *52nd Asilomar Conference on Signals, Systems, and Computers*. IEEE, Pacific Grove, CA, 1980–1984. https://doi.org/10.1109/ACSSC.2018.8645176

[20] Alireza Zaeemzadeh, Mohsen Joneidi, and Nazanin Rahnavard. 2017. Adaptive non-uniform compressive sampling for time-varying signals. IEEE, 1–6. https://doi.org/10.1109/CISS.2017.7926148

[21] Ramtin Zand, Kerem Y Camsari, Supriyo Datta, and Ronald F DeMara. 2018. Composable Probabilistic Inference Networks Using MRAM-based Stochastic Neurons. *arXiv preprint arXiv:1811.11390* (2018).

[22] Ramtin Zand, Kerem Yunus Camsari, Steven D. Pyle, Ibrahim Ahmed, Chris H. Kim, and Ronald F. DeMara. 2018. Low-Energy Deep Belief Networks Using Intrinsic Sigmoidal Spintronic-based Probabilistic Neurons. In *Proceedings of the 2018 on Great Lakes Symposium on VLSI (GLSVLSI '18)*. ACM, Chicago, IL, USA, 15–20. https://doi.org/10.1145/3194554.3194558

# Clockless Spin-based Look-Up Tables with Wide Read Margin

Soheil Salehi, Ramtin Zand, Ronald F. DeMara
Department of Electrical and Computer Engineering, University of Central Florida, Orlando, FL, 32816 USA

## ABSTRACT

In this paper, we develop a 6-input fracturable non-volatile Clockless LUT (C-LUT) using spin Hall effect (SHE)-based Magnetic Tunnel Junctions (MTJs) and provide a detailed comparison between the SHE-MTJ-based C-LUT and Spin Transfer Torque (STT)-MTJ-based C-LUT. The proposed C-LUT offers an attractive alternative for implementing combinational logic as well as sequential logic versus previous spin-based LUT designs in the literature. Foremost, C-LUT eliminates the sense amplifier typically employed by using a differential polarity dual MTJ design, as opposed to a static reference resistance MTJ. This realizes a much wider read margin and the Monte Carlo simulation of the proposed fracturable C-LUT indicates no read and write errors in the presence of a variety of process variations scenarios involving MOS transistors as well as MTJs. Additionally, simulation results indicate that the proposed C-LUT reduces the standby power dissipation by 5.4-fold compared to the SRAM-based LUT. Furthermore, the proposed SHE-MTJ-based C-LUT reduces the area by 1.3-fold and 2-fold compared to the SRAM-based LUT and the STT-MTJ-based C-LUT, respectively.

## CCS CONCEPTS

**• Hardware → Spintronics and magnetic technologies; Emerging architectures; Asynchronous circuits; Combinational circuits; Programmable logic elements; Process, voltage and temperature variations;**

## KEYWORDS

Reconfigurable Logic, Fracturable LUT, Magnetic Tunnel Junction, Spin-based Memory Cell, Spin Hall Effect, Spin Transfer Torque.

**ACM Reference Format:**
Soheil Salehi, Ramtin Zand, Ronald F. DeMara. 2019. Clockless Spin-based Look-Up Tables with Wide Read Margin.
In *Great Lakes Symposium on VLSI 2019 (GLSVLSI '19), May 9–11, 2019, Tysons Corner, VA, USA.* ACM, Washington, DC, USA, 4 pages. https://doi.org/10.1145/3299874.3318038

## 1 INTRODUCTION

Flexibility and runtime adaptability are two of the main motivations for the wide adoption of reconfigurable fabrics. Among the most commonly used reconfigurable fabrics, Field Programmable Gate Arrays (FPGA) have been the primary focus due to their flexibility that allows realization of logic elements at medium and fine granularities while incurring low non-recurring engineering costs and rapid deployment to market. Additionally, FPGAs have been researched as promising platform that can be utilized effectively to increase reliability in case of process-voltage-temperature variation [1]. The main challenge of static random access memory (SRAM)-based FPGAs is their increased area and power consumption to achieve flexible design. The main components of FPGAs are Look-Up Tables (LUTs) and switch boxes that are mainly consisted of SRAM cells [6]. However, SRAM-based LUTs incur limitations such as high static power, volatility, and low logic density.

Innovations using emerging devices within FPGAs have been sought to bridge the gaps needed to overcome the limitations of SRAM-based FPGAs. High-endurance non-volatile spin-based LUTs have been studied in the literature as promising alternatives to SRAM-based LUTs, Flash-based LUTs, and other state-of-the-art emerging LUTs such as resistive random access memory (RRAM)-based LUTs and phase change memory (PCM)-based LUTs [2, 4, 10–12, 14]. Spin-based devices offer non-volatility, near-zero static power, high endurance, and high integration density [9, 13]. The spin-based LUTs presented in the literature [2, 4, 10–12, 14] require separate read and write operations as well as a clock, which makes these LUTs a suitable candidate for sequential logic operations. However, the main challenge that has not been addressed in the literature is providing a spin-based LUT design for combinational logic operation without the need for a clock. Additionally, proposed spin-based LUTs proposed in the literature fail to maintain a wide sense margin and high reliability without incurring significant area and power dissipation overheads [2, 4, 10–12, 14]. In this paper, in order to address the aforementioned challenges, we develop a clockless 6-input fracturable non-volatile Combinational LUT (C-LUT) with wide read margin using spin Hall effect (SHE)-based Magnetic Tunnel Junction (MTJ) and provide a detailed comparison between the SHE-MRAM and Spin Transfer Torque (STT)-MRAM C-LUTs. Additionally, we provide detailed analysis on the reliability of our proposed C-LUT in the presence of Process Variation (PV).

## 2 REALIZING FRACTURABLE 6-INPUT CLOCKLESS LUT

The primary goal of using LUTs in the reconfigurable fabrics is for implementing combinational logic. Generally, $M$-input Boolean functions are implemented using LUTs that are considered a memory that has $2^M$ memory cells. The inputs are assigned using a select tree which is constructed with Pass Transistors and Transmission Gates (TGs) [15]. Most contemporary FPGAs, utilize fracturable 6-input LUTs in their design in order to be able to implement one 6-input boolean function or two 5-input boolean functions [7]. Fig. 1(a) depicts our proposed 6-input fracturable SHE-MRAM C-LUT and Fig. 1(b) illustrates the 6-input fracturable STT-MRAM C-LUT. In Fig. 1(a) and Fig. 1(b), where red color indicates the write path and black color indicates the read path. When the **WWL** and $\overline{\textbf{WWL}}$ signals are asserted, the Write TGs of each memory cell, **TGW1**


*GLSVLSI '19, May 9–11, 2019, Tysons Corner, VA, USA*

ACM ISBN 978-1-4503-6252-8/19/05....$15.00.
https://doi.org/10.1145/3299874.3318038

and **TGW2**, will turn on and using Bit Lines, $\mathbf{BL}_i$, and Source Lines, $\mathbf{SL}_i$, we write into both MTJs in each memory cell, $\mathbf{MTJ}_i$ and $\overline{\mathbf{MTJ}_i}$, so that they hold complementary values. If $\mathbf{MTJ}_i$ is in the *P* state then $\overline{\mathbf{MTJ}_i}$ will be in the *AP* state and vice versa. This will result in a wide read margin during the read operation.

After the termination of the write operation, in order to read the data stored in the MTJs, **RWL** and $\overline{\mathbf{RWL}}$ signals will be enabled, which results in activation of Read TGs of each memory cell, **TGR**. During the read operation, **PR** and **NR** transistors are turned on when **RWL** and $\overline{\mathbf{RWL}}$ are asserted, which provides the read path from **VDD** to **GND**. The source of **PR**, which is a PMOS transistor, is connected to **VDD** to provide strong one and the source of **NR**, which is an NMOS transistor, is connected to **GND** to provide strong zero. A voltage divider circuit is designed as a result of resistance difference between the $\mathbf{MTJ}_i$ and $\overline{\mathbf{MTJ}_i}$, and the divided voltage can be observed at the $\mathbf{D}_i$ nodes shown in Fig. 1(a) and Fig. 1(b). According to the select tree input signals, shown as **A**, **B**, **C**, **D**, **E**, and **F** in Fig. 1, using two inverters, the voltage on $\mathbf{D}_i$ nodes will be amplified to generate the required output. Since the values stored in the $\mathbf{MTJ}_i$ and $\overline{\mathbf{MTJ}_i}$ devices are complementary, using one MTJ device to retain the data value and the other as the reference value will result in a wide read margin from *AP* to *P* [8], which we leverage herein to increase the reliability of the read operation.

In the proposed C-LUT design there is no need for an external clock or a large sense amplifier circuit. Furthermore, the proposed fracturable C-LUT can perform as a single 6-input LUT or two 5-input LUTs. The Operation mode of the proposed LUT is controlled using **S5** and **S6** signals. If **S5** signal is enabled and **S6** is disabled, then the C-LUT will be operating as two 5-input LUTs and the outputs of the C-LUT will be **OUT0** and **OUT2**. On the other hand, if **S5** signal is disabled and **S6** signal is enabled, then the C-LUT will be operating as a 6-input LUT and **OUT1** will be the C-LUT's output. The proposed fracturable C-LUT provides significantly higher functional flexibility at the expense of slightly more power consumption as studied in Section 3.

## 3 SIMULATION FRAMEWORK, RESULTS, AND ANALYSIS

Herein, we use the HSPICE circuit simulator to validate the functionality of proposed C-LUT using 45nm CMOS technology and the STT-MRAM model developed by Kim *et al.* in [5]. Figure 2(a) and 2(b) show the transient response of the C-LUT implementing a 6-input OR operation for *ABCDEF* = "000000" and *ABCDEF* = "111111" input signals, respectively. In order to generate the current required for a write delay of less than 2ns, the write transistors are required to be enlarged 4-fold. As shown, the HSPICE simulations verify the correct functionality of our proposed C-LUT.

Table 1 lists comparison results between the SRAM-LUT and proposed C-LUT in terms of power consumption and delay. The results show more than 80% standby power reduction at the cost of increased write power which can be tolerated due to its infrequent occurrence of write operations in LUTs. There are three energy profiles in the FPGA LUT circuits: (1) Read energy consumption during the FPGA normal operation, (2) Standby energy for the LUTs that are not on the active datapath, which can constitute a significant portion of the FPGA fabric, and (3) write energy that is

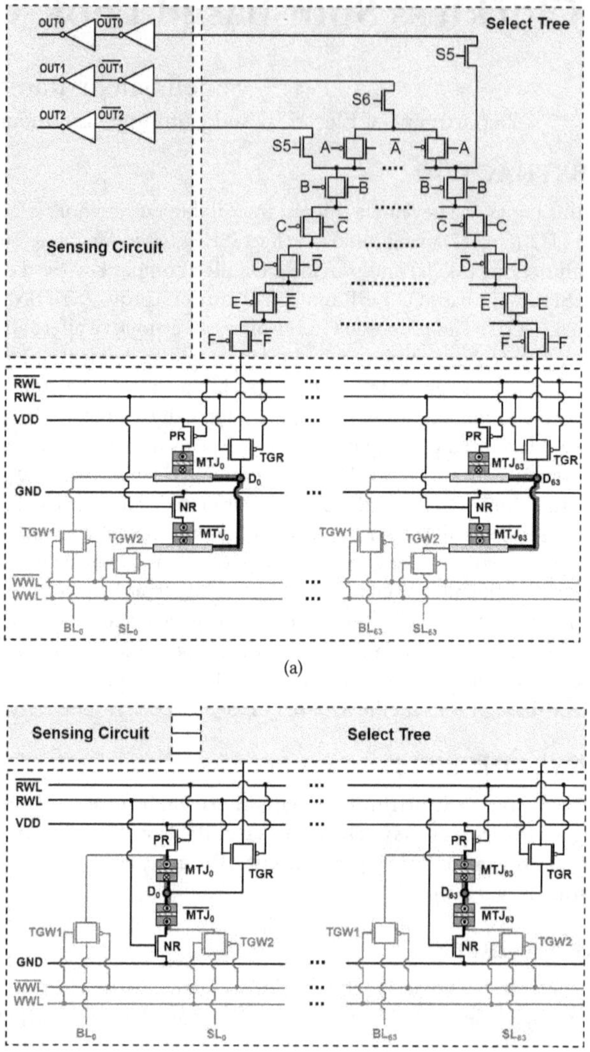


(a)

(b)

**Figure 1: The circuit-level diagram of the proposed 6-input fracturable Combinational Look-Up Table (C-LUT) using (a) SHE-MTJ devices and (b) STT-MTJ devices.**

**Table 1: Comparison between SRAM-LUT and MRAM-LUT.**

| | | Power ($\mu W$) | | | Delay | |
|---|---|---|---|---|---|---|
| | | Read | Write | Standby | Read | Write |
| SRAM LUT | Logic "0" | 2.58 | 28.4 | 1.5 | 30 ps | 20 ps |
| | Logic "1" | 7.55 | 27.7 | 1.85 | 30 ps | 20 ps |
| | Average | 5.06 | 25.08 | 1.67 | 30 ps | 20 ps |
| MRAM C-LUT | Logic "0" | 14.38 | 81.16 | 0.31 | 20 ps | 2 ns |
| | Logic "1" | 19.91 | 81.25 | 0.31 | 60 ps | 2 ns |
| | Average | 17.15 | 81.18 | 0.31 | 40 ps | 2 ns |

consumed during the LUTs' configuration operation which occurs

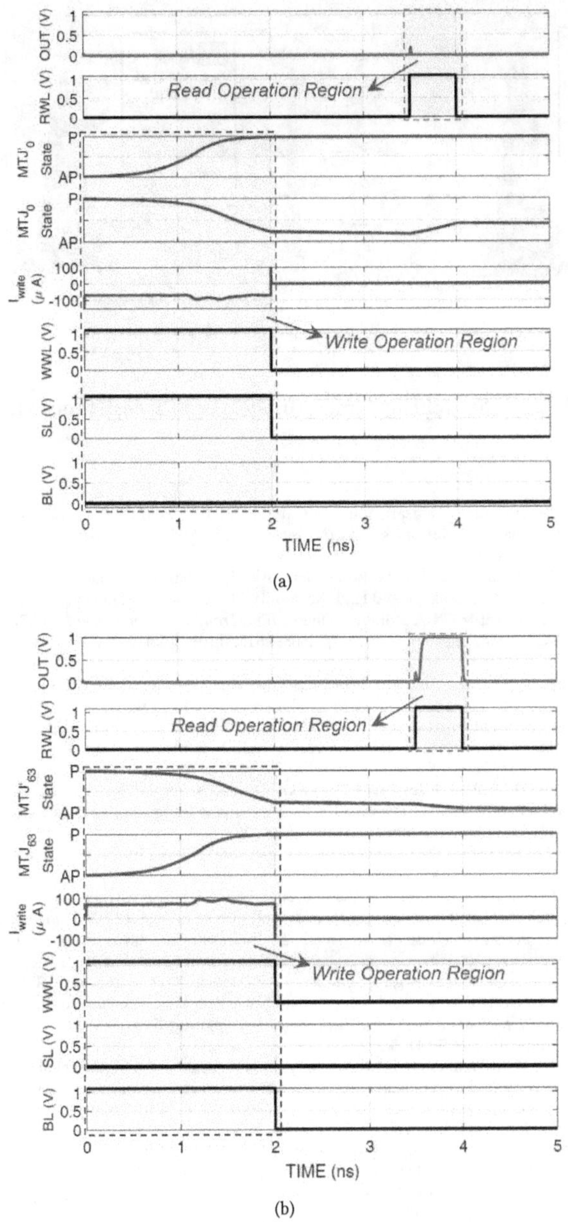


**Figure 2: Transient response of C-LUT implementing 6-input OR operation for (a)** *ABCDEF* = "000000" **input signal, and (b)** *ABCDEF* = "111111" **input signal.**

rarely. Table 2 provides an area and energy consumption comparison between SRAM-LUT and C-LUT. As listed, the structure of a 6-input MRAM-based C-LUT requires 1,547 MOS transistors plus 128 MTJs, which can be fabricated on top of the CMOS transistors incurring low area overhead, while the conventional 6-input SRAM-LUT includes 1,029 MOS transistors. This results in an area overhead of roughly 50% for C-LUT compared to SRAM-LUT, which is primarily induced by the write circuits. Thus, innovations are

**Table 2: Area and Energy Consumption comparison between SRAM LUT and MRAM C-LUT.**

| | Features | SRAM LUT | MRAM C-LUT |
|---|---|---|---|
| Device Count | Storage Cells | 384 MOS | 128MTJ |
| | Write/Control | 384 MOS | 256×4 + 256 MOS[(1)] |
| | Read | 261 MOS | 267 MOS |
| | Total | 1029 MOS | 1547 MOS + 128 MTJ |
| Average Energy Consumption | Read | 2.53 fJ | 8.58 fJ |
| | Write | 14 fJ | 162.36 fJ |

(1) Write transistors are 4× larger than minimum feature size.

**Table 3: Iso-Delay Area and Write Energy Consumption comparison between STT-MRAM and SHE-MRAM C-LUTs.**

| Features | | C-LUT | |
|---|---|---|---|
| | | STT-MRAM | SHE-MRAM |
| Device Count | Storage Cells | 128MTJ | 128MTJ |
| | Write/Control | (256×4)+256MOS [(1)] | 256+256MOS [(2)] |
| | Read | 267MOS | 267MOS |
| | Total | 1547MOS+128MTJ | 779MOS+128MTJ |
| Average Write Energy per Cell | | 162.3 fJ | 175.5 fJ |

(1) Write transistors are 4× larger than minimum feature size.
(2) Write transistors with minimum feature size are used.

sought to reduce the area and energy consumption of the MRAM cell's write circuit to mitigate these issues. Recently, SHE-MRAM cells have attracted considerable attentions as an alternative for the conventional STT-MRAMs. Herein, we have used the SHE-MRAM device model proposed by Camsari *et al.* [3] to realize a circuit-level simulation of our SHE-MRAM C-LUT. The results obtained exhibit that a TG-based write circuit with minimum-sized MOS transistors can produce the sufficient write current amplitude required for switching the SHE-MRAM's state in less than 2ns. Thus, table 3 provides an iso-delay comparison between STT-MRAM and SHE-MRAM C-LUT in terms of device count and write energy. As listed, the SHE-MRAM C-LUT can achieve more than 49% area reduction, while realizing comparable write energy consumption. Moreover, the SHE-MRAM C-LUT achieves at least 24% device count reduction compared to SRAM-LUT.

Furthermore, to analyze the reliability of the read and write operations of the proposed C-LUT, Monte Carlo (MC) simulation is performed to cover a wide range of PV scenarios that may occur in the fabricated device. The MC simulation is performed with 1,000 instances considering the effects of PV on CMOS peripheral circuit and the MTJs. In particular, variation of 10% for the MTJs' dimensions along with 10% variation on the threshold voltage and 1% variation on transistors dimentions are assessed. Fig. 3(a) depicts the distribution of the switching times for $T_{P-AP}$ and $T_{AP-P}$, Fig. 3(b) illustrates the distribution of MTJ resistances in $R_{AP}$ and $R_P$ states, and Fig. 3(c) shows the distribution of read, $I_{READ}$, and write, $I_{Write}$ currents for the 1,000 MC instances. According to the MC simulation results, C-LUT provides reliable write performance resulting in less than 0.001% write errors in 1,000 error-free MC instances. In particular, results of the MC simulation show that the

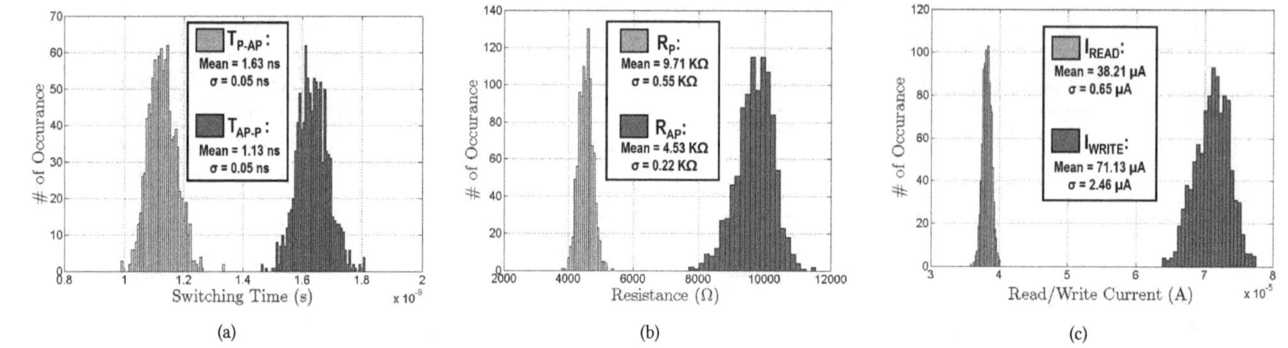


**Figure 3: Simulation Results of 1,000 MC instances for (a) $T_{P-AP}$ and $T_{AP-P}$ Switching Times, (b) $R_{AP}$ and $R_P$ resistance states, and (c) read, $I_{READ}$, and write, $I_{Write}$ currents.**

switching time for $P - AP$ is 1.63ns on average and the switching time for $AP - P$ is 1.13ns on average, which both fall under the 2ns duration of the write operation, as depicted in Fig. 3(a). Additionally, since the states of the MTJs are differential, they provide a wide read margin and as a result there are less than 0.001% read errors caused by PV based on the 1,000 error-free MC simulation results. Furthermore, our proposed C-LUT does not suffer from read disturbance due to the small read current compared to the write current as shown in Fig. 3(c). According to our MC simulation results, the read current is 38.21$\mu$A on average, which is significantly lower than the write current that is 71.13$\mu$A on average.

## 4 CONCLUSION

To overcome the conventional SRAM-LUT limitations such as high static power, volatility, and low logic density, we have proposed a novel LUT design using spin-based devices. The proposed C-LUT is a clockless design and a suitable candidate for combinational logic, which can also be combined with a flip-flop circuit to implement sequential logic. According to our simulation results, the standby power dissipation of the proposed C-LUT is 0.31$\mu$W, which is reduced by 5.4-fold compared to the SRAM-based LUT. Moreover, the structure of the proposed SHE-MRAM based C-LUT includes 250 and 768 fewer transistors compared to the SRAM-based LUT and the STT-MRAM based C-LUT, respectively. Additionally, according to the process variation reliability analysis, the C-LUT circuit exhibits $< 0.001\%$ error rate for read and write operations in presence of variations spanning both transistors and MTJs.

## ACKNOWLEDGEMENT

This work was supported in part by the National Science Foundation (NSF) through ECCS-1810256.

## REFERENCES


[1] Rawad Al-Haddad, Rashad S. Oreifej, Ramtin Zand, Abdel Ejnioui, and Ronald F. DeMara. 2015. Adaptive Mitigation of Radiation-Induced Errors and TDDB in Reconfigurable Logic Fabrics. In *2015 IEEE 24th North Atlantic Test Workshop*. IEEE, 23–32. https://doi.org/10.1109/NATW.2015.14

[2] Aliyar Attaran, Tyler David Sheaves, Praveen Kumar Mugula, and Hamid Mahmoodi. 2018. Static Design of Spin Transfer Torques Magnetic Look Up Tables for ASIC Designs. In *Proceedings of the 2018 on Great Lakes Symposium on VLSI - GLSVLSI '18*. ACM Press, New York, New York, USA, 507–510. https://doi.org/10.1145/3194554.3194651

[3] Kerem Yunus Camsari, Samiran Ganguly, and Supriyo Datta. 2015. Modular approach to spintronics. *Scientific reports* 5, 1 (9 2015), 10571. https://doi.org/10.1038/srep10571

[4] Kejie Huang, Yajun Ha, Rong Zhao, Akash Kumar, and Yong Lian. 2014. A Low Active Leakage and High Reliability Phase Change Memory (PCM) Based Non-Volatile FPGA Storage Element. *IEEE Transactions on Circuits and Systems I: Regular Papers* 61, 9 (9 2014), 2605–2613. https://doi.org/10.1109/TCSI.2014.2312499

[5] Jongyeon Kim, An Chen, Behtash Behin-Aein, Saurabh Kumar, Jian-Ping Wang, and Chris H. Kim. 2015. A technology-agnostic MTJ SPICE model with user-defined dimensions for STT-MRAM scalability studies. In *2015 IEEE Custom Integrated Circuits Conference (CICC)*. IEEE, 1–4. https://doi.org/10.1109/CICC.2015.7338407

[6] Ian Kuon, Russell Tessier, and Jonathan Rose. 2008. Fpga architecture: Survey and challenges. *Foundations and Trends in Electronic Design Automation* 2, 2 (2008), 135–253. https://doi.org/10.1561/1000000005

[7] Andrew Percey. 2007. Advantages of the Virtex-5 FPGA 6-Input LUT Architecture. (2007). www.BDTIC.com/XILINX

[8] Soheil Salehi and Ronald F. DeMara. 2018. BGIM: Bit-Grained Instant-on Memory Cell for Sleep Power Critical Mobile Applications. In *2018 IEEE 36th International Conference on Computer Design (ICCD)*. IEEE, 342–345. https://doi.org/10.1109/ICCD.2018.00058

[9] Soheil Salehi, Deliang Fan, and Ronald F Demara. 2017. Survey of STT-MRAM Cell Design Strategies: Taxonomy and Sense Amplifier Tradeoffs for Resiliency. *ACM Journal on Emerging Technologies in Computing Systems* 13, 3 (2017), 1–16. https://doi.org/10.1145/2997650

[10] Daisuke Suzuki and Takahiro Hanyu. 2019. Design of a highly reliable, high-speed MTJ-based lookup table circuit using fractured logic-in-memory structure. *Japanese Journal of Applied Physics* 58, SB (2 2019), SBBB10. https://doi.org/10.7567/1347-4065/aafd98

[11] Daisuke Suzuki, Yuhui Lin, Masanori Natsui, and Takahiro Hanyu. 2013. A 71%-Area-Reduced Six-Input Nonvolatile Lookup-Table Circuit Using a Three-Terminal Magnetic-Tunnel-Junction-Based Single-Ended Structure. *Japanese Journal of Applied Physics* 52, 4S (4 2013), 04CM04. https://doi.org/10.7567/JJAP.52.04CM04

[12] Xifan Tang, Gain Kim, Pierre-Emmanuel Gaillardon, and Giovanni De Micheli. 2016. A Study on the Programming Structures for RRAM-Based FPGA Architectures. *IEEE Transactions on Circuits and Systems I: Regular Papers* 63, 4 (4 2016), 503–516. https://doi.org/10.1109/TCSI.2016.2528079

[13] Hiroaki Yoda, Hideyuki Sugiyama, Tomoaki Inokuchi, Yuushi Kato, Yuichi Ohsawa, Keiko Abe, Naoharu Shimomura, Yoshiaki Saito, Satoshi Shirotori, Katsuhiko Koui, Buyandalai Altansargai, Souichi Oikawa, Mariko Shimizu, Mizue Ishikawa, Kazutaka Ikegami, Yuuzo Kamiguchi, Shinobu Fujita, and Atsushi Kurobe. 2017. High-Speed Voltage-Control Spintronics Memory (High-Speed VoCSM). In *2017 IEEE International Memory Workshop (IMW)*. IEEE, 1–4. https://doi.org/10.1109/IMW.2017.7939085

[14] Ramtin Zand and Ronald F DeMara. 2017. Radiation-hardened MRAM-based LUT for non-volatile FPGA soft error mitigation with multi-node upset tolerance. *Journal of Physics D: Applied Physics* 50, 50 (12 2017), 505002. https://doi.org/10.1088/1361-6463/aa9781

[15] Ramtin Zand, Arman Roohi, Soheil Salehi, and Ronald F. DeMara. 2016. Scalable Adaptive Spintronic Reconfigurable Logic Using Area-Matched MTJ Design. *IEEE Transactions on Circuits and Systems II: Express Briefs* 63, 7 (2016), 678–682. https://doi.org/10.1109/TCSII.2016.2532099

# A Hybrid Framework for Functional Verification using Reinforcement Learning and Deep Learning

Karunveer Singh, Rishabh Gupta, Vikram Gupta, Arash Fayyazi, Massoud Pedram, Shahin Nazarian
University of Southern California
Los Angeles CA USA
{karunves, rishabrg, vikramg, fayyazi, pedram, shahin.nazarian}@usc.edu

## ABSTRACT

In this paper, we propose a novel hybrid verification framework (HVF) which uses Reinforcement Learning (RL) and Deep Neural Networks (DNNs) to accelerate the verification of complex systems. More precisely, our HVF incorporates RL to generate all possible sequences of vectors needed to approach a target state as well as the corresponding path to the target state which contains a potential design error. Furthermore, HVF utilizes DNNs to accelerate the verification of complex data paths in the target states. We have tested our framework on several circuits including multi-core designs as well as bus-arbiters and confirmed its significant verification speedup when compared to prior work. For example, HVF provides a total speedup of 4.5x for a quad-core MIPS processor verification.

## CCS CONCEPTS

**• Computing methodologies → Reinforcement; • Hardware → Semi-formal verification;**

## KEYWORDS

Reinforcement Learning; Deep Neural Networks; SAT Solver; Assertions; Coverage Directed Test Generation

**ACM Reference format:**

Karunveer Singh, Rishabh Gupta, Vikram Gupta, Arash Fayyazi, Massoud Pedram, Shahin Nazarian. 2019. A Hybrid Framework for Functional Verification using Reinforcement Learning and Deep Learning. In Proceedings of 2019 Great Lakes Symposium on VLSI, Tysons Corner, VA, USA, May 9-11, 2019 (GLSVLSI'19), 4 pages. https://doi.org/10.1145/3299874.3318039

## 1. INTRODUCTION

Functional verification is a time intensive task, which becomes exponentially more difficult as the complexity of design increases. The product's time to market (TTM) is crucial for a design's success; hence, it is pertinent to reduce verification time. In addition, demand for complex circuits such as ASICs and System on Chips (SoCs) is ever increasing. Therefore, there is a need for advancements in verification approaches which can accelerate the error catching process. Recent work has shown that machine learning (ML) has the capability of reducing the execution time for solving certain problems in electronic design automation (EDA) and circuit recognition with applications in formal verification, etc. [2].

Simulation-based verification has been used as a complement to formal verification, especially for cases we lack detailed understanding of design specifications. Semi-formal verification [9] typically incorporates random test vector generation and coverage collection. ML is deployed for the stimuli generation for the design under verification (DUV) to identify test vectors with high probability of failing assertions [8] and converge towards the target coverage [5].

CDG [5] is superior to more traditional constraint-based random stimuli generation methods, thanks to its higher functional coverage. The neural network based framework presented in [8] is helpful in accelerating the CDG process but have some limitations. The major drawback of [8] is that it only provides vectors which will trigger the assertions. These vectors might not direct the design to the target state as the DNNs are not effective in finding out the interdependency of the vectors with the design states. The states and their transition conditions are equivalent to a decision-based graph representation. The graph-based verification methodology [1] solves the stimulus generation for deep state designs by traversing the decision graph. Therefore, the verification time is significantly reduced if instead of randomly generating test vectors, a sequence of vectors is generated to reach a target state.

The problem with the graph-based traversal techniques is that they are inefficient as they assume that design is static in nature [7]. However, the designs are modified throughout the product design cycle; hence, the design phases are dynamic. In this paper, we propose HVF (Hybrid Verification Framework), that incorporates a novel approach to cope with the dynamic conditions of complex sequential designs. Our approach is to deploy RL to filter the transitions which don't direct DUV to the target state. Then, RL generates test vectors to reach the target state and finally, we use DNNs to find the design error(s) in that state.


ACM ISBN 978-1-4503-6252-8/19/05...$15.00.
https://doi.org/10.1145/3299874.3318039

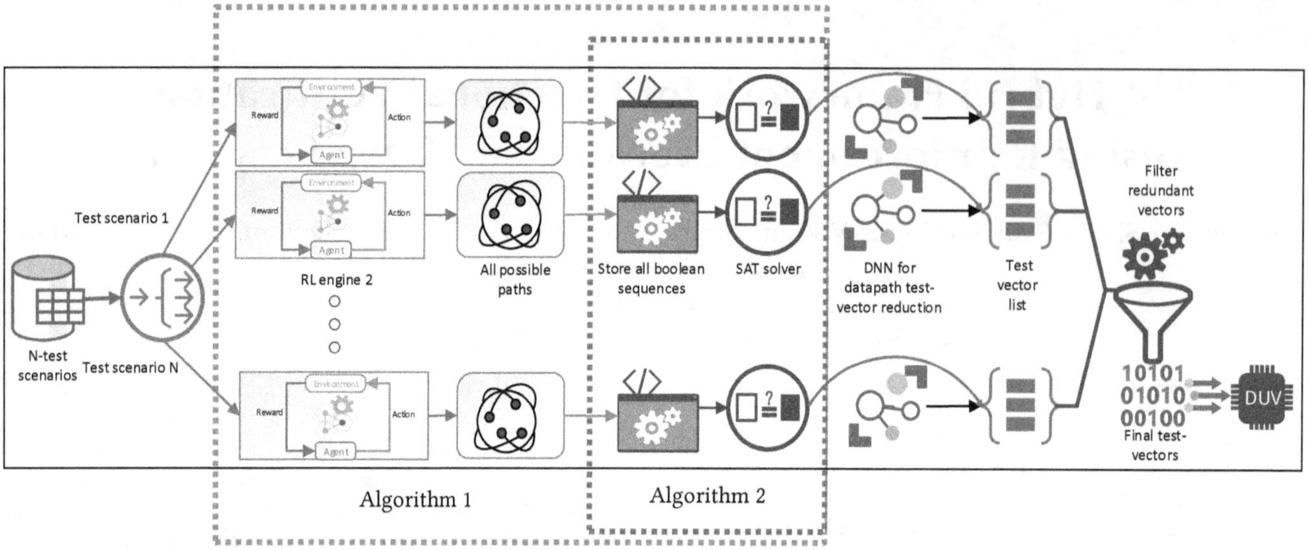


**Figure 1: Our HVF is fed with all possible test scenarios 1 to N (for target states 1 to N) to be processed in parallel. Each test scenario i corresponds to a target state i to be verified. For each scenario i an RL engine i explores all possible paths to target state i to learn the transition relational matrix $Q_i$. During the exploitation phase, all possible paths are stored in the Path matrix ($Path_i$) and passed to the SAT solver to get the transition vectors. Those vectors are then stored in the Transition Vector Sequence ($TVS_i$) list for target state i and then appended to the final TVS list ($TVS_{final}$). In parallel, DNNs are trained based on the outcomes of the random data fed to the combinational paths. The trained DNNs filter and append the input vectors to $TVS_{final}$. Finally, all the test vectors from all the parallel processes are collected to generate $TVS_{final}$ which is then fed to the DUV.**

Firstly, for the sequential part, depending upon the initial state and the target state, the proposed RL learns about the DUV and generates the sequences of transitions for all possible paths to the target state. After the RL agent has explored different paths to reach the target state, a learned-matrix is formed which stores all the explored Boolean transition conditions. We used a SAT solver to extract input vectors from learned-matrix to reach the target state. Once the target state is reached, our framework initializes the DNNs for verification of combinational path in the target state.

## 3. OUR PROPOSED FRAMEWORK

In this section, we present our HVF. We first explain the RL framework which we use for test sequence generation. Next, we describe how the verification framework interprets the test sequence and simultaneously initializes the DNNs for verification of the combinational design of the target state. Figure 1 depicts the flow of our HVF.

In complex sequential designs, there exist design errors which are deeply-rooted and require specific sequences of events to reach the target states. Neither the traditional constraint randomization nor the DNN based techniques can uncover such errors. We present a novel framework based on RL to identify sequences of vectors in order to reach the target states. Note that in the case of traditional CDG, as the design complexity increases, it becomes exponentially harder to cover all paths towards the target states, even if a complete state coverage was ensured. The RL framework solves this problem by providing sequences of vectors for all possible transitional paths thus making sure that all legal state transitions are verified.

### 3.1 Preprocessing and Matrix Generation

We transform the design spec to a Directed Graph (DG) where nodes are states. There is an edge between two nodes if there exists a legal transition determined by the design spec. Based on the DG we present the RL environment based on a matrix $R_i$ of size $N \times N$, where $N$ is the number of nodes in the DG. $R_{i_{jk}}$(element in $j^{th}$ row and $k^{th}$ column of $R_i$ matrix) has a value of -1 (i.e., the penalty value) for an illegal transition. The reward value of 100 (0) for the last (intermediate) legal transaction on the paths towards the target state are also empirically set. Note that the reward value for the last legal transition must be a large number. All parallel processes have different target states and also the corresponding $R_i$ matrices where $i$ is in range of 0 to number of target states.

### 3.2 RL Framework

We employed Q-learning-based RL. For the RL framework, the design spec is directly translated into the RL environment (i.e., $R_i$ matrix). We expect that the RL engines moves through the DUV and explore every possible alternative path to reach the target states. We empirically chose 170 epochs for the exploration part of our RL. The design is error-free if it can go into all the valid states specified in the design spec (see Algorithm 1). The Q matrix represents the resultant transition-relational matrix. It is initialized with zeros and is updated throughout exploration of the RL engine. The RL framework provides the all possible sequences of state-transitions by extracting the paths from the learned matrix (i.e., Q matrix) to the Path matrix, as in line 10 of Algorithm 1.

**Algorithm 1: RL approach for test vector generation**

**Input:** Set of target states: $S_{test} = \{(S_{0,initial}, S_{0,target}), (S_{1,initial}, S_{1,target}), \ldots, (S_{N,initial}, S_{N,target})\}$.
**Output:** Test vectors for target state transition

```
1   Initialize: Number of Epochs: N_E, Learning Rate: α
2               Discount Factor: γ
3   forall S_i in S_test do
4       Initialize Q_i matrix with zeros and rewards in R_i matrix
5       for each epoch in N_E do
6           Choose S_inext state from R_i using policy R-matrix
7           If S_i,next != S_i,target then
8               Update Q_i matrix
9       Initialize Path_i matrix
10      Path_i = ExtractPath (Q_i)
11      Initialize TVS_i (transition vector sequences) matrix
12      for all Transitions in Path_i do
13          TVS_i = getVectors (for each transition)
14      for each S_i in S_test do
15          TVS_final = append TVS_i
16  TVS_final = the list of all test sequences
17  return TVS_final
```

**Algorithm 2: SAT-based mapping transition relation**

**Function: getVectors()**
**Input:** State transition sequence: $Seq_{test} = \{(S_{curr}, S_{next})\}$.
**Output:** Transition vector sequence ($TVS_i$).

```
Initialize: Transition Action Matrix : TA
action = TA[S_curr][S_next]
TVS_i = miniSAT(action)
return TVS_i
```

## 3.3 Vector Extraction

Given the Path matrix ($Path_i$) the state transition sequence for target i is obtained (input to Algorithm 2). Given this state transition sequence a SAT solver (i.e., miniSAT in our work) is called to generate the vectors of the Boolean variables which satisfy the Boolean state transition expressions (which are already stored in transition action matrix, TA). The sequence of vectors to reach target state i is stored in $TVS_i$ (cf. Figure 1). The TVS lists for all test scenarios are appended into $TVS_{final}$ list (line 16 of Algorithm 1).

## 3.4 DNN Engine

We have adopted the neural network based framework of [8]. Note that our DNN engine of HVF runs in parallel with its RL framework. All assertions in the combinational path verification are grouped [3,6,8] by three factors namely the number of overlapping control signals, locality defined by the length of the shared data path and the number of common resources.

Each assertion group (AG) is analyzed based on a DNN, therefore the number of DNNs in our framework is equal to that of the AGs. Random sequences are generated and sent to the combinational design. Depending upon the assertion hits or misses, the vectors are labeled as passing or failing for an assertion group.

The DNNs are trained with the labeled transactions. Once each DNN is trained, test vectors are classified into valid and redundant vectors. Our DNNs drop the redundant vectors and collect the valid ones. In the target-state, the valid vectors are fed to the combinational path of the target states. The DNN tune the future transactions based on the outcome.

# 4. EXPERIMENTAL RESULTS

HVF has been tested on several circuits such as a bus arbiter similar to those of [4] but with extra states (to add to complexity) and multi-core processors, including a quad-core 5-stage MIPS processor which has a sequential instruction dispatcher and the cores are similar to those of the dual-core processor in [8]. The dispatcher dispatches instructions to different cores.

The RL framework (cf. Figure 1) learns the test vector sequences to the target states. There are 6 assertion groups, AG0-AG5, for a core, each of which having its own DNN. For DNNs, we adopt similar assertion grouping as discussed in [8]. Once the 6 DNNs are trained, their configuration can be used for other cores in parallel.

The Input layer of DNNs has 32 neurons since the processor has 32-bit instructions. Based on our experiments we have chosen two hidden layers having 128 neurons each. 1 neuron output is to test whether the input vector is triggering an assertion. We use ReLU (sigmoid) activation function for the hidden (output) layers.

The test scenarios (see section 3.1) are provided as test file to the RL engines, which generate the test vectors for each test scenario. The RL exploration time for a complex DUV can be a bottleneck, but that is mitigated by our parallel structure of the RL framework. Overall our framework outperforms the traditional CDG verification of a complex sequential design as illustrated in Figure 2. Three different test cases used in our evaluation are:

TEST1: Initial State = State A, Final State = State B
TEST2: Initial State = State A, Final State = State C
TEST3: Initial State = State A, Final State = State D

where State A: Core 1-2-3-4 working, State B: Core 1-2 Stall, Core 3-4 working, State C: Core 1-2-3 Stall, Core 4 working and State D: Core 1-2-3-4 Stall. Table 1 presents the comparison between a traditional CDG ( which was also used as a baseline in [8] ) and the RL framework of HVF in terms of producing the test vector sequences to reach the target states. As shown in Table 1, for X number of states (Design 1) the RL framework provides a significant improvement of 9x compared to traditional CDG.

**Table 1: Comparison of state transitions**

| | Number of states X | | | Number of states 2X | | |
|---|---|---|---|---|---|---|
| **Test Seq. #** | 1 | 2 | 3 | 1 | 2 | 3 |
| **Traditional CDG** | 18 | 16 | 9 | 242 | 40 | 45 |
| **HVF** | 2 | 3 | 4 | 6 | 5 | 4 |
| **Speedup** | 9x | 5.3x | 2x | 40.33x | 8x | 11.25x |

Similarly, the RL framework on the dispatcher with 2x number of states (Design 2) gives an improvement as high as 40x. Note that Design 1 is an instruction dispatcher, Design 2 is the same as Design 1, with 2x the number of states, while Design 3 is a bus arbiter. This improvement shows the scalability of our framework, as its RL framework learns from the environment and produces a sequence of vectors to reach the target state. However, the traditional CDG generates random vectors that may not result in reaching the target state.

Table 2 presents speedup of the RL framework of HVF over traditional CDG in terms of finding a target state. To be conservative, the RL time includes both exploration and exploitation times. The average speedup over all the three designs is 34.59x. In addition, the efficiency of RL framework in required number of transitions to find a target state is confirmed by testing it on Design 3. Table 3 shows maximum improvement of 27x in number of transitions required to reach the target state.

These results confirm significant increase in verification speedup as the complexity of sequential part grows. This is because the RL framework learns the vector sequences to reach the target states, whereas in the case of traditional CDG it would be exponentially expensive to randomly generate a vector sequence to reach a target state.

Once we have reached a target state using vectors provided by RL, trained DNNs start pruning data-path vectors by filtering out those vectors which have very low probability of triggering assertions. We randomly generated 60,000 vectors for creating training data. These vectors were then fed to the CPU data-path and respective outputs were stored. 75% of the data was used for training the network and rest for testing. Figure 2. shows the highest average assertion coverage improvement of 17.07x, for the DNN engine of HVF when compared to traditional CDG, for each core in the quad-core 5-stage MIPS processor.

Compared to the framework in [8], our HVF provides significant verification speedup. For example, a speedup of 4.5x was measured for the quad-core 5-stage MIPS processor. In addition to this speedup, HVF also provides error traces that lead to erroneous states.

**Table 2: RL framework speedup**

| | Design 1 | Design 2 | Design 3 |
|---|---|---|---|
| Speedup | 4.77x | 45x | 54x |

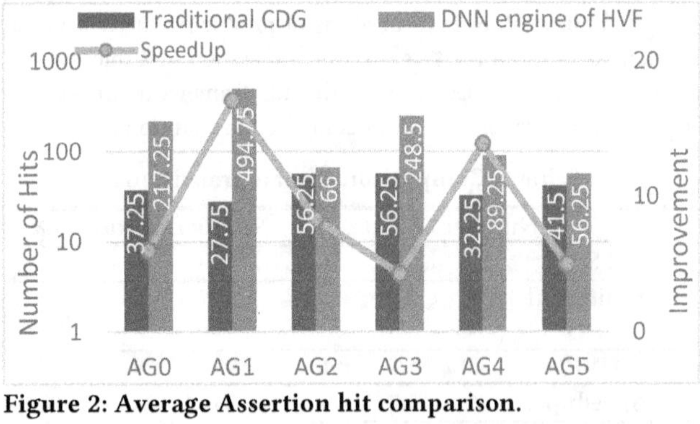


**Figure 2: Average Assertion hit comparison.**

**Table 3: Comparison of Number of state transitions after which target state is reached in Traditional CDG and HVF for a bus arbiter (Design 3)**

| | State 0 -> 6 | State 0 -> 7 | State 0 -> 5 |
|---|---|---|---|
| Traditional CDG | 21 | 45 | 54 |
| RL framework of HVF | 3 | 3 | 2 |
| Speedup | 7x | 15x | 27x |

## 5. CONCLUSION

Our verification framework integrates RL and DNNs into the CDG process to accelerate the verification process. The RL framework learns the sequential environment of DUV efficiently and provides the sequences of input vectors required to reach the target states. Once a target state is reached, the DNN engine verifies the combinational path.

Our experimental results confirm that our RL framework of HVF requires significantly fewer number of transitions compared to those of traditional CDG. Also, a total speedup of our 4.5x was confirmed when compared to the prior work based on neural networks.

As part of our future work, we plan to enhance our RL framework to be hierarchical such that it can utilize lower level RL engines for the sake of RL reusability across various designs with similar functional behavior.

## REFERENCES

[1] Randal E Bryant. 2001. *Graph-based algorithms for boolean function manipulation.*

[2] Arash Fayyazi, Soheil Shababi, Pierluigi Nuzzo, Shahin Nazarian, and Massoud Pedram. Deep Learning-Based Circuit Recognition Using Sparse Mapping and Level-Dependent Decaying Sum Circuit Representations.

[3] Marisabel Guevara, Benjamin Lubin, and Benjamin C. Lee. 2013. Navigating heterogeneous processors with market mechanisms. *Proc. - Int. Symp. High-Performance Comput. Archit.* (2013), 95–106. DOI:https://doi.org/10.1109/HPCA.2013.6522310

[4] Gary D Hachtel, Enrico Macii, Abelardo Pardo, and Fabio Somenzi. 1996. Markovian analysis of large finite state machines. *IEEE Trans. Comput. Des. Integr. Circuits Syst.* 15, 12 (1996), 1479–1493.

[5] Charalambos Ioannides and Kerstin I. Eder. 2012. Coverage-Directed Test Generation Automated by Machine Learning -- A Review. *ACM Trans. Des. Autom. Electron. Syst.* 17, 1 (2012), 1–21. DOI:https://doi.org/10.1145/2071356.2071363

[6] M H Neishaburi and Zeljko Zilic. 2010. Enabling efficient post-silicon debug by clustering of hardware-assertions. *2010 Des. Autom. Test Eur. Conf. Exhib. (DATE 2010)* (2010), 985–988. DOI:https://doi.org/10.1109/DATE.2010.5456904

[7] Péter Stefán, László Monostori, and Ferenc Erdélyi. 2001. Reinforcement learning for solving shortest-path and dynamic scheduling problems. *Proc. 3rd Int. Work. Emergent Synth. IWES* 1, 1 (2001), 83–88.

[8] Fanchao Wang, Hanbin Zhu, Pranjay Popli, Yao Xiao, Paul Bodgan, and Shahin Nazarian. 2018. Accelerating Coverage Directed Test Generation for Functional Verification: A Neural Network-based Framework. (2018). DOI:https://doi.org/10.1145/3194554.3194561

[9] William K. Lam. 2005. Hardware Design Verification: Simulation and Formal Method-Based Approaches. (2005).

# Digital and Analog-Mixed-Signal In-Memory Processing in CMOS SRAM

Akhilesh Jaiswal, Amogh Agrawal, Indranil Chakraborty, Mustafa Fayez Ali, and Kaushik Roy
School of Electrical and Computer Engineering, Purdue University
West Lafayette, IN, USA
{jaiswal,agrawa64,ichakra,ali102,kaushik}@purdue.edu

**ACM Reference Format:**
Akhilesh Jaiswal, Amogh Agrawal, Indranil Chakraborty, Mustafa Fayez Ali, and Kaushik Roy . 2019. Digital and Analog-Mixed-Signal In-Memory Processing in CMOS SRAM . In *Great Lakes Symposium on VLSI 2019 (GLSVLSI '19), May 9–11, 2019, Tysons Corner, VA, USA.* ACM, New York, NY, USA, 1 page. https://doi.org/10.1145/3299874.3319449

## 1 INTRODUCTION

Historically, Moore's Law, has been the key driving force for the ever increasing compute power on silicon chips. Architecturally, a key factor fueling the improvement in computing efficiency is due to the availability of large on-chip memory storage in form of SRAM arrays as a result of shrinking transistor sizes. The historic trend of *smaller* transistors and hence *larger* on-chip memories is slowing down recently. In sharp contrast to this slowdown, the demand for high throughput computations and associated energy-efficiency has escalated considerably in recent times. Researchers are in active pursuit of exploring alternate means to improve the computation throughput while also lowering the required energy consumption. *'In-Memory computing'* has emerged as a promising candidate to achieve both increased throughput along with decrease in energy consumption. SRAM based in-memory computations are of special interest due to the pervasive presence of large SRAM sub-arrays in state-of-the-art processors. One could, therefore, think of these in-memory enabled SRAM arrays as on-chip compute engines, thereby, exposing the end application to massive levels of parallelism.

## 2 SRAM BASED IN-MEMORY COMPUTING

Several proposals achieving various levels of compute parallelism within SRAM cells have been presented in the literature in recent times [1]-[8]. Interestingly, both digital [1]-[2] as well as analog-mixed-signal approaches [3]-[8] have been explored extensively. In general, digital approaches lead to accurate computations at the cost of reduced compute throughput. On the other hand, analog approaches lead to higher levels of data parallelism at the cost of approximate computations due to the inherent nature of analog-processing. Few representative strategies geared toward SRAM based in-memory computations are as follows:

(1) **Digital Bulk-Bit-wise Computations**: The generic approach toward bulk-bit-wise operations is to enable two memory rows, simultaneously, and read out a desired Boolean function of the constituent words through modified sensing circuits [1]-[2].
(2) **Analog-Mixed-Signal Binary Dot-Products**: Binary dot products comprise of bit-wise XNOR followed by population-count (pop-count: counting the number of '1's'). The usual approach here is to enable bulk-bit-wise operation and generate an analog voltage that is proportional to the pop-count in the resultant bit-stream. By sensing the analog voltage one can estimate the number of '1's' thereby accomplishing binary dot product operation [5]-[6].
(3) **Analog-Mixed-Signal Multi-bit Dot Products**: Multi-bit dot products require analog element-wise multiplication of two vectors followed by summation of the elements of the resulting vector. This summation of multiplications can be accomplished in 8T SRAM cells through current-mode computations wherein input vector voltages can be multiplied by effective conductance of the transistors through Ohm's Law and the resulting currents can be summed up in accordance to Kirchoff's Current Law [8].

Finally, due to the inherent approximate nature of analog processing, analog-mixed-signal schemes are suitable only for class of *error-resilient* applications as in machine learning. In contrast, digital in-memory computing can cater to a wider class of applications including both error-resilient as well as those that require accurate computations.

## 3 CONCLUSION

In this paper, we have highlighted three representative approaches with respect to in-memory computing in SRAM arrays ranging from strictly digital simple computations as in bulk bit-wise operations to massively parallel analog-mixed-signal computations involving accelerated multi-bit dot products estimations. It is important to note that the level of parallelism, the complexity of the required peripheral circuits and the approximation in computations increases when moving from digital to analog-mixed-signal in-memory computations.

## ACKNOWLEDGMENT

C-BRIC, one of six centers in JUMP, sponsored by SRC, DARPA, NSF, Intel Corporation and Vannevar Bush Fellowship.

## REFERENCES

[1] S. Jeloka, *et. al.* JSSCC, 2018. [2] A. Aggrawal *et. al.* TCAS-I, 2018. [3] S.K. Gonugondla, *et. al.* ISSCC, 2018. [4] J. Zhang *et. al.* JSSCC, 2017. [5] A. Biswas, *et. al.* ISSCC, 2018. [6] A. Agrawal *et. al.* arxiv, 2018. [7] Z. Jiang *et. al.* VLSI, 2018. [8] A. Jaiswal, *et. al.* arxiv, 2018.


*GLSVLSI '19, May 9–11, 2019, Tysons Corner, VA, USA*

ACM ISBN 978-1-4503-6252-8/19/05.
https://doi.org/10.1145/3299874.3319449

# Ferroelectric FET based In-Memory Computing for Few-Shot Learning

Ann Franchesca Laguna
alaguna@nd.edu
University of Notre Dame
Indiana, USA

Xunzhao Yin
xyin1@nd.edu
University of Notre Dame
Indiana, USA

Dayane Reis
dreis@nd.edu
University of Notre Dame
Indiana, USA

Michael Niemier
mniemier@nd.edu
University of Notre Dame
Indiana, USA

X. Sharon Hu
shu@nd.edu
University of Notre Dame
Indiana, USA

## ABSTRACT

As CMOS technology advances, the performance gap between the CPU and main memory has not improved. Furthermore, the hardware deployed for Internet of Things (IoT) applications need to process ever growing volumes of data, which can further exacerbate the "memory wall". Computing-in-memory (CiM) architectures, where logic and arithmetic operations are performed in memory, can significantly reduce energy and latency overheads associated with data transfer, and potentially alleviate processor-memory bottlenecks. In this paper, we consider the utility of ternary content addressable memory (TCAM) arrays and CiM arrays based on ferroelectric field effect transistors (FeFETs) to support emerging machine learning models that can learn new classes of data with significantly less training overhead – highly desirable in IoT applications. Architecturally, we use TCAM and CiM arrays to implement the external memory module in a memory enhanced neural network (MENN) – which can be used to minimize catastrophic forgetting – a major problem in applications such as lifelong and few-shot learning. As a representative example, we achieve 95.14% accuracy for a few-shot learning task with the Omniglot data set by using a combined $L_\infty$ and $L_1$ distance metric computed via a TCAM-CiM cascaded architecture (as opposed to 99.06% accuracy assuming a GPU backed by DRAM). While there is a slight drop in accuracy, the TCAM-CiM approach is 4.34X faster and 4.18X more energy efficient than a CMOS implementation for the same task. The ability of an FeFET to serve as both a compact logic and storage element helps to enable dense CiM and TCAM structures that drive the aforementioned improvements to application-level figures of merit (FOMs).

## CCS CONCEPTS

• **Computing methodologies → Online learning settings**; *Neural networks*; • **Hardware → Non-volatile memory**; *Arithmetic and datapath circuits.*

## KEYWORDS

MANN, neural networks, lifelong learning, few-shot learning, FeFET, TCAM, Compute-in-Memory

**ACM Reference Format:**

Ann Franchesca Laguna, Xunzhao Yin, Dayane Reis, Michael Niemier, and X. Sharon Hu. 2019. Ferroelectric FET based In-Memory Computing for Few-Shot Learning. In *Great Lakes Symposium on VLSI 2019 (GLSVLSI '19), May 9–11, 2019, Tysons Corner, VA, USA.* ACM, New York, NY, USA, 6 pages. https://doi.org/10.1145/3299874.3319450

## 1 INTRODUCTION

With the rapid expansion of Internet of Things (IoT) applications, there is an increasing need to develop machine learning (ML) algorithms that can **(i)** be readily trained with new classes of data, and **(ii)** perform sufficiently accurate, *local* inference to minimize both re-training and communication costs. The local re-training of a deployed ML model in the IoT is challenging given that edge devices typically operate in a resource constrained environment. Furthermore, models may need to be frequently re-trained based on new, locally observed data from new and unseen scenarios.

A memory enhanced neural network (MENN) [1–4] is promising in this scenario, as it can allow a neural network that was originally trained with a fixed set of classes to learn and identify new classes – all with just a few examples of each new class. That said, MENNs also require frequent distance metric calculations between a query vector (i.e., a given object to classify) and every entry in a network's memory (i.e., the set of learned classes). Furthermore, during training/inference, a MENN memory must be updated in a non-sequential/non-regular fashion (which does not map well to a GPGPU architecture, often a straightforward implementation choice for IoT applications) [5, 6]. Additionally, the aforementioned query comparisons are limited by memory bandwidth. In this paper, we leverage ternary content addressable memories (TCAMs) in conjunction with computing-in-memory (CiM) arrays to perform efficient distance metric calculations using $L_1$ and $L_\infty$ distance metrics as well as memory updates, and to support non-sequential writes of the external memory module used in MENNs.

TCAM and CiM architectures can help reduce the high data transfer overhead from an external memory to a processor by performing computations in the memory itself. TCAMs perform search operations in parallel over the entire memory – and can identify the memory words with the shortest Hamming distance to a query input in a single cycle. By using range encoding [7], a search operation that calculates the $L_\infty$ and $L_1$ distance between the memory


*GLSVLSI '19, May 9–11, 2019, Tysons Corner, VA, USA*

ACM ISBN 978-1-4503-6252-8/19/05…$15.00
https://doi.org/10.1145/3299874.3319450

words and the input data word can be realized for the inference. However, realizing a search operation with respect to an $L_1$ distance in a TCAM array can be computationally expensive [1] as it results in a much longer encoding than $L_\infty$. Alternatively, a CiM array can perform arithmetic operations such as additions (ADDs) and subtractions (SUBs) between two memory words inside the memory array [8, 9]. Thus, the word-wise arithmetic operations of CiM can be utilized to implement a search operation associated with an $L_1$ distance calculation. In essence, a search operation that employs an $L_\infty$ distance calculation can be implemented by a TCAM array, which can subsequently be followed by a CiM array-based computation that performs word-wise $L_1$ distance calculations. We show that such combined $L_1$ and $L_\infty$ based distance metric leads to minimal accuracy degradation compared with the cosine similarity metric while the corresponding TCAM and CiM design leads to much improved energy efficiency.

We consider hardware implementations of TCAM and CiM for the distance calculations and updates of a MENN. To date, TCAMs and CiMs based on various technologies such as CMOS, magnetic tunnel junction (MTJ), spin-transfer torque magnetic RAM (STT-MRAM), resitive RAM (ReRAM), etc. have all been proposed and studied [10–15]. Among these approaches, ferroelectric field effect transistors (FeFETs) stand out as a pathway for building both efficient TCAM and CiM arrays due to its three-terminal device structure, high $I_{on}/I_{off}$ ratio, and high off resistance [8, 16, 17]. In this work, we consider FeFET-based TCAM and CiM architectural combinations, and demonstrate energy efficiency and performance improvements over a GPU implementation. Our approach achieves a 4.34X speedup and 4.18X energy reduction over a conventional GPU approach with 95.14% 5-way 5-shot learning accuracy for the Omniglot dataset.

## 2 BACKGROUND

The primary focus of this paper is on combining FeFET-based TCAM and CiM designs for a MENN architecture which is used in one-shot learning applications. As a precursor to subsequent discussions, we provide a theoretical background of MENN in Sec. 2.1. Existing efforts with respect to TCAM arrays are discussed in Sec. 2.2. We then review related work with respect to CiM in Sec. 2.3, i.e., in terms of both technologies and computing capabilities. Finally, in Sec. 2.4 we describe the FeFET, our choice of the emerging device.

### 2.1 MENN for Few shot learning

The terms one-shot or few-shot learning refer to rapid learning from one/few examples. Given a set of support images with one/few image(s) per class and a query image, the goal of one/few shot learning is to be able to identify which support image the query image is most similar to. Thus, for the 3-way 1-shot classification[1] example in Fig. 1, the query image is most similar to the second support image. (For training, in a one/few shot learning task, the dataset is split such that the classes in the training set are disjoint from the classes in the test set.)

Augmenting a neural network with an external memory (i.e., outside of the neural network) can improve its abilities to "learn how to learn" and prevent catastrophic forgetting [18] – a common problem in one-shot learning. The training occurs as a series of

[1] *way* in Fig. 1 refers to the number of classes and *shot* refers to the number of images per class

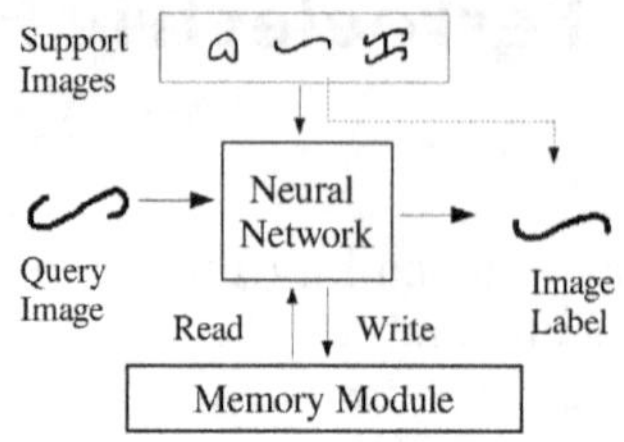


**Figure 1: MENN Overview with a 3-way 1-shot example.**

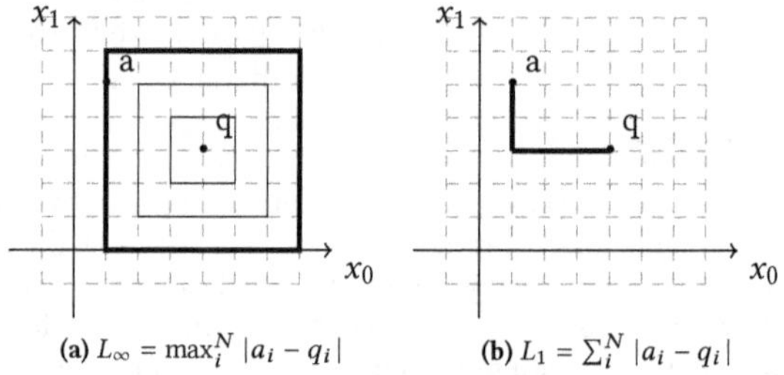


**Figure 2: Definition of $L_\infty$ and $L_1$ distance in the 2-D space.**

N-way K-shot examples. A traditional neural network updates its weights with a bias with the most recent example it has seen. It can therefore overfit on newer examples. Adding an external memory prevents this bias by caching information it has previously seen [19], which can be used by the neural network for a better generalization. Memory entries are then retrieved based on their similarity with a query vector.

There are two main operations in the external memory module: search and write/update [20]. The **search** operation is usually composed of a distance metric computation followed by a read. Cosine distance metric is commonly used in the MENN and represents the angular distance between two points to measure closeness with respect to the origin. Due to the high computational demand of evaluating cosine distance, $L_\infty$ (Fig. 2a) and $L_1$ (Fig. 2b) distance metrics can be considered as alternatives for measuring similarity between a query and the entries in the external memory module. Some MENN architectures perform weighted nearest neighbor search [3], and most MENN architectures limit the reads to the top k-nearest neighbors [21]. The top k-nearest neighbors may not necessarily be located in contiguous locations in the memory, resulting in sparse or non-sequential memory accesses. **Writing/Updating** to an external memory module also requires non-sequential memory accesses as new entries are added to the memory or as certain memory entries are replaced when the memory array reaches full capacity. A common practice for a MENN is to replace the oldest memory entry following the Least Recently Used (LRU) policy.

GPGPUs are currently widely used to implement MENNs. GPGPUs perform the best on sequential operations because they can perform operations while new data are being fetched. Non-sequential data-intensive operations in MENNs – such as search and write – have higher memory latencies and cannot take advantage of the GPU's compute capacity. These operations are hence limited by the memory bandwidth [5, 22]. Integrating computation with memory at finer granularities can mitigate data-transfer overhead with such operations. Below, we discuss CiM arrays and TCAM array functionality that could substantially reduce data transfer overhead.

## 2.2 Ternary Content Addressable Memories

TCAM is a special type of memory that can perform parallel searches across an entire memory array in a single step. The parallel search capability of a TCAM array makes it an ideal candidate for MENNs that demand massive distance metric calculations. Conventional MENNs perform floating point cosine distance calculations sequentially between the stored memory entries and the query vector for a search operation during inference, which is both time and energy consuming. By mapping floating point words to binary words, a TCAM array is able to perform Hamming distance calculations between the input query and all words in the memory in parallel to accomplish the search operation. This mapping function can be realized by using hashing [23] or range encoding [7]. In RENÉ [7], range encoding techniques are used to encode floating point data into binary reflected gray codes (BRGC). A nearest neighbor search based on the $L_\infty$ distance calculation (Fig. 2a), between the encoded words and the input word [7] can then be implemented.

A conventional CMOS TCAM typically employs two SRAMs to store ternary states. Other emerging devices such as ReRAMs and MTJs have also been used to build TCAMs [24]. These devices are non-volatile, and could encode binary states into variable resistances. The most common ReRAM-based TCAM design contains two transistors and two ReRAMs, and has been considered in the context of application spaces such as hyperdimensional computing [25]. That said, ReRAM cells may exhibit a rather low ratio between the two resistance states and a low off resistance, which can lead to high static power. ReRAM may also incur high write energy due to their current-driven write mechanisms. On contrast to CMOS- and ReRAM-based TCAM designs, FeFET-based TCAMs offer lower energy, delay and area overhead. FeFETs are also compatible with MOSFET processes.

## 2.3 Computing-in-Memory

CiM architectures aim to reduce the overheads associated with high volumes of data transfer from the memory to a processor, by exploiting the inherently large internal bandwidth of the memory to perform basic operations within the memory itself. Word-wise arithmetic operations — such as ADDs and SUBs — could be implemented either by a multiple step procedure [26] or by a single step as described in [27].

Besides traditional CMOS-based options [11, 28], CiM designs that employ emerging technologies such as STT-MRAM and ReRAM have been considered and offer desirable features such as high-density and nonvolatility. That said, there are challenges associated with memories that employ two terminal resistive devices such as STT-MRAM and ReRAM. Both the write energy and write latency of STT-MRAM and ReRAM cells are higher when compared to a conventional SRAM. Alternatively, FeFET devices can be used to build memory cells with high density, lower read/write latency compared to SRAM memories. In this work, we use in-memory word-wise ADDs as implemented in FeFET-CiM [27] to calculate $L_1$ distance metrics. (FeFET CiM designs will be discussed in more detail in Sec. 3.2).

## 2.4 Ferroelectric FET devices and model

A FeFET is structurally similar to a regular bulk MOSFET or FinFET, except that an additional layer of FE material is integrated in its gate stack. Recent fabricated demonstrations of ferroelectricity in

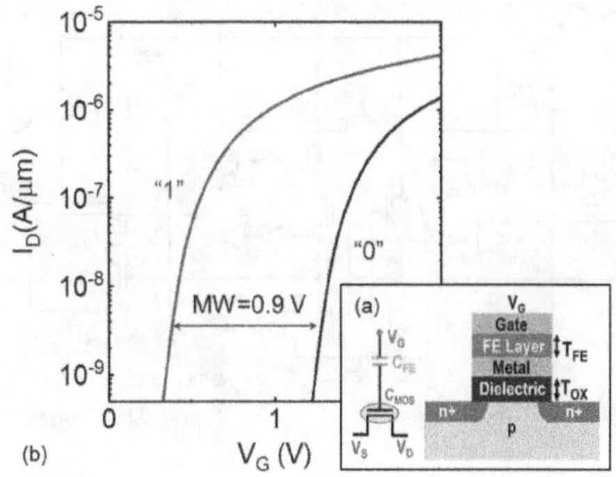


**Figure 3: (a) FeFET structure and its equivalent circuit representation; (b) simulated I-V curves.**

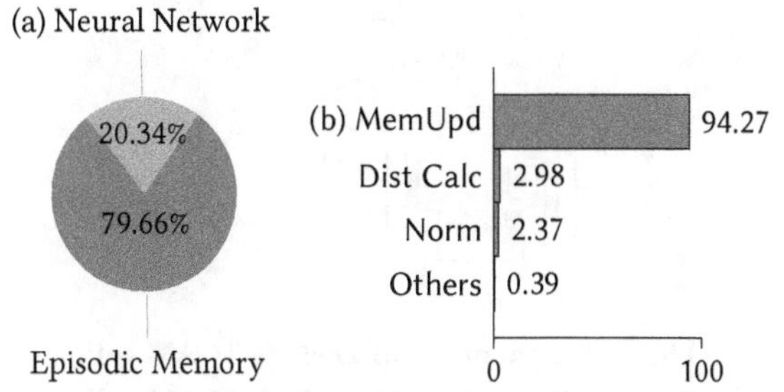


**Figure 4: Execution time distribution (a) between the neural network and (b) different operations of the episodic memory for one iteration of MENN on a 5-way 5-shot classification with 128x512 episodic memory during inference.**

hafnium zirconium oxide (HZO) [29], which is highly compatible with CMOS processes, has led to large-scale demonstrations of FeFETs, which opens up a path to industrial-scale realizations. A Preisach-based multi-domain model was developed and calibrated with experimental data of fabricated FeFET devices and informs the design efforts discussed here. Representative I-V characteristics are shown in Fig. 3. The multi-domain Preisach model captures the hysteretic characteristics of FeFETs that have been fabricated to date. The hysteretic characteristics and high $I_{ON}/I_{OFF}$ of FeFETs enable the device as a 1T storage element and a switch.

# 3 MENN DESIGN USING TCAM AND CIM

In this section, we discuss how to implement the external memory module of the MENN using TCAM and CiM designs. Sec. 3.1 discusses the neural network used in a MENN for a one-shot learning application considered here. Sec. 3.2 describes the FeFET-based CiM and TCAM designs that are used to perform the critical operations for MENN. Sec. 3.3 explains how TCAM and CiM support the distance calculations in a MENN.

## 3.1 MENN Design

As shown in Fig. 1, a MENN is composed of a neural network and an external memory module. Similar to [4], the neural network used in our work is composed of two 3x3 convolutional-ReLU layers that contain 64 filters each, a max-pooling layer, two 3x3 convolutional-ReLU layers that contain 128 filters each, and two fully connected (FC) layers. The output of the last FC layer forms the feature vector

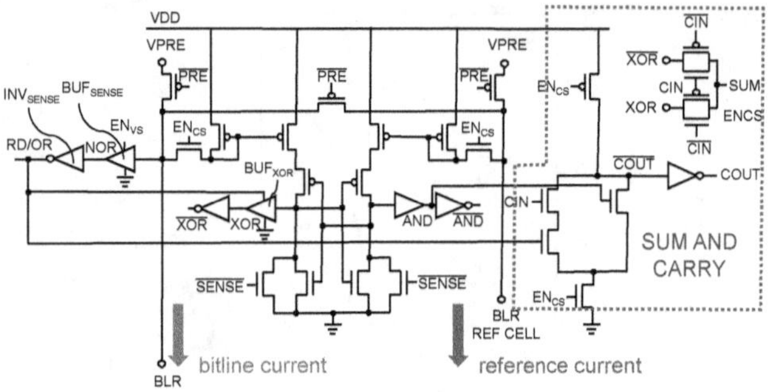


**Figure 5: FeFET-CiM Customized SA. The circuitry highlighted by the purple dotted outline leverages the results of bitwise operations to compute ADDs (Adapted from [8])**

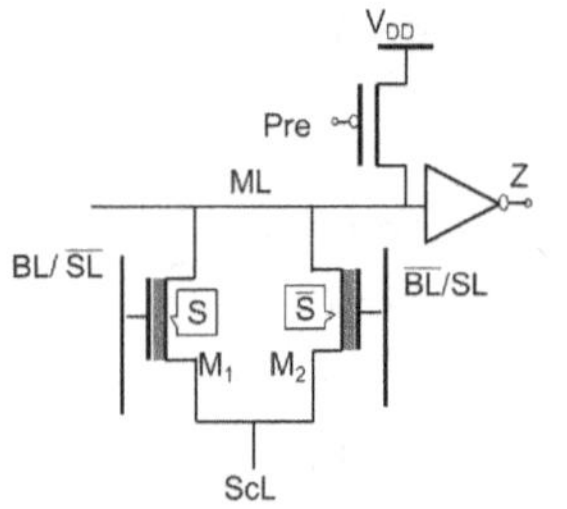


**Figure 6: Schematic of 2FeFET TCAM cell.**

**Table 1: Operations of 2FeFET TCAM cell.**

| $V_{\text{write}}$=4V $V_{\text{search}}$=1V | | $BL/\overline{SL}$ | $\overline{BL}/SL$ | $ScL$ | $S$ | $\overline{S}$ |
|---|---|---|---|---|---|---|
| Write '1' | Step 1 | $V_{\text{write}}$ | 0 | 0 | '1' | hold |
| | Step 2 | 0 | $-V_{\text{write}}$ | 0 | hold | '0' |
| Write '0' | Step 1 | $-V_{\text{write}}$ | 0 | 0 | '0' | hold |
| | Step 2 | 0 | $V_{\text{write}}$ | 0 | hold | '1' |
| Write *don't care* | | $-V_{\text{write}}$ | $-V_{\text{write}}$ | 0 | '0' | '0' |
| Search '1' | | 0 | $V_{\text{search}}$ | 0 | – | – |
| Search '0' | | $V_{\text{search}}$ | 0 | 0 | – | – |

that is delivered to the memory. The number of neurons in the last FC layer equals to the number of dimensions for each entry stored in the external memory module, where a dimension represents a feature. We evaluated the individual operations of the external memory as well as the execution time breakdown on the neural network and the memory module. During inference (Fig. 4(a)), optimizing the memory module becomes a greater priority as it takes the majority (79.66%) of computation time. Per Fig. 4(b), the most significant computation of comparison associated with the memory module is the memory update. (Distance calculations are the next most significant component, although they represent a smaller overall component of computation when compared to the memory update.)

## 3.2 Hardware Design

*3.2.1 FeFET TCAM.* Fig. 6 and Table 1 illustrate the schematic and the write and search operations of a 2 FeFET TCAM cell, respectively. The TCAM cell consists of two FeFETs, and the matchline $ML$ produces the $XNOR$ output between the stored bit $S$ and input data $SL$. Data bits are written in two steps into the two FeFETs in the TCAM cell. To write a logic '1', in the first step, $V_{\text{write}}$ is applied to $BL/\overline{SL}$ and 0 is applied to $ScL$ and $\overline{BL}/SL$. Thus, the gate-source voltage ($V_{GS}$) of $M_1$ is 4V, resulting in the switching of the FE polarization within the FeFET, and logic '1' is written into $S$. In the second step, $-V_{\text{write}}$ is applied to $\overline{BL}/SL$, and 0 is applied to $ScL$ and $BL/\overline{SL}$. Thus, $V_{GS}$ of $M_2$ is -4V and logic '0' is written into $\overline{S}$. To write a logic '0' into the TCAM cell, write voltages and 0 are applied as to write '0' into $S$, and '1' into $\overline{S}$, respectively. To write a *don't care* into the cell, logic '0' is written into the 2 FeFETs in one step. During the search operation, we first precharge $ML$ to high level $V_{DD}$. Then we apply $V_{\text{search}}/0$ to searchlines $SL/\overline{SL}$ to search logic '1', and apply $0/V_{\text{search}}$ to $SL/\overline{SL}$ to search logic '0'. When there is a mismatch, the $ML$ will discharge via the FeFET that stores logic '1'. Upon a match, $ML$ is not discharged and remains high, as two FeFETs turn off the discharge paths. In the *don't care* state, $ML$ remains high regardless of the input data, as both FeFETs store logic '0'.

*3.2.2 FeFET CiM.* Among the possible operations supported by FeFET-CiM [8], we are most interested in leveraging ADDs/SUBs between two words stored in memory. Below, we explain how ADD operations are accomplished in memory through a customized Sense Amplifier (SA). We note that the subtraction operation can be accomplished by the adder when we store one of the operands as a 2's complement. (inverted bits, with carry of the least significant bit set as 1).

The customized SA (depicted in Fig. 5) produces the results of in-memory bitwise operations, e.g. AND, OR, XOR/XNOR, that are in turn used to accomplish ADDs. The portion of Fig. 5 highlighted in purple in corresponds to a ripple-carry adder that is embedded in the customized SA. In this design, carry is computed through a dynamic logic-based circuit that is evaluated when we activate the control signal $EN_{CS}$, i.e. $EN_{CS} = 1$. With proper routing, the carry result ($C_{OUT}$) can be passed as an input ($C_{IN}$) to the subsequent bit of a word forming a *N-bit* carry propagation chain (where $N$ is the number of bits in a word). Word-wise sum is then computed through a pass transistor-based multiplex logic.

## 3.3 Hardware Implementation of External Memory Module

Memory operations in a MENN primarily need to identify relevant content and can be supported by hardware that perform efficient distance calculations. When considering distance metric calculations in a MENN, a cosine distance calculation requires numerous multiplication operations and data transfer. Alternatively, $L_\infty$ (Fig. 2a) is essentially the Hamming distance metric based on the range encoding, and can be performed efficiently in one step by a TCAM array due to its parallel search capability. Meanwhile, the CiM support $L_1$ distance calculations through in-memory word-wise additions/subtractions, without massive data transfer. In order to achieve a good trade off between the accuracy and hardware cost, we propose an approach that combines $L_\infty$ and $L_1$ using TCAM and CiM.

Per Fig. 7, the structure of the external memory module in a MENN is similar to that of a TCAM array, as both are composed of rows of memory entries. The external memory is composed of $d$ dimensions and $m$ entries. With a GPU, memory entries are stored as 32-bit floating point numbers. For the TCAM and CiM implementations, these entries are converted to a fixed-point representation as shown by the yellow path in Fig. 7(a) to 7(c). The binary dimension representations within each memory entry are then concatenated and stored in each TCAM row as shown in the red and blue path in Fig. 7(c) to 7(b). Note that the entries in the CiM are a replica of the

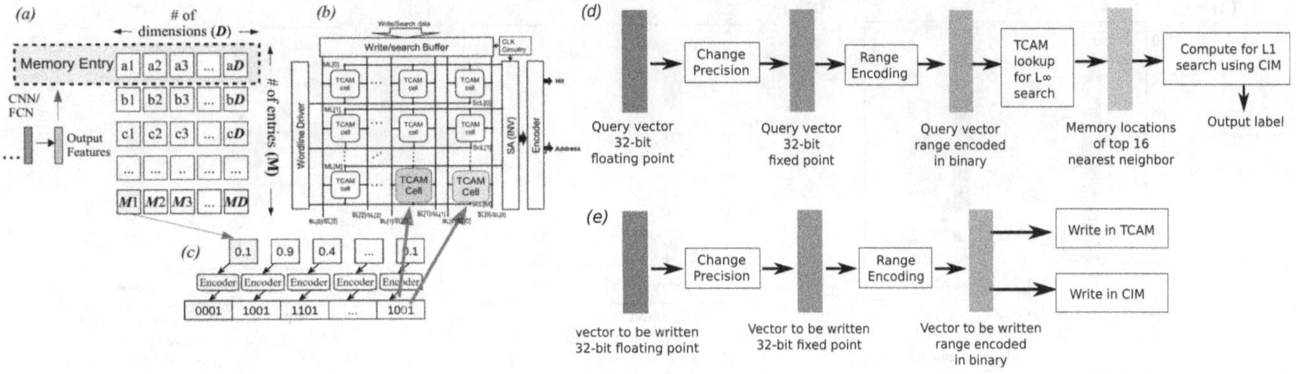

Figure 7: (a-c) Range encoding from external to TCAM: Each memory entry in the (a) external memory module is (c) encoded to a binary string. Each binary value is stored in a (b) TCAM cell. (d) The process of an external memory distance calculation combining TCAM and CiM (e) The process of a memory update for the TCAM and CiM in the context of MENN.

Table 2: Array Level Evaluation Summary.

| | Latency | Energy |
|---|---|---|
| Search | 3.55 ns | 1.80 fJ |
| Add | 3.77 ns | 5.42 fJ |
| Write | 10.00 ns | 0.09 fJ |

entries in the TCAM. Both the CiM and TCAM are updated during writes with the same memory entries.

The process of an external memory distance calculation is summarized below. As shown in Fig. 7(d), the 32-bit floating point entry is converted to a fixed point representation and then converted to a range encoded binary representation. The binary representations are stored in the TCAM and CiM arrays. The $L_\infty$ distance calculation is performed in the TCAM array to obtain the $K$ nearest neighbors. We then perform $L_1$ distance metric calculations on these $K$ nearest neighbors using the CiM array, and find the nearest neighbor entry based on the Hamming distance metric for improved accuracy. During a memory update, it is necessary to write on both the TCAM and CiM (Fig. 7(e)) to ensure that the entries in the CiM are a replica of the entries in the TCAM.

# 4 EVALUATION

The performance and energy efficiency of our proposed hardware implementations are evaluated at two levels: the array level and the application level. Sec. 4.1 summarizes energy and latency evaluation results for FeFET-based CiM and TCAM arrays. Sec. 4.2 considers energy and latency of the MENN external memory implemented by FeFET-based CiM and TCAM arrays at an application level.

## 4.1 Array Level

For energy/delay analysis, we use HSPICE simulations to evaluate the 2FeFET TCAM, as well as an FeFET-based CiM architecture that employs 1-FeFET memory cells. The arrays considered for both TCAM and CiM have 64 rows and 64 columns. The TCAM array schematic for evaluations includes the the output SAs, the clock signal and the input buffers. The FeFET-based CiM evaluation considers 1-FeFET memory cells and customized SAs that perform ADDs. Both TCAM array and 1-FeFET memory array simulations assume the multi-domain Preisach model for FeFETs [30]. The ASU PTM 45nm model [31] is employed for CMOS transistors. The energy and latency results for the CiM ADD calculation, and TCAM search and write operations are shown in Table 2.

## 4.2 Application Level

In a prior work [1], we evaluated the impact of reducing the number of bits used to represent the data and compared different distance metrics. We have found that a 4-bit fixed point $L_\infty$ is the simplest distance metric to implement with TCAM search operations. However, the TCAM implementation associated with $L_\infty$ distance metric suffers from lower accuracies for classification tasks as shown in Fig. 8(a). Thus, we introduced a combined TCAM and CiM approach to remove the offloading of the $L_1$ distance calculations to a GPU. First, the TCAM implementation is applied to perform the $L_\infty$ distance calculations between the memory words and input data and obtain a set of $K$ approximate entries [2] that are closest to the input data. Then the CiM array performs the $L_1$ distance calculation among those $K$ entries to find a solution with better accuracy. This approach results in significant performance and energy efficiency improvements versus a cosine distance GPU implementation (Fig. 8(b) and Fig. 8(c)). Fig. 8(a) shows the accuracies of different distance metric configurations at 32-bit precision on the 5-way 1-shot/5-shot classification task. It also considers the impact of floating point cosine and $L_1$ distance metrics on accuracy in a MENN when compared to fixed precision MENN with different distance metrics. Based on Amdahl's law and Fig. 4, our approach achieved an overall speedup and energy reduction of 4.34X and 4.18X, respectively.

# 5 CONCLUSION

We proposed to combine TCAM and CiM arrays to implement the external memory in a MENN for a one-shot learning application as opposed to a TCAM implementation that requires offloading $L_1$ calculations back to a GPU [1]. We then further made delay and energy evaluation comparison with a GPU approach. Our approach reduced the number of computations that must be performed on a GPU architecture (e.g., for cosine similarity metrics), and also addressed the memory bottleneck in terms of speed and size on the GPU. Furthermore, the simpler operations can give substantial speedup and energy reduction when implemented in hardware

[2] For the results on this paper, we used $K = 16$

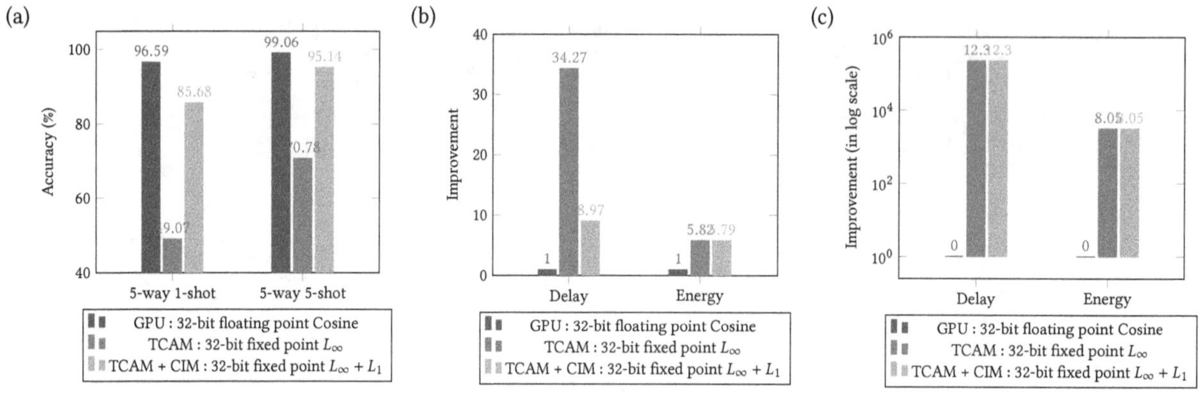


**Figure 8: Accuracy, delay and energy evaluations for 5-way 5-shot learning using Omniglot dataset for a 128x512 memory. (a) Accuracy evaluation for different distance calculations (b) Energy and delay evaluation for different distance calculations (c) Energy and delay evaluation for memory update.**

[7, 15]. Quantitative analysis of our approach suggests that the proposed approach can improve the MENN hardware [32] [33] by implementing the $L_\infty$ and $L_1$ distance calculations on TCAM and CiM designs, respectively. Compared with the conventional GPU based MENN that achieves 99.05% accuracy for Omniglot classification using floating point-based cosine distance metric, our approach still achieves a 95.14% classification accuracy for Omniglot classification tasks, with 4.34X and 4.18X speedups and energy reduction respectively over the conventional GPU-based MENN.

## ACKNOWLEDGMENTS

This work was supported in part by ASCENT, one of six centers in JUMP, a Semiconductor Research Corporation (SRC) program sponsored by DARPA.

## REFERENCES

[1] A. Laguna, et al. Design of hardware-friendly memory enhanced neural networks. In *Design, Automation Test in Europe Conference Exhibition (DATE), 2017*, March 2019.
[2] O. Vinyals, et al. Matching networks for one shot learning. *CoRR*, abs/1606.04080, 2016.
[3] A. Santoro, et al. One-shot learning with memory-augmented neural networks. *CoRR*, abs/1605.06065, 2016.
[4] L. Kaiser, et al. Learning to remember rare events. *CoRR*, abs/1703.03129, 2017.
[5] M. Pharr et al. *GPU Gems 2: Programming Techniques for High-Performance Graphics and General-Purpose Computation (Gpu Gems)*. Addison-Wesley Professional, 2005.
[6] Z. Lai, et al. Revisiting multi-pass scatter and gather on gpus. In *Proceedings of the 47th International Conference on Parallel Processing*, ICPP 2018, pages 25:1–25:11, New York, NY, USA, 2018. ACM.
[7] A. Bremler-Barr, et al. Encoding short ranges in tcam without expansion: Efficient algorithm and applications. *IEEE/ACM Transactions on Networking*, 26(2):835–850, April 2018.
[8] D. Reis, et al. Computing in Memory with FeFETs. In *ISLPED*, pages 24:1–24:6, New York, NY, USA, 2018. ACM.
[9] S. Jeloka, et al. A 28 nm configurable memory (tcam/bcam/sram) using push-rule 6t bit cell enabling logic-in-memory. *IEEE Journal of Solid-State Circuits*, 51(4):1009–1021, April 2016.
[10] Q. Dong, et al. A 0.3v vddmin 4+2t sram for searching and in-memory computing using 55nm ddc technology. In *2017 Symposium on VLSI Circuits*, pages C160–C161, June 2017.
[11] S. Jeloka, et al. A 28 nm configurable memory (tcam/bcam/sram) using push-rule 6t bit cell enabling logic-in-memory. *JSSC*, 51(4):1009–1021, 2016.
[12] J. Zhang, et al. In-memory computation of a machine learning classifier in a standard 6t sram array. *JSSC*, 52(4):915–924, 2017.
[13] K. Nii, et al. 13.6 a 28nm 400mhz 4-parallel 1.6gsearch/s 80mb ternary cam. In *2014 IEEE International Solid-State Circuits Conference Digest of Technical Papers (ISSCC)*, pages 240–241, Feb 2014.
[14] W. Kang, et al. In-memory processing paradigm for bitwise logic operations in stt-mram. *TMAG*, 53(11):1–4, 2017.
[15] D. Fujiki, et al. In-memory data parallel processor. In *Proceedings of the Twenty-Third International Conference on Architectural Support for Programming Languages and Operating Systems*, ASPLOS '18, pages 1–14, New York, NY, USA, 2018. ACM.
[16] A. Aziz, et al. Computing with ferroelectric fets: Devices, models, systems, and applications. In *2018 Design, Automation & Test in Europe Conference & Exhibition (DATE)*, pages 1289–1298. IEEE, 2018.
[17] X. Yin, et al. Design and benchmarking of ferroelectric fet based tcam. In *Proceedings of the Conference on Design, Automation & Test in Europe*, pages 1448–1453. European Design and Automation Association, 2017.
[18] S. Hochreiter, et al. Learning to learn using gradient descent. In *Artificial Neural Networks - ICANN 2001, International Conference Vienna, Austria, August 21-25, 2001 Proceedings*, pages 87–94, 2001.
[19] S. Hochreiter et al. Long short-term memory. *Neural Computation*, 9(8):1735–1780, 1997.
[20] A. Pritzel, et al. Neural episodic control. In *Proceedings of the 34th International Conference on Machine Learning, ICML 2017, Sydney, NSW, Australia, 6-11 August 2017*, pages 2827–2836, 2017.
[21] J. Weston, et al. Memory networks. *CoRR*, abs/1410.3916, 2014.
[22] M. Zhu, et al. Performance evaluation and optimization of hbm-enabled gpu for data-intensive applications. In *Design, Automation Test in Europe Conference Exhibition (DATE), 2017*, pages 1245–1248, March 2017.
[23] R. Shinde, et al. Similarity search and locality sensitive hashing using tcams. *CoRR*, abs/1006.3514, 2010.
[24] M.-F. Chang, et al. A 3t1r nonvolatile tcam using mlc reram with sub-1ns search time. In *Solid-State Circuits Conference-(ISSCC), 2015 IEEE International*, pages 1–3. IEEE, 2015.
[25] M. Imani, et al. Exploring hyperdimensional associative memory. In *International Symposium on High-Performance Computer Architecture*, pages 445–456. IEEE, 2017.
[26] N. Talati, et al. Logic design within memristive memories using memristor-aided logic (magic). *TNANO*, 15(4):635–650, 2016.
[27] D. Reis, et al. Computing in memory with fefets. In *Proceedings of the International Symposium on Low Power Electronics and Design*, ISLPED '18, pages 24:1–24:6, New York, NY, USA, 2018. ACM.
[28] S. Aga, et al. Compute caches. In *2017 IEEE International Symposium on High Performance Computer Architecture (HPCA)*, pages 481–492, Feb 2017.
[29] M. H. Lee, et al. Prospects for ferroelectric HfZrOx FETs with experimentally CET=0.98nm, SSfor=42mv/dec, SSrev=28mv/dec, switch-off <0.2v, and hysteresis-free strategies. In *2015 IEEE International Electron Devices Meeting (IEDM)*, pages 22.5.1–22.5.4, Dec 2015.
[30] K. Ni, et al. Critical role of interlayer in hf 0.5 zr 0.5 o 2 ferroelectric fet nonvolatile memory performance. *IEEE Transactions on Electron Devices*, 65(6):2461–2469, 2018.
[31] R. Vattikonda, et al. Modeling and minimization of pmos nbti effect for robust nanometer design. In *DAC*, 2006.
[32] V. Sze, et al. Efficient processing of deep neural networks: A tutorial and survey. *Proceedings of the IEEE*, 105(12):2295–2329, 2017.
[33] P. Chen, et al. Neurosim+: An integrated device-to-algorithm framework for benchmarking synaptic devices and array architectures. In *2017 IEEE International Electron Devices Meeting (IEDM)*, pages 6.1.1–6.1.4, Dec 2017.

# True In-memory Computing with the CRAM: From Technology to Applications

Masoud Zabihi[1], Zhengyang Zhao[1], Zamshed I. Chowdhury[1], Salonik Resch[1], Mahendra DC[2], Thomas Peterson[2], Ulya R. Karpuzcu[1], Jian-Ping Wang[1], Sachin S. Sapatnekar[1]
[1] Department of Electrical and Computer Engineering [2] School of Physics and Astronomy
University of Minnesota, Minneapolis, MN (USA)

## ABSTRACT

Big data applications are memory-intensive, and the cost of bringing data from the memory to the processor involves large overheads in energy and processing time. This has driven the push towards specialized accelerator units that can perform computations close to where the data is stored. Two approaches have been proposed:

- *near-memory computing* places computational units at the periphery of memory for fast data access.
- *true in-memory computing* uses the memory array to perform computations through simple reconfigurations.

Although there has been a great deal of recent interest in the area of in-memory computing, most solutions that are purported to fall into this class are really near-memory processors that perform computation near the edge of memory arrays/subarrays rather than inside it. We discuss a true in-memory computation platform in this presentation, the Computational Random Access Memory (CRAM). The CRAM enables this capability by making a small modification to a standard spintronics-based memory array. The CRAM-based approach is digital, unlike prior analog-like in-memory/near-memory solutions, which provides more robustness to process variations, particularly in immature technologies than analog schemes.

Our solution is based on spintronics technology, which is attractive because of its robustness, high endurance, and its trajectory towards fast improvement [2, 4]. The outline of the CRAM approach was first proposed in [3], operating primarily at the technology level with some expositions at the circuit level. The work was developed further to show system-level applications and performance estimations in [1] based on a spin-transfer-torque (STT) magnetic tunnel junction (MTJ). Next, in [5], a bridge was built between the two to provide an explicit link between CRAM technology, circuit implementations, and operation scheduling. Most recently, in [6], a redesigned CRAM was designed around a new MTJ based on the spin-Hall effect (SHE), providing greatly improved energy efficiency.

This talk provides an overview of several years of effort in developing the CRAM concept and surveys all of these efforts. The presentation covers alternatives at the technology level, followed by a description of how the in-memory computing array is designed, using the basic MTJ unit and some switches, to function both as a memory and a computational unit. This array is then used to build gates and arithmetic units by appropriately interconnecting memory cells, allowing high degrees of parallelism. Next, we show how complex arithmetic operations can be performed through appropriate scheduling (for adders, multipliers, dot products) and data placement of the operands. Finally, we demonstrate how this approach can be used to implement sample applications, such as neuromorphic inference engine and a 2D convolution, presenting results that benchmark the performance of these CRAMs against near-memory computation platforms. The performance gains can be atrributed to (a) highly efficient local processing within the memory, and (b) high levels of parallelism in rows of the memory.


*GLSVLSI '19, May 9–11, 2019, Tysons Corner, VA, USA*

ACM ISBN 978-1-4503-6252-8/19/05...$15.00
https://doi.org/10.1145/3299874.3319451

## CCS CONCEPTS

**• Computer systems organization → Special purpose systems; • Hardware → Non-volatile memory; Arithmetic and datapath circuits; Spintronics and magnetic technologies.**

## KEYWORDS

Spintronics, In-memory computing, CRAM, Memory bottleneck, STT-MRAM, SHE-MRAM, Spin-Hall effect, Neuromorphic computing, Adders, Multipliers, Nonvolatile memory, Convolution

**ACM Reference Format:**

Masoud Zabihi[1], Zhengyang Zhao[1], Zamshed I. Chowdhury[1], Salonik Resch[1], Mahendra DC[2], Thomas Peterson[2], Ulya R. Karpuzcu[1], Jian-Ping Wang[1], Sachin S. Sapatnekar[1]. 2019. True In-memory Computing with the CRAM: From Technology to Applications. In *Great Lakes Symposium on VLSI 2019 (GLSVLSI '19), May 9–11, 2019, Tysons Corner, VA, USA.* ACM, New York, NY, USA, 1 page. https://doi.org/10.1145/3299874.3319451

## ACKNOWLEDGMENTS

This work was supported in part by the DARPA Non-Volatile Logic program, NSF SPX Award CCF-1725420, and by C-SPIN, one of the six SRC STARnet Centers, sponsored by MARCO and DARPA.

## REFERENCES

[1] Z. Chowdhury, S. K. Khatamifard, M. Zabihi, J. D. Harms, Y. Lv, A. P. Lyle, J. P. Wang, S. Sapatnekar, and U. Karpuzcu. 2017. Efficient in-memory processing using spintronics. *IEEE Computer Architecture Letters* 17, 1 (Jan–Jun 2017), 42–46.

[2] A. Hirohata, H. Sukegawa, H. Yanagihara, I. Zutic, T. Seki, S. Mizukami, and R. Swaminathan. 2015. Roadmap for emerging materials for spintronic device applications. *IEEE Transactions on Magnetics* 51, 10 (Oct. 2015), 1–11.

[3] J. P. Wang and J. D. Harms. 2015. General structure for computational random access memory (CRAM). https://www.google.com/patents/US9224447 US Patent 9,224,447 B2.

[4] J. P. Wang, S. S. Sapatnekar, C. H. Kim, P. Crowell, S. Koester, S. Datta, K. Roy, A. Raghunathan, X. S. Hu, M. Niemier, A. Naeemi, C.-L. Chien, C. Ross, and R. Kawakami. 2017. A pathway to enable exponential scaling for the beyond-CMOS era. In *Proceedings of the ACM/ESDA/IEEE Design Automation Conference.* ACM, New York, NY.

[5] M. Zabihi, Z. Chowdhury, Z. Zhao, U. R. Karpuzu, J.-P. Wang, and S. S. Sapatnekar. 2018. In-memory processing on the spintronic CRAM: From hardware design to application mapping. *IEEE Transactions on Computers* (2018). https://doi.org/10.1109/TC.2018.2858251 (currently in IEEEXplore Early Access).

[6] M. Zabihi, Z. Zhao, Z. Chowdhury, M. Resch, T. Peterson, Mahendra DC, J.-P. Wang, U. Karpuzcu, and S. S. Sapatnekar. 2019. Using spin-Hall MTJs to build an energy-efficient in-memory computation platform. In *Proceedings of the IEEE International Symposium on Quality Electronic Design.* IEEE, Piscataway, NJ.

# An Overview of In-memory Processing with Emerging Non-volatile Memory for Data-intensive Applications

Bing Li*
bing.li.ece@duke.edu
ECE Dept., Duke University, US
Army Research Office, Research Triangle Park, US

Bonan Yan
ECE Dept., Duke University
Durham, North Carolina, US
bonan.yan@duke.edu

Hai "Helen" Li
ECE Dept., Duke University
Durham, North Carolina, US
hai.li@duke.edu

## ABSTRACT

The conventional von Neumann architecture has been revealed as a major performance and energy bottleneck for rising data-intensive applications. The decade-old idea of leveraging in-memory processing to eliminate substantial data movements has returned and led extensive research activities. The effectiveness of in-memory processing heavily relies on the memory scalability, which cannot be satisfied by traditional memory technologies. Emerging non-volatile memories (eNVMs) that pose appealing qualities such as excellent scaling and low energy consumption, on the other hand, have been heavily investigated and explored for realizing in-memory processing architecture. In this paper, we summarize the recent research progress in eNVM-based in-memory processing from various aspects, including the adopted memory technologies, locations of the in-memory processing in system, supported arithmetics, as well as applied applications.

## CCS CONCEPTS

• **Hardware → Memory and dense storage; Spintronics and magnetic technologies;** • **Computer systems organization →** *Other architectures.*

## KEYWORDS

Data-intensive applications, emerging non-volatile memory, in-memory processing

**ACM Reference Format:**
Bing Li, Bonan Yan, and Hai "Helen" Li. 2019. An Overview of In-memory Processing with Emerging Non-volatile Memory for Data-intensive Applications. In *Great Lakes Symposium on VLSI 2019 (GLSVLSI '19), May 9–11, 2019, Tysons Corner, VA, USA.* ACM, New York, NY, USA, 6 pages. https://doi.org/10.1145/3299874.3319452

## 1 INTRODUCTION

In current era with data explosion, deep neural network (DNN) models are used to process various applications that explore a large amount of information in different data formats. Executing such data-intensive applications on conventional *von Neumann* systems causes massive data movements between processors and memory elements and induces significant performance and energy overheads. After decades since it was proposed first time [1, 2], the concept of in-memory processing returns and evokes many innovative solutions. Different from the conventional computing paradigm where data and computing are decoupled, in-memory processing architecture pulls data close to processing elements to reduce the amount of data movement and minimize the computation cost.

Benefiting from the recent advances in processing integration and memory technologies, many in-memory processing architectures have been developed. These attempts can be cataloged into three groups: (1) processing close to memory, aka near-data processing (NDP); (2) processing in traditional memory; and (3) processing in emerging non-volatile memory (eNVM).

In enabling NDP, three-dimension (3D) integration is a key technology. For example, 3D DRAM is constituted by vertically stacking a set of DRAM dies on top of a CMOS logic die through through-silicon vias (TSVs). There are a number of 3D DRAM-based NDP platforms that exploit the logic die to perform simple but common operations in data-intensive applications [16, 29–34]. TSVs substantially shorten the distance between the logic and memory dies, increasing the data bandwidth and improving overall performance.

Processing in memory directly performs computations in memory arrays so as to reduce data movement to a large extent. Prior works exploit traditional memory technologies such as DRAM and SRAM to complete the frequent operations appearing in data-intensive applications [35–39]. However, as the scaling of traditional memory technologies is approaching the physical limit, it is

**Table 1: Emerging Non-volatile Memory Comparison**

| | SRAM | DRAM | STT-RAM | PCM | ReRAM |
|---|---|---|---|---|---|
| Cell Size ($F^2$) | >100 | 6-10 | 6-50 | 4-30 | ≤2 |
| Multibit | 1 | 1 | 1 | >2 | 2-7 |
| Endurance | $>10^{16}$ | $>10^{16}$ | $>10^{15}$ | $10^8$-$10^{15}$ | $10^8$-$10^{12}$ |
| Read Time (ns) | ~1 | ~110 | <10 | <10 | <10 |
| Write Time (ns) | ~1 | ~110 | <10 | 50 | <10 |
| Write Energy (J/bit) | $\sim 10^{-15}$ | $\sim 10^{-14}$ | $\sim 10^{-13}$ | $\sim 10^{-11}$ | $\sim 10^{-13}$ |

*Source:* [3–6]. *Note:* F represents the feature size.

*This author is supported by NAS Associate Fellowship Award.


ACM ISBN 978-1-4503-6252-8/19/05...$15.00
https://doi.org/10.1145/3299874.3319452

**Table 2: An Overview of In-memory Processing Designs**

| Works | | Types | Locations | Design Levels | Functions | Applications |
|---|---|---|---|---|---|---|
| Guo *et al.* [7] | 2010 | STT-RAM | Cache | Circuit; System | Logic; Arithmetic | Generic |
| AC-DIMM [8] | 2013 | | Main Memory | Circuit; System | Associative | Generic |
| Kang *et al.* [9] | 2017 | | - | Circuit | Logic | Bitmap |
| STT-CiM [10] | 2018 | | Scratchpad | Circuit; System | Logic; Addition; Vector | Generic |
| HielM [11] | 2018 | | - | Circuit; System | Logic | Encryption, Database |
| Pan *et al.* [12] | 2018 | | Co-processor | Circuit; System | Logic | Binary CNN |
| Cassinerio *et al.* [13] | 2013 | PCM | - | Device | Logic | - |
| Wright *et al.* [14, 15] | 2011, 2013 | | - | Device | Arithmetic | - |
| Hosseini *et al.* [16] | 2015 | | - | Device | Arithmetic | - |
| Pinatubo [17] | 2015 | | Main Memory | Circuit; System | Logic | Generic |
| Burr *et al.* [18, 19] | 2015 | | - | Circuit | MVM | DNN |
| Sebastian *et al.* [20] | 2017 | | - | Circuit | MVM | Unsupervised Learning |
| Le *et al.* [21, 22] | 2017, 2018 | | - | Circuit | MVM | Transfer Learning |
| MAGIC [23] | 2014 | ReRAM | Co-processor | Circuit | Logic; Arithmetic | Adder |
| Bojnordi *et al.*[24] | 2016 | | Co-processor | System | MVM | Boltzmann machine |
| ISAAC [25] | 2016 | | Co-processor | System | MVM | CNN |
| PipeLayer [26] | 2017 | | Co-processor | System | MVM | CNN |
| AtomLayer [27] | 2018 | | Co-processor | System | MVM | CNN |
| GraphR [28] | 2018 | | Co-processor | System | MVM | Graph |

*Note*: MVM – Matrix-Vector Multiplication; DNN – Deep Neural Network.

difficult to provide sufficient computing and storage capacity for data-intensive applications. Moreover, big cell size and high leakage power of traditional memory lead to large design area and energy consumption [40–42].

In recent years, eNVMs that demonstrate excellent scaling and near-zero leakage power are emerged as promising candidates for future trend. Table 1 compares traditional DRAM and SRAM with a few popular eNVM technologies, including spin-transfer torque RAM (STT-RAM), phase-change memory (PCM) and resistive RAM (ReRAM). Among these eNVM technologies, STT-RAM shows the fastest access speed and the lowest energy consumption while the cell area is relatively larger [41, 43]. Both PCMs [44, 45] and ReRAMs [46–48] can store multple logic bits in a single memory cell, demonstrating superior density with technology scaling. In addtion, they inherently support parallel data processing, which is uniquely beneficial to aforementioned data-intensive applications like DNNs. For the reason, extensive research efforts have been devoted to building in-memory processing using eNVM.

In this paper, we survey the recent progress in developing in-memory processing by leveraging the three mainstream eNVM technologies (STT-RAM. PCM and ReRAM). We present and discuss the difference and similarity of these works in terms of the supported functions, the location in architecture, the targeted applications, *etc.*

## 2 DESIGN OVERVIEW

Table 2 presents a summary of the latest eNVM-based in-memory processing designs reviewed in this paper. Each of them is classified according to the following five main categories.

- *Type* - The types of memory technologies adopted in these works: **STT-RAM, PCM** or **ReRAM**. Since the features of memories are different with each other, the selection of memory type determines the types of computation to some extent.
- *Location* - Where is the memory located in the computing architecture: **cache, main memory** or **scratchpad**? eNVMs can be used as storage and/or computing unit. Some works treat eNVM only as **co-processor** while some designate its location in memory hierarchy too.
- *Design Level* - The techniques in these works are carried out at different levels, such as **device, circuit** or **system**. Some works proposed the novel writing method to perform calculations in memory cells [13–16]. Some techniques are achieved through the modifications of the readout or write circuits associated with memory arrays. The system-level techniques would provide the interface and connection between the memory array and operation system so that the processing can be manipulated by applications.
- *Functions* - The function types in these works can be divided into the following groups: **logic, arithmetic, associative, vector** and **matrix-vector multiplication (MVM)**. A type of operation can be realized by different eNVMs, but the implementation details could vary significantly.
- *Applications* - Most works provide advanced functions to support most data-intensive applications, which are grouped

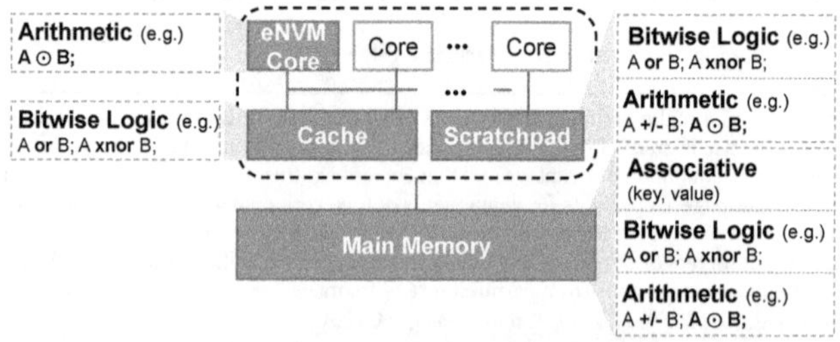


**Figure 1: Processing locations and function types.**

into **generic**. Some works carry out only the core operation in a number of applications such as **encryption, database**, and **CNN**. A few works complete simple and basic operations that are not designated to any targeted applications.

Figure 1 depicts a high-level view of the classifications based on the location of the in-memory processing in system (eNVM core, cache, scratchpad memory, or main memory) and the type of supported functions (bitwise logic, arithmetic, or associative).

# 3 ENVM-BASED IN-MEMORY PROCESSING

## 3.1 Spin-Torque Transfer RAM (STT-RAM)

STT-RAM consists of a magnetic tunnel junction (MTJ) device, which presents two resistance states depending on the relative magnetization orientation of the fixed and free ferromagnetic layers. Compared to other resistive memory devices, STT-RAM has faster write speed, lower write energy, and higher write endurance (refer Table 1). Due to the limited resistance difference between these distinct resistance states of MTJ, it is hard to implement multi-bit storage in STT-RAM cells. So most of STT-RAM-based in-memory processing designs focus on the bit-wise operations.

*3.1.1 Associative and combinational logic.* Early works exploit the high density of STT-RAM to complete the associative computing and combinational logic [7, 8]. These works achieve reduced cost relative to traditional memory technologies. For instance, **Guo *et al.*** [7] employ STT-RAM to construct *look-up table* (LUT) and further realize the computing by cascading multiple LUTs. As such, the floating-point units are replaced by STT-RAM-based LUTs. The work successfully demonstrates the improved power and performance brought by STT-RAM technology, compared to multi-core CPU platform.

*3.1.2 Bitwise logic operations.* Recent works [9–11, 49] explore the use of STT-RAM in accomplishing bitwise logic operations. Based on the basic logic function realization by STT-RAM, advanced operations are implemented. Kang *et al.* [9], STT-CiM [10] and HieIM [11] are taken as examples and introduced here.

**Kang *et al.*** [9] propose a STT-RAM chip which can process bitwise logic and store information. The operands reside in different rows of the same array. By simultaneously activating multiple rows, the bitwise operations are enabled and results are obtained through the modified readout periphery circuits, *i.e.* sense amplifier (SA). The functionality of one logic operation can be controlled by modifying the bit in one control row. The chip can benefit some particular applications which involve intensive bitwise logic operations such as *bitmap*. This work focuses on circuit design and functional evaluation.

**STT-CiM** [10] extends the supported functions from bitwise logic to basic arithmetic and vector operations. At circuit level, the row decoders and SAs are enhanced to enable logic functions. Additional logic gates are integrated into the sense circuits to realize arithmetic operations. Two row decoders are used to active multiple rows where operands are located. The connected multiplex circuits are controlled by select signals to determine the desired operation type. When processing vector function, the vector outputs from STT-RAM arrays will be fed into reduction units and switched to the scalar value. At array level, authors analyze the impact of process variation on the computing results and deploy error correction scheme to enhance the reliability. At architectural and system levels, this work extends the instruction set to convey the operation command from applications to memory array. Through the extensions across multiple levels together, STT-CiM can be placed next to processor as on-chip scratchpad memory and applied for various data-intensive applications such as text processing, data compression, and digits recognition.

**HieIM** [11] implements bulk bitwise operations in STT-RAM array too. Different from the above two designs, HieIM is more flexible and allows the computing to operate between any cells within the same array. Moreover, a data encryption engine based on HieIM is demonstrated, which consumes 51.5% lower energy than the CMOS-based ASIC counterpart.

*3.1.3 Neural networks.* Thanks to the evolution of DNN models, convolution in binary convolutional neural network (BCNN) can be replaced with bitwise operations such as XNOR and bit-count [50]. **Pan *et al.*** [12] build an accelerator based on multilevel STT-RAM (*i.e.* two-bit cell) for BCNN. STT-RAM arrays are programmable and can be switched between memory mode and bitwise operation mode. Thereby, multi-functional STT-RAM arrays are exploited to process convolutional layers. In this design, the two bits of one cell associates with inputs and weights, respectively so that the logic and add operations are carried out within one cell. This integrates the compuational STT-RAM array with an auxiliary processing unit (APU) which processes other computational layers in CNNs and implements the BCNN accelerator. Figure 2 illustrates the computing array and execution flows. Compared to other eNVM-based counterparts, the STT-RAM based accelerator achieves significant performance and energy improvement.

## 3.2 Phase Change Memory (PCM)

PCM can store more than one bit of data per cell, by diving the overall resistance range into a few levels. What's more, the cell conductance exhibits a linear increase along with the number of programming (more exactly, SET) pulses [51]. These key attributes of PCM are exploited to implement more complicate computations, such as the training of neural networks.

*3.2.1 Logic and basic arithmetic operations.* Phase change material manifests many physical attributes under various pulse amplitudes or duration, which have been exploited to realize computation. For example, **Cassinerio *et al.*** [13] leverage the resistance transition of phase change material and propose an initialize-compute-confirm scheme to implement Boolean logic operations within a single PCM cell. **Wright *et al.*** [14, 15] and **Hosseini *et al.*** [16] exploit the accumulative behavior of PCM material during programming and build an accumulator for arithmetic computations such as addition, subtraction, and parallel factoring. In these works, the partial and final results can be stored where computations are carried out. One single operation takes multiple cycles to complete as input operands sequentially enter. PCM cells are used to substitue for logic gates without revealing specific applications of interest.

**Sebastian *et al.*** [20] exploit the physical dynamics of PCM material and propose computational PCM to perform the temporal correlation detection between stochastic binary processes. One

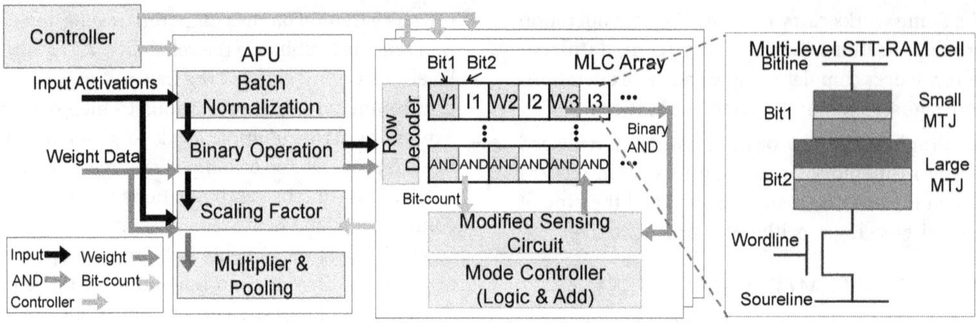


**Figure 2: The execution flow, computing array, and multilevel STT-RAM cell for convolutional layers of Binary CNN in [12].**

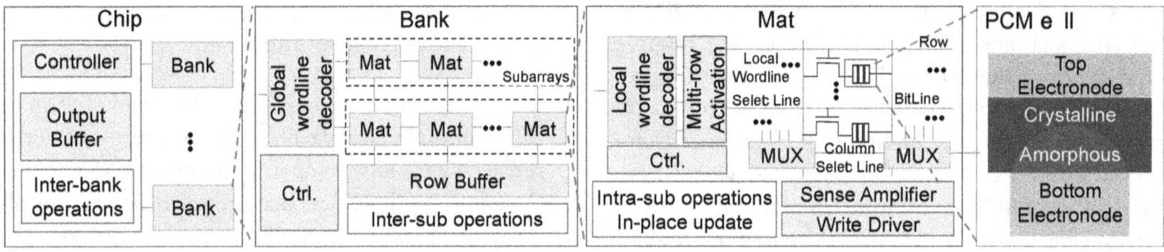


**Figure 3: Pinatubo [17] and PCM cell architecture.**

process is encoded into a SET pulse whose amplitude or duration is proportional to the instantaneous sum of all processes and enters the assigned PCM device. By comparing the conductance of each device, the correlated processes can be identified.

*3.2.2 Matrix-vector multiplications & machine learning.* Arranged in the crossbar structure, PCM devices can process analog matrix-vector multiplications, which have been intensively investigated [4, 18, 19, 21, 22, 52]. An element in an matrix can be corresponded to the conductance of a PCM device. With an PCM crossbar representing a matrix, the vector is encoded into the amplitudes or duration of voltage pulses applied along rows. Then, the currents along columns will be proportional to the results. The positive and negative elements of the matrix could be stored in a pair of PCM devices. When applying input signals to columns, the currents along rows denote the results of the vector multiplying with the transposed matrix. A 3-layer perceptron using PCMs trained with backpropagation on the MNIST database of handwritten digits can achieve the comparable accuracy with the software model [18, 19]. Moreover, leveraging PCM-based in-memory processing for other complicated tasks are demonstrated, such as compressed sensing recovery [22] and transfer learning [52].

*3.2.3 System-level bitwise operations.* **Pinatubo** [17] proposes a mechanism to perform bulk bitwise operations in PCM main memory. Read circuit and write driver are modified for Pinatubo processes logic functions. The operands are all stored in different rows in memory arrays. According to the locations that operands reside, Pinatubo has three computation modes: intra-subarray, inter-subarray and inter-bank (Figure 3). The rows associated with operands will be activated simultaneously when computing. Sense amplifiers are enhanced with more reference circuits to obtain the logic outputs which will be sent to I/O bus or another memory row. To bridge operating system and logic operations inside PCM, Pinatubo develops the programming model and run-time supports to ensure that operands are allocated to different memory rows. The design achieves 1.12× overall speedup, 1.11× overall energy saving over the conventional CPU.

## 3.3 Resistive RAM (ReRAM)

The attractive features of high resistances and multi-level cell storage make ReRAM stand out from other emerging memory technologies to construct dense and low-power computing systems [53]. A variety of ReRAM based computing systems have been proposed to demonstrate superior performances in different applications central to memory access reduction.

*3.3.1 Logic arithmetic operations.* **MAGIC** [23] proposes mechanisms to perform bitwise operations with the aid of binary ReRAM. These schemes enable the integration of fundamental logic gates as well as complex arithmetic units, *e.g.* multi-bit full adders, within a ReRAM array.

*3.3.2 Matrix-vector multiplications.* **ISAAC** [25] is an neural network accelerator based on ReRAM dot-product engine. In ISAAC, ReRAM crossbar arrays both store weights in DNN and perform MVM with analog current and analog/digital converters (*i.e.* DAC & ADC). Figure 4 shows the top-down view of ISAAC chip. A group of tiles are connected through on-chip network. Every tile is composed of eDARM buffers , several in-situ multiply-accumulators (IMA), output registers and the shift-adders. Pooling and activation units in tiles dedicate to the pooling and activation operations in neural network. Each IMA consists of a number of ReRAM crossbars, ADCs, the input/output registers, and shift-adders. ISAAC exploits this integration of storage and computation for saving data (especially weights in filters) movement. The deeply pipelined flow of ISAAC focuses on the optimization in neural network inference.

A number of ReRAM-based CNN accelerators are proposed for boosting the system performance in training [26, 27, 54]. For example, **PipeLayer** [26] balances the parallelism and throughput in training and inference based on both parallelism granularity and weight duplication. By eliminating the potential stalls as in

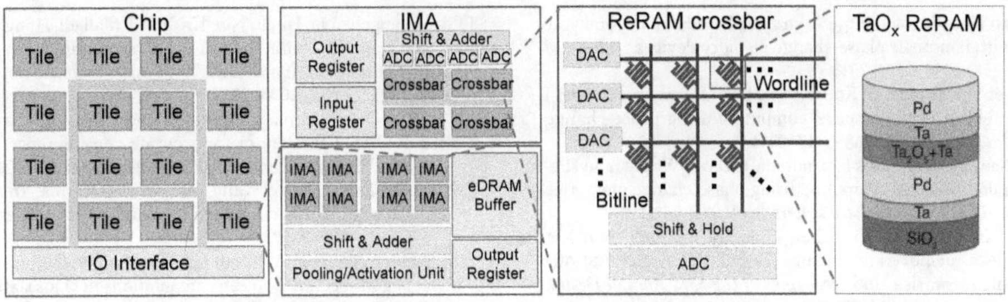


**Figure 4: ISAAC [25], ReRAM crossbar, and ReRAM cell architecture.**

ISAAC, PipeLayer yields an averagely 42.45× speedup and saves computation energy by 7.17× on average, compared to the massively parallel computing GPU platform. **AtomLayer** [27] attempts to provide a universal solution to enhance the efficiency during both training and inference. In this scheme, one network layer is executed at a time, *i.e.* atomic layer, to solve the issues brought by the highly pipelined operations, such as pipeline bubbles, long single-layer latency, and high cost of data buffers. AtomLayer revises the mapping scheme of weights to ReRAM arrays and data reuse and further reduces the on-chip data buffer access aside from the reduction of memory accesses. AtomLayer achieves 1.1× higher power efficiency than ISAAC in inference and 1.6× higher than PipeLayer in training, and its footprint shrinks 15× averagely with the reduction of on-chip buffers.

ReRAM array's parallel computing nature is capable of building accelerators for special computing models other than neural networks. **GraphR** [28] is a ReRAM-based graph processing accelerator to solve the poor locality and high-bandwidth requirement in graph processing. The ReRAM crossbar based graph engines offers low-cost hardware implementation to realize power-efficient graph processing acceleration.

Beyond convolutional computing engine, a number of works utilize ReRAM crossbars to support different computations and applications [24, 55–57]. For instance, **Bojnordi *et al.*** [24] implement the restricted Boltzmann machine with ReRAM arrays. The model of Boltzmann machine has been used to train deep neural networks with vast training samples. With the help of current summation circuit and reduction unit, large networks are reshaped to fit into ReRAM arrays, where in-situ computing operations are executed. Compared with conventional multi-core systems, ReRAM-based Boltzmann machine achieves 57× higher performance and 25× lower energy consumption without degrading the quality of solutions to optimization problems.

## 4 CONCLUSION

In this work, we gave an overview of recent works on eNVM-based in-memory processing that minimizes the cost of memory access and is expected to be meet the requirements of data-intensive applications. Emerging non-volatile memories (eNVMs) have advantages of low-power, high-density, superior scaling and inherent computing capability. Hence, numerous research works have been carried out to develop eNVM-based in-memory processing architectures. We summarize and discuss the types of eNVMs that have been adopted in in-memory processing designs, as well as a variety of implemented functions and supported applications. Because each type of eNVMs has distinct strengths and weaknesses, the selection of eNVM technology shall consider the specific requirements of applications. Following the progress of material science and device processing techniques, we anticipate continuous improvement in reliability, read/write speed, and energy efficiency of eNVM technologies. We believe the collaborative researches across various levels including device, circuit, system and applications, are essential to move eNVM-based in-memory processing towards commercial production.

## ACKNOWLEDGMENTS

Bing Li acknowledges the National Academy of Sciences (NAS), USA for awarding the NRC research fellowship. Any opinions, findings and conclusions or recommendations expressed in this material are those of the authors and do not necessarily reflect the views of NAS or their contractors.

## REFERENCES

[1] David Patterson, Thomas Anderson, Neal Cardwell, Richard Fromm, Kimberly Keeton, Christoforos Kozyrakis, Randi Thomas, and Katherine Yelick. A case for intelligent RAM. *IEEE Micro*, 17(2):34–44, 1997.

[2] Jeff Draper, Jacqueline Chame, Mary Hall, Craig Steele, Tim Barrett, Jeff LaCoss, John Granacki, Jaewook Shin, Chun Chen, Chang Woo Kang, et al. The architecture of the DIVAprocessing-in-memory chip. In *Proceedings of the 16th international conference on Supercomputing (ICS)*, pages 14–25, 2002.

[3] Micron Technology Inc. Ddr4 sdram system-power calculator, June 2016.

[4] Geoffrey W Burr, Matthew J Brightsky, Abu Sebastian, Huai-Yu Cheng, Jau-Yi Wu, Sangbum Kim, Norma E Sosa, Nikolaos Papandreou, Hsiang-Lan Lung, Haralampos Pozidis, et al. Recent progress in phase-change memory technology. *IEEE Journal on Emerging and Selected Topics in Circuits and Systems*, 6(2):146–162, 2016.

[5] Sparsh Mittal, Jeffrey S Vetter, and Dong Li. A survey of architectural approaches for managing embedded dram and non-volatile on-chip caches. *IEEE Transactions on Parallel and Distributed Systems*, page 14, 2015.

[6] Shimeng Yu and Pai-Yu Chen. Emerging memory technologies: recent trends and prospects. *IEEE Solid-State Circuits Magazine*, 8(2):43–56, 2016.

[7] Xiaochen Guo, Engin Ipek, and Tolga Soyata. Resistive computation: avoiding the power wall with low-leakage, stt-mram based computing. *ACM SIGARCH Computer Architecture News*, 38(3):371–382, 2010.

[8] Qing Guo, Xiaochen Guo, Ravi Patel, Engin Ipek, and Eby G Friedman. Ac-dimm: associative computing with stt-mram. *ACM SIGARCH Computer Architecture News*, 41(3):189–200, 2013.

[9] Wang Kang, Haotian Wang, Zhaohao Wang, Youguang Zhang, and Weisheng Zhao. In-memory processing paradigm for bitwise logic operations in stt–mram. *IEEE Transactions on Magnetics*, 53(11):1–4, 2017.

[10] Shubham Jain, Ashish Ranjan, Kaushik Roy, and Anand Raghunathan. Computing in memory with spin-transfer torque magnetic ram. *IEEE Transactions on Very Large Scale Integration (VLSI) Systems*, 26(3):470–483, 2018.

[11] Farhana Parveen, Zhezhi He, Shaahin Angizi, and Deliang Fan. Hielm: Highly flexible in-memory computing using stt mram. In *Design Automation Conference (ASP-DAC), 2018 23rd Asia and South Pacific*, pages 361–366. IEEE, 2018.

[12] Yu Pan, Peng Ouyang, Yinglin Zhao, Wang Kang, Shouyi Yin, Youguang Zhang, Weisheng Zhao, and Shaojun Wei. A multilevel cell stt-mram-based computing in-memory accelerator for binary convolutional neural network. *IEEE Transactions on Magnetics*, 54(99):1–5, 2018.

[13] M Cassinerio, N Ciocchini, and D Ielmini. Logic computation in phase change materials by threshold and memory switching. *Advanced Materials*, 25(41):5975–5980, 2013.

[14] C David Wright, Peiman Hosseini, and Jorge A Vazquez Diosdado. Beyond von-neumann computing with nanoscale phase-change memory devices. *Advanced Functional Materials*, 23(18):2248–2254, 2013.

[15] C David Wright, Yanwei Liu, Krisztian I Kohary, Mustafa M Aziz, and Robert J Hicken. Arithmetic and biologically-inspired computing using phase-change materials. *Advanced Materials*, 23(30):3408–3413, 2011.

[16] Peiman Hosseini, Abu Sebastian, Nikolaos Papandreou, C David Wright, and Harish Bhaskaran. Accumulation-based computing using phase-change memories with fet access devices. *IEEE Electron Device Letters*, 36(9):975–977, 2015.

[17] Shuangchen Li, Cong Xu, Qiaosha Zou, Jishen Zhao, Yu Lu, and Yuan Xie. Pinatubo: A processing-in-memory architecture for bulk bitwise operations in emerging non-volatile memories. In *Proceedings of the 53rd Annual Design Automation Conference*, page 173. ACM, 2016.

[18] Geoffrey W Burr, Robert M Shelby, Severin Sidler, Carmelo Di Nolfo, Junwoo Jang, Irem Boybat, Rohit S Shenoy, Pritish Narayanan, Kumar Virwani, Emanuele U Giacometti, et al. Experimental demonstration and tolerancing of a large-scale neural network (165 000 synapses) using phase-change memory as the synaptic weight element. *IEEE Transactions on Electron Devices*, 62(11):3498–3507, 2015.

[19] GW Burr, P Narayanan, RM Shelby, Severin Sidler, Irem Boybat, Carmelo di Nolfo, and Yusuf Leblebici. Large-scale neural networks implemented with non-volatile memory as the synaptic weight element: Comparative performance analysis (accuracy, speed, and power). In *Electron Devices Meeting (IEDM), 2015 IEEE International*, pages 4–4. IEEE, 2015.

[20] Abu Sebastian, Tomas Tuma, Nikolaos Papandreou, Manuel Le Gallo, Lukas Kull, Thomas Parnell, and Evangelos Eleftheriou. Temporal correlation detection using computational phase-change memory. *Nature Communications*, 8(1):1115, 2017.

[21] M Le Gallo, A Sebastian, G Cherubini, H Giefers, and E Eleftheriou. Compressed sensing recovery using computational memory. In *Electron Devices Meeting (IEDM), 2017 IEEE International*, pages 28–3. IEEE, 2017.

[22] Manuel Le Gallo, Abu Sebastian, Roland Mathis, Matteo Manica, Heiner Giefers, Tomas Tuma, Costas Bekas, Alessandro Curioni, and Evangelos Eleftheriou. Mixed-precision in-memory computing. *Nature Electronics*, 1(4):246, 2018.

[23] Shahar Kvatinsky, Dmitry Belousov, Slavik Liman, Guy Satat, Nimrod Wald, Eby G Friedman, Avinoam Kolodny, and Uri C Weiser. MagicâĂŤmemristor-aided logic. *IEEE Transactions on Circuits and Systems II: Express Briefs*, 61(11):895–899, 2014.

[24] Mahdi Nazm Bojnordi and Engin Ipek. Memristive boltzmann machine: A hardware accelerator for combinatorial optimization and deep learning. In *High Performance Computer Architecture (HPCA), 2016 IEEE International Symposium on*, pages 1–13. IEEE, 2016.

[25] Ali Shafiee, Anirban Nag, Naveen Muralimanohar, Rajeev Balasubramonian, John Paul Strachan, Miao Hu, R Stanley Williams, and Vivek Srikumar. Isaac: A convolutional neural network accelerator with in-situ analog arithmetic in crossbars. *ACM SIGARCH Computer Architecture News*, 44(3):14–26, 2016.

[26] Linghao Song, Xuehai Qian, Hai Li, and Yiran Chen. Pipelayer: A pipelined reram-based accelerator for deep learning. In *High Performance Computer Architecture (HPCA), 2017 IEEE International Symposium on*, pages 541–552. IEEE, 2017.

[27] Ximing Qiao, Xiong Cao, Huanrui Yang, Linghao Song, and Hai Li. Atomlayer: a universal reram-based cnn accelerator with atomic layer computation. In *Proceedings of the 55th Annual Design Automation Conference*, page 103. ACM, 2018.

[28] Linghao Song, Youwei Zhuo, Xuehai Qian, Hai Li, and Yiran Chen. Graphr: Accelerating graph processing using reram. In *High Performance Computer Architecture (HPCA), 2018 IEEE International Symposium on*, pages 531–543. IEEE, 2018.

[29] Seth H Pugsley, Jeffrey Jestes, Huihui Zhang, Rajeev Balasubramonian, Vijayalakshmi Srinivasan, Alper Buyuktosunoglu, Al Davis, and Feifei Li. Ndc: Analyzing the impact of 3d-stacked memory+ logic devices on mapreduce workloads. In *2014 IEEE International Symposium on Performance Analysis of Systems and Software (ISPASS)*, pages 190–200. IEEE, 2014.

[30] Amin Farmahini-Farahani, Jung Ho Ahn, Katherine Morrow, and Nam Sung Kim. Nda: Near-dram acceleration architecture leveraging commodity dram devices and standard memory modules. In *High Performance Computer Architecture (HPCA), 2015 IEEE 21st International Symposium on*, pages 283–295. IEEE, 2015.

[31] Dongping Zhang, Nuwan Jayasena, Alexander Lyashevsky, Joseph L Greathouse, Lifan Xu, and Michael Ignatowski. Top-pim: throughput-oriented programmable processing in memory. In *Proceedings of the 23rd international symposium on High-performance parallel and distributed computing*, pages 85–98. ACM, 2014.

[32] Mingyu Gao and Christos Kozyrakis. Hrl: Efficient and flexible reconfigurable logic for near-data processing. In *High Performance Computer Architecture (HPCA), 2016 IEEE International Symposium on*, pages 126–137. Ieee, 2016.

[33] Mingyu Gao, Jing Pu, Xuan Yang, Mark Horowitz, and Christos Kozyrakis. Tetris: Scalable and efficient neural network acceleration with 3d memory. *ACM SIGOPS Operating Systems Review*, 51(2):751–764, 2017.

[34] Duckhwan Kim, Jaeha Kung, Sek Chai, Sudhakar Yalamanchili, and Saibal Mukhopadhyay. Neurocube: A programmable digital neuromorphic architecture with high-density 3d memory. In *Computer Architecture (ISCA), 2016 ACM/IEEE 43rd Annual International Symposium on*, pages 380–392. IEEE, 2016.

[35] Shuangchen Li, Dimin Niu, Krishna T Malladi, Hongzhong Zheng, Bob Brennan, and Yuan Xie. Drisa: A dram-based reconfigurable in-situ accelerator. In *Proceedings of the 50th Annual IEEE/ACM International Symposium on Microarchitecture*, pages 288–301. ACM, 2017.

[36] Quan Deng, Lei Jiang, Youtao Zhang, Minxuan Zhang, and Jun Yang. Dracc: a dram based accelerator for accurate cnn inference. In *Proceedings of the 55th Annual Design Automation Conference*, page 168. ACM, 2018.

[37] Jintao Zhang, Zhuo Wang, and Naveen Verma. In-memory computation of a machine-learning classifier in a standard 6t sram array. *J. Solid-State Circuits*, 52(4):915–924, 2017.

[38] Amogh Agrawal, Akhilesh Jaiswal, Chankyu Lee, and Kaushik Roy. X-sram: Enabling in-memory boolean computations in cmos static random access memories. *IEEE Transactions on Circuits and Systems I: Regular Papers*, 65(99):1–14, 2018.

[39] Mingu Kang, Sujan K Gonugondla, Ameya Patil, and Naresh R Shanbhag. A multi-functional in-memory inference processor using a standard 6t sram array. *IEEE Journal of Solid-State Circuits*, 53(2):642–655, 2018.

[40] Minesh Patel, Jeremie S Kim, and Onur Mutlu. The reach profiler (reaper): Enabling the mitigation of dram retention failures via profiling at aggressive conditions. *ACM SIGARCH Computer Architecture News*, 45(2):255–268, 2017.

[41] Sang Phill Park, Sumeet Gupta, Niladri Mojumder, Anand Raghunathan, and Kaushik Roy. Future cache design using stt mrams for improved energy efficiency: devices, circuits and architecture. In *Proceedings of the 49th Annual Design Automation Conference*, pages 492–497. ACM, 2012.

[42] Sparsh Mittal. A survey of architectural techniques for improving cache power efficiency. *Sustainable Computing: Informatics and Systems*, 4(1):33–43, 2014.

[43] Nour Sayed, Rajendra Bishnoi, Fabian Oboril, and Mehdi B Tahoori. A cross-layer adaptive approach for performance and power optimization in stt-mram. In *2018 Design, Automation & Test in Europe Conference & Exhibition (DATE)*, pages 791–796. IEEE, 2018.

[44] T Nirschl, JB Philipp, TD Happ, Geoffrey W Burr, B Rajendran, M-H Lee, A Schrott, M Yang, M Breitwisch, C-F Chen, et al. Write strategies for 2 and 4-bit multi-level phase-change memory. In *Electron Devices Meeting, 2007. IEDM 2007. IEEE International*, pages 461–464. IEEE, 2007.

[45] Bing Li, Yu Hu, Ying Wang, Jing Ye, and Xiaowei Li. Power-utility-driven write management for mlc pcm. *ACM Journal on Emerging Technologies in Computing Systems (JETC)*, 13(3):50, 2017.

[46] H-S Philip Wong, Heng-Yuan Lee, Shimeng Yu, Yu-Sheng Chen, Yi Wu, Pang-Shiu Chen, Byoungil Lee, Frederick T Chen, and Ming-Jinn Tsai. Metal–oxide rram. *Proceedings of the IEEE*, 100(6):1951–1970, 2012.

[47] Cong Xu, Dimin Niu, Naveen Muralimanohar, Rajeev Balasubramonian, Tao Zhang, Shimeng Yu, and Yuan Xie. Overcoming the challenges of crossbar resistive memory architectures. In *2015 IEEE 21st International Symposium on High Performance Computer Architecture (HPCA)*, pages 476–488. IEEE, 2015.

[48] Bing Li, Bonan Yan, Chenchen Liu, and Hai Helen Li. Build reliable and efficient neuromorphic design with memristor technology. In *Proceedings of the 24th Asia and South Pacific Design Automation Conference*, pages 224–229. ACM, 2019.

[49] Akhilesh Jaiswal, Amogh Agrawal, and Kaushik Roy. In-situ, in-memory stateful vector logic operations based on voltage controlled magnetic anisotropy. *Scientific reports*, 8(1):5738, 2018.

[50] Mohammad Rastegari, Vicente Ordonez, Joseph Redmon, and Ali Farhadi. Xnor-net: Imagenet classification using binary convolutional neural networks. In *European Conference on Computer Vision*, pages 525–542. Springer, 2016.

[51] Abu Sebastian, Manuel Le Gallo, Geoffrey W. Burr, Sangbum Kim, Matthew BrightSky, and Evangelos Eleftheriou. Tutorial: Brain-inspired computing using phase-change memory devices. *Journal of Applied Physics*, 124(11):111101, 2018.

[52] Stefano Ambrogio, Pritish Narayanan, Hsinyu Tsai, Robert M Shelby, Irem Boybat, Carmelo Nolfo, Severin Sidler, Massimo Giordano, Martina Bodini, Nathan CP Farinha, et al. Equivalent-accuracy accelerated neural-network training using analogue memory. *Nature*, 558(7708):60, 2018.

[53] Bonan Yan, Chenchen Liu, Xiaoxiao Liu, Yiran Chen, and Hai Li. Understanding the trade-offs of device, circuit and application in reram-based neuromorphic computing systems. In *Electron Devices Meeting (IEDM), 2017 IEEE International*, pages 11–4. IEEE, 2017.

[54] Ming Cheng, Lixue Xia, Zhenhua Zhu, Yi Cai, Yuan Xie, Yu Wang, and Huazhong Yang. Time: A training-in-memory architecture for memristor-based deep neural networks. In *Proceedings of the 54th Annual Design Automation Conference 2017*, page 26. ACM, 2017.

[55] Bing Li, Linghao Song, Fan Chen, Xuehai Qian, Yiran Chen, and Hai Helen Li. Reram-based accelerator for deep learning. In *2018 Design, Automation & Test in Europe Conference & Exhibition (DATE)*, pages 815–820. IEEE, 2018.

[56] Shihui Yin, Xiaoyu Sun, Shimeng Yu, Jae-sun Seo, and Chaitali Chakrabarti. A parallel rram synaptic array architecture for energy-efficient recurrent neural networks. In *2018 IEEE International Workshop on Signal Processing Systems (SiPS)*, pages 13–18. IEEE, 2018.

[57] Zichen Fan, Ziru Li, Bing Li, Yiran Chen, and Hai Helen Li. Red: A reram-based deconvolution accelerator. In *2019 Design, Automation & Test in Europe Conference & Exhibition (DATE)*, 2019.

# Security Threats in Approximate Computing Systems

Pruthvy Yellu
Reliable and Secure Systems Laboratory
Department of Electrical and Computer Engineering
University of New Hampshire
py1007@wildcats.unh.edu

Novak Boskov
Adaptive and Secure Computing Systems Laboratory
Department of Electrical and Computer Engineering
Boston University
boskov@bu.edu

Michel A. Kinsy
Adaptive and Secure Computing Systems Laboratory
Department of Electrical and Computer Engineering
Boston University
mkinsy@bu.edu

Qiaoyan Yu
Reliable and Secure Systems Laboratory
Department of Electrical and Computer Engineering
University of New Hampshire
qiaoyan.yu@unh.edu

## ABSTRACT

Approximate computing systems improve energy efficiency and computation speed at the cost of reduced accuracy on system outputs. Existing efforts mainly explore the feasible approximation mechanisms and their implementation methods. There is limited work that investigates the security threats brought by approximate computing. To fill this gap, we first analyze the approximate mechanisms used in approximate system, software, storage, and arithmetic circuits, and then propose potential attacks that will challenge the integrity and security of approximate systems. Some illustrative examples are provided accordingly to showcase the consequences of the proposed new attacks.

## CCS CONCEPTS

• **Security and privacy** → **Security in hardware**; • **Hardware** → **Semiconductor memory**; **System-level fault tolerance**.

## KEYWORDS

Approximate computing, hardware security, error resilience, image processing, DRAM, SRAM, PCM, machine learning.

**ACM Reference Format:**

Pruthvy Yellu, Novak Boskov, Michel A. Kinsy, and Qiaoyan Yu. 2019. Security Threats in Approximate Computing Systems. In *Great Lakes Symposium on VLSI 2019 (GLSVLSI '19), May 9–11, 2019, Tysons Corner, VA, USA.* ACM, New York, NY, USA, 6 pages. https://doi.org/10.1145/3299874.3319453

## 1 INTRODUCTION

Traditionally, computation correctness has been at the forefront of computer systems design concerns - both at the software and hardware levels. However, there are many applications where the final output of the computation does not need to have high accuracy or full precision. For example, the encoding of audio files from an uncompressed pulse code modulation to a lossy format, such as MP3, can tolerate a non-exact translation. The analog signal actuated through the speaker membrane under the two formats sounds nearly identical to most listeners. Similarly, many neural networks already produce probability estimates when performing classification. In the aforementioned applications, minor errors in output probabilities can often be considered negligible. Moreover, many applications can exhibit full functional correctness even when computed in an approximated fashion. Some of these applications are image processing, computer vision, video streaming, machine learning, big data analysis, sensor data processing, and computation on aged devices [16, 19]. Approximate computing has emerged as a promising approach to improve energy efficiency. As a paradigm, it allows the computation to deviate from the reference or deterministic execution behavior.

As illustrated in Figure 1, the concept of approximate computing can be implemented with four different strategies: approximate systems, approximate software, approximate storage, and approximate arithmetic circuits. At the system level, approximate computing is realized using modified architectures where approximate accelerators and programmable processors are typically adopted [13, 24, 26]. With software-level approximation, power consumption is reduced by skipping the execution of the functions in a predicted part of the code [10, 18], by relaxing the constraints on synchronization timing and handshaking [15], by leveraging domain specific knowledge to simplify application algorithms [25], or by altering the implementation of algorithms for a specific function [4]. Techniques for approximate storage include applying different refresh rates on different memory blocks [20], loosening guard band of multi-level memory cells [23], and selective voltage scaling [5]. Circuit-level approximation techniques reduce the computation resolution or

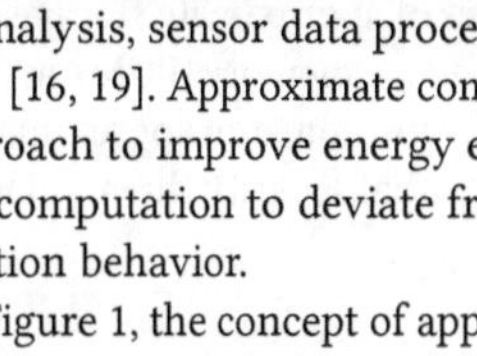


**Figure 1: Approximate computing strategies.**



*GLSVLSI '19, May 9–11, 2019, Tysons Corner, VA, USA*

ACM ISBN 978-1-4503-6252-8/19/05...$15.00
https://doi.org/10.1145/3299874.3319453

shorten the critical delay path to improve performance and energy efficiency [7, 12, 17].

Existing research efforts mainly focus on finding approximation mechanisms to trade off accuracy for delay/power/area. The security issues related to approximate computing are often overlooked. The work [21] initiates the investigation on the dark side of approximate computing and provides a brief analysis how a transition to the approximate computing paradigm would affect hardware security. In this work, we study the potential attack surfaces on approximate computing systems from circuit to software stacks. Indeed, approximate computing presents a particularly poignant security challenge, because it runs counter to emerging secure computer system design patterns. For example, attackers could (1) alter the original memory allocation map for precise memory and approximate memory blocks and then maliciously save critical data in the approximate memory block, which often does not have strong integrity check or authentication, (2) exploit the relaxation on design constraints (e.g., guard band) to incorrectly quantize analog input for digital critical data, or (3) tamper the memory controller to lose the original critical data (due to insufficient refresh frequency). More detailed discussions on the potential attack risks are presented in the later sections of this work.

The remainder of this work is organized as follows. In Section 2, we introduce security threats in the system-level framework for approximate computing. In Section 3, we propose the possible attack surfaces in three types of approximate storage, approximate DRAM, approximate phase change memory (PCM), and approximate SRAM. In Section 4, we briefly introduce an approximate arithmetic module and highlight the potential security threats. This work is concluded in Section 5.

## 2 GENERAL SYSTEM LEVEL APPROXIMATE COMPUTING FRAMEWORK

Broadly speaking, the steps in the computing system design cycle are functional description, functional specification, functional and implementation modeling, and physical implementation. The current secure computer system design patterns aim to eliminate or minimize any semantic gaps between these design steps, and implement strong module and state isolation. For example, both active side-channel attack (e.g., cache side-channel attack) and passive side-channel attack (e.g., thermal analysis) exploit gaps within these steps. Therefore, the push has been towards a greater semantic consistency between the different implementation steps to (a) avoid data leakage, (b) prevent an unauthorized party (users, processes, etc) from accessing services, resources data or discovering the existence of a critical piece of data, (c) check the integrity of computing processes, (d) monitor and control access to system resources, or (e) have predictable computing behaviors. The principle of approximate computing leaves or creates under-defined or under-specified behaviors - "Attack Gadget (AG)" - in the design at all levels. Figure 2 illustrates this problem.

Furthermore, in the light of recent micro-architecture security issues, it has become harder to claim that the undefined or under-specified behaviors of the system, which are being leveraged by approximate computing, could also be used for obfuscation to improve its resiliency. The current momentum is a move away from

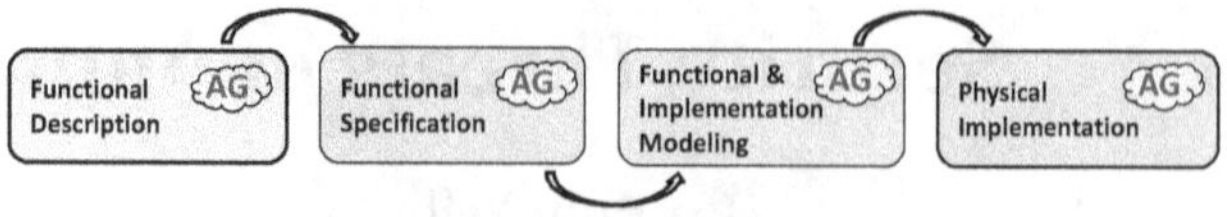


**Figure 2: Computing system design cycle steps.**

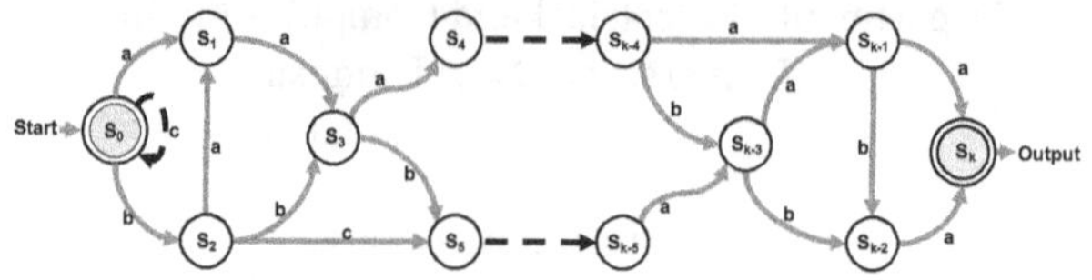


**Figure 3: Finite state machine (FSM) representation of the computer system.**

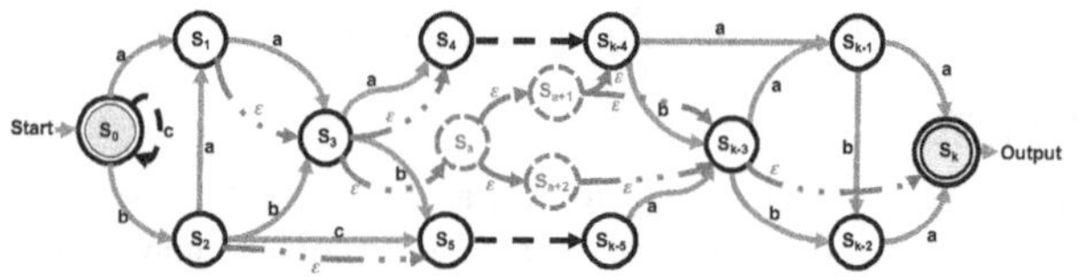


**Figure 4: States and transitions illustrating the approximate nature of the computing system either at the software/algorithmic level or hardware/device level.**

security by secrecy or obscurity towards a formally secure design paradigm. To illustrate this natural tension between approximation and security in computing, and without loss of generality, let us consider a simple finite state machine.

The canonical *finite state machine (FSM) - deterministic finite automaton (DFA)* definition can be described as a tuple

$$A = (Q, \Sigma, \delta, S_0, F)\,,$$

where

- $Q$ is a finite set of *states,*
- $\Sigma$ is a finite *alphabet,* in this illustrative case $\Sigma = \{a, b, c, \varepsilon, \boxed{d}, \boxed{T}\}$
- $\delta : Q \times \Sigma \rightarrow Q$ is the (total) *transition function,*
- $S_0 \in Q$ is the *initial state,* and
- $F \subseteq Q$ is the set of *final states.*

The *alphabet* and the transition set can be decomposed in this manner: $\Sigma = \Sigma^s \cup \Sigma^a \cup \Sigma^v$ where

- $\Sigma^s = \{a, b, c\}$ is the set of safe and deterministic *alphabet* and associated transitions, i.e., non-approximate transitions, shown in Figure 3,
- $\Sigma^a$ is the approximation *alphabet* denoted by $\varepsilon$ - in an approximation state could represent a software or hardware level mechanism - Figure 4.
- $\Sigma^v$ is the vulnerability *alphabet* set - $\Sigma^v = \{\boxed{d}, \boxed{T}\}$ - for a given system, $\boxed{T}$ denotes the set of possible attack triggers that can be used against the system, $\boxed{d}$ denotes the possible ways the attacker can manipulate the compute system when under attack - Figure 5.

From the system behavior analysis standpoint, the challenge is to decouple the approximation states from the vulnerable states. Approximation states provide a certain level of obfuscation to the attack states. Without the awareness of the states' intent, which often cannot be captured by system analysis tools, it is extremely difficult,

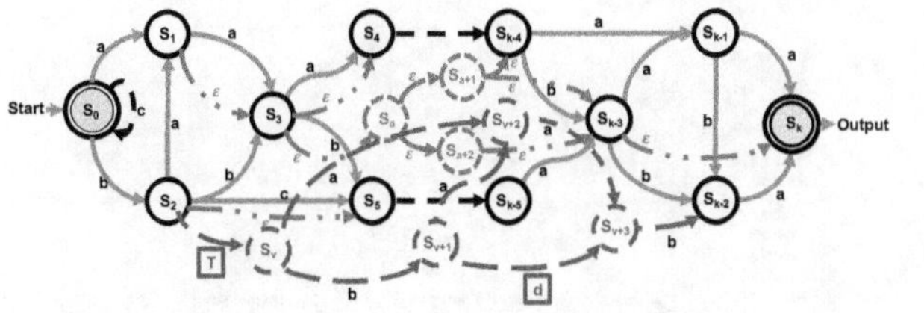

**Figure 5: Approximation states and attack states ambiguity.**

if not impossible, to isolate malicious states from the under-specified or under-determined or under-provisioned states - Figure 5.

# 3 SECURITY THREATS IN APPROXIMATE STORAGE

Power consumed by memory elements takes a large portion of system power. Approximate storage is emerging to be an effective way to achieve system-level energy efficiency. Unfortunately, approximate storage may incur new security threats over traditional precise memory.

## 3.1 Overview of Attacks on Approximate Storage

The use of approximate storage involves software and hardware, both of which could be the attack target. In Figure 6, we highlight some potential attack scenarios that could harm the integrity and reliability of approximate storage. The rest of this section summarizes the attack methods applicable on software and hardware for approximate storage.

To facilitate the use of approximate storage, the authors [9] add a new instruction (e.g. *LDx.a*) to the instruction set so that the compiler will know whether the destination is approximate memory or not. A compromised compiler could replace the instruction *LDx.a* with the regular instruction *LDx*, leading the system to experience unacceptable errors. The compiler and memory allocator need a memory map, which indicates the address range of different memory categories, to assign the registers, variables, and temporal storage space according to the acceptable error tolerance for each data segment. If the memory boundary between the precise memory and approximate memory is altered by an attacker, critical data could be stored in the approximate memory blocks. As a result, adversary may have an easy way to manipulate the data without being captured. One type of approximate storage achieves energy efficiency by relaxing the guard band for multi-level memory cells. The number of writing iterations guarantees the success of write operation. If an attacker maliciously modifies the number of writing iterations, the data stored in the approximate memory will be changed stealthily.

In the hardware component of approximate storage, the precision flag bit could be misinterpreted if the instruction decoder is sabotaged. Once the precision flag is ignored, the critical or approximate data will be sent to a wrong place. Some volatile memory components retains the same value only when the memory is refreshed periodically. A slower refresh rate would lead to the loss of the originally saved data. Any tampering on the refresh counter and refresh enable signal could ruin the memory content. Analog input needs to be converted to digital bits before it is saved in

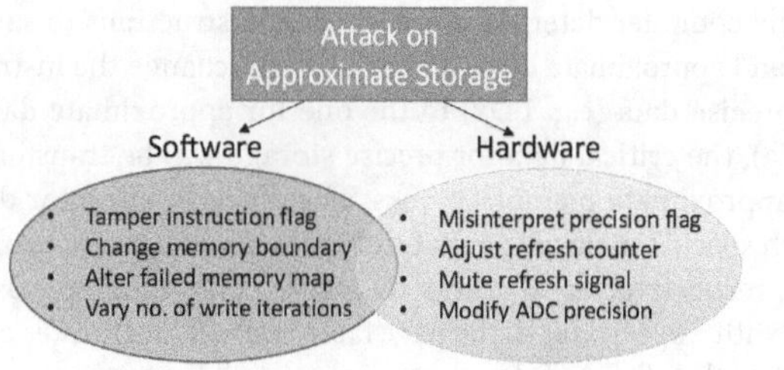


**Figure 6: Potential attacks on approximate storage.**

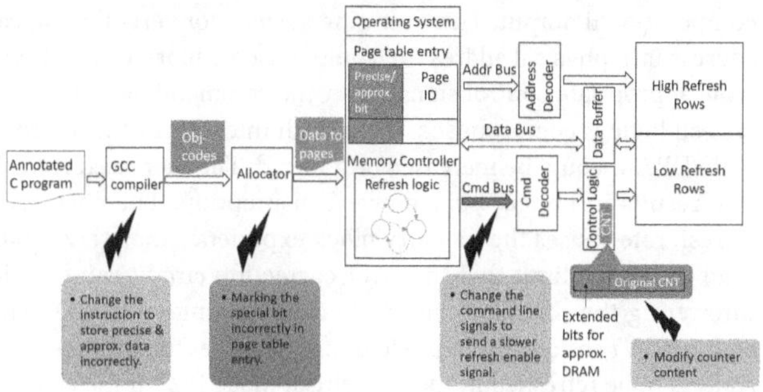


**Figure 7: Process flow of approximate DRAM storage.**

memory. Some types of approximate storage based on emerging memory vary the precision of Analog-to-Digital Converter (ADC) to reduce energy consumption. If an attacker takes charge of the ADC precision adjuster, the critical data will be saved with a lower precision than it should be, thus harming the system.

## 3.2 Attack on Approximate DRAM

*3.2.1 Approximation Mechanism.* A basic DRAM cell consists of an access transistor and a capacitor. When the DRAM cell is in the idle state, the capacitor starts to discharge. If the idle DRAM cell is not refreshed periodically on time, the logic value stored in that DRAM cell will be lost. As reported in [1], the power consumption for memory refresh is almost 50% of the total power consumed by DRAM. Moreover, write and read operations are prohibited during the period of memory refreshing. This fact limits the throughput of DRAM. To improve energy efficiency and throughput, approximate DRAM selectively reduces the refresh rate. The DRAM segment for precise storage is refreshed at every standard interval of time. In contrast, the DRAM blocks for approximate storage is refreshed with a slower rate, incurring storage error on some memory cells.

*3.2.2 Potential Attack Surfaces.* Despite of energy savings, approximate DRAM opens new exploration space for an adversary to implement new unique attacks. In Figure 7, we point out the vulnerable spots, where adversary could execute attacks in the process of storing and maintaining data in a memory with mixed precise and approximate DRAMs. Here, we assume that the application developer is trusted but the software and hardware that approximate DRAM involves are not trusted. Users annotate approximate and precise data in the high level description of the application. Main attacks on the software and hardware are summarized in Figure 7.

The compiler determines the specific instructions to save precise and approximate data. If attackers interchange the instruction for precise data (e.g. LDx) to the one for approximate data (e.g. LDx.a), the critical data for precise storage will be transferred to the approximate memory blocks. The memory allocator decides which specific memory pages to store the precise and approximate data, respectively, and marks the pages containing approximate data with a special bit in the page table entry. If an attacker can manipulate the allocator, the memory pages will be purposely marked with a different indication bit. For instance, loading precise data to the approximate memory will affect the accuracy of the final computational output. The operating system converts the logical address into physical address and guides the memory controller to issue appropriate control signals over the command bus. Once the refresh logic is compromised, the refresh interval for the approximate DRAM could be increased or reduced. The increased refresh rate results in unnecessary power consumption. The decreased refresh rate causes the memory block experience more error bits than the upper limit that the error correction circuit can handle. Interfering the command bus could cause timing violations. The counter *CNT* inside the control logic unit provides the next memory address to be refreshed in the self refresh mode [22]. If the counter hardware is tampered by an attacker, the DRAM blocks for precise and approximate storage will both suffer from the reduced memory refresh. Although precise DRAM typically has error correction circuit, the frequent usage of error correction will slow down the memory access speed and dramatic power increase. Due to the inappropriate refresh frequency, the approximate DRAM may not be able to achieve the acceptable precision.

*3.2.3 Attack Example.* A memory composed of precise and approximate DRAM cells will be refreshed in two modes: auto refresh and self refresh [22]. In the auto refresh mode, the external memory controller issues refresh commands. In the self refresh mode, the refresh commands are generated inside the DRAM module, and the counter in the control logic unit keeps track of the next address to be refreshed. The work [22] proposes to extend the counter CNT shown in Figure7 by adding $log_2(n)$ bits, where $n$ represents the ratio of standard refresh frequency to the lower refresh frequency for approximate DRAM. Once the MSB bits meet a pre-defined condition (e.g. all zeros), the approximate DRAM will be refreshed.

To sabotage the data saved in the precise DRAM, the attacker may only need to manipulate the configuration signal. As shown in Figure 8, once the configuration signal goes to high, the extended MSB bits of the refresh counter starts to increase. As a result, the memory refresh enable signal drops down earlier. Since the precise DRAM is not refreshed with the regular refresh rate, the data stored in the precise DRAM may lose charge and result in an uncorrectable error. We conducted a set of experiments to show the impact of attack induced by the reduced refresh rate on approximate DRAM storage. The image *Lena* shown in Figure 9(a) stored in the precise DRAM blocks was refreshed with an interval of 64ms before attack. When the configuration signal shown in Figure 8 is pulled up due to attack, the refresh happens every 60 seconds. We adopted the error rate reported in [11] and accordingly injected bit errors to the RGB values of the image pixels. Bit-flip and stuck-at-0 error models were applied in our error injection. The targeted image pixels could

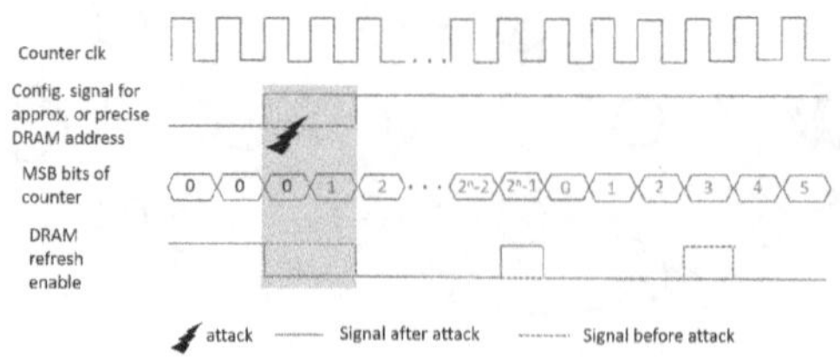


**Figure 8: Timing diagram for the DRAM with incorrect refresh frequency due to tampered memory counter.**

(a) (b) (c) (d)

**Figure 9: Impact of incorrect refresh rates on the output of approximate DRAM. (a) original, (b) random attack, (c) regional attack(bit-flip model), and (d) regional attack (stuck-at-0 model).**

be random or around in a region. Figures 9(b) and (c) show the impact of the random and regional errors on the recovered image, respectively. In this example, the attacker blurs the important characteristics of the critical image by manipulating the configuration signal for DRAM refreshing. If such an image is used for authentication, attacks on the approximate DRAM will significantly reduce the effort to pass authentication.

### 3.3 Attack on Approximate Phase Change Memory

*3.3.1 Approximation Mechanism.* Phase Change Memory (PCM) is a non-volatile memory. The voltage applied on the memory cell will turn the PCM material into either amorphous or crystalline. As the analog resistance presented by the PCM material can be quantized into multiple levels, the PCM is often observed as multi-level memory cells. PCM has been used as a media to implement approximate storage [23]. The main principle of approximation here is to reduce the size of guard band. As shown in Figure 10, the analog resistance is quantized into four levels to represent 2-bit information stored in a single PCM memory cell, and the approximate PCM relaxes the noise margin from a small $T_{precise}$ to a large $T_{approx}$ (i.e. the guard band of approximate PCM is less than that of precise PCM). To save power consumption, the number of writing iterations for approximate PCM is less than that for precise PCM [23]. Although the approximation technique [23] improves the speed of writing by 1.7× over the precise PCM, the reduced guard band and the less number of writing iterations make the approximate PCM vulnerable to security threats.

*3.3.2 Potential Attack Surfaces.* Based on the PCM writing procedure introduced in [23], we highlight the key steps of writing operation for approximate PCM in Figure 11. The possible attacks along the writing flow are proposed on the right side of Figure 11. The parameter $T_{approx}$ defines the noise margin. If the initialization of $T_{approx}$ is compromised, a precise PCM block will be turned

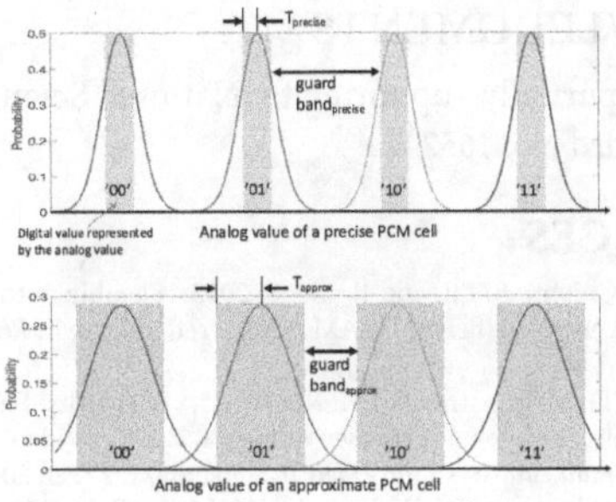


**Figure 10: Comparison of precise and approximate multi-level PCM cells.**

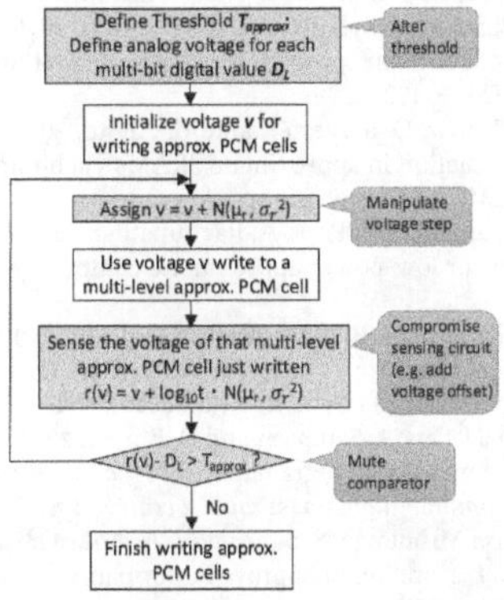


**Figure 11: Flowchart of PCM writing procedure with potential security attacks.**

into an approximate memory block. Consequently, the integrity of the critical data saved in the precise PCM will be affected. In the iterative writing procedure, the parameters $\mu_r$ and $\sigma_r$ are the mean and standard deviation of the error effect (due to insufficient writing voltage). The writing voltage $v$ increases incrementally in each writing iteration. When the noise function $N(\mu_r, \sigma_r^2)$ is under-estimated or overestimated, the voltage step will be manipulated by adversary and thus writing operation will fail. The determination of the number of writing iterations relies on the voltage difference sensed by the reading operation. If a voltage offset is stealthily introduced to the sensing logic, the content stored in the PCM can be modified arbitrarily. Or, the voltage comparator $(r(v) - D_L)$ is muted by the attacker so that he/she could overwrite confidential information, which is supposed to be saved in a precise PCM block.

*3.3.3 Attack Example.* We model the resistance distribution probability for the multi-level PCM cells shown in Figure 10, and set the threshold $T$ in a range of 60% to 90%. We consider the 90% case as precise PCM, and the other cases are approximate PCM. The attack implemented in this example consists of adding an offset to the output voltage from the PCM cells. Due to the voltage offset $\Delta$noise, the logic content saved in the PCM cell will be misinterpreted. When the resistance cannot be converted to the correct multi-bit state, we consider this to be a quantization error. As shown in Figure 12, the approximation mechanism incurs a higher quantization error rate than the precise case and the error rate further increases with the increasing noise. As presented in Figures 12(a) and (b), the imprecise writing makes the PCM more sensitive to a small noise. If the

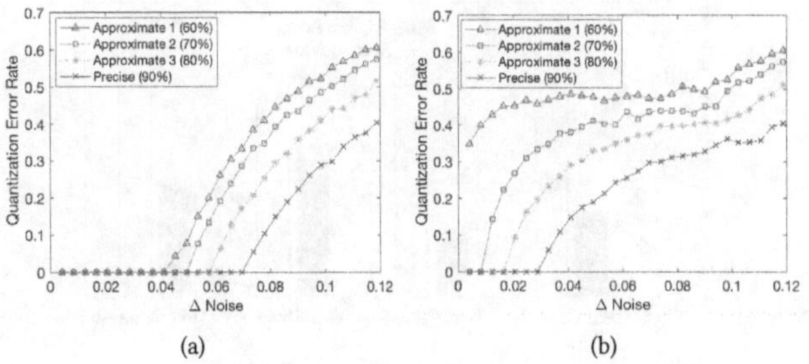


**Figure 12: Quantization error rate of a precise/approximate PCM cell written with (a) sufficient and (b) insufficient number of writing iterations.**

write and read operations in the approximate PCM are executed, the approximate PCM may suffer from more quantization errors.

## 3.4 Attack on Approximate SRAM

*3.4.1 Approximation Mechanism.* Approximate SRAM trades off accuracy and energy efficiency by scaling supply voltage. In the work [2], 8T SRAM cells are used to store the sign and exponent bits of floating-point numbers as 8T SRAM cells have better resilience than 6T SRAM cells against the noise. In contrast, 6T SRAM cells are utilized to save mantissa bits. Thus, even if the 6T SRAM cells experience read or write failures due to the lower supply voltage, the effect of scaled voltage on the SRAM quality is acceptable by some applications (e.g., image processing). The work [14] follows the similar approximate mechanism by replacing 8T SRAM cells with oversized 6T SRAM cells. A dual supply voltage technique is proposed in [3], where high and low voltages are applied to the precise and approximate SRAM cells, respectively. Alternatively, error correction code is implemented in the precise SRAM blocks to compensate for the errors induced by the overscaled supply voltage [6].

*3.4.2 Potential Attack Surfaces.* Attackers could exploit the over-scaled supply voltage technique in the work [6] to introduce more errors than what can be tolerated by the error correction code (ECC) available in the memory. The SRAM cells for the storage of ECC check bits may be the potential attack surface. Assume a hybrid precise and approximate SRAM is used to implement a cache memory, which is managed by a cache controller with the pre-knowledge of the hybrid SRAM map. If an attacker sabotages the SRAM map in the cache controller, critical data from the main memory could be loaded to the approximate SRAM cells, which have limited (or no) error correction capability. Or, data from the compromised main memory will be successfully transferred to the CPU via the cache.

# 4 SECURITY THREATS IN APPROXIMATE CIRCUIT

Circuit-level approximation techniques facilitate the system to reduce the computational power at the cost of decreased precision on the system output. In this section, we use an approximate adder as an illustrative example to present the potential security threats in approximate circuits.

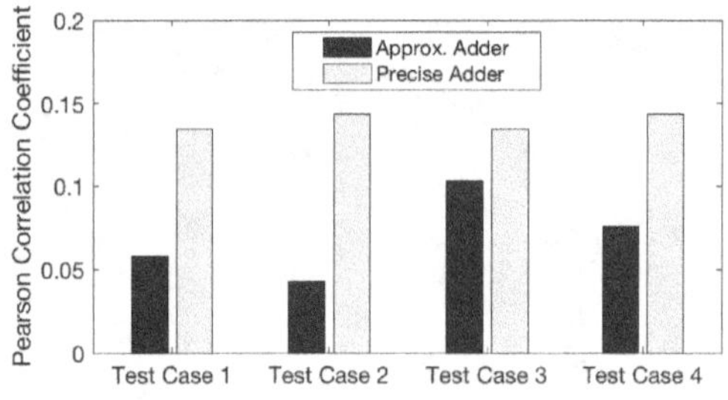


**Figure 13: Impact of approximation in adder circuit on Pearson correlation coefficient (PCC) between output and power.**

The power consumption and critical-path delay due to the carry-bit calculation is typically prominent in an adder. To minimize delay and also achieve energy efficiency, researchers redesign adder architecture or alter the truth table for addition operations to reduce the logic complexity and shorten the long path for carry propagation. The work [17] proposes to replace the original carry-in bit with an estimated one, which is based on the few input bits close to the current bit position. Depending on the number of bits used for carry estimation, the probability of getting the correct carry-in bit is in the range of 75% to 99.98% [17]. In the work [8], the truth table is modified in a way to achieve a better logic optimization. This type of approximation is feasible for floating-point additions in image processing applications, where the fractional part carried by the LSBs often time does not need precise calculation.

Adversaries could leverage the natural inaccuracy of the approximate adder to implement several attacks. If an attacker manipulates the adder inputs to persistently make the adder yield wrong outputs, the accumulated errors could trigger the system to utilize the fault-tolerance mechanism more often than usual. The use of the approximate adder may make verification process more challenging than the case of precise adders. If the verification is not exhaustive, the adversary could tamper the hardware implementation of approximate adders. The malicious modification on the approximate adder may not be detected by the side-channel analysis method. As a case study, we implemented two approximate adders and one precise adder, 8 bits per input, with an IBM 180nm CMOS technology, and compared the power correlation between the measured power and output-based power estimation. Hamming distance power model was used to estimate the power. As shown in Figure 13, the power correlation coefficient for the approximate adder is less than that for the precise adder. The test cases 1 and 2 were applied to an approximate adder with 25% output errors and the rest of the test cases were for the adder with 50% errors.

## 5 CONCLUSION

Approximate computing systems are emerging as an effective way to achieve energy efficiency without significantly sacrificing the accuracy. Despite of the promising benefits, the approximate mechanisms adopted in storage, arithmetic circuit, system architecture, and software stacks make approximate storage vulnerable to new security attacks. This work is one of the early efforts that comprehensively foresee the potential security threats on approximate computing systems.

## ACKNOWLEDGMENTS

This work is partially supported by National Science Foundation CAREER Award No. 1652474.

## REFERENCES

[1] I. Bhati, Z. Chishti, S. Lu, and B. Jacob. 2015. Flexible auto-refresh: Enabling scalable and energy-efficient DRAM refresh reductions. In *Proc. 2015 ISCA*. 235–246.

[2] I. J. Chang, D. Mohapatra, and K. Roy. 2011. A Priority-Based 6T/8T Hybrid SRAM Architecture for Aggressive Voltage Scaling in Video Applications. *IEEE Trans. on Circuits and Syst. for Video Technology* 21, 2 (Feb 2011), 101–112.

[3] M. Cho, J. Schlessman, W. Wolf, and S. Mukhopadhyay. 2011. Reconfigurable SRAM Architecture With Spatial Voltage Scaling for Low Power Mobile Multimedia Applications. *TVLSI* 19, 1 (Jan 2011), 161–165.

[4] H. Esmaeilzadeh, A. Sampson, L. Ceze, and D. Burger. 2013. Neural Acceleration for General-Purpose Approximate Programs. *IEEE Micro* 33, 3 (May 2013), 16–27.

[5] F. Frustaci, D. Blaauw, D. Sylvester, and M. Alioto. 2015. Better-than-voltage scaling energy reduction in approximate SRAMs via bit dropping and bit reuse. In *Proc. 2015 PATMOS*. 132–139.

[6] F. Frustaci, D. Blaauw, D. Sylvester, and M. Alioto. 2015. Better-than-voltage scaling energy reduction in approximate SRAMs via bit dropping and bit reuse. In *Proc. 2015 PATMOS*. 132–139.

[7] V. Gupta, D. Mohapatra, S. P. Park, A. Raghunathan, and K. Roy. 2011. IMPACT: IMPrecise adders for low-power approximate computing. In *Proc. 2011 ISLPED*. 409–414.

[8] V. Gupta, D. Mohapatra, A. Raghunathan, and K. Roy. 2013. Low-Power Digital Signal Processing Using Approximate Adders. *IEEE Trans. on Computer-Aided Design of Integr. Circuits and Syst.* 32, 1 (Jan 2013), 124–137.

[9] L. Ceze H. Esmaeilzadeh, A. Sampson and D. Burger. 2012. Architecture Support for Disciplined Approximate Programming. In *Proc. 7th Intl. Conf. on Architectural Support for Programming Languages and Operating Syst.* 301–312.

[10] H. Hoffmann, Sasa Misailovic, S. Sidiroglou, A. Agarwal, and Martin C. Rinard. 2009. Using Code Perforation to Improve Performance, Reduce Energy Consumption, and Respond to Failures.

[11] M. Jung, D. M. Mathew, C. Weis, and N. Wehn. 2016. Invited: Approximate computing with partially unreliable dynamic random access memory âĂŤ Approximate DRAM. In *Proc. 2016 DAC*. 1–4.

[12] S. Keshavarz and D. Holcomb. 2017. Privacy leakages in approximate adders. In *2017 ISCAS*. 1–4.

[13] D. S. Khudia, B. Zamirai, M. Samadi, and S. Mahlke. 2016. Quality Control for Approximate Accelerators by Error Prediction. *IEEE Design Test* 33, 1 (Feb 2016), 43–50.

[14] J. Kwon, I. J. Chang, I. Lee, H. Park, and J. Park. 2012. Heterogeneous SRAM Cell Sizing for Low-Power H.264 Applications. *TCAS-I* 59, 10 (Oct 2012), 2275–2284.

[15] J. Mengte, A. Raghunathan, S. Chakradhar, and S. Byna. 2010. Exploiting the forgiving nature of applications for scalable parallel execution. In *Proc. 2010 IPDPS*. 1–12.

[16] D. T. Nguyen, H. Kim, H. Lee, and I. Chang. 2018. An Approximate Memory Architecture for a Reduction of Refresh Power Consumption in Deep Learning Applications. In *Proc. 2018 ISCAS*. 1–5.

[17] N.Zhu, W. L. Goh, and K. S. Yeo. 2009. An enhanced low-power high-speed Adder For Error-Tolerant application. In *Proc. 2009 Intl. Symp. on Integr. Circuits*. 69–72.

[18] D. Palomino, M. Shafique, A. Susin, and J. Henkel. 2016. Thermal optimization using adaptive approximate computing for video coding. In *Proc. 2016 DATE*. 1207–1212.

[19] F. Qiao, N. Zhou, Y. Chen, and H. Yang. 2015. Approximate Computing in Chrominance Cache for Image/Video Processing. In *Proc. 2015 IEEE Intl. Conf. on Multimedia Big Data*. 180–183.

[20] A. Raha, S. Sutar, H. Jayakumar, and V. Raghunathan. 2017. Quality Configurable Approximate DRAM. *IEEE Trans. on Computers* 66, 7 (July 2017), 1172–1187.

[21] F. Regazzoni, C. Alippi, and I. Polian. 2018. Security: The Dark Side of Approximate Computing?. In *Proc. 2018 ICCAD*. 1–6.

[22] M. Thomas Benjamin G. Zorn S. Liu, P. Karthik. 2011. Flikker: saving DRAM refresh-power through critical data partitioning.

[23] A. Sampson, J. Nelson, K. Strauss, and L. Ceze. 2013. Approximate storage in solid-state memories. In *Proc. 2013 MICRO*. 25–36.

[24] S. Venkataramani, V. K. Chippa, S. T. Chakradhar, K. Roy, and A. Raghunathan. 2013. Quality programmable vector processors for approximate computing. In *Proc. 2013 MICRO*. 1–12.

[25] S. Venkataramani, A. Ranjan, K. Roy, and A. Raghunathan. 2014. AxNN: Energy-efficient neuromorphic systems using approximate computing. In *Proc. 2014 ISLPED*. 27–32.

[26] S. Xu and B. C. Schafer. 2017. Approximate Reconfigurable Hardware Accelerator: Adapting the Micro-Architecture to Dynamic Workloads. In *Proc. 2017 ICCD*. 113–120.

# Characterizing Approximate Adders and Multipliers Optimized under Different Design Constraints

Honglan Jiang
Institute of Microelectronics
Tsinghua University
Beijing, China
honglan@ualberta.ca

Francisco J. H. Santiago
Mohammad Saeed Ansari
University of Alberta
Edmonton, AB, Canada
{fh,ansari2}@ualberta.ca

Leibo Liu
Institute of Microelectronics
Tsinghua University
Beijing, China
liulb@tsinghua.edu.cn

Bruce F. Cockburn
University of Alberta
Edmonton, AB, Canada
cockburn@ualberta.ca

Fabrizio Lombardi
Northeastern University
Boston, MA, USA
lombardi@ece.neu.edu

Jie Han
University of Alberta
Edmonton, AB, Canada
jhan8@ualberta.ca

## ABSTRACT

Taking advantage of the error resilience in many applications as well as the perceptual limitations of humans, numerous approximate arithmetic circuits have been proposed that trade off accuracy for higher speed or lower power in emerging applications that exploit approximate computing. However, characterizing the various approximate designs for a specific application under certain performance constraints becomes a new challenge. In this paper, approximate adders and multipliers are evaluated and compared for a better understanding of their characteristics when the implementations are optimized for performance or power. Although simple truncation can effectively reduce the hardware of an arithmetic circuit, it is shown that some other designs perform better in speed, power and power-delay product. For instance, many approximate adders have a higher performance than a truncated adder. A truncated multiplier is faster but consumes a higher power than most approximate designs for achieving a similar mean error magnitude. The logarithmic multipliers are very fast and power-efficient at a lower accuracy. Approximate multipliers can also be generated by an automated process to be very efficient while ensuring a sufficiently high accuracy.

## KEYWORDS

approximate computing, adder, multiplier, speed, power

**ACM Reference Format:**
Honglan Jiang, Francisco J. H. Santiago, Mohammad Saeed Ansari, Leibo Liu, Bruce F. Cockburn, Fabrizio Lombardi, and Jie Han. 2019. Characterizing Approximate Adders and Multipliers Optimized under Different Design Constraints. In *GLSVLSI '19: ACM Great Lakes Symposium on VLSI, May 09–11, 2019, Washington, DC.* ACM, New York, NY, USA, 6 pages. https://doi.org/10.1145/1122445.1122456


*GLSVLSI '19, May 09–11, 2019, Washington, DC*

ACM ISBN 978-1-4503-9999-9/18/06...$15.00
https://doi.org/10.1145/1122445.1122456

## 1 INTRODUCTION

As a potential technique for implementing complex computations with reasonable speed and power consumption, approximate computing has been explored actively from circuits to programming languages. Among circuit designs, adders and multipliers have been a focus because they play a pivotal role in determining the performance and power dissipation of many compute-intensive applications [8]. Therefore a large variety of approximate adders and multipliers have been proposed. However, these designs usually seek tradeoffs among accuracy, performance and power consumption, i.e., a design may be very fast but with a low accuracy or high power, or a very power-efficient design may have a significantly low speed or accuracy. Also, different designs in the literature have been evaluated using different synthesis tools and technologies. These differences have made it difficult to choose a suitable approximate design for a specific application with designated purposes.

An evaluation and comparison of the accuracy and circuit characteristics was provided in [11] for approximate adders, multipliers and dividers. However, the circuit measurements were obtained without considering any design constraints and, hence, the generic power-delay product (PDP) metric was mainly used for hardware evaluation. At a similar PDP, it was concluded that a truncated arithmetic circuit results in a smaller error magnitude (in the mean relative error distance (MRED)) than most of the other approximate designs.

In this paper, rather than considering the overall measurement, high performance and power efficiency are respectively pursued as independent design metrics. For example, an approximate design with a high speed is useful for coping with aging-induced timing errors in adders and multipliers [1]. Also, high-performance arithmetic circuits are preferred in real-time machine learning systems [10]. For mobile and embedded devices, power-efficient arithmetic circuits would be key to the extended use given limited battery life. In this work, therefore, the approximate circuits are optimized for maximizing performance (through delay) or minimizing power (through area). Compared to previous studies, several recent approximate arithmetic designs are included for comparison and to provide new insights to approximate arithmetic circuit design.

## 2 SIMULATION METHODOLOGY

The accuracy of the approximate designs is evaluated through Monte Carlo simulations. The error distance (ED = $|M' - M|$) and the relative error distance (RED = $|\frac{ED}{M}|$) are then calculated, where $M'$ and $M$ are the approximate and accurate results, respectively [18]. The mean error distance (MED) is calculated by averaging all of the obtained EDs. The error characteristics of the approximate designs are assessed by the error rate (ER, the probability of producing an incorrect result), the normalized MED (NMED, the normalization of MED by the maximum output of the accurate design) and the MRED (the average value of all of the obtained REDs).

To assess the circuit characteristics, the approximate designs are implemented in VHDL and synthesized using the Synopsys Design Compiler (DC) in STMicro's 28-nm CMOS technology, with a supply voltage of 1.0 V at a temperature of 25°C. For a fair comparison, all designs use the same process, voltage and temperature with the same optimization option. To compare speed and power, the approximate circuits are synthesized under different constraints. The critical path delay of a design is constrained to the smallest value without a timing violation for the delay-optimized synthesis, whereas the area is minimized for the area-optimized synthesis. The DesignWare library and "ultra compile" are used in the synthesis for optimization. The critical path delay and area are reported by the Synopsys DC. Power dissipation is measured by the PrimeTime-PX tool with 10 million random input combinations.

## 3 APPROXIMATE ADDERS

Two basic adders for binary addition are the ripple-carry adder (RCA) and the carry lookahead adder (CLA). For an $n$-bit RCA, the delay and circuit complexity increase proportionally with $n$ (denoted by $O(n)$). The delay of an $n$-bit CLA is logarithmic in $n$ (or $O(log(n))$), thus significantly shorter than that of an $n$-bit RCA. However, a CLA requires a larger circuit area (in $O(nlog(n))$), which results in a higher power dissipation.

### 3.1 Review

*3.1.1 Speculative Adders.* In an $n$-bit speculative adder, $k$ ($k < n$) least significant bits (LSBs) are used to predict the carry input for each sum bit [22]. Thus, the critical path delay is reduced to $O(log(k))$ (for a parallel implementation such as the CLA, the same throughout this section unless otherwise noted). The almost correct adder (ACA) is designed to reduce the hardware overhead by sharing part of the carry-generation circuits [32].

*3.1.2 Segmented Adders.* A segmented adder is implemented by using several smaller adders operating in parallel. They include the equal segmentation adder (ESA) [26], the error-tolerant adder type II (ETAII) [36], the accuracy-configurable approximate adder (ACAA) [13] and the dithering adder [24]. The delays of the segmented adders grow with $O(log(k))$ and the circuit complexities grow with $O(nlog(k))$ for ESA and ETAII, and with $O((n-k)log(k))$ for ACAA [11].

*3.1.3 Carry Select Adders.* An $n$-bit carry select adder consists of $m = \lceil \frac{n}{k} \rceil$ blocks, and the carry input for each block is selected using different schemes in different designs. In the speculative carry select adder (SCSA), each block is made of two $k$-bit adders: adder0 with carry-in "0" and adder1 with carry-in "1"; the sum is selected by a multiplexer according to the carry-out of adder0 in the previous block [6]. SCSA and ETAII achieve the same accuracy for the same value of $k$ due to the same carry prediction function. For the carry skip adder (CSA), each block consists of a sub-carry generator and a sub-adder [14]. The carry-in of the $(i+1)^{th}$ sub-adder is determined by the propagate signals of the $i^{th}$ block, which enhances the carry prediction accuracy. In the carry speculative adder (CSPA), each block contains one sum generator, two internal carry generators and one carry predictor; fewer than $k$ input bits are used in a carry predictor [20]. In the consistent carry approximate adder (CCA), the carry prediction depends not only on its LSBs, but also on the higher bits [17]. The generate signals-exploited carry speculation adder (GCSA) has a similar structure as CSA and uses the generate signals for carry speculation [9]. In the gracefully-degrading accuracy-configurable adder (GDA), control signals are used to configure the accuracy by selecting an accurate or approximate carry-in signal using a multiplexer for each sub-adder [34]. In the carry cut-back adder (CCBA), the full carry propagation is prevented by a controlled multiplexer or an OR gate for a high-speed operation [5]. Although the critical path delays of the carry select adders vary, they generally grow with $O(log(k))$, where $k$ is the size of the sub-adder.

*3.1.4 Approximate Full Adders.* In this class of designs, the LSBs are implemented by approximate full adders. These adders include the simple use of OR gates (and one AND gate for carry propagation) in the lower-part-OR adder (LOA) [23], the approximate designs of the mirror adder [7] and the approximate XOR/XNOR-based full adders [33]. For the LOA, the critical path is approximately $O(log(n-l))$, where $l$ is the number of approximate LSBs. Finally, an adder whose $k$ LSBs are truncated is referred to as a truncated adder (TruA) that works with a lower precision. It is considered as a baseline design.

### 3.2 Evaluation

In this evaluation, 16-bit approximate adders are considered. For CSPA, the size of the carry predictor is $\lceil k/2 \rceil$. The global speculative carry for CCA is "0". All sub-adders are implemented as CLAs because most approximate adders are designed based on the CLA.

The simulation results show similar performance trends for the MRED and NMED of the approximate adders, so only the MRED is considered in the comparison. Figs. 1, 2 and 3 show the comparison of MRED, ER, delay (for delay-optimized synthesis), power (for area-optimized synthesis) and PDP.

Fig. 1 shows that, among the adders with small MREDs, LOA and ETAII are faster than the other designs, whereas CCA is the slowest followed by CSA. CSA-6 is not shown in the figures because it is accurate due to the precise carry generated for every block, so the ER and MRED of CSA-6 are 0. For a high MRED, ESA and CSPA are faster. When the same ER is considered, ETAII, SCSA and ACAA are among the fastest designs.

Fig. 2 shows that in terms of power consumption, CCBA, LOA and TruA are the most efficient designs, while ACA is very power consuming. However, CCBA, LOA and TruA have very high ERs. CSA has a rather low ER. For a similar ER, ETAII and ACAA are very power-efficient, while ACA consumes relatively high power.

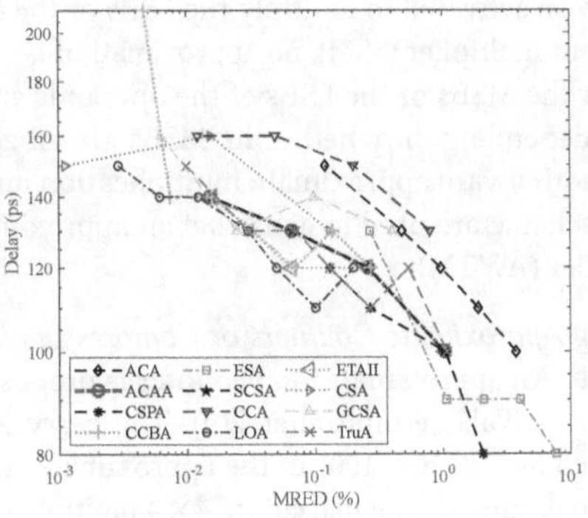


(a) MRED vs. Delay (delay-optimized)

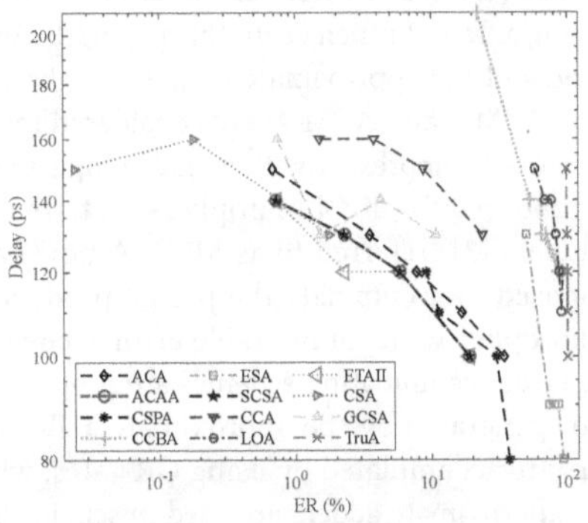


(b) ER vs. Delay (delay-optimized)

Figure 1: **A comparison of optimized delay for the approximate 16-bit adders using different error metrics. The parameter $k$ for LOA and TruA ranges from 3 to 9 from left to right, from 8 down to 3 for ESA and ACA, and from 6 down to 3 for the other adders from left to right. For CCBA, the configurations with the smallest PDPs are chosen for a similar MRED.**

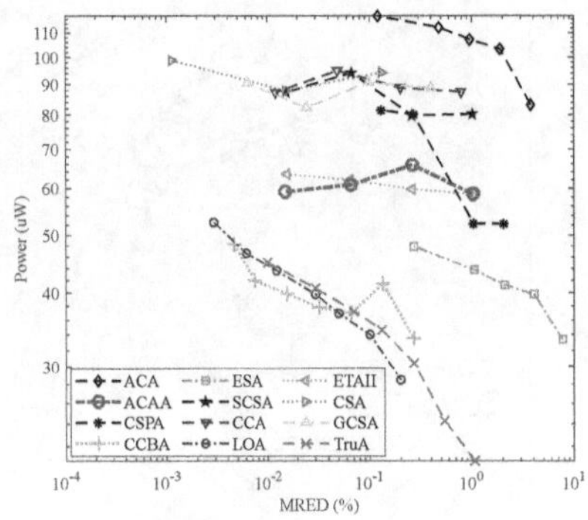


(a) MRED vs. Power (area-optimized)

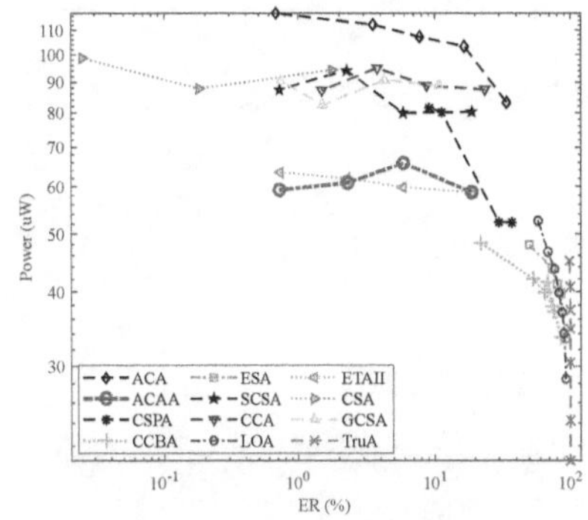


(b) ER vs. Power (area-optimized)

Figure 2: **A comparison of power for the area-optimized approximate 16-bit adders using different error metrics.**

As shown in Fig. 3, CCBA, LOA and TruA have smaller PDPs than the other designs for a similar MRED; ACA and CCA have larger PDPs. ETAII, SCSA, CSPA and GCSA show moderate PDPs. ESA has a rather small PDP, but a considerably larger ER and MRED. With the highest ERs, CCBA, LOA and TruA show the smallest PDPs for a moderate MRED. In fact, these approximate adders show a decent tradeoff in ED and hardware efficiency. In particular, they are useful in applications in which ER is not important. Consequently, truncation can be used to design a hardware-efficient approximate adder (albeit with a high ER). On the other hand, the carry select scheme is more effective for an approximate adder design to achieve a high accuracy.

**Table 1: Summary of approximate adders.**

| Adder | ER | ED | speed (delay-optimized) | power (area-optimized) | PDP |
|---|---|---|---|---|---|
| ACA | | high | | high | high |
| ESA | high | high | high | low | low |
| ETAII | | | | | |
| ACAA | | | | | |
| SCSA | | | | | |
| CSA | low | low | | | |
| CSPA | | high | high | | |
| CCA | | | low | | |
| GCSA | | | | | |
| CCBA | high | low | | low | low |
| LOA | high | low | | low | low |
| TruA | high | | | low | low |

Table 1 summarizes the different approximate adders, with their advantages and disadvantages highlighted (i.e., the metrics with moderate values are not shown). The MRED and NMED of approximate adders are represented by ED in the table.

## 4 APPROXIMATE MULTIPLIERS

Multiplication is implemented by partial product generation, accumulation and a final addition. A partial product is usually generated by an AND gate. The most common partial product accumulation structures are the Wallace and Dadda trees and the carry-save adder array. In a Wallace tree, the FAs (or half adders (HAs)) in each layer operate in parallel without carry propagation. Thus, for an $n \times n$ multiplier, the delay of the Wallace tree grows with $O(log(n))$. Also, the FAs in a Wallace tree can be considered to be (3:2) compressors and can be replaced by other counters or compressors (e.g. a (4:2) compressor) to further reduce the delay. The Dadda tree has a similar structure as the Wallace tree, but it uses as few adders as possible. In a carry-save adder array, the carry and sum signals generated by the FAs (or HAs) in a row are passed on to the FAs in the next row. FAs in a column operate in series. Hence the delay of an $n \times n$ carry-save adder array is approximately $O(n)$, longer than that of a Wallace tree. Five main methodologies are used for approximating an unsigned multiplier: approximation in generating the partial

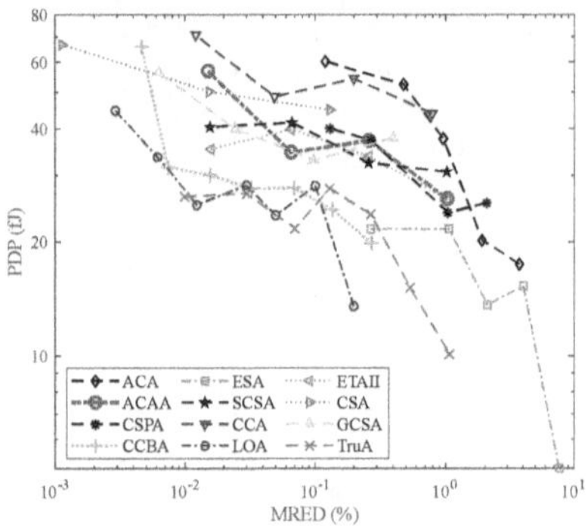


(a) MRED vs. PDP (delay-optimized)

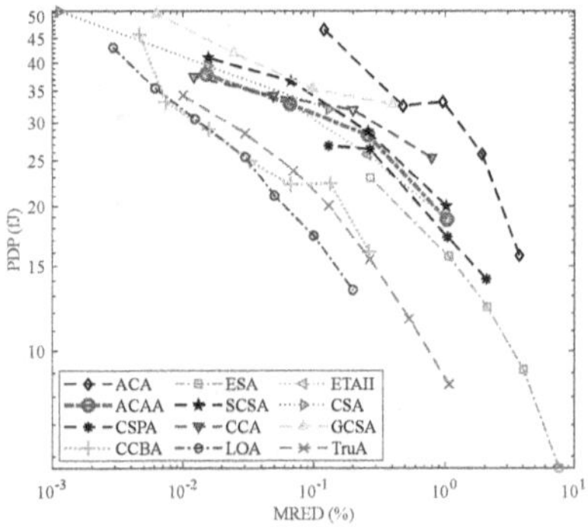


(b) MRED vs. PDP (area-optimized)

Figure 3: **A comparison of power-delay product (PDP) and MRED for the approximate 16-bit adders.**

products, approximation (including truncation) in the partial product tree, using approximate adders, counters or compressors in the partial product tree, using logarithmic approximation, and using an automated process such as a genetic programming method.

## 4.1 Review

*4.1.1 Approximation in Generating Partial Products.* In [15], the accurate $2 \times 2$ multiplication result "1001" is simplified to "111" to save one output bit when both the inputs are "11", which results in an approximate $2 \times 2$ multiplier. Larger approximate multipliers are then designed by using the approximate $2 \times 2$ multiplier, which is referred to as the underdesigned multiplier (UDM). UDM introduces an error when generating the partial products, however the accumulation remains accurate.

*4.1.2 Approximation in the Partial Product Tree.* The broken-array multiplier (BAM) omits some carry-save adders in an array multiplier in both the horizontal and vertical directions [23]. A more straightforward approach is to truncate some LSBs on the input operands and, thus, a smaller multiplier is used to process the remaining most significant bits (MSBs). This truncated multiplier (TruM) will be considered as a baseline design. In [35], partial product perforation is applied to different multiplier structures (PPAM), which ignores several consecutive rows of partial products (not necessarily starting from the LSB). The error tolerant multiplier (ETM) consists of a multiplication section and a non-multiplication section [16]. A control block is used to decide if the multiplication section is to be activated to multiply the LSBs or the MSBs. In the static segment multiplier (SSM), no approximation is applied to the LSBs; either the MSBs or the LSBs of the operands are accurately multiplied depending on whether its MSBs are all zeros [30]. In [4], a bit-width aware approximate multiplication and a carry-in prediction scheme are used to construct an approximate Wallace tree multiplier (AWTM).

*4.1.3 Using Approximate Counters or Compressors in the Partial Product Tree.* An approximate (4:2) counter is proposed for an inaccurate $4 \times 4$ Wallace multiplier [19]. The carry and sum are approximated as "10" for "100" in the approximate counter when all input signals are "1." The inaccurate $4 \times 4$ multiplier is then used to construct a larger multiplier that is referred to as ICM. In [27], two approximate (4:2) compressor designs are used in a Dadda multiplier with four different schemes. In this paper, the more accurate schemes 3 and 4 of the approximate compressor based multiplier (referred to as ACM-3 and ACM-4) are considered for comparison. An approximate 4:2 compressor with encoded inputs and improved accuracy is proposed for $4 \times 4$ multipliers that are used to build larger multipliers [3] (referred to as M16). A novel approximate adder is proposed to accumulate the partial products for the approximate multiplier with configurable error recovery [12]. Two approximate error accumulation schemes are proposed to compensate the error generated by the approximate adder. In scheme 1 (AM1), errors are accumulated by using OR gates, while both OR gates and the approximate adders are used in scheme 2 (AM2). The truncation of half LSBs in the partial products in AM1 and AM2 results in TAM1 and TAM2, respectively. In [31], approximate half adders, full adders and 4:2 compressors are utilized to accumulate the altered partial products; it is denoted as the USask design.

*4.1.4 Using Logarithmic Approximation.* By using the logarithm and anti-logarithm approximations of a binary number, [25] proposes a logarithmic multiplier (LM) implemented by shifting and addition; it is the baseline design for LMs. The accuracy of a LM is improved in [21] by using a set-one-adder (SOA) and in [2] by using an improved algorithm with exact and approximate adders (ILM-EA and ILM-AA).

*4.1.5 Using an Automated Process.* In [28], 471 $8 \times 8$ approximate multipliers are evolved by a multi-objective Cartesian genetic programming method, which are then used to construct $16 \times 16$ approximate multipliers [29] (i.e., BrnoA1, BrnoA2, BrnoA3 and BrnoA4 for different construction methods).

## 4.2 Evaluation

Monte Carlo simulation results for $16 \times 16$ multipliers show that most of the approximate designs result in large ERs close to 100%. However, ICM has a low ER of 5.45%; some configurations of BrnoA1, BrnoA2, BrnoA3 and BrnoA4 also show lower ERs than the other designs. Thus, MRED, NMED, delay (for delay-optimized synthesis), power (for area-optimized synthesis) and PDP (for both delay- and area-optimized syntheses) are jointly considered to evaluate the approximate multipliers, as shown in Figs. 4, 5 and 6.

Fig. 4 shows that BrnoA1 is the most accurate design with very small values of MRED and NMED because only one approximate $8 \times 8$ approximate multiplier is used to construct a $16 \times 16$ BrnoA1.

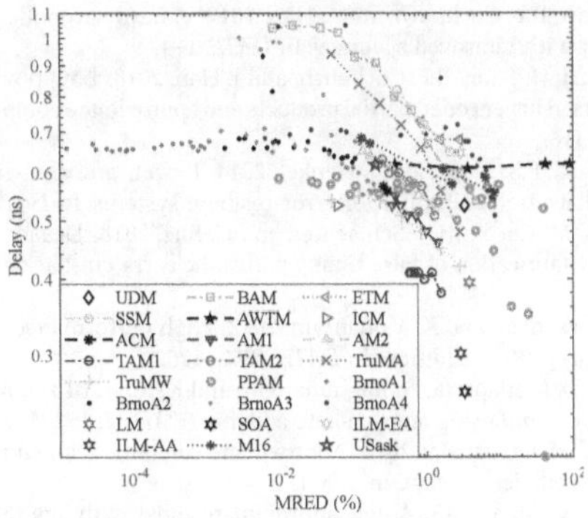


(a) MRED vs. Delay (delay-optimized)

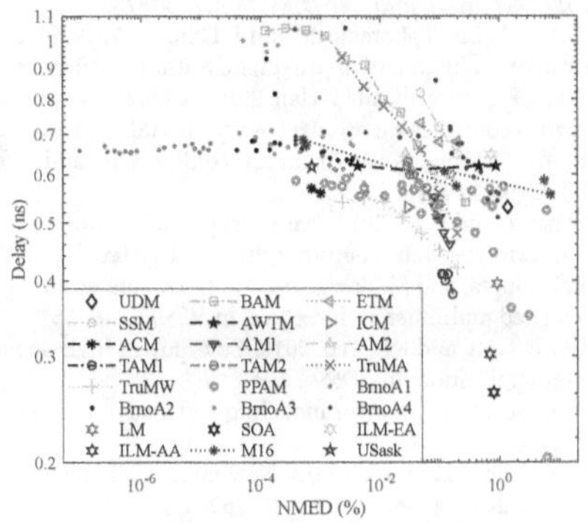


(b) NMED vs. Delay (delay-optimized)

Figure 4: **A comparison of optimized delay for the approximate 16×16 multipliers using different error metrics. The number of truncated LSBs for TruMA and TruMW is from 2 to 8 from left to right, and from 11 to 22 for BAM. The number of MSBs used for error compensation is from 16 to 10 for AM1, AM2, TAM1 and TAM2. The size of the accurate sub-multiplier is from 10 to 8 for ETM and SSM. The mode number is from 4 to 1 for AWTM, from 4 to 3 for ACM, and from 1 to 6 for M16. For BrnoA1, BrnoA2, BrnoA3 and BrnoA4, the configurations with the smallest PDPs are shown for a specific MRED, selected from 500 configurations for each design.**

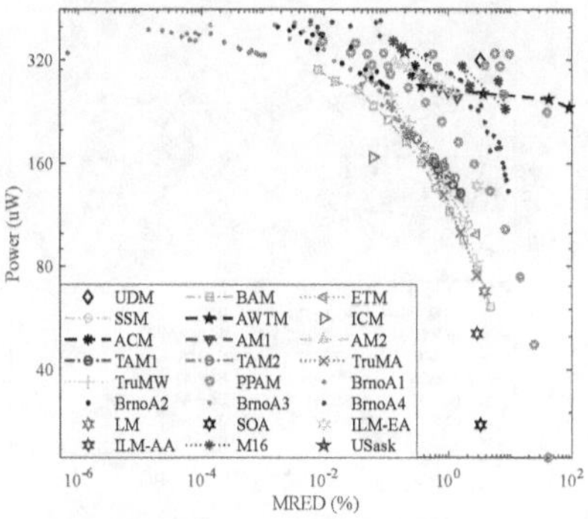


(a) MRED vs. Power (area-optimized)

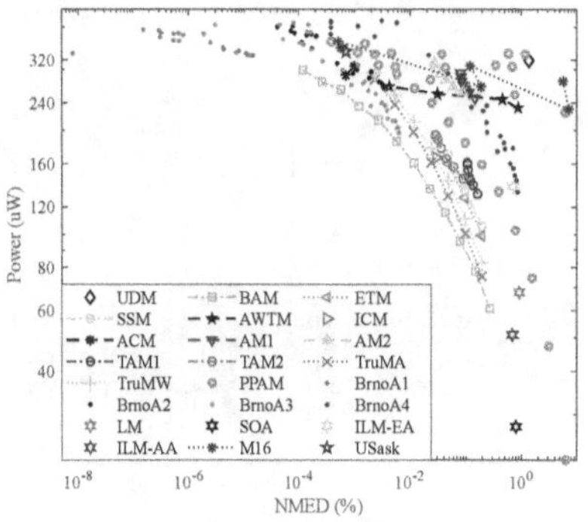


(b) NMED vs. Power (area-optimized)

Figure 5: **A comparison of power for the area-optimized approximate 16 × 16 multipliers considering MRED and NMED.**

ICM and the truncated Wallace multiplier (TruMW) are faster than the other designs for a low MRED and NMED, whereas TAM1, ILM-AA, SOA, PPAM are the fastest while the MRED and NMED are higher. AM1 is also very fast; however, BAM, SSM, ETM and the truncated array multiplier (TruMA) are relatively slow. As shown in Fig. 5, BAM is the most power-efficient followed by TruMA and BrnoA3, while UDM, AM1, AM2, M16 and BrnoA4 are relatively power-hungry. The power dissipation of TAM1 and TAM2 is in the medium range.

As shown in the delay-optimized results in Fig. 6(a), TAM1, BrnoA2 and BrnoA3 have smaller PDPs than other approximate designs (including TruMW) for a similar MRED. For the area-optimized results in Fig. 6(b), ICM, TAM1, TAM2 and BrnoA3 show smaller PDPs than other designs (including TruMA).

A summary of the accuracy and circuit characteristics for the approximate multipliers is shown in Table 2. Truncation is an effective scheme for a high-speed operation with a relatively low PDP. By using the logarithmic approximation, a multiplier tends to be

**Table 2: Summary of approximate multipliers.**

| Multiplier | MRED | NMED | speed (delay-optimized) | power (area-optimized) | PDP |
|---|---|---|---|---|---|
| UDM | high | high | | high | high |
| BAM | | | low | low | |
| PPAM | | | | | |
| ETM | | | low | | |
| SSM | | | low | | |
| AWTM | | | | | |
| ICM | low | | | | |
| ACM | | low | | high | |
| M16 | | | | high | high |
| AM1 | | | | high | |
| AM2 | | | | high | |
| TAM1 | | | high | | low |
| TAM2 | | | | | |
| USask | | low | | high | high |
| BrnoA1 | low | low | | high | |
| BrnoA2 | | | | | |
| BrnoA3 | | | | | |
| BrnoA4 | | | | | |
| LM | high | high | high | low | |
| SOA | high | high | high | low | low |
| ILM-EA | high | high | | | |
| ILM-AA | high | high | high | low | low |
| TruMA | | | | | low |
| TruMW | | | high | | |

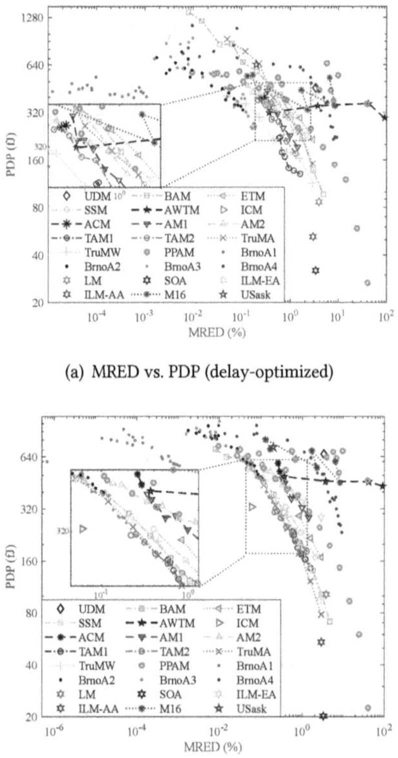


(a) MRED vs. PDP (delay-optimized)

(b) MRED vs. PDP (area-optimized)

Figure 6: **A comparison of power-delay product and MRED for the approximate** $16 \times 16$ **unsigned multipliers.**

hardware-efficient but with relatively low accuracy. The approximate multipliers designed using the automated process perform well when a high accuracy is required.

# 5 CONCLUSION

In this paper, designs of approximate adders and multipliers are evaluated in terms of accuracy and circuit characteristics. Specifically, the performance and power consumption are compared by obtaining the synthesis results under delay and area constraints.

The simulation results show that truncation is an effective scheme to improve the hardware efficiency of an arithmetic circuit. Most of the approximate adders in the literature are designed for a high-speed and low ER (e.g., 0.02% for CSA-5) by cutting off the carry propagation chain. A truncated adder has a high ER close to 100%; however, it has a lower power dissipation and lower PDP than most approximate designs at a similar MRED (except for LOA and CCBA). The performance (or speed) of a truncated adder is not as high as some approximate adders.

Unlike the adder, a truncated Wallace multiplier is faster than most approximate multipliers (except for ICM and TAM1), but with a higher power at a similar MRED. For a similar accuracy, BAM and BrnoA3 consume less power than a truncated multiplier. In terms of PDP, TAM1, TAM2, ICM, BrnoA2 and BrnoA3 have smaller values than a truncated multiplier for a given MRED.

# REFERENCES

[1] H. Amrouch, B. Khaleghi, and A. Gerstlauer. 2017. Towards aging-induced approximations. In *DAC*. 1–6.

[2] M.S. Ansari, B.F. Cockburn, and J. Han. 2019. A hardware-efficient logarithmic multiplier with improved accuracy. In *DATE*. 1–4.

[3] M.S. Ansari, H. Jiang, B.F. Cockburn, and J. Han. 2018. Low-power approximate multipliers using encoded partial products and approximate compressors. *JETCAS* 8, 3, 404–416.

[4] K. Bhardwaj, P.S. Mane, and J. Henkel. 2014. Power- and area-efficient approximate Wallace tree multiplier for error-resilient systems. In *ISQED*. 263–269.

[5] V. Camus, M. Cacciotti, J. Schlachter, and C. Enz. 2018. Design of approximate circuits by fabrication of false timing paths: the carry cut-back adder. *JETCAS* 8, 4, 746–757.

[6] Kai D., P. Varman, and K. Mohanram. 2012. High performance reliable variable latency carry select addition. In *DATE*. 1257–1262.

[7] V. Gupta, D. Mohapatra, A. Raghunathan, and K. Roy. 2013. Low-power digital signal processing using approximate adders. *TCAD* 32, 1, 124–137.

[8] J. Han and M. Orshansky. 2013. Approximate computing: an emerging paradigm for energy-efficient design. In *ETS*. 1–6.

[9] J. Hu and W. Qian. 2015. A new approximate adder with low relative error and correct sign calculation. In *DATE*. 1449–1454.

[10] G.B. Huang, Q.Y. Zhu, and C.K. Siew. 2006. Real-time learning capability of neural networks. *IEEE Trans. Neural Networks* 17, 4, 863–878.

[11] H. Jiang, C. Liu, L. Liu, F. Lombardi, and J. Han. 2017. A review, classification, and comparative evaluation of approximate arithmetic circuits. *JETC* 13, 4, 60.

[12] H. Jiang, C. Liu, F. Lombardi, and J. Han. 2019. Low-power approximate unsigned multipliers with configurable error recovery. *TCASI* 66, 1, 189–202.

[13] A.B. Kahng and S. Kang. 2012. Accuracy-configurable adder for approximate arithmetic designs. In *DAC*. 820–825.

[14] Y. Kim, Y. Zhang, and P. Li. 2013. An energy efficient approximate adder with carry skip for error resilient neuromorphic VLSI systems. In *ICCAD*. 130–137.

[15] P. Kulkarni, P. Gupta, and M. Ercegovac. 2011. Trading accuracy for power with an underdesigned multiplier architecture. In *VLSID*. 346–351.

[16] K.Y. Kyaw, W.L. Goh, and K.S. Yeo. 2010. Low-power high-speed multiplier for error-tolerant application. In *EDSSC*. 1–4.

[17] L. Li and H. Zhou. 2014. On error modeling and analysis of approximate adders. In *ICCAD*. 511–518.

[18] J. Liang, J. Han, and F. Lombardi. 2013. New metrics for the reliability of approximate and probabilistic adders. *TC* 62, 9, 1760–1771.

[19] C. Lin and I. Lin. 2013. High accuracy approximate multiplier with error correction. In *ICCD*. 33–38.

[20] I. Lin, Y. Yang, and C. Lin. 2015. High-performance low-power carry speculative addition with variable latency. *TVLSI* 23, 9, 1591–1603.

[21] W. Liu, J. Xu, D. Wang, C. Wang, P. Montuschi, and F. Lombardi. 2018. Design and evaluation of approximate logarithmic multipliers for low power error-tolerant applications. *TCASI* 65, 9, 2856–2868.

[22] S.L. Lu. 2004. Speeding up processing with approximation circuits. *Computer* 37, 3, 67–73.

[23] H.R. Mahdiani, A. Ahmadi, S.M. Fakhraie, and C. Lucas. 2010. Bio-inspired imprecise computational blocks for efficient VLSI implementation of soft-computing applications. *TCASI* 57, 4, 850–862.

[24] J. Miao, K. He, A. Gerstlauer, and M. Orshansky. 2012. Modeling and synthesis of quality-energy optimal approximate adders. In *ICCAD*. 728–735.

[25] J.N. Mitchell. 1962. Computer multiplication and division using binary logarithms. *IRE Trans. Electronic Computers* 4, 512–517.

[26] D. Mohapatra, V.K. Chippa, A Raghunathan, and K. Roy. 2011. Design of voltage-scalable meta-functions for approximate computing. In *DATE*. 1–6.

[27] A. Momeni, J. Han, P. Montuschi, and F. Lombardi. 2015. Design and analysis of approximate compressors for multiplication. *TC* 64, 4, 984–994.

[28] V. Mrazek, R. Hrbacek, Z. Vasicek, and L. Sekanina. 2017. EvoApprox8b: Library of approximate adders and multipliers for circuit design and benchmarking of approximation methods. In *DATE*. 258–261.

[29] V. Mrazek, Z. Vasicek, L. Sekanina, H. Jiang, and J. Han. 2018. Scalable construction of approximate multipliers with formally guaranteed worst case error. *TVLSI* 99, 2572–2576.

[30] S. Narayanamoorthy, H.A. Moghaddam, Z. Liu, T. Park, and N.S. Kim. 2015. Energy-efficient approximate multiplication for digital signal processing and classification applications. *TVLSI* 23, 6, 1180–1184.

[31] S. Venkatachalam and S.B. Ko. 2017. Design of power and area efficient approximate multipliers. *TVLSI* 25, 5, 1782–1786.

[32] A.K. Verma, P. Brisk, and P. Ienne. 2008. Variable latency speculative addition: a new paradigm for arithmetic circuit design. In *DATE*. 1250–1255.

[33] Z. Yang, A. Jain, J. Liang, J. Han, and F. Lombardi. 2013. Approximate XOR/XNOR-based adders for inexact computing. In *IEEE-NANO*. 690–693.

[34] R. Ye, T. Wang, F. Yuan, R. Kumar, and Q. Xu. 2013. On reconfiguration-oriented approximate adder design and its application. In *ICCAD*. 48–54.

[35] G. Zervakis, K. Tsoumanis, S. Xydis, D. Soudris, and K. Pekmestzi. 2016. Design-efficient approximate multiplication circuits through partial product perforation. *TVLSI* 24, 10, 3105–3117.

[36] N. Zhu, W.L. Goh, and K.S. Yeo. 2009. An enhanced low-power high-speed adder for error-tolerant application. In *ISIC 2009*. 69–72.

# Approximate Communication Strategies for Energy-Efficient and High Performance NoC: Opportunities and Challenges

Md Farhadur Reza
farhadurreza@vt.edu
Department of Electrical & Computer Engineering
Virginia Polytechnic Institute and State University
Blacksburg, VA

Paul Ampadu
ampadu@vt.edu
Department of Electrical & Computer Engineering
Virginia Polytechnic Institute and State University
Blacksburg, VA

## ABSTRACT

With the advancement and miniaturization of transistor technology, hundreds of cores can be integrated on a single chip. Network-on-Chips (NoCs) are the *de facto* on-chip communication fabrics for multi/many core systems because of their benefits over the traditional bus in terms of scalability, parallelism, and power efficiency. However, relative power consumption of NoC has been increasing with the increase in the number of cores on a chip, as communication costs much more time and energy than that of computation. Approximating computing concept can be applied in the NoC to reduce power consumption by approximating the communication data of emerging data-intensive applications, such as machine learning and big data analytics, that can tolerate errors. In this paper, we present an architecture for NoC approximation, and also provide preliminary results (which shows significant improvement) to support the importance of approximate communication solution for energy-efficient and high-performance NoC. Then we present various approximate communication solutions for reducing data movement in NoC. Finally, we discuss about the challenges and software and hardware overheads to adapt approximate technique in NoC, and also provide tentative solutions to address those challenges.

## CCS CONCEPTS

• **Computer systems organization → Multicore architectures;** • **Networks → Network on chip;** • **Hardware → Network on chip.**

## KEYWORDS

Approximate Communication; Error Tolerance/Threshold; Accuracy; Energy Consumption; Networks-on-Chip (NoCs)

**ACM Reference Format:**

Md Farhadur Reza and Paul Ampadu. 2019. Approximate Communication Strategies for Energy-Efficient and High Performance NoC: Opportunities and Challenges. In *Great Lakes Symposium on VLSI 2019 (GLSVLSI '19), May 9–11, 2019, Tysons Corner, VA, USA.* ACM, New York, NY, USA, 6 pages. https://doi.org/10.1145/3299874.3319455


ACM ISBN 978-1-4503-6252-8/19/05...$15.00
https://doi.org/10.1145/3299874.3319455

## 1 INTRODUCTION

Multi-core systems are moving towards the integration of hundreds of cores on a single chip to accomplish emerging applications through low-power highly parallel computing. Network-on-Chips (NoCs) have been adopted as a viable solution to manage complex interconnection and provide energy efficient performance in multi/many core systems. For example, a multi-core architecture on NoC is illustrated in Figure 1 where heterogeneous processor tiles are placed in a 2D grid. Each tile contains a processor (with distinct computation power), its local cache, a slice of the shared last-level cache, and a router (configured with different communication capacity) for data and control transmission between the tiles via varying bandwidth links. In multi-core NoC architecture, data flows from L1 and L2-caches of one core to another core, core to memory controller for memory traffic, etc.

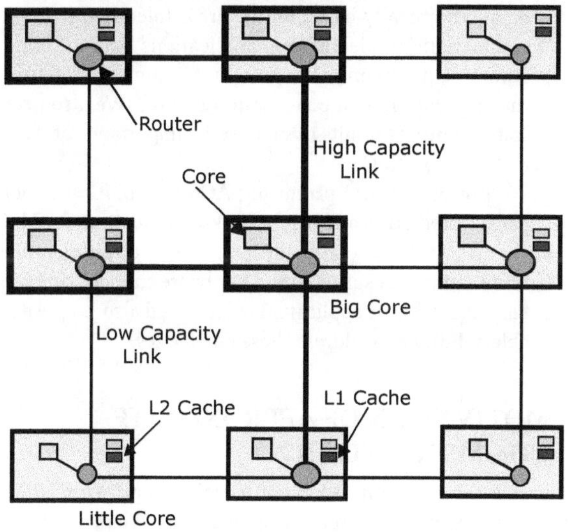


**Figure 1: Multi-Core NoC Architecture**

Computation has become more energy-efficient with the continued scaling of transistors. Billions of transistors can now be integrated on a single chip. However, interconnection energy efficiency/delay has not been scaled in the same way as that of transistor. For example, from 90*nm* to 7*nm* transistor technology, interconnection energy efficiency has been scaled down by only 1.6*X* compared to 6*X* scaling down of transistors (computation) [7]. Because of this disparity, energy consumption in the on-chip systems is increasingly being dominated by the interconnection delay [3].

NoC power consumption has been steadily increasing with the increase in the number of cores that are integrated on the chip. Research has shown that NoC power consumption can reach up to 30% of the overall chip power [14, 23, 24]. This high NoC power consumption challenge has led to many development in NoC architecture, for example, router architecture enhancement, adaptive routing algorithms, power/thermal-aware designs, etc.

Approximation, the focus of this paper, can reduce the communication workload to get low-power and high-throughput NoC. As the destination node does not need fully accurate data for computation, it presents an opportunity to reduce the data movement through NoC. There have been few works that focus on approximate communication (AComm) techniques [5, 8, 9, 25] for improving the communication efficiency in multi/many core systems. [5] defines the AComm as the application of approximate computing techniques to reduce the amount of communication between processing elements in large-scale parallel systems like multi/many core architectures. They explore the potential benefits of AComm for tackling the communication bottleneck issues in parallel multi-core systems by surveying three promising techniques : compression, relaxed synchronization, and value prediction.

The contributions of this paper are outlined below.

- We first present the motivation of AComm in NoC. Then we present NoC design challenges, and propose AComm technique to address those NoC challenges.
- We are presenting AComm technique to approximate the data dynamically based on the error tolerance (ET) of the applications, while different applications have different accuracy requirements. We present AComm architecture for the application of approximation in NoC. We also provide some empirical results to support the importance of AComm technique in NoC.
- We present several promising AComm solutions, such as packet prediction and error checking reduction, for NoC.
- We discuss the several challenges, such as error tolerance determination and software and hardware support, of AComm techniques for its application in NoC, and also propose probable solutions to address those challenges.

## 2 MOTIVATION OF APPROXIMATE COMMUNICATION

We discuss the communication bottleneck in multi-core NoC and error resiliency of data-intensive applications. We present the opportunity of AComm to improve the energy-efficiency and performance of NoC.

### 2.1 Communication Bottleneck

Communication is the major bottleneck to achieve high-parallelism in large-scale systems with many compute nodes (processing cores). Communication takes relatively more time compared to computation with the increase of the number of processing cores in the systems [3, 21]. Communication also consumes more energy compared to computation [3, 21, 28]. Furthermore, the error control techniques introduce more communication overhead and higher power consumption as were shown in [4, 12]. Therefore, it is essential to reduce the volume of data communication for energy-efficient and high-performance NoC.

### 2.2 Error Tolerance of Applications

Many emerging data intensive applications, such as machine learning (ML), pattern-recognition, image processing, and big data analytics, can tolerate errors with acceptable accuracies [5, 19, 27]. To extract the benefits out of this error resilient nature of these applications, approximate computing has emerged as an attractive computing technique by trading off computation accuracy for benefits in both performance and energy efficiency. We can apply the same concept of approximate computing in the communication by approximating the communication data, between compute nodes, needed for computation. For example, we can reduce the communication data volume to exploit the lower accuracy requirements of the data-intensive applications. ET is defined as the difference between actual and approximated data that is within (less than) that ET (error tolerance and error threshold used interchangeably in the paper). For example, for 10% ET, the data 32 as the approximate data of accurate data 35 will be accepted (as the difference of 3 is within the 10% ET). Approximation can reduce the communication workload to get low-power and high-throughput NoC. Some of the approximation techniques to improve the energy-efficiency and performance are: value prediction, data-protection reduction, and compressing data. As the destination node does not need fully accurate data for computation, it presents an opportunity to reduce the data movement through NoC.

## 3 NOC DESIGN CHALLENGES AND APPROXIMATE COMMUNICATION OPPORTUNITY

Energy-efficiency and high-performance are the major challenges in multi/many core NoC. Both of the challenges are discussed in detail in the following sections.

### 3.1 Energy Efficiency

Relative power consumption of NoC has been increasing with the increase in the number of cores in a chip, e.g., NoC consumes 36% of total chip power in 16-tile MIT Raw [23]. Power and temperature density, the dissipation by the per unit of area of chip, becomes important design factors in deep-submicron technologies. Power and thermal hotspots bring significant challenges in chip reliability, performance, cooling costs, and leakage power. Power consumption and temperature dissipation are directly proportional, for example, leakage power is exponentially related to temperature. Temperature of a node also affects (increases) by the neighbor active nodes. Thermal hot spots accelerate failure mechanisms such as electromigration, stress migration, and dielectric breakdown, which can cause permanent device failures [15]. High temperature also degrades performance, as the effective operating speed of devices decreases with increasing temperature. Therefore, power consumption becomes a critical issue in many-core on-chip networks.

As a significant power and thermal source, NoC resources can be configured dynamically to decrease pressure on the power and thermal budgets. Approximation can help this configuration process by reducing data movement based on the ET of the applications.

## 3.2 High Performance

As multi-core can provide multithreaded performance, performance can be increased indefinitely by increasing the number of cores theoretically. However, interconnection between cores imposes a limit on performance gain from multi-core systems [5, 7]. With the increase in number of cores, communication latency between distant nodes increases. Computational parallelism is hampered in multi-core systems as computation can be halted at a core by the data-dependent communication from the remote core or memory.

By approximating the packets in NoC, communication volume and/or number of communications can be reduced, and this will improve the packet latency. Processing elements (cores) can perform their computation quickly if the communication time of the data needed for computation reduces. Therefore, AComm can improve the computation speed and so can improve the parallelism in the system.

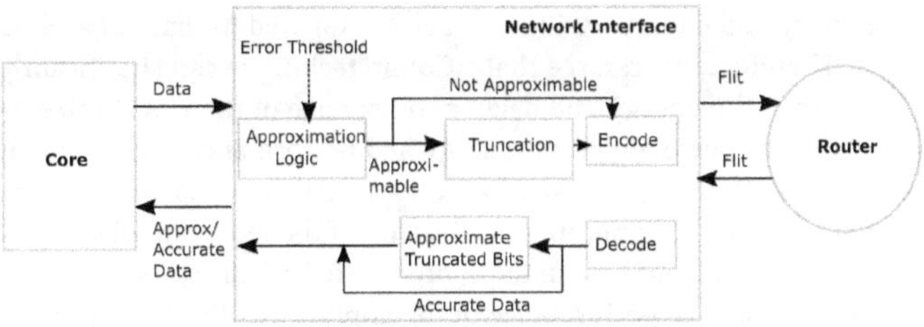


Figure 2: Approximate NoC Architecture

# 4 APPROXIMATE COMMUNICATION ARCHITECTURE

Figure 2 shows an approximate NoC architecture. We are presenting AComm technique to approximate the data dynamically based on the ET of the applications, while different applications have different accuracy requirements. Approximation is done in the network interface (NI) of the NoC, as NI is responsible for packetization/depacketization of data, flit fragmentation/ assembly for flow control, transmission error control, and other functions in NoC. NI-level approximation implementation makes the NoC applicable for any kind of processing elements (soft or hard block) in the multi/many core architectures, as modification (e.g., cache architecture) is not needed in processing elements. Approximation logic in NI finds out whether data packet can be approximated or not, based on the annotation of the code sections [13, 20] of packet communication. Approximation flag (in approximation logic) is used to identify whether the data packet is approximable (can be approximated) or the data needs full accuracy. Based on the annotation and ET of an application, we can approximate the communication data by truncating the data-bits to reduce data movement among cores. Data truncation technique has been adapted in this work for approximation in the NoC. Data truncation technique removes part of packet based on the accuracy requirements of applications. At the destination, NI will approximate the truncated bits before sending the packet to the processing elements. Finally, as approximation/truncation reduces data movement and resource utilization in the NoC, we can apply dynamic voltage and frequency scaling (DVFS) to the links and routers to improve the energy-efficiency of NoC. Voltage-levels of the router and links can be reduced at run-time based on the approximation of data packets, and this reduces communication energy consumption and improves the energy-efficiency of NoC. DVFS application based on the approximation can significantly reduce the power and thermal density, which are the major challenges of multi-core architectures. The operation flow Chart of the proposed AComm technique is shown in Figure 3.

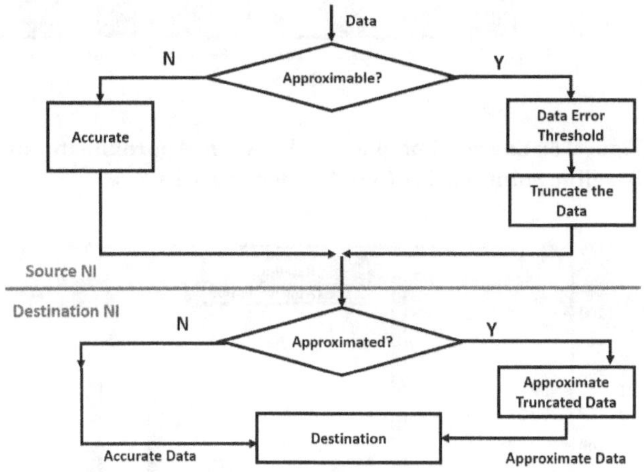


Figure 3: Flow Chart of Approximate Communication

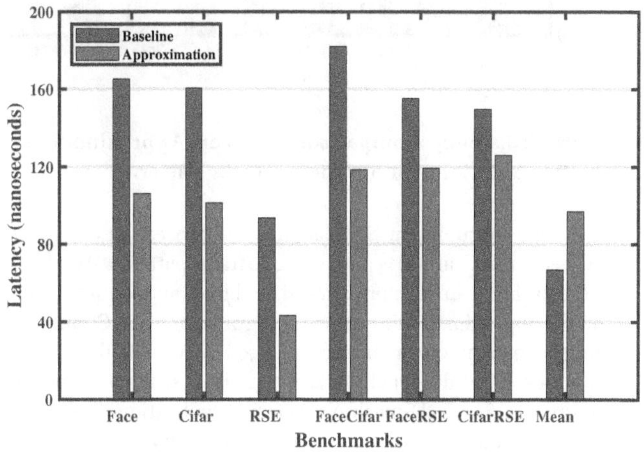


Figure 4: Latency Comparison between Approximate and Baseline Solutions for COSMIC Benchmarks

We simulate the proposed architecture using Garnet [1] on-chip network in gem5 platform [6]. Garnet/gem5 simulation configurations include: instruction set architecture = ALPHA , interconnect Frequency = 1GHz, no. of virtual networks (VN) = 3, no. of virtual channels (VC) per VN = 4, no. of buffers per VC = 4 and XY-routing [11]. DSENT [22] tool is integrated with gem5 to evaluate

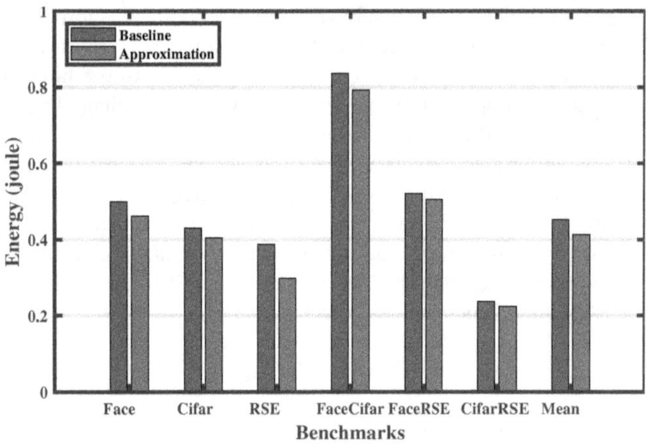


**Figure 5: Energy Comparison between Approximate and Baseline Solutions for COSMIC Benchmarks**

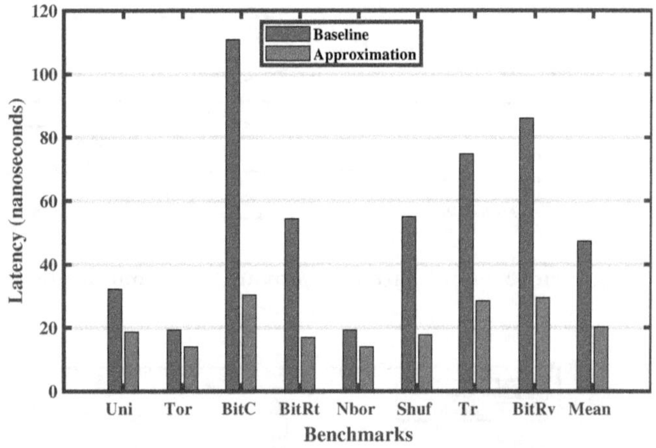


**Figure 6: Latency Comparison between Approximate and Baseline Solutions for Synthetic Traffic Patterns**

the energy consumption. Simulations were carried out using COSMIC benchmark suite [26] and synthetic traffic patterns. We assume all the packets can be approximated, and have applied 50% truncation for approximation to show the significance of AComm. The energy consumption and latency are used to evaluate the AComm technique. COSMIC benchmarks is simulated using 64-cores and routers in a $8 \times 8$ 2D-mesh NoC. Three applications from COSMIC are mapped in our simulations: face recognition, cifar, and reed-solomon code encoder (RS-Encoder). Face recognition (face), cifar, and RS-Encoder (RSE) application have 33, 33, and 141 tasks, respectively. We also mix the applications to simulate multiple applications in NoC. As shown in Figure 4 and 5, AComm improves latency and energy by 50% and 10% compared to that of baseline, because of the reduction of the data movement through approximation. Eight synthetic traffic patterns are simulated using 16-cores and routers in a $4 \times 4$ 2D-mesh NoC. Traffic patterns are: Uniform Random (Uni), Tornado (Tor), Bit-complement (BitC), Bit Rotation (BitRt), Neighbor (Nbor), Shuffle (Shuf), Transpose (Tr), and Bit

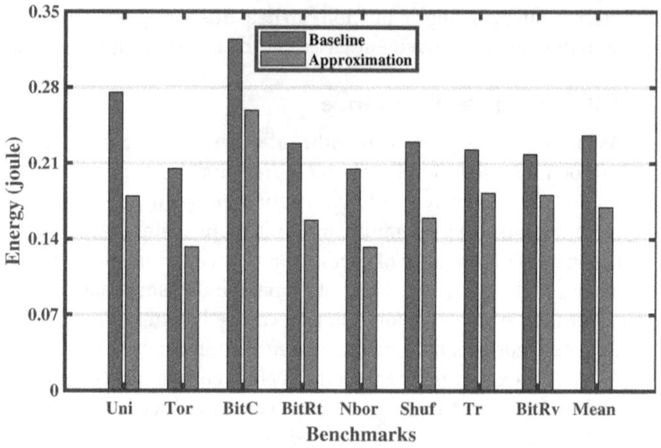


**Figure 7: Energy Comparison between Approximate and Baseline Solutions for Synthetic Traffic Patterns**

Reverse (BitRv). As shown in Figure 6 and 7, AComm improves latency and energy by 130% and 40% compared to that of baseline.

Therefore, we can see that AComm technique can significantly improve the energy and delay performance of the NoC, if the application is error-tolerant. Energy and performance improvement varies with the approximation ratio, which depends on the error-tolerance of the application(s). Because of the reduction of the data movement, throughput in the approximate NoC drops, but this may not hamper the performance of the application. But the output of the application needs to be within the ET to meet the accuracy requirements of the application. The output quality of an application can be measured by running the application separately on a host machine by cutting-off (truncating) the least significant bits of the variables in the approximable code sections (responsible for communication), and then we can compare the quality of approximate output and actual output of the application.

# 5 APPROXIMATE COMMUNICATION SOLUTIONS AND OPPORTUNITIES

We highlight several important AComm techniques for NoC.

## 5.1 Packet Prediction

Different packets in NoC face different latency because of shared resources of NoC. Some packets may face more congestion, and then can further introduce congestion for other packets. We can identify the packets that are introducing congestion in the NoC, and then predict those packets at the destination to reduce the number of communication packets and so to minimize congestion in NoC. Because of the packet prediction, core can continue their computation without waiting for the data to arrive from remote core or memory controller. For example, on a cache miss, core can predict the load value instead of fetching data from memory, which reduces the high cost of accessing memory [18]. This packet prediction technique can significantly reduce data movement in NoC, and can significantly increase parallelism in the NoC while reducing communication power consumption. ML can help to predict the packets (needed for computation) at the computing node. Here the advantage is that approximate packet prediction (for error tolerant applications) does not need the recovery mechanism for misprediction. The authors in [25] propose an approximation-based dynamic traffic regulation technique to reduce congestion in NoC. This technique drops a fraction of packet data before they are injected into network, based on the error resilience of application, and predicts the lost data in packet after being received in the destination node.

## 5.2 Data Approximation with Compression

Based on the ET, data can be approximated by approximating the precise value. Approximate pattern can be computed by calculating the allowed deviation from the precise values. Furthermore, data compression technique can be used in combination with the approximation to further compress the data patterns into more compact bits before they are stored or transmitted. Compression methods have been used to reduce data movement for high-performance and/or low-power NoC [8, 10, 16]. Frequent-pattern compression [2] and dictionary-based compression [16] are the state-of-the-art compression mechanisms. Compression reduces network traffic, benefits both latency and power. Compression increases the effective bandwidth of the links and routers of NoC. After the packet reaches the destination NI, the packet needs to be decompressed for the destination processing element. So, the compression mechanism needs both compressor and decompressor modules in every node, NI, of the NoC. Therefore, the compression techniques incurs additional latency and hardware overhead for its adaptation in NoC. The authors in [8] propose a hardware data approximation framework, namely Approx-NoC, with an online data error control mechanism for high performance NoCs. Approx-NoC reduces the transmission of approximately similar data in the NoC by delivering approximated versions of precise data using state-of-the-art compression mechanisms. [16] applies compression at run-time on the congested paths only if the compression improves NoC performance.

By approximating the cache, we can reduce both data storage and data movement in NoC. For example, by compressing the cache, we can store more data in the same cache size, which improves the memory system performance. The authors in [10] proposes cache compression mechanism, besides NI compression. As shown in [10], cache compression provides on an average 21% reduction in network latency and 7% reduction in power consumption due to the reduction in the communication. However, to apply the cache approximation in the multi-core architecture, cache banks in the IP block (e.g., core) need to be modified, which is not possible for hard IP blocks. Approximation (e.g. compression) in the NI, as proposed in this paper, does not require any modification in the cache banks. So, the NI approximation is applicable for any on-chip systems.

## 5.3 Error Detection and Correction Reduction

Error correction introduces additional checking to check the correctness of the packets in the destination. If there is any bit-error found in the output, then the source needs to resend the packet again to destination. This retransmission incurs additional energy consumption. Error checking requirements can be reduced for the applications that can tolerate errors. By truncating the data bits based on the ET requirements of applications, we can reduce the probability of re-transmission because of less number of error checking in the destinations.

In packet transmission, we can have both integer and floating-point packets based on the nature of application. An integer value has higher precision requirement than that of floating point value. That means we need to protect more bits of integer than that of floating point value. For example, to achieve 10% data ET for absolute data value 10, we need to protect 31 MSBs and 13 MSBs for integer and floating-point values, respectively. However, we can convert integer packet to floating point packet to reduce the error detection/correction length. This will reduce the error checking length in the destination and will result in less number of retransmission requirement due to errors. In the floating point data, as shown in Figure 8, 1-bit sign and 8-bits exponent are the critical information. Critical bits needs to be protected to maintain the quality of approximation. Other bits of the packet can be approximated based on the ET requirements of the application. We can truncate a part of the lower significant bits (LSBs) while protecting a part of most significant bits (MSBs). However, data packet conversion is needed in the destination. [9] uses an AComm approach, which reduces the probability of retransmission by reducing the number of protected bits checking for correctness at the destination, based on the error resiliency of the application.

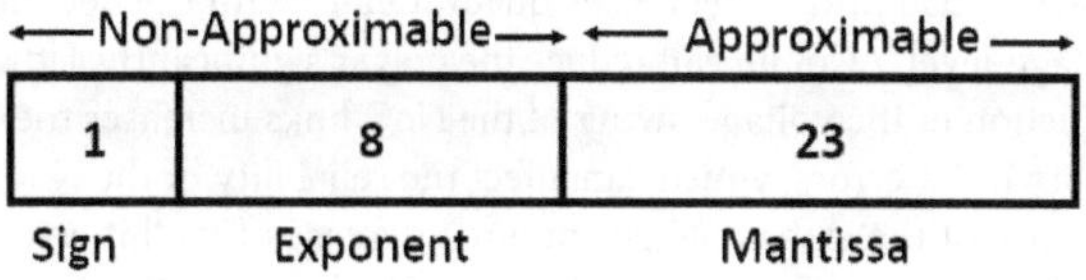


**Figure 8: Floating Point Data Approximation**

# 6 CHALLENGES OF APPROXIMATE COMMUNICATION

Approximate techniques need to overcome following challenges for its effective application in NoC.

## 6.1 Determination of Error Tolerance of Application

One major challenge in AComm is to determine the error tolerance (ET) requirement of an application. ET is the maximum acceptable accuracy loss of a value. One solution is to annotate the code sections of the application to find out the approximable and accurate (not approximable) data [13, 20]. Sensitivity analysis of an application can be done by running applications at different ETs, and determine the quality of the outputs (at different ETs). This sensitivity analysis can give us the picture of the extent of ET of an application. The ET requirement of an application can also suddenly change at run-time. Furthermore, different applications have different requirements on output quality, and it makes the task of determining ETs and applying approximation technique a challenging task.

## 6.2 Approximation Error and Machine Learning Solution

The major challenge of approximate techniques is to control the errors in the output. AComm error needs to be controlled to meet the output quality requirements of an application. Recent study [17] have shown that overall output quality varies with the change in the approximation error of the individual elements. Therefore, an AComm technique needs to control individual errors in each data packet while controlling output errors across the whole application. Different code sections of an application may require different accuracy requirements. Determination of approximation error takes time, and this time may not be feasible for approximate technique implementation in run-time systems. That's why, proactive technique is needed to determine errors with the AComm. To ensure the quality of the output, ML techniques, such as reinforcement learning (RL) and neural networks, can predict the approximation errors and take steps (train the predictor) to improve the accuracy. ML agent can be trained with errors for data packet approximation. For example, RL agent can continually monitor the approximation error in the packets, and train with the data sets collected during (online) experience. The implementation of ML can improve the AComm error while introduce new challenges (e.g., overhead).

### 6.3 Bit Error Rate

Links of the NoC consume a significant percentage of the overall NoC and chip power. Voltage-level of the links can be reduced by reducing the data movement through links by the AComm. As power consumption decreases quadratically with the decrease in voltage-level, AComm can reduce the power significantly. However, reduction of the voltage swing of the NoC links increases the probability of bit errors, which can affect the reliability of the NoC [12]. Because of the error resilient nature, increase of the bit error rate (BER) may not affect the application. However, BER needs to be controlled to keep the output error within the ET of an application.

### 6.4 Software and Hardware Overheads

The application of approximation incurs software and hardware overheads. Approximation error determination for different packets and applications incurs some overhead. Approximation also incurs extra cycles (latency) for applying approximation on the data. Hardware module is needed for AComm logic implementation. For example, approximate module is needed to truncate the data based on the ET of the data. Data packet conversion modules are needed for converting integer and floating point packets to reduce the bit-width of the data to be moved. Module is also needed for voltage and frequency scaling of links and routers. To apply ML for approximation error prediction, it (ML) needs hardware in terms of adder, multiplier and registers for calculating and storing data (for training and prediction). The implementation of approximation needs to be carefully designed so that overheads of approximation do not exceed the energy and performance gain.

## 7 CONCLUSIONS

We have proposed an architecture for approximate communication for error tolerant applications in NoC based multi/many core systems. Simulation results were presented to show the energy and delay performance improvement from approximation in NoC. We discussed several approximation communication solutions that have shown great promise to gain performance and energy improvement by reducing the number of packets and/or the size of the packets. Finally, we presented several challenges for the effective application of approximate communication techniques in NoC.

## REFERENCES

[1] N. Agarwal, T. Krishna, L. S. Peh, and N. K. Jha. 2009. GARNET: A detailed on-chip network model inside a full-system simulator. In *Proc. ISPASS*. 33–42. https://doi.org/10.1109/ISPASS.2009.4919636
[2] Alaa R. Alameldeen and David A. Wood. 2004. Frequent Pattern Compression: A Significance-Based Compression Scheme for L2 Caches.
[3] Keren Bergman et al. 2008. ExaScale Computing Study: Technology Challenges in Achieving Exascale Systems.
[4] Davide Bertozzi, Luca Benini, and Giovanni De Micheli. 2005. Error control schemes for on-chip communication links: the energy-reliability tradeoff. *IEEE TCAD* 24, 6 (2005), 818–831.
[5] Filipe Betzel et al. 2018. Approximate Communication: Techniques for Reducing Communication Bottlenecks in Large-Scale Parallel Systems. *ACM Comput. Surv.* 51, 1, Article 1 (Jan. 2018), 32 pages. https://doi.org/10.1145/3145812
[6] Nathan Binkert et al. 2011. The Gem5 Simulator. *SIGARCH Comput. Archit. News* 39, 2 (2011), 1–7. https://doi.org/10.1145/2024716.2024718
[7] S. Borkar. 2013. Exascale computing - A fact or a fiction?. In *Keynote at IPDPS*. https://doi.org/10.1109/IPDPS.2013.121
[8] Rahul Boyapati et al. 2017. APPROX-NOC: A Data Approximation Framework for Network-On-Chip Architectures. In *Proceedings of ISCA*. 666–677. https://doi.org/10.1145/3079856.3080241
[9] Y. Chen, M. F. Reza, and A. Louri. 2018. DEC-NOC: An Approximate Framework Based on Dynamic Error Control with Applications to Energy-Efficient NoCs. In *Proceedings of ICCD*. 480–487. https://doi.org/10.1109/ICCD.2018.00078
[10] R. Das et al. 2008. Performance and power optimization through data compression in Network-on-Chip architectures. In *Proceedings of HPCA*. 215–225. https://doi.org/10.1109/HPCA.2008.4658641
[11] Jose Duato, Sudhakar Yalamanchili, and Ni Lionel. 2002. *Interconnection Networks: An Engineering Approach.* Morgan Kaufmann Publishers Inc., San Francisco, CA, USA.
[12] Alireza Ejlali et al. 2010. Performability/energy tradeoff in error-control schemes for on-chip networks. *IEEE TVLSI* 18, 1 (2010), 1–14.
[13] Hadi Esmaeilzadeh, Adrian Sampson, Luis Ceze, and Doug Burger. 2012. Neural acceleration for general-purpose approximate programs. In *Proceedings of MICRO*. 449–460.
[14] Y. Hoskote et al. 2007. A 5-ghz mesh interconnect for a teraflops processor. *IEEE Micro* 27, 5 (2007), 51–61.
[15] JEDEC. 2008. Failure Mechanisms and Models for Semiconductor Devices, JEDEC publication JEP122C. http://www.jedec.org.
[16] Y. Jin, K. H. Yum, and E. J. Kim. 2008. Adaptive data compression for high-performance low-power on-chip networks. In *Proceedings of MICRO*. 354–363. https://doi.org/10.1109/MICRO.2008.4771804
[17] Daya S Khudia, Babak Zamirai, Mehrzad Samadi, and Scott Mahlke. 2015. Rumba: An online quality management system for approximate computing. In *Proceedings of ISCA*. 554–566.
[18] J. S. Miguel, M. Badr, and N. E. Jerger. 2014. Load Value Approximation. In *Proceedings of MICRO*. 127–139. https://doi.org/10.1109/MICRO.2014.22
[19] Sparsh Mittal. 2016. A survey of techniques for approximate computing. *ACM Computing Surveys (CSUR)* 48, 4 (2016), 62.
[20] Adrian Sampson et al. 2011. EnerJ: Approximate data types for safe and general low-power computation. In *ACM SIGPLAN Notices*, Vol. 46. 164–174.
[21] John Shalf, Sudip Dosanjh, and John Morrison. 2010. Exascale computing technology challenges. In *Proceedings of VECPAR*. 1–25.
[22] Chen Sun et al. 2012. DSENT - A Tool Connecting Emerging Photonics with Electronics for Opto-Electronic Networks-on-Chip Modeling. In *Proceedings of NOCS*. 201–210. https://doi.org/10.1109/NOCS.2012.31
[23] Michael Bedford Taylor et al. 2002. The Raw Microprocessor: A Computational Fabric for Software Circuits and General-Purpose Programs. *IEEE Micro* 22, 2 (2002), 25–35. https://doi.org/10.1109/MM.2002.997877
[24] Hangsheng Wang, Li-Shiuan Peh, and S. Malik. 2003. Power-driven design of router microarchitectures in on-chip networks. In *Proceedings of MICRO*. 105–116. https://doi.org/10.1109/MICRO.2003.1253187
[25] L. Wang, X. Wang, and Y. Wang. 2017. ABDTR: Approximation-Based Dynamic Traffic Regulation for Networks-on-Chip Systems. In *Proceedings of ICCD*. 153–160. https://doi.org/10.1109/ICCD.2017.31
[26] Zhe Wang et al. 2014. A Case Study on the Communication and Computation Behaviors of Real Applications in NoC-Based MPSoCs. In *Proc. ISVLSI*. 480–485. https://doi.org/10.1109/ISVLSI.2014.36
[27] Qiang Xu, Todd Mytkowicz, and Nam Sung Kim. 2016. Approximate computing: A survey. *IEEE Design & Test* 33, 1 (2016), 8–22.
[28] F. Zahn, S. Lammel, and H. FrÃűning. 2017. Early Experiences with Saving Energy in Direct Interconnection Networks. In *Proceedings of HiPINEB*. 33–40. https://doi.org/10.1109/HiPINEB.2017.10

# Information Hiding behind Approximate Computation

Ye Wang
School of Computer Science and Technology
Harbin Institute of Technology, Harbin, P.R.China
yewang@hit.edu.cn

Gang Qu
Department of Electrical and Computer Engineering and Institute of Systems Research
University of Maryland, College Park, USA
gangqu@umd.edu

Qian Xu
Department of Electrical and Computer Engineering and Institute of Systems Research
University of Maryland, College Park, USA
qxu1234@umd.edu

Jian Dong
School of Computer Science and Technology
Harbin Institute of Technology, Harbin, P.R.China
dan@hit.edu.cn

## ABSTRACT

There are many interesting advances in approximate computing recently targeting the energy efficiency in system design and execution. The basic idea is to trade computation accuracy for power and energy during all phases of the computation, from data to algorithm and hardware implementation. In this paper, we explore how to utilize approximate computing for security based information hiding. More specifically, we will demonstrate with examples the potential of embedding information in approximate hardware and approximate data, as well as during approximate computation. We analyze both the security vulnerabilities that this may cause and the potential security applications enabled by such information hiding. We argue that information could be hidden behind approximate computation without compromising the computation accuracy or energy efficiency.

## CCS Concepts

- Theory of computation~Rounding techniques
- Hardware~Arithmetic and datapath circuits

## Keywords

Information hiding, approximate computing, authentication, security, machine learning.

### ACM Reference format:

Ye Wang, Qian Xu, Gang Qu, and Jian Dong. 2019. Information Hiding behind Approximate Computation. In *Great Lakes Symposium on VLSI 2019 (GLSVLSI '19), May 9–11, 2019, Tysons Corner, VA, USA.* ACM, New York, NY, USA, 6 pages. DOI: 10.1145/3299874.3319456



*GLSVLSI '19, May 9–11, 2019, Tysons Corner, VA, USA*

ACM ISBN 978-1-4503-6252-8/19/05...$15.00
DOI: https://doi.org/10.1145/3299874.3319456

## 1. INTRODUCTION

Nowadays, with the explosive growth of data and computation scales, energy efficiency has become one of the most valuable indicators in modern computing system evaluation. In applications such as multimedia, image processing, data mining, and neuron network, results with some insignificant errors still can satisfy the accuracy requirements of practical tasks [1]. This observation has promoted the development of approximate computing (AC). AC is a design methodology that utilizes the error-resistant features of applications and trades partial precision of computing results for higher energy efficiency, which is used in many resource-saving computing systems.

Existing state-of-the-art AC technologies can be classified by where the approximation occurs and into the categories of software, compiler architecture, memory, and circuit [2]. Mostly, AC can be achieved by using a variety of strategies including voltage over-scaling (reducing the operating voltage of the system) [3], loop perforation (skipping some iterations of a loop) [4] and memorization reusing (reusing the previous results for similar functions or inputs) [5], etc. Inexact adders, multipliers, registers, and some other fine-designed approximate circuits have also been used as hardware accelerators. A more detailed review of AC will be provided in the next section.

Meanwhile, it has been noticed that AC can be valuable for potential security applications [6]. Because of the inherent advantages in data process, AC is advantageous for data-intensive applications that may contain massive confidential and privacy-sensitive data. So these applications must be enabled to withstand malicious attacks and design vulnerabilities. Compared with accurate calculation, AC usually utilizes inexact intermediate values in a running system or program and outputs approximate results with inevitable errors. In some situations, the error comes from artificial rounding, so on the one hand, the way how the data values are rounded can be utilized as an instrument of security. On the other hand, in the binary data representation, the "blank" bits (usually filled by 0's) created by rounding provide space for hiding information such as keys. This suggests that AC has the potential to provide lightweight security solutions without using additional complex security modules. But it still needs careful consideration to control the error introduced by AC in order not to sacrifice the energy efficiency while enhancing security.

Our main contribution in this paper is a systematic analysis of the potential of embedding information behind all stages of AC, which include the data used for AC, the hardware units (such as adder or multiplier) that perform the AC operation, and the AC algorithms that determine the computation load and result accuracy of the AC. Information hiding (IH) is a lightweight security method of embedding a piece of specific data into any artifacts (such as multimedia, algorithm, software, and circuits) in order to protect the artifact from illegal access, intellectual property extracting or other malicious attacks. Existing IH methods usually need additional modules for information embedding and extraction, and hence introduce changes or defects to the artifact and performance overhead (such as extra computation time and energy consumption). We show that there are various ways for IH behind the framework of AC that can support many security applications while maintaining acceptable result accuracy and energy efficiency.

The remainder of this paper is organized as follows: Section 2 provides a short survey on the existing AC and IH approaches. Section 3 mainly introduces our proposed information hiding principles with case studies on how to embed data in approximate hardware units, approximate data, and approximate computation algorithms. In Section 4, several security applications based on IH behind AC and their security analysis are presented. Section 5 concludes the paper with some discussion on future research directions.

# 2. RELATED WORK

In this section, we review the relevant work on approximate computing and information hiding.

## 2.1 Approximate Computing

The concept of trading computation accuracy for lower power and energy consumption has been around for a long time. In 2000, Qu and Potkonjak have proposed voltage scaling based approach to providing a required level of computation, not the maximal level, with minimal energy [7]. In 2003, Hua et al. applied this to multimedia data processing where they intentionally terminate the decoding of certain frames in order to conserve energy [1]. Surveys on more recent advances in approximate computing (AC) can be found in [2] and [8], where the principles of AC, existing frameworks and researches in both software level and hardware level have been systematic summarized.

Perhaps the most straightforward method to save energy in approximate arithmetic is to reduce carry operations in bit arithmetic. Based on this, new approximate arithmetic units are designed carefully and the bit width of operands can be adjusted accordingly. For example, in an error-tolerant adder [9], inputs are segmented into two parts: accurate part and inaccurate part. In the inaccurate part, starting from the leftmost position, every pair of corresponding bits from the two operands will be checked during each addition. If the two bits are not both 1, the algorithm will perform regular one-bit addition. Otherwise, all bits from that bit to the rightmost bit will be set to 1 and the checking process will stop. This algorithm can avoid carry operations on some low digital bits. In [10], Ye et al. illustrated a reconfiguration-oriented approximate adder design, which can trade accuracy with energy consumption. A Dynamic Range Unbiased Multiplier (DRUM) was proposed for AC in [11]. For saving energy, this technology truncates the LSBs dynamically so it enables designers to configure it to trade power and accuracy as desired, and its unbiased nature leads to the reduction of errors. In [3], Gao et al. proposed an Approximate Integer Format (AIF) and discussed how it can be used for all arithmetic operations. Basically, they select the most significant part of the operands for calculation during run time to reduce the number of bit operations on demand and thus achieve better energy saving (than the static input segmentation). They demonstrated that their AC algorithm only introduces negligible errors.

Besides the researches on arithmetic operations, AC can be implemented in many other ways. In [12], an approximate lookup table based accelerator was illustrated. The basic idea is to store selected function responses in a hierarchical lookup table in order to output results for similar functions without re-calculation. Liu et al. [13] studied iterative and non-iterative approximate logarithmic multipliers to reduce energy consumption and were able to get improvement in performance. AC has also found applications in the emerging deep learning and neuron network [8]. An accelerator-based on neuron network was proposed by Esmaeilzadeh et al. in [14]. This accelerator can train models to produce inaccurate results to replace the original sections of code executing in the core, which gains considerable energy saving by suffering from some acceptable error. Gupta et al. [15] designed a limited precision arithmetic unit applied in neuron network and proved this can significantly gain energy efficiency and computational throughput.

## 2.2 Information Hiding

While cryptography is to protect messages by encoding them and making them incomprehensible to hackers, information hiding technology tries to conceal the message in the cover media so that nobody will notice it. There exist a lot of cover medium that could help conceal and transmit information secretly. One of the most popular media is multimedia data where the traditional methods make minute changes to the original data subject to the human's imperfect visual and auditory systems. For example, the least significant bits of the digital media could be changed and noise signals can be manipulated to hide information without causing any noticeable degradation of the media's quality. More advanced multimedia information hiding techniques are able to embed secret behind the statistics of the data which are very challenging for adversary to remove or detect. State-of-the-art can be found in survey articles such as [17].

In computer software, information such as authorship can be embedded into programs as static or dynamic watermark [18]. Static watermark is embedded either in data format or in code format, and it will not change during the program execution process. Dynamic watermark, to the contrary, is stored during program execution, and watermark extraction may require a specific sequence of inputs or need data structures generated when program is in execution state.

In the VLSI field, information hiding is one of the most crucial concepts and powerful enabling technologies for many hardware security problems. Previously, it is well-known that digital watermarking and fingerprinting methods hide designer and user information into intellectual property (IP) for the purpose of IP identification and protection [19]. Indeed, other hot topics in hardware security and trust are also related to information hiding. For example, hardware Trojan can be considered as malicious functionality and/or information hidden in the circuit [20]; circuit obfuscation and gate camouflaging techniques attempt to hide design information from the reverse engineering attackers [21];

silicon physical unclonable function is a way to extract the fabrication variation information hidden in the chip [22].

In this paper, we will investigate the potential of information hiding in all stages of approximate computing, from the approximate hardware and data approximation to approximate algorithms and operations.

# 3. Information Hiding behind Approximate Computation

In this section, we elaborate our investigation of hiding information behind approximate computing. We will first investigate the possibility of embedding data in the current approximate computing framework hardware implementation. Then we will discuss how to do so by directly hiding data in the IEEE 754 data format with guaranteed error bound. Finally we will show how to hide information during the approximate computation operations.

## 3.1 Hiding Information in Approximate Hardware Units

The most commonly found approximate circuits are arithmetic units such as adders, multipliers, and dividers. We use the accuracy-configurable adder proposed in [19] as an example to illustrate how information might be hidden behind an approximate adder.

### *3.1.1 An Approximate Adder Example*

In [19], an approximate adder is proposed which can be used as both an accurate adder and an inaccurate approximate adder. Figure 1 illustrates how such adder works with 16-bit operands. Two 16-bit inputs A[15:0] and B[15:0] are added using three 8-bit adders as follow: first three 8-bit inputs are formed from each of the 16-bit inputs: {$A_H$[15:8], $A_M$[11:4], $A_L$[7:0]} and {$B_H$[15:8], $B_M$[11:4], $B_L$[7:0]}; then each pair of these three 8-bit values will be added by an 8-bit adder to produce $SUM_H$, $SUM_M$, and $SUM_L$; the result SUM is formed by using the high 4-bit from $SUM_H$ and $SUM_M$, and the 8-bit $SUM_L$, as well as the "carry" bit from $SUM_H$ as SUM[16]. Note that the calculation of the carry-ins SUM[16], SUM[15:12], and SUM[11:8] do not need to wait for the additional outcome of the lower bits. This reduces the timing of the critical path by 50%, and thus can save power and increase calculating speed.

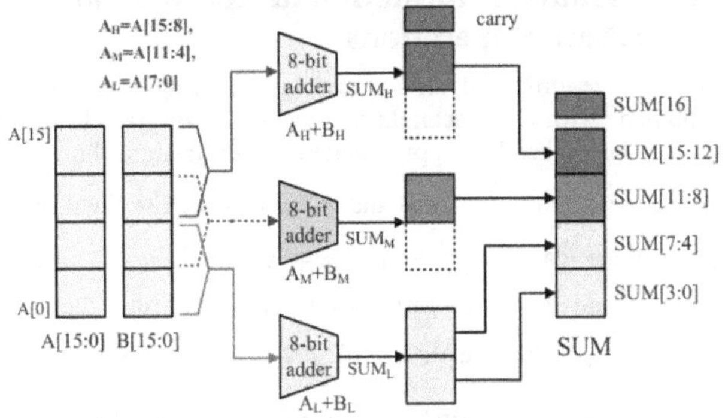


Figure 1. The accuracy-configurable adder ([19]).

The use of the middle 8-bit adder that creates $SUM_M$ increases the computation accuracy. Without this, the carry-out of SUM[7:0], which may be 0 and 1, will be discarded and hence results in an error roughly 50% of the time. However, when sub-adder is introduced, the probability of error will be reduced to 5.5% [19]. Furthermore, the authors also proposed an error detection and correction method which could increase the accuracy based on customers' requests. The error can be easily detected by checking whether the carry-out of each sub-adder is '1' or '0'. If a '1' is detected, error occurs and needs to be corrected by simply adding '1' to the approximate (inaccurate) output.

### *3.1.2 Hiding Information Using Approximate Adder*

In accordance with the approximate adder described above, we analyze potential methods to hide data behind this adder.

First, consider Figure 1, similar to SUM[11:8], the values in SUM[7:4] can come either from high 4 bits in $SUM_L$ (as shown in Figure 1) or the low 4 bits of $SUM_M$. The difference will be if the low 4 bits of $SUM_M$ is used, the carry from the calculation of SUM[3:0] will not be considered. However, this error occurs at the bit SUM[4], for a 16-bit data, an error in the $5^{th}$ least significant bit is normally negligible. In addition, when it is necessary, the error detection and correction circuit proposed in [19] can be used. This suggests that with little or no loss of accuracy or speed, there will be two different ways to implement SUM[7:4] segment of this approximate adder. A designer can then deliberately select one of the two to hide one bit of information. This bit can be easily extracted by providing a pair of inputs whose low 4 bits will produce a carry (while the error detection and correct circuit is disabled).

Second, for the 8 bits that are discarded from $SUM_H$ and $SUM_M$, since they are redundant and will not be used in any computation, normal circuit testing will not these signals. This creates some security complications, particularly at design time. For example, the designer can connect them to some registers or logic without being noticed. On one hand, this becomes the source of information leak or the trigger to some hardware Trojans circuit. On the other hand, the circuit designer could also take advantage of this to inject secret information into the circuit by deliberately constructing the values of the two operands so these 8 bits will be the information to be hidden.

Finally, we show how to hide some short message behind this approximate adder, more precisely adders $SUM_H$ and $SUM_M$. Suppose that we would like to hide a 4-bit message M = 1011, instead of computing A+B as Figure 1 depicts, we will compute $A_H+B_H+10$ using $SUM_H$ and $A_M+B_M+11$ using $SUM_M$. Note that 10 and 11 are the two higher bits and the two lower bits from message M, respectively. Apparently, this will over-calculate both $A_H+B_H$ and $A_M+B_M$. However, because in the final SUM, we do not use the last 4 bits of $SUM_H$ and $SUM_M$, this may not affect the accuracy of SUM.

For example, consider the operation 1234+2019, that is, A = 0000 0100 1101 0010, B = 0000 1111 1110 0011. We have $A_H+B_H$ = <u>0001</u> 1011; $A_M+B_M$ = 1 <u>0100</u> 1011; and $A_L+B_L$ = 1 <u>1011 0101</u>. As shown in Figure 1, the underlined parts give us the final SUM = 0001 0100 1011 0101, which is accurate. When message M = 1011 is embedded as described in the previous paragraph, we will compute $A_H+B_H+10$ = <u>0001</u> 1101 and $A_M+B_M+11$ = 1 <u>0100</u> 1110. Note that the underlined parts remain unchanged, so the adder with message M indeed gives the accurate SUM in this case.

In this example, the operations of $A_H+B_H+10$ and $A_M+B_M+11$ could be implemented directly with hardware logic. To reveal that the adder has been modified with the embedded message, deliberately selected operand values for A and B could force an incorrect SUM which can be used as a proof that $SUM_H$ and $SUM_M$

carry hidden information M = 1011. To ensure the accuracy of SUM, the error detection and correction circuitry proposed in [19] could be used.

## 3.2 Hiding Information in Approximate Data

Approximate computing algorithms specify how data and/or computation will be approximated. It is important to understand how data will be presented or the data format first. We focus on single precision floating point because of its ubiquitous application in real life energy-saving computing devices or systems such as IoT devices and mobile computing equipment. Our main study object is the IEEE 754, which is a widely-used, classic single-precision floating point format.

IEEE 754 represents single-precision floating point format through a 32-bit binary number, which is composed of one sign bit, 8 exponent bits and 23 mantissa bits [16]. The structure of this format is shown in Figure 2.

Figure 2. IEEE 754 format for single precision floating point. (redrawn from [6])

The value of an IEEE 754 number can be computed as

$$\left(-1^{Sign}\right) \times \left(1+Mantissa\right) \times 2^{Exponent-127} \qquad (3\text{-}1)$$

where *Sign* is one bit showing the sign of floating point, 0 for positive and 1 for negative; (*1+Mantissa*) is a real number in the interval of (1.0, 2.0), so essentially *Mantissa* is the fractional part represented in binary; *Exponent* is the exponent of 2 with a bias of $2^8$-1 = 127 obeying the IEEE standard of 32-bit single-precision format, so we need to subtract 127 when running the number system conversion. Consider the following IEEE 754 number, for example, 0,10000000,10010010000111111010000, the equivalent decimal value can be obtained as follows:

$$\left(-1^{0}\right) \times \left(1+0.570795059204...\right) \times 2^{128-127} \approx 1.570795059204 * 2$$
$$= 3.141590118408$$

From the structure of IEEE 754 format, we notice that the least significant bits (LSB) have little influence on the value it represents. This inspires us to truncate the last *p* bits and utilize these bit positions for information hiding (Figure 3). In the above example, if we reset the last 10 bits to 0, the translated decimal format will become 3.141357421875. This approximate output brings only 0.0074% error compared to the accurate result, which is totally negligible. One advantage of this method is that the error is bounded regardless of the value of the *security bits*. Theoretical analysis of this approximate operation gives us the following:

Figure 3. Security Embedding Format based on IEEE 754. (redrawn from [6])

**Theorem 1:** The error introduced by embedding an arbitrary value to the last p bits of an IEEE 754 format is less than $2^{p-23}$ of the original value.

**Proof:** For any IEEE 754 number *A*, we overwrite the last *p* bits as the security bits and noted this security embedding format as $A^s$. From equation 3-1, we have:

$$\begin{aligned} A &= \left(-1^{Sign}\right) \times \left(1+Mantissa\right) \times 2^{Exponent-127} \\ A^s &= \left(-1^{Sign}\right) \times \left(1+Mantissa'+Security\right) \times 2^{Exponent-127} \end{aligned} \qquad (3\text{-}2)$$

where *Mantissa'* is the approximate value of *Mantissa* by resetting the last *p* bits to 0. For simplicity, we note *Mantissa* as *M*, *Mantissa'* as *M'*, *Security* as *S* and *Exponent* as *E*, then the relative error can be represented as:

$$\begin{aligned} \frac{A\text{-}A^S}{A} &= \frac{\left(-1^{Sign}\right) \times 2^{E-127} \times \left[\left(1+M'+S\right) - \left(1+M\right)\right]}{\left(-1^{Sign}\right) \times 2^{E-127} \times \left(1+M\right)} \\ &= \frac{\left(1+M'+S\right) - \left(1+M\right)}{\left(1+M\right)} \\ &= \frac{M' - M + S}{1+M} \end{aligned} \qquad (3\text{-}3)$$

Note that *M'* is obtained by truncating the last p bits in *M*, so we have *M'*- *M* ≤0 and hence the following

$$\frac{A\text{-}A^S}{A} = \frac{M' - M + S}{1+M} \le \frac{S}{1+M} \le S \le 2^{p} \times 2^{-23} \qquad (3\text{-}4)$$

where the equal sign holds in the first inequality when *M=M'*, in the second inequality when *M*=0 and in the last inequality when the security bits are all 1's. In sum, this error bound is tight and we can approximate the bound as $2^{p-23}$ when $2^p >> 1$. ∎

From theorem 1, it is obvious that by carefully setting the parameter *p*, we can arbitrarily change the last p bits based on the security information within a known error bound. In another word, approximate computation under the IEEE 754 floating point format allows us to embed information during the computation.

## 3.3 Hiding Information in Approximate Computation Operations

As we have proposed an approximate floating point format combined with IH technology, we can now establish an information embedding approximate computing algorithm.

For any two real numbers *A* and *B*, we can rewrite them in the approximate data format: $A = A' \oplus K_A$ and $B = B' \oplus K_B$, where $A'$ and $B'$ are respectively created by resetting the last *p* bits of *A* and *B* by 0 in their IEEE 754 representations; $K_A$ and $K_B$ are the last p bits of *A* and *B*; ⊕ is the bitwise XOR operation.

As we have segmented the two numbers, any binary arithmetic operation *A•B* can be completed by following steps in order to perform AC and IH simultaneously.

1) Rewrite *A* and *B* in their approximate date format.

2) Compute $A' \bullet B'$ and rewrite the output as $O = O' \oplus K_{O'}$.

3) Generate a p-bit secret key $K_S = K_A \oplus K_B \oplus K_{O'} \oplus Key$, where $Key$ is a predefined or randomly generated p-bit binary number before this step.

4) Return $O = O' \oplus K_S$ as the final result of $A \bullet B$.

For example, when $A$=12.55, $B$=9.2019, and we choose $p$=10, $Key$=0101010101 to compute $A \times B$ using our algorithm. Following the above computing steps, we have:

1) $A$ = 0,10000010, 1001000110011,0011001101
$A'$= 0,10000010, 1001000110011,0000000000
$B$ = 0,10000010, 0010011001110,1011111011
$B'$= 0,10000010, 0010011001110,0000000000
$K_A$=0011001101, $K_B$= 0111000011

2) $A' \times B'$= 0,10000101,1100110111100,1000100001
$O'$= 0,10000101,1100110111100,0000000000
$K_{O'}$= 1000100001

3) $K_S$=$K_A \oplus K_B \oplus K_{O'} \oplus Key$ =1001111010

4) Output = 0,10000101,1100110111100,1001111010

After converting to decimal format, the final output in our approximate algorithm is 115.47359. Compared with the accurate result 115.48384, this output only incurs 0.008875% relative error, which can be nearly neglected in most applications.

Similarly, if we replace the $Key$ value by 0110110111, the approximate result with information hidden is 115.473816, whose error is only 0.00868% of the accurate result. As the final example, we replace the original $Key$ value by logical right shifting by 1 bit, which will be 0010101010. Follow the same procedure, we obtain the approximate result of 115.475624, whose error is 0.00711% of the accurate result. But more importantly, it is quite different from the result with the original $Key$ value.

# 4. Security Vulnerabilities in AC and Applications based on Information Hiding

In the previous section, we give several case studies on how information could be hidden behind the framework of AC. In this section, we discuss the security vulnerabilities this may cause and also list several security applications based on the IH technology we mentioned before. For each application, we will compare the IH approaches' advantages and disadvantages, potential threats, robustness, and possible countermeasures.

**Loss of Accuracy:** artificially hiding information into the AC framework might incur loss of accuracy (see the message embedding at the end of section 3.1.2 for example). Although most of the applications which AC can be applied to normally have certain level of tolerance to inaccurate results, it is important to note that for some applications, errors may add up quickly in particular for the case of biased AC algorithms (such as truncating the lower bits without proper compensation). So, the IH methods should be designed carefully to have no or guaranteed error.

**Hardware Trojans**: As we have described in the previous section, for AC algorithms and hardware units, when they do compute more than what the final result shows (e.g. truncating lower bits or using redundancy as in Figure 1), it may create a host for hardware Trojans. Furthermore, these Trojans would remain dormant until when they are triggered and since they are not part of the design, normal testing methods and the existing Trojan detection mechanisms may fail to catch them. A clearly specified requirement and documentation of the AC framework and a set of associated mechanisms to enforce them will be crucial.

**Information Removal**: There is a tradeoff between the robustness of the IH method and the loss of accuracy it may incur. In general, IH method that has no or little loss of computation accuracy is preferred. However, such method may not be robust and can be vulnerable to various simple attacks. For example, if information is hidden in the lower bits of the result, an aggressive truncation or post-processing of the result can easily remove or modify the embedded information.

**IP Watermarking:** IP Watermarking embeds the identification information of the author of the IP into the IP implementation such that this information can be extracted to claim the authorship. For IPs that has AC components, the IH methods discussed in the previous section can be considered as watermarking to defend against IP piracy. A well-designed watermarking method should be able to provide high confidence of IP authorship and remain robust against various removal and modification attacks. This becomes even more challenging because we also need a convenient mechanism to extract the embedded watermarking information. For example, if one implements the approximate adder in Figure 1 and decides to use the two alternative ways to construct SUM as the watermark, one way to extract the watermark is providing specific values A and B and observe the result SUM. This method is simple but still secure against attacks that treat the approximate adder as blackbox and do not perform circuit reverse engineering.

**Device Identification and Digital Fingerprinting:** IP watermark will be the same for all copies of the same IP. For situations when an individual IP or device needs to be identified, digital fingerprinting methods can be used. Basically, digital fingerprint is similar to digital watermark except that the embedded information (fingerprint) will be unique for each copy of the IP or device. In other words, the fingerprinted IPs can be considered as IPs watermarked with distinct watermarking information. Normally for digital fingerprints, a short message should be sufficient. For example, a 16-bit fingerprint will be able to distinguish $2^{16}$ = 65536 copies. The last method we discussed in section 3.1.2 could be a good candidate for this case.

**General Applications**: The IH methods in sections 3.2 and 3.3 enable us to hide any information into the approximate data and computation operations. One important advantage of these methods is that the embedded data can be totally unrelated to the desired AC and they will have no or guaranteed low impact to the AC results. The hidden information can be used for more general applications. As two examples, we mention that certain checksum or other pre-calculated values can be embedded (by the IH method in section 3.2) such that a run time attestation could be performed; and parity bits can be embedded to validate data integrity.

**More Vulnerabilities and Countermeasures:** To conclude this section, we mention two challenges for the proposed IH based security methods. First, most of these methods are passive defense method in the sense that the hidden information is static. It cannot evolve itself to respond to continuous attempts of attacks. In particular with the AC units as blackbox and users having full control of the input data and can observe the (approximate) output results with a rather clear idea of the expected (accurate) result, attackers can study the pairs of input and output values to reveal the hidden information. Second, the errors incurred by IH could be small and negligible. However, once the approximate result is used for further computation, the error may accumulate and therefore cause unacceptable loss of accuracy.

On the positive side, first, the many well-developed AC algorithms have successful ways to control the error bound, which can be utilized to our IH methods to balance the robustness and loss of accuracy. Second, intrinsic hardware features such as the Physical Unclonable Function (PUF) based on fabrication variation can be combined to enhance the robustness of the IH methods, in particular for device identification based applications.

## 5. CONCLUSIONS

In this paper, we go through all the stages of approximate computing where we can embed information. We first provide an example of an approximate adder and propose a method to hide information behind the adder. Then we introduce the standard floating point format and propose an enhanced version with security bits such that we could hide information in it. After that, we propose an approximate computing algorithm which helps embed information in the floating point format that we mentioned earlier and illustrate it in detail by giving an example. Finally, we make a full analysis of potential security vulnerabilities that we may encounter in hiding information in the approximate computing field and the corresponding possible countermeasures that we can use.

## REFERENCES

[1] Shaoxiong Hua, Gang Qu, and S.S. Bhattacharyya. 2003. Energy Reduction Techniques for Multimedia Applications with Tolerance to Deadline Misses. In Design Automation Conference (DAC'03), pp. 131-136.

[2] Qiang Xu, Todd Mytkowicz, and Nam Sung Kim. 2016. Approximate Computing: A Survey. IEEE Design and Test, 8-22.

[3] Mingze Gao, Qian Wang, Akshaya S Kankanhalli Nagendra, and Gang Qu. 2017. A Novel Data Format for Approximate Arithmetic Computing. In 22nd Asia and South Pacific Design Automation Conference.

[4] Stelios Sidiroglou-Douskos, Sasa Misailovic, Henry Hoffmann, and Martin Rinard. 2011. Managing performance vs. accuracy trade-offs with loop perforation. In ACM SIGSOFT symposium and the 13th European conference on Foundations of software engineering. 124–134.

[5] Abbas Rahimi, Luca Benini, and Rajesh K. Gupta. 2013. Spatial memoization: Concurrent instruction reuse to correct timing errors in SIMD architectures, IEEE Transactions on Circuits and Systems II: Express Briefs 60, 12 (2013), 847–851.

[6] Mingze Gao, Qian Wang, Md Tanvir Arafin, Yongqiang Lyu, and Gang Qu. 2017. Approximate Computing for Low Power and Security in the Internet of Things. IEEE Computer, Vol. 50, No. 6, pp. 27-34, June 2017.

[7] Gang Qu and M. Potkonjak. 2000. Energy Minimization with Guaranteed Quality of Service. International Symposium on Low Power Electronics and Design (ISLPED'00), pp. 43-48.

[8] Sparsh Mittal. 2016. A Survey of Techniques for Approximate Computing. ACM Computing Surveys (CSUR), 48(4), 62.

[9] Ning Zhu, Wang Ling Goh, Weija Zhang, Kiat Seng Yeo, and Zhi Hui Kong. 2010. Design of low-power high-speed truncation-error-tolerant adder and its application in digital signal processing. IEEE Transactions on Very Large Scale Integration, vol. 18, no. 8, 1225–1229.

[10] Rong Ye, Ting Wang, Feng Yuan, Rakesh Kumar, and Qiang Xu. 2013. On reconfiguration-oriented approximate adder design and its application. In Proceedings of the International Conference on Computer-Aided Design (ICCAD '13), 48-54.

[11] Soheil Hashemi, R. Iris Bahar, and Sherief Reda. 2015. DRUM: A dynamic range unbiased multiplier for approximate applications. In Proceedings of the IEEE/ACM international conference on computer-aided design. pp. 418-425

[12] Ye Tian, Ting Wang, Qian Zhang, and Qiang Xu. 2017. ApproxLUT: A novel approximate lookup table-based accelerator. In 2017 IEEE/ACM International Conference on Computer-Aided Design (ICCAD). IEEE, 2017: 438-443.

[13] Weiqiang Liu, Xu Jiahua, Danye Wang, Chenghua Wang, Paolo Montuschi, and Fabrizio Lombardi. 2017. Design and Evaluation of Approximate Logarithmic Multipliers for Low Power Error-Tolerant Applications. IEEE Transactions on Circuits and Systems I: Regular Papers, 1-13.

[14] Hadi Esmaeilzadeh, Adrian Sampson, Luis Ceze, and Doug Burger. 2012. Neural acceleration for general-purpose approximate programs. Proceedings of the 2012 45th Annual IEEE/ACM International Symposium on Microarchitecture, pp. 449–460.

[15] Suyog Gupta, Ankur Agrawal, Kailash Gopalakrishnan, and Pritish Narayanan. 2015. Deep learning with limited numerical precision. In International Conference on Machine Learning, 1737-1746.

[16] IEEE Std. 754-2008, IEEE Standard for Floating-Point Arithmetic, IEEE, 2008.

[17] Ruohan Meng, Qi Cui, and Chengsheng Yuan. 2018. A Survey of Image Information Hiding Algorithms Based on Deep Learning. Computer Modeling in Engineering & Sciences, 117(3), 425-454.

[18] Dalla Preda Mila and Michele Pasqua. 2019. Semantics-based software watermarking by abstract interpretation. Mathematical Structures in Computer Science, 29(2), 339-388.

[19] Andrew B. Kahng and Seokhyeong Kang. 2012. Accuracy-configurable adder for approximate arithmetic designs. In Proceedings of the 49th Annual Design Automation Conference 2012 Jun 3, 820-825.

[20] Yier Jin, Nathan Kupp, and Yiorgos Makris. 2009. Experiences in hardware Trojan design and implementation. In 2009 IEEE International Workshop on Hardware-Oriented Security and Trust, 50-57.

[21] Jeyavijayan Rajendran, Michael Sam, Ozgur Sinanoglu, and Ramesh Karri. Security Analysis of Integrated Circuit Camouflaging. In Proceedings of the 2013 ACM SIGSAC conference on Computer & communications security.

[22] Charles Herder, Meng-Day Yu, Farinaz Koushanfar, and Srinivas Devadas. 2014. Physical unclonable functions and applications: A tutorial. Proceedings of the IEEE, 102(8), 1126-1141.

# MLPrivacyGuard: Defeating Confidence Information based Model Inversion Attacks on Machine Learning Systems

Tiago A.O. Alves
tiago@ime.uerj.br
State University of Rio de Janeiro

Felipe M.G. França
felipe@cos.ufrj.br
Federal University of Rio de Janeiro

Sandip Kundu
kundu@umass.edu
University of Massachusetts, Amherst

## ABSTRACT

As services based on Machine Learning (ML) applications find increasing use, there is a growing risk of attack against such systems. Recently, adversarial machine learning has received a lot of attention, where an adversary is able to craft an input or manipulate an input to cause an ML system to misclassify. Another attack of concern is when an adversary with access to a ML model can reverse engineer attributes of a target class, creating a privacy concern, which is the subject of this paper. Such attacks use non-sensitive data obtainable by the adversary and the confidence levels returned by the ML model to infer sensitive attributes of the target user. Model Inversion attacks may be classified as white-box, where the ML model is known to the attacker, or black-box, where the adversary does not know the internals of the model. If the attacker has access to non-sensitive data of a target user, they can infer sensitive data by applying gradient ascent on the confidence returned by the model. Therefore, a black-box attack can be mounted by numerical approximations of the gradient to perform the gradient ascent. In this work, we present MLPrivacyGuard, a countermeasure against black-box model inversion attack is presented. This countermeasure consists of adding controlled noise to the output of the confidence function. It is important to preserve the accuracy of prediction/classification for the real users of the model while preventing attackers to infer sensitive data. This involves a trade-off between misclassification error and the effectiveness of defense. Based on experimental results, we demonstrate that when noise is injected with a long-tailed distribution, the objectives of low misclassification error with a strong defense can be attained as model inversion attacks are neutralized because numerical approximation of gradient ascent is unable to converge.

## CCS CONCEPTS

• **Security and privacy**;

## KEYWORDS

Neural Networks, Convolutional Neural Network, Adversarial Machine Learning, Model Inversion Attack



*GLSVLSI '19, June 30–July 5, 2019, Tysons Corner, VA, USA*



ACM ISBN 978-1-4503-6252-8/19/05...$15.00
https://doi.org/10.1145/3299874.3319457

**ACM Reference Format:**

Tiago A.O. Alves, Felipe M.G. França, and Sandip Kundu. 2019. MLPrivacyGuard: Defeating Confidence Information based Model Inversion Attacks on Machine Learning Systems. In *Great Lakes Symposium on VLSI 2019(GLSVLSI'19), June 30–July 5, 2019, Tysons Corner, VA, USA.* ACM, New York, NY, USA, 5 pages. https://doi.org/10.1145/3299874.3319457

## 1 INTRODUCTION

Machine learning (ML), and related advances like deep learning, have allowed computers to perform routine cognitive tasks by acquiring knowledge from carefully labeled training data. This has lead to proliferation of ML based services. Examples of such ML-services may be found in recommandation systems that learns from user preferences [4], medical diagnosis [5] and image classifiers [2]. As ML tools have become commodity applications, often the true value of such learning systems reside on the training data. This creates an incentive for adversaries to reverse engineer the training data from ML models or services. Normally, these functionalities are provided to users over web-services (WS), through which the user sends some input data and gets the outputs provided by the ML-service. Such outputs usually include some form of confidence levels for the prediction made by the ML model, which can be used by adversaries to obtain data from the training set using Model Inversion Attacks (MI) [3]. In the cases where the traning set of the ML model contains sensitive data, exposing the model via web-services may endanger the privacy of users or the overall security of companies and government agencies.

It has been demonstrated that ML models are vulnerable to attacks that cause breaches of privacy. Such attacks leak information to adversaries who should not have access to it. These attacks can be classified into two classes:

- **Model Stealing:** where an attacker exploits the access provided to the ML system to replicate its model [9]. This attack mainly poses a threat to intellectual property.
- **Model Inversion:** This kind of attack inverts the process of training data into a ML model. The threat in this case is potentially exposing data from the training set, which can contain private information, to the adversary.

The concepts introduced in [2, 3], comprise proof of the privacy threat posed by Model Inversion, as an adversary can exploit the confidence information to obtain data from the model.

Previous work by Fredrikson *et al.* [2, 3] shows that Model Inversion (MI) can infer sensitive information from datasets used to train models for drug dosage prediction, facial recognition and behavior prediction based on surveys. Their experiments provide insight on how an adversary can obtain sensitive features from subjects used to train the models using either *white-box* or *black-box* model inversion attacks.

In this work we focus on the prevention of black-box attacks that exploit confidence levels, as they are potentially more threatening, since the adversary does not need any knowledge about the model itself to infer sensitive data, as opposed to white-box attacks, where inversion is only feasible if the attacker has access to the inner workings of the trained model. Black-box MI attacks only require access to the model via an API (which can be published as a web-service) and the knowledge of non-sensitive features present in the training set. The attack is based on approximating an input feature vector $\mathbf{x} = (x_1, x_2, ..., x_n)$, where one or more elements of the vector are non-sensitive features in the training dataset known by the attacker, to maximize the confidence level of $f(\mathbf{x})$, the output of the model for the feature vector $\mathbf{x}$.

For instance, consider a model that classifies credit card transactions as legitimate or fraudlent bas on a training dataset of previous transactions. This training dataset may contain priviledged information about credit card holders if the model developers do not apply some kind of preprocessing to the data for anonymization [1]. Thus, if the model's functionality is exposed to users as a web-service that receives data about a credit card transaction and outputs a classification (either fradulent or not) for it with a corresponding level of confidence in such prediction, it is possible for an adversary to obtain sensitive data from the model using a black-box model attack. Considering that the attacker has access to non-sensitive information of some user, the model inversion would begin by instantiating a vector with these non-sensitive features and random variables for the senstitive ones. The attacker would then perform a numerical method for Gradient Ascent in order to obtain values for the sensitive features that maximize the confidence level of the prediction for the vector. The resulting vector will contain sensitive data used to train the model.

*MLPrivacyGuard*, the defensive solution introduced in this paper, is based on injecting small amounts of noise (error) to the confidence levels returned by the model. We show in our experimental results, that adopting long-tailed distributions for the size of the error achieves our goal of preventing black-box inversion attacks, while not disrupting the functionalities of the model for legitimate users.

The rest of the paper is organized as follows: *(i)* Section 2 presents related work; *(ii)* Section 2.2 discusses how the Model Inversion attacks work; Section 3 introduces MLPrivacyGuard; *(iii)* Section 4 contains experimental results and *(iv)* Section 5 summarizes our work.

# 2 RELATED WORK

In this section, we lay out an overview of previous work on Model Inversion as well as a formalization of ML models that we will use to describe our countermeasure. The nomenclature adopted in this paper is closely related to the work of Fredrikson *et al.*, for the sake of ease of comprehension of how our defense protects against the attacks proposed by them.

## 2.1 ML models

We consider an ML as a function $f : \mathbb{R}^n \mapsto \mathrm{Y}$ that maps $n$ features to a set of outputs Y. In cases where Y is finite, we refer to its elements as classes and $f$ is a classifier. If, $\mathrm{Y} = \mathbb{R}$, then $f$ is a regression model.

Classifiers such as the ones adopted for facial recognition first acquire a set of outputs, using the input features $\mathbf{v}$, via regression and then pick the output with the maximum confidence level. Thus, models like facial recognition start as regression models and end as classifiers, since the output will be the *class* (a unique identifier of the subject) and the confidence level in such classification, i.e. a real value in $[0, 1]$ that estimates the likelihood of the classification being correct.

A classifier is generated with a training set that contains input features for each subject and the *label*, name of the class, corresponding to that subject. In the case of facial recognition, the training dataset would contain different pictures with faces and the names of the individuals in each picture. The input users would send to the model are pictures of faces. The output would be the class (the name or other unique identifier for that person) and the confidence level, for the class that is the most likely match for the input picture. Following Fredrikson *et al.*, we decompose $f$ in two functions: $\tilde{f} : \mathbb{R}^n \mapsto [0, 1]^m$, where $n$ is the number of input features and $m$ is the number of classes, and $t : [0, 1]^m \mapsto [0, 1, .., m]$ represents the class with highest confidence for the given input. Hence, for a classifier with input $\mathbf{x}$, $\tilde{f}(\mathbf{x})$ are the confidence levels and $t(\tilde{f}(x))$ is the label to which $\mathbf{x}$ is mapped by the model.

## 2.2 Model Inversion

Fredrikson *et al.* [2, 3] introduced a new type of attack on ML systems that exposes sensitive information of users, called model inversion attacks. The attack aims for obtaining output values $\tilde{f}$ and $t$ related to the target user from the ML system. Then, by using these values the attacker is able to infer a set of sensitive features $\mathbf{x}$ which, when used as input for the model, corresponds to the user. This process is done by iteratively maximizing the confidence information returned by the model for the user's class.

Model inversion attacks can be classified either as white-box or black-box attacks. In the former it is necessary for the attacker to have access to the model itself, while in the latter the attacker just needs to know the outputs $\tilde{f}$ and $t$ for the given inputs. In the white-box attack, the knowledge about the inner workings of the model is used to differentiate $\tilde{f}$ and apply the derivative to *gradient descent* (GD) to maximize the confidence of the input vector matching a target label. On the other hand, black-box attacks assume no knowledge about the model, which would typically be the case of ML models provided via web-services, therefore the attacker must rely on numerical approximation of the gradient to perform GD. In this work we focus on black-box attacks because, intuitively, this would be the situation for an ML system that requires privacy of the dataset. In [3] the authors applied white-box attacks on a simple linear regression model used to predict inital dose of the drug Warfaring. They were able to show that, given a set of non-sensitive features of a subject in the dataset used to create to model, it is possible to obtain sensitive information about such subject. In [2] the authors present results acquired through black-box model inversion on face recognition ML systems.

In the context of this paper, we will present model inversion as attacks on classifier models, since our experimental results are based on this kind of ML. However, as mentioned earlier, model inversion can be applied to other types of ML systems. Algorithm

1 shows a general form of the model inversion attack, where the adversary wishes to infer sensitive information related to the class represented by $label$. We use the notation $\tilde{f}_{label}(\mathbf{x})$ to represent the output confidence that the input vector $\mathbf{x}$ matches the target class, represented by $label$. For instance, in the case of facial recognition, $label$ would be the name or some other unique identifier of a person whose facial features the attacker wants to obtain. The algorithm receives a vector $\mathbf{x} = (x_0, x_1, .., x_n)$, where some of the $x_i$'s may be non-sensitive data that the attacker could obtain about a target user, the rest is initialized with any value (random values, for instance). The goal of the attack is to maximize confidence (or minimize error) of the prediction up to a threshold. This is achieved by obtaining the gradient $\nabla \tilde{f}_{label}(\mathbf{x})$, multiplying it by a step-size $\alpha$ and adding the result to $x$. After convergence, the attack returns a new feature vector $x$, such that $t(\tilde{f}(x)) = label$, if the threshold picked was big enough.

**Algorithm 1** General Model Inversion Attack

**Require:** Initial vector $x$ with non-sensitive features and random value for sensitive features
**Ensure:** Output vector $x$ with inferred sensitive features
**while** $\tilde{f}_{label}(\mathbf{x})$ < THRESHOLD **do**
  $\mathbf{x} \leftarrow \mathbf{x} + \alpha \cdot \nabla \tilde{f}_{label}(\mathbf{x})$

## 3 PROPOSED APPROACH

In this section we introduce *MLPrivacyGuard*, a countermeasure to prevent model inversion attacks that does not require retraining or any kind of modification to the ML system's inner workings. MLPrivacyGuard relies on the injection of long-tailed distributed errors to the output $\tilde{f}$ of the model, so that a model inversion attack can not converge, whilst maintaining the functionality of the ML system reliable for legitimate users.

The idea behind MLPrivacyGuard is that when the confidence information has some level of randomness the model inversion attack is unable to converge in black-box systems. The reason for this is straightforward: since a black-box model inversion has to rely on numerical approximations of the gradient $\nabla \tilde{f}(\mathbf{x})$, which are obtained by numerical differentiation of $\tilde{f}$ on each of the features, the attack is unable to converge if the value of $\tilde{f}$ is nondeterministic. Meanwhile it is important to preserve correct classifications for legitimate users. As we will show in Section 4, this is guaranteed due to the distributions picked for the random erros. Since the errors have probability dense functions (PDF) which are long-tailed, the errors big enough to render missclassification are unlikely.

Furthermore, 50% of the times we multiply the error by $-1$, which yields a distribution of errors with mean equal to 0. Hence, the probability density functions (pdf) of distributions used in MLPrivacyGuard are shaped like Figure 1. This type of pdf, potentially yields a wavelike behaviour when model inversion is attempted against MLPrivacyGuard, as we will show in Section 4, thus hindering the ability of model inversion to perform its approximation.

Another positive aspect of our defense mechanism is that there is no need for re-training or any kind of modification in the ML model itself. Since we just inject noise in the confidence information

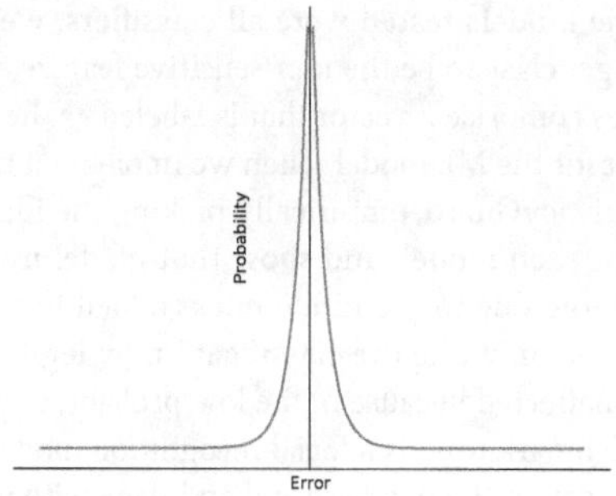


**Figure 1: Typical shape of a distribution adopted for error injection in MLPrivacyGuard.**

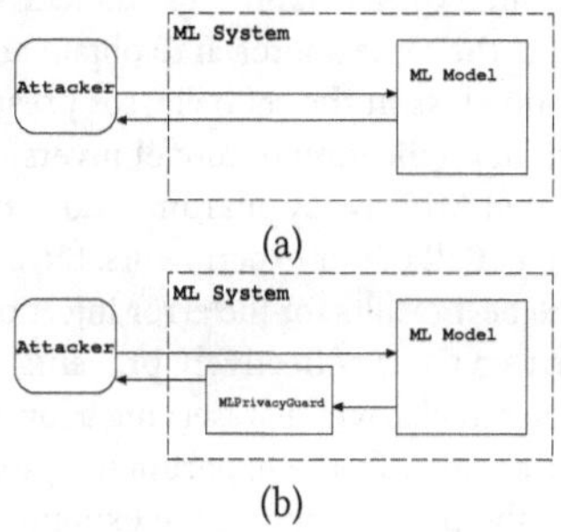


**Figure 2: Workflow description of model inversion without MLPrivacyGuard (a) and with MLPrivacyGuard implemented (b).**

returned by the model, this approach can potentially work on any ML model without. As we will show in Section 4, the provider of the model only has to chose the distribution ant its parameters parameters. This can be done empirically via experimentation for each model and dataset, as we show further in this work.

Figure 2 shows how MLPrivacyGuard is incorporated into the ML system to prevent black-box model inversion. The requests of the attacker are sent straight to the model as usual, while the output of the model is sent through the MLPrivacyGuard component, which in turn adds errors with long-tailed distributions. Thus, as we show in Section 4, the attacker is unable to achieve $\mathbf{x}$ that maximizes confidence. If instead of an attacker we have a legitimate user, the data-path is the same, but since the user only needs one request per input vector, the probability of misclassification caused by the error injected is very low, given that the right parameters for the error distribution were picked. In our experiments, the error size has exponential distribution, i.e. the absolute value of the error injected is $x$ with probability $\lambda e^{-\lambda x}$. Therefore, we only had to vary the value of $\lambda$ in Section 4.

## 4 EXPERIMENTAL SET-UP

To demonstrate the efficacy of our defense against model inversion, next we present a set of experiments executed on two different models. As our focus is on black-box model inversion, we implemented the attack using finite differences [8] to approximate the gradient $\nabla\tilde{f}$. Since the models tested were all classifiers, we consider the label of a target class to be the non-sensitive feature, while the sensitive features comprise a vector that is labeled as the target class if used as input for the ML model. Then we implement the error injection of MLPrivacyGuard, empirically picking the ideal long-tailed disriution for each model, and show that model inversion is not able to converge due to the randomness added to the confidence levels by the error, while the classification by legitimate remains practically unaffected because of the low probability of large errors. The first benchmark used is a facial recognition model that, given a name of a person in the database and an image with a face, outputs the distance between the given face and the face of the given person. In this benchmark we employed model inversion to minimize the distance (maximizing confidence) informed by the model, which renders an image that has the facial features of the targeted person. Our second benchmark is a classifier for the CIFAR-10 dataset; in this one we applied the same approach to obtain an image that gets labeled as a certain class in the set o classes present in CIFAR-10. After the successful application of model inversion on both models we implemented MLPrivacyGuard to add randomness to the confidence levels. For all of our experiments, the exponential distribution yielded the best results for the error injection. As our results will show, MLPrivacyGuard effectively prevents the convergence of model inversion attacks, while preserving a low misclassification rate for legitimate users. In the experiments presented, we only vary the value of the parameter $\lambda$ of the exponential distribution, since we adopt exponential distribution for all error injection. Thus, $1/\lambda$ represents the mean of the absolute value of the errors, as 50% of the errors are negative.

## 4.1 Facial Recognition

Facial recognition detects a face in an input image and verifies if the facial features present in the image correspond to an arbitrary person in the dataset. For this experiment, we considered the name of the person to be a non-sensitive feature, while the pixels of the image used as input comprise the vector **x**. Via numerical approximations, we are able to initialize a vector with random values for each pixel and converge it to an image that minimizes the distance between the facial features of the input and the face of the target person in the dataset. We chose to adopt the hamming distance of the input/target facial features because that is the output of the model used for this experiment. A value in the interval [0, 1] could be easily obtained using the softmax function, the results would be the same, but the visualization of the plot is better using the distance.

Figure 3 shows the attempt to converge (distance minimization) for a model inversion on a certain subject of the dataset, using different $\lambda$ parameters for the exponential distribution. The results allow us to pick the best value for $\lambda$ that prevents the attack, which intuitively is the one with the moving average (dashed lines) with slope closest to zero, since, as aforementioned, the mean error is zero. It is clear that $\lambda = 35$ renders the best results, so this value is chosen for MLPrivacyGuard in this benchmark. Note that when $\lambda = 40$, the attack stops in less than 5 iterations, because the mean $1/\lambda$ becomes so small that the errors injected do not prevent it.

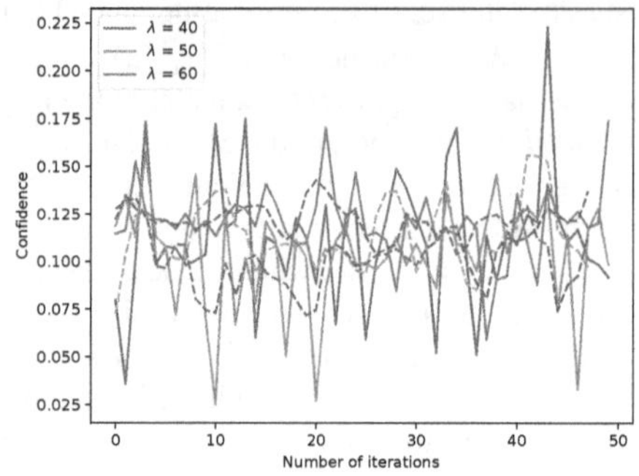


**Figure 3: Model Inversion Attack on Facial Recognition Benchmark. The best value for $\lambda$ is the one with the slope of the moving average closest to zero.**

The wavelike shape of the curve Distance vs. Number of iterations of the MI attack for the chosen $\lambda$ demonstrates that the attack can not converge. If we were to plot the same graph for the attack without MLPrivacyGuard, the curve would just show the hamming distance monotonically decreasing with the number of iterations of Algorithm 1.

Another important aspect, as stated before, is that the chosen $\lambda$ also preserves a low rate of misclassification. For this benchmark, with $\lambda = 40$ we obtained an increase of only 2% (from 4% to 6%) in the overall misclassification rate, which is acceptable for this application, even more so considering the absolute protection against model inversion that was obtained. The reason why the misclassification for users remains low while model inversion attacks are prevented is that the gradient approximation used by black-box model inversion attack calls the model function $O(n)$ times, where $n$ is the number of features in the vector, while a user just makes one call to the model to verify if the given image matches the target person.

## 4.2 CIFAR10 Image Classifier

The CIFAR-10 [6] dataset consists of 60000 32x32 RGB images in 10 classes, with 6000 images per class. For these experiments we applied model inversion on a CIFAR-10 classifier implemented in GluonCV [7]. We chose this classifier because of its simplicity, which allowed us to conduct experiments in feasible time. The feature vector $\mathbf{x} = (x_0, x_1, ..., x_{1024})$ is a representation of the image that should be labeled as the target class. Each $x_i$ corresponds to the grayscale intensity of a pixel of the input 32x32 image. The reason for using grayscale images in the experiments is also to reduce the running time of the experiments.

Model inversion was implemented by numerically differentianting $\tilde{f}_{label}$ (where *label* is a class of CIFAR-10) with respect to each pixel in **x**, which then comprises the approximation of $\nabla\tilde{f}_{label}(\mathbf{x})$. As we described in Algorithm 1, the approximated gradient is thus added to the feature vector until the confidence is high enough to guarantee that the image comprised by the pixels in **x** is classified by the model with the target label.

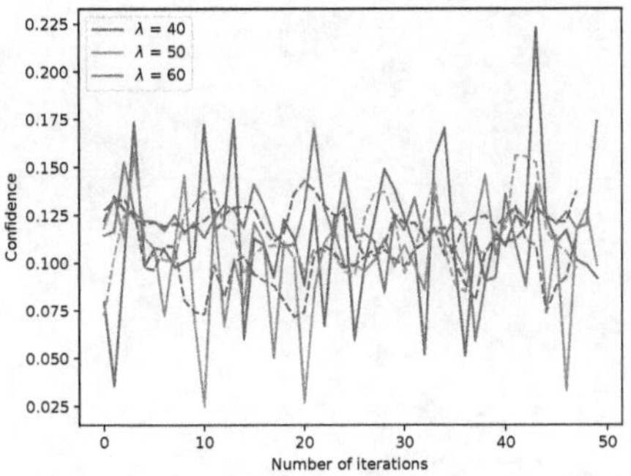


**Figure 4: Model Inversion Attack on CIFAR-10 classifier protected with MLPrivacyGuard with different values for $\lambda$.**

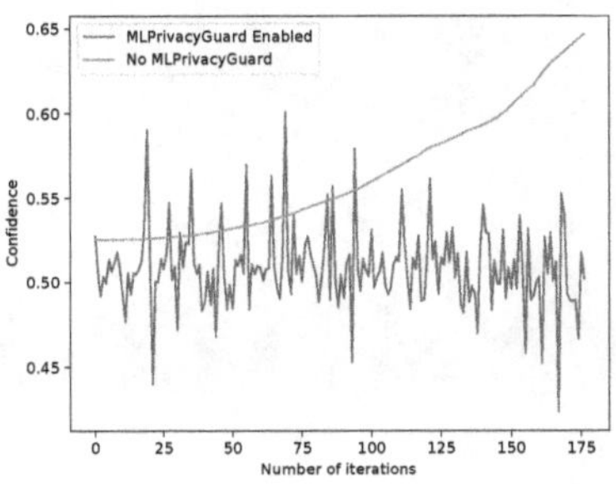


**Figure 5: Model Inversion Attack on CIFAR-10.**

MLPrivacyGuard here is also implemented using the exponential distribution and the parameter $\lambda$ is picked after running model inversion attempts with different values. Figure 4 shows the value of $\tilde{f}_{deer}(\mathbf{x})$, where *deer* is one of the classes in CIFAR-10, along the iterations of the loop in the attack.

We tested the misclassification rate for all the values of $\lambda$ in Figure 4. The results indicate that MLPrivacyGuard does not increase the probability of misclassification for any of these values, so we picked the one with the moving average closest to a constant function, namely, $\lambda = 60$. Figure 5 presents the effectiveness of the countermeasure when MLPrivacyGuard is enabled.

## 5 DISCUSSION

In this paper we introduced MLPrivacyGuard, a novel countermeasure against model inversion attacks. Our experimental results with image classification models (facial recognition and cifar-10 object classifier) show that MLPrivacyGuard does indeed prevent the attacks by addind errors with long-tailed distribution to the confidence levels returned by the ML system. This protection is due to the fact that the convergence curve of the model inversion attack is shaped like a wave when the best parameters for the distribution are chosen. The ideal parameters must keep the errors small enough to not jeopardize correct classification for legitimate users whilst yielding almost constant moving averages for the convergence attempts by adversaries. The values picked according to this criteria for the Facial Recognition and CIFAR-10 benchmarks were exponential distribution with $\lambda = 35$ and $\lambda = 60$, respectively.

It is also important to note that, for the chosen parameters, the misclassification rates were not affected by the errors injected by MLPrivacyGuard. This is due to the following facts:

- The probability of a large error being injected is small, since we adopt long-tailed distributions.
- Legitimate users only make one request to the model per input, so the effect of small errors is not significant.
- An attacker has to call the ML system $O(n)$ times to numerically approximate the gradient $\nabla\tilde{f}$ in a black-box model inversion attack, thus increasing the impact of errors.

MLPrivacyGuard is non-invasive, does not require retraining or any structural changes to the model; the attack is prevented simply by adding noise to the output $\nabla\tilde{f}$, making it attractive compared to solutions involving transformations and retraining. One pitfall of this approach is that it may be possible to make repeated calls with the same input to average the confidence noise to 0. However, such attacks are easily detected and defended by denial of services to the user.

## 6 CONCLUSION

Model inversion attack, where an adversary with access to a ML model can reverse engineer attributes of a target class, poses a threat to privacy of training data. In this paper, we presented MLPrivacyGuard, a countermeasure against black-box model inversion attack. MLPrivacyGuard adds controlled noise to the output of the confidence function that follows a long-tailed distribution. For the Facial Recognition and the CIFAR-10 classification benchmarks, the exponential distribution with $\lambda$ parameters equal to 35 and 60, respectively, were shown to increase the classification error rate at most by 2% while defeating adversarial model inversion attacks.

## REFERENCES

[1] Hervé Abdi and Lynne J. Williams. 2010. Principal Component Analysis. *WIREs Comput. Stat.* 2, 4 (July 2010), 433–459. https://doi.org/10.1002/wics.101
[2] Matt Fredrikson, Somesh Jha, and Thomas Ristenpart. 2015. Model Inversion Attacks That Exploit Confidence Information and Basic Countermeasures. (2015), 1322–1333. https://doi.org/10.1145/2810103.2813677
[3] Matthew Fredrikson, Eric Lantz, Somesh Jha, Simon Lin, David Page, and Thomas Ristenpart. 2014. Privacy in Pharmacogenetics: An End-to-end Case Study of Personalized Warfarin Dosing. In *Proceedings of the 23rd USENIX Conference on Security Symposium (SEC'14)*. USENIX Association, Berkeley, CA, USA, 17–32. http://dl.acm.org/citation.cfm?id=2671225.2671227
[4] Alexandros Karatzoglou and Balázs Hidasi. 2017. Deep Learning for Recommender Systems. In *Proceedings of the Eleventh ACM Conference on Recommender Systems (RecSys '17)*. ACM, New York, NY, USA, 396–397. https://doi.org/10.1145/3109859.3109933
[5] Igor Kononenko. 2001. Machine Learning for Medical Diagnosis: History, State of the Art and Perspective. *Artif. Intell. Med.* 23, 1 (Aug. 2001), 89–109. https://doi.org/10.1016/S0933-3657(01)00077-X
[6] Alex Krizhevsky. 2009. *Learning multiple layers of features from tiny images.* Technical Report.
[7] Giang Nguyen, Stefan Dlugolinsky, Martin Bobák, Viet Tran, Álvaro López García, Ignacio Heredia, Peter Malík, and Ladislav Hluchý. 2019. Machine Learning and Deep Learning frameworks and libraries for large-scale data mining: a survey. *Artificial Intelligence Review* (19 Jan 2019). https://doi.org/10.1007/s10462-018-09679-z
[8] L.M.M. Thomson. 2015. *The Calculus of Finite Differences.* Creative Media Partners, LLC. https://books.google.com/books?id=vi5AjgEACAAJ
[9] Florian Tramèr, Fan Zhang, Ari Juels, Michael K. Reiter, and Thomas Ristenpart. 2016. Stealing Machine Learning Models via Prediction APIs. In *Proceedings of the 25th USENIX Conference on Security Symposium (SEC'16)*. USENIX Association, Berkeley, CA, USA, 601–618. http://dl.acm.org/citation.cfm?id=3241094.3241142

# XNOR-SRAM: In-Bitcell Computing SRAM Macro based on Resistive Computing Mechanism

*Invited*

Zhewei Jiang
Electrical Engineering
Columbia University
New York, NY, US
zj2139@columbia.edu

Shihui Yin
School of ECEE
Arizona State Univ.
Tempe, AZ, US
syin11@asu.edu

Jae-sun Seo
School of ECEE
Arizona State Univ.
Tempe, AZ, US
jseo28@asu.edu

Mingoo Seok
Electrical Engineering
Columbia University
New York, NY, US
ms4415@columbia.edu

## ABSTRACT

We present an *in-memory computing* SRAM macro for binary neural networks. The memory macro computes XNOR-and-accumulate for binary/ternary deep convolutional neural networks on the bitline without row-by-row data access. It achieves 33X better energy and 300X better energy-delay-product than digital ASIC and achieves high accuracy in machine learning tasks (98.3% for MNIST and 85.7% for CIFAR-10 datasets).

## CCS CONCEPTS

• Hardware Accelerators • Analog computers • Dynamic Memory • Neural Networks

## KEYWORDS

In-memory computing, near-memory computing, machine learning accelerator, mixed-signal processing

**ACM Reference format:**

Zhewei Jiang, Shihui Yin, Jae-sun Seo, and Mingoo Seok. 2019. XNOR-SRAM: In-Bitcell Computing SRAM Macro based on Resistive Computing Mechanism. In *Proceedings of ACM GLSVLSI, Tyson Corners, VA, USA (GLSVLSI'19), 6 pages.*
DOI: 10.1145/3299874.3319458

## 1 Introduction

Edge computing is becoming ever more ubiquitous nowadays, driven by the rapid development of Internet-of-Things (IoT). Important features desirable in IoT are low latency, small data packets, and high security. These specifications are what made edge computing, as opposed to cloud computing, an important area for IoT engineering efforts. By virtue of performing the bulk of computation in the edge nodes, the amount of data for transmission is greatly reduced, and the security of the overall system is improved since much of the user-end information are neve transmitted. For much of the IoT edge computing needs, machine learning is a very important component.

Deep Neural Networks (DNNs) have unprecedentedly improved the accuracies in recognition tasks, which have a significant presence in IoT edge computing [1]. However, the arithmetic complexity, memory access, and the associated cost have limited the energy-efficiency of DNN deployment. For prevalent DNNs such as Convolutional Neural Networks (CNN), Multi-Layer Perceptron (MLP) or Recurrent Neural Networks (RNN), the bulk of DNN computations are multiply-and-accumulate and storage is dominated by weights. These two aspects are the most important vectors in tackling the edge node machine learning effort. To address the high computing cost, recent algorithms employ low-precision techniques where the weights and neuron activations are binarized to +1 or -1 [2-4]. In these Binary Neural Networks (BNN), the multiplication between weights and inputs/activations becomes an XNOR operation and the accumulation becomes bitcount of those XNOR results. With such computation reduction, data access can dominate the overall energy of CNN hardware [5]. Conventional data storage (e.g., SRAM) requires row-by-row accesses and fetching millions of weights in this manner consumes substantial energy and delay. To avoid this, recent works proposed the in-memory computing scheme, which performs computation on the bitline without reading out each row of memory [6-8], demonstrating large energy improvements.

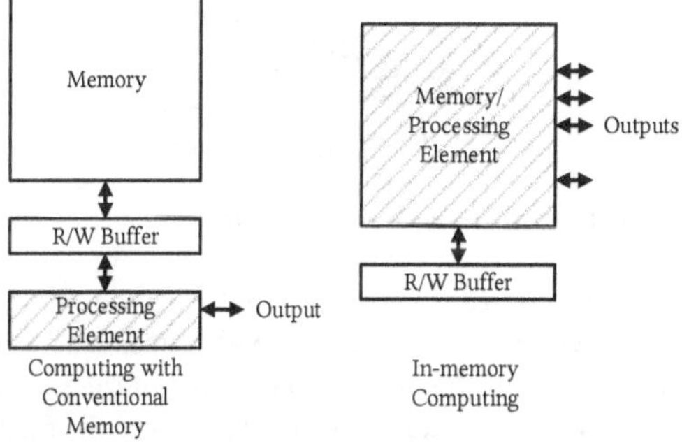


**Figure 1: Illustration of in-memory computing concept.**



*GLSVLSI '19, May 9–11, 2019, Tysons Corner, VA, USA*
© 2019 Association for Computing Machinery.
ACM ISBN 978-1-4503-6252-8/19/05 $15.00
https://doi.org/10.1145/3299874.3319458

As illustrated in Fig. 1, in-memory computing drastically improves the computing latency and throughput by eliminating the memory read bottleneck during high volume computation.

In this paper, we propose an in-memory mixed-signal SRAM macro titled XNOR-SRAM, which energy-efficiently computes XNOR-and-Accumulate (XAC) in binary/ternary DNNs. Our XNOR-SRAM performs a 256-input XAC without memory readout, via analog accumulation of bitwise XNOR results on the Read BitLine (RBL) voltage of the SRAM array, and digitizes the RBL voltage (VRBL) using a flash Analog-to-Digital Converter (ADC) embedded in the periphery. XNOR-SRAM supports binary weights (+1, -1) and binary inputs (+1, -1) as well as ternary inputs (+1, 0, -1). The 65 nm prototype [9] achieves 300X better Energy-Delay-Product (EDP) than digital ASIC in computing XAC. DNN/CNN classification using our macro achieves 98.3% accuracy for MNIST and 85.7% accuracy for CIFAR-10 dataset.

# 2 Architecture and Operation

## 2.1 Overview of major CNN/MLP computations

The basic building blocks of CNN are shown in Fig. 2. There are two types of layers in a typical CNN implementation, the convolutional layer and the fully connected layer. The network is composed of many convolutional layers that extract higher-level abstraction of input features and followed by several layers of fully connected layers, which determine the final classification result.

In the convolutional layer, filters composed of multiple channels of small kernels, which extract certain features, is 2D convolved with the input image and produce an output image (typically a 3D volume of many channels) that are then down-sampled via a pooling process, with max-pooling being the most common.

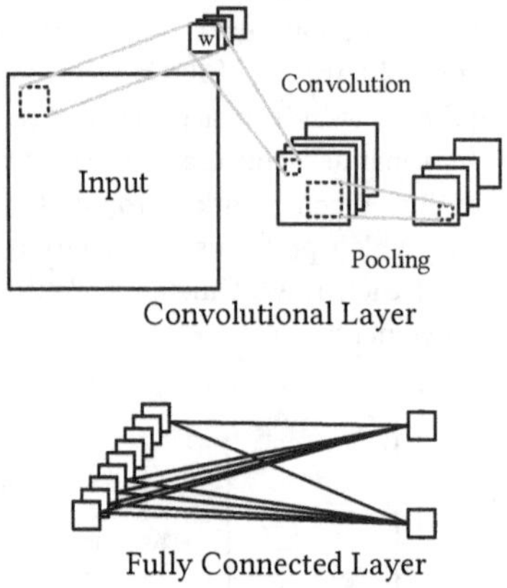


**Figure 2: Illustrations of basic CNN layers.**

In the fully-connected layers, the inputs are the features that have been down-sampled to a vector, each value being a channel. The weighted sum of this input is the output of the layer, which in turn becomes the input for the next layer until the final result. MLPs only consist of multiple fully-connected layers that are connected in series.

Both the convolutional and fully-connected layers in binary CNNs and MLPs are dominated by XAC operations with a high number of inputs. Additionally, machine learning algorithms are generally tolerant of degradation in intermediate computation. These two aspects make BNN a perfect application for in-memory mixed-signal computing for edge devices. BNN implementations based on in-memory computing can obtain a large improvement in energy, speed, and throughput, with minimal degradation in accuracy.

## 2.2 Architecture

Fig. 3 presents the proposed XNOR-SRAM architecture, which can map convolutional and fully-connected layers of binary/ternary CNNs and MLPs. The macro consists of a 256-by-64 custom SRAM array, a row decoder, an XNOR-mode WL driver, and a column periphery including an 11-level nonlinear flash ADC.

The XNOR-SRAM operates in either of two modes: memory mode and XNOR mode. In memory mode, it performs row-by-row digital read/write as regular memory circuits. In XNOR mode, it performs in-memory XAC computation with all rows asserted simultaneously. The XAC computation is computed in the analog domain.

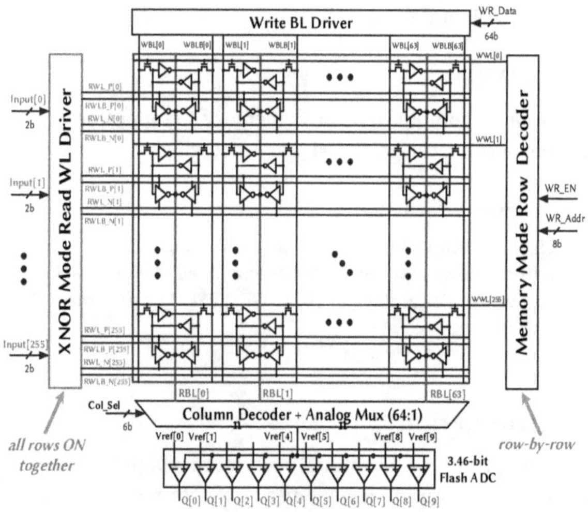


**Figure 3: XNOR-SRAM architecture.**

Fig. 4 shows the proposed 12T SRAM bitcell. T1 to T6 form a 6T SRAM cell; T7 to T10 form complimentary pull-up/-down (PU/PD) circuits for XNOR mode (and memory mode read); T11 and T12 power-gate the PU/PD circuits when the corresponding column is not enabled.

## 2.3 XNOR-SRAM Operation

In XNOR mode, the RWL (Read Word-Line) driver translates each ternary/binary input of the input vector to four RWLs according to Fig. 5. T7 to T10 in each bitcell in a selected column perform XNOR of the RWL (input/activation) and the weight stored in the bitcell.

As shown in Fig. 6, the XNOR output '+1' yields one strong PU by PMOS and one weak PU by NMOS; XNOR output '-1' results in one strong PD by NMOS and one weak PD by PMOS; XNOR output '0' is implemented by driving even rows of input '0' with strong PU/PD and odd rows of input '0' with weak PU/PD. The output '0' case yields the average strength of the '+1' and '-1' cases, as '0' inputs are randomly distributed in ternary CNNs.

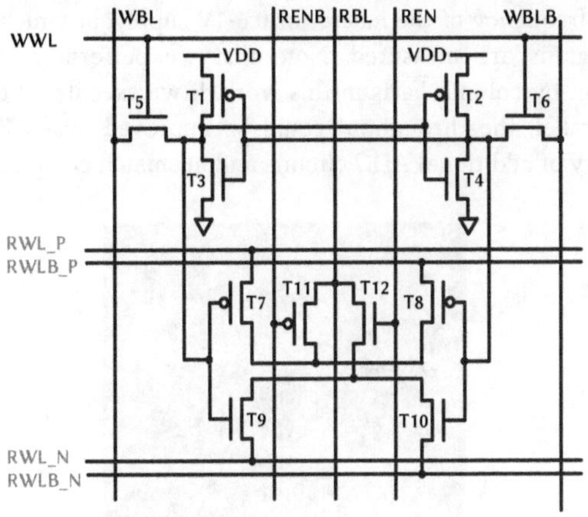


**Figure 4: XNOR-SRAM bitcell.**

| Input / RWL | +1 | -1 | 0 even row | 0 odd row |
|---|---|---|---|---|
| RWL_P | VDD | 0 | 0 | VDD |
| RWL_N | VDD | 0 | VDD | 0 |
| RWLB_P | 0 | VDD | 0 | VDD |
| RWLB_N | 0 | VDD | VDD | 0 |

**Figure 5: RWL control for XNOR operation.**

Parallel XNOR-output-controlled PU/PD paths from all bitcells in a column form a voltage divider, where RBL is the output. VRBL, therefore, becomes a monotonic transfer function of XAC (Fig. 7), and we can obtain the XAC result by digitizing VRBL with the ADC. The XAC mode computation is decoupled from the conventional read/write such that there is no risk of data being overwritten.

The embedded ADC plays a key role in the speed and DNN accuracy. We chose the flash ADC using strong-arm comparators for speed. We also investigated the required precision based on CIFAR-10 and MNIST datasets and found that employing 11 levels with nonlinear quantization using a Lloyd-Max algorithm based on statistical distribution yields satisfactory accuracy [10]. Fig. 7 shows the optimized references used for the 0.6V operation of XNOR-SRAM.

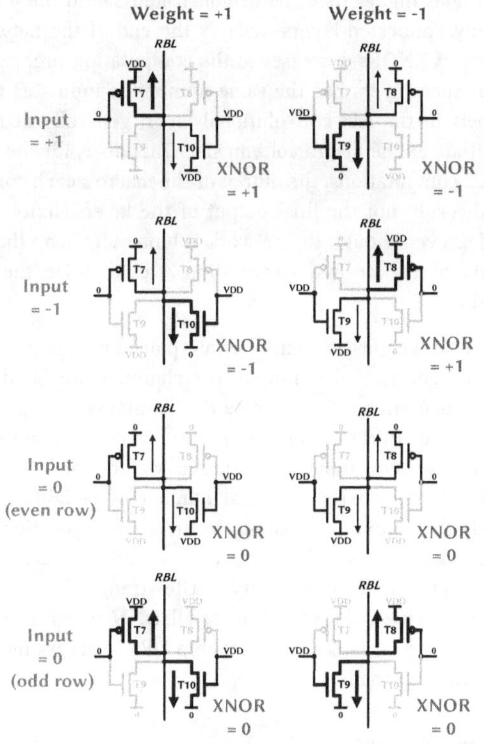


**Figure 6: Binary and ternary XNOR operations.**

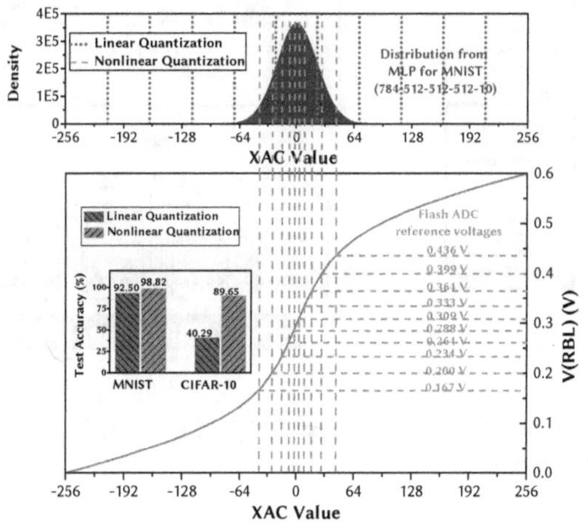


**Figure 7: XAC mapping on VRBL and nonlinear quantization.**

## 3 Mapping to BNN Layers

The macro computes generic XAC with a set amount of input terms. Efficiently mapping the desired network topology onto the macro is important for energy and latency savings.

For convolution layers, the number of XNOR terms is the total number of weights in a filter, i.e. kernel size multiplied by the channel count. Besides the first layer, which typically has few channels, the total bitcells needed are typical one or two magnitudes higher than the demonstrated 256 in the macro. For the fully connected layers towards the end of the network, the number of XNORs decreases as the computation progresses. The first of such layers has the same number of inputs as there are channels in the last convolutional layer, generally at the same magnitude as the macro column size. Therefore, for the majority of XAC computations, the output of the macro's each column is a partial result, not the final output of the layer. Hence the need for ADC even though the network is binary. To map the column outputs to the desired convolution, we organize the data as shown in Fig. 8.

The kernel weights in each filter are placed in separate memory macros. Following that format, the channels are filled in row-wise orientation. Each column contains weights from independent filters from the same layer, since all columns receive the same input. The unused weights will wait for its scheduled cycle if the the total number of weights in a filter exceeds the amount of memory in the above allocation scheme. This should, however, be avoided if possible to maximize filter reuse and minimize memory write traffic. In many edge computing cases, the condition of all DNN weights stored on-chip will be guaranteed since off-chip DRAM access incurs large energy/delay penalties.

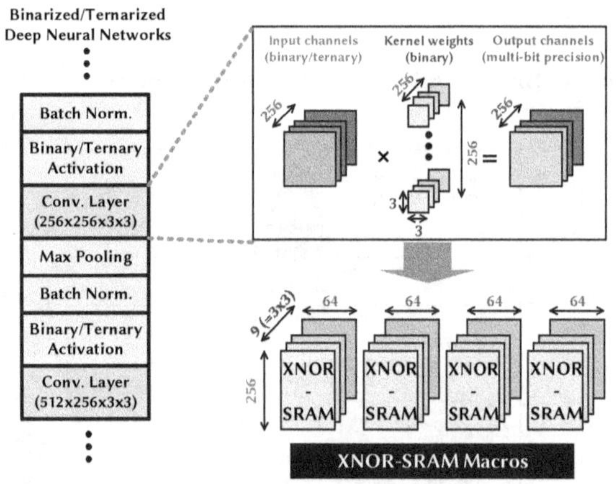


**Figure 8: Mapping binary CNNs onto multiple XNOR-SRAM macros.**

For fully-parallel computations, after each readout on the entire array, the ADC results are saved in scratchpads to be summed with the outputs of other memory macros or other cycles. For convolutional or fully connected layers that have fewer terms than the number of rows, the inputs are zero-padded. The output is binarized and serves as the result of the final convolution.

# 4 Measurements and Comparison

## 4.1 Power and delay measurements

We prototyped the proposed XNOR-SRAM in 65 nm CMOS (Fig. 9). Fig. 10 shows the power consumption of the column. Note the power is dependent on the XAC result. This is due to the nature of the voltage divider, where the least resistance occurs when the XAC output is zero. Unfortunately, the distribution of XAC outputs peaks around zero in typical DNNs.

At the supply of 1V, performing 64 operations of 256-input XAC at the worst energy case (all XAC outputs at zero), the XNOR-SRAM has a measured energy consumption of 235.5 pJ and latency of 54.21 ns. Fig. 11 shows the energy and the maximum clock frequency of the macro for 0.6-1V supply, at which similar EDP gains are measured. Note that we perform XAC on a column-by-column basis in this work. If we execute all columns in parallel, the throughput could be improved by ~64X at the penalty of additional ADC circuits and mismatch compensation.

**Figure 9: Die photo of 65 nm XNOR-SRAM macro.**

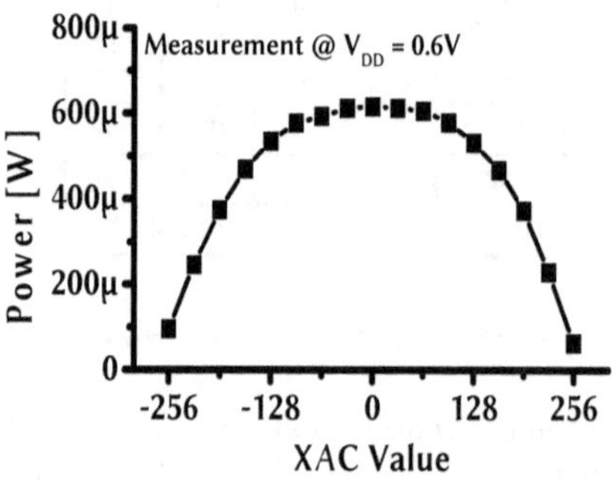


**Figure 10: Data-dependent XNOR-SRAM power consumption.**

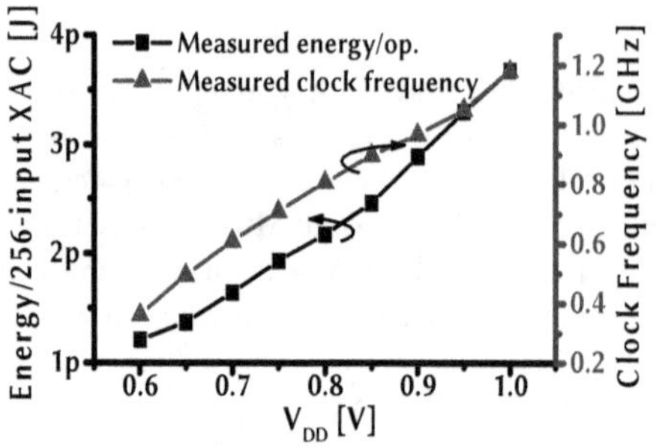


**Figure 11: Energy and delay scaling with supply.**

As a baseline comparison, we designed a well-crafted digital accelerator in 65 nm, which computes the same XAC but has to access weights from conventional SRAM. The post-layout simulation based on industrial 6T SRAMs, standard cells, and parasitic-annotated netlists at 1V supply (TT 25℃) shows the digital baseline consumes 7.81 nJ and 514 ns for the same XAC operations, 33X worse in energy and 300X worse in EDP than our macro also operating at 1V (Fig. 12).

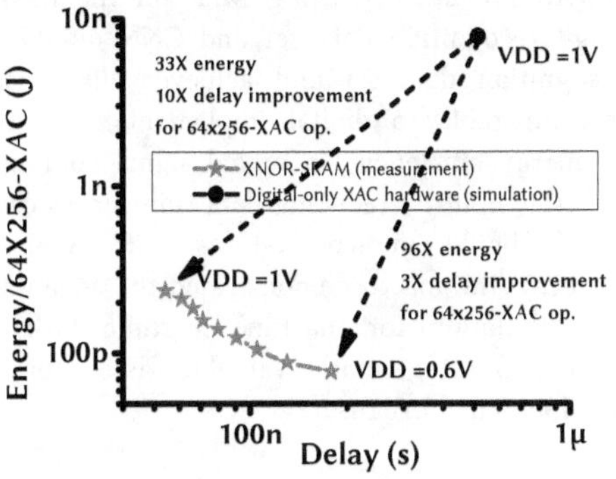


**Figure 12: Energy and delay comparison with conventional digital ASIC.**

The power and area breakdowns are presented in Fig. 13. The power is dominated by the driver power as the computation mechanism is current divider where the current is supplied by the driver source, and the area is mainly occupied by the SRAM array as the ADC is shared by 64 columns.

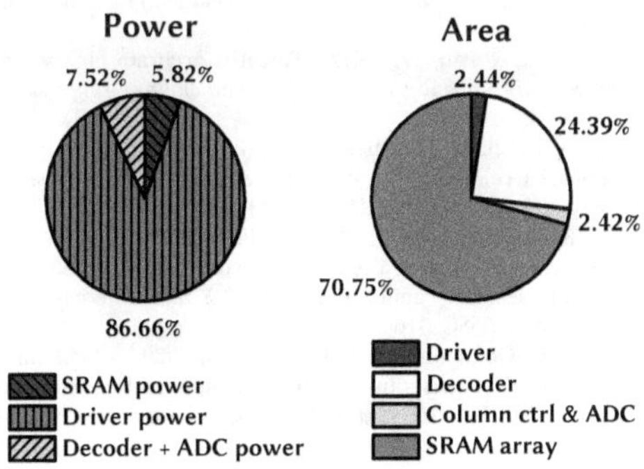


**Figure 13: Area and power breakdown.**

## 4.2 Non-idealities and mitigation approaches

The systematic strength imbalance between NMOS and PMOS can skew the transfer function. While this can be mitigated by setting the reference voltages according to the measured transfer curve, it is not optimal because extremely skewed transfer curve will negatively affect the ADC accuracy by decreasing the reference step. To maximize the difference between adjacent reference voltages for the ADC, the transfer function should have the least skewness.

We addressed this by biasing PMOS N-wells in the bitcell array at the marginal area/power penalty (Fig. 14). Given an optimal body bias, the transfer function passes the XAC output zero at half VDD.

Fig. 15 shows another measured non-ideality: VRBL variability resulted from process variation and parasitics across different columns and data patterns. For process variation, the operating principle of current based computation is at a disadvantage as dopant variation is more severe than geometric variations. The mitigation strategy here is implicit in the construction of the macro. As the number of bitcells increase, the variability decreases quadratically [11].

The most significant source of error is parasitics. While the bitcells themselves are designed to match resistance in all paths, bitcells in different rows may have varied resistance PU/PD paths, due to different lengths of RBL segments to the ADC. This is also minimized implicitly via a statistical convenience. As input/activations are distributed randomly, there is a deterministic skew that is implicitly captured by the transfer function. The variation on this curve is much less than the worst case distribution that cluster inputs. Furthermore, the highest variation (20mV standard deviation) occurred at the lowest XAC value of zero, which has the least impact on final DNN outputs and accuracy.

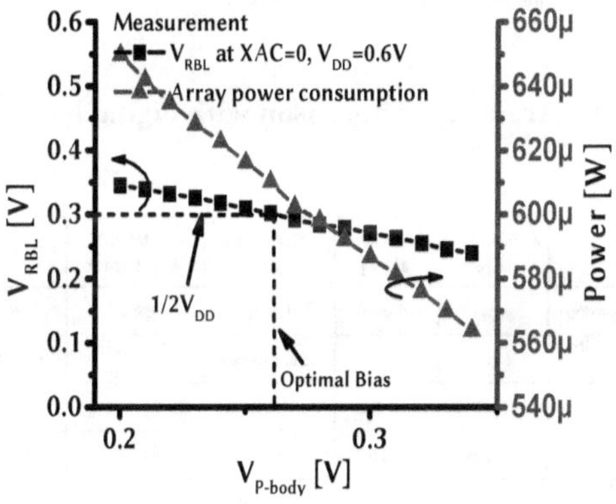


**Figure 14: Body bias tuning for P/N mismatch.**

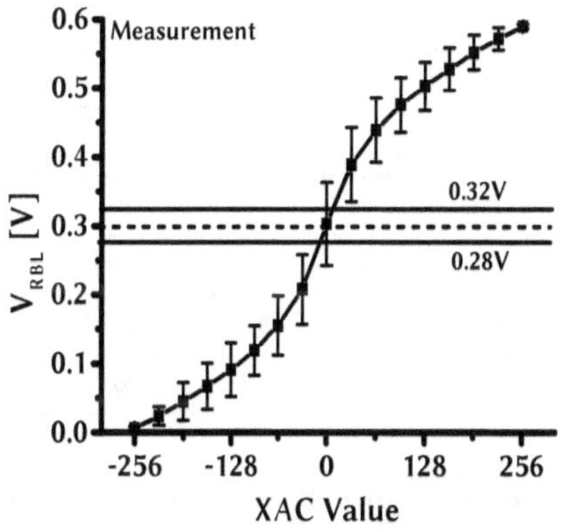


**Figure 15: Transfer function variability.**

Using our macro, we evaluated the accuracy for MNIST and CIFAR-10 datasets (Fig. 16). For MNIST, a MLP with three hidden layers, each with 512 neurons, is used. CNN for CIFAR-10 has six convolutional layers and three fully-connected layers [3]. Starting from the first hidden layer of the MLP/CNN, our macro computes 256-input XACs for MAC/convolution operations. Accumulation of XAC outputs, pooling, and batch normalization are performed in the digital simulation with bit precisions of 12, 12, and 10, respectively. The DNNs with our macro (with ideal digital simulation) achieve 98.3% (98.8%) accuracy for MNIST and 85.7% (90.7%) for CIFAR-10.

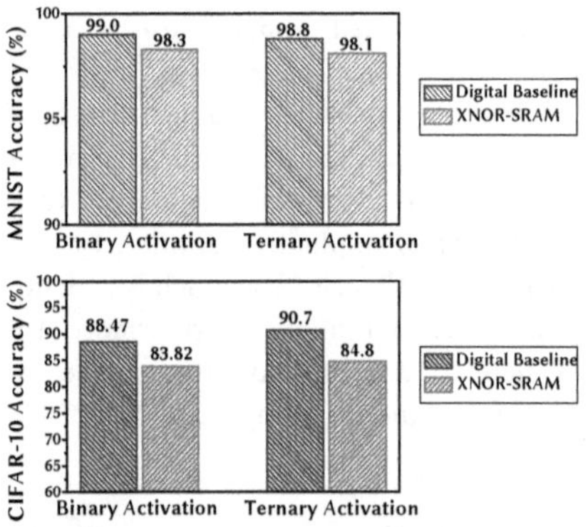


**Figure 16: Accuracy comparison with digital baseline.**

| | *A. Biswas et al.* [6] | M. Kang *et al.* [7] | J. Zhang *et al.* [8] | Digital XAC Accelerator | This work |
|---|---|---|---|---|---|
| **Technology** | 65nm LP | 65nm | 130nm | 65nm | 65nm |
| **SRAM bitcell area** | 4 μm² | 2.11x0.92 μm² | 1.26x3.44 μm² | Off-the-shelf 6T, <0.1μm² | 1.45x2.7 μm² |
| **Array size** | 256x64 | 512x256 | 128x128 | 256x64 | 256x64 |
| **Supply voltage** | 0.9-1.2V | 1V and 0.75V | 1.2V (WL: <0.4V) | 1.0V | 0.6-1.0V |
| **Column sensing** | CSH ADC | Differential SA | Differential SA | Digital adder | **Flash ADC** |
| **Supported operation/algorithm** | DCNN (1-b weight, 5-b input) | Random forest classifier | Ada-Boost (1-b weight, 5-b inputs) | DCNN (1-b weight, binary/ ternary input) | **DCNN (1-b weight, binary/ ternary input)** |
| **Energy per operation (operation)** | 3.6pJ (Convolution) | 19.4 nJ/ decision (64-tree decision) | 2.84 fJ (Dot product) | 28.3 fJ (1.0V) (ternary XNOR / acc.) | **2.48-7.19 fJ (0.6-1.0V)** (ternary XNOR / acc.) |
| **Reported EDP gain** | 60X | 6.8X | 175X | 1X | **288-330X (0.6-1.0V)** |
| **MNIST accuracy** | 96% | N/A | 90% | 98.8% | **98.3%** |
| **CIFAR-10 accuracy** | N/A | N/A | N/A | 90.7% | **85.7%** |
| **KUL traffic sign accuracy** | N/A | 94% | N/A | N/A | N/A |

**Figure 17: Comparison with prior in-memory computing works.**

As shown in Fig. 17, our macro improves EDP by 300X over digital hardware performing the same XAC operations while improving classification accuracy significantly over prior in-memory computing hardware [6-8].

## 5 Conclusion

This paper presents XNOR-SRAM, an in-memory binary/ternary convolution macro for accelerating neural networks. We demonstrated functionality using MLP on the MNIST hand-written digit recognition data set and CNN on the CIFAR-10 object recognition data set and achieved high classification accuracy comparable to digital implementations. The macro improves energy efficiency via mixed signal computation and improves throughput by reducing data transfer, as compared to conventional digital implementations with Von Neumann memory access. The macro demonstrated the advantages of in-memory computation for machine learning tasks and will become an increasing more valuable asset for the edge computing dominated IoT future.

## ACKNOWLEDGMENTS

The work is supported in part by Wei Family Private Foundation and Catalyst Foundation.

## REFERENCES

[1] Mohammadi, M., Al-Fuqaha, A., Sorour, S., & Guizani, M. (2018). Deep learning for IoT big data and streaming analytics: A survey. *IEEE Communications Surveys & Tutorials*, 20(4), 2923-2960.

[2] M. Rastegari, V. Ordonez, J. Redmon, A. Farhadi, (2016). Xnor-net: Imagenet classification using binary convolutional neural networks. In *European Conference on Computer Vision*, 525-542.

[3] I. Hubara, M. Courbariaux, D. Soudry, R. El-Yaniv, Y. Bengio, (2016). Binarized neural networks. In *Advances in neural information processing systems*, 4107-4115.

[4] Lin, X., Zhao, C., & Pan, W. (2017). Towards accurate binary convolutional neural network. *In Advances in Neural Information Processing Systems* (pp. 345-353).

[5] Y. H. Chen, T. Krishna, J. S. Emer, V. Sze, (2017). Eyeriss: An energy-efficient reconfigurable accelerator for deep convolutional neural networks. *IEEE Journal of Solid-State Circuits*, 52(1), 127-138.

[6] Biswas, A., & Chandrakasan, A. P. (2018, February). Conv-RAM: An energy-efficient SRAM with embedded convolution computation for low-power CNN-based machine learning applications. *In 2018 IEEE International Solid-State Circuits Conference-(ISSCC)* (pp. 488-490). IEEE.

[7] M. Kang, S. K. Gonugondla, N. R. Shanbhag, (2017, September). A 19.4 nJ/decision 364K decisions/s in-memory random forest classifier in 6T SRAM array. *In IEEE ESSCIRC 2017-43rd IEEE European Solid-State Circuits Conference*, 263-266.

[8] J. Zhang, Z. Wang, N. Verma, (2017). In-memory computation of a machine-learning classifier in a standard 6T SRAM array. *IEEE Journal of Solid-State Circuits*, 52(4), 915-924.

[9] Jiang, Z., Yin, S., Seok, M., & Seo, J. S. (2018, June). XNOR-SRAM: In-Memory Computing SRAM Macro for Binary/Ternary Deep Neural Networks. *In 2018 IEEE Symposium on VLSI Technology* (pp. 173-174). IEEE.

[10] Lloyd, S. (1982). Least squares quantization in PCM. *IEEE transactions on information theory*, 28(2), 129-137.

[11] Borkar, S. (2005). Designing reliable systems from unreliable components: the challenges of transistor variability and degradation. *IEEE Micro*, 25(6), 10-16.

# Efficient Process-in-Memory Architecture Design for Unsupervised GAN-based Deep Learning using ReRAM

Fan Chen, Linghao Song, Hai "Helen" Li
Department of Electrical and Computer Engineering, Duke University, Durham, North Carolina, USA
{fan.chen,linghao.song,hai.li}@duke.edu

## ABSTRACT

The ending of Moore's Law makes domain-specific architecture as the future of computing. The most representative is the emergence of various deep learning accelerators. Among the proposed solutions, resistive random access memory (ReRAM) based process-in-memory (PIM) architecture is anticipated as a promising candidate because ReRAM has the capability of both data storage and in-situ computation. However, we found that existing solutions are unable to efficiently support the computational needs required by the training of unsupervised generative adversarial networks (GANs), due to the lack of the following two features: 1) Computation efficiency: GAN utilizes a new operator, called transposed convolution. It inserts massive zeros in its input before a convolution operation, resulting in significant resource under-utilization; 2) Data traffic: The data intensive training process of GANs often incurs structural heavy data traffic as well as frequent massive data swaps. Our research follows the PIM strategy by leveraging the energy-efficiency of ReRAM arrays for vector-matrix multiplication to enhance the performance and energy efficiency. Specifically, we propose a novel computation deformation technique that can skip zero-insertions in transposed convolution for computation efficiency improvement. Moreover, we explore an efficient pipelined training procedure to reduce on-chip memory access. The implementation of related circuits and architecture is also discussed. At the end, we present our perspective on the future trend and opportunities of deep learning accelerators.

## CCS CONCEPTS

• **Hardware → Hardware accelerators.**

## KEYWORDS

GAN; process-in-memory; ReRAM; unsupervised learning

**ACM Reference Format:**

Fan Chen, Linghao Song, Hai "Helen" Li. 2019. Efficient Process-in-Memory Architecture Design for Unsupervised GAN-based Deep Learning using ReRAM. In *Great Lakes Symposium on VLSI 2019 (GLSVLSI '19), May 9–11, 2019, Tysons Corner, VA, USA.* ACM, New York, NY, USA, 6 pages. https://doi.org/10.1145/3299874.3319482



*GLSVLSI '19, May 9–11, 2019, Tysons Corner, VA, USA*



ACM ISBN 978-1-4503-6252-8/19/05...$15.00
https://doi.org/10.1145/3299874.3319482

## 1 INTRODUCTION

Generative adversarial network (GAN) based unsupervised deep learning has recently been extensively deployed in various modern computer vision tasks [11, 12, 20]. GANs have demonstrated great potential in extending deep learning into a wider range of domains [8, 13, 30] where sufficient labeled training data is generally unavailable or at least costly to obtain. In contrast to traditional supervised learning which requires a large amount of labeled training data, GANs are capable to learn reusable feature representations from unlabeled samples. In a GAN model, two deep neural networks (DNNs) – a generator and a discriminator, are simultaneously trained against each other via an adversarial process: the generator captures the data distribution and attempts to generate synthetic samples, while the discriminator implements a binary classifier to differentiates the samples generated by a generator against real data. This learning process is performed iteratively until we obtain a generator with strong generative capability and a discriminator with high classification accuracy.

Given the abundant DNN accelerator designs [4, 5, 22, 23], it was believed that the computational needs of GANs can be accommodated by conventional DNN accelerators. As such, for a long period, there was a lack of hardware accelerators for GAN execution. By studying the algorithmic characteristics of GAN models, researchers realized that the training process of GANs involves a special mathematical operator (e.g. transposed convolution), more complex training phases, and massive computation and data movement. These problems, however, have been exacerbated in recent years because of the continuously increasing trend of deploying larger and deeper networks in GANs, e.g. 101-layer ResNet generator and discriminator [12].

Although some designs [24, 28, 29] have recently been proposed for GANs acceleration, these solutions are subject to various constraints. For instance, the dataflow optimization approach in [24] limits the shape and structure of the generator and/or discriminator being trained in a GAN model and fails to support many popular GAN variations. FlexiGAN [28] and GANAX [29] require a sophisticated interleaving MIMD and SIMD microarchitecture to support their proposed dataflow. In this paper, we present our research on efficient architecture design for GANs. We utilize the energy efficiency of the emerging resistive random access memory (ReRAM) array for vector-matrix multiplication, and the design follows the Process-In-Memory (PIM) concept to improve performance and energy efficiency. Specifically, we propose a novel computation deformation technique that can skip zero-insertions in transposed convolution for computation efficiency. Moreover, we explore an efficient pipelined training procedure to reduce on-chip memory access. In summary, we make the following key contributions:

- We completely eliminate inserted zeros in transposed convolution by a novel computation deformation. The optimized computing model exhibits improved computation efficiency and resource utilization.
- We analyze the general training process in GAN and proposed a pipeline architecture that improves system throughput by leveraging structural layer-wise computation. The architecture uses ReRAM array to perform calculations directly, without the need for additional processing units. The ReRAM memory is also used as buffers to store intermediate results. This design greatly reduces data movement and energy consumption by preventing data from being transferred across the memory hierarchy.
- To further improve the training efficiency, we propose *spatial parallelism* and *computation sharing* by exploring the data dependency and the trade-off between parallelism and hardware resource.
- We use various applications and the most recent GAN models on distinct benchmarks to evaluate the effectiveness of the proposed design. Our experimental results show significant acceleration and energy savings compared to prior arts.

## 2 BACKGROUND

In this section, we describe the background of GAN and some of the concepts involved in its development. We also briefly introduce the emerging ReRAM memory and its basic operations.

### 2.1 GAN Basics

GAN is an unsupervised training paradigm based on an adversarial game between a generator (G) and a discriminator (D) as illustrated in Figure 1. Both D and G typically are modeled as DNNs and trained simultaneously. In general, G is optimized to produce good samples from noise to simulate real data distribution, while D is a binary classifier trained by distinguishing between real samples and generated samples. The objective of GAN training can be represented as a minimax game with these two players:

$$\min_{G}\max_{D} V(D,G) = E_{x\sim P_{data}}[logD(x)] + E_{z\sim P_z}[log(1-D(G(z)))] \quad (1)$$

In image processing, most of the GAN variations are (or at least partially) based on the deep convolutional generative adversarial networks (DCGAN) [20]. Therefore, DCGAN is the targe model for GAN acceleration. In DCGAN, D uses discriminative convolutions to "downsample" the input to produce a classification. Instead, G takes a uniform noise distribution as input, then projects it onto a small spatial extent convolutional representation with many feature maps which serves as the beginning of a series of transposed convolutional (TCONV) layers. The results are eventually converted into high-dimension images. Different from traditional convolution operation (CONV), TCONV inserts many zeros into its input feature maps and then performs the up-sampling convolutional computation. The output feature maps of TCONV are larger than its input. TCONV can essentially be implemented using the CONV operator. However, it requires adding several columns and rows of zeros to the inputs, resulting in severe resource under-utilization.

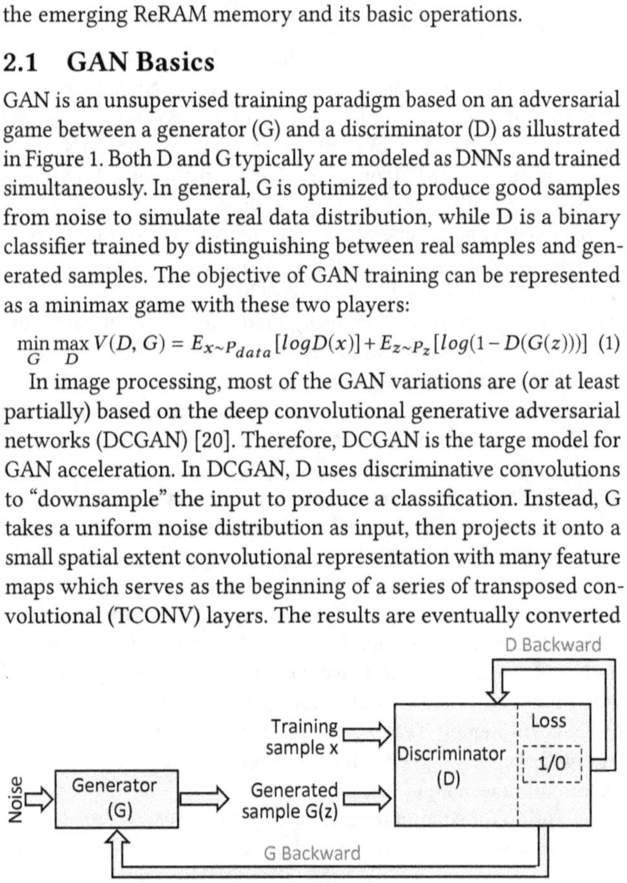


Figure 1: A GAN system.

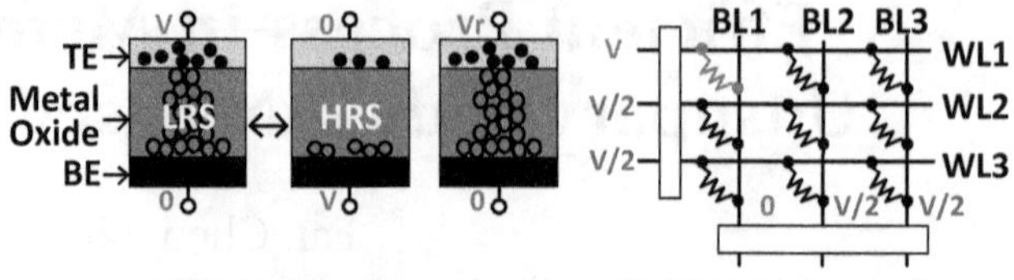


(a) ReRAM cell. (b) 2D ReRAM crossbar.

Figure 2: The ReRAM basics.

Activation layers are typically cascaded after convolutional layers to act as a threshold by performing a non-linear function. The batch normalization layer is another important component. It is applied before activation layers to stabilize the training process of GANs.

### 2.2 ReRAM Basics

ReRAM is an emerging type of non-volatile memory that stores information with cell resistances. As demonstrated in Figure 2(a), each ReRAM cell has a metal oxide layer sandwiched between top electrode (TE) and bottom electrode (BE). The resistance of a ReRAM cell can be programmed by applying a current or voltage with proper pulse-width or magnitude between TE and BE. The data stored in a cell can be represented by the resistance level accordingly: a low resistance state (LRS) denotes logic bit '1', while a high resistance state (HRS) represents logic bit '0'. For read operations, a small sense voltage is applied across the device, and then the cell resistance can be determined based on the magnitude of the detected current to further obtain a corresponding logic value stored in the cell.

Recent work has demonstrated a high density ReRAM crossbar implementation. Figure 2(b) illustrates the array biasing scheme when writing '1' on a $3 \times 3$ ReRAM crossbar array. The wordline (WL) and bitline (BL) of the selected cell are driven to $V$ and 0 respectively, while unselected WLs and BLs are set to $V/2$. To write a '0', the biasing polarity must be alternated. For a read, the selected WL is charge to a small read voltage $V_r$ and the current changes on the corresponding BL will be sensed to determine the resistance.

## 3 PRIOR ARTS

A major challenge in GAN acceleration is the high demand for computing resource and large data transfer because a GAN model consists of two DNNs. Moreover, GANs training involves more complex operations and more computing phases compared to traditional supervised deep learning. For instance, a direct adoption of the accelerator PipeLayer [23] designed for CNN training to implement GAN consumes 3× latency and hardware compared to its CNN counterpart. Moreover, existing schemes mainly focus on accelerating discriminative convolution. The generator core leverages TCONV, a fundamentally different operator that first inserts many zeros into its input feature maps and then performs the up-sampling CONV computation. This operator manifests unique challenges for hardware acceleration, which is not well studied in prior arts.

**Table 1: Comparison of GAN Accelerators**

| Accelerator | Year | Description | Architecture Optimization |
|---|---|---|---|
| [32] | 2017 | TCONV acceleration on FPGA | reversing loop; stride hole skipping |
| FCN-engine [27] | 2018 | CMOS TCONV inference accelerator | reschedule TCONV data path with on-chip buffer |
| Red [10] | 2019 | ReRAM TCONV inference accelerator | pixel-wise mapping; zero-skipping data flow |
| [24] | 2018 | CMOS GAN accelerator | time multiplexed design; zero skipping |
| FlexiGAN [28] | 2018 | GAN acceleration on FPGA | TCONV computation reorder; architecture optimizer on FPGA |
| GANAX [29] | 2018 | CMOS GAN acclerator | TCONV computation reorder; MIMD-SIMD; decoupled access/execute $\mu$engine |

We summarize recent works on GAN acceleration in Table 1. The work in [32] attempted to accelerate TCONV on FPGA. FCN-engine [27] and Red [10] implemented a fully convolutional accelerator that can handle both CONV and TCONV operations using CMOS and ReRAM, respectively. These three works only focus on inference task but do not support the more sophisticated and intensive training function. Song et al. [24] proposes a CMOS-based GAN training accelerator where zero operands can be skipped by carefully mapping the network onto its process elements (PEs). The proposed dataflow, however, imposes strong limitations on the shape and topology of G and/or D, making it less flexible to serve various GAN variations. FlexiGAN [28] and GANAX [29] reorder the output computation and allocate computing rows with similar patterns of zeros to adjacent PEs for efficient TCONV execution. To support such reorganized dataflow, these two works propose specific architectures to realize interleaving MIMD and SIMD operations on FPGA and ASIC, respectively. FlexiGAN [28] and GANAX [29] both implement decoupled access and execute micro-engines, resulting in increased design complexity.

# 4 EFFICIENT PIM ARCHITECTURE FOR GAN

In this section, we present our research on two ReRAM-based accelerator architectures for GANs, namely ReGAN [2] and ZARA [3]. We analyze the GAN training process and then present ReGAN – a training architecture that implements both the inter-layer and intro-layer parallelism in a pipelined fashion for improving the throughput. Our latest work, ZARA, focuses on optimizing the GAN calculation model and completely eliminating the insertion of zeros in the TCONV convolution so as to improve computational efficiency and alleviate under-utilization of resources.

## 4.1 Training Process

Figure 3 demonstrates the complex training phases in a three-layer GAN. A discriminator and a generator are both modeled as a DNN and are alternately trained until they reach equilibrium or meet predetermined constraints. D is trained to differentiate generated fake samples from genuine data. The dataflow of training D with

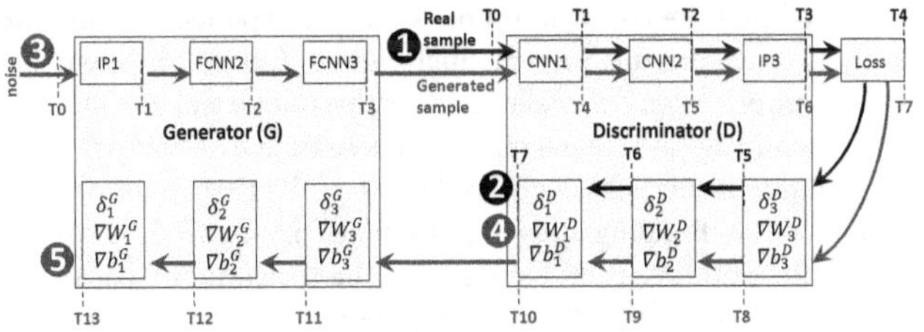


**Figure 3: Training processes in a GAN [2].**

real samples is denoted by ❶~❷. When a training sample enters the first layer in D at $T0$, it continuously flows through all layers in D in the forward direction. A loss function is then calculated at $T4$ based on the exact label ('1' for the training sample). Finally, the error and partial derivatives are propagated back to the first layer of D and stored. This process requires 7 logical cycles.

The data stream of training D with the generated samples is represented by ❸~❹. Here, G is connected to D to form a large network. G maps a random vector to a sample with the same dimension as a real sample. The sample is processed through all layers in D, and a loss function is finally executed using the exact label ('0' for the generated sample). Similarly, the partial derivative propagates back to the first layer of D at $T10$. In $T11$, the two sets of previously calculated and stored derivatives are added together and used to update the weight of D. It takes a total of $7 + 10 + 1 = 18$ cycles. In this process, G is used but not updated.

G is optimized to generate samples that simulate the distribution of real data, thereby tricking D into misprediction. The data stream is represented by ❸~❺, which is similar to ❸~❹, except that: 1) The error is calculated in $T7$ using a different label ('1' for the generated sample), since the target of G is to mislead D; 2) The error is always propagated back to the first layer of G; and 3) The weight of G is updated in $T14$, while D is fixed. Thus, it takes 14 cycles to process one sample with G. Note that the cycles in Figure 3 (e.g. $T0$, $T1$, ...) are logical cycles, which could take several physical clock cycles depending on the implementation details.

## 4.2 Pipelined Design & Compute Optimization

In practice, the training data are processed in batches of size $B$ (e.g., 64 or 128). $B$ is a hyperparameter which controls the number of training samples to process before updating the internal weights of a DNN. For example, when performing DNN training with $B =$ 64, 64 inputs in the same batch are processed continuously. The backpropagation error caused by each input is stored and applied only at the end of the batch. There is no dependency among the data inputs in a same batch. The training process can be essentially pipelined to increase system throughput.

We use the same GAN model as demonstrated in Figure 3 to explain the pipelined training execution in ReGAN. Assuming the discriminator has $L_D$ layers, the generator has $L_G$ layers, and batch size is $B$. In order to update D, we first feed the real samples into D in a pipelined fashion. Both the forward and backward path take $L_D$ cycles. It also consumes 1 cycle for calculating the loss function and $B - 1$ cycles to drain the previous batch from the pipeline. Therefore, it takes a total of $L_D + L_D + 1 + B - 1$ cycles. To train D on generated fake samples, it takes $L_G + L_D + L_D + 1 + B - 1$. Finally, 1 addtional cycle is required to update D. Similarly, training

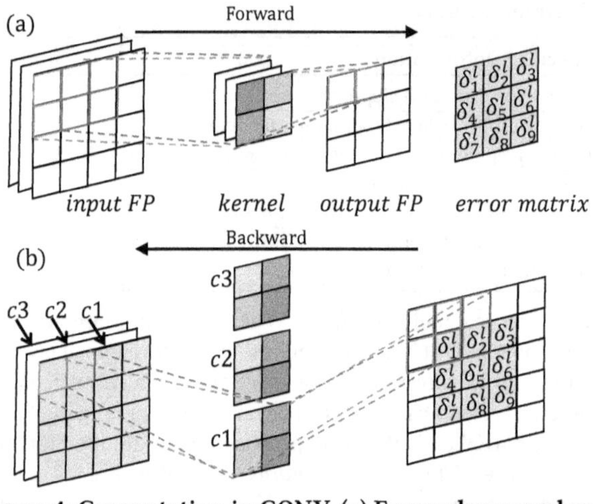


**Figure 4: Computation in CONV. (a) Forward pass and error matrix; (b) Error backpropagation.**

G requires $2L_G + 2L_D + B + 1$ cycles. As a comparison, if the training process is performed without a pipeline, D and G training consume $(4L_D + L_G + 2)\times B$ cycles and $(2L_G + 2L_D + 1)\times B$ cycles, respectively. Furthermore, ReGAN proposes *spatial parallelism* and *computation sharing* to further optimize pipeline performance. The design principle behind both solutions is to take advantage of the trade-off between system performance and hardware requirement.

**Spatial parallelism (SP).** Since D remains unchanged in ❶~❷ and ❸~❹, we can duplicate D for two copies and perform training processes ❶~❷ and ❸~❹ in parallel. In this way, the total latency is as the same as the latency of ❸~❹ for the spatial parallelism hides the latency of ❶~❷.

**Computation sharing (CS).** The data stream of training D with generated samples (❸~❹) and training G (❸~❺) share the same forward path. However, they are distinguished from the definition of loss function, and hence have different backpropagation data path. With this observation, we propose to co-train D and G by duplicating the memory for intermediate computation storage (e.g. memory to store the error and partial derivatives). In this case, the training of D and G share the forward path $T0 - T6$. At cycle $T7$, two backward branches are computed in parallel. The weights of G are updated at T14 and D can be updated at $T11$.

## 4.3 Dataflow Optimization

Table 2 summarizes the symbols used to explain the GAN calculation. Note that $\circ$ denotes elementwise multiplication. We do not provide the complete description of these parameters or mathematical model of the GAN training process due to page limits. We recommend interested readers to refer [23] and [2].

Figure 4(a) visualizes the main calculations of the forward path in CONV corresponding to Equations (1) and (2) in Table 2. As shown,

**Table 2: Notations used for explaining GAN training process.**

| Symbols/equations | | Description |
|---|---|---|
| $u_l = W_l d_{l-1} + b_l$ | (1) | forward function |
| $d_l = h(u_l)$ | (2) | activation function |
| $\delta_{l-1} = {W_l}^T \delta_l \circ h'(u_l)$ | (3) | error backpropagation |
| $\nabla W_l = d_{l-1}{\delta_l}^T$ | (4) | weight partial derivative |
| $\nabla b_l = \delta_l$ | (5) | bias partial derivative |

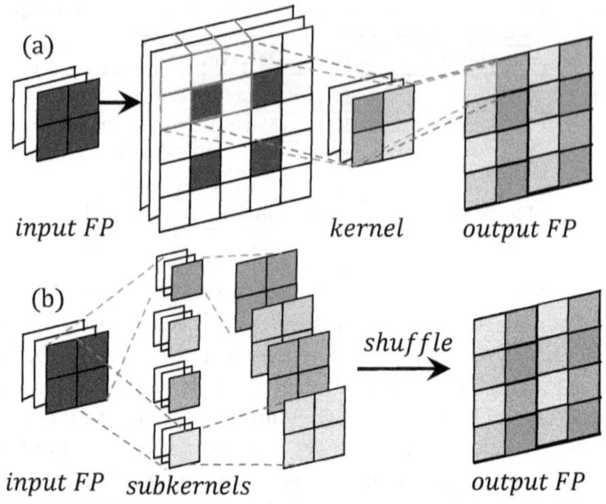


**Figure 5: (a) TCONV operation; (b) TCONV deformation.**

a set of kernels are convoluted with the input or the output of the previous layer. The sliding convolution window is repeated for all possible positions in the input feature map (FP), and the results are stored in the output FP. These results are then used as the inputs of the following layer. Once the forward layerwise computation finished, a *cost function* $J$ is defined to quantitatively evaluate the difference between the network output and its expected output. The error for layer $l$ is defined as $\delta_l = \frac{\partial J}{\partial b_l}$ which will be propagated backwards to the previous layer as depicted in Figure 4(b). The backpropagation process can be described by Equation (3)~(5) in Table 2.

Compared to CONV, TCONV first transforms its input to a larger representation by zero paddings around the image and zero insertions between adjacent rows/columns and then performs CONV on the expanded input. For instance, Figure 5(a) illustrates the zero-insertion step for a $2 \times 2$ input FP with $stride = 1$ and $padding = 1$. A kernel convolves with this transformed input FP and correspondingly generate an output FP with a size of $4 \times 4$. In this example, 21 zeros are inserted, that is, only 4/25 the source operands are valid input and contributes to the final results. Previous work have shown that executing GAN by following conventional convolution dataflow illustrated in Figure 5(a) leads to a low computational efficiency because generally more than 60% of the computations are multiplications and additions with zero operands due to the zero-insertion step in TCONV [29].

To address this issue, we propose ZARA – an ReRAM-based GAN accelerator. Through the novel deformation of TCONV, ZARA can completely skip over zero-insertions in both forward and backward computation phases. Taking the example in Figure 5(a), we observed that the convolution between the expanded FP and the kernels only contains four distinct valid patterns. The elements in odd output rows only related to a subset of kernel weights (e.g. the second row in this example), whereas the even output rows use a different kernel weights subset (e.g. the first row) for their computations. Building upon this observation, we introduce a series of dataflow optimization covers both the forward and backward phases in TCONV to mitigate the aforementioned inefficiency in TCONV execution. For simplicity, we only demonstrate the data optimization in a forward phase in Figure 5(b).

**Table 3: Benchmarks (C: convolution layer; T: transposed convolution layer; F: fully connected layer.).**

| ReGAN | | | | ZARA | | | |
|---|---|---|---|---|---|---|---|
| **Model** | **Dataset** | **D Topology** | **G Topo.** | **Model** | **Dataset** | **D Topo.** | **G Topo.** |
| MLP1 | mnist [15] | 2/4-layer MLP | 2/4-layer MLP | FCN [27] | POSVAL VOC [9] | 5C2F | N/A |
| MLP2 | mnist [15] | 3C1F | 4-layer MLP | DCGAN [20] | LSUN [31] | 4C1F | 1F4T |
| GAN1 | CIFAR-10 [14] | 4C1F | 1F4T | iGAN [21] | CIFAR-10 [14] | 3C1F | 1F3T |
| GAN2 | celebA [18]/LSUN [31] | 5C1F | 1F5T | 3DGAN [26] | IKEA [16] | 5C1F | 1F4T |
| ResnetGAN | CIFAR-10 [14] | [12] | [12] | ArtGAN [25] | CIFAR-10 [14] | 6C1F | 1F5T |

## 4.4 Hardware Implementation

Normally, ReRAM-based DNN accelerators use ReRAM arrays as precessing units for vector-matrix multiplication. As demonstrated in Figure 6, the weight matrix is written as cell conductance states in the crossbar. Input FPs are applied to the WLs as voltage levels. In this way, all BLs in the crossbar produce the current sums simultaneously with the same voltage along WLs, and hence a vector-matrix multiplication is performed in each step. . Representative ReRAM-based DNN accelerators include PRIME [7], ISAAC [22], and PipeLayer [23].

Similar to [7, 23], ReGAN [2] partitions the ReRAM main memory into three regions: *memory subarrays* for data storage, *full function subarrays* for both in-site VMM and data storage, and *buffer subarrays* for storing the intermediate results between layers (e.g., generated images, data required for compute partial derivatives, etc.). The *buffer subarrays* are connected to the *full function subarrays* through private high-throughput local data ports, so that buffer accesses do not consume the bandwidth of memory subarrays. It is worth mentioning that we adopted the spike-based scheme [17] in ReGAN to minimize the energy overhead of power-hungry analog-digital converters. ReGAN realizes the non-linear activation function by using a *look-up table.* Moreover, we implemented various function units (e.g. *substractor, shift & add, etc.*) to support the related computation involved during the training process.

ZARA leverages the ReRAM crossbar to perform in-memory GAN execution. However, different from ReGAN, ZARA is a domain-specific standalone accelerator. More specific, ZARA aims to solve the inconsistent computational delay caused by TCONV deformation, which breaks the pipeline execution model. A *mapper* and a *scheduler* are designed to effectively map and schedule the operations of the optimized dataflow onto PEs to eliminate the inconsistency in execution time. ZARA PIM is implemented in a tiled computation architecture. The top level is ZARA nodes. Each ZARA node consists of a ReRAM memory to store input/output values, a *mapper* and a *scheduler* that map the optimized dataflow onto target PEs and control the computation flow respectively, an IO interface to communicate with other ZARA nodes, and a number of PEs connected via on-chip mesh. Each PE contains multiple vector-matrix multipliers, a ReRAM buffer to cache temporal data, activation units to perform nonlinear function, and output register to aggregate results, all connected with a shared bus. A PE also has simple algorithm and logic units (sALU). The crossbar arrays within a vector-matrix multipliers share a driver by global wordline. At a time, only one crossbar array in a vector-matrix multipliers can be activated and used to perform in-situ VMM. The results can be selected via a bitline multiplex. The details of these components are described in [3].

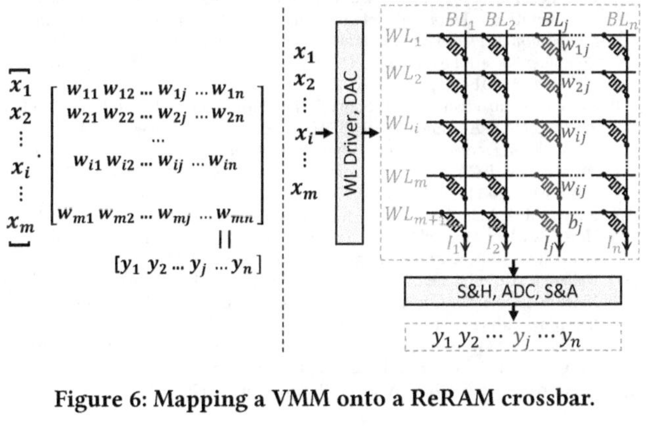


**Figure 6: Mapping a VMM onto a ReRAM crossbar.**

# 5 EVALUATION

Table 3 summarizes the topological structures of evaluated networks and dataset in ReGAN [2] and ZARA [3]. To evaluate ReGAN, we built four MLP GANs which has a multiLayer perceptron (MLP) generator and a MLP/CNN discriminator. We test them on mnist [15]. For CIFAR-10 [14] and LSUN [31], we built a symmetric GAN with four CNN/FCNN layers in G/D. In particular, we also selected the 101-layer ResNet GAN in [12] as benchmarks on CIFAR-10 [14]. For CelebA [18] and LSUN [31], we built a five-layer CNN/FNN GAN as benchmarks. We compare ReGAN against the GTX1080 GPU platform. Our experimental results show that ReGAN can achieve 240× performance speedup compared to GPU platform averagely, with an average energy saving of 94×.

We evaluated the ZARA architecture against four counterparts [2, 23, 27, 29] using five state-of-the-art GANs. For comparison purpose, we also include fully convolution network [27] in evaluation. Experimental results show that ZARA can improve the training performance of GAN by averagely 1.6 × ~23× over CMOS-based GAN accelerators. Compared to state-of-the-art ReRAM-based accelerator designs, ZARA also provides 1.15 × ~2.1× performance improvement.

# 6 DISCUSSION AND FUTURE WORK

In recent years, we have seen a continuously increasing trend of deploying emerging frameworks such as generative adversarial networks with hierarchical structure into various complex application domains. These models are often trained and tested with huge dataset, and therefore, consume high computation and storage resources. Moreover, data processing in these models often incurs heavy data traffic as well as frequent massive data interaction, which makes the memory wall issue even worse. Almost all of the current machine learning acceleration schemes, however, focus on the execution of DNN inference but pay less attention on the more sophisticated and intensive training phases.

In this paper, we review the current advance in accelerator designs for GANs and point out their limitations. Then we introduce our solutions. Different from previous research, we use ReRAM-based in-memory computation since ReRAM is capable of both computation and storage, significantly reducing the data movement. ReGAN [2] explored an efficient pipelined training procedure to reduce on-chip memory access. *Spatial parallelism* and *computation sharing* were proposed to further improve performance. ZARA [3] proposed a novel computation deformation technique that can skip zero-insertions in TCONV. A dataflow mapper and an operation scheduler were also implemented to support the proposed execution model.

There is still much work unsolved on ReRAM-based GANs acceleration. For example, many current studies on ReRAM-based accelerators assume ideal ReRAM cells. However, real devices suffers from severe process variations [19], circuit noise [1] and short retention time and endurance [6] issues. How to realize reliable accelerators using the real device model is a common challenge, not only for ReRAM-based designs but also all emerging memory based solutions. We are encouraged by the broad design space enabled by ReRAM crossbar arrays and we also intend to explore the future opportunity of performing GANs learning in end devices because it would be desirable to have the intelligent edge devices capable of adaptively learning and tuning their parameters to achieve a desirable accuracy.

## ACKNOWLEDGMENTS

This work was supported in part by NSF 1725456, NSF 1744082 and DOE DE-SC0017030. Any opinions, findings and conclusions or recommendations expressed in this material are those of the authors and do not necessarily reflect the views of grant agencies or their contractors.

## REFERENCES

[1] Stefano Ambrogio, Simone Balatti, A Cubeta, A Calderoni, N Ramaswamy, and Daniele Ielmini. 2013. Understanding switching variability and random telegraph noise in resistive RAM. In *2013 IEEE International Electron Devices Meeting*.

[2] F. Chen, L. Song, and Y. Chen. 2018. ReGAN: A pipelined ReRAM-based accelerator for generative adversarial networks. In *2018 23rd Asia and South Pacific Design Automation Conference (ASP-DAC)*.

[3] Fan Chen, Linghao Song, and Yiran Chen. 2019. ZARA: A Novel Zero-free Dataflow Accelerator for Generative Adversarial Networks in 3D ReRAM. In *Proceedings of the 56th annual design automation conference*. ACM.

[4] Tianshi Chen, Zidong Du, Ninghui Sun, Jia Wang, Chengyong Wu, Yunji Chen, and Olivier Temam. 2014. DianNao: A Small-footprint High-throughput Accelerator for Ubiquitous Machine-learning. In *Proceedings of the 19th International Conference on Architectural Support for Programming Languages and Operating Systems (ASPLOS '14)*.

[5] Y. Chen, T. Krishna, J. S. Emer, and V. Sze. 2017. Eyeriss: An Energy-Efficient Reconfigurable Accelerator for Deep Convolutional Neural Networks. *IEEE Journal of Solid-State Circuits* (2017).

[6] Yang Yin Chen, Ludovic Goux, Sergiu Clima, Bogdan Govoreanu, Robin Degraeve, Gouri Sankar Kar, Andrea Fantini, Guido Groeseneken, Dirk J Wouters, and Malgorzata Jurczak. 2013. Endurance/retention trade-off on HfO2/metal cap 1T1R bipolar RRAM. *IEEE Transactions on electron devices* (2013).

[7] P. Chi, S. Li, C. Xu, T. Zhang, J. Zhao, Y. Liu, Y. Wang, and Y. Xie. 2016. PRIME: A Novel Processing-in-Memory Architecture for Neural Network Computation in ReRAM-Based Main Memory. In *2016 ACM/IEEE 43rd Annual International Symposium on Computer Architecture (ISCA)*.

[8] Ahmed Elgammal, Bingchen Liu, Mohamed Elhoseiny, and Marian Mazzone. 2017. CAN: Creative Adversarial Networks, Generating "Art" by Learning About Styles and Deviating from Style Norms. *arXiv e-prints* (2017), arXiv:1706.07068.

[9] M. Everingham, S. M. A. Eslami, L. Van Gool, C. K. I. Williams, J. Winn, and A. Zisserman. 2015. The Pascal Visual Object Classes Challenge: A Retrospective. *International Journal of Computer Vision* (2015).

[10] Zichen Fan, Ziru Li, Bing Li, Yiran Chen, and Helen Hai Li. 2019. RED: A ReRAM-based Deconvolution Accelerator. In *2019 Design, Automation & Test in Europe Conference & Exhibition (DATE)*.

[11] Ian Goodfellow, Jean Pouget-Abadie, Mehdi Mirza, Bing Xu, David Warde-Farley, Sherjil Ozair, Aaron Courville, and Yoshua Bengio. 2014. Generative Adversarial Nets. In *Advances in Neural Information Processing Systems 27*. Curran Associates, Inc., 2672–2680.

[12] Ishaan Gulrajani, Faruk Ahmed, Martin Arjovsky, Vincent Dumoulin, and Aaron Courville. 2017. Improved Training of Wasserstein GANs. *arXiv e-prints* (2017), arXiv:1704.00028.

[13] Taeksoo Kim, Moonsu Cha, Hyunsoo Kim, Jung Kwon Lee, and Jiwon Kim. 2017. Learning to Discover Cross-Domain Relations with Generative Adversarial Networks. In *Proceedings of the 34th International Conference on Machine Learning (Proceedings of Machine Learning Research)*.

[14] A. Krizhevsky and G. Hinton. 2009. Learning multiple layers of features from tiny images. In *Technical report, University of Toronto*.

[15] Y. LeCun. 1998. In *Proceedings of the 56th annual design automation conference*. http://yann.lecun.com/exdb/mnist/

[16] J. J. Lim, H. Pirsiavash, and A. Torralba. 2013. Parsing IKEA Objects: Fine Pose Estimation. In *2013 IEEE International Conference on Computer Vision*.

[17] C. Liu, B. Yan, C. Yang, L. Song, Z. Li, B. Liu, Y. Chen, H. Li, and and. 2015. A spiking neuromorphic design with resistive crossbar. In *2015 52nd ACM/EDAC/IEEE Design Automation Conference (DAC)*.

[18] Ziwei Liu, Ping Luo, Xiaogang Wang, and Xiaoou Tang. 2015. Deep Learning Face Attributes in the Wild. In *The IEEE International Conference on Computer Vision (ICCV)*.

[19] Dimin Niu, Yiran Chen, Cong Xu, and Yuan Xie. 2010. Impact of process variations on emerging memristor. In *Proceedings of the 47th Design Automation Conference*.

[20] Alec Radford, Luke Metz, and Soumith Chintala. 2016. Unsupervised Representation Learning with Deep Convolutional Generative Adversarial Networks. *CoRR* abs/1511.06434 (2016).

[21] Tim Salimans, Ian Goodfellow, Wojciech Zaremba, Vicki Cheung, Alec Radford, and Xi Chen. 2016. Improved Techniques for Training GANs. *ArXiv e-prints* (2016), arXiv:1606.03498.

[22] A. Shafiee, A. Nag, N. Muralimanohar, R. Balasubramonian, J. P. Strachan, M. Hu, R. S. Williams, and V. Srikumar. 2016. ISAAC: A Convolutional Neural Network Accelerator with In-Situ Analog Arithmetic in Crossbars. In *2016 ACM/IEEE 43rd Annual International Symposium on Computer Architecture (ISCA)*.

[23] L. Song, X. Qian, H. Li, and Y. Chen. 2017. PipeLayer: A Pipelined ReRAM-Based Accelerator for Deep Learning. In *2017 IEEE International Symposium on High Performance Computer Architecture (HPCA)*.

[24] M. Song, J. Zhang, H. Chen, and T. Li. 2018. Towards Efficient Microarchitectural Design for Accelerating Unsupervised GAN-Based Deep Learning. In *2018 IEEE International Symposium on High Performance Computer Architecture (HPCA)*.

[25] Wei Ren Tan, Chee Seng Chan, Hernan Aguirre, and Kiyoshi Tanaka. 2017. ArtGAN: Artwork Synthesis with Conditional Categorical GANs. *ArXiv e-prints* (Feb. 2017), arXiv:1702.03410.

[26] Jiajun Wu, Chengkai Zhang, Tianfan Xue, William T Freeman, and Joshua B Tenenbaum. 2016. Learning a probabilistic latent space of object shapes via 3d generative-adversarial modeling. In *Advances in Neural Information Processing Systems*. 82–90.

[27] Dawen Xu, Kaijie Tu, Ying Wang, Cheng Liu, Bingsheng He, and Huawei Li. 2018. FCN-engine: Accelerating Deconvolutional Layers in Classic CNN Processors. In *ICCAD*.

[28] A. Yazdanbakhsh, M. Brzozowski, B. Khaleghi, S. Ghodrati, K. Samadi, N. Kim, and H. Esmaeilzadeh. 2018. FlexiGAN: An End-to-End Solution for FPGA Acceleration of Generative Adversarial Networks. In *2018 IEEE 26th Annual International Symposium on Field-Programmable Custom Computing Machines (FCCM)*. IEEE Computer Society, Los Alamitos, CA, USA, 65–72. DOI: http://dx.doi.org/10.1109/FCCM.2018.00019

[29] Amir Yazdanbakhsh, Kambiz Samadi, Nam Sung Kim, and Hadi Esmaeilzadeh. 2018. GANAX: A Unified MIMD-SIMD Acceleration for Generative Adversarial Networks. In *Proceedings of the 45th Annual International Symposium on Computer Architecture (ISCA '18)*. IEEE Press, Piscataway, NJ, USA, 650–661. DOI: http://dx.doi.org/10.1109/ISCA.2018.00060

[30] Raymond A. Yeh, Chen Chen, Teck Yian Lim, Alexander G. Schwing, Mark Hasegawa-Johnson, and Minh N. Do. 2016. Semantic Image Inpainting with Deep Generative Models. *arXiv e-prints* (2016), arXiv:1607.07539.

[31] Fisher Yu, Ari Seff, Yinda Zhang, Shuran Song, Thomas Funkhouser, and Jianxiong Xiao. 2015. LSUN: Construction of a Large-scale Image Dataset using Deep Learning with Humans in the Loop. *arXiv e-prints* (2015), arXiv:1506.03365.

[32] Xinyu Zhang, Srinjoy Das, Ojash Neopane, and Ken Kreutz- Delgado. 2017. A Design Methodology for Efficient Implementation of Deconvolutional Neural Networks on an FPGA. *ArXiv e-prints* (2017), arXiv:1705.02583.

# DigitalPIM: Digital-based Processing In-Memory for Big Data Acceleration

Mohsen Imani, Saransh Gupta, Yeseong Kim, Minxuan Zhou, Tajana Rosing
CSE Department, UC San Diego, La Jolla, CA 92093, USA
{moimani, sgupta, yek048, miz087, tajana}@ucsd.edu

## ABSTRACT

In this work, we design, DigitalPIM, a Digital-based Processing In-Memory platform capable of accelerating fundamental big data algorithms in real time with orders of magnitude more energy efficient operation. Unlike the existing near-data processing approach such as HMC 2.0, which utilizes additional low-power processing cores next to memory blocks, the proposed platform implements the entire algorithm directly in memory blocks without using extra processing units. In our platform, each memory block supports the essential operations including: bitwise operation, addition/multiplication, and search operation internally in memory without reading any values out of the block. This significantly mitigates the processing costs of the new architecture, while providing high scalability and parallelism for performing the extensive computations. We exploit these essential operations to accelerate popular big data applications entirely in memory such as machine learning algorithms, query processing, and graph processing. Our evaluations show that for all tested applications, the performance can be accelerated significantly by eliminating the memory access bottleneck.

## CCS CONCEPTS

• **Computer systems organization → Architectures**; • **Hardware → Emerging technologies**; *Electronic design automation*;

## KEYWORDS

Processing in Memory; Non-volatile memories; Energy efficiency; Big data acceleration

**ACM Reference Format:**
Mohsen Imani, Saransh Gupta, Yeseong Kim, Minxuan Zhou, Tajana Rosing. 2019. DigitalPIM: Digital-based Processing In-Memory for Big Data Acceleration. In *Great Lakes Symposium on VLSI 2019 (GLSVLSI '19), May 9–11, 2019, Tysons Corner, VA, USA.* ACM, New York, NY, USA, 6 pages. https://doi.org/10.1145/3299874.3319483

## 1 INTRODUCTION

We live in a world where technological advances are continually creating more data than what we can cope with. With the emergence of the Internet of Things, sensory and embedded devices will generate massive data streams demanding services that pose huge technical challenges due to limited device resources. Today IoT applications typically analyze raw data by running machine learning algorithms in data centers. Sending all the data to the cloud for processing is not scalable, cannot guarantee a real-time response, and is often not desirable due to privacy and security concerns. Much of IoT data processing will need to run at least partly on the devices at the edge of the internet. However, running data-intensive workloads with large datasets on traditional cores results in high energy consumption and slow processing speed due to a large amount of data movement between memory and processing units. Although new processor technology has evolved to serve computationally complex tasks in a more efficient way, data movement costs between processor and memory still hinder the higher efficiency of application performance. In addition, applications in this area involve diverse data analytic procedures which needs to be significantly accelerated while handling a large amount of data. Our work seeks to build systems capable of responding to the diverse needs in real time with orders of magnitude more energy efficient operation.


*GLSVLSI '19, May 9–11, 2019, Tysons Corner, VA, USA*

ACM ISBN 978-1-4503-6252-8/19/05...$15.00
https://doi.org/10.1145/3299874.3319483

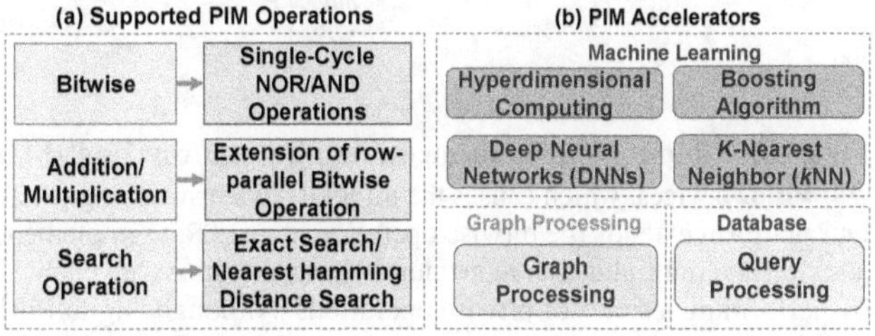


**Figure 1: The list of supported operations and (b) the list of applications accelerated by the proposed DigitalPIM platform.**

In this work, we propose, DigitalPIM, a novel Digital-based Processing In-Memory (PIM) platform which accelerates the fundamental operations and diverse data analytic procedures. The DigitalPIM supports fundamental block-parallel operations inside memory, e.g., addition, multiplication or bitwise computations. This capability is implemented on a crossbar memory which stored data point of an application. Since a large amount of data is not required to be sent to the processing cores for computation, the performance can be accelerated significantly by avoiding the memory access bottleneck. To fully get the advantage of DigitalPIM for popular data processing procedures and machine learning algorithms, we design specialized accelerator. Our platform can process several applications including machine learning, graph and query processing entirely in-memory without using any processing cores.

## 2 DIGITAL-BASED PIM

### 2.1 DigitalPIM Overview

In this work, we present processing in-memory architecture to enable hardware accelerations for popular big data applications. We exploit a conventional crossbar memory to enable essential operations in memory. Figure 1a shows the list of operations supported by DigitalPIM platform. The first supported operation by DigitalPIM is bitwise operation. In contrast to prior works that compute bitwise operation on the sense amplifier of each memory block [1], our design supports bitwise operations internally in memory without even reading the values out of the block. Prior work enabled the bitwise operation by exploiting the analog/resistive characteristic of

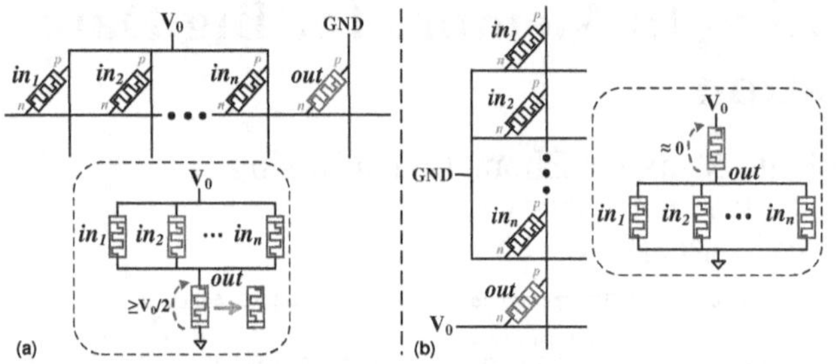


**Figure 2: $n$-input NOR implementation in (a) a row and (b) a column [3].**

memristor devices, which causes the internal device switching [2, 3]. Our platform extends the bitwise operation, e.g., NOR, to implement addition and multiplication in memory. These operations are enabled by performing a series of bitwise operations. Although DigitalPIM addition and multiplication are much slower than CMOS logics, the high parallelism of the PIM operations results in a higher overall DigitalPIM throughput as compared to the CMOS-based logics. In other words, DigitalPIM performs the computation in a row-parallel way, resulting in about 1K parallel addition/multiplication on memory with 1K rows. DigitalPIM also supports search operation internally in memory. During the search, blocks configured as content addressable memory (CAM). Conventionally CAM blocks are only used for exact matching. Here, we extend the search operation such that CAMs can also find a row with the nearest Hamming distance or the nearest absolute distance with query data.

DigitalPIM exploits the PIM-supported operations to accelerates diverse data-intensive applications partially or entirely in-memory. Figure 1b shows the list of applications accelerated by our proposed DigitalPIM architecture. Our platform can accelerate different machine learning including deep neural networks, AdaBoost, k-nearest neighbor applications entirely in memory without using any processing cores. DigitalPIM can also accelerate graph and query processing algorithms, along with a set of Hyperdimensional (HD) computing algorithms that support classification on a wide range of data types.

## 2.2 DigitalPIM Supported Operations

**Bitwise Operations:** We exploit the analog characteristic of memristor devices to support bit-parallel or row-parallel bitwise operation internally in memory. Work in [2, 4] showed that crossbar memory can internally support NOR-based operation between the $N$ selected rows or columns of the memory, as shown in Figure 2. This operation happens by activating $N$ columns (rows) of the memory at the same time and connecting the target column (row) which store the results of NOR operation to a zero voltage. This enables the internal NOR operation between the selected columns (rows) to be written directly on the selected output column (row).

Our work, FELIX [3], exploits the bipolar nature of the voltage controlled ReRAM devices to enable NOR, NOT, Min, NAND, and OR in a single cycle in crossbar memory. The benefits from FELIX are muti-fold. Not only it is 1.86× faster and 2.21× more energy efficient but also requires 1.68× lower memory as compared to the fastest digital PIM technique. The addition and multiplication are supported in crossbar memory by performing a series of sequential FELIX operations. In FELIX, multiple NOR/NAND gates are combined together to implement any logic operation, including but not limited to XOR, majority, and implication. For example, AND operation can be implemented with two sequential NAND operations. In a different approach to PIM, researchers have tried to exploit sense amplifiers to read out data locally and process it. Our works in MPIM [1] and LUPIS [5] modified memory sense amplifiers to enable bitwise operations like AND, OR, XOR, etc. The sense amplifier based techniques trade energy and area for better performance as compared to a relatively slower PIM execution.

**Addition/Multiplication:** The basic logic functions supported by MAGIC and FELIX can be extended to implement addition and multiplication. An implementation of addition proposed by FELIX combines XOR and majority operations [3]. A 1-bit adder can be represented by,

$$S = A \oplus B \oplus C_{in}, \tag{1a}$$

$$C_{out} = A.B + B.C + C.A = MajNA, B, C_{in}, \tag{1b}$$

where A, B, and $C_{in}$ are 1-bit inputs while S and $C_{out}$ are the generated sum and carry bits respectively. Here, S is implemented as two serial in-memory XOR operations. $C_{out}$, on the other hand, can be executed by inverting the output of . Hence, S takes a total of 4 cycles and 2 additional memristors, while $C_{out}$ needs 2 cycles and 2 additional memristors. Further, multiplication is implemented by multiple additions and shift operations. A naive implementation of multiplication would result in a lot of data movement due to shifts. Our work in [6] proposed the first digital PIM-based multiplication. It dealt with the data movement overhead by sub-dividing memory blocks using interconnects which allowed bit-shifts without reading out data and also accelerated PIM multiplication. The work in [7] takes another approach where it does not accelerate an individual multiplication significantly but makes it highly parallelizable. Work in [8] exploited DigitalPIM operations to support floating point operation in memory and extended them to accelerate deep neural network training.

**Search:** Our work, MPIM [1], supports a block-serial row parallel Hamming distance based operations. We proposed ReCAM [9], which can be configured to perform the closest distance search operation inside the memory. Although it does not implement binary distance search but it is a close approximation. However, many applications require a binary distance based comparison. We proposed NVQuery [10, 11] which enabled, for the first time, exact binary distance search in memory. It achieved it by using smart voltage application techniques to exploit the differential discharging time of capacitance. We used it to enable complex functions, including but not limited to sorting, compare, aggregation, and prediction. These functions have huge time complexities when implemented on traditional hardware.

# 3 MACHINE LEARNING ACCELERATORS

In this section, we describe how we fully leverage the advantages of DigitalPIM for large scale data processing and machine learning applications by designing specialized PIM accelerator blocks. In machine learning, we look at four important classes of algorithms: hyperdimensional computing, deep learning, AdaBoost, and k-Nearest Neighbor algorithms.

## 3.1 Hyperdimensional Computing Acceleration

The brain's circuits are massive in terms of numbers of neurons and synapses, suggesting that large circuits are fundamental to the brain's computing. Brain-inspired hyperdimensional (HD) computing explores this idea by looking at computing with ultra-wide words high-dimensional vectors, or hypervectors [12–14]. Figure 3a shows the overview structure of HD computing for classification example. The first step is to encode data into hypervectors. The goal of the encoder is to map key input data to a single hypervector and then combine these for all of the data points in a class to generate a unique hypervector representing each class. Each class hypervector is a long

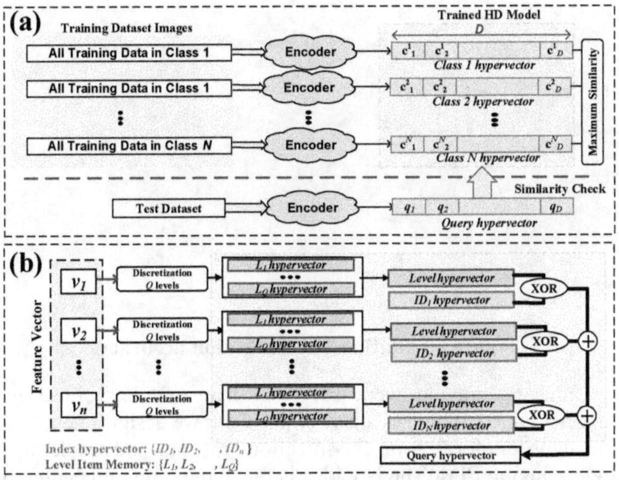

**Figure 3: (a) overview of HD computing during classification. (b) The details of the encoding functionality in HD computing [3].**

vector with $D$ dimension with binary (0, 1) elements. Associative memory stores the trained hypervectors for all classes. Once the data is encoded and clustered into appropriate categories, various types of operations can be implemented, but at the heart of all implementations is a search for a category match. HD classifies an unknown input data by encoding it to a hypervector using the same encoder used for training. The query hypervector has binary elements and the same dimensions as the class hypervectors. Then, this hypervector is broadcast to the associative memory module for comparing with a set of learned class hypervectors. The associative memory returns the closest match. We exploit such architectural insights to develop scalable and efficient encoder and associative memories that can accelerate HD computing as discussed next.

**Encoder**: Figure 3b shows the functionality of the encoding module in HD computing. HD encoder generates m random hypervectors representing each feature level $(L_1, L_2, \cdots, L_m)$. These hypervectors use only binary elements, with information randomly distributed over all $D$ dimensions (e.g. $D = 10,000$). To consider the impact of feature position, HD computing assigns a unique position hypervectors. For a feature vector with $n$ elements, HD generates $n$ $P$ position hypervectors. The $P$ is another randomly generated hypervector with the same dimensionality as the level hypervector, $D$, and specifies the effect of feature position in the final hypervector. In this way, the hypervectors are combined together using element-wise XOR of the position and level hypervectors, and then summing the resulting hypervectors over all features. We map all these operations in PIM-enabled memory [3]. We perform $n$ PIM XORs (one for each ID) and generate $n$ outputs. For the first $n$ iterations, we select one ID and XOR it with one of the Ls in every iteration. For a pair of ID and L, PIM XOR can be computed in parallel for all dimensions. We then add the generated $n$ elements serially, three bits at a time. If $X_1$, $X_2$,... $X_n$ are the vectors to be added together, we first add $X_1$, $X_2$, and $X_3$ to generate $S_1$ and $C_1$. We then add $X_4$, $X_5$, and $\{C_1, S_1\}$ to generate $S_2$ and $C_2$, and so on till we have added all XOR results. The addition of $n$ 1-bit elements results in an output with $p = \lceil log_2 n \rceil$ bits. We implement this PIM-based HD encoding while ensuring optimal storage, whose details can be found in [3].

**Associative memory:** is in charge of storing all class hypervectors. Our design stores all available classes in an associative memory as a trained HD model. In inference, when an unknown input digit is loaded into the system, our design uses a similar encoding to generate the *query hypervector*. Then, associative memory finds the closest match between a set of learned hypervectors and a query hypervector by using a distance metric. Depending on the data representation, HD can use different similarity metrics. Here we consider Hamming distance to find the most similar class. The state-of-the-art associative memories are not able to compare vectors with dimensionality in thousands [9, 15]. They also lack techniques for uniformly tolerating errors in any vector component and hence cannot efficiently exploit the holographic feature of hypervectors. Further, most of them are implemented as a content addressable memory (CAM) and so are not able to find the minimum distance. We designed new architectures for hyperdimensional associative memory that can facilitate energy-efficient, fast, and scalable search operations [13]. Our proposed CAM exploits the analog discharging current of different CAM rows to identify a CAM row with the minimum mismatches with the query hypervector. In other words, our design uses a tree-based structure of a Loser-Takes-All (LTA) blocks to identify a CAM row (a class) with the minimum Hamming distance. These analog HD designs linearly scale with the number of dimensions in the hypervectors while exploring a large design space at orders of magnitude higher efficiency [13].

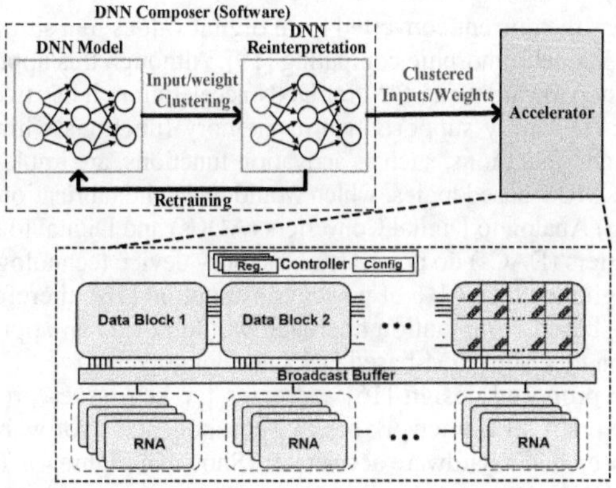

**Figure 4: The overview of the proposed DNN acceleration framework [16].**

## 3.2 Deep Neural Network Acceleration:

We present a novel PIM accelerator for DNNs that supports all DNN functionality in memory [16]. Figure 4 shows an overview of the proposed framework. Our framework first analyzes the computation flow of a DNN model and encodes key DNN operations for a specialized PIM-enabled accelerator. It identifies the representative parameters, i.e., weights and input values, for each neuron using clustering algorithms. The other key operations, like activation functions, are also modeled to enable in-memory processing. The key idea underlying our design is that even though the operations of a DNN are continuous, they can be approximated as step-wise functions without losing the quality of inference. Thus, we can create lookup tables that store the finite pre-computed values, and map them into specialized memory blocks capable of computation.

Prior work proposed PIM-based neural network accelerators which keep the input data and trained weights inside memory [17, 18]. For example, the work in [18] showed that memristor devices can model multiplications and additions for each neuron. Authors of [18] store trained weights of each neuron as device resistance values, and pass the current converted from digital values in a similar way to spiking neuromorphic computing [19]. Although this approach is a first step toward using PIM for DNN acceleration, it has two major issues: (i) it only supports two in-memory functions while other important operations, such as activation functions, are implemented using CMOS-based logics, which would make the fabrication expensive. (ii) Analog to Digital Converters (ADCs) and Digital to Analog Converters (DACs) do not scale as memory device technology does, although they take 61% of power consumption [18]; therefore, the analog-based computation approach would not be an appropriate solution to design PIM-based DNN accelerators.

Our proposed design [16] addresses the key issues present in prior work. Our framework has two components: a software DNN composer, and a hardware accelerator (Shown in Figure 4). The role of the DNN composer is to convert each neural network operation into tables which can be stored in the accelerator memory blocks for processing in memory. In an offline stage, starting with a given DNN model, the DNN composer analyzes weights and inputs of each neuron and generates a new DNN model which is compatible with the proposed PIM-based accelerator. The newly constructed DNN model is repeatedly revised through multiple retraining procedures. The final model is stored into the accelerator for online inference. Our framework supports three layers of popularly used for designing DNNs: fully-connected, convolution, and pooling layers. We group the computation tasks of the networks into four operations: multiplication, addition, activation function, and pooling.

Considering the model of a single neuron, our approach works based on the encoded input/weight [16], since the DNN composer selects the best representatives inputs/weights by analyzing the network. Therefore, the multiplication can be implemented by simply accessing the pre-evaluated multiplication values. Then, the results of multiplication can locally accumulate in memory without using any processing cores. Our design approximately models the activation function using a lookup table. Finally, we utilize another lookup table with a similar structure to encode the output of the activation function. We exploit the fact that the weights of a network are computed during testing. These constant weights can be preprocessed and encoded in a way suitable for in-memory processing. Since pre-processing is done only once, its latency is negligible in comparison to the speedup provided during the testing phase. Our evaluation shows that our approach [16] achieves 68.4×, 49.5× energy efficiency improvement and 48.1×, 10.9× speedup as compared to ISAAC [18] and PipeLayer [20], the state-of-the-art DNN accelerators, while ensuring less than 0.5% of quality loss.

### 3.3 Adaptive Boosting Acceleration

One of the methods for classification is to exploit decision rules which are automatically generated by learning algorithms such as ID3, C4.5, and CART [21]. The simple decision rules and trees can be combined to create more accurate and sophisticated decisions with meta-learning algorithms. AdaBoost (Adaptive Boosting) is one of the best meta-learning algorithms. In our previous work, we designed a novel hardware accelerator, which accelerates the decision rule computations inside memory for visual object recognition tasks [22]. The proposed design accelerates both the image feature extraction and boosting-based learning algorithm, which are key subtasks of the state-of-the-art image recognition approaches. We show in [22] that our design successfully performs practical image recognition tasks, including text, face, pedestrian, and vehicle recognition with 0.3% of accuracy loss due to approximation.

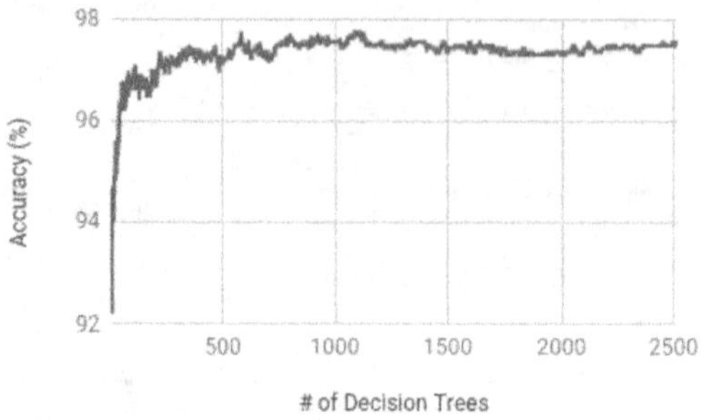


**Figure 5: AdaBoost classification accuracy.**

Unlike the previous work that relies on the existence of learning models trained offline, as a part of this work we design a new training algorithm for general classification problems and accelerate it by leveraging PIM. The key idea is that the training procedure of the decision trees can be decomposed into two steps: i) generating multiple candidates of decision rules, and ii) evaluating the expected accuracy of each decision rule to find the optimal rule. Evaluating a decision rule can be implemented using the similarity search operations that the PIM technique supports. Thus, by mapping multiple memory blocks for each decision candidate, we can perform the evaluation procedure in a block-parallel way, thus quickly identifying the best rule. To verify that our classification method is able to handle general classification problems, we implemented our idea in software and conducted an initial analysis by classifying human activities from smartphone-based sensors. As shown in Figure 5, the modified AdaBoost training method can create the first decision tree with 92% accuracy, and by combining multiple decision rules (on x-axis), we can further increase the accuracy by 98% for human activity classification.

### 3.4 K-Nearest Neighbor Acceleration

Nearest neighbor search problem arises in numerous fields of applications, including pattern recognition, statistical classification, biology, computer vision, etc. The nearest search computation is highly parallelizable for datasets on the order of tens of megabytes. Running analysis of more massive datasets on existing general purpose processors results in significant performance overhead due to a large number of data movements across the memory hierarchy. For example, to process 1 billion candidate points, one query needs 150 GFLOPs computation and 500G of data communication [23]. We propose to design a K-Nearest Neighbor accelerator [24] consisting of ternary content addressable memory (TCAM) blocks which enable in-memory nearest search. Our design exploits dynamic voltage scaling and analog detector circuitry to find kNN data based on the Hamming distance. It overcomes energy and performance issues in traditional computing systems by utilizing multiple TCAMs to search for the nearest neighbor data in parallel. We also design a new search-based accelerator which supports the nearest search with different distance metrics. The proposed memory is a configurable architecture which could take any similarity metric.

## 4 GRAPH PROCESSING & DATABASE ACCELERATOR

We have also used PIM to accelerate graph and query processing algorithms completely in-memory without using any processing cores. In the following, we explain the details of the different design implementation.

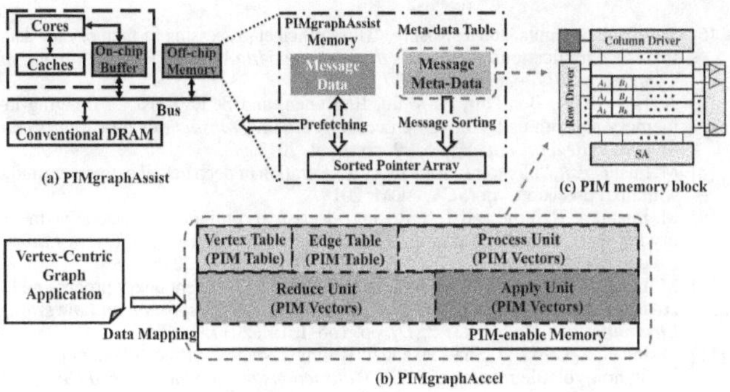


**Figure 6: The architecture overview of PIMgraphAssist and PIMgraphAccel. [30]**

## 4.1 Graph Processing Acceleration

Large-scale graph processing is becoming more and more important in the big data era. Framework-based models are widely used to represent most graph processing applications which run on different computing platforms. However, such large-scale graph applications are not handled efficiently by conventional architecture because of the irregular structure of graph data. For instance, widely used message passing vertex-centric model [25] has random memory access patterns because the destination of each message depends on the structure of the graph which is very irregular. Several accelerators have been proposed to improve the memory performance of hardware when processing graph applications. For instance, Tesseract [26] utilizes near-data computing based on 3D DRAM to build a scalable architecture for efficiently processing message-passing based graph applications. GraphPIM [27] offloads synchronization operations to memory to reduce the overhead of atomic operations. However, the inefficient data movement still exists in all these works because most operations are handled by processing cores. There are also some customized accelerators for graph processing, like Graphicionado [28] and work done by Ozdal et al. [29]. These ASIC designs reduce the impact of random memory accesses by special on-chip memory architectures which adds a lot of hardware complexity and does not scale well with larger graph data sizes. In contrast, we plan to utilize novel PIM technologies to minimize the inefficiency caused by the conventional memory hierarchy in graph processing. Specifically, we propose two different accelerators for graph processing: a PIM-based accelerator assistant for vertex-centric graph processing, and a general graph processing accelerator which translates the whole graph application into in-memory operations with high-degree parallelism.

**PIMgraphAssist:** Our proposed accelerator assistant is a heterogeneous memory component added in the conventional memory hierarchy. PIMgraphAssist consists of an on-chip buffer and an off-chip PIM memory as shown in Figure 6. The off-chip PIM memory has an associative memory and a normal memory. The associative memory supports fast in-memory search operations and stores meta-data of generated messages of application, while the normal memory stores contents of messages. For each message processed in the application, we write the message into the off-chip memory without accessing conventional memory hierarchy (including on-chip caches). The meta-data table stores an entry for each message, and each entry consists of source vertex, the destination vertex, and the address of message in the normal memory. Then, the accelerator sorts all the messages based on the order that the program requires by utilizing efficient associative searches in the meta-data table. The sorting process generates a pointer array and a two-level prefetching scheme is designed to efficiently send sorted results to the on-chip buffer. Specifically, PIMgraphAssist uses a streaming prefetching when accessing the pointer array and an indirect prefetching for each pointer fetched. The performance gain of our proposed PIM accelerator is due to two reasons: the random memory access will no longer cause high cache miss rates because all corresponding memory accesses are directly forwarded to PIM-based accelerator, and the processor can prefetch the sorted messages which maximize the memory bandwidth. Our design can be used for existing message passing based graph processing software frameworks by introducing memory load and store API for all messages generated.

**PIMgraphAccel:** Our PIM-based accelerator maps each phase of graph processing to in-memory operations by leveraging a large amount of processing memory blocks that can compute simultaneously. A typical vertex-centric graph processing framework has three phases: process, reduce and apply. In the process phase, all active vertices process messages based on their current application-specific status data and edge information. Then, all vertices receiving messages collect the message received and reduce them into a new temporary value based on an application-specific function during the reduce phase. In the apply phase, each vertex updates its status data based on the computed temporary values. In such a framework, there is a great potential of parallelism which cannot be fully exploited by conventional architecture because of data movement and an insufficient number of processing cores. For example, all operations during the process phase can be handled simultaneously. Furthermore, reduce and apply operations on different vertices can also be parallelized because there is no data dependency. Based on this observation, we design a graph processing accelerator PIMgraphAccel, by leveraging PIM architecture supporting various operations. Each function unit has a heterogeneous PIM architecture handling different tasks by PIM blocks. Specifically, we store the application-specific property (e.g., distance value in single-source-shortest-path) in PIM blocks supporting normal PIM operations like addition and bit-wise operations. These PIM blocks can compute several properties stored in the same row by one PIM command. In addition to row-level parallelism, different PIM blocks can perform computations simultaneously to provide block-level parallelism. We utilize PIM blocks to enable fast associative search to accelerate meta-data look-up in graph processing, like fetching active vertices list. Furthermore, we design several techniques to maximize the parallelism of PIM operations. PIMgraphAccel utilizes in-memory associative searches to schedule computations which can be parallelized during run-time. A new circuit design is proposed to enable parallel in-memory compare-and-swap (CAS) operations. We expect to significantly improve the performance of framework-based graph processing application by utilizing extensive parallelism and efficient in-memory data movements. To extend the lifetime of the proposed accelerator, we also design an endurance management mechanism specific to graph processing to evenly distribute write operations to different NVM parts.

## 4.2 Query Processing Acceleration

Data management systems (DMS) are used for collecting and analyzing large amounts of data for web applications and end users. The execution time of DMS queries increases at least linearly and sometimes exponentially as more records are stored on a server due to hardware and software limitations. Our recent work proposed a non-volatile memory-based query processing accelerator, called NVQuery [10], that supports a wide range of query functionalities including aggregation functions, prediction functions, bitwise operations, addition, exact, and nearest distance search operations. Our experimental evaluation using common SQL queries shows that, as compared to the state-of-the-art query accelerators [31], NVQuery can achieve 26.2× energy-delay product improvement while providing similar accuracy. However, it does not support some commonly used query functions.

We also proposed NVQuery+ [11] that support different types of functions which are costly to process on conventional core including: Between and Join which are used frequently in a query system. These functions are very costly to compute on conventional systems. On the other hand, NVQuery+ exploits its in-memory architecture to accelerate three different types of Joins, namely inner, right, and left, efficiently. We enable these extra functionalities by changing the memory structure to support functionalities such as sort and in-memory addition. Furthermore, our design support two types of parallelization in memory: row level parallelism, which allows multiple additions performs in a single memory block and block-level parallelism which increases the overall throughput of PIM. In addition, we extend the idea of NVQuery+ to approximate query processor by applying voltage overscaling on the memory block and enabling approximate in-memory multiplication. In this mode, the query operations can be implemented in an approximate mode within a controllable level of accuracy. This design adaptively balances the level of energy efficiency and quality of computation based on the accuracy requirement.

# 5 CONCLUSION

Running data-intensive workloads with large datasets on traditional cores results in high energy consumption and slow processing speed due to a large amount of data movement between memory and processing units. In this work, we built a platform capable of responding to our needs in real time with orders of magnitude more energy efficient operation. We propose a Processing In-Memory platform which accelerates fundamental operations and diverse data analytic procedures. Instead of sending a large amount of data to the processing cores for computation, our platform performs a large part of computation tasks inside the memory, thus the application performance can be accelerated significantly by avoiding the memory access bottleneck. Our platform accelerates general real-world big applications including machine learning applications, graph processing, and query processing.

# ACKNOWLEDGMENT

This work was partially supported by CRISP, one of six centers in JUMP, an SRC program sponsored by DARPA, and also NSF grants #1730158 and #1527034.

# REFERENCES

[1] M. Imani, Y. Kim, and T. Rosing, "Mpim: Multi-purpose in-memory processing using configurable resistive memory," in *2017 22nd Asia and South Pacific Design Automation Conference (ASP-DAC)*, pp. 757–763, IEEE, 2017.
[2] S. Kvatinsky, D. Belousov, S. Liman, G. Satat, N. Wald, E. G. Friedman, A. Kolodny, and U. C. Weiser, "MagicâĂŤmemristor-aided logic," *IEEE Transactions on Circuits and Systems II: Express Briefs*, vol. 61, no. 11, pp. 895–899, 2014.
[3] S. Gupta, M. Imani, and T. Rosing, "Felix: Fast and energy-efficient logic in memory," in *2018 IEEE/ACM International Conference on Computer-Aided Design (ICCAD)*, pp. 1–7, IEEE, 2018.
[4] N. Talati, S. Gupta, P. Mane, and S. Kvatinsky, "Logic design within memristive memories using memristor-aided logic (magic)," *IEEE Transactions on Nanotechnology*, vol. 15, no. 4, pp. 635–650, 2016.
[5] J. Sim, M. Imani, W. Choi, Y. Kim, and T. Rosing, "Lupis: latch-up based ultra efficient processing in-memory system," in *2018 19th International Symposium on Quality Electronic Design (ISQED)*, pp. 55–60, IEEE, 2018.
[6] M. Imani, S. Gupta, and T. Rosing, "Ultra-efficient processing in-memory for data intensive applications," in *Proceedings of the 54th Annual Design Automation Conference 2017*, p. 6, ACM, 2017.
[7] A. Haj-Ali, R. Ben-Hur, N. Wald, R. Ronen, and S. Kvatinsky, "Imaging-in-memory algorithms for image processing," *IEEE Transactions on Circuits and Systems I: Regular Papers*, no. 99, pp. 1–14, 2018.
[8] M. Imani *et al.*, "Floatpim: In-memory acceleration of deep neural network training with high precision," in *ISCA*, ACM, 2019.
[9] M. Imani, A. Rahimi, and T. S. Rosing, "Resistive configurable associative memory for approximate computing," in *2016 Design, Automation & Test in Europe Conference & Exhibition (DATE)*, pp. 1327–1332, IEEE, 2016.
[10] M. Imani, S. Gupta, A. Arredondo, and T. Rosing, "Efficient query processing in crossbar memory," in *2017 IEEE/ACM International Symposium on Low Power Electronics and Design (ISLPED)*, pp. 1–6, IEEE, 2017.
[11] M. Imani, S. Gupta, S. Sharma, and T. Rosing, "Nvquery: Efficient query processing in non-volatile memory," *IEEE Transactions on Computer-Aided Design of Integrated Circuits and Systems*, 2018.
[12] P. Kanerva, "Hyperdimensional computing: An introduction to computing in distributed representation with high-dimensional random vectors," *Cognitive Computation*, vol. 1, no. 2, pp. 139–159, 2009.
[13] M. Imani, A. Rahimi, D. Kong, T. Rosing, and J. M. Rabaey, "Exploring hyperdimensional associative memory," in *2017 IEEE International Symposium on High Performance Computer Architecture (HPCA)*, pp. 445–456, IEEE, 2017.
[14] M. Imani, C. Huang, D. Kong, and T. Rosing, "Hierarchical hyperdimensional computing for energy efficient classification," in *2018 55th ACM/ESDA/IEEE Design Automation Conference (DAC)*, pp. 1–6, IEEE, 2018.
[15] T. Kohonen, *Associative memory: A system-theoretical approach*, vol. 17. Springer Science & Business Media, 2012.
[16] M. Imani, M. Samragh, Y. Kim, S. Gupta, F. Koushanfar, and T. Rosing, "Rapidnn: In-memory deep neural network acceleration framework," *arXiv preprint arXiv:1806.05794*, 2018.
[17] P. Chi, S. Li, C. Xu, T. Zhang, J. Zhao, Y. Liu, Y. Wang, and Y. Xie, "Prime: A novel processing-in-memory architecture for neural network computation in reram-based main memory," in *ACM SIGARCH Computer Architecture News*, vol. 44, pp. 27–39, IEEE Press, 2016.
[18] A. Shafiee, A. Nag, N. Muralimanohar, R. Balasubramonian, J. P. Strachan, M. Hu, R. S. Williams, and V. Srikumar, "Isaac: A convolutional neural network accelerator with in-situ analog arithmetic in crossbars," *ACM SIGARCH Computer Architecture News*, vol. 44, no. 3, pp. 14–26, 2016.
[19] T. Serrano-Gotarredona, T. Masquelier, T. Prodromakis, G. Indiveri, and B. Linares-Barranco, "Stdp and stdp variations with memristors for spiking neuromorphic learning systems," *Frontiers in neuroscience*, vol. 7, p. 2, 2013.
[20] L. Song, X. Qian, H. Li, and Y. Chen, "Pipelayer: A pipelined reram-based accelerator for deep learning," in *2017 IEEE International Symposium on High Performance Computer Architecture (HPCA)*, pp. 541–552, IEEE, 2017.
[21] J. R. Quinlan, *C4. 5: programs for machine learning*. Elsevier, 2014.
[22] Y. Kim, M. Imani, and T. Rosing, "Orchard: Visual object recognition accelerator based on approximate in-memory processing," in *2017 IEEE/ACM International Conference on Computer-Aided Design (ICCAD)*, pp. 25–32, IEEE, 2017.
[23] Y. Deng and B. Manjunath, "Content-based search of video using color, texture, and motion," in *Proceedings of International Conference on Image Processing*, vol. 2, pp. 534–537, IEEE, 1997.
[24] M. Imani, Y. Kim, and T. Rosing, "Ngine: Ultra-efficient nearest neighbor accelerator based on in-memory computing," in *2017 IEEE International Conference on Rebooting Computing (ICRC)*, pp. 1–8, IEEE, 2017.
[25] G. Malewicz *et al.*, "Pregel: a system for large-scale graph processing," in *Proceedings of the 2010 ACM SIGMOD International Conference on Management of data*, pp. 135–146, ACM, 2010.
[26] J. Ahn, S. Hong, S. Yoo, O. Mutlu, and K. Choi, "A scalable processing-in-memory accelerator for parallel graph processing," *ACM SIGARCH Computer Architecture News*, vol. 43, no. 3, pp. 105–117, 2016.
[27] L. Nai, R. Hadidi, J. Sim, H. Kim, P. Kumar, and H. Kim, "Graphpim: Enabling instruction-level pim offloading in graph computing frameworks," in *2017 IEEE International symposium on high performance computer architecture (HPCA)*, pp. 457–468, IEEE, 2017.
[28] T. J. Ham, L. Wu, N. Sundaram, N. Satish, and M. Martonosi, "Graphicionado: A high-performance and energy-efficient accelerator for graph analytics," in *2016 49th Annual IEEE/ACM International Symposium on Microarchitecture (MICRO)*, pp. 1–13, IEEE, 2016.
[29] M. M. Ozdal, S. Yesil, T. Kim, A. Ayupov, J. Greth, S. Burns, and O. Ozturk, "Energy efficient architecture for graph analytics accelerators," in *2016 ACM/IEEE 43rd Annual International Symposium on Computer Architecture (ISCA)*, pp. 166–177, IEEE, 2016.
[30] M. Zhou, M. Imani, S. Gupta, and T. Rosing, "Gas: A heterogeneous memory architecture for graph processing," in *Proceedings of the International Symposium on Low Power Electronics and Design*, p. 27, ACM, 2018.
[31] N. Potti and J. M. Patel, "Daq: a new paradigm for approximate query processing," *Proceedings of the VLDB Endowment*, vol. 8, no. 9, pp. 898–909, 2015.

# In-memory Processing based on Time-domain Circuit

Yuyao Kong
Southeast University
Nanjing, Jiangsu, China
yuyao_kong@seu.edu.cn

Jun Yang
Southeast University
Nanjing, Jiangsu, China
dragon@seu.edu.cn

## ABSTRACT

Deep Neural Networks (DNN) have emerged as a dominant algorithm for machine learning (ML). High performance and extreme energy efficiency are critical for deployments of DNN, especially in mobile platforms such as autonomous vehicles, cameras, and other devices of internet of things. However, DNNs lead to massive data movement and memory accesses, which prevents it from being integrated into always-on Internet-of-Things (IoT) devices. Recently, computing in-memory (CIM) architectures embeds analog computation circuits in/near the memory arrays. It significantly reduces data movement energy. This paper summarizes the most recent novel methods on the CIM architectures based on the time-domain computation. Compared with voltage-domain and frequency-domain analog computing method, time-domain computation provides more flexibility, higher accuracy and greater scalability for larger neural networks. Thereafter, the first in-memory binary weight network (BWN) processor based on pulse-width modulation in which the feature is stored in memory is also presented. This work significantly reduces memory accesses (4x), and achieves state-of-the-art peak energy efficiency of 119.7TOPS/W.

## KEYWORDS

Computing in-memory, Time-domain, BWN

**ACM Reference Format:**

Yuyao Kong, Jun Yang. 2019. In-memory Processing based on Time-domain Circuit. In *GLSVLSI '19: 2019 Great Lakes Symposium on VLSI*, May 9–11, 2019, Washington, D.C., USA. 4 pages. https://doi.org/10.1145/3299874.3319484

## 1 Background

Deep neural networks (DNN) have evolved to the state-of-the-art technique for a broad range of tasks, such as computer vision, speech recognition, automatic translation, advertisement recommendation. However, as the neural networks develop rapidly, the large number of weights requires a considerable storage volume and memory bandwidth. For instance, AlexNet needs over 200 MB to store the weights, while the VGG-16 over 500 MB. As a result, the large number of weights incurs an intensive amount of computation and memory accesses. Therefore, it remains a magnificent challenge to, efficiently process large-scale neural networks with limited resources.

In order to address such a challenge, many DNN accelerators have been proposed. The implementation of DNN accelerators can be classified into three major categories by the signal used to do processing; they are digital, analog, and mixed analog/digital platforms.

1) Digital: Four categories of digital systems are widely used to implement DNN accelerators. The first one is field programmable gate arrays (FPGAs). FPGAs have been frequently utilized as neural network accelerators to achieve speed-up over CPU-based solutions. However, FPGAs are not suitable for low-power applications due to their large footprint and power consumption. Besides FPGAs, ASIC is the second candidate to implement DNNs. They are always highly optimized for a specific DNN model. The third class is the customized Digital Signal Processors (DSPs) with specified instruction sets. For example, S. Zhang, et al. proposed Cambricon-X [1]. It is capable of accelerating both dense and sparse DNNs. Performance-wise, Cambricon-X achieves 544 GOP/s throughput, while improves energy efficiency by 6.43x as compared to the prior works. The last approach is using coarse grained reconfigurable architecture (CGRA) to accelerate DNNs. It provides high design flexibility and energy efficiency. For example, Yin, et al. [2] proposed a reconfigurable heterogeneous DNN accelerator. It consists two arrays, while each consists of 16x16 processing elements (PE). Each PE supports adaptive bit-width to fit different bit-widths between different neural layers. This accelerator achieves 1.27TOPS/W at most in throughput and outperforms the state-of-the-art up to 5.2X in energy efficiency.

2) Analog: Similar to FPGAs for digital systems, specific field programmable analog arrays (FPAAs) to accelerate DNNs have been proposed. Such FPAAs contain programmable components to implement neurons, synapses, and interconnects between them. They are suitable to implement neuromorphic systems as they share some common characteristics, such as conservation of charge, amplification and integration. However, FPAAs suffer from the unreliability in analog systems.

3) Mixed Analog/Digital: Mixed analog/digital circuits can address some issues of the pure analog systems. On top of that mixed analog/digital systems can be used to accelerate DNNs. For


*GLSVLSI '19, May 9–11, 2019, Washington, D.C., USA*

ACM ISBN 978-1-4503-6252-8/19/05...$15.00
https://doi.org/10.1145/3299874.3319484

instance, YodaNN [3] was proposed to accelerate the binary weight network (BWN), where weight is represented by either 1 or -1. YodaNN is a flexible convolutional engine supporting different sizes of CNN kernels in the range from 1×1 to 7×7. It adopts a latch-based standard cell memory (SCM) architecture for on-chip data storage; it provides a better voltage scalability and energy efficiency. As a result, it significantly improves the energy efficiency (61.2 TOPS/W at 0.6V).

## 2 Motivation

In conventional von Neumann architecture, which is composed of separate memories and computation units, requires a large amount of data movement. Such bottleneck prevents Machine Learning (ML) and the Internet of Things (IoT) from applying to always-on devices. Meanwhile, data are represented as multi-bit digital signals in digital domain computation. These signals switch frequently between each clock cycle. As a result, the frequent capacitance charging and discharging consumes considerable dynamic power. Figure 1 shows the breakdown of power consumed by a typical DNN accelerator based on von Neumann architecture, and the energy consumption of Multiplication and Accumulation (MAC) units and memory access consumes 92% of the overall power [4]. The mixed-signal architecture with the separated memory and analog processor effectively reduces the power consumption of the MAC units by implementing them with the analog circuits. Nevertheless, the memory accesses still dominate the energy and latency costs. Recently, the computing in-memory (CIM) architecture is a promising candidate as an alternative to von Neumann architecture. It embeds analog computation circuit in/near the memory arrays. As a result, it significantly reduces the number of memory accesses and then the incurred energy consumption. However, CIM still suffers from limited flexibility and reliability. How to addresses these issues remains a challenge for such CIM architectures.

The remainder of this section will present the state of the art of the analog signal processing based on voltage- and frequency-domain, respectively.

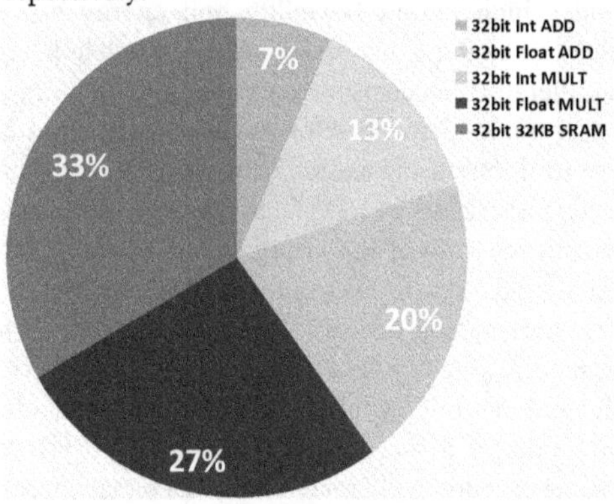


**Figure 1: Power breakdown of a typical DNN accelerator in von Neumann architecture.**

### 2.1 Voltage-domain based analog processing

Most analog compute techniques are based on voltage-domain (i.e., using voltage as the processing signal). These techniques typically utilize charge manipulation schemes to realize efficient computations in neural network accelerators. For instance, A. Biswas et al. [5] (Figure 2) use features of the DNNs to control the discharging time of the computing bit-cell array. Thereby the feature data is represented as the voltage that remains on the local bit-lines (BL). A local multiply-and-average (MAV) circuit evaluates the average of local BL and passes the voltage to the positive and negative voltage rails depending on the input weight. The difference between two rails is fed to a charge-sharing based ADC to obtain the digital outputs of the multiply-and-accumulate (MAC) computation.

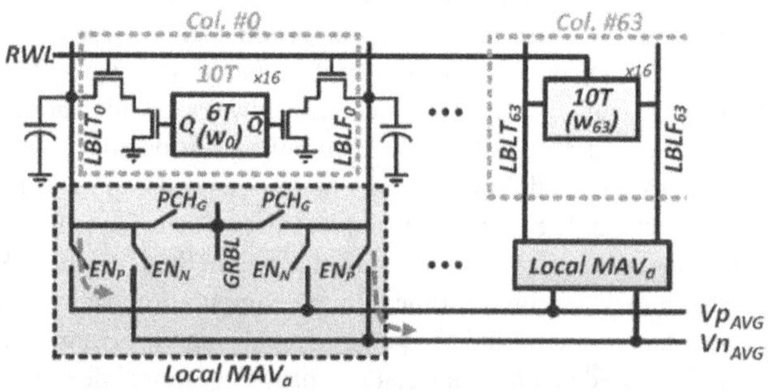


**Figure 2: Voltage-domain Processing.**

However, the voltage-domain MAC designs need enough voltage headroom and power/area–hungry ADCs/DACs. It limits the circuit's voltage scalability and the MAC energy efficiency.

### 2.2 Frequency-domain based analog processing

Another major style of analog processing used to accelerate DNNs is based on frequency-domain (i.e., using frequency of signals to do computation). Authors of [6] proposed a frequency-modulation-based approach to realize MAC computations, as shown in figure 3. Each value of the feature map is represented by a pulse. The value of each weight controls an oscillator to generate a clock with different frequencies. The final MAC result is processed by an up/down counter; this counter is driven by a sample clock whose frequency depends on the value of the weight. However, such a design needs to control the value of frequency very accurately. As a result, it cannot maximize the performance potential of the frequency-domain techniques.

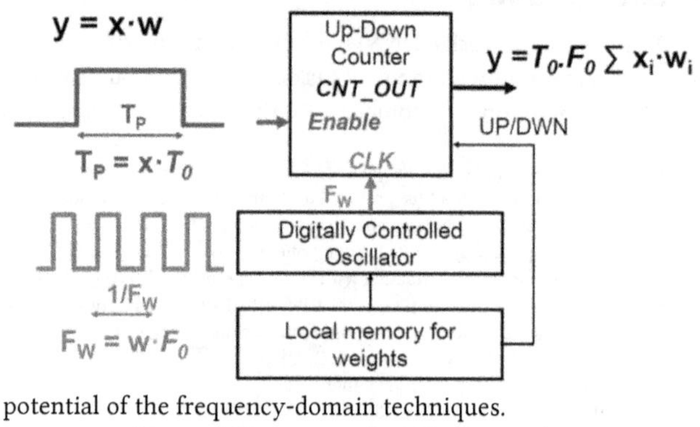


**Figure 3: Frequency-domain Processing.**

## 3 Time-domain processing

In time-domain signal processing, the multi-bit digital data is represented as the pulse width or the circuit path latency. Comparing with voltage-domain and frequency-domain processing, time-domain processing consumes less dynamic energy due to its less capacitance and signal-toggling activity.

### 3.1 Path Latency Based Processing

D. Miyashita et al. [7] proposed a DNN accelerator for BWN. Two circuit paths with a short and long latency are used to represent the positive and negative value of each weight, respectively. The binary MAC result is obtained by comparing the rising edge arrival time of these two pulses. In addition, L.R. Everson et al. [8] proposed graph processing accelerator. It uses the entire memory array as the vertices of the graph algorithm, and inserts a delay cell of each edge between every two vertices. A pulse is propagated between the vertices through the delay cells. Each vertex senses and stores the direction of the first arrival pulse. Next, it prevents other pulses from overwriting it. And then propagates it to neighboring vertices. The shortest path can be traced from start point to the target.

The path latency processing method can easily by only comparing the propagation delay of each pulse. Thus it is difficult to extend into large-scale high-precision networks.

### 3.2 Pulse Accumulation

In [9], A. Sayal et al. presented the pulse accumulation method to realize the MAC operations in CNN. Features are represented by the pulse with different widths, as similar as the method in [5]. The bi-directional memory delay line (MDL) is controlled by the input weight. Positive value makes clockwise propagation, while negative valus makes anti-clockwise propagation. During the untenable time, MDL behaves like a latch to store the pulse. On top of that, it can store/add/subtract different pulses in each clock cycle. The final MAC result is obtained from the up/down edge triggered counter. This method represents the digital result as the pulse width and has better time scalability. It is more suitable for network requiring high data precision.

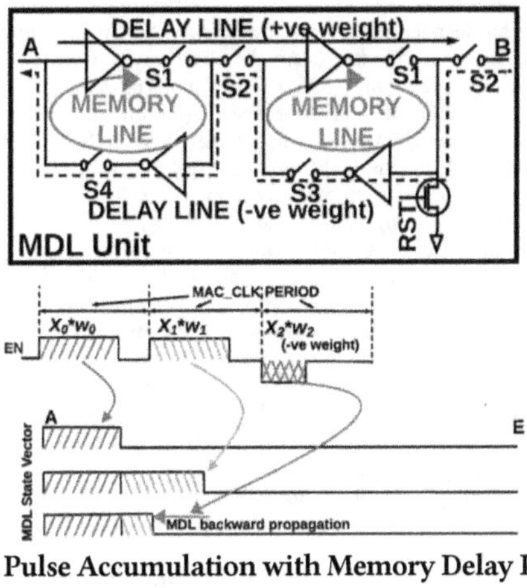


**Figure 4: Pulse Accumulation with Memory Delay Line Unit.**

### 3.3 Pulse Width Modulation

Our prior work has presented an energy-efficient in-memory BWN architecture with pulse-width modulation [10]. A conventional in-memory implementation, which merges weight memory and the analog computing circuit together, still requires large feature data movement. Considering the BWN, feature memory access is larger than that of weights. This work proposed architecture has 2 key points: 1) It combines feature, weight, and computing together, like a sandwich 2) Considering the area overhead, the computing circuit must be small enough. So a pulse-width modulation method is also presented.

With the above two points, as the figure 5 shown, weight shifting - convolution is a basic operation. The input feature map can be reused until weight shifting to the end. Thus, it significantly reduces memory access

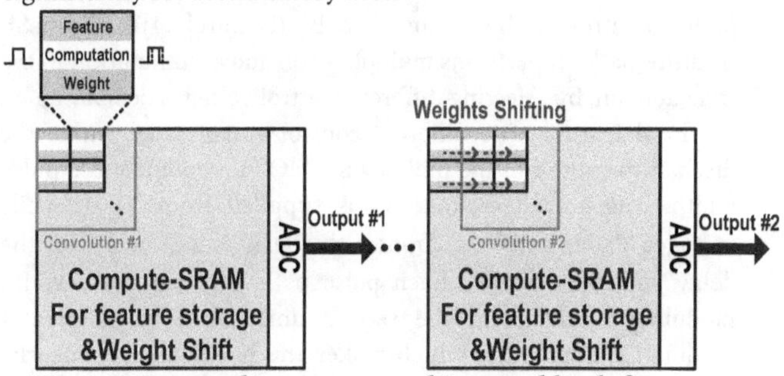


**Figure 5: Proposed in-memory architecture blends feature, weight memory with computing circuit together.**

Figure 6 shows the overall architecture. It is consisted of a controller for operating configuration, a weight pre-processing unit to reduce weight complexity, a post-processing unit including an accumulation memory, and the sandwich-shaped computing SRAM(Sandwich-RAM). The Sandwich-RAM can work in two modes: 1) Memory Mode: the memory array can be written in feature map and weight like a traditional SRAM. The Sandwich-RAM constitutes by 8T bitcell array for feature storage and shift pulse-latch for weight storage and shifting. 2) Computation mode: The main function of the Sandwich-RAM is executing the convolution on the loaded features and weight based on the pulse width modulation unit. Each block comprises of 6×8b 8T bitcell to store 6 feature data. The computation circuit and the weight data is shared between 6 features. One feature is selected for computation at a time, and other features can be updated during the computation. After one convolution, the weight is shifted to the adjacent blocks for the next calculation, repeating as such until all convolutions with the stored feature map are computed. In addition, the Sandwich-RAM can be divided into 4 or 16 independent computation parts depending on different network, in order to increase Sandwich-RAM utilization.

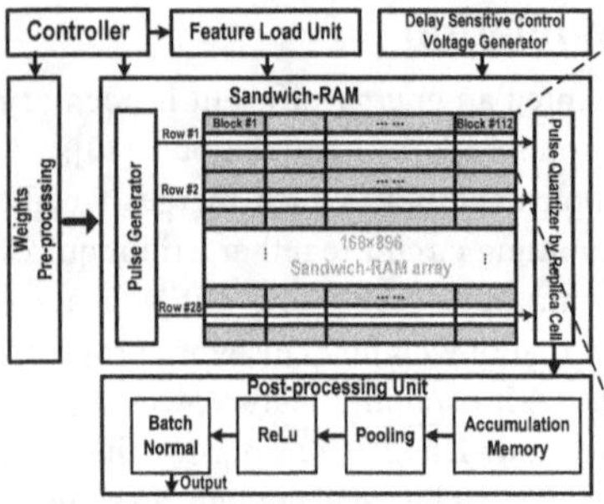


**Figure 6: Pulse Accumulation with Memory Delay Line Unit.**

A fixed-width pulse is generated on the left side of Sandwich-RAM, modulated by each pulse-width modulation unit (PWMU) and quantized on the right. The PWMU is small enough to realize efficient computation. As figure 7 shown, the PWMU has two paths controlled by feature MSB (Feature[7:4]) and LSB (Feature[3:0]). It performs multiplication and accumulation in the time domain, by selecting different control voltages depending on the local feature. The different control voltages determine the discharging speed of the pull down NMOS to modulate the pulse width. The control voltage $V_1$ is supplied from VDD, while voltages $V_2$, $V_3$ and $V_4$ guarantee the delay is 2, 3 or 4× of the delay controlled by $V_1$. Each pulse path has two pulse width modulation units, and the second unit has 4 times greater modulation capability, which makes the pulse change linearly. There are two modulation paths controlled by the input weight: positive values make pulses wider, while negative values make them narrower. In conventional in-memory architecture, the computation array can only operate on a row-by-row or column-by-column mode, which results in low utilization for variant network size. The PWMU has a bypass path, which has no effect on the pulse. The bypass path makes this analog processing more flexible and suitable for different network.

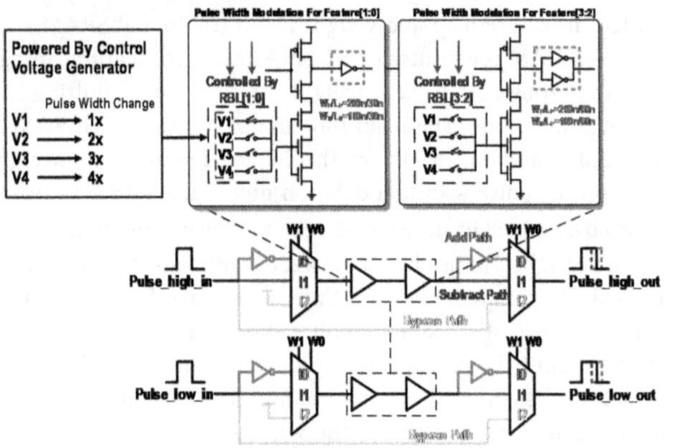


**Figure 7: Time-domain manipulation schemes based on Pulse Width Modulation Unit.**

Analog computing circuit is greatly affected by the global PVT variation and voltage fluctuation. In order to get more accurate computing results, the Delay Sensitive Control Voltage Generator (DSCVG) and Pulse Quantizer by Replica Cell (PQRC) are presented, which dynamically adjust the control voltage and sample clock. As figure 8 shown, the modulation capability remains great linearity in PVT variation. The MAC result is represented as the final pulse width and sampled using the PQRC to reduce the floatability of results. This work is fabricated in a 28nm CMOS technology, and reach peak energy efficiency of 119.7 TOPS/W at 0.6V.

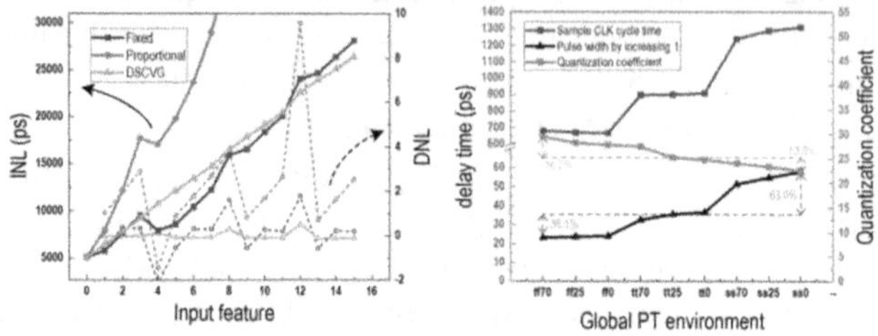


**Figure 8: (a) the modulation linear graph. (b) Quantizer results floatation by PQRC.**

# 6 CONCLUSIONS

CIM architectures effectively reduce the energy consumption of memory access and are promising to alleviate or even remove the von Neumann bottleneck. The design of analog computing circuits is the key to the CIM architecture. They should be flexible and stable enough. Time-domain analog signal processing is a promising candidate to implement such analogy circuits at present. It provides a better scalability and consumes less energy. However, the analog signal processing method still faces some challenges such as computation errors due to PVT variation and limited analog-to-digital converter (ADC) accuracy. Once these challenges are properly addressed, time-domain-based CIM architectures are stepping further to accelerate the high-precision DNNs.

# ACKNOWLEDGMENTS

This work was supported by the National Natural Science Foundation of China (NO. 61474022) and the National Science and Technology Project under Grant. 2018ZX01031101-005.

# REFERENCES

[1] S. Zhang, et al, "Cambricon-X: An accelerator for sparse neural networks," in IEEE/ACM International Symposium on Microarchitecture. IEEE, 2016.

[2] S. Yin, et al, "A 1.06-to-5.09 TOPS/W reconfigurable hybrid-neural-network processor for deep learning applications," in VLSI Circuits, Symposium , 2017.

[3] Renzo Andri, et al., "YodaNN: An Architecture for Ultralow Power Binary-Weight CNN Acceleration", TCAD, vol. 37, no.1, pp. 48-60, Jan. 2018.

[4] Han S, et al., "EIE: Efficient Inference Engine on Compressed Deep Neural Network," in ACM SIGARCH Computer Architecture News, 2016.

[5] A. Biswas, et al., "Conv-RAM: An Energy-Efficient SRAM with Embedded Convolution Computation for Low-Power CNN-Based Machine Learning Applications," ISSCC, pp. 488-489, 2018.

[6] A. Amravati, et al., "A 55nm Time-Domain Mixed-Signal Neuromorphic Accelerator With Stochastic Synapses and Embedded Reinforcement Learning For Autonomous Micro-Robots," ISSCC, pp. 124-126, 2018.

[7] D. Miyashita, et al., "A Neuromorphic Chip Optimized for Deep Learning and CMOS Technology with Time-Domain Analog and Digital Mixed-Signal Processing," JSSC, vol. 52, no. 10, pp. 2679-2689, Oct. 2017..

[8] L. R. Everson, et al., "A 40×40 Four-Neighbor Time-Based In- Memory Computing Graph ASIC Chip Featuring Wavefront Expansion and 2D Gradient Control," ISSCC, pp. 50-52, 2019

[9] A. Sayal, et al., "All-Digital Time-Domain CNN Engine Using Bidirectional Memory Delay Lines for Energy-Efficient Edge Computing," ISSCC, pp. 228-230, 2019.

[10] J. Yang, et al., "Sandwich-RAM: An Energy-Efficient In-Memory BWN Architecture with Pulse-Width Modulation," ISSCC, pp. 394-396 , 2019.

# An Overview of Thermal Challenges and Opportunities for Monolithic 3D ICs

Prachi Shukla
Boston University
Boston, USA
prachis@bu.edu

Ayse K. Coskun
Boston Univeristy
Boston, USA
acoskun@bu.edu

Vasilis F. Pavlidis
University of Manchester
Manchester, UK
pavlidis@cs.man.ac.uk

Emre Salman
Stony Brook University (SUNY)
Stony Brook, USA
emre.salman@stonybrook.edu

## ABSTRACT

Monolithic 3D (MONO3D) is a three-dimensional integration technology that can overcome some of the fundamental limitations faced by traditional, two-dimensional scaling. This paper analyzes the unique thermal characteristics of MONO3D ICs by simulating a two-tier flip-chip MONO3D IC and highlights the primary differences in comparison to a similarly-sized flip-chip TSV-based 3D IC. Specifically, we perform architectural-level thermal simulations for both technologies and demonstrate that vertical thermal coupling is stronger in MONO3D ICs, leading to lower upper tier temperatures. We also investigate the significance of lateral versus vertical flow of heat in MONO3D ICs. We simulate different hot spot scenarios in a two-tier MONO3D IC and show that although the lateral heat flow is limited as compared to TSV-based 3D ICs, ignoring this mechanism can cause nonnegligible error (~ 4 °C) in temperature estimation, particularly for layers farther from the heat sink. In addition, we show that with increasing interconnect utilization (due to the contribution of Joule heating to overall temperature), the on-chip temperatures and the significance of lateral heat flow within the two-tier MONO3D IC also increase. Finally, we discuss potential opportunities in MONO3D ICs to enhance their thermal integrity.

## KEYWORDS

Monolithic 3D, thermal integrity, vertical thermal coupling, lateral heat spreading

**ACM Reference Format:**

Prachi Shukla, Ayse K. Coskun, Vasilis F. Pavlidis, and Emre Salman. 2019. An Overview of Thermal Challenges and Opportunities for Monolithic 3D ICs. In *Great Lakes Symposium on VLSI 2019 (GLSVLSI '19), May 9–11, 2019, Tysons Corner, VA, USA,* 6 pages. https://doi.org/10.1145/3299874.3319485


*GLSVLSI '19, May 9–11, 2019, Tysons Corner, VA, USA*

ACM ISBN 978-1-4503-6252-8/19/05...$15.00
https://doi.org/10.1145/3299874.3319485

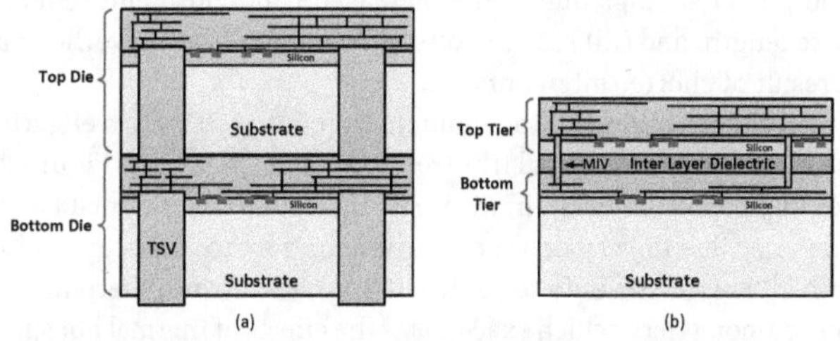


**Figure 1: Two 3D integration technologies: (a) TSV-based 3D integration, and (b) MONO3D integration with MIVs**

## 1 INTRODUCTION

Two-dimensional scaling of transistors is reaching its limits due to factors such as (i) lithographic challenges, (ii) increasing power densities and related thermal challenges, (iii) on-chip communication overhead as metal wires typically scale less than scaling of transistors, and (iv) increasing manufacturing cost [8]. Three-dimensional integrated circuits (3D ICs) are highly promising as they can mitigate the interconnect related challenges and provide a significant boost in performance and power, while also reducing the chip footprint as compared to two-dimensional ICs.

Two major types of 3D integration are sequential MONO3D process and through silicon vias (TSV)-based 3D process, as illustrated in Fig. 1 [15]. MONO3D is an emerging 3D integration technology where the tiers are fabricated sequentially and interconnected using nanoscale monolithic inter-tier vias (MIVs). Sequential integration in MONO3D results in thin tiers (~ 500 nm) that are separated by an inter-layer dielectric (ILD) ($SiO_2$) with a thickness in the range of tens of nanometers [18].

Alternatively, in TSV-based 3D ICs, the tiers originate from separately fabricated wafers. As such, each tier is substantially thicker compared to MONO3D ICs. These tiers are interconnected using micrometer scale TSVs and are integrated with a thick insulating bonding layer [18]. This significant difference between the size of a TSV (several micrometers) and an MIV (nanometers) not only affects the integration density, but also the chip-level power and performance characteristics. For example, a practical TSV with several micrometers of diameter exhibits a capacitance in the range of tens of femtofarads, which is equivalent to approximately 100 gates (with fanout of two) in a relatively old 45 nm technology node [20, 25]. In the 7 nm technology node, a TSV is equivalent to approximately several thousand gates, thereby consuming significant dynamic power and causing *RC* delay. Furthermore, the keep-out zone around a TSV (i.e., region that should be free of transistors due to undesirable TSV effects such as stress and threshold voltage variation) exacerbates these issues.

Thus, Mono3D ICs with MIVs not only reduce the overall footprint and increase integration density, but also significantly enhance the power and performance characteristics. For example, a two-tier Mono3D IC has been shown to potentially achieve up to a 50% reduction in die size and ~50% reduction in power compared to its 2D counterpart at the same feature size, providing advantages equivalent to a generation of dimensional scaling [1, 12, 26, 28]. The key advantages of Mono3D ICs can be summarized as: (i) smaller chip footprint, (ii) significant performance enhancements and power savings due to the increased bandwidth and reduced wire length, and (iii) reduced on-chip communication overhead as a result of shorter interconnects.

A primary and well-known limitation facing 3D ICs is effective heat dissipation, particularly from the upper tiers (see Figure 2a for upper/bottom tiers). In Mono3D ICs, additional thermal issues can arise due to very dense device integration, routing congestion (which may contribute to Joule heating), and strong thermal coupling among tiers, which exacerbates the effects of thermal hot spots. These factors differentiate Mono3D technology from TSV-based 3D ICs. Furthermore, Mono3D process requires low temperature fabrication steps to protect the devices within the bottom tier. To withstand higher temperatures on the bottom tier, tungsten-based interconnects have been proposed [2]. However, such methods also increase the vertical thermal resistance and lead to performance degradation and higher on-chip temperatures [14, 19].

Overall, Mono3D ICs face unique thermal issues during both fabrication and design stages. This paper discusses these thermal challenges and also the opportunities to mitigate them. The main contributions of this work are as follows:

(1) We model and compare Mono3D and TSV-based two-tier 3D ICs in terms of inter-tier thermal coupling. We further investigate the effects of thermal coupling on circuit temperatures for these technologies.
(2) We present an architectural-level thermal analysis on the lateral and vertical heat flow in a two-tier Mono3D IC. We show that lateral heat flow plays an important role with increasing distance from the heat sink and in scenarios with high-density hot spots on the upper tier.
(3) We model different utilization levels of the interconnects to represent various application behaviors (slightly, moderately, and highly parallel), and calculate the effect that such application scenarios have on circuit temperature and lateral versus vertical heat flow.

The rest of the paper is organized as follows. Section 2 briefly discusses the differences between Mono3D and TSV-based 3D integration technologies, followed by a summary of recent work on thermal management in Mono3D ICs. In Section 3, we investigate the unique thermal issues faced by Mono3D ICs. We then discuss a few opportunities to enhance thermal integrity of Mono3D ICs in Section 4. Finally, we conclude in Section 5.

## 2 BACKGROUND

In the following subsections, we discuss how Mono3D differs from TSV-based 3D ICs. We also describe the recent work in Mono3D ICs with a focus on thermal issues.

### 2.1 Mono3D versus TSV-based 3D Integration

Mono3D and TSV-based 3D integration technologies differ in many aspects. In TSV-based 3D technology, the device layers are thicker (tens of $\mu m$) because each device layer (tier) has its own substrate. Although the thicker substrates improve the lateral heat spreading, they also result in high vertical thermal resistance. In addition, the TSVs exhibit large physical dimensions (5-100 $\mu m$) and facilitate the flow of heat vertically. However, the presence of a thick bonding layer (~ 2.5 $\mu$m) between the device layers impedes the flow of heat both vertically and laterally from the upper tier to the bottom tier, thereby, degrading the overall conductivity of the 3D IC [18].

On the other hand, the device layers in Mono3D ICs are much thinner (100-500 *nm*) due to which the lateral heat spreading capability reduces, thereby resulting in higher-density hot spots. In addition, the size of the MIVs is similar to conventional metal vias (*nm*) and therefore facilitate significantly denser device integration in Mono3D ICs. This dense integration, however, may cause routing congestion and exacerbated Joule heating [3, 27].

### 2.2 Thermal Management in Mono3D ICs

Recent works in Mono3D ICs have focused on alleviating the thermal challenges stated in the previous section. Samal *et al.* show that optimizing PDN design styles can increase thermal conductivity in Mono3D ICs and further lead to reduction in on-chip temperature by up to 5% [17]. Wei *et al.* further show that ignoring PDNs in thermal models can result in overestimation of steady-state temperature in Mono3D ICs [24]. Iqbal *et al.* propose the use of nano pillars for extracting heat from selected hot spot regions without interfering with the vias [9]. Such techniques improve thermal conductivity, thus, coupling, which allows heat to flow faster. In another work, Samal *et al.* show that the lateral flow of heat is negligible in Mono3D ICs and then build a non-linear regression model for temperature estimation of the tiers [18]. However, their thermal analysis lacks a wide coverage of different power profiles.

Tier partitioning and floorplanning are also important design optimization decisions for Mono3D ICs with implications on temperature. Kim *et al.* propose four-tier partitioning methods, in which a 2D placement policy is applied to an initial 2D design to partition cells recursively and build a four tier Mono3D design with MIVs [10]. Another 3D placement technique minimizes wire length while reducing routing congestion [13]. Pletea *et al.* provide a logic and memory partitioning scheme for Mono3D ICs with large memories using 2D EDA tools [16]. Another recent approach uses simulated annealing to iteratively partition the cells into different tiers while minimizing wire length [6]. Guler *et al.* utilize simulated annealing to floorplan circuits with Mono3D technology at diverse integration granularities (block, gate, and transistor levels) [7]. Their floorplanner creates a hybrid Mono3D design that minimizes the area, wire length, and power consumption.

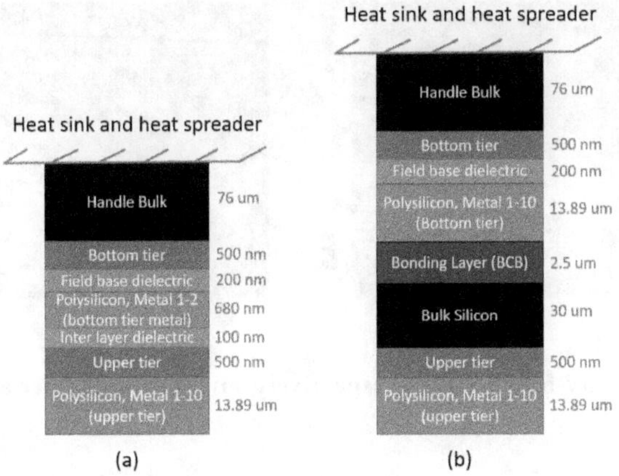


**Figure 2: Cross-section of a flip-chip stack for (a) two-tier MONO3D IC, (b) two-tier TSV-based 3D IC. These structures are input into the thermal simulator for thermal analysis.**

# 3 INSIGHTS ON MONO3D THERMAL ANALYSIS AND THERMAL INTEGRITY

In this section, we present architectural-level insights on thermal challenges faced by the MONO3D integration technology. We begin by comparing a two-tier Mono3D IC to a TSV-based 3D IC to investigate and quantify the distinct thermal characteristics of these technologies. We then analyze further the lateral and vertical heat flow in MONO3D ICs under different hot spot scenarios. In addition, we investigate the effect of different interconnect utilization levels on lateral versus vertical heat flow and on-chip temperatures. All of the analyses in this paper are performed using the architectural-level HotSpot-6.0 thermal simulator [22].

## 3.1 Inter-Tier Thermal Coupling in MONO3D versus TSV-based 3D

In this section, we study the differences in the thermal characteristics of TSV-based and MONO3D ICs. For this study, we model a flip-chip two-tier MONO3D and TSV-based 3D IC in HotSpot-6.0, with a heat sink mounted on top of the bottom tier (see Figure 2). We model all of the metal layers of both tiers in the MONO3D IC since each layer has comparable thickness. For a fair comparison between the two ICs, we also model the metal layers in the TSV-based 3D IC. In addition, HotSpot-6.0 supports features for heterogeneous modeling within a layer in a chip stack [11]. We use this functionality to model the TSVs along with silicon in the upper tier. However, we do not model the MIVs in the MONO3D IC since the size of the MIVs in the nanometer range is not practical for architecture-level analysis. Furthermore, ignoring MIVs underestimates the vertical heat flow in MONO3D technology, ensuring that our model presents a pessimistic analysis. Investigating the impact of MIV on temperature characteristics remains as future work that focuses on layout-level temperature estimation.

To study the thermal behavior of the two ICs, we model a 10 mm × 10 mm chip. Further, we model the TSVs as 4 TSV arrays, each of dimension 5 mm x 200 $\mu$m × 33 $\mu$m (length × width × height), passing through the upper tier, bulk silicon, and bonding layer. We

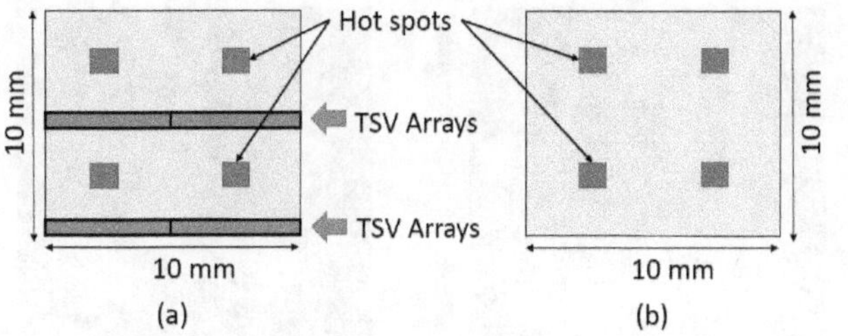


**Figure 3: Top view of the upper tiers with four hot spots in (a) TSV-based 3D IC, and (b) MONO3D IC.**

then place a hot spot at the center of the bottom tier and 4 hot spots in the upper tier. All of the hot spots are of size 400 $\mu$m × 400 $\mu$m. The bottom and the upper tiers consume a background power density of 25 and 30 W/cm$^2$, respectively. In addition, we assign 5% of the total power consumed by the tiers to the interconnects. Of that 5%, we assign 20% to the TSVs. The power densities are selected to ensure that the on-chip temperatures do not exceed 110 °C [23]. Since hot spot power densities in future processors are expected to reach up to 2 $kW/cm^2$, we assign each hot spot a power density of 750 W/cm$^2$ (to keep maximum on-chip temperature below 110 °C) [21]. The steady-state thermal maps obtained from the HotSpot thermal simulations are shown in Figure 4. The figures also illustrate the lateral heat spreading between the hot spots and cooler regions of the chip.

As shown in Figures 4a and 4b, hot spots in the upper tier reach very high temperatures (~ 109 °C) in the TSV-based 3D IC. The same locations on the bottom tier are approximately 38 °C cooler, thus, indicating weak vertical thermal coupling between the tiers. There are two main reasons for the observed weak vertical thermal coupling: (i) distance of the upper tier from the heat sink, and (ii) presence of an insulating bonding layer between the tiers. Note that the hot spot at the center of the bottom tier has a negligible effect on the center of the upper tier. This is because the vertical heat flow path from the bottom tier to the heat sink exhibits a lower thermal resistance due to the shorter distance and absence of an insulating layer.

On the other hand, Figures 4c and 4d illustrate that hot spots on the upper tier of MONO3D IC lead to similar hot spots on the bottom tier, reaching a temperature of ~ 77 °C. Overall, the temperature distribution among the two tiers varies up to only ~ 4 °C, while the temperature difference in TSV-based 3D IC reaches up to 38 °C. Note that the hot spots in MONO3D IC are more localized than those in TSV-based IC, thus, demonstrating that MONO3D technology exhibits lower lateral thermal coupling within a tier. Despite the reduced lateral thermal coupling in MONO3D IC, the maximum on-chip temperature is lower due to the stronger vertical inter-tier coupling as compared to TSV-based 3D IC. This, as a result, indicates enhanced overall thermal coupling in MONO3D ICs.

## 3.2 Significance of Lateral versus Vertical Heat Flow in MONO3D ICs

In this section, we explore the significance of lateral versus vertical heat flow in MONO3D ICs. The chip stack used for this analysis is the same as shown in Figure 2a. We use the HotSpot simulator to

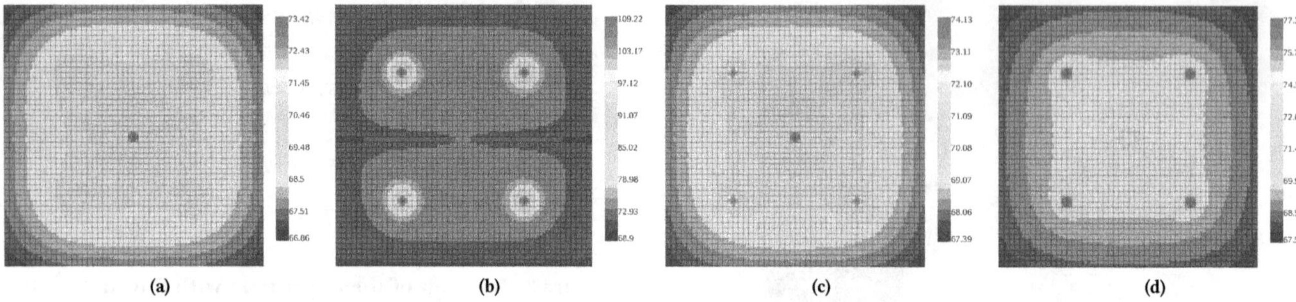


**Figure 4: Thermal maps of (a) bottom tier and (b) upper tier of the TSV-based 3D IC, respectively, and (c) bottom tier and (d) upper tier of the MONO3D IC, respectively.**

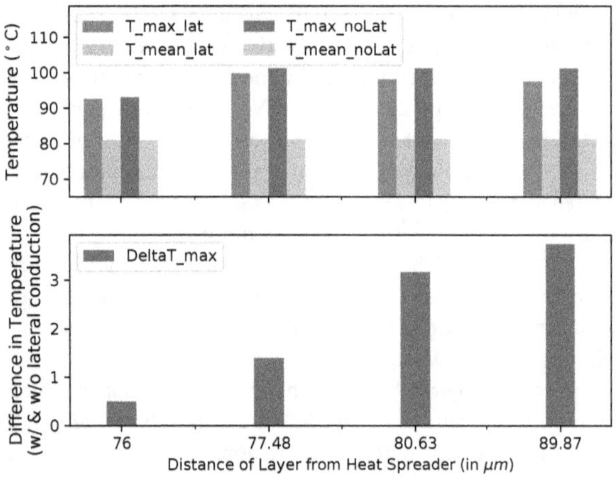


**Figure 5: Effect on chip temperature and lateral heat flow modeling when a single hot spot is at the center of each tier.**

evaluate the induced errors in on-chip temperatures when lateral modeling is turned off for the nanoscale layers. We simulate two scenarios for this study. In the first scenario, we simulate a 10 mm × 10 mm chip with a single hot spot at the center of each tier. Each hot spot is of size 200 $\mu$m × 200 $\mu$m with a power density of 1,600 W/cm$^2$. We set the background power density of the upper and bottom tiers to 50 and 40 W/cm$^2$, respectively. We report the maximum and mean temperatures across the two cases of modeling, i.e., with lateral modeling turned on and turned off. As shown in Figure 5, the maximum difference in on-chip temperature can reach $\sim 4$ °C for layers that are at $\sim 90$ $\mu$m distance from the heat sink. This difference is highest at the hot spot locations and the area around the hot spots. Note that the bottom and the upper tiers are at a distance of 76 and 77.48 $\mu$m from the heat spreader, respectively.

In the second scenario, we simulate two 10 mm × 10 mm chips (see Figure 6) with hot spots consuming $\sim$ 10% of the total chip area. In both chips, we place hot spots in the upper tier to produce high on-chip temperatures. The background power density of the upper and bottom tiers is set to 25 and 20 W/cm$^2$, respectively, while the hot spot power density is set to 1,000 W/cm$^2$. The size of each hot spot in the chip with scattered hot spots is 200 $\mu$m × 200 $\mu$m. The first chip with lumped hot spots results in higher on-chip temperatures, while the second chip with scattered hot

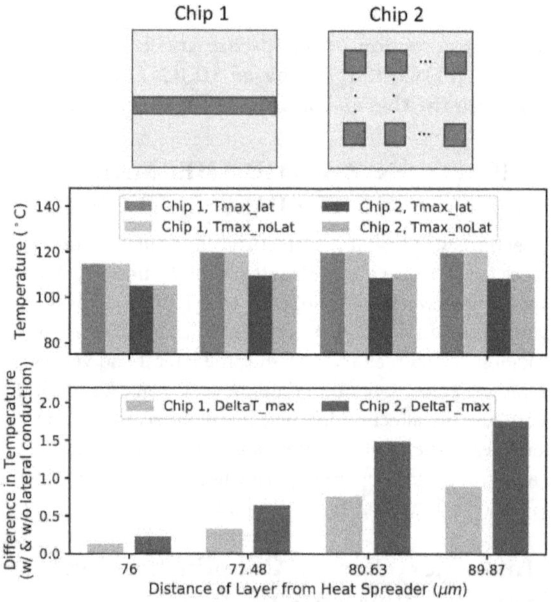


**Figure 6: Top view of the upper tier with 10% hot spot area. Chip 1 contains lumped hot spots, while chip 2 contains scattered hot spots. The graphs show maximum on-chip temperatures and significance of lateral heat flow modeling in chips 1 and 2.**

spots (i.e., with high power density spread across the chip) has lower temperature owing to higher lateral heat flow from hotter to cooler regions. When lateral modeling is turned off, the second chip is expected to show higher inaccuracy in on-chip temperature, as illustrated in Figure 6. According to this figure, for the layers away from the heat sink, the inaccuracy in on-chip temperatures increases to several degrees. Furthermore, the inaccuracy is observed to be the highest ($\sim$ 2 °C) in the areas next to the hot spots.

## 3.3 Thermal Impact of Interconnect Utilization in MONO3D ICs

In this section, we investigate the thermal impact of various interconnect utilization levels on lateral and vertical heat flow as well as on-chip temperatures. The utilization level of the interconnects is representative of the extent of parallelism within an application.

To perform this analysis, we first fix the total power budget of the MONO3D chip stack. We then vary the ratios of power distribution between the active tiers and the interconnects. We then run thermal simulations using HotSpot-6.0 to analyze how these utilization levels affect the thermal profile and lateral versus vertical heat flow in a MONO3D IC.

We set the power profile of the MONO3D IC to ensure that the maximum on-chip temperature does not exceed ~ 110 °C. We set the total power budget to 90 Watts and vary the ratio of power assigned to the interconnects versus the active tiers. The ratio represents three kinds of application behaviour: light (30:70), moderate (50:50) and extensive (70:30) parallelism. We then distribute the interconnect power linearly between metal layers 1-8, with metal 8 consuming the highest power. We test two hot spot scenarios: (i) high density hot spots at the center of both the tiers, and (ii) multiple high density hot spots in the upper tier alone (one at the center and four at the center of each quadrant of the upper tier). Each hot spot, in both the scenarios, is of size 400 $\mu$m × 400 $\mu$m.

In the scenario with a single hot spot on each tier, we set the hot spot power density to 1,300, 1,500, and 1,700 W/cm$^2$. For the multiple hot spot scenario, we set each hot spot power density to 1,600, 1,800 and 2,000 W/cm$^2$. We then run thermal simulations with HotSpot to obtain the steady-state thermal profile of the chip. Figures 7 and 8 show the on-chip temperature and the significance of modeling lateral heat flow with increasing distance from the heat sink, as the metal utilization increases from 30% to 70%. In both scenarios, we find that as the interconnect power increases, the difference in temperatures between w/ and w/o lateral heat flow modeling slightly increases. In addition, with increasing metal utilization, the maximum on-chip temperature also increases slightly (~ 1.2 °C). This behavior is because metal layers of the upper tier comprise global interconnect layers, which exhibit higher vertical thermal resistance. As a result, ignoring lateral heat flow induces a greater error in the reported temperatures of the MONO3D IC. Note that this error increases with increasing distance from the heat sink, showing that lateral heat flow modeling is relatively more important for layers that are farther away from the heat sink. In addition, due to strong vertical thermal coupling, the increase in maximum on-chip temperature is less. Furthermore, with lateral modeling enabled, it takes ~ 18 minutes to run a steady-state HotSpot simulation for a two-tier MONO3D IC with 100 × 100 grids (per layer), while it takes ~ 13 minutes to simulate the same MONO3D IC with lateral modeling disabled.

# 4 OPPORTUNITIES TO ENHANCE THERMAL INTEGRITY IN MONO3D ICS

Some of the unique MONO3D technology characteristics can be leveraged to mitigate thermal issues. For example, the bottom tier in existing MONO3D processes has limited number of metal layers (typically in the range of 2 to 3) since additional metal layers introduce significant fabrication challenges for top tier devices [4, 5]. Thus, a majority of the hot spots are expected to be within the top tier. Furthermore, logic gates within the bottom tier are likely to rely on the metal layers located within the top tier, particularly for global interconnections. Joule heating will therefore be more dominant within the top tier. These characteristics can be leveraged

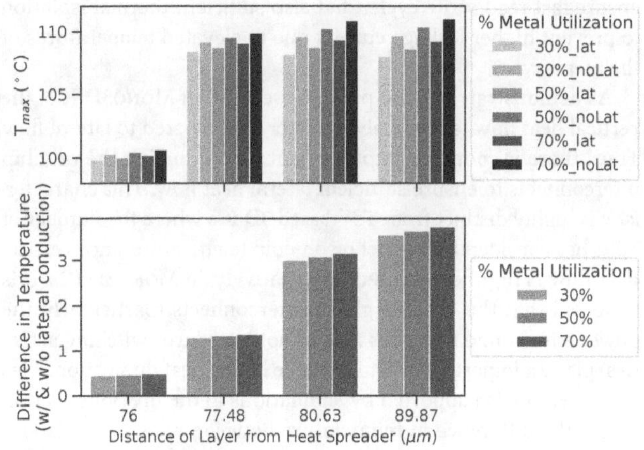


**Figure 7: Single hot spot scenario (hot spot power density = 1,700 W/cm$^2$): Significance of lateral heat flow modeling with increasing metal utilization.**

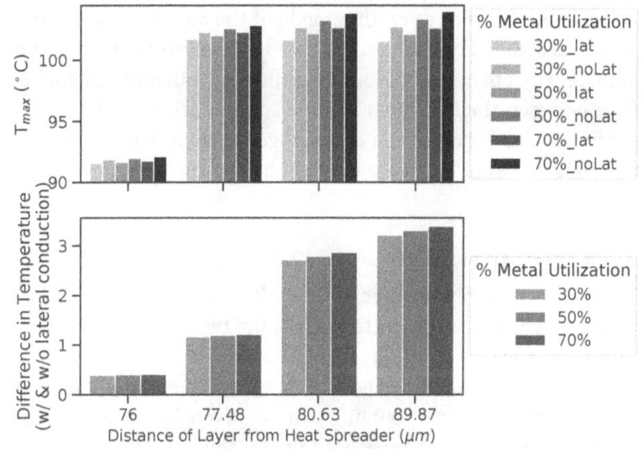


**Figure 8: Multiple hot spot scenario (hot spot power density = 2,000 W/cm$^2$): Significance of lateral heat flow modeling with increasing metal utilization.**

to reduce computational complexity of temperature analysis by nonuniform grid sizes depending upon the tier.

Furthermore, unlike TSV-based 3D ICs, MONO3D technology permits circuit partition at different granularities (transistor-level, gate-level, and block-level) with important implications to on-chip temperature. For example, a transistor-level partitioning can achieve the highest integration density, but it can also cause hot spots that span multiple tiers since an aggressor block that generates significant heat needs to be partitioned into two tiers. This flexibility in partitioning can be utilized to develop a thermally-optimum distribution of transistor-, gate-, and block-level partitioning for a MONO3D chip, given a set of system-level parameters. This approach can play a key role to mitigate the effects of strong inter-tier thermal coupling while also ensuring interconnect latency constraints. A typical example is to partition a processing unit with memory where the two elements should have spatial proximity to ensure fast read/write cycles, but also sufficient thermal isolation to prevent higher leakage current due to elevated temperatures of the memory.

As demonstrated in the previous section, in MONO3D ICs, the vertical heat flow is relatively stronger as compared to lateral flow. Thus, there is room for improvement by optimizing the on-chip interconnects to ensure sufficient lateral heat flow. This characteristic is highly distinct from TSV-based 3D ICs where the number of TSVs has considerable impact on on-chip temperature since vertical heat flow is highly restricted. Alternatively, in MONO3D ICs, it is expected that the on-chip global interconnects (particularly the power and ground networks that do not introduce switching activities) play an important role to enhance lateral heat dissipation. This characteristic is supported by simulations in the previous section where the difference in temperature between w/ and w/o lateral heat flow modeling increases with increasing interconnect power.

The strong vertical thermal coupling and limited lateral coupling also motivate thermally-aware design-time and runtime optimizations specific to MONO3D. For example, a floorplanning technique can co-optimize both tiers together to avoid placing high-density blocks in the same vertical line. Similarly, runtime techniques (such as task allocation or operating mode of the cores) can also be designed to avoid very high temperatures by monitoring the cores on both tiers together. In addition, we demonstrate that the lateral heat flow between the hot spots and the cooler region in MONO3D is confined. This behavior can be leveraged in floorplanning because two neighbouring hot spots may not have a significant impact on one another.

## 5 CONCLUSIONS

We model a flip-chip two-tier MONO3D IC and a TSV-based 3D IC to compare the thermal characteristics of the two technologies. These models include the metal layers, bulk silicon, active tiers, bonding layer and ILD. It is observed that MONO3D technology exhibits strong vertical thermal coupling with relatively homogeneous temperature distribution across both the bottom and the upper tiers. This characteristic is in contrast with the TSV-based 3D IC, where the upper tier reaches very high temperatures due to the presence of the bonding layer and a longer resistive path to the heat sink. We also demonstrate that despite the limited lateral flow of heat in MONO3D (due to thin tiers), ignoring lateral heat propagation for the layers farther from the heat sink can lead to inaccuracies in estimating the on-chip temperatures (up to $\sim 4\ ^{\circ}$C). In addition, as the interconnect utilization increases (i.e., more Joule heating due to metal layers), both the maximum on-chip temperature and the significance of modeling lateral heat flow slightly increase. Finally, we discuss opportunities to enhance thermal integrity in MONO3D ICs by leveraging some of its unique characteristics.

## ACKNOWLEDGMENTS

This project has been partially funded by the NSF CRI (CI-NEW) grant #1730316.

## REFERENCES

[1] Why Monolithic 3D? http://www.monolithic3d.com/why-monolithic-3d.html
[2] P. Batude et al. 2008. Enabling 3D Monolithic Integration. *ECS Transactions* 16, 8 (2008), 47–54.
[3] P. Batude et al. 2009. GeOI and SOI 3D monolithic cell integrations for high density applications. In *IEEE Symposium on VLSI Technology*. 166–167.
[4] P. Batude et al. 2014. 3D sequential integration opportunities and technology optimization. In *IEEE Proc. of International Interconnect Technology Conference*. 373–376.
[5] P. Batude et al. 2015. 3DVLSI with CoolCube process: An alternative path to scaling. In *IEEE Symposium on VLSI Technology*. T48–T49.
[6] G. Berhault et al. 2016. 3DIP: An iterative partitioning tool for monolithic 3D IC. In *IEEE Proc. of International 3D Systems Integration Conference (3DIC)*. 1–5.
[7] A. Guler and N. K. Jha. 2018. Hybrid monolithic 3D IC floorplanner. *IEEE Transactions on Very Large Scale Integration (VLSI) Systems* 26, 10 (Oct. 2018), 1868–1880.
[8] R. Ho, K. W. Mai, and M. A. Horowitz. 2001. The future of wires. *Proc. of the IEEE* 89, 4 (2001), 490–504.
[9] M. A. Iqbal and M. Rahman. 2017. New thermal management approach for transistor-level 3-D integtration. In *IEEE Proc. of SOI-3D-Subthreshold Microelectronics Technology Unified Conference (S3S)*. 1–3.
[10] K. M. Kim et al. 2016. Four-tier monolithic 3D ICs: Tier partitioning methodology and power benefit study. In *ACM Proc. of International Symposium on Low Power Electronics and Design (ISLPED)*. 70–75.
[11] J. Meng, K. Kawakami, and A. K. Coskun. 2012. Optimizing energy efficiency of 3D multicore systems with stacked DRAM under power and thermal constraints. In *ACM Proc. of Design Automation Conference (DAC)*. 648–655.
[12] Z. Or-Bach. 2013. The monolithic 3D advantage: Monolithic 3D is far more than just an alternative to 0.7 x scaling. In *IEEE Proc. of the International 3D Systems Integration Conference (3DIC)*. 1–7.
[13] S. Panth, K. Samadi, Y. Du, and S. K. Lim. 2015. Placement-driven partitioning for congestion mitigation in monolithic 3D IC designs. *IEEE Transactions on Computer-Aided Design of Integrated Circuits and Systems (TCAD)* 34, 4 (Apr. 2015), 540–553.
[14] G. Pares et al. 2011. Through silicon via technology using tungsten metallization. In *IEEE Proc. of International Conference on IC Design & Technology*. 1–4.
[15] V. F. Pavlidis, I. Savidis, and E. G. Friedman. 2017. *Three-dimensional integrated circuit design*. Newnes.
[16] I. Pletea, Z. Wurman, Z. Or-Bach, and V. Sontea. 2015. Monolithic 3D layout using 2D EDA for embedded memory-rich designs. In *IEEE Proc. of SOI-3D-Subthreshold Microelectronics Technology Unified Conference (S3S)*. 1–2.
[17] S. K. Samal et al. 2014. Full chip impact study of power delivery network designs in monolithic 3D ICs. In *IEEE/ACM Proc. of International Conference on Computer-Aided Design (ICCAD)*. 565–572.
[18] S. K. Samal et al. 2016. Adaptive regression-based thermal modeling and optimization for monolithic 3D ICs. *IEEE Transactions on Computer-Aided Design of Integrated Circuits and Systems* 35, 10 (Oct. 2016), 1707–1720.
[19] S. K. Samal et al. 2016. Tier partitioning strategy to mitigate BEOL degradation and cost issues in monolithic 3D ICs. In *ACM Proc. of International Conference on Computer-Aided Design (ICCAD)*. 129.
[20] S. M. Satheesh and E. Salman. 2012. Power distribution in TSV-based 3D processor-memory stacks. *IEEE Journal on Emerging and Selected Topics in Circuits and Systems* 2, 4 (Dec. 2012), 692–703.
[21] M. Schultz et al. 2016. Embedded two-phase cooling of large three-dimensional compatible chips with radial channels. *Journal of Electronic Packaging* 138, 2 (Apr. 2016), 021005.
[22] K. Skadron et al. 2003. Temperature-aware microarchitecture. In *IEEE Proc. of International Symposium on Computer Architecture (ISCA)*. 2–13.
[23] G. J. Snyder et al. 2006. Hot spot cooling using embedded thermoelectric coolers. In *IEEE Semiconductor Thermal Measurement And Management Symposium*. 135–143.
[24] H. Wei et al. 2012. Cooling three-dimensional integrated circuits using power delivery networks. In *IEEE International Electron Devices Meeting*. 14–2.
[25] Q. Xie et al. 2015. Performance comparisons between 7-nm FinFET and conventional bulk CMOS standard cell libraries. *IEEE Transactions on Circuits and Systems II: Express Briefs* 62, 8 (Aug. 2015), 761–765.
[26] C. Yan, S. Kontak, H. Wang, and E. Salman. 2017. Open source cell library Mono3D to develop large-scale monolithic 3D integrated circuits. In *IEEE Proc. of International Symposium on Circuits and Systems*. 1–4.
[27] C. Yan and E. Salman. 2017. Routing congestion aware cell library development for monolithic 3D ICs. In *International Conference on Rebooting Computing*. 1–4.
[28] C. Yan and E. Salman. 2018. Mono3D: Open source cell library for monolithic 3D integrated circuits. *IEEE Transactions on Circuits and Systems I: Regular Papers* 65, 3 (Mar. 2018), 1075–1085.

# Logic Monolithic 3D ICs: PPA Benefits and EDA Tools Necessary

Sai Surya Kiran Pentapati
sai.pentapati@gatech.edu
Georgia Institute of Technology
Atlanta, Georgia

Da Eun Shim
daeun@gatech.edu
Georgia Institute of Technology
Atlanta, Georgia

Sung Kyu Lim
limsk@ece.gatech.edu
Georgia Institute of Technology
Atlanta, Georgia

## ABSTRACT

Monolithic 3D (M3D) ICs provide a way to achieve high performance and low power designs within the same technology node, thereby bypassing the need for transistor scaling. M3D ICs have multiple 2D tiers sequentially fabricated on top of each other and connected through Monolithic Inter-tier vias (MIVs) which go from the top metal of the bottom die to the top metal of the top die. MIVs go through the dielectric separation between tiers and the active layer of the top die. The traditional APR tools only support place and route optimization in 2D IC designs and thus cannot handle the M3D designs. This paper provides a survey of all the efforts done to implement commercial quality M3D ICs using 2D APR tools and the benefit of M3D ICs over traditional 2D ICs.

## CCS CONCEPTS

• **Hardware → 3D integrated circuits**; Software tools for EDA.

## KEYWORDS

Monolithic 3D ICs, EDA tools, Design flows for Logic M3D ICs

**ACM Reference Format:**
Sai Surya Kiran Pentapati, Da Eun Shim, and Sung Kyu Lim. 2019. Logic Monolithic 3D ICs: PPA Benefits and EDA Tools Necessary. In *Great Lakes Symposium on VLSI 2019 (GLSVLSI '19), May 9–11, 2019, Tysons Corner, VA, USA.* ACM, New York, NY, USA, 6 pages. https://doi.org/10.1145/3299874.3319486

## 1 INTRODUCTION

In order to support ever growing features in modern-day mobile devices and computers, there is an increased demand of high performance hardware. Traditionally transistor scaling has been employed to meet such demands, but it is becoming increasingly difficult to continue on with the traditional approach due to physical limitations in achieving gate-lengths that are few nanometers wide and constraints in the lithography process. 3D ICs show promising PPA improvement compared to 2D ICs within the same technology node. By splitting a 2D design into multiple dies and reducing the footprint of the chip, 3D ICs reduce the distance between a pair of cells.

There have been efforts to use 3D integration in different fields of electronics design. For example, 3D NAND Flash memories are now mass-produced by companies such as Samsung and Micron with more than ninety stacked cell layers[1]. SRAM and other large memory structures have a relatively uniform structure that are based on repeating arrays which makes it easier to design in 3D manually. Logic design on the other hand requires a lot of automated optimization of different inter-dependent constraints and thus it is not possible to design a near-optimal logic 3D design manually. A 3D IC has multiple dies that are connected using vias from the bottom die to the top die.

3D designs can be differentiated into block-level, transistor-level, and gate-level 3D designs based on the granularity of 3D integration. Transistor level 3D designs require us to generate our own 3D standard cell layouts as done in [10]. Block level 3D designs can only improve the inter-block communication which limits the benefits of 3D and leaves less room for improvement. Gate level 3D designs enjoy the freedom of being able to use existing standard cells while being able to target all the nets in a design. Based on the fabrication technology, different levels of 3D integration are possible. Monolithic 3D ICs support the highest level of 3D connection density[2] and thus we will use M3D to achieve gate-level 3D ICs. M3D ICs are fabricated by processing each tier sequentially. The Front-End-Of-Line (FEOL) of the bottom tier is first grown followed by the Back-End-Of-Line (BEOL) of the bottom tier. This is then followed by FEOL of top tier containing its active layer and finally the BEOL of top tier. The standard Copper metals in BEOL of the bottom tier puts a limit on the maximum temperature to 450°C to be used in later steps to ensure stability. High temperature processes (>500°C) in the top tier also degrades the bottom tier transistor performance due to dopant de-activation. During normal semiconductor fabrication, processes like dopant activation is carried out using spike-annealing at 1050°C. Authors in paper [8] show that it is possible to perform dopant activation using solid phase epitaxial regrowth(SPER) at 450°C. There are also processes such as spacer formation, selective epitaxy that require temperatures of 600-650°C which are over the temperature limit.

In the following sections of the paper, we will present the different tool flows developed for optimizing gate-level M3D designs and how these flows handle M3D designs using commercial 2D EDA tools. We also talk about the characteristics of an ideal M3D flow and issues faced by M3D designs.

## 2 RTL-TO-GDSII TOOL FLOWS FOR M3D ICS

Current EDA tools only offer optimization for 2D designs and require special tricks to optimize M3D designs. The most important difference between 2D and M3D designs is that M3D designs has die-to-die connections inside the chip boundary whereas a 2D die


*GLSVLSI '19, May 9–11, 2019, Tysons Corner, VA, USA*

ACM ISBN 978-1-4503-6252-8/19/05...$15.00
https://doi.org/10.1145/3299874.3319486

only has IO pins on the edges of the die. We review the following RTL-to-GDSII tool flows:

- Shrunk2D [11]
- Compact2D [9]
- Cascade2D [3]

## 2.1 Shrunk2D

Shrunk2D is the first RTL-to-GDSII tool flow that creates near-optimal M3D designs using 2D EDA tools. In the Shrunk2D flow, the width and height of the standard cells are first shrunk by a factor of $1/\sqrt{2} = 0.707$ thereby halving the area of standard cells (Hence the name Shrunk2D). With the shrunk dimensions, all the cells fit in a floorplan half the area of a 2D floorplan with the same cell density of a normal 2D design. With the halved footprint, the distance between cells in an M3D design is approximately 0.707 of 2D designs which gives a theoretical wirelength savings of 30%. The shrunk design can be treated as a proxy for M3D design because the cell distances are almost equal to that of the M3D design (ignoring the z-direction distances which are relatively short). At this stage, the design is still considered 2D and all the optimization capabilities of a commercial EDA tool such as cell sizing, buffer insertion, removal, routing, power optimization, timing closure etc., can be leveraged. The next step is to transform it to a 3D design without

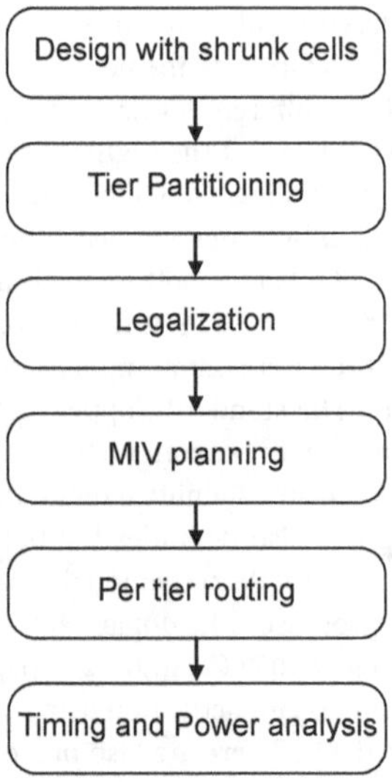


**Figure 1: Shrunk2D flow as described in [11]**

losing the optimization done by EDA tools. In this step, the cells are expanded back to their original sizes without changing the cell locations. This creates many overlaps among close-by cells which are resolved through a bin-based tier partitioning method. The floorplan is divided into grids and the cells in each grid/bin are partitioned into two tiers while minimizing the number of connections between the tiers using the Fiduccia-Mathheyses(FM) algorithm. This step removes most of the overlaps but there a few overlaps still remain in each tier which are then removed by legalization. The bin-based partitioning alleviates the loss of placement context from shrunk2D optimization by having small bins. Authors in [6] show that the average displacement of cells during legalization is directly proportional to the size of each grid which affects the PPA. If the bin size is too small so that it contains only a couple cells, FM can only optimize the cut-size of the nets among those cells which results in 3D overhead and a degradation in the whole chip PPA. On the other extreme, having a single bin for the entire design can minimize the number of 3D connections but can leave many overlaps unresolved. This will have a very high impact on run-time of FM and cell displacements during legalization. After the tier-partitioning, a netlist for each tier and a top level netlist that contains both tiers are created. MIV locations are then found with the help of EDA tools. A 3D tech LEF is created with the metal layer information of both tiers as well as the MIV cut layer that connects the two tiers. Then, cells from both tiers are projected on a single die and the pins are assigned to their respective tier metal layers. Routing is performed on all the 3D nets and the locations of vias between the top metal of the bottom tier and the bottom metal of the top tier are the locations of the MIVs. These locations are saved and treated as IO pin locations for each tier. Each tier is treated as a 2D die and die-by-die routing is performed. Sign-off timing analysis is done using tempus/Prime-time considering both dies as a whole with the help of a top level netlist. This gives us the final commercially viable M3D design.

The intermediate shrunk2D design has some shortcomings as a proxy for 3D designs. In the original shrunk2D flow presented in the paper [11], the wire widths and pitches are scaled by a factor of 0.707 to allow for routing on a smaller footprint. In this case, the authors did not consider the change in wire parasitics due to the geometry scaling. In paper [7] this issue is addressed to create better RC-lookup tables so that the parasitics in the shrunk2D stage mirror the parasitics in the M3D design. Correct parasitic estimation is necessary for EDA engines to optimize M3D designs. Another drawback is that the shrunk2D flow does not provide optimization after tier partitioning meaning that the cell movement during legalization and the routing overhead of 3D nets are not considered. When we refer to the shrunk2D flow in the paper we simply refer to the original shrunk2D flow without the parasitic adjustments.

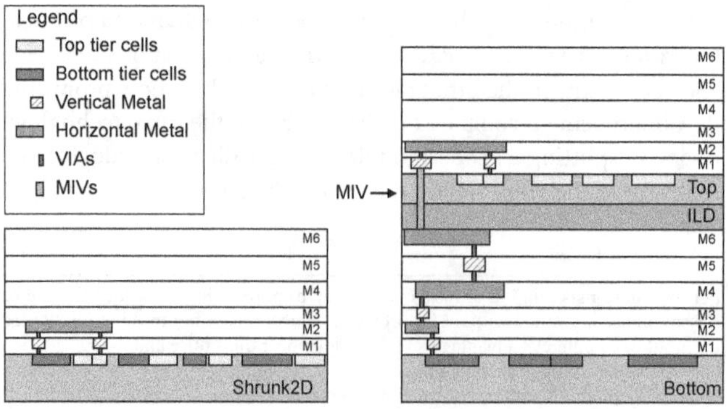


**Figure 2: Routing overhead of a 3D net**

## 2.2 Compact2D

Compact2D is another RTL-to-GDSII tool flow. It has an advantage over shrunk2D as it does not need to shrink cells which removes the need for one-technology node lower licenses for EDA tools. While the shrunk2D flow is based on the assumption that cells in M3D are on average 0.707x closer, compact2D goes one step further uses the fact that closer cells and smaller wirelengths implies smaller parasitics. This means the wire load in M3D is on average 0.707x times the wire load in 2D. Thus, compact2D simply scales the RC parasitics without shrinking any geometry. As EDA tools perform optimization based on the output load and the connectivity of cells, compact2D employs scaling of RC parasitics to mimic the M3D design. Once the design is optimized, the cells are then mapped to a halved footprint by linearly scaling the x,y coordinates by 0.707. Then we have a complete cell placement in a half-footprint of the 2D design with overlaps that are resolved in the same fashion as shrunk2D using bin-based partitioning.

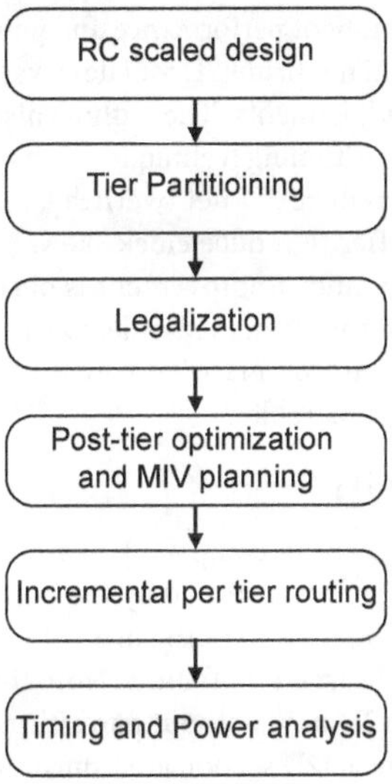


**Figure 3: Compact2D flow as described in [9] for F2F 3D ICs**

The second big improvement of compact2D is in the MIV planning stage, as it re-optimizes the whole design after tier-partitioning to consider the cell movement during legalization and the 3D net overhead. This particular step is called post-tier optimization and is the most important addition in compact2D. In the case of shrunk2D, placing cells on a single half-footprint die creates overlaps in the MIV planning stage. Compact2D employs placement row splitting during it's MIV planning stage to prevent overlaps. The standard cell row and cell heights are halved and by assigning every odd row to cells from one tier and even row to the other tier, the overlaps are completely removed. The pin locations stay the same as they are before halving the cells and therefore lie outside cell boundaries. With this placement row splitting, optimization engines can run without any issues. The design is therefore optimized with 3D overhead and 3D metal layer structure in consideration and is a better proxy for the final M3D design. Routing is saved for each tier in a DEF format. Each tier is then loaded with routing and MIV locations as IO ports and incremental routing is done for each tier to get a final commercial quality M3D design. Note that, in [9] the authors designed the compact2D flow for face-to-face bonded 3D ICs but it can also be used for monolithic 3D ICs.

The main drawback in compact2D is that the scaling factor of 0.707 is not accurate as not all nets scale exactly by a factor of 0.707 in M3D. The scaling factor should be modified depending on the design as wirelength savings can vary. Also, to get a true proxy of 3D parasitics a net-by-net scaling factor control is necessary which cannot be determined until the 3D design is completed.

## 2.3 Cascade2D

Cascade2D is a different type of 3D RTL-to-GDSII flow where the z-location(tier assignment) of the cells are determined before performing x-y optimization unlike the previous two flows. The authors present the following methods to determine the z-location:

- Decided by the designer based on the micro-architecture of the RTL
- Implement 2D design and perform tier partitioning based on the 2D results

The first option completely leaves the partitioning choice up to the designer. In case it is not feasible, the second alternative is chosen. Based on 2D design results, the authors first fix the critical timing paths on different tiers to minimize the distance between the cells within these paths. Next, the remaining cells are partitioned to maximize the number of timing paths crossing between the tiers with the cell area balance in consideration. After deciding the tier assignment, the next step is MIV planning where MIV locations are decided. This is again done in a different manner from both shrunk2D and compact2D. In cascade2D, the top tier is first designed independently of the bottom tier with MIV port locations placed on top of its respective receiving or driving cell to decrease the distance between MIV and cell-pin. This still leaves the locations of MIVs that are directly connected to IO ports to be decided. Using the MIV port locations calculated from the top tier design, the bottom tier is then optimized independently to fix the locations of the remaining MIVs by placing them on top of their connected cells on the bottom tier. Fixing the predetermined MIV locations from the top tier helps guide the placement of bottom tier cells. After this stage, only the MIV locations are preserved while discarding the routing and cell information.

A 2D floorplan is then made with two partitions side by side where each partition represents a tier. Partitions and blockages are set so that cell locations and routing of each tier is contained in their respective partitions. The connections between tier partitions are made by adding layers on top of the metals used for die-by-die routing. These additional metal layers have zero resistance and capacitance as they are used just for connectivity in the cascade2D footprint and are replaced by MIVs in direct contact in the final M3D design. All the wiring done in these additional metals is only for inter-die routing and has zero delay wire (dummy wires). Anchor cells, which are buffers with zero delay-power, are placed at the MIV locations in each partition. For the anchor cells on the bottom tier, both input and output pins are located on the top metal layer as the landing metal of MIVs is the top metal layer for the bottom tier. For the top tier, two configurations of anchor cells are designed:

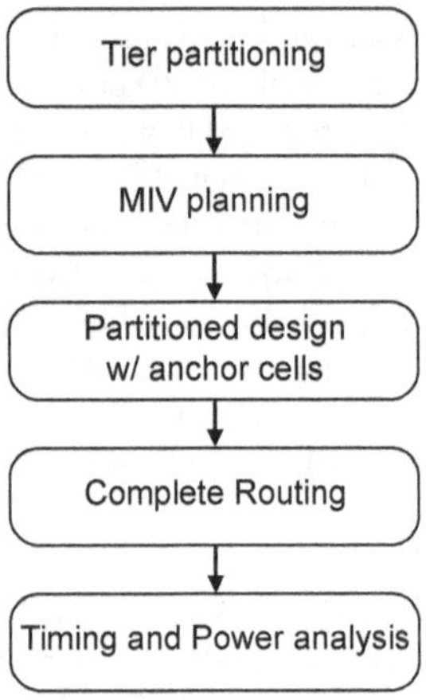


**Figure 4: Cascade2D flow as described in [3]**

receiving anchor cells (for MIVs connected to the input pin of a top tier cell), driving anchor cells (for MIVs connected to the output pin of the top tier cell). The receiving anchor cell has the input pin on the top metal as it receives a connecting net from the bottom tier partition. The output pin is located on the bottom-most metal of the top tier, which is the landing metal for MIVs in M3D design. The driving anchor cell receives a connection to the input pin located on the bottom metal and is connected to the bottom tier through the output pin that is located on top metal layer of the top tier. These anchor cells act as wormhole connections between the bottom metal of the top tier, where MIVs are connected in M3D designs, to the top metal which is used to connect to bottom tier partition in a Cascade2D design. This setup allows use of EDA optimization tools for routing and placement of the cells in both partitions as a whole.

## 2.4 Ideal Gate-level M3D Flow

There are three main aspects in a 2D IC design: Cell Placement, Clock tree layout, Routing. Optimizations are performed after each of the stages. Similarly in a 3D IC design, all three stages along with the ability to perform optimizations should remain possible for an optimized design.

Cell Placement: The flow should be able to optimize x,y,z locations simultaneously. This placement should be done based on timing and power of the design. The z-location determination is akin to the tier partitioning strategies from the tool flows discussed previously. All flows used some heuristics to find the z-location without considering the complete M3D tech LEF and M3D net overheads.

Clock tree layout: Clock tree is an important part of 2D IC design. The design of clock tree aims to reduce clock skew and improve overall timing. In the M3D flows described previously, the clock tree is designed before tier-partitioning which may not translate to the best 3D clock tree. Thus, the clock tree should be optimized with both tiers and the total metal stack in consideration.

Routing: Routing should be performed on the whole design (both tiers) at the same time. Compact2D and cascade2D flow allow for complete routing and have the perfect characteristics of an ideal 3D routing stage. In cascade2D the MIV planning is done die-by-die separately and thus the MIV planning stage is not ideal.

Optimizations: The ability to change cell locations, cell sizes, add and remove buffers at each stage of the design should be supported. All the tool flows have this ability to some extent. However, in the case of the shrunk2D flow, this type of optimization is not supported after tier partitioning. Compact2D has this ability all through-out the design stages but after tier partitioning it does not allow for cells to change tiers. Cascade2D also has this ability to the same extent as compact2D.

The ability to handle incremental updates such as ECO routing and re-optimization after manual buffer insertion, deletion, and tier changing while considering the two levels of M3D design as a whole should be supported. These features are useful for manual changes to the design after initial M3D design.

# 3 PPA BENEFITS OF THE M3D TOOL FLOWS

## 3.1 Shrunk2D

A comprehensive study of performance and power benefits of M3D ICs was done in [7]. The shrunk2D tool flow was used and improved through parasitic adjustments. The authors also incorporate other timing aware tier partitioning techniques such as placing long wires on a single tier to reduce 3D net overhead, and fixing clock tree buffers to a single tier to reduce clock skew. Using nangate45nm, up to 15.6% performance improvement is observed from Table 1. At iso-performance the authors also demonstrated power benefits ranging from as low as 5.6% in rocket-core to as high as 40% savings in LDPC as depicted in Table 2.

## 3.2 Compact2D

The main improvement in compact2D was post-tier partitioning optimization. This is demonstrated by the improvement in timing of M3D designs compared to both shrunk2D-based M3D and 2D designs which is observed in Table 3. Note that the shrunk2D is the original shrunk2D flow without parasitic adjustments. All the numbers in the compact2D section are from designs using a dual-Vt commercial-grade 28nm PDK.

Compared to 2D ICs, compact2D based F2F 3D designs show 5.7% to 26.8% iso-performance power improvements at the 28nm technology node as can be seen in Table 3. Please note that the results are not from M3D ICs where the die integration is front-to-back but are from the wafer bonded front-to-front fabrication considered in the paper. This table still shows the improvement of compact2D in improving timing due to its post-tier optimization with little overhead on power.

## 3.3 Cascade2D

All the results in Table 4 regarding cascade2D are from [3]. The authors use a foundry based 28nm planar PDK as their technology node. Shrunk2D has higher wirelength savings as it starts with placing cells closely. Cascade2D does tier partition first based on architecture aware heuristics and has lower wirelength savings than shrunk2D. However, the main improvement is in the cell area savings where cascade2D beats shrunk2D because of its choice of tier partitioning and all around optimization of both tiers in M3D. Standard cell area contributes to a higher portion of total

**Table 1: Max Performance Results of shrunk2D with Parasitic Adjustment as shown in [7]**

| parameters | rocket-core | | | ride-core | | | AES-128 | | | LDPC | | |
|---|---|---|---|---|---|---|---|---|---|---|---|---|
| | 2D | M3D | | 2D | M3D | | 2D | M3D | | 2D | M3D | |
| footprint | 0.384 | 0.188 | (-51.0%) | 0.523 | 0.256 | (-52.4%) | 0.390 | 0.191 | (-51.0%) | 0.228 | 0.112 | (-51.0%) |
| eff freq(MHz) | **783.3** | **905** | (15.5%) | **524** | **550.0** | (5.0%) | **1,388** | **1,585** | (14.2%) | **716** | **828** | (15.6%) |
| total power | 156.7 | 175.2 | (11.8%) | 147.8 | 149.8 | (1.4%) | 177.0 | 207.9 | (17.5%) | 219.4 | 252.1 | (14.9%) |
| target freq(MHz) | 813 | 938 | (15.4%) | 530 | 562 | (5.9%) | 1,375 | 1,750 | (27.3%) | 750 | 875 | (16.7%) |

**Table 2: Iso-performance power comparison of the M3D designs implemented with baseline shrunk-2D flow (S2D-base) and shrunk-2D flow with parasitic adjustment(S2D-PA). The percentage values in the M3D designs are w.r.t. their 2D counterparts. From [7]**

| designs | paramaters | M3D /w S2D-base | M3D /w S2D-PA |
|---|---|---|---|
| rocket -core | sw. pwr | -9.1% | -11.8% |
| | int. pwr | -1.4% | -3.1% |
| | lkg. pwr | -2.7% | -6.8% |
| | **tot. pwr** | -3.5% | -5.6% |
| ride -core | sw. pwr | -16.7% | -23.0% |
| | int. pwr | -3.4% | -10.0% |
| | lkg. pwr | -4.8% | -14.2% |
| | **tot. pwr** | -9.2% | -15.7% |
| AES -128 | sw. pwr | -7.6% | -12.2% |
| | int. pwr | -1.7% | -6.6% |
| | lkg. pwr | -3.0% | -13.5% |
| | **tot. pwr** | -4.1% | -9.0% |
| LDPC | sw. pwr | -41.9% | -47.5% |
| | int. pwr | -21.4% | -30.2% |
| | lkg. pwr | -22.2% | -32.7% |
| | **tot. pwr** | -33.5% | -40.5% |

**Table 3: Iso-performance power comparison of the F2F designs of OpenSparc T2 core implemented with original shrunk-2D design flow (S2D) and Compact-2D(C2D) Flow. The percentage values in the F2F designs are w.r.t. their 2D counterparts. From [9]**

| designs | paramaters | F2F /w S2D | F2F /w C2D |
|---|---|---|---|
| OpenSPARC -T2 core | **tot. pwr** | -11.0% | -11.1% |
| | tot. neg. slack | -1.7% | 83.6% |
| | tot. pos. slack | 8.0% | 9.5% |
| | tot WL | -23.4% | -24.8% |

power in cell dominant circuits and in improved technology nodes, cascade2D becomes more powerful in such cases.

# 4 FACTORS IMPACTING OF M3D ICS

## 4.1 Issues caused by sequential fabrication

As discussed before Monolithic 3D ICs use sequential fabrication that allow the use of MIVs with a high 3D interconnect density. As sequential fabrication either needs low temperature processes for the top tier FEOL or tungsten based bottom tier BEOL, one of the tiers will experience degradation either due to weak cells on the top tier or high resistance wires on the bottom tier. The authors of [12] have developed BEOL/FEOL degradation aware tier-partitioning strategies to minimize the impact of this degradation. They use shrunk2D as their baseline flow and in the case of FEOL degradation, the tier partitioning is done in such a way that cells with most available slack are assigned to the top tier. This helps in combating the timing degradation that arises due to slow top tier cells. In the case of BEOL degradation due to tungsten wires, the authors assign long wires to be routed exclusively on the top tier where the interconnects are still based on Copper.

The degradation aware tier-partitioning methods are just heuristics and are not the best possible optimization. Compact2D can exploit the commercial router capabilities to combat BEOL degradation. During the post tier-partitioning optimization of compact2D, the timing-aware routing is done by EDA tools where it can utilize the top tier BEOL when the bottom tier BEOL is degraded to improve timing on critical paths. This produces both degradation aware MIV locations, and die-by-die routing. Tier partitioning can also be improved in case of FEOL degradation by the cell slack based partitioning method mentioned in the previous paragraph. This adds to the benefit of timing aware 3D routing.

**Table 4: Iso-performance power comparison of the M3D designs of a commercial in-order processor implemented with original shrunk-2D design flow (S2D) and Cascade-2D Flow. The percentage values in the M3D designs are w.r.t. their 2D counterparts. From [3]**

| designs | paramaters | M3D /w S2D | M3D /w Cascade2D |
|---|---|---|---|
| 32-bit application processor | tot. WL | -19.3% | -11.9% |
| | std. cell area | -7.6% | -9.5% |
| | sw. pwr | -13.4% | -13.0% |
| | int. pwr | -4.8% | -14.5% |
| | lkg. pwr | -7.7% | -9.5% |
| | **tot. pwr** | -9.3% | -13.4% |

## 4.2 Power Delivery in M3D ICs

Power delivery in M3D is a challenge because we do not have C4 bumps on the bottom tier due to the sequential nature of M3D fabrication. As M3D designs have half the footprint of 2D designs, the maximum number of C4 bumps in M3D also halves. This almost doubles the current drawn from each bump increasing the IR-drop. For the top tier Power Delivery Network (PDN), the current is drawn from the C4 bumps as usual, but for the bottom tier the current is delivered through power MIVs (array of MIVs). This structure means that the PDN of top and bottom tiers are in series and the IR-drop of the bottom tier is added to the already higher IR-drop in the top tier. The authors in [5] shows the static and dynamic IR-drop in M3D ICs compared to 2D ICs. According to the authors, the static instance based IR-drop in 3D ICs is almost twice that of 2D ICs. However, the dynamic IR-drop in 3D ICs is only 11.3% higher than that of 2D ICs on average. This is attributed to the higher density of decap cell placement in 3D design as they can be placed in both top and bottom tiers. It is also observed that the voltage spiking reduces in 3D due to the increased resistance of the PDN.

### 4.3 Thermal issues in M3D designs

Thermal hotspot is another issue in M3D designs as they have a higher power density compared to 2D ICs. It is also difficult for the heat in the bottom tier to dissipate as it is surrounded by a thick dielectric on the bottom and top tier. Heat from the bottom tier is hence only efficiently dissipated through the routing metals and the PDN to the top tier where it can be dumped into the cooling system. This makes the operating temperature of 3D ICs higher than 2D ICs. The authors in [13] used commercial thermal analysis tools with the help of some in-house scripts to perform thermal analysis. They also reduced the temperature by 5% through optimization of the PDN to improve heat flow without violating the IR-drop limit.

### 4.4 Frequency impact on power Benefits of M3D ICs

Higher frequency gives better power savings in M3D design. This is simply due to the fact that a higher frequency design in 2D needs stronger cells and has more timing critical paths. This allows more optimizations in 3D ICs where it can reduce wirelengths and cell sizes as lower wire-load needs lower driving strength cells. The authors in [4] explored the impact of frequency and technology node on M3D power benefits. The results can be seen in Figure 5.

### 4.5 PPA benefits at various technology nodes

Technology node plays an important part in determining the impact of M3D benefit on any design. This is mostly because the portion of pin capacitance increases in advanced technology nodes based on FinFETs where transistors have vertical gates placed close to each other. This increases the cross-coupling capacitance between the fins. Figure 5 shows the impact of technology node and frequency on power savings on OpenSparc T2 SoC design. The M3D designs are obtained using the shrunk2D tool flow. 28nm planar foundry-based PDK, 14nm FinFET based PDK, predictive 7nm FinFET based technologies are considered.

## 5 CONCLUSIONS

From the results we can conclude that M3D designs show better performance/power numbers compared to traditional 2D designs. The three M3D design flows presented show power benefits ranging from 5% to 40% based on the technologies and benchmarks. A performance improvement of up to 15% is also demonstrated. Developing better power delivery networks and cooling solutions are crucial and can effect the overall M3D quality. With the observations made, M3D can be a viable option for improving PPA of

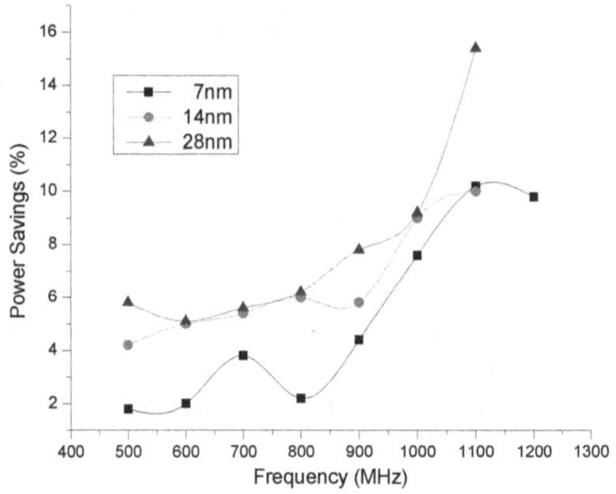


**Figure 5: Impact of frequency and technology node on M3D Power savings [4]**

designs in absence of technology scaling. Therefore, it would be important to develop a true 3D tool to realize the complete benefits of 3D designs.

## 6 ACKNOWLEDGMENTS

This research is funded by the DARPA ERI 3DSOC Program under Award HR001118C0096.

## REFERENCES

[1] 3Dnand:Samsung. "https://news.samsung.com/us/samsung-fifth-generation-v-nand-mass-production/".
[2] E. Beyne. The 3-d interconnect technology landscape. *IEEE Design and Test*, 33:8–20, 2016.
[3] K. Chang et al. Cascade2D: A design-aware partitioning approach to monolithic 3D IC with 2D commercial tools. In *Proc. IEEE Int. Conf. on Computer-Aided Design*, 2016.
[4] K. Chang et al. Match-making for Monolithic 3D IC: Finding the Right Technology Node. In *Proc. ACM Design Automation Conf.*, 2016.
[5] K. Chang et al. Frequency and Time Domain Analysis of Power Delivery Network for Monolithic 3D ICs. In *Proc. Int. Symp. on Low Power Electronics and Design*, 2017.
[6] K. Chang et al. Full-chip Monolithic 3D IC Design and Power Performance Analysis with ASAP7 Library. In *Proc. IEEE Int. Conf. on Computer-Aided Design*, 2017.
[7] K. Chang, S. Pentapati, D. E. Shim, and S. K. Lim. Road to High-Performance 3D ICs: Performance Optimization Methodologies for Monolithic 3D ICs. In *Proc. Int. Symp. on Low Power Electronics and Design*, 2018.
[8] F. L. et al. Methodology for thermal budget reduction of sper down to 450c for 3d sequential integration. *Nuclear Instruments and Methods in Physics Research Section B: Beam Interactions with Materials and Atoms*, 370(14-18), 2016.
[9] B. W. Ku, K. Chang, and S. K. Lim. Compact-2D: A Physical Design Methodology to Build Commercial-Quality Face-to-Face-Bonded 3D ICs. In *Proc. Int. Symp. on Physical Design*, 2018.
[10] Y.-J. Lee and S. K. Lim. Ultra High Density Logic Designs Using Transistor-Level Monolithic 3D Integration. In *Proc. IEEE Int. Conf. on Computer-Aided Design*, 2012.
[11] S. A. Panth, K. Samadi, Y. Du, and S. K. Lim. Shrunk-2D: A Physical Design Methodology to Build Commercial-Quality Monolithic 3D ICs. *IEEE Trans. on Computer-Aided Design of Int. Circuits and Systems*, 2017.
[12] S. K. Samal et al. Tier Partitioning Strategy to Mitigate BEOL Degradation and Cost Issues in Monolithic 3D ICs. In *Proc. IEEE Int. Conf. on Computer-Aided Design*, 2016.
[13] S. K. Samal, K. Samadi, P. Kamal, Y. Du, and S. K. Lim. Full chip impact study of power delivery network designs in monolithic 3D ICs. In *Proc. IEEE Int. Conf. on Computer-Aided Design*, 2014.

# Investigation and Trade-offs in 3DIC Partitioning Methodologies

Nikolaos Sketopoulos
EECE Department, University of Thessaly
Volos, Greece
sketopou@eece.uth.gr

Christos P. Sotiriou
EECE Department, University of Thessaly
Volos, Greece
chsotiriou@eece.uth.gr

Vasileios Samaras
EECE Department, University of Thessaly
Volos, Greece
vsamaras@eece.uth.gr

## ABSTRACT

In this work, we compare alternative 3DIC partitioning methodologies, in terms of slack, number of inter-tier vias, Tier Area Ratio (TAR) and HPWL design parameters. The popular 3DIC post-placement, bin-based Fiducia-Mattheyses (FM) partitioning flow is used as a baseline for comparison. While the latter does produce a minimum number of inter-tier vias, for a specified FM area balance, their number cannot be directly constrained. This behaviour motivated us to investigate a different 3DIC partitioning scheme, based on post-placement 3D legalisation, where the legaliser is capable of spreading cells across all available tiers for minimum displacement or HPWL. In contrast to bin-based FM, in 3D legalisation, the number of inter-tier vias can be directly constrained, albeit at the expense of TAR. The 3D legalisation partitioning scheme can expose a continuous trade off between the available number of inter-tier vias and design parameters. An unconstrained number of vias, which produce the best 3D gains in design parameters, while constraining the number of vias will trade them off with lower 3D gains. Results for three 3DIC partitioning flows are presented, on four OpenCores benchmarks, and the achieved trade offs between number of inter-tier vias and slack, TAR and HPWL parameters, per flow, are described.

## KEYWORDS

3DIC, partitioning, legalisation

**ACM Reference Format:**

Nikolaos Sketopoulos, Christos P. Sotiriou, and Vasileios Samaras. 2019. Investigation and Trade-offs in 3DIC Partitioning Methodologies. In *Great Lakes Symposium on VLSI 2019 (GLSVLSI '19), May 9–11, 2019, Tysons Corner, VA, USA.* ACM, New York, NY, USA, 5 pages. https://doi.org/10.1145/3299874.3319487

## 1 INTRODUCTION

3DICs present a new opportunity for improved Power, Performance and Area (PPA) metrics [8]. Originally, 3DICs were based on packaging integration using Through-Silicon Vias (TSVs). TSVs support limited inter-tier integration density [2], as TSV pitch is limited between 5$\mu$m and 10$\mu$m. The emerging alternative 3D technology is Monolithic 3D, where multiple tiers are fabricated sequentially, offering very high inter-tier integration density, with sub-micron Monolithic Inter-tier Vias (MIVs) pitch [1]. In addition, recent advances in Wafer-to-Wafer bonding [3], for Stacked Die 3DICs, *i.e.* parallel integration, indeed provide high density connectivity, with Hybrid Bond pad pitches between 1.4$\mu$m and 1.8$\mu$m. Thus, the available 3DIC number of inter-tier vias depends on both the 3DIC technology used, *e.g.* TSV-based 3DIC, Monolithic (sequential) or Stacked Die (parallel integration), as well as the relative size ratio between standard cells and tier to tier connections.

Several 3DIC partitioning techniques start off with Shrunk 2D placement and perform post Shrunk 2D partitioning across typically two tiers [5, 7]. This approach allows them to be 2D placement aware. Shrunk 2D placement places cells in half of the original area, *i.e.* a multiplication factor of $\sqrt{2}$ for width and height. Post Shrunk 2D placement, bin-based Fiduccia-Mattheyses (FM) has been commonly used in the literature to partition cells among two 3D tiers [7]. FM aims for minimum cutsize, *i.e.* minimum number of inter-tier vias. However, despite aiming at minimum cutsize, the resultant cutsize, *i.e.* number of inter-tier vias, cannot be directly constrained in bin-based FM. An alternative perspective to graph-based partitioning methods, similar to FM, is 3D legalisation. In the latter, the legalisation algorithm, post Shrunk 2D spreads cells among multiple tiers, using as cost function the minimum displacement or minimum HPWL, and has a global cutsize view. Both bin-based FM and 3D legalisation affect the tier area balance, which is traded-off with the number of inter-tier vias. One implication is that, if the area of the 3DIC tiers is not balanced, one of the tiers may be larger than half the original 2D area. In this work, we compare these two alternative 3DIC partitioning flows in terms of all Quality of Results (QoR) parameters, including slack, number of inter-tier vias, Tier Area Ratio (TAR) and HPWL. Our contribution is the comparative analysis between 3D flows, for four benchmark circuits from OpenCores, implemented in a 3DIC customised version of a NANGATE 45nm technology library.

## 2 3D FLOWS

In this work, we implement and compare three 3DIC flows, Figure 1. All of them begin post Shrunk 2D placement. The first flow uses bin-based FM, followed by 2D legalisation,


*GLSVLSI '19, May 9–11, 2019, Tysons Corner, VA, USA*

ACM ISBN 978-1-4503-6252-8/19/05...$15.00
https://doi.org/10.1145/3299874.3319487

performed on each tier separately. The second flow applies 3D legalisation on the Shrunk 2D placement, without any inter-tier via constraint, targeting minimum displacement or minimum HPWL, or a combination of the two. The third flow, applies Constrained 3D legalisation, imposing a number of inter-tier via constraints, to 3D legalisation. The last step for all three flows, is timing-driven In-Place Optimisation (IPO), performed per tier, while the other tier cells are fixed.

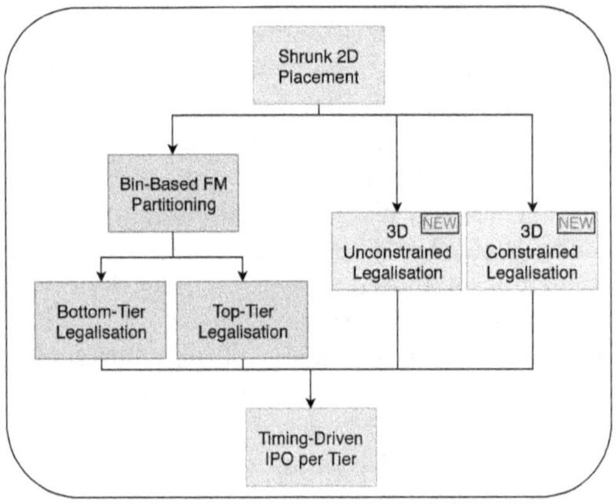


**Figure 1: 3D Flows investigated in this work**

## 2.1 Bin-based FM

Bin-based FM is a placement-aware partitioning scheme [7]. There are two possibilities for bin-based FM. A completely local FM, per bin, with bin cutsize being the cost function, where nets that span beyond the bin are ignored. This is a **greedy** approach, achieving $O(C)$ complexity [7], assuming a fixed bin size, with $C$ being the total number of design components. This complexity also stems from the fact that the number of nets per bin are effectively fixed. Another possibility is bin-based, yet global cutsize FM, where FM is performed on a bin by bin basis, yet all nets are considered. The related complexity is, however, $O(C \times N)$, as no reduction in complexity is achieved. This approach is not greedy, as by considering all nets, the global cutsize, and not the bin cutsize, is minimised. Thus, global cutsize FM has a global view, but is of higher computational complexity. Out of the two FM versions, in this work we decided to implement global cutsize FM, to assess its scalability, cutsize and 3D QoR results and compare against 3D legalisation. It is straightforward to modify our version to be greedy, bin-based FM.

In our global cutsize, bin-based FM implementation, bins are partitioned sequentially. FM cutsize is computed incrementally, per move, and once a cell is assigned to a tier, it becomes locked and cannot move between tiers again. Once all of a bin's cells have been examined, the next bin is partitioned. The area balance factor is per bin. As the FM cutsize view is global, cutsize monotonically decreases, as bins are partitioned. We have noticed that bin sizes affect cutsize, as in [4], and execution time significantly. If bin size is small, cutsize will be large, yet execution time will be reduced. On the other hand, as bin size increases, cutsizes tend to decrease, yet execution time also increases.

## 2.2 3D Legalisation

3D legalisation is essentially a form of partitioning. The 3D legalisation algorithm legalises, and simultaneously partitions cells across multiple tiers, by identifying the minimum displacement, or minimum HPWL position, or a combination of the two, considering all tiers, per cell. One advantage of this approach is that it is not limited to two tiers. Tier to tier spacing and tier index are used to incorporate z-distance into cell displacement and net 3D HPWL. We used the Abax [9] algorithm for 3D legalisation, which we also constrained with respect to the maximum number of inter-tier vias.

*2.2.1 Unconstrained 3D Legalisation.* Unconstrained 3D legalisation focuses on achieving optimal 3D HPWL reduction. Thus, the results of this approach may effectively serve as an upper bound for 3D gains, and also produce a required cutsize, *i.e.* number of inter-tier vias, for achieving these gains. Consequently, we use Unconstrained 3D as a reference point for comparison.

*2.2.2 Constrained 3D Legalisation.* The 3D legalisation algorithm may be constrained, by imposing an upper bound for the maximum allowed number of inter-tier vias, $V$. The advantage of 3D legalisation over bin-based FM, is that the former can guarantee that the bound is satisfied, albeit at the expense of TAR. Thus, by sweeping the maximum number of inter-tier vias constraint, a trade-off curve between the number of inter-tier vias and 3D gains may be obtained. Such a bound is highly relevant for Stacked Die 3D, where the number of Hybrid Bond pads is constrained, *e.g.* 1 Hybrid Bond pad every $1.4\mu$m.

To guarantee the inter-tier via bound, $V$, the sequential 3D legalisation algorithm [9] is modified to perform a limited number of different tier, 3D assignment moves. These moves are spread uniformly across the legalisation process. Algorithm 1 describes the modified Constrained 3D legalisation algorithm.

With $N$ the total number of cells to be legalised, $N$ sequential legalisation operations are required. For a $V$ via constraint, we modify the original algorithm to consider a 3D legalisation move, every $\frac{N}{V}$ moves, as shown in lines 4-5. A 3D legalisation move tentatively legalises the current cell on all available tiers $T$, considering 3D displacement or 3D HPWL cost, or a combination of the two, and performs the minimum cost legalisation move, lines 8-11. Thus, a cell will end up on a different tier to $T_0$, only if lower cost is achieved. Default, 2D legalisation is performed otherwise, lines 15-17. In this way, we guarantee that only a maximum of $V$ cells is moved into another tier, line 6.

Ultimately, the maximum number $V$, of cells legalised on one tier, is not necessarily correlated directly to the number of inter-tier vias, as each cell may be connected to multiple nets. Thus, the outcome of constraint $V$ will be a slightly

**Algorithm 1:** Constrained 3D Legalisation

```
Input: Netlist Cells (N), Inter-tier Vias Bound (V), Tiers (T)
Output: Legal Placement with Minimum Cost
best_cost = ∞;
i = 1;
for each cell c_i in N do
    do_3D_legalisation = i mod |N|/V;
    if (do_3D_legalisation == 0) then
        for each tier T_i in T do
            Legalise c_i on tier T_i;
            3D_cost = compute_3D_cost();
            if (3D_cost < best_cost) then
                Update best_cost and best solution;

        end
    else
        Legalise c_i on tier T_0;
        2D_cost = compute_2D_cost();
        Update best_cost and best solution;
    i = i + 1;
end
```

different inter-tier via value, $T$, which may be measured and controlled, during or post 3D legalisation.

By specifying different number of inter-tier via constraints, it is feasible to use Constrained 3D legalisation to explore the solution space between the bin-based FM solution, *i.e.* cutsize lower bound, and the Unconstrained 3D legalisation, *i.e.* cutsize upper bound, and evaluate 3D QoR results in terms of slack, number of inter-tier vias, TAR and HPWL. This evaluation is described in the following section.

# 3 EXPERIMENTAL RESULTS

To compare the three 3DIC partitioning methodologies, we used the 45nm nanoCAS library [10], which is a 3D variation of the 45nm NANGATE library, featuring explicitly defined top and bottom tier cells. This feature allows us to keep the cells of a specific tier fixed, while timing-driven optimisation is performed for the other tier. In terms of wire delay, for the specific 45nm library, 1 Fanout-of-4 (FO4) inverter gate delay is proportional to 300$\mu$m RC wire delay. Thus, RC delay is not as significant for the library we used, as in more advanced technology nodes, *i.e.* 20$n$m and below, where the designs are wire delay dominated and not gate delay dominated, as in our case.

We selected four OpenCores benchmarks [6] for the comparison, and used the Cadence Innovus EDA tool for physical design. An Intel Xeon 4114 CPU machine was used, clocked at 2.2GHz, for running our custom 3DIC partitioning tool, as well as Innovus. 2D and Shrunk 2D placement is performed using Innovus, the latter performed by shrinking all cells to single site width. Post Shrunk 2D, we utilise our custom tool, and after tier partitioning, we move the design back to Innovus for timing-driven IPO. For bin-based FM partitioning, fixed bins of 20$\mu$m width, 20$\mu$m height are used. The 3D legaliser was used in displacement mode.

Table 1 reports the inter-tier vias constraint to relative HPWL trade-off, for 3D legalisation, where the 100% value corresponds to Unconstrained 3D legalisation. The latter achieves the smallest HPWL value, while imposed cutsize constraints increase HPWL. Stricter constraints lead to higher

**Table 1: 3D Legalisation: Inter-tier Vias vs. 3D HPWL Ratio**

| Benchmark | Cutsize | Cutsize Constraint | | | | | |
|---|---|---|---|---|---|---|---|
| | | 100% | 90% | 60% | 40% | 30% | 20% |
| | | 3D HPWL Ratio | | | | | |
| *pid* | 3361 | **1.00** | 1.50 | 1.82 | 1.79 | 1.77 | 1.69 |
| *aes* | 5755 | **1.00** | 1.20 | 1.59 | 1.62 | 1.69 | 1.70 |
| *aes128* | 7334 | **1.00** | 1.55 | 1.98 | 1.99 | 2.56 | 1.87 |
| *ldpc* | 51599 | **1.00** | 1.00 | 1.96 | 2.08 | 2.11 | 2.07 |

HPWL results, *e.g.* `ldpc` benchmark's HPWL doubles, for a 40% cutsize constraint (60% cutsize reduction), compared to the Unconstrained 3D legalisation result. However, this trend is not monotonic, particularly for small inter-tier vias constraint value, *e.g.* 20%. At this point, HPWL may be improved, *e.g* benchmarks `aes128` and `ldpc`, as more and more of the design will be assigned to a single tier.

Figures 2, 3 illustrate HPWL results for a range of cutsize constraints for the `pid` and `ldpc` benchmarks. Similarly to the results presented on Table 1, graphs illustrate that stricter constraints may lead to higher HPWL values. However, this trend is not monotonic. The non-monotonicity of the Constrained 3D legaliser curves stems from the specific selection of $\frac{N}{V}$ legalisation moves, which it depends on $V$, as well as the fact that our current 3D legaliser implementation does not check global cutsize, per move.

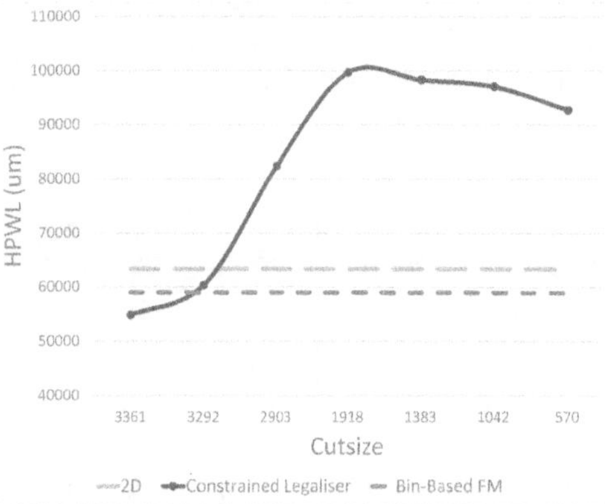


**Figure 2: HPWL vs. Cutsize for the *pid* Benchmark**

Tables 2 and 3 present comparative results, post the 3D tier partitioning and timing driven IPO for the three 3D flows, *i.e.* the Constrained and Unconstrained 3D legaliser, the bin-based FM baseline, and the original 2D design. Parameters compared, for each benchmark, include slack, number of inter-tier vias (cutsize), total routed WireLength (WL), as reported by the P&R tool, and Tier Area Ratio (TAR). For the Constrained 3D legaliser, we used three cutsize constraints, *i.e.* 90%, 60% and 30%, relative to the cutsize value achieved by the Unconstrained 3D legaliser. Slack values in the tables do not follow a uniform trend, for the benchmarks selected and 45nm library used. This is the case, as IPO operations significantly change the design slack profile. Further on, we

**Table 2: 3DIC Methodologies Comparison**

| Benchmark | Unconstrained 3D-Legaliser | | | | Bin-Based FM (Global Cutsize) | | | | 2D | |
|---|---|---|---|---|---|---|---|---|---|---|
| | Total WL (um) | Inter-tier Vias Num. | Slack Ratio | Pre-IPO Tier Area Ratio | Total WL (um) | Inter-tier Vias Num. | Slack Ratio | Pre-IPO Tier Area Ratio | Total WL (um) | Slack Ratio |
| *pid* | 6.80E+04 | 3361 | 1.005 | 1.308 | 5.16E+04 | 840 | 0.985 | 1.027 | 7.10E+04 | 1.00 |
| *aes* | 1.89E+05 | 5755 | 1.143 | 1.276 | 1.50E+05 | 1825 | 1.063 | 1.204 | 1.57E+05 | 1.00 |
| *aes128* | 1.45E+05 | 7334 | 1.061 | 1.455 | 2.01E+05 | 2083 | 2.418 | 0.984 | 1.90E+05 | 1.00 |
| *ldpc* | 3.17E+06 | 51599 | 1.049 | 1.153 | 2.55E+06 | 18462 | 0.936 | 1.159 | 3.41E+06 | 1.00 |
| AVG | 8.92E+05 | - | **1.065** | - | 7.38E+05 | - | **1.351** | - | 9.57E+05 | **1.00** |

**Table 3: Constrained 3D-Legaliser Results**

| Benchmark | Total WL (um) | Inter-tier Vias Num. | Slack Ratio | Pre-IPO Tier Area Ratio | 2D Slack Ratio |
|---|---|---|---|---|---|
| *pid* | 7.23E+04 | 3000 (90%) | 1.002 | 2.385 | 1.00 |
| | 7.38E+04 | 2000 (60%) | 1.052 | 5.647 | |
| | 6.77E+04 | 1000 (30%) | 1.003 | 12.943 | |
| *aes* | 1.87E+05 | 5000 (90%) | 1.101 | 2.066 | 1.00 |
| | 2.07E+05 | 3500 (60%) | 1.017 | 5.151 | |
| | 2.16E+05 | 1800 (30%) | 1.045 | 12.186 | |
| *aes128* | 1.95E+05 | 6600 (90%) | 1.041 | 2.138 | 1.00 |
| | 2.05E+05 | 4400 (60%) | 0.867 | 5.157 | |
| | 2.02E+05 | 2200 (30%) | 0.949 | 12.387 | |
| *ldpc* | 3.24E+06 | 46500 (90%) | 1.091 | 2.062 | 1.00 |
| | 3.13E+06 | 31000 (60%) | 1.073 | 8.049 | |
| | 3.18E+06 | 15500 (30%) | 1.055 | 12.061 | |
| AVG | 9.14E+05 | - | **0.927** | - | **1.00** |

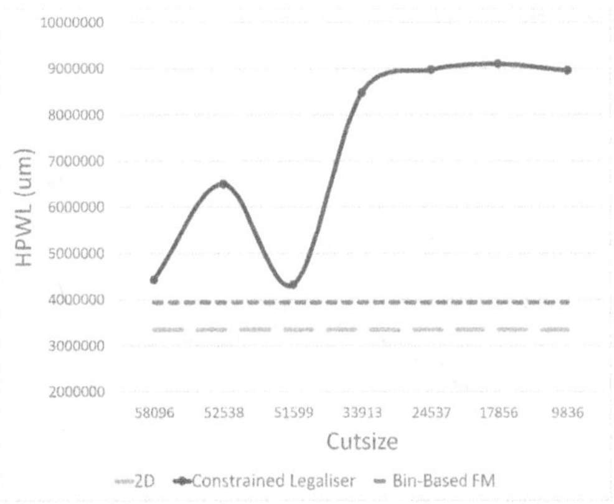


**Figure 3: HPWL vs. Cutsize for the *ldpc* Benchmark**

do not observe a 1-1 correspondence between total WL and slack. For example, benchmark **aes128** has higher total 3D WL, for the bin-based FM flow, compared to 2D WL, but better slack. In fact, this benchmark produces the best slack ratio, 2.418, compared to 2D. With respect to TAR measurements, bin-based FM exhibits excellent area balance, as area balance is a a feature built into the FM algorithm. The Unconstrained 3D legaliser does not take area balance into account, thus its TAR reaches a value of approximately 1.5, *e.g.* for the **aes128** benchmark. The Constrained 3D legaliser exhibits high TAR values for the same reason. The smaller the cutsize constraint, the more likely it is that more cells end up on the same tier, thus TAR is likely to rise as the cutsize constraint becomes stricter, *i.e.* smaller.

3D legalisation and bin-based, global cutsize FM exhibit a significant difference in execution time, as Table 4 presents. For instance, the execution time of bin-based FM for **ldpc** is about 1 hour, whereas 3D legalisation takes less than 1 minute. This is the reason why a greedy bin-based FM version is considered more appropriate, however its resultant cutsize will not be globally optimal, and is thus likely to be higher than the value presented here.

**Table 4: Execution Time Comparison**

| Benchmark | Constrained 3D-Legaliser (s) | Unconstrained 3D-Legaliser (s) | Bin-Based FM (Global Cutsize) (s) |
|---|---|---|---|
| *pid* | 0.18 | 0.24 | 4.15 |
| | 0.31 | | |
| | 0.26 | | |
| *aes* | 0.54 | 0.54 | 17.6 |
| | 0.72 | | |
| | 0.80 | | |
| *aes128* | 1.78 | 1.46 | 87.36 |
| | 2.93 | | |
| | 2.69 | | |
| *ldpc* | 32.94 | 47.92 | 3452.11 |
| | 48.93 | | |
| | 39.90 | | |

Figures 4 (a), (b) and (c), (d) and (e) and (f) and (g), illustrate **aes128** benchmark layouts for 2D, Unconstrained Legalisation, Constrained 3D legalisation with 2200 inter-tier vias, and bin-based FM flows respectively. Unconstrained 3D legalisation and bin-based FM produce balanced TAR, while Constrained 3D legalisation is highly imbalanced. This TAR imbalance will require a core area larger than half the original core area, and this is why Figures 4 (d), (e) are drawn larger.

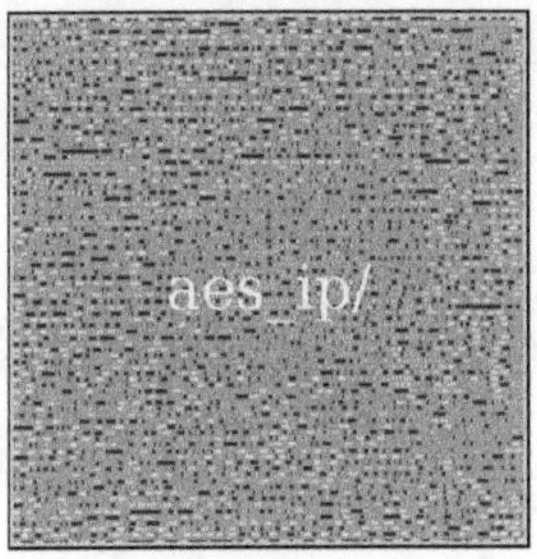


(a) 2D

(b) Unconstrained 3D Legalisation - Top Tier

(c) Unconstrained 3D Legalisation - Bottom Tier

(d) Constrained 3D Legalisation - Top Tier

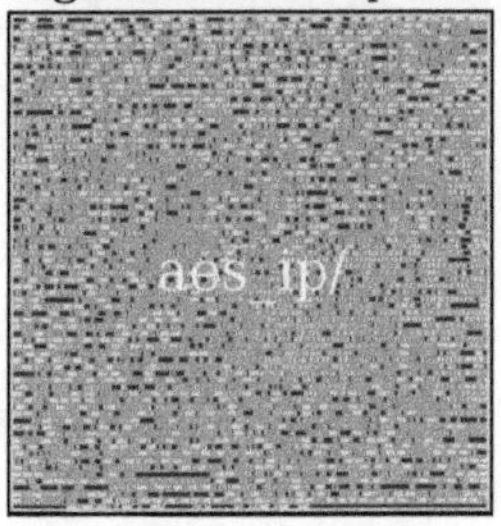


(e) Constrained 3D Legalisation - Bottom Tier

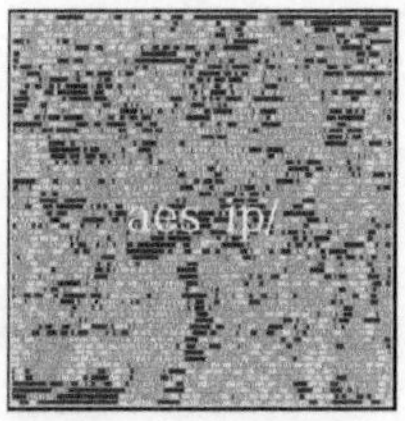


(f) Bin-Based FM - Top Tier

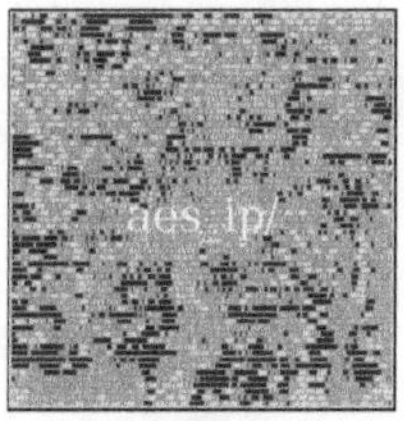


(g) Bin-Based FM - Bottom Tier

**Figure 4: *aes128* Benchmark 3DIC Flows Comparative Layouts**

# 4 CONCLUSIONS AND FUTURE WORK

We investigated three 3DIC tier partitioning flows, contrasting post-placement bin-based, global cutsize FM partitioning, and 3D legalisation, both without and with an inter-tier number of vias constraint. Post tier partitioning, we performed timing-driven IPO, to also compare slack. We used a 45nm library, with small wire delay, *i.e.* 1 FO4 inverter gate delay is proportional to 300$\mu$m RC wire delay. Results show that even for such a library, 3DIC can potentially produce better slack and smaller total routed WL, on average, compared to 2D. Comparative analysis between the flows shows that bin-based FM is able to guarantee TAR, and achieves a small cutsize, yet does not always produce better slack or total WL value, compared to 3D legalisation. The former also has significantly higher execution time than the 3D legaliser, and leads us to believe that greedy, bin-based FM is a good alternative to global cutsize FM. Constraining the 3D legaliser indeed produces a tradeoff between number of inter-tier vias and total WL, but more importantly significantly affects TAR. In terms of future work, we would like to also add Greedy bin-based FM to our 3DIC flows, and evaluate more designs and smaller scale technology libraries, *i.e.* smaller than 45nm.

# REFERENCES

[1] Perrine Batude, Thomas Ernst, Julien Arcamone, Gregory Arndt, Perceval Coudrain, and Pierre-Emmanuel Gaillardon. 2012. 3-D sequential integration: A key enabling technology for heterogeneous co-integration of new function with CMOS. *IEEE Journal on Emerging and Selected Topics in Circuits and Systems* 2, 4 (2012), 714–722.

[2] Xiangyu Dong, Jishen Zhao, and Yuan Xie. 2010. Fabrication cost analysis and cost-aware design space exploration for 3-D ICs. *IEEE Transactions on Computer-Aided Design of Integrated Circuits and Systems* 29, 12 (2010), 1959–1972.

[3] EVG Group. 2017. IMEC and EVG demonstrate for the first time 1.8$\mu$m pitch overlay accuracy for wafer bonding. https://www.evgroup.com/en/about/news/201701imec/.

[4] Bon Woong Ku, Kyungwook Chang, and Sung Kyu Lim. 2018. Compact-2D: A Physical Design Methodology to build Commercial-quality face-to-face-bonded 3D ICs. In *Proceedings of the 2018 International Symposium on Physical Design.* ACM, 90–97.

[5] Bon Woong Ku, Peter Debacker, Dragomir Milojevic, Praveen Raghavan, Diederik Verkest, Aaron Thean, and Sung Kyu Lim. 2016. Physical design solutions to tackle FEOL/BEOL degradation in gate-level monolithic 3D ICs. In *Proceedings of the 2016 International Symposium on Low Power Electronics and Design.* ACM, 76–81.

[6] OpenCores. 2019. OpenCores Open IP Community. https://opencores.org/.

[7] Shreepad Panth, Kambiz Samadi, Yang Du, and Sung Kyu Lim. 2014. Placement-Driven Partitioning for Congestion Mitigation in Monolithic 3D IC Designs. In *Proceedings of the 2014 International Symposium on Physical Design (ISPD).*

[8] Vasilis F Pavlidis, Ioannis Savidis, and Eby G Friedman. 2017. *Three-dimensional integrated circuit design.* Newnes.

[9] Nikolaos Sketopoulos, Christos Sotiriou, and Stavros Simoglou. 2018. Abax: 2D/3D legaliser supporting Look-ahead Legalisation and Blockage strategies. In *Proceedings of the 2018 Design Automation and Test In Europe (DATE).* IEEE, 1469–1472.

[10] Chen Yan and Emre Salman. 2018. Mono3D: Open source cell library for monolithic 3-D integrated circuits. *IEEE Transactions on Circuits and Systems I: Regular Papers* 65, 3 (2018), 1075–1085.

# Test and Design-for-Testability Solutions for Monolithic 3D Integrated Circuits

Abhishek Koneru
abhishek.koneru@duke.edu
Department of Electrical and Computer Engineering, Duke University
Durham, NC

Krishnendu Chakrabarty
krish@duke.edu
Department of Electrical and Computer Engineering, Duke University
Durham, NC

## ABSTRACT

M3D integration can result in reduced area and higher performance when compared to 3D die stacking. Due to the benefits of M3D integration, there is growing interest in industry towards the adoption of this technology. However, test challenges for M3D integration have remained largely unexplored. We present three key test challenges for M3D integration: (i) performance variations due to high-density integration, (ii) defect analysis and modeling, and (iii) defect isolation and yield enhancement. For each test challenge, we motivate the need to study its impact on an M3D IC, analyze the effectiveness of existing test solutions, and propose new solutions.

## CCS CONCEPTS

• **Hardware → Design for testability**; *Fault models and test metrics*; 3D integrated circuits.

## KEYWORDS

Monolithic 3D; design-for-test; built-in-self-test; defect modeling

**ACM Reference Format:**
Abhishek Koneru and Krishnendu Chakrabarty. 2019. Test and Design-for-Testability Solutions for Monolithic 3D Integrated Circuits. In *Great Lakes Symposium on VLSI 2019 (GLSVLSI '19), May 9–11, 2019, Tysons Corner, VA, USA.* ACM, New York, NY, USA, 6 pages. https://doi.org/10.1145/3299874.3319488

## 1 INTRODUCTION

Three-dimensional (3D) integration is a promising way to achieve high-performance ICs with more functionality and reduced die footprint. Today's 3D integration process is primarily based on die/wafer stacking since it does not require substantial changes to the existing fabrication flow. In this process, separately manufactured dies/wafers are integrated onto the same package, and through-silicon-vias (TSVs) are used to connect dies to each other. Considerable research efforts have therefore been directed towards the development of TSV-based 3D stacking technology [2, 9], and products based on this technology have been successfully introduced into the market, e.g., the AMD Fiji chip [12]. However, the keep-out-zone (KOZ) required for TSVs and limitations on the die alignment precision impose limits on the device integration density that can be achieved using TSV-based 3D stacking. A minimum KOZ of 3 μm is required for ICs fabricated at the 20 nm technology node [11], and the die alignment precision is currently limited to 0.5 μm [1].

Monolithic 3D (M3D) integration is an emerging technology in which transistors are processed layer-by-layer on the same wafer. Sequential integration of transistor layers enables high-density vertical interconnects, known as inter-layer vias (ILVs). The size and pitch of an ILV is typically one to two orders of magnitude smaller than those of a through-silicon via (TSV) [6]. Therefore, M3D integration can result in significantly reduced area and higher performance when compared to 3D die stacking.

Due to the above benefits of M3D integration, there is a growing interest in industry towards the adoption of this technology [3, 7, 8]. In order to ensure that M3D integration is primed for use when industry is ready to adopt it, researchers have started investigating solutions to various problems related to the design and fabrication of M3D ICs. For instance, a low-temperature process to fabricate high-performance top transistor layers without degrading the performance of bottom transistor layers was proposed in [6]. Design techniques to reduce the interconnect length, critical path delay, and die area were presented in [10, 20]. Despite these advances, test challenges for M3D integration received much less attention.

In this paper, we present three key test challenges for M3D integration: (i) performance variations due to high-density integration, (ii) defect analysis and modeling, and (iii) defect isolation and yield enhancement. We describe how the first two challenges were addressed in [13, 15, 17]. We quantified the impact of electrostatic coupling and wafer-bonding defects on the threshold voltage of a top-layer transistor in an M3D IC. In addition, we showed that wafer-bonding defects can lead to a change in the resistance of ILVs, and in some cases, lead to an open in an ILV or a short between two ILVs. We also studied the impact of these defects on path delays and on the effectiveness of delay-test patterns for large benchmarks. Our results show that the timing characteristics of an M3D IC can be significantly altered due to coupling and wafer-bonding defects if the thickness of its inter-layer dielectric is less than 100 nm.

Next, we describe a DfT solution for M3D ICs based on dedicated test layers to address challenge (iii) [16, 18, 19]. We have evaluated the cost associated with the proposed DfT solution and compare it with that for a potential DfT solution based on the proposed IEEE Std. P1838. Our results show that the proposed DfT solution is more cost-efficient than the P1838-based DfT solution for a wide range of ILV density, ILV yield, and defect density. We also present


ACM ISBN 978-1-4503-6252-8/19/05...$15.00
https://doi.org/10.1145/3299874.3319488

a test scheduling and optimization technique for wafer-level testing of M3D ICs.

Finally, we describe an ILV built-in self-test (BIST) solution for M3D ICs to address isolation of ILV defects and yield enhancement [14]. In this ILV BIST solution, interface-register cells in a test layer are stitched into a TRC using their functional outputs and the ILVs. We show that the proposed solution detects all hard opens and shorts in the ILVs. We validate the detection of all hard opens and shorts using HSpice simulations.

The rest of the paper is organized as follows. Section II provides an overview of M3D technology. Section III presents key test challenges. Section IV presents the analysis of coupling and wafer-bonding defects. Section V presents a DfT solution based on dedicated test layers. Section VI presents an ILV BIST solution. Finally, Section VI concludes the paper.

## 2 M3D TECHNOLOGY AND DESIGN OVERVIEW

M3D integration involves sequential processing of transistor layers on the same wafer. First, the bottom-layer transistors and their associated interconnects are processed using a standard high-temperature process, e.g., silicon-on-insulator (SOI), FinFET, or bulk CMOS technology. Next, a thin silicon layer is created over the bottom layer. The top-layer transistors are then processed under a strict thermal budget. Finally, ILVs are processed to connect the two layers. The last three steps are repeated to fabricate additional layers.

Sequential integration of device layers would not have been possible without the development of: (i) a low-temperature process to create a thin silicon film over the bottom layer, and (ii) a process to realize top-layer transistors without damaging the underlying interconnects and degrading the properties of the bottom-layer transistors. Several approaches have been proposed in the literature to create a thin silicon film at low temperatures: (i) thin-film polysilicon deposition (which is based on the method used to create thin-film transistors and is currently for 3D-NAND flash memories), (ii) pulsed-laser crystallization of amorphous silicon, (iii) excimer laser crystallization, (iv) epitaxial layer transfer (ELTRAN), (v) wafer bonding followed by grinding and etchback, and (vi) modified Smart-Cut process.

An M3D IC can be partitioned at the core-level, at the block-level, at the gate-level, and at the transistor-level. Core-level and block-level design-partitioning approaches do not fully utilize the high integration density offered by M3D. In the transistor-level design partitioning approach, the P-channel and N-channel transistors are placed on different layers, thereby allowing the fabrication process to be optimized separately for each layer. In the gate-level design partitioning approach, all the transistors in a standard cell are fabricated in one layer. Note that 3D standard cells have to be designed for transistor-level M3D integration. However, existing design automation tools can be reused to place and route these 3D standard cells [20]. On the other hand, 3D-aware physical layout tools are required for gate-level design partitioning [4].

## 3 TEST CHALLENGES FOR M3D ICS

In this section, we first present three test challenges for M3D integration.

### 3.1 Timing Variations due to High-Density Integration

In order to realize high-density vertical interconnects, the inter-layer dielectric (ILD) thickness in M3D ICs is being aggressively scaled [7, 20], which leads to electrostatic coupling between device layers. Electrostatic coupling was first observed in SOI transistors in which the front- and back-gates compete to induce charge in the silicon film (body); therefore, the electrical state of the silicon film at any point in time depends on the bias at both these gates. As a result, transistor parameters such as the threshold voltage and drain current depend on the bias at both these gates. Transistors in non-bottom layers in an M3D IC are SOI transistors since those layers are separated from their underneath layer by a dielectric. Therefore, transistors in non-bottom layers can be influenced by transistors underneath them.

### 3.2 Defect Analysis and Modeling

The condition of the bonding surfaces plays a crucial role in achieving a defect-free bond during the wafer-bonding step in the fabrication of an M3D IC. Oxide layers are the prime candidates for bonding surfaces due to the presence of hydroxyl (OH) groups that lead to high bond strengths. These oxide layers also act as the ILD. Therefore, defects that arise during the wafer-bonding step can impact the top-layer transistors, as well as the ILVs. It is important to understand and analyze wafer-bonding defects, and develop methods to test for these defects. The defects during the wafer-bonding process occur at the bond interface. Defects can often be attributed to voids, delaminations, and foreign particles. The size of these defects can be in the mm to nm range.

### 3.3 Defect Isolation and Yield Enhancement

Industry presentations have highlighted concerns about defects that may arise in the bottom layer in an M3D IC when additional layers are processed [3]. In addition, non-bottom layers are susceptible to process variations [22] and electrostatic coupling, and the ILVs are prone to defects that arise during wafer bonding. Therefore, there is a need for low-cost design-for-test (DfT) solutions to enable defect isolation and yield enhancement.

The proposed IEEE Std P1838 can potentially be extended for M3D ICs. However, the overhead due to this register at the boundary of every layer can be significant since the number of ILVs in M3D ICs is expected to be an order of magnitude higher compared to TSV-based 3D ICs [6]. Although the extension of P1838 to M3D enables reuse of methods developed for TSV-based 3D ICs, new test solutions are needed due to the significant differences between M3D and TSV-based 3D in terms of design, fabrication, failure modes, and test constraints [6]. Moreover, a die (including the TSVs) can be tested pre-bond and a known-good die can be used for a TSV-based 3D stack [21]. On the other hand, ILVs are absent in the uppermost layer during partial-assembly test. For layers other than the top layer, there is no functional interface through which tests can be applied. The ILVs are not fabricated until the next silicon layer is assembled and the front-end is processed. Therefore, even if we insert probe pads on the uppermost layer, the logic connected to the ILVs will still remain untested. Wrapper cells are required for each ILV in order to test the connected logic. However, since the number of ILVs in an M3D IC can be very large, the area overhead due to wrapper cells for each ILV will be high.

## 4 ANALYSIS OF COUPLING AND WAFER-BONDING DEFECTS

In order to stufy the problem of timing variations in M3D, we have analyzed electrostatic coupling between device layers in M3D ICs and quantify its impact on circuit timing [13]. Due to the coupling between the top and bottom transistor layers, the threshold voltage of a transistor in the top layer can differ considerably from that of a conventional transistor (SOI or bulk CMOS), and depends on the bias and properties of the back gate. We carried out detailed device simulations to understand the impact of coupling on the threshold voltage of a top-layer transistor for both transistor- and gate-level integration. Simulations were performed using Silvaco Atlas, a physics-based numerical device simulator.

We simulated two device structures using Atlas: (i) an asymmetric double-gate SOI transistor to study the impact of coupling in transistor-level M3D integration, and (ii) an asymmetric double-gate SOI transistor in which the front- and back-gates are independent of each other to study the impact of coupling in gate-level M3D integration. The values of various parameters for the devices in our simulations were obtained from [6]. In our simulations, we have included physical models such as Shockley-Read-Hall recombination, Lombardi's mobility, and Selberherr's impact ionization.

We analyzed the change in threshold voltage ($|\Delta V_{th}|$) from that of a conventional SOI transistor due to coupling. The threshold voltage values are calculated from $I_D - V_{FG}$ plots using the constant current threshold voltage extraction method for a drain-source bias of 100 mV. In this method, threshold voltage of a device is the gate-source voltage at which the drain current is equal to a constant current ($I_{D0}$) multiplied by the ratio of gate width to gate length. The value of $I_{D0}$ is process dependent, and it typically ranges between 50 and 500 nA. In this paper, the value of $I_{D0}$ was chosen to be 300 nA for N-channel and 70 nA for P-channel transistors.

Figure 1(a) shows the $|\Delta V_{th}|$ of a double-gated device created to simulate a top-tier transistor in the case of transistor-level M3D integration. For both N-channel and P-channel double-gate transistors, the $|\Delta V_{th}|$ was obtained to be 51 mV for an ILD thickness of 23 nm. However, for an ILD thickness of 100 nm, the $|\Delta V_{th}|$ reduces to 7 mV and 9 mV for N-channel and P-channel transistors, respectively. Therefore, we conclude that for ILD thicknesses greater than 100 nm, the impact of the bottom tier on threshold voltage of a top-tier transistor in transistor-level M3D is minimal. For ILD thickness less than 50 nm, the impact of coupling on threshold voltage of a top-tier transistor is significant, and cannot be ignored.

Figure 1(b) shows the $|\Delta V_{th}|$ of a double-gated device created to simulate a top-tier transistor in the case of gate-level M3D integration. For the N-channel double-gate transistor, the $|\Delta V_{th}|$ was obtained to be 44 mV and 65 mV for a back-gate (metal line from the bottom tier) voltage of 0V and 1V, respectively. However, for an ILD thickness of 100 nm, the $|\Delta V_{th}|$ reduces to 9 mV and 13 mV for a back-gate voltage of 0 V and 1 V, respectively. Similarly, for the P-channel double-gate transistor, we observe that the impact of a metal line from the bottom tier on the threshold voltage of a top-tier transistor is minimal for ILD thickness greater than 100 nm. Therefore, we conclude that for ILD thickness greater than 100 nm, coupling between the top and bottom tiers is minimal. For ILD thickness less than 50 nm, the impact of coupling on threshold voltage of a top-tier transistor is significant, and cannot be ignored.

We also studied the impact of wafer-bonding defects on the threshold voltage of a top-layer transistor and on the ILVs [15, 17]. If a void is present in the back-gate dielectric of a double-gate transistor, the back-gate capacitance will be lower compared to the defect-free case, since the dielectric constant of air is lower than that of a dielectric material. The effective back-gate dielectric capacitance can be expressed as the capacitance of the void in series with the capacitance of the dielectric layers above and below the void:

$$\frac{1}{C_{effective}} = \frac{t'_{box}}{\epsilon_{ox}} + \frac{t_{void}}{\epsilon_{void}} + \frac{t''_{box}}{\epsilon_{ox}} \tag{1}$$

where $t_{box}$ is the thickness of the back-gate dielectric in the absence of a void, $t'_{box}$ and $t''_{box}$ are the thicknesses of the dielectric layers above and below the void, respectively, $t'_{void}$ is the thickness of the void, and $\epsilon_{ox}$ and $\epsilon_{air}$ are the dielectric constants of the ILD and void, respectively. From (1), we can conclude that the effective back-gate dielectric capacitance ($C_{effective}$) will be less than the capacitance of the back-gate dielectric in the absence of a void ($t_{box}/\epsilon_{ox}$) since $\epsilon_{void} < \epsilon_{ox}$.

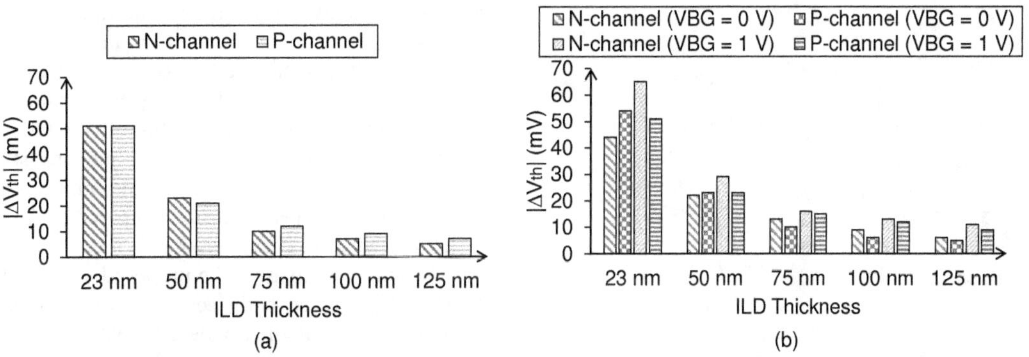


**Figure 1: Threshold voltage change from that of a conventional SOI transistor for: (a) transistor-level M3D, and (b) gate-level M3D.**

## 5 DFT SOLUTION BASED ON DEDICATED TEST LAYERS

In this section, we present a new DfT solution for M3D ICs based on dedicated test layers, which are inserted between functional layers [16, 18, 19]. These layers provide controllability and observability to signals at the interfaces of functional layers. The main features of a test layer are: (1) a low-bandwidth serial interface, and a higher-bandwidth parallel interface, (2) dedicated probe pads on all layers, except the top layer, to enable partial-assembly testing, and (3) test structures to enable modular testing of the assembled layers.

An overview of the architecture is presented in Fig. 2. The figure shows an example M3D IC consisting of two functional layers and two test layers. The test layer for the uppermost functional layer is optional, and the IEEE 1149.1 boundary scan can be placed in the uppermost functional layer itself. A limited number of additional pins are required for boundary scan, of which two (TDI and TDO) are shown. The functional layers have intra-layer DfT such as scan-chains, test data CoDeCs, IEEE Std wrappers, and test-access mechanisms (TAMs). However, all the layer-level DfT is located in the test layer, thus facilitating the reuse of test structures.

The placement of test structures for modular testing of M3D ICs on a separate layer is realistic since M3D integration enables significantly higher integration density compared to TSV-based 3D integration. Such high device density is achieved by using an extremely thin inter-layer dielectric (ILD) and silicon layers [6]. The dedicated test layers can be manufactured using a mature technology to reduce the impact on cost due to the additional processing steps.

A register is added to the test layer to control and observe the signals at the interface of two functional layers. We refer to this register as the interface register. By placing the interface register on a dedicated test layer, we are not adding any test structures to the functional layer apart from conventional test structures. Note that the proposed solution will not replace scan-based test. It will just

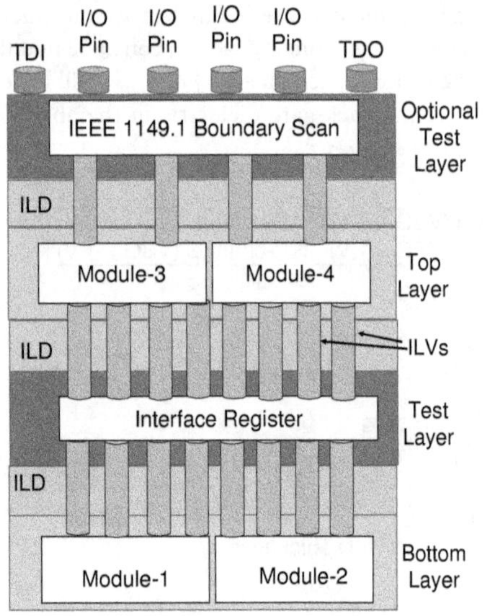


**Figure 2: Overview of the proposed DfT solution.**

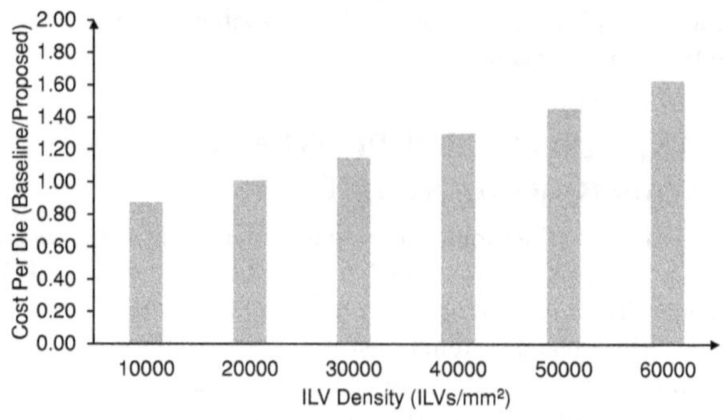


**Figure 3: Cost ratio obtained for multiplier as function of ILV density.**

aid in pinpointing faulty ILVs. Moreover, the impact on functional performance due to the interface register is not significant since the structure of an interface register is similar to that of a IEEE Std. 1500 wrapper. The operating modes supported by a test layer are:

1. *Partial-assembly test*: test access via dedicated probe pads;
2. *Post-assembly test*: test access via external I/O pins;
3. *Primary test*: test the functional layer for which the test layer forms the primary interface;
4. *Secondary test*: test the functional layer for which the test layer forms the secondary interface;
5. *Bypass*: only the bypass register is included in the test access chain;
6. *Interconnect test*: test the interface register;
7. *Turn*: the test-access mechanism (TAM) turns upwards from the test layer;
8. *Elevate*: the TAM goes downwards towards the next layer.

The cost-per-die in M3D is impacted by the addition of DfT structures. The DfT structures can be placed on the functional layer, e.g., IEEE Std P1838 extension to M3D, or on a dedicated test layer. In order to justify the practicality of the proposed method, we have evaluated the DfT cost in [16, 19]. We derive a detailed cost model by modifying the cost models for wafer-to-wafer stacked 3D ICs to account for the additional steps involved in M3D integration. We then carefully analyze and quantify the impact of the above test solution on yield and cost.

We compare the cost of the proposed DfT solution with the cost of a potential solution based on P1838. We perform the cost comparison analysis for a 128-bit multiplier benchmark. In [22], block-level partitioning of these benchmarks into two layers was performed. The partitioning tool assumes that both the layers have identical transistors and interconnects. The floor-planning algorithm considers inter-layer variation in M3D ICs and minimizes the weighted sum of wirelength, area, and longest path delay. The floor-planning algorithm does not minimize the number of ILVs since the ILVs are smaller in size compared to TSVs.

In [19], we have evaluated the ratio of the cost for the P1838-based solution to that for the proposed solution for a two-layer M3D IC. Fig. 3 presents the cost ratio for a multiplier benchmark obtained by varying the ILV density. We observe that the cost per die of the proposed method is lower compared to that of the P1838-based method for all values of ILV density greater than 20,000 ILVs/mm$^2$. Therefore, the proposed solution is more cost-efficient than the P1838-based solution for all values of ILV density greater than 20,000 ILVs/mm$^2$.

# 6 INTER-LAYER INTERCONNECT BIST

Although ILVs are comparable in size and pitch to conventional vias, they differ significantly in terms of fabrication steps and yield. The yield for processing ILVs is speculated to be much lower compared to a conventional via. Yield learning is especially important for a new technology such as M3D integration. Due to aggressive scaling of ILD thickness, the ILVs are prone to shorts, opens, and delay defects [15, 17]. Incomplete metal filling or voids in an ILV increase resistance and impact circuit timing [5, 17]. Large voids in the ILV can result in an open path, thereby causing a catastrophic failure. Impurities may increase resistance and interconnect delay. ILVs are also affected by voids that arise in the ILD since they are processed after the wafer-bonding step. Such voids lead to an increase in ILV resistance. If the size of a void in the ILD is large enough to impact two neighboring ILVs, then it leads to a resistive short between the two ILVs. The resistance of the defect depends on the thickness of the void.

Conventional scan-based test pattern generation cannot be re-used to test ILVs since they do not provide the diagnostic resolution to diagnose and characterize ILV faults. We may not be able to pinpoint to a specific ILV using conventional scan-based diagnosis since it may produce large number of candidates for one failure. Pre-bond TSV testing methods is infeasible for ILVs since bare ILVs cannot be be exposed, and the state-of-the-art wafer-probe technology cannot support the pitch requirement for ILVs (100 nm to 200 nm). Techniques proposed to carry out post-bond TSV testing can be extended to M3D for post-assembly testing. For example, the proposed IEEE Std. P1838 [21], which defines a standardized architecture to test the TSVs, can be extended to M3D and used to test the ILVs. However, a wrapper cell has to be inserted at both ends of a TSV in order to test that TSV using P1838. A similar memory element is needed at both ends of an ILV in order to test an ILV by extending P1838 to M3D ICs. However, the overhead due to the insertion of memory elements on all ILVs can be significant since the number of ILVs in M3D ICs is expected to be an order of magnitude higher compared to TSV-based 3D ICs.

We present a post-assembly ILV BIST solution [14]. The proposed ILV BIST solution enables stand-alone testing of the ILVs without incurring significant area overhead. In the proposed solution, interface-register cells are stitched into a TRC using their functional outputs and ILVs. Fig. 4 shows a four-bit TRC formed using interface-register cells. ILVs connected to the input and output of an interface-register cell are defined as the inbound and outbound ILVs, respectively. In a TRC, the inverse of the output of the last cell is connected to the input of the first cell. Such a counter circulates a stream of ones followed by zeros around the ring. For example, in a counter with an initial register value of 0000, the repeating pattern is: 0000, 1000, 1100, 1110, 1111, 0111, 0011, 0001, and 0000. Once a TRC is initialized to a specific pattern, the pattern in the counter repeats every $2N$ clock cycles, where $N$ is the number of cells in the counter. We show later that we can detect all opens and shorts in the ILVs by using these patterns. We also evaluate the size of the delay defect that can be detected by using a TRC.

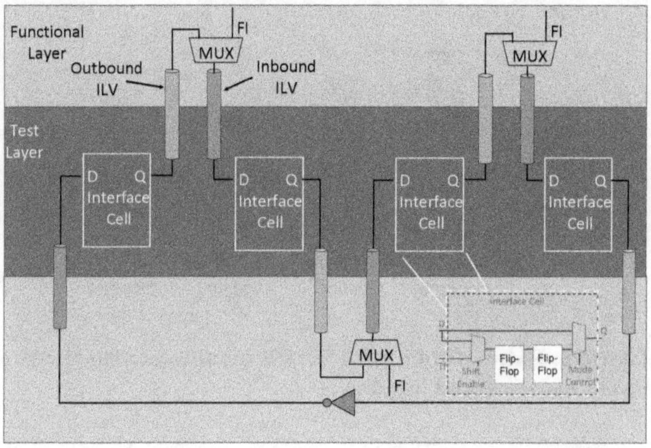


**Figure 4: Illustration of a four-bit TRC using interface cells.**

In order to implement a TRC using interface-register cells, we need to connect an outbound ILV to an inbound ILV. In an M3D IC, the number of inbound ILVs (to a layer) is typically not equal to the number of outbound ILVs (to a layer). However, we need to match an inbound ILV with an outbound ILV to stitch the interface cells into a TRC. Therefore, we cluster the inbound (outbound) ILVs when the number of inbound (outbound) ILVs is greater than outbound (inbound) ILVs such that the total number of clusters matches the outbound (inbound) ILV count. The additional hardware required to cluster ILVs is described in [14].

If the ILVs are treated as nodes in a graph and an edge between two nodes is used to denote a valid connection between two ILVs (inbound ILV and outbound ILV), then the resultant graph is bipartite. A *bipartite graph* is a graph whose vertices can be divided into two disjoint and independent sets such that every edge connects a vertex in one set to one in another. The Manhattan distance between an inbound ILV and an outbound ILV is used to represent the weight of an edge between the corresponding ILVs. The wire-length minimization problem then maps to finding a minimum cost Hamiltonian circuit in the weighted bipartite graph. The wire-length minimization problem is different from scan-chain routing problem since we can only visit an input (output) ILV from an output (input) ILV. There is no such constraint for the scan-chain routing problem, which has traditionally been mapped to the traveling-salesman problem. In [14], we showed that the weighted Hamiltonian circuit problem is NP-Complete for complete bipartite graphs.

We have proposed an efficient heuristic to solve the wire-length minimization problem. The proposed heuristic can be used to carry out wire-length optimization during the physical design phase of an M3D IC. First, we balance the number of inbound and outbound ILVs by carrying out $k$-means clustering on the set that has higher number of nodes. For each cluster, we identify ILVs which receive inverted value from the driver interface cell for this cluster using graph coloring. To construct a graph for a given cluster, we represent each ILV in that cluster by a node. We then insert an edge between two nodes if the distance between the corresponding ILVs is less than a given threshold. The threshold for ILV spacing is used to identify ILVs which are likely to have a short between them. If the spacing between ILVs is greater than the defined threshold, those ILVs are less likely to have a short between. In the graph-coloring

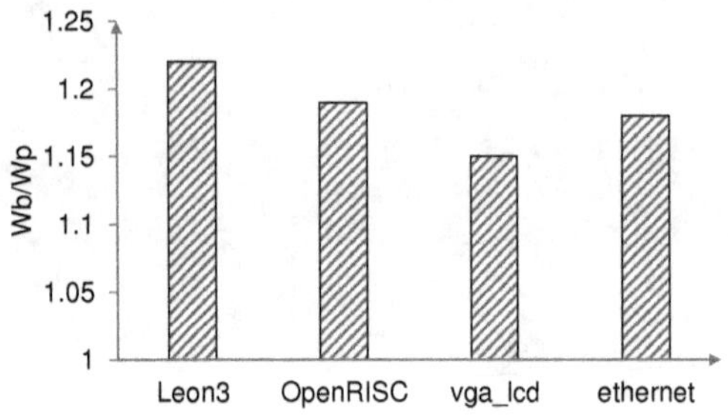


**Figure 5: Ratio of total wire length obtained using the proposed heuristic and baseline.**

step, we enforce the algorithm to use only two colors since the ILVs can only be of two types: (i) receive input directly from driver, and (ii) receive inverted value of input from driver. This constraint may lead to two adjacent ILVs having the same color and result in coverage loss. However, accepting the coverage loss is a more practical solution since re-balancing the clusters every time we obtain a graph coloring with more than two colors will make the run time of the heuristic prohibitively large.

Next, we represent each cluster by a representative node at the center of the cluster. We then construct a balanced-complete-weighted bipartite graph using the resulting set of input and outbound ILVs. Next, we find a Hamiltonian circuit in the balanced bipartite graph by using a well-known heuristic proposed in . In this heuristic, a minimum-cost matching consisting of edges that connect input and outbound ILVs is found using a heuristic for maximum-weighted bipartite matching. A minimum-cost tour that visits all the inbound ILVs is also found using a heuristic for the traveling salesman problem. The resulting Hamiltonian circuit consists of visiting the inbound ILVs in the sequence specified by the tour and using the matching edges to make sure that an outbound ILV is visited after an inbound ILV.

We utilize four IWLS'05 benchmarks to evaluate the effectiveness of the proposed algorithm. These benchmarks were implemented using the Arizona State Predictive PDK (ASAP) 7 nm technology library. We used Cadence RTL compiler to carry out synthesis and Cadence Innovus to carry out placement and routing. We used six metal layers of the metal stack from ASAP 7 nm library for routing the benchmark. The location of signal ILVs obtained from the place-and-route step is used as input to the wirelength-minimization heuristic.

We generate the distance matrices for each benchmark based on the ILV locations. Once the distance matrices are generated, they are provided as input to the proposed heuristic implemented in a Python script, and the Hamiltonian circuit that corresponds to a tour of ILVs with minimum wire length is generated. We define a baseline method in which we start at a random ILV and pick the ILV that is visited next in a greedy manner, i.e., an output (input) ILV nearest to an input (output) ILV. The total wirelength required to form the TRC using the proposed method and baseline method are denoted by $W_p$ and $W_b$, respectively. Fig. 5 shows the results in terms of the ratio $W_b/W_p$. It can be seen that $W_b$ is 15% to 22% larger than $W_p$. Therefore, the proposed algorithm reduces the total wire length required to form the TRC.

## 7 CONCLUSIONS

We have presented the first comprehensive test solutions for emerging M3D integrated circuits. In this work, we have identified and addressed some of the key challenges related to testing of M3D ICs. Novel DfT solutions have been presented to carry out modular testing of M3D ICs. We have also addressed some of the key challenges related to defect isolation and yield enhancement. We have also made advances in modeling of electrostatic coupling and wafer-bonding defects.

## ACKNOWLEDGMENTS

We thank Dr. Sukeshwar Kannan from Lightmatter for contributions to the work on analysis of wafer-bonding defects and DfT solution based on dedicated test layers.

## REFERENCES

[1] [n. d.]. International Technology Roadmap for Semiconductors. http://www.itrs2.net/. ([n. d.]).
[2] D. H. Kim et al. 2015. Design and Analysis of 3D-MAPS (3D Massively Parallel Processor with Stacked Memory). *IEEE Trans. Comput.* 64, 1 (Jan 2015), 112–125.
[3] K. Arabi et al. 2015. 3D VLSI: A Scalable Integration Beyond 2D. In *ISPD.* 1–7.
[4] O. Billoint et al. 2015. A Comprehensive Study of Monolithic 3D Cell on Cell Design Using Commercial 2D Tool. In *DATE.* 1192–1196.
[5] O. D. Patterson et al. 2006. Detection of Resistive Shorts and Opens using Voltage Contrast Inspection. In *Advanced Semiconductor Manufacturing Conference.* 327–333.
[6] P. Batude et al. 2012. 3-D Sequential Integration: A Key Enabling Technology for Heterogeneous Co-Integration of New Function With CMOS. *IEEE J. Emerging and Selected Topics in Circuits and Sys.* 2, 4 (Dec 2012), 714–722.
[7] P. Batude et al. 2012. 3-D Sequential Integration: A Key Enabling Technology for Heterogeneous Co-Integration of New Function With CMOS. *IEEE JETCAS* 2, 4 (Dec 2012), 714–722.
[8] P. Batude et al. 2015. 3DVLSI with CoolCube process: An alternative path to scaling. In *VLSIT.* T48–T49.
[9] P. Coudrain et al. 2013. 3D Integration of CMOS image sensor with coprocessor using TSV last and micro-bumps technologies. In *ECTC.* 674–682.
[10] S. Bobba et al. 2011. CELONCEL: Effective Design Technique for 3-D Monolithic Integration targeting High Performance Integrated Circuits. In *ASP-DAC.* 336–343.
[11] S. Kannan et al. 2015. Device performance analysis on 20nm technology thin wafers in a 3D package. In *IRPS.*
[12] J. Rearick. 2015. New Paradigm Shift in 3-D Design and Testing. *ITC 3D Test Workshop.* (2015).
[13] A. Koneru and K. Chakrabarty. 2016. Analysis of Electrostatic Coupling in Monolithic 3D Integrated Circuits and its Impact on Delay Testing. In *ETS.*
[14] A. Koneru and K. Chakrabarty. 2018. An Inter-Layer Interconnect BIST Solution for Monolithic 3D ICs. In *VTS.* 1–6.
[15] Abhishek Koneru, Sukeshwar Kannan, and Krishnendu Chakrabarty. 2016. Impact of Wafer-Bonding Defects on Monolithic 3D Integrated Circuits. In *EPEPS.*
[16] Abhishek Koneru, Sukeshwar Kannan, and Krishnendu Chakrabarty. 2017. A Design-for-Test Solution for Monolithic 3D Integrated Circuits. *ICCD* 00 (2017), 685–688.
[17] Abhishek Koneru, Sukeshwar Kannan, and Krishnendu Chakrabarty. 2017. Impact of Electrostatic Coupling and Wafer-Bonding Defects on Delay Testing of Monolithic 3D Integrated Circuits. *JETC* (2017).
[18] A. Koneru, S. Kannan, and K. Chakrabarty. 2017. Testing monolithic three dimensional integrated circuits. (Nov. 2017). US Patent Application no. 15/801,380.
[19] A. Koneru, S. Kannan, and K. Chakrabarty. 2018. A Design-for-Test Solution Based on Dedicated Test Layers and Test Scheduling for Monolithic 3D Integrated Circuits. *TCAD* (2018).
[20] Y.-J. Lee and S. K. Lim. 2013. Ultrahigh Density Logic Designs Using Monolithic 3-D Integration. *IEEE Trans. CAD* (Dec 2013).
[21] E. J. Marinissen, T. McLaurin, and Hailong Jiao. 2016. IEEE Std P1838: DfT standard-under-development for 2.5D-, 3D-, and 5.5D-SICs. In *ETS.* 1–10.
[22] S. Panth, K. Samadi, Y. Du, and S. K. Lim. 2014. Power-performance study of block-level monolithic 3D-ICs considering inter-tier performance variations. In *DAC.* 1–6.

# N3XT Monolithic 3D Energy-Efficient Computing Systems

Mohamed M. Sabry Aly
SCSE, Nanyang Technological University, Singapore
msabry@ntu.edu.sg

## ABSTRACT

The world's appetite for analyzing massive amounts of structured and unstructured data has grown dramatically. The computational demands of these abundant-data applications far exceed the capabilities of today's computing systems. The N3XT (Nano-Engineered Computing Systems Technology) approach overcomes this challenge through: (i) new logic devices such as carbon nanotube field-effect transistors, (ii) high-density non-volatile memory, and (iii) ultra-dense monolithic 3D integration of thin layers of logic and memory devices that are fabricated at low temperature. N3XT hardware prototypes demonstrate the practicality of this approach. We evaluate the benefits of N3XT using a simulation framework calibrated using experimental measurements, which also enables the analysis of a several device and integration technologies. N3XT improves the system-level energy-delay product of common implementations of abundant-data workloads by three orders of magnitude compared to conventional architectures.


*GLSVLSI '19, May 9–11, 2019, Tysons Corner, VA, USA.*

ACM ISBN 978-1-4503-6252-8/19/05.
DOI: https://doi.org/10.1145/3299874.3319489

## CCS Concepts/ACM Classifiers

• Hardware~3D integrated circuits
• Hardware~Non-volatile memory
• Hardware~Analysis and design of emerging devices and systems
• Hardware~Carbon based electronic

## Author Keywords

Monolithic 3D; Carbon Nanotubes; Resistive RAM

# How to Generate Robust Keys from Noisy DRAMs?

Nima Karimian
San Jose State University
nima.karimian@sjsu.edu

Fatemeh Tehranipoor
San Francisco State University
tehranipoor@sfsu.edu

## ABSTRACT

Security primitives based on Dynamic Random Access Memory (DRAM) can provide cost-efficient and practical security solutions, especially for resource-constrained devices, such as hardware used in the Internet of Things (IoT), as DRAMs are an intrinsic part of most contemporary computer systems [1]. Over the past few years, DRAM-based physical unclonable functions became very popular among researchers in this field. However, similar to other types of PUFs, DRAM PUF reliability for authentication and key generation is highly dependent on its resistance against the environmental noises such as Temperature variation, Voltage variations, and Device aging. This paper addresses the challenges related to the reliability and robustness of DRAM PUFs under noisy environments. In this paper we apply a new approach (Quantization) that extracts keys from DRAM startup values with a high reliability and stability rate. This quantization technique identifies suitable features from power-up values of DRAM memories and quantize them into binary bits using tunable parameters that control and predict the environmental noises. Our experimental result shows a high reliability and min-entropy rate for relatively large number of DRAM key bits.

## KEYWORDS

DRAM PUF, Quantization, Noise.

**ACM Reference Format:**

Nima Karimian and Fatemeh Tehranipoor. 2019. How to Generate Robust Keys from Noisy DRAMs?. In *Proceedings of ACM Great Lakes Symposium on VLSI (GLSVLSI)., May 9-11, Tyson's Corner, VA.* ACM, New York, NY, USA. 5 pages. https://doi.org/10.1145/3299874.3319494

## 1 INTRODUCTION AND OBJECTIVES

A physically unclonable function (PUF) is an irreversible probabilistic function that produces a random bit string. PUFs have been widely proposed as hardware security primitives to provide device identification, authentication, and key generation [2]. However, one big challenge is how a PUF key/ID can be extracted during enrollment process in noisy environmental conditions. Over the past few years, various types of DRAM-based PUFs have been proposed with researchers from all over the world. DRAMs seem to have a number of additional advantages regarding their usage for the implementation of security primitives, such as their presence in most contemporary computer systems, their large storage size, and the easy way in which they can be accessed, even at run-time. In particular, their large storage size can guarantee both the existence of an adequate amount of entropy [3] and that a part of them can be used, for a limited amount of time, exclusively as a dedicated security primitive, while the system is running. Similarly, a DRAM PUF reliability for authentication and key generation is highly dependent on its resistance against the following noises and related challenges: Temperature variation, Voltage variations, and Device aging [4]. These environmental noises impact on the stability of PUF. Not only that, the existing neighboring bit selection [5] will pain a large penalty for unused bits during enrollment. Due to the noise in these PUFs, generating binary values using this approach can result in a high error. Often, error correction codes (ECC) [6] are considered as a potential solution for addressing the stability of PUFs. However, ECC methods are usually very intensive in terms of the amount of overhead they add to the design. As a result, it may not be possible to find a potential and robust algorithm to fully resolve the aforementioned issues.

In this paper, we are focused on improving the reliability of key generation based on DRAM PUFs. To overcome the aforementioned challenges and drawbacks, in this paper, we apply a new key generation approach based on quantization scheme [19] [20] that extracts key bits from DRAM startup values [16] [17] with a very high reliability and entropy rate. Note that the quantized DRAM PUF is based on raw data of DRAMs (startup values-decimal format). Our technique identifies suitable features from power-up values of DRAM memories and quantize them into binary bits using tunable parameters that control and predict the environmental noises. Generally, converting analog measurement DRAM startup values to binary strings is also known in the field of biometrics. The proposed approach, several parameters affected by temperature [18] and measurement noise is used to trade off reliability and uniqueness key bits. Our approach for quantizing features to two bits is most clearly illustrated in Figure 1. The population probability density function (PDF) of a feature is shown in black. The PDFs for the same feature in genuine subjects are shown in blue. Our technique will mitigate error indicated in red color and select reliable bits in enrollment from DRAM startup values.

Our main contributions are as follows:

1). **DRAM Startup Value Collection:** It has been noted that the cells of DRAMs keep different values ('0's and '1's) at startup in a similar way to SRAM cells. We had tested 3 Commercial-Of-The-Shelf (COTS) DRAM and collected their power up values.

2). **Quantization Approach**: We apply a new framework for key generation of DRAM PUFs that incorporates statistical information of the memory cells value, their locations and parameters trade off reliability and entropy. This technique is able to quantize the most reliable features (DRAM cell values) of each PUF into more than one bit, thus extending the length of keys possible from DRAM


*GLSVLSI '19, May 9–11, 2019, Tysons Corner, VA, USA*

ACM ISBN 978-1-4503-6252-8/19/05...$15.00.
DOI: https://doi.org/10.1145/3299874.3319494

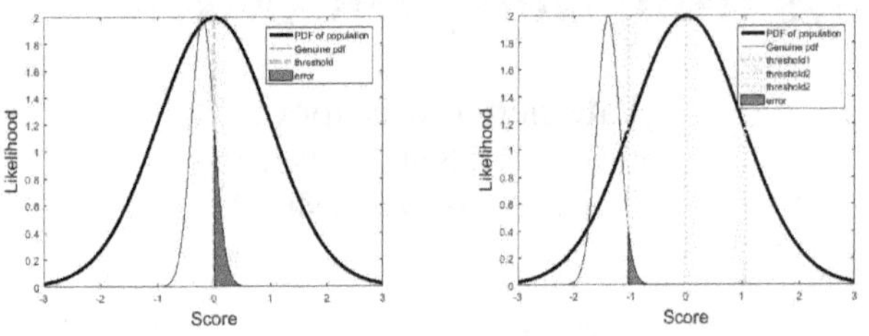

(a) (b)

**Figure 1: General quantization scheme; (a). one-bit and (b). two bit**

PUF while still balancing entropy and reliability.

3). **Application of Our Quantization Technique for all Types of PUFs**: Although, we only applied this quantization technique to DRAM-based PUFs, it can be easily used for other types of PUFs as well.

The rest of the paper is organized as follows. Section II show the background of DRAM PUFs and quantization techniques. In Section III, we describe DRAM-based PUF. We discuss our key generation approach using quantization technique and results in Section IV. Finally, in Section V, conclusions and future works are provided.

## 2 LITERATURE REVIEW

Memory elements are inherent components of most modern computer systems, therefore allowing for cost-efficient PUF implementations, especially in resource-constrained devices, such as IoT hardware [7] [8]. Additionally, DRAM PUFs based on the startup values of the DRAM offer a significantly larger amount of entropy than SRAM PUFs because of the much larger size of DRAMs found in most modern computer systems [16]. Moreover, DRAM decay-based PUFs can also offer run-time access to their responses, addressing in this way one of the major shortcomings of the SRAM PUF [9]. Furthermore, the most recent implementation of the DRAM latency-based PUF can offer a significantly lower evaluation time than the DRAM decay-based PUF, therefore making evaluation practical in all cases [10]. Finally, the row hammer PUF is an implementation that can significantly increase the entropy extracted from the decay characteristic of DRAMs [11].

There exists a couple of research related to our work on other types of PUFs. In 2011, Schaumont et al. proposed an identity-mapping function that expands the set of CRPs of a ring-oscillator PUF (RO-PUF) with low area cost. The CRPs generated through this function exhibit strong PUF qualities in terms of uniqueness and reliability [12]. In 2014, Potkonjak et al. proposed a quantized Public PUF (PPUF) and showed that increasing the number of quanta improves the matching probability up to a point, after which the quantization intervals begin to overlap, thereby reducing the matching probability [13]. Authors in [20] proposed a quantization scheme to extract bit strings from the MEMS analog measurements. They provided upper and lower bounds for the minimum entropy of the bit strings derived from the measurements and analyzed the intra- and inter-class distributions across the operation range of the MEMS device. To the best of our knowledge, we are the first group applying quantization technique to DRAM-based PUFs to improve its reliability and entropy.

## 3 DRAM-BASED PUF AND EXPERIMENTAL SETUP

Hardware-based security primitives exploit inherent characteristics of hardware in order to extract entropy, in the form of random and unique outputs, which can be used for the implementation of cryptographic solutions. These outputs can be robust, in which case they can be used for identification and authentication [14], or unstable, in which case they can be used in cryptography as random one-time keys and nonces. Manufacturing variations cause minor imperfections in commodity hardware, such as DRAMs, which can serve to create inherent characteristics in a random and unique way in each individual hardware instance [15]. Therefore, while such imperfections do not affect the correct operation of hardware, they can be exploited for the implementation of security primitives. Researchers have identified a number of inherent characteristics in DRAMs that can be leveraged for the implementation of hardware-based security primitives. In particular, it has been noted that the cells of DRAMs may assume different values at startup [16] in a similar way to SRAM cells. In this case, the startup charge of the capacitor of each individual cell (in a 1T1C DRAM) may be slightly above the Vdd/2 threshold value (Figure 2 (a)-top), or slightly below it (Figure 2 (a)-bottom), a situation that leads to the cell's value being interpreted as logical one or logical zero, respectively, if the cell is a true cell, and vice versa, if the cell is an anti-cell. Figure 2 (a) provides an overview of how voltage moves, in each of the two cases, through the DRAM circuitry presented in Figure 2 (b), when the cells are read. The cells are previously untouched, not having been written by the system or the user.

We collected the data from DRAMs under various environmental operating conditions. There are various parameters that can affect PUF stability, such as PV, PUF activity, temperature, and supply voltage. Others have proposed PUFs that take into account both process and environmental variations such as crosstalk, which magnifies chip-to-chip signature randomness and uniqueness [21]. One of the advantages of our work is the stability evaluation against different operating conditions for more than one DRAM. We did all the experiments for three DRAMs, which we will call them DRAM1, DRAM2, and DRAM3. We explored the differences between reliable and unreliable DRAM cell values and the impact of operating conditions on them. To make a PUF highly reliable across its lifetime, unstable bits that are easily flipped by different operating conditions should not be used.

We used three 1-Mbit HM51100AL CMOS DRAMs [22] in dual in-line package (DIP) packages. Our setup essentially consists of four parts: 1). data acquisition experimental setup, the FPGA-based development board (Spartan 6 FPGA); 2). the power supply and digital storage oscilloscope; 3). the breadboard-based circuit (extension circuit); and 4) the host PC. During data collection, the power supply supplies voltage to the extension circuit (off-chip DRAMs) that is mounted on the breadboard and we check the voltage levels using the oscilloscope. The communication between the host PC and the FPGA is composed of two connections: 1). USB connection, which is used for FPGA configuration download; 2). a high density

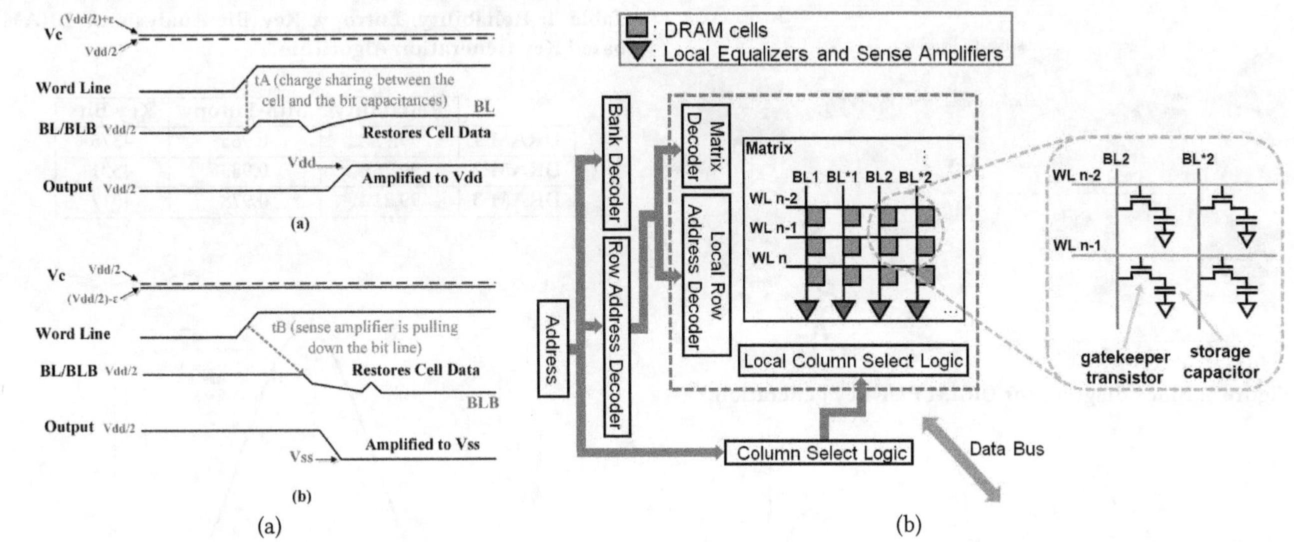


**Figure 2: Timing diagram of a DRAM cell, biased to Vdd (top) or Vss (bottom) at startup (a); DRAM memory cells (b)**

serial connector, which is used for data communication among the PC software, ISE Design Suit 14.7, and the software running on the FPGA (developed using Xilinx EDK). In other words, the FPGA was programmed to control the test sequence supplied to the DRAM chip and transmit the outputs of the DRAM to a computer using an on-board USB-UART module.

# 4 DRAM PUF KEY GENERATION USING QUANTIZATION

## 4.1 Overview of the Proposed Approach

In this paper, we apply a new technique for key generation approach using quantization. Note that the quantized DRAM PUF is based on raw data of DRAMs (startup values-decimal format). The approach has several salient features. First, the most reliable features (startup values of DRAM cells are collected in decimal form) for each DRAM are determined by an enrollment step and only those cells (features) are used for key generation. Note that we only use the cells that are stable under different operating conditions (such as normal condition, high temperature, low temperature, high voltage, low voltage and aging). Additionally, by stable bit we mean the cell bits that do not change under various environmental conditions. In short, the bit cells are selected based on various operating conditions in and across DRAM. Note that this will result in different key lengths per DRAM since the process variation impact is vary from one chip to another. Additionally, next we apply "neighboring bit selection" technique. In details, for DRAM memory cells, we can have a grid for memory rows and columns that can give us a very good picture of the cell distribution in the memory array. Thus, spatial correlations (neighborhood stable cells) can be made in both x- and y-directions. In all, the algorithm uses spatial information within the DRAMs to infer the stability of a bit cell. In other words, stable neighbors provide better reliability than random selection (features are selected). Next, each feature that is selected as reliable can be quantized into one or more bits. This can increase the key length provided there is enough margin to do so. Third, both the reliable DRAM cells and bit length for each feature are stored as helper data to re-generate the key later on. Note that the helper data only specifies the memory cells and does not leak information in our approach. The feature space is quantized in such a way that every possible bit combination is equally likely for a feature. For instance, when quantizing to one bit, the probability of '0' and '1' are equal. When quantizing to two bits, the probability of '00', '01', '11', and '10' are equal.

Figure 3 demonstrates the flow for the registration enrollment and key generation processes in our approach. During enrollment phase, the startup value of DRAM cells is collected using FPGA. Then the feature extraction (in this case DRAM memory cell's value) is used for quantization step. Next, quantization scheme is used to to generate unique, reliable, and high entropy key bits from each DRAM memory. Since the selected memory cells as features may differ from one chip to another, the indices corresponding to the selected features must also be stored as helper data for later use. During reconstruction, an enrolled DRAM chip supplies a startup values of cell to the system. The helper data is used to select the reliable features and quantize them to form the key bits. The key can be used to verify the chip by comparing it to a database in the manufacturer side.

## 4.2 Quantization Scheme and Results

Figure 4 demonstrates the general quantization concept where each feature is converted to one or more bits. It is assumed that samples from the entire DRAM chips are able to characterize the background probability density function (PDF) of every feature. The background PDF is considered Gaussian with zero mean and unit standard deviation, i.e., $\mathcal{N}(0, 1)$. As illustrated in Figure 4, each feature can be quantized based on the number of bins ($b$) selected. In the case of two bins, the feature can be encoded into binary $[0, 1]$ based on which side of the threshold (dash line) it lies. In the case

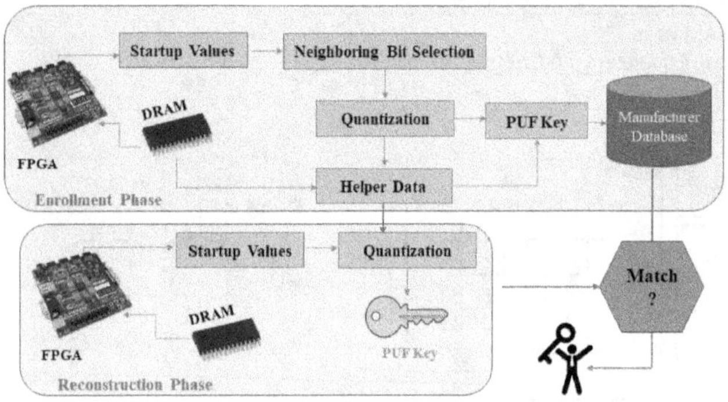


**Figure 3: Block diagram for DRAM PUF key generation.**

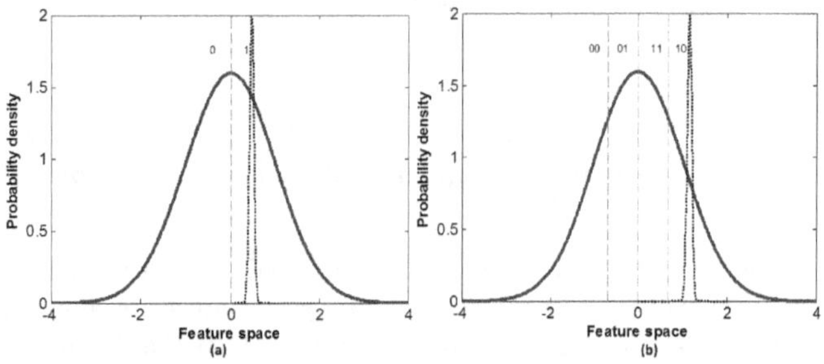


**Figure 4: Fixed quantization boundaries of DRAM features (stable cell's value) for (a) one bit and (b) two bits quantization.**

of four bins, a feature is encoded into [00, 01, 11, 10] and so forth. The solid signal is a visualization of the probability distribution of DRAM cells for among three chips. The dotted signal refers to the probability distribution of the same feature (selected memory cells in DRAMs) under various environmental conditions for a specific DRAM.

While DRAM PUFs have their advantages, keys generated from DRAM may suffer from environment noise, internal instability, and so on. In addition, keys generated from DRAM should be uniformly random (i.e., possess high entropy) in order to remain resistant to attack. In order to overcome these detriments, we have developed a statistical approach to mitigate the intra-subject variance while preserving privacy and generating long keys. Our approach begins with an initialization phase. Startup value are extracted from off chip DRAM from a large population of DRAM memory. Statistics for each startup value are used to determine thresholds and boundaries to quantize the feature into one or more key bits. The number of bits depends on the parameters and statistics, and can vary from DRAM bit cells to another. Boundaries and thresholds for a one-bit quantization are shown in Figure5. The boundaries (B0, B1) and threshold are calculated based on control parameters and the collected statistics. Once these boundaries are determined, users can be enrolled. Since certain features may be reliable for some but unreliable for others, our approach will only use reliable features from each DRAM chip. Thus, the key length per DRAM varies. Reliable features are determined with respect to the thresholds

**Table 1: Reliability, Entropy, Key Bit Analysis of DRAM based Key Generation Algorithm.**

| | Reliability | Min-Entopy | Key Bits |
|---|---|---|---|
| **DRAM 1** | 99.91% | 0.965 | 4376 |
| **DRAM 2** | 99.78% | 0.953 | 4321 |
| **DRAM 3** | 99.21% | 0.978 | 4017 |

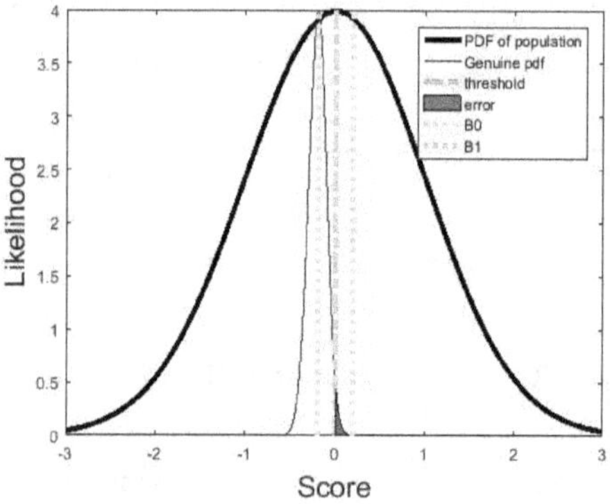


**Figure 5: Proposed DRAM cells selection and key generation.**

obtained during initialization. The DRAM startup value selected for a DRAM memory are stored as helper data for each enrolled DRAM chip. The thresholds and helper data from initialization and enrollment phases are used with the supplied DRAM memory startup value to handle key regeneration at run-time.

We compare the quality of keys generated DRAM 1, DRAM 2 and DRAM 3 by two evaluation criteria: **Reliability**: is the bitwise similarities between enrolled key and regenerated keys; **Min-entropy**: is a randomness indicator. We desire both reliability and entropy close to 1 for a good quality. We present the results in Table 1. As can be seen, DRAM-1 has the highest reliability (99.91%) with entropy rate of 0.965. The reliability of DRAM-2 and DRAM-3 is 99.78% and 99.21% with entropy of 0.953 and 0.978, respectively. Based on our result in Table1, DRAM-1 provides the highest number of key bits as well, 4376. In summary, DRAM 1 provides both the longest key and reliability while DRAM 3 exhibits the highest bit entropy. Although we used this quantization technique on DRAM-based PUF, we have confident that it is applicable for other types of PUFs too.

**Comparison with the previous work:** In [16], we applied a bit selection algorithm to generate the most stable bits among DRAM cells. Our results shows that the maximum reliability we could achieved was around 97.9% for DRAM-1, 97.7% for DRAM-2 and 96.9% for DRAM-3 for 2048 key bits length (16* 128-bit keys). Using the quantization scheme, we were able to improve the result in terms of entropy and entropy to the highest value for more than 4000 key bit length.

## 5 CONCLUSION

In this paper we applied a solution (quantization approach) to the results of our investigation on addressing the challenges related reliability of DRAM PUFs under noisy conditions. In more detail, we apply a new framework for key generation of DRAM PUFs that incorporates statistical information of the memory cells value, their locations and parameters trade off reliability and entropy. This technique is able to quantize the most reliable features of each PUF into more than one bit, thus extending the length of keys possible from DRAM PUF while still balancing entropy and reliability. Our experimental result shows a high reliability and min-entropy rate for relatively large number of DRAM key bits. Through our solution one would know that the keys/IDs produced from a startup value based DRAM PUF is trustworthy and robust. We are confident that this quantization technique is applicable to other types of PUFs.

## REFERENCES

[1] Hassan, Qusay F., and Sajjad A. Madani. Internet of things: Challenges, advances, and applications. Chapman and Hall/CRC, 2017.
[2] Gassend, Blaise, Dwaine Clarke, Marten Van Dijk, and Srinivas Devadas. "Silicon physical random functions." In Proceedings of the 9th ACM conference on Computer and communications security, pp. 148-160. ACM, 2002.
[3] Tehranipoor, Fatemeh, Wei Yan, and John A. Chandy. "Robust hardware true random number generators using DRAM remanence effects." In 2016 IEEE International Symposium on Hardware Oriented Security and Trust (HOST), pp. 79-84. IEEE, 2016.
[4] Tehranipoor, F., Karimian, N., Yan, W. and Chandy, J.A., 2017, May. Investigation of DRAM PUFs reliability under device accelerated aging effects. In 2017 IEEE International Symposium on Circuits and Systems (ISCAS) (pp. 1-4). IEEE.
[5] Xiao, Kan, Md Tauhidur Rahman, Domenic Forte, Yu Huang, Mei Su, and Mohammad Tehranipoor. "Bit selection algorithm suitable for high-volume production of SRAM-PUF." In 2014 IEEE International Symposium on Hardware-Oriented Security and Trust (HOST), pp. 101-106. IEEE, 2014.
[6] Yan, Wei, Fatemeh Tehranipoor, and John A. Chandy. "Puf-based fuzzy authentication without error correcting codes." IEEE Transactions on Computer-Aided Design of Integrated Circuits and Systems 36, no. 9 (2017): 1445-1457
[7] Katzenbeisser, S.; Kocabas, U.; Rozic, V.; Sadeghi, A.R.; Verbauwhede, I.; Wachsmann, C. "PUFs: Myth, Fact or Busted A Security Evaluation of Physically Unclonable Functions (PUFs) Cast in Silicon", In International Workshop on Cryptographic Hardware and Embedded Systems; Springer: Berlin, Germany, 2012; pp. 283301.
[8] Tehranipoor, F.; Karimian, N.;Wortman, P. A.; Haque, A.; Fahrny, J.; Chandy, J. A.; Exploring Methods of Authentication for the Internet of Things. In Internet of Things: Challenges, Advances, and Applications; Hassan, Q.F., Khan, A.R., Madani, S.A., Eds.; CRC Press: Boca Raton, FL, USA, 2017.
[9] Xiong, W.; Schaller, A.; Anagnostopoulos, N.A.; Saleem, M.U.; Gabmeyer, S.; Katzenbeisser, S.; Szefer, J. Run-Time Accessible DRAM PUFs in Commodity Devices. In International Conference on Cryptographic Hardware and Embedded Systems; Springer: Berlin, Germany, 2016; pp. 432453.
[10] Kim, J.S.; Patel, M.; Hassan, H.; Mutlu, O. The DRAM Latency PUF: Quickly Evaluating Physical Unclonable Functions by Exploiting the Latency-Reliability Tradeoff in Modern DRAM Devices. In Proceedings of the 24th International Symposium on High-Performance Computer Architecture (HPCA), Vienna, Austria, 2428 February 2018.
[11] Schaller, A.; Xiong, W.; Anagnostopoulos, N.A.; Saleem, M.U.; Gabmeyer, S.; Katzenbeisser, S.; Szefer, J. Intrinsic Rowhammer PUFs: Leveraging the Rowhammer Effect for Improved Security. In Proceedings of the 2017 IEEE International Symposium on Hardware Oriented Security and Trust (HOST), McLean, VA, USA, 15 May 2017; pp. 17.
[12] Maiti, Abhranil, Inyoung Kim, and Patrick Schaumont. "A robust physical unclonable function with enhanced challenge-response set." IEEE Transactions on Information Forensics and Security 7, no. 1 (2012): 333-345.
[13] Potkonjak, Miodrag, and Vishwa Goudar. "Public physical unclonable functions." Proceedings of the IEEE 102, no. 8 (2014): 1142-1156.
[14] Yan, Wei, Fatemeh Tehranipoor, and John A. Chandy. "A novel way to authenticate untrusted integrated circuits." In Proceedings of the IEEE/ACM International Conference on Computer-Aided Design, pp. 132-138. IEEE Press, 2015.
[15] Anagnostopoulos, N., Katzenbeisser, S., Chandy, J. and Tehranipoor, F., 2018. An Overview of DRAM-Based Security Primitives. Cryptography, 2(2), p.7.
[16] Tehranipoor, Fatemeh, Nima Karimian, Wei Yan, and John A. Chandy. "DRAM-based intrinsic physically unclonable functions for system level security and authentication." IEEE Transactions on Very Large Scale Integration (VLSI) Systems 25, no. 3 (2017): 1085-1097.
[17] Tehranipoor, F., Karimian, N., Xiao, K. and Chandy, J., 2015, May. DRAM based intrinsic physical unclonable functions for system level security. In Proceedings of the 25th edition on Great Lakes Symposium on VLSI (pp. 15-20). ACM.
[18] Anagnostopoulos, Nikolaos Athanasios, Tolga Arul, Yufan Fan, Christian Hatzfeld, Fatemeh Tehranipoor, and Stefan Katzenbeisser. "Addressing the Effects of Temperature Variations on Intrinsic Memory-Based Physical Unclonable Functions." crypto day matters 28 (2018).
[19] Karimian, N., Guo, Z., Tehranipoor, M. and Forte, D., 2017. Highly reliable key generation from electrocardiogram (ECG). IEEE Transactions on Biomedical Engineering, 64(6), pp.1400-1411.
[20] Willers, Oliver, Christopher Huth, Jorge Guajardo, and Helmut Seidel. "MEMS gyroscopes as physical unclonable functions." In Proceedings of the 2016 ACM SIGSAC Conference on Computer and Communications Security, pp. 591-602. ACM, 2016.
[21] X. Wang and M. Tehranipoor, Novel physical unclonable function with process and environmental variations, in Proc. Design, Autom. Test Eur. Conf. Exhibit. (DATE), Mar. 2010, pp. 10651070.
[22] Jameco Part Number 42219, (2015). [Online]. Available: http://www.jameco.com/Jameco/Products/ProdDS/42219.pdf

# Threats on Logic Locking: A Decade Later

Kimia Zamiri Azar, Hadi Mardani Kamali, Houman Homayoun, Avesta Sasan
George Mason University, Fairfax, VA, USA
{kzamiria,hmardani,hhomayou,asasan}@gmu.edu

## ABSTRACT

To reduce the cost of ICs and to meet the market's demand, a considerable portion of manufacturing supply chain, including silicon fabrication, packaging and testing may be pushed offshore. Utilizing a global IC manufacturing supply chain, and inclusion of non-trusted parties in the supply chain has raised concerns over security and trust related challenges including those of overproduction, counterfeiting, IP piracy, and Hardware Trojans to name a few. To reduce the risk of IC manufacturing in an untrusted and globally distributed supply chain, the researchers have proposed various locking and obfuscation mechanisms for hiding the functionality of the ICs during the manufacturing, that requires the activation of the IP after fabrication using the key value(s) that is only known to the IP/IC owner. At the same time, many such proposed obfuscation and locking mechanisms are broken with attacks that exploit the inherent vulnerabilities in such solutions. The past decade of research in this area, has resulted in many such defense and attack solutions. In this paper, we review a decade of research on hardware obfuscation from an attacker perspective, elaborate on attack and defense lessons learned, and discuss future directions that could be exploited for building stronger defenses.

## KEYWORDS

Reverse Engineering, Logic Locking, SAT Attack, SMT Attack

**ACM Reference Format:**
Kimia Zamiri Azar, Hadi Mardani Kamali, Houman Homayoun, Avesta Sasan. 2019. Threats on Logic Locking: A Decade Later. In *Great Lakes Symposium on VLSI 2019 (GLSVLSI '19), May 9–11, 2019, Tysons Corner, VA, USA.* https://doi.org/10.1145/3299874.3319495

## 1 INTRODUCTION

The increasing cost of IC manufacturing has pushed several stages of the semiconductor device's manufacturing supply chain offshore [33]. However, many of these offshore facilities are identified as untrusted entities. Processing and fabrication of ICs in an untrusted supply chain poses a number of challenging security threats such as IP piracy and IC overproduction [14]. To counter these threats, various hardware design-for-trust techniques have been proposed. The term *logic locking, a.k.a.* hardware obfuscation, surfaced in 2008 by EPIC [6], in which a limited programmability was introduced into a netlist by means of inserting additional key programmable gates (KG)s at design time. After fabrication, the functionality of the IC is programmed by loading the correct key values. The key inputs could be stored in, and loaded from, an on-chip tamper-proof memory [21]. The purpose of inserting KGs is to hide the IC's functionality from untrusted foundries. Since the functionality of a design is locked with a secret key, the attacker cannot learn


*GLSVLSI '19, May 9–11, 2019, Tysons Corner, VA, USA*

ACM ISBN 978-1-4503-6252-8/19/05...$15.00
https://doi.org/10.1145/3299874.3319495

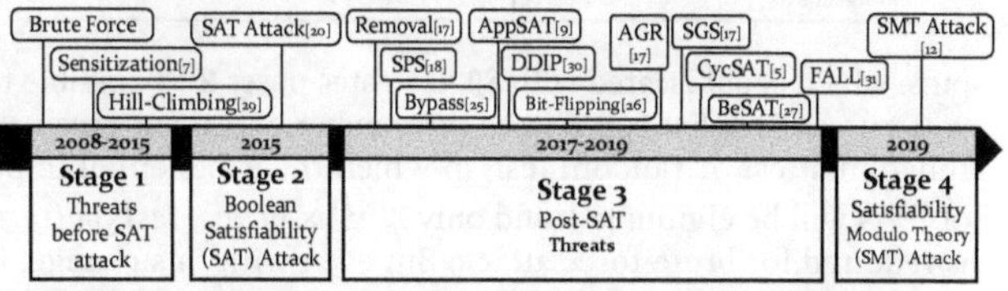


**Figure 1: Categorization of attacks against logic locking schemes.**

the functionality of the locked netlist after reverse engineering. Insertion of $n$ KGs hides the ICs functionality between $2^n$ different circuit possibilities, each generated by a different key. The correct functionality will be recovered when the loaded $n$-bit key is correct.

EPIC, however did not end the threat against IP piracy (or other related concerns), as this solution and many other obfuscation solutions that were proposed over the last decade were broken using various carefully crafted attacks. A decade of research in this area, has resulted in a wide range of defense [1, 3, 4, 7, 8, 10, 13, 15, 16, 19, 23, 24, 28, 32] and attack solutions [2, 5, 7, 9, 12, 17, 18, 20, 22, 25–27, 29–31]. In this paper, we review many of these obfuscation solutions, explain and reviewing most notable attack mechanisms, summarize and compare the effectiveness of obfuscation solutions against these attacks, and describe the strength and weaknesses of various obfuscation and attack solutions. As illustrated in Fig. 1, the defense and attack solutions related to hardware obfuscation, based on functionality, capability, effectiveness and time-line are categorized into four categories: (1) *Test-Inspired Attacks* that were mostly inspired from test concepts and attempted to discover the obfuscation key value based on the location of KGs, described in Section 2. (2) SAT Attack, formulation and revelation of which significantly affected the direction and presumed assumptions of the hardware obfuscation research community, explained in Section 3. (3) Post-SAT Attacks where the focus of hardware security researchers changed to the design of an attack against obfuscation solutions that resist the SAT attack, explained in 4. And (4) SMT Attack as a universal attack platform capable of instantiating many theory solvers to act as pre- post- or co- processors to the SAT solver, described in Section 5. We conclude the paper in Section 6 by summarizing the effectiveness of attacks discussed in this paper and provide a short discussion on new opportunities related to designing secure logic locking solutions.

## 2 STAGE 1: TEST-BASED ATTACKS

### 2.1 Brute Force Attack

The *brute force* attack is the most intuitive attack against obfuscated circuits. This attack exhaustively search for the correct key by testing all key and input values. For instance, assuming that adversary has access to the reverse-engineered netlist, and considering that the circuit has four *PI*s ( $i_{0..4}$) and two *KI*s ($k_{0..1}$), an exhaustive search may result in applying of $2^{2+4} = 64$ test patterns (in the worst case) and checking the output against an activated (functionally correct) chip to verify correctness. Based on the number of primary inputs ($|PI|$) and the number of key bits ($|KI|$), the number of possible test patterns is ($2^{|PI|+|KI|}$). Hence, the search space for a brute force attack is extremely large, making the attack even for small circuits and small number of keys unfeasible in a reasonable amount of time. For example, a small circuit with 20 input

Table 1: Classification of KGs in Sensitization Attack.

| Term | Description | Strategy used by attacker |
|---|---|---|
| **Runs of KGs** | Back-to-Back KGs | Replacing by a Single KG |
| **Isolated KGs** | No Path between KGs | Finding Unique Pattern per KG (Golden Pattern (GP)) |
| **Dominating KGs** | $k1$ is on Every Path between $k0$ and $PO$s | Muting $k0$, Sensitizing $k1$ |
| **Concurrently Mutable Convergent KGs** | Convergent at a Third Gate Both can be Propagated to $PO$s | Muting $k0/k1$, Sensitizing $k1/k0$ |
| **Sequentially Mutable Convergent KGs** | Convergent at a Third Gate One can be Propagated to $PO$s | Determining $k1$ by GP, Update the Netlist, Target $k0$ |
| **Non-Mutable Convergent KGs** | Convergent at a Third Gate None can be Propagated to $PO$s | Brute Force Attack |

pins, which is obfuscated with 80 key gates poses $2^{100}$ possible test pattern. An attacker can reduce the number of test patterns using functional test or random test, in which the exponential impact of $|PI|$s will be eliminated, and only $2^{|KI|} \times (func\_test\_patterns)$ is required for brute force attack. But even with this change, the attack time is exponential with respect to the number of key gates. EPIC [6] used a random KG insertion policy referred to as random logic locking (RLL). Using RLL, EPIC reasoned that by replacing a small percentage of gates (or insertion of KGs), the obfuscation can resist brute force attacks.

## 2.2 Sensitization Attack

After introducing EPIC [6], Rajendran *et al.* [7] proposed a *sensitization* attack, which determines individual key values, in a time linear to the |KI|, by applying patterns that sensitize key values to the output. As its name implies, sensitization of an internal wire (key bit) **L** to an output **O** means that the value of **L** can be propagated to **O** and thus any change on **L** is observable on **O**. After determining an input pattern that propagates the value of the key-bit to the output, the attacker applies the input pattern to a functional IC (An IC activated and programmed with the correct key that could be obtained from market). The correct key value will be propagated to an output by applying this pattern to the functional IC. The attacker observe and record this output as the value of the sensitized key-bit. The propagation of a key-bit to the output is heavily depending on the location of the KGs, hence, they classify KGs based on their location and discuss corresponding attack strategies for each case. The summary of strategies and techniques used in the sensitization attack is reflected in Table 1. To prevent sensitization attack they proposed SLL, in which the KGs are inserted in locations with maximum mutual interference. In SLL the attacker cannot sensitize the key-bit values to a primary output. Similar to SLL, several prior-art methods in the literature, including fault-analysis (FLL), LUT-based locking, etc. [1, 3, 7, 8, 24], tried to maximize the complexity of obfuscation using different KGs replacement strategies.

## 2.3 Random-based Hill-Climbing Attack

Plaza *et al.* [29] developed a new algorithmic attack that uses test patterns and observe responses. Unlike sensitization attack [7], their proposed approach does not require netlist access. They propose a randomized local key-searching algorithm to search the key that can satisfy a subset of correct input/output patterns. The algorithm proposed in [29] is iterative in nature. At first, it selects random value for key bits and then at each iteration, the key bits, which are selected randomly, are toggled one by one. The target is to minimize the frequency of differences between the observed and expected responses. Hence, a random key candidate is gradually improved based on observed test responses. If no solution is found in one iteration, the algorithm resets the key to a new random key value. However, the complexity of this attack quickly increases with increasing number of KGs.

# 3 STAGE 2: SAT ATTACK

In 2015, Subramanyan *et al.* [20] proposed a new and powerful attack using Boolean satisfiability (SAT) solver, called SAT attack,

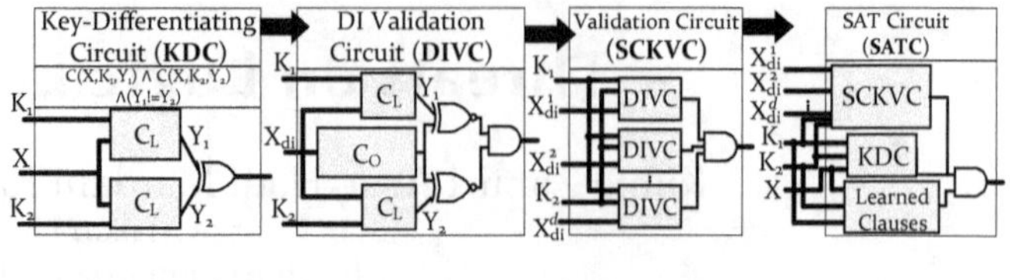


Figure 2: SAT Attack Iterative Flow.

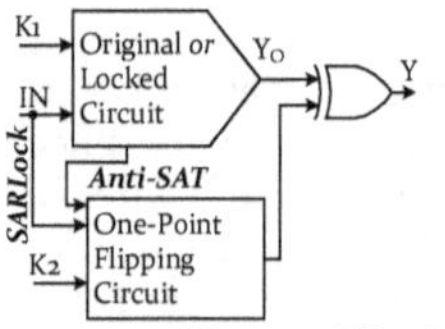


| $Y_O$ | IN | k=0 | k=1 | k=2 | k=3 | k=4 | k=5 | k=6 | k=7 |
|---|---|---|---|---|---|---|---|---|---|
| ✓ | 0 | ✓ | ✓ | ✓ | ✓ | ✗ | ✓ | ✓ | ✓ |
| ✓ | 1 | ✗ | ✓ | ✓ | ✓ | ✓ | ✓ | ✓ | ✓ |
| ✓ | 2 | ✓ | ✓ | ✗ | ✓ | ✓ | ✓ | ✓ | ✓ |
| ✓ | 3 | ✓ | ✓ | ✓ | ✓ | ✓ | ✗ | ✓ | ✓ |
| ✓ | 4 | ✓ | ✓ | ✓ | ✓ | ✓ | ✓ | ✓ | ✓ |
| ✓ | 5 | ✓ | ✓ | ✓ | ✓ | ✓ | ✓ | ✗ | ✓ |
| ✓ | 6 | ✓ | ✓ | ✓ | ✓ | ✓ | ✓ | ✓ | ✗ |
| ✓ | 7 | ✓ | ✓ | ✓ | ✗ | ✓ | ✓ | ✓ | ✓ |

Figure 3: Flipping Structure of SARLock and Anti-SAT.

that effectively and quickly broke all previously proposed logic locking techniques. As an *"oracle-guided"* attack, SAT attack requires a reverse-engineered but locked netlist ($C_L$), and a functionally activated chip ($C_O$). A circuit view of steps taken in a SAT attack is shown in Fig. 2. For this attack, the attacker first replicate the obfuscated circuit and builds a double circuit which is used for finding an input ($X_d[i]$) that for two different key values generates two different outputs. Such input is referred to as Discriminating Input Pattern(DIP). Each $X_d[i]$ is used to create a DI validation circuit (DIVC). The validation circuit, as shown in Fig. 2 assures that for a previously found $X_d[i]$, two different keys generate the same output value. Each iteration of the SAT attack finds a new ($X_d[i]$), and add a new DI validation circuit. The DIVCs are ANDed together to form a Set of Correct Key Validation Circuit (SCKVC). In each iteration, the SAT solver try to find a new $X_d[i]$ and two key values that satisfy the double circuit (KDC) and the Validation Circuit (SCKVC). The key values and the $X_d[i]$, as illustrated in Alg. 1 (line 5), is found by a SAT query. This means the new key generate two different values for the new $X_d[i]$, but generate the same value for all previously found $X_d$s for both key values. This process continues until the SAT solver cannot find a new $X_d[i]$ (line 4). At this point any key that generates the correct output for the set of found $X_d$s is the correct key (line 9).

**Algorithm 1** SAT-based Attack Algorithm [20]

```
1: function SAT_ATTACK(Circuit C_L, Circuit C_O)
2:     i ← 0; F_0 ← C_L(X, K_1, Y_1) ∧ C_L(X, K_2, Y_2);
3:     while SAT(F_i ∧ (Y_1 ≠ Y_2)) do
4:         X_d[i] ← sat_assignment (F_i ∧(Y_1 ≠Y_2)); Y_d[i] ← C_O(X_d[i]);
5:         F_{i+1} ← F_i ∧ C_L(X_d[i], K_1, Y_d[i]) ∧ C_L(X_d[i], K_2, Y_d[i]); i ← i+1;
6:     K* ← sat_assignment_{K_1} (F_i);
```

For all prior obfuscation schemes, even those resistant to sensitization attack, the SAT attack was able to rule out a significant number of key values at each iterations (by finding each DIP). Hence, In order to thwart SAT attack, the first attempted approach was to weaken the strength of the DIPs to reduce its pruning power. SARLock [15] and Anti-SAT [32] were the first prior-art methods that accomplished this. Both SARLock and Anti-SAT engaged one-point flipping function, demonstrated in Fig. 3. Using this obfuscation scheme, each DIP is able to rule out only one incorrect key. Hence, the SAT attack requires to apply all $2^{|KI|}$ to retrieve the correct functionality. However, this method results in obfuscation circuits that for all but one output work as the original circuit, and the output corruption upon application of a wrong key is quite low.

# 4 STAGE 3: POST-SAT ATTACKS

As discussed, the proposed SAT-resilient solutions suffered from low output corruption. This however could have been addressed by combining a SAT-hard solution with a traditional obfuscation solution, such as RLL or SLL, that exhibits high level of output corruption. Although SAT-resilient logic locking schemes provided a defense against SAT attack, researchers found new vulnerabilities associated with this class of obfuscation techniques resulting in the development of many new attacks on the presumed SAT-hard logic locking schemes described in this section.

## 4.1 Removal Attack

As shown in Fig 3, in bare implementation of one-point flipping circuit, the locking circuitry is completely decoupled from the original circuit. A removal attack identifies and removes/bypasses the locking circuitry to retrieve the original circuit and to remove dependence on key values [17]. The removal attack, presented in [17], was used to detect and remove SARLock [15]. In presence of removal attack, researchers investigated SAT-hard solutions that are hard to detect (preventing removal by pure structural analysis), an example of which was Anti-SAT [32].

## 4.2 Signal Probability Skew (SPS) Attack

The Signal Probability Skew (SPS) attack [18] leverages the structural traces in Anti-SAT block to identify and isolate the Anti-SAT block [32]. *Signal probability skew* (SPS) of a signal $x$ is defined as $s = P_r[x = 1] - 0.5$, where $P_r[x = 1]$ indicates the probability that signal $x$ is 1. The range of $s$ is $[-0.5, 0.5]$. If the SPS of signal $x$ is closer to zero, an attacker have lower chance of guessing the signal value by random. For a 2-input gate, the signal probability skew is the difference between the signal probability of its input wires. The flipping-circuit in the Anti-SAT is constructed using two complementary circuits, $g$ and $\overline{g}$, in which the number of input vectors that make the function $g$ equal to 1 ($p$) is either close to 1 or $2^n - 1$. These two complementary circuits converge at an AND gate $G$. Considering this structure, the *absolute difference of the signal probability skew* (ADS) of the inputs of gate $G$ is quite large, noting that the SAT resilience is ensured by this skewed $p$. Algorithm 2 shows the SPS attack, which identifies the Anti-SAT block's output by computing signal probabilities and searching for the skew(s) of arriving signals to a gate in a given netlist.

**Algorithm 2** SPS Attack Algorithm [18]

```
function SPS_ATTACK(Circuit C_L)
    ADS_arr ← {};
    for each gate ∈ C_L do
        ADS_arr(gate_i) ← Compute_ADS(C_L, gate_i);
    G ← Find_Maximum(ADS_arr);
    Y ← Find_value_from_skew(G);          ▷ Correct value of Anti_SAT output
    C_Lock ← remove_TFI(C_L, G, Y);       ▷ Transitive FanIn of the gate G
    return C_Lock                         ▷ C_Lock: C_L after removing Anti_SAT block
```

## 4.3 Bypass Attack

Although SARLock and Anti-SAT break the SAT attack, their respective output corruptibility is very low if they are not mixed with traditional logic locking, such as SLL. Observing and relying on the very low level of output corruption in such SAT-hard solutions, the bypass attack [25] was introduced. The bypass attack instantiates two copies of the obfuscated netlist using two randomly selected keys, and build a miter circuit that evaluates to 1 only when the output of two circuits is different. The miter circuit is then fed to a SAT solver looking for such inputs. The SAT returns with minimum of two inputs for which the outputs are different. These input patterns are tested using an activated IC (golden IC) validating the correct output. Then a bypass circuit is constructed using a comparator that is stitched to the primary output of the netlist which is unlocked using the selected random key, to retrieve the correct functionality if that input pattern is applied. The Bypass attack works well when the SAT-hard solution is not mixed with traditional logic locking mechanism since its overhead increases very quickly as output corruption of logic locking increases. This observation motivated researchers to look at possibilities of approximate attacks to retrieve the key values associated to non SAT-hard obfuscation solutions that are mixed with SAT-hard solutions.

## 4.4 AppSAT Attack

So far, defences solution to mitigate the SAT attack, are based on the assumption that the attacker needs an exact attack on logic locking. However, Shamsi *et al.* [9] proposed a new attack (AppSAT), which relax this constraint. AppSAT shown in Algorithm 3, is an approximate attack on logic locking based on the SAT attack and random testing. The authors use *probably-approximate-correct* (PAC) model for formulating approximate learning problem. The exact SAT attack continues to find DIPs until no more DIPs can be found. However, the AppSAT will be terminated in any early step in which the error falls below the certain limit. If this condition happens, the key value will be considered as an approximate key with specified error rate; otherwise, the random sampling that resulted in a disagreement will be added to a SAT formula as a new constraint. In AppSAT, heuristic methods for estimating the error is used for large functions, to avoid any computation complexity.

## 4.5 Double-DIP Attack

Double-DIP [30] is another approximate attack, shown in Algorithm 4. Double-DIP is an extension of SAT attack in which during each iteration, the discriminating input should eliminate at least two wrong keys. To illustrate its effectiveness, researchers used double-DIP to target SARLock+SSL, representing a compound of SAT-hard and high output corruption obfuscation. When the double-DIP attack terminates, the key of the traditional logic locking (SSL) is guaranteed to be correct. As a result, the compound logic locking will be reduced to a single SAT attack resilient technique, that could then be attacked using bypass attack.

**Algorithm 3** AppSAT Attack Algorithm [9]

```
function APPSAT_ATTACK(Circuit C_L, Circuit C_O)
    i ← 0; F_0 ← C_L(X, K_1, Y_1) ∧ C_L(X, K_2, Y_2);
    while SAT(F_i ∧ (Y_1 ≠ Y_2)) do
        X_d[i] ← sat_assignment (F_i∧(Y_1 ≠Y_2)); Y_d[i] ← C_O(X_d[i]);
        F_{i+1} ← F_i ∧ C_L(X_d[i], K_1, Y_d[i]) ∧ C_L(X_d[i], K_2, Y_d[i]); i ← i+1;
        every n rounds do
        for each (x ∈ Random Patterns) do
            if C_L(X, K_1, Y) ≠ C_O(X) then
                FailedPatterns ← FailedPatterns + 1;
                F_{i+1} ← F_{i+1} ∧ (C_L(X, K_1, Y) = C_O(X)); i ← i+1;
        if error < ErrorThreshold then
            return K_1 as an approximate key
    K* ← sat_assignment_{K_1} (F_i);
```

**Algorithm 4** Double-DIP Attack Algorithm [30]

```
function DOUBLEDIP_ATTACK(Circuit C_L, Circuit C_O)
    i ← 0; F_0 ← C_L(X, K_1, Y_1) ∧ C_L(X, K_2, Y_2) ∧ C_L(X, K_3, Y_1) ∧ C_L(X, K_4, Y_2);
    while SAT(F_i ∧ (Y_1 ≠ Y_2)) ∧ (K_1 ≠ K_3)) ∧ (K_2 ≠ K_4)) do
        X_d[i] ← sat_assignment (F_i∧(Y_1 ≠Y_2)) ∧ (K_1 ≠ K_3)) ∧ (K_2 ≠ K_4));
        Y_d[i] ← C_O(X_d[i]);
        F_{i+1} ← F_i ∧_{j=1}^{4} C_L(X_d[i], K_j, Y_d[i]); i ← i+1;
    K* ← sat_assignment_{K_1} (F_i);
```

## 4.6 Bit-Flipping Attack

The Bit-flipping attack [26] is yet another attack against compound logic locking schemes in which a SAT-hard solution such as SARLock is combined with a traditional logic locking to guarantee both high error rates and resilience to the SAT-based attack. In Bit-flipping attack, the keys are first separated into two groups ($k_1$ and $k_2$) by counting DIPs for two keys with hamming distance equal to one. The attack is motivated from the observation that in traditional logic locking, wrong key causes substantial wrong input-output pattern. However, the error rate of bit-flipping function is usually very small. As shown in Algorithm 5, after separation of keys, this attack fixes SAT-resilient keys, $k_2$, as a random number, and uses a SAT solver to find the correct key values for $k_1$. After finding $k_1$, the bypass attack is applied to retrieve the original circuit.

**Algorithm 5** Bit-flipping Attack Algorithm [26]

```
function BITFLIPPING_ATTACK(Circuit C_L, Circuit C_O)
    for each j < Fixed-iteration do
        K_A ← a random key;
        for each bit b ∈ K_A do
            K_B ← K_A while bit b flipped;
            i ← 0; F_0 ← C_L(X, K_A, Y_A) ∧ C_L(X, K_B, Y_B);
            while SAT(F_i ∧ (Y_A ≠ Y_B)) do
                X_d[i] ← sat_assignment (F_i∧(Y_A ≠Y_B));
                F_{i+1} ← F_i ∧ (X ≠ X_d[i]); i ← i+1;
                if i > Threshold then
                    b is in K_1,
                    break;
        j ← j + 1;
    K_2 ← all key bits / K_1;          ▷ Seperation is Done. Then, fix K_2 as a random number.
    K_1 ← SAT_ATTACK (C_L, C_O);                        ▷ Find Traditional Keys using SAT.
    C*_L ← update_netlist(C_L | K_1)
    return (BYPASS_ATTACK(C*_L));
```

## 4.7 AppSAT Guided Removal Attack

AppSAT Guided Removal (AGR) attack targets compound logic locking, particularly Anti-SAT + traditional logic locking [17]. This attack integrates AppSAT with a simple structural analysis of the locked netlist (a post-processing steps). Unlike AppSAT, the AGR attack recovers the correct key. In this attack, first the AppSAT is used to find the key of the traditional obfuscation scheme (used as a part of compound lock). Then, AGR targets the remaining key bits belong to the SAT-resilient logic locking, such as Anti-SAT block, through a simple structural analysis. As shown in Algorithm 6, in the post-processing steps, AGR finds the gate ($G$) at which most of the Anti-SAT key bits converge. AGR finds $G$ by tracing the transitive fanout of the Anti-SAT key inputs, where all the Anti-SAT key bits converge. The ratio of key bits converging at each of the inputs of the gate $G$, are close to 0.5, which is shown as the *selected property* in line 7 of Algorithm 6. AGR identifies the candidates for gate $G$ by checking this property for all gates in the circuit, and then sort these candidate based on the number of key inputs that converge at a gate and pick the gate $G$ from all candidates, which has the most number of key inputs converge to that gate. Then the attacker re-synthesize the design with the constant value for the output of $G$ gate and retrieving the correct functionality.

**Algorithm 6** AGR Attack Algorithm [17]

```
1:  function AGR_ATTACK(Circuit C_L, Circuit C_O)
2:      #Cand ← num_gates(C_L)
3:      while (#Cand > 1 and !Timeout) do
4:          AppSAT_Attack();                                              ▷ 4 times
5:          Candidates ← {};
6:          for each gate ∈ C_L do
7:              if gate_i has the selected property then
8:                  Candidates ← Candidates + 1;
9:      G ← Find_Max_key_count(Candidates);
10:     C_Lock ← remove_TFI(C_L, G);          ▷ remove Transitive FanIn of the gate G
11:     return C_Lock;                   ▷ C_Lock: C_L after removing Anti_SAT block
```

## 4.8 Sensitization Guided SAT Attack

While the one-point flipping circuit in Anti-SAT and SARLock are completely decoupled from the original netlist, Li *et al.* [13] proposed the AND-tree Insertion (ATI), as a SAT-resilient logic locking, which embeds AND trees inside the original netlist. It not only makes all aforementioned attack less effective, it also decreases the implementation overhead. Additionally, the input of AND-tree are camouflaged by inserting INV/BUF camouflaged gates, which can be replaced with the XOR/XNOR gates in order to lock the AND-tree. However, this defense was broken by a new attack that

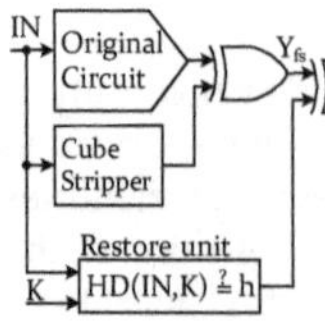


| $Y_{fs}$ | IN | k=0 | k=1 | k=2 | k=3 | k=4 | k=5 | k=6 | k=7 |
|---|---|---|---|---|---|---|---|---|---|
| ✓ | 0 | ✓ | ✓ | ✓ | ✓ | ✗ | ✓ | ✓ | ✓ |
| ✓ | 1 | ✗ | ✓ | ✓ | ✓ | ✓ | ✓ | ✓ | ✓ |
| ✓ | 2 | ✓ | ✓ | ✗ | ✓ | ✓ | ✓ | ✓ | ✓ |
| ✓ | 3 | ✓ | ✓ | ✓ | ✓ | ✓ | ✗ | ✓ | ✓ |
| ✗ | 4 | ✗ | ✓ | ✗ | ✗ | ✗ | ✗ | ✗ | ✗ |
| ✓ | 5 | ✓ | ✓ | ✓ | ✓ | ✓ | ✓ | ✗ | ✓ |
| ✓ | 6 | ✓ | ✓ | ✓ | ✓ | ✓ | ✓ | ✓ | ✗ |
| ✓ | 7 | ✓ | ✓ | ✓ | ✗ | ✓ | ✓ | ✓ | ✓ |

**Figure 4: SFLL-HD while $h = 0$.**

was coined as Sensitization Guided SAT (SGS) attack [17]. The SGS attack is carried out in two stages: (1) *sensitization* that exploits bias in input patterns which allows an attacker to apply only a subset of DIPs, i.e., those that bring unique values to the AND-tree inputs. (2) *SAT attack* using the patterns discovered in the first stage.

## 4.9 Functional Analysis Attack

Aiming to provide a defense that resists all previously formulated attacks led to the introduction of Stripped-Functionality Logic Locking (SFLL) [16]. In SFLL the original circuit is modified for at-least one input pattern (cube) using a *cube stripping unit*, demonstrated in Fig. 4. As shown, $Y_{fs}$ is the output of the stripped circuit, in which the output corresponding to at-least one input pattern is flipped. The restore unit not only generates the flip signal for one input pattern per each wrong key, it also restores the stripped output, (e.g. $IN = 4$ in Fig. 4) to recover the correct functionality on $Y$. Note that applying removal attack on restore unit recovers $Y_{fs}$, which is not the correct functionality. In addition, SFLL-HD is able to protect $\binom{k}{h}$ input patterns that are of Hamming Distance (HD) $h$ from the $k$-bit secret key, and accordingly uses Hamming Distance checker as a restore unit (e.g. $h = 0$ in Fig. 4 is also called TTLock [19]).

Although SFLL was resilient against all previously formulated attacks, it was exploited using a newly formulated attack, called Functional Analysis on Logic Locking (FALL) attack [31]. In this attack model, the adversary is assumed to be a malicious foundry that knows the locking algorithm and its parameters, e.g. $h$ in SFLL-HD. A FALL attack is carried out in three main stages and relies on structural and functional analyses to determine potential key values of a locked circuit. First, FALL attack tries to find all nodes which are the results of comparing an input value with a key input. It is done by a comparator identification. Such nodes ($nodes_{RU}$), which contains these particular comparators, are very likely to be part of the functionality restoration unit. The set of all inputs that appear in these comparators, should be in the fan-in cone of the cube stripping unit. Then, it finds a set of all gates whose fan-in-cone is identical to the members of $nodes_{RU}$. This set of gates must contain the output of the cube stripping unit. Second, the attacker applies functional analysis on the candidate nodes suggested by and collected from the first stage to identify suspected key values. Broadly speaking, the attacker uses functional properties of the cube stripping function used in SFLL, to determines the values of the keys. Based on the author's view, this function has three specific properties. So, they have proposed three attacks algorithms on SFLL, which exploit unateness and Hamming distance properties of the cube stripping functions. The input of these algorithm is circuit node $c$, that computed from the first stage, and the algorithm checks if $c$ behaves as a Hamming distance calculator in the cube stripping unit of SFLL-HD. If the attack is successful, the return value is the protected cube. Third, they have proposed a SAT-based key confirmation algorithm using a list of suspected key values and I/O oracle access, that verifies whether one of the suspected key values computed from the second stage, is correct.

## 4.10 CycSAT Attack

Considering the strength of all previously formulated attacks, some of the researchers started seeking solutions that fundamentally violated the assumptions of these attacks with respect to the nature of locked circuits. One of such attempts was the introduction of cyclic logic locking [10][23], was first proposed in [10]. In this obfuscation technique each deliberately established cycle is designed to have more than one way to open. The requirement for having more than one way to open each cycle assures that even if the original netlist has no cycle by itself, the cycles remains irreducible by means of structural analysis. The cyclic obfuscation resulted in an obfuscation with high level of output corruption, while it was able to break the SAT attack either by 1) trapping it in an infinite loop, or 2) forcing it to exit with a wrong key depending on weather the introduced cycles make the circuit stateful or oscillating.

The promise of secure cyclic obfuscation was shortly after broken by CycSAT attack [5]. In CycSAT, the key combinations that result in formation of cycles are found in a pre-processing step. These conditions are then translated into problem augmenting CNF formulas, denoted as cycle avoidance clauses, satisfaction of which guarantee no cycle in the netlist. The cycle avoidance clauses are then added to the original SAT circuit CNF and the SAT attack is executed. The validity of this attack, however, was challenged in [23], as researchers illustrated that the pre-processing time for CycSAT attack is linearly dependent on the number of cycles in the netlist. Hence, by building an exponential relation between the number of feedback, and the number of cycles in the design, the pre-processing step of CycSAT will face exponential runtime.

### 4.11 Behavioral SAT (BeSAT) Attack

Inability to analyze all cycles in the prepossessing step of CycSAT results in missing cycles in the pre-processing step of CycSAT, leading to building a statefull or oscillating circuit, trapping the SAT stage of the CycSAT attack. BeSAT [27] remedies this shortcoming by augmenting the CycSAT attack with a run-time behavioral analysis. As shown in Algorithm 7, by performing behavioral analysis at each SAT iteration, BeSAT detects repeated DIPs when the SAT is trapped in an infinite loop. Also, when SAT cannot find any new DIP, a ternary-based SAT is used to verify the returned key as a correct one, preventing the SAT from exiting with an invalid key.

**Algorithm 7** BeSAT Attack on Cyclic Locked Circuits [27]

```
function BeSAT_Attack(Circuit C_L, Circuit C_O)
    W = (w_0, w_1, ...w_m) ← FindFeedback(C_L);
    for each (w_i ∈ W) do
        F(w_i, w'_i) ← no_ structural_ path(w_i);
    i ← 0; NC(K)=∧_{i=0}^{m} F(w_i, w'_i)
    C*_L(X, K, Y) ← C_L(X, K, Y) ∧ NC(K); F_0 ← C*_L(X, K_1, Y_1) ∧ C*_L(X, K_2, Y_2);
    while SAT(F_i ∧ (Y_1 ≠ Y_2)) do
        X_d[i] ← sat_assignment (F_i ∧(Y_1 ≠Y_2)); Y_d[i] ← C_O(X_d[i]);
        F_{i+1} ← F_i ∧ C_L(X_d[i], K_1, Y_d[i]) ∧ C_L(X_d[i], K_2, Y_d[i]);
        if (X_d[i] in DIP) and (C_L(X_d[i], K_1) ≠ Y_d[i])) then
            F_{i+1} ← F_{i+1} ∧ (K_1 ≠ K̂_1) ∧ (K_2 ≠ K̂_1);
        else if (X_d[i] in DIP) and (C_L(X_d[i], K_2) ≠ Y_d[i]) then
            F_{i+1} ← F_{i+1} ∧ (K_1 ≠ K̂_2) ∧ (K_2 ≠ K̂_2);
        i ← i+1;
    while SAT_{K_1}(F_i) do                                  ▹ Correct Key: K̂_c
        if Ternary_SAT(F_i, K_c) then
            F_i ← F_i ∧ (K_1 ≠ K̂_c)
        else
            K* ← K̂_c; break;
```

## 5 STAGE 4: SMT ATTACK

As discussed previously, many of the attacks proposed at post-SAT attack stage were formulated by adding a pre-processing step to the original SAT attack, and/or extending the SAT attack to co-process and check additional features in each iteration. In other terms, to break many of the post-SAT era obfuscation techniques, attackers relied on compound attacks by combining SAT solvers by pre-processors (e.g. in CycSAT) and co-processors (e.g. in BeSAT) to extend its modeling reach. Motivated by this trend, the need for having pre- co- and post- processors along with a SAT solver in an attack was realized and addressed in [12] and a new and extremely powerful attack, coined as Satisfiability Module Theory (SMT) attack was introduced. The strength of SMT attack, as the superset of SAT attack, comes from its ability to combine SAT and Theory solvers. The SMT attack could be invoked with any number and combination of theory solvers, and a SAT solver, which allow the attacker to express constraints that are difficult or even impossible to express using CNF, including timing, delay, power, arithmetic, graph and many other first-order theories in general. To showcase the modeling capability of SMT attack, the authors used the SMT attack 1) to break a new breed of obfuscation that relied on locking the delay information in netlist (by generating setup and hold violations), 2) to formulate an accelerated attack (to reduce the attack time) with means of approximate exit (if trapped with SAT hard solutions).

In pursuit of obfuscation schemes that could not be attacked by SAT motivated attackers, some researchers tried to extend the locking mechanism to aspects of a circuit's function that cannot be translated to CNF. For example, Xie *et al.* proposed a timing obfuscation scheme, denoted as delay logic locking (DLL), in [28]. The Goal of DLL obfuscation scheme is introducing setup and hold violation if the correct key is not applied. In this case, the obfuscation attempts to change both logical and behavioral (timing) properties. A functionally-correct but timing-incorrect key will result in timing violations, leading to circuit malfunctions. Considering that timing is not translatable to CNF, the SAT solver remains oblivious to the keys used for timing obfuscation. Authors in [12], however, illustrated that the SMT attack could easily deploy a graph theory solver, provide timing constraints to the theory solver (in terms of required min and max delay to meet the hold and setup time), and use the theory solver in parallel with the internal SAT solver to break both logic and delay obfuscation. They additionally show that the theory solver could be initiated as a pre-processor (Eager SMT approach) or as a co-processor (Lazy SMT approach) to break the same problem, showcasing the strength of SMT attack. The *lazy* mode of this attack is illustrated in Algorithm 8. Although at about the same time Chakraborty proposed TimingSAT to attack the DLL [2], similar to many prior SAT-based attack, it was by deploying a pre-processor for analysis of graph timing, and generating helper clauses for the subsequent call to the SAT attack.

**Algorithm 8** SMT Attack on DLL (Lazy Approach) [12]

```
function SMTLazy_Attack(Circuit C_L, Circuit C_O)
    C*_L ← toBOOLEAN(C_L);                             ▹ Replace TDK with Buffer
    i ← 0; F ← C*_L(X, K_1, Y_1) ∧ C*_L(X, K_2, Y_2);
    G*_L ← toGRAPH(C_L);                               ▹ Wires = Edges, Gates = Vertices
    F_T ← GenTCE(G*_L)                                 ▹ Theory Learned Clauses
    F_SMT ← F ∧ F_T;                                   ▹ SMT Clauses
    while SMT(F_SMT) do                                ▹ X_d[i], K_1, K_2, CC
        Y_d[i] ← C_O(X_d[i]); F ← F ∧ C*_L(X_d[i], K_1, Y_d[i]) ∧ C*_L(X_d[i], K_2, Y_d[i]);
        F_SMT ← F ∧ CC; i ← i+1;
    K* ← smt_assignment_{K_1}(F_SMT);
```

```
    function GenTCE(Graph G*_L)
        Inputs ← find_start_points(G*_L); Outputs ← find_end_points(G*_L); T_CE(K) ← [];
        for each ((Sp, Ep) ∈ (Inputs, outputs)) do
            Upper(Sp,Ep)(K) ← !(distance_leq(Sp, Ep, t_cd));      ▹ Hold Violation
            Lower(Sp,Ep)(K) ← distance_leq(Sp, Ep, t_p);          ▹ Setup Violation
            Range(Sp,Ep)(K) ← Lower(Sp,Ep)(K) ∧ Upper(Sp,Ep)(K);
            T_CE(K) ← T_CE(K) ∪ Range(Sp,Ep)(K);
        return T_CE(K)
```

The ability of SMT solver to instantiate and integrate different theory solver makes it a suitable attack platform for modeling and formulating very strong attacks. As an example of the strength of SMT attack, the authors in [12] formulated and presented an accelerated SMT attack with ability of detecting the presence of SAT-hard obfuscation and switching to an accelerated approximate attack. As shown in Algorithm 9, this was done by invoking a *BitVector* theory solver to constrain the SMT solver for finding keys that result in highest output corruption first. This could be done by constraining the required HD between the output of double circuit when two different keys for the same discriminating input is being tested. The required HD starts from a large value, and every time that the SMT solver return UNSAT, the constraint is relaxed until HD of 1 is reached. This leads to the guaranteed discovery of keys for traditional logic locking first. After $N$ tries (*Rep* in Algorithm 9) for HD of 1, the SMT attack exits, notes that there exist a SAT-hard obfuscation, which now could be addressed by the Bypass attack.

**Algorithm 9** Accelerated SMT Attack on Compound Locking [12]

```
function AccSMT_Attack(Circuit C_L, Circuit C_O)
    i ← 0; HD_h ← sizeof(output); HD_l ← HD_h - 1;
    TimeOut ← 20; Rep ← 20; HD_R ← 1; R_cnt ← 0;
    C*_L ← toBOOLEAN(C_L);                                  ▷ Everything is Boolean.
    F ← C*_L(X, K1, Y1) ∧ C*_L(X, K2, Y2);
    BV*_L ← toBITVECTOR(C_L);                          ▷ Define BITVECTOR on output.
    BVs*_L(X, K1, K2) ← ONEs(BV*_L(X, K1) ⊕ BV*_L(X, K2));
    F_T ← (BVs*_L(X, K1, K2) ⩾ HD_l) ∧ (BVs*_L(X, K1, K2) ⩽ HD_h);
    F_SMT ← F ∧ F_T;                                                ▷ SMT Clauses
    while HD_l ⩾ 1 do
        while SMT(F_SMT | TimeOut) do                          ▷ X_d[i], K1, K2, CC
            Y_d[i] ← C_O(X_d[i]);
            F ← F ∧ C*_L(X_d[i], K1, Y_d[i]) ∧ C*_L(X_d[i], K2, Y_d[i]); F_SMT ← F ∧ CC;
            if HD_l ⩽ HD_R then
                if R_cnt == Rep then
                    break;
                R_cnt++;
        HD_l--;
    K* ← smt_assignment_K1(F_SMT);
```

## 6 DISCUSSION & OPPORTUNITIES

Table 2 compares the effectiveness of the attacks discussed in this paper against most notable obfuscation schemes. As illustrated the combination of FALL, Bypass and SMT attack can break all existing solutions, pointing us to a need for a new direction for generating non-bypassable SMT hard obfuscation solutions. The dilemma is that SAT-hard solutions have extremely low output corruption, and are prone to Bypass, FALL, Removal and SPS attack. On the other hand, the traditional logic locking schemes have high output corruption, but could be easily broken with SAT/SMT attack. The compound logic locking solutions that combine the SAT-hard solutions for resistance against SAT and SMT attack, and traditional logic locking for resistance against Bypass, FALL, Removal and SPS attack are also prone to approximate SAT and SMT attacks. What is really desired, is a SMT-hard logic locking scheme with high degree of output corruption. As a step in this direction, few very recent research papers have focused on increasing the execution time of each SAT/SMT iteration rather than the total execution time [4, 11]. The Full-Lock in [4] is argued that the strength of SAT/SMT solvers come from their *Conflict-Driven Clause Learning* (CDCL) ability, which is resulted by recursively calling *Davis-Putnam-Logemann-Loveland* (DPLL) algorithm. Hence, the Full-Lock creates an obfuscation method that results in very deep recursive call trees. They argue that the SAT/SMT attack execution time can be expresses by formula 1, in which $N$ denotes the number of iterations (DIPs) of the SAT/SMT attack, $T_{DPLL}(\Phi)$ is the execution time of recursive calls for DPLL algorithm on CNF $\Phi$, and $t$ is the execution time of the remaining book keeping code executed at each iteration.

$$T_{Attack} = \sum_{i=1}^{N} T(i) = \sum_{i=1}^{N} (t + T_{DPLL}(\Phi)) = \sum_{i=1}^{N}\sum_{j=1}^{M} (T_{DPLL}^{Avg}) \simeq MN \times T_{DPLL}^{Avg} \quad (1)$$

Authors argue that $M$ in formula 1 denotes the number of recursive DPLL calls. Accordingly, the execution time of SAT attack could also become unfeasible by building an exponential relation between the percentage gate inserted (area overhead) and M. The strong aspect of this alternative solution is that (1) the problems posed at each iteration of SAT/SMT attack is a SAT-hard problem, (2) the output corruption of this methods is significantly higher than obfuscating solution relying on increasing the $N$, (3) it is not susceptible to SPS, removal, bypass, approximate attack, to name a few. The hardness of SAT/SMT attack in the solution posed by Full-Lock cannot be assessed/formulated similar to that of SFLL. Moving towards this new direction for generating SAT-hard problems with high level of output corruption can be generalized more, where an obfuscation solution in this direction can engineer the number of recursive calls, pushing the number of recursive call to be an exponential function of added gates counts (area overhead).

**Table 2: Comparison of proposed attacks/defenses.**

| Attacks \ Defenses | RLL [6] | FLL [8] | SLL [7] | Anti-SAT [32] | SARLock [15] | Compound [15] | SFLL [16] | Cyclic [10] | SRCLock [23] | DLL [28] |
|---|---|---|---|---|---|---|---|---|---|---|
| **Brute Force** | ✗ | ✗ | ✗ | ✗ | ✗ | ✗ | ✗ | ✗ | ✗ | ✗ |
| **Sensitization[7]** | ✓ | ✓ | ✗ | ✗ | ✗ | ✗ | ✗ | ✗ | ✗ | ✗ |
| **Hill-Climbing[29]** | ✓ | ✓ | ✗ | ✗ | ✗ | ✗ | ✗ | ✗ | ✗ | ✗ |
| **SAT[20]** | ✓ | ✓ | ✓ | ✗ | ✗ | ✗ | ✗ | ✗ | ✗ | ✗ |
| **SPS+Removal[17][18]** | ✗ | ✗ | ✗ | ✓ | ✓ | ✗ | ✗ | ✗ | ✗ | ✗ |
| **Bypass[25]** | ✗ | ✗ | ✗ | ✓ | ✓ | ✗ | ✗ | ✗ | ✗ | ✗ |
| **AppSAT[9]** | ✓ | ✓ | ✓ | ✗ | ✗ | P | ✗ | ✗ | ✗ | ✗ |
| **Double-DIP[30]** | ✓ | ✓ | ✓ | ✗ | ✗ | P | ✗ | ✗ | ✗ | ✗ |
| **Bit-Flipping[26]** | ✓ | ✓ | ✓ | ✓ | ✓ | ✓ | ✗ | ✗ | ✗ | ✗ |
| **AGR[17]** | ✓ | ✓ | ✓ | ✓ | ✓ | ✓ | ✗ | ✗ | ✗ | ✗ |
| **FALL[31]** | ✗ | ✗ | ✗ | ✗ | ✗ | ✗ | ✓ | ✗ | ✗ | ✗ |
| **CycSAT[5]** | ✓ | ✓ | ✓ | ✗ | ✗ | ✗ | ✗ | ✓ | ✗ | ✗ |
| **BeSAT[27]** | ✓ | ✓ | ✓ | ✗ | ✗ | ✗ | ✗ | ✓ | ✗ | ✗ |
| **TimingSAT[2]** | ✓ | ✓ | ✓ | ✗ | ✗ | ✗ | ✗ | ✗ | ✗ | ✓ |
| **SMT[12]** | ✓ | ✓ | ✓ | ✗ | ✗ | P | ✗ | ✓ | ✓ | ✓ |

✓: Attack Success, ✗: Fail to Attack, **P**: Only removes the key to the traditional locking in Compound Defense.

## REFERENCES

[1] A. Baumgarten *et al.* 2010. Preventing IC piracy using reconfigurable logic barriers. *IEEE Design & Test of Computers* 27, 1 (2010), 66–75.

[2] A. Chakraborty *et al.* 2018. TimingSAT: timing profile embedded SAT attack. In *ICCAD*. 6.

[3] H. M. Kamali *et al.* 2018. LUT-lock: A novel LUT-based logic obfuscation for FPGA-bitstream and ASIC-hardware protection. In *ISVLSI*. 405–410.

[4] H. M. Kamali *et al.* 2019. Full-Lock: Hard Distributions of SAT Instances for Obfuscating Circuits using Fully Configurable Logic and Routing Blocks. In *DAC*. 6.

[5] H. Zhou *et al.* 2017. CycSAT: SAT-based attack on cyclic logic encryptions. In *ICCAD*. 49–56.

[6] J. Roy *et al.* 2010. Ending piracy of integrated circuits. *Computer* 43, 10 (2010), 30–38.

[7] J. Rajendran *et al.* 2012. Security analysis of logic obfuscation. In *DAC*. 83–89.

[8] J. Rajendran *et al.* 2015. Fault analysis-based logic encryption. *IEEE Trans. on Comp.* 64, 2 (2015), 410–424.

[9] K. Shamsi *et al.* 2017. AppSAT: Approximately deobfuscating integrated circuits. In *HOST*. 95–100.

[10] K. Shamsi *et al.* 2017. Cyclic obfuscation for creating sat-unresolvable circuits. In *GLSVLSI*. 173–178.

[11] K. Shamsi *et al.* 2018. Cross-Lock: Dense Layout-Level Interconnect Locking using Cross-bar Architectures. In *GLSVLSI*. 147–152.

[12] K. Z. Azar *et al.* 2019. SMT Attack: Next Generation Attack on Obfuscated Circuits with Capabilities and Performance Beyond the SAT Attacks. *IACR Trans. on CHES (TCHES)* (2019), 97–122.

[13] M. Li *et al.* 2017. Provably secure camouflaging strategy for IC protection. *IEEE Trans. on CAD (TCAD)* (2017).

[14] M. Rostami *et al.* 2014. A primer on hardware security: Models, methods, and metrics. *Proc. IEEE* 102, 8 (2014), 1283–1295.

[15] M. Yasin *et al.* 2016. SARLock: SAT Attack Resistant Logic Locking. In *HOST*. 236–241.

[16] M. Yasin *et. al.* 2017. Provably-secure logic locking: From theory to practice. In *ACM-CCS*. 1601–1618.

[17] M. Yasin *et al.* 2017. Removal attacks on logic locking and camouflaging techniques. *IEEE Trans. on Emerging Topics in Computing* 1 (2017), 1–1.

[18] M. Yasin *et al.* 2017. Security analysis of anti-sat. In *ASP-DAC*. 342–347.

[19] M. Yasin *et al.* 2017. What to lock?: Functional and parametric locking. In *GLSVLSI*. 351–356.

[20] P. Subramanyan *et al.* 2015. Evaluating the security of logic encryption algorithms. In *HOST*. 137–143.

[21] P. Tuyls *et al.* 2006. Read-proof hardware from protective coatings. In *CHES*. 369–383.

[22] S. Roshanisefat *et al.* 2018. Benchmarking the capabilities and limitations of SAT solvers in defeating obfuscation schemes. In *IOLTS*. 275–280.

[23] S. Roshanisefat *et al.* 2018. SRCLock: SAT-Resistant Cyclic Logic Locking for Protecting the Hardware. In *GLSVLSI*. 153–158.

[24] T. Winograd *et al.* 2016. Hybrid STT-CMOS designs for reverse-engineering prevention. In *DAC*. 6.

[25] X. Xu *et al.* 2017. Novel bypass attack and BDD-based tradeoff analysis against all known logic locking attacks. In *CHES*. 189–210.

[26] Y. Shen *et al.* 2018. SAT-based bit-flipping attack on logic encryptions. In *DATE*. 629–632.

[27] Y. Shen *et al.* 2019. BeSAT: behavioral SAT-based attack on cyclic logic encryption. In *ASP-DAC*. ACM, 657–662.

[28] Y. Xie *et al.* 2017. Delay locking: Security enhancement of logic locking against ic counterfeiting and overproduction. In *DAC*. 9.

[29] S. M. Plaza and I. L. Markov. 2015. Solving the third-shift problem in IC piracy with test-aware logic locking. *IEEE Trans. on CAD (TCAD)* 34, 6 (2015), 961–971.

[30] Y. Shen and H. Zhou. 2017. Double dip: Re-evaluating security of logic encryption algorithms. In *GLSVLSI*. 179–184.

[31] D. Sirone and P. Subramanyan. 2018. Functional Analysis Attacks on Logic Locking. *arXiv preprint arXiv:1811.12088* (2018).

[32] Y. Xie and A. Srivastava. 2016. Mitigating sat attack on logic locking. In *CHES*. 127–146.

[33] A. yeh. 2012. Trends in the global IC design service market. *DIGITIMES research* (2012).

# On Custom LUT-based Obfuscation

Gaurav Kolhe, Sai Manoj P D, Setareh Rafatirad, Avesta Sasan, Houman Homayoun
George Mason University, Fairfax, VA, USA
{gkolhe,spudukot,srafatir,asasan,hhomayou}@gmu.edu

Hamid Mahmoodi
LogiMem Corporation
San Francisco, CA, USA
mahmoodi@logimem.com

## ABSTRACT

Logic obfuscation yields hardware security against various threats, such as Intellectual Property (IP) piracy and reverse engineering. Evolving Boolean satisfiability (SAT) attacks have challenged the hardware security assurance rendered by various obfuscation methods. Recent works have centered on using re-configurable components such as Look-Up-Tables (LUTs) to enhance resiliency against SAT attacks. Resiliency against SAT attack is guaranteed when the size of LUT (number of inputs) is large. However, this incurs significant power, area and performance overheads. To address this challenge, this work proposes logic encryption based on customized LUT to make this practical. We propose two variants of the customized LUT based obfuscation: LUT+MUX based obfuscation, securing the design through routing obfuscation by MUX (multiplexer) and logic obfuscation of LUTs; and LUT+LUT based obfuscation, benefiting from LUT based obfuscation reinforced with additional logic/routing obfuscation. We evaluate the hardware security and overheads of the proposed two variants of customized LUT-based obfuscation on various benchmarks. Proposed customized LUT-based obfuscation breaks the security, power, and area trade-offs. The proposed solution is shown to be robust against SAT-attacks and power analysis-based side-channel attacks with 8× reduced area and 3× reduced power on an average compared to state-of-the-art LUT-based obfuscation.

## KEYWORDS

Reverse Engineering, hardware obfuscation, logic encryption, STT-LUT, LUT obfuscation, SAT-attack.

**ACM Reference Format:**

Gaurav Kolhe, Sai Manoj P D, Setareh Rafatirad, Avesta Sasan, Houman Homayoun and Hamid Mahmoodi. 2019. On Custom LUT-based Obfuscation. In *Great Lakes Symposium on VLSI 2019 (GLSVLSI '19), May 9–11, 2019, Tysons Corner, VA, USA.* ACM, New York, NY, USA, 6 pages. https://doi.org/10.1145/3299874.3319496

## 1 INTRODUCTION

To minimize the increasing fabrication costs and design complexity of Integrated Circuits (ICs), IC companies are becoming fabless [10] and have started employing third party Intellectual property modules (IPs) to meet the reduced time-to-market constraints and minimize the design flow efforts. Despite economic benefits, this trend poses significant challenges to hardware security assurance in various forms such as reverse engineering (RE) [4, 7, 15, 16].

In order to thwart these security threats, many hardware design-for-trust techniques have been introduced; split manufacturing [12], IC camouflaging [5], and logic locking [26] to name a few. Among multiple aforementioned techniques, logic locking can thwart the majority of the attacks at any phase in the IC Production chain [26]. This is because the logic locking requires keys to unlock the correct functionality of the design. In addition, as a part of the post-manufacturing process, the activation of the IC (providing correct keys) will be accomplished in a trusted regime after fabrication to hide the functionality from the untrusted foundry, and attackers. Having key-programmable gates allow the designer or user to control the functionality using these key inputs.

Although introducing logic locking schemes have enhanced the security of the design, through advent of advanced Boolean satisfiability (SAT) based attack [2, 19] also known as "oracle-guided" threat model shows that by applying a few stimuli to the design and monitoring the output, the key value and functionality of an IC could be extracted in the order of a few minutes.

Numerous logic locking techniques [22, 23] have been proposed to improve the resiliency against SAT-attack. However, many of these techniques are vulnerable to other RE practises such as removal and SPS (Signal Probability Skew) attacks [24, 25]. Among the proposed logic locking schemes, some recent obfuscation methods focus on using configurable barriers, such as Look-Up-Tables (LUTs), as a key-programmable logic to achieve resiliency against attacks like SAT [1, 8]. Despite the achieved resiliency, the incurred area and power overheads with such LUT-based obfuscation acclimatizes the feasibility of implementation. Even employing emerging Spin-Transfer-Torque (STT) based LUTs that provides much higher density, performance, and near zero leakage power compared to CMOS-based LUTs, does not address the area and power overhead problem [20].

In this work, first, we study the previously proposed LUT-based obfuscation schemes [1, 3, 8, 20], and discuss the challenges to make them resilient against SAT-attack. To make LUT-based obfuscation a practical solution, we need to 1) radically reduce the design overhead, and 2) do not compromise the security benefits. Unfortunately, these two goals are contradictory with general LUT-based obfuscation. To address the design overhead, we propose a customized LUT design that not only benefits from configurable barriers for obfuscation but also mitigates the incurred area and power overheads of previous works. Two different variants of the proposed customized LUT is presented in this work for security: LUT+MUX based obfuscation, and LUT+LUT based obfuscation that benefits from re-configurability of the LUT along with the routing obfuscation supplemented by additional MUX/LUT. This


*GLSVLSI '19, May 9–11, 2019, Tysons Corner, VA, USA*

ACM ISBN 978-1-4503-6252-8/19/05...$15.00
https://doi.org/10.1145/3299874.3319496

blend of two obfuscation techniques assist in elevating security provided by logic obfuscation while concurrently creating SAT-hard instances.

The proposed customized LUT-based obfuscation is rigorously tested for various metrics such as power, performance, area. The contributions of this work are outlined as follows:

- To address the design overhead of LUT-based obfuscation, we propose a customized LUT-based obfuscation, where LUT is the crucial element in providing security, as replacing a gate with LUT realizes $2^{2^n}$ logical function where $n$ is the LUT size.
- Two variants of customized LUT are proposed: LUT+MUX and LUT+LUT. LUT+MUX enhances the security through the confluence of routing obfuscation (by MUX) and logic obfuscation (by LUT). Similarly, LUT+LUT fortifies the logic obfuscation by adding an extra layer of routing/logic obfuscation.
- The proposed customized LUT breaks the design parameters and security trade-offs and is optimized for power, performance, area, and security simultaneously, whereas state-of-the-art works are optimized for either security or power, performance, and area.

# 2 BACKGROUND AND RELATED WORK

## 2.1 Logic Obfuscation

Logic obfuscation referred as logic locking [26] is a hardware security solution that facilitates to hide the IP using key-programmable logic gates to combat against RE and other hardware threats. The activation of the obfuscated IP must be accomplished in a trusted regime before releasing the product into the market. During the activation phase, the correct key is applied to these key-programmable gates to recover the correct functionality of the IC/IP. In addition, the correct key will be stored in a tamper-proof memory.

## 2.2 SAT-Attack and SAT-resilient Obfuscation

Although logic locking schemes try to minimize the probability of determining the correct key by the attacker, introducing SAT-attack shows that these schemes can be broken as fast as in a few minutes [19]. To perform a SAT-attack, attacker requires an access to the functional IC along with the extracted obfuscated netlist. By searching for the Distinguishing Input Patterns (DIP) which is applied as the input to the obfuscated circuit, produces different outputs ($Y_i$) when different key values are applied. This DIP is used to distinguish between the set of correct and incorrect keys. The number of DIPs discovered during the SAT-based attack is equal to the number of iterations needed to unlock the obfuscated design.

Different SAT-hard schemes such as [22, 23] are proposed to curb the SAT-attack. The motive of these defenses is to increase the number of DIPs required to prune the correct key. These type of defenses are mostly point function, where the number of iterations needed can be increased up to $2^{n-1}$. Hence, the queries that SAT-attack must make and apply grows exponentially as the size of the key ($n$) increases. To overcome such obfuscation variants, SAT-attack such as AppSAT and Double-DIP [17, 18] are proposed. Furthermore, new obfuscation schemes that focus on non-Boolean behavior of circuits [21], that are not convertible to a SAT circuit are proposed for SAT resilience. Some of such defenses include adding cycles into the design [14]. Adding cycles into the design may cause SAT-attack to get stuck in the infinite loop, however, advanced SAT-based attacks such as cycSAT [27], SMT-attack [2] can extract the correct key despite employing such defenses.

Recently proposed obfuscation schemes relying on the concept of polymorphism [11, 13] facilitate to configure the Boolean function at run-time. However, polymorphic Memristor-CMOS gate based implementations are limited to only 2 logical functions, while giant spin-Hall effect (GSHE) is reconfigurable to 16 Boolean functions. While converting the obfuscated circuit to SAT representation using [11, 13], one can replace obfuscated gates using MUX which lets us choose between different functions implemented by GSHE and polymorphic Memristor-CMOS devices. Our simulations have shown that the above obfuscation schemes [11, 13] on C7552 circuit with as much as 50% obfuscation coverage, the reverse engineering (RE) time using SAT solver is found to be less than 5 days.

## 2.3 Obfuscation Using Look-Up-Tables

Look-up-tables (LUTs) built using STT can be used as a means of obfuscation. When a gate is replaced with a LUT, only the IP holder knows the function implemented by the LUT. As the content of the LUT is stored in tamper-proof memory, unauthorized users do not have access to the configuration of the LUT and cannot RE the IP. With the increase in LUT size, the functionality of the obfuscated logic can become complex, leading to increased robustness against SAT and other attacks. In this type of obfuscation, the partial part of the circuit is mapped to the LUT.

There has been some prevalent research using LUTs for logic obfuscation. The work in [3] proposes obfuscation and discusses multiple replacement strategies to secure the design, but falls short in providing the resiliency against SAT-based attacks. Three different LUT replacement policies are discussed in [20], which suggests that using STT based LUT could reduce the Power, Performance, and Area (PPA) overhead. Despite depicting low overheads, similar to the aforementioned works [3], the work in [20] also does not guarantee resiliency against state-of-the-art SAT-attack. The primitive in [8] has shown robustness against SAT-attack but does not evaluate the PPA overheads, which are equally critical in hardware design.

One of the most straightforward approaches in LUT-based obfuscation is to increase the number of LUTs. However, this does not guarantee the best security promises. It is observed that using larger LUTs enhance the security by an exponential margin because, the SAT-attack replaces the LUTs with deeper MUX trees, and the time to find the correct key grows exponentially. An example of obfuscation is demonstrated in Figure 1. The gates to be replaced are identified and are further replaced by LUT of size 8. However, this adds large power and area overheads.

Another solution to circumvent utilizing large LUTs is the choice of replacement policies. However, replacement policies alone do not solve the area and power overhead challenges, as these policies cannot reduce the size of LUT beyond a certain limit. For example, we observe that for a circuit like C7552, security can be achieved against SAT-based attack by replacing 1% of the gates in the random fashion with LUT size 12. However, when we use better replacement policy such as Algorithm 1, even with a LUT size of 8, a similar level of resiliency against SAT-attack can be achieved. Nevertheless, the PPA incurred by the relatively lower LUT size 8 is still very large and unacceptable. We observe that for circuit C7552, when 1% of the gates are obfuscated with LUT of size 8 using improved replacement strategy, the power and area overhead are 7× and 38× higher compared to original C7552 un-obfuscated circuit.

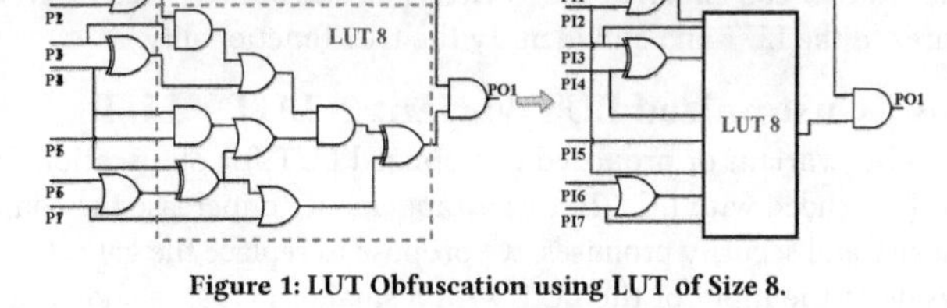


**Figure 1: LUT Obfuscation using LUT of Size 8.**

# 3 PROPOSED CUSTOMIZED LOGIC OBFUSCATION

In this section, we present the proposed customized LUT which offers secure obfuscation along with a significant reduction in the area and power overheads. We form the rationale for using STT technology for proposed LUT obfuscation followed by the replacement policies. This section further delves into the implementation of customized LUT Variant using STT-LUT along with additional MUX and LUT. We propose LUT+MUX based obfuscation for CMOS compatible devices benefiting using the fewer non-volatile (NV) elements while LUT+LUT can be used for emerging technology.

## 3.1 STT-LUT based Obfuscation

For obfuscation, we rely on STT-LUTs because of the following reasons. The employed design of STT-LUT is similar to that in [20].

- The configuration bits are stored in the Magnetic Tunnel Junction (MTJ), which are inserted between metal layers. The stored bits are highly susceptible and will be lost during RE, thus making it nearly impossible for the attacker to retrieve the configuration bits and determine the functionality of the LUT.
- STT based LUT provides higher integration density than SRAMs along with high endurance and retention time.
- MTJs hav near-zero leakage, and have soft error resilience.
- STT-LUT is highly integrative in CMOS fabrication process. The work in [20] has shown the feasibility to create the full-custom design and optimize one-bit MTJ latch cell using the Synopsys generic 28nm process for fabrication purposes.

Compared to static CMOS design, the timing overhead can be mitigated when employing the LUT-based obfuscation using STT-LUTs. As the ASIC standard cells are static in nature, the STT-LUT has implemented in a way that the path from LUT inputs to the LUT output is a MUX. This allows the designers to implement such type of STT-LUTs to be written in synthesizable RTL code for Electronic Design Automation (EDA) and optimization.

## 3.2 Gate Replacement Policy

In this work, we have used a replacement policy that is discussed in Algorithm 1 to reduce the size of the LUT needed for obfuscation. However other replacement policies can also be applied [8]. We start the Design Space Exploration (DSE) by obfuscating 1% of the gates with varying LUT size (from 2 to 15) to produce desired attack resiliency. The gate replacement algorithm used to find the gates for replacement is formulated in the Algorithm 1.

**Algorithm 1** Gate Replacement Policy

```
Remove the Sequential Element                          ▷ PO: Primary Outputs
Convert the Netlist to Graph Representation
for each (PO in Output_cone) do
    for each (gate in PO) do
        tag_key(PO)
        gate_obfuscation_gate_count += 1
Sort (Output Cone, gate_obfuscation_count, descending)
find Combination of PO where (gate_obfuscation_count > target_number)
while (obfuscated_gate_count < targated_number) do
    for each gate in Combination_Output_Cone do
        if parent_gate not replaced by LUT then
            Replace_LUT (gate, LUT_size)
    obfuscated_gate_count += 1
s = SAT_Attack (obfuscated_netlist)
PPA = DC_Compiler (obfuscated_netlist)
Normalize (S, PPA)
Calculate (S/PPA)
```

In this gate replacement policy, we choose gates such that the output corruptibility is low. When the output corruptibility is high i.e., the probability of having the hamming distance between the outputs of locked and activated IC greater than 1, it enables the SAT-attack to discover conflict clauses easily, which in turn enables SAT solver to eliminate the incorrect keys. On the other hand, when the output corruptibility is low, SAT solver requires more iterations to learn the underlying clauses for assigning a satisfying assignment. This increases the complexity by a significant margin. Along with this replacement policy, the gates are replaced such that LUTs are never connected to each other directly in back-to-back manner. Avoiding connecting the LUTs in this manner ensures only one single valid key for the circuit [8]. The number of output cones being selected for obfuscation depends on the number of gates that are being targeted for the obfuscation. To summarize, this algorithm finds the combination of output cone such that maximum number of gates are selected for obfuscation while less number of output cones are affected. If the resiliency against SAT-attack [19] can't be achieved with the selected number of gates even at higher LUT sizes, the obfuscated gate count are further increased. The gates to be replaced are again obtained using Algorithm 1. The selected gates are then replaced with, different sizes of the LUTs.

By iteratively sweeping the LUT size and gate count, we obtain the power, area and delay overheads along with the security metric. By calculating the S/PPA metric (Security per unit Power, Performance, and Area overhead) for each run, we find the optimal configuration that achieves the maximum robustness against SAT and other attacks with lower overheads. A large value of S/PPA indicates higher security assurance with lower PPA overheads. For further mitigating the overheads, We propose two variants of the customized LUT-based obfuscation..

## 3.3 Customized LUT Variant 1: LUT with MUXes

In, a SAT solver the clause to variable ratio (CVR) is one of the important metrics for qualitatively evaluating the security. For instance, to be proven as SAT-hard, the CVR needs to be around 4.2

[9]. However, when the clauses are short, there are many satisfying assignments and the clauses are said to be under-constrained. On the other hand, long clauses are over-constrained (contradictions can often be easily found), facilitating determining a large number of DIPs. The SAT solver uses the DPLL (Davis Putnam Logemann Loveland) method for backtracking, and with an increasing ratio of clauses to the variable the computational cost of DPLL calls decreases monotonically. Hence, one needs to determine a trade-off between the clause and variables.

In this work, we have chosen MUX to be integrated with LUTs for enhanced security. The rationale can be explained as follows: MUX has 4 clauses thereby using the MUX for obfuscation assists in averaging clause/variable ratio in the Conjunctive Normal Form (CNF) to 4. Furthermore, symmetric problems pose a great difficulty to SAT solver in finding a solution [6]. By effectively using the LUTs with MUX, one can formulate symmetry, to increase the SAT-hardness. In this work, we limit the size of the MUX to 2 for ensuring minimum PPA overheads. By employing the LUT + MUX configuration, the design benefits from both LUT and Routing obfuscation. As the LUT is a fully reconfigurable logical block, adding MUX tree increases the number of ways LUT can be configured, which significantly increase the key search space. Further, in SAT, the LUTs are represented using MUX, and hence combining MUX with LUT of size $n$, increases the depth of the MUX tree, thereby creating even harder SAT-instances.

Once the optimal LUT size and gates for replacement are determined, we replace the LUT using the proposed customized LUT +MUX to address the power and area overhead challenges. For example, it is observed that by using LUT size 8, the design can be made resilient to the SAT-attack however, leveraging LUT size 8 for obfuscation, the design suffers from the hefty design overheads. We address the PPA overhead issue by replacing the LUT size of 8 with smaller LUT of size 4 with an additional 4-2:1 MUX tree at the input of LUT size 4. Figure 2 demonstrate the gate replacement using LUT+MUX based obfuscation. While trading the size of the LUT, the size of the MUX tree has to be determined. We therefore iteratively reduce the LUT size while increasing the number of MUX to find the configuration which has a higher S/PPA.

Figure 2 shows the obfuscation using proposed LUT + MUX design. Gates are selected for replacement using Algorithm 1 and the gates are replaced by LUT Size of 4. In addition, 2:1 MUXes are added to configure 4-input LUTs in $2^4 \times 2^{2^4}$ ways. By utilizing this type of configuration, one can ensure high resiliency against SAT-attack while using a LUT size of 4 and lower PPA overheads. The additional dummy wires that create the confusion can be routed anywhere from the circuit while making sure we do not introduce cycles.

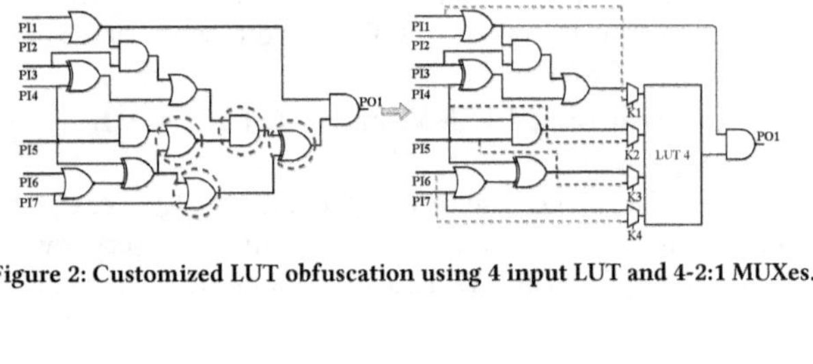

**Figure 2: Customized LUT obfuscation using 4 input LUT and 4-2:1 MUXes.**

Perhaps one can use switch-box instead of MUXes for creating routing obfuscation. However, attacker can eliminate a few permutations formed by m×n switch-box, thus reducing the search space. For instance, by creating a 4×4 switch-box at the input of the LUT, the switch-box can be configured in 16 different ways, however, the attacker can eliminate this switch-box and directly feed these 4 wires to the LUT and still identify the true functionality.

### 3.4 Customized LUT Variant 2: LUT + LUT

Another variant of proposed customized LUT for obfuscation is LUT cascaded with LUT. In this arrangement, to increase the complexity and security promises, we propose to replace the gates that reside at the input of the LUT with a smaller LUTs, as shown in Figure 3 (a). The main motive behind this is to increase the possible ways in which the larger LUT can be configured. The newly added smaller LUTs can take the form of a MUX or some arbitrary logical function. In order to translate LUT+MUX strategy to LUT+LUT, one needs to replace each of the 2:1 MUXes with a LUT of size 2. Note that it is stated that back-to-back implementation of the LUTs increases the number of correct combination [8], therefore we refrain from replacing two back-to-back gates with LUT+LUT or even LUT+MUX.

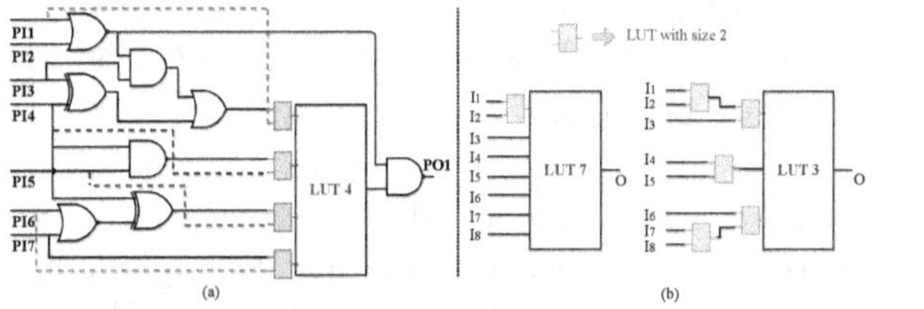

**Figure 3: (a) Customized LUT Obfuscation using LUT Size 4 and LUT Size 2. (b) Different LUT+LUT configuration**

Since, the LUT can take $2^{2^n}$ possible forms, and by adding the extra m-LUT, the total number of possible combinations becomes $m \times 2^{2^2} \times 2^{2^n}$ with the size of smaller LUT fixed to 2. This is chosen to keep the overhead margin as low as possible. The Figure 3 (b) shows the different configuration of the LUT+LUT that can replace the LUT Size 8 with the proposed method.

## 4 EXPERIMENTAL EVALUATION

### 4.1 Experimental Setup

To demonstrate and test the capabilities of the proposed customized LUTs, we are using a cluster computing environment which consists of 50 nodes, totaling 1060 cores and over 3TB of memory. We allocated a maximum of 128GB to each run of the SAT solvers. It is assumed that an attacker (fab or end-user) has no access to tamper-proof memory, however, all other flip-flops in the design can be accessed using the scan-chain that are implemented for the design-for-test. Uninterruptedly the experiments are run with a time-out of 10 days, which is higher than the time-out used in recent SAT-hard works. As the SAT solvers does not have the support for the LUTs, we construct the LUTs using the 2:1 MUXes [8].

The benchmarks that are employed for validating the proposed customized LUT-based obfuscation and its details are presented in Table 1 along with the gate count. The evaluated benchmarks comprise of 2 combinational and 5 sequential circuits.

As discussed, the proposed customized-LUT employs STT-LUTs for obfuscation to alleviate the overheads. To obfuscate with STT-LUTs, we define the STT based LUT as a Verilog module, and identified gates in the netlist are replaced by these modules. The logic library of NV latch is used to re-synthesize the design putting do-not-touch on the STT-LUT gate, to prevent them from being replaced during the subsequent rounds of synthesis.

DSE is used to find the best S/PPA ratio by varying LUT Size and gate count to obfuscate. For instance, as shown in Table 2, the LUT size 8 achieves the highest S/PPA for C7552, hence LUT size 8 is chosen as an optimal size for obfuscating C7552 circuit. For the purpose of experimentation, the constraint on the obfuscation is set such that, the design should remains resilient against the SAT-attack for 10 consecutive days. Using LUT size 8, we can achieve the resiliency for 10 days, and this is the reason, we refrain from using the LUT size 9. Further to reduce hefty PPA overheads, we have replaced the 8 input LUT with the proposed LUT+MUX techniques, so that it matches the overall input size of 8 with LUT of size 4 and 4 2:1 MUXes. In case of the LUT+LUT technique, LUT size 8 is replaced with LUT size 3 with 5 2-input LUTs as shown in Figure 3(b). The same LUT configuration is followed in all experiments.

**Table 1: Benchmark Summary**

| Benchmark | Synthesized Gate Count | Selected Gate Count | Source |
|---|---|---|---|
| C2670 | 430 | 12 | ISCAS'85 |
| C7552 | 1296 | 15 | ISCAS'85 |
| B12 | 2780 | 28 | ISCAS'89 |
| AES | 9511 | 50 | OpenCores |
| FIR | 14971 | 50 | CEP |
| IIR | 17054 | 50 | CEP |
| DES | 25450 | 50 | OpenCores |

## 4.2 Security Analysis Against SAT-Attack

The execution time of the SAT solver with traditional LUT-based obfuscation for C7552 benchmark is presented in Table 2. For traditional obfuscation, the LUT size is varied. The final LUT size is fixed to 8, as it achieves the best S/PPA metric. Using the proposed obfuscation technique, we can replace LUT 8 with smaller LUT size. It can be seen from Table 3, that LUT+MUX with LUT size of 4 and LUT+LUT using LUT size 3 makes it impossible to decode the key in the provided time-out of 10 days, but with traditional LUT obfuscation it can be done in the range of few seconds to minutes. Due to leveraging lower sizes of LUT for obfuscation, the proposed LUT-based obfuscation incurs 8× lower area with 3× lower power compared to traditional obfuscation. The ∞ denotes time-out i.e., SAT solver was unable to find the keys within 10 days. Customized obfuscation using LUT+LUT relies on lower LUT sizes, thus further minimizing the PPA overheads. Figure 3 also shows deobfuscation time for various configuration of Size of LUT + number of (2 input MUX/LUT).

**Table 2: Impact of LUT Size on S/PPA metric**

| LUT Size | 8 | 7 | 6 | 5 | 4 | 3 | 2 |
|---|---|---|---|---|---|---|---|
| S/PPA | 34.57 | 0.002 | 0.004 | 0.007 | 0.0017 | 0.02445 | 0 |

There have been several methods proposed for logic obfuscation in the recent year. The most recent and prominent one, which is closesr to the proposed obfuscation is GSHE [11]. Therefore, in this paper we are comparing our proposed custom LUT-based obfuscation with two other methods: 1) standard LUT-based and 2) GSHE. Table 4 demonstrates the empirical results obtained using the proposed LUT-based obfuscation (with two variants) and the traditional LUT-based obfuscation using LUT Size of 8. Table 4 also shows the de-obfuscation time using the method proposed in [11] while obfuscating 10% of the design. As [11] did not report the timing and power, we only compare the SAT execution time.

**Table 3: SAT-attack execution time using different LUT sizes on C7552 circuit**

| | | | | | | | | |
|---|---|---|---|---|---|---|---|---|
| Traditional LUT-Obfuscation | LUT Size used for Obfuscation | 8 | 7 | 6 | 5 | 4 | 3 | 2 |
| | SAT Execution time for LUT Obf. | ∞ | 612.3 | 363.2 | 224.8 | 121.7 | 87.3167 | 0.598 |
| Proposed Custom LUT-Based Obfuscation | SAT Execution time for LUT+MUX Obf. | - | ∞ | ∞ | ∞ | ∞ | 14549 | 7.85 |
| | SAT Execution time for LUT+LUT Obf. | - | ∞ | ∞ | ∞ | ∞ | ∞ | 2642.8 |
| | Customized LUT Configuration | - | 7+1 | 6+2 | 5+3 | 4+4 | 3+5 | 2+6 |

From Table 4, one can observe nearly 8× and 3× reduction in area and power overheads on average compared to traditional LUT-based obfuscation. It is also evident that LUT+LUT further mitigates the PPA overhead while utilizing lower LUT Sizes. In terms of resilience to the SAT-attack, one can observe that the proposed customized LUT-based solution secures the IC against SAT-attack with the time-out of 10 days (represented as ∞), whereas with the traditional LUT-based obfuscation, the IC can be reverse engineered in the range of seconds to a few minutes. The work in [11] despite having 10% obfuscation fails to demonstrate the resiliency against the SAT-solver. With the proposed LUT+MUX and LUT+LUT based obfuscation, even small circuits such as "C2670" can be hardened against SAT-attack. As the circuit size is small (only 430 gates), the overhead added by LUTs is significant. However, with larger and more practical circuits like AES, DES it can be observed that the overhead added by the proposed technique is small and justifiable which renders this technique a practical solution for rendering SAT-resilient designs. It is also important to note that the obfuscated circuit is normally a small part of a large millions or billions gates design. Therefore the extra 1~3× overhead on a small 10K~1M gates design results in a very small overall design overhead. While both variants of proposed customized LUT achieve similar SAT-hardness, LUT+LUT yields lower overhead while LUT+MUX requires less number of expensive NV memory elements. To secure the design for longer time-span, the designer can utilize the DSE to find the optimized LUT size and number of gates to be obfuscated to achieve the resiliency. Further the bigger LUT size can be replaced with the proposed methods to relieve the hefty overheads.

## 4.3 Side Channel Attack Vulnerabilities and Prevention

The secret key in this technique is the configuration bits that are stored in the non-volatile latches (NV-latches). The NV-latches are idle during run-time and their power consumption is leakage only and is independent of their states due to their differential design. Hence, the latches themselves do not directly generate any side channel signature such as the power or temperature map of the chip. However, the power of the MUX of the customized LUT and its fan-out cone depends on the LUT content, which could be a source of vulnerability for side-channel attack. If the attacker is given an option to reprogram the LUTs, an attacker may attempt to configure the LUTs with different keys and compare the power of the chip at each configuration with the power of a reference chip that has the

**Table 4: The impact of Different methodology on de-obfuscation time (in seconds) along with power and area overhead for different benchmarks**

| Benchmarks | De-Obfuscation time using SAT-attack | | | | Impact on Area Overhead* | | | Impact on Power Overhead* | | |
|---|---|---|---|---|---|---|---|---|---|---|
| | GSHE (Obf. Coverage = 10%) | LUT Obf. | Proposed Obf | | LUT Obf. | Proposed Obf | | LUT Obf. | Proposed Obf | |
| | | | LUT + MUX | LUT + LUT | | LUT + MUX | LUT + LUT | | LUT + MUX | LUT + LUT |
| C2670 | 19.8 | 79.8 | ∞ | ∞ | 95.06x | 7.51x | 6.80x | 15.14x | 2.28x | 1.96x |
| C7552 | 29.6 | 121.7 | ∞ | ∞ | 38.63x | 3.65x | 3.21x | 6.39x | 1.48x | 1.14x |
| B12 | 31.8 | 150.7 | ∞ | ∞ | 27.56x | 2.81x | 2.04x | 4.48x | 1.41x | 1.09x |
| FIR | 745.5 | 28342.6 | ∞ | ∞ | 9.42x | 1.63x | 2.06x | 2.62x | 1.31x | 1.19x |
| IIR | 654.6 | 95838.4 | ∞ | ∞ | 8.21x | 1.57x | 1.36x | 2.32x | 1.22x | 1.18x |
| AES | 950.6 | 98637.5 | ∞ | ∞ | 11.63x | 1.89x | 1.59x | 3.45x | 1.76x | 1.65x |
| DES | 1438.7 | 154429 | ∞ | ∞ | 7.50x | 1.51x | 1.29x | 1.90x | 1.10x | 1.05x |

For LUT obfuscation, the size of the LUT used is 8, while proposed method (1) LUT + MUX use LUT Size 4 along with 4-MUX and (2) LUT + LUT uses LUT Size 3 with 5-LUT of Size 2 for replacing LUT Size 8. The number of gates obfuscated is reported in Table 1. However, for GSHE obfuscation 10% of gates are encrypted in random fashion. The SAT-deobfuscation time is given in seconds. * Figures represent the area and power overheads in comparison to the implementation of the circuit/design with no obfuscation.

correct configuration already programmed in. The proposed customized LUT-based solution increases the number of permutations to $2^{2^n}$, where $n$ is the size of LUT. As the side-channel attacks are compute-intensive and require precise measurements, one can argue that by achieving SAT-attack resilience, sufficient side-channel attack resilience can also be achieved. Nonetheless, there are solutions possible for integrating additional security mechanisms in place to make the aforementioned side-channel attack more difficult. The simplest option is to apply encryption to the configuration bits so that the bits given to the on-chip programmer get decrypted before being written into the LUTs. The encryption/decryption key will be generated by an on-chip PUF and is unique to each chip so it cannot be guessed or attacked. Such solutions will be integrated with the proposed customized-LUT as a part of future research.

### 4.4 Resiliency to Other Attacks

The proposed customized LUT-based obfuscation is also resilient to the removal attacks. One cannot remove the LUT or MUX as removing them can strip the functionality of the circuit. The layout of the LUT is visually similar and nothing can be inferred by visual inspection. Though the Electron Microscopy (EM) can be applied for read-out data during run-time, the technology is currently not mature enough to reverse engineer switching elements [11].

## 5 CONCLUSIONS

In this work, we have introduced obfuscation using Customized LUT to mitigate the design overhead while not compromising the security. Further, to enhance the resilience against SAT-attack and make it a practical solution, we propose to employ LUTs in conjunction with MUX that facilitates routing based obfuscation or using an extra layer of LUT for increased depth of MUX for SAT-attack, therefore, making it resilient to power analysis-based side-channel attacks and EM-based reverse engineering attacks. Our experimental results show that with the proposed customized LUT-based obfuscation, higher robustness can be achieved against SAT-attack. Furthermore, nearly 3× power and 8× area overheads can be reduced on an average, compared to the state-of-the-art defenses. LUT+MUX offer competitive resiliency compared to LUT+LUT based obfuscation while using fewer NV-elements, while LUT+LUT technique benefits the IP holder from lower design overhead perspective.

## REFERENCES

[1] A. Attaran, Tyler D. Sheaves, and P. Kumar et.al. Mugula. 2018. Static Design of Spin Transfer Torques Magnetic Look Up Tables for ASIC Designs. In *GLSVLSI.*

[2] Kimia Azar, Hadi Kamali, Houman Homayoun, and Avesta Sasan. 2019. SMT Attack: Next Generation Attack on Obfuscated Circuits with Capabilities and Performance Beyond the SAT Attacks. In *Conf. on CHES.*

[3] Alex Baumgarten, Akhilesh Tyagi, and J Zambreno. 2010. Preventing IC piracy using reconfigurable logic barriers. *IEEE Design & Test of Computers* (2010).

[4] Ferdinand Brasser and et. al. 2018. Hardware-Assisted Security: Understanding Security Vulnerabilities and Emerging Attacks for Better Defenses. In *International Conference on Compilers, Architecture, and Synthesis for Embedded Systems.*

[5] R. P. Cocchi, J. P. Baukus, L. W. Chow, and B. J. Wang. 2014. Circuit camouflage integration for hardware IP protection. In *ACM/IEEE Design Automation Conf.*

[6] J. Crawford, M. Ginsberg, and et.al. Luks. 1996. Symmetry-breaking Predicates for Search Problems. In *Proceedings of the International Conference on Principles of Knowledge Representation and Reasoning.*

[7] Ramesh Karri, Jeyavijayan Rajendran, Kurt Rosenfeld, and Mohammad Tehranipoor. 2010. Trustworthy hardware: Identifying and classifying hardware trojans. *Trans. Computer* (2010).

[8] H. Mardani, K. Zamiri, and et.al. Gaj, K. 2018. LUT-Lock: A Novel LUT-Based Logic Obfuscation for FPGA-Bitstream and ASIC-Hardware Protection. In *IEEE Computer Society Annual Symposium on VLSI (ISVLSI).*

[9] Eugene N., Alex D., and Yoav S. et.al. [n. d.]. Understanding Random SAT: Beyond the Clauses-to-Variables Ratio. In *In Proc. of CP-04.*

[10] Department of Defense. 2005. Defense science board task force on high performance microchip supply. (2005). https://www.acq.osd.mil/dsb/reports/2000s/ADA435563.pdf

[11] S. Patnaik, N. Rangarajan, and J. Knechtel et.al. 2018. Advancing hardware security using polymorphic and stochastic spin-hall effect devices. In *Design, Automation Test in Europe Conference Exhibition (DATE).*

[12] J. Rajendran, O. Sinanoglu, and R. Karri. 2013. Is split manufacturing secure?. In *Design, Automation Test in Europe Conference Exhibition (DATE).*

[13] A. Rezaei, Y. Shen, S. Kong, and J. Gu et.al. 2018. Cyclic locking and memristor-based obfuscation against CycSAT and inside foundry attacks. In *Design, Automation Test in Europe Conference Exhibition (DATE).*

[14] S. Roshanisefat, H. Mardani, and A. Sasan. 2018. SRCLock: SAT-Resistant Cyclic Logic Locking for Protecting the Hardware. In *Proceedings of the 2018 on Great Lakes Symposium on VLSI.*

[15] Masoud Rostami, Farinaz Koushanfar, and Ramesh Karri. 2014. A primer on hardware security: Models, methods, and metrics. *Proc. IEEE* (2014).

[16] Hossein Sayadi, Nisarg Patel, and Sai Manoj et.al. 2018. Ensemble Learning for Effective Run-time Hardware-based Malware Detection: A Comprehensive Analysis and Classification. In *Design Automation Conference.*

[17] K. Shamsi, M. Li, and T. Meade et.al. 2017. AppSAT: Approximately deobfuscating integrated circuits. In *IEEE International Symposium on Hardware Oriented Security and Trust (HOST).*

[18] Y. Shen and H. Zhou. 2017. Double DIP: Re-Evaluating Security of Logic Encryption Algorithms. In *Proceedings of the on Great Lakes Symposium on VLSI.*

[19] P. Subramanyan, S. Ray, and S. Malik. 2015. Evaluating the security of logic encryption algorithms. In *Hardware Oriented Security and Trust (HOST), 2015 IEEE International Symposium on.*

[20] T. Winograd, H. Salmani, and H. et.al. Mahmoodi. 2016. Hybrid STT-CMOS designs for reverse-engineering prevention. In *Proceedings of the 53rd Annual Design Automation Conference.*

[21] Y. Xie and A. Srivastava. 2017. Delay locking: Security enhancement of logic locking against IC counterfeiting and overproduction. In *ACM/EDAC/IEEE Design Automation Conference (DAC).*

[22] Y. Xie and A. Srivastava. 2018. Anti-SAT: Mitigating SAT Attack on Logic Locking. *IEEE Trans. on Computer-Aided Design of Integrated Circuits and Systems* (2018).

[23] M. Yasin, B. Mazumdar, and J. J. V. Rajendran et.al. 2016. SARLock: SAT attack resistant logic locking. In *IEEE International Symposium on Hardware Oriented Security and Trust (HOST).*

[24] M. Yasin, B. Mazumdar, and O. Sinanoglu et.al. 2017. Security analysis of Anti-SAT. In *Asia and South Pacific Design Automation Conference (ASP-DAC).*

[25] M. Yasin, B. Mazumdar, O. Sinanoglu, and J. Rajendran. 2018. Removal Attacks on Logic Locking and Camouflaging Techniques. *IEEE Transactions on Emerging Topics in Computing* (2018).

[26] M. Yasin, J. J. Rajendran, and et.al. O. Sinanoglu. 2016. On Improving the Security of Logic Locking. *IEEE Transactions on Computer-Aided Design of Integrated Circuits and Systems* (2016).

[27] H. Zhou, R. Jiang, and S. Kong. 2017. CycSAT: SAT-based attack on cyclic logic encryptions. In *IEEE/ACM International Conference on Computer-Aided Design.*

# Securing Analog Mixed-Signal Integrated Circuits Through Shared Dependencies

Kyle Juretus*
Drexel University
Philadelphia, Pennsylvania 19104
kjj39@drexel.edu

Vaibhav Venugopal Rao*
Drexel University
Philadelphia, Pennsylvania 19104
vv85@drexel.edu

Ioannis Savidis
Drexel University
Philadelphia, Pennsylvania 19104
isavidis@coe.drexel.edu

## ABSTRACT

The transition to a horizontal integrated circuit (IC) design flow has raised concerns regarding the security and protection of IC intellectual property (IP). Obfuscation of an IC has been explored as a potential methodology to protect IP in both the digital and analog domains in isolation. However, novel methods are required for analog mixed-signal circuits that both enhance the current disjoint implementations of analog and digital security measures and prevent an independent adversarial attack of each domain. This paper demonstrates the vulnerabilities of implementing disjointed obfuscation techniques to protect analog mixed-signal ICs. In addition, a novel methodology is developed to generate functional and behavioral dependencies between the analog and digital domains that results in an increase in the adversarial key search space. The dependencies between the analog and digital keys result in a 3x increase in the number of iterations required to complete the SAT attack. An analysis of best practices is also provided to aid in the implementation of security measures for analog mixed-signal circuits.

## KEYWORDS

logic locking, parameter locking, SAT attack, hardware security

**ACM Reference Format:**

Kyle Juretus, Vaibhav Venugopal Rao, and Ioannis Savidis. 2019. Securing Analog Mixed-Signal Integrated Circuits Through Shared Dependencies. In *Great Lakes Symposium on VLSI 2019 (GLSVLSI '19), May 9–11, 2019, Tysons Corner, VA, USA.* ACM, New York, NY, USA, 6 pages. https://doi.org/10.1145/3299874.3319497

## 1 INTRODUCTION

Malicious modifications to integrated circuits (ICs) represent a serious threat to the security of the entire computing stack, with back doors [1] and a variety of counterfeit ICs [2, 3] having already been discovered within military ICs. The security threats at the hardware level are expected to increase as the IC manufacturing flow transitions to a horizontal model, where manufacturing, testing, and intellectual property (IP) are procured from third-parties [3]. Untrusted third-parties within the IC design flow possess the ability to steal IP, counterfeit and overproduce ICs, and insert harmful circuit modifications (hardware Trojans).

According to a report by Information Handling Services (IHS) Markit [4], the top five most counterfeit types of semiconductors include analog ICs, microprocessors, memory, programmable logic ICs, and discrete transistors, which represents an annual potential risk of approximately $169 billion to the semiconductor supply chain [4]. To address the pertinent security issues of IP theft, overproduction, reverse engineering, counterfeiting, Trojan insertion, and data hacking effectively, hardware level design-for-trust techniques including logic locking [5–7], watermarking [8, 9], camouflaging [10], and IC metering [11] have been proposed. The majority of hardware security measures are only applicable to digital circuits and are not suitable for implementation on analog circuits.

The security of analog mixed-signal (AMS) circuits, however, is of importance as 25% of the reported counterfeit incidences [4] occur in AMS systems. In addition, there is a large increase in demand for analog mixed-signal circuits with varied capabilities due to a growing demand for Internet of Things (IoT) devices, which are used in a wide array of applications from household products to defense systems. According to an IHS report, the number of IoT devices is estimated to increase by around 200% from 2019 to 2025 [12]. As more and more IoT devices are produced, securing the circuits against hardware security threats including counterfeiting, overproduction, reverse engineering, and Trojan insertion becomes challenging. As AMS systems are vulnerable to a wide range of threat vectors, the unsecured analog circuit blocks also present an exploitable point of entry to the IC even when the digital IP is protected.

To address the growing need of protecting AMS IP, this paper proposes a novel methodology to concurrently secure both analog and digital circuit blocks. The analog block is protected with a parameter based obfuscation technique [13] that masks the dimensions of the transistors used to implement vital components of the analog circuit. The analog circuit only operates as intended when the correct key is applied. The digital portion of the AMS circuit is protected with two different logic locking strategies; the XOR methodology [5] and the modified logic cone methodology [14]. The correct functionality of the digital block is also dependent on the application of the correct key to the circuit.

An analysis of the security of independently locked analog and digital circuit blocks is provided. An attack that isolates the analog and digital circuit blocks is described, limiting the effective key space of the secured circuit. The analog and digital blocks are modified to include correlated key dependencies within the circuit, which results in an increase in the level of difficulty to attack the IC.

*These authors contributed equally to this work



*GLSVLSI '19, May 9–11, 2019, Tysons Corner, VA, USA*

ACM ISBN 978-1-4503-6252-8/19/05...$15.00
https://doi.org/10.1145/3299874.3319497

Both the analog and digital circuits are attacked with a satisfiability modulo theory (SMT) based technique that explores the logical and functional search space generated by a 16-bit key, where the attack is characterized by the number of iterations required to determine the correct key. The primary contributions of this paper include:

(1) protection of analog mixed-signal circuits by obfuscating both the analog and digital sub-components,
(2) an analysis of the security of the analog mixed-signal circuit using a SMT based search space exploration technique, and
(3) the development of a novel methodology to generate functional and behavioral dependencies between the analog and digital domains that results in an increase in the adversarial key search space.

The paper is organized as follows. Recent techniques to protect digital, analog, and AMS circuits are described in Section 2. The assumed threat model is provided in Section 3. An overview of the proposed obfuscation technique and the implementation of the technique on an AMS circuit is described in Section 4.1 and 4.2, respectively. The limitation of independently securing analog and digital blocks is analyzed in Section 4.3. A methodology to generate dependencies between the analog and digital circuit blocks is described in Section 5. Best practices to secure AMS circuits are described in Section 6. Some concluding remarks are provided in Section 7.

## 2 PRIOR RESEARCH ON CIRCUIT OBFUSCATION

An overview of prior research to secure digital, analog, and AMS circuits is provided in this section.

### 2.1 Digital Logic Locking

Extensive research on logic locking techniques that protect digital IP have previously been reported. There are two distinct categories of digital logic locking techniques: 1) methods that obfuscate within the logic cone, and 2) the addition of circuitry that produces errors in circuit functionality when an incorrect key is applied. Techniques that insert XOR/XNOR [5], LUT [6], and MUX [7] based secure gates within the original logic cone have been developed. Optimization of circuit locking techniques to lower the overhead in power, area, and performance [15, 16] and selection algorithms to determine the optimal insertion point of the secure gates in the circuit [7, 17–19] have also been reported.

The SAT attack proposed in [20] resulted in the development of techniques that add additional circuitry to increase the total number of distinguishing input patterns (DIPs) needed to successfully execute the SAT attack [14, 21–24]. However, while the methodologies provide a provable means to quantify the number of iterations required to execute the SAT attack, some of the methods are vulnerable to the removal of the added circuitry [25]. To prevent removal attacks, more recent techniques, such as described in [14] and [24], alter the original logical functionality of the IC and implement added circuitry to rectify the altered minterms when the correct key is applied.

### 2.2 Analog Logic Locking

A key-based locking/unlocking mechanism for a sense amplifier circuit is proposed in [26]. A memristor-based voltage divider is implemented to provide a variable voltage bias to the body of the transistors of the sense amplifier. A memristor crossbar structure allows for the programming of the voltage divider, which results in the correct circuit functionality only when the correct 16-bit key is applied. The practical application of the method is limited as memristors are not readily available and the fabrication of the memristors is incompatible with standard CMOS processes.

The current mirror based combinational locking technique proposed in [27] utilizes transistors of different sizes to mask the current gains of the analog circuit. Based on the applied key sequence, a range of current values are set. A satisfiability modulo theory (SMT) based algorithm is used to generate a unique key. The primary disadvantage of current mirror based combinational locking is that the technique is limited to masking the biasing currents of an analog circuit.

Key based performance locking of analog circuits is proposed in [13, 27, 28], where locking circuitry is inserted into an analog IC to mask biasing conditions, gains, operating frequencies, and performance parameters. In the parameter obfuscation technique proposed in [13] and [28], the sizes of the transistors used to set the optimal biasing conditions are masked using parallel (vector) and mesh-based transistor arrays. Based on the applied key, a subset of the transistors in the vector or mesh are activated to produce an overall effective transistor width over length ratio $(\frac{W}{L})_{eff}$. Proper analog circuit functionality is only achieved when the correct key is applied. The SMT based search space exploration methodology proposed in [29] is applied to ensure that only a single correct key exists that sets the optimal circuit performances and that incorrect keys result in significant degradation in the performance of the analog circuit blocks (i.e. eliminate keys that set "good enough" performance values).

### 2.3 AMS Logic Locking

The logic locking methodologies described in [30] and [31] obfuscate the digital part of the mixed-signal IC. Specifically, the stripped-functionality logic locking (SFLL) [14] technique is implemented on the digital portion of the circuit to lock the entire mixed-signal IC. Digital circuitry responsible for the post-silicon tuning of the analog circuits is obfuscated using the SFLL logic locking technique in [31]. The primary disadvantage of only obfuscating the digital portion of an AMS IC is that no protection is offered to the purely analog blocks. In addition, all prior work to secure AMS circuits applied techniques that independently protect the analog and/or digital blocks. An analysis of applying disjoint security measures to the analog and digital circuit blocks of an AMS IC is, therefore, provided in Section 4.3. In addition, a methodology to generate a functional and behavioral dependency between the analog and digital circuit domains is developed in Section 5 that increases the security and effective key space of the IC.

## 3 THREAT MODEL

The threat model for this work assumes that an adversary possesses the tools and knowledge necessary to reverse engineer the IC and produce an extracted locked netlist representation of the circuit. To obtain the logically functional representation of the circuit, an adversary must determine the correct keys for the obfuscated portions of the IC. In addition, an adversary is assumed to possess an activated IC, which is used to obtain input-output pairs that allow for the efficient pruning of the key space when applying a SAT based attack [20]. An adversary is assumed to have access to a second activated IC, which is used to modify a subset of the applied key bits. The adversary also has complete access to the scan chain of the IC, which allows for the read-out of the internal circuit state.

# 4 VULNERABILITIES OF INDEPENDENTLY SECURED ANALOG AND DIGITAL CIRCUIT BLOCKS

Research on protecting ICs from a multitude of threats has resulted in methodologies to independently secure analog and digital circuits. In a typical AMS IC pipeline, multiple components of the circuit must be secured against reverse engineering. A discussion on potential vulnerabilities of independently securing the analog and digital blocks is provided in this section. An overview of the AMS pipeline used as an example throughout the paper is described in Section 4.1. A description of the implemented obfuscation technique is provided in Section 4.2. An analysis of an attack to determine the key of the analog and digital circuits through isolation of each block is described in Section 4.3.

## 4.1 Proposed AMS Circuit Implementation

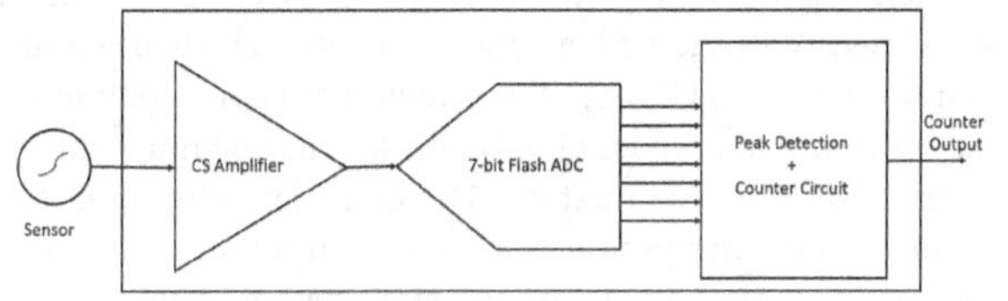


**Figure 1: AMS circuit obfuscated with the proposed technique.**

A peak detection and counting circuit is considered, which consists of an analog front end, analog-to-digital converter, and digital back end as shown in Fig. 1. The peak detection and counting circuitry is applicable to a wide-range of applications including heart-rate monitoring devices, mass spectrometers, X-ray machines, and image processing applications. The analog front end consists of a common-source amplifier with a diode connected load used in the detection and amplification of a low-voltage output signal from a sensor. The output of the amplifier is applied to a 7-bit flash analog-to-digital converter (ADC). The output of the ADC is connected to a back-end digital computation block comprising of a peak detection circuit and a counter. The two most significant output bits from the ADC, referred to as Bit-1 (B1) and Bit-2 (B2), are applied to the peak detection circuit, where a bit flip from 0 to 1 on B1 implies the detection of a peak over a set threshold voltage and a bit flip from 1 to 0 of B2 returns the circuit to an active detection state.

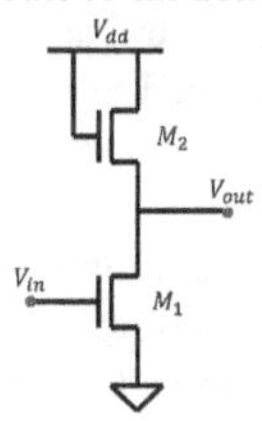


**Figure 2: Schematic of the common-source amplifier with diode-connected load.**

### 4.1.1 *Common Source Amplifier With Diode-Connected Load.*

The schematic of the proposed common-source (CS) amplifier is shown in Fig. 2. Due to challenges in fabricating large on-chip resistors that fall within a tight tolerance, diode connected loads are preferred. The gain of the common source amplifier is given by

$$A_v = -\frac{1}{1+\eta}\sqrt{\frac{\left(\frac{W}{L}\right)_1}{\left(\frac{W}{L}\right)_2}}, \quad (1)$$

where $\eta$ is the back-gate transconductance parameter and $(\frac{W}{L})_1$ and $(\frac{W}{L})_2$ represent the width over length ratios of transistors $M_1$ and $M_2$, respectively. From (1), the amplifier gain is neither a function of the bias current nor the input signal, which results in a linear amplifier gain, tolerance to input and output voltage level fluctuations, a high input resistance, and a high open loop-gain. In addition, the gain of the amplifier is a function of the transistor sizes, which provides a direct design parameter available to obfuscate the amplifier gain. In the proposed obfuscated circuit, the common-source amplifier is designed to produce a gain of 8x when biased by a DC voltage of 0.45 V for an input signal with a peak-to-peak amplitude of no more than 0.04 V.

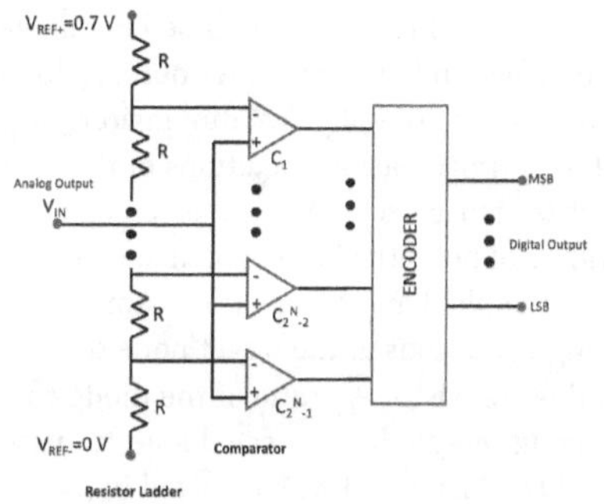


**Figure 3: Schematic representation of the flash ADC.**

### 4.1.2 *7-Bit Flash Analog-to-Digital Converter.*

The amplified signal is digitized using a 7-bit flash ADC as shown in Fig. 3. The ADC consists of a $2^N$ resistive divider providing the reference voltage for the $2^N - 1$ comparators. A logic 1 is produced when the analog voltage is higher than the set reference voltage applied to the comparator. Otherwise the output from the individual comparators is a 0. The combined outputs from all the comparators results in a thermometer code, which is then translated to the appropriate digital output code using an encoder.

### 4.1.3 *Peak Detection and Counting Circuit.*

The peak detection circuit connected to the output of the ADC is set to a voltage threshold of 0.6125 V, which determines if the most significant bit of the ADC (B1) transitions to a logic *1*. A state machine diagram of the circuit is shown in Fig. 4, where state *S1* signifies the system is waiting for the detection of a peak and *S2* signifies the state of the system once a peak has been detected. The circuit only detects another peak after the voltage falls below a second set threshold (0.525 V for the designed circuit), which is represented by the second most significant bit of the ADC (B2).

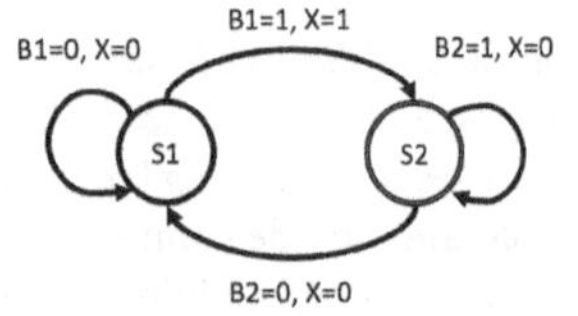


Figure 4: FSM of the peak detection and counting circuit.

Once a peak is detected, the output signal $X$ is used to advance a 3-bit counter. By monitoring the output of the counter, the circuit is able to detect peak bursts or signal abnormalities if a large number of peaks are observed over a bounded period of time.

## 4.2 Implementation of the Obfuscation Techniques

Obfuscation techniques are implemented on both the analog and digital blocks of the circuit. The 7-bit flash ADC is the only unobfuscated block of the IC. The parameter obfuscating technique proposed in [13] is applied to the analog circuit with a 10-bit key. The digital circuit is obfuscated with a 6-bit key using a combination of XOR-based logic encryption [5] and stripped functionality logic locking (SFLL) [14]. The total key length applied to the circuit is 16-bits.

*4.2.1 Analog Circuit Obfuscation.* The gain of the common source amplifier is masked using the vector-based parameter obfuscation technique described in [13]. Parameter obfuscation is a key based technique that targets the physical dimensions of the transistors used to set the optimal biasing conditions of the circuit. The width of a transistor is obfuscated and, based on an applied key sequence, provides a range of potential biasing points. Only when the correct key sequence is applied and certain transistor(s) are active, are the correct biasing conditions at the target node set.

The effective transistor $\frac{W}{L}$ ratio of the diode connected load is masked by using ten diode-connected load transistors each with different sized transistor widths connected in parallel. Each of the ten transistors is either activated or remains deactivated based on a digital key applied through a decryption block implemented using pass transistor logic. From (1), the gain of the CS amplifier is inversely proportional to the square-root of the $\frac{W}{L}$ ratio of transistor $M_2$. The desired transistor width is only set when the correct key is applied, which produces the target amplifier gain $A_v$ [13].

*4.2.2 Digital Circuit Obfuscation.* The digital circuitry is obfuscated with two separate techniques. The first is an implementation of XOR based logic locking [5] within the counter of the digital block. The selection strategy for the XOR based locking technique was random and two XOR gates were inserted within the counter circuit. The second technique is applied to the logic cone within the peak detection circuit, where the circuit is modified for a single minterm input. The circuit implemented in [14] that produces a zero Hamming distance from the inputs of the digital block and the applied key is utilized to correct the flipped minterm.

The circuit characterizing the Hamming distance compares four key inputs and four inputs from the peak detection circuit. The four monitored inputs include B1 and B2 from the output of the ADC and the two outputs from the registers of the state machine shown in Fig. 4. The added security of the circuit is, therefore, bounded by $2^4$ distinguishing input patterns (DIPs), where the number of DIPs is correlated to the size of the circuit being secured.

## 4.3 Attacking AMS Blocks in Isolation

The system level schematic shown in Fig. 1 includes a 10-bit key applied to the CS amplifier and a 6-bit key applied to the digital peak detection and counter circuit. When protecting both circuit blocks, the objective is to include obfuscated circuitry that adds to the overall security of the IC, which is bounded by a key space of $2^{16}$ combinations. However, if not properly implemented, an adversary is able to isolate the analog and digital circuit blocks, which allows for the independent determination of both the key for the CS amplifier and the key for the digital peak detection and counter circuit. Two techniques to isolate the analog and digital blocks are described: 1) using saturating conditions of the analog circuit block (Section 4.3.1) and 2) partially altering the keys of an activated IC (4.3.2).

*4.3.1 Saturation Conditions of the Analog Circuit.* The CS amplifier of the AMS circuit produces two responses that are known independent of the key. The first response is a result of applying a 0 V input to the CS amplifier. Independent of the applied gain set by the key, the output of the amplifier remains 0.45 V (the DC offset). A logic *0* is produced at the input of the digital circuit for both B1 and B2, which results in the generation of SAT based constraints that more efficiently attack the key space. The second response is due to the saturation of the CS amplifier, which results in an output of 1.8 V, the set power supply voltage (VDD) for the 180 nm technology node used for SPICE simulation. Therefore, applying VDD to the input of the amplifier produces a known output of VDD. DIPs are, therefore, generated for the digital circuit when an all one input is applied to the peak detection circuit. Applying the known logic zero and logic one constraints results in the SAT attack determining the key of the digital circuit in four iterations. Once the digital key is determined, the analog key is now vulnerable to an isolation attack, essentially reducing the key space to $2^{10}$ combinations from the maximum possible combinations of $2^{16}$.

*4.3.2 Partial Activated IC by Applying Semi-Correct Key.* As part of the threat model described in Section 3, an adversary is assumed to possess access to a second activated IC. The second activated IC allows for partial key modifications, whether applied solely to the digital or analog portions of the circuit. For example, consider an adversary attempting to attack the key of the analog block in isolation. The adversary must determine a set of key values and inputs to the peak detection and counter circuit that exposes the value of the ADC bits (sensitizes the ADC bits). The miter circuit of the AMS circuit shown in Fig. 1 is utilized to determine an input pattern that is dependent on the value of B1 at the output of the digital block. The key inputs and scan chain inputs of the digital circuit are modified and applied to the second activated IC, which allows for the correct determination of the B1 bit based on the input voltage applied to the CS amplifier. The adversary is, therefore, able to set a voltage input to the amplifier that results in the switching of the output of the digital circuit. Inputting a voltage (0 V and VDD) as a constraint to the circuit eliminates all but the correct key, which allows the adversary to decrypt the analog block and reduce the key search space from a maximum of $2^{16}$ combinations to $2^6$.

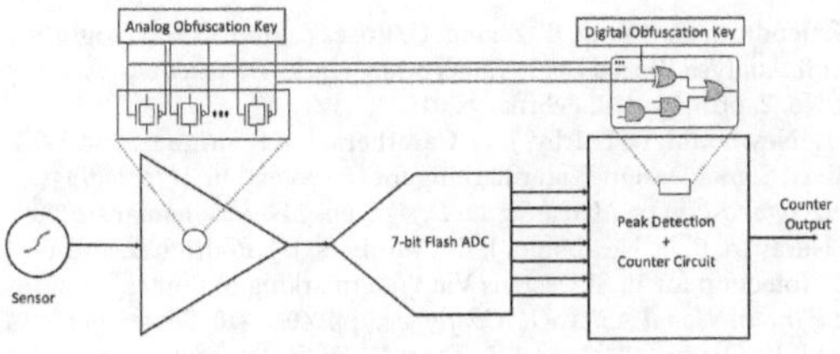


**Figure 5: AMS circuit topology with dependencies between the analog and the digital blocks. The key for the digital circuit block is now dependent on the key set for the analog circuit.**

The opposite condition also applies, where the adversary simply determines the output of the ADC that isolates the digital portion of the AMS circuit. The adversary applies a SMT solver to determine input and key conditions to the analog block that result in the desired ADC outputs, at which point the activated response of the digital system is obtained. The conventional SAT attack is then executed on the digital block of the circuit. For each determined DIP of the digital block by the SAT solver, the circuit input and key inputs to the analog block are determined such that the target B1 and B2 values are generated. Executing the described attack on the given AMS circuit requires only three iterations of the SAT attack to determine the correct digital key.

# 5 ADDING KEY DEPENDENCIES BETWEEN ANALOG AND DIGITAL CIRCUIT BLOCKS OF AN AMS CIRCUIT

An attack on a secured AMS circuit that isolates the digital and analog blocks by applying saturating inputs and/or partial key modifications on an activated IC is demonstrated in Section 4. The generation of key dependencies between the AMS circuit blocks is described in this section, which results in an increase in the difficulty of determining the key of an AMS circuit when isolating the digital and analog blocks.

To correlate the key response of the analog and digital circuits, an XOR gate with two key inputs, one from the analog circuit and the other from the digital block, is used. The system model shown in Fig. 1 is now altered to that shown in Fig. 5, with the added correlation between the keys of the analog and digital blocks shown in red dashed lines (interconnects between the analog obfuscation key and digital obfuscation key in Fig. 5).

To implement the interdependence between the analog and digital blocks, four random pairs of analog and digital key bits are chosen and XORed together. By including the correlated keys, the circuit is no longer vulnerable to the attack described in Section 4 that exploits saturating zero and one inputs to trim the key space. Instead, eight valid digital keys remain after the application of the saturating conditions. Essentially, the SAT attack is able to deduce that the analog and digital keys are either equal or inverses of one another, but is not able to determine the value of either key.

Execution of the partial key attack described in Section 4.3.2 no longer results in the determination of the key of the digital block as the output is also dependent on the analog key bits. As an example, consider applying the SAT solver to generate a condition that outputs a value of *1110000* by the ADC. Even though the output of the ADC is known, the generated analog key is also provided to the digital block, which results in a functionally incorrect output from the IC. The adversary is, therefore, forced to concurrently consider the analog and digital blocks of the IC to determine the key.

To attack the linked blocks, the saturating conditions are first applied. The key space is constrained to eight possible digital key values, which reduces the key space from $2^{16}$ to $2^{13}$ combinations. A SMT based attack is then applied to the analog portion of the AMS circuit by generating a miter circuit that is inputted to a satisfiability modulo theory (SMT) solver. The SMT solver allows for the mathematical expression of the gain equation of the CS amplifier. Simply applying a miter circuit with analog parameters includes challenges as a floating point value differing by a single least significant bit (LSB) generates an undesired but valid miter circuit constraint. To eliminate a larger set of keys per generated DIP, a range of applied voltages is applied to the activated IC. As an example, consider a DIP generated with an input voltage of approximately 0.0378 V and the internal state registers in the digital block set to *01110*. The saturating conditions of the circuit are first checked for the given internal register state. The circuit switches one of the output register values of the counter for the operating range of the amplifier (less than 0.04 V). Since the output switches based on the applied input to the CS amplifier alone, an adversary knows that the obfuscated gain of the amplifier is vulnerable to attack. To exploit the condition that an applied voltage within the operating input voltage range of the amplifier switches B1 or B2 from a logic *0* to a *1*, the initial input voltage of the DIP (0.0378 V in this example) is varied by ±30% to determine if the logical output of B1 and B2 changes. The ±30% range on either side of the applied input voltage to the ADC generated by the DIP can be constrained more aggressively. A larger range provides a greater probability to observe the change at the output of the circuit, but results in a less constrained key space. A smaller range more effectively constrains the key space, but results in greater difficulty in determining the toggle voltage of B1 and B2. For the implemented peak-detection circuit, three DIPs with a 30% search margin are sufficient to constrain the AMS circuit to return the correct key. The attack on the entire AMS circuit required 12 iterations of the SAT solver, which was substantially greater than the three total iterations required when attacking the analog block in isolation or the four total iterations when independently attacking the digital block.

As AMS circuits require protecting digital and analog IP, an assurance that the added security is not vulnerable to isolation attacks is needed. The proposed method that links the keys of the analog and digital sub-blocks resulted in a significant enhancement of the security of the implemented circuit.

# 6 SECURING AMS SYSTEMS

The analysis of the security of the AMS peak detection circuit indicates multiple considerations to account for when concurrently securing analog and digital circuit blocks. The following design criteria is provided as a guide to properly secure AMS circuits:

(1) The analog and digital circuit blocks must be evaluated for input-output combinations that are independent of the applied key. For the AMS circuit in this paper, an input voltage of 0 V sensitizes and isolates the digital circuit block as shown

in Section 4.3.1. To avoid such conditions, the generated digital key must account for saturating DIPs, or the AMS circuit must be dependent on the key for all the possible inputs.

(2) Independently securing digital and analog blocks must be avoided. Therefore, a technique is proposed in the paper to link the analog and digital keys. Such dependencies prevent an adversary from extracting circuit information by partially altering the key of an activated IC, which is discussed in Section 4.3.2.

(3) Ensure that the scan chain and internal testing points are inaccessible to adversaries. The AMS pipeline was highly susceptible to attack as every register within the digital block was accessible. The observability of all of the registers permits access to the ADC output, which results in increased isolation of the analog and digital circuit blocks. Obfuscation, or limitation, of the scan chain and testing circuits is needed to prevent an adversary from efficiently determining the key used for logic locking.

## 7 CONCLUSIONS

This paper proposes a novel obfuscation methodology to protect AMS circuits against IP piracy and theft by implementing logic and performance locking techniques on the digital and analog domains, respectively. Security analysis utilizing a SMT-based attack on an obfuscated peak detection circuit is performed, indicating a vulnerability when independently implementing obfuscating techniques in the analog and digital circuit sub-blocks. Both saturating conditions of the analog block and application of a partial key to an activated IC allow for the determination of the keys for each circuit block in isolation. To force an adversary to concurrently consider the keys of both circuit blocks, the key inputs between the analog and digital blocks are linked. The interconnection of the keys from the two blocks results in a 3x increase in the number of DIPs required to determine the key of the AMS circuit. Accounting for the security of the entire AMS circuit as opposed to the individual circuit blocks is, therefore, critical when designing an AMS system.

## ACKNOWLEDGMENTS

This research is supported in part by the Air Force Office of Scientific Research, National Defense Science and Engineering Graduate (NDSEG) Fellowship, 32 CFR 168a, Drexel Ventures Innovation Fund, and the National Science Foundation under Grant CNS-1648878 and Grant CNS-1751032.

## REFERENCES

[1] S. Skorobogatov and C. Woods, "Breakthrough Silicon Scanning Discovers Backdoor in Military Chip," *Proceedings of the International Conference on Cryptographic Hardware and Embedded Systems*, pp. 23–40, September 2012.
[2] U.S Department of Commerce, "Defense Industrial Base Assessment: Counterfeit Electronics," 2010.
[3] 112th Congress, "Inquiry into Counterfeit Electronic Parts in the Department of Defense Supply Chain," May 2012.
[4] IHS Technology Press Release, "Top 5 Most Counterfeited Parts Represent A $169 Billion Potential Challenge for Global Semiconductor Market," April 2012.
[5] J. A. Roy, F. Koushanfar, and I. L. Markov, "Ending Piracy of Integrated Circuits," *Computer*, Vol. 43, No. 10, pp. 30–38, October 2010.
[6] A. Baumgarten, A. Tyagi, and J. Zambreno, "Preventing IC Piracy Using Reconfigurable Logic Barriers," *IEEE Design and Test of Computers*, Vol. 27, No. 1, pp. 66–75, February 2010.
[7] J. Rajendran, H. Zhang, C. Zhang, G. Rose, Y. Pino, O. Sinanoglu, and R. Karri, "Fault Analysis-Based Logic Encryption," *IEEE Transactions on Computers*, Vol. 64, No. 2, pp. 410–424, February 2015.
[8] R. D. Newbould, D. L. Irby, J. D. Carothers, J. J. Rodriguez, and W. T. Holman., "Mixed Signal Design Watermarking for IP Protection," *Proceedings of the Southwest Symposium on Mixed-Signal Design*, pp. 249–265, January 2003.
[9] N. Narayan, R. D. Newbould, J. D. Carothers, J. J. Rodriguez, and W. T. Holman, "IP Protection for VLSI Designs Via Watermarking of Routes," *Proceedings of the IEEE International ASIC/SOC Conference*, pp. 406–410, September 2001.
[10] M. Li, K. Shamsi, T. Meade, Z. Zhao, B. Yu, Y. Jin, and D. Pan, "Provably Secure Camouflaging Strategy for IC Protection," *Proceedings of the IEEE/ACM International Conference on Computer-Aided Design*, pp. 1–8, November 2016.
[11] F. Koushanfar, "Provably Secure Active IC Metering Techniques for Piracy Avoidance and Digital Rights Management," *IEEE Transactions on Information Forensics and Security*, Vol. 7, No. 1, pp. 51–63, February 2012.
[12] IHS Markit, "IoT Trend Watch 2018," 2018.
[13] V. V. Rao and I. Savidis, "Protecting Analog Circuits with Parameter Biasing Obfuscation," *Proceedings of the IEEE Latin American Test Symposium (LATS)*, pp. 1–6, March 2017.
[14] M. Yasin, A. Sengupta, M. T. Nabeel, M. Ashraf, J. Rajendran, and O. Sinanoglu, "Provably-Secure Logic Locking: From Theory To Practice," *Proceedings of the ACM SIGSAC Conference on Computer and Communications Security*, pp. 1601–1618, November 2017.
[15] K. Juretus and I. Savidis, "Reduced Overhead Gate Level Logic Encryption," *Proceedings of the IEEE/ACM Great Lakes Symposium on VLSI*, pp. 15–20, May 2016.
[16] K. Juretus and I. Savidis, "Reducing Logic Encryption Overhead Through Gate Level Key Insertion," *Proceedings of the IEEE International Conference on Circuits and Systems*, pp. 1714–1717, May 2016.
[17] S. Dupuis, P. S. Ba, G. Di Natale, M. L. Flottes, and B. Rouzeyre, "A Novel Hardware Logic Encryption Technique for Thwarting Illegal Overproduction and Hardware Trojans," *Proceeding of the IEEE International On-Line Testing Symposium*, pp. 49–54, July 2014.
[18] M. Yasin, J. Rajendran, O. Sinanoglu, and R. Karri, "On Improving the Security of Logic Locking," *IEEE Transactions on Computer-Aided Design of Integrated Circuits and Systems*, Vol. 35, No. 9, pp. 1411–1424, September 2016.
[19] K. Juretus and I. Savidis, "Increasing the SAT Attack Resiliency of In-Cone Logic Locking," *Proceedings of the IEEE International Symposium on Circuits and Systems*, pp. 1–5, May 2019.
[20] P. Subramanyan, S. Ray, and S. Malik, "Evaluating the Security of Logic Encryption Algorithms," *Proceedings of the IEEE International Symposium on Hardware Oriented Security and Trust*, pp. 137–143, May 2015.
[21] Y. Xie and A. Srivastava, "Mitigating SAT Attack on Logic Locking," *Proceedings of the International Conference on Cryptographic Hardware and Embedded Systems*, pp. 127–146, June 2016.
[22] M. Yasin, B. Mazumdar, J. Rajendran, and O. Sinanoglu, "SARLock: SAT Attack Resistant Logic Locking," *Proceedings of the IEEE International Symposium on Hardware Oriented Security and Trust*, pp. 236–241, May 2016.
[23] M. Li, K. Shamsi, T. Meade, Z. Zhao, B. Yu, Y. Jin, and D. Z. Pan, "Provably Secure Camouflaging Strategy for IC Protection," *IEEE Transactions on Computer-Aided Design of Integrated Circuits and Systems*, pp. 1–14, September 2018.
[24] K. Juretus and I. Savidis, "Time Domain Sequential Locking for Increased Security," *Proceedings of the IEEE International Symposium on Circuits and Systems*, pp. 1–5, May 2018.
[25] M. Yasin, B. Mazumdar, O. Sinanoglu, and J. Rajendran, "Removal Attacks on Logic Locking and Camouflaging Techniques," *IEEE Transactions on Emerging Topics in Computing*, Vol. 64, No. 9, September 2017.
[26] D. H. K. Hoe, J. Rajendran, and R. Karri, "Towards Secure Analog Designs: A Secure Sense Amplifier Using Memristors," *Proceedings of the IEEE Computer Society Annual Symposium on VLSI*, pp. 516–521, July 2014.
[27] J. Wang, C. Shi, A. Sanabria-Borbon, E. Sanchez-Sinencio, and J. Hu, "Thwarting Analog IC Piracy Via Combinational Locking," *Proceedings of the IEEE International Test Conference (ITC)*, pp. 1–10, October 2017.
[28] V. V. Rao and I. Savidis, "Mesh Based Obfuscation of Analog Circuit Properties," *Proceedings of the IEEE International Symposium on Circuits and Systems*, pp. 1–5, May 2019.
[29] V. V. Rao and I. Savidis, "Transistor Sizing for Parameter Obfuscation of Analog Circuits Using Satisfiability Modulo Theory," *Proceedings of the IEEE Asia Pacific Conference on Circuits and Systems (APCCAS)*, pp. 102–106, October 2018.
[30] J. Leonhard, M. Yasin, S. Turk, M. T. Nabeel, R. C. Avot M. M. Louërat, O. Sinanoglu H. Aboushady, and H. G. Stratigopoulos, "MixLock: Securing Mixed-Signal Circuits via Logic Locking," *Proceedings of the IEEE Design, Automation Test in Europe Conference Exhibition*, p. PP, March 2019.
[31] N. G. Jayasankaran, A. S. Borbon, E. Sanchez-Sinencio, J. Hu, and J. Rajendran, "Towards Provably-secure Analog and Mixed-signal Locking Against Overproduction," *Proceedings of the International Conference on Computer-Aided Design*, pp. 1–8, November 2018.

# Design Methodology for Embedded Approximate Artificial Neural Networks

Adarsha Balaji[†], Salim Ullah[‡], Anup Das[†], and Akash Kumar[‡]

[†] Drexel University, Philadelphia, USA
[‡] Technische Universität Dresden, Germany

## ABSTRACT

Artificial neural networks (ANNs) have demonstrated significant promise while implementing recognition and classification applications. The implementation of pre-trained ANNs on embedded systems requires representation of data and design parameters in low-precision fixed-point formats; which often requires retraining of the network. For such implementations, the multiply-accumulate operation is the main reason for resultant high resource and energy requirements. To address these challenges, we present *Rox-ANN*, a design methodology for implementing ANNs using processing elements (PEs) designed with low-precision fixed-point numbers and high performance and reduced-area approximate multipliers on FPGAs. The trained design parameters of the ANN are analyzed and clustered to optimize the total number of approximate multipliers required in the design. With our methodology, we achieve insignificant loss in application accuracy. We evaluated the design using a LeNet based implementation of the MNIST digit recognition application. The results show a 65.6%, 55.1% and 18.9% reduction in area, energy consumption and latency for a PE using 8-bit precision weights and activations and approximate arithmetic units, when compared to 16-bit full precision, accurate arithmetic PEs.

## CCS CONCEPTS

• **Computing methodologies → Neural networks**; *Classification and regression trees*; • **Computer systems organization → Embedded hardware**; • **Hardware → Neural systems.**

## KEYWORDS

Artificial neural networks (ANNs), approximate computing, FPGA

**ACM Reference Format:**

Adarsha Balaji, Salim Ullah, Anup Das, and Akash Kumar. 2019. Design Methodology for Embedded Approximate Artificial Neural Networks. In *Proc. of the Great Lakes Symposium on VLSI 2019 (GLSVLSI '19), May 9–11, 2019, Tysons Corner, VA, USA*. ACM, NY, NY, USA. 6 pages. https://doi.org/10.1145/3299874.3319490


ACM ISBN 978-1-4503-6252-8/19/05...$15.00
https://doi.org/10.1145/3299874.3319490

## 1 INTRODUCTION

Inspired by the human brain, artificial neural networks (ANNs) are computational models built using a system of interconnected computing nodes called neurons. Each neuron is associated with two input parameters, a weight vector (w) and an input vector (x). The output $g_j$ of a neuron is defined by

$$g_i = \sigma\Big(\sum_{j=0}^{N-1} w_{i,j}x_i - \phi\Big) \quad (1)$$

where, $\sigma()$ is the activation function, N is the fan-in of the neuron j, $w_{ij}$ is the weight of the synapse between the i-th and the j-th neurons, respectively, and $\phi$ is the bias added to the weighted sum. The function first computes the weighted sum of all its inputs, and then performs a non-linear activation on the computed sum to generate $g_i$.

Utilizing these neurons, ANN models consist of an input layer, one or more hidden layers and an output layer. Depending on the interconnect patterns of the neurons and the activation functions used, neural network models are broadly classified into feed-forward neural networks (FNN), recurrent neural networks (RNN) and convolutional neural networks (CNN). Figure. 1 shows the architecture of an FNN. During the training and inference phases, every neuron in the network computes a weighted sum of its corresponding inputs and utilizes a non-linear activation function to produce its output, as shown in Eq. 1.

Recent advances in ANNs have seen their large scale incorporation in a diverse set of applications such as synthesis, classification and recognition [4][10]. To achieve higher accuracy, present implementations of ANNs are made larger and more complex. Due to the massive number of multiply-accumulate (MAC) operations, used to compute the weighted sum at each neuron, training of ANNs is

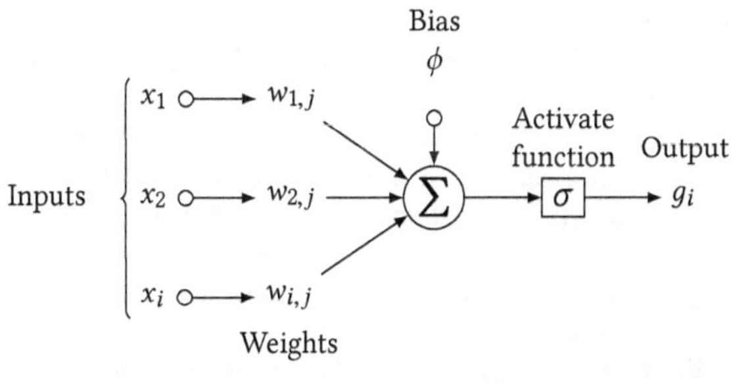


**Figure 1: Design of an Artificial Neuron.**

performed, preferably, using massive parallel computing platforms, such as Graphics processing units (GPUs).

For the utilization of ANNs in embedded systems, the ASIC-based ANN hardware accelerators aim to provide high performance and energy-efficient *inference engines*. As ANNs are naturally designed to be error resilient [18], several approximation techniques have been proposed in literature to optimize the hardware implementations of ANN to reduce energy consumption and improve the overall efficiency. These implementations, such as [2, 7, 9, 12, 17], mainly consider the quantization of data, such as activations and weights, to reduce the resources and energy demands of the implementations.

Besides using quantized data, some recent works have also explored the utilization of approximate arithmetic components for enhancing the performance of ASIC-based ANN accelerators. Du et al. [5] propose the use of approximate multipliers to design inexact neurons in neural networks. The multipliers proposed in this design use a logic minimization algorithm to reduce the runtime latency of the multiply operation. The proposed model exploits the error-tolerance of ANNs to achieve significant energy, latency and area gains. Venkataramani et al. [15] proposed a methodology of identifying error-resilient neurons based on the back-propagation gradients. For the error-resilient neurons, an approximation using precision modification and piecewise-linear approximation of activation function was applied to create an approximate neural network. Since training is by itself an error-healing process, after creating the approximate version, the NN is retrained. They also proposed a neuromorphic processing engine platform to determine the best trade-off between the precision and energy. In a similar approach, Zhang et al. [18] propose a method to identify critical neurons in a proposed architecture. The authors present a theoretical approach to detect critical neurons by studying the effect of small errors, introduced at the input, on the neuron's computation. The neurons are then ranked according to their criticality and three separate approximation techniques are introduced, memory access reduction, data and weight quantization and approximate arithmetic circuits.

However, ASIC-based hardware accelerators are constrained by their inability to support different types of neural networks and the limited size of the inferred network. To address these limitations, efforts have been made to implement reconfigurable ANN architectures and accelerators. Eyeriss [3] is a reconfigurable accelerator designed for CNNs that minimizes the energy cost for data movement. Considering the flexibility, high-parallelism and reconfigurability of FPGAs, recent works have also considered FPGA-based ANN accelerators [6, 11, 13, 16, 17]. However, many of the state-of-the-art FPGA-based implementations, such as [17], utilize High-level Synthesis Tools (HLS), such as provided by Vivado, to generate synthesizable RTL. However, the limitation of Vivado HLS to use only Vivado-provided IPs during the generation of RTL, makes it difficult to incorporate custom approximate IPs (arithmetic units) in the generated RTL. Other FPGA-based ANN accelerators, such as [6, 16] do not consider the approximate arithmetic modules during their proposed implementations.

In this paper we propose *RoxANN*, a methodology to design area and energy efficient ANN hardware using approximate arithmetic units on FPGAs. The methodology includes:

- the design of ANN processing elements (PEs) that support the utilization of approximate multipliers, thereby achieving significant area and energy savings;
- the use of quantized activations and weights to reduces the memory demand on the FPGA;
- a weight clustering technique, used post training, to incorporate weight sharing. With a fixed number of shared weights, we propose the use of *constant multipliers* in PEs, significantly reducing the area and resource demand on the FPGA.

The remainder of this work is organized as follows. We introduce our *Rox-ANN* design methodology in Section 2. We present our evaluation methodology in Section 3. We compare our approach against a fully precise and accurate ANN hardware implementation in Section 4. Finally, we conclude the paper in Section 5.

## 2 DESIGN METHODOLOGY

In this section, we present the FPGA-based Rox-ANN methodology. First, we propose the design of a generic processing element that supports the use of accurate/approximate arithmetic units, such as adders and multipliers, to compute the partial weighted sum of neurons. Next, we demonstrate the use of quantized activations and weights on the training and implementations phase of the neural network. Finally, we present a clustering based approach, used after the training phase of the neural network, to minimize the number of distinct weights on the network.

### 2.1 Processing Element

The proposed design of a generic PE, as shown in Figure 2, is optimized for the state-of-the-art Xilinx FPGAs (with 6-input lookup tables), however, it can also be implemented on FPGAs from other vendors, such as those provided by Intel. As described in Fig. 2(a), the neurons in the hidden layer and output layer of an ANN compute the weighted sum of all its corresponding activations. In a layered architecture, such as a Multilayer Perceptron (MLP), neurons that belong to the same hidden layer share all the inputs from the previous layer, stored in a vector $x$, and contains a weight for every synaptic connection, stored in a vector $w$. Each processing element consists of two dual-port block random access memories (BRAMs); one to store a subset of the activations $\hat{x}$ and the other to store a subset of the weights $\hat{w}$, respectively. The size of the BRAM can be configured based on the architecture of target FPGA platform, design constraints—such as energy, area and latency—and the size and type of neural network architecture being implemented on the FPGA.

Each PE contains two multipliers and two adders as shown in Fig. 2. Each multiplier and adder pair computes the partial weighted sum of the inputs $\hat{x}$ and the corresponding weights $\hat{w}$. The design of the PE is configurable, based on the demands and constraints of the neural network. Fig. 2(b) and Fig. 2(c) show two possible configurations of the proposed PE. The PE in Fig. 2(b) can compute the partial weighted sum of *two* separate neurons, with each multiplier-adder pair used to represent a single neuron. The two multiplier-adder pairs in a PE can also be configured to represent a single neuron as shown in Fig. 2(c). The configuration in Fig. 2(c) will have double the throughput of the design in Figure 2(b) for a single neuron. Similarly, depending upon target FPGA platform

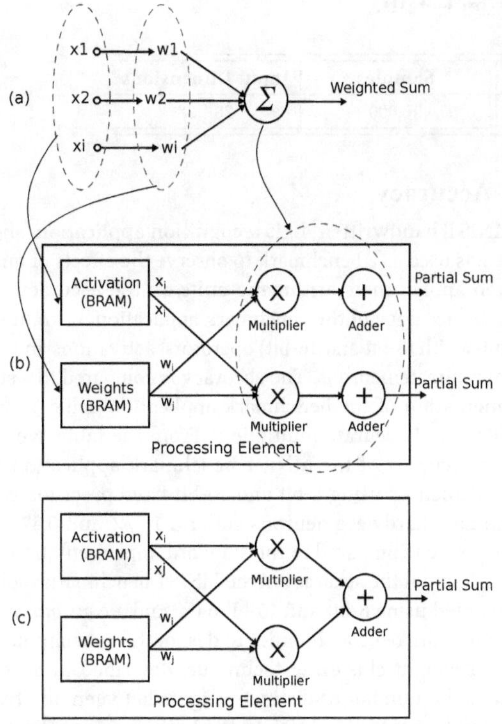


**Figure 2: Implementation of a single processing element on the FPGA to compute the partial sum of single or multiple neurons.**

and design requirements, a layer/neuron can be implemented by multiple concurrently executing PEs. This flexibility allows the designer to choose a PE configuration based on design constraints.

The proposed methodology also supports approximate and constant multipliers for the PE implementation. The modular and RTL based implementation of the proposed PE makes it very easy to instantiate high performance approximate multipliers, such as those provided in [14], to meet the implementation's performance constraints. The utilization of approximate multipliers, for PE implementation, also results in overall area savings, which can be used for instantiating more PEs on a smaller FPGA platform with limited resources. As discussed in Section 2.3, we perform weight clustering to significantly reduce the total number of distinct weights for a layer. Utilizing the resultant fixed clustered weights, our proposed methodology can configure the PE to use constant multipliers. With constant multipliers, there is no need to store the weight vector $w$ and only one single BRAM is used by a PE. Besides significantly reducing the overall resource utilization of a PE, the constant multipliers-based PE offer very high performance as compared to the accurate/approximate multipliers-based PE implementations.

## 2.2 Data Quantization

Standard implementations of ANNs use 32-bit, or word-size floating point operators, activations and weights during the training and inference phases [1]. In order to reduce the memory required to

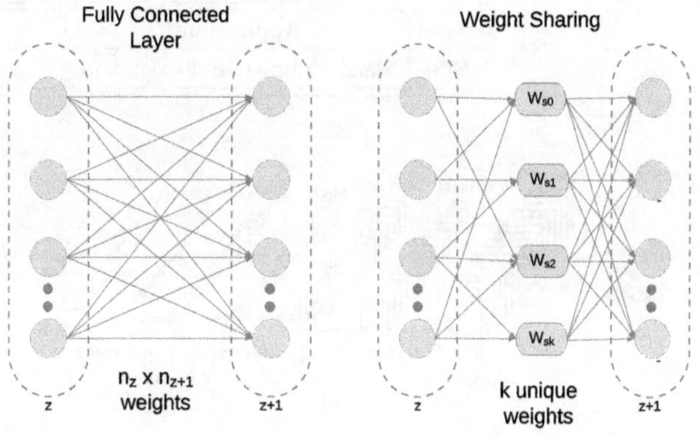


**Figure 3: Proposed Weight Sharing technique compared to a Fully Connected layer.**

store the weights, intermediate outputs and the memory accesses, we use 8-bit and 16-bit fixed point arithmetic operators, weights and activations during the training and inference of the neural network. Several works in literature [2] [8] have shown that quantization of operators and data, even below 8-bits, have little to no effect on the accuracy of the ANN application.

To validate this, we re-train and infer a standard MNIST handwritten digit recognition benchmark using 8-bit and 16-bit fixed precision operator. For the 8-bit and 16-bit fixed point operators, we use 1 bit and 2 bits for the integer part, respectively and 7-bits and 14-bits for the fractional part, respectively. It is important to note that the output of the arithmetic operator is truncated down to 8 and 16-bits respectively.

## 2.3 Weight Clustering

In a fully connected neural network, the number of weighted synapses between any two layers is represented as $n_z$ x $n_{z+1}$, where $z$ is the layer number and $n$ is the number of neurons in the given layer. In order to reduce the memory required to store the respective weights on the PE and to minimize the latency due to memory reads, we propose a layer-wise, clustering based, *weight sharing technique*, to reduce the number of unique weights in the network.

We propose the use of Kmeans, an unsupervised learning algorithm, to divide a one-dimensional weight matrix $W_{z,z+1}$ into k clusters, where k determines the number of unique weights. The objective of the k-means algorithm is to minimize the sum of distances of every weight in a cluster to the cluster centroid $C_k$. The distance between the weight and the centroid $C_k$ is computed as the *Euclidean distance.* Post clustering, weights belonging to a cluster k are replaced by the centroids $C_k$ the respective cluster. Therefore, the centroid weight $C_k$ is shared by all the synapses in the cluster $k$. Figure 3 shows the weight clustering technique used between two hidden layers of a fully connected network.

With the weights reduced to $k$ fixed values, we propose the use of constant multipliers to design the PE. The use of constant multipliers significantly reduces the area and runtime latency of a single PE. This can be attributed to the exclusion of the redundant

**Table 1: Dataset and Application Details.**

| Dataset | Application | Source | Samples | Input Dimensions |
|---|---|---|---|---|
| MNIST | Hand Writing Digit Recognition | NYU | 10,000 | 28 * 28 |

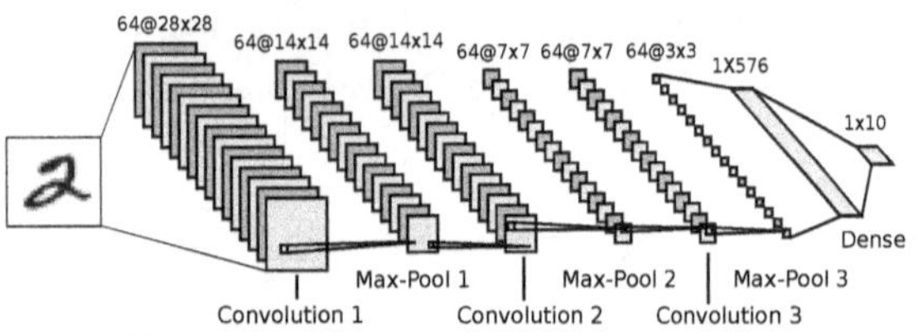


**Figure 4: LeNet based MNIST digit recognition application.**

BRAM used to store weights, the reduced number memory reads and the size of a constant multiplier.

## 3 EXPERIMENTAL SETUP

To evaluate the performance and efficiency of the proposed Rox-ANN design methodology, we have used VHDL, Xilinx Vivado 17.4 and Xilinx Artix-7 AC701 evaluation platform (xc7a200tfbg676-2 device) for the implementation of proposed PE design. We have used the 2-neurons configuration of the PE, shown in Fig. 2(b), for describing the effects of utilizing accurate, approximate and constant multipliers on area utilization, critical path delay and energy consumption. For EDP calculations, Vivado Simulator and Power Analyzer tools have been used.

We evaluate the following metrics.

*Application Accuracy.* The classification accuracy of the benchmark application when retrained using quantized activations and weights, and approximate arithmetic units.

*Energy Consumption.* The static and dynamic energy consumed by the proposed PE is mainly attributed to the size of the BRAMs and the arithmetic units used to design the PE.

*Area Overhead.* The area (number of utilized LUTs) of a PE's implementation is also mainly defined by the size of BRAM and choice of arithmetic units.

*Latency.* The latency of the designed PE is measured as the critical path delay for a single multiply-accumulate (MAC) operation.

We perform experiments on the LeNet based implementation of the MNIST digit recognition application. Figure 4 shows the architecture of the neural network used to train and infer the MNIST digit recognition application. Table 1 shows the details of the MNIST dataset.

## 4 RESULTS

In this section, we present results that demonstrate the accuracy obtained and also the energy efficiency, reduced latency and area reduction achieved using the Rox-ANN design.

### 4.1 Accuracy

The MNIST handwritten digit recognition application, shown in Figure 4, is used as a benchmark to observe the effects of quantized data and approximate arithmetic units on the accuracy. Table 2 shows the accuracy of the benchmark application, re-trained using fixed bit-width (8-bit and 16-bit) operators, activations and weights and approximate neurons. The accuracy is compared to a standard implementation of the benchmark application using 32-bit float point data and accurate multipliers. From the table, we observe that the accuracy of the MNIST benchmark application trained and implemented using 8-bit and 16-bit fixed precision data and approximate hardware neurons suffer a 1.77% and 0.37% loss in accuracy when compared to the standard implementation.

Table 3 shows the accuracy of the MNIST benchmark application, implemented using 8-bit and 16-bit data, and a *constant multiplier* based hardware neuron. In order to design the constant multiplier, we use a weight clustering technique, described in Section 2.3, to reduce the number of distinct weights between any two fully connected layers of the ANN. In the benchmark application, we introduce constant multiplier based PEs to implement the dense layers of the LeNet architecture. In Table 3, we observe a marginal drop in application accuracy with a reduction in the number of constant multipliers used to implement the dense layers.

### 4.2 Performance Metrics of Processing Element

The proposed PE design, shown in Fig. 2(b), has been implemented using two different quantization schemes and utilizing accurate, approximate and constant multipliers. For accurate and approximate multipliers-based PEs, both neurons (in a single PE) reads 576 different activations (vector $x$) and corresponding weights (vector $w$) from the associated BRAMs. For constant multipliers-based PE design, the clustered weights define the constant multipliers, and hence, only the activations (vector $x$) is read from a single associate BRAM. Table 4 shows the area, energy consumption and latency of the *four* proposed configurations of the PE. The results demonstrate that the use of approximate PEs designed using *Rox-ANN* have a significant impact on the area, energy and latency of an ANN implementation, when compared to accurate multipliers-based PE implementation. For accurate multipliers-based PE, our methodology utilizes Vivado speed-optimized multiplier IPs. For implementing approximate signed multipliers, we have used 8×8 and 16×16 precision-reduced multipliers. For these multipliers, the two LSBs of each input operand have been truncated to use 6×6 and 14×14 multiplier IPs (provided by Vivado) to implement precision-reduced 8×8 and 16×16 multipliers respectively. An accurate 8×8 multiplier occupies 75 LUTs, whereas 42 LUTs are occupied by a precision-reduced 8×8 approximate mutiplier. From Fig. 5 we see that the use of 8-bit approximate arithmetic units achieves a 65.6%, 55.1%, and 18.9% reduction in the area, energy consumption and latency for a single PE when compared to a fully-accurate PE. The

**Table 2: Experimental Statistics for Approximate Arithmetic Neurons**

| Dataset | Fixed Bit-Width Implementation | | Float-Point Implementation | |
|---|---|---|---|---|
| | Configuration | Accuracy | Configuration | Accuracy |
| MNIST | S_8 | 97.33 % | S_32 | 99. 10 % |
| | S_16 | 98.73% | | |

**Table 3: Experimental Statistics for Constant Multiplier Approach.**

| Dataset | Fixed Bit-Width Implementation | | | Float-Point Implementation | | |
|---|---|---|---|---|---|---|
| | Configuration | Clusters | Accuracy | Configuration | Clusters | Accuracy |
| MNIST | S_8 | 4 | 96.41% | S_32 | 1 | 99.10 % |
| | | 8 | 96.93% | | | |
| | | 16 | 97.19% | | | |
| | S_16 | 4 | 97.28% | | | |
| | | 8 | 97.94% | | | |
| | | 16 | 98.21% | | | |

**Table 4: Area, Energy and Latency of the proposed PEs.**

| PE Design | Area (LUTs) | Multiplier Area (LUTs) | Energy (pJ) | Latency (ns) |
|---|---|---|---|---|
| 8-bit Accurate | 1233 | 75 | 3.18 | 9.65 |
| 16-bit Accurate | 2488 | 287 | 4.83 | 11.34 |
| 8-bit Approximate | 856 | 42 | 2.17 | 9.20 |
| 16-bit Approximate | 2181 | 220 | 4.84 | 10.69 |
| 8-bit Constant | 150 | 19 | 2.30 | 7.59 |
| 16-bit Constant | 256 | 52 | 3.04 | 8.70 |

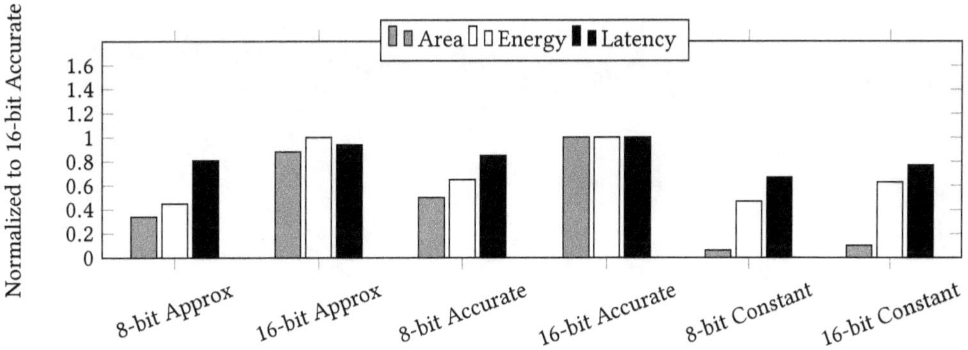


**Figure 5: Area, Energy and Latency of the proposed PEs, normalized to the 16-bit Accurate PE.**

performance of the ANN can be further improved by incorporating constant multipliers based PEs in the design of the fully-connected layers of the ANN. PEs designed using 8×8 and 16×16 constant multipliers demonstrate a 95.08% and 89.98% reduction in area respectively, and a 33.05 % and 23.3% reduction in critical path delay, respectively, when compared to a 16-bit accurate PE. The LUTs occupied by 8×8 and 16×16 constant multipliers are 19 and 52 respectively.

## 5 CONCLUSION

Approximate computing is a design paradigm used to reduce the resources required to implement artificial neural networks (ANNs) on hardware. In this paper, we present Rox-ANN, an FPGA-based methodology to design processing elements (PEs) that supports the use of approximation techniques, such as approximate arithmetic units and quantized data, to implement artificial neural networks (ANNs). With the proposed PEs, we demonstrate a 65.6%, 55.1% and 18.9% reduction in area, energy consumption and latency for a 8-bit approximate PE when compared to a PE designed using 16-bit accurate arithmetic units. Furthermore, we propose a technique to implement a fully-connected layer of an ANN using constant-multipliers based PEs.

## REFERENCES


[1] Murat Alçın, İhsan Pehlivan, and İsmail Koyuncu. 2016. Hardware design and implementation of a novel ANN-based chaotic generator in FPGA. *Optik* 127, 13 (2016), 5500–5505.

[2] Tianshi Chen, Zidong Du, Ninghui Sun, Jia Wang, Chengyong Wu, Yunji Chen, and Olivier Temam. 2014. Diannao: A small-footprint high-throughput accelerator for ubiquitous machine-learning. In *ACM Sigplan Notices*, Vol. 49. ACM, 269–284.

[3] Yu-Hsin Chen, Tushar Krishna, Joel S Emer, and Vivienne Sze. 2017. Eyeriss: An energy-efficient reconfigurable accelerator for deep convolutional neural networks. *IEEE Journal of Solid-State Circuits* 52, 1 (2017), 127–138.

[4] George E Dahl, Dong Yu, Li Deng, and Alex Acero. 2012. Context-dependent pre-trained deep neural networks for large-vocabulary speech recognition. *IEEE Transactions on audio, speech, and language processing* 20, 1 (2012), 30–42.

[5] Zidong Du, Krishna Palem, Avinash Lingamneni, Olivier Temam, Yunji Chen, and Chengyong Wu. 2014. Leveraging the error resilience of machine-learning applications for designing highly energy efficient accelerators. In *2014 19th Asia and South Pacific Design Automation Conference (ASP-DAC)*. IEEE, 201–206.

[6] K. Guo, L. Sui, J. Qiu, J. Yu, J. Wang, S. Yao, S. Han, Y. Wang, and H. Yang. 2018. Angel-Eye: A Complete Design Flow for Mapping CNN Onto Embedded FPGA. *IEEE Transactions on Computer-Aided Design of Integrated Circuits and Systems* 37, 1 (Jan 2018), 35–47. https://doi.org/10.1109/TCAD.2017.2705069

[7] Itay Hubara, Matthieu Courbariaux, Daniel Soudry, Ran El-Yaniv, and Yoshua Bengio. 2017. Quantized neural networks: Training neural networks with low precision weights and activations. *The Journal of Machine Learning Research* 18, 1 (2017), 6869–6898.

[8] Kyuyeon Hwang and Wonyong Sung. 2014. Fixed-point feedforward deep neural network design using weights+ 1, 0, and- 1. In *2014 IEEE Workshop on Signal Processing Systems (SiPS)*. IEEE, 1–6.

[9] Patrick Judd, Jorge Albericio, Tayler Hetherington, Tor Aamodt, Natalie Enright Jerger, Raquel Urtasun, and Andreas Moshovos. 2015. Reduced-precision strategies for bounded memory in deep neural nets. *arXiv preprint arXiv:1511.05236* (2015).

[10] Alex Krizhevsky, Ilya Sutskever, and Geoffrey E Hinton. 2012. Imagenet classification with deep convolutional neural networks. In *Advances in neural information processing systems*. 1097–1105.

[11] UroÅą Lotric and Patricio Bulic. 2012. Applicability of approximate multipliers in hardware neural networks. *Neurocomputing* 96 (2012), 57–65.

[12] Mohammad Rastegari, Vicente Ordonez, Joseph Redmon, and Ali Farhadi. 2016. XNOR-Net: ImageNet Classification Using Binary Convolutional Neural Networks. *CoRR* abs/1603.05279 (2016). arXiv:1603.05279 http://arxiv.org/abs/1603.05279

[13] Mohammad Samragh, Mohammad Ghasemzadeh, and Farinaz Koushanfar. 2017. Customizing neural networks for efficient fpga implementation. In *2017 IEEE 25th Annual International Symposium on Field-Programmable Custom Computing Machines (FCCM)*. IEEE, 85–92.

[14] Salim Ullah, Sanjeev Sripadraj Murthy, and Akash Kumar. 2018. SMApproxlib: Library of FPGA-based Approximate Multipliers. In *Proceedings of the 55th Annual Design Automation Conference (DAC '18)*. ACM, New York, NY, USA, Article 157, 6 pages. https://doi.org/10.1145/3195970.3196115

[15] Swagath Venkataramani, Ashish Ranjan, Kaushik Roy, and Anand Raghunathan. 2014. AxNN: energy-efficient neuromorphic systems using approximate computing. In *Proceedings of the 2014 international symposium on Low power electronics and design*. 27–32.

[16] Y. Wang, J. Xu, Y. Han, H. Li, and X. Li. 2016. DeepBurning: Automatic generation of FPGA-based learning accelerators for the Neural Network family. In *2016 53nd ACM/EDAC/IEEE Design Automation Conference (DAC)*. 1–6. https://doi.org/10.1145/2897937.2898002

[17] Chen Zhang, Peng Li, Guangyu Sun, Yijin Guan, Bingjun Xiao, and Jason Cong. 2015. Optimizing FPGA-based Accelerator Design for Deep Convolutional Neural Networks. In *Proceedings of the 2015 ACM/SIGDA International Symposium on Field-Programmable Gate Arrays (FPGA '15)*. ACM, New York, NY, USA, 161–170. https://doi.org/10.1145/2684746.2689060

[18] Qian Zhang, Ting Wang, Ye Tian, Feng Yuan, and Qiang Xu. 2015. ApproxANN: An approximate computing framework for artificial neural network. In *Proceedings of the 2015 DATE*. 701–706.

# Exploration of Segmented Bus As Scalable Global Interconnect for Neuromorphic Computing

Adarsha Balaji[†], Yuefeng Wu[‡], Anup Das[†], Francky Catthoor[II], and Siebren Schaafsma[‡]

[†] Drexel University, Philadelphia, USA
[‡] Stichting IMEC Nederland, Eindhoven, Netherlands
[II] IMEC Belgium and KU Leuven

## ABSTRACT

Spiking Neural Networks (SNNs) are efficient computation models for spatio-temporal pattern recognition on resource and power constrained platforms. Dedicated SNN hardware, also called neuromorphic hardware, can further reduce the energy consumption of these platforms. A neuromorphic hardware consists of crossbars, which are arrangements of input and output neurons with fully-connected synapses. Time-multiplexed interconnects are used to communicate spikes between crossbars. When a SNN model is mapped on multiple crossbars, the time-multiplexed interconnect increases spike latency and energy consumption, and disorders spike arrivals at output neurons, which reduces application accuracy. In this paper, we propose segmented bus interconnect for global synapses in a neuromorphic architecture. The objective is to reduce power consumption and enable parallel processing compared to traditional time-multiplexed interconnects. The fundamental idea for the segmented bus is to partition a single bus into several segments, with the segmentation switches controlled by software. We evaluate the scalability of segmented bus using synthetic applications. Our results show that segmented bus reduces the latency and energy consumption of the global synapse network significantly with respect to state-of-the-art techniques.

## CCS CONCEPTS

• **Hardware → Emerging architectures**; **Neural systems**; *Interconnect.*

## KEYWORDS

Spiking neural networks (SNNs), segmented bus, spike latency

**ACM Reference Format:**
Adarsha Balaji, Yuefeng Wu, Anup Das, Francky Catthoor, and Siebren Schaafsma. 2019. Exploration of Segmented Bus As Scalable Global Interconnect for Neuromorphic Computing. In *Great Lakes Symposium on VLSI 2019 (GLSVLSI'19), May 9–11, 2019, Tysons Corner, VA, USA.* ACM, NY, NY, USA. 6 pages. https://doi.org/10.1145/3299874.3319491


ACM ISBN 978-1-4503-6252-8/19/05...$15.00
https://doi.org/10.1145/3299874.3319491

## 1 INTRODUCTION

Spiking Neural Networks (SNNs) [17] are widely-used computation models for spatio-temporal pattern recognition [9]. In a SNN, neurons communicate with each other by sending short impulses of infinitesimally small duration, called *spikes*. Spikes are communicated via synaptic weights, which are adjusted during training of SNNs. Dedicated SNN hardware, also called neuromorphic hardware [12], are used to execute SNNs. A neuromorphic hardware consists of crossbars, which are arrangements of input and output neurons with fully-connected synapses. Time-multiplexed interconnects are used to communicate spikes between crossbars. In the context of neuromorphic computing, SNN synapses that map inside crossbars are called **local** synapses, while those that map on the time-multiplexed interconnect are called **global** synapses.

Due to the sharing of the time-multiplexed interconnect amongst all global synapses, the interconnect becomes the performance and energy bottleneck, especially for SNNs with large number of neurons and synapses. In our earlier work [7], we observe that the hand written digit recognition application [9] (with 894 neurons and 79.4K synapses), when mapped on a neuromorphic hardware (with four 256-neurons crossbars arranged in a 2x2 mesh), the energy consumption of the global synapses contributes to over 60% of the total energy consumption of the hardware. Additionally, the spike congestion and latency on the time-multiplexed interconnect increases inter-spike interval distortion, and spike disorder, each of which reduces the application's accuracy. Our previous work reported an accuracy loss of ≈ 10% for the hand written digit recognition application compared to when the application is analyzed using software simulations.

To address these limitations, several interconnect topologies are explored recently to assess their suitability for neuromorphic computing. Examples include the networks-on-chip (NoCs), which is used in TrueNorth [1], the multi-stage NoCs, which is used in CxQuad [12], and the toroidal mesh, which is used in SpiNNaker [14]. In Figure 1, we illustrate how the spike latency on global synapses of a NoC-based neuromorphic hardware increases as we increase the number of neurons. This exponential growth of latency reduces an application's accuracy. We observe a similar trend for all interconnect networks that are currently used in neuromorphic hardware. These results clearly motivate us to investigate a scalable interconnect architecture for global synapses of a neuromorphic hardware.

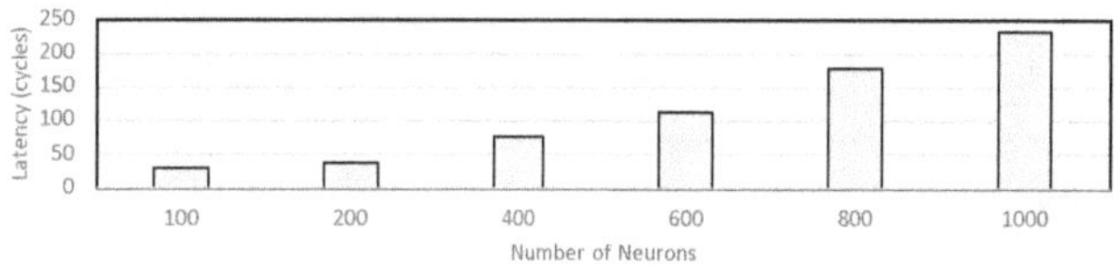


**Figure 1: Significant increase of spike latency with increase in the number of neurons.**

In this work, we propose to use a segmented bus approach [5] for the global synapse communication in neuromorphic hardware platforms, which we illustrate in Figure 5. Conceptually, a segmented bus is a parallel bus, where each individual bus lane is partitioned into several segments using segmentation switches. Segmented bus improves (1) energy efficiency, by allowing two communicating crossbars to utilize only a segment, rather than the entire bus, and (2) parallel processing, by concurrently communicating spikes through non-overlapping segments. We show that segmented bus reduces spike latency by 67%, and energy consumption by 57%.

The remainder of this work is organized as follows. We provide background on SNNs and segmented bus in Section 2. We introduce our segmented bus-based neuromorphic hardware design in Section 3. We present our evaluation methodology in Section 4. We compare against state-of-the-art in Section 5. Finally, we provide related works in Section 6, and conclude the paper in Section 7.

# 2 BACKGROUND

## 2.1 Background on SNNs and Neuromorphic Hardware

In this section we introduce SNNs, and provide an overview of their execution on a neuromorphic hardware. In Figure 2, we illustrate how neurons are interconnected in SNNs. Input $x_1, x_2, \cdots, x_n$ are used to excite the input neurons, which are connected to an output neuron using synaptic weights $w_1, w_2, \cdots, w_n$. The output neuron integrates the spikes at its input, and generates an output spike when its membrane potential exceeds a threshold $\theta_i$. In this figure we illustrate how the input spikes (blue) are integrated to generate two output spikes (red).

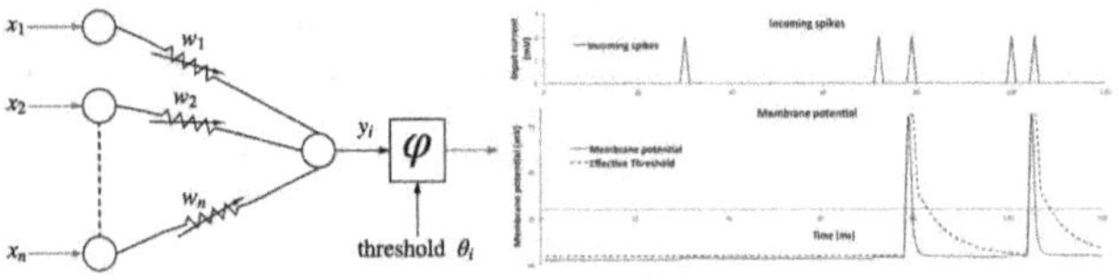


**Figure 2: An illustration of SNN, with n input neurons feeding spikes to an output neuron.**

In deep neural network architectures, (spiking) neurons are organized into layers. A typical deep SNN architecture consists of one input layer, one or more hidden layers, and one output layer. SNNs learn to perform tasks by considering examples from the field, without being exclusively programmed with any task-specific rules. To this end, synaptic weights in a SNN are adjusted for specific training examples to generate the desired spike train in the output layer neurons, a process known as the **training** of SNNs. Once trained, SNNs are deployed for **inference** with in-field or unseen data. An application's accuracy is assessed either from inter-spike interval times, or from the spike rate of output spike trains.

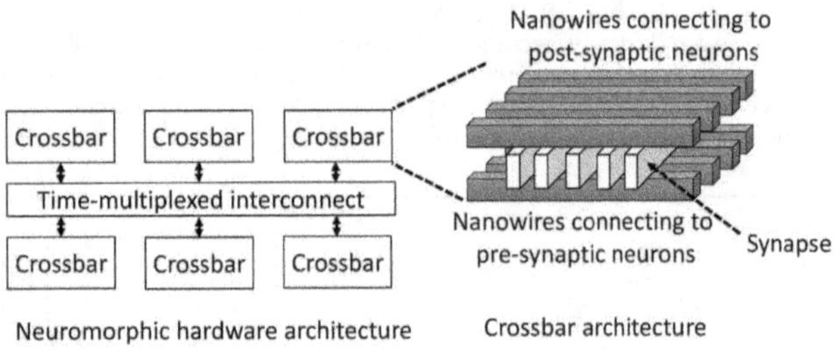


**Figure 3: An illustration of crossbar-based neuromorphic hardware with time-multiplexed interconnect.**

SNNs are executed on neuromorphic hardware, which consists of crossbars interconnected using a time-multiplexed interconnect, which we illustrate in Figure 3. To limit energy consumption of crossbars, their sizes are constrained. Typically, a crossbar can accommodate between 128 and 256 neurons. For a large application, such as the handwritten digit recognition, spikes on the global synapse (those that map on the time-multiplexed interconnect) end up with non-zero communication latency. The accuracy therefore deviates significantly from what is analyzed using software simulations (which assume zero spike latency).

## 2.2 Background on Segmented Bus

Segmented bus architecture for on-chip interconnect is proposed to reduce power consumption and enable parallel processing compared to traditional bus architecture. The fundamental idea for the segmented bus is to partition each individual bus lanes of a parallel bus into several segments [5], where interconnections between segments are bridged and controlled by switches. In Figure 4, we illustrate segmented bus with 8 devices, partitioned into 3 segments.

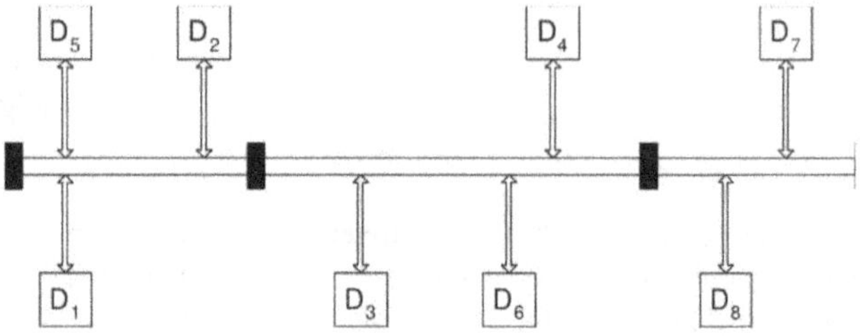


**Figure 4: An illustration of segmented bus with 8 devices divided into 3 segments.**

Segmented bus offers the following key advantages that we exploit in this work.

- **Power Efficiency:** Due to the segmentation, node-to-node communications on the bus do not need to wake and utilize the entire bus, reducing power consumption significantly.
- **Parallel Processing:** Communications staying within the scope of a single segment can be concurrently executed after partitioning, facilitating parallel processing.
- **Scalability:** More nodes can be ported to the segmented bus with relatively shortened length of the bus since the nodes can connect to different segments. This increases scalability.

# 3 SEGMENTED BUS BASED NEUROMORPHIC HARDWARE

## 3.1 High-level Overview

In Figure 5, we present a high-level overview of our neuromorphic hardware design. Observe the similarity of this design with that of the generic neuromorphic hardware, which we illustrate in Figure 3. At a high-level, the time-multiplexed interconnect in Fiigure 3 is replaced by the segmented bus architecture, and a new block is added for the coordination and control of the switches. The segmented bus communicate spike packets using one or more segments in the bus. Based on this understanding, we now present a detailed design of our segmented bus based neuromorphic hardware.

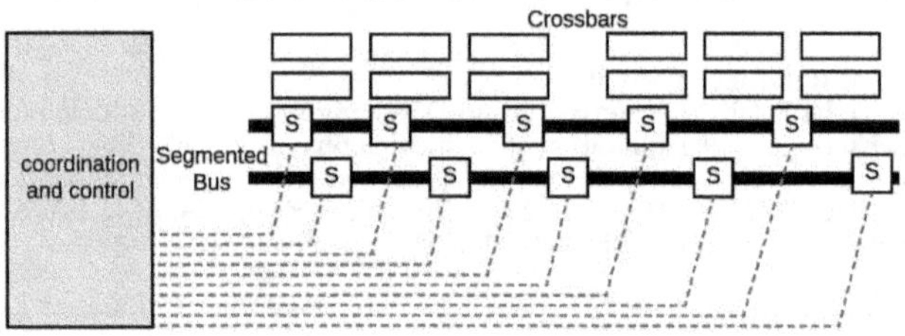


**Figure 5: Segmented bus-based neuromorphic hardware.**

## 3.2 Detailed Design

We integrated our segmented bus implementation inside the Noxim simulator [4]. Following are the details of the components that we implement for segmented bus.

*3.2.1 Spike Representation.* Address-event representation (AER) is a communication protocol originally proposed as a method to communicate sparse neural events between neuromorphic crossbars [3]. Massive interconnections among individual neurons or neuron clusters are allocated to the reduced number of channels by time division multiplexing. According to the AER protocol, each spike is represented by its location and spiking time.

In Figure 6, we provide a simple example of AER protocol. The sender generates 4 spikes from Neurone 1, 2, 0, 1 successively. The encoder that implements AER protocol compresses the spikes in one channel (bus) connected to the decoder at receiver's side. The spikes are distinguished based on the source neuron ID and spiking time. The decoder restores the spikes from the stream and allocates them to designated receivers.

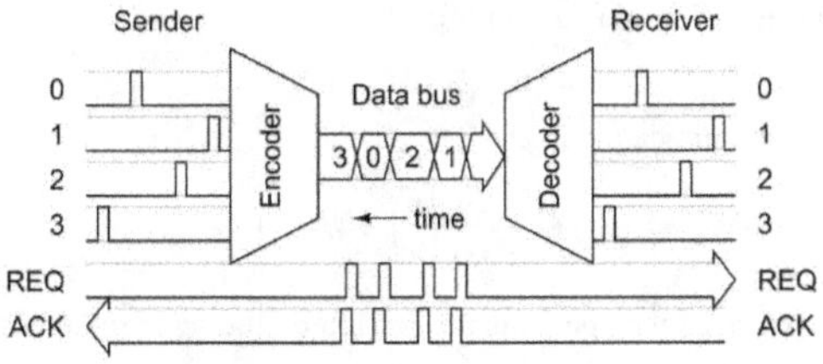


**Figure 6: A example of AER protocol [3].**

For fully connected networks, assuming that there are $N$ neurons in the input layer and $N$ neurons in the output layer, there should be $N^2$ connections without AER, while only $(2 \cdot N + 1)$ connections with AER protocol (the extra 1 is for the connection of the bus in the middle). Clearly, AER protocol reduces the complexity to $O(N)$, compared to $O(N^2)$ in the default scenario. We therefore, use AER protocol for our design.

*3.2.2 Arbitration.* We use segment arbiters (SA) to arbitrate spike packets within a segment (intra-segment arbitration), and central arbiters (CA) to arbitrate spike packets across segments (i.e., inter-segment arbitration). In our architecture, only one crossbar can act as a master for a given segment, and multicast spike packets to a subset of the crossbars attached to the segment. Apart from giving control to the master crossbar, the SA is also responsible to notify CA when a inter-segment communication is needed, such is the case when a crossbar needs to communicate spike packet to another crossbar located at a different segment. CA is responsible to coordinate inter-segment communications and resolve collisions.

However, arbitration increases spike communication latency. To address this limitation, we analyze all spike communications offline, and program the arbiters for run-time use. This is to eliminate any arbitration related latency during inference. To achieve this, we introduce externally controllable switches, which connect crossbars to the segment, and determine the spike flow directions and connectivity. The overall flow of our neuromorphic approach is as follows. Once a SNN is trained using the training set, the trained SNN is analyzed with test data, which are representative of the SNN's input for in-field operations. Using the spike communication information, we use an offline approach to partition the segmented bus into multiple segments for parallel use, and program the switches to facilitate spike communication between a pair of crossbars. Since, no run-time control is necessary in our approach, the design of our switch can be simplified. In Figure 7, we show the simplified design of our switch, which we use in our neuromorphic hardware. The design consists of 6 NOT gates, which can be enabled or disabled. A switch can communicate spikes in three directions on a segment: direction A (west), direction B (east), &, direction C (north). In our design, the north direction is reserved for communicating with a crossbar within the segment. In Figure 7, we also illustrate the control signals necessary to configure the direction of spike propagation, which we generate based on the offline analysis with the test data. Our CA design is implemented in software. However, to facilitate inter-segment communication, we use two-way switches, which are similar in design to the three-way segmentation switches of Figure 7 with the exception of two directions instead of three.

*3.2.3 Communication Protocol.* In our segmented bus design, we use circuit switching protocol. Generally speaking, in a circuit switching network, a dedicated communication channel is established before any two nodes can communicate. In the light of directly channeled connection, the quality of

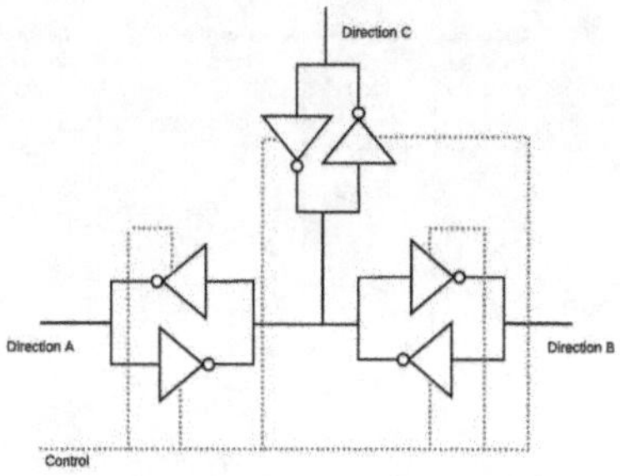


**Figure 7: Segmentation switches.**

service (QoS) can be guaranteed at a cost of additional latency due to channel establishment. However, in our design, the channels (i.e., the segments) are pre-established using offline analysis, so latency is not an issue. The only challenge in our design is a communication channel between a pair of crossbars, which has not been analyzed offline. If such a channel can be established using the existing configurations, then there will be no impact. Otherwise, spikes packets can get blocked, failing to find an appropriate path from source to destination. This could lead to an accuracy drop. In our design, we analyze such impact at run-time and reconfigure the segmented bus arbiters periodically to incorporate unseen communication patterns.

*3.2.4 Spike Collision Resolution.* We consider the following two classes of spike collisions in our proposed architecture:

- multi-master spike collision within a segment, and
- spike collision across the segments.

The first type of collision occurs when there are more than one master crossbars in a segment, and they both generate spike at the same time. The spikes will collide at a switch, and the switch may discard one of the spikes randomly. The second type of collision occurs when a spike from another segment arrives at the same time when a spike is generated by the master in the segment. In this case also, the switch at which the two spikes collide, will discard one of the spikes randomly. These two types of collision can occur independently, as well as simultaneously, and result in spike loss, which leads to an accuracy loss.

To address both these problems, a time-multiplexing-based scheduler is developed based on the fact that the temporal length of spikes for inter-neuron communication is typically longer than one clock cycle, mostly 1-2 orders higher. In this mechanism, each spike has its own hard deadline to arrive at its destination. It is set as the generation time of the next spike to the destination plus the length of the spike. In digital neuromorphic systems, each spike event is normally allocated one full clock cycle. As long as the spike arrives at the clock cycle no later than its hard deadline, there is no accuracy impact. Our scheduler implements exactly so. The underlying time multiplexing mechanism entails dynamic change of the connectivity among the master and slave crossbars in the bus architecture every cycle in a time-multiplexed fashion. We propose a mapping algorithm to reassign masters and slaves dynamically with low overhead and processing time, reusing established segments from previous cycles as much as possible. We demonstrate this time multiplexing mechanism in Figure 8. There are two spike sources, which generate spike 0:0 and 1:0 at the same time. From the reception perspective, these spikes arrive before their deadlines, which is the generation time of Spike 0:1 added with their identical length. However, Spike 0:1 actually arrives at the destination after the generation time of Spike 1:1 and therefore, misses its deadline.

We now present our evaluation methodology, together with comparison with state-of-the-art.

# 4 EVALUATION METHODOLOGY

We build our simulation environment with the following system components.

- **CARLsim** [6] : A GPU accelerated simulator used to train and test SNN-based applications. CARLsim reports spike times for every synapse in the SNN.
- **Noxim** [4] : A trace-driven and cycle-accurate interconnect simulator for multiprocessor systems. We extend it (1) to incorporate crossbar-based neuromorphic hardware, (2) to communicate spikes

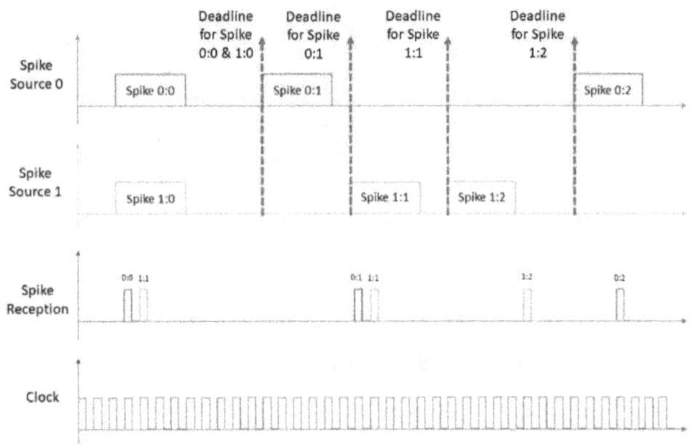


**Figure 8: An example of time division multiplexing.**

| Apps | Synapse | Topology | Apps | Synapse | Topology |
|---|---|---|---|---|---|
| Synth100 | 2,400 | FeedForward (40, 40, 20) | Synth600 | 87,500 | FeedForward (250, 250, 100) |
| Synth200 | 3,200 | FeedForward (80, 80, 40) | Synth700 | 100,000 | FeedForward (300, 300, 100) |
| Synth300 | 21,600 | FeedForward (120, 120, 60) | Synth800 | 150,000 | FeedForward (300, 300, 200) |
| Synth400 | 37,500 | FeedForward (150, 150, 100) | Synth900 | 180,000 | FeedForward (300, 300, 300) |
| Synth500 | 60,000 | FeedForward (200, 200, 100) | Synth1000 | 240,000 | FeedForward (400, 400, 200) |

**Table 1: Synthetic applications we use to evaluate our design.**

(rather than data packets), and (3) to generate key performance statistics such as energy consumption, spike latency, ISI distortion, and spike disorder. In our mechanism, the spike timing information from CARLsim is used as trace and is input to Noxim to generate the performance statistics.

- **CxQuad** [12]: We configure Noxim++ to model the CxQuad neuromorphic hardware at 65nm technology nodes with 256 neurons per crossbar. We extract the latency and energy numbers of each crossbar from silicon data [12]. We also use the analytical performance and energy model of interconnect network at 65nm technology. Finally, we use predictive technology mapping (PTM) [18] to scale technology parameters to 28nm nodes.

We compare our design with the *Baseline* system, which uses time-division multiplexing based NoCs for spike communication on the global synapses using the packet switching technique. We evaluate 10 synthetic applications, with number of neurons between 100 and 1000. These applications are indicated in Table 1.

We evaluate the following metrics.

*Energy Consumption.* In our design, energy is mainly consumed by switches to relay the spikes, and is estimated to be proportional to the number of switch hops the spike travels through.

*Area Overhead.* Area overhead is estimated to be proportional to the total number of switches on all occupied buses.

*Latency.* The latency in our design is due to two components: switch hop and time division multiplexing. The switch hop latency is obtained by multiplying the switch latency with the number of hops a spike takes to reach its destination. The time division multiplexing related latency is computed as follows.

In our segmented bus simulators, which we integrate in Noxim, the length of each spike is set to one clock cycle. In our proposed solution for time division multiplexing, the duration of concurrent spikes will be extended. The length of the extension is related to the number of overlapping connection groups on the bus. We consider that there are $n$ overlapping connection groups mapped onto one bus and each concurrent spike will consume one additional time unit. When there is no multiplexing, the latency is $L = 0$. With one multiplexing, the total latency is

$$L = 1 \cdot \binom{n}{2} \tag{1}$$

With two multiplexing, the total latency is

$$L = 2 \cdot \binom{n}{3} \tag{2}$$

Considering all possible multiplexing scenarios, the total latency is

$$L = 1 \cdot \binom{n}{2} + 2 \cdot \binom{n}{3} + \cdots + (n-1) \cdot \binom{n}{n} = \sum_{k=2}^{n} (k-1) \cdot \binom{n}{k} \tag{3}$$

The above equation can be simplified to

$$L = (n-2) \cdot 2^{n-1} + 1 \tag{4}$$

The total communication is given by

$$C = \sum_{k=1}^{n} \binom{n}{k} = 2^n - 1 \tag{5}$$

The worst-case latency per communication on the segmented bus

$$\begin{aligned} L_{TDM} &= \frac{\text{Total Latency}}{\text{Total Communication}} \\ &= \frac{n}{2 - \frac{1}{2^{n-1}}} - 1 \end{aligned} \tag{6}$$

To estimate the impact of time multiplexing on the overall latency, we simulate Equation 6 for different values of $n$, i.e., the number of overlapping segments mapped on to a bus. In Figure 9, we report these results. We make the following two observations.

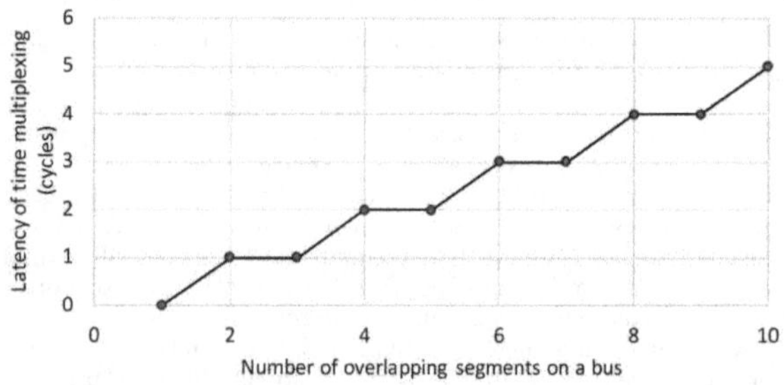


**Figure 9: Increase in latency due to time multiplexing, with increase in the number of overlapping segments.**

First, as the number of overlapping segments increases, there is an increase in the latency. Even for $n = 10$, the latency due to multiplexing is only 5 cycles, which is less than 3% of the total latency on the bus. Second, if there are no overlapping segments i.e., there are no intra-segment and inter-segment conflicts, the latency due to time multiplexing is 0. This is the case with the result for $n = 1$. These results clearly demonstrate that segmented bus has much reduced latency for spike communication in the context of a neuromorphic hardware.

## 5 RESULTS

In this section, we present detailed results of our design.

### 5.1 Comparison of Spike Latency on the Global Synapses

In Figure 10, we plot the spike latency of our design normalized to the Baseline system for all our evaluated workloads. We make the following key observations from this figure.

First, between the Baseline and our segmented bus-based design, our design achieves lower latency. This is because, the segmented bus splits a single bus into multiple segments, with each segment operating mostly independently of one another. The reduced interference reduces the latency

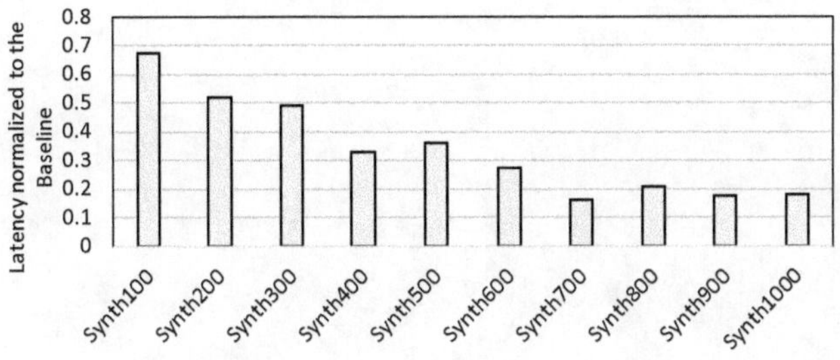


**Figure 10: Latency, normalized to the Baseline.**

significantly compared to a NoC, where the spike congestion on some of the paths can be large. We observe that our design achieves 67% lower latency on average for these evaluated workloads. Second, the latency improvement increases for larger SNNs. We observe that our improvement for synth900 and synth1000 is 85% lower than that of a NoC. This significant improvement is due to three factors. **First**, with large SNNs, the number of spikes on global synapses is considerably large, increasing the spike traffic on almost every path in a NoC. The routing algorithm therefore, cannot find paths with lower congestion. Segmented bus does not suffer from this limitation because communications among a pair of crossbars happen within a segment. Only in rare instances are spikes communicate across multiple segments. **Second**, our partition algorithm takes the spike patterns into account to create the segments such that the latency is deterministic to a larger degree than in a NoC. **Third**, the switches we introduce in our design do not require any routing tables, which reduces the latency compared to NoCs, where each switch has to store the routing table to decide which direction a packet is to be routed. By fixing the routing offline, we reduce the switching overhead significantly, which reduces the latency.

### 5.2 Comparison of Energy Consumption of Global Synapses

In Figure 11, we report the energy consumption on the global interconnect normalized to the baseline for all our evaluated workloads. We make the following key observations.

First, between he Baseline and our segmented bus-based design, our design achieves lower energy consumption on the global synapses by an average 57%. This reduction is due to two factors: spikes in our design only uses a specific segment, rather than a complete bus, and the segmentation switches we designed are lightweight and do not contain power hungry routing tables. We observe that the switches consume 5X lower energy than the equivalent switches in a NoC. Second, as we increase the size of the SNNs, the number of spikes increases, which increases the energy consumption, both for a traditional NoC, and for our segmented bus. However, we still achieve much lower energy footprint, average 50% lower energy than NoC for synth900 and synth1000 applications.

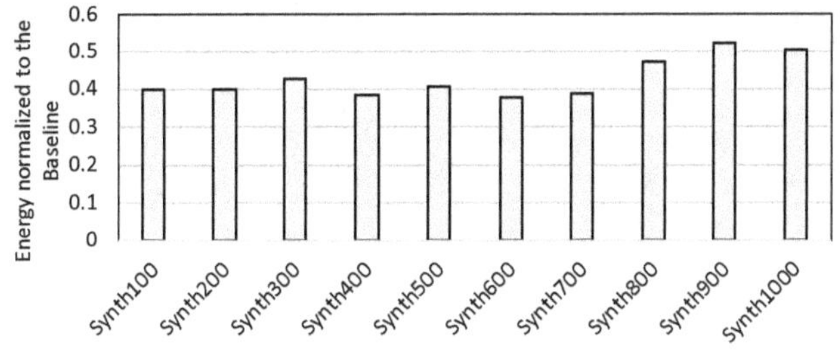


**Figure 11: Energy consumption, normalized to the Baseline.**

## 6 RELATED WORKS

Most earlier works for neuromorphic hardware is based on the assumption that the global interconnect is one of the traditional ones used for multiprocessor systems – NoCs [2], multi-stage NoCs [15], and mesh [11]. In [13], the authors propose a technique to map convolutional neural networks (non spiking) on crossbar-based hardware using a simple bus as the interconnect. In [10], the authors propose PACMAN to map spiking neural networks on SpiNNaker [14], which is based on mesh interconnect. In [16], authors propose to prune the synaptic connections on TrueNorth [1] system. In [7, 8], authors propose mapping strategies for spiking neural networks on CxQuad [12], which uses multi-stage NoCs.

To our knowledge, this is the first paper that evaluates the interconnect choice for spiking neural network, and explicitly develops strategies to minimize latency and energy consumption.

## 7 CONCLUSION

In this paper we propose segmented bus based neuromorphic hardware. The objective is to partition spiking neural networks (SNNs) into local synapses, which maps onto crossbars in the hardware, and global synapses, which maps on the segmented bus. We propose to offline analyze the spike communication based on test data for a given SNN-based application. Based on such analysis, we place segmentation switches in the bus to allow parallel segments to continue operations, without requiring the entire bus to be allocated for a given section. With synthetic applications, we verify that segmented bus allows to reduce latency by 67%, and energy consumption by 57%, with respect to NoC-based hardware. We further observe that reduction of latency directly translates to a reduction of inter-spike interval distortion, which improves application accuracy. Our continuing work further investigates the opportunity of energy reduction in a segmented bus architecture through proper switch placement.

## ACKNOWLEDGMENT

This work is supported by EU-H2020 grant NeuRAM3 Cube (NEUral computing aRchitectures in Advanced Monolithic 3D-VLSI nano-technologies) and ITEA3 proposal PARTNER (Patient-care Advancement with Responsive Technologies aNd Engagement togetheR).

## REFERENCES

[1] Filipp Akopyan et al. 2015. TrueNorth: Design and tool flow of a 65 mW 1 million neuron programmable neurosynaptic chip. *IEEE TCAD* (2015).
[2] Luca Benini and Giovanni De Micheli. 2002. Networks on chip: A new paradigm for systems on chip design. In *DATE*.
[3] Kwabena A Boahen. 1998. Communicating neuronal ensembles between neuromorphic chips. In *Neuromorphic systems engineering*.
[4] Vincenzo Catania et al. 2015. Noxim: An open, extensible and cycle-accurate network on chip simulator. In *ASAP*.
[5] J. Chen et al. 1999. Segmented bus design for low-power systems. *IEEE TVLSI* (1999).
[6] T. Chou et al. 2018. CARLsim 4: An Open Source Library for Large Scale, Biologically Detailed Spiking Neural Network Simulation using Heterogeneous Clusters. In *IJCNN*.
[7] A. Das et al. 2018. Mapping of local and global synapses on spiking neuromorphic hardware. In *DATE*.
[8] Anup Das and Akash Kumar. 2018. Dataflow-Based Mapping of Spiking Neural Networks on Neuromorphic Hardware. In *GLSVLSI*.
[9] P. Diehl et al. 2015. Unsupervised learning of digit recognition using spike-timing-dependent plasticity. *Frontiers in computational neuroscience* (2015).
[10] Francesco Galluppi et al. 2012. A hierachical configuration system for a massively parallel neural hardware platform. In *CF*.
[11] Yatin Hoskote et al. 2007. A 5-GHz mesh interconnect for a teraflops processor. *IEEE Micro* (2007).
[12] Giacomo Indiveri et al. 2015. Neuromorphic architectures for spiking deep neural networks. In *IEDM*.
[13] Yu Ji et al. 2016. NEUTRAMS: Neural network transformation and co-design under neuromorphic hardware constraints. In *MICRO*.
[14] Muhammad Mukaram Khan et al. 2008. SpiNNaker: mapping neural networks onto a massively-parallel chip multiprocessor. In *IJCNN*.
[15] Hee-choul Lee. 2002. Multi-stage interconnection network for high speed packet switching. US Patent 6,335,930.
[16] Xiaoxiao Liu et al. 2018. Neu-NoC: A high-efficient interconnection network for accelerated neuromorphic systems. In *ASP-DAC*.
[17] Wolfgang Maass. 1997. Networks of spiking neurons: the third generation of neural network models. *Neural networks* 10, 9 (1997), 1659–1671.
[18] Wei Zhao and Yu Cao. 2006. New generation of predictive technology model for sub-45 nm early design exploration. *IEEE TED* (2006).

# ADMM-based Weight Pruning for Real-Time Deep Learning Acceleration on Mobile Devices

Hongjia Li
li.hongjia@husky.neu.edu
Northeastern University
Boston, USA

Ning Liu
Xiaolong Ma
Sheng Lin
Northeastern University
Boston, USA

Shaokai Ye
Tianyun Zhang
Syracuse University
Syracuse, USA

Xue Lin
xue.lin@northeastern.edu
Northeastern University
Boston, USA

Wenyao Xu
wenyaoxu@buffalo.edu
University at Buffalo
Buffalo, USA

Yanzhi Wang
yanz.wang@northeastern.edu
Northeastern University
Boston, USA

## ABSTRACT

Deep learning solutions are being increasingly deployed in mobile applications, at least for the inference phase. Due to the large model size and computational requirements, model compression for deep neural networks (DNNs) becomes necessary, especially considering the real-time requirement in embedded systems. In this paper, we extend the prior work on systematic DNN weight pruning using ADMM (Alternating Direction Method of Multipliers). We integrate ADMM regularization with masked mapping/retraining, thereby guaranteeing solution feasibility and providing high solution quality. Besides superior performance on representative DNN benchmarks (e.g., AlexNet, ResNet), we focus on two new applications facial emotion detection and eye tracking, and develop a top-down framework of DNN training, model compression, and acceleration in mobile devices. Experimental results show that with negligible accuracy degradation, the proposed method can achieve significant storage/memory reduction and speedup in mobile devices.

## CCS CONCEPTS

• **Computing methodologies → Neural networks; Real-time simulation;**

## KEYWORDS

Mobile devices, neural networks, acceleration, real-time

**ACM Reference Format:**

Hongjia Li, Ning Liu, Xiaolong Ma, Sheng Lin, Shaokai Ye, Tianyun Zhang, Xue Lin, Wenyao Xu, and Yanzhi Wang. 2019. ADMM-based Weight Pruning for Real-Time Deep Learning Acceleration on Mobile Devices. In *Great Lakes Symposium on VLSI 2019 (GLSVLSI '19), May 9–11, 2019, Tysons Corner, VA, USA.* ACM, New York, NY, USA, 6 pages. https://doi.org/10.1145/3299874.3319492



*GLSVLSI '19, May 9–11, 2019, Tysons Corner, VA, USA*



ACM ISBN 978-1-4503-6252-8/19/05...$15.00
https://doi.org/10.1145/3299874.3319492

## 1 INTRODUCTION

Recently, deep learning has been expanded into many new application fields, such as automatic drive system, 3D printing detection, and medical imaging and diagnosis [15, 19, 25]. As an example for the latter application, deep neural networks (DNNs) can be trained for the detection of facial expressions and performing eye tracking for the patients [6, 16]. By extracting complex and high-level features from large-scale data, DNNs can achieve a high accuracy and provide significant help and convenience for both doctors and patients.

DNNs are typically trained in an offline manner, and are often deployed in low-power, embedded, or mobile devices during inference. One of the major challenges is the large model size and computational requirement, which makes it difficult for real-time implementation in mobile devices. To overcome this challenge, many efforts have been devoted to DNN model compression from both industry and academia. One pioneering work [9] adopts an iterative heuristic for DNN weight pruning, achieving good pruning results: 9× weight reduction in AlexNet [17] and 12× in LeNet-5 [18]. Despite the promising results, the compression gain mainly focuses on the fully-connected (FC) layers, and the pruning ratio is limited on convolutional (CONV) layers (e.g., 2.7× for CONV layers in AlexNet). This limitation needs to be overcome as CONV layers become the most computationally intensive layers in current DNNs [11, 17].

Later weight pruning work extend to (i) use more sophisticated heuristic such as both weight prune and grow [4, 8], (ii) strike a desirable tradeoff between pruning ratio and accuracy, and (iii) incorporate regularity or structure in weight pruning framework [12, 26]. To partially overcome the heuristic nature, recently, a systematic DNN weight pruning framework has been proposed in [27], based on the powerful ADMM (Alternating Direction Methods of Multipliers) technique [1]. This work formulates the DNN weight pruning problem as a mathematical optimization problem, and observes the compatibility between the combinatorial constraints (associated with weight pruning) with ADMM. It achieves improved weight pruning results, 21× on AlexNet and 71.2× on LeNet-5, with no accuracy loss. However, this work adopts a direct application of ADMM, and lacks rigorous guarantee on feasibility (satisfying all constraints) and solution quality due to the non-convex objective function.

Using [27] as the starting point, this work first develops a systematic, algorithmic DNN weight pruning framework, with an integration of ADMM regularization and masked mapping/retraining steps. In this way the solution feasibility can be guaranteed and solution quality (test accuracy) can be improved. The proposed framework outperforms prior work on representative benchmarks such as AlexNet and LeNet-5, and also achieves 18× weight reduction on ResNet-50 [11], which is widely accepted to be difficult for compression. We further incorporate structured pruning [26], including filter-wise, channel-wise, and filter shape-wise sparsities, into the ADMM regularization framework, thereby facilitating high parallelism and hardware implementations.

Deep learning solutions are being increasingly deployed in mobile applications, at least for the inference phase[20]. Due to the large model size and computational requirements, model compression for deep neural networks (DNNs) becomes necessary, especially considering the real-time requirement in embedded systems. For real-world and real-time applications, we apply the proposed framework on two medical-related applications and implement on different embedded systems. The first application is the facial emotion recognition [6]. The second application is eye tracking [16]. DNNs for both applications are mainly CONV layers. The first application uses the FER-2013 dataset [6], and we prune 78.33% of total weights with (almost) no accuracy loss. We can achieve 97.2% weight reduction in the second application. For inference acceleration in mobile devices, we use sparse matrices and *dictionary of keys*[5] for weight representation and computation after pruning, and perform testing on three mobile devices. We achieve 10x speedup and 13.2x speedup on these two applications, respectively, when testing on mobile devices. Our models are released at the anonymous link https://bit.ly/2P1ehdb.

# 2 A SYSTEMATIC WEIGHT PRUNING FRAMEWORK USING ADMM

## 2.1 Systematic View of Weight Pruning

Similar to [27], we provide a systematic view of DNN weight pruning during training as an optimization problem. Consider a general $N$-layer DNN. Sets of weights and biases of the $i$-th (CONV or FC) layer are denoted by $\mathbf{W}_i$ and $\mathbf{b}_i$, respectively. Let us denote the loss function of the $N$-layer DNN as $f\big(\{\mathbf{W}_i\}_{i=1}^N, \{\mathbf{b}_i\}_{i=1}^N\big)$. Then the overall problem is defined as

$$\begin{aligned} &\underset{\{\mathbf{W}_i\},\{\mathbf{b}_i\}}{\text{minimize}}\ f\big(\{\mathbf{W}_i\}_{i=1}^N, \{\mathbf{b}_i\}_{i=1}^N\big),\\ &\text{subject to } \mathbf{W}_i \in \mathcal{S}_i,\ i = 1, \ldots, N. \end{aligned} \tag{1}$$

The set $\mathcal{S}_i = \big\{\mathbf{W}_i \big| \text{card}(\text{supp}(\mathbf{W}_i)) \le \alpha_i\big\}$ reflects constraint for weight pruning, where 'card' refers to cardinality and 'supp' refers to support set. Elements in $\mathcal{S}_i$ are $\mathbf{W}_i$ solutions, satisfying that the number of non-zero elements in $\mathbf{W}_i$ is limited by $\alpha_i$ for layer $i$. Because of such combinatorial constraints, problem (1) cannot be solved using conventional stochastic gradient descent which assumes no hard constraints. This is key reason that prior work use heuristic methods to get rid of these constraints. To overcome this limitation, a key observation is that such form of combinatorial constraints is compatible with ADMM technique.

## 2.2 Connection to ADMM

ADMM [23, 24] is a powerful optimization tool, by decomposing an original problem into two subproblems that can be solved separately and iteratively. Consider optimization problem

$$\min_{\mathbf{x}}\ f(\mathbf{x}) + g(\mathbf{x}). \tag{2}$$

In ADMM, the problem is first re-written as

$$\min_{\mathbf{x},\mathbf{z}}\ f(\mathbf{x}) + g(\mathbf{z}), \quad \text{subject to } \mathbf{x} = \mathbf{z}. \tag{3}$$

Next, by using augmented Lagrangian [1], the above problem is decomposed into two subproblems on $\mathbf{x}$ and $\mathbf{z}$. The first is $\min_{\mathbf{x}} f(\mathbf{x}) + q_1(\mathbf{x}|\mathbf{z})$, where $q_1(\mathbf{x}|\mathbf{z})$ is a quadratic function of $\mathbf{x}$ with fixed $\mathbf{z}$. Subproblem 2 is $\min_{\mathbf{z}} g(\mathbf{z}) + q_2(\mathbf{z}|\mathbf{x})$, where $q_2(\mathbf{z}|\mathbf{x})$ is a quadratic function on $\mathbf{z}$ with fixed $\mathbf{x}$. The two subproblems will be solved iteratively until convergence is achieved [23, 24].

ADMM is conventionally utilized to accelerate convergence of convex optimization problems. The optimality and fast convergence have been proven for convex problems [1, 23]. As a special property, ADMM can effectively deal with a subset of combinatorial constraints and yields optimal (or at least high quality) solutions [14, 21]. Our observation is that associated constraints in DNN weight pruning belong to this subset. More specifically, we use indicator functions to incorporate combinatorial constraints into objective function. The indicator functions are $g_i(\mathbf{W}_i) = \begin{cases} 0 & \text{if } \mathbf{W}_i \in \mathcal{S}_i \\ +\infty & \text{otherwise} \end{cases}$.

Then problem (1) becomes:

$$\underset{\{\mathbf{W}_i\},\{\mathbf{b}_i\}}{\text{minimize}}\ f\big(\{\mathbf{W}_i\}_{i=1}^N, \{\mathbf{b}_i\}_{i=1}^N\big) + \sum_{i=1}^N g_i(\mathbf{W}_i) \tag{4}$$

Despite the compatibility of the combinatorial constraints with ADMM, there is difficulty in using ADMM directly due to the non-convex nature of the objective function in (1). Therefore, special mechanisms are needed to guarantee the *solution feasibility* and *solution quality*.

## 2.3 Systematic DNN Weight Pruning

Instead of direct application of ADMM, we develop an integrated framework of *ADMM regularization* and *masked mapping and retraining* as showed in Algorithm 1. We guarantee solution feasibility (satisfying all constraints) and provide high quality (maintaining test accuracy).

The ADMM regularization starts from a DNN model without compression. By incorporating auxiliary variables $\mathbf{Z}_i$'s, and dual variables $\mathbf{U}_i$'s, we decompose (4) into two subproblems, and iteratively solves them until convergence. The first subproblem is

$$\underset{\{\mathbf{W}_i\},\{\mathbf{b}_i\}}{\text{minimize}}\ f\big(\{\mathbf{W}_i\}_{i=1}^N, \{\mathbf{b}_i\}_{i=1}^N\big) + \sum_{i=1}^N \frac{\rho_i}{2}\|\mathbf{W}_i - \mathbf{Z}_i^k + \mathbf{U}_i^k\|_F^2. \tag{5}$$

The first term in (5) is the differentiable (non-convex) loss function of the DNN, while the other quadratic terms are differentiable and convex. As a result, this subproblem can be solved by stochastic gradient descent similar to the one that would be used to train the original DNN.

The second subproblem is

$$\underset{\{\mathbf{Z}_i\}}{\text{minimize}} \sum_{i=1}^{N} g_i(\mathbf{Z}_i) + \sum_{i=1}^{N} \frac{\rho_i}{2} \|\mathbf{W}_i^{k+1} - \mathbf{Z}_i + \mathbf{U}_i^k\|_F^2. \quad (6)$$

The optimal, analytical solution is the Euclidean projection of $\mathbf{W}_i^{k+1} + \mathbf{U}_i^k$ onto the set $S_i$. Since $\alpha_i$ is the desired number of weights after pruning in the $i$-th layer, we can prove that the Euclidean projection results in keeping $\alpha_i$ elements in $\mathbf{W}_i^{k+1} + \mathbf{U}_i^k$ with the largest magnitudes and setting the remaining weights to zeros. After both subproblems solved, we update the dual variables $\mathbf{U}_i$ as Eqn. (7) and complete one iteration in ADMM regularization.

$$\mathbf{U}_i^{k+1} = \mathbf{U}_i^k + \mathbf{W}_i^{k+1} - \mathbf{Z}_i^{k+1} \quad (7)$$

*Masked Mapping and Retraining:* We extend the formulation in [27] by introducing masked mapping and retraining step. After ADMM regularization, we obtain intermediate $\mathbf{W}_i$ solutions. In this step, we first perform the said Euclidean projection (mapping) to guarantee that at most $\alpha_i$ weights in each layer are non-zero. Next, we mask the zero weights and retrain the DNN with non-zero weights using training sets (while keeping the masked weights 0). In this way test accuracy can be partially restored.

Algorithm 1 shows the pseudo-codes of the proposed weight pruning training algorithm, in which *ADMM_ITERA TION* is normally set as $\frac{1}{10}$ of *MAX_ITERATION_FOR_SGD*.

**Algorithm 1:** Systematic Weight Pruning Training Algorithm using ADMM

```
Initialize training hyperparameters;
for CURRENT_ITERATION <
  MAX_ITERATION_FOR_SGD do
    Solve(Eqn. (5));
    if CURRENT_ITERATION % ADMM_ITERATION == 0
     then
        Solve(Eqn. (6));
        Solve dual update according to Eqn. (7);
    end
end
Masked mapping;
Retrain the pruned model;
```

**Feasibility and Solution Quality:** One can observe that constraints on weight pruning are satisfied through the mapping step and that the retraining process restores the accuracy loss of mapping. ADMM regularization acts as a smart, adaptive DNN regularization (see Eqn. (5)), where the regularization targets are dynamically updated in each iteration by solving subproblem 2 (optimally and analytically). This is one key reason that this method outperforms many prior works on DNN weight pruning based on fixed regularization [26], where regularization targets are not updated.

**Sample Results on Representative DNNs:** Sparse matrices are employed for representing the pruned weights due to the reduced space complexity (by storing only the non-zero entries and index to the next non-zero entry) and associated computation savings. We have performed testing on representative DNNs, LeNet-5 [18] for MNIST dataset, and AlexNet [17] and ResNet-50 [11] for ImageNet dataset. As shown in Table 1, we achieve 167x reduction in number of weights in LeNet-5, 31x in AlexNet, and 15x in ResNet-50, with (almost) no accuracy loss. These results consistently outperform prior arts especially on ResNet, which is difficult for pruning in prior work.

**Table 1: Sample results on representative DNNs**

| Network | Method | Accuracy Loss | Weights | Pruning Rate |
|---|---|---|---|---|
| LeNet-5 (99.2%) | Network Pruning [10] | 0.0% | 34.5K | 12.5x |
| | Direct ADMM[27] | 0.0% | 6.05K | 71.2x |
| | **Our Proposed Method** | 0.2% | 2.58K | **167x** |
| AlexNet (80.2%) | Network Pruning [10] | 0.0% | 6.7M | 9x |
| | NEST [4] | 0.0% | 3.9M | 15.7x |
| | Direct ADMM[27] | 0.0% | 2.9M | 21x |
| | **Our Proposed Method** | 0.1% | 1.9M | **31x** |
| ResNet-50 (92.4%) | Fine-grained Pruning [22] | 0.1% | 12.6M | 2.6x |
| | **Our Proposed Method** | 0.4% | 2.18M | **15x** |
| | | 0.8% | 1.82M | **18x** |

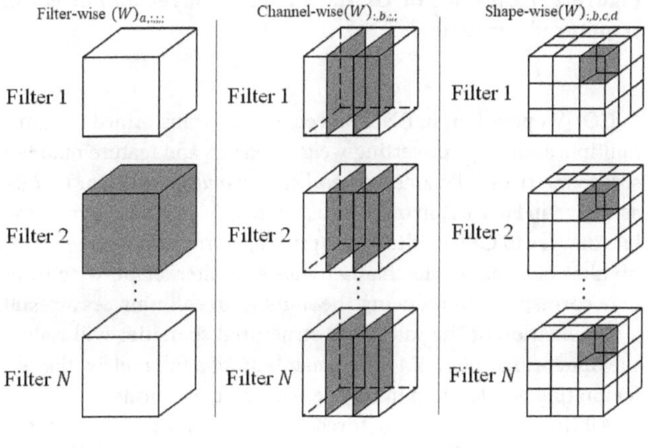


**Figure 1: Examples of filter-wise, channel-wise and shape-wise structured sparsities.**

## 2.4 Incorporating Structures in Weight Pruning

As discussed before, the DNN after weight pruning is an irregular, sparse neural network, and sparse matrices with indices are utilized for weight storage. One clear disadvantage is the limitation on parallelism degree and therefore degradation in hardware performance as also observed in [26]. Prior work (e.g., [26]) incorporates regularity or "structures" in DNN weight pruning in order to solve this problem, but lacks a systematic approach to achieve this goal.

We make an observation that structured pruning is compatible with the ADMM-based weight pruning framework, and therefore can be solved systematically. We use CONV layers (the most computationally intensive in current DNNs [11, 17]) as an illustrative example while FC layers can be treated similarly. There are three types of structured sparsities, *filter-wise*, *channel-wise*, and *shape-wise* sparsities as shown in Figure 1.

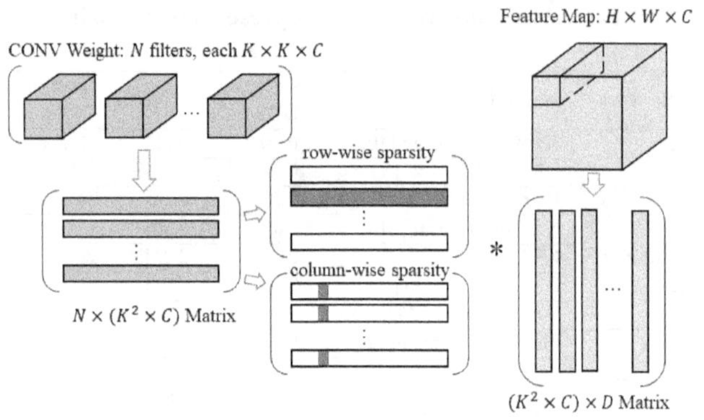


**Figure 2: Examples of GEMM in CONV layer and effect of structured sparsities.**

CONV operations in DNNs are commonly transformed to matrix multiplications by converting weight tensors and feature map tensors to matrices [3], named *general matrix multiplication* or GEMM, as shown in Figure 2, in order to facilitate implementation from mobile devices to GPUs. Filter-wise pruning corresponds to reducing number of rows, while channel-wise and filter shape-wise prunings correspond to reducing the number of columns. As a result, a combination of the said three structured sparsities will reduce the dimension in GEMM while maintaining a full matrix, thereby facilitating acceleration in mobile/hardware platforms.

All the above three structured pruning scenarios can be incorporated into the ADMM regularization framework. For filter-wise sparsity as an example, the constraint set $S_i$ will indicate that the number of nonzero filters in $\mathbf{W}_i$ is less than a predefined value. For channel-wise sparsity, constraint set $S_i$ will indicate that the number of nonzero channels in $\mathbf{W}_i$ is less than a predefined value. In this way structured pruning will replace the second subproblem in (6), and the optimal Euclidean mapping will be derived accordingly. The first subproblem in (5) and the masked mapping/retraining step will maintain the same form (and solution method).

## 3 MOBILE IMPLEMENTATION/ ACCELERATION OF PRUNED DNNS

In this section, we describe mobile implementation/ acceleration of the inference phase of pruned DNNs. As shown in Figure 3, there are four high-level modules on Android-based platforms: model constructor, parameters loader, dataset loader and inference engine. In the first module, the network architecture will be constructed and through parameters import, pre-trained weights and bias will be loaded. In the third module, the test data are loaded through camera or files and we perform inference in the last module through C++ interface.

Since GEMM is utilized for CONV layer computation in mobile systems, and CONV layer is the most computationally intensive layer, we adopt sparse matrices in GEMM based on the weight pruning results. Specifically, the computational complexity is reduced from $O(N^3)$ to $O(K \cdot N)$, where $N$ is weight matrix dimension, and $K$ is the number of non-zero elements in the matrix. We implement sparse matrix computation in a bottom-up manner from C++ array

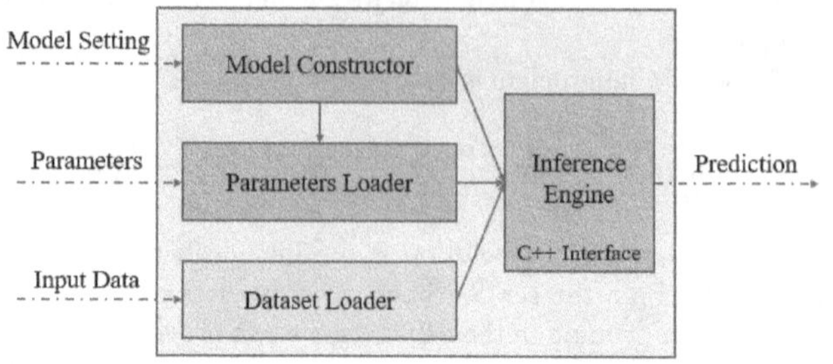


**Figure 3: Building blocks of software implementation.**

template, instead of existing libraries (e.g., *OpenCV* [2], *Eigen* [7]). This is because of the limited scalability of the mobile version of such libraries to support large-scale DNNs.

The DNN inference acceleration algorithm is shown in Algorithm 2, focusing on GEMM acceleration for a specific layer. In each layer, the input matrix and weight matrix in GEMM are denoted by $\mathbf{X}$ and $\mathbf{W}$, respectively. The bias vector is $\mathbf{b}$. To accelerate the computation, the structure of the weight matrix $\mathbf{W}$ is transformed to the sparse matrix structure denoted as $\mathbf{W}'$, in which *Dictionary of Keys* is adopted to efficiently construct and represent. *Step 5* to *12* show the details of the general multiplication of the dense input matrix $\mathbf{X}$ and the sparse weight matrix $\mathbf{W}'$. The dimensionality of $\mathbf{W}'$ is $K \times 3$.

**Algorithm 2:** Pruned Model Inference Algorithm on Mobile Devices (focusing on GEMM for one layer)

```
1  Input: m × n matrix X;
2  Parameters: W, b;
3  Output: matrix Y;
   /* convert dense matrix to sparse matrix */
4  W' ← W;
   /* sparse matrix * dense matrix operation */
5  for index ← 0 until K do
6      row ← W'_{index,0};
7      col ← W'_{index,1};
8      value ← W'_{index,2};
9      for j ← 0 until n do
10         Y_{row,j} ← Y_{row,j} + value * X_{col,j};
11     end
12 end
13 Y ← Y + b;
14 Return Y;
```

## 4 EXPERIMENTAL RESULTS AND DISCUSSIONS

In this section, we perform evaluation on two medical related applications, starting from DNN construction, systematic weight pruning using ADMM, and finally implementation of DNN inference on

**Table 2: Platforms under test and specifications.**

| Platform | Android | Primary CPU | Companion CPU | CPU Architecture | GPU | RAM (GB) |
|---|---|---|---|---|---|---|
| Huawei Honor 6X | 7 (Nougat) | 4 × 2.1GHz Cortex-A53 | 4 × 1.7GHZ Cortex-A53 | ARMv8-A | Mali T830 | 3 |
| LG Nexus 5X | 8.1 (Oreo) | 4 × 1.4 GHz Cortex-A53 | 2 × 1.8GHz Cortex-A57 | ARMv8-A | Adreno 418 | 2 |
| Huawei Honor 10 | 8.1 (Oreo) | 4 × 2.4 GHz Cortex-A73 | 4 × 1.8 GHz Cortex-A53 | ARMv8-A | Mali-G72 MP12 | 6 |

multiple mobile devices to evaluate the applicability of the inference phase. Table 2 summarizes the specifications of test mobile platforms.

The performance evaluation includes two aspects: (a) storage reduction due to the reduced DNN model size, (b) inference acceleration (running time reduction). The largest portion of inference time is from GEMM operation, which will benefit from sparse matrices. We compare the run-time cost of GEMM as well as the overall run-time.

## 4.1 Case I: Facial Emotion Recognition

Facial emotion recognition is utilized in many fields such as medical, entertainment and security. For this application, FER-2013 face database [6] is used to train and test the DNN model. The dataset comprises a total of 35,887 pre-cropped, 48-by-48-pixel grayscale images of faces each labeled with one of the 7 emotion classes: anger, disgust, fear, happiness, sadness, surprise, and neutral. Due to the small portion of the disgust class, the dataset is merged into six classes including angry, fear, happy, sad, surprise, and neutral [13].

A typical DNN is constructed, comprising 9 CONV layers with one max-pooling after every three CONV layers. There are 32, 64, and 218 filters in these three CONV-layer groups, respectively. In addition, 2 FC layers are constructed followed by a softmax layer in the end. Table 3 shows the weight pruning result. Our pruning algorithm can achieve a high compression ratio by 4.6x without accuracy loss.

**Table 3: Weight Pruning Result on Facial Emotion Recognition Model**

| Layer | Weights | Weights after prune | Matrices sparsity |
|---|---|---|---|
| conv1 | 288 | 230 | 20% |
| conv2 | 9216 | 3687 | 60% |
| conv3 | 9216 | 2765 | 70% |
| conv4 | 18432 | 3687 | 80% |
| conv5 | 36864 | 7373 | 80% |
| conv6 | 36864 | 5530 | 85% |
| conv7 | 73728 | 11060 | 85% |
| conv8 | 147456 | 22119 | 85% |
| conv9 | 147456 | 22119 | 85% |
| fc1 | 294912 | 88474 | 70% |
| fc2 | 4096 | 1639 | 60% |
| fc3 | 384 | 154 | 60% |
| Total | 778912 | 168837 | 78.33% |

In Table 4, the overall performance is shown including the accuracy and inference time on various mobile systems. According to the results, the overall acceleration of the pruned model can achieve up to 10x, while the GEMM acceleration can achieve up to 22x compared with the non-pruned model. The actual speedup is even higher than the pruning ratio, due to two reasons: (i) we focus more on the pruning of computationally intensive CONV layers than FC layers, and (ii) the bandwidth requirement is also reduced besides computation reduction.

**Table 4: Performance of Facial Emotion Recognition Model on Mobile Devices**

| | | Model | Pruned model | Speedup |
|---|---|---|---|---|
| Accuracy | | 58.2056% | 58.0663% | - |
| Honor 6X | Overall | 0.971s | 0.133s | 7.3x |
| | GEMM | 0.925s | 0.082s | 11.3x |
| Nexus 5X | Overall | 0.161s | 0.015s | 10x |
| | GEMM | 0.137s | 0.006s | 22x |
| Honor 10 | Overall | 0.304s | 0.046s | 6.6x |
| | GEMM | 0.283s | 0.025s | 11.3x |

## 4.2 Case II: Eye Tracking

Eye tracking is one widely used application in many areas such as human-computer interaction, medical diagnoses, psychological studies and computer vision. To implement the weight pruned eye tracking model for embedded systems, we use GazeCapture, a large-scale mobile eye tracking dataset, containing data from over 1,450 people with almost 2.5M frames [16].

The eye tracking DNN model takes as input the detected and cropped portions of the original frame, including left eye, right eye, and face images (all of size 224 x 224). Additionally, the face grid is considered as another input, with a binary mask to indicate the location and size of the head within the frame (of size 25 x 25). The output is the distance, in centimeters, from the camera. The whole model consists of 13 CONV layers and 7 FC layers. Compared with typical DNN, the eye tracking network has a more complicated architecture. It consists of three small typical DNNs taking inputs from the right eye, left eye and face respectively. The outputs get concatenated and go through 7 FC layers along with the input from face grid. The details of model structure are demonstrated in [16]. The network architecture also shows a big impact on the overall real-time speedup.

After applying our weight pruning method, the weight reduction result is shown in Table 5. The overall pruning ratio can achieve 36x. The total number of weights is reduced from 718K to 19K. The performance on three mobile devices is demonstrated in the following Table 6. The pruned model achieves up to 13x speedup compared with the non-pruned model, especially, the GEMM computing time gets accelerated up to 28x.

**Table 5: Weight Pruning Result of Eye Tracking Model**

| Layer | Weights | Weights after prune | Matrices sparsity |
|---|---|---|---|
| conv-e1 | 4875 | 3413 | 30% |
| conv-e2 | 102400 | 512 | 99.5% |
| conv-e3 | 73728 | 369 | 99.5% |
| conv-e4 | 8192 | 1229 | 85% |
| conv-f1 | 4875 | 3413 | 30% |
| conv-f2 | 102400 | 512 | 99.5% |
| conv-f3 | 73728 | 369 | 99.5% |
| conv-f4 | 8192 | 1229 | 85% |
| fc-e1 | 65536 | 3933 | 94% |
| fc-f1 | 32768 | 656 | 98% |
| fc-f2 | 8192 | 1475 | 82% |
| fc-fg1 | 160000 | 800 | 99.5% |
| fc-fg2 | 32768 | 984 | 97% |
| fc1 | 40960 | 615 | 98.5% |
| fc2 | 256 | 256 | - |
| Total | 718870 | 19765 | 97.25% |

**Table 6: Performance of Eye Tracking Model on Mobile Devices**

| | | Model | Pruned model | Speedup |
|---|---|---|---|---|
| Accuracy | | 92.97% | 91.47% | - |
| Honor 6X | Overall | 0.563s | 0.043s | 13.2x |
| | GEMM | 0.541s | 0.019s | 28.8x |
| Nexus 5X | Overall | 0.070s | 0.009s | 7.5x |
| | GEMM | 0.065s | 0.002s | 28x |
| Honor 10 | Overall | 0.142s | 0.018s | 7.7x |
| | GEMM | 0.131s | 0.007s | 17.4x |

## 5 CONCLUSION

In this paper, we extend the prior work on systematic DNN weight pruning using ADMM. We integrate ADMM regularization with masked mapping/retraining, thereby guaranteeing solution feasibility and providing high solution quality. We develop two new applications: facial emotion detection and eye tracking, and propose a top-down framework of DNN training, model compression, and acceleration in mobile devices. The proposed method shows significant storage/memory reduction and speedup measured on mobile devices.

## ACKNOWLEDGMENTS

This work is funded by the National Science Foundation Awards CNS-1704662 and CNS-1739748.

## REFERENCES


[1] Stephen Boyd, Neal Parikh, Eric Chu, Borja Peleato, Jonathan Eckstein, et al. 2011. Distributed optimization and statistical learning via the alternating direction method of multipliers. *Foundations and Trends® in Machine learning* 3, 1 (2011), 1–122.

[2] G. Bradski. 2000. The OpenCV Library. *Dr. Dobb's Journal of Software Tools* (2000).

[3] Sharan Chetlur, Cliff Woolley, Philippe Vandermersch, Jonathan Cohen, John Tran, Bryan Catanzaro, and Evan Shelhamer. 2014. cudnn: Efficient primitives for deep learning. *arXiv preprint arXiv:1410.0759* (2014).

[4] Xiaoliang Dai, Hongxu Yin, and Niraj K Jha. 2017. NeST: a neural network synthesis tool based on a grow-and-prune paradigm. *arXiv preprint arXiv:1711.02017* (2017).

[5] Gene H Golub and Charles F Van Loan. 2012. *Matrix computations*. Vol. 3. JHU press.

[6] Ian J Goodfellow, Dumitru Erhan, Pierre Luc Carrier, Aaron Courville, Mehdi Mirza, Ben Hamner, Will Cukierski, Yichuan Tang, David Thaler, Dong-Hyun Lee, et al. 2013. Challenges in representation learning: A report on three machine learning contests. In *International Conference on Neural Information Processing*. Springer, 117–124.

[7] Gaël Guennebaud, Benoît Jacob, et al. 2010. Eigen v3. http://eigen.tuxfamily.org. (2010).

[8] Yiwen Guo, Anbang Yao, and Yurong Chen. 2016. Dynamic network surgery for efficient dnns. In *Advances In Neural Information Processing Systems*. 1379–1387.

[9] Song Han, Huizi Mao, and William J Dally. 2015. Deep compression: Compressing deep neural networks with pruning, trained quantization and huffman coding. *arXiv preprint arXiv:1510.00149* (2015).

[10] Song Han, Jeff Pool, John Tran, and William Dally. 2015. Learning both weights and connections for efficient neural network. In *Advances in neural information processing systems*. 1135–1143.

[11] Kaiming He, Xiangyu Zhang, Shaoqing Ren, and Jian Sun. 2016. Deep residual learning for image recognition. In *Proceedings of the IEEE conference on computer vision and pattern recognition*. 770–778.

[12] Yihui He, Xiangyu Zhang, and Jian Sun. 2017. Channel pruning for accelerating very deep neural networks. In *International Conference on Computer Vision (ICCV)*, Vol. 2.

[13] Jostine Ho. 2016. Facial Emotion Recognition. https://github.com/JostineHo/mememoji. (2016).

[14] Mingyi Hong, Zhi-Quan Luo, and Meisam Razaviyayn. 2016. Convergence analysis of alternating direction method of multipliers for a family of nonconvex problems. *SIAM Journal on Optimization* 26, 1 (2016), 337–364.

[15] Joel Janai, Fatma Güney, Aseem Behl, and Andreas Geiger. 2017. Computer vision for autonomous vehicles: Problems, datasets and state-of-the-art. *arXiv preprint arXiv:1704.05519* (2017).

[16] Kyle Krafka, Aditya Khosla, Petr Kellnhofer, Harini Kannan, Suchendra Bhandarkar, Wojciech Matusik, and Antonio Torralba. 2016. Eye Tracking for Everyone. In *IEEE Conference on Computer Vision and Pattern Recognition (CVPR)*.

[17] Alex Krizhevsky, Ilya Sutskever, and Geoffrey E Hinton. 2012. Imagenet classification with deep convolutional neural networks. In *Advances in neural information processing systems*. 1097–1105.

[18] Yann LeCun, Léon Bottou, Yoshua Bengio, and Patrick Haffner. 1998. Gradient-based learning applied to document recognition. *Proc. IEEE* 86, 11 (1998), 2278–2324.

[19] Zhe Li, Xiaolong Ma, Hongjia Li, Qiyuan An, Aditya Singh Rathore, Qinru Qiu, Wenyao Xu, and Yanzhi Wang. 2018. C3PO: Database and Benchmark for Early-stage Malicious Activity Detection in 3D Printing. *arXiv preprint arXiv:1803.07544* (2018).

[20] Sheng Lin, Ning Liu, Mahdi Nazemi, Hongjia Li, Caiwen Ding, Yanzhi Wang, and Massoud Pedram. 2018. FFT-based deep learning deployment in embedded systems. In *2018 Design, Automation & Test in Europe Conference & Exhibition (DATE)*. IEEE, 1045–1050.

[21] Sijia Liu, Jie Chen, Pin-Yu Chen, and Alfred O Hero. 2017. Zeroth-order online alternating direction method of multipliers: Convergence analysis and applications. *arXiv preprint arXiv:1710.07804* (2017).

[22] Huizi Mao, Song Han, Jeff Pool, Wenshuo Li, Xingyu Liu, Yu Wang, and William J Dally. 2017. Exploring the regularity of sparse structure in convolutional neural networks. *arXiv preprint arXiv:1705.08922* (2017).

[23] Hua Ouyang, Niao He, Long Tran, and Alexander Gray. 2013. Stochastic alternating direction method of multipliers. In *International Conference on Machine Learning*. 80–88.

[24] Taiji Suzuki. 2013. Dual averaging and proximal gradient descent for online alternating direction multiplier method. In *International Conference on Machine Learning*. 392–400.

[25] Xiaosong Wang, Yifan Peng, Le Lu, Zhiyong Lu, Mohammadhadi Bagheri, and Ronald M Summers. 2017. Chestx-ray8: Hospital-scale chest x-ray database and benchmarks on weakly-supervised classification and localization of common thorax diseases. In *Proceedings of the IEEE Conference on Computer Vision and Pattern Recognition*. 2097–2106.

[26] Wei Wen, Chunpeng Wu, Yandan Wang, Yiran Chen, and Hai Li. 2016. Learning structured sparsity in deep neural networks. In *Advances in Neural Information Processing Systems*. 2074–2082.

[27] Tianyun Zhang, Shaokai Ye, Kaiqi Zhang, Jian Tang, Wujie Wen, Makan Fardad, and Yanzhi Wang. 2018. A systematic DNN weight pruning framework using alternating direction method of multipliers. *arXiv preprint arXiv:1804.03294* (2018).

# On the use of Deep Autoencoders for Efficient Embedded Reinforcement Learning

Bharat Prakash
University of Maryland
Baltimore County

Mark Horton
University of Maryland
Baltimore County

Nicholas R. Waytowich
US Army Research Laboratory

William David Hairston
US Army Research Laboratory

Tim Oates
University of Maryland
Baltimore County

Tinoosh Mohsenin
University of Maryland
Baltimore County

## ABSTRACT

In autonomous embedded systems, it is often vital to reduce the amount of actions taken in the real world and energy required to learn a policy. Training reinforcement learning agents from high dimensional image representations can be very expensive and time consuming. Autoencoders are deep neural network used to compress high dimensional data such as pixelated images into small latent representations. This compression model is vital to efficiently learn policies, especially when learning on embedded systems. We have implemented this model on the NVIDIA Jetson TX2 embedded GPU, and evaluated the power consumption, throughput, and energy consumption of the autoencoders for various CPU/GPU core combinations, frequencies, and model parameters. Additionally, we have shown the reconstructions generated by the autoencoder to analyze the quality of the generated compressed representation and also the performance of the reinforcement learning agent. Finally, we have presented an assessment of the viability of training these models on embedded systems and their usefulness in developing autonomous policies. Using autoencoders, we were able to achieve 4-5 × improved performance compared to a baseline RL agent with a convolutional feature extractor, while using less than 2W of power.

## KEYWORDS

Autoencoders, Neural networks, Reinforcement learning, Embedded devices, Deep learning

**ACM Reference Format:**

Bharat Prakash, Mark Horton, Nicholas R. Waytowich, William David Hairston, Tim Oates, and Tinoosh Mohsenin. 2019. On the use of Deep Autoencoders for Efficient Embedded Reinforcement Learning. In *Great Lakes Symposium on VLSI 2019 (GLSVLSI '19), May 9–11, 2019, Tysons Corner, VA, USA.* ACM, New York, NY, USA, 6 pages. https://doi.org/10.1145/3299874.3319493

## 1 INTRODUCTION

Recently, deep reinforcement learning algorithms have provided an effective approach to automating tasks which previously could only be performed by humans. The most popular modern reinforcement learning algorithms use deep neural networks and backpropagation in order to maximize a reward function which indicates how well the agent is performing in the environment. However, when these algorithms are applied to high-dimensional data such as pixelated images, they implicitly must learn to extract useful features from an environment. This feature extraction requires the training of large convolutional layers, which learn to detect shapes in the training samples. Deep convolutional networks used in tasks such as reinforcement learning and image classification are notoriously power intensive, requiring optimization and specialized hardware in order to be viable for embedded applications [4]. Training these networks is time intensive and often requires very large datasets. When training reinforcement learning algorithms for real life tasks such as autonomous driving, it is impractical to collect large datasets of images while taking the actions suggested by a partially trained reinforcement learning algorithm, which is likely to lead to crashes and costly outcomes. However, learning to detect important visual features does not necessarily require taking undirected actions, and can happen outside of the context of reinforcement learning. For this reason, an autoencoder can be used to compress high-dimensional visual inputs into a more compressed representation which can be used in a smaller network that requires far fewer iterations to learn an effective policy.

In order to preserve the safety of our agent and expedite the training of the autoencoder, we are using a methodology in which a large number of samples are gathered by a human expert, exported to a powerful GPU server, and used to train an autoencoder which is then imported onto the embedded GPU and used to perform compression and reinforcement learning in real time. The authors of "Learning to Drive Smoothly in Minutes" and the associated github repository [7] provided an implementation of this methodology in the Donkey Car environment, which we will use to demonstrate its potential viability in embedded real-world tasks. For example, if we were training a self-driving car, we would have a human driving and collecting video, export the video to a GPU server, train an autoencoder to compress and reconstruct the video frames, import the encoder parameters back into the self-driving car's embedded GPU, and then we would perform standard reinforcement learning on the compressed version of images captured by the camera. This way, the autonomous car would learn a driving policy significantly faster and with significantly fewer crashes than if we were to train a deep convolutional neural network end to end. In this paper, we will demonstrate the viability of using this architecture in real


*GLSVLSI '19, May 9–11, 2019, Tysons Corner, VA, USA*

ACM ISBN 978-1-4503-6252-8/19/05...$15.00
https://doi.org/10.1145/3299874.3319493

**Figure 1: Donkey Car Environment**

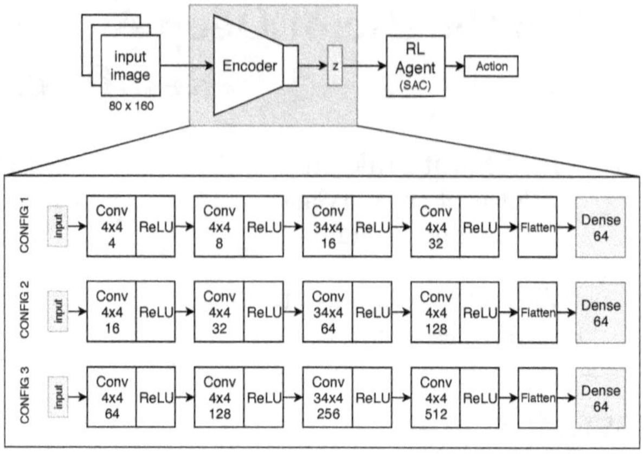


**Figure 2: Proposed Architecture - The input image is encoded using the pre-trained encoder to obtain the latent representation. This is then used by the Soft Actor Critic RL agent to output the actions. It also shows the 3 different configurations of the encoder with increasing trainable parameters**

time on an embedded system to choose an optimal action from frames of video captured by the camera. Additionally, we will vary different parameters in our encoder in an attempt to reduce its computational cost, increase the accumulated reward of the policy network, and decrease the number of iterations needed to achieve a satisfactory reward. We believe that this architecture presents an effective approach to performing faster and safer reinforcement learning on embedded devices. We also believe that by optimizing our autoencoder architecture, we can reduce the amount of power and time needed to reach a successful policy, and we can improve the peak performance of our agent.

## 2 RELATED WORK

Over the past several years, there has been significant interest in performing reinforcement learning in high-dimensional visual environments. This gained traction starting with Deepmind's landmark paper in which they were able to successfully play Atari games using pixelated images as the input to a Deep Q-Network [6]. Since then, there has been promise that self-driving cars, autonomous drones, and smart robotic systems would be soon to follow. However, despite innovations to the underlying reinforcement learning algorithms [10], [5], [9], engineers have often struggled to apply these algorithms to real-life domains.

Modern reinforcement learning algorithms require vast amounts of data to learn policies in complex environments, resulting in costly real-world actions. The amount of data needed varies between different reinforcement learning algorithms, so we are using the Soft Actor Critic (SAC) [3] algorithm used in [7] for its ability to learn high-quality policies with a small number of samples. This will be of vital importance when training on a sensitive embedded system. Unlike many other state of the art reinforcement learning algorithms, SAC is off-policy, meaning that it can learn from a random set of environment interactions, instead of a specific sequential set as is required by on-policy algorithms. This is critical in embedded environments, because on-policy algorithms are bottlenecked by the rate at which an agent can take actions, which is often much lower in physical systems such as autonomous vehicles than in simulated environments such as videogames. Additionally, the ability to learn from previously taken actions improves the sample efficiency of this algorithm, meaning that fewer dangerous steps need to be taken by the agent in order to learn an effective policy. Finally, this algorithm has a high degree of stability, meaning that there is a low variation in the reward achieved during different training cycles, making it ideal for performance tests.

Training the deep convolutional networks commonly used for reinforcement learning is often power and time intensive, requiring substantial hardware and offline training. In order to address these issues, engineers have often opted to produce high-fidelity simulations in order to train networks offline , or explicitly extract a small set of meaningful, hand-crafted features from a high dimensional environment so that training can be done quickly on a smaller network online. These approaches can expand reinforcement learning to more domains, but producing simulations and manually extracting features both require human labor and expertise, and often fail to generalize to environments with more complex dynamics and features. In these cases when it becomes excessively burdensome to explicitly model environments, autoencoders can replace human experts and learn compressed representations of high dimensional environments without supervision [2]. These compressed representations can either be used to produce simulations and train offline [2], or train smaller networks online learning from compressed representations [1, 11, 12]. While it is not a novel idea to use autoencoders to accelerate reinforcement learning, we have not found substantial work focused applying these models to embedded learning tasks where power and environment interactions are valuable, limited resources.

An autoencoder is a simple concept: a neural network which is trained to output a close approximation of its input. Generally, these models consist of an encoder, which maps a high dimensional input such as an image into a reduced vector of latent variables, and a decoder, which uses this reduced representation to generate a reconstruction of the original high-dimensional input. There are many variations of this model, but we will focus on the Variational Autoencoders (VAE) in particular. Variational Autoencoders have been used in a number of reinforcement learning tasks for its ability to do substantial unsupervised compression and partial disentanglement [2]. The variational autoencoder is an autoencoder in which guassian noise is added to the latent space, and each variable in the latent space is incentivized to conform to a multidimensional gaussian distribution with predetermined parameters.

Although they can create small, easy to work with representations of large input data, convolutional autoencoders themselves are generally large, power-intensive models. While one can avoid much of this burden by training the autoencoder offline and leaving the only online training for the policy network, it is still necessary to perform inference on the encoder at each time step in order to compress the sample. Therefore, we will also explore variations we can make to the encoder architecture and the corresponding effects it will have on the performance of the reinforcement learning algorithm, the energy required to encode a frame of video, and the latency associated with this encoding. We will also explore the effect of the number of filters on all of these performance parameters. Using this information, we will analyse the viability of this approach to information compression and reinforcement learning on an embedded Nvidia Jetson TX2 platform.

## 3 METHODS

In this section, we will explain the architecture of our autoencoder and reinforcement learning algorithm. This includes a description of the environment in Section 3.1., the collecton of training data for the autoencoder in section 3.2, and the training of the RL agent in Section 3.3.

### 3.1 Environment

We have used the Donkey Car Simulator [7] as our test environment in which our RL agent acts. This simulator, shown in Figure 1, is built on the the Unity game platform and can be easily interacted with via python libraries. The agent is a toy car with the goal of maximizing speed while staying on the track. The input to the agent is a 120x160 image from the car's camera and the action space is [steering, throttle] where these are continuous values. The reward function we get from the environment is a function of cross track error (*cte*). Cross track error measures the distance between the center of the track and car. The shaped reward we use to train the reinforcement learning agent is $reward = 1 - (abs(cte)/max\_cte) * speed$ where $max\_cte$ is a normalizing constant.

### 3.2 Pre-Training the Autoencoder

The first step in the process is to collect data to train the autoencoder. We collected these images using a human driver who controlled the car for a fixed number of steps until we obtained the required number of images.

We collected 5000 images using the human driver and then trained a variational autoencoder with the objective of re-constructing the original image fed to the network. The autoencoder was trained for 100 epochs. Performing the task of reconstruction with a bottleneck in the network forces the encoder to compress the original image to a lower dimensional vector in the latent space. We do not need to use the embedded device for this step, so it can be performed offline on a more powerful server.

We repeated this process with various architectures of the variational autoencoders by changing the filter sizes and observing how the performance varies in terms of encoding, power consumption, and the performance of the reinforcement agent trained in the latent space. We show this in more detail in the following sections.

### 3.3 Training the RL Agent

The RL agent is trained using the Soft actor critic(SAC) algorithm with the following reward function:

- reward = -10 - w1 x throttle (when getting off track)
- reward = +1 + w2 x throttle (when on track)
- w1 and w2 are hyperparameters which can be tuned

During training, the input images are compressed by the encoder of the variation autoencoder in order to obtain the latent vector. The RL agent, instead of receiving the high dimensional image, will receive the compressed representation from the encoder. This means that the RL agent can be a simple feed forward neural network, which will train much quicker than its larger convolutional counterpart.

This architecture is especially beneficial for embedded devices since we also see lower power consumption while training compared to the full RL agent with a CNN feature extractor.

The basic architecture and the configurations are shown in Figure 2. We can see that the input image is passed to the pre-trained encoder which gives us the compressed representation of the image. This is then passed to the RL agent to learn a policy and output the actions. The actions in our case are throttle and steering values. An episode ends when the car goes off track and the weights of the RL agent are updated at the end of each episode. The RL agent is trained for 150 episodes and we repeat this with different configurations of the autoencoder.

## 4 EXPERIMENTS AND RESULTS

This section will detail the experiments we performed with different configurations of the variational autoencoder as well as the results for each configuration. We also show the power consumption and energy efficiency on Nvidia TX2 for different CPU and GPU frequency combinations.

### 4.1 VAE configurations

We experimented with various configurations of the VAE by varying the number of convolutional filters in each layer as shown in Figure 2. In the first set of experiments, we changed the number of filters in the convolutional layer thereby increasing the number of trainable parameters from from 38k, 274k to 3.15M. Figure 3 shows how the quality of the reconstruction from the autoencoder changes as we increase the number of parameters. We also measured the quality of reconstruction by calculating Mean Squared Error (MSE) and Peak Signal to Noise Ratio (PSNR) and visually showing reconstructions from each configuration. Table 1 shows the MSE and PSNR values for the 3 selected configurations, and Figure 3 shows the reconstructions generated by each VAE.

One can visually observe in Figure 3 that config 3 produced sharper reconstructions than config 2. This is reaffirmed by the the MSE and PSNR metrics in Table 1, which both show quantitatively

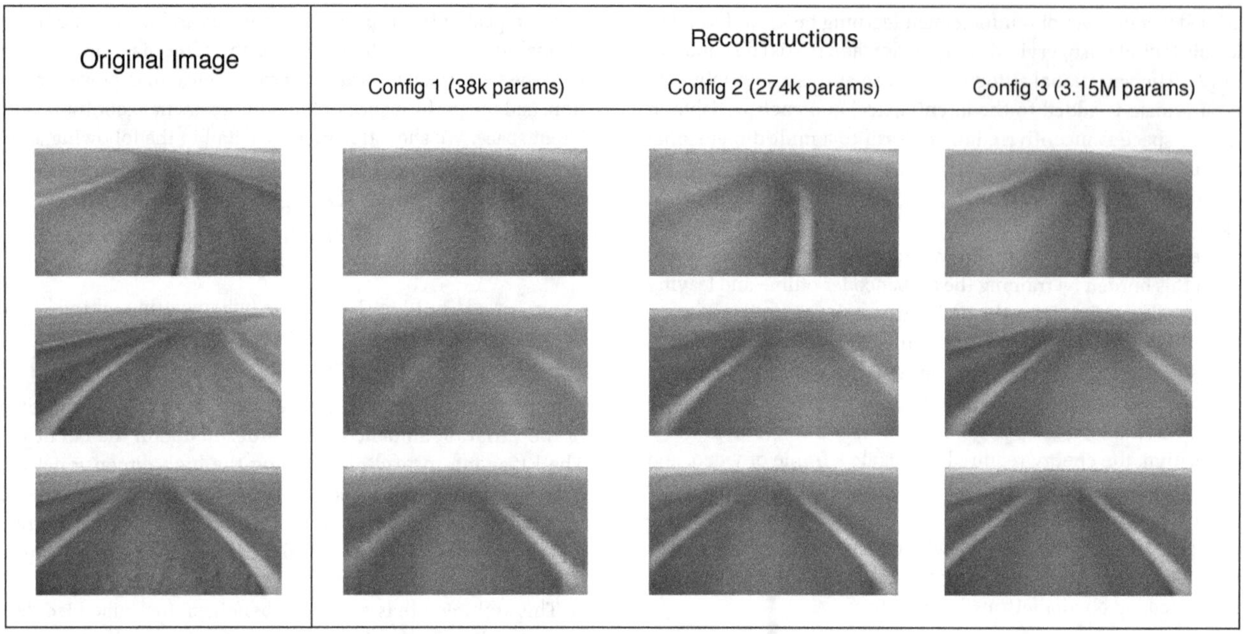


**Figure 3: Autoencoder image reconstructions for different configurations. This shows how reconstruction quality improves as we increase the number of parameters. This implies that we obtain more detailed latent space representations as we increase the number of parameters.**

that the quality of reconstructions increases as the number of parameters in the encoder increases. Although there is a quantitative difference in reconstruction quality, visual inspection would indicate that config 3 and config 2 both seem to be able to effectively encode the position of the agent on the road as well as the shape of nearby segments of the road.

## 4.2 Reinforcement Learning (RL) Performance

In order to test the effects the various VAE architecures have on policy learning, we trained an RL agent with each of the three pre-trained autoencoders. As a baseline, we also trained the RL agent without a pre-trained autoencoder, using only the raw images, to show the benefits that using an autoencoder has on learning.

This policy network for the baseline RL agent has a CNN feature extractor followed by fully connected layers. In contrast, the policy network in our architecture consists of just fully connected layers and its input is the low dimensional encoded vector from the pre-trained encoder. We measure its performance in terms of episode

| # Parameters | Config 1<br>38 k | Config 2<br>274 k* | Config 3<br>3.15 M |
|---|---|---|---|
| MSE | 43.48 | 23.48* | 18.52 |
| PSNR | 31.74 | 34.429* | 36.52 |

**Table 1: Autoencoder Performance for different configurations.**

rewards. The reward is a function of the distance travelled by the car and its speed while staying on the track.

We trained the RL agent for 150 episodes and evaluated the agent every 5 episodes, then repeated this process using the three different VAE configurations. In Figure 4, we show the episode rewards for these configurations. Here, we can observe that the policy learned in the latent space is better and faster than the policy learned in the high dimensional image space (no VAE). When learning from the latent representation, the episode reward reached 2500 after 150 episodes while the baseline RL agent stays around 400. The baseline agent requires more steps to achieve the same performance as our agent. After 50 episodes, the latent space reinforcement learning algorithm was able to produce a viable policy while the standard reinforcement learner made little noticeable progress. There are a few important caveats to this conclusion however. First of all, the standard reinforcement learning algorithm will generally match or exceed the reward generated by the autoencoder method given a long enough time horizon. Additionally, before the autoencoder can be trained, we must use a human driver to in order to generate a set of training data for the autoencoder. Finally, the set of information extracted by an autoencoder is necessarily larger than the information needed to perform reinforcement learning, meaning that a raw reinforcement learner may require a smaller architecture with fewer parameters. However, when using comparable architectures, the reinforcement learner which incorporates an autoencoder can train a viable policy with many fewer dangerous interactions in the environment than with a standard reinforcement learner.

In Figure 4, we also demonstrate how changing size of the autoencoder effects the performance of the agent. Over the set of

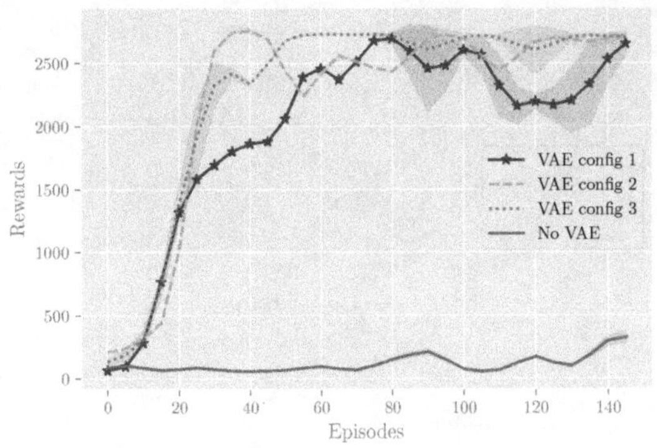


**Figure 4: Episode Rewards - This shows the episode rewards accumulated while training the RL agent using different VAE configurations and also without the VAE. We observe that the RL agent learns considerably faster when trained with pre-trained encoders. Also, we see how the performance varies when we increase the number of convolutional filters in our VAEs.**

experiments we performed, we found that we could not meaningfully distinguish the performance of config 2 and config 3 in training a reinforcement learning algorithm. The performance of each of these varied between experiments because of stochasticity introduced by retraining the autoencoders and reinforcement learning algorithm from scratch. However, we found that config 1 consistently took longer to approach it peak reward. In this case, config 2 and 3 both surpassed a reward of 2000 after roughly 20-30 episodes while config 1 required 40-50 episodes. This result seems to be consistent with the detail generated in the reconstructions of each config as show in Figure 3. In this figure we see slight visual differences in the reconstructions generated by config 2 and config 3. However, they were both able to effectively encode the position of the agent on the road and the shape of the road, which are the two most important factors to consider when deciding on an action. However, neither of these are nearly as clear in the config 1 reconstruction, which is likely why the reinforcement learner learning from config 1 embeddings struggled relative to the other two. Interestingly, even the config 1 reinforcment learner was able to achieve high rewards over a longer time horizon, meaning that even this configuration was encoding substantial information relevant to the agent.

## 4.3 Embedded Hardware Metrics

We measured power consumption and energy efficiency of these models on the Embedded Nvidia TX2 platform in order to demonstrate the feasibility of such architectures on embedded devices. We performed tests on the TX2 with different combinations of GPU and CPU frequencies. Figure 5 shows these metrics where we measure the power, energy efficiency, frame rate and performance for the three autoencoder configurations. As shown in Figure 5, even the largest configuration that we tested consumes about 3 watts at the 586 MHz GPU frequency, while being able to process more than 60 frames per second. This frame rate is more than sufficient for most embedded navigation and control tasks, and 3 watts of power is a small percentage of the power consumed by electric cars and drones, which are often targeted platforms for autonomous embedded systems.

Additionally, we conducted similar hardware experiments with config 2 to find the CPU/GPU frequencies that result in optimal implementation. We choose Config 2 because the RL agent performance of Config 2 and Config 3 are very similar even though Config 2 has significantly less parameters. Table 2 shows the Power, frame rate and energy efficiency for the various combinations of CPU and GPU frequencies on the NVIDIA TX2. In the experiments that we did, the frame rate requirements were fixed to be 60 FPS. From Table 2 we see that a few combinations are able to achieve this frame rate. It also shows 2 combinations where no GPU were used. It either failed to achieve 60 FPS or the power consumption and energy efficiency was above 3 W. The ideal combination we found was CPU 1.4 GHz and GPU 1.3 GHz/586 Mhz which are among those that meet the frame rate of 60 FPS and consume 1.8 W or less.

# 5 CONCLUSIONS AND FUTURE WORKS

Through our experiments, we have demonstrated the usefulness of autoencoders for compression in embedded reinforcement learning tasks. Using this architecture, we can significantly reduce the time needed to produce a viable policy while also preserving a sufficiently high throughput and low power to perform a large number of embedded reinforcement learning tasks. There are significant steps that one could take to further improve the sample efficiency and safety of these methods. For example, one could use the compressed representation generated by the variational autoencoder to learn to model the dynamics on an environment, and subsequently train a policy completely in a simulation, further increasing the safety of the training process [2]. Additionally, fear based methods provide a way to reduce dangerous environment interactions by using human inputs [8]. We chose to use a more simple reinforcement learner because it would be the most broadly applicable method and thus a good way to compare different autoencoder configurations. However, the incorporation of these methods could significantly increase sample efficiency in some cases. Future work will also include the deploying and testing of our embedded models on robotic systems as quadrotors or ground robots.

# 6 ACKNOWLEDGMENTS

This project was sponsored by the U.S. Army Research Laboratory under Cooperative Agreement Number W911NF-10-2-0022. The views and conclusions contained in this document are those of the authors and should not be interpreted as representing the official policies, either expressed or implied, of the U.S. Government. The U.S. Government is authorized to reproduce and distribute reprints for Government purposes notwithstanding any copyright notation herein.

# REFERENCES

[1] Vinicius G. Goecks, Gregory M. Gremillion, Vernon J. Lawhern, John Valasek, and Nicholas R. Waytowich. 2019. Efficiently Combining Human Demonstrations and Interventions for Safe Training of Autonomous Systems in Real Time. *AAAI Conference on Artificial Intelligence* (2019).

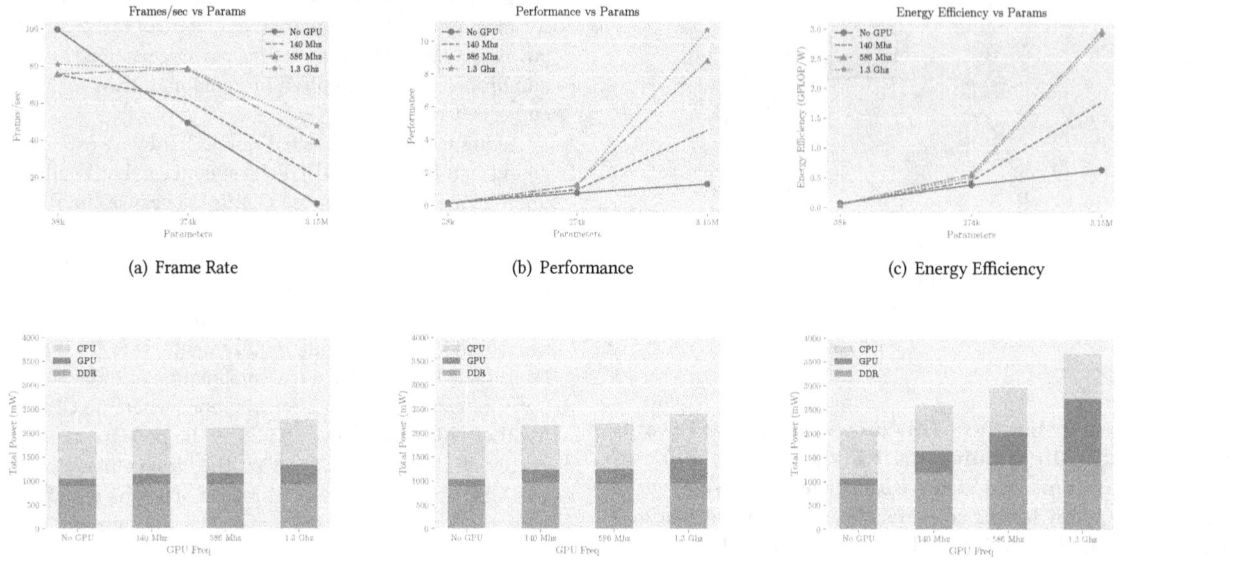


(a) Frame Rate (b) Performance (c) Energy Efficiency

(d) Power - Config 1 (e) Power - Config 2 (f) Power - Config 3

**Figure 5: This figure shows how the Power, Energy, Frame Rate and Performance change for different configurations of the autoencoder**

| CPU Freq | GPU Freq | Power (mW) | | | | Time/frame(ms) | Frame Rate | Performance (GFLOP/S) | Energy(J) | Energy Eff (GFLOPS/W) |
|---|---|---|---|---|---|---|---|---|---|---|
| | | CPU | GPU | DDR | Total | | | | | |
| 345. MHz | 140 MHz | 230 | 198.5 | 372.5 | 801.0 | 72.9 | 13.7 | 0.219 | 0.058 | 0.273 |
| | 586 MHz | 230 | 199.4 | 804.7 | 1234.1 | 65.1 | 15.4 | 0.245 | 0.080 | 1.98 |
| | 1.3 GHz | 230 | 33.5 | 804.1 | 1369.5 | 62.7 | 15.9 | 0.254 | 0.086 | 0.186 |
| 1.4 GHz | 140 MHz | 537 | 244.2 | 917.6 | 1698.8 | 19.4 | 51.6 | 0.823 | 0.033 | 0.484 |
| | **586 MHz** | **537** | **261.8** | **915.5** | **1714.3** | **16.8** | **59.6** | **0.949** | **0.029** | **0.554** |
| | **1.3 GHz** | **537** | **416.1** | **917.8** | **1870.9** | **16.7** | **60.1** | **0.957** | **0.031** | **0.512** |
| 2 GHz | 140 MHz | 931.8 | 288.5 | 966.2 | 2186.5 | 16.9 | 59.1 | 0.941 | 0.037 | 0.431 |
| | 586 MHz | 935.8 | 323.3 | 955.9 | 2214.9 | 12.9 | 77.4 | 1.234 | 0.029 | 0.557 |
| | 1.3 GHz | 933.1 | 545.6 | 953.9 | 2432.6 | 12.7 | 78.7 | 1.255 | 0.031 | 0.516 |
| 2 GHz | No GPU | 997.0 | 153 | 882.5 | 2032.5 | 20.3 | 49.2 | 0.785 | 0.041 | 0.386 |
| 2 GHz (4 cores) | | 2158.3 | 178.5 | 1031.1 | 3367.9 | 15.8 | 63.4 | 1.016 | 0.053 | 0.302 |

**Table 2: Hardware performance of Config 2 with different combinations of CPU and GPU frequencies**


[2] David Ha and Jürgen Schmidhuber. 2018. World models. *arXiv preprint arXiv:1803.10122* (2018).

[3] Tuomas Haarnoja, Aurick Zhou, Pieter Abbeel, and Sergey Levine. 2018. Soft actor-critic: Off-policy maximum entropy deep reinforcement learning with a stochastic actor. *arXiv preprint arXiv:1801.01290* (2018).

[4] Ali Jafari, Ashwinkumar Ganesan, Chetan Sai Kumar Thalisetty, Varun Sivasubramanian, Tim Oates, and Tinoosh Mohsenin. 2018. Sensornet: A scalable and low-power deep convolutional neural network for multimodal data classification. *IEEE Transactions on Circuits and Systems I: Regular Papers* 99 (2018), 1–14.

[5] Volodymyr Mnih, Adria Puigdomenech Badia, Mehdi Mirza, Alex Graves, Timothy Lillicrap, Tim Harley, David Silver, and Koray Kavukcuoglu. 2016. Asynchronous methods for deep reinforcement learning. In *International conference on machine learning*. 1928–1937.

[6] Volodymyr Mnih, Koray Kavukcuoglu, David Silver, Andrei A Rusu, Joel Veness, Marc G Bellemare, Alex Graves, Martin Riedmiller, Andreas K Fidjeland, Georg Ostrovski, et al. 2015. Human-level control through deep reinforcement learning. *Nature* 518, 7540 (2015), 529.

[7] Antonin Raffin and Roma Sokolkov. 2019. Learning to Drive Smoothly in Minutes. https://github.com/araffin/learning-to-drive-in-5-minutes/. (2019).

[8] William Saunders, Girish Sastry, Andreas Stuhlmueller, and Owain Evans. 2017. Trial without Error: Towards Safe Reinforcement Learning via Human Intervention. (jul 2017). arXiv:1707.05173 http://arxiv.org/abs/1707.05173

[9] John Schulman, Filip Wolski, Prafulla Dhariwal, Alec Radford, and Oleg Klimov. 2017. Proximal policy optimization algorithms. *arXiv preprint arXiv:1707.06347* (2017).

[10] Richard S Sutton, David A McAllester, Satinder P Singh, and Yishay Mansour. 2000. Policy gradient methods for reinforcement learning with function approximation. In *Advances in neural information processing systems*. 1057–1063.

[11] Garrett Warnell, Nicholas Waytowich, Vernon Lawhern, and Peter Stone. 2018. Deep TAMER: Interactive Agent Shaping in High-Dimensional State Spaces. *AAAI Conference on Artificial Intelligence* (2018), 1545–1553. https://aaai.org/ocs/index.php/AAAI/AAAI18/paper/view/16200

[12] Nicholas R. Waytowich, Vinicius G. Goecks, and Vernon J. Lawhern. 2018. Cycle-of-Learning for Autonomous Systems from Human Interaction. *CoRR* abs/1808.09572v1 (2018). arXiv:1808.09572v1 https://arxiv.org/abs/1808.09572v1

# Tuning Track-based NVM Caches for Low-Power IoT Devices

Hoda Aghaei Khouzani and Chengmo Yang
University of Delaware
Newark, DE, USA
hoda,chengmo@udel.edu

## ABSTRACT

Track-based non-volatile memories, such as Domain Wall Memory (DWM) and Skyrmion, are promising candidates to be used as CPU caches due to their ultra-high density and low-static power. However, the access latency and energy of these devices are highly affected by the number of shift operation performed. Existing track-based NVM cache designs place logically-adjacent blocks close to each other, resulting in extra shift operations performed to access the data. This paper makes the observation that the block access pattern in cache is typically repetitive with a stride of $N$. Such pattern motivates us to propose a new cache block placement for track-based NVMs, aiming at reducing the number of shift operations throughout program execution.

## CCS CONCEPTS

• **Hardware → Non-volatile memory**; **Emerging architectures**; • **Computer systems organization** → *Embedded hardware.*

## KEYWORDS

Non-volatile memories; Cache; Low power design; Internet-of-Things

**ACM Reference Format:**
Hoda Aghaei Khouzani and Chengmo Yang. 2019. Tuning Track-based NVM Caches for Low-Power IoT Devices. In *Great Lakes Symposium on VLSI 2019 (GLSVLSI '19), May 9–11, 2019, Tysons Corner, VA, USA.* ACM, New York, NY, USA, 6 pages. https://doi.org/10.1145/3299874.3319335

## 1 INTRODUCTION

Internet-of-Things (IoT) devices, as they are usually small and battery-dependent, bring extra challenges to system design, especially to on-chip cache design. Built with SRAM technology, caches contribute to 80% of chip area and more than 50% of chip power consumption [11]. As SRAM is limited by scalability and high static power, researchers started to explore the use of emerging non-volatile memory (NVM) technologies in IoT devices. Track-based NVM technologies, such as Domain Wall Memory (DWM) [17, 21] and Skyrmion [12], are promising alternatives given their ultra-high density and low static power. The main challenge in employing them in IoT devices, however, is their sequential access structure which considerably affects the access latency and energy of IoT devices. In particular, track-based memories store several bits of data on track-shaped materials and deploy a limited number of access ports at fixed positions on each track. To read/write data from/to a track, it is necessary to shift the track to align the target bit with the appropriate access port.


*GLSVLSI '19, May 9–11, 2019, Tysons Corner, VA, USA*

ACM ISBN 978-1-4503-6252-8/19/05.
https://doi.org/10.1145/3299874.3319335

The goal of this work is to minimize the number of shift operations in a track-based NVM when its is employed as the on-chip cache for IoT devices. In general, the cache access latency depends on three parameters, *Hit time*, *Miss rate*, and *Miss penalty* [8]. The two latter are affected by the size of cache, cache replacement policy, and the access latency of lower-level components in the memory hierarchy. The former is directly impacted by the access latency of data on the cache, which further depends on the organization and data layout in a track-based NVM device. Although some works have proposed to employ track-based NVMs as CPU caches [13, 21, 23], none of them have examined the impact of different cache layouts on the number of shift operations and the resultant *Hit time*, which is the main focus of this work.

Our observation is that the *Hit time* is largely influenced by the access pattern to the different sets and different ways of a cache, as well as the order of their placement on track-based NVMs. To explore the design space of track-based NVM caches and identify the best solution for IoT devices, this work makes three contributions. First, it thoroughly analyzes the access behavior of representative benchmarks, extracting the most common access patterns to different cache sets and the different ways within the same set. Second, it compares three existing layouts of track-based NVM caches, namely, *way-based data placement*, *way stride based data placement*, and *set-based data placement*, and finds that these designs place data blocks with high locality on positions served through one access port, thus serializing their accesses and engendering more shift operations. Finally, a new NVM cache organization called *set stride based data placement* is proposed, capable of accessing data with high locality through dependent and synchronized access ports, thus reducing the number of shift operations and improving cache access latency.

The rest of the paper is organized as follows: Section 2 briefly introduces track-based NVM devices and reviews related work on using them as on-caches. Section 3 compares the different layouts of track-based NVM caches, pinpoints their shortcomings, and presents the proposed set stride based NVM cache organization. Section 4 presents the results of our experimental studies, while Section 5 concludes the paper.

## 2 PRELIMINARIES

### 2.1 Track-based NVMs

Track-based non-volatile memories, also known as Racetrack memories, have demonstrated a great potential to store vast amount of data in limited space. The two most well-known track-based NVMs are Domain Wall Memory (DWM) and Magnetic Skyrmion Memory (Skyrmion), both of which store data on hundreds of millions of

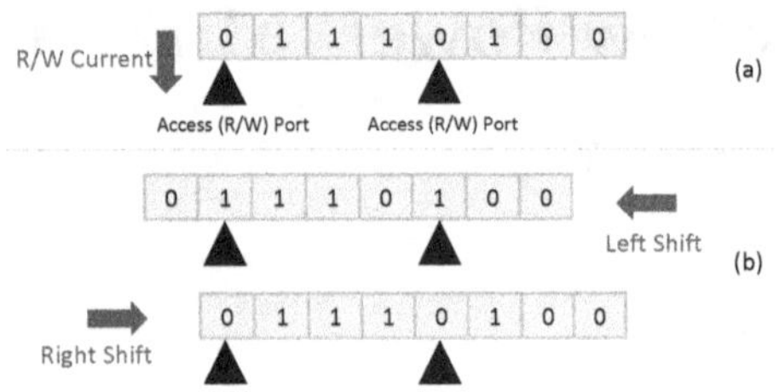


**Figure 1: Track-based NVM access structure**

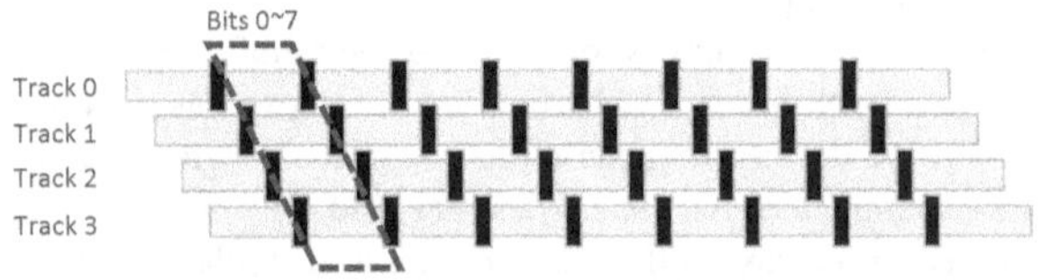


**Figure 2: Structure of Macro Unit $MU_{64\_32\_4}$. Each track has 64 domains, the MU contains 32 access ports and 4 tracks.**

ferromagnetic nanowires on a silicon substrate called *tracks* [22]. A track contains several magnetized regions each of which represents a bit, shown in Figure 1. The difference between the two technologies is that DWM codes the information using the direction of magnetic field, while the Skyrmion uses presence/absence of the skyrmion to represent 1/0 [20].

Regardless of the methodology of storing data, both technologies adopt a track-based structure and places multiple access (R/W) ports at fixed positions on the track for reading/writing data. Each access port serves only a fixed chunk of positions on a track and can read/write one bit at a time. To access any bit on a track, it should be aligned with its predetermined access port. Bits are shifted forward or backward using current-induced pulses [16] or spin orbit torque methods [26] applied at either end of the track, as shown in Figure 1. In such a structure, bits on the distance equal to the distance of neighboring access ports can be accessed simultaneously. The overall access latency and energy are non-uniform and proportional to the number of shift operations. Therefore, designing the cache/memory architectures in a way that mitigates the adverse impact of shift operations is desirable.

In track-based NVMs, the width of R/W access port is usually larger than the track width. To enhance area utilization and increase storage density, multiple tracks can be overlapped to form a Macro Unit (MU) [19], shown in Figure 2. MU is the basic building block of a track-based NVM array. Its configuration, denoted as $MU_{ND\_NP\_NRT}$, is defined by three parameters: the number of bits on each track (*ND*), the number of access ports in an MU (*NP*), and the number of tracks in an MU (*NRT*). Two research studies investigated different MU configurations [10, 25]. They both found that the organization of $MU_{64\_32\_4}$ is the best configuration balancing area, performance, and energy. This is adopted as the default configuration in this work.

Although Skyrmion is shown to be a more stable technology throughout the shift process, more research studies evolved around DWM which is introduced earlier than Skyrmion. From an architectural perspective, however, the two devices are similar, and the proposed cache organization can be applied to both of them.

## 2.2 Related Work

As track-based NVMs offer ultra-high density and short read/write latency comparable to SRAM, researchers have examined their usage at different levels of memory hierarchy, from main memory [5, 10] to on-chip caches [13, 23] and even the register file and stack in the processing units [6, 14].

Most of previous works try to tackle the adverse impact on latency and energy induced by the sequential access structure. A study in [7] shows that optimizing the number of shift operations through data placement is NP-complete. Hence, a compiler-based heuristic algorithm is proposed to generate near-optimal solution. In [10], DWM is used as main memory, and data access latency is reduced through transposing the rows and columns in the memory sub-arrays. The work in [5] optimizes DWM main memory for storing the performance-critical page table. The state of pagetable entry (PTE) is determined base on the access port position prior to reading the PTE. The scratchpad memory in [9] combines DWM cells with STT-RAM cells to take advantage of the high density of the former and the short latency of the latter. In [14], DWM is used to build GPGPU's register file. The work alleviates the impact of shifts through register remapping and wrap scheduling. The work in [6] designs and optimizes a DWM-based stack architecture for low-power IoT devices.

TapeCache [21] is the earliest proposed DWM-based cache. It employs a circuit/architecture co-design technique to mitigate the adverse impact of shift operations on the latency and energy. It also equips each track with extra read-only ports to further reduce the performance-critical read latency. Aiming to improving the TapeCache, several schemes are proposed subsequently. The cache design in [13] places data blocks of the same set at stride *d* positions (*d* is the distance between two neighboring access ports) so that they can be accessed at the same time. The workload-oriented cache in [18] uses different track configurations. Each track combines a different number of read-only and R/W ports and is tailored to a specific data access pattern. The work in [24] reduces the number of shift operations by utilizing compression techniques to reduce the number of bits to traverse.

A study on the current used for shift operations reveals that higher currents increase the velocity but leads to higher power consumption [15]. This trade-off is the basis for the cache design proposed in [15] which adopts three different types of shift and write operations (fast, medium, and slow) to balance performance and energy. A dual-level private cache is proposed in [23] which combines L1 and L2 caches into a single physical component. The cells aligned to the access port constitute the L1 cache, whereas the remaining cells constitute the L2 cache. This design allows L1 to be accessed without any shift operation and naturally offers inclusion and eviction properties. Upon an L1 miss, the track is shifted to align the new data with the access port, which is equivalent to promoting the data from L2 to L1 and evicting the data previously in L1 to L2.

# 3 CACHE LAYOUT EXPLORATION

## 3.1 Envisioned IoT Cache Hierarchy

Many forms of ARM architectures are embraced by embedded and IoT devices due to their low cost, small footprint, and low power consumption compared to expensive cores such as Intel Xeon. ARM

**Table 1: Cache Configuration, based on ARM Cortex A Series [2].**

| | Cache size | Associativity | Block size |
|---|---|---|---|
| iL1 | 32KB | 8 | 64B |
| dL1 | 32KB | 8 | 64B |
| L2 | 256KB | 4 | 64B |
| L3 | 8MB | 16 | 64B |

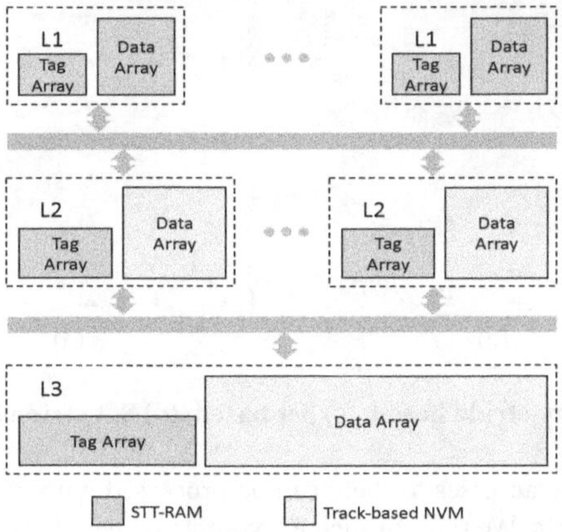


**Figure 3: Envisioned IoT Cache Hierarchy**

CPUs have different cache configurations, ranging form Qualcomm Scorpion [3] with two levels of caches to Apple Cyclone [1] with three levels of caches. This study focuses on the designs with three levels of caches, as two-level cache architectures can be a subset of them. Table 1 outlines the cache configurations used in this study.

Figure 3 presents the technologies to be used in the envisioned IoT cache hierarchy. This work employs track-based memories for lower-level caches, namely, L2 and L3 caches. L1 cache is not one of the target for these technologies as its *Hit time* is critical and should be within one CPU cycle ideally. Track-based NVMs, however, cannot fulfill such requirement due to their varying access latency. Instead, it is more desirable to utilize STT-MRAM, which has smaller capacity but faster and uniform access latency to build the L1 cache, as shown in Figure 3. On the other hand, for L2 and L3 caches, which are orders of magnitude larger and whose *Hit time* is much less critical than the *Miss rate*, it is preferable to utilize track-based NVM devices which offer much more storage density than STT-MRAM.

For a similar reason, this work focuses on examining the access latency and energy of the data array rather than the tag array. To accelerate the tag matching process in modern caches, the tag array is typically implemented as content-addressable memory (CAM), allowing all the tags in a cache set to be read and compared against the requested tag in parallel. As the size of the tag array is much smaller than the data array, implementing it in STT-MRAM rather than track-based NVM happens to be a better design choice.

## 3.2 Existing Cache Layout Comparison

In the most straightforward manner, track-based caches can be organized in the same way as traditional SRAM caches. Bits of one cache line can be placed on the same track, while adjacent tracks can accommodate different cache lines within the same set. To read/write any cache line, $d$ shifts need to be performed, with $d$ equal to the distance between two neighboring access ports. This is due to the sequential access structure of track-based NVMs which is explained in Section 2.1.

Aiming at reducing the latency overhead induced by the sequential access structure, a few schemes start re-organizing the layout of data over track-based NVM caches [13, 21]. Their goal is to reduce the temporal dependency between the bits that are accessed through one access port. These schemes organize cache lines of the same set vertically on the same group of tracks. As shown in Figures 4(a) and 4(b), the same bit position on $n$ tracks are used to store the different bits of a cache line, with $n$ equal to the size of the cache line. Consequently, the $i^{th}$ ($0 \leq i < n$) bits of all the cache lines within the same cache set are written on the $i^{th}$ track. The advantage of such layouts is that all the bits of one cache line can be read/written simultaneously. Yet to align the target cache line to the access ports, all the $n$ tracks need to shifted. The number of shifts required per track ranges from 0 to $d - 1$. This number cannot be higher than $d$ which is the distance between two neighboring access ports. If the distance between two cache lines on the same track is larger than $d - 1$, the number of shifts will be $distance\%d$.

While both layouts allow concurrent accesses to all the bits of one cache line, the difference lies in their strategies on placing cache lines of the same set. In the *way based placement* [21], shown in Figure 4(a), all the different ways of one cache set are written next to each other, while in the *way stride based placement* [13], shown in Figure 4(b), they are placed at stride $d$ positions. In these schemes, the number of shifts to access a cache lines depends on the physical distance between the *to-be-accessed* line and the *most-recently-accessed* line. From this perspective, the second layout has an advantage as it offers the potential to reduce the adverse impact induced by the dependency between the cache lines of the same set. More specifically, if two consecutive accesses target two lines in the same cache set (e.g., Set0Way0 and Set0Way1), in the layout shown in Figure 4(a), $n$ tracks have to be shifted one unit to align the first access port on each track (0 to $n - 1$) to Set0Way1, while in the layout shown in Figure 4(b), no shift is needed since both Set0Way0 and Set0Way1 are aligned respectively with the first and second access ports on tracks 0 to $n - 1$.

## 3.3 Common Access Pattern Identification

Although consecutive accesses to the same set follow high locality pattern, not all the consecutive accesses are directed to the same set. To identify the most common access pattern, we conducted an investigation over the sets of accesses to the L2 and L3 caches. We analyzed the access patterns of 20 benchmarks in SPEC 2006 set using the cache configuration in table 1 [2]. We used Pin [4] to implement instruction and data L1 caches, and collected traces of the addresses of cache lines missed in and evicted from the L1 cache. These traces were fed into an event-driven simulator, developed to analyze the access pattern in L2 and L3 caches. Traces were grouped to simulate a multi-process environment.

We collected and analyzed the distance between the sets of every two consecutive accesses to L2 and L3 caches. The results of the L2 cache are shown in Table 2. On average, only 42% of the consecutive accesses are directed to the same cache set, meaning that the intra-set locality that the *way stride based placement* aims to exploit is

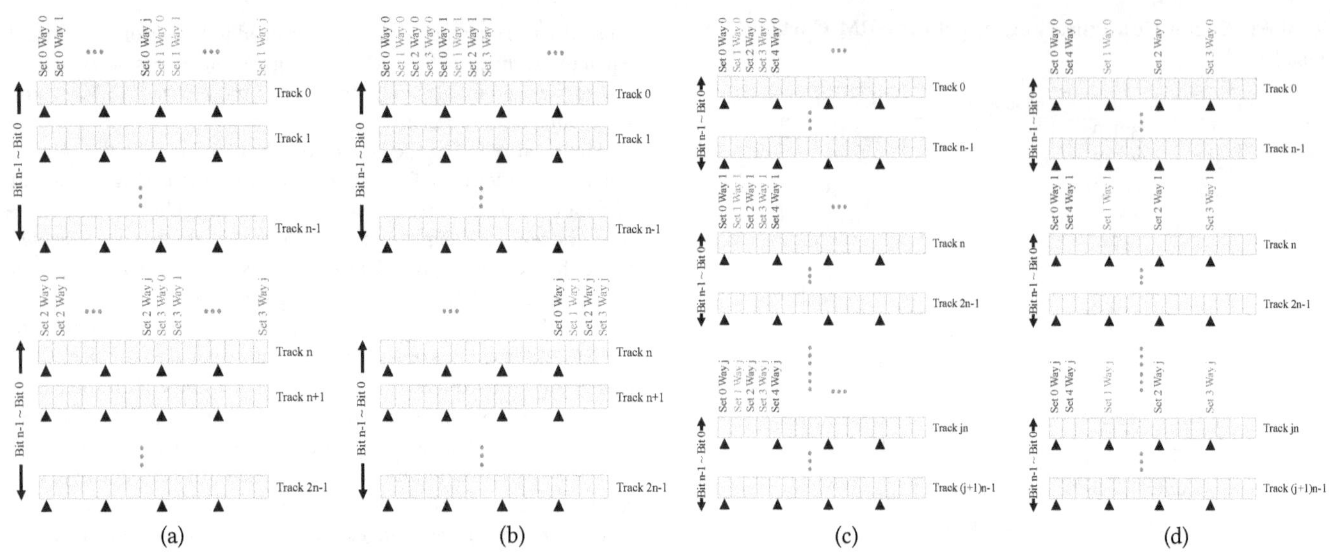

Figure 4: Four different NVM cache organizations: (a) Way based, (b) Way stride based, (c) Set based, (d) Set stride based.

Table 2: Percentage of consecutive L2 accesses to cache sets with distance of i, $0 \leq i < 8$

| Benchmark | distance between sets | | |
|---|---|---|---|
| | 0 | 1~7 | total |
| astar | 42.34% | 23.31% | 65.65% |
| bwave | 42.56% | 29.85% | 72.41% |
| cactusADM | 7.34% | 33.38% | 40.72% |
| calculix | 33.36% | 34.28% | 67.64% |
| gamess | 41.63% | 33.65% | 75.27% |
| gcc | 50.77% | 34.09% | 84.86% |
| GemsFDTD | 42.38% | 22.74% | 65.12% |
| gobmk | 63.20% | 35.71% | 98.91% |
| gromacs | 44.75% | 23.64% | 68.38% |
| h264ref | 52.64% | 33.03% | 85.66% |
| hmmer | 38.59% | 21.01% | 59.60% |
| leslie3d | 50.11% | 26.75% | 76.86% |
| libquantum | 50.71% | 42.84% | 93.55% |
| mcf | 52.51% | 23.74% | 76.26% |
| milc | 50.83% | 27.30% | 78.13% |
| omnetpp | 19.02% | 10.26% | 29.28% |
| sjeng | 36.59% | 33.77% | 70.36% |
| soplex | 53.67% | 17.13% | 70.80% |
| tonto | 41.33% | 29.51% | 70.84% |
| zeusmp | 30.72% | 20.04% | 50.76% |
| Average | 42.25% | 27.80% | 70.05% |

limited to 42% of all the accesses. For the L3 cache, this value is much smaller; less than one percent of the consecutive accesses are to the same set. Our study also shows that most benchmarks have inter-set locality. As shown in Table 2, about 28% of consecutive accesses are to sets with distance less than 7. This motivate us to propose a set based placement to exploit inter-set locality.

## 3.4 Proposed Set Based Placement

Instead of placing cache lines of the same set on the same track, an alternative is to place these lines in different groups of tracks, so that the accesses to them can be processed with independent access ports. We refer to such a layout as *set based placement.* An example is shown in Figure 4(c). In such a layout, $t$ sets share the same group of tracks, with $t$ denoting the number of bits on a track. This implies that accesses to the sets whose distance is more than $t$ are independent, since these sets are managed through different groups of tracks.

In the *set based placement*, accessing two consecutive sets with distance $d$ (e.g., Set0Way0 and Set4Way0 in Figure 4(c)) requires no extra shift, while accessing two adjacent sets (e.g., Set0Way0 and Set1Way0 in Figure 4(c)) requires one shift on each of the $n$ tracks. As accesses to adjacent sets are more common due to the well-known spatial locality property, it is preferable to place adjacent sets at distance $d$ positions on the same track. We refer to such a layout as *set stride based placement*, as shown in Figure 4(d). In this layout, the consecutive accesses with set distance of $0 \leq i < p$ can be performed without extra shifts. $p$ is the number of access ports on a track and $p = t/d$. For example, in Figure 4(d), sets 0 to 3 are served with access ports 0 to 3 respectively, Once any of them is aligned to its corresponding access port, all of them can be accessed without the need for extra shifts.

According to the studies of track-based NVM array configurations in [10, 25], the best configuration is $MU_{64\_32\_4}$, meaning that each Marco Unit (MU) contains 4 tracks, each track consists of 64 domains and has 8 access ports. Meanwhile, Table 2 shows that on average, 70% of consecutive accesses are to sets with distance of $0 \leq i < 8$. This implies that the proposed *set stride based placement* can reduce the number of shifts by up to 70% in total.

# 4 EVALUATION

## 4.1 Experimental Setup

A cache simulator incorporating the four cache layout placements in figure 4 has been developed, including four private L2 caches and one shared L3 cache. The evaluation set includes 20 SPEC 2006 benchmarks, which are relatively memory-intensive and engender

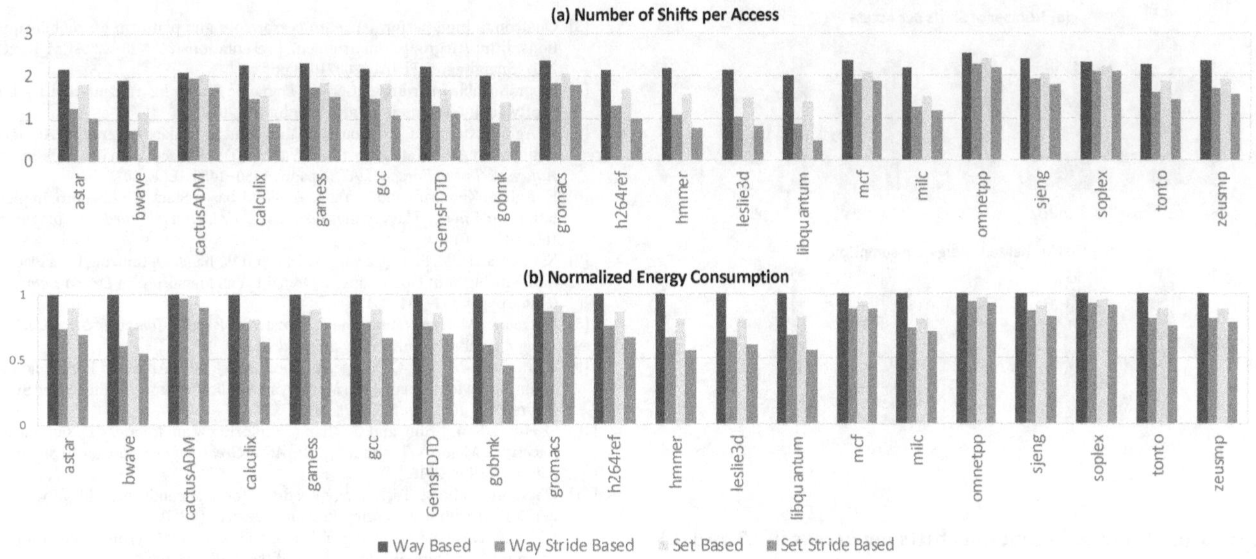


**Figure 5: (a) Average number of shifts per access in L2 and (b) Dynamic energy consumption of L2.**

**Table 3: Groups of benchmarks**

| | Benchmarks |
|---|---|
| Group1 | bwave, gamess, gcc, mcf |
| Group2 | cactusADM, gromacs, milc, zeusmp |
| Group3 | calculix, gobmk, leslie3d, soplex |
| Group4 | GemsFDTD, hmmer, libquantum, sjeng |
| Group5 | astar, h264ref, omnetpp, tonto |

non-trivial amount of accesses to the cache hierarchy. Traces of L1 cache misses and writebacks (thus generating read and write accesses to the L2 cache) are extracted using Pin[4], including the access address, the operation type (read or eviction), and the corresponding instruction count used to simulate the execution time. Extracted traces are grouped to simulate a multi-process environment and are fed to the developed simulator as inputs. Table 3 shows the groups of benchmarks.

The cache configuration used in the study is based on ARM Cortex A series [2], and is summarized in Table 1. The array of track-based NVM is $MU_{64\_32\_4}$, reported in [10] as the most efficient MU that balances area, performance, and energy.

## 4.2 Results Analysis

*4.2.1 Shift per Access.* The number of shift operations performed in the track-based NVM cache for the four investigated layouts are collected. The distance between the appropriate access port and the position to access determines the number of shift operations. Note that, per each access to a cache block (which is the unit of read and write) with size $n$, $n$ different tracks are shifted simultaneously and they all contribute to energy consumption.

Figures 5(a) and 6(a) show the average number of shift operations performed per access in the four different layouts for L2 and L3 caches, respectively. The lower the value, the shorter the latency, the lower the power consumption. The ideal case is to perform no shift per each access.

Figure 5(a) shows that in the L2 cache, the *set stride based placement* decreases the average number of shift operations per access to 1.25 which is 44%, 18%, and 31%, better than *way based placement, way stride based placement,* and *set based placement,* respectively. For some benchmarks such as *bwave, gobmk,* and *libquantum,* the *set stride based placement* reduces the average number of shift operations per access to less than 1, meaning that most of the consecutive accesses are to the sets with distance between 0 to 7. This is inline with the values reported in table 2, where the rates of consecutive accesses with such attribute are above 70%. For benchmarks such as *gamess,* although the rate of neighboring consecutive accesses is also above 70%, the number of shift operations per access is not less than 1. The reason could lie into the fact that these logically-adjacent sets might be mapped to different groups of tracks, because each group of tracks can only accommodate 64 sets. As a result, the *set stride based placement* cannot take advantage of the locality in the access pattern to the maximum extent.

Figure 6(a) shows that in the L3 cache, on average the *set stride based placement* decreases the required number of shift operations per access by 50%, 5% and 15%, compared to *way based placement, way stride based placement,* and *set based placement,* respectively. Since multiple programs share the L3 cache, their access patterns can disturb each other as sharing a cache set increases the chance that different ways in those sets are targeted. As a result, the improvement achieved by *set stride based placement* over *set based placement* and *way stride based placement* is reduced.

*4.2.2 Energy Consumption.* The dynamic energy consumed in L2 and L3 caches is calculated as follows:

$$Energy = (N_{Read} \times E_{Read} + N_{Write} \times E_{Write} + N_{Shift} \times E_{Shift}) \times Block\_Size \quad (1)$$

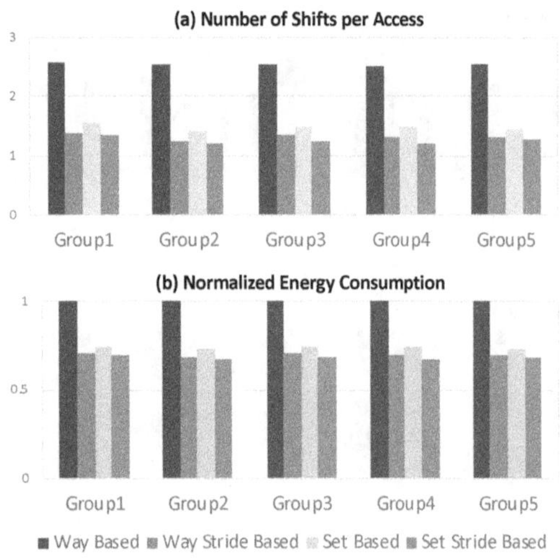


**Figure 6: (a) Average number of shifts per access in L3 and (b) Dynamic energy consumption in L3.**

Here, $E_{Read}$, $E_{Write}$, and $E_{Shift}$ represent the energy consumed by reading, writing, and shifting one bit, which are 0.037nJ, 0.46nJ, and 0.31nJ, respectively [19].

Figures 5(b) and 6(b) show the dynamic energy consumed in the four different layouts for L2 and L3 caches, respectively. All values are normalized to the energy consumption of *way based placement*. The lower the value, the lower the energy consumption. The reduction in energy consumption follows the same trend as the reduction of shift operation. In the L2 cache, the *set stride based placement* is able to reduce the total energy by 28%, 9%, and 18% more than *way based placement*, *way stride based placement*, and *set based placement*, respectively. These results confirm that the impact of shift operations on the energy consumption is significant. In the L3 cache, the *set stride based placement* achieves 31%, 2%, and 8% more energy reduction than *way based placement*, *way stride based placement*, and *set based placement*, respectively.

## 5 CONCLUSION

This paper has explored the use of track-based NVM caches in IoT devices, aiming at designing the most energy efficient cache organization. It has been observed that, while existing NVM cache layouts aim at exploiting the access locality within a cache set, their potential energy benefit is limited as consecutive accesses to the same set are limited. Instead, this paper proposed to explore the access locality across cache sets with a new cache layout, called *set stride based placement*. This layout places the cache lines within the same set on non-overlapping group of tracks, while logically-adjacent sets are aligned to access ports on the same track. Experimental results show that the proposed cache layout decreases the number of shift operations by 44%, 18%, and 31% than *way based placement*, *way stride based placement*, and *set based placement*, respectively.

## REFERENCES


[1] Apple A8 SoC: A more powerful cyclone. https://www.tomshardware.com/reviews/apple-iphone-6-plus-review,3976-5.html.

[2] ARM Architecture. http://infocenter.arm.com/help/index.jsp.

[3] Qualcomm high performance processor core and platform for mobile applications. http://rtcgroup.com/arm/2007/presentations/253%20-%20ARM_DevCon_2007_Snapdragon_FINAL_20071004.pdf.

[4] Programmable Instrumentation - A Dynamic Binary Instrumentation Tool. http://software.intel.com/en-us/articles/pintool, 2012.

[5] H. Aghaei Khouzani, P. Fotouhi, C. Yang, and G. R. Gao. Leveraging Access Port Positions to Accelerate Page Table Walk in DWM-based Main Memory. In *Design Autom. & Test in Europe (DATE)*, pages 1450–1455. IEEE, 2017.

[6] H. Aghaei Khouzani and C. Yang. A DWM-based Stack Architecture Implementation for Energy Harvesting Systems. *ACM Trans. Embedded Comput. Syst.*, 16(5s):155, 2017.

[7] X. Chen, E. H.-M. Sha, Q. Zhuge, P. Dai, and W. Jiang. Optimizing Data Placement for Reducing Shift Operations on Domain Wall Memories. In *Design Autom. Conf. (DAC)*, pages 139–144, 2015.

[8] M. Dubois, M. Annavaram, and P. Stenstrom. *Parallel Computer Organization and Design*. cambridge university press, 2012.

[9] S. Gu, E. H.-M. Sha, Q. Zhuge, Y. Chen, and J. Hu. Area and Performance Co-optimization for Domain Wall Memory in Application-specific Embedded Systems. In *Design Autom. Conf. (DAC)*, 2015.

[10] Q. Hu, G. Sun, J. Shu, and C. Zhang. Exploring Main Memory Design Based on Racetrack Memory Technology. In *ACM Great Lakes Symp. on VLSI (GLVLSI)*, pages 397–402, 2016.

[11] ITRS. International Technology Roadmap for Semiconductors. http://www.itrs2.net/2013-itrs.html. Emerging Research Devices (ERD).

[12] W. Kang, Y. Huang, X. Zhang, Y. Zhou, and W. Zhao. Skyrmion-Electronics: An Overview and Outlook. *Proceedings of the IEEE*, 104(10):2040–2061, 2016.

[13] S. S. N. Larimi, M. Kamal, A. Afzali-Kusha, and H. Mahmoodi. Power and Energy Reduction of Racetrack-based Caches by Exploiting Shared Shift Operations. In *Intl. Conf. VLSI & System-on-Chip (VLSI-SoC)*, pages 1–6, 2016.

[14] M. Mao, W. Wen, Y. Zhang, Y. Chen, and H. Li. Exploration of GPGPU Register File Architecture Using Domain-wall-shift-write based Racetrack Memory. In *Design Autom. Conf. (DAC)*, 2014.

[15] S. Motaman and S. Ghosh. Adaptive Write and Shift Current Modulation for Process Variation Tolerance in Domain Wall Caches. *IEEE Trans. VLSI Syst.*, 24(3):944–953, 2016.

[16] S. Motaman, A. Iyengar, and S. Ghosh. Domain Wall Memory- Layout, Circuit and Synergistic Systems. *IEEE Trans. on Nanotechnology*, 14, Mar. 2015.

[17] S. S. Parkin, M. Hayashi, and L. Thomas. Magnetic Domain-Wall Racetrack Memory. *Science*, 320:109–194, Apr. 2008.

[18] Z. Sun, X. Bi, A. K. Jones, and H. Li. Design Exploration of Racetrack Lower-level Caches. In *Proc. Intl. Symp. Low Power Electron. & Design (ISLPED)*, pages 263–266, 2014.

[19] Z. Sun, W. Wu, and H. Li. Cross-Layer Racetrack Memory Design for Ultra High Density and Low Power Consumption. In *Design Autom. Conf. (DAC)*, 2013.

[20] R. Tomasello, V. Puliafito, E. Martinez, A. Manchon, M. Ricci, M. Carpentieri, and G. Finocchio. Performance of Synthetic Anti-ferromagnetic Racetrack Memory: Domain Wall versus Skyrmion. *J. of Physics D: Applied Physics*, 50(32):325–302, 2017.

[21] R. Venkatesan, V. Kozhikkottu, C. Augustine, A. Raychowdhury, K. Roy, and A. Raghunathan. TapeCache: A High Density, Energy Efficient Cache Based on Domain Wall Memory. In *Proc. Intl. Symp. Low Power Electron. & Design (ISLPED)*, 2012.

[22] X. Xing, P. W. Pong, and Y. Zhou. Skyrmion Domain Wall Collision and Domain Wall-gated Skyrmion Logic. *Physical Review B*, 94(5):054–408, 2016.

[23] H. Xu, Y. Alkabani, R. Melhem, and A. K. Jones. FusedCache: A Naturally Inclusive, Racetrack Memory, Dual-level Private Cache. *IEEE Trans. on Multi-Scale Comput. Syst.*, 2(2):69–82, 2016.

[24] H. Xu, Y. Li, R. Melhem, and A. K. Jones. Multilane Racetrack Caches: Improving Efficiency through Compression and Independent Shifting. In *Asia & South Pacific Design Autom. Conf. (ASP-DAC)*, pages 417–422, 2015.

[25] H. Zhang, C. Zhang, Q. Hu, C. Yang, and J. Shu. Performance Analysis on Structure of Racetrack Memory. In *Asia & South Pacific Design Autom. Conf. (ASP-DAC)*, pages 367–374, 2018.

[26] Y. Zhang, W. Zhao, J.-O. Klein, C. Chappert, and D. Ravelosona. Peristaltic Perpendicular-magnetic-anisotropy Racetrack Memory based on Chiral Domain Wall Motions. *J. of Physics D: Applied Physics*, 48, Feb. 2015.

# Dynamic Computation Migration at the Edge: Is There an Optimal Choice?

Sina Shahhosseini[1], Iman Azimi[2], Arman Anzanpour[2], Axel Jantsch[3], Pasi Liljeberg[2], Nikil Dutt[1], and Amir M. Rahmani[1,3]
[1]University of California Irvine, Irvine, CA, USA
[2]University of Turku, Turku, Finland
[3]TU Wien, Vienna, Austria
{sshahhos, dutt, a.rahmani}@uci.edu, {imaazi, armanz, pakrli}@utu.fi, axel.jantsch@tuwien.ac.at

## ABSTRACT

In the era of Fog computing where one can decide to compute certain time-critical tasks at the edge of the network, designers often encounter a question whether the sensor layer provides the optimal response time for a service, or the Fog layer, or their combination. In this context, minimizing the total response time using computation migration is a communication-computation co-optimization problem as the response time does not depend only on the computational capacity of each side. In this paper, we aim at investigating this question and addressing it in certain situations. We formulate this question as a static or dynamic computation migration problem depending on whether certain communication and computation characteristics of the underlying system is known at design-time or not. We first propose a static approach to find the optimal computation migration strategy using models known at design-time. We then make a more realistic assumption that several sources of variation can affect the system's response latency (e.g., the change in computation time, bandwidth, transmission channel reliability, etc.), and propose a dynamic computation migration approach which can adaptively identify the latency optimal computation layer at runtime. We evaluate our solution using a case-study of artificial neural network based arrhythmia classification using a simulation environment as well as a real test-bed.

## KEYWORDS

Internet of Things, Fog Computing, Computation Migration

**ACM Reference Format:**

Sina Shahhosseini, Iman Azimi, Arman Anzanpour, Axel Jantsch, Pasi Liljeberg, Nikil Dutt, and Amir M. Rahmani. 2019. Dynamic Computation Migration at the Edge: Is There an Optimal Choice?. In *Proc. of GLSVLSI (GLSVLSI '19), May 9–11, 2019, Tysons Corner, VA, USA.* ACM, NY, NY, USA. 6 pages. DOI: https://doi.org/10.1145/3299874.3319336

## 1 INTRODUCTION

The number of IoT-enabled sensor devices are growing rapidly as we are entering the Internet-of-Things (IoT) era [1]. Today, a variety of sensor devices such as wearables are capable of interacting with the Internet, offering smart and connected solutions [2]. According to Cisco, 500 billion devices will be connected to the Internet by 2030, resulting in an exponential increase in the scale and the complexity of existing computing and communication systems [3].

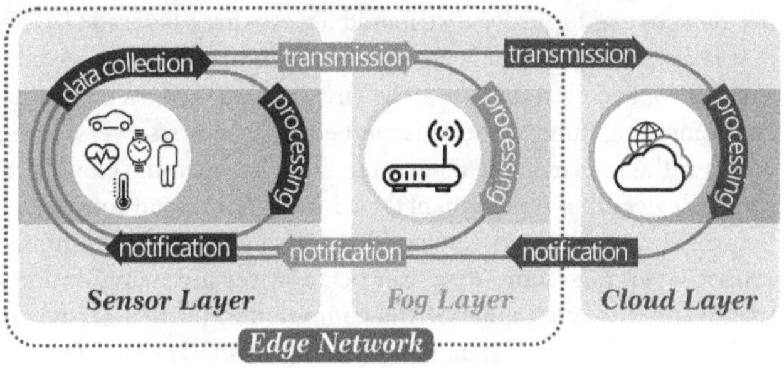


**Figure 1: IoT System Architecture**

Modern IoT systems often comprise of three main layers [1] as shown in Figure 1. At the first layer, a local sensor network is in charge of collecting sensory data and sending it to the next layer of interconnected smart gateways, also known as Fog layer [4]. This layer is a bridge between the cloud layer (i.e., the third layer) and the sensor network. It provides a set of services at the edge of the network to reduce latency and increase availability. Third is the cloud layer which includes data storage and analytics.

The resource constraints in sensor nodes in terms of computation and energy is often handled by offloading computation from sensor devices to the upper layers (i.e., Fog/Cloud). It has been shown that migrating the computation from sensor nodes to gateways or cloud can help the system to improve performance and energy consumption [4]. This is based on the assumption that the response time is mostly determined by the computation time and shifting the computation towards more powerful units can help reduce the total response time. However, this may not be always the case since such migration is a communication-computation co-optimization problem. More precisely, the response time of an application is not only a function of the execution time but also it depends on the transmission time when the computation of collected data is performed at the upper layers [5]. Therefore, any significant increase in transmission time leads to an increase in response time. Thus, a complex system under continuous change, application interference, environmental uncertainty needs to be dynamically controlled w.r.t. computational assignments of each layer to minimize response time and offer performance guarantees [6].


*GLSVLSI '19, May 9–11, 2019, Tysons Corner, VA, USA*

ACM ISBN 978-1-4503-6252-8/19/05.
https://doi.org/10.1145/3299874.3319336

The key contribution of this paper is twofold. We first present an abstract taxonomy of IoT applications and study the impact of full and partial computation migration at the edge on some of application classes to see if there is a static (design-time) optimal solution to this problem. Based on the observations made in the first part, we then propose a proof-of-concept dynamic computation migration approach for the edge sensor nodes and gateways considering the changes in the system characteristics and environment.

## 2 SYSTEM ARCHITECTURE AND APPLICATION CHARACTERISTICS

IoT devices are typically distributed across three layers [1]. The first layer is the physical layer, which is comprised of sensors that can sense and collect data from the environment. The second is the Fog computing (interconnected smart edge gateways/servers) layer, which is the intermediate computing layer between the cloud and sensor devices that complement the advantages of cloud computing by providing additional services that operate more closely to the sensor layer. Fog computing can perform certain computations mainly to take over some of the computation burden of sensor nodes and/or bringing latency-sensitive cloud analytics to the edge [4]. Another potential advantages of Fog computing is a significant reduction in the volume of data that needs to be transferred to the next layer(s) resulting in reduced transmission latency [7–10]. The third layer is the cloud layer providing unconstrained computing and storage resources. In this paper, we focus on the computation migration at the edge network referring to how data is process in the sensor layer and/or the Fog layer.

Response time is the total time which takes to respond to a request for a service. In a typical IoT architecture, a device in the sensor layer consists of one or more sensors and actuators. The sensors are responsible for collecting a set of data and the actuators are responsible for performing some specific actions (e.g., commands, notifications, etc.) according to collected data. In such systems, the data processing unit needs to analyze the data and decide the corresponding action. Here, the response time is the time difference between the moment when enough data for decision-making is gathered on the sensor node memory and the moment when a node has the actuation command ready-to-execute in hand [5]. Based on this scenario, the processing can happen on the sensor node microprocessor, gateway device processing unit, cloud server processors, or on a combination of these. Assuming that an IoT device is capable of sensing, local processing, and notification (e.g., a smart watches, smart home appliances, surveillance cameras, etc.) and it runs all the processes locally, the total response time is simply the time it needs to process and analyze the collected data:

$$Response\ Time_{total} = T_{comp}^{Sensor} \tag{1}$$

In contrast, if the sensor outsources all the computation to gateway(s) at the Fog layer, the total response time will include the data transmission time from the sensor device to the next layer and vice versa. Therefore, in the case of a two-layer sensor-gateway scenario the total response time is:

$$Response\ Time_{total} = T_{tran}^{stog} + T_{comp}^{Gateway} + T_{tran}^{gtos} \tag{2}$$

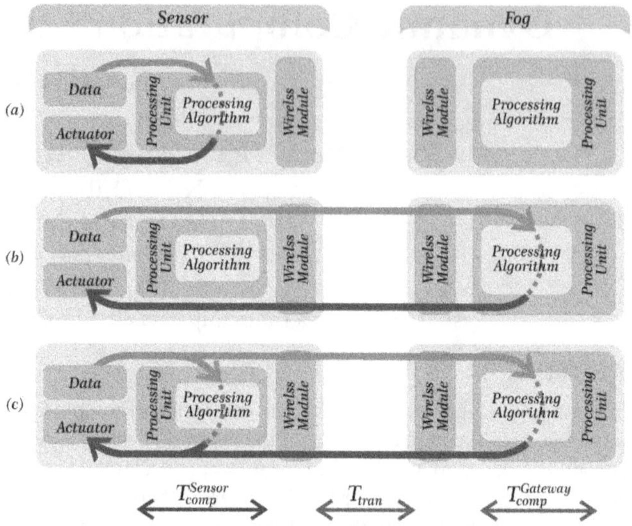


**Figure 2: The data flow and response time calculation based on the computation scheme, a) Full computation at the Fog layer, b) Full computation at the sensor layer, and c) Partial computation at both sensor and Fog layer.**

where $t_{tran}^{stog}$ and $t_{tran}^{gtos}$ are the sensor to gateway and gateway to sensor transmission time, respectively, and $T_{comp}^{Gateway}$ is the computation time needed on the gateway to complete the task.

If the processing load is distributed across multiple layers, Equation 2 will change. For instance, for a 2-layer sensor-gateway scenario, the response time will be as follows:

$$Response\ Time_{total} = T_{comp}^{Sensor} + T_{tran}^{stog} + T_{comp}^{Gateway} + T_{tran}^{gtos} \tag{3}$$

where $T_{comp}^{Sensor}$ is the computation time needed on the sensor to complete a portion of a task while $T_{comp}^{Gateway}$ is the time needed to complete the remaining of the task. The ways response time is calculated in all these schemes are shown in Figure 2.

In addition, there exists another application characteristic which is often neglected during design space exploration. In IoT applications, the ratio of a generated data to the input data can vary, which significantly affects the response time. We define this characteristic as Output-Input Data Generation (OIDG) ratio and classify IoT applications based on it as follows:

(1) **Class 1:** Applications with extremely low OIDG ratio such as machine learning inference where a large fraction of input data is classified into often a handful of classes ($OIDG << 1$).
(2) **Class 2:** Applications with low OIDG ratio such as compression, down-sampling, etc. ($OIDG < 1$).
(3) **Class 3:** Applications with OIDG ratio of almost equal to 1, such as noise filtering ($OIDG \approx 1$).
(4) **Class 4:** Applications with high OIDG ratio such as encryption ($OIDG > 1$).

We discuss in the following section how these classes can impact the total response time when mapped to a layered IoT architecture. It should be noted that an IoT application, depending on its structure and use case, can be partitioned using two different ways:

(1) **Data-driven Partitioning:** In this case, data is divided into several partitions and these partitions are distributed among computing units. Each unit keeps the entire application code while computing a portion of data, similar to the scenarios shown in Figure 2. Partitioning of high dimension data presented in [11] can be an appropriate example of such method.
(2) **Task-driven Partitioning:** In this method, a multi-task application is partitioned into (parallel) tasks, and each task or a set of task is mapped to a computation unit. As an example of this method, an approach for partitioning convolutional neural network across edge devices is presented in [12].

In this paper, we focus on data-driven partitioning.

# 3 STATIC COMPUTATION MIGRATION

There exists a rich literature on how to offload computation from one layer to another or how to partition IoT applications temporally or spatially across different computations layers [12–14]. An example could be the work presented by Xu *et al.* [15] examining the effect of partitioning layers of a deep neural network between a mobile gateway and a battery powered IoT device on the overall response time.

Although executing an IoT application fully in the sensor node or in the Fog layer can both have several advantages and disadvantages, a proper decision cannot be made without considering the characteristics of the communication channel among them. In this section, we assume the inter-layer communication characteristics are static and known a priori and make an attempt to propose a partitioning approach for both full and partial computation migration scenarios. In the next section, we make a more realistic assumption by including the unpredictable nature of network latency in our problem formulation.

## 3.1 Full Computation Migration

Data is inherently generated at the sensor layer, but when there are constraints to process it locally, the data is migrated to the next layer (e.g., the edge server/gateway). In contrast to *data migration* to the next layer, which moves data to computation, *computation migration* refers to the scenario when computation is moved to data (e.g., to a sensor device). *Computation migration* and *data migration* are complementary which means one of them performs well when other one does not. However, different degrees of network and application latency can determine which scheme is the optimal solution in terms of performance and energy consumption. Assume that computing $v$ bits of data on a sensor takes:

$$T_{comp}^{Sensor}(v) \tag{4}$$

and computing the same $v$ bits of data on a gateway takes:

$$T_{comp}^{Gateway}(v) \tag{5}$$

Since the communication characteristics of the network are assumed to be static, the transmission time of $v$ bits is:

$$T_{tran}(v) \tag{6}$$

where $v$ is the number of transferred bits. Also consider that an application processes $v$ bits raw data and produces $v'$ bits as an output. Taking the above equations, the response time of computing the raw data on the sensor is obtained by the following formula:

$$T_{res}^{Sensor}(v) = T_{comp}^{Sensor}(v) \tag{7}$$

The response time of computing the raw data on the gateway is obtained by following formula:

$$T_{res}^{Gateway}(v, v') = T_{comp}^{Gateway}(v) + T_{tran}(v) + T_{tran}(v') \tag{8}$$

In Class 1 IoT applications, as the volume of generated data is very negligible, it can be removed and the the response time can be estimated using the following formula:

$$T_{res}^{Gateway}(v) = T_{comp}^{Gateway}(v) + T_{tran}(v) \tag{9}$$

In a static full computation migration approach, the lower response time at each side is simply the optimal solution. Therefore, the system determines the computation scheme by identifying the one leading to a shortest response time. For example, if at a given network latency $T_{res}^{Sensor}(v) > T_{res}^{Gateway}(v)$, then, the $v$ bits of raw data are processed at the gateway layer, and the $v'$ bits of output is transferred to the gateway. Full computation migration works well when $v'$ is much less than $v$ (i.e., Class 1 application).

## 3.2 Partial Computation Migration

Although the previous solution allocates all computations to the sensor-side or the Fog-side, there are specific applications in which dividing the processing between the sensor and gateway results in a lower latency. In such a data-driven partitioning, we process $R$ portion of data on the sensor-side and the rest (1-$R$) on the Fog-side. For Class 1 applications, the result of processing ($v'$) is very small in size and can be excluded from the transmission traffic. Therefore, the response time would be:

$$T_{res}^{Total}(v) = RT_{comp}^{Sensor}(v) + (1-R)T_{comp}^{Gateway}(v) + (1-R)T_{tran}(v) \tag{10}$$

We take the ratios between the components of this equation into account to have a better view of the solution and find the situation where the partial migration leads to lower response time. We consider sensor computation time to be $\alpha$ times and the transmission time $\beta$ times longer than the gateway computation time:

$$T_{comp}^{Sensor} = \alpha T_{comp}^{Gateway} \tag{11}$$

$$T_{tran} = \beta T_{comp}^{Gateway} \tag{12}$$

We expect a gateway to process data faster than a sensor, but the transmission time can be shorter or longer than gateway's computation time, therefore $\alpha > 1$ and $\beta > 0$. In this case the total response time would be:

$$T_{res}^{Total} = R\alpha T_{comp}^{Gateway} + (1-R)T_{comp}^{Gateway} + (1-R)\beta T_{comp}^{Gateway} \tag{13}$$

We are interested in finding the relation between $\alpha$ and $\beta$, therefore, we simplify Equation 13 by considering $T_{res}^{Total}/T_{comp}^{Gateway}$ as a linear function of $\beta$:

$$T_{res}^{Total}/T_{comp}^{Gateway} = (R\alpha + 1 - R) + (1-R)\beta \tag{14}$$

For different $R$ values, the resulting functions are a group of lines intersecting at [$\alpha$-1, $\alpha$ $T_{comp}^{Gateway}$]. As shown in Figure 3 (a), when the transmission time is smaller than $\alpha$-1 times of the gateway

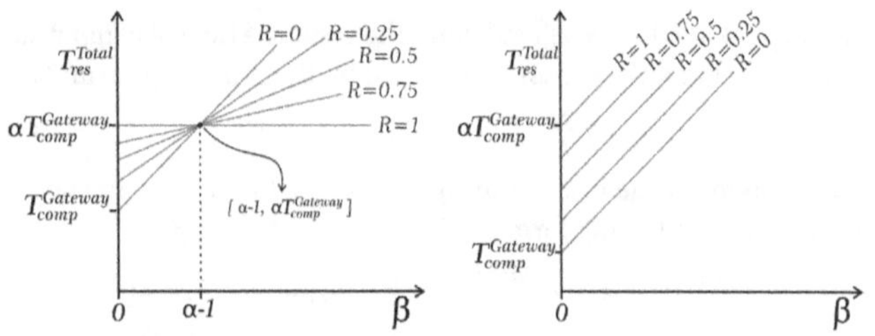


(a) Class 1 (b) Class 3

**Figure 3: The parametric graph of total response time equation in Class 1 and Class 3 Applications.**

computation time, performing a part of the calculation in the sensor node results in a shorter response time.

For Class 3 applications, the size of processed and unprocessed data is almost the same. Therefore, the response time would be:

$$T_{res}^{Total}(v) = RT_{comp}^{Sensor}(v) + (1 - R)T_{comp}^{Gateway}(v) + T_{tran}(v) \quad (15)$$

Using similar coefficients for the sensor computation time and the transmission time would result in:

$$T_{res}^{Total}/T_{comp}^{Gateway} = (R\alpha + 1 - R) + \beta \quad (16)$$

As shown in Figure 3 (b), in Class 3 applications, any R value between 0 and 1 results in a response time between $T_{comp}^{Gateway}$+$\beta$ and $\alpha.T_{comp}^{Gateway}$+$\beta$; but the shortest response time belongs to a setting that performs all computations on the gateway (R = 0).

The aforementioned shows that the total response time is a function of $\beta$ which is the transmission time coefficient. In other words, in a static partial computation migration scenario, the transmission rate defines the computation migration ratio which is the key to minimize the response time.

## 4 DYNAMIC COMPUTATION MIGRATION

An important challenge when using static computation migration is the variations in the system's behavior at run-time, in particular w.r.t. communication characteristics. Several sources of variation can affect the system's response latency such as the change in computation time, bandwidth, transmission channel reliability, and transmission latency due to the system's mobility and environmental changes. An alternative approach for such dynamic systems is to dynamically incorporate system's behaviour and context into the computation migration decision-making.

The Observe, Decide, and Act (ODA) control loop paradigm [16] is a proper strategy in this context to leverage real-time observations to dynamically tune system configuration. A classic ODA loop measures the system state and/or context (Observe), performs a decision-making w.r.t. the measurements (Decide), and applies possible changes (Act). In this section, we propose an ODA closed-loop dynamic computation migration approach implemented in the Fog layer to decide the optimal computation layer at runtime.

Our proof-of-concept dynamic computation migration approach is detailed in Algorithm 1. The algorithm assumes two computation status (i.e., $C_{status}$) as "computation at the sensor node" and "computation at the Fog layer" which is a simple flag indicating where computation is currently performed. If needed, the system

**Algorithm 1** The dynamic computation migration algorithm

**Initialize:**
  $T_{comp}^{sensor} \leftarrow$ estimate computation time at the sensor node
  $C_{status} \leftarrow$ computation at the sensor node
**while** system is on **do**
  $T_{comp}^{gateway} \leftarrow$ estimate computation time at the Fog layer
  $T_{tran} \leftarrow$ measure transmission time between the sensor node and the Fog layer
  **if** $C_{status}$ = computation at the sensor node **then**
    **if** $T_{comp}^{sensor} - \Delta/2 > T_{tran} + T_{comp}^{gateway}$ **then**
      $C_{status} \leftarrow$ computation at the Fog layer
    **end if**
  **else if** $C_{status}$ = computation at the Fog layer **then**
    **if** $T_{comp}^{sensor} + \Delta/2 < T_{tran} + T_{comp}^{gateway}$ **then**
      $C_{status} \leftarrow$ computation on the sensor node
    **end if**
  **end if**
**end while**

dynamically changes the status based on 3 parameters to minimize the total response time. The first parameter is the computation time at the sensor ($T_{comp}^{sensor}$). This parameter is often fixed and can be measured at design-time. In contrast, the computation time at the Fog layer ($T_{comp}^{gateway}$), as the second parameter, can vary as it relies on the amount of computation capacity available at the moment. Therefore, it needs to be estimated at runtime. The third parameter is the transmission time between the sensor node and the Fog layer ($T_{tran}$). $T_{tran}$ highly depends on several parameters such as distance, interference, objects in the environment, just to mention a few. There are well-established methods to estimate the network latency at runtime, for instance based on packet loss probability.

Our straightforward proof-of-concept algorithm iteratively measures/estimates $T_{comp}^{gateway}$ and $T_{tran}$ values at runtime and compares their sum against the ($T_{comp}^{sensor}$ value to determine the layer with the lower response time. To avoid unnecessary oscillations of computation migration between layers, it uses a simple threshold-based (i.e., soft margin $\Delta$) strategy. It should be noted that our approach is proposed as a proof-of-concept, and more advanced and efficient control approaches (e.g., predictive modeling) can be used to make smarter decisions.

## 5 EXPERIMENTAL RESULTS

We present the evaluation of our proposed dynamic full computation migration approach in this section. We first present a case study which requires a rapid response in decision making. Then, we perform the evaluations in two different settings.

### 5.1 Case Study: Neural Network-based Arrhythmia Classification

We use a real-time arrhythmia classification approach as an exemplar for a time-critical health application, where the state of a patient's health deterioration is estimated via Electrocardiogram (ECG) signals. The approach is enabled via an IoT-based system to perform ubiquitous health monitoring in everyday settings for

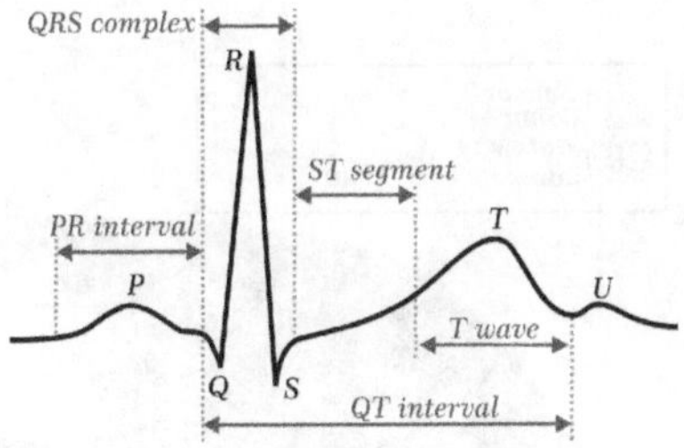


**Figure 4: An ECG cycle with the 5 features**

| | Raspberry Pi 3 Model B | HP Compaq 8200 Elite |
|---|---|---|
| Processor | Quad-core Broadcom BCM2837 64bit | Quad-core Core i3 2100 |
| Architecture | ARMv8-A | Intel Core |
| Speed | 1.2 GHz | 3.10 GHz |
| RAM | 1 GB | 16GB |
| External Storage | 16 GB fast eMMC | 250GB SATA HDD |

**Table 1: The device specifications**

patients suffering from cardiovascular diseases. Such a system continuously acquires health data (i.e., ECG signal) from a user, implements a decision making (i.e., the classification approach), and sends the health decision to the user. These situations demand a rapid response time to alert the possibility of deterioration in health state, which in turn requires a reduction in response time.

We use "Long-Term ST Database" available on Physiobank [17], including normal ECG signals (patient with a normal health condition) and ECG signals showing arrhythmia (patient with a critical health condition). A binary classification is performed on the data, by which the normal ECG signals and ECG signals with arrhythmia are distinguished. The classifier in this approach is an Artificial Neural Network (ANN) method with one hidden layer and rectified linear unit (ReLU) as the activation function. The classifier is trained exploiting 12 hours of ECG signals, i.e., 6 hours of normal ECG and 6 hours of ECG with arrhythmia. In this regard, we, first, extract 5 different attributes from the ECG signal as QRS complex duration, ST segment duration, T wave duration, PR interval and QT interval [18]. Figure 4 shows an ECG cycle with the 5 features. The feature extraction is implemented via a cross-correlation between the ECG signal and a Triangular signal. Afterwards, the features are fed to the classifier.

In the following, the case study is evaluated first in a real-hardware setting and then in a more comprehensive simulation-based environments to assess the efficiency of our proposed dynamic full computation migration approach.

## 5.2 Evaluation on a Real Testbed

We conduct an experiment to indicate the dynamic full computation migration in a real-time health monitoring system. The system includes a sensor node and a gateway device, each of which is able to implement the decision-making approach. In the following, the details of our setup is presented.

*5.2.1 Setup.* We exploit a Raspberry Pi 3 as the sensor node and an HP Compaq 8200 Elite Linux machine as the gateway device. The latter device is equipped with a Quad-core Corei3 2100 CPU and 16GB RAM, which is considerably more powerful than the sensor node. The specifications of both devices are indicated in Table 1. Both the sensor and gateway devices run Apache web servers with PHP interpreters installed and are interconnected with a WiFi network. The reply duration of an HTTP request is used to measure the data transmission time.

Data collection is emulated in this setup, leveraging the existing dataset (i.e., "Long-Term ST Database"). The pre-recoreded data with 250 Hz sampling frequency are stored in files in the MicroSD card of the Raspberry Pi 3. Each file includes a 5-second window of (ECG) signal. The files are sequentially analyzed at the sensor node or transmitted to the gateway device. For the decision making, the binary classification is performed on the data (each segment).

*5.2.2 Measurements.* The dynamic computation migration is carried out to minimize the system's response time. In this regard, two different settings can be selected to perform the computation (i.e., decision making): at the sensor node or at the gateway device.

In the first setting, the sensor node performs the data collection and decision making (i.e., binary classification). Then, the decision is delivered to the user. As the senor node is attached to the user, the response time only includes $T^{sensor}_{comp}$: the computation time of the decision making at the sensor node. Running the classifier in 1000 iterations, $\alpha$ equals to $86.67 \pm 3.61$ ms.

In the second setting, the sensor node is in charge of the data collection and sending the data to the gateway device. The gateway performs the classification and sends the decision back to the user. The response time contains (1) data transmission time from the sensor node to the gateway device, (2) $T^{gateway}_{comp}$: computation time of the decision making at the gateway device , and (3) data transmission time from the gateway device to the sensor node. We consider (1) and (3) as the $T_{tran}$. Data flows in the two settings are indicated in Figure 2 (a) and (b). $T^{gateway}_{comp}$ equals to $18.39 \pm 0.63$ ms in this setup (measured in 1000 iterations). $T_{tran}$ is not a fixed value and highly depends on the distance between the sensor node and gateway device. $T_{tran}$ equals to $31.88 \pm 4.92$ ms when the sensor node is close to the gateway (i.e., $< 2$ meters). The value rises when the distance increases. High packet loss ratio in data transmission in long distances is one of the main reasons for such changes.

The response time of the two settings is indicated in Figure 5. When the two devices are close, the response time will be lower if the classification is performed at the gateway. However, when the distance exceeds 2.5 meters, the response time will be larger then the one of the first setting. The gateway dynamically generates a procedure for the system to reduce the response time, determining if the decision making should be performed at the sensor layer or at the gateway device. In this regard, a service is implemented at the gateway device, selecting one of the settings based to Algorithm 1.

## 5.3 Simulation-based Evaluation

We conduct an experiment to evaluate the dynamic full computation migration method in a more flexible simulation environment. To this end, we use open-source Cooja Simulator [19]. For our simulations, a Sky mote as a sensor device and an ARM A9-Cortex processor as a gateway device are used. The behavior of a gateway sensor is modeled and simulated in MATLAB with Star topology. In

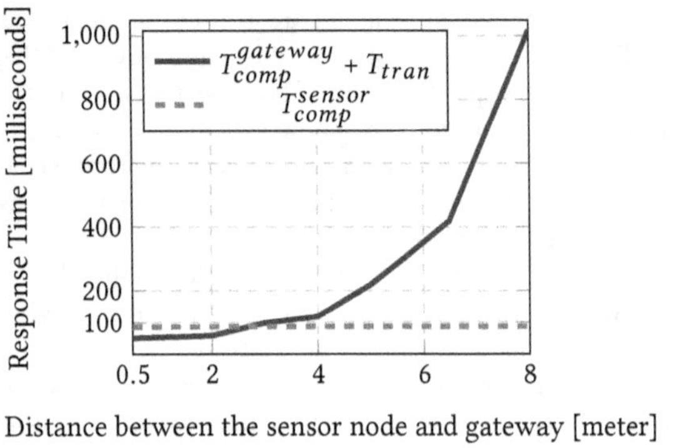


**Figure 5: Response time of the system when the classification is performed at the gateway and at the sensor node.**

the Star topology, all nodes are connected to a central connection point, such as a gateway.

The experiment shows a sensor-gateway pair running a neural network application (emulating our case study) using two scenarios: running on the sensor node or running on the gateway. The response time is measured with different packet loss ratio and the results are shown in Figure 6. As can be seen from the figure, the response time is almost constant when the application is computing fully at sensor layer, and increasing the packet loss ratio does not significantly increase the response time. However, as the gateway is more computationally powerful then the sensor node, when the packet loss is negligible the gateway response time is lower than sensor response time at the same packet loss ratio.

The experiments also evaluate the response time of a more complex system with many connected sensors to a gateway. Increasing the number of sensors can lead to a rise in response time in the Fog computing scheme if the we consider limited resources at the Fog layer. Whereas, increasing the number of sensors does not affect the response time in the sensor computing scheme. Thus, as shown in Figure 6, by increasing the number of sensors connected to the gateway, the Gateway response time exceeds the sensor response time. A dynamic computation migration solution can adapt to these variations at runtime by estimating the response time and finding the layer for computation which leads to the shortest response time.

## 6 CONCLUSIONS

This paper investigated the communication-computation co-design aspect of computation migration for the edge network of a typical 3-layer IoT architecture. Since the total response time does not depend only on the computational capacity of each layer, we presented a communication-computation co-optimization formulation to minimize the total response time. Furthermore, due to the uncertainty in network parameters and the number of IoT sensors, an absolute computation scheme is not an optimal solution. Therefore we also proposed a dynamic solution for computation migration at the edge. We evaluated our proposed scheme through several experiments using a real-time health monitoring application for arrhythmia classification from real-time ECG signals. Experiments show the optimal solution varies based on the network latency and the number of connected sensors to the Fog layer.

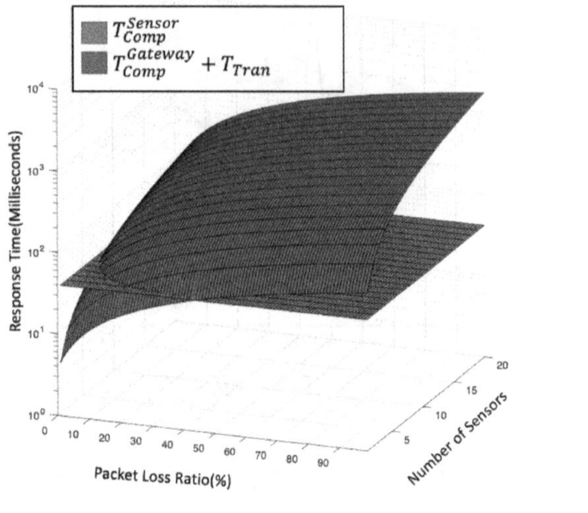


**Figure 6: Response Time for different number of sensors and packet loss ratio (plotted based on the interpolation of a large set of discrete simulation results)**

## 7 ACKNOWLEDGMENTS

This material is based upon work supported partially by the US National Science Foundation (NSF) WiFiUS grant CNS-1702950 and Academy of Finland grants 311764 and 311304.

## REFERENCES

[1] L. Atzori et al. The internet of things: A survey. *Computer networks*, 54(15), 2010.
[2] F. Firouzi et al. Internet-of-Things and big data for smarter healthcare: From device to architecture, applications and analytics. *FGCS*, 2018.
[3] CISCO. *Internet of Things At a Glance*, 2016. https://www.cisco.com/c/dam/en/us/products/collateral/se/internet-of-things/at-a-glance-c45-731471.pdf.
[4] A.M. Rahmani et al. *Fog Computing in the Internet of Things - Intelligence at the Edge*. Springer, 2017.
[5] M.R. Nakhkash et al. Analysis of Performance and Energy Consumption of Wearable Devices and Mobile Gateways in IoT Applications. In *COINS*, 2019.
[6] C. Perera et al. Context Aware Computing for The Internet of Things: A Survey. *IEEE Communications Surveys Tutorials*, 16(1):414–54, 2014.
[7] R. Roman et al. A survey and analysis of security threats and challenges. *Future Generation Computer Systems*, 78, 2018.
[8] D. Amiri *et al.* Edge-Assisted Sensor Control in Healthcare IoT. In *IEEE GLOBECOM*, 2018.
[9] I. Azimi *et al.* Hich: Hierarchical fog-assisted computing architecture for healthcare iot. *ACM Transactions on Embedded Computing Systems*, 16(5), 2017.
[10] I. Azimi et al. Empowering healthcare iot systems with hierarchical edge-based deep learning. In *IEEE/ACM CHASE*, 2019.
[11] J. Zhou et al. An efficient multidimensional fusion algorithm for IoT data based on partitioning. *Tsinghua Science and Technology*, 18(4):369–78, 2013.
[12] S. Dey et al. Partitioning of CNN Models for Execution on Fog Devices. In *1st ACM Int. Workshop on Smart Cities and Fog Computing*, pages 19–24, 2018.
[13] T.N. Gia et al. Fog Computing in Body Sensor Networks: An Energy Efficient Approach. In *IEEE Int. Body Sensor Networks Conference*, 2015.
[14] A.M. Rahmani et al. Exploiting smart e-health gateways at the edge of healthcare Internet-of-Things: a Fog computing approach. *Future Generation Computer Systems*, 78(2):641–58, 2018.
[15] M. Xu et al. Enabling cooperative inference of deep learning on wearables and smartphones. *CoRR*, abs/1712.03073, 2017.
[16] H. Hoffmann et al. SEEC: A Framework for Self-aware Computing. Technical report, MIT, 2010.
[17] F. Jager et al. Long-term st database: a reference for the development and evaluation of automated ischaemia detectors and for the study of the dynamics of myocardial ischaemia. *Medical & Biological Engineering & Computing*, 2003.
[18] J.T. Catalano. *Guide to ECG Analysis*. Lippincott Williams & Wilkins, 2002.
[19] Osterlind, F. and others. Cross-level sensor network simulation with COOJA. *Proceedings. 2006 31st IEEE Conf. on Local Computer Networks*, 2006.

# Solving Energy and Cybersecurity Constraints in IoT Devices Using Energy Recovery Computing

Himanshu Thapliyal and Zachary Kahleifeh
VLSI Emerging Design And Nano Things Security Lab (VEDANTS-Lab)
Department of Electrical and Computer Engineering
University of Kentucky, Lexington, KY, USA
hthapliyal@uky.edu

## ABSTRACT

With the growth of Internet-of-Things (IoT), the potential threat vectors for malicious cyber and hardware attacks are rapidly expanding. As the IoT paradigm emerges, there are challenging requirements to design energy-efficient and secure systems. To address these challenges, we illustrate energy recovery computing as a potential solution to design low-energy hardware security primitives for IoT devices. Energy Recovery (ER) is a circuit design technique in which circuits recycle the charge stored in the load capacitor. This overview provides example applications of ER computing in (i) low-energy and Differential Power Analysis (DPA) resistant design, (ii) low-energy Physically Unclonable Function (PUF), and (iii) hardware trojan detection.

## CCS CONCEPTS

• **Security and privacy → Security in hardware.**

## KEYWORDS

Hardware Security, Low-Power, DPA attack, Physically Unclonable Functions, Hardware Trojan

**ACM Reference Format:**
Himanshu Thapliyal and Zachary Kahleifeh. 2019. Solving Energy and Cybersecurity Constraints in IoT Devices Using Energy Recovery Computing. In *Great Lakes Symposium on VLSI 2019 (GLSVLSI '19), May 9–11, 2019, Tysons Corner, VA, USA.* ACM, New York, NY, USA, 6 pages. https://doi.org/10.1145/3299874.3319337

## 1 INTRODUCTION

Internet of Things (IoT) devices have application in smart home, medical devices, vehicles, cyber-physical systems and consumer electronics systems [24]. The IoT devices operate at low frequencies and have an extremely limited energy and power budget. Therefore, low energy computing paradigms are worth considering when designing resource constrained IoT devices. Lightweight cryptography (LWC) provides cryptographic solutions for resource-constrained IoT devices [14, 16]. However, the secret information stored in LWC-based IoT devices is vulnerable and can be revealed by side-channel attacks such as Differential Power Analysis (DPA) [30]. DPA is used to reveal the keys from cryptosystems by statistically analyzing the power consumption [10]. The challenge in IoT devices is that low-energy lightweight cryptographic (LWC) operations that are DPA-resistant are needed because their energy and power budget is extremely limited. DPA can extract the key stored in the hardware by correlating the instantaneous power consumed by the device with the input data. Hiding and masking are the two principal DPA countermeasures that can usually increase the energy consumption of LWC circuits as compared to their implementation without DPA-resistance. Hence, there is a trade-off between an increase in DPA-resistance and energy consumption of the cryptographic operation in an IoT device.

IC piracy, IC counterfeiting, malicious modifications, reverse engineering and IC recycling are major hardware security threats in IoT devices [25]. Physical Unclonable Functions (PUFs) can solve security problems such as IC piracy, IC counterfeiting, secure authentication and key management. PUFs use the inherent variations in the manufacturing process of an IC to create unique and unclonable IDs. However, the computations performed in PUFs are vulnerable to power analysis based side-channel attacks. Therefore, low-energy security solutions must be developed for side channel resistant cryptographic hardware and PUFs for IoT devices. Further, hardware Trojan (HT) based hardware attack introduces the malicious modifications of a circuit during the design or fabrication [3, 17]. HTs have already been detected in military chips and therefore can also be considered a major security threat in IoT devices [20].

Energy Recovery (ER) is a circuit design technique to design low-energy hardware. Energy recovery (ER) circuits recycle the charge stored in the load capacitor. Because of their ability to recycle the charge, ER circuits have lower energy consumption as compared to conventional CMOS [23]. ER circuits operate energy efficiently at low frequencies. Therefore, ER computing is an ideal choice for designing low-energy IoT-based devices operating at low frequencies, for example, RFID operates at 13.56 MHz. Energy recovery computing (ER-Computing) uses power clocks to recycle the charge stored in the load capacitor. Because of recycling of charge, ER computing has reduced dynamic switching energy loss [1]. Fig. 1 shows the charging/discharging of the load capacitors in an ER circuit. The energy dissipated in an energy recovery circuit [23] is given as,

$$E_{diss} = \frac{RC}{T} CV_{dd}^2 \tag{1}$$

where T is the charging/discharging time of the capacitor, C is the load capacitor, $V_{dd}$ is the full swing of the power clock. If T ≫ 2RC


*GLSVLSI '19, May 9–11, 2019, Tysons Corner, VA, USA*

ACM ISBN 978-1-4503-6252-8/19/05.
https://doi.org/10.1145/3299874.3319337

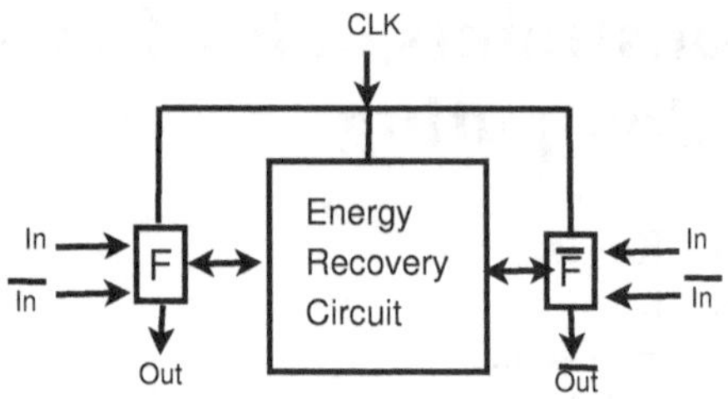


**Figure 1: Structure of energy recovery circuits.**

(time constant), then the energy dissipated by the energy recovery circuit is less than the conventional CMOS circuit.

Figure 2 shows the current traces of the inverter implemented using a conventional CMOS logic, a dual rail CMOS logic and a DPA secure adiabatic logic family. From the Figure 2 (a), we can see that the conventional CMOS based inverter has non-uniform current traces flowing in the circuit for various input transitions. Figure 2 (b) shows the current traces of a dual rail CMOS logic to thwart DPA attack. Though the dual rail CMOS based inverter has uniform current traces, the peak current traces is higher than the CMOS logic. Higher the peak traces, higher the power consumption of the circuit. Figure 2 (c) shows the DPA resistant ER-logic implementation of the inverter. DPA resistant ER-logic implementation of inverter has lower peak traces than the conventional CMOS based inverter and also has uniform current traces. The uniform and lowering of peak current traces would help energy recovery computing to solve hardware security problems in IoT devices where power and energy consumption are the most important parameter in the design [12, 27].

This overview illustrates the application of ER logic in IoT devices towards: (i) low-energy and Differential Power Analysis (DPA) resistant design, (ii) low-energy Physically Unclonable Function (PUF), and (iii) hardware trojan detection. A case study of DPA attacks on the benchmark circuits for PRESENT crypto algorithm is performed. From our simulations, we have found that EE-SPFAL [7] (Energy recovery: ER)-based one round of PRESENT algorithm with a 4-phase power clock generator consumes only 43% of energy as compared to the standard CMOS-based design. Further, the security of PRESENT S-box has been evaluated by performing a DPA attack through SPICE simulations. The Measurement To Disclosure (MTD) results are used to validate the claim that the EE-SPFAL based implementation of PRESENT-80 provides higher security as compared to the CMOS based implementation. We recently presented a low-power ER based PUF (ER-PUF) [11], the design of which is also discussed in this paper. SPICE simulations show that ER-PUF has $0.39\mu$Watt of power consumption to generate a response bit and satisfies the security metrics of reliability, uniqueness and uniformity, etc. Further, we are using the Differential Power Analysis (DPA) resistant energy recovery circuits for HT detection in IoT devices [9]. DPA resistant ER gates consume uniform and less power compared to conventional CMOS logic gates. We assume that the insertion of a CMOS gate in the DPA resistant ER circuits will produce a power glitch due to non-synchronization of the power clock. The non-uniform power consumption can be used to detect smaller trojans in DPA resistant ER logic circuits. ER computing based HT detection does not require a golden chip for the detection of HT. Two benchmark circuits, C17 and carry save adder, are used to illustrate the proposed approach of ER computing based HT detection.

This overview is organized as follows: Section II presents the application of ER computing in low-energy and DPA resistant PRESENT-80. Section III discusses the application of ER computing to design low-energy physically unclonable function. Section IV presents energy recovery based hardware trojan detection. Section V concludes the paper.

## 2 ENERGY RECOVERY COMPUTING BASED LOW-ENERGY AND DPA RESISTANT PRESENT-80

To improve security and to reduce the energy consumed by energy recovery circuits, we have proposed a novel energy recovery logic family called Energy Efficient Secure Positive Feedback Adiabatic Logic (EE-SPFAL) [7] that has lower energy consumption compared to existing approaches and is resistant to power analysis attacks by breaking the correlation between the current consumption and the input data. Fig. 6 shows the proposed EE-SPFAL XOR gate. Fig. 7 shows the uniform current (μA) consumed by the proposed SPGAL XOR gate at 45nm. Fig. 8 shows that the energy consumed during each cycle of the EE-SPFAL buffer is less than the equivalent CMOS buffer. Further, we have performed a preliminary comparative study on CMOS-based and ER-based DPA countermeasures as illustrated in Table 1. We have used the S-box in PRESENT which is a 4x4 bit S-box as the benchmark circuit [19]. As can be observed from Table 1, ER-based DPA countermeasures consume significantly less energy per cycle compared to CMOS-based DPA countermeasures. For example, the PRESENT S-box based on the energy recovery logic (EE-SPFAL) consumes 4.22 fJ per cycle at the frequency of 12.5 MHz. Further, from their simulation result, conventional CMOS-based PRESENT S-box circuit consumes 38.93 fJ of energy per cycle. Therefore, the energy recovery-based S-Box of PRESENT has energy saving factor (ESF) of 9.22 where ESF is defined as the ratio of energy consumed in CMOS-based PRESENT S-BOX and energy consumed in EE-SPFAL-based PRESENT S-BOX.

Further, we have implemented a 4-phase power clock generator and integrated it with the customized design of one round of PRESENT algorithm. From our simulations, we have found that EE-SPFAL (Energy recovery: ER)-based one round of PRESENT algorithm with a 4-phase power clock generator consumes only 43% of energy as compared to the standard CMOS-based design (Energy Consumption using ER Computing=134.3 fJ and Energy Consumption using CMOS=310.62 fJ). Similar results have been validated through silicon prototype in the existing literature which have illustrated that the ER circuits can have 1.5 to 4 times less energy dissipation compared to standard CMOS.

The ultra-low-energy consumption of energy recovery (ER) logic families along with their DPA-resistant property makes ER logic an ideal choice for implementing low-energy IoT devices. Further, SPFAL-based S-box circuit has uniform power consumption and is resistant to DPA attack as the correct key is hidden in EE-SPFAL-based S-Box circuit (Fig. 6). The correlation coefficient of the EE-SPFAL-based S-Box circuit is very low ($10^{-4}$). The secret key in

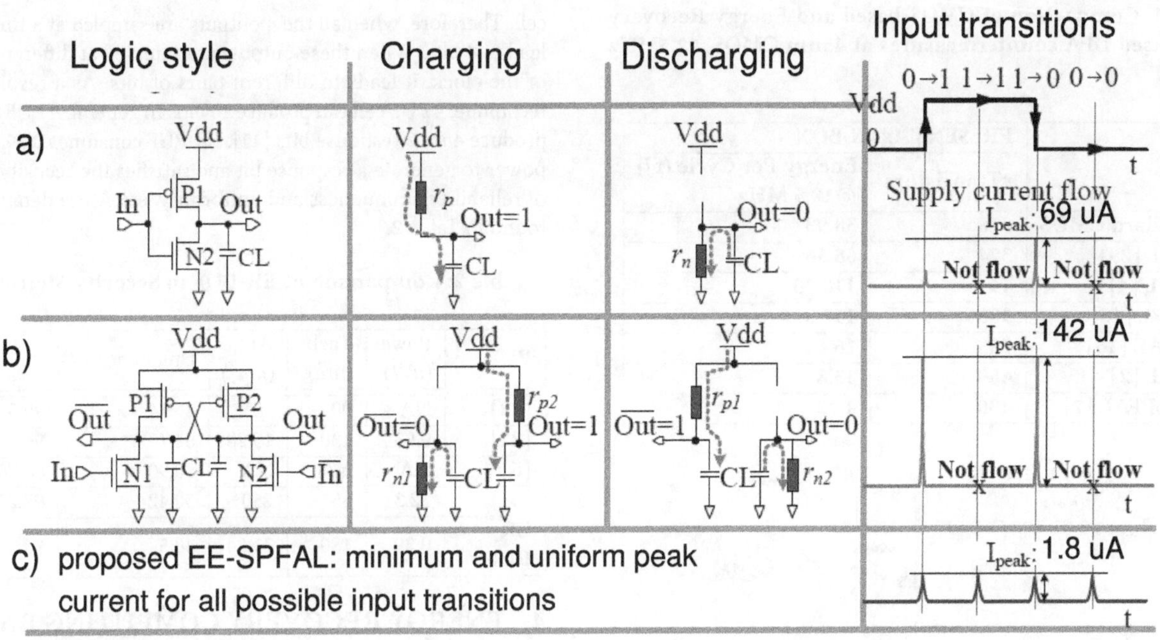


**Figure 2: Current traces of an inverter implemented using a) conventional CMOS logic b) CMOS based DPA resistant family c) energy recovery based DPA resistant family.**

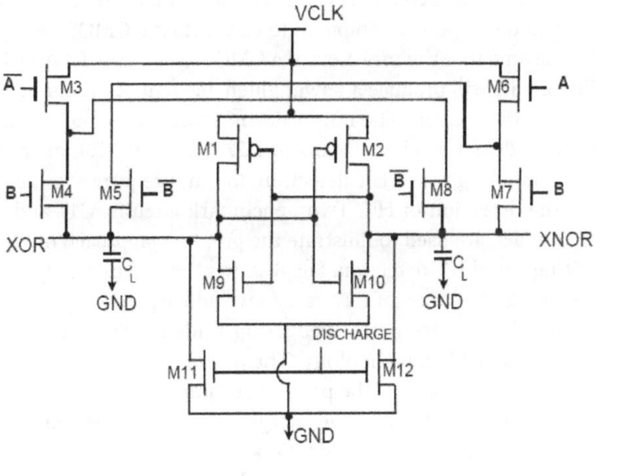


**Figure 3: EE-SPFAL XOR gate [7].**

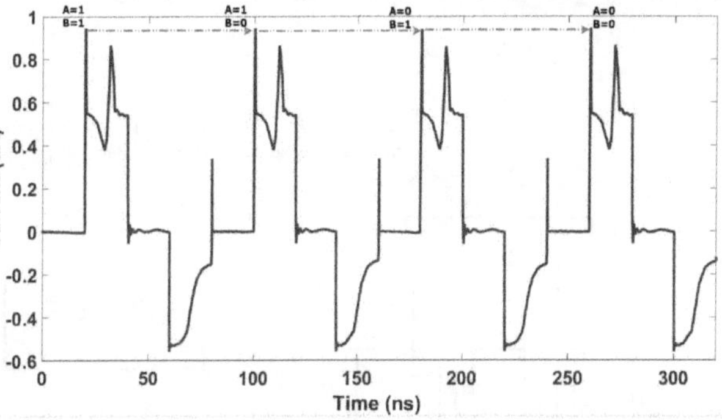


**Figure 4: Uniform current in EESPFAL.**

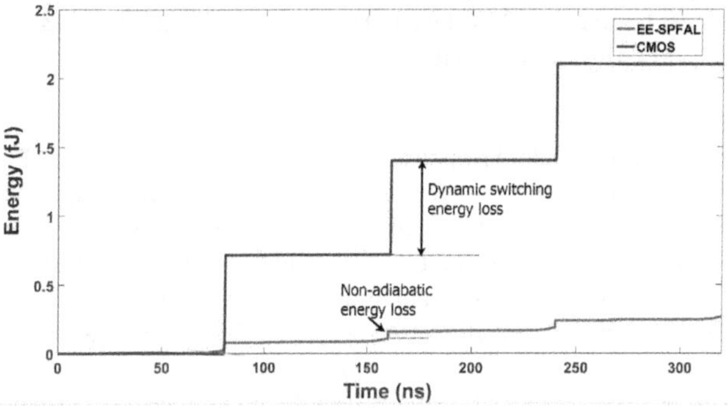


**Figure 5: CMOS and EE-SPFAL buffers energy consumption per cycle.**

CMOS design was revealed using only 6130 input traces while the secret key was not revealed in the EE-SPFAL-based PRESENT even after more than 50,000 input traces. The result indicates that the EE-SPFAL-based S-Box circuit is more secure than the CMOS-based design.

## 3 ENERGY RECOVERY COMPUTING BASED PHYSICALLY UNCLONABLE FUNCTION (ER-PUF)

Energy Recovery computing based PUF (ER-PUF) uses the threshold mismatch present in the cross-coupled inverter based latch to

**Table 1: Comparison of CMOS-based and Energy Recovery (ER) based DPA countermeasures at 45nm CMOS, 12.5MHz and 1fF**

| | PRESENT 4x4 S-BOX | |
|---|---|---|
| | #Transistors | Energy Per Cycle (fJ) @12.5 MHz |
| Standard CMOS | 216 | 38.93 |
| SABL [29] | 374 | 68.56 |
| TPDL [4] | 441 | 116.75 |
| MDPL [18] | 1056 | 117.375 |
| CSSAL [15] | 783 | 16 |
| SQAL [2] | 459 | 13.8 |
| EE-SPFAL [7] | 430 | 4.22 |

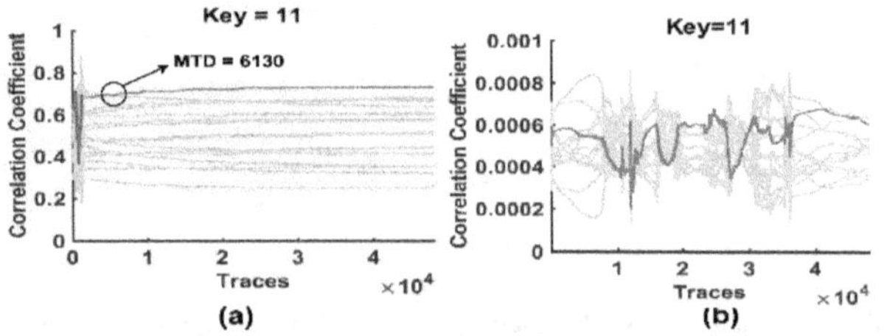


**Figure 6: DPA attack on PRESENT S-Box implemented using (a) standard CMOS, and (b) Energy Recovery logic.**

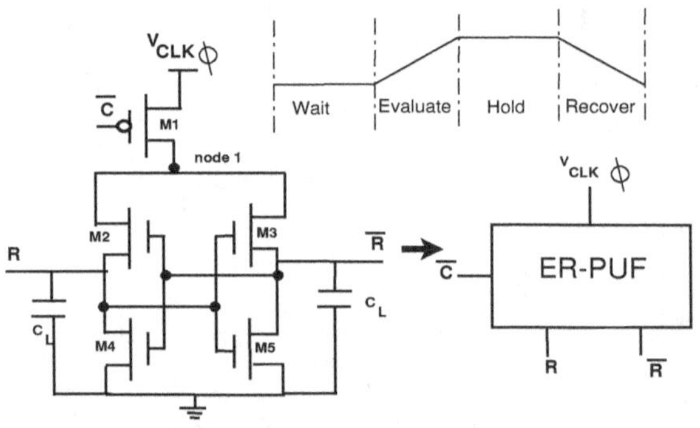


**Figure 7: Schematic of ER-PUF cell [11]. M1 transistor is the sleep transistor. The latch structure is designed using M2, M3, M4 and M5 transistors.**

generate the random response bit [11]. The proposed adiabatic PUF employs the energy recovery concept to conserve the energy from one logical operation to the next, and uses the four phase adiabatic clocking scheme to generate a large number of challenge response pairs. The schematic diagram of the proposed ER-PUF is shown in Fig. 7. More details on the operation of the ER-PUF can be found in [11].

Four phase clocks (wait, evaluate, hold and recovery) are used in ER-PUF to recover energy and to produce more response bits. In ER-PUF, each cell produces 4 repetitive random bits. Therefore, it will be difficult for the attackers to model ER-PUF. Further, each cell has a phase difference of 90 degrees with respect to the adjacent cell. Therefore, when all the 4 outputs are sampled at a time it will lead to 4 bits. When these outputs are sampled at different phases of the clock, it leads to different pairs of bits. As a result of this technique, 4 PUF cell can produce 16 bits. In general, $n$ PUF cells can produce $4n$ $x$ 2 response bits [11]. ER-PUF consumes 0.39$\mu$Watt of power to generate a response bit and satisfies the security metrics of reliability, uniqueness and uniformity, etc. More details can be found in Table 2.

**Table 2: Comparison of ER-PUF in Security Metrics [11]**

| PUF | Power ($\mu$W) | Tech (nm) | Area ($\mu m^2$) | Uniqueness(%) | Reliability(%) |
|---|---|---|---|---|---|
| [22] | NA | 90 | NA | 46.14 | 99.52 |
| [21] | 0.93 | 130 | 15.288 | 64.70 | 96.96 |
| [6] | NA | NA | NA | 50.90 | 98.70 |
| [5] | 32.3 | 65 | 250 | 50.42 | 97.22 |
| ER-PUF | 0.39 | 180 | 31.24 | 40.5 | 96.2 |

# 4 ENERGY RECOVERY COMPUTING BASED HARDWARE TROJAN DETECTION

We are using the Differential Power Analysis (DPA) resistant energy recovery circuits for HT detection in IoT devices [9]. Side-channel analysis based trojan detection is one the possible approach for hardware trojan detection [17]. DPA resistant ER gates consume uniform and less power compared to conventional CMOS logic gates. We assume that the insertion of a CMOS gate in the DPA resistant ER circuits will produce a power glitch due to non-synchronization of the power clock. The non-uniform power consumption can be used to detect smaller trojans in DPA resistant ER logic circuits. ER computing based HT detection does not require a golden chip for the detection of HT. Two benchmark circuits, C17 and carry save adder, are used to illustrate the proposed approach of ER computing based HT detection. Fig. 8 shows the schematic of 'infected benchmark circuits' of C17 carry save adder [13].

Simulations are performed using Cadence Spectre simulator with 45nm CMOS technology. The power reported for EE-SPFAL based circuits includes the power consumption in the power clock generator. Table 3 shows the energy per cylcle of the conventional CMOS and EE-SPFAL based C17 benchmark and CSA circuit. EE-SPFAL based C17 and CSA circuits have 52% and 33% less energy consumption as compared to the conventional CMOS circuits.

| Circuit | CMOS | EE-SPFAL | energy savings |
|---|---|---|---|
| C17 | 4.5fJ | 2.1fJ | 52% |
| CSA | 12.9fJ | 8.5 fJ | 33% |

**Table 3: CMOS vs EE-SPFAL Energy Per Cycle**

The power difference between 'golden' and 'infected' circuits in CMOS and EE-SPFAL logic is illustrated in Fig. 9. The CMOS based golden and the infected circuits of C17 and CSA have 44% and 22% difference in power consumption. However, EE-SPFAL based golden and the infected circuits of C17 and CSA circuit have 85% and

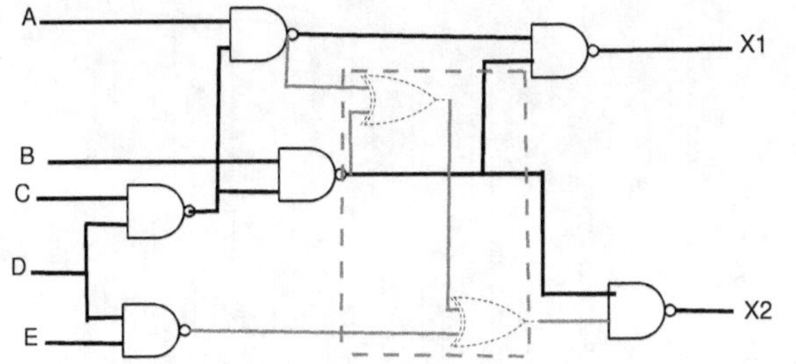

(a) C17 Circuit (Infected)

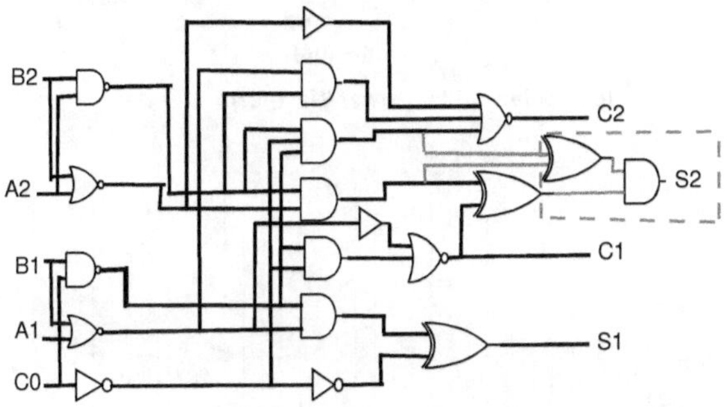

(b) Carry Save Adder Circuit (Infected)

**Figure 8: C17 and Carry Save Adder Infected Circuits (Trojan circuit represented by red lines)**

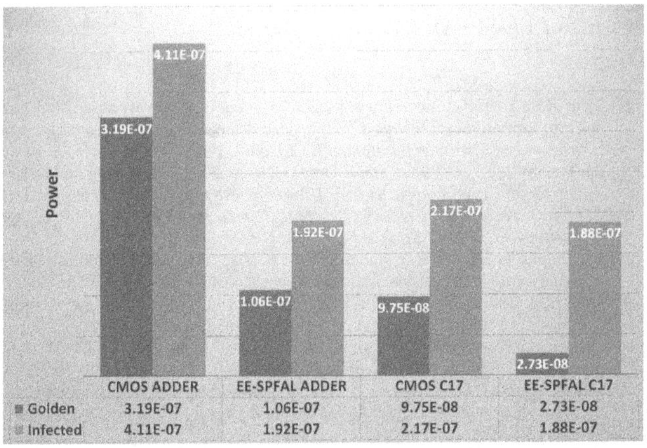


**Figure 9: Differences in Power consumption of Golden and Infected circuits.**

50% difference in power consumption. Fig. 10 presents the power consumption of the EE-SPFAL based C17 and adder circuit with and without trojan. From Fig. 10 (a) and (c), the 'golden' EE-SPFAL based C17 and CSA circuits have uniform power consumption. Further, as can be observed from the Fig. 10 (b) and (d) the 'infected' EE-SPFAL based C17 and CSA circuits have non-uniform power consumption.

## 5 CONCLUSION

IoT devices have an extremely limited energy and power budget. Moreover, the secret information stored in IoT devices can be revealed by side-channel attacks. We have provided the perspective on the use of energy recovery computing as an potential choice for designing low-energy and secure IoT devices which operate at low frequency. We have shown a low-power and DPA resistant lightweight cryptographic circuits using energy recovery logic. A study on the design of low-power PUF using energy-recovery logic is illustrated. Further, we illustrate the application of ER computing towards Hardware Trojans (HTs) detection without a golden (non-trojan). The applications of energy recovery (ER) computing in FinFET, Tunnel FET and emerging technologies could also be explored to develop ultra-low-energy and secure solutions [8, 26, 28] for embedded computing. In conclusion, energy recovery (ER) computing has a potential to be adopted as a mainstream computing paradigm to solve energy and cybersecurity constraints in IoT devices.

## REFERENCES

[1] William C Athas, Lars J Svensson, Jefferey G Koller, Nestoras Tzartzanis, and E Ying-Chin Chou. 1994. Low-power digital systems based on adiabatic-switching principles. *IEEE Transactions on Very Large Scale Integration (VLSI) Systems* 2, 4 (1994), 398–407.

[2] M. Avital, H. Dagan, I. Levi, O. Keren, and A. Fish. 2015. DPA-Secured Quasi-Adiabatic Logic (SQAL) for Low-Power Passive RFID Tags Employing S-Boxes. *IEEE Transactions on Circuits and Systems I: Regular Papers* 62, 1 (Jan 2015), 149–156. https://doi.org/10.1109/TCSI.2014.2359720

[3] Swarup Bhunia, Michael S Hsiao, Mainak Banga, and Seetharam Narasimhan. 2014. Hardware Trojan attacks: threat analysis and countermeasures. *Proc. IEEE* 102, 8 (2014), 1229–1247.

[4] Marco Bucci, Luca Giancane, Raimondo Luzzi, and Alessandro Trifiletti. 2006. Three-Phase Dual-Rail Pre-charge Logic. In *Cryptographic Hardware and Embedded Systems - CHES 2006*, Louis Goubin and Mitsuru Matsui (Eds.). Springer Berlin Heidelberg, Berlin, Heidelberg, 232–241.

[5] Yuan Cao, Le Zhang, Chip-Hong Chang, and Shoushun Chen. 2015. A Low-power Hybrid RO PUF with Improved Thermal Stability for Lightweight Applications. (2015).

[6] Qingqing Chen, György Csaba, Paolo Lugli, Ulf Schlichtmann, and Ulrich Rührmair. 2011. The bistable ring puf: A new architecture for strong physical unclonable functions. In *Hardware-Oriented Security and Trust (HOST), 2011 IEEE International Symposium on*. IEEE, 134–141.

[7] S. Dinesh Kumar, H. Thapliyal, and A. Mohammad. 2018. EE-SPFAL: A Novel Energy-Efficient Secure Positive Feedback Adiabatic Logic for DPA Resistant RFID and Smart Card. *IEEE Transactions on Emerging Topics in Computing* (2018), 1–1. https://doi.org/10.1109/TETC.2016.2645128

[8] S. Dinesh Kumar, H. Thapliyal, and A. Mohammad. 2018. FinSAL: FinFET-Based Secure Adiabatic Logic for Energy-Efficient and DPA Resistant IoT Devices. *IEEE Transactions on Computer-Aided Design of Integrated Circuits and Systems* 37, 1 (Jan 2018), 110–122. https://doi.org/10.1109/TCAD.2017.2685588

[9] Z. Kahleifeh, S. Dinesh Kumar, and H. Thapliyal. 2018. Hardware Trojan Detection in Implantable Medical Devices Using Adiabatic Computing. In *2018 IEEE International Conference on Rebooting Computing (ICRC)*. 1–6. https://doi.org/10.1109/ICRC.2018.8638602

[10] Paul Kocher, Joshua Jaffe, and Benjamin Jun. 1999. Differential power analysis. In *Annual International Cryptology Conference*. Springer, 388–397.

[11] S Dinesh Kumar and Himanshu Thapliyal. 2016. Qualpuf: A novel quasi-adiabatic logic based physical unclonable function. In *Proceedings of the 11th Annual Cyber and Information Security Research Conference*. ACM, 24.

[12] S Dinesh Kumar, Himanshu Thapliyal, Azhar Mohammad, and Kalyan S Perumalla. 2017. Design exploration of a symmetric pass gate adiabatic logic for energy-efficient and secure hardware. *Integration, the VLSI Journal* 58 (2017), 369–377.

[13] Karthikeyan Lingasubramanian, Ranveer Kumar, Nagendra Babu Gunti, and Thomas Morris. 2018. Study of hardware trojans based security vulnerabilities in cyber physical systems. In *Consumer Electronics (ICCE), 2018 IEEE International Conference on*. IEEE, 1–6.

[14] Kerry McKay, Lawrence Bassham, Meltem Sönmez Turan, and Nicky Mouha. 2016. *Report on lightweight cryptography*. Technical Report. National Institute of Standards and Technology.

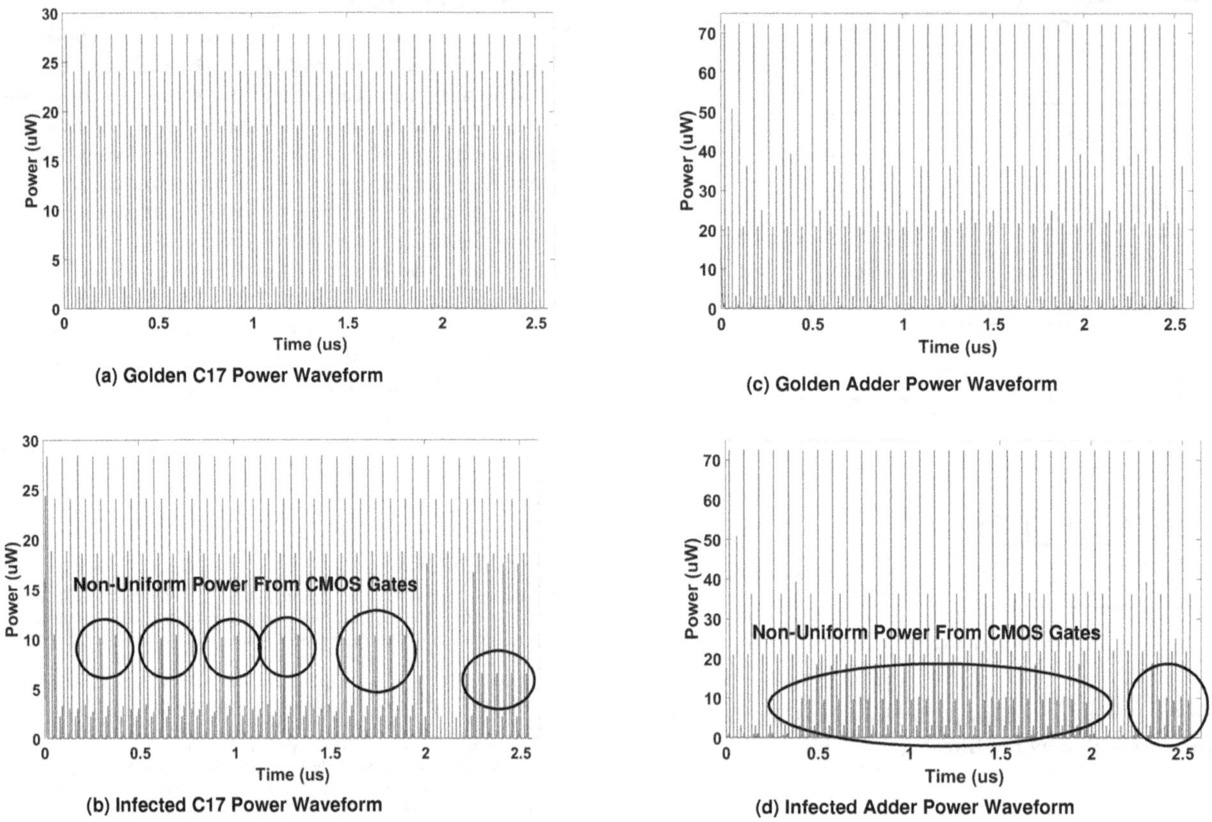


**Figure 10: Golden vs Infected Power Waveforms of EE-SPFAL C17 and Adder.**


[15] C. Monteiro, Y. Takahashi, and T. Sekine. 2014. An LSI implementation of a bit-parallel cellular multiplier over GF(24) using secure charge-sharing symmetric adiabatic logic. In *2014 IEEE International Symposium on Circuits and Systems (ISCAS)*. 826–829. https://doi.org/10.1109/ISCAS.2014.6865263

[16] Amir Moradi and Axel Poschmann. 2010. Lightweight cryptography and DPA countermeasures: A survey. In *Financial Cryptography and Data Security*. Springer, 68–79.

[17] Seetharam Narasimhan, Dongdong Du, Rajat Subhra Chakraborty, Somnath Paul, Francis Wolff, Christos Papachristou, Kaushik Roy, and Swarup Bhunia. 2010. Multiple-parameter side-channel analysis: A non-invasive hardware Trojan detection approach. In *Hardware-Oriented Security and Trust (HOST), 2010 IEEE International Symposium on*. IEEE, 13–18.

[18] Thomas Popp and Stefan Mangard. 2005. Masked Dual-Rail Pre-charge Logic: DPA-Resistance Without Routing Constraints. In *Cryptographic Hardware and Embedded Systems – CHES 2005*, Josyula R. Rao and Berk Sunar (Eds.). Springer Berlin Heidelberg, Berlin, Heidelberg, 172–186.

[19] Axel York Poschmann. 2009. Lightweight cryptography: cryptographic engineering for a pervasive world. In *PH. D. THESIS*. Citeseer.

[20] Sergei Skorobogatov and Christopher Woods. 2012. Breakthrough silicon scanning discovers backdoor in military chip. In *International Workshop on Cryptographic Hardware and Embedded Systems*. Springer, 23–40.

[21] Ying Su, Jeremy Holleman, and Brian P Otis. 2008. A digital 1.6 pJ/bit chip identification circuit using process variations. *Solid-State Circuits, IEEE Journal of* 43, 1 (2008), 69–77.

[22] G Edward Suh and Srinivas Devadas. 2007. Physical unclonable functions for device authentication and secret key generation. In *Proceedings of the 44th annual Design Automation Conference*. ACM, 9–14.

[23] Philip Teichmann. 2011. *Adiabatic logic: future trend and system level perspective*. Vol. 34. Springer Science & Business Media.

[24] Himanshu Thapliyal. 2018. Internet of Things-Based Consumer Electronics: Reviewing Existing Consumer Electronic Devices, Systems, and Platforms and Exploring New Research Paradigms. *IEEE Consumer Electronics Magazine* 7, 1 (2018), 66–67.

[25] Himanshu Thapliyal and S Dinesh Kumar. 2018. Energy-recovery based hardware security primitives for low-power embedded devices. In *2018 IEEE International Conference on Consumer Electronics (ICCE)*. IEEE, 1–6.

[26] H. Thapliyal, T. S. S. Varun, and S. Dinesh Kumar. 2017. Low-Power and Secure Lightweight Cryptography Via TFET-Based Energy Recovery Circuits. In *2017 IEEE International Conference on Rebooting Computing (ICRC)*. 1–4. https://doi.org/10.1109/ICRC.2017.8123640

[27] H. Thapliyal, T. S. S. Varun, and S. D. Kumar. 2017. Adiabatic Computing Based Low-Power and DPA-Resistant Lightweight Cryptography for IoT Devices. In *2017 IEEE Computer Society Annual Symposium on VLSI (ISVLSI)*. 621–626. https://doi.org/10.1109/ISVLSI.2017.115

[28] Himanshu Thapliyal, T. S. S. Varun, and S. Dinesh Kumar. 2017. UTB-SOI Based Adiabatic Computing for Low-power and Secure IoT Devices. In *Proceedings of the 12th Annual Conference on Cyber and Information Security Research (CISRC '17)*. ACM, New York, NY, USA, Article 16, 4 pages. https://doi.org/10.1145/3064814.3064825

[29] K. Tiri and I. Verbauwhede. 2004. Charge recycling sense amplifier based logic: securing low power security ICs against DPA [differential power analysis]. In *Proceedings of the 30th European Solid-State Circuits Conference*. 179–182. https://doi.org/10.1109/ESSCIR.2004.1356647

[30] Ingrid Verbauwhede. 2016. VLSI design methods for low power embedded encryption. In *2016 International Great Lakes Symposium on VLSI (GLSVLSI)*. IEEE, 7–7.

# Right-Provisioned IoT Edge Computing: An Overview

Tosiron Adegbija
tosiron@email.arizona.edu
Department of Electrical & Computer Engineering
University of Arizona, Tucson, AZ, USA

Roman Lysecky
rlysecky@ece.arizona.edu
Department of Electrical & Computer Engineering
University of Arizona, Tucson, AZ, USA

Vinu Vijay Kumar
vinuv@google.com
Google
Mountain View, CA

## ABSTRACT

Edge computing on the Internet of Things (IoT) is an increasingly popular paradigm in which computation is moved closer to the data source (i.e., edge devices). Edge computing mitigates the overheads of cloud-based computing arising from increased response time, communication bandwidth, data security and privacy, energy consumption, etc. However, given the potentially stringent resource constraints and functional requirements of emerging IoT devices, edge computing must neither be over- or under-provisioned for its stated purpose. In this paper, we present an overview of the problem of *right-provisioned IoT edge computing*, wherein IoT devices are equipped with resources that are 'just enough,' even when 'just enough' may not be clearly defined at design time. We highlight a few research directions and key challenges that must be addressed to enable right-provisioned IoT edge computing.

## CCS CONCEPTS

• **Computer systems organization → Embedded systems; Processors and memory architectures;**

## KEYWORDS

Internet of Things; edge computing; low-power embedded systems; right-provisioned; adaptable computing; high-level synthesis; memory hierarchy; computation migration; IoT security.

**ACM Reference format:**
Tosiron Adegbija, Roman Lysecky, and Vinu Vijay Kumar. 2019. Right-Provisioned IoT Edge Computing: An Overview. In *Proceedings of Great Lakes Symposium on VLSI 2019, Tysons Corner, VA, USA, May 9–11, 2019 (GLSVLSI '19),* 6 pages.
https://doi.org/10.1145/3299874.3319338

## 1 INTRODUCTION

Unlike on the Internet, where most of the data is generated by humans, on the Internet of Things (IoT), most of the data will be generated by 'things' or edge devices. Considering that the IoT continues to grow rapidly, with billions of devices that span a wide variety of applications and domains, the challenge of efficiently processing the vast amounts of data produced by IoT devices will become even more pressing [1]. *Edge computing* [2] has emerged as a paradigm in which computation is moved closer to the edge devices of the IoT network, in order to reduce the overheads concomitant to the bandwidth and latency challenges of transmitting data to the cloud for computations. In this paper, we distinguish edge computing as computation on the edge devices [3], as opposed to fog computing or mobile edge computing (MEC), where computation is performed at base stations or routers [2, 4].

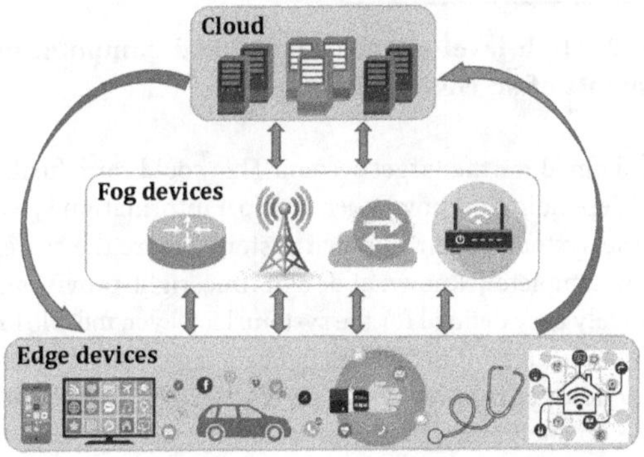


**Figure 1: Overview of the Internet of Things (IoT) devices and where computations can be performed, ranging from edge devices to cloud devices.**

As illustrated in Figure 1, computations can be performed on the fog devices, or even closer to the data source on the edge devices. However, moving computations closer to the edge devices is especially challenging because edge devices usually have stringent resource constraints (e.g., physical size, energy) and functional requirements (e.g., response time, application execution) that necessitate that the computational resources are *right-provisioned* for the individual device, system, or application.

*Right-provisioned IoT edge computing* implies that the edge device is neither under-provisioned nor over-provisioned for the requisite functions. When under-provisioned, the device is unable to satisfy its functional requirements; for instance, response time is high, or worse, a hard deadline may be violated [5]. On the other hand, when over-provisioned, the device wastes resources and incurs unnecessary overheads (e.g., cost, size, energy consumption). As such, the provisioning of computational resources must be 'just enough' for all its functional requirements, including computations, communications, security, etc.

To achieve right-provisioned IoT edge computing, several challenges must be addressed. First, considering that right-provisioning could be very nuanced for different systems and applications—a right-provisioned system for one application may be severely under- or over-provisioned for another—right-provisioning must first be


*GLSVLSI '19, May 9–11, 2019, Tysons Corner, VA, USA*

ACM ISBN 978-1-4503-6252-8/19/05.
https://doi.org/10.1145/3299874.3319338

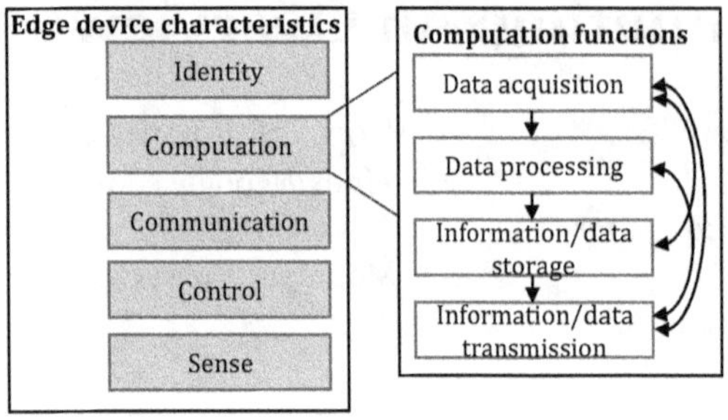


**Figure 2: High-level characteristics and computational requirements of an edge device.**

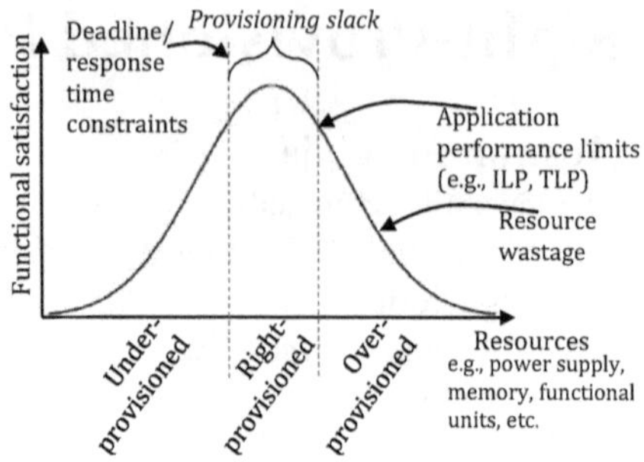


**Figure 3: Defining right-provisioning.**

clearly defined for the target system. This could raise further challenges, depending on how much a priori information is available about the system. Given a known system, where the system's behavior is completely known at design time, right-provisioning can be relatively easy defined for the system. However, most IoT devices involve some variability, where applications, system inputs, objective functions, or user requirements may change drastically during runtime. In such systems, the provisioning must be adaptable to dynamically changing runtime requirements, without introducing substantial overheads from the adaptability.

This paper provides an overview of the problem of right-provisioned IoT edge computing. We explore what it means for an IoT device to be right-provisioned with respect to its computational capabilities and explore some of the nuances of right-provisioning. We also highlight some recent work and a few research challenges that need to be addressed to enable right-provisioned computing in emerging IoT edge devices.

## 2 DEFINING RIGHT-PROVISIONED IOT EDGE COMPUTING

Figure 2 presents a high-level summary of the general characteristics of edge devices and their key computational functions. These characteristics and functions may also apply to fog devices, but for brevity, we simply refer to edge devices in the rest of this paper. The major characteristics, which have been discussed in detail in prior work, include *unique identity* (e.g., IPv6 addressing) [6], *communication* (e.g., Bluetooth, WiFi) [7], *control* (e.g., actuation) [8], *sense* (via various sensors) [9], and *computation* (e.g., microcontrollers, microprocessors) [10]. This paper focuses on right-provisioning for the computation functions, which can further be broken down into *data acquisition, data processing, information or data storage*, and *information or data transmission.* Details of these functions have been presented in prior work (e.g., [3, 10]).

The first step to designing right-provisioned edge devices is to understand what it means for the device to be right-provisioned for its target application, given the required computation functions. At this point, we draw a distinction between *optimization* and right-provisioning. Optimization implies that the system is designed to achieve the *best possible* results given the system constraints, e.g., minimize the energy consumption without degrading the performance beyond a given threshold. Right-provisioning, on the other hand, means that the best results need not be achieved as long as the device's functional requirements are fully satisfied.

Understanding the device requirements is very challenging due to the wide variety of devices and applications that exist on the IoT. In general, right-provisioning may also involve allowing for some *provisioning slack.* That is, the system does not necessarily have to be *perfectly* provisioned, as long as its functional requirements are met. Figure 3 illustrates this idea. The system resources (e.g., power supply, memory, functional units) are under-provisioned when they are unable to satisfy the applications' functional requirements, such as a deadline or response time constraint.

For instance, consider a task that must complete in time $ts$. Assuming a soft deadline requirement [11], which allows the task to be completed within a given slack $ls$ beyond the deadline, without any system failure, the system is considered right-provisioned as long as its computational resources allow the task to be completed within $(t + l)$s. The system is considered over-provisioned when additional resources, beyond what is required to achieve $(t + l)$s, do not result in any functional benefits to the system. For instance, a system may be over-provisioned with out-of-order execution resources if the application has limited instruction level parallelism (ILP) and the application's instructions must execute in order [12]. In some cases, the slack produced by the over-provisioned system may be leveraged for other applications, whereas in other cases, the over-provisioning is simply tantamount to resource wastage.

Therefore, an edge device is right-provisioned if the available resources $R$ are such that $r \leq R \leq (r + s)$, where $r$ is the resource requirement to achieve the system's minimum functional requirements, and $s$ is the provisioning slack and may be bounded by the system's design constraints. Both $r$ and $s$ can be generalized to any functional requirements, such as energy, response time, etc. It is clear that right-provisioning is difficult to define, given the variety of applications, systems, and requirements. The next two subsections attempt to further define some of the nuances of right-provisioned edge computing.

### 2.1 Granularity of Right-Provisioning

One of the first questions that must be answered when designing a right-provisioned edge device is the execution granularity for which the device is provisioned. We define four alternatives for execution granularity, namely, *task-specific, application-specific, domain-specific*, and *general purpose.* Task-specific (or phase-based) right-provisioning refers to a case where an edge device is right-provisioned for a specific task, kernel, or application phase. For example, inference tasks, such as audio sensing, which are commonly executed by edge devices (e.g., wearables) represent a good candidate for task-specific right-provisioning [13].

Application-specific right-provisioning refers to satisfying the requirements of a specific application. For example, prior work (e.g. [3]) has proposed edge devices specifically for ECG applications in the Internet of Medical Things (IoMT). Domain-specific right-provisioning refers to satisfying the requirements of a domain of applications, which would likely have a similar set of characteristics or functional requirements. For example, Yamaga et al. [14] propose an approximate-ReRAM that uses deep neural network (DNN) for image recognition applications. While domain-specific right-provisioning may not satisfy the functional requirements of individual applications, unlike application-specific right-provisioning, the domain-specific approach allows for better application flexibility and may be better overall for a system that executes a variety of similar applications. Finally, general-purpose right-provisioning involves equipping the edge device with resources to satisfy a wide variety of tasks and applications, without necessary being right-provisioned for a single task, application, or domain [13]. Depending on the target edge device, the various granularities of right-provisioning can be achieved in various ways as we discuss in the following subsection.

### 2.2 Static vs. Dynamic Right-Provisioning

Edge devices can be provisioned either *statically* or *dynamically*. A statically right-provisioned edge device is designed with the appropriate computing resources, which remain static throughout the device's lifetime. There is a wide variety of systems that enable statically right-provisioned edge devices, ranging from application-specific integrated circuits (ASICs) [15] to CPUs that are specifically tuned for the executing applications or a group of applications [16]. Most current edge devices are statically provisioned. For instance, the FitBit features a low-power ARM Cortex M3 microcontroller, and the NEST thermostat features the higher-performance ARM Cortex A8 processor for its machine learning functions. In both cases, the computing resources remain static throughout the devices' lifetime, regardless of what task is being executed. In order for an edge device to be statically right-provisioned, the system must be fully known at design time. That is, the applications must be known and must not be subject to substantial runtime changes (e.g., changes in execution requirements due to new inputs). As such, static right-provisioning is easiest for devices that only execute a single application or a small group of applications whose characteristics are known a priori.

A dynamically right-provisioned edge device, on the other hand, allows the system resources to be dynamically adapted to the runtime functional requirements of executing tasks. Dynamic provisioning is especially important since most applications exhibit variability in runtime behavior due to the applications' characteristics, new inputs, user requirements, etc. For instance, dynamic voltage and frequency scaling (DVFS) is a popular technique that allows the clock frequency (or voltage) to be dynamically adapted to different runtime requirements, in order to reduce energy consumption or meet task deadlines [17].

Dynamic provisioning has the advantage that, unlike static provisioning, various runtime requirements can be satisfied by the edge device. For example, for an edge device that executes multiple applications with different levels of thread-level parallelism, the device can be provisioned with a multicore CPU such that cores can be powered off, depending on the number of parallel threads present in an application. Furthermore, parts of various components (e.g., cache resources, functional units, etc.) can be shut down, depending on the applications' execution requirements. Dynamic right-provisioning can also be achieved using heterogeneous resources, wherein tasks can be dynamically scheduled to the resource that most closely satisfies each task's requirement [16]. While there is a large body of work on dynamic provisioning for a wide variety of general-purpose applications, there still remains much research to be done on novel low-overhead techniques to enable adaptability for IoT edge devices, given the stringent design constraints of these devices.

## 3 OPEN RESEARCH CHALLENGES

In this section, we highlight a few important open research challenges for right-provisioned IoT edge computing. We note that these challenges are not exhaustive; they represent a variety of research directions in which there is much ongoing research, but still contain several gaps that need further investigations and improvement to fully enable right-provisioned IoT edge computing.

### 3.1 High-Level Synthesis for Right-Provisioning

One of the driving forces for right-provisioned IoT edge computing will be application-specific systems that adhere to specific timing, resource, and functional requirements. While several system-level hardware design methods exist, current techniques typically trade off productivity for timing precision. Hardware description language (HDLs), such as Verilog and VHDL, require designers to specify system behaviors for each clock cycle (i.e., cycle-accurate description). While these methods allow precise timing specification, design productivity is low.

To increase designer productivity, high-level synthesis (HLS) approaches use high-level languages (e.g., C, C++) to specify system functionality and automatically generate hardware implementations [18]. However, high-level languages rely on the implied order of operations, as opposed to explicitly defined and precise timing. Thus, timing must be inferred from the structure or manually added through tool-specific annotations, thereby leading to computations that may behave differently than the equivalent software [19].

Given these drawbacks of current HLS techniques, new approaches are required to enable the rapid design and optimization of hardware components for IoT edge devices that satisfy their functional requirements and adhere to their timing and resource constraints. We refer to these required new HLS approaches as *timing-driven high-level synthesis (TD-HLS)*. Figure 4 provides an overview of a TD-HLS methodology for designing timing-driven low-power right-provisioned edge devices. The initial goal is to select clock domain and frequencies for each of the system's individual components, such that the combined latencies are less than the overall latency constraint, while satisfying power constraints. During system specification, designers can specify end-to-end latency constraints for a system-level composition of components.

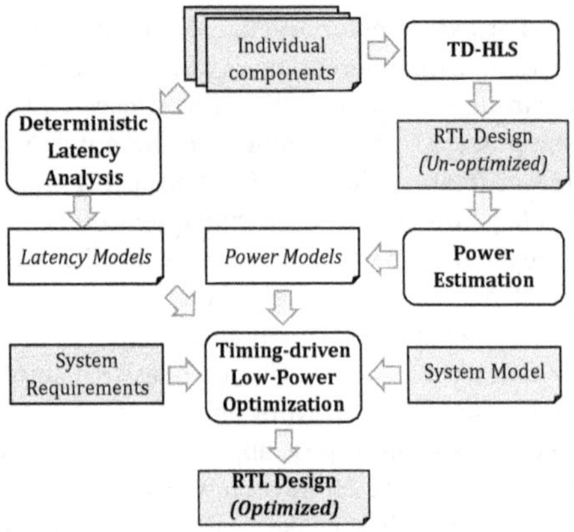


**Figure 4: Overview of the Timing-Driven High Level Synthesis (TD-HLS) approach.**

Given the synthesized RTL design, commercial tools for FPGAs or ASICs can be used to create power models for each individual component that relate power consumption to the execution frequency. The latency and power model can then be utilized to determine a right-provisioned frequency mapping that meets the system's latency and/or energy constraints.

There are several open problems that must be addressed towards achieving the required TD-HLS techniques. For instance, emerging HLS approaches must provide formal design, synthesis, and optimization frameworks that support synthesizable precisely-timed system models that enable the explicit and integrated specification of precise timing behaviors for various kinds of computation.

Furthermore, these new HLS approaches must be capable of automatically extracting component-level and system-level synthesis constraints required to seamlessly integrate with existing performance-driven HLS tools/approaches. Finally, the new HLS approaches must support design methods, event-driven communication, and self-clock gating for optimizing energy consumption, given system requirements and constraints.

## 3.2 Computation Migration

One of the most important decisions that must be made in edge computing is *how much* computing *should* and *can* be performed at the edge. While the conventional wisdom is that migrating computations from edge devices to the fog or cloud can improve the IoT system's overall performance and energy consumption [20], a right-provisioned edge device may further alleviate the performance and energy overheads of transferring data between the edge device and other layers (fog or cloud).

From the perspective of the edge device, there are two extremes of computation migration with various tradeoffs. On one extreme, a *zero computation migration* or *local execution* scheme could be used, where all the computations are performed on the edge device. This scheme lends itself to the lowest response time, since it eliminates the latency overheads of transmitting data to the fog or cloud. However, performing all the computations on the edge device may result in prohibitive overhead with respect to energy and form factor. On the other extreme, a *full computation migration* or *full offloading* [21] scheme could be used, where the edge device collects data and transmits all the data to the cloud where all the computations are performed. A happy medium between both extremes is the *partial computation migration* or *partial offloading* [22] scheme where some computations are performed on the edge device, while the rest is transmitted to the fog (or cloud).

There is a growing body of work that studies different computation migration schemes for different applications [4, 23]. For example, Xu et al [24] studied the response time effects of partitioning different components of a deep neural network (DNN) between an edge device and a mobile gateway (fog). However, there is still much room for research into understanding whether or not there is an optimal choice for computation migration, given the system constraints and functional requirements. Understanding the best computation migration scheme to achieve right-provisioning for the target system is a challenging communication-computation co-optimization problem, since the best scheme depends on both the computation resources on the edge device and the communication medium. For instance, while computing on fog devices may be faster or more energy efficient than computing on the edge device, the transmission time to move data between the edge device and the fog may negate the speed or energy benefits of computing on fog devices.

Furthermore, a formulation of the best scheme also depends on how well-known the system is at design time. If the applications, computation resources, and communication characteristics are well-known at design time, the best computation migration scheme may be accurately defined a priori. However, in most realistic systems, some of the required information may be unknown at design time or the systems may change during runtime due to application interference, environmental uncertainty, mobility, or even dynamic functional requirements and constraints. As such, *dynamic computation migration* schemes may be required to adaptively determine where computations must be performed in order to satisfy the functional requirements and system constraints.

## 3.3 Threat Detection, Mitigation, and Resilience

IoT edge devices are especially vulnerable to security threats due to several intrinsic characteristics, such as mobility, connectivity, scale, resource constraints, complexity, etc. Edge devices are susceptible to several kinds of threats including side-channel attacks (e.g., differential power analysis (DPA) [25]) and hardware-based vulnerabilities (e.g., IC piracy, IC counterfeiting, reverse engineering [26]). As alluded to throughout this paper, IoT edge devices also typically have stringent functional requirements and limited computational resources. As such, resources for achieving security and privacy are usually limited. Furthermore, achieving security must not detract from the computational resources required for satisfying the devices' functional requirements. Thus, security mechanisms for edge computing must also be right-provisioned, such that they do not waste resources, but are also sufficient for the security requirements of individual devices or applications. It is important that emerging security mechanisms are designed to be both proactive (i.e., able to prevent intrusions) and reactive (i.e., able to detect and mitigate the effect of intrusions). In addition, the security functions must be performed while ensuring continuity of operations.

Several efforts have been made to develop novel techniques for detecting and mitigating threats in IoT devices. For example, Kumar et al. [27] present the design of an energy-efficient secure positive feedback adiabatic logic (EE-SPEAL) to enable the design of DPA-resistant IoT circuits, while saving energy compared to traditional CMOS circuits. Carreon et al. [28] present a probabilistic approach for estimating the presence of malware for individual operations and sequences of operations in an embedded system, including thresholds to minimize false positives based on training data.

There is still much room for research on efficient security mechanisms that can non-invasively detect threats, observe anomalous execution behavior, isolate the system components/data that are affected by the detected threat, and allow the device to operate in a mode that isolates threats (e.g., by disabling affected components). These detection and mitigation methods must be appropriately provisioned for the specific IoT edge device based on the available computing resources and constraints. In addition, similar to computation migration, security functions may need to be distributed across different levels of the IoT system. For instance, given an edge device with limited resources, the runtime threat detection can be customized to use a simple model for defining the normal system execution behaviors, which would allow energy-efficient threat detection but with a lower accuracy. In contrast, a gateway (fog) device with higher computational capabilities and energy resources can be customized to use a more robust model and machine learning algorithms for threat detection, using aggregated data across multiple edge devices.

### 3.4 Right-Provisioned Energy Supply

Energy efficiency is probably one of the most researched topics with respect to edge devices and remains a daunting challenge as a result of several characteristics, including, limited battery resources, small form factor, scale, mobility, real-time requirements, etc. Several emerging technologies offer much promise for right-provisioned energy supply in edge devices. One such technology is *energy harvesting* [17], which converts power from ambient sources, such as mechanical motion, electromagnetic radiation, etc., into electrical power. For instance, in a wearable device (e.g., smartwatch), the mechanical energy produced by the motion of a human body can be converted into electric energy [29]. As such, energy harvesting capability serves as a renewable energy source, thereby mitigating the need for reliance on batteries for energy. Important directions for right-provisioned energy supply for edge devices include novel approaches for self-powered devices, low-overhead energy storage mechanisms, and techniques for coping with the unpredictability of energy harvesting mechanisms. A framework for maximizing energy efficiency under ultra-low power harvesting scenarios is presented in [30]. Furthermore, new advances must take into account the variability of power and longevity requirements for the different devices and applications, and the fact that these requirements may vary during runtime [31].

Another technology trend that warrants further investigation with respect to edge devices is dark silicon [32]. Dark silicon is an undesirable feature of thermal and current limited modern designs. It can also be an unavoidable byproduct of a platform-based design approach to amortizing design costs over a family of products. A good strategy to take advantage of the inevitability of dark silicon is to divide the design into highly power-efficient always-powered infrastructure regions, and energy efficient but not necessarily power optimal dark regions. The dark silicon regions are enabled on demand non-concurrently based on use cases. The dark silicon regions would be designed to a 'Joule/compute-operation' metric and include right-provisioned complex processing and techniques such as lossy compression, etc. that are power inefficient, but minimize overall energy due to reduced demand on the always powered infrastructure. A model-free reinforcement learning (RL) approach for optimizing power efficiency and lowering energy delay product is presented in [33].

### 3.5 Adaptable Memories

As can be inferred from Figure 2, one of the most important components of an IoT device is the memory subsystem. At different stages of an edge device's lifecycle, different kinds of data (e.g., raw data, intermediate data, processed information) must be stored or cached for quick access. As such, the memory subsystem has significant implications for several system functions and characteristics, including performance, energy consumption, form factor, etc.

Memory design and optimization techniques for a wide variety of systems and objectives (e.g., energy reduction) is a well-studied research area. However, IoT edge devices have some intrinsic characteristics that can be explored and exploited for further improving the memory subsystem design. For example, some IoT applications are error-tolerant, meaning that a right-provisioned memory subsystem for edge devices executing such applications need not be error-free [3]. However, the applications' error tolerance must be carefully analyzed in order to design memory subsystems that satisfy the requisite functional requirements. Alternatively, hybrid memory systems—featuring both error-free and error-prone memory segments—can be utilized for edge devices that execute applications with different runtime requirements [34].

An emerging class of memories that offer much promise for designing right-provisioned edge devices are non-volatile memories (NVMs) [35]. NVMs (e.g., STT-RAM, flash, PCM, etc.) offer several advantages, including non-volatility (beneficial for designing non-volatile processors that can restore the system state when the device loses power), high density (beneficial for size), and low-static power (beneficial for low energy consumption) [29, 36]. There are several on-going research efforts towards exploiting emerging NVM technologies for IoT applications. For instance, Ueki et al. [37] developed a ReRAM-based memory architecture for IoT applications, demonstrating its low-power benefits. Ghoneim et al. [38] review how NVMs' ultra-dense and ultra-low-power characteristics can be leveraged in designing physically flexible electronic systems for IoT applications.

An important area of research that still warrants further studies involves understanding the variable runtime execution characteristics of IoT applications. Given these variable characteristics, new approaches are also required to design adaptable memories and memory management techniques that allow the memory resources to be dynamically adapted to the applications' requirements. An example of a promising NVM technology for right-provisioned IoT edge computing is the *racetrack memory*, which also offers the aforementioned advantages of NVMs. Racetrack memory, like other NVMs, further offers the advantage of flexibility, since it has several device level design parameters [39]. These parameters must be explored for right-provisioning for a variety of IoT devices. Similarly, there has also been much prior research into relaxing the retention time of NVMs (e.g., STT-RAM) to trade off the non-volatility for higher energy efficiency. However, given that applications' retention time requirements are highly variable [40], much work still remains to be done to study the applications' requirements and designing adaptable NVM architectures that satisfy those requirements.

## 4 CONCLUSIONS

This paper presented an overview of the challenge of right-provisioned IoT edge computing. We defined right-provisioned IoT edge computing as a paradigm in which IoT devices are equipped with 'just enough' computing capability to satisfy their functional requirements and resource constraints. We highlighted a few research directions that must be addressed, with respect to high-level synthesis, energy supply, memory, and computation migration. We hope that this paper will motivate researchers to address some of these challenges in order to further spur the growth of the IoT.

## REFERENCES


[1] H. Sundmaeker, P. Guillemin, P. Friess, and S. Woelfflé, *Vision and challenges for realising the Internet of Things*. EUR-OP, 2010, vol. 20, no. 10.

[2] B. Varghese, N. Wang, S. Barbhuiya, P. Kilpatrick, and D. S. Nikolopoulos, "Challenges and opportunities in edge computing," in *2016 IEEE International Conference on Smart Cloud (SmartCloud)*. IEEE, 2016, pp. 20–26.

[3] F. Samie, L. Bauer, and J. Henkel, "Iot technologies for embedded computing: A survey," in *Proceedings of the Eleventh IEEE/ACM/IFIP International Conference on Hardware/Software Codesign and System Synthesis*. ACM, 2016, p. 8.

[4] P. Mach and Z. Becvar, "Mobile edge computing: A survey on architecture and computation offloading," *IEEE Communications Surveys & Tutorials*, vol. 19, no. 3, pp. 1628–1656, 2017.

[5] J.-E. Kim, T. Abdelzaher, L. Sha, A. Bar-Noy, R. Hobbs, and W. Dron, "On maximizing quality of information for the internet of things: A real-time scheduling perspective," in *2016 IEEE 22nd International Conference on Embedded and Real-Time Computing Systems and Applications (RTCSA)*. IEEE, 2016, pp. 202–211.

[6] T. Savolainen, J. Soininen, and B. Silverajan, "Ipv6 addressing strategies for iot," *IEEE Sensors Journal*, vol. 13, no. 10, pp. 3511–3519, 2013.

[7] S. Al-Sarawi, M. Anbar, K. Alieyan, and M. Alzubaidi, "Internet of things (iot) communication protocols," in *2017 8th International Conference on Information Technology (ICIT)*. IEEE, 2017, pp. 685–690.

[8] C. Shi, J. Liu, H. Liu, and Y. Chen, "Smart user authentication through actuation of daily activities leveraging wifi-enabled iot," in *Proceedings of the 18th ACM International Symposium on Mobile Ad Hoc Networking and Computing*. ACM, 2017, p. 5.

[9] S.-T. Khang, J. W. Yu, and W.-S. Lee, "Compact folded dipole rectenna with rf-based energy harvesting for iot smart sensors," *Electronics Letters*, vol. 51, no. 12, pp. 926–928, 2015.

[10] T. Adegbija, A. Rogacs, C. Patel, and A. Gordon-Ross, "Microprocessor optimizations for the internet of things: A survey," *IEEE Transactions on Computer-Aided Design of Integrated Circuits and Systems*, 2017.

[11] Y. Mao, C. You, J. Zhang, K. Huang, and K. B. Letaief, "A survey on mobile edge computing: The communication perspective," *IEEE Communications Surveys & Tutorials*, vol. 19, no. 4, pp. 2322–2358, 2017.

[12] T. Adegbija, A. Rogacs, C. Patel, and A. Gordon-Ross, "Enabling right-provisioned microprocessor architectures for the internet of things," in *International Mechanical Engineering Congress and Exposition*. ASME, 2015.

[13] N. D. Lane, S. Bhattacharya, P. Georgiev, C. Forlivesi, and F. Kawsar, "An early resource characterization of deep learning on wearables, smartphones and internet-of-things devices," in *Proceedings of the 2015 international workshop on internet of things towards applications*. ACM, 2015, pp. 7–12.

[14] Y. Yamaga, Y. Deguchi, S. Fukuyama, and K. Takeuchi, "5x reliability enhanced 40nm taox approximate-reram with domain-specific computing for real-time image recognition of iot edge devices," in *2018 IEEE Symposium on VLSI Technology*. IEEE, 2018, pp. 109–110.

[15] S. Lerner and B. Taskin, "Workload-aware asic flow for lifetime improvement of multi-core iot processors," in *2017 18th International Symposium on Quality Electronic Design (ISQED)*. IEEE, 2017, pp. 379–384.

[16] Z. Wang, Y. Liu, Y. Sun, Y. Li, D. Zhang, and H. Yang, "An energy-efficient heterogeneous dual-core processor for internet of things," in *2015 IEEE international symposium on circuits and systems (ISCAS)*. IEEE, 2015, pp. 2301–2304.

[17] H. Jayakumar, K. Lee, W. S. Lee, A. Raha, Y. Kim, and V. Raghunathan, "Powering the internet of things," in *Proceedings of the 2014 international symposium on Low power electronics and design*. ACM, 2014, pp. 375–380.

[18] G. Martin and G. Smith, "High-level synthesis: Past, present, and future," *IEEE Design & Test of Computers*, vol. 26, no. 4, pp. 18–25, 2009.

[19] A. Agarwal, M. C. Ng *et al.*, "A comparative evaluation of high-level hardware synthesis using reed–solomon decoder," *IEEE Embedded Systems Letters*, vol. 2, no. 3, pp. 72–76, 2010.

[20] A. M. Rahmani, P. Liljeberg, J.-S. Preden, and A. Jantsch, *Fog computing in the internet of things: Intelligence at the edge*. Springer, 2017.

[21] K. Kumar and Y.-H. Lu, "Cloud computing for mobile users: Can offloading computation save energy?" *Computer*, no. 4, pp. 51–56, 2010.

[22] Y. Wang, M. Sheng, X. Wang, L. Wang, and J. Li, "Mobile-edge computing: Partial computation offloading using dynamic voltage scaling," *IEEE Transactions on Communications*, vol. 64, no. 10, pp. 4268–4282, 2016.

[23] S. Dey, A. Mukherjee, A. Pal, and P. Balamuralidhar, "Partitioning of cnn models for execution on fog devices," in *Proceedings of the 1st ACM International Workshop on Smart Cities and Fog Computing*. ACM, 2018, pp. 19–24.

[24] M. Xu, F. Qian, and S. Pushp, "Enabling cooperative inference of deep learning on wearables and smartphones," *arXiv preprint arXiv:1712.03073*, 2017.

[25] I. Verbauwhede, "Vlsi design methods for low power embedded encryption," in *2016 International Great Lakes Symposium on VLSI (GLSVLSI)*. IEEE, 2016, pp. 7–7.

[26] T. Xu, J. B. Wendt, and M. Potkonjak, "Security of iot systems: Design challenges and opportunities," in *Proceedings of the 2014 IEEE/ACM International Conference on Computer-Aided Design*. IEEE Press, 2014, pp. 417–423.

[27] S. D. Kumar, H. Thapliyal, and A. Mohammad, "Ee-spfal: A novel energy-efficient secure positive feedback adiabatic logic for dpa resistant rfid and smart card," *IEEE Transactions on Emerging Topics in Computing*, 2016.

[28] N. A. Carreon, S. Lu, and R. Lysecky, "Hardware-based probabilistic threat detection and estimation for embedded systems," in *2018 IEEE 36th International Conference on Computer Design (ICCD)*. IEEE, 2018, pp. 522–529.

[29] H. Jayakumar, A. Raha, Y. Kim, S. Sutar, W. S. Lee, and V. Raghunathan, "Energy-efficient system design for iot devices," in *2016 21st Asia and South Pacific Design Automation Conference (ASP-DAC)*. IEEE, 2016, pp. 298–301.

[30] C. Pan, M. Xie, and J. Hu, "Enzyme: An energy-efficient transient computing paradigm for ultralow self-powered iot edge devices," *IEEE Transactions on Computer-Aided Design of Integrated Circuits and Systems*, vol. 37, no. 11, pp. 2440–2450, Nov 2018.

[31] J. Lee, Y. Zhang, Q. Dong, W. Lim, M. Saligane, Y. Kim, S. Jeong, J. Lim, M. Yasuda, S. Miyoshi, M. Kawaminami, D. Blaauw, and D. Sylvester, "19.2 a 6.4pj/cycle self-tuning cortex-m0 iot processor based on leakage-ratio measurement for energy-optimal operation across wide-range pvt variation," in *2019 IEEE International Solid- State Circuits Conference - (ISSCC)*, Feb 2019, pp. 314–315.

[32] M. B. Taylor, "Is dark silicon useful? harnessing the four horsemen of the coming dark silicon apocalypse," in *DAC Design Automation Conference 2012*. IEEE, 2012, pp. 1131–1136.

[33] S. Yue, D. Zhu, Y. Wang, and M. Pedram, "Reinforcement learning based dynamic power management with a hybrid power supply," in *2012 IEEE 30th International Conference on Computer Design (ICCD)*, Sep. 2012, pp. 81–86.

[34] D. Bortolotti, H. Mamaghanian, A. Bartolini, M. Ashouei, J. Stuijt, D. Atienza, P. Vandergheynst, and L. Benini, "Approximate compressed sensing: ultra-low power biosignal processing via aggressive voltage scaling on a hybrid memory multi-core processor," in *Proceedings of the 2014 international symposium on Low power electronics and design*. ACM, 2014, pp. 45–50.

[35] X. Li, K. Ma, S. George, J. Sampson, and V. Narayanan, "Enabling internet-of-things with opportunities brought by emerging devices, circuits and architectures," in *IFIP/IEEE International Conference on Very Large Scale Integration-System on a Chip*. Springer, 2016, pp. 1–23.

[36] K. Ma, X. Li, J. Li, Y. Liu, Y. Xie, J. Sampson, M. T. Kandemir, and V. Narayanan, "Incidental computing on iot nonvolatile processors," in *Proceedings of the 50th Annual IEEE/ACM International Symposium on Microarchitecture*. ACM, 2017, pp. 204–218.

[37] M. Ueki, K. Takeuchi, T. Yamamoto, A. Tanabe, N. Ikarashi, M. Saitoh, T. Nagumo, H. Sunamura, M. Narihiro, K. Uejima *et al.*, "Low-power embedded reram technology for iot applications," in *2015 Symposium on VLSI Technology (VLSI Technology)*. IEEE, 2015, pp. T108–T109.

[38] M. Ghoneim and M. Hussain, "Review on physically flexible nonvolatile memory for internet of everything electronics," *Electronics*, vol. 4, no. 3, pp. 424–479, 2015.

[39] H. Zhang, C. Zhang, Q. Hu, C. Yang, and J. Shu, "Performance analysis on structure of racetrack memory," in *2018 23rd Asia and South Pacific Design Automation Conference (ASP-DAC)*. IEEE, 2018, pp. 367–374.

[40] K. Kuan and T. Adegbija, "Lars: Logically adaptable retention time sttram cache for embedded systems," in *Design, Automation & Test in Europe Conference & Exhibition, 2018. DATE'18*. IEEE Computer Society, 2018.

# Secure Computing Systems Design Through Formal Micro-Contracts

Michel A. Kinsy
Adaptive and Secure Computing Systems Laboratory
Department of Electrical and Computer Engineering
Boston University
mkinsy@bu.edu

Novak Boskov
Adaptive and Secure Computing Systems Laboratory
Department of Electrical and Computer Engineering
Boston University
boskov@bu.edu

## ABSTRACT

Two enduring concepts in computer system design are abstraction levels and layered composition. The design generally takes a layered approach where each layer implements a different abstraction of the system. The layers communicate through interfaces that are designed to support functional specification of the system as a whole. Traditionally, these layers and interfaces have primarily focused on functionality and efficiency – performance, power and area. Security-related issues are often overlooked or deferred until later in the design cycle or applied as add-ons when some security features are explicitly required. The challenge with this approach is that chasing security implications of certain design decisions along the multiple layers is a complex and error-prone task. Therefore, in this work, we are introducing the notion of "security micro-contracts" or simply "micro-contracts". We propose a novel secure computer systems design approach through minimal contracts – micro-contracts – between adjacent layers. These contracts have strict structures that contain security-relevant details of each connected layer and the secure properties that have to be preserved to assure confidentiality, integrity and availability of the data of interest. Micro-contracts may be used as (i) basic formalism for proving security properties of computing systems both in the software and hardware layers and across them or (ii) run time security policy checks.

## CCS CONCEPTS

• **Security and privacy → Formal security models; Hardware-based security protocols.**

## KEYWORDS

security, secure system design, micro-contracts, formal methods, layered composition, abstract level.

**ACM Reference Format:**
Michel A. Kinsy and Novak Boskov. 2019. Secure Computing Systems Design Through Formal Micro-Contracts. In *Great Lakes Symposium on VLSI 2019 (GLSVLSI '19), May 9–11, 2019, Tysons Corner, VA, USA.* ACM, New York, NY, USA, 6 pages. https://doi.org/10.1145/3299874.3319447


ACM ISBN 978-1-4503-6252-8/19/05.
https://doi.org/10.1145/3299874.3319447

## 1 INTRODUCTION

The partitioning of computing systems into layers originates from the need for abstraction. Abstraction-based design enables system designers to cope with the ever-increasing complexity of the system. One of the benefits that abstraction brings into the design fold is the principle of *separation of concerns*. This principle gives us the mechanisms to achieve modularity. We usually specify module internals separately from the interfaces between modules through which the communication flows in order to implement desired functionality of the whole system. Interfaces tend to be minimal and clear in order to allow for different internal implementations of adjacent layers. However, the abstraction has also failed to establish strong security guarantees across these levels [5].

In the process of defining the interfaces, some details of the design that are considered non-essential to the functionality of the system are abstracted out, and are not necessarily preserved across the interfaces. This abstraction technique has traditionally worked. In fact, it is adopted across the full computing system stack, from instruction set architectures (ISAs) and memory subsystems to high level application programming interfaces (APIs). However, this abstraction process sometimes removes or misses important contextual or security-related information. Essentially, the process may create semantic gaps or widen them.

Through the analysis of known security vulnerabilities, one can distinguish three major classes. In this work, we use these classes to illustrate the space of possible vulnerabilities and to introduce the notion of "micro-contracts".

One class of security vulnerabilities is caused by *human error*. We usually refer to this class of vulnerabilities as security bugs. Security bugs happen when a programmer or designer of the system makes design mistakes mostly due to the weight of inherent system's complexity. In this case, security threats normally can be precluded by applying existing well-known mitigations, e.g., best software/hardware development practices. This class of vulnerabilities happens in a variety of real-world cases such as wrongly ordered pointer dereferencing causing privilege escalation in Linux kernel [12] and poor application of the *separation of concerns* principle in OpenSSH library that allows for connecting unauthorized clients to the server [11]. This ubiquitous class of security vulnerabilities encompasses a large portion of the vulnerabilities in publicly available databases such as Common Vulnerabilities and Exposures (CVE) and National Vulnerability Database (NVD). Provided that vulnerabilities are correctly documented and timely published, needed solutions are usually developed in a tolerable time frame. These solutions may require diverse set of actions including design changes but normally do not rely on massive abstraction modifications.

The second vulnerability class stems from *misuse of the existing abstractions.* For example, a programmer may unintentionally establish its security guards on the basis of optimization-unstable code in C/C++ [15]. This may happen when a security-related logic is on a control flow path removed through an optimization. For instance, the correctness of a compiler optimization is judged in accordance with functionality and performance, not necessarily its security. In other words, when a piece of code is pruned by the compiler, program's functionality is guaranteed to remain the same while security properties as intended by the programmer may be violated. Consequently, a program that expresses some security guard in its source code may not contain the same guard in its binary. Similar security vulnerabilities may also happen with other programming languages and runtime environments with more complex and dynamic behaviors like Java [8].

Both vulnerability classes — i.e., caused by human errors and by abstraction misuse — may be partially or completely mitigated by applying static analysis techniques. The human error vulnerability class is straightforward and its resolution has been the object of many research efforts. The case of abstraction misuse is more subtle to analyze. However, there are known common abstraction misuse patterns that can be described and guarded against within the abstraction itself. Thus, some vulnerabilities within this class can be partially or completely mitigated. For example, according to the C programming language standard, there are 77 examples of undefined behavior in the core language description [4]. In general, if there is a known list of abstraction misuses, one can erect guards as part of the abstraction construction to prevent abuses, and consequently, security holes. For instance, at the programming language level, through its compiler, one can detect "negative" semantic constructs and add rewrite rules to cover cases of undefined behavior [3]. One simple approach is for the compiler to halt the compilation process when it detects an undefined behavior and alert the programmer. Using the compiler's error message, the programmer can rewrite their program to retain desired security-related properties.

The third class is the security vulnerabilities *inherent to the abstraction* itself. These vulnerabilities are generally hard or even impossible to solve without significant redesigning of abstraction. Even if the designer uses the abstraction in a correct and consistent manner, security threats are not neutralized. One such a case is speculative execution side-channel based attacks [7]. Speculative execution timing side-channel based attacks may be considered an inherent security vulnerability tied to the abstraction view that the programmer and the compiler have of the processor. Specifically, this view is an isolated, sequential execution of the program statements/instructions as opposed to a pipelined, speculative, multi-threaded, multi-program execution environment.

The CPU micro-architecture implements the abstraction given through the ISA on one end, while for example compilers implement the same abstraction on the software side. By the virtue of abstraction both layers have freedom to implement their internals independently as long as the abstraction itself remains intact. For example, CPUs minimize time per cycle and cycles per instruction abstracting out micro-architectural features such as speculative execution and caches. These features are usually not exposed through the ISA as the interface corresponding to the abstraction. That is, an adjacent layer that uses ISA (e.g., a compiler) does not distinguish loads and stores that cause a cache hit from those which cause a cache miss. The properties of instructions other than their functionality are normally absent from the abstraction. One of such absent properties that an attacker may use to obtain sensitive information is timing. An attacker may measure the time difference of cache hits and cache misses to infer the data. Since timing of the instructions is not described in the ISA and since an attacker can use this information to affect the confidentiality of the system, we consider this class of vulnerabilities as inherent to the abstraction. However, the three classes are not mutually exclusive and a single vulnerability may belong to more than one class.

## 2 RELATED WORK

Various approaches have been used in the study of security property preservation targeting the different layers of computing abstractions. Some approaches focus on guarding the compilation process from attacks in low-level co-linked components [13]. Other researchers have tackled security implications of undefined behavior in programming languages by also taking into account the internal machine states to bridge the gap between security and the correctness. For example, D'Silva et al. [2] study security effects by extending source machine, a formalism used in studying compiler correctness. Some other approaches [3, 15] consider all the undefinedness in C as potential security holes and give rewrite rules to catch all the standard-prescribed undefined behaviors or use other techniques to discover it.

Multi-layer approaches are particularly interesting from the perspective of this work. In some approaches, the authors chose to implement a subset of C [1] on top of capability hardware [16] and investigate the preservation of security properties through memory object model [10]. With other techniques the focus was more on enforcing end-to-end security policies starting from high-level languages as described by Sabelfeld and Myers [14]. Mcilroy et. al. [9] recently took on the problem of understanding microarchitectural side channels and the formal analysis of their security implications.

## 3 GENERAL FRAMEWORK FOR MICRO-CONTRACTS

Micro-contracts are designed as a unified framework to tackle all three classes of vulnerabilities in a formal and security-centric manner. The solutions for known vulnerabilities that we are aware of normally mitigate each vulnerability using a relatively unique method. However, they do not describe security implications of the mitigations themselves. The solutions are normally demonstrated on minimal examples contained in vulnerability databases. Their implementation in complex systems usually requires numerous other changes whose security implications are studied separately from the vulnerability being mitigated.

For example, compilers rely on ISA of the underlying processor. They usually perform various optimizations without taking into account implementation details of instructions nor the high level intent of the programmer. One such optimization is *strength reduction* which can modify two previously equally time intensive branches to two branches that have observable difference in execution time. In this case, the difference is caused by compiler's decision to replace expressions with static values that do not consume any execution time or to change time complexity of the calculation. Further, an attacker may time branches and infer security sensitive information [2]. Even though some of the security implications of this kind may be tackled by disabling certain optimizations in the compiler, it may also cause an unacceptable runtime overhead. Having these constraints in mind, the programmer is forced to make an ad-hoc performance-security trade-off. The programmer can apply the separation of concern principle and separate critical code portions from the rest of the program. When the separation into critical functions (or even files) is done, the programmer can use specific compiler options to suspend particular optimizations on the critical code portions. In practice, this process usually requires a programmer that understands not only the motivation for the particular compiler optimization but also its internal implementation in the specific compiler. Furthermore, the programmer has to understand details of the compiler's infrastructure to properly apply optimization restrictions.

The approaches similar to the previous one may be useful as ad-hoc solutions. However, the approaches may also be considered as intermingling multiple abstractions through bypassing the high level interface of the programming language imposed by the standard and implemented by the compiler. The programmer is expected to explicitly use compiler's internals in order to achieve the desired program behavior. This poses a violation of computing system modularity and thus impedes reasoning about the complex systems' behavior. Consequentially, tracing security implications of certain design decisions becomes harder.

We propose micro-contracts, a strictly defined, minimal and modular framework for ensuring the security of layered computing systems. Micro-contracts are security-centric in the sense that they consider security of the whole system as the strict boundaries imposed to the functionality. This framework is also data-centric in the sense that it focuses on expressing desired security-related properties of the data instead of describing the internals of security preserving functions of the system's parts.

### 3.1 Design

Micro-contracts are designed as a framework for security analysis and policy enforcement in complex computing systems divided into layers. Policies are formed on the basis of the concrete attacks being analyzed. A general overview of the micro-contracts framework is given in Figure 1.

A micro-contract represents a security-related agreement between two adjacent layers in the computing stack. The two adjacent layers are represented as $CSL_i$ and $CSL_{i+1}$ and may denote e.g., high level programming language and its compiler, respectively. $CSL_i$ describes higher level intents of the programmer while the compiler produces the binary image that is executed. In general, *CSLs* are given through their abstractions such as a programming language standard or an ISA of a CPU.

Security policies from layer $CSL_i$ are translated in $CSL_{i+1}$ by some function $f : SP_k^{CSL_i} \rightarrow SP_k^{CSL_{i+1}}$. As we explain in §4, some

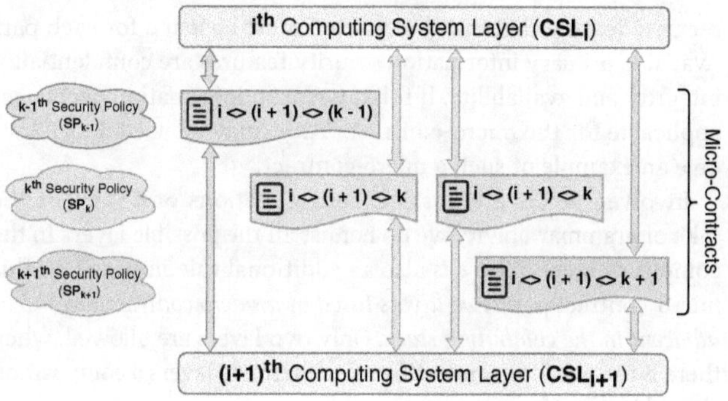


**Figure 1: Overview of the micro-contracts framework.**

properties of $SP_k$ may be lost after the application of function $f$ while some other properties may be added. To preserve security properties originally expressed in $SP_k$ while it gets passed down the layers, one has to characterize the translation ($f$). A micro-contract is the tool that helps us to describe the translation with regards to the security property that we want to enforce. Additionally, it offers the mechanism for the analysis of the security implications of the design decisions made on different layers of the computing system. A security policy may be enforced by many micro-contracts while a single micro-contract should be related to only one security policy. Relations between security policies should be studied through the composition of micro-contracts. Normally, we have multiple micro-contracts between two layers. Micro-contracts must conform to the strict structure given in Figure 2. This structure is logical rather than syntactical and may be implemented in different syntaxes as well as in the form of ontologies. For the sake of simplicity, in this work we give the examples using a language similar to YAML.

```
information ::= "information: " (info-descriptor
                                  | "Any") ;
info-descriptor ::= {ID primary-concept} ;
primary-concept ::= "primary concept:"
                    ("confidentiality"
                     | "integrity"
                     | "availability") ;
involved-layers ::= "involved layers:" {layer} ;
layer ::= "compiler"
          | "programming language"
          | "microarchitecture" ;
layer-concepts ::= "layer concepts:" {layer-concept} ;
layer-concept ::= ID
                  "belongs to:" layer
                  "defined as:" definition
                  "criteria:" criteria ;
definition ::= (* available definitions *) ;
criteria ::= (* criteria expressions *) ;
```

**Figure 2: Partial general micro-contract grammar in extended Backus-Naur form.**

The specification of micro-contracts has three major parts: *information, involved layers* and *layer concepts*. The information part is aimed to express the data that is compromised in the attack for which the mitigation is enforced within the security policy. Each part of the information can be described separately. The primary security feature that may be violated must be listed for each part. Available primary information security features are confidentiality, integrity and availability. If for any reason information part is not applicable for the micro-contract, "Any" may be used. In §4.2 we give an example of such a micro-contract.

Involved layers are possible concretizations of *CSLs*. For the sake of grammar brevity we do not list all the possible layers in the computing stack. There is also an additional rule imposed on this micro-contract part: *two layers listed in a micro contract have to be adjacent in the computing stack.* Only two layers are allowed, when there is the need for connecting more then two layers a composition should be used.

Layer concepts are the central part of a micro-contract. Each layer concept represents a layer abstraction's part crucial for the enforcement of the security policy. Layer concepts are internally distinguished using identifiers. Each layer explicitly lists the abstraction that it belongs to. It also declares the way it is defined in the native layer. Some important kinds of definitions are: property (specific ability of a layer), internal (internal layer concept), simple data (numbers, strings etc.) and auxiliary definitions. The last kind represents the predicates that have to be defined by the author of the micro contract for the involved layer. In the examples in §4 we use only one auxiliary definition — `grammar`. In one case it represents the grammatical rule in programming language C while in other it represents grammatical rule in RISC-V ISA.

The criteria part of layer concepts is given in the form of condition that is used to decide whether particular layer concept must be enforced. It may contain auxiliary predicates that have to be implementable in the native concepts of the corresponding layer. For example, in §4.2 we use `contains(expression, variable)` auxiliary predicate from the compiler layer. Since all compilers have the notion of expressions and variables, the auxiliary predicate is easily implemented.

## 3.2 Composition of Micro-Contracts

Often, it is not enough to track the security implications only to the adjacent layer but also deeper along the computing stack. In this case, micro-contracts provide the mechanism of multi-layer composition. This kind of composition is aimed at tracking the enforcement of security policies along the computing system stack.

As shown in Figure 3, we connect two or more layers by inserting at least one micro-contract between each two layers. The mapping represented by the arrows in Figure 3 is now:

$$f : SP_k^{CSL_{i-1}} \to SP_k^{CSL_i} \to SP_k^{CSL_{i+1}}$$

However, not all the micro-contracts can compose so as to preserve desired security property. Thus, we define the following rule:

> *Two micro-contracts can compose iff the conjunction of their criteria is satisfiable.*

Criteria of a micro-contract, denoted as $MC_j^{crit}$, is given as a logical expression $MC_j^{crit} \equiv \alpha \to (\beta \wedge \gamma)$ where $\alpha$, $\beta$ and $\gamma$ represent constituents of the criteria expression in $MC_j^{crit}$.

Assume that we compose $MC_j$ with $MC_{j+1}$ and that:

$$MC_{j+1}^{crit} \equiv (\alpha \to \delta) \wedge (\delta \to (\neg\gamma \wedge \beta))$$

Then, the criteria of composition becomes:

$$MC_j^{crit} \wedge MC_{j+1}^{crit} \equiv \alpha \to (\beta \wedge \gamma) \wedge (\alpha \to \delta) \wedge (\delta \to (\neg\gamma \wedge \beta))$$

This composition is satisfiable for $\langle \alpha, \beta, \gamma, \delta \rangle := \langle \bot, \top, \bot, \top \rangle$ meaning that $MC_j$ can compose with $MC_{j+1}$ so as to preserve security policies expressed by the micro-contracts. If the composition criteria were unsatisfiable that would indicate that two micro-contracts cannot compose in the security-preserving manner.

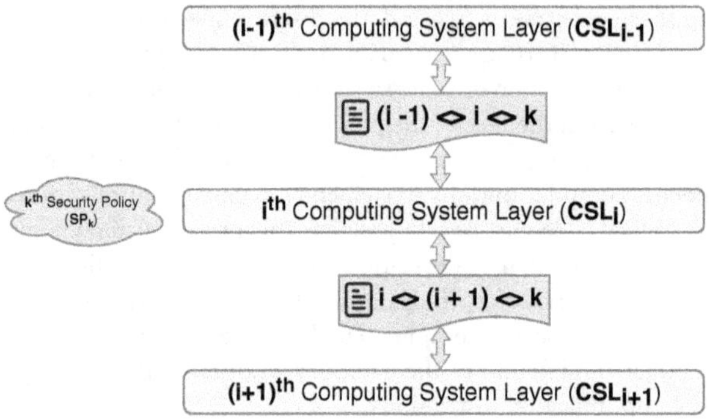


**Figure 3: Multi-layer composition of micro-contracts.**

# 4 ILLUSTRATIVE EXAMPLES

To illustrate the spirit of micro-contracts we give two examples of their usage on two distinct layer joints. The first one is a timing side channel attack opened by the strength reduction compiler optimization [2, III C]. This example describes a micro-contract that lies between high level code in programming language C and its compiler. The second example is Spectre1.1 speculative buffer overflow attack [6]. For the sake of illustration we present a hypothetical micro-contract that tackles Spectre1.1 on the joint between ISA and microarchitecture.

## 4.1 A Strength Reduction Micro-Contract

A simple example of strength reduction is implementation of multiplication using bit shift operations. For example, an expression that contains multiplication by 2 can be reduced to a functionally equivalent yet less processor intensive expression that uses left shift by one. Thus, expressions in the form `expr*63+23` can be rewritten as `(expr<<6)-expr+23` for any `expr` representing an integer.

Even though strength reduction can substantially improve the performance of various arithmetic expressions especially in loops, it may have hazardous security implications. Sometimes, programmers intentionally try to make branches equally computationally intensive in order to hide the information about what branch has been taken. In this case, strength reduction may open a timing side channel through which sensitive information can be leaked [2].

In the Figure 5 we give an example of a micro-contract to tackle the vulnerability incurred by strength reduction optimization in the compiler. This micro-contract pertains the information contained in the critical variable. The primary security feature that is compromised in this kind of attack is the confidentiality of the cryptographic key stored in the critical variable. In practice, we want to maximally hide the key from the attacker. Since attacker may utilize the time difference between branches, it may be better to leave the branches that handle the key in the original form expressed by the programmer. We assume that the programmer is aware of the timing side channels and is able to apply some of the known measures to make branches as closely computationally intensive as possible. Having said that, the security analyst may decide to use the following policy:

> *The programmer should declare keys using the* KEY_DECL *pragma. Compiler is not allowed to apply strength reduction on branches that contain computation that involves keys.*

In Figure 4 we show C code snippet that uses the KEY_DECL pragma on declaration of variable that holds the key at line 2. The programmer's idea is to avoid the timing difference between branches in line 5 and 7 by using one multiplication and one subtraction in both cases. Such written code should not exhibit any timing differences between the two branches.

```
1  int crypt(int x) {
2      #pragma KEY_DECL
3      int key = 0x23;
4      if (x == 0xDEAD) {
5          key = key * 7 - 5;
6      } else {
7          key = 2 * 17 - 3
8      }
9      return key;
10 }
```

**Figure 4: An example of a micro-contract-abiding C implementation of a toy cryptographic function.**

```
information:
    - critical_variable
        primary concept: confidentiality
involved layers:
    - programming language
    - compiler
layer concepts:
    - critical_variable:
        belongs to: programming language
        defined as: grammar("#pragma KEY_DECL")
        criteria: Always
    - expression:
        belongs to: compiler
        defined as: internal
        criteria: Always
    - strength_reduction:
        belongs to: compiler
        defined as: property
        criteria:
            if contains(expression, critical_variable)
               then absent
               else present
```

**Figure 5: An example of a micro-contract for mitigating timing side channel attacks allowed by the strength reduction compiler optimization.**

This is an example of the micro-contract between the programming language and the compiler. Such a contract may be implemented between e.g. C11 programming language and the LLVM compiler.

The layer concepts involved in the micro-contract are the critical variable, condition and strength reduction. The critical variable belongs to the programming language. This practically means that the designers of the micro-contract decided to extend C programming language with a technique for marking critical variables. The idiomatic way of doing so in C is by defining a pragma which will then have a generic pragma syntax `#pragma KEY_DECL`. `expression` is the primitive concept that belongs to compiler and is defined as its internal. This means that a compiler internally contains the notion of expression that can be given to disposal of micro-contracts. `Strength_reduction` is the concept that belongs to compiler and is defined as property. This means that the micro-contract uses it as the capability of the compiler that can be instrumented. The way a micro-contract instruments the property is given by the criteria. In this case, the micro-contract turns off strength reduction by declaring it absent in the cases when the expression contains the critical variable.

The mechanism for checking whether some variable is contained in the expression is normally present in the compiler's framework because it is needed even in the fundamental scope resolution.

It is important to mention that the vulnerabilities that are incurred by compiler optimizations can involve other optimizations such as common subexpression elimination or peephole optimizations. To tackle these vulnerabilities, the security analysts may decide to extend their policy and design one contract that describes the extended policy. However, the micro-contracts framework is designed to embrace minimal contracts and advocate the approaches with their composition.

## 4.2 A Spectre1.1 Micro-Contract

Spectre1.1, as introduced by Kiriansky and Waldspurger, is a Spectre [7] variant that uses speculative store instruction execution in modern superscalar processors to induce buffer overflows. Speculative store may be utilized to cause an out-of-bounds write that overwrites the return address of the function in which a vulnerable code portion resides. From that moment on, the attack resembles return-oriented-programming and can even invoke the critical part of Spectre1.0 gadget if present to leak sensitive information.

However, an important prerequisite of Spectre1.1 is pointed out by its authors. The speculative window must be wide enough to admit all the payload gadgets plus the instructions that lie between the vulnerable conditional branch and the indirect return instruction that is being attacked. If the wrong prediction is discovered before the return, the corrupt data needed for the attack will be invalidated and the attack will fail. For our purposes, we will assume that the security analyst that works on mitigating the critical vulnerability decided to approach the problem using the following policy:

> *Branches that lead to basic blocks with small number of instructions are more vulnerable to Spectre1.1. Instruction set defines* `sb*` *(short branch) instructions for all the branching conditions.* `sb*` *branches are branches that do not allow speculation window wider than* $IC_{short}$ *instructions.*

Since the policy is given in the terms of ISA and does not refer to any higher layers (e.g. compiler), the micro-contract corresponding to the policy will lie between ISA and the microarchitecture. There is a multitude of such micro-contracts that may be constructed. We are giving one in Figure 6 as an illustrative example.

Layer concepts involved in the micro-contract from Figure 6 are maximal number of instructions in short branches (IC_short), short branch itself and speculation. IC_short belongs to ISA. This practically means that ISA is being extended to include this information. It is defined as a number. Since this is primitive concept needed for more complex ones, it should always be enforced by the micro-contract. Short_branch_eq is a more complex concept present on the level of ISA. It is defined grammatically as a regular instruction similar to BEQ (branch if equal). For the purpose of this example, we use RISC-V-like instruction syntax. However, the concept is general and supports any concrete ISA for which the author can provide corresponding grammar definition. Finally, this concept has to be enforced by the micro-contract when instruction count of the branch is smaller than the maximal number of instructions in short branches.

The speculation part represents the processor's ability to speculatively execute instructions. It is clearly a property of the microarchitecture itself. The criteria under which the micro-contract enforces speculation to be turned off is short_branch_eq. When short_branch_eq is enforced on the ISA level then speculation is suspended. This particular part of the micro-contract illustrates the logical junction between two abstractions without intermingling their internals.

It is also important to note that sb* is not completely covered by the micro-contract in Figure 6. However, the criteria for all the branch instructions is considered to be the same. Thus, extension of this micro-contract to cover all the branches would just add simple grammatical definitions for the other five RISC-V branch counterparts (BNE.s, BLT.s, BGE.s, BLTU.s and BGU.s) while other parts would remain the same. For the sake of convenience, future versions of the micro-contracts framework will provide the support for concise expressions of repeating parts. One of the possible approaches is inheritance of the layer concepts. However, the ontological information contained in a more concise version of the micro-contract is exactly the same as in its extended version.

Additionally, we may need to construct a finely-grained mechanism for tackling security implications of Spectre1.1 further up the computing stack. That is, we may be interested in analyzing the security of our system through reasoning about the high level concept such as cryptographic keys given to the system as variables of a program. To do so, we need to design the chain of micro-contracts so as to cover upper layers such as e.g. assembler, linker, compiler and the programming language itself. The micro-contracts framework embraces writing multiple micro-contracts that chain to each other all the way down to the microarchitecture. Therefore, we eliminate a portion of the complexity of non-trivial computing systems that impedes our reasoning about information security.

## 5 CONCLUSION

In this paper we introduced the micro-contracts framework as a formal, minimal and modular methodology for enforcing security policies over multiple layers of computing systems. We discussed the building blocks of a micro-contract as well as the internal structure. Afterwards, we described multi-layer composition of multiple micro-contracts and introduced the concept of composability. Finally, we demonstrated the usability of the introduced concepts through the design of the micro-contracts among different layers.

```
information:
    - Any
involved layers:
    - ISA
    - microarchitecture
layer concepts:
    - IC_short:
        belongs to: ISA
        defined as: number
        criteria: Always
    - short_branch_eq:
        belongs to: ISA
        defined as: grammar("BEQ.s rs1, rs2, imm")
        criteria: instruction_count() > IC_short
    - speculation:
        belongs to: microarchitecture
        defined as: property
        criteria: if short_branch_eq then absent
                                       else present
```

**Figure 6: An example of micro-contract for mitigating Spectre1.1 attack.**

We focused on guarding against timing side channel attacks introduced by strength reduction compiler optimization and Spectre1.1. We envision micro-contracts as a sound methodology for studying cross-layer security implications of both future attacks and their mitigations.

## REFERENCES


[1] David Chisnall, Colin Rothwell, Robert N.M. Watson, Jonathan Woodruff, Munraj Vadera, Simon W. Moore, Michael Roe, Brooks Davis, and Peter G. Neumann. 2015. Beyond the PDP-11. *ACM SIGARCH Computer Architecture News* 43, 1 (Mar 2015), 117–130.

[2] Vijay D'Silva, Mathias Payer, and Dawn Song. 2015. The Correctness-Security Gap in Compiler Optimization. *2015 IEEE Security and Privacy Workshops* (May 2015).

[3] Chris Hathhorn, Chucky Ellison, and Grigore Roşu. 2015. Defining the undefinedness of C. *ACM SIGPLAN Notices* 50, 6 (Jun 2015), 336–345.

[4] ISO/IEC JTC1/SC22/WG14. 2011. *Information technology - Programming languages - C.* ISO/IEC 9899:2011. International Organization for Standardization.

[5] M. A. Kinsy, S. Khadka, M. Isakov, and A. Farrukh. 2017. Hermes: Secure heterogeneous multicore architecture design. In *2017 IEEE International Symposium on Hardware Oriented Security and Trust (HOST)*. 14–20.

[6] Vladimir Kiriansky and Carl Waldspurger. 2018. Speculative Buffer Overflows: Attacks and Defenses. arXiv:cs.CR/1807.03757

[7] Paul Kocher, Jann Horn, Anders Fogh, , Daniel Genkin, Daniel Gruss, Werner Haas, Mike Hamburg, Moritz Lipp, Stefan Mangard, Thomas Prescher, Michael Schwarz, and Yuval Yarom. 2019. Spectre Attacks: Exploiting Speculative Execution. In *40th IEEE Symposium on Security and Privacy (S&P'19)*.

[8] V. Benjamin Livshits and Monica S. Lam. 2005. Finding Security Vulnerabilities in Java Applications with Static Analysis. In *Proceedings of the 14th Conference on USENIX Security Symposium - Volume 14 (SSYM'05)*. USENIX Association, Berkeley, CA, USA, 18–18.

[9] Ross Mcilroy, Jaroslav Sevcik, Tobias Tebbi, Ben L. Titzer, and Toon Verwaest. 2019. Spectre is here to stay: An analysis of side-channels and speculative execution. arXiv:cs.PL/1902.05178

[10] Kayvan Memarian, Justus Matthiesen, James Lingard, Kyndylan Nienhuis, David Chisnall, Robert N. M. Watson, and Peter Sewell. 2016. Into the depths of C: elaborating the de facto standards. *ACM SIGPLAN Notices* 51, 6 (Jun 2016), 1–15.

[11] MITRE. 2009. CVE-2009-1897.

[12] MITRE. 2018. CVE-2018-10933.

[13] Marco Patrignani and Deepak Garg. 2017. Secure Compilation and Hyperproperty Preservation. *2017 IEEE 30th Computer Security Foundations Symposium (CSF)* (Aug 2017).

[14] Andrei Sabelfeld and Andrew C Myers. 2003. Language-based information-flow security. *IEEE Journal on selected areas in communications* 21, 1 (2003), 5–19.

[15] Xi Wang, Nickolai Zeldovich, M. Frans Kaashoek, and Armando Solar-Lezama. 2013. Towards optimization-safe systems. *Proceedings of the Twenty-Fourth ACM Symposium on Operating Systems Principles - SOSP '13* (2013).

[16] Robert N.M. Watson, Jonathan Woodruff, Peter G. Neumann, Simon W. Moore, Jonathan Anderson, David Chisnall, Nirav Dave, Brooks Davis, Khilan Gudka, Ben Laurie, and et al. 2015. CHERI: A Hybrid Capability-System Architecture for Scalable Software Compartmentalization. *2015 IEEE Symposium on Security and Privacy* (May 2015).

# Author Index

# NOTES